Conte

CHAPTER 4
Analysis of Financial Statements 105

CHAPTER 5
Time Value of Money 148

BRIGHAM HOUSTON

FUNDAMENTALS OF FINANCIAL MANAGEMENT
CONCISE EDITION

10E

EUGENE F. BRIGHAM
University of Florida

JOEL F. HOUSTON
University of Florida

CENGAGE

Australia • Brazil • Mexico • Singapore • United Kingdom • United States

CENGAGE

Fundamentals of Financial Management:
Concise, 10th Edition
Eugene F. Brigham and Joel F. Houston

Senior Vice President, Higher Ed Product, Content, and Market Development: Erin Joyner

VP, Product Management: Mike Schenk

Sr. Product Team Manager: Joe Sabatino

Content Manager: Christopher Valentine

Learning Designer: Brittany Waitt

Product Assistant: Renee Schnee

Marketing Manager: Christopher Walz

Marketing Coordinator: Sean Messer

Production Service: MPS Limited

Art Director: Chris Doughman

Text Designer: Imbue Design/Kim Torbeck

Cover Designer: Chris Doughman

Cover Image: Eugene Moerman/Shutterstock.com

Intellectual Property Analyst: Reba Frederics

Intellectual Property Project Manager: Carly Belcher

Part Opener image: hfzimages/Shutterstock.com

Design Element images: Sylverarts Vectors /Shutterstock.com, 3RUS/Shutterstock.com

Library of Congress Control Number: 2018965082

ISBN: 978-1-337-90257-1

Cengage
20 Channel Center Street
Boston, MA 02210
USA

Cengage is a leading provider of customized learning solutions with employees residing in nearly 40 different countries and sales in more than 125 countries around the world. Find your local representative at **www.cengage.com.**

Cengage products are represented in Canada by Nelson Education, Ltd.

To learn more about Cengage platforms and services, register or access your online learning solution, or purchase materials for your course, visit **www.cengage.com.**

Printed in the United States of America
Print Number: 01 Print Year: 2019

Brief Contents

Appendixes

Preface

When the first edition of *Fundamentals* was published 41 years ago, we wanted to provide an introductory text that students would find interesting and easy to understand. *Fundamentals* immediately became the leading undergraduate finance text, and it has maintained that position ever since. However, over the years, as *Fundamentals* got larger and larger, we heard more and more often that it was difficult to cover the entire book in a single term. These concerns led us to create *Fundamentals of Financial Management Concise* 24 years ago. When designing *Concise*, we had in mind those instructors who wanted to retain *Fundamentals'* depth and level but eliminate some less essential topics. As is the case with *Fundamentals*, our continuing goal is to produce a book and ancillary package that sets a new standard for finance textbooks.

Finance is an exciting and continually changing field. Since the last edition, many important changes have occurred within the global financial environment. In the midst of this changing environment, it is certainly an interesting time to be a finance student. In this latest edition, we highlight and analyze the events leading to these changes from a financial perspective. Although the financial environment is ever changing, the tried-and-true principles that the book has emphasized over the past four decades are now more important than ever.

Structure of the Book

Our target audience is a student taking his or her first, and perhaps only, finance course. Some of these students will decide to major in finance and go on to take courses in investments, money and capital markets, and advanced corporate finance. Others will choose marketing, management, or some other nonfinance business major. Still others will major in areas other than business and take finance plus a few other business courses to gain information that will help them in law, real estate, or other fields.

Our challenge has been to provide a book that serves all of these audiences well. We focus on the core principles of finance, including the basic topics of time value of money, risk analysis, and valuation. In each case, we address these topics from two points of view: (1) that of an investor who is seeking to make intelligent investment choices and (2) that of a business manager trying to maximize the value of his or her firm's stock. Both investors and managers need to understand the same set of principles, so the core topics are important to students regardless of what they choose to do after they finish the course.

In planning the book's structure, we first listed the core topics in finance that are important to virtually everyone. Included were an overview of financial markets, methods used to estimate the cash flows that determine asset values, the time value of money, the determinants of interest rates, the basics of risk analysis, and the basics of bond and stock valuation procedures. We cover these core topics in the first nine chapters. Next, because most students in the course will probably work for a business firm, we want to show them how the core ideas are implemented in practice. Therefore, we go on to discuss cost of capital, capital budgeting, capital structure, dividend policy, working capital management, financial forecasting, and international operations.

Non-finance majors sometimes wonder why they need to learn finance. As we have structured the book, it quickly becomes obvious to everyone why they need to understand time value, risk, markets, and valuation. Virtually all students enrolled in the basic course expect at some point to have money to invest, and they quickly realize that the knowledge gained from Chapters 1 through 9 will help them make better investment decisions. Moreover, students who plan to go into the business world soon realize that their own success requires that their firms be successful, and the topics covered in Chapters 10 through 17 will be helpful here. For example, good capital budgeting decisions require accurate forecasts from people in sales, marketing, production, and human resources, and non-financial people need to understand how their actions affect the firm's profits and future performance.

Organization of the Chapters: A Valuation Focus

As we discuss in Chapter 1, in an enterprise system such as that of the United States, the primary goal of financial management is to maximize their firms' values. At the same time, we stress that managers should not do "whatever it takes" to increase the firm's stock price. Managers have a responsibility to behave ethically, and when striving to maximize value, they must abide by constraints such as not polluting the environment, not engaging in unfair labor practices, not breaking the antitrust laws, and the like. In Chapter 1, we discuss the concept of valuation, explain how it depends on future cash flows and risk, and show why value maximization is good for society in general. This valuation theme runs throughout the text.

Stock and bond values are determined in the financial markets, so an understanding of those markets is essential to anyone involved with finance. Therefore, Chapter 2 covers the major types of financial markets, the rates of return that investors have historically earned on different types of securities, and the risks inherent in these securities. This information is important for anyone working in finance, and it is also important for anyone who has or hopes to own any financial assets. In this chapter, we also highlight how this environment has changed in the aftermath of the financial crisis.

Asset values depend in a fundamental way on earnings and cash flows as reported in the accounting statements. Therefore, we review those statements in Chapter 3 and then, in Chapter 4, show how accounting data can be analyzed and used to measure how well a company has operated in the past and how well it is likely to perform in the future.

Chapter 5 covers the time value of money (TVM), perhaps the most fundamental concept in finance. The basic valuation model, which ties together cash flows, risk, and interest rates, is based on TVM concepts, and these concepts are used throughout the remainder of the book. Therefore, students should allocate plenty of time to studying Chapter 5.

Chapter 6 deals with interest rates, a key determinant of asset values. We discuss how interest rates are affected by risk, inflation, liquidity, the supply of and demand for capital in the economy, and the actions of the Federal Reserve. The discussion of interest rates leads directly to the topics of bonds in Chapter 7 and stocks in Chapters 8 and 9, where we show how these securities (and all other financial assets) are valued using the basic TVM model.

The background material provided in Chapters 1 through 9 is essential to both investors and corporate managers. These are finance topics, not business or corporate finance topics as those terms are commonly used. Thus, Chapters 1 through 9 concentrate on the concepts and models used to establish values, whereas Chapters 10 through 17 focus on specific actions managers can take to maximize their firms' values.

Because most business students don't plan to specialize in finance, they might think the business finance chapters are not particularly relevant to them. This is most decidedly not true, and in the later chapters we show that all really important business decisions involve every one of a firm's departments—marketing, accounting, production, and so on. Thus, although a topic such as capital budgeting can be thought of as a financial issue, marketing people provide inputs on likely unit sales and sales prices, manufacturing people provide inputs on costs, and so on. Moreover, capital budgeting decisions influence the size of the firm, its products, its profits, and its stock price, and those factors affect all of the firm's employees, from the CEO to the mail room staff.

Innovations for the Tenth Edition

A great deal has happened in the financial markets and corporate America since the 9th edition was published. In this Tenth Edition, we have made several important changes to reflect this dynamic environment. Here is a brief summary of the more significant changes.

1. Today's students are tomorrow's business and government leaders, and it is essential that they understand the key principles of finance and the important role that financial markets and institutions have on our economy. Since the last edition, a number of key events have significantly influenced the financial markets and finance in general. Over the last few years, we have witnessed continued sluggishness but steady improvement in the world economy, a dramatic reduction in oil prices, the surprise election of President Donald J. Trump in November 2016, and continued unrest overseas. At the same time, the Federal Reserve has begun to slowly increase interest rates in the aftermath of its aggressive policy of quantitative easing that had pushed interest rates to the lowest levels in years. We have also witnessed between August 2014 and August 2018 the continued dramatic run-up in the U.S. stock market to record-high levels. Throughout the Tenth Edition, we discuss these events and their implications for financial markets and corporate managers, and we use these examples to illustrate the importance of the key concepts covered in *Concise* for investors, businesses, and even government officials.
2. In December 2017, Congress passed the Tax Cuts and Jobs Act. We have described the act's key features and have highlighted its important impacts throughout the text. More specifically, in Chapter 3 (Financial Statements, Cash Flow, and Taxes), we incorporate the act's effects in our newly revised illustrative financial statements and in our discussion of individual and corporate tax rates and tax provisions. In Chapter 10 (The Cost of Capital), we discuss a firm's capital components and the new law's impact on a firm's after-tax cost of debt and therefore its WACC. In Chapter 12 (Cash Flow Estimation and Risk Analysis), we illustrate the act's impact on a project's free cash flows due to immediate 100% expensing of certain new and used business assets and the lower corporate tax rate. In Chapter 13 (Capital Structure and Leverage), we illustrate the lower corporate tax rate's impact on a firm's optimal capital structure. In Chapter 14 (Distributions to Shareholders: Dividends and Share Repurchases), we discuss the change in corporate dividend exclusion percentages. In Chapter 16 (Financial Planning

and Forecasting), we illustrate the lower corporate tax rate's impact on a firm's forecasted financial statements and related forecasted ratios. Finally, we have also revised the relevant end-of-chapter problems and have updated our various ancillaries to take into account the effects of the recent act.

3. In the Tenth Edition, we also continue to highlight the important influences of increased globalization and changing technology. These influences have created new opportunities, but they have also generated new sources of risk for individuals and businesses. Notably, since the last edition, we have seen the phenomenal increase in the stock prices of the FANG (Facebook, Amazon, Netflix, and Google's parent Alphabet). We have also witnessed the initial public offerings of SNAP and Alibaba, the disrupting forces of Uber and Airbnb, the continued rise of Bitcoin and other cryptocurrencies, and several high-profile mergers.
4. Instructors and students continually impress upon us the importance of having interesting and relevant real-world examples. Throughout the Tenth Edition we have added several new examples where recent events help illustrate the key concepts covered in the text. We have added a number of new boxes discussing chapter concepts impacting real-world companies, such as Chapter 2: "Lower Fees Motivate Investors to Move Toward Index Funds"; Chapter 3: "Congress Passes Sweeping Tax Reform Act in 2017"; Chapter 3: "Corporate Tax Rates Around the World"; Chapter 4: "Household Debt Burdens Have Declined in Recent Years"; Chapter 17: "Brexit Shakes Europe"; and Chapter 17: "President Trump Announces New Tariffs." We have also expanded and updated the many tables where we present real-world data, and we have updated our Taking a Closer Look Problems. Finally, as is always the case, we have made significant changes to many of the opening vignettes that precede each chapter.
5. Behavioral finance theory continues to have an important influence on the academic literature and it has in many ways reshaped the way that many of us think about financial markets and corporate finance. In addition, we continue to highlight the importance of securitization, the role of derivatives, and the increasing importance of hedge funds, mutual funds, and private equity firms.
6. We have added a discussion on traditional and Roth IRAs.
7. In Chapter 3, we revised the definition of operating working capital. Following real-world practices and the increase in the number of companies with extremely large cash holdings, we now exclude excess cash from our calculation of operating current assets. In response to this change, we also now allow for non-operating assets in our estimates of stock valuation in Chapter 9.
8. We updated the exchange rate data in Chapter 17 to reflect what's currently going on in the world. All figures and text discussion have been updated accordingly, including "Hungry for a Big Mac? Go to Egypt," "Stock Market Indexes Around the World," and "Investing in International Stocks" boxes.

Digital Solutions for the Tenth Edition

Changing technology and new ideas have had an exciting and dramatic influence on the ways we teach finance. Innovative instructors are developing and utilizing different classroom strategies, and new technology has allowed us to present key material in a more interesting and interactive fashion. As textbook authors, we think these new developments are tremendously exciting, and we have worked closely with our publisher's top team of innovative content and media developers, who have created a whole new set of revolutionary products for the Tenth Edition.

MINDTAP™

MindTap™, Cengage Learning's fully online, highly personalized learning experience combines readings, multimedia activities, and assessments into a singular Learning Path. MindTap™ guides students through their course with ease and engagement with a learning path that includes an Interactive Chapter Reading, Problem Demonstrations, Blueprint Problems, Excel Online Problems, and Homework Assignments powered by Aplia. These homework problems include rich explanations and instant grading, with opportunities to try another algorithmic version of the problem to bolster confidence with problem solving. Instructors can personalize the Learning Path for their students by customizing the robust suite of the Tenth Edition resources and adding their own content via apps that integrate into the MindTap™ framework seamlessly with Learning Management Systems.

EXCEL ONLINE PROBLEMS

Microsoft Excel Online activities provide students with an opportunity to work auto-gradable, algorithmic homework problems directly in their browser using Excel Online. Students receive instant feedback on their Excel work, including "by hand" calculations and a solution file containing a recommended way of solving the problem. Students' Excel work is saved in real time in the cloud; is platform, device, and browser independent; and is always accessible with their homework without cumbersome file uploads and downloads. This unique integration represents a direct collaboration between Cengage and Microsoft to strengthen and support the development of Microsoft Office education skills for success in the workplace.

ATP

Adaptive Test Prep allows students to create practice quizzes covering multiple chapters in a low stakes environment. Students receive immediate feedback so they know where they need additional help, and the test bank–like questions prepare students for what to expect on the exam. With many questions offered per chapter, students can create multiple unique practice quizzes within MindTap™.

EXPLORING FINANCE

Exploring Finance offers instructors and students interactive visualizations that engage with "lean forward" interactivity. Exploring Finance offers instructors visual, interactive tools that they can use to help students "see" the financial concept being presented directly within MindTap™.

FINANCE IN ACTION

MindTap™ offers a series of Finance in Action analytical cases that assess students' higher level of understanding, critical thinking, and decision making.

BLUEPRINT PROBLEMS

Written by the authors and located within MindTap™, Blueprints teach students the fundamental finance concepts and their associated building blocks—going beyond memorization. By going through the problems step by step, they reinforce foundational concepts and allow students to demonstrate their understanding of the problem-solving process and business impact of each topic. Blueprints include rich feedback and explanations, providing students with an excellent learning resource to solidify their understanding.

CONCEPTCLIPS

Embedded throughout the new interactive eReader, finance ConceptClips present fundamental key topics to students in an entertaining and memorable way via short animated video clips. Developed by Mike Brandl of The Ohio State University, these vocabulary animations provide students with a memorable auditory and visual representation of the important terminology for the course.

EVEN MORE PROBLEM WALK-THROUGHS

More than 150 Problem Walk-Through videos are embedded in the new interactive MindTap™ eReader and online homework. Each video walks students through solving a problem from start to finish, and students can play and replay the tutorials as they work through homework assignments or prepare for quizzes and tests, almost as though they had an instructor by their side the whole time.

COGNERO™ TESTING SOFTWARE

Cengage Learning Testing Powered by Cognero™ is a flexible, online system that allows you to author, edit, and manage test bank content from multiple Cengage Learning solutions, create multiple test versions in an instant, and deliver tests from your LMS, your classroom, or wherever you want. Revised to reflect concepts covered in the Tenth Edition, the Cognero™ Test Bank is tagged according to Tier I (AACSB Business Program Interdisciplinary Learning Outcomes) and Tier II (Finance specific) topic, Bloom's Taxonomy, and difficulty level. In addition to these changes, we have also significantly updated and improved our more traditional ancillary package, which includes the Instructor's Manual, Test Bank, Excel Chapter Models, Excel Chapter Integrated Case Models, Excel Spreadsheet Problem Models, and PowerPoints for Chapter Integrated Cases.

Acknowledgments

The book reflects the efforts of a great many people, both those who worked on *Concise* and our related books in the past and those who worked specifically on this Tenth Edition. First, we would like to thank Dana Aberwald Clark, who worked closely with us at every stage of the revision—her assistance was absolutely invaluable.

Our colleagues John Banko, Roy Crum, Jim Keys, Andy Naranjo, M. Nimalendran, Jay Ritter, Mike Ryngaert, Craig Tapley, and Carolyn Takeda Brown have given us many useful suggestions over the years regarding the ancillaries and many parts of the book, including the integrated cases. We also benefited from the work of Mike Ehrhardt and Phillip Daves of the University of Tennessee, who worked with us on companion books.

We would also like to thank the following professors, whose reviews and comments on this and our earlier books contributed to this edition:

Rebecca Abraham
Robert Abraham
Joe Adamo
Robert Adams
Mike Adler
Cyrus Aleseyed
Sharif Ahkam
Syed Ahmad
Ed Altman
Bruce Anderson
Ron Anderson
Tom Anderson
John Andrews
Bob Angell
Vince Apilado
Harvey Arbalaez
Kavous Ardalan
Henry Arnold
Tom Arnold
Bob Aubey
Gil Babcock
Peter Bacon
Chung Baek
Bruce Bagamery
Kent Baker
Robert J. Balik
Tom Bankston
Babu Baradwaj
Les Barenbaum
Charles Barngrover
Sam Basu
Deborah Bauer
Greg Bauer
Laura A. Beal
David Becher
Bill Beedles
Brian Belt
Moshe Ben-Horim
Gary Benesh
Bill Beranek
Tom Berry
Al Berryman
Will Bertin
Scott Besley
Dan Best
Mark S. Bettner
Roger Bey
Gilbert W. Bickum
Dalton Bigbee
John Bildersee
Kenneth G. Bishop
Laurence E. Blose
Russ Boisjoly
Bob Boldin
Keith Boles
Michael Bond
Elizabeth Booth
Geof Booth
Waldo Born
Brian Boscaljon
Steven Bouchard
Kenneth Boudreaux
Rick Boulware
Helen Bowers
Oswald Bowlin
Don Boyd
G. Michael Boyd
Pat Boyer
Joe Brandt
Elizabeth Brannigan
Mary Broske
Christopher Brown
David T. Brown
Kate Brown
Larry Brown
Todd A. Brown
Bill Brueggeman
Paul Bursik
Alva Butcher
Bill Campsey
W. Thomas Carls
Bob Carlson
Severin Carlson
David Cary
Steve Celec
Mary Chaffin
Rajesh Chakrabarti
Charles Chan
Don Chance
Antony Chang
Susan Chaplinsky
K. C. Chen
Jay Choi
S. K. Choudhary
Lal Chugh
Peter Clarke
Maclyn Clouse
Thomas S. Coe
Bruce Collins
Mitch Conover
Margaret Considine
Phil Cooley
Joe Copeland
David Cordell
Marsha Cornett
M. P. Corrigan
John Cotner
Charles Cox
David Crary
John Crockett Jr.
Julie Dahlquist
Brent Dalrymple
Bill Damon
Morris Danielson
Joel Dauten
Steve Dawson
Sankar De
Fred Dellva
Jim DeMello
Chad Denson
James Desreumaux
Thomas Devaney
Bodie Dickerson
Bernard Dill
Gregg Dimkoff
Les Dlabay
Nathan Dong
Mark Dorfman
Tom Downs
Frank Draper
Anne M. Drougas
Gene Drzycimski
David A. Dubofsky
Dean Dudley
David Durst
Ed Dyl
Fred J. Ebeid
Daniel Ebels
Richard Edelman
Charles Edwards
Scott Ehrhorn
U. Elike
John Ellis
George Engler
Suzanne Erickson
Dave Ewert
John Ezzell
Olubunmi Faleye
L. Franklin Fant
John Farns
John Farris
David Feller
Richard J. Fendler
Michael Ferri
Jim Filkins
John Finnerty
Robert Fiore
Susan Fischer
Peggy Fletcher
Steven Flint
Russ Fogler
Jennifer Foo
Jennifer Frazier
Dan French
Harry Gallatin
Partha Gangopadhyay
John Garfinkel
Michael Garlington
David Garraty
Sharon H. Garrison
Jim Garven
Adam Gehr Jr.
Jim Gentry
Sudip Ghosh
Wafica Ghoul
Erasmo Giambona
Armand Gilinsky Jr.
Philip Glasgo
Rudyard Goode
Raymond Gorman
Walt Goulet
Bernie Grablowsky
Theoharry Grammatikos
Georg Grassmueck
Greg Gregoriou
Owen Gregory
Ed Grossnickle
John Groth
Alan Grunewald
Manak Gupta
Darryl Gurley
Sam Hadaway
Don Hakala
Gerald Hamsmith
Mahfuzul Haque
William Hardin
John Harris
Mary Hartman
Paul Hastings
Bob Haugen
Steve Hawke
Stevenson Hawkey
Del Hawley
Eric M. Haye
Robert Hehre
Jeff Heinfeldt
Brian Henderson
Kath Henebry
David Heskel
George Hettenhouse
Hans Heymann
Kendall Hill
Roger Hill
Tom Hindelang
Linda Hittle
Ralph Hocking
Robert P. Hoffman
J. Ronald Hoffmeister
Robert Hollinger
Jim Horrigan
John Houston
John Howe
Keith Howe
Stephen Huffman
Steve Isberg
Jim Jackson

Kevin T. Jacques
Keith Jakob
Vahan Janjigian
Narayanan Jayaraman
Benjamas Jirasakuldech
Zhenhn Jin
Kose John
Craig Johnson
Keith Johnson
Ramon Johnson
Steve Johnson
Ray Jones
Frank Jordan
Manuel Jose
Sally Joyner
Alfred Kahl
Gus Kalogeras
Rajiv Kalra
Ravi Kamath
John Kaminarides
Ashok Kapoor
Howard Keen
Michael Keenan
Bill Kennedy
Peppi M. Kenny
Carol Kiefer
Joe Kiernan
Richard Kish
Robert Kleiman
Erich Knehans
Don Knight
Ladd Kochman
Dorothy Koehl
Jaroslaw Komarynsky
Duncan Kretovich
Harold Krogh
Charles Kroncke
Don Kummer
Robert A. Kunkel
Reinhold Lamb
Christopher J. Lambert
Joan Lamm
Larry Lang
David Lange
P. Lange
Howard Lanser
Alex Lau
Catherine Lau
Edward Lawrence
Martin Lawrence
Jerry M. Leabman
Rick LeCompte
Alice Lee
Wayne Lee
Jim LePage
Vance Lesseig
David E. LeTourneau
Denise Letterman
Jules Levine
John Lewis
Jason Lin
Chuck Linke
Yi Liu
Bill Lloyd
Susan Long
Robert L. Losey
Nancy L. Lumpkin
Yulong Ma
Fraser MacHaffie
Judy Maese
Bob Magee
Ileen Malitz
Bob Malko
Phil Malone
Abbas Mamoozadeh
Terry Maness
Chris Manning
Surendra Mansinghka
Timothy Manuel
Barry Marchman
Brian Maris
Terry Martell
David Martin
D. J. Masson
John Mathys
Ralph May
John McAlhany
Andy McCollough
Ambrose McCoy
Thomas McCue
Bill McDaniel
John McDowell
Charles McKinney
Robyn McLaughlin
James McNulty
Jeanette Medewitz-Diamond
Jamshid Mehran
Larry Merville
Rick Meyer
Jim Millar
Ed Miller
John Miller
Jill Misuraca
John Mitchell
Carol Moerdyk
Bob Moore
Scott B. Moore
Jose F. Moreno
Matthew Morey
Barry Morris
Gene Morris
Dianne R. Morrison
John K. Mullen
Chris Muscarella
David Nachman
Tim Nantell
Don Nast
Edward Nelling
Bill Nelson
Bob Nelson
Tom C. Nelson
William Nelson
Duong Nguyen
Bob Niendorf
Bruce Niendorf
Ben Nonnally Jr.
Tom O'Brien
William O'Connell
Dennis O'Connor
John O'Donnell
Jim Olsen
Robert Olsen
Dean Olson
Napoleon Overton
R. Daniel Pace
Darshana Palkar
Jim Pappas
Stephen Parrish
Helen Pawlowski
Barron Peake
Michael Pescow
Glenn Petry
Jim Pettijohn
Rich Pettit
Dick Pettway
Aaron Phillips
Hugo Phillips
Michael Phillips
H. R. Pickett
John Pinkerton
Gerald Pogue
Eugene Poindexter
R. Potter
Franklin Potts
R. Powell
Dianna Preece
Chris Prestopino
John Primus
Jerry Prock
Howard Puckett
Herbert Quigley
George Racette
Bob Radcliffe
David Rakowski
Narendar V. Rao
Allen Rappaport
Charles R. Rayhorn
Bill Rentz
Thomas Rhee
Ken Riener
Charles Rini
John Ritchie
Bill Rives
Pietra Rivoli
Antonio Rodriguez
James Rosenfeld
Stuart Rosenstein
E. N. Roussakis
Dexter Rowell
Saurav Roychoudhury
John Rozycki
Arlyn R. Rubash
Marjorie Rubash
Bob Ryan
Jim Sachlis
Abdul Sadik
Travis Sapp
Salil Sarkar
Thomas Scampini
Kevin Scanlon
Frederick Schadeler
Patricia L. Schaeff
David Schalow
Mary Jane Scheuer
David Schirm
Harold Schleef
Tom Schmidt
Oliver Schnusenberg
Robert Schwebach
Carol Schweser
John Settle
Alan Severn
James Sfiridis
Sol Shalit
Eliot H. Sherman
Frederic Shipley
Dilip Shome
Ron Shrieves
Neil Sicherman
J. B. Silvers
Sudhir Singh
Clay Singleton
Amit Sinha
Joe Sinkey
Stacy Sirmans
Greg Smersh
Jaye Smith
Patricia Smith
Patricia Matisz Smith
Dean S. Sommers
Don Sorensen
David Speairs
Michal Spivey
Ken Stanley
Kenneth Stanton
Ed Stendardi
Alan Stephens
Don Stevens
Glenn L. Stevens
Jerry Stevens
Lowell E. Stockstill
Glen Strasburg

David Suk
Katherine Sullivan
Kathie Sullivan
Timothy G. Sullivan
Philip Swensen
Bruce Swenson
Ernest Swift
Paul Swink
Eugene Swinnerton
Gary Tallman
Dular Talukdar
Dennis Tanner
T. Craig Tapley
Russ Taussig
John Teall
Richard Teweles
Ted Teweles
Madeline Thimmes
Samantha Thapa
Francis D. Thomas
Andrew Thompson
John Thompson
Thomas H. Thompson
Arlene Thurman
Dogan Tirtirogu
Janet Todd
Holland J. Toles
William Tozer
Emery Trahan
George Trivoli
Eric Tsai
George Tsetsekos
David Tufte
David Upton
Lloyd Valentine
Howard Van Auken
Pretorious Van den Dool
Pieter Vandenberg
Paul Vanderheiden
David O. Vang
JoAnn Vaughan
Jim Verbrugge
Patrick Vincent
Steve Vinson
Susan Visscher
John Wachowicz
Joe Walker
John Walker
Mike Walker
Elizabeth J. Wark
Sam Weaver
Marsha Weber
Al Webster
Shelton Weeks
Kuo-Chiang Wei
Bill Welch
Fred Weston
Richard Whiston
Jeffrey Whitworth
Norm Williams
Frank Winfrey
Tony Wingler
Ed Wolfe
Criss Woodruff
Don Woods
Yangru Wu
Robert Wyatt
Steve Wyatt
Sheng Yang
Elizabeth Yobaccio
Michael Yonan
David Zalewski
John Zietlow
Dennis Zocco
Sijing Zong
Kent Zumwalt

Special thanks are due to Shirley Love, Idaho State University, who wrote some chapter boxes relating to small-business issues; to Emery Trahan and Paul Bolster, Northeastern University, for their contributions; to Dilip Shome, Virginia Polytechnic Institute, who helped greatly with the capital structure chapter; to Dave Brown and Mike Ryngaert, University of Florida, who helped us with the bankruptcy material; to Roy Crum, Andy Naranjo, and Subu Venkataraman, who worked with us on the international materials; to Mike Ryngaert who helped us with the new tax material; to Scott Below, East Carolina University, who developed the website information and references; to Laurie and Stan Eakins of East Carolina, who developed the Excel tutorial materials on the website; to Larry Wolken, Texas A&M University, who offered his hard work and advice for the development of the Lecture Presentation Software; to Burhan Kawosa, Wright State University, who created many of the Problem Walk-Through videos; and to Christopher Buzzard who helped us develop the Excel models, the website, and the PowerPoint presentations. Finally, we also want to acknowledge the contributions of the late Chris Barry, who wrote some of the chapter boxes in earlier editions.

Finally, the Cengage Learning staff, especially Joe Sabatino, Chris Valentine, Brittany Waitt, Chris Walz, Mark Hopkinson, Sean Messer, and Renee Schnee, helped greatly with all phases of the book's development and production.

Errors in the Textbook

At this point, most authors make a statement such as this: "We appreciate all the help we received from the people listed above; but any remaining errors are, of course, our own responsibility." And generally there are more than enough remaining errors! Having experienced difficulties with errors ourselves, both as students and instructors, we resolved to avoid this problem in *Concise*. As a result of our detection procedures, we are convinced that few errors remain, but primarily because we want to detect any errors that may have slipped by so that we can correct them in subsequent printings, we decided to offer a reward of $10 to the first person who reports an error in the printed textbook or the corresponding e-book. For the purpose of this reward, errors are defined as misspelled words, nonrounding numerical errors, incorrect statements, and any other error that inhibits comprehension. Typesetting problems such as irregular spacing and differences of opinion regarding grammatical or punctuation conventions do not qualify for this reward. Given the ever changing nature of the World Wide Web, changes in web addresses also do not qualify as errors, although we would like to learn about them. Finally, any qualifying error that has follow-through effects is counted as two errors only. Please report any errors to Joel Houston through e-mail at bhconcise@gmail.com or by regular mail at the address at the end of the Preface.

Conclusion

Finance is, in a real sense, the cornerstone of the enterprise system—good financial management is vitally important to the economic health of all firms and hence to the nation and the world. Because of its importance, finance should be widely and thoroughly understood, but this is easier said than done. The field is complex, and it undergoes constant change due to shifts in economic conditions. All of this makes finance stimulating and exciting, but challenging and sometimes perplexing. We sincerely hope that this Tenth Edition of *Concise* will meet its own challenge by contributing to a better understanding of our financial system.

EUGENE F. BRIGHAM
JOEL F. HOUSTON
Warrington College of Business
University of Florida
P.O. Box 117168
Gainesville, FL 32611-7168

bhconcise@gmail.com

November 2018

About the Authors

Eugene F. Brigham University of Florida

Dr. Eugene F. Brigham is Graduate Research Professor Emeritus at the University of Florida, where he has taught since 1971. Dr. Brigham received his MBA and PhD from the University of California–Berkeley and his undergraduate degree from the University of North Carolina. Prior to joining the University of Florida, Dr. Brigham held teaching positions at the University of Connecticut, the University of Wisconsin, and the University of California–Los Angeles. Dr. Brigham has served as president of the Financial Management Association and has written many journal articles on the cost of capital, capital structure, and other aspects of financial management. He has authored or coauthored 10 textbooks on managerial finance and managerial economics that are used at more than 1,000 universities in the United States and have been translated into 11 languages worldwide. He has testified as an expert witness in numerous electric, gas, and telephone rate cases at both federal and state levels. He has served as a consultant to many corporations and government agencies, including the Federal Reserve Board, the Federal Home Loan Bank Board, the U.S. Office of Telecommunications Policy, and the RAND Corporation. He spends his spare time on the golf course, enjoying time with his family and dogs, and tackling outdoor adventure activities, such as biking through Alaska.

Joel F. Houston University of Florida

Joel F. Houston holds the Eugene F. Brigham Chair in Finance at the University of Florida. He received his MA and PhD from the Wharton School at the University of Pennsylvania, and his undergraduate degree from Franklin and Marshall College. Prior to his appointment at the University of Florida, Dr. Houston was an economist at the Federal Reserve Bank of Philadelphia. His research is primarily in the areas of corporate finance and financial institutions, and his work has been published in a number of top journals including the *Journal of Finance, Journal of Financial Economics, Journal of Business, Journal of Financial and Quantitative Analysis,* and *Financial Management*. Professor Houston also currently serves as an associate editor for the *Journal of Money, Credit and Banking, Journal of Financial Services Research,* and *Journal of Financial Economic Policy*. Since arriving at the University of Florida in 1987, he has received 20 teaching awards and has been actively involved in both undergraduate and graduate education. In addition to coauthoring leading textbooks in financial management, Dr. Houston has participated in management education programs for the PURC/World Bank Program, Southern Company, Exelon Corporation, and Volume Services America. He enjoys playing golf, working out, and spending time with his wife (Sherry), two children (Chris and Meredith), daughter-in-law (Renae), and grandson (Teddy). He is an avid sports fan who follows the Florida Gators and the Pittsburgh Steelers, Pirates, and Penguins.

part 1

Introduction to Financial Management

CHAPTERS

An Overview of Financial Management

CHAPTER 1

Philip Lange/Shutterstock.com

Striking the Right Balance

In 1776, Adam Smith described how an "invisible hand" guides companies as they strive for profits, and that hand leads them to decisions that benefit society. Smith's insights led him to conclude that profit maximization is the right goal for a business and that the free enterprise system is best for society. But the world has changed since 1776. Firms today are much larger, they operate globally, they have thousands of employees, and they are owned by millions of stockholders. This makes us wonder if the "invisible hand" still provides reliable guidance: Should companies still try to maximize profits, or should they take a broader view and more balanced actions designed to benefit customers, employees, suppliers, and society as a whole?

Many academics and finance professionals today subscribe to the following modified version of Adam Smith's theory:

- A firm's principal financial goal should be to maximize the wealth of its stockholders, which means maximizing the value of its stock.
- Free enterprise is still the best economic system for society as a whole. Under the free enterprise framework, companies develop products and services that people want and that benefit society.
- However, some constraints are needed—firms should not be allowed to pollute the air and water, to engage in unfair employment practices, or to create monopolies that exploit consumers.

These constraints take a number of different forms. The first set of constraints is the costs that are assessed on companies if they take actions that harm society. Another set of constraints arises through the political process, where society imposes a wide range of regulations that are designed to keep companies from engaging in practices that are harmful to society. Properly imposed, these costs fairly transfer value to suffering parties and help create incentives that help prevent similar events from occurring in the future.

The financial crisis in 2007 and 2008 dramatically illustrates these points. We witnessed many Wall Street firms engaging in extremely risky activities that pushed the financial system to the brink of collapse. Saving the financial system required a bailout of the banks and other financial companies, and that bailout imposed huge costs on taxpayers and helped push the economy into a deep recession. Apart from the huge costs imposed on society, the financial firms also paid a heavy price—a number of leading financial institutions saw a huge drop in their stock price, some failed and went out of business, and many Wall Street executives lost their jobs.

Arguably, these costs are not enough to prevent another financial crisis from occurring. Many maintain that the events surrounding the financial crisis illustrate that markets don't always work the way they should and that there is a need for stronger regulation of the financial sector. For example, in his recent books, Nobel Laureate Joseph Stiglitz makes a strong case for enhanced regulation. At the same time, others with a different political persuasion continue to express concerns about the costs of excessive regulation.

Beyond the financial crisis, there is a broader question of whether laws and regulations are enough to compel firms to act in society's interest. An increasing number of companies continue to recognize the need to maximize shareholder value, but they also see their mission as more than just making money for shareholders. Google's parent company Alphabet's motto is "Do the right thing—follow the law, act honorably, and treat each other with respect." Consistent with this mission, the company has its own in-house foundation that each year makes large investments in a wide range of philanthropic ventures worldwide.

Microsoft is another good example of a company that has earned a well-developed reputation for taking steps to be socially responsible. On its corporate blog, the company recently released its 2017 Corporate Social Responsibility Report. In this report, Microsoft highlighted its broader mission:

> We continue to be guided by our mission to **empower every person and every organization on the planet to achieve more**. The breadth and depth of our mission unlock unprecedented opportunity as technology transforms every industry and has the power to make a difference in the lives of everyone. We strive to create local opportunity, growth and impact in every community and country around the world. Our platforms and tools enable creativity in all of us, and help drive small-business productivity, large business competitiveness and public-sector efficiency. They also support new startups, improve educational and health outcomes, and empower human ingenuity. Our sense of purpose lies in our customers' success.

The report goes on to say:

> Our mission to empower every person and every organization on the planet extends to our corporate social responsibility efforts. We strive to use our technology, grants, employees and voice to improve people's lives by enabling access to the benefits and opportunities that technology offers.

For nearly the past two decades, Microsoft's co-founder Bill Gates and his wife, Melinda Gates, have also dedicated the bulk of their time, money, and energy to the Bill & Melinda Gates Foundation, which has made notable investments aimed at attacking some of society's toughest problems on a global level. In its 2016 annual report, the Foundation reports an endowment of over $40 billion and indicates that it had made $41.3 billion in grant payments through the end of 2016. The Foundation has also attracted a well-known benefactor in Warren Buffett, who announced in 2006 that he was going to give a significant portion of his fortune to the Gates Foundation. To date, Buffett has already contributed more than $19 billion, and he has pledged considerably more over time.

While many companies and individuals have taken very significant steps to demonstrate their commitments to being socially responsible, corporate managers frequently face a tough balancing act. Realistically, there will still be cases where companies face conflicts between their various constituencies—for example, a company may enhance shareholder value by laying off some workers, or a change in policy may improve the environment but reduce shareholder value. We also have seen recent examples where leading tech companies such as Facebook and Google have come under fire for their handling of their users' private information. In each of these instances, managers have to balance these competing interests and different managers will clearly make different choices. At the end of the day, all companies struggle to find the right balance. Enlightened managers recognize that there is more to life than money, but it often takes money to do good things.

Sources: Kevin J. Delaney, "Google: From 'Don't Be Evil' to How to Do Good," *The Wall Street Journal*, January 18, 2008, pp. B1–B2; Joseph E. Stiglitz, *FreeFall: America, Free Markets, and the Sinking of the World Economy* (New York: W.W. Norton, 2010); Joseph E. Stiglitz, *The Price of Inequality* (New York: W.W. Norton, 2012); "Microsoft 2017 Corporate Social Responsibility Report," www.microsoft.com/en-us/about/corporate-responsibility/reports-hub, October 16, 2017; and "Gates Foundation Fact Sheet," www.gatesfoundation.org/Who-We-Are/General-Information/Foundation-Factsheet.

PUTTING THINGS IN PERSPECTIVE

This chapter will give you an idea of what financial management is all about. We begin the chapter by describing how finance is related to the overall business environment, by pointing out that finance prepares students for jobs in different fields of business, and by discussing the different forms of business organization. For corporations, management's goal should be to maximize shareholder wealth, which means maximizing the value of the stock. When we say "maximizing the value of the stock," we mean the "true, long-run value," which may be different from the current stock price. In the chapter, we discuss how firms must provide the right incentives for managers to focus on long-run value maximization. Good managers understand the importance of ethics, and they recognize that maximizing long-run value is consistent with being socially responsible.

When you finish this chapter, you should be able to do the following:

- **Explain the role of finance and the different types of jobs in finance.**
- **Identify the advantages and disadvantages of different forms of business organization.**
- **Explain the links between stock price, intrinsic value, and executive compensation.**
- **Identify the potential conflicts that arise within the firm between stockholders and managers and between stockholders and bondholders, and discuss the techniques that firms can use to mitigate these potential conflicts.**
- **Discuss the importance of business ethics and the consequences of unethical behavior.**

1-1 What Is Finance?

Finance is defined by *Webster's Dictionary* as "the system that includes the circulation of money, the granting of credit, the making of investments, and the provision of banking facilities." Finance has many facets, which makes it difficult to provide one concise definition. The discussion in this section will give you an idea of what finance professionals do and what you might do if you enter the finance field after you graduate.

1-1A AREAS OF FINANCE

Finance as taught in universities is generally divided into three areas: (1) financial management, (2) capital markets, and (3) investments.

Financial management, also called corporate finance, focuses on decisions relating to how much and what types of assets to acquire, how to raise the capital needed to purchase assets, and how to run the firm so as to maximize its value. The same principles apply to both for-profit and not-for-profit organizations, and as the title suggests, much of this book is concerned with financial management.

Capital markets relate to the markets where interest rates, along with stock and bond prices, are determined. Also studied here are the financial institutions that supply capital to businesses. Banks, investment banks, stockbrokers, mutual funds, insurance companies, and the like bring together "savers" who have money to invest and businesses, individuals, and other entities that need capital for various purposes. Governmental organizations such as the Federal Reserve System, which regulates banks and controls the supply of money, and the Securities and Exchange Commission (SEC), which regulates the trading of stocks and bonds in public markets, are also studied as part of capital markets.

Investments relate to decisions concerning stocks and bonds and include a number of activities: (1) *Security analysis* deals with finding the proper values of individual securities (i.e., stocks and bonds). (2) *Portfolio theory* deals with the best way to structure portfolios, or "baskets," of stocks and bonds. Rational investors want to hold diversified portfolios in order to limit risks, so choosing a properly balanced portfolio is an important issue for any investor. (3) *Market analysis* deals with the issue of whether stock and bond markets at any given time are "too high," "too low," or "about right." Included in market analysis is *behavioral finance,* where investor psychology is examined in an effort to determine whether stock prices have been bid up to unreasonable heights in a speculative bubble or driven down to unreasonable lows in a fit of irrational pessimism.

Although we separate these three areas, they are closely interconnected. Banking is studied under capital markets, but a bank lending officer evaluating a business' loan request must understand corporate finance to make a sound decision. Similarly, a corporate treasurer negotiating with a banker must understand banking if the treasurer is to borrow on "reasonable" terms. Moreover, a security analyst trying to determine a stock's true value must understand corporate finance and capital markets to do his or her job. In addition, financial decisions of all types depend on the level of interest rates; so all people in corporate finance, investments, and banking must know something about interest rates and the way they are determined. Because of these interdependencies, we cover all three areas in this book.

1-1B FINANCE WITHIN AN ORGANIZATION

Most businesses and not-for-profit organizations have an organization chart similar to the one shown in Figure 1.1. The board of directors is the top governing body, and the chairperson of the board is generally the highest-ranking individual. The chief executive officer (CEO) comes next, but note that the chairperson of the board often also serves as the CEO. Below the CEO comes the chief operating officer (COO), who is often also designated as a firm's president. The COO directs the firm's operations, which include marketing, manufacturing, sales, and other operating departments. The chief financial officer (CFO), who is generally a senior vice president and the third-ranking officer, is in charge of accounting, finance, credit policy, decisions regarding asset acquisitions, and investor relations, which involves communications with stockholders and the press.

The duties of the CFO have broadened over the years. CFO magazine's online service, ***ww2.cfo.com****, is an excellent source of timely finance articles intended to help the CFO manage those new responsibilities.*

If the firm is publicly owned, the CEO and the CFO must both certify to the SEC that reports released to stockholders, and especially the annual report, are accurate. If inaccuracies later emerge, the CEO and the CFO could be fined or even jailed. This requirement was instituted in 2002 as a part of the **Sarbanes-Oxley Act**. The act was passed by Congress in the wake of a series of corporate scandals involving now-defunct companies such as Enron and WorldCom, where investors, workers, and suppliers lost billions of dollars due to false information released by those companies.

Sarbanes-Oxley Act
A law passed by Congress that requires the CEO and CFO to certify that their firm's financial statements are accurate.

1-1C FINANCE VERSUS ECONOMICS AND ACCOUNTING

Finance, as we know it today, grew out of economics and accounting. Economists developed the notion that an asset's value is based on the future cash flows the asset will provide, and accountants provided information regarding the likely size of those cash flows. People who work in finance need knowledge of both economics and accounting. Figure 1.1 illustrates that in the modern corporation, the accounting department typically falls under the control of the CFO. This further illustrates the link among finance, economics, and accounting.

FIGURE 1.1 Finance within the Organization

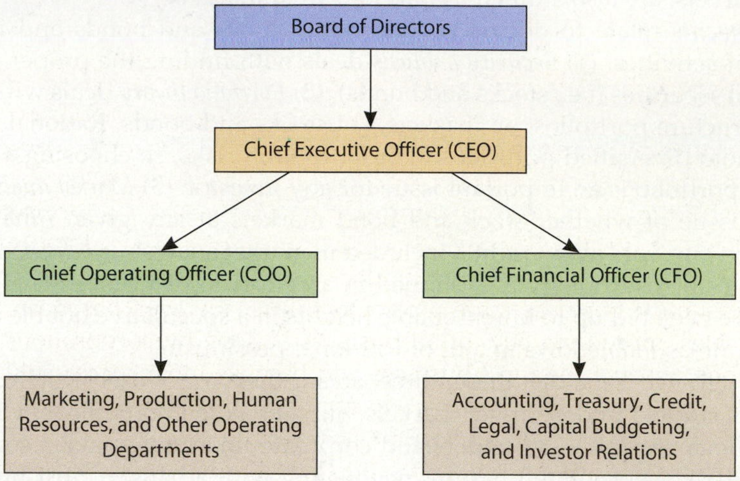

Self*Test*

What three areas of finance does this book cover? Are these areas independent of one another, or are they interrelated in the sense that someone working in one area should know something about each of the other areas? Explain.

Who is the CFO, and where does this individual fit into the corporate hierarchy? What are some of his or her responsibilities?

Does it make sense for not-for-profit organizations such as hospitals and universities to have CFOs? Why or why not?

What is the relationship among economics, finance, and accounting?

1-2 Jobs in Finance

To find information about different finance careers, go to ***allbusinessschools.com/business-careers/finance/job-description****. This website provides information about different finance areas.*

Finance prepares students for jobs in banking, investments, insurance, corporations, and government. Accounting students need to know marketing, management, and human resources; they also need to understand finance, for it affects decisions in all those areas. For example, marketing people propose advertising programs, but those programs are examined by finance people to judge the effects of the advertising on the firm's profitability. So to be effective in marketing, one needs to have a basic knowledge of finance. The same holds for management—indeed, most important management decisions are evaluated in terms of their effects on the firm's value.

It is also worth noting that finance is important to individuals regardless of their jobs. Some years ago most employees received pensions from their employers upon retirement, so managing one's personal investments was not critically important. That's no longer true. Most firms today provide "defined contribution" pension plans, where each year the company puts a specified amount of money into an account that belongs to the employee. The employee must decide how those funds are to be invested—how much should be divided among stocks, bonds, or money funds—and how much risk they're willing to take with their stock and bond investments. These decisions have a major effect on people's lives, and the concepts covered in this book can improve decision-making skills.

***efinancialcareers.com** provides finance career news and advice including information on who's hiring in finance and accounting fields.*

1-3 Forms of Business Organization

The basics of financial management are the same for all businesses, large or small, regardless of how they are organized. Still, a firm's legal structure affects its operations and thus should be recognized. There are four main forms of business organizations: (1) proprietorships, (2) partnerships, (3) corporations, and (4) limited liability companies (LLCs) and limited liability partnerships (LLPs). In terms of numbers, most businesses are proprietorships. However, based on the dollar value of sales, more than 80% of all business is done by corporations.[1] Because corporations conduct the most business and because most successful businesses eventually convert to corporations, we focus on them in this book. Still, it is important to understand the legal differences between types of firms.

Proprietorship
An unincorporated business owned by one individual.

A **proprietorship** is an unincorporated business owned by one individual. Going into business as a sole proprietor is easy—a person begins business operations. Proprietorships have three important advantages: (1) They are easy and inexpensive to form. (2) They are subject to few government regulations. (3) They are subject to lower income taxes than are corporations. However, proprietorships also have three important limitations: (1) Proprietors have unlimited personal liability for the business' debts, so they can lose more than the amount of money they invested in the company. You might invest $10,000 to start a business but be sued for $1 million if, during company time, one of your employees runs over someone with a car. (2) The life of the business is limited to the life of the individual who created it, and to bring in new equity, investors require a change in the structure of the business. (3) Because of the first two points, proprietorships have difficulty obtaining large sums of capital; hence, proprietorships are used primarily for small businesses. However, businesses are frequently started as proprietorships and then converted to corporations when their growth results in the disadvantages outweighing the advantages.

Partnership
An unincorporated business owned by two or more persons.

A **partnership** is a legal arrangement between two or more people who decide to do business together. Partnerships are similar to proprietorships in that they can be established relatively easily and inexpensively. Moreover, the firm's income is allocated on a pro rata basis to the partners and is taxed on an individual basis. This allows the firm to avoid the corporate income tax. However, all of the partners are generally subject to unlimited personal liability, which means that if a partnership goes bankrupt and any partner is unable to meet his or her pro rata share of the firm's liabilities, the remaining partners will be responsible for making good on the unsatisfied claims. Thus, the actions of a Texas partner can bring ruin to a millionaire New York partner who had nothing to do with the actions that led to the downfall of the company. Unlimited liability makes it difficult for partnerships to raise large amounts of capital.[2]

---

[1]Refer to *ProQuest Statistical Abstract of the United States: 2017 Online Edition*, Table 768: Number of Tax Returns, Receipts, and Net Income by Type of Business: 1990 to 2013.

[2]Originally, there were just straightforward partnerships, but over the years lawyers have created a number of variations. We leave the variations to courses on business law, but we note that the variations are generally designed to limit the liabilities of some of the partners. For example, a *limited partnership* has a general partner, who has unlimited liability, and one or more limited partners, whose liability is limited to the amount of their investment. This sounds great from the standpoint of limited liability, but the limited partners must cede sole control to the general partner, which means that they have almost no say in the way the firm is managed. With a corporation, the owners (stockholders) have limited liability, but they also have the right to vote and thus change management if they think that a change is in order. Note too that LLCs and LLPs, discussed later in this section, are increasingly used in lieu of partnerships.

Corporation
A legal entity created by a state, separate and distinct from its owners and managers, having unlimited life, easy transferability of ownership, and limited liability.

A **corporation** is a legal entity created by a state, and it is separate and distinct from its owners and managers. It is this separation that limits stockholders' losses to the amount they invested in the firm—the corporation can lose all of its money, but its owners can lose only the funds that they invested in the company. Corporations also have unlimited lives, and it is easier to transfer shares of stock in a corporation than one's interest in an unincorporated business. These factors make it much easier for corporations to raise the capital necessary to operate large businesses. Thus, companies such as Hewlett-Packard and Microsoft generally begin as proprietorships or partnerships, but at some point they find it advantageous to become a corporation.

S Corporations
A special designation that allows small businesses that meet qualifications to be taxed as if they were a proprietorship or a partnership rather than a corporation.

A major drawback to corporations is taxes. Most corporations' earnings are subject to double taxation—the corporation's earnings are taxed, and then when its after-tax earnings are paid out as dividends, those earnings are taxed again as personal income to the stockholders. However, as an aid to small businesses, Congress created **S corporations**, which are taxed as if they were proprietorships or partnerships; thus, they are exempt from the corporate income tax.[3] To qualify for S corporation status, a firm can have no more than 100 stockholders, which limits their use to relatively small, privately owned firms. Larger corporations are known as *C corporations*. The vast majority of small corporations elect S status and retain that status until they decide to sell stock to the public, at which time they become C corporations.

Limited Liability Company (LLC)
A popular type of organization that is a hybrid between a partnership and a corporation.

Limited Liability Partnership (LLP)
Similar to an LLC but used for professional firms in the fields of accounting, law, and architecture. It provides personal asset protection from business debts and liabilities but is taxed as a partnership.

A **limited liability company (LLC)** is a popular type of organization that is a hybrid between a partnership and a corporation. A **limited liability partnership (LLP)** is similar to an LLC. LLPs are used for professional firms in the fields of accounting, law, and architecture, while LLCs are used by other businesses. Similar to corporations, LLCs and LLPs provide limited liability protection, but they are taxed as partnerships. Further, unlike limited partnerships, where the general partner has full control of the business, the investors in an LLC or LLP have votes in proportion to their ownership interest. LLCs and LLPs have been gaining in popularity in recent years, but large companies still find it advantageous to be C corporations because of the advantages in raising capital to support growth. LLCs/LLPs were dreamed up by lawyers; they are often structured in very complicated ways, and their legal protections often vary by state. So, it is necessary to hire a good lawyer when establishing one.

When deciding on its form of organization, a firm must trade off the advantages of incorporation against double taxation. However, for the following reasons, the value of any business other than a relatively small one will probably be maximized if it is organized as a corporation:

1. Limited liability reduces the risks borne by investors, and, other things held constant, the lower the firm's risk, the higher its value.
2. A firm's value is dependent on its growth opportunities, which are dependent on its ability to attract capital. Because corporations can attract capital more easily than other types of businesses, they are better able to take advantage of growth opportunities.

---

[3]Under the new tax law and until January 1, 2026, pass-through entities (S corporations, partnerships, and proprietorships) can deduct 20% of their qualified business income (QBI), which is the net amount of income, gain, deduction, and loss with respect to the trade or business. QBI doesn't include investment-related income or loss. This deduction phases out beginning at $157,500 of income for single taxpayers and $315,000 for couples filing jointly. While the lowered tax rate from 35% to 21% for C corporations is attractive, double taxation remains an issue for them. So, if the bulk of the profits will be taken out of the business and distributed to owners rather than being reinvested in the business, a pass-through entity will be preferable. S corporations are still advantageous in many situations. For more details, refer to Nellie Akalp, "How the New Tax Law Will Affect Your Clients' S Corporations," *Accounting Today* (www.accountingtoday.com), February 6, 2018.

3. The value of an asset also depends on its liquidity, which means the time and effort it takes to sell the asset for cash at a fair market value. Because the stock of a corporation is easier to transfer to a potential buyer than is an interest in a proprietorship or partnership, and because more investors are willing to invest in stocks than in partnerships (with their potential unlimited liability), a corporate investment is relatively liquid. This too enhances the value of a corporation.

Self*Test*

What are the key differences among proprietorships, partnerships, and corporations?

How are LLCs and LLPs related to the other forms of organization?

What is an S corporation, and what is its advantage over a C corporation? Why don't firms such as IBM, GE, and Microsoft choose S corporation status?

What are some reasons why the value of a business other than a small one is generally maximized when it is organized as a corporation?

1-4 The Main Financial Goal: Creating Value for Investors

In public corporations, managers and employees work on behalf of the shareholders who own the business, and therefore they have an obligation to pursue policies that promote stockholder value. While many companies focus on maximizing a broad range of financial objectives, such as growth, earnings per share, and market share, these goals should not take precedence over the main financial goal, which is to create value for investors. Keep in mind that a company's stockholders are not just an abstract group—they represent individuals and organizations who have chosen to invest their hard-earned cash into the company and who are looking for a return on their investment in order to meet their long-term financial goals, which might be saving for retirement, a new home, or a child's education. In addition to financial goals, the firm also has nonfinancial goals, which we will discuss in Section 1-7.

If a manager is to maximize stockholder wealth, he or she must know how that wealth is determined. Throughout this book, we shall see that the value of any asset is the present value of the stream of cash flows that the asset provides to its owners over time. We discuss stock valuation in depth in Chapter 9, where we see that stock prices are based on cash flows expected in future years, not just in the current year. Thus, stock price maximization requires us to take a long-run view of operations. At the same time, managerial actions that affect a company's value may not immediately be reflected in the company's stock price.

1-4A DETERMINANTS OF VALUE

Figure 1.2 illustrates the situation. The top box indicates that managerial actions, combined with the economy, taxes, and political conditions, influence the level and riskiness of the company's future cash flows, which ultimately determine the company's stock price. As you might expect, investors like higher expected cash flows, but they dislike risk; so the larger the expected cash flows and the lower the perceived risk, the higher the stock's price.

FIGURE 1.2 Determinants of Intrinsic Values and Stock Prices

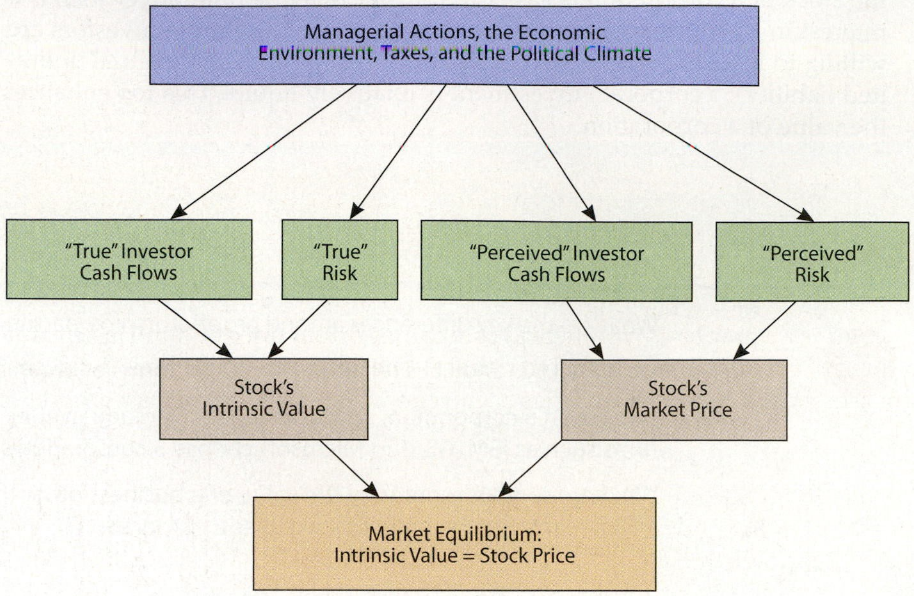

Intrinsic Value
An estimate of a stock's "true" value based on accurate risk and return data. The intrinsic value can be estimated, but not measured precisely.

Market Price
The stock value based on perceived but possibly incorrect information as seen by the marginal investor.

Marginal Investor
An investor whose views determine the actual stock price.

Equilibrium
The situation in which the actual market price equals the intrinsic value, so investors are indifferent between buying and selling a stock.

The second row of boxes differentiates what we call "true" expected cash flows and "true" risk from "perceived" cash flows and "perceived" risk. By "true," we mean the cash flows and risk that investors would expect if they had all of the information that existed about a company. "Perceived" means what investors expect, given the limited information they have. To illustrate, in early 2001, investors had information that caused them to think Enron was highly profitable and would enjoy high and rising future profits. They also thought that actual results would be close to the expected levels and hence that Enron's risk was low. However, true estimates of Enron's profits, which were known by its executives, but not the investing public, were much lower; Enron's true situation was extremely risky.

The third row of boxes shows that each stock has an **intrinsic value**, which is an estimate of the stock's "true" value as calculated by a competent analyst who has the best available data, and a **market price**, which is the actual market price based on perceived but possibly incorrect information as seen by the **marginal investor**.[4] Not all investors agree, so it is the "marginal" investor who determines the actual price.

When a stock's actual market price is equal to its intrinsic value, the stock is in **equilibrium**, which is shown in the bottom box in Figure 1.2. When equilibrium exists, there is no pressure for a change in the stock's price. Market prices can—and do—differ from intrinsic values; eventually, however, as the future unfolds, the two values tend to converge.

[4]Investors at the margin are the ones who actually set stock prices. Some stockholders think that a stock at its current price is a good deal, and they would buy more if they had more money. Others think that the stock is priced too high, so they would not buy it unless the price dropped sharply. Still others think that the current stock price is about where it should be; so they would buy more if the price fell slightly, sell it if the price rose slightly, and maintain their current holdings unless something were to change. These are the marginal investors, and it is their view that determines the current stock price. We discuss this point in more depth in Chapter 9, where we discuss the stock market in detail.

1-4B INTRINSIC VALUE

Actual stock prices are easy to determine—they can be found on the Internet and are published in newspapers every day. However, intrinsic values are estimates, and different analysts with different data and different views about the future form different estimates of a stock's intrinsic value. *Indeed, estimating intrinsic values is what security analysis is all about and is what distinguishes successful from unsuccessful investors.* Investing would be easy, profitable, and essentially riskless if we knew all stocks' intrinsic values—but, of course, we don't. We can estimate intrinsic values, but we can't be sure that we are right. A firm's managers have the best information about the firm's future prospects, so managers' estimates of intrinsic values are generally better than those of outside investors. However, even managers can be wrong.

Figure 1.3 graphs a hypothetical company's actual price and intrinsic value as estimated by its management over time.[5] The intrinsic value rises because the firm retains and reinvests earnings each year, which tends to increase profits. The value jumped dramatically in Year 20, when a research and development (R&D) breakthrough raised management's estimate of future profits before investors had this information. The actual stock price tended to move up and down with the estimated intrinsic value, but investor optimism and pessimism, along with imperfect knowledge about the true intrinsic value, led to deviations between the actual prices and intrinsic values.

Intrinsic value is a long-run concept. *Management's goal should be to take actions designed to maximize the firm's intrinsic value, not its current market price.*

FIGURE 1.3 Graph of Actual Prices versus Intrinsic Values

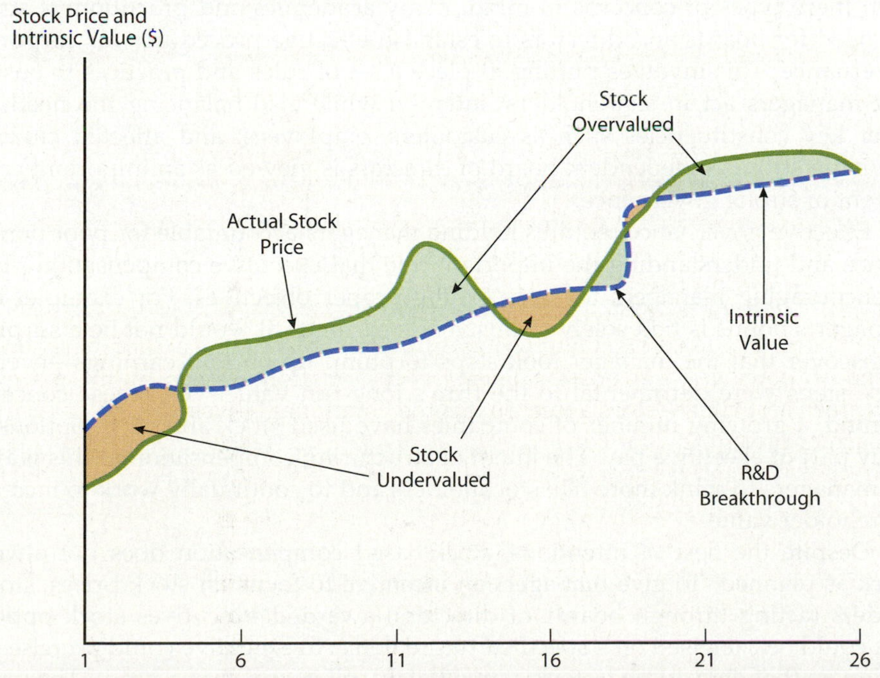

[5]We emphasize that the intrinsic value is an estimate and that different analysts have different estimates for a company at any given time. Managers should also estimate their firm's intrinsic value and then take actions to maximize that value. They should try to help outside security analysts improve their intrinsic value estimates by providing accurate information about the company's financial position and operations, but without releasing information that would help its competitors.

Note, though, that maximizing the intrinsic value will maximize the *average* price over the long run, but not necessarily the current price at each point in time. For example, management might make an investment that lowers profits for the current year but raises expected future profits. If investors are not aware of the true situation, the stock price will be held down by the low current profit even though the intrinsic value was actually raised. Management should provide information that helps investors make better estimates of the firm's intrinsic value, which will keep the stock price closer to its equilibrium level. However, there are times when management cannot divulge the true situation because doing so would provide information that helps its competitors.[6]

1-4C CONSEQUENCES OF HAVING A SHORT-RUN FOCUS

Ideally, managers adhere to this long-run focus, but there are numerous examples in recent years where the focus for many companies shifted to the short run. Perhaps most notably, prior to the recent financial crisis, many Wall Street executives received huge bonuses for engaging in risky transactions that generated short-term profits. Subsequently, the value of these transactions collapsed, causing many of these Wall Street firms to seek a massive government bailout.

Apart from the recent problems on Wall Street, there have been other examples where managers have focused on short-run profits to the detriment of long-term value. For example, Wells Fargo implemented incentives to reward employees for signing up customers to new accounts. Unfortunately, to obtain bonuses some employees created fake accounts or signed up customers for unauthorized credit cards. This led to the firing of thousands of employees, as well as its CEO and other senior managers, and millions of dollars in fines for Wells Fargo. In addition, the Fed has limited Wells Fargo's growth so total assets are no greater than the year end 2017 total until the bank repairs its culture and cleans up its act. With these types of concerns in mind, many academics and practitioners stress the need for boards and directors to establish effective procedures for **corporate governance**. This involves putting in place a set of rules and practices to ensure that managers act in shareholders' interests while also balancing the needs of other key constituencies such as customers, employees, and affected citizens. Having a strong, independent board of directors is viewed as an important component of strong governance.

Corporate Governance
Establishment of rules and practices by Board of Directors to ensure that managers act in shareholders' interests while balancing the needs of other key constituencies.

Effective governance requires holding managers accountable for poor performance and understanding the important role that executive compensation plays in encouraging managers to focus on the proper objectives. For example, if a manager's bonus is tied solely to this year's earnings, it would not be a surprise to discover that the manager took steps to pump up current earnings—even if those steps were detrimental to the firm's long-run value. With these concerns in mind, a growing number of companies have used stock and stock options as a key part of executive pay. The intent of structuring compensation in this way is for managers to think more like stockholders and to continually work to increase shareholder value.

Despite the best of intentions, stock-based compensation does not always work as planned. To give managers an incentive to focus on stock prices, stockholders (acting through boards of directors) awarded executives stock options that could be exercised on a specified future date. An executive could exercise the option on that date, receive stock, immediately sell it, and earn a profit. The profit

[6]As we discuss in Chapter 2, many academics believe that stock prices embody all publicly available information—hence, that stock prices are typically reasonably close to their intrinsic values and thus at or close to equilibrium. However, almost no one doubts that managers have better information than the public at large, that at times stock prices and equilibrium values diverge, and thus that stocks can be temporarily undervalued or overvalued (as we suggest in Figure 1.3).

was based on the stock price on the option exercise date, which led some managers to try to maximize the stock price on that specific date, not over the long run. That, in turn, led to some horrible abuses. Projects that looked good from a long-run perspective were turned down because they would penalize profits in the short run and thus lower the stock price on the option exercise day. Even worse, some managers deliberately overstated profits, temporarily boosted the stock price, exercised their options, sold the inflated stock, and left outside stockholders "holding the bag" when the true situation was revealed.

Self*Test*

What's the difference between a stock's current market price and its intrinsic value?

Do stocks have known and "provable" intrinsic values, or might different people reach different conclusions about intrinsic values? Explain.

Should managers estimate intrinsic values or leave that to outside security analysts? Explain.

If a firm could maximize either its current market price or its intrinsic value, what would stockholders (as a group) want managers to do? Explain.

Should a firm's managers help investors improve their estimates of the firm's intrinsic value? Explain.

1-5 Stockholder–Manager Conflicts[7]

It has long been recognized that managers' personal goals may compete with shareholder wealth maximization. In particular, managers might be more interested in maximizing their own wealth than their stockholders' wealth; therefore, managers might pay themselves excessive salaries.

Effective executive compensation plans motivate managers to act in their stockholders' best interests. Useful motivational tools include (1) reasonable compensation packages, (2) firing of managers who don't perform well, and (3) the threat of hostile takeovers.

1-5A COMPENSATION PACKAGES

Compensation packages should be sufficient to attract and retain able managers, but they should not go beyond what is needed. Compensation policies need to be consistent over time. Also, compensation should be structured so that managers are rewarded on the basis of the stock's performance over the long run, not the stock's price on an option exercise date. This means that options (or direct stock awards) should be phased in over a number of years so that managers have an incentive to keep the stock price high over time. When the intrinsic value can be measured in an objective and verifiable manner, performance pay can be based on changes in intrinsic value. However, because intrinsic value is not observable, compensation must be based on the stock's market price—but the price used should be an average over time rather than on a specific date.

---

[7] Conflicts between stockholders and managers, which are discussed in this section, and conflicts between stockholders and debtholders, which are discussed in the next section, are studied under the heading of "agency theory" in finance literature. The classic work on agency theory is Michael C. Jensen and William H. Meckling, "Theory of the Firm, Managerial Behavior, Agency Costs, and Ownership Structure," *Journal of Financial Economics*, vol. 3, no. 4 (October 1976), pp. 305–360.

ARE CEOs OVERPAID?

A recent *Wall Street Journal* analysis of 133 S&P 500 companies, found that the median CEO received $11.6 million in total compensation (which includes salaries, bonuses, and long-term incentives such as stock options) in 2017. Compared to 2016, total CEO compensation for these executives rose 9.9%, reflecting strong corporate performances and stock market gains in 2017. During this same year, shareholder returns in this sample were over 19%, while the average worker's pay was up roughly 2.5%. It is interesting to note that while median CEO pay has risen, most of the gains came from stock awards, as cash compensation grew modestly and companies reduced stock option grants.

Media scrutiny and investor concerns about excessive compensation have led some companies to limit the compensation paid to their top executives. A further concern is the "Say on Pay" provisions in the 2010 Dodd-Frank Act, which give shareholders an ability to vote on whether they approve of the CEO's compensation package. While these votes are nonbinding, they have put pressure on firms who want to avoid the negative publicity surrounding a shareholder vote to reject the pay plan. Because of these provisions, a substantial part of a CEO's pay is now tied to performance. Indeed, it's interesting to note that a typical CEO pay package consists of 32% cash, 60% stock and options, 2% perks, and 6% toward pensions and other forms of deferred compensation.

Average compensation levels are significantly higher than they were a decade or two ago. The large shifts in CEO compensation over time can often be attributed to the increased importance of stock options.[8] On the plus side, stock options provide CEOs with a powerful incentive to raise their companies' stock prices. Indeed, most observers believe there is a strong causal relationship between CEO compensation procedures and stock price performance.

Other critics argue that although performance incentives are entirely appropriate as a method of compensation, the overall level of CEO compensation is just too high. The critics ask such questions as these: Would these CEOs have been unwilling to take their jobs if they had been offered only half as many stock options? Would they have put forth less effort, and would their firms' stock prices have not increased as much? It is hard to say. Other critics lament that the exercise of stock options has dramatically increased the compensation of not only truly excellent CEOs, but it has also dramatically increased the compensation of some pretty average CEOs, who were lucky enough to have had the job during a stock market boom that raised the stock prices of even poor-performing companies. In addition, huge CEO salaries are widening the gap between top executives and middle management salaries leading to employee discontent and declining employee morale and loyalty.

As the current survey indicates, the shift to better align CEO pay with corporate performance is modest. Stock returns and corporate financial results are only two factors impacting CEO pay. The correlation between executive compensation and firm performance is not always strong. Other factors that influence CEO pay are the size of the firm (larger companies pay their CEOs more) and the type of industry (energy companies pay their CEOs more).

Sources: Louis Lavelle, Frederick F. Jespersen, and Michael Arndt, "Executive Pay," *BusinessWeek*, April 15, 2002, pp. 80–86; Jason Zweig, "A Chance to Veto a CEO's Bonus," *The Wall Street Journal* (www.wsj.com), January 29, 2011; Emily Chasan, "Early Say-On-Pay Results Show Rising Support, Few Failures," *The Wall Street Journal* (www.wsj.com), April 2, 2014; and Theo Francis and Joann S. Lublin, "CEO Pay Reached New High in 2017," *The Wall Street Journal* (www.wsj.com), March 22, 2018, pp. B1, B8.

1-5B DIRECT STOCKHOLDER INTERVENTION

Years ago most stock was owned by individuals. Today, however, the majority of stock is owned by institutional investors such as insurance companies, pension funds, hedge funds, and mutual funds, and private equity groups are ready and able to step in and take over underperforming firms. These institutional money managers have the clout to exercise considerable influence over firms' operations. Given their importance, they have access to managers and

[8] Over the past few years, a small number of CEOs have attracted attention by announcing that they are only going to accept a $1 cash salary. A recent study finds that shareholders of these firms don't do particularly well, but the CEOs' total compensation doesn't suffer since they instead receive offsetting compensation in the form of stock and stock options. Refer to Gilberto R. Loureiro, Anil K. Makhija, and Dan Zhang, "The Ruse of a One-Dollar CEO Salary," Charles A. Dice Center Working Paper No. 2011-7 and Fisher College of Business Working Paper No. 2011-03-007, January 10, 2014. The paper is available at ssrn.com/abstract=1571823.

can make suggestions about how the business should be run. In effect, institutional investors such as CalPERS (California Public Employees' Retirement System, with $300 billion of assets) and TIAA-CREF (Teachers Insurance and Annuity Association-College Retirement Equities Fund, a retirement plan originally set up for professors at private colleges that now has more than $600 billion of assets) act as lobbyists for the body of stockholders. When such large stockholders speak, companies listen. For example, Coca-Cola Co. revised its compensation package after hearing negative feedback from its largest stockholder, Warren Buffett.[9]

At the same time, any shareholder who has owned $2,000 of a company's stock for 1 year can sponsor a proposal that may be voted on at the annual stockholders' meeting, even if management opposes the proposal.[10] Although shareholder-sponsored proposals are nonbinding, the results of such votes are heard by top management.

There has been an ongoing debate regarding how much influence shareholders should have through the proxy process. As a result of the passage of the Dodd-Frank Act, the SEC was given authority to make rules regarding shareholder access to company proxy materials. On August 25, 2010, the SEC adopted changes to federal proxy rules to give shareholders the right to nominate directors to a company's board. Rule 14a-11 under the 1934 SEC Act requires public companies to permit any shareholder owning at least 3% of a public company's voting stock for at least 3 years to include director nominations in the company's proxy materials.

Years ago, the probability of a large firm's management being ousted by its stockholders was so remote that it posed little threat. Most firms' shares were so widely distributed and the CEO had so much control over the voting mechanism that it was virtually impossible for dissident stockholders to get the votes needed to overthrow a management team. However, that situation has changed. In recent years, the top executives of Uber, Mattel, Citigroup, AT&T, Coca-Cola, Merrill Lynch, Fannie Mae, General Motors, Peugeot, IBM, Target, and Xerox, to name a few, were forced out due to poor corporate performance.

Relatedly, a recent article in *The Wall Street Journal* documents the growing importance of shareholder activists. It points out that in 2014, activists established a record level of influence when they were granted a board seat in 73% of the proxy fights that occurred that year. Likewise, a 2015 cover story in *The Economist* highlights the important role that activists play in ensuring that managers act in shareholders' interests—their article labels these activists as "Capitalism's Unlikely Heroes." In another high-profile example, GE became one of a small group of companies that has voluntarily made it easier for shareholders to secure a board seat. GE's new plan allows shareholder groups holding at least 3% of the company's stock to directly nominate candidates for its board.[11]

---

[9]Anupreeta Das, Mike Esterl, and Joann S. Lublin, "Buffett Pressures Coca-Cola over Executive Pay," *The Wall Street Journal* (www.wsj.com), April 30, 2014; and Mark Melin, "Coca-Cola Changes Pay Plan, Warren Buffett Influence Credited," *ValueWalk* (www.valuewalk.com), October 1, 2014.

[10]Under current guidelines, shareholder proposals are restricted to governance issues, and shareholders are not allowed to vote directly on items that are considered to be "operating issues." However, the SEC recently adopted rules (resulting from the passage of the Dodd-Frank Act) mandating an advisory vote on CEO compensation at least once every 3 years.

[11]Refer to David Benoit, "Activists Are on a Roll, with More to Come," *The Wall Street Journal* (www.wsj.com), January 1, 2015; "Capitalism's Unlikely Heroes," *The Economist* (www.economist.com), February 7, 2015; and Ted Mann and Joann S. Lublin, "GE to Allow Proxy Access for Big Investors," *The Wall Street Journal* (www.wsj.com), February 11, 2015.

1-5C MANAGERS' RESPONSE

Corporate Raiders
Individuals who target corporations for takeover because they are undervalued.

Hostile Takeover
The acquisition of a company over the opposition of its management.

If a firm's stock is undervalued, **corporate raiders** will see it as a bargain and will attempt to capture the firm in a **hostile takeover**. If the raid is successful, the target's executives will almost certainly be fired. This situation gives managers a strong incentive to take actions to maximize their stock's price. In the words of one executive, "If you want to keep your job, never let your stock become a bargain."

Note that the price managers should be trying to maximize is not the price on a specific day. Rather, it is the average price over the long run, which will be maximized if management focuses on the stock's intrinsic value. However, managers must communicate effectively with stockholders (without divulging information that would aid their competitors) to keep the actual price close to the intrinsic value. It's bad for stockholders and managers when the intrinsic value is high but the actual price is low. In that situation, a raider may swoop in, buy the company at a bargain price, and fire the managers. To repeat our earlier message:

> *Managers should try to maximize their stock's intrinsic value and then communicate effectively with stockholders. That will cause the intrinsic value to be high and the actual stock price to remain close to the intrinsic value over time.*

Because the intrinsic value cannot be observed, it is impossible to know whether it is really being maximized. Still, as we will discuss in Chapter 9, there are procedures for estimating a stock's intrinsic value. Managers can use these valuation models to analyze alternative courses of action and thus see how these actions are likely to impact the firm's value. This type of value-based management is not precise, but it is the best way to run a business.

Self*Test*

What are three techniques stockholders can use to motivate managers to maximize their stock's long-run price?

Should managers focus directly on the stock's actual market price or its intrinsic value, or are both important? Explain.

1-6 Stockholder–Debtholder Conflicts

Conflicts can also arise between stockholders and debtholders. Debtholders, which include the company's bankers and its bondholders, generally receive fixed payments regardless of how well the company does, while stockholders do better when the company does better. This situation leads to conflicts between these two groups, to the extent that stockholders are typically more willing to take on risky projects.[12]

To illustrate this problem, consider the example in Table 1.1, where a company has raised \$2,000 in capital, \$1,000 from bondholders, and \$1,000 from stockholders. To keep things simple, we assume that the bonds have a 1-year maturity and pay an 8% annual interest rate. The company's current plan is to

[12]We are assuming here that managers make decisions on behalf of stockholders, so saying that there are conflicts between stockholders and debtholders is the same as saying there are conflicts between managers and debtholders.

TABLE 1.1 Stockholder-Debtholder Conflict Example

Project L:

	Money Invested Today	Market Conditions 1 Year from Now: GOOD	Market Conditions 1 Year from Now: BAD	Expected Cash Flow	Expected Return
Cash flow to firm		$2,400	$2,000	$2,200	
Bondholders' portion	$1,000	1,080	1,080	1,080	8.00%
Stockholders' portion	1,000	1,320	920	1,120	12.00

Project H:

	Money Invested Today	Market Conditions 1 Year from Now: GOOD	Market Conditions 1 Year from Now: BAD	Expected Cash Flow	Expected Return
Cash flow to firm		$4,400	$0	$2,200	
Bondholders' portion	$1,000	1,080	0	540	–46.00%
Stockholders' portion	1,000	3,320	0	1,660	66.00

invest its $2,000 in Project L, a relatively low-risk project that is expected to be worth $2,400 one year from now if the market is good and $2,000 if the market is bad. There is a 50% chance that the market will be good and a 50% chance the market will be bad. In either case, there will be enough cash to pay the bondholders their money back plus the 8% annual interest rate that they were promised. The stockholders will receive whatever is left over after the bondholders have been paid. As expected, because they are paid last, the stockholders are bearing more risk (their payoff depends on the market), but they are also earning a higher expected return.

Now assume that the company discovers another project (Project H) that has considerably more risk. Project H has the same expected cash flow as Project L, but it will produce cash flows of $4,400 if the market is good but $0 if the market is bad. Clearly, the bondholders would not be interested in Project H, because they wouldn't receive any additional benefits if the market is good and they would lose everything if the market is bad. Notice, however, that Project H provides a higher rate of return for stockholders than Project L, because they capture all of the extra benefits if the market turns out to be good. While Project H is clearly riskier, in some circumstances managers acting on behalf of the stockholders may decide that the higher expected return is enough to justify the additional risk, and they would proceed with Project H despite the strong objections of the bondholders.

Notice, however, that astute bondholders understand that managers and stockholders may have an incentive to shift to riskier projects. Recognizing this incentive, they will view the bonds as being riskier and will demand a higher rate of return, and in some cases the perceived risk may be so great that they will not invest in the company, unless the managers can credibly convince bondholders that the company will not pursue excessively risky projects.

Another type of stockholder–debtholder conflict arises over the use of additional debt. As we see later in this book, the more debt a firm uses to finance a given amount of assets, the riskier the firm becomes. For example, if a firm has

$100 million of assets and finances them with $5 million of bonds and $95 million of common stock, things have to go terribly badly before the bondholders suffer a loss. On the other hand, if the firm uses $95 million of bonds and $5 million of stock, the bondholders suffer a loss even if the value of the assets declines only slightly.

Bondholders attempt to protect themselves by including *covenants* in the bond agreements that limit firms' use of additional debt and constrain managers' actions in other ways. We address these issues later in this book, but they are quite important and everyone should be aware of them.

Self*Test*

Why might conflicts arise between stockholders and debtholders?

How might astute bondholders react if stockholders take on risky projects?

How can bondholders protect themselves from managers' actions that negatively impact bondholders?

1-7 Balancing Shareholder Interests and the Interests of Society

Shareholder Wealth Maximization
The primary financial goal for managers of publicly owned companies implies that decisions should be made to maximize the long-run value of the firm's common stock.

Throughout this book, we focus primarily on publicly owned companies; hence, we operate on the assumption that management's primary financial goal is **shareholder wealth maximization**. At the same time, the managers know that this does not mean maximize shareholder value "at all costs." Managers have an obligation to behave ethically, and they must follow the laws and other society-imposed constraints that we discussed in the opening vignette to this chapter.

To understand how corporate managers balance the interests of society and shareholders, it is helpful to first look at those issues from the perspective of a sole proprietor. Consider Larry Jackson, the owner of a local sporting goods store. Jackson is in business to make money, but he likes to take time off to play golf on Fridays. He also has a few employees who are no longer very productive, but he keeps them on the payroll out of friendship and loyalty. Jackson is running the business in a way that is consistent with his own personal goals. He knows that he could make more money if he didn't play golf or if he replaced some of his employees. But he is comfortable with his choices—and because it is his business, he is free to make those choices.

By contrast, Linda Smith is CEO of a large corporation. Smith manages the company; however, most of the stock is owned by shareholders who purchased it because they were looking for an investment that would help them retire, send their children to college, pay for a long-anticipated trip, and so forth. The shareholders elected a board of directors, which then selected Smith to run the company. Smith and the firm's other managers are working on behalf of the shareholders, and they were hired to pursue policies that enhance shareholder value.

Most managers understand that maximizing shareholder value does not mean that they are free to ignore the larger interests of society. Consider, for example, what would happen if Linda Smith narrowly focused on creating shareholder value, but in the process her company was unresponsive to its employees and customers, hostile to its local community, and indifferent to the effects its

INVESTING IN SOCIALLY RESPONSIBLE FUNDS

The same societal pressures that have encouraged consumers to buy products of companies that they believe to be socially responsible have also led some investors to search for ways to limit their investments to firms they deem to be socially responsible. Indeed, today there are a large number of mutual funds that only invest in companies that meet specified social goals. Each of these socially responsible funds applies different criteria, but typically they consider a company's environmental record, its commitment to social causes, and its employee relations. Many of these funds also avoid investments in companies that are involved with alcohol, tobacco, gambling, and nuclear power. Investment performance varies among funds from year to year. The accompanying chart compares the past performance of a representative socially responsible fund, the Domini Impact Equity Investor Fund, with that of the S&P 500 during the past 20+ years. Although the general shape of each is similar, in the last 15 years or so the S&P 500 has outperformed this fund.

A recent article in *The Wall Street Journal* cites a study that suggests that investors may be able to profit by buying stocks that other investors choose to avoid. The study by professors Elroy Dimson, Paul Marsh, and Mike Staunton of the London Business School found that over the past century, U.S. tobacco stocks have dramatically outperformed the overall market. As a possible explanation, the article provides a quote from one of the authors:[13]

> "It appears that when the people who abhor such stocks have shunned them, they have depressed the share prices but haven't managed to destroy the industries," Prof. Marsh says. "So investors who don't have the same scruples have been able to pick up [these stocks] at a cheaper price."

Recent Performance of Domini Impact Equity Investor Fund versus S&P 500

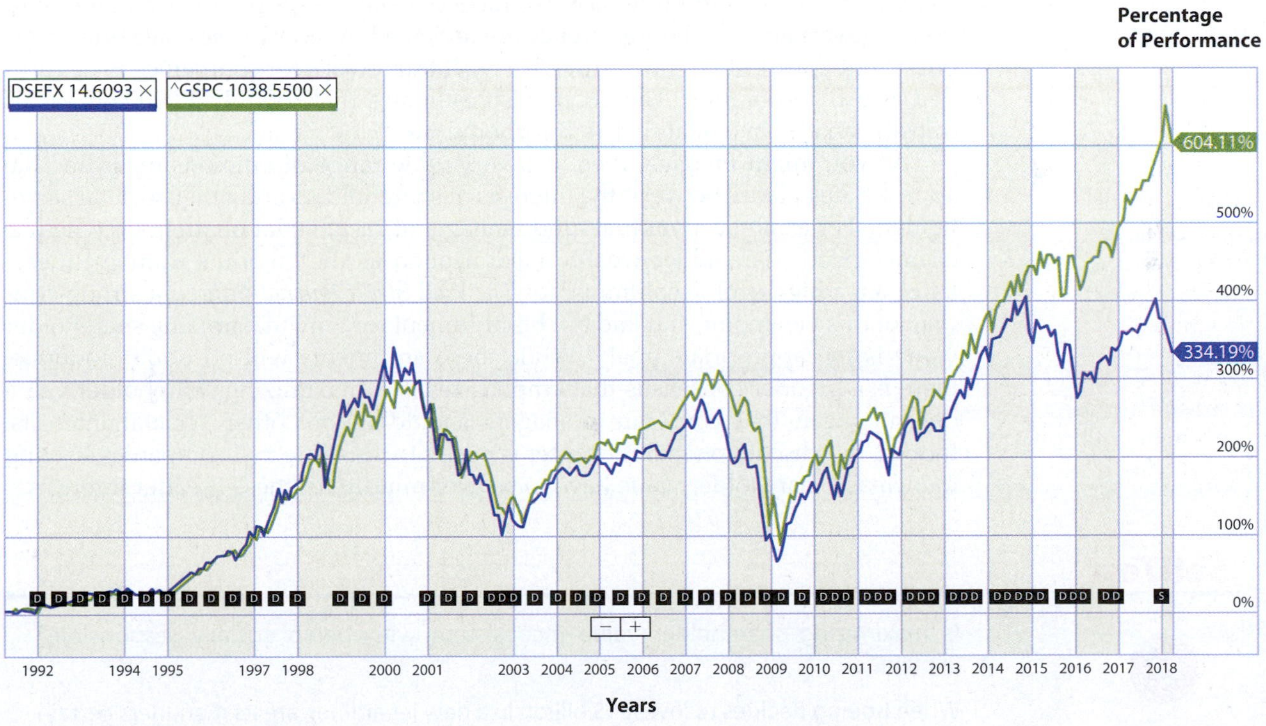

Source: finance.yahoo.com, March 27, 2018.

actions had on the environment. In all likelihood, society would impose a wide range of costs on the company. It may find it hard to attract top-notch employees, its products may be boycotted, it may face additional lawsuits and regulations, and it may be confronted with negative publicity. These costs would ultimately

[13]Refer to Jason Zweig, " 'Sin-Vestors' Can Reap Smoking-Hot Returns," *The Wall Street Journal* (www.wsj.com), February 13, 2015.

lead to a reduction in shareholder value. So clearly, when taking steps to maximize shareholder value, enlightened managers need to also keep in mind these society-imposed constraints.[14]

From a broader perspective, firms have a number of different departments, including marketing, accounting, production, human resources, and finance. The finance department's principal task is to evaluate proposed decisions and judge how they will affect the stock price and thus shareholder wealth. For example, suppose the production manager wants to replace some old equipment with new automated machinery that will reduce labor costs. The finance staff will evaluate that proposal and determine whether the savings seem to be worth the cost. Similarly, if marketing wants to spend $10 million of advertising during the Super Bowl, the financial staff will evaluate the proposal, look at the probable increase in sales, and reach a conclusion as to whether the money spent will lead to a higher stock price. Most significant decisions are evaluated in terms of their financial consequences, but astute managers recognize that they also need to take into account how these decisions affect society at large.

Interestingly, some companies have taken more explicit steps to recognize the broader needs of society. A fairly small but rapidly growing number of companies have become certified as "B" or "benefit" corporations. While these companies are still focused on making a profit, they are committed to putting other stakeholders such as employees, customers, and their communities on an equal footing with shareholders. In order to qualify as a B corporation, the company must subject itself to an annual audit in which its practices regarding social responsibility, corporate governance, and transparency are reviewed. A recent *Time* magazine article points out that 26 states now provide a legal framework for companies to be certified as a B corporation. The article also estimates that roughly 1,200 companies (mostly small) have qualified as B corporations.[15]

As you might imagine, there is a very wide range of opinions regarding the appropriate balance between the interests of shareholders and other societal stakeholders. For example, a mutual fund manager attracted a lot of attention when he characterized shareholder wealth maximization as the "world's dumbest idea." Later on, a high-profile columnist for *The Wall Street Journal* offered a strong criticism of this viewpoint, and laid out his argument for why maximizing shareholder value is the appropriate goal.[16] While these arguments will no doubt continue, there is a broader consensus that emphasizes that maximizing shareholder value doesn't mean that corporate managers should ignore other societal interests. Indeed, our discussion in this chapter is meant to illustrate that companies striving to increase shareholder value have to be ever mindful of these broader interests.

Self*Test*

Is maximizing shareholder value inconsistent with being socially responsible? Explain.

When Boeing decides to invest $5 billion in a new jet airliner, are its managers certain of the project's effects on Boeing's future profits and stock price? Explain.

---

[14]A recent study highlights the various factors that motivate corporate managers to make socially responsible investments. Refer to Richard Borghesi, Joel F. Houston, and Andy Naranjo, "Corporate Socially Responsible Investments: CEO Altruism, Reputation, and Shareholder Interests," *Journal of Corporate Finance*, vol. 26 (June 2014), pp. 164–181.

[15]Refer to Bill Saporito, "Making Good, Plus a Profit: A New Type of Company Lures Activist Entrepreneurs," *Time*, March 23, 2015, p. 22.

[16]Refer to Holman W. Jenkins, Jr., "Are Shareholders Obsolete?" *The Wall Street Journal* (www.wsj.com), January 2, 2015.

1-8 Business Ethics

As a result of the financial scandals occurring during the past decade, there has been a strong push to improve *business ethics.* This is occurring on many fronts—actions begun by former New York Attorney General and former Governor Elliot Spitzer and others who sued companies for improper acts; Congress's passing of the Sarbanes-Oxley Act of 2002 to impose sanctions on executives who sign financial statements later found to be false; Congress's passing of the Dodd-Frank Act to implement an aggressive overhaul of the U.S. financial regulatory system aimed at preventing reckless actions that would cause another financial crisis; and business schools trying to inform students about proper versus improper business actions.

As noted earlier, companies benefit from having good reputations and are penalized by having bad ones; the same is true for individuals. Reputations reflect the extent to which firms and people are ethical. *Ethics* is defined in *Webster's Dictionary* as "standards of conduct or moral behavior." Business ethics can be thought of as a company's attitude and conduct toward its employees, customers, community, and stockholders. A firm's commitment to business ethics can be measured by the tendency of its employees, from the top down, to adhere to laws, regulations, and moral standards relating to product safety and quality, fair employment practices, fair marketing and selling practices, the use of confidential information for personal gain, community involvement, and the use of illegal payments to obtain business.

For the past 12 years, Ethisphere, an organization based out of Scottsdale, Arizona, has focused on evaluating ethical business practices and has published a list of "The World's Most Ethical Companies." It honors companies that promote ethical business standards and practices internally, enable managers and employees to make good choices, and shape industry standards by introducing best practices. Those companies that have made the list in every year are Aflac, Deere & Company, Ecolab, Fluor Corporation, GE, International Paper, Kao Corporation, Milliken & Company, Pepsico, Starbucks, Texas Instruments, UPS, and Xerox.[17]

1-8A WHAT COMPANIES ARE DOING

Most firms today have strong written codes of ethical behavior; companies also conduct training programs to ensure that employees understand proper behavior in different situations. When conflicts arise involving profits and ethics, ethical considerations sometimes are so obviously important that they dominate. In other cases, however, the right choice is not clear. For example, suppose that Norfolk Southern's managers know that its coal trains are polluting the air, but the amount of pollution is within legal limits, and further reduction would be costly. Are the managers ethically bound to reduce pollution? Similarly, several years ago Merck's research indicated that its Vioxx pain medicine might be causing heart attacks. However, the evidence was not overly strong, and the product was clearly helping some patients. Over time, additional tests produced stronger evidence that Vioxx did pose a health risk. What should Merck have done, and when should Merck have done it? If the company released negative but perhaps incorrect information, this announcement would have hurt sales and possibly prevented some patients benefitting from the product. If the company delayed the release of this additional information, more patients might have suffered irreversible harm. At what point should Merck have made the potential problem known to the public? There are no obvious answers to questions such as these, but companies must deal with them, and a failure to handle them properly can lead to severe consequences.

[17]"The World's Most Ethical Companies 2018," www.ethisphere.com, February 12, 2018.

1-8B CONSEQUENCES OF UNETHICAL BEHAVIOR

Over the past few years, ethical lapses have led to a number of bankruptcies. The collapses of Enron and WorldCom as well as the accounting firm Arthur Andersen dramatically illustrate how unethical behavior can lead to a firm's rapid decline. In all three cases, top executives came under fire because of misleading accounting practices that led to overstated profits. Enron and WorldCom executives were busily selling their stock at the same time they were recommending the stock to employees and outside investors. These executives reaped millions before the stock declined, while lower-level employees and outside investors were left "holding the bag." Some of these executives are now in jail, and Enron's CEO had a fatal heart attack while awaiting sentencing after being found guilty of conspiracy and fraud. Moreover, Merrill Lynch and Citigroup, which were accused of facilitating these frauds, were fined hundreds of millions of dollars.

In other cases, companies avoid bankruptcy but face a damaging blow to their reputation. Safety concerns tarnished Toyota's once sterling reputation for reliability. Ethical questions were raised regarding when the company's senior management became aware of the problems and whether they were forthcoming in sharing these concerns with the public. Similarly, GM agreed to pay a $900 million settlement for its delay in addressing defective ignition switches, which have been connected to 57 deaths and the recall of 2.6 million vehicles.

Likewise, in April 2010, the SEC brought forth a civil fraud suit against Goldman Sachs. The SEC contended that Goldman Sachs misled its investors when it created and marketed securities that were backed by subprime mortgages. In July 2010, Goldman Sachs ultimately reached a settlement where it agreed to pay $550 million. While just one example, many believe that too many Wall Street executives in recent years have been willing to compromise their ethics. In May 2011, Raj Rajaratnam, the founder of the hedge fund Galleon Group LLC, was convicted of securities fraud and conspiracy in one of the government's largest insider trading cases. Mr. Rajaratnam traded on information (worth approximately $63.8 million) from insiders at technology companies and others in the hedge fund industry. On October 13, 2011, he was sentenced to 11 years in prison. On March 14, 2014, the Federal Deposit Insurance Corporation (FDIC) sued 16 big banks (including Bank of America, Citigroup, and JPMorgan Chase) for actively manipulating the London Interbank Offered Rate (the LIBOR rate) to make additional profits on their trades. This is particularly important because the LIBOR rate is used to set the terms in many financial contracts. The banks are accused of rigging LIBOR from August 2007 to mid-2011. Five of the banks, Barclays, RBS, UBS, Deutsche Bank, and Rabobank of the Netherlands, together have paid $5 billion to settle the charges and avoid criminal prosecution if they meet certain conditions.

More recently, Mylan, a pharmaceutical company, agreed to pay the U.S. Department of Justice a $465 million settlement for overcharging Medicaid for its allergy shot EPIPen. In early 2018, Theranos founder Elizabeth Holmes agreed to a settlement with the SEC after being charged with fraud. The settlement included a financial penalty, eliminated her voting control of the company, and barred her for 10 years from serving as an officer or director of a public company. In another high-profile case, Wells Fargo fired its CEO, other senior managers, and 5,000 employees, and paid $185 million in government fines and customer refunds because employees created fake accounts and signed up customers for unauthorized credit cards to reach sales quotas for bonuses. The Fed has placed an additional penalty on Wells Fargo by limiting its growth. These recent problems are not unique to U.S. companies. Volkswagen (VW) recently admitted to selling cars that were installed with software to cheat emissions tests. Approximately 11 million cars worldwide, including 8 million in Europe, have the software installed in them. VW has set aside 6.7 billion euros (roughly $7.6 billion) to cover the cost of recalling millions of cars, which resulted in its first quarterly loss (third quarter, 2015) in 15 years.

Its CEO resigned and several of its top executives were fired because of this scandal. In another recent scandal, Canadian drug maker Valeant has been accused of improper accounting and predatory price hikes to boost its growth. In addition, it appears that Philidor (an undisclosed affiliate of Valeant) may have changed patients' prescriptions to push Valeant's high-priced drugs. Near the end of 2016, two Philidor executives (one of whom had been an executive with Valeant) had been arrested and charged with a multimillion-dollar fraud and kickback scheme.

A firm's CEO is the face of the corporation. When a CEO is accused of illegal activity, the Board of Directors conducts an independent investigation, and if the allegation is verified, it takes corrective action. In most cases, the CEO is terminated. It's much less obvious what the board should do when the CEO is accused of questionable, but not illegal, behavior. When a CEO is accused of misconduct, the board must investigate the situation, take proactive steps to ensure that the situation is properly dealt with, and, most importantly, ensure that the corporate reputation, culture, and long-term performance are not damaged.[18]

The perception of widespread improper actions has caused many investors to lose faith in American business and to turn away from the stock market, which makes it difficult for firms to raise the capital they need to grow, create jobs, and stimulate the economy. So, unethical actions can have adverse consequences far beyond the companies that perpetrate them.

All this raises a question: Are *companies* unethical, or is it just a few of their employees? That was a central issue that came up in the case of Arthur Andersen, the accounting firm that audited Enron, WorldCom, and several other companies that committed accounting fraud. Evidence showed that relatively few of Andersen's accountants helped perpetrate the frauds. Its top managers argued that while a few rogue employees did bad things, most of the firm's 85,000 employees, and the firm itself, were innocent. The U.S. Justice Department disagreed, concluding that the firm was guilty because it fostered a climate where unethical behavior was permitted and that Andersen used an incentive system that made such behavior profitable to both the perpetrators and the firm. As a result, Andersen was put out of business, its partners lost millions of dollars, and its 85,000 employees lost their jobs. In most other cases, individuals, rather than firms, were tried, and though the firms survived, they suffered damage to their reputations, which greatly lowered their future profit potential and value.

1-8C HOW SHOULD EMPLOYEES DEAL WITH UNETHICAL BEHAVIOR?

Far too often the desire for stock options, bonuses, and promotions drives managers to take unethical actions such as fudging the books to make profits in the manager's division look good, holding back information about bad products that would depress sales, and failing to take costly but needed measures to protect the environment. Generally, these acts don't rise to the level of an Enron or a WorldCom, but they are still bad. If questionable things are going on, who should take action and what should that action be? Obviously, in situations such as Enron and WorldCom, where fraud was being perpetrated at or close to the top, senior managers knew about the illegal activities. In other cases, the problem is caused by a mid-level manager trying to boost his or her unit's profits and thus his or her bonus. In all cases, though, at least some lower-level employees are aware of what's happening; they may even be ordered to take fraudulent actions. Should the lower-level employees obey their boss's orders; refuse to obey those orders; or report the situation to a higher authority, such as the company's board of directors, the company's auditors, or a federal prosecutor?

---

[18]David Larcker and Brian Tayan, "We Studied 38 Incidents of CEO Bad Behavior and Measured Their Consequences," *Harvard Business Review* (www.hbr.org), June 9, 2016.

As you might imagine, these issues are often tricky and judgment comes into play when deciding on what action to take and when to take it. If a lower-level employee thinks that a product should be pulled, but the boss disagrees, what should the employee do? If an employee decides to report the problem, trouble may ensue regardless of the merits of the case. If the alarm is false, the company will have been harmed, and nothing will have been gained. In that case, the employee will probably be fired. Even if the employee is right, his or her career may still be ruined because many companies (or at least bosses) don't like "disloyal, troublemaking" employees.

Such situations arise fairly often, ranging from accounting fraud to product liability, sexual harassment, and environmental cases. Employees jeopardize their jobs if they come forward over their bosses' objections. However, if they don't speak up, they may suffer emotional problems and contribute to the downfall of their companies and the accompanying loss of jobs and savings. Moreover, if employees obey orders regarding actions they know are illegal, they may end up going to jail. Indeed, in most of the scandals that have gone to trial, the lower-level people who physically entered the bad data received longer jail sentences than the bosses who presumably gave the directives. So employees can be "stuck between a rock and a hard place," that is, doing what they should do and possibly losing their jobs versus going along with the boss and possibly ending up in jail. This discussion shows why ethics is such an important consideration in business and in business schools—and why we are concerned with it in this book.

Self*Test*

How would you define *business ethics*?

Can a firm's executive compensation plan lead to unethical behavior? Explain.

Unethical acts are generally committed by unethical people. What are some things companies can do to help ensure that their employees act ethically?

TYING IT ALL TOGETHER

This chapter provides a broad overview of financial management. *Management's primary goal should be to maximize the long-run value of the stock, which means the intrinsic value as measured by the stock's price over time.* To maximize value, firms must develop products that consumers want, produce the products efficiently, sell them at competitive prices, and observe laws relating to corporate behavior. If firms are successful at maximizing the stock's value, they will also be contributing to social welfare and citizens' well-being.

Businesses can be organized as proprietorships, partnerships, corporations, limited liability companies (LLCs), or limited liability partnerships (LLPs). The vast majority of all business is done by corporations, and the most successful firms become corporations, which explains the focus on corporations in this book.

The primary tasks of the CFO are (1) to make sure the accounting system provides "good" numbers for internal decision making and for investors, (2) to ensure that the firm is financed in the proper manner, (3) to evaluate the operating units to make sure they are performing in an optimal manner, and (4) to evaluate all proposed capital expenditures to make sure they will increase the firm's value. In the remainder of this book, we discuss exactly how financial managers carry out these tasks.

Self-Test Questions And Problems

(Solutions Appear in Appendix A)

ST-1 **KEY TERMS** Define each of the following terms:

a. Sarbanes-Oxley Act
b. Proprietorship; partnership; corporation
c. S corporation; limited liability company (LLC); limited liability partnership (LLP)
d. Intrinsic value; market price
e. Marginal investor; equilibrium
f. Corporate governance
g. Corporate raider; hostile takeover
h. Stockholder wealth maximization
i. Business ethics

Questions

1-1 What is a firm's intrinsic value? Its current stock price? Is the stock's "true" long-run value more closely related to its intrinsic value or to its current price?

1-2 When is a stock said to be in equilibrium? Why might a stock at any point in time not be in equilibrium?

1-3 Suppose three honest individuals gave you their estimates of Stock X's intrinsic value. One person is your current roommate, the second person is a professional security analyst with an excellent reputation on Wall Street, and the third person is Company X's CFO. If the three estimates differed, in which one would you have the most confidence? Why?

1-4 Is it better for a firm's actual stock price in the market to be under, over, or equal to its intrinsic value? Would your answer be the same from the standpoints of stockholders in general and a CEO who is about to exercise a million dollars in options and then retire? Explain.

1-5 If a company's board of directors wants management to maximize shareholder wealth, should the CEO's compensation be set as a fixed dollar amount, or should the compensation depend on how well the firm performs? If it is to be based on performance, how should performance be measured? Would it be easier to measure performance by the growth rate in reported profits or the growth rate in the stock's intrinsic value? Which would be the better performance measure? Why?

1-6 What are the various forms of business organization? What are the advantages and disadvantages of each?

1-7 Should stockholder wealth maximization be thought of as a long-term or a short-term goal? For example, if one action increases a firm's stock price from a current level of $20 to $25 in 6 months and then to $30 in 5 years, but another action keeps the stock at $20 for several years but then increases it to $40 in 5 years, which action would be better? Think of some specific corporate actions that have these general tendencies.

1-8 What are some actions that stockholders can take to ensure that management's and stockholders' interests are aligned?

1-9 The president of Southern Semiconductor Corporation (SSC) made this statement in the company's annual report: "SSC's primary goal is to increase the value of our common stockholders' equity." Later in the report, the following announcements were made:

a. The company contributed $1.5 million to the symphony orchestra in Birmingham, Alabama, its headquarters city.
b. The company is spending $500 million to open a new plant and expand operations in China. No profits will be produced by the Chinese operation for 4 years, so earnings will be depressed during this period versus what they would have been had the decision been made not to expand in China.
c. The company holds about half of its assets in the form of U.S. Treasury bonds, and it keeps these funds available for use in emergencies. In the future, though, SSC plans to shift its emergency funds from Treasury bonds to common stocks.

Discuss how SSC's stockholders might view each of these actions and how the actions might affect the stock price.

1-10 Investors generally can make one vote for each share of stock they hold. TIAA-CREF is the largest institutional shareholder in the United States; therefore, it holds many shares and has more votes than any other organization. Traditionally, this fund has acted as a passive investor, just going along with management. However, in 1993, it mailed a notice to all 1,500 companies whose stocks it held that henceforth it planned to actively intervene if, in its opinion, management was not performing well. Its goal was to improve corporate performance to boost the prices of the stocks it held. It also wanted to encourage corporate boards to appoint a majority of independent (outside) directors, and it stated that it would vote against any directors of firms that "don't have an effective, independent board that can challenge the CEO."

In the past, TIAA-CREF responded to poor performance by "voting with its feet," which means selling stocks that were not doing well. However, by 1993, that position had become difficult to maintain for two reasons. First, the fund invested a large part of its assets in "index funds," which hold stocks in accordance with their percentage value in the broad stock market. Furthermore, TIAA-CREF owns such large blocks of stocks in many companies that if it tried to sell out, doing so would severely depress the prices of those stocks. Thus, TIAA-CREF is locked in to a large extent, which led to its decision to become a more active investor.

a. Is TIAA-CREF an ordinary shareholder? Explain.

b. Due to its asset size, TIAA-CREF owns many shares in a number of companies. The fund's management plans to vote those shares. However, TIAA-CREF is owned by many thousands of investors. Should the fund's managers vote its shares, or should it pass those votes, on a pro rata basis, back to its own shareholders? Explain.

1-11 Edmund Enterprises recently made a large investment to upgrade its technology. Although these improvements won't have much effect on performance in the short run, they are expected to reduce future costs significantly. What effect will this investment have on Edmund Enterprises' earnings per share this year? What effect might this investment have on the company's intrinsic value and stock price?

1-12 Suppose you were a member of Company X's board of directors and chairperson of the company's compensation committee. What factors should your committee consider when setting the CEO's compensation? Should the compensation consist of a dollar salary, stock options that depend on the firm's performance, or a mix of the two? If "performance" is to be considered, how should it be measured? Think of both theoretical and practical (i.e., measurement) considerations. If you were also a vice president of Company X, might your actions be different than if you were the CEO of some other company?

1-13 Suppose you are a director of an energy company that has three divisions—natural gas, oil, and retail (gas stations). These divisions operate independently from one another, but all division managers report to the firm's CEO. If you were on the compensation committee, as discussed in Question 1-12, and your committee was asked to set the compensation for the three division managers, would you use the same criteria as that used for the firm's CEO? Explain your reasoning.

1-14 Bedrock Company has $70 million in debt and $30 million in equity. The debt matures in 1 year and has a 10% interest rate, so the company is promising to pay back $77 million to its debtholders 1 year from now.

The company is considering two possible investments, each of which will require an up-front cost of $100 million. Each investment will last for 1 year, and the payoff from each investment depends on the strength of the overall economy. There is a 50% chance that the economy will be weak and a 50% chance it will be strong.

Here are the expected payoffs (all dollars are in millions) from the two investments:

	Payoff in 1 Year If the Economy Is Weak	Payoff in 1 Year If the Economy Is Strong	Expected Payoff
Investment L	$90.00	$130.00	$110.00
Investment H	50.00	170.00	110.00

Note that the two projects have the same expected payoff, but Project H has higher risk. The debtholders always get paid first and the stockholders receive any money that is available after the debtholders have been paid.

Assume that if the company doesn't have enough funds to pay off its debtholders 1 year from now, then Bedrock will declare bankruptcy. If bankruptcy is declared, the debtholders will receive all available funds, and the stockholders will receive nothing.

a. Assume that the company selects Investment L. What is the expected payoff to the firm's debtholders? What is the expected payoff to the firm's stockholders?
b. Assume that the company selects Investment H. What is the expected payoff to the firm's debtholders? What is the expected payoff to the firm's stockholders?
c. Would the debtholders prefer that the company's managers select Project L or Project H? Briefly explain your reason.
d. Explain why the company's managers, acting on behalf of the stockholders, might select Project H, even though it has greater risk.
e. What actions can debtholders take to protect their interests?

Financial Markets and Institutions

CHAPTER 2

Jemal Countess/Getty Images Entertainment/Getty Images

The Economy Depends on a Strong Financial System

History shows that a strong financial system is a necessary ingredient for a growing and prosperous economy. Companies raising capital to finance capital expenditures and investors saving to accumulate funds for future use require well-functioning financial markets and institutions.

Over the past few decades, changing technology and improving communications have increased cross-border transactions and expanded the scope and efficiency of the global financial system. Companies routinely raise funds throughout the world to finance projects all around the globe. Likewise, with the click of a mouse an individual investor in Pittsburgh can deposit funds in a European bank or purchase a mutual fund that invests in Chinese securities.

These innovations helped spur global economic growth by providing capital to an increasing number of individuals throughout the world. Along the way, the financial industry attracted a lot of talented people who created, marketed, and traded a large number of new financial products. However, despite their benefits many of these same factors led to excesses that culminated in the financial crisis of 2007 and 2008.

In the aftermath of the crisis, the financial sector is slowly recovering, but its effects continue to linger. The crisis also reaffirmed how changes in the value of financial assets can quickly spill over and affect other parts of the economy. For example, a 2014 article in *The Wall Street Journal* described how a dramatic drop in many of the leading hot tech stocks (Facebook, King Digital Entertainment, Netflix, Yelp, and Twitter) suddenly made it more difficult for new start-ups to raise money in the initial public offering (IPO) market. In the following three years, at least two of the stocks (Netflix and Facebook) sharply rebounded and generated large returns for their investors.

In recent years, there have been a few other high-profile IPOs. For example, in January 2015 the burger chain Shake Shack had a stronger than expected IPO—although the stock's price has fallen sharply in the three years following its public offering. But, arguably the most dramatic event was when the Chinese online retailer Alibaba raised $25 billion in September 2014. This turned out to be the largest global IPO in history. More recently, Snapchat's parent company (Snap) went public in March 2017 to considerable fanfare—although, in the year or so after its IPO, it struggled to stay above its original offering price. Most recently, Dropbox went public on March 23, 2018, and saw its share price increase by 36% to a market value of $11.2 billion. It remains to be seen whether this enthusiasm and price can be sustained.

At the same time, a number of other high-profile "unicorns" (a term first coined by venture capitalist Aileen Lee to describe start-ups valued at more than a billion dollars) have successfully raised private funds and have so far resisted the urge to go public. These companies include Uber, Airbnb, and Palintir—all of which have been valued at $20 billion or more.

While these recent events have attracted a lot of attention, it is important to understand that almost all companies have been affected by changing technology and globalization. More generally, managers and investors don't operate in a vacuum—they make decisions within a large and complex financial environment. This environment includes financial markets and institutions, tax and regulatory policies, and the state of the economy. The environment both determines the available financial alternatives and affects the outcome of various decisions. Thus, it is crucial that investors and financial managers have a good understanding of the environment in which they operate.

Sources: Peter Cohan, "After 36% Pop, Don't Rush into Dropbox Stock," *Forbes* (www.forbes.com), March 26, 2018; Michael J. De La Merced, "Shake Shack More Than Doubles Its I.P.O. Price in Market Debut," *The New York Times* (dealbook.nytimes.com), January 30, 2015; Mike Isaac and Michael J. De La Merced, "Uber Closes $1.6 Billion in Financing," *The New York Times* (dealbook.nytimes.com), January 21, 2015; Ryan Mac, "Alibaba Claims Title for Largest Global IPO Ever with Extra Share Sales," *Forbes* (www.forbes.com), September 22, 2014; and Scott Austin, Chris Canipe, and Sarah Slobin, "The Billion Dollar Startup Club," *The Wall Street Journal* (graphics.wsj.com/billion-dollar-club/), February 18, 2015.

PUTTING THINGS IN PERSPECTIVE

In Chapter 1, we saw that a firm's primary financial goal is to maximize long-run shareholder value. Shareholder value is ultimately determined in the financial markets; so if financial managers are to make good decisions, they must understand how these markets operate. In addition, individuals make personal investment decisions; so they too need to know something about financial markets and the institutions that operate in those markets. Therefore, in this chapter, we describe the markets where capital is raised, securities are traded, and stock prices are established, as well as the institutions that operate in these markets. We will also discuss the concept of market efficiency and demonstrate how efficient markets help promote the effective allocation of capital.

In recent years, the dramatic price swings in the financial markets that have become increasingly common have led many to question whether markets are always efficient. In response, there has been increased interest in *behavioral finance theory*. This theory focuses on how psychological factors influence individual decisions (sometimes in perverse ways), and the resulting impact these decisions have on financial markets.

*For additional information regarding the financial crisis, students can refer to **stlouisfed.org/Financial-Crisis**. Another good source can be found at **fcic.law.stanford.edu**, which focuses on the Financial Crisis Inquiry Commission.*

When you finish this chapter, you should be able to do the following:

- **Identify the different types of financial markets and financial institutions, and explain how these markets and institutions enhance capital allocation.**
- **Explain how the stock market operates, and list the distinctions between the different types of stock markets.**

- **Explain how the stock market has performed in recent years.**
- **Discuss the importance of market efficiency, and explain why some markets are more efficient than others.**
- **Develop a simple understanding of behavioral finance.**

2-1 The Capital Allocation Process

Businesses, individuals, and governments often need to raise capital. For example, Carolina Power & Light Energy (CP&L) forecasts an increase in the demand for electricity in North and South Carolina, so it will build a new power plant to meet those needs. Because CP&L's bank account does not contain the $1 billion necessary to pay for the plant, the company must raise this capital in the financial markets. Similarly, the proprietor of a San Francisco hardware store wants to expand into appliances. Where will he get the money to buy the initial inventory of TV sets, washers, and freezers? Or suppose the Johnson family wants to buy a home that costs $200,000, but they have only $50,000 in savings. Where will they obtain the additional $150,000? The city of New York needs $200 million to build a new sewer plant. Where can it obtain this money? Finally, the federal government needs more money than it receives from taxes. Where will the extra money come from?

On the other hand, some individuals and firms have incomes that exceed their current expenditures, in which case they have funds available to invest. For example, Carol Hawk has an income of $36,000, but her expenses are only $30,000. That leaves her with $6,000 to invest. Similarly, Microsoft has accumulated roughly $142.78 billion of cash and marketable securities. What can Microsoft do with this money until it is needed in the business?

People and organizations with surplus funds are saving today in order to accumulate funds for some future use. Members of a household might save to pay for their children's education and the parents' retirement, while a business might save to fund future investments. Those with surplus funds expect to earn a return on their investments, while people and organizations that need capital understand that they must pay interest to those who provide that capital.

In a well-functioning economy, capital flows efficiently from those with surplus capital to those who need it. This transfer can take place in the three ways described in Figure 2.1.

1. *Direct transfers* of money and securities, as shown in the top section, occur when a business sells its stocks or bonds directly to savers, without going through any type of financial institution. The business delivers its securities to savers, who, in turn, give the firm the money it needs. This procedure is used mainly by small firms, and relatively little capital is raised by direct transfers.
2. As shown in the middle section, transfers may also go through an investment bank (IB) such as Morgan Stanley, which *underwrites* the issue. An underwriter facilitates the issuance of securities. The company sells its stocks or bonds to the investment bank, which then sells these same securities to savers. The businesses' securities and the savers' money merely "pass through" the investment bank. However, because the investment bank buys and holds the securities for a period of time, it is taking a risk—it may not be able to resell the securities to savers for as much as it paid. Because new securities are involved and the corporation receives the sale proceeds, this transaction is called a *primary market transaction.*
3. Transfers can also be made through a *financial intermediary* such as a bank, an insurance company, or a mutual fund. Here the intermediary obtains funds from savers in exchange for its securities. The intermediary uses this money to buy and hold businesses' securities, and the savers hold the intermediary's

FIGURE 2.1 Diagram of the Capital Formation Process for Business

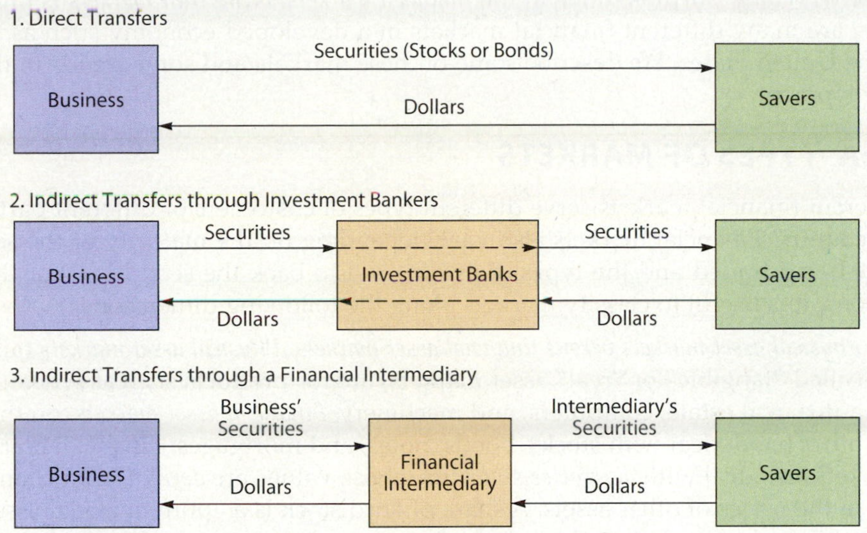

securities. For example, a saver deposits dollars in a bank, receiving a certificate of deposit; then the bank lends the money to a business in the form of a mortgage loan. Thus, intermediaries literally create new forms of capital—in this case, certificates of deposit, which are safer and more liquid than mortgages and thus better for most savers to hold. The existence of intermediaries greatly increases the efficiency of money and capital markets.

Often the entity needing capital is a business (and specifically a corporation), but it is easy to visualize the demander of capital being a home purchaser, a small business, or a government unit. For example, if your uncle lends you money to fund a new business, a direct transfer of funds will occur. Alternatively, if you borrow money to purchase a home, you will probably raise the funds through a financial intermediary such as your local commercial bank or mortgage banker. That banker could sell your mortgage to an investment bank, which then might use it as collateral for a bond that is purchased by a pension fund.

In a global context, economic development is highly correlated with the level and efficiency of financial markets and institutions.[1] It is difficult, if not impossible, for an economy to reach its full potential if it doesn't have access to a well-functioning financial system. In a well-developed economy like that of the United States, an extensive set of markets and institutions has evolved over time to facilitate the efficient allocation of capital. To raise capital efficiently, managers must understand how these markets and institutions work, and individuals need to know how the markets and institutions work to earn high rates of returns on their savings.

Self*Test*

Name three ways capital is transferred between savers and borrowers.

Why are efficient capital markets necessary for economic growth?

[1]For a detailed review of the evidence linking financial development to economic growth, see Ross Levine, "Finance and Growth: Theory and Evidence," Chapter 12 in *Handbook of Economic Growth*, edited by Philippe Aghion and Steven Durlauf (Amsterdam: Elsevier Science, 2005).

2-2 Financial Markets

People and organizations wanting to borrow money are brought together with those who have surplus funds in the *financial markets*. Note that *markets* is plural; there are many different financial markets in a developed economy such as that of the United States. We describe some of these markets and some trends in their development.

2-2A TYPES OF MARKETS

Different financial markets serve different types of customers or different parts of the country. Financial markets also vary depending on the maturity of the securities being traded and the types of assets used to back the securities. For these reasons, it is useful to classify markets along the following dimensions:

1. *Physical asset markets versus financial asset markets. Physical asset markets* (also called "tangible" or "real" asset markets) are for products such as wheat, autos, real estate, computers, and machinery. *Financial asset markets*, on the other hand, deal with stocks, bonds, notes, and mortgages. Financial markets also deal with *derivative securities* whose values are *derived* from changes in the prices of other assets. A share of Ford stock is a "pure financial asset," while an option to buy Ford shares is a derivative security whose value depends on the price of Ford stock.

Spot Markets
The markets in which assets are bought or sold for "on-the-spot" delivery.

Futures Markets
The markets in which participants agree today to buy or sell an asset at some future date.

Money Markets
The financial markets in which funds are borrowed or loaned for short periods (less than one year).

Capital Markets
The financial markets for stocks and for intermediate- or long-term debt (one year or longer).

Primary Markets
Markets in which corporations raise capital by issuing new securities.

Secondary Markets
Markets in which securities and other financial assets are traded among investors after they have been issued by corporations.

2. *Spot markets versus futures markets.* **Spot markets** are markets in which assets are bought or sold for "on-the-spot" delivery (literally, within a few days). **Futures markets** are markets in which participants agree today to buy or sell an asset at some future date. For example, a farmer may enter into a futures contract in which he agrees today to sell 5,000 bushels of soybeans 6 months from now at a price of $10.275 a bushel. To continue that example, a food processor that needs soybeans in the future may enter into a futures contract in which it agrees to buy soybeans 6 months from now. Such a transaction can reduce, or *hedge*, the risks faced by both the farmer and the food processor.
3. *Money markets versus capital markets.* **Money markets** are the markets for short-term, highly liquid debt securities. The New York, London, and Tokyo money markets are among the world's largest. **Capital markets** are the markets for intermediate- or long-term debt and corporate stocks. The New York Stock Exchange, where the stocks of the largest U.S. corporations are traded, is a prime example of a capital market. There is no hard-and-fast rule, but in a description of debt markets, *short-term* generally means less than 1 year, *intermediate-term* means 1 to 10 years, and *long-term* means more than 10 years.
4. *Primary markets versus secondary markets.* **Primary markets** are the markets in which corporations raise new capital. If GE were to sell a new issue of common stock to raise capital, a primary market transaction would take place. The corporation selling the newly created stock, GE, receives the proceeds from the sale in a primary market transaction. **Secondary markets** are markets in which existing, already outstanding securities are traded among investors. Thus, if Jane Doe decided to buy 1,000 shares of GE stock, the purchase would occur in the secondary market. The New York Stock Exchange is a secondary market because it deals in outstanding, as opposed to newly issued, stocks and bonds. Secondary markets also exist for mortgages, other types of loans, and other financial assets. The corporation whose securities are being traded is not involved in a secondary market transaction and thus does not receive funds from such a sale.

5. *Private markets versus public markets.* **Private markets**, where transactions are negotiated directly between two or more parties, are differentiated from **public markets**, where standardized contracts are traded on organized exchanges. Bank loans and private debt placements with insurance companies are examples of private market transactions. Because these transactions are private, they may be structured in any manner to which the relevant parties agree. By contrast, securities that are traded in public markets (for example, common stock and corporate bonds) are held by a large number of individuals. These securities must have fairly standardized contractual features because public investors do not generally have the time and expertise to negotiate unique, nonstandardized contracts. Broad ownership and standardization result in publicly traded securities being more liquid than tailor-made, uniquely negotiated securities.

Private Markets
Markets in which transactions are worked out directly between two or more parties.

Public Markets
Markets in which standardized contracts are traded on organized exchanges.

Other classifications could be made, but this breakdown shows that there are many types of financial markets. Also note that the distinctions among markets are often blurred and unimportant except as a general point of reference. For example, it makes little difference if a firm borrows for 11, 12, or 13 months, that is, whether the transaction is a "money" or "capital" market transaction. You should be aware of the important differences among types of markets, but don't be overly concerned about trying to distinguish them at the boundaries.

A healthy economy is dependent on efficient funds transfers from people who are net savers to firms and individuals who need capital. Without efficient transfers, the economy could not function: Carolina Power & Light Energy could not raise capital, so Raleigh's citizens would have no electricity; the Johnson family would not have adequate housing; Carol Hawk would have no place to invest her savings; and so forth. Obviously, the level of employment and productivity (i.e., the standard of living) would be much lower. Therefore, it is essential that financial markets function efficiently—not only quickly, but also inexpensively.

Table 2.1 is a listing of the most important instruments traded in the various financial markets. The instruments are arranged in ascending order of typical length of maturity. As we go through this book, we will look in more detail at many of the instruments listed in Table 2.1. For example, we will see that there are many varieties of corporate bonds, ranging from "plain vanilla" bonds to bonds that can be converted to common stocks to bonds whose interest payments vary depending on the inflation rate. Still, the table provides an overview of the characteristics and costs of the instruments traded in the major financial markets.

2-2B RECENT TRENDS

Financial markets have experienced many changes in recent years. Technological advances in computers and telecommunications, along with the globalization of banking and commerce, have led to deregulation, which has increased competition throughout the world. As a result, there are more efficient, internationally linked markets, which are far more complex than what existed a few years ago. While these developments have been largely positive, they have also created problems for policymakers. With these concerns in mind, Congress and regulators have moved to reregulate parts of the financial sector. The box titled "Changing Technology Has Transformed Financial Markets" on page 36 illustrates some dramatic examples of how changing technology has transformed financial markets in recent years.

Globalization has exposed the need for greater cooperation among regulators at the international level, but the task is not easy. Factors that complicate coordination include (1) the different structures in nations' banking and securities

TABLE 2.1 Summary of Major Market Instruments, Market Participants, and Security Characteristics

				Security Characteristics	
Instrument (1)	**Market (2)**	**Major Participants (3)**	**Riskiness (4)**	**Original Maturity (5)**	**Interest Rate on 3/26/18[a] (6)**
U.S. Treasury bills	Money	Sold by U.S. Treasury to finance federal expenditures	Default-free, close to riskless	91 days to 1 year	1.76%
Commercial paper	Money	Issued by financially secure firms to large investors	Low default risk	Up to 270 days	1.92%
Negotiable certificates of deposit (CDs)	Money	Issued by major money-center commercial banks to large investors	Default risk depends on the strength of the issuing bank	Up to 1 year	0.88%
Money market mutual funds	Money	Invest in Treasury bills, CDs, and commercial paper; held by individuals and businesses	Low degree of risk	No specific maturity (instant liquidity)	0.35%
Consumer credit, including credit card debt	Money	Issued by banks, credit unions, and finance companies to individuals	Risk is variable	Variable	Variable, but average APR is 13.09% to 23.59%
U.S. Treasury notes and bonds	Capital	Issued by U.S. government	No default risk, but price will decline if interest rates rise; hence, there is some risk	2 to 30 years	2.32% on 2-year to 3.07% on 30-year bonds
Mortgages	Capital	Loans to individuals and businesses secured by real estate; bought by banks and other institutions	Risk is variable; risk is high in the case of subprime loans	Up to 30 years	4.20% adjustable 5-year rate, 4.45% 30-year fixed rate
State and local government bonds	Capital	Issued by state and local governments; held by individuals and institutional investors	Riskier than U.S. government securities but exempt from most taxes	Up to 30 years	2.90% to 3.45% on 20-year AAA-rated to A-rated bonds

TABLE 2.1 Summary of Major Market Instruments, Market Participants, and Security Characteristics (*Continued*)

Instrument (1)	Market (2)	Major Participants (3)	Security Characteristics: Riskiness (4)	Security Characteristics: Original Maturity (5)	Security Characteristics: Interest Rate on 3/26/18[a] (6)
Corporate bonds	Capital	Issued by corporations; held by individuals and institutional investors	Riskier than U.S. government securities but less risky than preferred and common stocks; varying degree of risk within bonds depends on strength of issuer	Up to 40 years[b]	3.89% on 20-year AAA bonds, 4.15% on 20-year A bonds
Leases	Capital	Similar to debt in that firms can lease assets rather than borrow and then buy the assets	Risk similar to corporate bonds	Generally 3 to 20 years	Similar to bond yields
Preferred stocks	Capital	Issued by corporations to individuals and institutional investors	Generally riskier than corporate bonds but less risky than common stock	Unlimited	5.75% to 9.5%
Common stocks[c]	Capital	Issued by corporations to individuals and institutional investors	Riskier than bonds and preferred stock; risk varies from company to company	Unlimited	NA

Notes:

[a]The yields reported are from *The Wall Street Journal* (www.wsj.com), March 26, 2018, Board of Governors of the Federal Reserve System, "Selected Interest Rates (Daily)," www.federalreserve.gov/releases/H15/update; "FDIC Weekly National Rates and Rate Caps," FDIC (www.fdic.gov/regulations/resources/rates/); "and Municipal Market Yields," FMS Bonds, Inc. (www.fmsbonds.com/market-yields/).

[b]A few corporations have issued 100-year bonds; however, the majority has issued bonds with maturities that are less than 40 years.

[c]While common stocks do not pay interest, they are expected to provide a "return" in the form of dividends and capital gains. Historically, stock returns have averaged between 9% and 12% a year, but they can be much higher or lower in a given year. Of course, if you purchase a stock, your actual return may be considerably higher or lower than these historical averages.

Changing Technology Has Transformed Financial Markets

In recent years, changing technology has created numerous innovations and has dramatically transformed the operation of financial markets. Here are just a few interesting examples:

- Changing technology has created a whole class of firms that use computer algorithms to buy and sell securities, often at speeds less than a second. The trades conducted by these high-frequency trading (HFT) firms now represent a very significant fraction of the total trading volume in a given day. Proponents argue that these HFT firms generate liquidity, which helps reduce transactions costs and makes it easier for other investors to get in and out of the market. Critics argue that these activities can create market instability and that HFT firms often engage in trades that are self-serving to their own interests, to the detriment of other investors. A recent best-selling book by Michael Lewis, titled *Flash Boys*, attracted a lot of attention for its highly critical depiction of HFT firms.
- Changing technology has allowed some individuals and firms to bypass intermediaries and directly raise money from investors to help fund various projects. This activity is referred to as *crowdfunding*. Two leading examples of these platforms include Kickstarter and Indiegogo.[2]
- Many financial firms have created "robo-advisors" that utilize algorithmic technology to create relatively low-cost optimal investment portfolios for investors based on important factors such as their investment horizon and their tolerance for risk. These products have begun to have a disruptive effect on many human advisors, who are often more expensive. At the same time, astute financial advisors continue to find ways to add value and to incorporate technology in ways that benefit both them and their clients.
- Changing technology has changed the way that many people pay for transactions. Many of us rarely use cash anymore and instead often rely on debit and credit cards for payment. Others often use electronic commerce services such as PayPal to make online payments. More recently, there has been a growing interest in Bitcoin and other cryptocurrencies that involve no intermediary and have no fees.[3] The following chart from *The Wall Street Journal* illustrates the recent dramatic swings in Bitcoin's value. In March 2017, Bitcoin was trading at just over $1,000. The price surged to a high of $19,501 by mid-December. In the subsequent 3 months, the currency steadily fell in value and was trading just under $7,000 at the end of March 2018. Although intriguing, many are concerned that the lack of regulation makes Bitcoin and other cryptocurrencies an attractive vehicle for illegal transactions.[4]

- While many debate the true value of Bitcoin, even many of its skeptics believe that its underlying blockchain technology has the potential to be transformative. A 2015 article in *The Economist* provides an excellent early summary of the promise of this technology. Here's a relevant quote from that article:

  > But most unfair of all is that bitcoin's shady image causes people to overlook the extraordinary potential of the "blockchain", the technology that underpins it. This innovation carries a significance stretching far beyond cryptocurrency. The blockchain lets people who have no particular confidence in each other collaborate without having to go through a neutral central authority. Simply put, it is a machine for creating trust.

  Professor David Yermack of NYU, a leading academic expert on blockchain, believes that this technology will have profound effects for the accounting and financial system in the years ahead. His website (http://www.stern.nyu.edu/faculty/bio/david-yermack) is an excellent resource if you are looking for more details.

Sources: "The Trust Machine: The Technology Behind Bitcoin Could Transform How the Economy Works," *The Economist* (www.economist.com), October 31, 2015; and Steven Johnson, "Beyond the Bitcoin Bubble," *The New York Times* (www.nytimes.com), January 16, 2018.

[2] For a discussion of the role that these groups play in the funding process, see "Where Do Crowdfunding Platforms Fit in Venture Capital?" *The Wall Street Journal* (blogs.wsj.com), May 2, 2014.

[3] For a concise review of Bitcoin, see Tal Yellin, Dominic Aratari, and Jose Pagliery, "What Is Bitcoin?" *CNN Money* (money.cnn.com), January 2014.

[4] Despite these concerns, many believe that Bitcoin would become an important part of the global economy. See, for example, a recent article by Paul Vigna and Michael J. Casey, "BitBeat: The Fed's Surprisingly Warm Take on Bitcoin," *The Wall Street Journal* (blogs.wsj.com), May 19, 2014.

industries, (2) the trend toward financial services conglomerates, which obscures developments in various market segments, and (3) the reluctance of individual countries to give up control over their national monetary policies. Still, regulators are unanimous about the need to close the gaps in the supervision of worldwide markets.

Another important long-standing trend over the past few decades has been the increased use of **derivatives**. A derivative is any security whose value is *derived* from the price of some other "underlying" asset. An option to buy IBM stock is a derivative, as is a contract to buy Japanese yen 6 months from now. The value of the IBM option depends on the price of IBM's stock and the value of the Japanese yen "future" depends on the exchange rate between yen and dollars. The market for derivatives has grown dramatically over time, providing investors with new opportunities but also exposing them to new risks.

Derivatives
Any financial asset whose value is derived from the value of some other "underlying" asset.

To illustrate the growing importance of derivatives, consider the case of *credit default swaps (CDS)*.[5] Credit default swaps are contracts that offer protection against the default of a particular security. Suppose a bank wants to protect itself against the default of one of its borrowers. The bank could enter into a credit default swap where it agrees to make regular payments to another financial institution. In return, that financial institution agrees to insure the bank against losses that would occur if the borrower defaulted. The CDS market grew from less than $1 trillion at the beginning of 2001 to over $60 trillion by the end of 2007 (the beginning of the financial crisis). Almost 10 years later, the market is only at $10 trillion due to the impact of the financial crisis and tougher regulations on banks. However, the CDS market is currently experiencing renewed growth due to recent market volatility.[6]

Derivatives can be used to reduce risks or to speculate. Suppose a wheat processor's costs rise and its net income falls when the price of wheat rises. The processor could reduce its risk by purchasing derivatives—wheat futures—whose value increases when the price of wheat rises. This is a *hedging operation*, and its purpose is to reduce risk exposure. Speculation, on the other hand, is done in the hope of high returns, but it raises risk exposure. For example, several years ago Procter & Gamble disclosed that it lost $150 million on derivative investments. More recently, losses on mortgage-related derivatives helped contribute to the credit collapse in 2008.

If a bank or any other company reports that it invests in derivatives, how can one tell if the derivatives are held as a hedge against something like an increase in the price of wheat or as a speculative bet that wheat prices will rise? The answer is that it is very difficult to tell how derivatives are affecting the firm's risk profile. In the case of financial institutions, things are even more complicated—the derivatives are generally based on changes in interest rates, foreign exchange rates, or stock prices, and a large international bank might have tens of thousands of separate derivative contracts. The size and complexity of these transactions concern regulators, academics, and members of Congress. Former Fed Chairperson Alan Greenspan noted that in theory, derivatives should allow companies to better manage risk but that it is not clear whether recent innovations have increased or decreased the inherent stability of the financial system.

---

[5]A 2010 article in *The New York Times* reported that this market had grown from $900 billion in 2000 to more than $30 trillion in 2008. The article also describes how credit default swaps helped contribute to the 2007–2008 financial crises in the United States and Europe. Refer to "Times Topics: Credit Default Swaps," *The New York Times* (topics.nytimes.com), March 10, 2010.

[6]Chris White, "The Rise and Fall of the Hottest Financial Product in the World," *Business Insider* (www.businessinsider.com), August 15, 2016; and Philip Stafford and Joe Rennison, "Credit Default Swaps Activity Heats Up," *Financial Times* (www.ft.com), February 4, 2016.

Self*Test*

Distinguish between physical asset markets and financial asset markets.

What's the difference between spot markets and futures markets?

Distinguish between money markets and capital markets.

What's the difference between primary markets and secondary markets?

Differentiate between private and public markets.

Why are financial markets essential for a healthy economy and economic growth?

2-3 Financial Institutions

Direct funds transfers are common among individuals and small businesses and in economies where financial markets and institutions are less developed. But large businesses in developed economies generally find it more efficient to enlist the services of a financial institution when it comes time to raise capital.

In the United States and other developed nations, a set of highly efficient financial intermediaries has evolved. Their original roles were generally quite specific, and regulation prevented them from diversifying. However, in recent years regulations against diversification have been largely removed; today, the differences between institutions have become blurred. Still, there remains a degree of institutional identity. Therefore, it is useful to understand the major categories of financial institutions. Keep in mind, though, that one company can own a number of subsidiaries that engage in the different functions described next.

Investment Bank
An organization that underwrites and distributes new investment securities and helps businesses obtain financing.

1. **Investment banks** traditionally help companies raise capital. They (1) help corporations design securities with features that are currently attractive to investors, (2) buy these securities from the corporation, and (3) resell them to savers. Because the investment bank generally guarantees that the firm will raise the needed capital, the investment bankers are also called *underwriters*. The credit crisis has had a dramatic effect on the investment banking industry. Bear Stearns collapsed and was later acquired by JPMorgan, Lehman Brothers went bankrupt, and Merrill Lynch was forced to sell out to Bank of America. The two "surviving" major investment banks (Morgan Stanley and Goldman Sachs) received Federal Reserve approval to become commercial bank holding companies.

Commercial Bank
The traditional department store of finance serving a variety of savers and borrowers.

2. **Commercial banks**, such as Bank of America, Citibank, Wells Fargo, and JPMorgan Chase, are the traditional "department stores of finance" because they serve a variety of savers and borrowers. Historically, commercial banks were the major institutions that handled checking accounts and through which the Federal Reserve System expanded or contracted the money supply. Today, however, several other institutions also provide checking services and significantly influence the money supply. Note too that the larger banks are generally part of financial services corporations as described next.[7]

Financial Services Corporation
A firm that offers a wide range of financial services, including investment banking, brokerage operations, insurance, and commercial banking.

3. **Financial services corporations** are large conglomerates that combine many different financial institutions within a single corporation. Most financial services corporations started in one area but have now diversified to cover most of the financial spectrum. For example, Citigroup owns Citibank (a commercial bank), an investment bank, a securities brokerage organization, insurance companies, and leasing companies.

[7]Two other institutions that were important a few years ago were *savings and loan associations* and *mutual savings banks*. Most of these organizations have now been merged into commercial banks.

4. *Credit unions* are cooperative associations whose members are supposed to have a common bond, such as being employees of the same firm. Members' savings are loaned only to other members, generally for auto purchases, home improvement loans, and home mortgages. Credit unions are often the cheapest source of funds available to individual borrowers.
5. *Pension funds* are retirement plans funded by corporations or government agencies for their workers and administered primarily by the trust departments of commercial banks or by life insurance companies. Pension funds invest primarily in bonds, stocks, mortgages, and real estate.
6. *Life insurance companies* take savings in the form of annual premiums; invest these funds in stocks, bonds, real estate, and mortgages; and make payments to the beneficiaries of the insured parties. In recent years, life insurance companies have also offered a variety of tax-deferred savings plans designed to provide benefits to participants when they retire.
7. **Mutual funds** are corporations that accept money from savers and then use these funds to buy stocks, long-term bonds, or short-term debt instruments issued by businesses or government units. These organizations pool funds and thus reduce risks by diversification. They also achieve economies of scale in analyzing securities, managing portfolios, and buying and selling securities. Different funds are designed to meet the objectives of different types of savers. Hence, there are bond funds for those who prefer safety, stock funds for savers who are willing to accept significant risks in the hope of higher returns, and **money market funds** that are used as interest-bearing checking accounts.

   Another important distinction exists between actively managed funds and indexed funds. *Actively managed funds* try to outperform the overall markets, whereas *indexed funds* are designed to simply replicate the performance of a specific market index. For example, the portfolio manager of an actively managed stock fund uses his or her expertise to select what he or she thinks will be the best-performing stocks over a given time period. By contrast, an index fund that tracks the S&P 500 index will simply hold the basket of stocks that comprise the S&P 500. Both types of funds provide investors with valuable diversification, but actively managed funds typically have much higher fees—in large part, because of the extra costs involved in trying to select stocks that will (hopefully) outperform the market. In any given year, the very best actively managed funds will outperform the market index, but many will do worse than the overall market—even before taking into account their higher fees. Furthermore, it is extremely difficult to predict which actively managed funds will beat the market in a particular year. For this reason, many academics and practitioners have encouraged investors to rely more heavily on indexed funds.[8]

   There are literally thousands of different mutual funds with dozens of different goals and purposes. Excellent information on the objectives and past performances of the various funds are provided in publications such as *Value Line Investment Survey* and *Morningstar Mutual Funds,* which are available in most libraries and on the Internet.
8. *Exchange Traded Funds (ETFs)* are similar to regular mutual funds and are often operated by mutual fund companies. ETFs buy a portfolio of stocks of a certain type—for example, the S&P 500 or media companies or Chinese companies—and then sell their own shares to the public. ETF shares are generally traded in the public markets, so an investor who wants to invest in the Chinese market, for example, can buy shares in an ETF that holds stocks

Mutual Funds
Organizations that pool investor funds to purchase financial instruments and thus reduce risks through diversification.

Money Market Funds
Mutual funds that invest in short-term, low-risk securities and allow investors to write checks against their accounts.

[8]Refer to Mark Hulbert, "The Index Funds Win Again," *The New York Times* (www.nytimes.com), February 21, 2009; and Rick Ferri, "Index Fund Portfolios Reign Superior," *Forbes* (www.forbes.com), August 20, 2012.

TABLE 2.2 The 10 Largest Exchange Traded Funds (March 2018)

Symbol	Fund Name	Assets Under Management (Billions of Dollars)	Underlying Index
SPY	SPDR S&P 500 ETF	$250.60	S&P 500
IVV	iShares Core S&P 500 ETF	138.81	S&P 500
VTI	Vanguard Total Stock Market ETF	91.18	CRSP U.S. Total Market
VOO	Vanguard S&P 500 ETF	85.77	S&P 500
EFA	iShares MSCI EAFE ETF	77.53	MSCI EAFE
VEA	Vanguard FTSE Developed Markets ETF	69.49	MSCI EAFE
VWO	Vanguard FTSE Emerging Markets ETF	68.13	FTSE Emerging
QQQ	PowerShares QQQ ETF	60.25	NASDAQ 100
IEFA	iShares Core MSCI EAFE ETF	55.85	MSCI EAFE Investable Market Index
AGG	ishares Core U.S. Aggregate Bond ETF	54.57	Barclays Capital U.S. Aggregate Bond

Source: etfdb.com/compare/market-cap/

in that particular market. Table 2.2 provides a list of the top ETFs in early March 2018 ranked according to the ETF's assets under management (AUM).

9. *Hedge funds* are also similar to mutual funds because they accept money from savers and use the funds to buy various securities, but there are some important differences. While mutual funds (and ETFs) are registered and regulated by the Securities and Exchange Commission (SEC), hedge funds are largely unregulated. This difference in regulation stems from the fact that mutual funds typically target small investors, whereas hedge funds typically have large minimum investments (often exceeding $1 million) and are marketed primarily to institutions and individuals with high net worths. Hedge funds received their name because they traditionally were used when an individual was trying to hedge risks. For example, a hedge fund manager who believes that interest rate differentials between corporate and Treasury bonds are too large might simultaneously buy a portfolio of corporate bonds and sell a portfolio of Treasury bonds. In this case, the portfolio would be "hedged" against overall movements in interest rates, but it would perform especially well if the spread between these securities became smaller.

   However, some hedge funds take on risks that are considerably higher than that of an average individual stock or mutual fund. For example, Paulson & Company, a firm that profited during the 2008 subprime mortgage crisis, has lost more than half of its hedge fund's assets during the last 9 years. In fact, Paulson Partners Fund, a merger arbitrage strategy fund, has lost 42% of its value over the past 4 years, while Paulson Partners Enhanced Fund declined by 35% in 2017 and by 49% in 2016. The fund made a big bet on Valeant, a Canadian pharmaceutical company that has recently been accused of improper accounting and predatory price hikes, and it invested in other struggling pharmaceutical companies. The fund's estimated losses could total $4 billion. In fact, during 2016, John Paulson, the hedge fund manager, actually pledged personal holdings as additional collateral for a line of credit to help bolster the fund.[9]

   Table 2.3 lists the 10 largest hedge funds for 2017. As evidence of their growing importance, each of these funds controls more than $100 billion

[9]Refer to GuruFocus.com, "John Paulson Invests in Entertainment in 4th Quarter," *Forbes* (www.forbes.com), February 20, 2018; and Nathan Reiff, "The Biggest Hedge Fund Failures of 2016," *Investopedia* (www.investopedia.com), January 6, 2017.

LOWER FEES MOTIVATE INVESTORS TO MOVE TOWARD INDEX FUNDS

In the text, we point out that actively managed funds and hedge funds often have considerably higher fees than passive investment products that include index funds and ETFs. A passive fund generally costs less because you don't have to pay a group of often expensive fund managers to try to beat the market—instead, the fund is just simply replicating the given market using technology. If anything, increased competition and improving technology have further accelerated the drop in passive investment fees. For example, a 2017 *Wall Street Journal* article utilizing Morningstar data reports that the average annual cost per $10,000 invested in an actively managed U.S. stock fund is $81—which is more than five times higher than the $14 average cost for passively managed U.S. stock funds. Moreover, more than 100 passive mutual funds and exchange traded funds charge less than $10 for every $10,000 invested.

As you might expect this gap in fees has led many investors to shift their money toward passive products. Morningstar's Annual Funds Flow report illustrates active versus passive U.S. equity flows from 2006 through 2017:

Further strengthening the case for passive investments is the historical evidence, which has convincingly shown that the average actively managed fund typically fails to produce higher returns than the corresponding index funds. So, investors in actively managed products are often paying more for poorer relative performance. Keep in mind, however, that in any given year, the best-performing actively managed funds will outperform the corresponding index. The challenge, however, is to find funds that consistently beat the overall market.

Relatedly, Warren Buffet attracted a lot of attention in 2007 when he made a "million-dollar bet" with Ted Seides, co-manager of the asset-management firm Protégé Partners. Each party put $500,000 toward charity and the bet concerned which of two hypothetical investments would generate the highest performance over the following 10 years. Buffet's investment was in a low-cost S&P 500 index fund managed by Vanguard. Seides chose instead to invest in five hedge funds. In February 2018, Buffett reported the final results in his 2017 letter to shareholders: the index fund rose 125.8%, which translates into an average annual compounded return of 8.5%. By contrast, the five hedge funds' returns during the 10-year period ranged from 2.8% to 87.7%, with annual returns ranging between 0.3% to 6.5%.

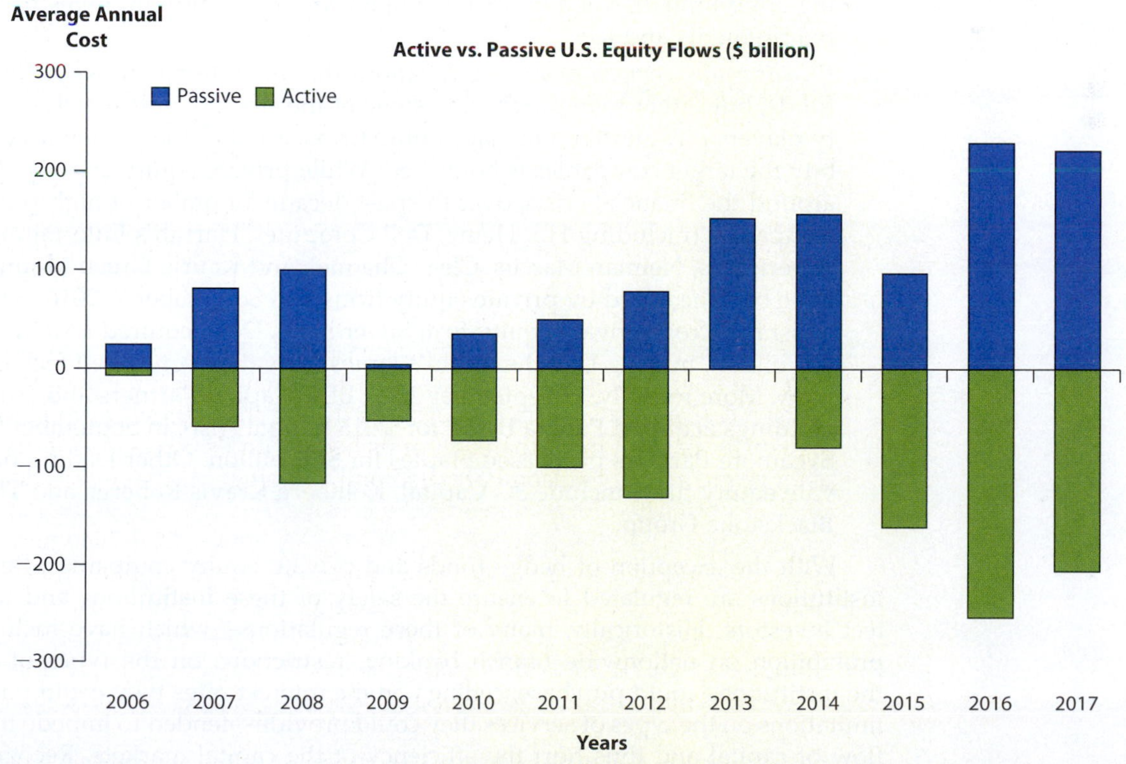

Source: Morningstar Direct Asset Flows

Sources: Bernice Napach, "Passive Investments Drive Record Fund Flows in 2017: Morningstar," *ThinkAdvisor* (www.thinkadvisor.com), January 29, 2018; Carol J. Loomis, "Warren Buffett Scorches the Hedge Funds," *Fortune* (www.fortune.com), February 25, 2017; Jason Zweig and Sarah Krouse, "Fees on Mutual Funds and ETFs Tumble Toward Zero," *The Wall Street Journal* (www.wsj.com), January 26, 2016; and Warren Buffett's Annual Letter to Berkshire Hathaway Shareholders (www.berkshirehathaway.com/letters/2017ltr.pdf), February 24, 2018.

TABLE 2.3 The 10 Largest Hedge Funds (2017)

Fund	Assets under Management (Billions of Dollars)
Nomura Asset Management Co. LTD.	$416.0
Bridgewater Associates, LP	239.3
Millennium Management LLC	207.6
Samsung Asset Management Company, LTD.	182.2
Citadel Advisors LLC	152.7
Nikko Asset Management Co. LTD.	148.0
Apollo Capital Management, LP	125.5
Pictet Asset Management SA	122.8
Vanguard Asset Management LTD.	120.2
The Carlyle Group	101.9

Source: Ian Rayner, "Biggest Hedge Funds by Assets Under Management July 2017," (www.raynergobran.com), July 9, 2017.

in assets. While hedge funds have grown tremendously over the past two decades, the road has been a bit bumpy in recent years. Hedge fund assets under management fell sharply after the financial crisis, and it wasn't until 2013 that they once again reached their pre-crisis levels. At the same time, many hedge funds have come under fire for their high fees and sub-optimal performance. They have also faced increased competition from other products and investment advisors. In the midst of this challenging environment, some funds have reduced their minimum investment requirements and fees.

10. *Private equity companies* are organizations that operate much like hedge funds, but rather than purchasing some of the stock of a firm, private equity players buy and then manage entire firms. Most of the money used to buy the target companies is borrowed. While private equity activity slowed around the financial crisis, over the past decade a number of high-profile companies (including H.J. Heinz, Dell Computer, Harrah's Entertainment, Albertson's, Neiman Marcus, Clear Channel, and Keurig Green Mountain) have been acquired by private equity firms. On September 7, 2016, with assistance from private equity firm Silver Lake, Dell acquired EMC for $60 billion, making Dell the world's largest privately controlled tech company. More recently, in September 2017, BDT Capital Partners and JAB Holdings acquired Panera Bread for $7.16 billion. Also, in September 2017, Sycamore Partners purchased Staples for $6.9 billion. Other leading private equity firms include 3G Capital, Kohlberg Kravis Roberts, and The Blackstone Group.

With the exception of hedge funds and private equity companies, financial institutions are regulated to ensure the safety of these institutions and to protect investors. Historically, many of these regulations—which have included a prohibition on nationwide branch banking, restrictions on the types of assets the institutions could purchase, ceilings on the interest rates they could pay, and limitations on the types of services they could provide—tended to impede the free flow of capital and thus hurt the efficiency of the capital markets. Recognizing this fact, policymakers took several steps during the 1980s and 1990s to deregulate financial services companies. For example, the restriction barring nationwide branching by banks was eliminated in 1999.

Many believed that excessive deregulation and insufficient supervision of the financial sector were partially responsible for the 2007–2008 financial crisis.

Largest Banks and Underwriters **TABLE 2.4**

Panel A: U.S. Bank Holding Companies[a]	**Panel B: World Banking Companies**[b]	**Panel C: Leading Global IPO Underwriters**[c]
JPMorgan Chase & Co.	Industrial & Commercial Bank of China Ltd. (China)	Morgan Stanley
Bank of America Corp.	China Construction Bank Corporation (China)	JPMorgan
Wells Fargo & Co.	Agricultural Bank of China Ltd (China)	Citi
Citigroup Inc.	Bank of China Ltd. (China)	Credit Suisse
Goldman Sachs Group, Inc.	BNP Paribas SA (France)	Goldman Sachs
Morgan Stanley	JPMorgan Chase Bank National Association (USA)	UBS
U.S. Bancorp	China Development Bank (China)	BofA Merrill Lynch
PNC Financial Services Group, Inc.	Japan Post Bank Co. Ltd. (Japan)	Deutsche Bank
TD Group US Holdings LLC	The Bank of Tokyo-Mitsubishi UFJ Ltd. (Japan)	CITIC Group Corp. Ltd.
Bank of New York Mellon Corp.	Wells Fargo Bank National Association (USA)	Barclays

Notes:
[a]Ranked by total assets as of December 31, 2017.
Source: National Information Center (www.ffiec.gov/nicpubweb/nicweb/HCSGreaterThan10B.aspx).
[b]Ranked by total assets from balance sheet information available on January 30, 2018.
Source: https://accuity.com/resources/bank-rankings/.
[c]Ranked by dollar amount raised through new IPO issues in 2017. For this ranking, the lead underwriter (manager) is given credit for the entire issue.
Source: Thomson Reuters, "Global Equity Capital Markets Review: Managing Underwriters, Full Year 2017," (https://www.thomsonreuters.co.jp/content/dam/openweb/documents/pdf/japan/market-review/2017/ecm-4q-2017-e.pdf), December 31, 2017, p. 3.

With these concerns in mind, Congress passed the Dodd-Frank Act. The legislation's main goals were to create a new agency for consumer protection, work to increase the transparency of derivative transactions, and force financial institutions to take steps to limit excessive risk taking and to hold more capital. Since its enactment, the effectiveness of Dodd-Frank has been vigorously debated. Some have argued that it has effectively accomplished its main goals—while others (including President Trump) contend that it has imposed significant compliance costs on the financial services industry and have called for its repeal. In fact, the Senate is due to pass legislation in 2018 to ease regulatory scrutiny for community and regional banks.[10]

Panel A of Table 2.4 lists the 10 largest U.S. bank holding companies, and Panel B shows the leading world banking companies. Among the world's

[10]Alan S. Blinder, "Washington Protects Wall Street at Ordinary Citizens' Expense," *The Wall Street Journal* (www.wsj.com), February 12, 2017; Dave Michaels, "Trump's Man for the SEC: Time to Ease Regulation," *The Wall Street Journal* (www.wsj.com), February 19, 2017; and Renae Merle, "The 5 Ways the Senate Plans to Roll Back Regulations on Wall Street," *The Washington Post* (www.washingtonpost.com), March 6, 2018.

10 largest, only two are based in the United States. While U.S. banks have grown dramatically as a result of recent mergers, they are still small by global standards. Panel C of the table lists the 10 leading global IPO underwriters in terms of dollar volume of new equity issues. Five of the top underwriters are also listed as major commercial banks or are part of bank holding companies shown in Panels A and B, which confirms the continued blurring of distinctions between different types of financial institutions.

SECURITIZATION HAS DRAMATICALLY TRANSFORMED THE BANKING INDUSTRY

At one time, commercial banking was a simpler business than it is today. A typical bank received money from its depositors and used it to make loans. In the vast majority of cases, the banker held the loan on its books until it matured. Because they originated the loan and continued to hold it on their books, the banks generally knew the risks involved. However, because banks often had limited funding, there was a cap on the number of loans they could hold on their books. And because most of the loans were made to individuals and businesses in their local market, banks were less able to spread their risk.

To address these concerns, financial engineers came up with the idea of securitizing loans. This is a process whereby an agent (such as an investment bank) creates an entity that buys a large number of loans from a wide range of banks and then issues securities that are backed by the loan payments. Securitization began in the 1970s when government-backed entities purchased pools of home mortgages and then issued securities backed by the cash flows from the diversified portfolio of mortgages. In many respects, securitization was a tremendous innovation. Banks no longer had to hold their mortgages, so they could quickly convert the originated loan to cash, enabling them to redeploy their capital to make other loans. At the same time, the newly created securities gave investors an opportunity to invest in a diversified portfolio of home mortgages. In addition, these securities traded on the open market so that investors were able to easily buy and sell them as their circumstances and views of the mortgage markets changed over time.

Over the last few decades, this process has accelerated. Bankers have securitized different types of loans into all types of different securities. One notable example is *collateralized debt obligations (CDOs)*, where an entity issues several classes of securities backed by a portfolio of loans. For example, an investment bank purchases $100 million of mortgage loans from banks and mortgage brokers throughout the country. The investment bank uses the collateral to create $100 million in new securities, which are divided into three classes (often referred to as *tranches*). The Class A bonds have the first claim on the cash flows from the mortgages. Because they have the first claim, they are the least risky and are rated AAA by the rating agencies. The Class B bonds get paid after the Class A bonds are paid, but they too will generally have a high rating. Finally, the Class C bonds get paid. Because they are last in line, they will have the highest risk, but they will also sell for the lowest price. If the underlying mortgages perform well, the C bonds will realize the highest returns, but they will suffer the most if the underlying mortgages don't perform well.

CDOs backed by pools of higher risk (subprime) mortgages played a major role in the 2007–2008 financial crisis. During the housing boom, financial institutions and mortgage brokers originated a large number of new mortgages, and investment bankers hungry for fees were more than happy to create new CDOs backed by these subprime mortgages. The securities created through these CDOs were sold primarily to other commercial and investment banks and to other financial institutions, such as hedge funds, mutual funds, and pension funds. Buoyed by the mistaken belief that housing prices would never fall, many viewed these securities as solid investments, and they received additional comfort from the fact that they were highly rated.

When the housing market collapsed, the value of these securities plummeted, destroying the balance sheets of many financial institutions. Making matters worse, it became very hard to value these securities because they were backed by such a large, diverse pool of mortgages. Not sure what they had on their books, many institutions tried to sell these securities at the same time, and the "rush to the exit" further depressed prices, causing the cycle to deepen.

Following the crisis, many have looked to reform the securitization business, and others have criticized the rating agencies for routinely assigning high credit ratings to what in hindsight were extremely risky securities. At the same time, an article in *Barron's* highlights the important role that securitization plays in the capital markets and raises concerns that the economy won't thrive again until the securitization business recovers.

Source: David Adler, "A Flat Dow for 10 Years? Why It Could Happen," *Barron's* (www.barrons.com), December 28, 2009.

Self*Test*

What's the difference between a commercial bank and an investment bank?

List the major types of financial institutions, and briefly describe the primary function of each.

What are some important differences between mutual funds, Exchange Traded Funds, and hedge funds? How are they similar?

2-4 The Stock Market

As noted earlier, outstanding, previously issued securities are traded in the secondary markets. Approximately 75% of U.S. stocks are owned by long-term investors, while only 25% are held by short-term investors.[11] By far, the most active secondary market—and the most important one to financial managers—is the *stock market,* where the prices of firms' stocks are established. Because the primary goal of financial managers is to maximize shareholder wealth, knowledge of the stock market is important to anyone involved in managing a business.

There are a number of different stock markets. The two leaders are NYSE and NASDAQ. Stocks are traded using a variety of market procedures, but there are two basic types: (1) *physical location exchanges,* which include the NYSE and several regional stock exchanges, and (2) *electronic dealer-based markets,* which include the NASDAQ, the less formal over-the-counter market, and the recently developed electronic communications networks (ECNs). (See the box titled "The NYSE and NASDAQ Go Global.") Because the physical location exchanges are easier to describe and understand, we discuss them first.

2-4A PHYSICAL LOCATION STOCK EXCHANGES

Physical location exchanges are tangible entities. Each of the larger exchanges occupies its own building, allows a limited number of people to trade on its floor, and has an elected governing body—its board of governors. Members of the NYSE formerly had "seats" on the exchange, although everybody stood. Today the seats have been exchanged for trading licenses, which are auctioned to member organizations and cost about $50,000 per year. Most of the larger investment banks operate *brokerage departments.* They purchase seats on the exchanges and designate one or more of their officers as members. The exchanges are open on all normal working days, with the members meeting in a large room equipped with telephones and other electronic equipment that enable each member to communicate with his or her firm's offices throughout the country.

Physical Location Exchanges
Formal organizations having tangible physical locations that conduct auction markets in designated ("listed") securities.

Like other markets, security exchanges facilitate communication between buyers and sellers. For example, Goldman Sachs (the fifth-largest brokerage firm) might receive an order from a customer who wants to buy shares of GE stock. Simultaneously, Morgan Stanley (the largest brokerage firm) might receive an order from a customer wanting to sell shares of GE. Each broker communicates electronically with the firm's representative on the NYSE.

[11] Refer to Rebecca Darr and Tim Koller, "How to Build an Alliance Against Corporate Short-Termism," McKinsey & Company (www.mckinsey.com), January 2017.

GLOBAL PERSPECTIVES

The NYSE and NASDAQ Go Global

Advances in computers and telecommunications that spurred consolidation in the financial services industry have also promoted online trading systems that bypass the traditional exchanges. These systems, which are known as *electronic communications networks (ECNs)*, use electronic technology to bring buyers and sellers together. The rise of ECNs accelerated the move toward 24-hour trading. U.S. investors who wanted to trade after the U.S. markets closed could utilize an ECN, thus bypassing the NYSE and NASDAQ.

Recognizing the new threat, the NYSE and NASDAQ took action. First, both exchanges went public, which enabled them to use their stock as "currency" that could be used to buy ECNs and other exchanges across the globe. For example, NASDAQ acquired the Philadelphia Stock Exchange, several ECNs, and 15% of the London Stock Exchange. NASDAQ has continued acquiring companies. On February 25, 2016, NASDAQ acquired Marketwired to strengthen its global corporate services. And, on June 30, 2016, NASDAQ acquired International Securities Exchange (ISE) to strengthen its equities options business. The NYSE also looked for acquisition targets, including a merger with the largest European exchange, Euronext, to form NYSE Euronext and then acquiring the American Stock Exchange (AMEX).

However, NYSE Euronext itself became a takeover target, when it was acquired by the Intercontinental Exchange (ICE) on November 3, 2013. The deal combined ICE's futures, over-the-counter, and derivatives trading with the NYSE's stock trading. On June 24, 2014, ICE spun off Euronext. On January 31, 2017, the NYSE acquired National Stock Exchange, which gives the NYSE Group an additional U.S. exchange license. Also, the NYSE has announced plans to allow trading of all U.S. stocks and exchange traded funds on its trading floor. Most of the U.S. stock exchanges already allow trading of any security, no matter where it is listed. NYSE's move is seen to be a response to IEX Group Inc., an upstart trading company wanting to level the playing field between ultra-fast traders and traditional investors.

These actions illustrate the growing importance of global trading, especially electronic trading. Indeed, many pundits have concluded that the floor traders who buy and sell stocks on the NYSE and other physical exchanges will soon become a thing of the past. That may or may not be true, but it is clear that stock trading will continue to undergo dramatic changes in the upcoming years. To find a wealth of up-to-date information on the NYSE and NASDAQ, go to Google (or another search engine) and do NYSE history and NASDAQ history searches.

Sources: John McCrank and Luke Jeffs, "ICE to Buy NYSE Euronext for $8.2 Billion," www.reuters.com, December 20, 2012; Inti Landauro, "ICE Plans Euronext IPO," *The Wall Street Journal* (www.wsj.com), May 27, 2014; Alex Gavrish, "Euronext NV: Recent Spin-Off Warrants Further Monitoring," *ValueWalk* (www.valuewalk.com), August 25, 2014; "Nasdaq Reaches 52-Week High on Compelling Acquisitions," www.nasdaq.com, March 14, 2016; "NYSE Agrees to Acquire National Stock Exchange," *Business Wire* (www.businesswire.com), December 14, 2016; and Alexander Osipovich, "NYSE to Open Floor Trading to Stocks Listed at Rival Exchanges," *The Wall Street Journal* (www.wsj.com), January 11, 2017.

Other brokers throughout the country are also communicating with their own exchange members. The exchange members with *sell orders* offer the shares for sale, and they are bid for by the members with *buy orders*. Thus, the exchanges operate as *auction markets*.[12]

[12]The NYSE is actually a modified auction market wherein people (through their brokers) bid for stocks. Originally—in 1792—brokers would literally shout, "I have 100 shares of Erie for sale; how much am I offered?" and then sell to the highest bidder. If a broker had a buy order, he or she would shout, "I want to buy 100 shares of Erie; who'll sell at the best price?" The same general situation still exists, although the exchanges now have members known as *specialists* who facilitate the trading process by keeping an inventory of shares of the stocks in which they specialize. If a buy order comes in at a time when no sell order arrives, the specialist will sell some inventory. Similarly, if a sell order comes in, the specialist will buy and add to inventory. The specialist sets a *bid price* (the price the specialist will pay for the stock) and an *ask price* (the price at which shares will be sold out of inventory). The bid and ask prices are set at levels designed to keep the inventory in balance. If many buy orders start coming in because of favorable developments, or many sell orders come in because of unfavorable events, the specialist will raise or lower prices to keep supply and demand in balance. Bid prices are somewhat lower than ask prices, with the difference, or *spread*, representing the specialist's profit margin. Special facilities are available to help institutional investors such as mutual or pension funds sell large blocks of stock without depressing their prices. In essence, brokerage houses that cater to institutional clients will purchase blocks (defined as 10,000 or more shares) and then resell the stock to other institutions or individuals. Also, when a firm has a major announcement that is likely to cause its stock price to change sharply, it will ask the exchange to halt trading in its stock until the announcement has been made and the resulting information has been digested by investors.

2-4B OVER-THE-COUNTER (OTC) AND THE NASDAQ STOCK MARKETS

Although the stocks of most large companies trade on the NYSE, a larger number of stocks trade off the exchange in what was traditionally referred to as the **over-the-counter (OTC) market**. An explanation of the term *over-the-counter* will help clarify how this term arose. As noted earlier, the exchanges operate as auction markets—buy and sell orders come in more or less simultaneously, and exchange members match these orders. When a stock is traded infrequently, perhaps because the firm is new or small, few buy and sell orders come in, and matching them within a reasonable amount of time is difficult. To avoid this problem, some brokerage firms maintain an inventory of such stocks and stand prepared to make a market for them. These "dealers" buy when individual investors want to sell, and they sell part of their inventory when investors want to buy. At one time, the inventory of securities was kept in a safe, and the stocks, when bought and sold, were literally passed over the counter.

Over-the-Counter (OTC) Market
A large collection of brokers and dealers, connected electronically by telephones and computers, that provides for trading in unlisted securities.

Today these markets are often referred to as **dealer markets**. A dealer market includes all facilities that are needed to conduct security transactions, but the transactions are not made on the physical location exchanges. The dealer market system consists of (1) the relatively few *dealers* who hold inventories of these securities and who are said to "make a market" in these securities, (2) the thousands of brokers who act as *agents* in bringing the dealers together with investors, and (3) the computers, terminals, and electronic networks that provide a communication link between dealers and brokers. The dealers who make a market in a particular stock quote the price at which they will pay for the stock (the *bid price*) and the price at which they will sell shares (the *ask price*). Each dealer's prices, which are adjusted as supply and demand conditions change, can be seen on computer screens across the world. The *bid-ask spread*, which is the difference between bid and ask prices, represents the dealer's markup, or profit. The dealer's risk increases when the stock is more volatile or when the stock trades infrequently. Generally, we would expect volatile, infrequently traded stocks to have wider spreads in order to compensate the dealers for assuming the risk of holding them in inventory.

Dealer Markets
Include all facilities that are needed to conduct security transactions not conducted on the physical location exchanges.

Brokers and dealers who participate in the OTC market are members of a self-regulatory body known as the *Financial Industry Regulatory Authority (FINRA)*, which licenses brokers and oversees trading practices. The computerized network used by FINRA is known as NASDAQ, which originally stood for "National Association of Securities Dealers Automated Quotations."

NASDAQ started as a quotation system, but it has grown to become an organized securities market with its own listing requirements. Over the past decade, the competition between the NYSE and NASDAQ has become increasingly fierce. As noted earlier, the NASDAQ has invested in the London Stock Exchange and other market makers, while the NYSE merged with Euronext (which was later spun off) and was purchased by Intercontinental Exchange—further adding to the competition. Because most of the larger companies trade on the NYSE, the market capitalization of NYSE-traded stocks is much higher than for stocks traded on NASDAQ. As of June 30, 2017, the market cap of listed companies on the NYSE was over $21.3 trillion and those listed companies had over 453 billion shares outstanding.[13]

Interestingly, many high-tech companies such as Microsoft, Google (now Alphabet Inc.), and Intel have remained on NASDAQ even though they meet the listing requirements of the NYSE. At the same time, however, other high-tech companies have left NASDAQ for the NYSE. Despite these defections, NASDAQ's growth over the past decade has been impressive. In the years ahead, competition between NASDAQ and NYSE will no doubt remain fierce.

---

[13]Refer to "NYSE Group Shares Outstanding and Market Capitalization of Companies Listed, 2017," (www.nyxdata.com/nysedata/asp/factbook/viewer_edition.asp?mode=tables&key=333&category=5), March 29, 2018.

SelfTest

What are the differences between the physical location exchanges and the NASDAQ stock market?

What is the bid-ask spread?

2-5 The Market for Common Stock

Closely Held Corporation
A corporation that is owned by a few individuals who are typically associated with the firm's management.

Publicly Owned Corporation
A corporation that is owned by a relatively large number of individuals who are not actively involved in the firm's management.

Some companies are so small that their common stocks are not actively traded; they are owned by relatively few people, usually the companies' managers. These firms are said to be *privately owned*, or **closely held, corporations**; their stock is called *closely held stock*. In contrast, the stocks of most large companies are owned by thousands of investors, most of whom are not active in management. These companies are called **publicly owned corporations**, and their stock is called *publicly held stock*.

2-5A TYPES OF STOCK MARKET TRANSACTIONS

We can classify stock market transactions into three distinct categories:

1. *Outstanding shares of established publicly owned companies that are traded: the secondary market.* Allied Food Products, the company we study in Chapters 3 and 4, has 75 million shares of stock outstanding. If the owner of 100 shares sells his or her stock, the trade is said to have occurred in the *secondary market*. Thus, the market for outstanding shares, or *used shares*, is the secondary market. The company receives no new money when sales occur in this market.
2. *Additional shares sold by established publicly owned companies: the primary market.* If Allied Food decides to sell (or issue) an additional 1 million shares to raise new equity capital, this transaction is said to occur in the *primary market*.[14]
3. *Initial public offerings made by privately held firms: the IPO market.* Whenever stock in a closely held corporation is offered to the public for the first time, the company is said to be **going public**. The market for stock that is just being offered to the public is called the **initial public offering (IPO) market**. In the summer of 2004, Google sold shares to the public for the first time at $85 per share. By March 2018, its parent company's stock (Alphabet Inc.) was selling for more than $1,030. Another noteworthy deal was when General Motors (GM) went public as part of its reorganization following its government bailout. Other high-profile recent IPOs include LinkedIn Corp, Alibaba, Facebook, Twitter, Snap (the parent company of Snapchat), and Dropbox.

Going Public
The act of selling stock to the public at large by a closely held corporation or its principal stockholders.

Initial Public Offering (IPO) Market
The market for stocks of companies that are in the process of going public.

The number of new IPOs rises and falls with the stock market. When the market is strong, many companies go public to bring in new capital and to give their founders an opportunity to cash out some of their shares. As you might expect, not all IPOs are well received. The most striking example is Facebook, which had the largest and highest-profile IPO of 2012. Amid much fanfare, the company went public on May 18, 2012, at a price of $38 per share. In the 2 weeks after the IPO, the stock had fallen to below $28, and just a few months later in September,

---

[14]Allied has 90 million shares authorized but only 75 million outstanding; thus, it has 15 million authorized but unissued shares. If it had no authorized but unissued shares, management could increase the authorized shares by obtaining stockholders' approval, which would generally be granted without any arguments.

INITIAL BUZZ SURROUNDING IPOs DOESN'T ALWAYS TRANSLATE INTO LONG-LASTING SUCCESS

A recent article in *Fortune* cautions IPO investors: "Don't be fooled by the drama of first-day performance." The article suggests that there is not always a strong correlation between the market's initial reaction to an IPO and the stock's longer-run performance. As a case in point, *Fortune* compares the post-IPO performance of Facebook and Twitter. As we mention in the text, Facebook's stock slid sharply in the aftermath of its IPO. However, since then Facebook's stock has impressively rebounded. By contrast, Twitter's IPO generated a lot of initial buzz, but since then the stock has languished. In late March 2018, its share price hovered around $29.00. The following chart illustrates Twitter's post-IPO struggles and highlights the major events the company faced after going public.

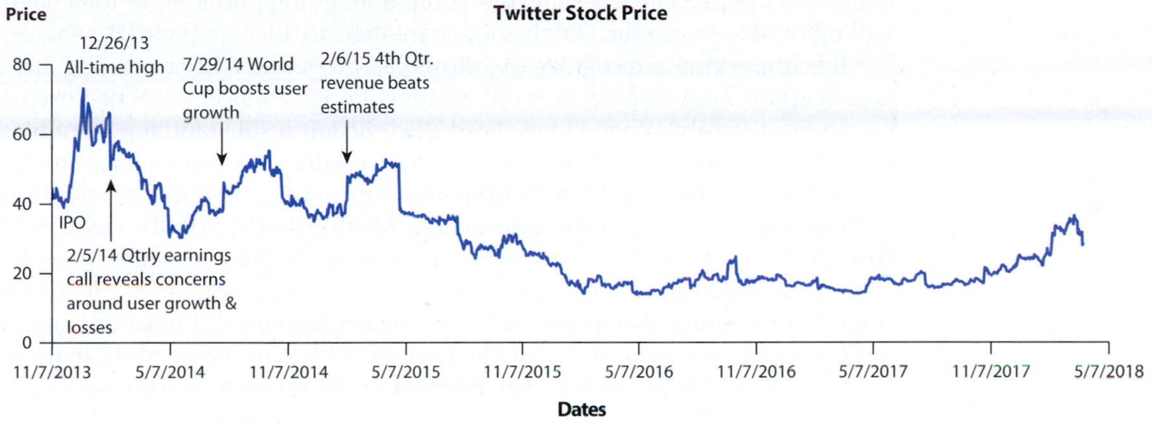

Source: Erin Griffith, "The Tale of Two IPOs: Facebook and Twitter," *Fortune* (www.fortune.com), February 19, 2015; and finance.yahoo.com for daily historical prices.

the price reached a low of $17.55. By year-end 2012, the stock rebounded to $26.62, which was still 30% below the initial offering price. So, although Facebook raised a lot of money through its IPO, its initial investors did not quickly realize the big return that many were looking to capture. However, it is important to note that despite its rocky start, investors who continued to hold Facebook stock did quite well. In contrast, the box titled "Initial Buzz Surrounding IPOs Doesn't Always Translate into Long-Lasting Success" demonstrates Twitter's disappointing post-IPO performance, despite a much higher first-day return. These experiences led many analysts to ask the following question in early 2017 following Snap's IPO: "Is Snap the next Facebook or the next Twitter"?[15] As mentioned earlier in the chapter, Dropbox's share price rose 36% on its first day of trading; however, whether this enthusiasm is sustainable and translates into even higher returns is anyone's guess.

For information on IPOs, refer to Professor Jay Ritter's (University of Florida) web page ***site.warrington.ufl.edu/ritter/ipo-data/****.*

Even if you are able to identify a "hot" issue, it is often difficult to purchase shares in the initial offering. These deals are often *oversubscribed,* which means that the demand for shares at the offering price exceeds the number of shares issued. In such instances, investment bankers favor large institutional investors (who are their best customers), and small investors find it hard, if not impossible, to get in on the ground floor. They can buy the stock in the aftermarket, but evidence suggests that when an investor does not get in on the ground floor, over the long run

[15]Mathew Ingram, "Is Snap the Next Facebook or the Next Twitter?" *Fortune* (www.fortune.com), February 2, 2017.

IPOs often underperform the overall market.[16] Other critics point out that when an IPO's price dramatically jumps the first day of trading, this implies that the underwriter set the price too low and failed to maximize the issuer's potential proceeds by "leaving money on the table."[17]

Google's highly publicized IPO attracted attention both because of its size (Google raised $1.67 billion in stock) and because of the way the sale was conducted. Rather than having the offer price set by its investment bankers, Google conducted a Dutch auction, where individual investors placed bids for shares directly. In a *Dutch auction,* the actual transaction price is set at the highest price (the clearing price) that causes all of the offered shares to be sold. Investors who set their bids at or above the clearing price received all of the shares they subscribed to at the offer price, which turned out to be $85. While Google's IPO was in many ways precedent setting, few companies going public since then have been willing or able to use the Dutch auction method to allocate their IPO shares.

It is important to recognize that firms can go public without raising any additional capital. For example, the Ford Motor Company was once owned exclusively by the Ford family. When Henry Ford died, he left a substantial part of his stock to the Ford Foundation. When the Foundation later sold some of the stock to the general public, the Ford Motor Company went public, even though the company itself raised no capital in the transaction. Most recently, Spotify went public on April 3, 2018—through the first *direct listing* of an NYSE company. Direct listings differ from traditional IPOs in that no new shares are issued, so all shares sold come from existing shareholders. In this regard, Spotify did not raise any capital in the transaction, but it did provide a useful vehicle for some of its shareholders to "cash in" and make shares available to a wider range of investors.[18]

Self*Test*

Differentiate between closely held and publicly owned corporations.

Differentiate between primary and secondary markets.

What is an IPO?

What is a Dutch auction, and what company used this procedure for its IPO?

2-6 Stock Markets and Returns

Anyone who has invested in the stock market knows that there can be (and generally are) large differences between *expected* and *realized* prices and returns. Figure 2.2 shows how total realized portfolio returns have varied from year to year. As logic would suggest (and as is demonstrated in Chapter 9), a stock's expected return as estimated by investors at the margin is always positive; otherwise, investors would not buy the stock. However, as Figure 2.2 shows, in some years, actual returns are negative.

[16]See Jay R. Ritter, "The Long-Run Performance of Initial Public Offerings," *Journal of Finance*, vol. 46, no. 1 (March 1991), pp. 3–27. Professor Ritter's summary of more recent IPO data is provided in the following article: Miriam Gottfried, "Reaping IPO Riches Isn't a Snap," *The Wall Street Journal*, March 9, 2017, p. B12.

[17]See, for example, the online column by Professor Hersh Shefrin, "Why Twitter's IPO Was Really a Failure," *Forbes* (www.forbes.com), November 8, 2013.

[18]Bob Pisani, "As Spotify Nears Its Direct Listing on NYSE, Traders Brace for Uncertainty," *CNBC* (www.cnbc.com), March 28, 2018.

FIGURE 2.2 S&P 500 Index, Total Returns: Dividend Yield + Capital Gain or Loss, 1968–2017

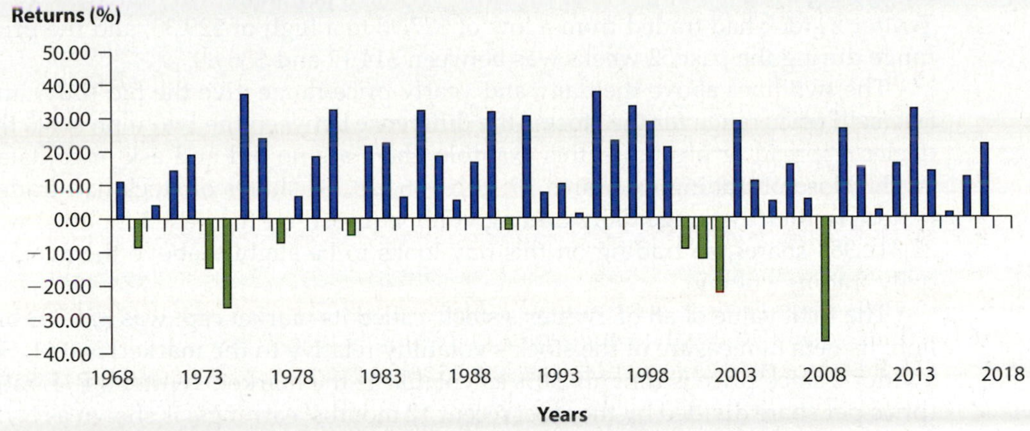

Source: Data taken from various issues of *The Wall Street Journal* "Investment Scoreboard" section and "S&P 500 Annual Total Return Historical Data," (ycharts.com/indicators/sandp_500_total_return_annual), March 29, 2018.

2-6A STOCK MARKET REPORTING

Up until a few years ago, the best source of stock quotations was the business section of daily newspapers such as *The Wall Street Journal*. One problem with newspapers, however, is that they report yesterday's prices. Now it is possible to obtain quotes throughout the day from a wide variety of Internet sources. One of the best is Yahoo!'s finance.yahoo.com; Figure 2.3 shows a detailed quote for Twitter, Inc. (TWTR) for March 29, 2018. As the heading shows, Twitter is traded on the NYSE under the symbol TWTR. The information right below the company name and ticker symbol shows the stock price quote at the close of the market at

FIGURE 2.3 Stock Quote for Twitter, Inc., March 29, 2018

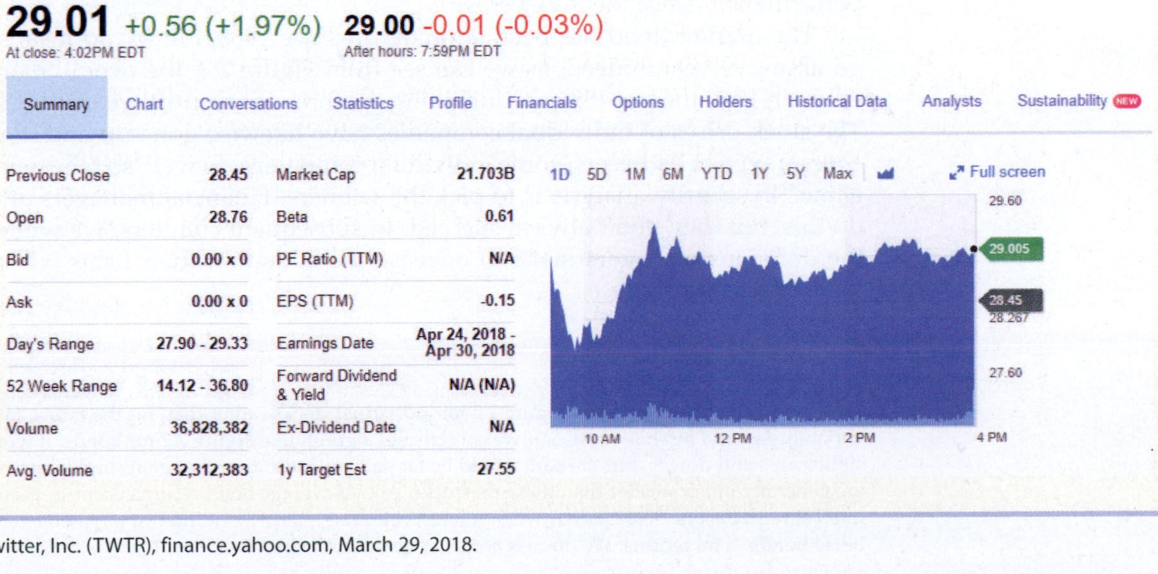

Source: Twitter, Inc. (TWTR), finance.yahoo.com, March 29, 2018.

4:02 p.m. EDT of $29.01, which is up $0.56 (or +1.97%) from the previous day's close. (Note that the after-hours price at 7:59 p.m. of $29.00 is also shown.) Twitter stock closed on Wednesday, March 28, 2018, at $28.45 per share, and it opened for trading on Thursday, March 29, 2018, at $28.76 per share. On March 29, 2018, Twitter's stock had traded from a low of $27.90 to a high of $29.33, and the price range during the past 52 weeks was between $14.12 and $36.80.

The two lines above the daily and yearly price range give the bid (buy) and ask (sell) price range for the stock—the difference between the two represents the dealer's spread or profit. (In this example, there are no bid and ask price data.) At the close of trading on March 29, 2018, 36,828,382 shares of stock had traded hands. Twitter's average daily trading volume (based on the past 3 months) was 32,312,383 shares, so trading on this day looks to be slightly above the average daily trading volume.

The total value of all of Twitter's stock, called its market cap, was $21.703 billion. Its beta (a measure of the stock's volatility relative to the market) is 0.61. So, Twitter's stock price is roughly 60% as volatile as the market. Twitter's P/E ratio (price per share divided by the most recent 12 months' earnings) is shown as N/A (not applicable), as earnings per share were very small and negative—so a meaningful number could not be calculated. Its earnings per share for the most recent 12 months was −$0.15. The firm's next earnings announcement is estimated between April 24 and April 30. The 1-year target estimate represents the median 1-year target price as forecasted by analysts covering the stock. It is estimated at $27.55. Twitter doesn't pay a dividend so the dividend and yield information is shown as N/A.

In Figure 2.3, the chart to the right plots the stock price during the day; however, the links above the chart allow you to pick different time intervals for plotting data. As you can see, Yahoo! provides a great deal of information in its detailed quote, and even more detail is available on the screen page below the basic quote information.

2-6B STOCK MARKET RETURNS

In Chapters 8 and 9, we discuss in detail how a stock's rate of return is calculated, what the connection is between risk and returns, and what techniques analysts use to value stocks. However, it is useful at this point to give you an idea of how stocks have performed in recent years. Figure 2.2 shows how the returns on large U.S. stocks have varied over the past years, and the box titled "Measuring the Market" provides information on the major U.S. stock market indices and their performances since the mid-1990s.

The market trend has been strongly up since 1968, but by no means does it go up every year. Indeed, as we can see from Figure 2.2, the overall market was down in 10 of the last 48 years, including the three consecutive years of 2000–2002. The stock prices of individual companies have likewise gone up and down.[19] Of course, even in bad years, some individual companies do well; so "the name of the game" in security analysis is to pick the winners. Financial managers attempt to do this, but they don't always succeed. In subsequent chapters, we will examine the decisions managers make to increase the odds that their firms will perform well in the marketplace.

[19]If we constructed a graph like Figure 2.2 for individual stocks rather than for the index, far greater variability would be shown. Also, if we constructed a graph like Figure 2.2 for bonds, it would have similar ups and downs, but the bars would be far smaller, indicating that gains and losses on bonds are generally much smaller than those on stocks. Above-average bond returns occur in years when interest rates decline, losses occur when interest rates rise sharply, but interest payments tend to stabilize bonds' total returns. We discuss bonds in detail in Chapter 7.

MEASURING THE MARKET

Stock market indexes are designed to show the performance of the stock market. However, there are many stock indexes, and it is difficult to determine which index best reflects market actions. Some are designed to represent the entire stock market, some track the returns of certain industry sectors, and others track the returns of small-cap, mid-cap, or large-cap stocks. In addition, there are indexes for different countries. We discuss here the three leading U.S. indexes. These indexes are used as a benchmark for comparing individual stocks with the overall market, for measuring the trend in stock prices over time, and for determining how various economic factors affect the market.

Dow Jones Industrial Average

Unveiled in 1896 by Charles H. Dow, the Dow Jones Industrial Average (DJIA) began with just 10 stocks, was expanded in 1916 to 20 stocks, and then was increased to 30 stocks in 1928, when the editors of *The Wall Street Journal* began adjusting the index for stock splits and making periodic substitutions. In 2015, Apple replaced AT&T on the DJIA, recognizing the importance of computer technology and social media companies. In 2018, Walgreens Boots Alliance Inc. replaced GE on the DJIA, recognizing the importance of the consumer and health care sectors in the economy. Today the DJIA still includes 30 companies. They represent about a fifth of the market value of all U.S. stocks, and all are leading companies in their industries and widely held by individual and institutional investors.

S&P 500 Index

Created in 1926, the S&P 500 Index is widely regarded as the standard for measuring large-cap U.S. stock market performance. The stocks in the S&P 500 are selected by the Standard & Poor's Index Committee, and they are the leading companies in the leading industries. It is weighted by each stock's market value, so the largest companies have the greatest influence. The S&P 500 is one of the most commonly used benchmarks for the U.S. stock market. Index funds designed to mirror the same performance of the index have grown in number and size over the last decade. The number of index funds has more than quadrupled in the last decade, and assets in stock index funds have grown over 85% during the past 5 years.

NASDAQ Composite Index

The NASDAQ Composite Index measures the performance of all stocks listed on the NASDAQ. Currently, it includes approximately 2,700 companies, and because many companies in the technology sector are traded on the computer-based NASDAQ exchange, this index is generally regarded as an economic indicator of the high-tech industry. Apple, Microsoft, Google (now known as Alphabet Inc.), Facebook, and Intel are the five largest NASDAQ companies, and they make up a high percentage of the index's value-weighted market capitalization. For this reason, substantial movements in the same direction by these five companies can move the entire index.

Recent Performance

The accompanying figure plots the value that an investor would now have if he or she had invested $1 in each of the three indexes on January 1, 1995, through January 1, 2018. The returns on the three indexes are compared with an investment strategy that invests only in 1-year Treasury bills (T-bills). During the last 23 years, the average annualized returns of these indexes ranged from 8.22% for the S&P 500 to 10.46% for the NASDAQ. (The Dow's annualized return during this same period was 8.71%).

Growth of a $1 Investment Made on January 1, 1995, through January 1, 2018

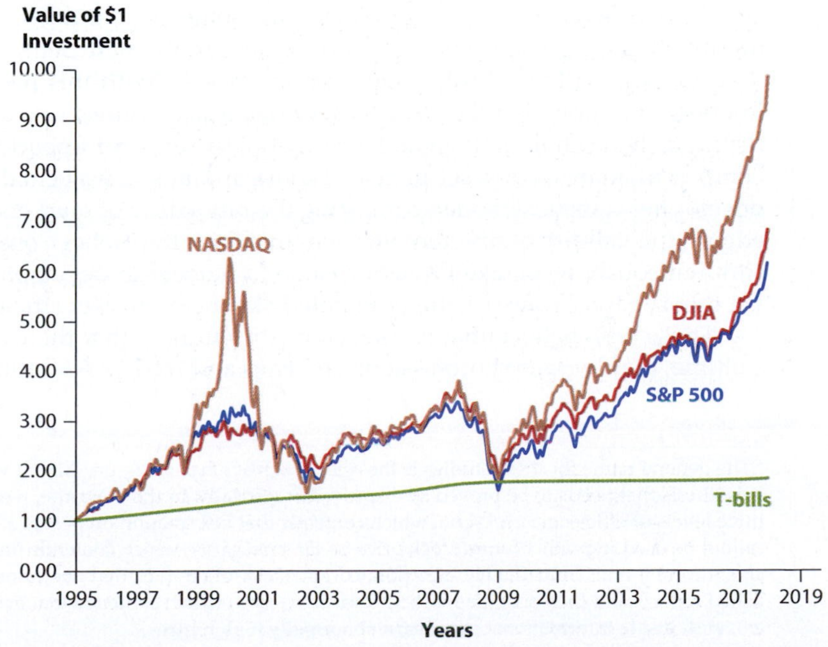

Self*Test*

Would you expect a portfolio that consisted of the NYSE stocks to be more or less risky than a portfolio of NASDAQ stocks?

If we constructed a chart like Figure 2.2 for a typical S&P 500 stock, do you think it would show more or less volatility? Explain.

2-7 Stock Market Efficiency

To begin this section, consider the following definitions:

- *Market price:* The current price of a stock. For example, the Internet showed that on one day, Twitter's stock traded at $29.01. The market price had varied from $27.90 to $29.33 during that same day as buy and sell orders came in.
- *Intrinsic value:* The price at which the stock would sell if all investors had all knowable information about a stock. This concept was discussed in Chapter 1, where we saw that a stock's intrinsic value is based on its expected future cash flows and its risk. Moreover, the market price tends to fluctuate around the intrinsic value, and the intrinsic value changes over time as the company succeeds or fails with new projects, competitors enter or exit the market, and so forth. We can guess (or estimate) Twitter's intrinsic value, but different analysts will reach somewhat different conclusions.
- *Equilibrium price:* The price that balances buy and sell orders at any given time. When a stock is in equilibrium, the price remains relatively stable until new information becomes available and causes the price to change.
- *Efficient market:* A market in which prices are close to intrinsic values and stocks seem to be in equilibrium.

When markets are efficient, investors can buy and sell stocks and be confident that they are getting good prices. When markets are inefficient, investors may be afraid to invest and may put their money "under the pillow," which will lead to a poor allocation of capital and economic stagnation. From an economic standpoint, market efficiency is good.

Academics and financial professionals have studied the issue of market efficiency extensively.[20] As generally happens, some people think that markets are highly efficient, some think that markets are highly inefficient, and others think that the issue is too complex for a simple answer. With this point in mind, it is interesting to note that the 2013 Nobel Prize in Economics was awarded to three distinguished scholars (Eugene Fama, Lars Hansen, and Robert Shiller) for their "empirical analysis of asset prices." Professor Hansen was cited for his work in developing statistical models for testing the rationality of markets. Also, acknowledging the validity of different views in this area, the Nobel Committee saw fit to simultaneously recognize Professor Fama (a pioneer in developing efficient market theory) and Professor Shiller (a noted skeptic of market efficiency).

Those who believe that markets are efficient note that there are 100,000 or so fulltime, highly trained professional analysts and traders operating in the market.

[20]The general name for these studies is the *efficient markets hypothesis*, or *EMH*. It was, and still is, a hypothesis that needs to be proved or disproved empirically. In the literature, researchers identified three levels of efficiency: *weak form*, which contends that information on past stock price movements cannot be used to predict future stock prices; *semi-strong form*, which contends that all publicly available information is immediately incorporated into stock prices (i.e., that one cannot analyze published reports and then beat the market); and *strong form*, which contends that even company insiders, with inside information, cannot earn abnormally high returns.

Many have PhDs in physics, chemistry, and other technical fields in addition to advanced degrees in finance. Moreover, there are fewer than 3,000 major stocks; so if each analyst followed 30 stocks (which is about right, as analysts tend to focus on a specific industry), on average, 1,000 analysts would be following each stock. Further, these analysts work for organizations such as Goldman Sachs, JPMorgan Chase, and Deutsche Bank or for Warren Buffett and other billionaire investors who have billions of dollars available to take advantage of bargains. Also, the SEC has disclosure rules that, combined with electronic information networks, means that new information about a stock is received by all analysts at about the same time, causing almost instantaneous revaluations. All of these factors help markets to be efficient and cause stock prices to move toward their intrinsic values.

However, other people point to data that suggest that markets are not very efficient. For example, on May 6, 2010, the Dow Jones Index fell nearly 1,000 points only to rebound rapidly by the end of the day.[21] In 2000, Internet stocks rose to phenomenally high prices, and then fell to zero or close to it the following year. No truly important news was announced that could have caused either of these changes; if the market was efficient, it's hard to see how such drastic changes could have occurred. Another situation that causes people to question market efficiency is the apparent ability of some analysts to consistently outperform the market over long periods. Warren Buffett comes to mind, but there are others. If markets are truly efficient, then each stock's price should be close to its intrinsic value. That would make it hard for any analyst to consistently pick stocks that outperform the market.

The diagram below sums up where most observers seem to be today. There is an "efficiency continuum," with the market for some companies' stocks being highly efficient and the market for other stocks being highly inefficient. The key factor is the size of the company—the larger the firm, the more analysts tend to follow it and thus the faster new information is likely to be reflected in the stock's price. Also, different companies communicate better with analysts and investors, and the better the communications, the more efficient the market for the stock. In an inefficient market, it might be possible to purchase the company's stock at a low price and then be able to turn around and sell it at a higher price making a profit. This is called *arbitrage*.

Efficiency Continuum

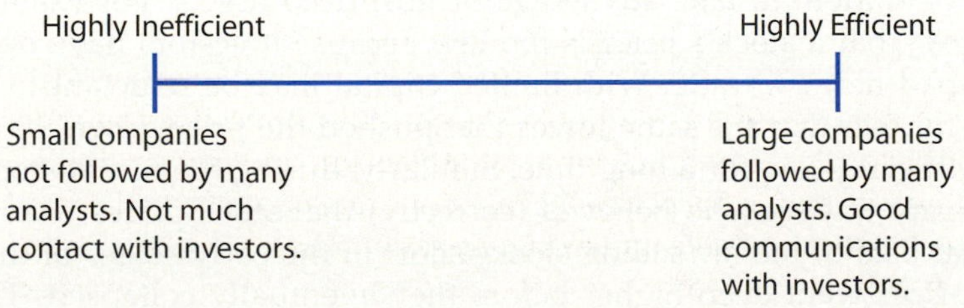

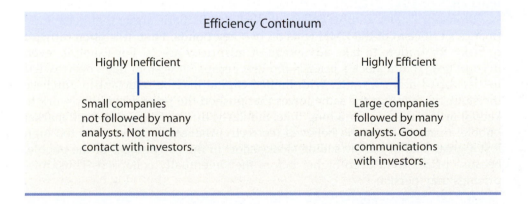

As an investor, would you prefer to purchase a stock whose price was determined in an efficient or an inefficient market? If you thought you knew something that others didn't know, you might prefer inefficient markets. But if you thought that those physics PhDs with unlimited buying power and access to company CEOs might know more than you, you would probably prefer efficient markets, where the

[21]Regulators are investigating the causes of this dramatic decline, and are particularly focusing on the role played by computerized trading. Refer to Tom Lauricella, Scott Patterson, and Carolyn Cui, "Computer Trading Is Eyed," *The Wall Street Journal* (www.wsj.com), May 8, 2010.

price you paid was likely to be the "right" price. From an economic standpoint, it is good to have efficient markets in which everyone is willing to participate. So the SEC and other regulatory agencies should do everything they can to encourage market efficiency.

Thus far we have been discussing the market for individual stocks. But the notion of efficiency applies to the pricing of all assets. For example, the dramatic rise and subsequent collapse of housing prices in many U.S. markets suggests that there was a lot of inefficiency in these markets. It is also important to realize that the level of market efficiency also varies over time. In one respect, we might expect that lower transactions costs and the increasing number of analysts would cause markets to become increasingly efficient over time. However, the recent housing bubble and the previous bubble for Internet stocks provides some contrary evidence. Indeed, these recent events have caused many experts to look for alternative reasons for this apparent irrational behavior. A lot of their research looks for psychologically based explanations, which we discuss in the next section.

2-7A BEHAVIORAL FINANCE THEORY

The *efficient markets hypothesis (EMH)* remains one of the cornerstones of modern finance theory. It implies that, on average, asset prices are about equal to their intrinsic values. The logic behind the EMH is straightforward. If a stock's price is "too low," rational traders will quickly take advantage of this opportunity and buy the stock, pushing prices up to the proper level. Likewise, if prices are "too high," rational traders will sell the stock, pushing the price down to its equilibrium level. Proponents of the EMH argue that these forces keep prices from being systematically wrong.

Although the logic behind the EMH is compelling, many events in the real world seem inconsistent with the hypothesis, which has spurred a growing field called *behavioral finance*. Rather than assuming that investors are rational, behavioral finance theorists borrow insights from psychology to better understand how irrational behavior can be sustained over time. Pioneers in this field include psychologists Daniel Kahneman, Amos Tversky, and Richard Thaler. Their work has encouraged a growing number of scholars to work in this promising area of research.[22]

Professor Thaler and his colleague Nicholas Barberis argue that behavioral finance's criticism of the EMH rests on two key points. First, it is often difficult or risky for traders to take advantage of mispriced assets. For example, even if you know that a stock's price is too low because investors have overreacted to recent bad news, a trader with limited capital may be reluctant to purchase the stock for fear that the same forces that pushed the price down may work to keep it artificially low for a long time. Similarly, during the recent stock market bubble, many traders who believed (correctly) that stock prices were too high lost a great deal of money selling stocks short in the early stages of the bubble, because prices went even higher before they eventually collapsed. Thus, mispricings may persist.

[22]Five noteworthy sources for students interested in behavioral finance are George Akerlof and Robert Shiller, *Animal Spirits: How Human Psychology Drives the Economy, and Why It Matters for Global Capitalism* (Princeton, NJ: Princeton University Press, 2009); Richard Thaler and Cass Sunstein, *Nudge: Improving Decisions about Health, Wealth, and Happiness* (New Haven, CT: Yale University Press, 2008); Richard H. Thaler, Editor, *Advances in Behavioral Finance* (New York: Russell Sage Foundation, 1993); Hersh Shefrin, "Behavioral Corporate Finance," *Journal of Applied Corporate Finance*, vol. 14, no. 3 (Fall 2001), pp. 113–125; and Nicholas Barberis and Richard Thaler, "A Survey of Behavioral Finance," Chapter 18 in *Handbook of the Economics of Finance*, edited by George Constantinides, Milt Harris, and René Stulz (New York: Elsevier/North-Holland, 2003). Students interested in learning more about the efficient markets hypothesis should consult Burton G. Malkiel, *A Random Walk Down Wall Street: The Time-Tested Strategy for Successful Investing*, 9th edition (New York: W.W. Norton, 2007).

The second point deals with why mispricings can occur in the first place. Here insights from psychology come into play. For example, Kahneman and Tversky suggested that individuals view potential losses and gains differently. If you ask average individuals whether they would rather have $500 with certainty or flip a fair coin and receive $1,000 if a head comes up and nothing if a tail comes up, most would prefer the certain $500, which suggests an aversion to risk. However, if you ask people whether they would rather pay $500 with certainty or flip a coin and pay $1,000 if it's a head and nothing if it's a tail, most would indicate that they prefer to flip the coin. Other studies suggest that people's willingness to take a gamble depends on recent performance. Gamblers who are ahead tend to take on more risk, whereas those who are behind tend to become more conservative.

These experiments suggest that investors and managers behave differently in down markets than they do in up markets, which might explain why those who made money early in the stock market bubble continued to invest their money in the market even as prices went ever higher. Other evidence suggests that individuals tend to overestimate their true abilities. For example, a large majority of people (upward of 90% in some studies) believe that they have above-average driving ability and above-average ability to get along with others. Barberis and Thaler point out:

> *Overconfidence may in part stem from two other biases, self-attribution bias and hindsight bias. Self-attribution bias refers to people's tendency to ascribe any success they have in some activity to their own talents, while blaming failure on bad luck rather than on their ineptitude. Doing this repeatedly will lead people to the pleasing, but erroneous, conclusion that they are very talented. For example, investors might become overconfident after several quarters of investing success [Gervais and Odean (2001)]. Hindsight bias is the tendency of people to believe, after an event has occurred, that they predicted it before it happened. If people think they predicted the past better than they actually did, they may also believe that they can predict the future better than they actually can.*[23]

Behavioral finance has been studied in both the corporate finance and investments areas. For example, Mark Grinblatt and Matti Keloharju conducted a recent study demonstrating that investors who are characterized as being overconfident and prone to "seeking sensations" trade more frequently.[24] Likewise, a study by Ulrike Malmendier of Stanford and Geoffrey Tate of Wharton found that overconfidence leads managers to overestimate their ability and thus the profitability of their projects.[25] This may explain why so many corporate projects fail to live up to their stated expectations.

2-7B CONCLUSIONS ABOUT MARKET EFFICIENCY

As noted previously, if the stock market is efficient, it is a waste of time for most people to seek bargains by analyzing published data on stocks. That follows because if stock prices already reflect all publicly available information, they will be fairly priced, and a person can beat the market only with luck or inside information. So rather than spending time and money trying to find undervalued stocks, it would be better to buy an index fund designed to match the overall

[23]Nicholas Barberis and Richard Thaler, "A Survey of Behavioral Finance," Chapter 18 in *Handbook of the Economics of Finance*, edited by George Constantinides, Milt Harris, and René Stulz (New York: Elsevier/North-Holland, 2003).

[24]Mark Grinblatt and Matti Keloharju: "Sensation Seeking, Overconfidence, and Trading Activity," *The Journal of Finance*, vol. LXIV, no. 2 (April 2009), pp. 549–578.

[25]Ulrike Malmendier and Geoffrey Tate, "CEO Overconfidence and Corporate Investment," Stanford Graduate School of Business Research Paper #1799, June 2004.

market as reflected in an index such as the S&P 500. However, if we worked for an institution with billions of dollars, we would try to find undervalued stocks or companies because even a small undervaluation would amount to a great deal of money when investing millions rather than thousands. Also, markets are more efficient for individual stocks than for entire companies; so for investors with enough capital, it does make sense to seek out badly managed companies that can be acquired and improved. Note, though, that a number of private equity players are doing exactly that; so the market for entire companies may soon be as efficient as that for individual stocks.

However, even if markets are efficient and all stocks and companies are fairly priced, an investor should still be careful when selecting stocks for his or her portfolio. Most importantly, the portfolio should be diversified, with a mix of stocks from various industries along with some bonds and other fixed-income securities. We will discuss diversification in greater detail in Chapter 8, but it is an important consideration for most individual investors.

Self*Test*

What does it mean for a market to be "efficient"?

Is the market for all stocks equally efficient? Explain.

Why is it good for the economy that markets be efficient?

Is it possible that the market for individual stocks could be highly efficient, but the market for whole companies could be less efficient? Explain.

What is arbitrage?

What is behavioral finance? What are the implications of behavioral finance for market efficiency?

TYING IT ALL TOGETHER

In this chapter, we provided a brief overview of how capital is allocated and discussed the financial markets, instruments, and institutions used in the allocation process. We discussed physical location exchanges and electronic markets for common stocks, stock market reporting, and stock indexes. We demonstrated that security prices are volatile—investors expect to make money, which they generally do over time—but losses can be large in any given year. Finally, we discussed the efficiency of the stock market and developments in behavioral finance. After reading this chapter, you should have a general understanding of the financial environment in which businesses and individuals operate, realize that actual returns are often different from expected returns, and be able to read stock market quotations from business newspapers or various Internet sites. You should also recognize that the theory of financial markets is a "work in progress," and much work remains to be done.

Self-Test Questions And Problems

(Solutions Appear in Appendix A)

ST-1 **KEY TERMS** Define each of the following terms:

a. Spot markets; futures markets
b. Money markets; capital markets
c. Primary markets; secondary markets
d. Private markets; public markets
e. Derivatives
f. Investment banks (IBs); commercial banks; financial services corporations
g. Mutual funds; money market funds
h. Exchange traded funds; hedge funds; private equity companies
i. Physical location exchanges; over-the-counter (OTC) market; dealer market
j. Closely held corporation; publicly owned corporation
k. Going public; initial public offering (IPO) market
l. Efficient markets hypothesis (EMH); arbitrage
m. Behavioral finance

Questions

2-1 How does a cost-efficient capital market help reduce the prices of goods and services?

2-2 Describe the different ways in which capital can be transferred from suppliers of capital to those who are demanding capital.

2-3 Is an initial public offering an example of a primary or a secondary market transaction? Explain.

2-4 Indicate whether the following instruments are examples of money market or capital market securities.

a. U.S. Treasury bills
b. Long-term corporate bonds
c. Common stocks
d. Preferred stocks
e. Dealer commercial paper

2-5 What would happen to the U.S. standard of living if people lost faith in the safety of the financial institutions? Explain.

2-6 What types of changes have financial markets experienced during the last two decades? Have they been perceived as positive or negative changes? Explain.

2-7 Differentiate between dealer markets and stock markets that have a physical location.

2-8 Identify and briefly compare the two leading stock exchanges in the United States today.

2-9 Briefly explain what is meant by the term *efficiency continuum.*

2-10 Explain whether the following statements are true or false.

a. Derivative transactions are designed to increase risk and are used almost exclusively by speculators who are looking to capture high returns.
b. Hedge funds typically have large minimum investments and are marketed to institutions and individuals with high net worths.
c. Hedge funds have traditionally been highly regulated.
d. The New York Stock Exchange is an example of a stock exchange that has a physical location.
e. A larger bid-ask spread means that the dealer will realize a lower profit.

INTEGRATED CASE

SMYTH BARRY & COMPANY

2-1 FINANCIAL MARKETS AND INSTITUTIONS Assume that you recently graduated with a degree in finance and have just reported to work as an investment adviser at the brokerage firm of Smyth Barry & Co. Your first assignment is to explain the nature of the U.S. financial markets to Michelle Varga, a professional tennis player who recently came to the United States from Mexico. Varga is a highly ranked tennis player who expects to invest substantial amounts of money through Smyth Barry. She is very bright; therefore, she would like to understand in general terms what will happen to her money. Your boss has developed the following questions that you must use to explain the U.S. financial system to Varga.

a. What are the three primary ways in which capital is transferred between savers and borrowers? Describe each one.

b. What is a market? Differentiate between the following types of markets: physical asset markets versus financial asset markets, spot markets versus futures markets, money markets versus capital markets, primary markets versus secondary markets, and public markets versus private markets.

c. Why are financial markets essential for a healthy economy and economic growth?

d. What are derivatives? How can derivatives be used to reduce risk? Can derivatives be used to increase risk? Explain.

e. Briefly describe each of the following financial institutions: investment banks, commercial banks, financial services corporations, pension funds, mutual funds, exchange traded funds, hedge funds, and private equity companies.

f. What are the two leading stock markets? Describe the two basic types of stock markets.

g. If Apple decided to issue additional common stock, and Varga purchased 100 shares of this stock from Smyth Barry, the underwriter, would this transaction be a primary or a secondary market transaction? Would it make a difference if Varga purchased previously outstanding Apple stock in the dealer market? Explain.

h. What is an initial public offering (IPO)?

i. What does it mean for a market to be efficient? Explain why some stock prices may be more efficient than others.

j. After your consultation with Michelle, she wants to discuss these two possible stock purchases:

   1. While in the waiting room of your office, she overheard an analyst on a financial TV network say that a particular medical research company just received FDA approval for one of its products. On the basis of this "hot" information, Michelle wants to buy many shares of that company's stock. Assuming the stock market is highly efficient, what advice would you give her?

   2. She has read a number of newspaper articles about a huge IPO being carried out by a leading technology company. She wants to purchase as many shares in the IPO as possible and would even be willing to buy the shares in the open market immediately after the issue. What advice do you have for her?

k. How does behavioral finance explain the real-world inconsistencies of the efficient markets hypothesis (EMH)?

part

2

Fundamental Concepts in Financial Management

CHAPTERS

Financial Statements, Cash Flow, and Taxes

CHAPTER

3

Tupungato/Dreamstime.com

Unlocking the Valuable Information in Financial Statements

In Chapter 1, we said that managers should make decisions that enhance long-term shareholder value, and they should be less concerned about short-term accounting measures such as earnings per share. With that important point in mind, you might reasonably wonder why are we now going to talk about accounting and financial statements. The simple answer is financial statements convey a lot of useful information that helps corporate managers assess the company's strengths and weaknesses and gauge the expected impact of various proposals. Good managers must have a solid understanding of the key financial statements. Outsiders also rely heavily on financial statements when deciding whether they want to buy the company's stock, lend money to the company, or enter into a long-term business relationship with the company.

At first glance, financial statements can be overwhelming—but if we know what we are looking for, we can quickly learn a great deal about a company after a quick review of its financial statements. Looking at the balance sheet we can see how large a company is, the types of assets it holds, and how it finances those assets. Looking at the income statement, we can see if the company's sales increased or declined and whether the company made a profit. Glancing at the statement of cash flows, we can see if the company made any new investments, if it raised funds through financing, repurchased debt or equity, or paid dividends.

For example, in early 2018, Dunkin' Brands Group released its fourth quarter and annual financial statements for 2017. The company announced that its annual adjusted earnings per share increased 7.5% to $2.43. Its reported sales for the fiscal year were $860.5 million, which was just under 4% higher than sales for 2016. The company also announced a 7.75% increase in its quarterly dividend. In its statement, the company also mentioned that same-store quarterly sales were up 0.8%

for its Dunkin' Donuts' stores and up 5.1% for its Baskin-Robbins stores. Reviewing the company's 2017 annual report at the end of its fiscal year (December 31, 2017), Dunkin' Brands showed total assets of $3.94 billion and total liabilities of $3.93 billion on its balance sheet—indicating that the book value of the company's equity was only slightly positive. Finally, looking at the statement of cash flows, we see that Dunkin' generated $277 million from its operating activities, and used $14 million for its investing activities. The company also generated $419 million from its financing activities; most notably, the company raised $1.4 billion in new long-term debt, but nearly a billion of these funds were used to repay other existing debt, to pay dividends, and to repurchase some shares of common stock. It follows that the company's overall cash position increased by $682 million during 2017.

While we can learn a lot from a quick tour of the financial statements, a good financial analyst does not just accept these numbers at face value. The analyst digs deeper to see what's really driving the numbers and uses his or her intuition and knowledge of the industry to help assess the company's future direction. Keep in mind that just because a company reports great numbers doesn't mean that you should purchase the stock. In the case of Dunkin' Brands, its stock price fell more than 3% despite posting fourth quarter earnings that were better than analysts' forecasts. Analysts have mixed feelings about the stock's future direction. It's these types of disagreements that make finance interesting, and as always, time will tell whether the optimists (the bulls) or the pessimists (the bears) are correct.

Sources: "Dunkin' Brands Reports Fourth Quarter and Fiscal Year 2017 Results," http://investor.dunkinbrands.com/news-releases/news-release-details/dunkin-brands-reports-fourth-quarter-and-fiscal-year-2017, February 6, 2018; and Sarah Whitten, "Dunkin' Brands Shares Slip on Soft Sales in US," *CNBC* (www.cnbc.com), February 6, 2018.

PUTTING THINGS IN PERSPECTIVE

A manager's primary goal is to maximize shareholder value, which is based on the firm's future cash flows. But how do managers decide which actions are most likely to increase those flows, and how do investors estimate future cash flows? The answers to both questions lie in a study of financial statements that publicly traded firms must provide to investors. Here *investors* include both institutions (banks, insurance companies, pension funds, and the like) and individuals like you.

Much of the material in this chapter deals with concepts you covered in a basic accounting course. However, the information is important enough to warrant a review. Also, in accounting you probably focused on how accounting statements are made; the focus here is on how investors and managers *interpret* and use them. Accounting is the basic language of business, so everyone engaged in business needs a good working knowledge of it. It is used to "keep score"; if investors and managers do not know the score, they won't know whether their actions are appropriate. If you took midterm exams but were not told your scores, you would have a difficult time knowing whether you needed to improve. The same idea holds in business. If a firm's managers—whether they work in marketing, human resources, production, or finance—do not understand financial statements, they will not be able to judge the effects of their actions, which will make it hard for the firm to survive, much less to have a maximum value.

When you finish this chapter you should be able to do the following:

- **List each of the key financial statements and identify the kinds of information they provide to corporate managers and investors.**
- **Estimate a firm's free cash flow and explain why free cash flow has such an important effect on firm value.**
- **Discuss the major features of the federal income tax system and changes due to the passage of the "Tax Cuts and Jobs Act."**

3-1 Financial Statements and Reports

Annual Report
A report issued annually by a corporation to its stockholders. It contains basic financial statements as well as management's analysis of the firm's past operations and future prospects.

The **annual report** is the most important report that corporations issue to stockholders, and it contains two types of information.[1] First, there is a verbal section, often presented as a letter from the chairperson, which describes the firm's operating results during the past year and discusses new developments that will affect future operations. Second, the report provides these four basic financial statements:

1. The *balance sheet,* which shows what assets the company owns and who has claims on those assets as of a given date—for example, December 31, 2019.
2. The *income statement,* which shows the firm's sales and costs (and thus profits) during some past period—for example, 2019.
3. The *statement of cash flows,* which shows how much cash the firm began the year with, how much cash it ended up with, and what it did to increase or decrease its cash.
4. The *statement of stockholders' equity,* which shows the amount of equity the stockholders had at the start of the year, the items that increased or decreased equity, and the equity at the end of the year.

These statements are related to one another, and, taken together, they provide an accounting picture of the firm's operations and financial position.

The quantitative and verbal materials are equally important. The firm's financial statements report *what has actually happened* to its assets, earnings, and dividends over the past few years, whereas management's verbal statements attempt to explain why things turned out the way they did and what might happen in the future.

For discussion purposes, we use data for Allied Food Products, a processor and distributor of a wide variety of food products, to illustrate the basic financial statements. Allied was formed in 1985, when several regional firms merged; it has grown steadily while earning a reputation as one of the best firms in its industry. Allied's earnings dropped from $152.3 million in 2018 to $146.3 million in 2019. Management reported that the drop resulted from losses associated with a drought as well as increased costs due to a 3-month strike. However, management then went on to describe a more optimistic picture for the future, stating that full operations had been resumed, that several unprofitable businesses had been eliminated, and that 2020 profits were expected to rise sharply. Of course, an increase in profitability may not occur, and analysts should compare management's past statements with subsequent results. In any event, *the information contained in the annual report can be used to help forecast future earnings and dividends.* Therefore, investors are very interested in this report.

We should note that Allied's financial statements are relatively simple and straightforward; we also omitted some details often shown in the statements. Allied finances with only debt and common stock—it has no preferred stock, convertibles, or complex derivative securities. Also, the firm has made no acquisitions that resulted in goodwill that must be carried on the balance sheet. We deliberately chose such a company because this is an introductory text; as such, we want to explain the basics of financial analysis, not wander into arcane accounting matters that are best left to accounting and security analysis courses. We do point out some of the pitfalls that can be encountered when trying to interpret accounting statements, but we leave it to advanced courses to cover the intricacies of accounting.

[1]Firms also provide quarterly reports, but these are much less comprehensive than the annual report. In addition, larger firms file even more detailed statements with the Securities and Exchange Commission (SEC), giving breakdowns for each major division or subsidiary. These reports, called *10-K reports,* are made available to stockholders upon request to a company's corporate secretary. In this chapter, we focus on annual data—balance sheets at the ends of years and income statements for entire years rather than for shorter time periods.

GLOBAL PERSPECTIVES

Global Accounting Standards: Will It Ever Happen?

For the past decade, global accounting standards to improve financial reporting to investors and users of that information seemed all but certain. In 2005, the EU required the adoption of International Financial Reporting Standards (IFRS), and in 2007, the SEC eliminated the requirement for companies reporting under IFRS to reconcile their financial statements to U.S. Generally Accepted Accounting Principles (GAAP). To date, 120 countries have adopted IFRS. However, on July 13, 2012, the SEC staff issued a report that failed to recommend IFRS for U.S. adoption. The ultimate decision will be up to the SEC. On December 6, 2014, at an AICPA (American Institute of Certified Public Accountants) national conference, the SEC chief accountant at that time, James Schnurr, stated that he was open to dialogue about the best way to achieve high-quality financial information and comparability, but there is currently no sign that the United States will be adopting IFRS anytime soon.

The effort to internationalize accounting standards began in 1973 with the formation of the International Accounting Standards Committee. However, in 1998, it became apparent that a full-time rule-making body with global representation was necessary; so the International Accounting Standards Board (IASB) was established. The IASB was charged with the responsibility for creating a set of IFRS. The "convergence" process began in earnest in September 2002 with the "Norwalk Agreement," in which the Financial Accounting Standards Board (FASB) and IASB undertook a short-term project to remove individual differences between the FASB's U.S. GAAP and IFRS and agreed to coordinate their activities. The process was meant to narrow gaps between the two standards, with the intention of making the transition for companies simpler and less expensive. Some progress has been made, but differences still remain.

Obviously, the globalization of accounting standards is a huge endeavor—one that involves compromises between the IASB and FASB. However, in recent years the momentum behind this goal has diminished. Despite the best of intentions, progress toward consolidation was slowed by the 2007–2008 financial crisis and the resulting global recession. In addition, it has become apparent that the cost to companies, both large and small, for switching from GAAP to IFRS will be significant. Another reason for resistance to convergence is the principles-based IFRS approach fails to offer guidance as compared to the rules-based U.S. standards. Finally, the SEC has been given the task of implementing the Dodd-Frank financial reform law—limiting its ability to focus on adopting global accounting standards.

The United States is an important economy, and without its participation it will be difficult to truly have global accounting standards. In the meantime, it is important for companies and analysts that evaluate businesses in different countries to have a full understanding of the key differences between the various global accounting standards.

Sources: Nicolas Pologeorgis, "The Impact of Combining the U.S. GAAP and IFRS," *Investopedia* (www.investopedia.com), March 12, 2018; David M. Katz "The Path to Global Standards?" *CFO.com*, January 28, 2011; "Global Accounting Standards: Closing the GAAP," *The Economist* (economist.com), vol. 404, July 21, 2012; Joe Adler, "Is Effort to Unify Accounting Regimes Falling Apart?" *American Banker*, vol. 177, no. 145, July 30, 2012; Kathleen Hoffelder, "SEC Report Backs Away from Convergence," *CFO Magazine* (cfo.com/magazine), September 1, 2012; Ken Tysiac, "Still in Flux: Future of IFRS in U.S. Remains Unclear after SEC Report," *Journal of Accountancy* (journalofaccountancy.com), September 2012; and Tammy Whitehouse, "Ten Years on, Convergence Movement Starting to Wane," *Compliance Week* (complianceweek.com), October 2, 2012.

Self*Test*

What is the annual report, and what two types of information does it provide?

What four financial statements are typically included in the annual report?

Why is the annual report of great interest to investors?

3-2 The Balance Sheet

Balance Sheet
A statement of a firm's financial position at a specific point in time.

The **balance sheet** is a "snapshot" of a firm's position at a specific point in time. Figure 3.1 shows the layout of a typical balance sheet. The left side of the statement shows the assets that the company owns, and the right side shows the firm's liabilities and *stockholders' equity*, which are claims against the firm's assets. As Figure 3.1 shows, assets are divided into two major categories: current assets and fixed, or long-term, assets. Current assets consist of assets that should be converted to cash within one year, and they include cash and cash equivalents, accounts receivable,

FIGURE 3.1 A Typical Balance Sheet

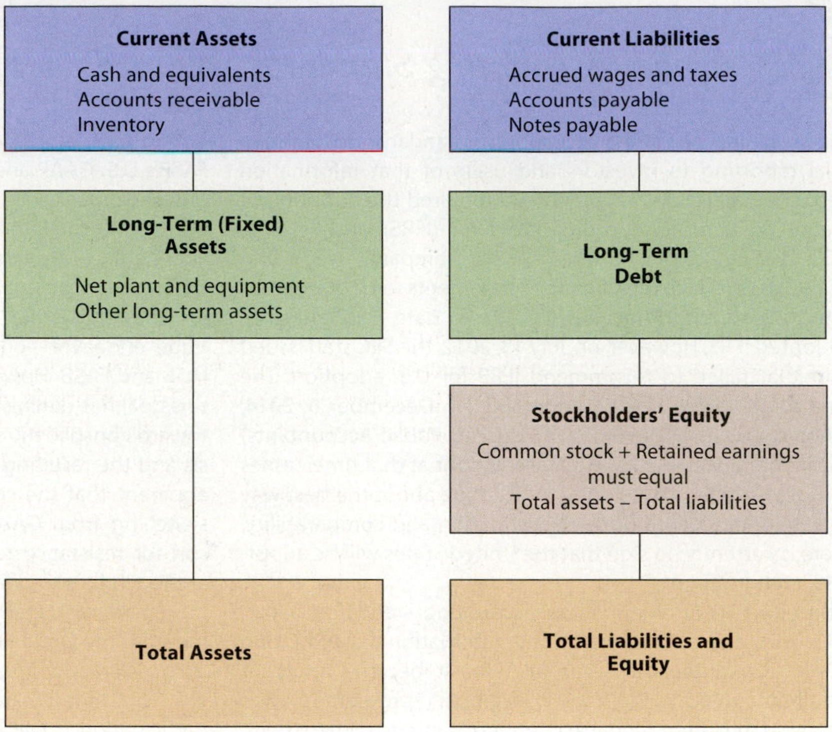

Note: This is the typical layout of a balance sheet for one year. When balance sheets for two or more years are shown, assets are listed in the top section, and liabilities and equity in the bottom section. See Table 3.1 for an illustration.

and inventory.[2] Long-term assets are assets expected to be used for more than one year; they include plant and equipment in addition to intellectual property such as patents and copyrights. Plant and equipment is generally reported net of accumulated depreciation. Allied's long-term assets consist entirely of net plant and equipment, and we often refer to them as "net fixed assets."

The claims against assets are of two basic types—liabilities (or money the company owes to others) and stockholders' equity. Current liabilities consist of claims that must be paid off within one year, including accounts payable, accruals (total of accrued wages and accrued taxes), and notes payable to banks and other short-term lenders that are due within one year. Long-term debt includes bonds that mature in more than a year.

Stockholders' Equity
It represents the amount that stockholders paid the company when shares were purchased and the amount of earnings the company has retained since its origination.

Stockholders' equity can be thought of in two ways. First, it is the amount that stockholders paid to the company when they bought shares the company sold to raise capital, in addition to all of the earnings the company has retained over the years:[3]

$$\text{Stockholders' equity} = \text{Paid-in capital} + \text{Retained earnings}$$

[2]Allied and most other companies hold some currency in addition to a bank checking account. They may also hold short-term interest-bearing securities that can be sold and thus converted to cash immediately with a simple telephone call. These securities are called "cash equivalents," and they are generally included with checking account balances for financial reporting purposes. If a company owns stocks or other marketable securities that it regards as short-term investments, these items will be shown separately on the balance sheet. Allied does not hold any marketable securities other than cash equivalents.

[3]On Allied's balance sheet, we simply show a common stock line representing the "paid-in" capital of stockholders when they purchased common shares of stock.

The **retained earnings** are not just the earnings retained in the latest year—they are the cumulative total of all of the earnings the company has earned and retained during its life.

Retained Earnings
They represent the cumulative total of all earnings kept by the company during its life.

Stockholders' equity can also be thought of as a residual:

Stockholders' equity = Total assets − Total liabilities

If Allied had invested surplus funds in bonds backed by subprime mortgages and the bonds' value fell below their purchase price, the true value of the firm's assets would have declined. The amount of its liabilities would not have changed—the firm would still owe the amount it had promised to pay its creditors. Therefore, the reported value of the common equity must decline. The accountants would make a series of entries, and the result would be a reduction in retained earnings—and thus in common equity. In the end, assets would equal liabilities and equity, and the balance sheet would balance. This example shows why common stock is more risky than bonds—any mistake that management makes has a big impact on the stockholders. Of course, gains from good decisions also go to the stockholders; so with risk come possible rewards.

Assets on the balance sheet are listed by the length of time before they will be converted to cash (inventories and accounts receivable) or used by the firm (fixed assets). Similarly, claims are listed in the order in which they must be paid: Accounts payable must generally be paid within a few days, accruals must also be paid promptly, notes payable to banks must be paid within 1 year, and so forth, down to the stockholders' equity accounts, which represent ownership and need never be "paid off."

3-2A ALLIED'S BALANCE SHEET

Table 3.1 shows Allied's year-end balance sheets for 2019 and 2018. From the 2019 statement, we see that Allied had $2 billion of assets—half current and half long term. These assets were financed with $310 million of current liabilities, $750 million of long-term debt, and $940 million of common equity. Comparing the balance sheets for 2019 and 2018, we see that Allied's assets grew by $320 million and its liabilities and equity necessarily grew by that same amount. Assets must, of course, equal liabilities and equity; otherwise, the balance sheet does not balance.

resource

Students can download the Excel chapter models from the textbook's student companion site on cengage.com. Once downloaded onto your computer, retrieve the Chapter 3 Excel model and follow along as you read this chapter.

Several additional points about the balance sheet should be noted:

1. *Cash versus other assets.* Although assets are reported in dollar terms, only the cash and equivalents account represents actual spendable money. Accounts receivable represent credit sales that have not yet been collected. Inventories show the cost of raw materials, work in process, and finished goods. Net fixed assets represent the cost of the buildings and equipment used in operations minus the depreciation that has been taken on these assets. At the end of 2019, Allied has $10 million of cash; hence, it could write checks totaling that amount. The noncash assets should generate cash over time, but they do not represent cash in hand. And the cash they would bring in if they were sold today could be higher or lower than the values reported on the balance sheet.
2. *Working capital.* Current assets are often called **working capital** because these assets "turn over"; that is, they are used and then replaced throughout the year. When Allied buys inventory items on credit, its suppliers, in effect, lend it the money used to finance the inventory items. Allied could have borrowed from its bank or sold stock to obtain the money, but it received the funds from its suppliers. These loans are shown as accounts payable, and they typically are "free" in the sense that they do not bear interest. Similarly, Allied pays its workers every two weeks and pays taxes quarterly; so

Working Capital
Current assets.

TABLE 3.1 Allied Food Products: December 31 Balance Sheets (millions of dollars)

	2019	2018
Assets		
Current assets:		
Cash and equivalents	$ 10	$ 80
Accounts receivable	375	315
Inventories	615	415
Total current assets	$1,000	$ 810
Net fixed assets:		
Net plant and equipment (cost minus depreciation)	1,000	870
Other assets expected to last more than a year	0	0
Total assets	$2,000	$1,680
Liabilities and Equity		
Current liabilities:		
Accounts payable	$ 60	$ 30
Accruals	140	130
Notes payable	110	60
Total current liabilities	$ 310	$ 220
Long-term bonds	750	580
Total liabilities	$1,060	$ 800
Common equity:		
Common stock (75,000,000 shares)	$ 130	$ 130
Retained earnings	810	750
Total common equity	$ 940	$ 880
Total liabilities and equity	$2,000	$1,680

Notes:

1. Inventories can be valued by several different methods, and the method chosen can affect both the balance sheet value and the cost of goods sold, and thus net income, as reported on the income statement. Similarly, companies can use different depreciation methods for financial reporting. The methods used must be reported in the notes to the financial statements, and security analysts can make adjustments when they compare companies if they think the differences are material.
2. Book value per share: Total common equity/Shares outstanding = $940/75 = $12.53.
3. A relatively few firms use preferred stock, which we discuss in Chapter 9. Preferred stock can take several different forms, but it is generally like debt because it pays a fixed amount each year. However, it is like common stock because a failure to pay the preferred dividend does not expose the firm to bankruptcy. If a firm does use preferred stock, it is shown on the balance sheet between total debt and common stock. There is no set rule on how preferred stock should be treated when financial ratios are calculated—it could be considered as debt or as equity. Bondholders often think of it as equity, while stockholders think of it as debt because it is a fixed charge. In truth, preferred stock is a hybrid, somewhere between debt and common equity.

Allied's labor force and taxing authorities provide it with loans equal to its accrued wages and taxes. In addition to these "free" sources of short-term credit, Allied borrows from its bank on a short-term basis. These bank loans are shown as notes payable. Although accounts payable and accruals do not bear interest, Allied pays interest on funds obtained from the bank. The total of accounts payable, accruals, and notes payable represent current liabilities on its balance sheet. If we subtract current liabilities from current assets, the difference is called **net working capital:**

Net Working Capital
Current assets minus current liabilities.

Net working capital = Current assets − Current liabilities
= $1,000 − $310 = $690 million

Net Operating Working Capital (NOWC)
Operating current assets minus operating current liabilities.

Current liabilities include accounts payable, accruals, and notes payable to the bank. Financial analysts often make an important distinction between net working capital (NWC) and **net operating working capital (NOWC)**. NOWC differs from

NWC in two important ways. First, NOWC makes a distinction between cash that is used for operating purposes and "excess" cash that is being held for other purposes. Thus, when calculating NOWC, analysts make an estimate of excess cash and subtract this from the company's current assets to get the company's operating current assets. Second, when looking at a company's current liabilities, analysts distinguish between its "free" liabilities (accruals and accounts payable) and its interest-bearing notes payable. These interest-bearing liabilities are typically treated as a financing cost, rather than an operating cost, which explains why they are not included as part of the company's operating current liabilities. Given these two adjustments, NOWC is calculated as follows:

$$\text{Net operating working capital (NOWC)} = \text{Operating current assets} - \text{Operating current liabilities} \qquad (3.1)$$

$$= \left(\text{Current assets} - \text{Excess cash}\right) - \left(\text{Current liabilities} - \text{Notes payable}\right)$$

$$= (\$1{,}000 - \$0) - (\$310 - \$110) = \$800 \text{ million}$$

Note that since Allied's cash holdings in 2019 are fairly small ($10 million), we are assuming that all of its cash is being held for operating purposes and that it has no excess cash. If we had instead assumed that all of Allied's $10 million in cash is held for non-operating purposes, then this $10 million in excess cash would be subtracted from its current assets, and its NOWC would be calculated as $790 million instead of the $800 million calculated earlier. Although the difference for Allied is fairly small, assumptions about the level of excess cash become much more important when analyzing companies with very large cash holdings. For example, on December 31, 2017, Microsoft had more than $140 billion in cash and short-term investments. In this case, it matters considerably whether the cash is treated as operating cash or excess cash. To keep things simple, when relevant, we will indicate what portion of the cash is assumed to be excess cash.

quick question

QUESTION:

Refer to Allied's balance sheets shown in Table 3.1 to answer the following questions:

a. What was Allied's net working capital on December 31, 2018?

b. What was Allied's net operating working capital on December 31, 2018? Once again, assume Allied has no excess cash in 2018.

ANSWER:

a. $\text{Net working capital}_{2018} = \text{Current assets}_{2018} - \text{Current liabilities}_{2018}$

$\text{Net working capital}_{2018} = \$810 - \$220 = \mathbf{\$590\ million}$

b. $$\text{Net operating working capital}_{2018} = \left(\text{Current assets}_{2018} - \text{Excess cash}_{2018}\right) - \left(\text{Current liabilities}_{2018} - \text{Notes payable}_{2018}\right)$$

$$\text{Net operating working capital}_{2018} = (\$810 - \$0) - (\$220 - \$60)$$

$$\text{Net operating working capital}_{2018} = \$810 - \$160 = \mathbf{\$650\ million}$$

3. *Total debt versus total liabilities.* A company's total debt includes both its short-term and long-term interest-bearing liabilities. Total liabilities equal total debt plus the company's "free" (non-interest bearing) liabilities. Allied's short-term debt is shown as notes payable on its balance sheet:[4]

$$\text{Total debt} = \text{Short-term debt} + \text{Long-term debt}$$
$$= \$110 + \$750 = \$860 \text{ million}$$
$$\text{Total liabilities} = \text{Total debt} + (\text{Accounts payable} + \text{Accruals})$$
$$= \$860 + (\$60 + \$140) = \$1{,}060 \text{ million} = \$1.06 \text{ billion}$$

4. *Other sources of funds.* Most companies (including Allied) finance their assets with a combination of short-term debt, long-term debt, and common equity. Some companies also use "hybrid" securities such as preferred stock, convertible bonds, and long-term leases. Preferred stock is a hybrid between common stock and debt, while convertible bonds are debt securities that give the bondholder an option to exchange their bonds for shares of common stock. In the event of bankruptcy, debt is paid off first, and then preferred stock. Common stock is last, receiving a payment only when something remains after the debt and preferred stock are paid off.[5]
5. *Depreciation.* Most companies prepare two sets of financial statements—one is based on Internal Revenue Service (IRS) rules and is used to calculate taxes; the other is based on GAAP and is used for reporting to investors. Firms often use straight-line depreciation for stockholder reporting because the financial statements will report higher earnings to shareholders than would accelerated depreciation methods. Firms use the prescribed IRS depreciation method for taxes. Prior to the new tax legislation, firms used MACRS depreciation, an accelerated depreciation method to calculate depreciation—which lowered taxable income, lowered taxes, and increased cash flows. However, under the new tax law, 100% of the costs of certain new and used assets can be immediately expensed. There is a sunset to this provision; we will discuss depreciation

quick question

QUESTION:

Refer to Allied's balance sheets shown in Table 3.1. What was Allied's total debt on December 31, 2018?

ANSWER:

$\text{Total debt}_{2018} = \text{Short-term debt}_{2018} + \text{Long-term debt}_{2018}$

$\text{Total debt}_{2018} = \$60 + \$580 = \mathbf{\$640\ million}$

[4]Companies also include the portion of their long-term bonds that is currently due as part of short-term debt.

[5]These other forms of financing are discussed in greater detail in Chapter 20, "Hybrid Financing: Preferred Stock, Warrants, and Convertibles," from E. F. Brigham and P. R. Daves, *Intermediate Financial Management*, 13th edition (Mason, OH: Cengage Learning, 2019).

in greater detail later in Section 3-9 when we discuss taxes and later in the book when we discuss capital budgeting. Allied uses its tax depreciation method for both sets of financial statements.[6]

6. *Market values versus book values.* Companies generally use GAAP to determine the values reported on their balance sheets. In most cases, these accounting numbers (or "book values") are different from what the assets would sell for if they were offered for sale (or "market values"). For example, Allied purchased its headquarters in Chicago in 1991. Under GAAP, the company must report the value of this asset at its historical cost (what it originally paid for the building in 1991) less accumulated depreciation. Given that Chicago real estate prices have increased over the last 26 years (even considering the impact of the recent recession on real estate values), the market value of the building is higher than its book value. Other assets' market values also differ from their book values.

   We can also see from Table 3.1 that the book value of Allied's common equity at the end of 2019 was $940 million. Because 75 million shares were outstanding, the book value per share was $940/75 = $12.53. However, the market value of the common stock was $23.06. As is true for most companies in 2019, shareholders are willing to pay more than book value for Allied's stock. This occurs in part because the values of assets have increased due to inflation and in part because shareholders expect earnings to grow. Allied, like most other companies, has learned how to make investments that will increase future profits.

   Apple provides an example of a company with very strong future prospects, and as a result, in early April 2018 its market value was more than six times its book value. On the other hand, if a company has problems, its market value can fall below its book value. For example, at this same point in time, Genworth Financial, an insurance company that has been struggling in recent years, saw its stock trading around $2.80 a share when its book value per share approximated $28.

7. *Time dimension.* The balance sheet is a snapshot of the firm's financial position *at a point in time*—for example, on December 31, 2019. Thus, we see that on December 31, 2018, Allied had $80 million of cash, but that balance fell to $10 million by year-end 2019. The balance sheet changes every day as inventories rise and fall, as bank loans are increased or decreased, and so forth. A company such as Allied, whose business is seasonal, experiences especially large balance sheet changes during the year. Its inventories are low just before the harvest season but high just after the fall crops have been harvested and processed. Similarly, most retailers have large inventories just before Christmas but low inventories (and high accounts receivable) just after Christmas. We will examine the effects of these changes in Chapter 4, when we compare companies' financial statements and evaluate their performance.

---

[6]Having the ability to immediately expense 100% of an asset's cost lowers taxable income, which reduces taxes. Due to the time value of money, it is better to delay taxes. Either accelerated or straight-line depreciation methods can be used for stockholder reporting. Allied is a relatively conservative company; hence, it uses its tax depreciation for stockholder reporting. Had Allied elected to use straight line for stockholder reporting, its 2019 depreciation expense would have been $25 million lower, the $1 billion shown for "net plant" on its balance sheet would have been $25 million higher, and its reported income would also have been higher.

Depreciation is also important in capital budgeting, where we make decisions regarding new investments in fixed assets. We will have more to say about depreciation in Chapter 12, when we discuss capital budgeting.

THE BALANCE SHEET OF AN AVERAGE AMERICAN HOUSEHOLD

Balance sheets are not unique to corporations. Every entity—including state and local governments, nonprofit agencies, and individual households—has a balance sheet.

We can learn a lot about a household's financial well-being by looking at its balance sheet. Although obviously every household is different, economists can use available data to estimate the balance sheet of an average American household.

For example, in 2009, James Kwak posted his calculations of the average household balance sheet on his popular website *The Baseline Scenario* (baselinescenario.com), which provides interesting commentary on a variety of current economic and financial issues. The underlying data for his calculations came from the Federal Reserve Board's *Survey of Consumer Finances.*

A summary of Kwak's calculations for 2004, 2007, and 2009 is shown in the following table. Although his calculations were only meant to give a broad picture of recent trends, they produce some interesting findings:

- The largest asset of the average household is its primary residence.
- The average American household does not have a large amount of savings in place for retirement.
- Perhaps somewhat surprisingly, average household debt levels have not increased dramatically in recent years.
- Average household net worth increased slightly from 2004 to 2007, but declined sharply from 2007 to 2009. The decline in net worth was due to two reasons: The sharp decline in the housing market reduced the value of the average home and the sharp decline in the stock market reduced the value of the average amount of retirement savings.

Likewise, a Federal Reserve study (*2010 Survey of Consumer Finances*) highlighted the deterioration in household finances due to the financial crisis and resulting recession. The average family's pre-tax income fell 5.6%, and the average family's net worth dropped nearly 40% during the period 2007–2010. Indeed, at the end of 2010, the average family's net worth stood at the same level that was observed in 1992—so in effect, the recent decline wiped out about 18 years' worth of savings and investment.

Although not broken down on a per-household level, updated information on aggregate household finances is on the Federal Reserve website. For example, numbers released in December 2017 indicate that aggregate household balance sheets have strengthened somewhat since 2010. Indeed, household net worth from 2010 through 2017 increased by almost 57%. These improvements reflect that many households have made progress in reducing their debt level. Household levels of net worth have also improved because of the surge in home prices and the large run-up in the stock market during this time period.[7]

At the same time, it is very important to realize that these aggregate improvements in net worth have not been shared equally across households. Indeed, many are concerned that the gains over the past few decades have accrued largely to those who are already quite wealthy. According to a report from the Organization for Economic Cooperation and Development, the richest 10% of American households earn 28% of overall income; however, the 10% wealthiest U.S. households have 76% of all the wealth in America. Thus, when evaluating the current state of American households, it is important to consider both the level of overall wealth as well as the distribution of household income and wealth.

	2004	2007	2009
Income	$ 47,500	$ 47,300	$ 47,300
Assets			
Bank accounts	3,300	2,700	2,700
Retirement savings	19,000	23,900	17,900
Vehicles	14,400	14,600	14,600
Primary residence	148,300	150,000	125,400
Total assets	$185,000	$191,200	$160,600
Liabilities			
Mortgage on primary residence	$ 84,800	$ 88,700	$ 88,700
Installment loans	11,800	12,800	12,800
Credit cards	2,400	2,400	2,400
Total liabilities	$ 99,000	$103,900	$103,900
Net worth	$ 86,000	$ 87,300	$ 56,700

Note: See Kwak's posting on *The Baseline Scenario* for more details about the methods that he used in his calculations.

Sources: James Kwak, "Tracking the Household Balance Sheet," *The Baseline Scenario* (baselinescenario.com), February 15, 2009; William R. Emmons and Bryan J. Noeth, "Unsteady Progress: Income Trends in the Federal Reserve's Survey of Consumer Finances," Federal Reserve Bank of St. Louis, *In the Balance*, no. 2, 2012 (www.stlouisfed.org); Charles Riley, "Family Net Worth Plummets Nearly 40%," *CNN Money* (money.cnn.com), June 12, 2012; "Financial Accounts of the United States, Third Quarter, 2017," *Federal Reserve Statistical Release,* December 7, 2017; and Christopher Ingraham, "If You Thought Income Inequality Was Bad, Get a Load of Wealth Inequality," *The Washington Post* (www.washingtonpost.com), May 21, 2015.

[7]Refer to "Recent Developments in Household Net Worth and Domestic Nonfinancial Debt," Financial Accounts of the United States, Third Quarter, 2017, *Federal Reserve Statistical Release* (www.federalreserve.gov/releases/z1/current/html/introductory_text.htm), December 7, 2017.

Self*Test*

What is the balance sheet, and what information does it provide?

How is the order in which items are shown on the balance sheet determined?

Explain in words the difference between net working capital and net operating working capital.

Explain in words the difference between total debt and total liabilities.

What items on Allied's December 31 balance sheet would probably be different from its June 30 values? Would these differences be as large if Allied were a grocery chain rather than a food processor? Explain.

3-3 The Income Statement

Table 3.2 shows Allied's 2018 and 2019 **income statements**. Net sales are shown at the top of the statement; then operating costs, interest, and taxes are subtracted to obtain the net income available to common shareholders. We also show earnings and dividends per share, in addition to some other data, at the bottom of Table 3.2. Earnings per share (EPS) is often called "the bottom line," denoting that of all items on the income statement, EPS is the one that is most important to stockholders. Allied earned \$1.95 per share in 2019, down from \$2.03 in 2018. In spite of the decline in earnings, the firm still increased the dividend from \$1.06 to \$1.15.

Income Statements
Reports summarizing a firm's revenues, expenses, and profits during a reporting period, generally a quarter or a year.

A typical stockholder focuses on the reported EPS, but professional security analysts and managers differentiate between *operating* and *non-operating* income. **Operating income** is derived from the firm's regular core business—in Allied's case, from producing and selling food products. Moreover, it is calculated before deducting interest expenses and taxes, which are considered to be non-operating costs. Operating income is also called EBIT, or earnings before interest and taxes. Here is its equation:

Operating Income
Earnings from operations before interest and taxes (i.e., EBIT).

$$\begin{aligned}\text{Operating income (or EBIT)} &= \text{Sales revenues} - \text{Operating costs} \\ &= \$3{,}000 - \$2{,}722 \\ &= \$278 \text{ million}\end{aligned} \qquad (3.2)$$

This figure must, of course, match the one reported on the income statement.

Different firms have different amounts of debt, different tax carryforwards, and different amounts of non-operating assets such as marketable securities. These differences can cause two companies with identical operations to report significantly different net incomes. For example, suppose two companies have identical sales, operating costs, and assets. However, one company uses some debt, and the other uses only common equity. Despite their identical operating performances, the company with no debt (and therefore no interest expense) would report a higher net income because no interest was deducted from its operating income. Consequently, if you want to compare two companies' operating performances, it is best to focus on their operating income.[8]

[8]Operating income is important for several reasons. Managers are generally compensated based on the performance of the units they manage. A division manager can control his or her division's performance, but not the firm's capital structure policy or other corporate decisions. Second, if one firm is considering acquiring another, it will be interested in the value of the target firm's operations; that value is determined by the target firm's operating income. Third, operating income is normally more stable than total income, as total income can be heavily influenced by write-offs of bonds backed by subprime mortgages and the like. Therefore, analysts focus on operating income when they estimate firms' long-run stock values.

TABLE 3.2 Allied Food Products: Income Statements for Years Ending December 31 (millions of dollars, except for per-share data)

	2019	2018
Net sales	$3,000.0	$2,850.0
Operating costs except depreciation and amortization	2,622.0	2,497.0
Depreciation and amortization	100.0	90.0
Total operating costs	$2,722.0	$2,587.0
Operating income, or earnings before interest and taxes (EBIT)	$ 278.0	$ 263.0
Less interest	83.0	60.0
Earnings before taxes (EBT)	$ 195.0	$ 203.0
Taxes (25%)	48.8	50.8
Net income	$ 146.3	$ 152.3
Here are some related items:		
Total dividends	$ 86.3	$ 79.5
Addition to retained earnings = Net income − Total dividends	$ 60.0	$ 72.8
Per-share data:		
Common stock price	$ 23.06	$ 26.00
Earnings per share (EPS)[a]	$ 1.95	$ 2.03
Dividends per share (DPS)[a]	$ 1.15	$ 1.06
Book value per share (BVPS)[a]	$ 12.53	$ 11.73

Note:
[a]Allied has 75 million shares of common stock outstanding. Note that EPS is based on net income available to common stockholders. Calculations of EPS, DPS, and BVPS for 2019 are as follows:

$$\text{Earnings per share} = \text{EPS} = \frac{\text{Net income}}{\text{Common shares outstanding}} = \frac{\$146{,}300{,}000}{75{,}000{,}000} = \$1.95$$

$$\text{Dividends per share} = \text{DPS} = \frac{\text{Dividends paid to common stockholders}}{\text{Common shares outstanding}} = \frac{\$86{,}300{,}000}{75{,}000{,}000} = \$1.15$$

$$\text{Book value per share} = \text{BVPS} = \frac{\text{Total common equity}}{\text{Common shares outstanding}} = \frac{\$940{,}000{,}000}{75{,}000{,}000} = \$12.53$$

When a firm has options or convertibles outstanding or it recently has issued new common stock, a more comprehensive EPS, "diluted EPS," is calculated. Its calculation is a bit more complicated, but you may refer to any financial accounting text for a discussion.

From Allied's income statement, we see that its operating income increased from $263 million in 2018 to $278 million in 2019, or by $15 million. However, its 2019 net income declined. This decline occurred because it increased its debt in 2019, and the $23 million increase in interest lowered its net income.

Depreciation
The charge to reflect the cost of assets depleted in the production process. Depreciation is not a cash outlay.

Amortization
A noncash charge similar to depreciation except that it represents a decline in value of intangible assets.

Taking a closer look at the income statement, we see that depreciation and amortization are important components of operating costs. Recall from accounting that **depreciation** is an annual charge against income that reflects the estimated dollar cost of the capital equipment and other tangible assets that were depleted in the production process. **Amortization** amounts to the same thing except that it represents the decline in value of intangible assets such as patents, copyrights, trademarks, and goodwill. Because depreciation and amortization are so similar, they are generally lumped together for purposes of financial analysis on the income statement and for other purposes. They both write off, or allocate, the costs of assets over their useful lives.

Even though depreciation and amortization are reported as costs on the income statements, they are not cash expenses—cash was spent in the past, when the assets being written off were acquired, but no cash is paid out to cover depreciation and amortization. Therefore, managers, security analysts, and bank loan officers who are concerned with the amount of cash a company is generating often calculate **EBITDA**, an acronym for earnings before interest, taxes, depreciation, and amortization. Allied has no amortization charges, so Allied's depreciation and amortization expense consists entirely of depreciation. In 2019, Allied's EBITDA was $378 million.

EBITDA
An acronym for earnings before interest, taxes, depreciation, and amortization.

Although the balance sheet represents a snapshot in time, the income statement reports on operations *over a period of time.* For example, during 2019, Allied had sales of $3 billion and its net income was $146.3 million. Income statements are prepared monthly, quarterly, and annually. The quarterly and annual statements are reported to investors, while the monthly statements are used internally by managers for planning and control purposes.

Finally, note that the income statement is tied to the balance sheet through the retained earnings account on the balance sheet. Net income as reported on the income statement less dividends paid is the retained earnings for the year (e.g., 2019). Those retained earnings are added to the cumulative retained earnings from prior years to obtain the year-end 2019 balance for retained earnings. The retained earnings for the year are also reported in the statement of stockholders' equity. All four of the statements provided in the annual report are interrelated.

Self*Test*

Why is earnings per share called "the bottom line"? What is EBIT, or operating income?

What is EBITDA?

Which is more like a snapshot of the firm's operations—the balance sheet or the income statement? Explain your answer.

3-4 Statement of Cash Flows

Net income as reported on the income statement is not cash, and in finance, "cash is king." Management's goal is to maximize the firm's intrinsic value, and the value of any asset, including a share of stock, is based on the cash flows the asset is expected to produce. Therefore, managers strive to maximize the cash flows available to investors. The **statement of cash flows**, as shown in Table 3.3, is the accounting report that shows how much cash the firm is generating. The statement is divided into four sections, and we explain it on a line-by-line basis.[9]

Statement of Cash Flows
A report that shows how items that affect the balance sheet and income statement affect the firm's cash flows.

Here is a line-by-line explanation of the statement shown in Table 3.3:

a. *Operating activities.* This section deals with items that occur as part of normal ongoing operations.

b. *Net income.* The first operating activity is net income, which is the first source of cash. If all sales were for cash, if all costs required immediate cash payments, and if the firm were in a static situation, net income would equal cash from operations. However, these conditions don't hold, so net income is not equal to cash from operations. Adjustments shown in the remainder of the statement must be made.

---

[9] Allied's statement of cash flows is relatively simple because it is a relatively uncomplicated company. Many cash flow statements are more complex, but if you understand Table 3.3, you should be able to follow more complex statements.

TABLE 3.3 Allied Food Products: Statement of Cash Flows for 2019 (millions of dollars)

		2019
a.	**I. Operating Activities**	
b.	Net income	$ 146.3
c.	Depreciation and amortization	100.0
d.	Increase in inventories	(200.0)
e.	Increase in accounts receivable	(60.0)
f.	Increase in accounts payable	30.0
g.	Increase in accrued wages and taxes	10.0
h.	Net cash provided by (used in) operating activities	$ 26.3
i.	**II. Investing Activities**	
j.	Additions to property, plant, and equipment	($230.0)
k.	Net cash used in investing activities	($230.0)
l.	**III. Financing Activities**	
m.	Increase in notes payable	$ 50.0
n.	Increase in bonds	170.0
o.	Payment of dividends to stockholders	(86.3)
p.	Net cash provided by financing activities	$ 133.8
q.	**IV. Summary**	
r.	Net decrease in cash (Net sum of I, II, and III)	($ 70.0)
s.	Cash and equivalents at the beginning of the year	80.0
t.	Cash and equivalents at the end of the year	$ 10.0

Note: Here and throughout the book parentheses are sometimes used to denote negative numbers.

c. *Depreciation and amortization.* The first adjustment relates to depreciation and amortization. Allied's accountants subtracted depreciation (it has no amortization expense), which is a noncash charge, when they calculated net income. Therefore, depreciation must be added back to net income when cash flow is determined.

d. *Increase in inventories.* To make or buy inventory items, the firm must use cash. It may receive some of this cash as loans from its suppliers and workers (payables and accruals), but ultimately, any increase in inventories requires cash. Allied increased its inventories by $200 million in 2019. That amount is shown in parentheses on line d because it is negative (i.e., a use of cash). If Allied had reduced its inventories, it would have generated positive cash.

e. *Increase in accounts receivable.* If Allied chooses to sell on credit when it makes a sale, it will not immediately get the cash that it would have received had it not extended credit. To stay in business, it must replace the inventory that it sold on credit, but it won't yet have received cash from the credit sale. So if the firm's accounts receivable increase, this will amount to a use of cash. Allied's receivables rose by $60 million in 2019, and that use of cash is shown as a negative number on line e. If Allied had reduced its receivables, this would be shown as a positive cash flow. (Once cash is received for the sale, the accompanying accounts receivable will be eliminated.)

f. *Increase in accounts payable.* Accounts payable represent a loan from suppliers. Allied bought goods on credit, and its payables increased by $30 million this year. That is treated as a $30 million increase in cash on line f. If Allied had reduced its payables, that would have required, or used, cash. Note that as Allied grows, it will purchase more inventories. That will give rise to additional payables, which will reduce the amount of new outside funds required to finance inventory growth.

g. *Increase in accrued wages and taxes.* The same logic applies to accruals as to accounts payable. Allied's accruals increased by $10 million this year, which means that in 2019, it borrowed an additional $10 million from its workers and taxing authorities. So this represents a $10 million cash inflow.

h. *Net cash provided by operating activities.* All of the previous items are part of normal operations—they arise as a result of doing business. When we sum them, we obtain the net cash flow from operations. Allied had positive flows from net income, depreciation, and increases in payables and accruals, but it used cash to increase inventories and to carry receivables. The net result was that operations led to a $26.3 million net cash inflow.

i. *Investing activities.* All activities involving long-term assets are covered in this section. It also includes the purchase and sale of short-term investments, other than trading securities, and lending and collecting on notes receivables. Allied had only one investment activity—the acquisition of some fixed assets, as shown on line j. If Allied had sold some fixed assets, its accountants would have reported it in this section as a positive amount (i.e., as a cash inflow).

j. *Additions to property, plant, and equipment.* Allied spent $230 million on fixed assets during the current year. This is an outflow; therefore, it is shown in parentheses. If Allied had sold some of its fixed assets, this would have been a cash inflow.[10]

k. *Net cash used in investing activities.* Because Allied had only one investment activity, the total on this line is the same as that on the previous line.

l. *Financing activities.* Allied's financing activities are shown in this section.

m. *Increase in notes payable.* Allied borrowed an additional $50 million from its bank this year, which was a cash inflow. When Allied repays the loan, this will be an outflow.

n. *Increase in bonds (long-term debt).* Allied borrowed an additional $170 million from long-term investors this year, issuing bonds in exchange for cash. This is shown as an inflow. When the bonds are repaid by the firm some years hence, this will be an outflow.

o. *Payment of dividends to stockholders.* Dividends are paid in cash, and the $86.3 million that Allied paid to stockholders is shown as a negative amount.

p. *Net cash provided by financing activities.* The sum of the three financing entries, which is a positive $133.8 million, is shown here. These funds, along with the small positive operating cash flow, were used to help pay for the $230 million of new plant and equipment.

q. *Summary.* This section summarizes the change in cash and cash equivalents over the year.

r. *Net decrease in cash.* The net sum of the operating activities, investing activities, and financing activities is shown here. These activities resulted in a $70 million net decrease in cash during 2019, mainly due to expenditures on new fixed assets.

s. *Cash and equivalents at the beginning of the year.* Allied began the year with $80 million of cash, which is shown here.

t. *Cash and equivalents at the end of the year.* Allied ended the year with $10 million of cash, the $80 million it started with minus the $70 million net decrease that occurred during the year. Clearly, Allied's cash position is weaker than it was at the beginning of the year.

---

[10]The number on line j is "gross" investment, or total expenditures. It is also equal to the change in net plant and equipment (from the balance sheet) plus depreciation, as shown on line c: Gross investment = Net investment + Depreciation = $130 + $100 = $230.

Allied's statement of cash flows should be of concern to its managers and investors. The company had a small positive operating cash flow that didn't begin to cover its fixed assets investment requirements. So the large investment in fixed assets was covered by borrowing and reducing its beginning balances of cash and equivalents. However, the firm can't continue to do this indefinitely. In the long run, Section I needs to show larger positive operating cash flows. In addition, we would expect Section II to show expenditures on fixed assets that are about equal to (1) its depreciation charges (to replace worn out fixed assets), along with (2) some additional expenditures to provide for growth. Section III would normally show some net borrowing in addition to a "reasonable" amount of dividends.[11] Finally, Section IV should show a reasonably stable year-to-year cash balance. These conditions don't hold for Allied, so some actions should be taken to correct the situation. We will consider corrective actions in Chapter 4, when we analyze the firm's financial statements.

Self*Test*

What is the statement of cash flows, and what are some questions it answers?

Identify and briefly explain the four sections shown in the statement of cash flows.

If during the year a company has high cash flows from its operations, does this mean that cash on its balance sheet will be higher at the end of the year than it was at the beginning of the year? Explain.

3-5 Statement of Stockholders' Equity

Statement of Stockholders' Equity
A statement that shows by how much a firm's equity changed during the year and why this change occurred.

Changes in stockholders' equity during the accounting period are reported in the **statement of stockholders' equity**. Table 3.4 shows that Allied earned $146.3 million during 2019, paid out $86.3 million in common dividends, and plowed $60 million back into the business. Thus, the balance sheet item "Retained earnings" increased from $750 million at year-end 2018 to $810 million at year-end 2019.[12]

Note that "retained earnings" represents a *claim against assets*, not assets per se. Stockholders allow management to retain earnings and reinvest them in the business, use retained earnings for additions to plant and equipment, add to inventories, and the like. Companies *do not* just pile up cash in a bank account. *Thus, retained earnings as reported on the balance sheet do not represent cash and are not "available" for dividends or anything else.*[13]

[11]The average company pays out about one-third of its earnings as dividends, but there is a great deal of variation between companies, depending on each company's needs for retained earnings to support growth. As you can see, Allied currently pays a much larger portion of its earnings as dividends. We cover dividends in detail in Chapter 14.

[12]If they had been applicable, columns would have been used to show Additional Paid-in Capital and Treasury Stock. Also, additional rows would have contained information on such things as new issues of stock, treasury stock acquired or reissued, stock options exercised, and unrealized foreign exchange gains or losses.

[13]Cash (as of the balance sheet date) is found in the cash account, an asset account. A positive number in the retained earnings account indicates only that the firm has in the past earned income and has not paid it all out as dividends. Even though a company reports record earnings and shows an increase in retained earnings, it still may be short of cash if it is using its available cash to purchase current and fixed assets to support growth. The same situation holds for individuals. You might own a new BMW (no loan), many clothes, and an expensive stereo (hence, have a high net worth), but if you had only $0.23 in your pocket plus $5.00 in your checking account, you would still be short of cash.

TABLE 3.4

Allied Food Products: Statement of Stockholders' Equity, December 31, 2019 (millions of dollars)

	COMMON STOCK			
	Shares (000)	**Amount**	**Retained Earnings**	**Total Stockholders' Equity**
Balances, December 31, 2018	75,000	$130.0	$750.0	$880.0
2019 Net income			146.3	
Cash dividends			(86.3)	
Addition to retained earnings				60.0
Balances, December 31, 2019	75,000	$130.0	$810.0	$940.0

Self*Test*

What information does the statement of stockholders' equity provide?

Why do changes in retained earnings occur?

Explain why the following statement is true: The retained earnings account reported on the balance sheet does not represent cash and is not "available" for dividend payments or anything else.

3-6 Uses and Limitations of Financial Statements

As we mentioned in the opening vignette to this chapter, financial statements provide a great deal of useful information. You can inspect the statements and answer a number of important questions such as these: How large is the company? Is it growing? Is it making or losing money? Is it generating cash through its operations, or are operations actually losing cash?

At the same time, investors need to be cautious when they review financial statements. Although companies are required to follow GAAP, managers still have a lot of discretion in deciding how and when to report certain transactions.

Consequently, two firms in exactly the same situation may report financial statements that convey different impressions about their financial strength. Some variations may stem from legitimate differences of opinion about the correct way to record transactions. In other cases, managers may choose to report numbers in a manner that helps them present either higher or more stable earnings over time. As long as they follow GAAP, such actions are legal, but these differences make it difficult for investors to compare companies and gauge their true performances. In particular, watch out if senior managers receive bonuses or other compensation based on earnings in the short run—they may try to boost short-term reported income to boost their bonuses.

Unfortunately, there have also been cases where managers disregarded GAAP and reported fraudulent statements. One blatant example of cheating involved WorldCom, which reported asset values that exceeded their true value by about $11 billion. This led to an understatement of costs and a corresponding overstatement of profits. Enron is another high-profile example. It overstated the value of certain assets, reported those artificial value increases as profits, and transferred the assets to subsidiary companies to hide the true facts. Enron's and WorldCom's investors eventually learned what was happening, and the companies were forced into bankruptcy. Many of their top executives went to jail, the accounting firm that audited their books was forced out of business, and investors lost billions of dollars.

After the Enron and WorldCom fiascos, Congress in 2002 passed the Sarbanes-Oxley Act (SOX), which required companies to improve their internal auditing standards and required the CEO and CFO to certify that the financial statements were properly prepared. The SOX bill also created a new watchdog organization to help make sure that the outside accounting firms were doing their jobs.

More recently, a serious debate has arisen regarding the appropriate accounting for complicated investments held by financial institutions. In the recent financial crisis, many of these investments (particularly those related to subprime mortgages) turned out to be worth a lot less than their stated book value. Currently, regulators and other policy makers are struggling to come up with the best way to account for and regulate many of these "toxic assets."[14]

Finally, keep in mind that even if investors receive accurate accounting data, it is cash flows, not accounting income, that matters most. Similarly, as we shall see in Chapters 11 and 12, when managers make capital budgeting decisions on which projects to accept, their focus should be on cash flow.

SelfTest

Can investors be confident that if the financial statements of different companies are accurate and are prepared in accordance with GAAP, the data reported by one company will be comparable to the data provided by another?

Why might different companies account for similar transactions in different ways?

3-7 Free Cash Flow

Free Cash Flow (FCF)
The amount of cash that could be withdrawn without harming a firm's ability to operate and to produce future cash flows.

Thus far, we have focused on financial statements as they are prepared by accountants. However, accounting statements are designed primarily for use by creditors and tax collectors, not for managers and stock analysts. Therefore, corporate decision makers and security analysts often modify accounting data to meet their needs. The most important modification is the concept of **free cash flow (FCF)**, defined as "the amount of cash that could be withdrawn without harming a firm's ability to operate and to produce future cash flows." Here is the equation used to calculate free cash flow:

$$\text{FCF} = \left[\text{EBIT}(1 - \text{T}) + \begin{matrix}\text{Depreciation}\\ \text{and amortization}\end{matrix}\right] - \left[\begin{matrix}\text{Capital}\\ \text{expenditures}\end{matrix} + \begin{matrix}\Delta\text{Net operating}\\ \text{working capital}\end{matrix}\right] \quad (3.3)$$

Net Operating Profit After Taxes (NOPAT)
The profit a company would generate if it had no debt and held only operating assets.

The first term represents the amount of cash that the firm generates from its current operations. EBIT (1 − T) is often referred to as **NOPAT**, or **net operating profit after taxes**. Depreciation and amortization are added back because these are noncash expenses that reduce EBIT but do not reduce the amount of cash the company has available to pay its investors. The second bracketed term indicates

[14]On May 12, 2011, the FASB and IASB jointly issued new guidance regarding how fair value measurement should be applied where its use is already required. It does not extend the use of fair value accounting.

the amount of cash that the company is investing in its fixed assets (capital expenditures) and operating working capital in order to sustain ongoing operations. A positive level of FCF indicates that the firm is generating more than enough cash to finance current investments in fixed assets and working capital. By contrast, negative free cash flow means that the company does not have sufficient internal funds to finance investments in fixed assets and working capital, and that it will have to raise new money in the capital markets in order to pay for these investments.

Consider the case of Home Depot. The first bracketed term in Equation 3.3 represents the amount of cash that Home Depot is generating from its existing stores. The second bracketed term represents the amount of cash that the company is spending this period to construct new stores. When Home Depot opens a new store, it needs cash to purchase the land and construct the building—these are capital expenditures, and they lead to a corresponding increase in the firm's fixed assets on the balance sheet. However, when it opens a new store, the company also needs to increase its net operating working capital. In particular, the company needs to stock the store with new inventory. Part of this inventory may be financed through accounts payable—for example, a supplier might ship Home Depot some flashlights today and allow Home Depot to pay for them later. In this case, there would be no increase in net operating working capital because the increase in current assets exactly equals the increase in current liabilities. Other portions of their inventory may not have offsetting accounts payable, so there will be an increase in net operating working capital, and the company must come up with the cash today in order to pay for this increase. Putting everything together, the company as a whole is generating positive free cash flow if the money generated from operating existing stores exceeds the money required to build new stores.

Looking at Allied's key financial statements, we can collect the pieces that we need to calculate its free cash flow. First, we can obtain Allied's EBIT and depreciation and amortization expense from the income statement. Looking at Table 3.2, we see that Allied's 2019 operating income (EBIT) was $278 million. Because Allied's tax rate is 25%, it follows that its NOPAT = EBIT(1 − T) = $278(1 − 0.25) = $208.5 million. We also see that Allied's depreciation and amortization expense in 2019 was $100 million.

Allied's capital expenditures (the cash used to purchase new fixed assets) can be found under the investment activities on the Statement of Cash Flows. Looking at Table 3.3, we see that Allied's capital expenditures in 2019 totaled $230 million.[15] Finally, we need to calculate the change in net operating working capital (ΔNOWC). Recall that NOWC is operating current assets (where operating current assets equal current assets minus excess cash) minus operating current liabilities (where operating current liabilities are calculated as current liabilities minus notes payable). We showed earlier that Allied's NOWC for 2019 was:

$$\text{NOWC}_{2019} = (\$1{,}000 - \$0) - (\$310 - \$110) = \$800 \text{ million}$$

[15]Alternatively, we can calculate Allied's capital expenditures by looking at changes in net fixed assets on the balance sheet between 2018 and 2019 and then adding back depreciation and amortization for 2019. In this example, Allied's net fixed assets increased $130 million (from $870 million in 2018 to $1 billion in 2019), and its depreciation and amortization totaled $100 million in 2019. Consequently, gross capital expenditures were $130 million + $100 million = $230 million.

Likewise, assuming once again that Allied had no excess cash in 2018, its NOWC for 2018 can be calculated as:

$$\textbf{NOWC}_{2018} = (\$810 - \$0) - (\$220 - \$60) = \$650 \text{ million}$$

Thus, Allied's change in net operating working capital (ΔNOWC) = $150 million ($800 million − $650 million). Putting everything together, we can now calculate Allied's 2019 free cash flow:

$$\text{FCF} = \left[\text{EBIT}(1 - \text{T}) + \begin{matrix}\text{Depreciation}\\ \text{and amortization}\end{matrix}\right] - \left[\begin{matrix}\text{Capital}\\ \text{expenditures}\end{matrix} + \begin{matrix}\Delta\text{Net operating}\\ \text{working capital}\end{matrix}\right]$$

$$\begin{aligned}\text{FCF}_{2019} &= [\$208.5 + \$100] - [\$230 + \$150] \\ &= -\$71.5 \text{ million}\end{aligned}$$

Allied's FCF is negative, which is not good. Note, though, that the negative FCF is largely attributable to the $230 million expenditure for a new processing plant. This plant is large enough to meet production for several years, so another new plant will not be needed until 2023. Therefore, Allied's FCF for 2020 and the next few years should increase, which means that Allied's financial situation is not as bad as the negative FCF might suggest.

Most rapidly growing companies have negative FCFs—the fixed assets and working capital needed to support a firm's rapid growth generally exceed cash flows from its existing operations. This is not bad, provided a firm's new investments are eventually profitable and contribute to its FCF.

Many analysts regard FCF as being the single most important number that can be developed from accounting statements, even more important than net income. After all, FCF shows how much cash the firm can distribute to its investors. We discuss FCF again in Chapter 9, which covers stock valuation, and in Chapters 11 and 12, which cover capital budgeting.

quick question

QUESTION:

A company has EBIT of $30 million, depreciation of $5 million, and a 25% tax rate. It needs to spend $10 million on new fixed assets and $15 million to increase its operating current assets. It expects its accounts payable to increase by $2 million, its accruals to increase by $3 million, and its notes payable to increase by $8 million. The firm's current liabilities consist of only accounts payable, accruals, and notes payable. What is its free cash flow?

ANSWER:

First, you need to determine the ΔNet operating working capital (ΔNOWC):

$$\begin{aligned}\Delta\text{NOWC} &= \Delta\text{Operating current assets} - \Delta\text{Operating current liabilities}\\ \Delta\text{NOWC} &= \Delta\text{Operating current assets} - (\Delta\text{Current liabilities} - \Delta\text{Notes payable})\\ \Delta\text{NOWC} &= \$15 - (\$13 - \$8)\\ \Delta\text{NOWC} &= \$15 - \$5 = \$10 \text{ million}\end{aligned}$$

Now, you can solve for free cash flow (FCF):

$$\begin{aligned}\text{FCF} &= [\text{EBIT}(1 - \text{T}) + \text{Depreciation and amortization}] - [\text{Capital expenditures} + \Delta\text{NOWC}]\\ \text{FCF} &= [\$30(1 - 0.25) + \$5] - [\$10 + \$10]\\ \text{FCF} &= [\$22.5 + \$5] - \$20\\ \text{FCF} &= \mathbf{\$7.5 \text{ million}}\end{aligned}$$

FREE CASH FLOW IS IMPORTANT FOR BUSINESSES BOTH SMALL AND LARGE

Free cash flow is important to large companies like Allied Foods. Security analysts use FCF to help estimate the value of the stock, and Allied's managers use it to assess the value of proposed capital budgeting projects and potential merger candidates. Note, though, that the concept is also relevant for small businesses.

Assume that your aunt and uncle own a small pizza shop and that their accountant prepares their financial statements. The income statement shows their annual accounting profits. Although they are certainly interested in this number, what they probably care more about is how much money they can take out of the business each year to maintain their standard of living. Let's assume that the shop's net income for 2019 was $75,000. However, your aunt and uncle had to spend $50,000 to refurbish the kitchen and restrooms.

So although the business is generating a great deal of "profit," your aunt and uncle can't take much money out because they have to put money back into the pizza shop. Stated another way, their free cash flow is much less than their net income. The required investments could be so large that they even exceed the money made from selling pizza. In this case, your aunt and uncle's free cash flow would be negative. If so, this means they must find funds from other sources just to maintain their pizza business.

As astute business owners, your aunt and uncle recognize that their restaurant investments, such as updating the kitchen and restrooms, are nonrecurring, and if nothing else happens unexpectedly, your aunt and uncle should be able to take more cash out of the business in future years, when their free cash flow increases. But some businesses never seem to produce cash for their owners—they consistently generate positive net income, but this net income is swamped by the amount of cash that has to be plowed back into the business.

Thus, when it comes to valuing the pizza shop (or any business small or large), what really matters is the amount of free cash flow that the business generates over time. Looking ahead, your aunt and uncle face competition from national chains that are moving into the area. To meet the competition, your aunt and uncle will have to modernize the dining room. This will again drain cash from the business and reduce its free cash flow, although the hope is that it will enable them to increase sales and free cash flow in the years ahead. As we will see in Chapters 11 and 12, which cover capital budgeting, evaluating projects require us to estimate whether the future increases in free cash flow are sufficient to more than offset the initial project cost. Therefore, the free cash flow calculation is critical to a firm's capital budgeting analysis.

Self*Test*

What is free cash flow (FCF)?

Why is FCF an important determinant of a firm's value?

3-8 MVA and EVA

Items reported on the financial statements reflect historical, in-the-past, values, not current market values, and there are often substantial differences between the two. Changes in interest rates and inflation affect the market value of the company's assets and liabilities but often have no effect on the corresponding book values shown in the financial statements. Perhaps, more importantly, the market's assessment of value takes into account its ongoing assessment of current operations as well as future opportunities. For example, it cost Microsoft very little to develop its first operating system, but that system turned out to be worth many billions that were not shown on its balance sheet. For a given level of debt, these increases in asset value also lead to a corresponding increase in the market value of equity.

To illustrate, consider the following situation. A firm was started with $1 million of assets at book value (historical cost), $500,000 of which was provided by bondholders, and $500,000 by stockholders (50,000 shares purchased at $10 per share). However, this firm became very successful; the market value of the firm's equity is now worth $19.5 million, and its current stock price is $19,500,000/50,000 = $390 per share. Clearly the firm's managers have done a marvelous job for the stockholders.

The accounting statements do not reflect market values, so they are not sufficient for purposes of evaluating managers' performance. To help fill this void, financial analysts have developed two additional performance measures, the first of which is **MVA**, or **market value added**.[16] MVA is simply the difference between the market value of a firm's equity and the book value as shown on the balance sheet, with market value found by multiplying the stock price by the number of shares outstanding. For our hypothetical firm, MVA is $19.5 million − $0.5 million = $19 million.

Market Value Added (MVA)
The excess of the market value of equity over its book value.

For Allied, which has 75 million shares outstanding and a stock price of $23.06, the market value of the equity is $1,729.5 million versus a book value, as shown on the balance sheet in Table 3.1, of $940 million. Therefore, Allied's MVA is $1,729.5 − $940 = $789.5 million. This $789.5 million represents the difference between the money Allied's stockholders have invested in the corporation since its founding—including retained earnings—versus the cash they could receive if they sold the business. The higher its MVA, the better the job management is doing for the firm's shareholders. Boards of directors often look at MVA when deciding on the compensation a firm's managers deserve. Note, though, that just as all ships rise in a rising tide, most firms' stock prices rise in a rising stock market, so a positive MVA may not be entirely attributable to management performance.

A related concept, **economic value added (EVA)**, sometimes called "economic profit," is closely related to MVA and is found as follows:[17]

Economic Value Added (EVA)
Excess of NOPAT over capital costs.

$$\text{EVA} = \begin{matrix}\text{Net operating profit}\\ \text{after taxes}\\ \text{(NOPAT)}\end{matrix} - \begin{matrix}\text{Annual dollar}\\ \text{cost of}\\ \text{capital}\end{matrix} \qquad \textbf{3.4}$$

$$= \text{EBIT}(1 - \text{T}) - \left(\begin{matrix}\text{Total}\\ \text{invested}\\ \text{capital}\end{matrix} \times \begin{matrix}\text{After-tax}\\ \text{percentage}\\ \text{cost of capital}\end{matrix}\right)$$

Companies create value (and realize positive EVA) if the benefits of their investments exceed the cost of raising the necessary capital. Total invested capital represents the amount of money that the company has raised from debt, equity, and any other sources of capital (such as preferred stock).[18] The annual dollar cost of capital is total invested capital multiplied by the after-tax percentage cost of this capital. So, for example, if the company has raised $1 million in capital, and the current cost of capital is 10%, the annual dollar cost of capital would be $100,000. The funds raised from this capital are invested in a variety of net fixed assets and net operating working capital. In any given year, NOPAT is the amount of money that these investments have generated for the company's investors after paying for operating costs and taxes—in this regard it represents the benefits of capital investments.

EVA is an estimate of a business's true economic profit for a given year, and it often differs sharply from accounting net income. The main reason for this

[16]The concepts of EVA and MVA were developed by Joel Stern and Bennett Stewart, co-founders of the consulting firm Stern Stewart & Company. Stern Stewart copyrighted the terms *MVA* and *EVA*, so other consulting firms have given other names to these values. Still, MVA and EVA are the terms most commonly used in practice. For more on MVA and EVA, see G. Bennett Stewart, *The Quest for Value* (New York: HarperCollins, 1991, 1999).

[17]Another top consulting company, McKinsey & Company, uses the term *economic profit*. Its definition of economic profit is:

$$(\text{Total invested capital}) \times (\text{Return on invested capital} - \text{Cost of capital})$$

Because the return on invested capital is [EBIT(1 − T)]/Total invested capital, you can show with a little bit of algebra that EVA and economic profit are identical.

[18]Note that some analysts (as the citation in this note shows) take out excess cash when calculating total invested capital. However, we are going to keep things simple and use the standard definition in this text. For a further discussion, refer to news.morningstar.com/classroom2/course.asp?docid=145095&page=9.

difference is that although accounting income takes into account the cost of debt (the company's interest expense), it does not deduct for the cost of equity capital. By contrast, EVA takes into account the total dollar cost of all capital, which includes both the cost of debt and equity capital.

If EVA is positive, then after-tax operating income exceeds the cost of the capital needed to produce that income, and management's actions are adding value for stockholders. Positive EVA on an annual basis will help ensure that MVA is also positive. Note that whereas MVA applies to the entire firm, EVA can be determined for divisions as well as for the company as a whole, so it is useful as a guide to "reasonable" compensation for divisional as well as top corporate managers.

Self*Test*

Define the terms *market value added (MVA)* and *economic value added (EVA)*.

How does EVA differ from accounting net income?

3-9 Income Taxes

Individuals and corporations pay out a significant portion of their income as taxes, so taxes are important in both personal and corporate decisions. We summarize the key aspects of the U.S. tax system for individuals in this section and for corporations in the next section, using 2018 data. The details of our tax laws change fairly often, and indeed President Trump signed a new tax bill, the Tax Cuts and Jobs Act, into law on December 22, 2017. Some of the provisions in the law are set to sunset, and it remains possible that key features discussed in this section may change over time.

*The IRS website is **www.irs.gov**. Here you can find current filing information and current credits and deductions information, and order needed forms and publications.*

CONGRESS PASSES SWEEPING TAX REFORM ACT IN 2017

In December 2017, Congress passed and President Trump signed the Tax Cuts and Jobs Act, which enacted the most sweeping changes to the tax code since 1986. The new tax legislation impacts both individuals and corporations. Here is a quick summary of the bill's key provisions, and we provide sources at the end of this box so that you may read the bill's provisions in greater detail.

Major Changes to the Individual Tax Code

First, we provide a summary of the bill's major changes to the individual tax code. It is important to recognize that all of the individual provisions listed below will sunset at the end of 2025. Moreover, there is a significant chance that future Congresses may change at least some of these provisions.

- The bill lowered **the maximum tax rate from 39.6% to 37%.**
- The bill eliminated **the personal exemption for taxpayers and their dependents.**
- The bill sharply **raised the standard deduction for all individuals and married couples.** The standard deduction is the amount that taxpayers can apply as a deduction against their taxable income. Typically, households have two choices: They can either take the standard deduction and file a very simple tax form with no other deductions allowed, or they can itemize their deductions in a more complicated tax form. Most households take the standard deduction, and itemizers tend to be those who have very large allowable deductions such as large mortgage payments, charitable donations, and medical expenses. The new bill nearly doubled the standard deduction to $12,000 for individuals and to $24,000 for married couples.
- The bill **limited mortgage interest deductions.** Taxpayers may only deduct interest on up to $750,000 of principal. In addition, taxpayers can no longer deduct interest on home equity loans.
- The bill **limited deductions for state and local taxes.**
- The **individual alternative minimum tax (AMT) was kept**; although these amounts were increased and continue to be indexed for inflation.
- The bill **eliminated miscellaneous itemized deductions.**
- The bill **doubles the estate tax exclusion amount to $10 million**, and this amount will continue to be indexed for inflation.

Implications of These Changes

- Most households received a tax cut, either due to the increase in the standard deduction and/or due to the drop in marginal tax rates. Analysts disagree about what portion of this increase in after-tax income will be spent or saved. The answer will influence the bill's overall economic impact and its effect on interest rates.
- The Congressional Budget Office reported that the bill will increase the federal deficit over time, which is likely to lead to further upward pressure on interest rates.
- The increase in the standard deduction will likely cause many taxpayers to stop itemizing their deductions, which would simplify the filing of taxes for many households.
- The tax bill could potentially lead to higher taxes for itemizing households living in high-tax-rate states, where the curtailment of the state and local tax deductions may more than offset the increase in the standard deduction. A likely spillover effect is that households living in higher-tax-rate states will experience an increase in the cost of state and local government, which may put pressure on those state governments to cut expenditures and tax rates.
- There are likely to be a large number of other (in many cases unintended) spillover effects. For example, charitable organizations may see an increase in giving because of the overall increase in after-tax income. But at the same time, fewer households are likely to itemize, which may cause them to curtail giving because they will no longer be able to deduct their charitable expenses (because they have opted for the standard deduction).

Major Changes to the Corporate Tax Code

Next, we summarize the bill's major changes to the corporate tax code. While most of these provisions will not automatically sunset over time, as we discuss next, some will evolve or be eliminated over time. Once again, there is also the chance that they may be altered over time by future Congresses.

- The bill **established a flat 21% corporate tax rate**. The impetus for lowering the corporate tax rate was to make U.S. companies more competitive—with the hope of creating jobs.
- The bill **permits an immediate 100% expensing of certain new and used business assets** placed into service after September 27, 2017 and before January 1, 2023. This "bonus" percentage declines to 80% after January 1, 2023, and before January 1, 2027. This provision sunsets on January 1, 2027. The main reason for this provision was to spur new investment in plant and equipment.
- The bill **repealed the corporate alternative minimum tax (AMT)**.
- The bill **eliminated the net operating loss (NOL) carry-back provision and changed the carryforward provision so that NOLs can be carried forward indefinitely**. However, the carryforward in any one year is limited to the lower of the NOL or 80% of the firm's taxable income for that year.
- The new tax bill **limits the corporate interest deduction on debt to 30% of income** (measured as EBITDA for 2018–2021 and as EBIT thereafter). The reason for this provision was to discourage companies from taking on too much debt. Companies with average sales of $25 million or less during the past 3 years are exempt from this provision.
- The bill will **provide a one-time repatriation tax holiday for firms with money parked overseas**. Firms will be taxed 15.5% on cash and equivalents and 8% on noncash and liquid assets such as equipment abroad purchased with foreign profits. The lower rate is meant to motivate firms to bring cash home and to use it here in the United States.
- The bill **changed the corporate dividend exclusion** from 70% to 50% for less than 20%-owned subsidiaries and from 80% to 65% for less than 80%-owned subsidiaries.

Implications of These Changes

- The lower corporate tax rates will make U.S. companies more globally competitive, and they may also spur some companies to repatriate their income back to the United States.
- The lower tax rate also reduces the value of the tax deduction associated with debt financing. This effect will likely reduce the percentage of debt financing and lead to an increase in the average company's cost of capital.
- The lower corporate tax rate increases most companies' after-tax free cash flows.
- The combination of higher after-tax free cash flows and the expensing of business assets mean that more projects have a positive net present value (NPV), which will encourage more investment.
- The bill took away many corporate deductions but lowered the tax rate, so companies were impacted differently. Those companies with fewer deductions were more favorably impacted by the new lower corporate tax rate than those with more deductions.

This is just a summary of the bill's key features. In Chapters 12 and 13, we will consider in more detail how these changes will affect firms' capital budgeting and capital structure decisions.

Sources: "Analysis of the Final Tax Reform Bill," (https://www.cooley.com), December 20, 2017; Phillip Daves, "Web Extension 1C: The 2017/18 Tax Reform and Its Impact on Corporate Finance," *Intermediate Financial Management*, 13th edition (Mason: OH, Cengage Learning, 2019); Kimberly Amadeo, "Trump's Tax Plan and How It Affects You," *The Balance* (www.thebalance.com), April 9, 2018; Wendy Connick, "What's in the Final Version of the Tax Cuts and Jobs Act," *The Motley Fool* (www.fool.com), January 3, 2018; and Ben Casselman, "Federal Tax Cuts Leave States in a Bind," *The New York Times* (www.nytimes.com), May 12, 2018. Refer to Congress.gov (https://www.congress.gov/bill/115th-Congress/house-bill/1) for the actual bill and all its provisions.

3-9A INDIVIDUAL TAXES

Individuals pay taxes on wages and salaries, on investment income (dividends, interest, and profits from the sale of securities), and on the profits of proprietorships and partnerships. The tax rates are **progressive**—that is, the higher one's income, the larger the percentage paid in taxes. Table 3.5 provides the 2018 tax rates that taxpayers will pay for tax returns due April 15, 2019.

Progressive
A tax system where the tax rate is higher on higher incomes. The personal income tax in the United States, which ranges from 0% on the lowest incomes to 37% on the highest incomes, is progressive.

Taxable income is defined as "gross income less a set of exemptions and deductions." When filing a tax return in 2019 for the tax year 2018, taxpayers no longer receive an exemption for each dependent, including the taxpayer, because the personal exemption was eliminated with the passage of the new tax bill. Certain expenses can still be deducted and thus be used to reduce taxable income—but some have been either reduced or eliminated. For example, for mortgages begun after December 31, 2017, taxpayers can only deduct interest on up to $750,000 of principal, but the interest deduction for home equity loans has been eliminated. Also, the tax law eliminates most itemized deductions; however, deductions for charitable contributions, retirement savings, and student loan interest remain. Taxpayers may now only claim an itemized deduction up to $10,000 (for couples filing jointly) and $5,000 (for single taxpayers) for a combination of state and local property, income, and sales taxes. Finally, the standard deduction (which is taken

TABLE 3.5 2018 Individual Tax Rates

Single Individuals

If Your Taxable Income Is	You Pay This Amount on the Base of the Bracket	Plus This Percentage on the Excess over the Base (Marginal Rate)	Average Tax Rate at Top of Bracket
Up to $9,525	$0.00	10.0%	10.0%
$9,525–$38,700	952.50	12.0	11.5
$38,700–$82,500	4,453.50	22.0	17.1
$82,500–$157,500	14,089.50	24.0	20.4
$157,500–$200,000	32,089.50	32.0	22.8
$200,000–$500,000	45,689.50	35.0	30.1
Over $500,000	150,689.50	37.0	37.0

Married Couples Filing Joint Returns

If Your Taxable Income Is	You Pay This Amount on the Base of the Bracket	Plus This Percentage on the Excess over the Base (Marginal Rate)	Average Tax Rate at Top of Bracket
Up to $19,050	$0.00	10.0%	10.0%
$19,050–$77,400	1,905.00	12.0	11.5
$77,400–$165,000	8,907.00	22.0	17.1
$165,000–$315,000	28,179.00	24.0	20.4
$315,000–$400,000	64,179.00	32.0	22.8
$400,000–$600,000	91,379.00	35.0	26.9
Over $600,000	161,379.00	37.0	37.0

Notes:
1. These are the 2018 tax rates that will be paid on tax returns due April 15, 2019. The income ranges at which each tax rate takes effect are indexed with inflation, so they change each year.
2. The average tax rates are always below the marginal rates, but in 2018 the average at the top of the brackets approaches 37% as taxable income rises without limit.
3. In 2018, the personal exemption for the taxpayer and dependents was eliminated. With the deduction limitation on state and local property, income, and sales taxes and the existence of payroll taxes (Social Security and Medicare taxes), the 2018 effective tax rate will be higher than 37%.

if itemized deductions are below this amount) has been increased to $12,000 for single individuals and $24,000 for married couples filing jointly.

Marginal Tax Rate
The tax rate applicable to the last unit of a person's income.

The **marginal tax rate** is defined as "the tax rate on the last dollar of income." Marginal rates begin at 10% and rise to 37%. Note, though, that when consideration is given to Social Security and Medicare taxes, and to state taxes, the marginal tax rate may actually exceed 45%. Average tax rates can be calculated from the data in Table 3.5. For example, if a single individual had taxable income of $40,000, his or her tax bill would be $4,453.50 + ($40,000 − $38,700)(0.22) = $4,453.50 + $286.00 = $4,739.50. Her **average tax rate** would be $4,739.50/$40,000 = 11.85% versus a marginal rate of 22%. If she received a raise of $1,000, bringing her income to $41,000, she would have to pay $220 of it as taxes, so her after-tax raise would be $780.

Average Tax Rate
Taxes paid divided by taxable income.

Note too that *interest income* received by individuals from corporate securities is added to other income and thus is taxed at federal rates going up to 37%, plus state taxes.[19] *Capital gains and losses,* on the other hand, are treated differently. Assets such as stocks, bonds, and real estate are defined as *capital assets.* When you buy a capital asset and later sell it for more than you paid, you earn a profit that is called a **capital gain**; when you suffer a loss, it is called a **capital loss**. If you held the asset for a year or less, you will have a *short-term capital gain or loss,* while if you held it for more than a year, you will have a *long-term capital gain or loss.* Thus, if you buy 100 shares of Disney stock for $100 per share and sell them for $110 per share, you have a capital gain of 100 × $10, or $1,000. However, if you sell the stock for $90 per share, you will have a $1,000 capital loss. Depending on how long you hold the stock, you will have a short-term or long-term capital gain or loss.[20] If you sell the stock for exactly $100 per share, you make neither a gain nor a loss, so no tax is due.

Capital Gain
The profit from the sale of a capital asset for more than its purchase price.

Capital Loss
The loss from the sale of a capital asset for less than its purchase price.

A short-term capital gain is taxed at the same rate as ordinary income. However, long-term capital gains are taxed differently. For most taxpayers, the rate on long-term capital gains is only 15%.[21] Thus, if in 2018, you were an individual taxpayer with an income of $300,000, any short-term capital gains you earned would be taxed just like ordinary income, but your long-term capital gains would only be taxed at 15%. However, the tax rate on long-term capital gains is 20% for single taxpayers with income greater than $425,800 and married couples filing jointly with income greater than $479,000. In addition, high-income taxpayers may incur a 3.8% unearned income Medicare contribution tax applied to their capital gains and other net investment income. So, the highest tax rate that could apply on short-term capital gains that are taxed at ordinary rates is 40.8%, compared to 23.8% on long-term capital gains. Even for individuals at these high income levels, the tax rate on long-term capital gains remains considerably lower than the tax rate on ordinary income.

Beginning in 2013, the maximum tax rate on *qualified dividends* increased to 20% for taxpayers in the 39.6% tax bracket.[22] However, for most taxpayers the top tax rate on qualified dividends is 15%.[23] Because corporations pay dividends

[19]Under U.S. tax laws, interest on most state and local government bonds, called municipals or "munis," is not subject to federal income taxes. This has a significant effect on the values of munis and on their rates of return. We discuss rates and returns in Chapter 8.

[20]If you have a *net* capital loss (your capital losses exceed your capital gains) for the year, you can deduct up to $3,000 of this loss against your other income (for example, salary, interest, and dividends).

[21]The long-term capital gains tax rates are 0%, 15%, and 20%. For single taxpayers with income up to $38,600 and married couples filing jointly with income up to $77,200, the long-term capital gains tax rate is 0%. For single individuals with income between $38,600 and $425,800 and married couples filing jointly with income between $77,200 and $479,000, the long-term capital gains tax rate is 15%. For income above these levels, the long-term capital gains tax rate is 20%.

[22]For a dividend to be "qualified," the investor must have owned the stock for more than 60 days during a 121-day period that begins 60 days prior to the ex-dividend date. We discuss dividends in Chapter 14; however, for now, understand that the ex-dividend date is the date when the right to the current dividend leaves the stock.

[23]The qualified dividend tax rates are 0%, 15%, and 20% and these rates correspond to the same income levels as previously provided for the long-term capital gains tax rates.

out of earnings that have already been taxed, there is *double taxation of corporate income*—income is first taxed at the corporate rate; then, when what is left is paid out as dividends, it is taxed again. This double taxation motivated Congress to tax dividends at a lower rate than the rate on ordinary income.

Tax rates on dividends and capital gains have varied over time, but they have generally been lower than rates on ordinary income. Congress wants the economy to grow. For growth, we need investment in productive assets, and low capital gains and dividend tax rates encourage investment. Individuals with money to invest understand the tax advantages associated with making equity investments in newly formed companies versus buying bonds, so new ventures have an easier time attracting capital under the tax system. All in all, lower capital gains and dividend tax rates stimulate capital formation and investment.

As you might imagine, over the years Congress has frequently adjusted the tax code for individuals to promote certain activities. For example, Individual Retirement Accounts (IRAs) have encouraged individuals to save more for retirement. There are two main types of IRAs, **Traditional IRAs** and **Roth IRAs**. In each case, investors receive valuable tax benefits as long as the money is held in their account until age 59½. Qualified contributions to a Traditional IRA are tax deductible, and the income and capital gains on the investments within the account are not taxed until the money is withdrawn after age 59½. On the other hand, contributions to a Roth IRA are not tax deductible (they come out of after-tax dollars), but from that point forward, neither the future income nor the capital gains from the investments are taxed. In each case, investors in IRAs face penalties if they withdraw funds before age 59½, unless there is a qualifying exception—for example, investors in a Roth IRA can withdraw up to $10,000 from their account to help pay for a first-time home without facing a penalty.

Traditional IRAs
Individual retirement arrangements in which qualified contributions are tax deductible and income and capital gains on investments within the account are not taxed until the money is withdrawn after age 59½.

Roth IRAs
Individual retirement arrangements in which contributions are not tax deductible but the future income and capital gains within these accounts are not taxed if the money is withdrawn after age 59½.

As a very rough rule of thumb, Roth IRAs are more attractive for those individuals who believe that their tax rates will increase over time—either because they think their income will increase as they age and/or because they think Congress will raise overall tax rates in the future. For this reason, many younger investors who expect higher pay (and therefore higher tax rates!) over time tend to select Roth IRAs. Indeed, a Vanguard analyst in a recent article in *The Wall Street Journal* estimates that investors under 30 years old allocate 92% of their IRA funds into Roth accounts. But as you might expect, one size doesn't fit all, and it is important to review the specific eligibility requirements, potential penalties, and distribution policies before making any investments. Fortunately, there are a lot of great online resources that summarize the relative benefits and drawbacks with both Traditional and Roth IRAs.[24]

One other tax feature should be addressed—the **Alternative Minimum Tax (AMT)**. The AMT was created in 1969 because Congress learned that 155 millionaires with high incomes paid no taxes because they had so many tax shelters from items such as depreciation on real estate and municipal bond interest. Under the AMT law, people must calculate their tax under the "regular" system and then under the AMT system, where many deductions are added back to income and then taxed at a special AMT rate. For many years, the AMT was not indexed for inflation, and literally millions of taxpayers found themselves subject to this very complex tax.[25]

Alternative Minimum Tax (AMT)
Created by Congress to make it more difficult for wealthy individuals to avoid paying taxes through the use of various deductions.

Single taxpayers earning more than $200,000 and married taxpayers earning more than $250,000 will incur an additional 0.9% Medicare tax and a 3.8% net investment income tax on certain types of investment income. These taxes, originally enacted by the Affordable Care Act, were left untouched by the new tax law legislation.

[24]For additional information regarding IRAs refer to Laura Saunders, "Is a Roth Account Right for You?" *The Wall Street Journal* (www.wsj.com), December 19, 2014; and David Wolpe, "All about IRAs," *The Motley Fool* (www.fool.com/money/allaboutiras/allaboutiras.htm).

[25]Beginning in 2013, the AMT exemption amounts are indexed to inflation. In 2018, the AMT exemption amounts are $70,300 (with the exemption phase-out at $500,000) for single taxpayers and $109,400 (with the exemption phase-out at $1,000,000) for those married and filing jointly. The new tax law repealed the corporate AMT.

3-9B CORPORATE TAXES

The corporate tax structure is simple. The new tax law lowered the corporate tax rate to one single flat rate of 21%. Because of state and local tax rates, in this textbook we will use a federal-plus-state corporate tax rate of 25%. To illustrate, if a firm had $65,000 of taxable income and we assume a federal-plus-state corporate tax rate of 25%, its tax bill would be $16,250:

$$\text{Taxes} = \$65,000\,(0.25) = \$16,250.$$

Interest and Dividends Received by a Corporation

Corporations earn most of their income from operations, but they may also own securities—bonds and stocks—and receive interest and dividend income. Interest income received by a corporation is taxed as ordinary income at the lower corporate flat rate. *However, dividends are taxed more favorably: 50% of dividends received is excluded from taxable income, whereas the remaining 50% is taxed at the flat corporate tax*

CORPORATE TAX RATES AROUND THE WORLD

In the text, we describe some key elements of the new tax legislation. The impetus for passing this legislation was to lower tax rates for both individuals and corporations and to spur the creation of jobs with the lower corporate tax rate. The concern was that U.S. companies pay much higher rates than their global competitors—and they did prior to the passage of the new tax bill. The new lower flat rate of 21% is much more in line with other corporate tax rates around the world, as shown in the following table. This table shows the full impact of effective corporate tax rates that consider federal and state and local tax rates for 2016, 2017, and 2018, so that's why the U.S. rate is above 21% in 2018. As you can see, the 2018 U.S. corporate tax rate is no longer one of the highest shown.

Sample of Corporate Tax Rates around the World

Country	2016 Tax Rate	2017 Tax Rate	2018 Tax Rate
Australia	30.00%	30.00%	30.00%
Canada	26.50	26.50	26.50
Denmark	22.00	22.00	22.00
France	33.30	33.33	33.00
Germany	29.72	29.79	30.00
Hong Kong	16.50	16.50	16.50
Ireland	12.50	12.50	12.50
Japan	30.86	30.86	30.86
Mexico	30.00	30.00	30.00
Russia	20.00	20.00	20.00
Saudi Arabia	20.00	20.00	20.00
South Africa	28.00	28.00	28.00
Spain	25.00	25.00	25.00
United Kingdom	20.00	19.00	19.00
United States	**40.00**	**40.00**	**27.00**

Source: "Corporate Tax Rates Table," (https://home.kpmg.com/xx/en/home/services/tax/tax-tools-and-resources/tax-rates-online/corporate-tax-rates-table.html).

rate.[26] Thus, a corporation would normally pay only (0.5)(0.25) = 0.125 = 12.5% of its dividend income as taxes. If this firm had $10,000 in pretax dividend income, its after-tax dividend income would be $8,750:

$$\text{After-tax income} = \text{Pretax income}(1 - T) = \$10{,}000(1 - 0.125) = \$8{,}750$$

The rationale behind this exclusion is that when a corporation receives dividends and then pays out its own after-tax income as dividends to its stockholders, the dividends received are subjected to triple taxation: (1) The original corporation is taxed. (2) The second corporation is taxed on the dividends it receives. (3) The individuals who receive the final dividends are taxed again. This explains the 50% intercorporate dividend exclusion.

Suppose a firm has excess cash that it does not need for operations, and it plans to invest this cash in marketable securities. The tax factor favors stocks, which pay dividends, rather than bonds, which pay interest. For example, suppose Allied had $100,000 to invest, and it could buy bonds that paid 8% interest, or $8,000 per year, or stock that paid 7% in dividends, or $7,000. Remember, Allied's federal-plus-state corporate tax rate is 25%. Therefore, if Allied bought bonds and received interest, its tax on the $8,000 of interest would be 0.25($8,000) = $2,000, and its after-tax income would be $6,000. If it bought stock, its tax would be $7,000(0.125) = $875, and its after-tax income would be $6,125. *Other factors might lead Allied to invest in bonds, but when the investor is a corporation, the tax factor favors stock investments.*

Interest and Dividends Paid by a Corporation

A firm like Allied can finance its operations with either debt or stock. If a firm uses debt, it must pay interest, whereas if it uses stock, it is expected to pay dividends. *Interest paid can be deducted from operating income to obtain taxable income, but the deduction is limited to 30% of earnings before interest, taxes, and depreciation (EBITDA) for the years from 2018 through 2021—and starting in 2022 the deduction is limited to 30% of earnings before interest and taxes (EBIT).*[27] *Companies with average annual gross receipts of $25 million or less for the prior 3 years are exempt from this limitation. However, dividends paid cannot be deducted.* Therefore, Allied would need $1 of pretax income to pay $1 of interest, but because it has a 25% federal-plus-state corporate tax rate, it must earn $1.33 of pretax income to pay $1 of dividends:

$$\begin{array}{l}\text{Pretax income needed} \\ \text{to pay \$1 of dividends}\end{array} = \frac{\$1}{1 - \text{Tax rate}} = \frac{\$1}{0.75} = \$1.33$$

Working backward, if Allied has $1.33 in pretax income, it must pay $0.33 in taxes [(0.25)($1.33) = $0.33]. This leaves it with after-tax income of $1.00.

Table 3.6 shows the situation for a firm with $10 million of assets, sales of $5 million, and $1.5 million of earnings before interest and taxes (EBIT). The company's average annual gross receipts are less than $25 million and have been for the prior 3 years, so the firm is exempt from the interest deduction limitation. As shown in column 1, if the firm were financed entirely by bonds and if it made interest payments of $1.5 million, its taxable income would be zero, taxes would be zero, and its investors would receive the entire $1.5 million. (The term *investors* includes both stockholders and bondholders.) However, as shown in column 2, if the firm had

[26]The exclusion depends on the percentage of the paying company's stock the receiving company owns. If it owns 100% (hence, the payer is a wholly owned subsidiary), all of the dividend will be excluded. If it owns less than 80% of the subsidiary, then 65% of the dividend will be excluded. If it owns less than 20%, which is the case if the stock held is just an investment, 50% will be excluded. In this text, we assume that the stock is held just for investment, so we assume that the company owns less than 20% of the stock, so the applicable dividend exclusion is 50%. Also, state tax rules vary, but in our example, we assume that Allied also has a state tax exclusion.

[27]Note that disallowed interest deductions can be carried forward indefinitely. We discuss carryforwards in a later section.

TABLE 3.6 Returns to Investors under Bond and Stock Financing

	Use Bonds (1)	Use Stocks (2)
Sales	$5,000,000	$5,000,000
Operating costs	3,500,000	3,500,000
Earnings before interest and taxes (EBIT)	$1,500,000	$1,500,000
Interest	1,500,000	0
Taxable income	$ 0	$1,500,000
Federal-plus-state taxes (25%)	0	375,000
After-tax income	$ 0	$1,125,000
Income to investors	$1,500,000	$1,125,000
Rate of return on $10 million of assets	15.0%	11.25%

no debt and was therefore financed entirely by stock, all of the $1.5 million of EBIT would be taxable income to the corporation, the tax would be $1,500,000(0.25) = $375,000, and investors would receive only $1.125 million versus $1.5 million under debt financing. Therefore, the rate of return to investors on their $10 million investment is much higher when debt is used.

Of course, it is generally not possible to finance exclusively with debt, and the risk of doing so would offset the benefits of the higher expected income. *Still, the fact that interest is a deductible expense—even though the deduction may be limited—has a profound effect on the way businesses are financed—the corporate tax system favors debt financing over equity financing.* This point is discussed in more detail in Chapters 10 and 13.[28]

Corporate Capital Gains

Before 1987, corporate long-term capital gains were taxed at lower rates than corporate ordinary income; so the situation was similar for corporations and individuals. Currently, though, corporations' capital gains are taxed at the same flat corporate tax rate as their operating income.

Corporate Loss Carryforward

Carryforward
Ordinary corporate operating losses can be carried forward indefinitely to offset taxable income in a given year.

Ordinary corporate operating losses can be carried forward (**carryforward**) indefinitely. The carryforward deduction is limited to the lessor of the total available net operating loss (NOL) or 80% of the taxable income for the year to which the carryforward will be applied.

To illustrate, suppose in 2019, Company X lost $12 million. Also, assume that in 2020 and 2021, Company X is profitable and has taxable income of $10 million in each year. (Of course, we won't have this information ahead of time, we're simply illustrating how carryforwards will be applied in future years for this company.) As shown in Table 3.7, Company X would use the carryforward feature in 2020 to adjust its profits and calculate its adjusted tax liability. The loss that can be carried forward in 2020 is the lesser of the actual loss, $12 million in this case, or 80% of the 2020 taxable income. Because 80% of the 2020 taxable income is $8 million, Company X can carry forward $8 million of its 2019 loss to adjust its 2020 profits. Taxes owed for 2020 would be calculated as $500,000 ([0.25][$2,000,000]). Because not all of the 2019 loss has been used, Company X can carry forward the remaining $4 million loss to use in future years. In 2021, the firm has taxable income of $10 million, so we can use the remaining carryforward to adjust the firm's 2021 profits. Because all of the carryforward available is less than 80% of the 2021 taxable income, Company X's profits will be reduced by $4 million, so its adjusted 2021 profit is $6 million and its

[28]A company could, in theory, refrain from paying dividends to help prevent its stockholders from having to pay taxes on dividends received. The IRS has a rule against the *improper accumulation of retained earnings*. However, in our experience, it is easy for firms to justify retaining earnings, and we have never seen a firm have a problem with the improper accumulation rule.

Calculation of Loss Carryforward for 2020–2021 Using a $12 Million 2019 Loss — **TABLE 3.7**

	2020	2021
Taxable income	$10,000,000	$10,000,000
Carryforward credit	8,000,000	4,000,000
Adjusted profit	$ 2,000,000	$ 6,000,000
Taxes owed (25%)	$ 500,000	$ 1,500,000
2019 loss	$12,000,000	$12,000,000
Carryforward loss used	8,000,000	12,000,000
Carryforward loss still available	$ 4,000,000	$ 0

tax liability is $1.5 million. At this point, the entire 2019 loss carryforward has been used, so no carryforward remains in our example. However, carryforwards can be extended indefinitely, so if an amount remained, it would be applied to the next year using the same steps as we did here to adjust the firm's profits and lower its tax liability for that year. The purpose of permitting this loss treatment is to avoid penalizing corporations whose incomes fluctuate substantially from year to year.

Consolidated Corporate Tax Returns

If a corporation owns 80% or more of another corporation's stock, it can aggregate income and file one consolidated tax return. This allows the losses of one company to be used to offset the profits of another. (Similarly, one division's losses can be used to offset another division's profits.) No business wants to incur losses, but tax offsets make it more feasible for large, multidivisional corporations to undertake risky new ventures or ventures that will suffer losses during a developmental period.

Taxation of Small Businesses: S Corporations

As we noted in Chapter 1, the Tax Code allows small businesses that meet certain conditions to be set up as corporations and thus receive the benefits of the corporate form of organization—especially limited liability—but they are still taxed as proprietorships or partnerships rather than as corporations. These corporations are called **S corporations**. (Regular corporations are called C corporations.) If a corporation elects to set up as an S corporation, all of its income is reported as personal income by its stockholders, on a pro rata basis, and thus is taxed at the stockholders' individual rates. Because the income is taxed only once, this is an important benefit to the owners of small corporations in which all or most of the income earned each year will be distributed as dividends. The situation is similar for LLCs.

S Corporation
A small corporation that, under Subchapter S of the Internal Revenue Code, elects to be taxed as a proprietorship or a partnership yet retains limited liability and other benefits of the corporate form of organization.

Depreciation

Depreciation plays an important role in income tax calculations—the larger the depreciation, the lower the taxable income, the lower the tax bill, and thus the higher the operating cash flow. Under the new tax legislation, 100% of the cost of certain new and used business assets may be immediately expensed if placed into service after September 27, 2017, and before January 1, 2023. For assets placed into service after January 1, 2023, but before January 1, 2027, only 80% of the asset's cost may be immediately expensed. Immediate expensing is eliminated after January 1, 2027. This "bonus" depreciation is typically for assets with lives less than 20 years. Nonresidential real property not subject to "bonus" depreciation falls under the alternative depreciation system and is depreciated straight line over 40 years. We will discuss depreciation in greater detail and how depreciation affects income and cash flows when we study capital budgeting.

SelfTest

Explain this statement: Our tax rates are progressive.

What's the difference between individual marginal and average tax rates?

What's the AMT, and what is its purpose?

What's a muni bond, and how are these bonds taxed?

What are long-term capital gains? Are they taxed like other income? Explain.

How does our tax system influence the use of debt financing by corporations?

What is the logic behind allowing tax loss carryforwards?

Differentiate between S and C corporations.

TYING IT ALL TOGETHER

The primary purposes of this chapter were to describe the basic financial statements, to present background information on cash flows, to differentiate between cash flow and accounting income, and to provide an overview of the federal income tax system. In the next chapter, we build on this information to analyze a firm's financial statements and to determine its financial health.

Self-Test Questions And Problems

(Solutions Appear in Appendix A)

ST-1 **KEY TERMS** Define each of the following terms:

a. Annual report; balance sheet; income statement; statement of cash flows; statement of stockholders' equity
b. Stockholders' equity; retained earnings; working capital; net working capital; net operating working capital (NOWC); total debt
c. Depreciation; amortization; operating income; EBITDA; free cash flow (FCF)
d. Net operating profit after taxes (NOPAT)
e. Market value added (MVA); economic value added (EVA)
f. Progressive tax; marginal tax rate; average tax rate
g. Tax loss carryforward; alternative minimum tax (AMT)
h. Traditional IRAs; Roth IRAs
i. Capital gain (loss)
j. S corporation

ST-2 **NET INCOME AND CASH FLOW** Last year Rattner Robotics had $5 million in operating income (EBIT). Its depreciation expense was $1 million, its interest expense was $1 million, and its corporate tax rate was 25%. At year-end, it had $14 million in operating current assets, $3 million in accounts payable, $1 million in accruals, $2 million in notes payable, and $15 million in net plant and equipment. Assume Rattner has no excess cash. Rattner uses only debt and common equity to fund its operations. (In other words, Rattner has no preferred stock on its balance sheet.) Rattner had no other current liabilities. Assume that Rattner's only noncash item was depreciation.

a. What was the company's net income?
b. What was its net operating working capital (NOWC)?
c. What was its net working capital (NWC)?
d. Rattner had $12 million in net plant and equipment the prior year. Its net operating working capital has remained constant over time. What is the company's free cash flow (FCF) for the year that just ended?
e. Rattner has 500,000 common shares outstanding, and the common stock amount on the balance sheet is $5 million. The company has not issued or repurchased common stock during the year. Last year's balance in retained earnings was $11.2 million, and the firm paid out dividends of $1.8 million during the year. Develop Rattner's end-of-year statement of stockholders' equity.
f. If the firm's stock price at year-end is $52, what is the firm's market value added (MVA)?
g. If the firm's after-tax percentage cost of capital is 9%, what is the firm's EVA at year-end?

Questions

3-1 What four financial statements are contained in most annual reports?

3-2 Who are some of the basic users of financial statements, and how do they use them?

3-3 If a "typical" firm reports $20 million of retained earnings on its balance sheet, could its directors declare a $20 million cash dividend without having any qualms about what they were doing? Explain your answer.

3-4 Explain the following statement: Although the balance sheet can be thought of as a snapshot of a firm's financial position *at a point in time,* the income statement reports on operations *over a period of time.*

3-5 Financial statements are based on generally accepted accounting principles (GAAP) and are audited by CPA firms. Do investors need to worry about the validity of those statements? Explain your answer.

3-6 Refer to the box titled, "The Balance Sheet of an Average American Household," when answering parts a and b.

a. Based on this evidence, did the financial position of the average household improved during 2004–2007? During 2007–2010? During 2010–2017? Explain your answers.
b. What do you think the average household balance sheet looks like today? Explain your answer.

3-7 What is free cash flow? If you were an investor, why might you be more interested in free cash flow than net income?

3-8 Would it be possible for a company to report negative free cash flow and still be highly valued by investors; that is, could a negative free cash flow ever be viewed optimistically by investors? Explain your answer.

3-9 How are management's actions incorporated in EVA and MVA? How are EVA and MVA interconnected?

3-10 Explain the following statement: Our tax rates are progressive.

3-11 What does *double taxation of corporate income* mean? Could income ever be subject to *triple* taxation? Explain your answer.

3-12 How does the deductibility of interest and dividends by the paying corporation affect the choice of financing (i.e., the use of debt versus equity)?

Problems

Easy Problems 1-8

3-1 **BALANCE SHEET** The assets of Dallas & Associates consist entirely of current assets and net plant and equipment, and the firm has no excess cash. The firm has total assets of $2.5 million and net plant and equipment equals $2 million. It has notes payable of $150,000, long-term debt of $750,000, and total common equity of $1.5 million. The firm does have accounts payable and accruals on its balance sheet. The firm only finances with debt and common equity, so it has no preferred stock on its balance sheet.

a. What is the company's total debt?
b. What is the amount of total liabilities and equity that appears on the firm's balance sheet?
c. What is the balance of current assets on the firm's balance sheet?
d. What is the balance of current liabilities on the firm's balance sheet?
e. What is the amount of accounts payable and accruals on its balance sheet? (*Hint:* Consider this as a single line item on the firm's balance sheet.)
f. What is the firm's net working capital?
g. What is the firm's net operating working capital?
h. What is the explanation for the difference in your answers to parts f and g?

3-2 **INCOME STATEMENT** Byron Books Inc. recently reported $15 million of net income. Its EBIT was $20.8 million, and its tax rate was 25%. What was its interest expense? (*Hint*: Write out the headings for an income statement, and fill in the known values. Then divide $15 million of net income by (1−T) = 0.75 to find the pretax income. The difference between EBIT and taxable income must be interest expense. Use this same procedure to complete similar problems.)

3-3 **INCOME STATEMENT** Patterson Brothers recently reported an EBITDA of $7.5 million and net income of $2.625 million. It had $1.5 million of interest expense, and its corporate tax rate was 25%. What was its charge for depreciation and amortization?

3-4 **STATEMENT OF STOCKHOLDERS' EQUITY** In its most recent financial statements, Nessler Inc. reported $75 million of net income and $825 million of retained earnings. The previous retained earnings were $784 million. How much in dividends were paid to shareholders during the year? Assume that all dividends declared were actually paid.

3-5 **MVA** Harper Industries has $900 million of common equity on its balance sheet, its stock price is $80 per share, and its market value added (MVA) is $50 million. How many common shares are currently outstanding?

3-6 **MVA** Over the years, Masterson Corporation's stockholders have provided $34,000,000 of capital when they purchased new issues of stock and allowed management to retain some of the firm's earnings. The firm now has 2,000,000 shares of common stock outstanding, and the shares sell at a price of $28 per share. How much value has Masterson's management added to stockholder wealth over the years, that is, what is Masterson's MVA?

3-7 **EVA** Barton Industries has operating income for the year of $3,500,000 and a 25% tax rate. Its total invested capital is $20,000,000 and its after-tax percentage cost of capital is 8%. What is the firm's EVA?

3-8 **PERSONAL TAXES** Susan and Stan Britton are a married couple who file a joint income tax return, where the tax rates are based on the tax tables presented in the chapter. Assume that their taxable income this year was $375,000.

a. What is their federal tax liability?
b. What is their marginal tax rate?
c. What is their average tax rate?

Intermediate Problems 9–14

3-9 **BALANCE SHEET** Which of the following actions are most likely to directly increase cash as shown on a firm's balance sheet? Explain and state the assumptions that underlie your answer.

a. It issues $4 million of new common stock.
b. It buys new plant and equipment at a cost of $3 million.
c. It reports a large loss for the year.
d. It increases the dividends paid on its common stock.

3-10 **STATEMENT OF STOCKHOLDERS' EQUITY** Electronics World Inc. paid out $22.4 million in total common dividends and reported $144.7 million of retained earnings at year-end. The prior year's retained earnings were $95.5 million. What was the net income? Assume that all dividends declared were actually paid.

3-11 **EVA** For 2019, Gourmet Kitchen Products reported $22 million of sales and $19 million of operating costs (including depreciation). The company has $15 million of total invested capital. Its after-tax cost of capital is 10%, and its federal-plus-state income tax rate was 25%. What was the firm's economic value added (EVA), that is, how much value did management add to stockholders' wealth during 2019?

3-12 **STATEMENT OF CASH FLOWS** Hampton Industries had $39,000 in cash at year-end 2018 and $11,000 in cash at year-end 2019. The firm invested in property, plant, and equipment totaling $210,000—the majority having a useful life greater than 20 years and falling under the alternative depreciation system. Cash flow from financing activities totaled +$120,000.

a. What was the cash flow from operating activities?

b. If accruals increased by $15,000, receivables and inventories increased by $50,000, and depreciation and amortization totaled $25,000, what was the firm's net income?

3-13 **STATEMENT OF CASH FLOWS** You have just been hired as a financial analyst for Barrington Industries. Unfortunately, company headquarters (where all of the firm's records are kept) has been destroyed by fire. So, your first job will be to recreate the firm's cash flow statement for the year just ended. The firm had $100,000 in the bank at the end of the prior year, and its working capital accounts except cash remained constant during the year. It earned $5 million in net income during the year but paid $800,000 in dividends to common shareholders. Throughout the year, the firm purchased $5.5 million of property, plant, and equipment—the majority having a useful life of more than 20 years and falling under the alternative depreciation system. You have just spoken to the firm's accountants and learned that annual depreciation expense for the year is $450,000. The purchase price for the property, plant, and equipment represents additions before depreciation. Finally, you have determined that the only financing done by the firm was to issue long-term debt of $1 million at a 6% interest rate. What was the firm's end-of-year cash balance? Recreate the firm's cash flow statement to arrive at your answer.

3-14 **FREE CASH FLOW** Arlington Corporation's financial statements (dollars and shares are in millions) are provided here.

Balance Sheets as of December 31

	2019	2018
Assets		
Cash and equivalents	$ 15,000	$ 14,000
Accounts receivable	35,000	30,000
Inventories	33,320	27,000
Total current assets	$ 83,320	$ 71,000
Net plant and equipment	48,000	46,000
Total assets	$131,320	$ 117,000
Liabilities and Equity		
Accounts payable	$ 10,100	$ 9,000
Accruals	8,000	6,000
Notes payable	7,000	5,050
Total current liabilities	$ 25,100	$ 20,050
Long-term bonds	20,000	20,000
Total liabilities	$ 45,100	$ 40,050
Common stock (4,000 shares)	40,000	40,000
Retained earnings	46,220	36,950
Common equity	$ 86,220	$ 76,950
Total liabilities and equity	$131,320	$ 117,000

Income Statement for Year Ending December 31, 2019

Sales	$210,000
Operating costs excluding depreciation and amortization	160,000
EBITDA	$ 50,000
Depreciation and amortization	6,000
EBIT	$ 44,000
Interest	5,350
EBT	$ 38,650
Taxes (25%)	9,663
Net income	$ 28,988
Dividends paid	$ 19,718

a. What was net operating working capital for 2018 and 2019? Assume that all cash is excess cash; i.e., this cash is not needed for operating purposes.
b. What was Arlington's 2019 free cash flow?
c. Construct Arlington's 2019 statement of stockholders' equity.
d. What was Arlington's 2019 EVA? Assume that its after-tax cost of capital is 10%.
e. What was Arlington's MVA at year-end 2019? Assume that its stock price at December 31, 2019 was $25.

Challenging Problems 15–18

3-15 INCOME STATEMENT Edmonds Industries is forecasting the following income statement:

Sales	$10,000,000
Operating costs excluding depreciation and amortization	5,500,000
EBITDA	$ 4,500,000
Depreciation and amortization	1,200,000
EBIT	$ 3,300,000
Interest	500,000
EBT	$ 2,800,000
Taxes (25%)	700,000
Net income	$ 2,100,000

The CEO would like to see higher sales and a forecasted net income of $3,000,000. Assume that operating costs (excluding depreciation and amortization) are 55% of sales and that depreciation and amortization and interest expenses will increase by 6%. The tax rate, which is 25%, will remain the same. (Note that while the tax rate remains constant, the taxes paid will change.) What level of sales would generate $3,000,000 in net income?

3-16 FINANCIAL STATEMENTS The Davidson Corporation's balance sheet and income statement are provided here.

Davidson Corporation: Balance Sheet as of December 31, 2019 (millions of dollars)

Assets		Liabilities and Equity	
Cash and equivalents	$ 15	Accounts payable	$ 120
Accounts receivable	515	Accruals	280
Inventories	880	Notes payable	220
Total current assets	$1,410	Total current liabilities	$ 620
Net plant and equipment	2,590	Long-term bonds	1,520
		Total liabilities	$2,140
		Common stock (100 million shares)	260
		Retained earnings	1,600
		Common equity	$1,860
Total assets	$4,000	Total liabilities and equity	$4,000

Davidson Corporation: Income Statement for Year Ending December 31, 2019 (millions of dollars)

Sales	$ 6,250
Operating costs excluding depreciation and amortization	5,230
EBITDA	$ 1,020
Depreciation and amortization	220
EBIT	$ 800
Interest	180
EBT	$ 620
Taxes (25%)	155
Net income	$ 465
Common dividends paid	$ 183
Earnings per share	$ 4.65

a. Construct the statement of stockholders' equity for December 31, 2019. No common stock was issued during 2019.
b. How much money has been reinvested in the firm over the years?
c. At the present time, how large a check could be written without it bouncing?
d. How much money must be paid to current creditors within the next year?

3-17 **FREE CASH FLOW** Financial information for Powell Panther Corporation is shown here.

Powell Panther Corporation: Income Statements for Year Ending December 31 (millions of dollars)

	2019	2018
Sales	$ 1,200.0	$1,000.0
Operating costs excluding depreciation and amortization	1,020.0	850.0
EBITDA	$ 180.0	$ 150.0
Depreciation and amortization	30.0	25.0
Earnings before interest and taxes (EBIT)	$ 150.0	$ 125.0
Interest	21.7	20.2
Earnings before taxes (EBT)	$ 128.3	$ 104.8
Taxes (25%)	32.1	26.2
Net income	$ 96.2	$ 78.6
Common dividends	$ 79.7	$ 61.3

Powell Panther Corporation: Balance Sheets as of December 31 (millions of dollars)

	2019	2018
Assets		
Cash and equivalents	$ 12.0	$ 10.0
Accounts receivable	180.0	150.0
Inventories	180.0	200.0
Total current assets	$ 372.0	$ 360.0
Net plant and equipment	300.0	250.0
Total assets	$ 672.0	$ 610.0
Liabilities and Equity		
Accounts payable	$108.0	$ 90.0
Accruals	72.0	60.0
Notes payable	67.0	51.5
Total current liabilities	$247.0	$ 201.5
Long-term bonds	150.0	150.0
Total liabilities	$397.0	$ 351.5
Common stock (50 million shares)	50.0	50.0
Retained earnings	225.0	208.5
Common equity	$275.0	$ 258.5
Total liabilities and equity	$672.0	$ 610.0

a. What was net operating working capital for 2018 and 2019? Assume the firm has no excess cash.
b. What was the 2019 free cash flow?
c. How would you explain the large increase in 2019 dividends?

3-18 **PERSONAL TAXES** Mary Jarvis is a single individual who is working on filing her tax return for the previous year. She has assembled the following relevant information:

- She received $82,000 in salary.
- She received $12,000 of dividend income.
- She received $5,000 of interest income on Home Depot bonds.
- She received $22,000 from the sale of Disney stock that was purchased 2 years prior to the sale at a cost of $9,000.

- She received $10,000 from the sale of Google stock that was purchased 6 months prior to the sale at a cost of $7,500.
- Mary only has allowable itemized deductions of $7,500, so she will take the standard deduction of $12,000. The standard deduction is subtracted from her gross income from her gross income to determine her taxable income.

Assume that her tax rates are based on the tax tables presented in the chapter.

a. What is Mary's federal tax liability?
b. What is her marginal tax rate?
c. What is her average tax rate?

Comprehensive/Spreadsheet Problem

3-19 FINANCIAL STATEMENTS, CASH FLOW, AND TAXES Laiho Industries's 2018 and 2019 balance sheets (in thousands of dollars) are shown.

	2019	2018
Cash	$102,850	$ 89,725
Accounts receivable	103,365	85,527
Inventories	38,444	34,982
Total current assets	$244,659	$210,234
Net fixed assets	67,165	42,436
Total assets	$311,824	$252,670
Accounts payable	$ 30,761	$ 23,110
Accruals	30,477	22,656
Notes payable	16,717	14,217
Total current liabilities	$ 77,955	$ 59,983
Long-term debt	76,264	63,914
Total liabilities	$154,219	$123,897
Common stock	100,000	90,000
Retained earnings	57,605	38,773
Total common equity	$157,605	$128,773
Total liabilities and equity	$311,824	$252,670

a. Sales for 2019 were $455,150,000, and EBITDA was 15% of sales. Furthermore, depreciation and amortization were 18% of net fixed assets, interest was $8,583,000, the corporate tax rate was 25%, and Laiho pays 47.25% of its net income as dividends. Given this information, construct the firm's 2019 income statement.
b. Construct the statement of stockholders' equity for the year ending December 31, 2019, and the 2019 statement of cash flows.
c. Calculate 2018 and 2019 net operating working capital (NOWC) and 2019 free cash flow (FCF). Assume the firm has no excess cash.
d. If Laiho increased its dividend payout ratio, what effect would this have on corporate taxes paid? What effect would this have on taxes paid by the company's shareholders?
e. Assume that the firm's after-tax cost of capital is 10.5%. What is the firm's 2019 EVA?
f. Assume that the firm's stock price is $22 per share and that at year-end 2019 the firm has 10 million shares outstanding. What is the firm's MVA at year-end 2019?

INTEGRATED CASE

D'LEON INC., PART I

3-20 **FINANCIAL STATEMENTS AND TAXES** Donna Jamison, a 2014 graduate of the University of Florida, with 4 years of banking experience, was recently brought in as assistant to the chairperson of the board of D'Leon Inc., a small food producer that operates in north Florida and whose specialty is high-quality pecan and other nut products sold in the snack foods market. D'Leon's president, Al Watkins, decided in 2018 to undertake a major expansion and to "go national" in competition with Frito-Lay, Eagle, and other major snack foods companies. Watkins believed that D'Leon's products were of higher quality than the competition's, that this quality differential would enable it to charge a premium price, and that the end result would be greatly increased sales, profits, and stock price.

The company doubled its plant capacity, opened new sales offices outside its home territory, and launched an expensive advertising campaign. D'Leon's results were not satisfactory, to put it mildly. Its board of directors, which consisted of its president, vice president, and major stockholders (all of whom were local businesspeople), was most upset when directors learned how the expansion was going. Unhappy suppliers were being paid late, and the bank was complaining about the deteriorating situation and threatening to cut off credit. As a result, Watkins was informed that changes would have to be made—and quickly; otherwise, he would be fired. Also, at the board's insistence, Donna Jamison was brought in and given the job of assistant to Fred Campo, a retired banker who was D'Leon's chairperson and largest stockholder. Campo agreed to give up a few of his golfing days and help nurse the company back to health, with Jamison's help.

Jamison began by gathering the financial statements and other data given in Tables IC 3.1, IC 3.2, IC 3.3, and IC 3.4. Assume that you are Jamison's assistant. You must help her answer the following questions for Campo. (Note: We will continue with this case in Chapter 4, and you will feel more comfortable with the analysis there. But answering these questions will help prepare you for Chapter 4. Provide clear explanations.)

a. What effect did the expansion have on sales, after-tax operating income, net operating working capital (NOWC), and net income?

b. What effect did the company's expansion have on its free cash flow?

c. D'Leon purchases materials on 30-day terms, meaning that it is supposed to pay for purchases within 30 days of receipt. Judging from its 2019 balance sheet, do you think that D'Leon pays suppliers on time? Provide an explanation and include a discussion about what problems might occur if suppliers are not paid in a timely manner.

d. D'Leon spends money for labor, materials, and fixed assets (depreciation) to make products—and spends still more money to sell those products. Then the firm makes sales that result in receivables, which eventually result in cash inflows. Does it appear that D'Leon's sales price exceeds its costs per unit sold? How does this affect the cash balance?

e. Suppose D'Leon's sales manager told the sales staff to start offering 60-day credit terms rather than the 30-day terms now being offered. D'Leon's competitors react by offering similar terms, so sales remain constant. What effect would this have on the cash account? How would the cash account be affected if sales doubled as a result of the credit policy change?

f. Can you imagine a situation in which the sales price exceeds the cost of producing and selling a unit of output, yet a dramatic increase in sales volume causes the cash balance to decline? Explain.

g. Did D'Leon finance its expansion program with internally generated funds (additions to retained earnings plus depreciation) or with external capital? How does the choice of financing affect the company's financial strength?

h. Refer to Tables IC 3.2 and IC 3.4. Suppose D'Leon broke even in 2019 in the sense that sales revenues equaled total operating costs plus interest charges. Would the asset expansion have caused the company to experience a cash shortage that required it to raise external capital? Explain.

i. The new tax law calls for immediate expensing of certain qualified business assets rather than depreciating them over a longer time period. How will that affect (1) a company's physical stock of assets, (2) a firm's balance sheet account for fixed assets, (3) a company's reported net income, and (4) a company's cash position? In your responses, assume that the same depreciation method is used for stockholder reporting and for tax calculations and that the accounting change has no effect on assets' physical lives.

j. Explain how earnings per share, dividends per share, and book value per share are calculated and what they mean. Why does the market price per share not equal the book value per share?

k. Explain briefly the tax treatment of (1) interest and dividends paid, (2) interest earned and dividends received, (3) capital gains, and (4) tax loss carryforwards. How might each of these items affect D'Leon's taxes?

TABLE IC 3.1 Balance Sheets

	2019	2018
Assets		
Cash[a]	$ 7,282	$ 57,600
Accounts receivable	632,160	351,200
Inventories	1,287,360	715,200
Total current assets	$1,926,802	$1,124,000
Net fixed assets	939,790	344,800
Total assets	$2,866,592	$1,468,800
Liabilities and Equity		
Accounts payable	$ 524,160	$ 145,600
Accruals	489,600	136,000
Notes payable	636,808	200,000
Total current liabilities	$1,650,568	$ 481,600
Long-term debt	723,432	323,432
Common stock (100,000 shares)	460,000	460,000
Retained earnings	32,592	203,768
Total equity	$ 492,592	$ 663,768
Total liabilities and equity	$2,866,592	$1,468,800

[a]Assume that all cash is excess cash; i.e., this cash is not needed for operating purposes.

TABLE IC 3.2 Income Statements

	2019	2018
Sales	$6,126,796	$ 3,432,000
Cost of goods sold	5,528,000	2,864,000
Other expenses	519,988	358,672
Total operating costs excluding depreciation and amortization	$6,047,988	$ 3,222,672
Depreciation and amortization	116,960	18,900
EBIT	($ 38,152)	$ 190,428
Interest expense	122,024[a]	43,828
EBT	($ 160,176)	$ 146,600
Taxes (25%)	0[b]	36,650
Net income	($ 160,176)	$ 109,950
EPS	($ 1.602)	$ 1.100
DPS	$ 0.110	$ 0.275
Book value per share	$ 4.926	$ 6.638
Stock price	$ 2.25	$ 8.50
Shares outstanding	100,000	100,000
Tax rate	25.00%	25.00%
Lease payments	$ 40,000	$ 40,000
Sinking fund payments	0	0

[a]D'Leon Inc.'s annual gross receipts have been less than $25 million for the past three years, so it's exempt from the interest expense deduction limitation.

[b]The 2019 net operating loss (NOL) can be carried forward indefinitely to lower taxable income and taxes in future years, but no tax credit (refund) is received in the current year. Refer back to Section 3-9, where we demonstrated how tax loss carryforwards are handled.

TABLE IC 3.3

Statement of Stockholders' Equity, 2019

	Common Stock			
	Shares	**Amount**	**Retained Earnings**	**Total Stockholders' Equity**
Balances, December 31, 2018	100,000	$460,000	$ 203,768	$ 663,768
2019 Net income			(160,176)	
Cash dividends			(11,000)	
Addition (subtraction) to retained earnings				(171,176)
Balances, December 31, 2019	100,000	$460,000	$ 32,592	$ 492,592

TABLE IC 3.4

Statement of Cash Flows, 2019

Operating Activities	
Net income	($ 160,176)
Depreciation and amortization	116,960
Increase in accounts payable	378,560
Increase in accruals	353,600
Increase in accounts receivable	(280,960)
Increase in inventories	(572,160)
Net cash provided by operating activities	($ 164,176)
Investing Activities	
Additions to property, plant, and equipment	($ 711,950)
Net cash used in investing activities	($ 711,950)
Financing Activities	
Increase in notes payable	$ 436,808
Increase in long-term debt	400,000
Payment of cash dividends	(11,000)
Net cash provided by financing activities	$ 825,808
Summary	
Net decrease in cash	($ 50,318)
Cash at beginning of year	57,600
Cash at end of year	$ 7,282

TAKING A CLOSER LOOK

Exploring Dunkin' Brands Group's Financial Statements

Use online resources to work on this chapter's questions. Please note that website information changes over time, and these changes may limit your ability to answer some of these questions.

Dunkin' Brands Group, Inc. operates under the Dunkin' Donuts and Baskin-Robbins brands worldwide and has about 12,000 Dunkin' Donuts and 7,600 Baskin-Robbins restaurants.

Using financial websites such as finance.yahoo.com and money.msn.com, you can access a wealth of financial information for companies such as Dunkin' Brands. By entering the company's ticker symbol, DNKN, you will be able to access a great deal of useful information, including a summary of what Dunkin' Brands does (Profile), a chart of its recent stock price (Summary), EPS estimates (Analysts), recent news stories (Summary), and a list of key financial data and ratios (Statistics).

In researching a company's operating performance, a good place to start is the recent stock price performance. From an interactive chart, you can obtain a chart of the company's stock price performance and compare it to the overall market (as measured by the S&P 500 index) between 2011 and 2018. As you can see, Dunkin' Brands has had its ups and downs. But the company's overall performance has been strong during the past 5 years, following the market trend, but generally underperforming the market the past 2 years or so.

You can also find Dunkin' Brands' recent financial statements (Financials). Typically, you can find annual balance sheets, income statements, and cash flow statements for 3 years. Quarterly information is also available.

Discussion Questions

1. Looking at the most recent year available, what is the amount of total assets on Dunkin' Brands' balance sheet? What percentage is fixed assets, such as plant and equipment? What percentage is current assets? How much has the company grown over the years that are shown?
2. Does Dunkin' Brands have very much long-term debt? What are the chief ways in which Dunkin' Brands has financed assets?
3. Looking at the statement of cash flows, what factors can explain the change in the company's cash position over the last couple of years?
4. Looking at the income statement, what are the company's most recent sales and net income? Over the past several years, what has been the sales growth rate? What has been the growth rate in net income?
5. Over the past few years, has there been a strong correlation between stock price performance and reported earnings? Explain. (*Hint:* Change the Interactive Stock Chart so that it corresponds to the same number of years shown for the financial statements.)

Analysis of Financial Statements

CHAPTER 4

AP Images/Charles Sykes

Can You Make Money Analyzing Stocks?

For many years, a debate has raged over this question. Some argue that the stock market is highly efficient and that all available information regarding a stock is already reflected in its price. The "efficient market advocates" point out that there are thousands of smart, well-trained analysts working for institutions with billions of dollars. These analysts have access to the latest information, and they spring into action—buying or selling—as soon as a firm releases any information that has a bearing on its future profits. The "efficient market advocates" also point out that few mutual funds, which hire good people and pay them well, actually beat the averages. If these experts earn only average returns, how can the rest of us expect to beat the market?

Others disagree, arguing that analysis can pay off. They point out that some fund managers perform better than average year after year. Also, they note that some "activist" investors analyze firms carefully, identify those with weaknesses that appear to be correctable, and then persuade their managers to take actions to improve the firms' performances.

Arguably, the world's best-known investor is Warren Buffett. Through his company Berkshire Hathaway, Buffett has made significant investments in a number of well-known companies, including Coca-Cola, American Express, DIRECTV, IBM, and Wells Fargo. Buffett is well known for taking a long-run view of things. His value-investing approach, which borrows heavily from the ideas espoused decades ago by Benjamin Graham, looks for stocks trading at prices that are significantly lower than their estimated intrinsic value. Value investors rely heavily on the type of analysis described in this chapter to assess a company's strengths and weaknesses and to derive the key inputs for their estimates of intrinsic value.

Berkshire Hathaway's performance under Buffett's management has been nothing short of amazing. Between 1965 and 2017 with Buffett at the helm, Berkshire Hathaway provided its investors with a staggering total return of

2,404,748%, which translates into a compound annual return of 20.9%! And so far, Buffett is showing no signs of slowing down. From January 2015 to early April 2018, the stock jumped another 35%, once again outperforming the overall market during the same time period.

Always looking for new opportunities, in June 2013, Berkshire Hathaway partnered with private equity firm 3G Capital and acquired H.J. Heinz Company for $28 billion. A year later in November 2014, Buffett saw what he thought was another good opportunity. In that transaction, Berkshire purchased the Duracell battery unit from Procter and Gamble. In March 2015, he once again combined forces with 3G Capital to help finance the merger between Heinz and Kraft Foods. In each case, Buffett purchased a well-established brand that he believes has even greater potential for improvement. Even more recently, Berkshire Hathaway attracted headlines by making a big bet on Apple in the fourth quarter of 2016. The company increased its investment in Apple from 15 million shares to 57 million shares. Since this investment, Apple's stock price has soared, and a recent *Forbes* magazine article suggests that assuming the company did not make any changes to its position, it had made more than $1 billion from its investment in Apple over just a few short months! That said, at least one expert has taken a different view and has argued that the long-run prospects for Apple are not as strong as many believe. Most recently, in October 2017, Berkshire Hathaway purchased a 38.6% partnership interest in Pilot Flying J, one of the nation's leading travel-center operators. Berkshire Hathaway plans to become the company's biggest shareholder in 6 years, with an 80% ownership stake at that time.

So, although many people regard financial statements as "just accounting," they really are much more. As you will see in this chapter, these statements provide a wealth of information that can be used for a wide variety of purposes by managers, investors, lenders, customers, suppliers, and regulators. An analysis of its statements can highlight a company's strengths and shortcomings, and this information can be used by management to improve the company's performance and by others to predict future results.

Sources: "Berkshire's Performance vs. the S&P 500," Warren Buffett's 2017 Annual Letter to Shareholders (www.berkshirehathaway.com/letters/2017ltr.pdf), February 24, 2018; Ed Hammond and Noah Buhayar, "Buffett's Berkshire Hathaway Buys Stake in Pilot Flying J," *Bloomberg* (www.bloomberg.com/news), October 3, 2017; Jonathan Stempel and Devika Krishna Kumar, "Buffett's Berkshire Hathaway Buys P&G's Duracell," *Reuters* (www.reuters.com), November 13, 2014; and Lauren Gensler, "Warren Buffett Nearly Quadruples Stake in Apple," *Forbes* (www.forbes.com), February 14, 2017.

PUTTING THINGS IN PERSPECTIVE

The primary goal of financial management is to maximize shareholders' wealth, not accounting measures such as net income or earnings per share (EPS). However, accounting data influence stock prices, and these data can be used to see why a company is performing the way it is and where it is heading. Chapter 3 described the key financial statements and showed how they change as a firm's operations change. Now, in Chapter 4, we show how the statements are used by managers to improve the firm's stock price, by lenders to evaluate the likelihood that borrowers will be able to pay off loans, and by security analysts to forecast earnings, dividends, and stock prices.

If management is to maximize a firm's value, it must take advantage of the firm's strengths and correct its weaknesses. Financial analysis involves (1) comparing the firm's performance to that of other firms in the same industry and (2) evaluating trends in the firm's financial position over time. These studies help managers identify deficiencies and take corrective actions. In this chapter, we focus on how managers and investors evaluate a firm's financial position. Then, in later chapters, we examine the types of actions managers can take to improve future performance and thus increase the firm's stock price.

When you finish this chapter, you should be able to do the following:

- **Explain what ratio analysis is.**
- **List the five groups of ratios and identify, calculate, and interpret the key ratios in each group.**

- **Discuss each ratio's relationship to the balance sheet and income statement.**
- **Discuss why return on equity (ROE) is the key ratio under management's control and how the other ratios impact ROE, and explain how to use the DuPont equation for improving ROE.**
- **Compare a firm's ratios with those of other firms (benchmarking) and analyze a given firm's ratios over time (trend analysis).**
- **Discuss the tendency of ratios to fluctuate over time (which may or may not be problematic), explain how they can be influenced by accounting practices as well as other factors, and explain why they must be used with care.**

4-1 Ratio Analysis

Ratios help us evaluate financial statements. For example, at the end of 2019, Allied Food Products had $860 million of interest-bearing debt and interest charges of $83 million, while Midwest Products had $52 million of interest-bearing debt and interest charges of $4 million. Which company is stronger? The burden of these debts and the companies' ability to repay them can best be evaluated by comparing each firm's total debt to its total capital and comparing interest expense to the income and cash available to pay that interest. Ratios are used to make such comparisons. We calculate Allied's ratios for 2019 using data from the balance sheets and income statements given in Tables 3.1 and 3.2. We also evaluate the ratios relative to food industry averages, using data in millions of dollars.[1] As you will see, we can calculate many different ratios, with different ones used to examine different aspects of the firm's operations. You will get to know some ratios by name, but it's better to understand what they are designed to do than to memorize names and equations.

resource

Students can download the Excel chapter models from the textbook's student companion site on cengage .com. Once downloaded onto your computer, retrieve the Chapter 4 Excel model and follow along as you read this chapter.

We divide the ratios into five categories:

1. *Liquidity ratios*, which give an idea of the firm's ability to pay off debts that are maturing within a year.
2. *Asset management ratios*, which give an idea of how efficiently the firm is using its assets.
3. *Debt management ratios*, which give an idea of how the firm has financed its assets as well as the firm's ability to repay its long-term debt.
4. *Profitability ratios*, which give an idea of how profitably the firm is operating and utilizing its assets.
5. *Market value ratios*, which give an idea of what investors think about the firm and its future prospects.

---

[1]Financial statement data for most publicly traded firms can be obtained from the Internet. One site that provides this information is Yahoo! Finance (finance.yahoo.com). This website provides financial statements, which can be copied to an Excel file and used to create your own ratios, but it also provides calculated ratios.

In addition to the ratios discussed in this chapter, financial analysts often employ a tool known as *common size analysis*. To form a *common size balance sheet*, simply divide each asset, liability, and equity item by total assets and then express the results as percentages. To develop a *common size income statement*, divide each income statement item by sales. The resultant percentage statements can be compared with statements of larger or smaller firms or with those of the same firm over time. One would normally obtain the basic statements from a source such as Yahoo! Finance and copy them to Excel, so constructing common size statements is quite easy. Note too that industry average data are generally given as percentages, which make them easy to compare with a firm's own common size statements. We provide Allied Food Products's common size statements in Web Appendix 4A.

Satisfactory liquidity ratios are necessary if the firm is to continue operating. Good asset management ratios are necessary for the firm to keep its costs low and thus its net income high. Debt management ratios indicate how risky the firm is and how much of its operating income must be paid to bondholders rather than stockholders. Profitability ratios combine the asset and debt management categories and show their effects on ROE. Finally, market value ratios tell us what investors think about the company and its prospects.

All of the ratios are important, but different ones are more important for some companies than for others. For example, if a firm borrowed too much in the past and its debt now threatens to drive it into bankruptcy, the debt ratios are key. Similarly, if a firm expanded too rapidly and now finds itself with excess inventory and manufacturing capacity, the asset management ratios take center stage. The ROE is always important, but a high ROE depends on maintaining liquidity, on efficient asset management, and on the proper use of debt. Managers are, of course, vitally concerned with the stock price, but managers have little direct control over the stock market's performance; they do, however, have control over their firm's ROE. So ROE tends to be the main focal point.

4-2 Liquidity Ratios

The liquidity ratios help answer this question: Will the firm be able to pay off its debts as they come due and thus remain a viable organization? If the answer is no, liquidity must be addressed.

A **liquid asset** is one that trades in an active market and thus can be quickly converted to cash at the going market price. As shown in Table 3.1, Allied has $310 million of current liabilities that must be paid off within the coming year. Will it have trouble meeting that obligation? A full liquidity analysis requires the use of a cash budget, which we discuss in Chapter 15; however, by relating cash and other current assets to current liabilities, ratio analysis provides a quick and easy-to-use measure of liquidity. Two of the most commonly used **liquidity ratios** are discussed in this section.

Liquid Asset
An asset that can be converted to cash quickly without having to reduce the asset's price very much.

Liquidity Ratios
Ratios that show the relationship of a firm's cash and other current assets to its current liabilities.

Current Ratio
This ratio is calculated by dividing current assets by current liabilities. It indicates the extent to which current liabilities are covered by those assets expected to be converted to cash in the near future.

4-2A CURRENT RATIO

The primary liquidity ratio is the **current ratio**, which is calculated by dividing current assets by current liabilities:

$$\text{Current ratio} = \frac{\text{Current assets}}{\text{Current liabilities}}$$

$$= \frac{\$1{,}000}{\$310} = 3.2\times$$

$$\text{Industry average} = 4.2\times$$

Current assets include cash, marketable securities, accounts receivable, and inventories. Allied's current liabilities consist of accounts payable, accrued wages and taxes, and short-term notes payable to its bank, all of which are due within 1 year.

If a company is having financial difficulty, it typically begins to pay its accounts payable more slowly and to borrow more from its bank, both of which increase current liabilities. If current liabilities are rising faster than current assets,

FINANCIAL ANALYSIS ON THE INTERNET

A wide range of valuable financial information is available on the Internet. With just a couple of clicks, an investor can find the key financial statements for most publicly traded companies.

Suppose you are thinking of buying some Disney stock, and you want to analyze its recent performance. Here's a partial (but by no means complete) list of sites you can access to get started:

- One source is Yahoo! Finance (finance.yahoo.com). Here you will find updated market information along with links to a variety of research sites. Enter a stock's ticker symbol, and you will see the stock's current price along with recent news about the company. Click "Statistics" to find a report on the company's key financial ratios. Links to the company's financials (income statement, balance sheet, and statement of cash flows) can also be found. Yahoo! Finance also has a list of insider transactions (which can be found under Holders) that tell you whether a company's CEO and other key insiders are buying or selling the company's stock. In addition, the site has a message board (which can be found under Conversations) where investors share opinions about the company. Note also that, in most cases, a complete listing of a firm's SEC filings can be found at the SEC website (sec.gov).
- Two other websites with similar information are Google Finance (google.com/finance) and MSN Money (msn.com/en-us/money/markets). After entering a stock's ticker symbol, you will see the current stock price and a list of recent news stories. At the MSN Money website, you will find links to a company's financial statements and key ratios, as well as other information including analyst ratings, historical charts, earnings estimates, and a summary of insider transactions.
- Other sources for up-to-date market information are CNN Money (money.cnn.com), Zacks Investment Research (zacks.com), and MarketWatch (marketwatch.com), part of The Wall Street Journal Digital Network. On these sites, you also can obtain stock quotes, financial statements, company profiles, and charts of a firm's stock price over time.
- CNBC (cnbc.com) is another good source of financial information. Here, you enter a firm's ticker symbol to obtain the firm's stock price and fundamentals like its market cap, beta, and dividend yield. You can also chart a firm's stock price and obtain news about the company, earnings history and estimates, industry peer comparisons, quarterly or annual financial statements, and a summary of ownership.
- Seekingalpha.com provides stock price quotes; fundamentals like EPS, P/E, and dividend yield information as well as stock price charts. In addition, you can obtain breaking news on any stocks you've listed in your portfolio or any that you wish to follow.
- If you're looking for data on bond yields, key money rates, and currency rates, Bloomberg (bloomberg.com) is an excellent source for this type of information.
- Another good place to look is Reuters (reuters.com). Here you can find links to analysts' research reports along with the key financial statements.
- A valuable subscriber website from Value Line Investment Survey (valueline.com) provides industry-specific and detailed company income statement data, capital structure data, returns data, EPS, book value per share, cash flow per share, and other investment data.
- If you're interested in obtaining baseline values on individual stocks, you will find ValuePro (valuepro.net) helpful. It identifies key financial numbers used to obtain a stock's value and allows the user to make changes and see their impact on the stock's value.
- After accumulating all of this information, you may want to look at a site that provides opinions regarding the direction of the overall market and a particular stock. Two popular sites are The Motley Fool (fool.com) and The Street (thestreet.com).
- A popular source is The Wall Street Journal website (www.wsj.com). It is a great resource, but you have to subscribe to access the full range of materials.

When analyzing ratios using different sources, it is important that you understand how each source calculates a particular ratio. Differences among sources could be attributable to timing differences (using an average number versus a trailing 12-month number) or to different definitions. It is quite possible that, if you were to examine the same ratio for a particular company, you might see different values for the same ratio depending on the source chosen. You can often click "Help" within the particular website and search for the site's specific finance glossary to determine how ratios are defined. Keep this in mind when conducting ratio analysis.

This list is just a small subset of the information available online and available to you to work the end-of-chapter Internet exercises, "Taking a Closer Look". Sites come and go and change their content over time. In addition, new and interesting sites are constantly being added to the Internet.

the current ratio will fall, and this is a sign of possible trouble. Allied's current ratio is 3.2, which is well below the industry average of 4.2. Therefore, its liquidity position is somewhat weak, but by no means desperate.[2]

Although industry average figures are discussed later in some detail, note that an industry average is not a magic number that all firms should strive to maintain; in fact, some very well managed firms may be above the average, while other good firms are below it. However, if a firm's ratios are far removed from the averages for its industry, an analyst should be concerned about why this variance occurs. Thus, a deviation from the industry average should signal the analyst (or management) to check further. Note too that a high current ratio generally indicates a very strong, safe liquidity position; it might also indicate that the firm has too much old inventory that will have to be written off and too many old accounts receivable that may turn into bad debts. Or the high current ratio might indicate that the firm has too much cash, receivables, and inventory relative to its sales, in which case these assets are not being managed efficiently. So it is always necessary to thoroughly examine the full set of ratios before forming a judgment as to how well the firm is performing.

4-2B QUICK, OR ACID TEST, RATIO

Quick (Acid Test) Ratio
This ratio is calculated by deducting inventories from current assets and then dividing the remainder by current liabilities.

The second liquidity ratio is the **quick**, or **acid test**, **ratio**, which is calculated by deducting inventories from current assets and then dividing the remainder by current liabilities:

$$\text{Quick, or acid test, ratio} = \frac{\text{Current assets} - \text{Inventories}}{\text{Current liabilities}}$$

$$= \frac{\$385}{\$310} = 1.2\times$$

$$\text{Industry average} = 2.2\times$$

Inventories are typically the least liquid of a firm's current assets, and if sales slow down, they might not be converted to cash as quickly as expected.[3] Also, inventories are the assets on which losses are most likely to occur in the event of liquidation. Therefore, the quick ratio, which measures the firm's ability to pay off short-term obligations without relying on the sale of inventories, is important.

The industry average quick ratio is 2.2, so Allied's 1.2 ratio is relatively low. Still, if the accounts receivable can be collected, the company can pay off its current liabilities even if it has trouble disposing of its inventories.

---

[2]Because current assets should be convertible to cash within a year, it is likely that they could be liquidated at close to their stated value. With a current ratio of 3.2, Allied could liquidate current assets at only 31% of book value and still pay off current creditors in full: $1/3.2 = 0.31$, or 31%. Note also that $0.31(\$1{,}000) = \$310$, the current liabilities balance.

[3]Some companies also report "Other current assets" on their balance sheet. Our definition of the quick ratio would implicitly assume that these other current assets could be easily converted to cash. As an alternative measure, some analysts define the quick ratio as

(Cash and equivalents + Accounts receivable)/Current liabilities

This alternative measure assumes that the other current assets cannot be easily converted to cash. In the case of Allied, because it has no other current assets, the two measures would yield the same number.

Self*Test*

What are the characteristics of a liquid asset? Give examples of some liquid assets.

What question are the two liquidity ratios designed to answer?

Which is the least liquid of the firm's current assets?

A company has current liabilities of $500 million, and its current ratio is 2.0. What is the total of its current assets? **($1,000 million)** If this firm's quick ratio is 1.6, how much inventory does it have? **($200 million)** (*Hint:* To answer this problem and some of the other problems in this chapter, write out the equation for the ratio in the question, insert the given data, and solve for the missing value.) Examples:

Current ratio = 2.0 = CA/CL = CA/$500, so CA = 2($500) = $1,000.
Quick ratio = 1.6 = (CA − Inventories)/CL = ($1,000 − Inventories)/$500, so $1,000 − Inventories = 1.6($500) and Inventories = $1,000 − $800 = $200.

4-3 Asset Management Ratios

The second group of ratios, the **asset management ratios**, measure how effectively the firm is managing its assets. These ratios answer this question: Does the amount of each type of asset seem reasonable, too high, or too low in view of current and projected sales? These ratios are important because when Allied and other companies acquire assets, they must obtain capital from banks or other sources and capital is expensive. Therefore, if Allied has too many assets, its cost of capital will be too high, which will depress its profits. On the other hand, if its assets are too low, profitable sales will be lost. So Allied must strike a balance between too many and too few assets, and the asset management ratios will help it strike this proper balance.

Asset Management Ratios
A set of ratios that measure how effectively a firm is managing its assets.

4-3A INVENTORY TURNOVER RATIO

"Turnover ratios" divide sales by some asset: Sales/Various assets. As the name implies, these ratios show how many times the particular asset is "turned over" during the year. Here is the **inventory turnover ratio**:

Inventory Turnover Ratio
This ratio is calculated by dividing sales by inventories. It indicates how many times inventory is turned over during the year.

$$\textbf{Inventory turnover ratio} = \frac{\textbf{Sales}}{\textbf{Inventories}}$$

$$= \frac{\$3{,}000}{\$615} = 4.9\times$$

$$\textbf{Industry average} = 10.9\times$$

As a rough approximation, each item of Allied's inventory is sold and restocked, or "turned over," 4.9 times per year. *Turnover* is a term that originated many years ago with the old Yankee peddler who would load up his wagon with pots and pans, and then go off on his route to peddle his wares. The merchandise was called working capital because it was what he actually sold, or "turned over," to produce his profits, whereas his "turnover" was the number of trips he took each year. Annual sales divided by inventory equaled turnover, or trips per year. If he made 10 trips per year, stocked 100 pots and pans, and made a gross profit of $5 per item, his annual gross profit was (100)($5)(10) = $5,000. If he went faster and made 20 trips per year, his gross profit doubled, other things held constant. So his turnover directly affected his profits.

Allied's inventory turnover of 4.9 is much lower than the industry average of 10.9. This suggests that it is holding too much inventory. Excess inventory is, of course, unproductive and represents an investment with a low or zero rate of return. Allied's low inventory turnover ratio also makes us question its current ratio. With such a low turnover, the firm may be holding obsolete goods that are not worth their stated value.[4]

Note that sales occur over the entire year, whereas the inventory figure is for one point in time. For this reason, it might be better to use an average inventory measure.[5] If the business is highly seasonal or if there has been a strong upward or downward sales trend during the year, it is especially useful to make an adjustment. Allied's sales are not growing especially fast though, and to maintain comparability with industry averages, we used year-end rather than average inventories.

4-3B DAYS SALES OUTSTANDING

Days Sales Outstanding (DSO) Ratio
This ratio is calculated by dividing accounts receivable by average sales per day. It indicates the average length of time the firm must wait after making a sale before it receives cash.

Accounts receivable are evaluated by the **days sales outstanding (DSO) ratio**, also called the average collection period (ACP).[6] It is calculated by dividing accounts receivable by the average daily sales to find how many days' sales are tied up in receivables. Thus, the DSO represents the average length of time the firm must wait after making a sale before receiving cash. Allied has 46 days' sales outstanding, well above the 36-day industry average:

$$\text{DSO} = \begin{array}{c}\text{Days}\\ \text{sales}\\ \text{outstanding}\end{array} = \frac{\text{Receivables}}{\text{Average sales per day}} = \frac{\text{Receivables}}{\text{Annual sales/365}}$$

$$= \frac{\$375}{\$3{,}000/365} = \frac{\$375}{\$8.2192} = 45.625 \text{ days} \approx 46 \text{ days}$$

$$\text{Industry average} = 36 \text{ days}$$

The DSO can be compared with the industry average, but it is also evaluated by comparing it with Allied's credit terms. Allied's credit policy calls for payment within 30 days. So the fact that 46 days' sales are outstanding, not 30 days', indicates that Allied's customers, on average, are not paying their bills on time. This deprives the company of funds that could be used to reduce bank loans or some other type of costly capital. Moreover, the high average DSO indicates that if some customers are paying on time, quite a few must be paying very late. Late-paying customers often default, so their receivables may end up as bad debts that can never be collected.[7] Note too that the trend in the DSO over the past few years has

---

[4]Our measure of inventory turnover is frequently used by established compilers of financial ratio statistics such as *Value Line* (valueline.com) and *Morningstar* (morningstar.com). However, you should recognize that other sources calculate inventory using cost of goods sold in place of sales in the formula's numerator. The rationale for this alternative measure is that sales are stated at market prices; so if inventories are carried at cost, as they generally are, the calculated turnover overstates the true turnover ratio. Therefore, it might be more appropriate to use cost of goods sold in place of sales in the formula's numerator. When evaluating and comparing financial ratios from various sources, it is important to understand how those sources are specifically calculating financial ratios.

[5]Preferably, the average inventory value should be calculated by summing the monthly figures during the year and dividing by 12. If monthly data are not available, the beginning and ending figures can be added and then divided by 2. Both methods adjust for growth but not for seasonal effects.

[6]We could use the receivables turnover to evaluate receivables. Allied's receivables turnover is $3,000/$375 = 8×. However, the DSO ratio is easier to interpret and judge.

[7]For example, if further analysis along the lines suggested in Part 6 of this text (Working Capital Management, Forecasting, and Multinational Financial Management) indicates that 85% of the customers pay in 30 days, for the DSO to average 46 days, the remaining 15% must be paying, on average, in 136.67 days. Paying that late suggests financial difficulties. A DSO of 46 days would alert a good analyst of the need to dig deeper.

been rising, but the credit policy has not been changed. This reinforces our belief that Allied's credit manager should take steps to collect receivables faster.

4-3C FIXED ASSETS TURNOVER RATIO

The **fixed assets turnover ratio**, which is the ratio of sales to net fixed assets, measures how effectively the firm uses its plant and equipment:

Fixed Assets Turnover Ratio
The ratio of sales to net fixed assets. It measures how effectively the firm uses its plant and equipment.

$$\text{Fixed assets turnover ratio} = \frac{\text{Sales}}{\text{Net fixed assets}} = \frac{\$3{,}000}{\$1{,}000} = 3.0\times$$

$$\text{Industry average} = 2.8\times$$

Allied's ratio of 3.0 times is slightly above the 2.8 industry average, indicating that it is using its fixed assets at least as intensively as other firms in the industry. Therefore, Allied seems to have about the right amount of fixed assets relative to its sales.

Potential problems may arise when interpreting the fixed assets turnover ratio. Recall that fixed assets are shown on the balance sheet at their historical costs less depreciation. Inflation has caused the value of many assets that were purchased in the past to be seriously understated. Therefore, if we compare an old firm whose fixed assets have been depreciated with a new company with similar operations that acquired its fixed assets only recently, the old firm will probably have the higher fixed assets turnover ratio. However, this would be more reflective of the age of the assets than of inefficiency on the part of the new firm. The accounting profession is trying to develop procedures for making financial statements reflect current values rather than historical values, which would help us make better comparisons. However, at the moment, the problem still exists; so financial analysts must recognize this problem and deal with it judgmentally. In Allied's case, the issue is not serious because all firms in the industry have been expanding at about the same rate; hence, the balance sheets of the comparison firms are reasonably comparable.[8]

4-3D TOTAL ASSETS TURNOVER RATIO

The final asset management ratio, the **total assets turnover ratio**, measures the turnover of all of the firm's assets, and it is calculated by dividing sales by total assets:

Total Assets Turnover Ratio
This ratio is calculated by dividing sales by total assets. It measures how effectively the firm uses its total assets.

$$\text{Total assets turnover ratio} = \frac{\text{Sales}}{\text{Total assets}} = \frac{\$3{,}000}{\$2{,}000} = 1.5\times$$

$$\text{Industry average} = 1.8\times$$

Allied's ratio is somewhat below the industry average, indicating that it is not generating enough sales given its total assets. We just saw that Allied's fixed assets turnover is in line with the industry average; so the problem is with its current assets, inventories, and accounts receivable, whose ratios were below the industry standards. Inventories should be reduced and receivables collected faster, which would improve operations.

---

[8]Refer to FASB Accounting Standards Codification Topic 255, Changing Prices, for a discussion of the effects of inflation on financial statements. ASC 255 references FAS 89, Financial Reporting and Changing Prices, issued in December 1986.

SelfTest

Write the equations for four ratios that are used to measure how effectively a firm manages its assets.

If one firm is growing rapidly and another is not, how might this distort a comparison of their inventory turnover ratios?

If you wanted to evaluate a firm's DSO, with what could you compare it?

How might the different ages of firms distort comparisons of their fixed assets turnover ratios?

A firm has annual sales of $100 million, $20 million of inventory, and $30 million of accounts receivable. What is its inventory turnover ratio? **(5×)** What is its DSO? **(109.5 days)**

4-4 Debt Management Ratios

Debt Management Ratios
A set of ratios that measure how effectively a firm manages its debt.

The use of debt will increase, or "leverage up," a firm's ROE if the firm earns more on its assets than the interest rate it pays on debt. However, debt exposes the firm to more risk than if it financed only with equity. In this section we discuss **debt management ratios**.

Table 4.1 illustrates the potential benefits and risks associated with debt.[9] Here we analyze two companies that are identical except for how they are financed. Firm U (for *Unleveraged*) has no debt; thus, it uses 100% common equity. Firm L (for *Leveraged*) obtained 50% of its capital as debt at an interest rate of 10%. We will also assume that Firm L meets the IRS requirements so that it is exempt from the interest deduction limitation. Both firms have $100 of assets, and their sales are expected to range from a high of $150 down to $75 depending on business conditions. Some of their operating costs (e.g., rent and the president's salary) are fixed and will be the same regardless of the level of sales, while other costs (e.g., manufacturing labor and materials costs) vary with sales.[10]

Notice that everything is the same in the table for the leveraged and unleveraged firms down through operating income—thus, their EBITs are the same in each state of the economy. However, things differ below operating income. Firm U has no debt, it pays no interest, its taxable income is the same as its operating income, it pays a 25% state and federal tax rate, and its net income ranges from $33.75 under good conditions down to $0 under bad conditions. When U's net income is divided by its common equity, its ROEs range from 33.75% to 0% depending on the state of the economy.

Firm L has the same EBIT as U under each state of the economy, but L uses $50 of debt with a 10% interest rate; so it has $5 of interest charges regardless of the economy. This $5 is deducted from EBIT to arrive at taxable income, taxes are taken out, and the result is net income, which ranges from $30 to −$5 depending

[9]We discuss ROE in more depth later in this chapter, and we examine the effects of leverage in detail in Chapter 13. The relationship between various debt management ratios and bond ratings is discussed in Chapter 7.

[10]The financial statements do not show the breakdown between fixed and variable operating costs, but companies can and do make this breakdown for internal purposes. Of course, the distinction is not always clear because a fixed cost in the very short run can become a variable cost over a longer time horizon. It's interesting to note that companies are moving toward making more of their costs variable, using such techniques as increasing bonuses rather than base salaries, switching to profit-sharing plans rather than fixed pension plans, and outsourcing various operations.

TABLE 4.1

The Effects of Financial Leverage

Firm U—Unleveraged (No Debt)

Current assets	$ 50	Debt	$ 0
Fixed assets	50	Common equity	100
Total assets	$100	Total liabilities and equity	$100

		State of the Economy		
		Good	**Expected**	**Bad**
Sales revenues		$150.00	$100.00	$ 75.00
Operating costs	Fixed	45.00	45.00	45.00
	Variable	60.00	40.00	30.00
Total operating costs		105.00	85.00	75.00
Operating income (EBIT)		$ 45.00	$ 15.00	$ 0.00
Interest (Rate = 10%)		0.00	0.00	0.00
Earnings before taxes (EBT)		$ 45.00	$ 15.00	$ 0.00
Taxes (Rate = 25%)		11.25	3.75	0.00
Net income (NI)		$ 33.75	$ 11.25	$ 0.00
ROE_U		33.75%	11.25%	0.00%

Firm L—Leveraged (Some Debt)

Current assets	$ 50	Debt	$ 50
Fixed assets	50	Common equity	50
Total assets	$100	Total liabilities and equity	$ 100

		State of the Economy		
		Good	**Expected**	**Bad**
Sales revenues		$150.00	$100.00	$ 75.00
Operating costs	Fixed	45.00	45.00	45.00
	Variable	60.00	40.00	30.00
Total operating costs		105.00	85.00	75.00
Operating income (EBIT)		$ 45.00	$ 15.00	$ 0.00
Interest (Rate = 10%)		5.00	5.00	5.00
Earnings before taxes (EBT)		$ 40.00	$ 10.00	−$ 5.00
Taxes (Rate = 25%)		10.00	2.50	0.00
Net income (NI)		$ 30.00	$ 7.50	−$ 5.00
ROE_L		60.00%	15.00%	−10.00%

on conditions.[11] At first, it looks as though Firm U is better off under all conditions, but this is not correct—we need to consider how much the two firms' stockholders have invested. Firm L's stockholders have put up only $50; so when that investment is divided into net income, we see that their ROE under good conditions is a whopping 60% (versus 33.75% for U) and is 15% (versus 11.25% for U) under expected conditions. However, L's ROE falls to −10% under bad conditions, which means that Firm L would go bankrupt if those conditions persisted for several years.

Thus, firms with relatively high debt ratios typically have higher expected returns when the economy is normal, but experience lower returns and possibly

[11]As we discussed in the last chapter, firms can carry forward losses indefinitely. Assuming the firm has taxable income in future years, the net operating loss would be used to reduce taxable income and thus taxes in future years. An example of carryforwards was shown in Chapter 3.

face bankruptcy if the economy goes into a recession. Therefore, decisions about the use of debt require firms to balance higher expected returns against increased risk. Determining the optimal amount of debt is a complicated process, and we defer a discussion of that subject until Chapter 13. For now, we simply look at two procedures that analysts use to examine the firm's debt: (1) They check the balance sheet to determine the proportion of total funds represented by debt. (2) They review the income statement to see the extent to which interest is covered by operating profits.

4-4A TOTAL DEBT TO TOTAL CAPITAL

Total Debt to Total Capital
The ratio of total debt to total capital; it measures the percentage of the firm's capital provided by debtholders.

The ratio of **total debt to total capital** measures the percentage of the firm's capital provided by debtholders:

$$\frac{\text{Total debt}}{\text{Total capital}} = \frac{\text{Total debt}}{\text{Total debt} + \text{Equity}}$$

$$= \frac{\$110 + \$750}{\$1{,}800} = \frac{\$860}{\$1{,}800} = 47.8\%$$

$$\text{Industry average} = 36.4\%$$

Recall from Chapter 3 that total debt includes all short-term and long-term interest-bearing debt, but it does not include operating items such as accounts payable and accruals. Allied has total debt of \$860 million, which consists of \$110 million in short-term notes payable and \$750 million in long-term bonds. Its total capital is \$1.80 billion: \$860 million of debt plus \$940 million in total equity. To keep things simple, unless we say otherwise, we will generally refer to the total debt to total capital ratio as the company's *debt ratio*.[12] Creditors prefer low debt ratios because the lower the ratio, the greater the cushion against creditors' losses in the event of liquidation. Stockholders, on the other hand, may want more leverage because it can magnify expected earnings, as we saw in Table 4.1.

Allied's debt ratio is 47.8%, which means that its creditors have supplied roughly half of its total funds. As we will discuss in Chapter 13, a number of factors affect a company's optimal debt ratio. Nevertheless, the fact that Allied's debt ratio exceeds the industry average by a large amount raises a red flag, and this will make it relatively costly for Allied to borrow additional funds without first raising more equity. Creditors will be reluctant to lend the firm more money, and management would probably be subjecting the firm to too high a risk of bankruptcy if it sought to borrow a substantial amount of additional funds.

4-4B TIMES-INTEREST-EARNED RATIO

Times-Interest-Earned (TIE) Ratio
The ratio of earnings before interest and taxes (EBIT) to interest charges; a measure of the firm's ability to meet its annual interest payments.

The **times-interest-earned (TIE) ratio** is determined by dividing earnings before interest and taxes (EBIT in Table 3.2) by the interest charges:

$$\text{Times-interest-earned (TIE) ratio} = \frac{\text{EBIT}}{\text{Interest charges}}$$

$$= \frac{\$278}{\$83} = 3.3\times$$

$$\text{Industry average} = 6.0\times$$

---

[12]Two other debt ratios are often used in financial analysis:

1. Some analysts like to look at a broader debt ratio that includes all total liabilities (including accounts payables and accruals) divided by total assets. For Allied, the total liabilities-to-assets ratio is 53% (\$1,060 million divided by \$2,000 million), while the industry average is 40%.
2. Another measure, the debt-to-equity ratio equals total debt divided by total equity. Allied's debt-to-equity ratio is \$860 million/\$940 million = 91.5%.

HOUSEHOLD DEBT BURDENS HAVE DECLINED IN RECENT YEARS

The Federal Reserve keeps track of household financial obligations as a percentage of disposable personal income. In many respects, this ratio is similar to the times-interest-earned ratio, but it looks at debt burdens from the perspective of households. The Fed's measure of household financial obligations includes mortgage and consumer debt payments along with other responsibilities such as rent and property taxes. As you can see from the following graph, this ratio rises and falls over time—it steadily increased from the early 1990s until the financial crisis of 2007–2008. Following the crisis, there has been a sharp drop in household debt levels. Two factors explain this trend. First, after the crisis many households have become more conservative and have taken steps to repair their household balance sheets. Another reason is that banks and other lending institutions have been less willing to provide credit to households. This reluctance has arisen because banks are only now recovering from the large losses they suffered during the crisis. This weakness in their own balance sheets coupled with more stringent regulations has led many banks to scale back their consumer lending.

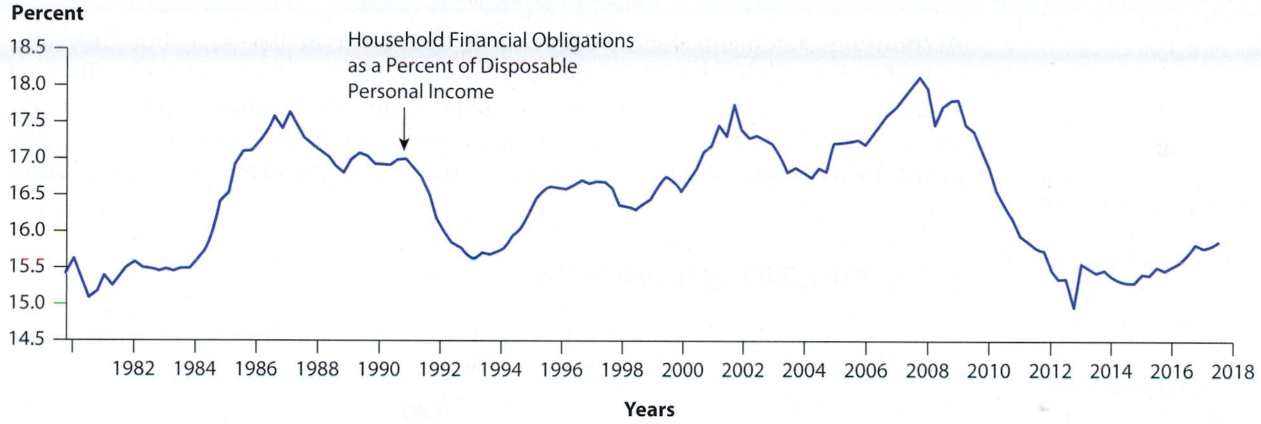

Source: FRED, Federal Reserve Bank of St. Louis, (https://fred.stlouisfed.org/series/FODSP), January 9, 2018. Data are shown from January 1, 1980 to July 1, 2017.

The TIE ratio measures the extent to which operating income can decline before the firm is unable to meet its annual interest costs. Failure to pay interest will bring legal action by the firm's creditors and probably result in bankruptcy. Note that earnings before interest and taxes, rather than net income, are used in the numerator. Because interest is paid with pretax dollars, the firm's ability to pay current interest is not affected by taxes.

Allied's interest is covered 3.3 times. The industry average is 6 times, so Allied is covering its interest charges by a much lower margin of safety than the average firm in the industry. Thus, the TIE ratio reinforces our conclusion from the debt ratio, namely, that Allied would face difficulties if it attempted to borrow additional money.[13]

[13]Another commonly used debt management ratio, using earnings before interest, taxes, depreciation, and amortization (EBITDA), is the EBITDA coverage ratio calculated as

$$\text{EBITDA coverage ratio} = \frac{\text{EBITDA} + \text{Lease payments}}{\text{Interest} + \text{Principal payments} + \text{Lease payments}}$$

This ratio is more complete than the TIE ratio because it recognizes that depreciation and amortization expenses are not cash expenses, and thus are available to service debt, and that lease payments and principal repayments on debt are fixed charges. For more on this ratio, see E. F. Brigham and P. R. Daves, *Intermediate Financial Management,* 13th edition (Mason, OH: Cengage Learning, 2019), Chapter 7.

SelfTest

How does the use of financial leverage affect stockholders' control position?

How does the U.S. tax structure influence a firm's willingness to finance with debt?

How does the decision to use debt involve a risk-versus-return trade-off?

Explain the following statement: Analysts look at both balance sheet and income statement ratios when appraising a firm's financial condition.

Name two ratios that are used to measure financial leverage and write their equations.

4-5 Profitability Ratios

Accounting statements reflect events that happened in the past, but they also provide clues about what's really important—that is, what's likely to happen in the future. The liquidity, asset management, and debt ratios covered thus far tell us something about the firm's policies and operations. Now we turn to the **profitability ratios**, which reflect the net result of all of the firm's financing policies and operating decisions.

Profitability Ratios
A group of ratios that show the combined effects of liquidity, asset management, and debt on operating results.

4-5A OPERATING MARGIN

Operating Margin
This ratio measures operating income, or EBIT, per dollar of sales; it is calculated by dividing operating income by sales.

The **operating margin**, calculated by dividing operating income (EBIT) by sales, gives the operating profit per dollar of sales:

$$\text{Operating margin} = \frac{\text{EBIT}}{\text{Sales}} = \frac{\$278}{\$3{,}000} = 9.3\%$$

$$\text{Industry average} = 10.0\%$$

Allied's 9.3% operating margin is below the industry average of 10.0%. This subpar result indicates that Allied's operating costs are too high. This is consistent with the low inventory turnover and high days sales outstanding ratios that we calculated earlier.

4-5B PROFIT MARGIN

Profit Margin
This ratio measures net income per dollar of sales and is calculated by dividing net income by sales.

The **profit margin**, also sometimes called the *net profit margin*, is calculated by dividing net income by sales:

$$\text{Profit margin} = \frac{\text{Net income}}{\text{Sales}} = \frac{\$146.3}{\$3{,}000} = 4.9\%$$

$$\text{Industry average} = 6.0\%$$

Allied's 4.9% profit margin is below the industry average of 6.0%, and this subpar result occurred for two reasons. First, Allied's operating margin was below the industry average because of the firm's high operating costs. Second, the profit margin is negatively impacted by Allied's heavy use of debt. To see this second point, recognize that net income is *after interest*. Suppose two firms have identical operations in the sense that their sales, operating costs, and operating income are identical. However, one firm uses more debt; hence, it has higher interest charges. Those interest charges pull down its net income, and because sales are identical, the result is a relatively low profit margin for the firm with more debt. We see then that Allied's operating inefficiency and its high debt ratio combine to lower its profit margin below the food processing industry average. It also follows that when two companies have the same operating margin but different debt ratios, we can expect the company with a higher debt ratio to have a lower profit margin.

Note too that while a high return on sales is good, we must also be concerned with turnover. If a firm sets a very high price on its products, it may earn a high return on each sale but fail to make many sales. It might generate a high profit margin but realize low sales, and hence experience a low net income. We will see shortly how, through the use of the DuPont equation, profit margins, the use of debt, and turnover ratios interact to affect overall stockholder returns.

4-5C Return on Total Assets

Net income divided by total assets gives us the **return on total assets (ROA)**:

Return on Total Assets (ROA)
The ratio of net income to total assets; it measures the rate of return on the firm's assets.

$$\text{Return on total assets (ROA)} = \frac{\text{Net income}}{\text{Total assets}}$$

$$= \frac{\$146.3}{\$2{,}000} = 7.3\%$$

$$\text{Industry average} = 10.8\%$$

Allied's 7.3% return is well below the 10.8% industry average. This is not good—it is obviously better to have a higher than a lower return on assets. Note, though, that a low ROA can result from a conscious decision to use a great deal of debt, in which case high interest expenses will cause net income to be relatively low. That is part of the reason for Allied's low ROA. Never forget—you must look at a number of ratios, see what each suggests, and then look at the overall situation before you judge the performance of a company and consider what actions it should undertake to improve.

4-5D Return on Common Equity

Another important accounting ratio is the **return on common equity (ROE)**, which is found as follows:

Return on Common Equity (ROE)
The ratio of net income to common equity; it measures the rate of return on common stockholders' investment.

$$\text{Return on common equity (ROE)} = \frac{\text{Net income}}{\text{Common equity}}$$

$$= \frac{\$146.3}{\$940} = 15.6\%$$

$$\text{Industry average} = 18.7\%$$

Stockholders expect to earn a return on their money, and this ratio tells how well they are doing in an accounting sense. Allied's 15.6% return is below the 18.7% industry average, but not as far below as the return on total assets. This somewhat better ROE results from the company's greater use of debt, a point discussed earlier in the chapter.

4-5E Return on Invested Capital

The **return on invested capital (ROIC)** measures the total return that the company has provided for its investors:

Return on Invested Capital (ROIC)
The ratio of after-tax operating income to total invested capital; it measures the total return that the company has provided for its investors.

$$\text{Return on invested capital (ROIC)} = \frac{\text{EBIT}(1 - \text{T})}{\text{Total invested capital}}$$

$$= \frac{\text{EBIT}(1 - \text{T})}{\text{Debt} + \text{Equity}} = \frac{\$208.5}{\$1{,}800} = 11.6\%$$

$$\text{Industry average} = 13.2\%$$

ROIC differs from ROA in two ways. First, its return is based on total invested capital rather than total assets. Second, in the numerator it uses after-tax operating income (NOPAT) rather than net income. The key difference is that net income subtracts the company's after-tax interest expense and therefore represents the total amount of income available to shareholders, while NOPAT is the amount of funds available to pay both stockholders and debtholders.

quick question

QUESTION:

A company has $20 billion of sales and $1 billion of net income. Its total assets are $10 billion. The company's total assets equal total invested capital, and its capital consists of half debt and half common equity. The firm's interest rate is 5%, and its tax rate is 25%.

1. What is its profit margin?
2. What is its ROA?
3. What is its ROE?
4. What is its ROIC?
5. Would this firm's ROA increase if it used less leverage? (The size of the firm does not change.)

ANSWER:

a. $\text{Profit margin} = \frac{\text{Net income}}{\text{Sales}} = \frac{\$1\text{ billion}}{\$20\text{ billion}} = 5\%.$

b. $\text{ROA} = \frac{\text{Net income}}{\text{Total assets}} = \frac{\$1\text{ billion}}{\$10\text{ billion}} = 10\%.$

c. $\text{ROE} = \frac{\text{Net income}}{\text{Common equity}} = \frac{\$1\text{ billion}}{\$5\text{ billion}} = 20\%.$

d. First, we need to calculate the firm's EBIT by working up the firm's income statement:

EBIT	$1,583,333,333	EBT + Interest
Interest	250,000,000	0.05 × 0.5 × $10,000,000,000
EBT	$1,333,333,333	$1,000,000,000/(1 − 0.25)
Taxes (25%)	333,333,333	EBT × 0.25
Net income	$1,000,000,000	

$$\text{ROIC} = \frac{\text{EBIT}(1 - \text{T})}{\text{Total invested capital}} = \frac{\$1{,}583{,}333{,}333(0.75)}{\$10{,}000{,}000{,}000} = 11.9\%$$

e. If the company used less debt, it would increase net income because interest expense would be reduced. Because assets would not change and net income increases, ROA will increase.

4-5F BASIC EARNING POWER (BEP) RATIO

Basic Earning Power (BEP) Ratio
This ratio indicates the ability of the firm's assets to generate operating income; it is calculated by dividing EBIT by total assets.

The **basic earning power (BEP) ratio** is calculated by dividing operating income (EBIT) by total assets:

$$\textbf{Basic earning power (BEP)} = \frac{\textbf{EBIT}}{\textbf{Total assets}}$$
$$= \frac{\$278}{\$2{,}000} = 13.9\%$$
$$\textbf{Industry average} = 18.0\%$$

This ratio shows the raw earning power of the firm's assets before the influence of taxes and debt, and it is useful when comparing firms with different debt and tax situations. Because of its low turnover ratios and poor profit margin on sales, Allied has a lower BEP ratio than the average food processing company.

SelfTest

Identify six profitability ratios, and write their equations.

Why does the use of debt lower the profit margin and the ROA?

Using more debt lowers profits and thus the ROA. Why doesn't debt have the same negative effect on the ROE?

A company has a 10% ROA. Assume that a company's total assets equal total invested capital, and that the company has no debt, so its total invested capital equals total equity. What are the company's ROE and ROIC? **(10%, 10%)**

4-6 Market Value Ratios

ROE reflects the effects of all of the other ratios, and it is the single best accounting measure of performance. Investors like a high ROE, and high ROEs are correlated with high stock prices. However, other things come into play. For example, financial leverage generally increases the ROE but also increases the firm's risk; so if a high ROE is achieved by using a great deal of debt, the stock price might end up lower than if the firm had been using less debt and had a lower ROE. We use the final set of ratios—the **market value ratios**, which relate the stock price to earnings and book value price—to help address this situation. If the liquidity, asset management, debt management, and profitability ratios all look good, and if investors think these ratios will continue to look good in the future, the market value ratios will be high; the stock price will be as high as can be expected; and management will be judged as having done a good job.

Market Value Ratios
Ratios that relate the firm's stock price to its earnings and book value per share.

The market value ratios are used in three primary ways: (1) by investors when they are deciding to buy or sell a stock, (2) by investment bankers when they are setting the share price for a new stock issue (an IPO), and (3) by firms when they are deciding how much to offer for another firm in a potential merger.

4-6A PRICE/EARNINGS RATIO

The **price/earnings (P/E) ratio** shows how much investors are willing to pay per dollar of reported profits. Allied's stock sells for \$23.06; so with an EPS of \$1.95, its P/E ratio is 11.8×:

Price/Earnings (P/E) Ratio
The ratio of the price per share to earnings per share; shows the dollar amount investors will pay for \$1 of current earnings.

$$\text{Price/Earnings (P/E) ratio} = \frac{\text{Price per share}}{\text{Earnings per share}}$$

$$= \frac{\$23.06}{\$1.95} = 11.8\times$$

$$\text{Industry average} = 13.6\times$$

As we will see in Chapter 9, P/E ratios are relatively high for firms with strong growth prospects and little risk but low for slowly growing and risky firms. Allied's P/E ratio is below its industry average; so this suggests that the company is regarded as being relatively risky, as having poor growth prospects, or both.[14]

P/E ratios vary considerably over time and across firms.[15] In early April 2018, the S&P 500's P/E ratio was 25.04×. At this same point in time, Apple Inc. had a P/E of 17.30×, while Amazon, the world's highest-grossing online retailer, had a P/E of 227.27×. Moreover, AFLAC, a supplemental health and life insurer and a stable company in an industry that has been impacted by the Affordable Care Act and related uncertainties, has a P/E ratio of 7.52×.

4-6B MARKET/BOOK RATIO

The ratio of a stock's market price to its book value gives another indication of how investors regard the company. Companies that are well regarded by investors—which means low risk and high growth—have high M/B ratios. For Allied, we first find its book value per share:

$$\text{Book value per share} = \frac{\text{Common equity}}{\text{Shares outstanding}} = \frac{\$940}{75} = \$12.53$$

Market/Book (M/B) Ratio
The ratio of a stock's market price to its book value.

We then divide the market price per share by the book value per share to get the **market/book (M/B) ratio**, which for Allied is 1.8×:

$$\text{Market/Book(M/B) ratio} = \frac{\text{Market price per share}}{\text{Book value per share}} = \frac{\$23.06}{\$12.53} = 1.8\times$$

$$\text{Industry average} = 2.6\times$$

Investors are willing to pay less for a dollar of Allied's book value than for one of an average food processing company. This is consistent with our other findings. M/B ratios typically exceed 1.0, which means that investors are willing to pay more for stocks than the accounting book values of the stocks. This situation occurs primarily because asset values, as reported by accountants on corporate balance sheets, do not reflect either inflation or goodwill. Assets purchased years ago at pre-inflation prices are carried at their original costs even though inflation might have caused their actual values to rise substantially; successful companies' values rise above their historical costs, whereas unsuccessful ones have low M/B ratios.[16] This point is demonstrated by Alphabet Inc. (now the parent of Google) and MetLife, Inc.: In early April 2018, Alphabet's M/B ratio was 4.59× while MetLife's was only 0.80×. Alphabet's stockholders now have $4.59 in market value per $1.00 of equity, whereas MetLife's stockholders have only $0.80 for each dollar they invested.

---

[14]Security analysts also look at the price-to-free-cash-flow ratio. In addition, analysts consider the PEG, or P/E-to-growth, ratio where the P/E is divided by the firm's forecasted growth rate. Allied's growth rate as forecasted by a number of security analysts for the next 5 years is 6.0%, so its PEG = 11.8/6.0 = 2.0×. The lower the ratio, the better; most firms have ratios in the range of 1.0× to 2.0×. We note, though, that P/E ratios jump around from year to year because earnings and forecasted growth rates fluctuate. Like other ratios, PEG ratios are interesting, but must be interpreted with care and judgment.

[15]On his website (www.econ.yale.edu/~shiller/data.htm), Professor Robert Shiller reports the annual P/E ratio of the overall stock market dating back to 1871. His calculations show that the historical average P/E ratio for the market has been 16.8×, and it has ranged from 4.8× to 44.2×.

[16]The second point is known as *survivor bias.* Successful companies survive and are reflected in the averages, whereas unsuccessful companies vanish, and their low numbers are not reflected in the averages.

4-6C ENTERPRISE VALUE/EBITDA RATIO

In recent years, a lot of analysts have begun to focus intently on another key ratio, the **enterprise value/EBITDA (EV/EBITDA) ratio**. Unlike the P/E and the market/book ratios, both of which focus on the relative market value of the company's equity, the EV/EBITDA ratio looks at the relative market value of all the company's key financial claims. One benefit of this approach is that unlike the P/E ratio, the EV/EBITDA ratio is not heavily influenced by the company's debt and tax situations.[17] For Allied, we first find its enterprise value (in millions of dollars):

Enterprise Value/ EBITDA (EV/EBITDA) Ratio
The ratio of a firm's enterprise value relative to its EBITDA.

$$\text{Enterprise value (EV)}_{2019} = \text{Market value of equity} + \text{Market value of total debt} + \text{Market value of other financial claims} - \text{(Cash and equivalents)}$$

$$= (\$23.06 \times 75) + (\$110 + \$750) + \$0 - \$10$$
$$= \$1{,}729.5 + \$860 + \$0 - \$10$$
$$= \$2{,}579.5 \text{ million}$$

Total debt in this calculation includes long-term debt plus short-term interest-bearing debt. In addition, for simplicity, we are assuming that Allied's debt is priced at par, so the market value of its debt is assumed to equal its book value. (This is a common assumption.)

This measure of enterprise value subtracts out the company's cash holdings. This adjustment makes it easier to compare companies with very different levels of excess cash. For example, if we didn't make this assumption, a company with large cash holdings but inefficient operations would mistakenly appear to be outperforming a peer that is much more efficient but has less cash on hand.

Finally, we divide Allied's enterprise value by the company's 2019 EBITDA of $378 million (which we calculated in Chapter 3, Section 3-3). So, we calculate Allied's EV/EBITDA ratio as follows:

$$\text{EV/EBITDA}_{2019} = \$2{,}579.5 \text{ million}/\$378 \text{ million}$$
$$= 6.8\times$$

$$\text{Industry average} = 9.2\times$$

As you can see, Allied's EV/EBITDA ratio is significantly lower than the industry average. This reinforces our other calculations, indicating that the firm's operations are not run as efficiently as they could be.

*Self*Test

Describe the three ratios discussed in this section and write their equations.

In what sense do these market value ratios reflect investors' opinions about a stock's risk and expected future growth?

What does the price/earnings (P/E) ratio show? If one firm's P/E ratio is lower than that of another firm, what factors might explain the difference?

How is book value per share calculated? Explain how inflation and R&D programs might cause book values to deviate from market values.

[17]It is similar in spirit to the motivation behind the basic earning power measure.

4-7 Tying the Ratios Together: The DuPont Equation

DuPont Equation
A formula that shows that the rate of return on equity can be found as the product of profit margin, total assets turnover, and the equity multiplier. It shows the relationships among asset management, debt management, and profitability ratios.

We have discussed many ratios, so it would be useful to see how they work together to determine the ROE. For this, we use the **DuPont equation**, a formula developed by the chemical giant's financial staff in the 1920s. It is shown here for Allied and the food processing industry:

$$
\begin{aligned}
\text{ROE} &= \text{ROA} \times \text{Equity multiplier} \\
&= \text{Profit margin} \times \text{Total assets turnover} \times \text{Equity multiplier} \\
&= \frac{\text{Net income}}{\text{Sales}} \times \frac{\text{Sales}}{\text{Total assets}} \times \frac{\text{Total assets}}{\text{Total common equity}} \\
&= \frac{\$146.3}{\$3{,}000} \times \frac{\$3{,}000}{\$2{,}000} \times \frac{\$2{,}000}{\$940} \\
&= 4.88\% \times 1.5 \text{ times} \times 2.13 \text{ times} = 15.6\% \\
\text{Industry} &= 6.0\% \times 1.8 \text{ times} \times 1.73 \text{ times} = 18.7\%
\end{aligned}
\qquad (4.1)
$$

- The first term, the profit margin, tells us how much the firm earns on its sales. This ratio depends primarily on costs and sales prices—if a firm can command a premium price and hold down its costs, its profit margin will be high, which will help its ROE.
- The second term is the total assets turnover. It is a "multiplier" that tells us how many times the profit margin is earned each year—Allied earned 4.88% on each dollar of sales, and its assets were turned over 1.5 times each year; so its return on assets was 4.88% × 1.5 = 7.3%. Note, though, that this entire 7.3% belongs to the common stockholders—the bondholders earned a return in the form of interest, and that interest was deducted before we calculated net income to stockholders. So the whole 7.3% return on assets belongs to the stockholders. Therefore, the return on assets must be adjusted upward to obtain the return on equity.
- That brings us to the third term, the equity multiplier, which is the adjustment factor. Allied's assets are 2.13 times its equity, so we must multiply the 7.3% return on assets by the 2.13× equity multiplier to arrive at its ROE of 15.6%.[18]

Note that ROE as calculated using the DuPont equation is identical to Allied's ROE, 15.6%, which we calculated earlier. What's the point of going through all of the steps required to implement the DuPont equation to find ROE? The answer is that the DuPont equation helps us see *why* Allied's ROE is only 15.6% versus 18.7% for the industry. First, its profit margin is below average, which indicates that its costs are not being controlled as well as they should be and that it cannot charge premium prices. In addition, because it uses more debt than most companies, its high interest charges also reduce its profit margin. Second, its total assets turnover is below the industry average, which indicates that it has more assets than it needs. Finally, because its equity multiplier is relatively high, its heavy use of debt offsets to some extent its low profit margin and turnover. However, the high debt ratio exposes Allied to above-average bankruptcy risk; so it might want to cut back on its financial leverage. But if it reduced its debt to the same level as

[18]The equity multiplier relates to the firm's use of debt. The industry equity multiplier can be obtained by using the industry ROE and ROA. The equity multiplier = Total assets divided by common equity. ROE = Net income/Common equity, and ROA = Net income/Total assets. So, ROE ÷ ROA = Equity multiplier as shown here:

$$\frac{\text{ROE}}{\text{ROA}} = \frac{\text{NI}}{\text{Equity}} \div \frac{\text{NI}}{\text{Assets}} = \frac{\text{NI}}{\text{Equity}} \times \frac{\text{Assets}}{\text{NI}} = \frac{\text{Assets}}{\text{Equity}} = \text{Equity multiplier}$$

MICROSOFT EXCEL: A TRULY ESSENTIAL TOOL

Microsoft Excel is an essential tool for anyone dealing with business issues—not just finance and accounting professionals but also lawyers, marketers, auto sales managers, government employees, and many others. Indeed, anyone who works with numbers will be more efficient and productive if they know the basics of Excel, so it's a necessity for anyone who hopes to hold a managerial position.

As you go through this book, you will see that Excel is used in four main ways:

1. *As a financial calculator.* Excel can add, subtract, multiply, and divide, and it can retain results from one operation for use in subsequent operations. For example, we created the financial statements in Chapter 3 with Excel, and we use it to analyze those statements in the current chapter. We could have done this with a calculator or pencil and paper, but it was a lot easier with Excel. As we will see throughout the text, Excel also has a large number of built-in financial functions that can be used to simply calculate the answers to a wide range of financial problems. For example, using Excel, it is straightforward to calculate the return on an investment, the price of a bond, or the value of a project.

2. *To modify the work when things change.* Suppose your boss asked you to create the statements in Chapter 3, but when you finished she said, "Thanks, but the accounting department just informed us that inventories in 2019 were overstated by $100 million, which means that total assets were also overstated. To make the balance sheet balance, we must reduce retained earnings, common equity, and total claims against assets. Please make those adjustments and give me a revised set of statements before the board meeting tomorrow morning."

If you were working with a calculator, you'd be looking at an all-nighter, but with Excel you could make just one change—reduce 2019 inventories by $100 million—and Excel would instantly revise the statements. If your company had two people working on problems like this, who would get promoted and who would get a pink slip?

3. *Sensitivity analysis.* We use ratios to analyze financial statements and assess how well a company is managed, and if weaknesses are detected management can make changes to improve the situation. For example, Allied's return on equity (ROE), a key determinant of its stock price, is below the industry average. ROE depends on a number of factors, including the level of inventories, and using Excel one can see how ROE would change if inventories were increased or decreased. Then, management can investigate alternative inventory policies to see how they would impact profits and the ROE. In theory, one could do this analysis with a calculator, but this would be inefficient, and in a competitive world efficiency is essential to survival.

4. *Risk assessments.* Sensitivity analysis can be used to assess the risk inherent in different policies. For example, *forecasted* returns on equity are generally higher if a firm increases its debt, but the more debt the firm carries, the worse the effects of an economic downturn. We can use Excel to quantify the effects of changing economic conditions with different amounts of debt, and thus the probability that the firm will go bankrupt in a recession. Many firms learned about this during the 2007–2009 recession, so the survivors are now more interested than ever in risk models.

This listing gives you an idea of what Excel can do and why it is important in business today. We illustrate it throughout the book, and you should make an effort to understand how to use it. The Excel chapter models can be found on the student companion site on cengage.com. You will find an understanding of Excel very helpful when you begin interviewing for a job.[19]

the average firm in its industry without any other changes, its ROE would decline significantly, to $4.88\% \times 1.5 \times 1.73 = 12.66\%$.[20]

Allied's management can use the DuPont equation to help identify ways to improve its performance. Focusing on the profit margin, its marketing people can study the effects of raising sales prices or of introducing new products with higher margins. Its cost accountants can study various expense items and, working with engineers, purchasing agents, and other operating personnel, seek ways to cut costs.

[19]It is often impractical for professors to test students on their ability to integrate Excel into financial management, so some students conclude that knowing more about Excel won't help them on tests and thus they ignore it. That's unfortunate, and we can only say that there's more to school than grades alone, and in the long run knowing something about Excel is one of the most valuable tools you can learn in school.

[20]The ROE reduction would actually be somewhat less because if debt were lowered, interest payments would also decline, which would raise Allied's profit margin. Allied's analysts determined that the net effect of a reduction in debt would still be a significant reduction in ROE.

The credit manager can investigate ways to speed up collections, which would reduce accounts receivable and therefore improve the quality of the total assets turnover ratio. And the financial staff can analyze the effects of alternative debt policies, showing how changes in leverage would affect both the expected ROE and the risk of bankruptcy.

As a result of this analysis, Ellen Jackson, Allied's chief executive officer (CEO), undertook a series of moves that are expected to cut operating costs by more than 20%. Jackson and Allied's other executives have a strong incentive to improve the firm's financial performance—their compensation depends on how well the company operates.

Self*Test*

Write the equation for the DuPont equation.

What is the equity multiplier, and why is it used?

How can management use the DuPont equation to analyze ways of improving the firm's performance?

4-8 Potential Misuses of ROE

Although ROE is an important measure of performance, we know that managers should strive to maximize shareholder wealth. If a firm takes steps that improve its ROE, does that mean that shareholder wealth will also be increased? The answer is "not necessarily." Indeed, three problems are likely to arise if a firm relies too heavily on ROE to measure performance.

First, ROE does not consider risk. Shareholders care about ROE, but they also care about risk. To illustrate, consider two divisions within the same firm. Division S has stable cash flows and a predictable 15% ROE. Division R has a 16% expected ROE, but its cash flows are quite risky; so the expected ROE may not materialize. If managers were compensated solely on the basis of ROE and if the expected ROEs were actually achieved during the coming year, Division R's manager would receive a higher bonus than S's, even though S might actually be creating more value for shareholders as a result of its lower risk. Similarly, financial leverage can increase expected ROE, but more leverage means higher risk; so raising ROE through the use of leverage may not be good.

Second, ROE does not consider the amount of invested capital. To illustrate, consider a company that is choosing between two mutually exclusive projects. Project A calls for investing $50,000 at an expected ROE of 50%, while Project B calls for investing $1,000,000 at a 45% ROE. The projects are equally risky, and the company's cost of capital is 10%. Project A has the higher ROE, but it is much smaller. Project B should be chosen because it would add more to shareholder wealth.

Third, a focus on ROE can cause managers to turn down profitable projects. For example, suppose you manage a division of a large firm and the firm determines bonuses solely on the basis of ROE. You project that your division's ROE for the year will be an impressive 45%. Now you have an opportunity to invest in a large, low-risk project with an estimated ROE of 35%, which is well above the firm's 10% cost of capital. Even though this project is extremely profitable, you might still be reluctant to undertake it because it would reduce your division's average ROE and therefore your year-end bonus.

ECONOMIC VALUE ADDED (EVA) VERSUS NET INCOME

As we mentioned in Chapter 3, economic value added (EVA) is a measure of how much management has added to shareholders' wealth during the year. To better understand the idea behind EVA, let's look at Allied's 2019 numbers (in millions). Allied's total invested capital consists of \$110 of notes payable, \$750 of long-term debt, and \$940 of common equity, totaling \$1,800. Debt represents 47.78% of this total, and common equity is 52.22% of this total. Later in the text we discuss how to calculate the cost of Allied's capital. But for now, to simplify things, we estimate its capital cost at 10%. Thus, the firm's total dollar cost of capital (which includes both debt and common equity) per year is 0.10 × \$1,800 = \$180.

Now let's look at Allied's income statement. Its operating income, EBIT, is \$278, and its interest expense is \$83. Therefore, its taxable income is \$278 − \$83 = \$195. Taxes equal 25% of taxable income, or 0.25 (\$195) = \$48.8; so the firm's net income is \$146.3. Its return on equity, ROE, is \$146.3/\$940 = 15.6%.

Given this data, we can now calculate Allied's EVA. The basic formula for EVA (as discussed in Chapter 3) is as follows:

$$\text{EVA} = \text{EBIT}(1-T) - \left(\begin{array}{c}\text{Total}\\ \text{invested capital}\end{array}\right) \times \left(\begin{array}{c}\text{After-tax}\\ \text{cost of capital}\end{array}\right)$$

$$= \$278(1-0.25) - (\$1{,}800)(0.10)$$

$$= \$208.5 - \$180$$

$$= \$28.5$$

This positive EVA indicates that Allied's shareholders actually earned \$28.5 million more than they could have earned by investing in other stocks with the same risk as Allied. To see where this \$28.5 comes from, let's trace what happened to the money:

- The firm generated \$278 of operating income.
- \$48.8 went to the government to pay taxes, leaving \$229.3 available for investors—stockholders and bondholders.
- \$83 went to the bondholders in the form of interest payments, thus leaving \$146.3 for the stockholders.
- However, Allied's shareholders must also earn a return on the equity capital they have invested in the firm, because they could have invested in other companies of comparable risk. We call this the cost of Allied's equity.
- Once Allied's shareholders are "paid" their return, the firm has an additional \$28.5 million—that's the economic value management added. Allied's management created *positive* wealth because it provided shareholders with a higher return than they could have earned on alternative investments with the same risk as Allied's stock.
- In practice, it is often necessary to make several adjustments to arrive at a "better" measure of EVA. The adjustments deal with non-operating assets, leased assets, depreciation, and other accounting details that we leave for discussion in advanced finance courses.

The Connection between ROE and EVA

EVA is different from traditional accounting profit *because EVA reflects the cost of equity as well as the cost of debt.* Indeed, using the previous example, we could also express EVA as net income minus the dollar cost of equity:

$$\text{EVA} = \text{Net income} - (\text{Equity} \times \text{Cost of equity})$$

This preceding expression could be rewritten as follows:

$$\text{EVA} = (\text{Equity})(\text{Net income/Equity} - \text{Cost of equity})$$

which can be rewritten as

$$\text{EVA} = \text{Equity}(\text{ROE} - \text{Cost of equity})$$

This last expression implies that EVA depends on three factors: rate of return, as reflected in ROE; risk, which affects the cost of equity; and size, which is measured by the equity employed. Recall that earlier in this chapter, we said that shareholder value depends on risk, return, and capital invested. This final equation illustrates that point.

These three examples suggest that a project's ROE must be combined with its size and risk to determine its effect on shareholder value, as we illustrate in the following diagram:

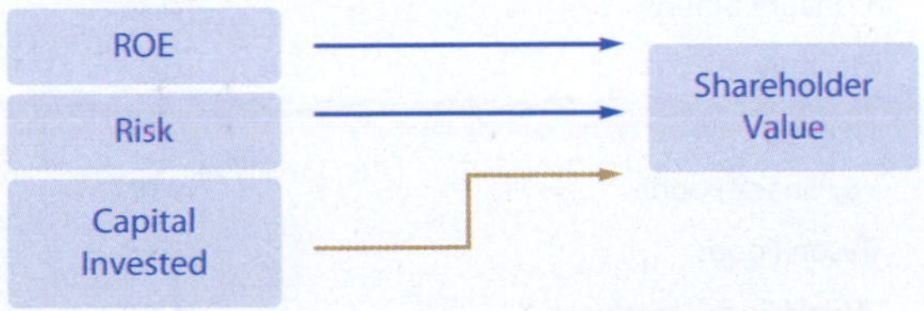

We will discuss this in more depth when we consider capital budgeting, where we look in detail at how projects are selected to maximize shareholder value.

Self*Test*

If a firm takes steps that increase its expected future ROE, does this necessarily mean that the stock price will also increase? Explain.

4-9 Using Financial Ratios to Assess Performance

Although financial ratios help us evaluate financial statements, it is often hard to evaluate a company by just looking at the ratios. For example, if you see that a company has a current ratio of 1.2, it is hard to know if that is good or bad, unless you put the ratio in its proper perspective. Allied's management could look at industry averages; it could compare itself to specific companies or "benchmarks"; and it can analyze the trends in each ratio. We look at all three approaches in this section.

4-9A COMPARISON TO INDUSTRY AVERAGE

As we have done for Allied, one way to assess performance is to compare the company's key ratios to the industry averages. Table 4.2 provides a summary of the ratios we have discussed in this chapter. This table is useful as a quick reference, and the calculated ratios and accompanying comments give a good sense of Allied's strengths and weaknesses relative to the average food processing company. To give you a further sense of some "real-world" ratios, Table 4.3 provides a list of ratios for a number of different industries in early April 2018.

4-9B BENCHMARKING

Benchmarking
The process of comparing a particular company with a subset of top competitors in its industry.

Ratio analysis involves comparisons with industry average figures, but Allied and many other firms also compare themselves with a subset of top competitors in their industry. This is called **benchmarking**, and the companies used for the comparison are called benchmark companies. Allied's management benchmarks against Campbell Soup, a leading manufacturer of canned soups; Tyson Foods, a processor of chicken, beef, and pork products; J&J Snack Foods, a manufacturer of nutritional snack foods; Conagra Brands, a packaged food company that supplies entrees, sauces, frozen potatoes, and other vegetables to commercial customers; Flowers Foods, a producer of bakery and snack-food goods; Hershey Foods, a producer of chocolates and non-chocolate confectionary products; and Kellogg Company, a manufacturer of ready-to-eat cereals and convenience foods. Ratios are calculated for each company, then listed in descending order as shown in the following table for the profit margin (the firms' latest 12 months' results reported by Yahoo! Finance [finance.yahoo.com]) as of April 9, 2018:

Company	Profit Margin
Campbell Soup	13.41%
Conagra Brands	11.36
Hershey	10.42
Kellogg	9.82
J&J Snack Foods	9.06
Tyson Foods	7.15
Allied Food Products	**4.88**
Flowers Foods	3.83

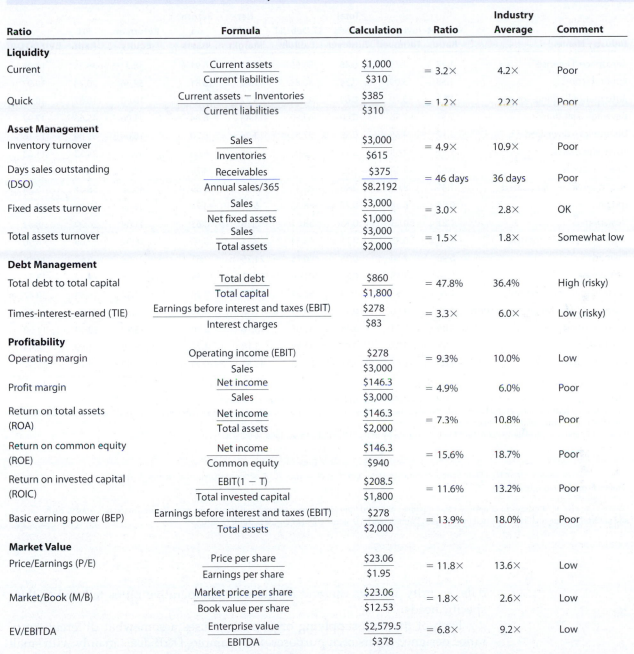

TABLE 4.2 Allied Food Products: Summary of Financial Ratios (millions of dollars)

Ratio	Formula	Calculation	Ratio	Industry Average	Comment
Liquidity					
Current	$\frac{\text{Current assets}}{\text{Current liabilities}}$	$\frac{\$1,000}{\$310}$	= 3.2×	4.2×	Poor
Quick	$\frac{\text{Current assets} - \text{Inventories}}{\text{Current liabilities}}$	$\frac{\$385}{\$310}$	= 1.2×	2.2×	Poor
Asset Management					
Inventory turnover	$\frac{\text{Sales}}{\text{Inventories}}$	$\frac{\$3,000}{\$615}$	= 4.9×	10.9×	Poor
Days sales outstanding (DSO)	$\frac{\text{Receivables}}{\text{Annual sales/365}}$	$\frac{\$375}{\$8.2192}$	= 46 days	36 days	Poor
Fixed assets turnover	$\frac{\text{Sales}}{\text{Net fixed assets}}$	$\frac{\$3,000}{\$1,000}$	= 3.0×	2.8×	OK
Total assets turnover	$\frac{\text{Sales}}{\text{Total assets}}$	$\frac{\$3,000}{\$2,000}$	= 1.5×	1.8×	Somewhat low
Debt Management					
Total debt to total capital	$\frac{\text{Total debt}}{\text{Total capital}}$	$\frac{\$860}{\$1,800}$	= 47.8%	36.4%	High (risky)
Times-interest-earned (TIE)	$\frac{\text{Earnings before interest and taxes (EBIT)}}{\text{Interest charges}}$	$\frac{\$278}{\$83}$	= 3.3×	6.0×	Low (risky)
Profitability					
Operating margin	$\frac{\text{Operating income (EBIT)}}{\text{Sales}}$	$\frac{\$278}{\$3,000}$	= 9.3%	10.0%	Low
Profit margin	$\frac{\text{Net income}}{\text{Sales}}$	$\frac{\$146.3}{\$3,000}$	= 4.9%	6.0%	Poor
Return on total assets (ROA)	$\frac{\text{Net income}}{\text{Total assets}}$	$\frac{\$146.3}{\$2,000}$	= 7.3%	10.8%	Poor
Return on common equity (ROE)	$\frac{\text{Net income}}{\text{Common equity}}$	$\frac{\$146.3}{\$940}$	= 15.6%	18.7%	Poor
Return on invested capital (ROIC)	$\frac{\text{EBIT}(1 - \text{T})}{\text{Total invested capital}}$	$\frac{\$208.5}{\$1,800}$	= 11.6%	13.2%	Poor
Basic earning power (BEP)	$\frac{\text{Earnings before interest and taxes (EBIT)}}{\text{Total assets}}$	$\frac{\$278}{\$2,000}$	= 13.9%	18.0%	Poor
Market Value					
Price/Earnings (P/E)	$\frac{\text{Price per share}}{\text{Earnings per share}}$	$\frac{\$23.06}{\$1.95}$	= 11.8×	13.6×	Low
Market/Book (M/B)	$\frac{\text{Market price per share}}{\text{Book value per share}}$	$\frac{\$23.06}{\$12.53}$	= 1.8×	2.6×	Low
EV/EBITDA	$\frac{\text{Enterprise value}}{\text{EBITDA}}$	$\frac{\$2,579.5}{\$378}$	= 6.8×	9.2×	Low

The benchmarking setup makes it easy for Allied's management to see exactly where it stands relative to the competition. As the data show, Allied is near the bottom of its benchmark group relative to its profit margin, so it has lots of room for improvement. Other ratios are analyzed similarly.

Comparative ratios are available from a number of sources, including both Yahoo! Finance and MSN Money. Useful ratios are also compiled by Value Line, Dun and Bradstreet (D&B), and the Risk Management Association, which is the national association of bank loan officers. Also, financial statement data for thousands of publicly owned corporations are available on other Internet sites, and as brokerage houses, banks, and other financial institutions have access to these

TABLE 4.3 Key Financial Ratios for Selected Industries[a]

Industry Name	Current Ratio	Inventory Turnover[b]	Total Assets Turnover	LT Debt/LT Capital[c]	Net Profit Margin	Return on Assets	Return on Equity	P/E Ratio	EV/EBITDA[d]
Aerospace/Defense	1.27	2.73	0.88	56.90%	7.83%	6.91%	48.21%	28.25	13.96
Apparel stores	1.58	5.09	2.34	40.83	7.20	16.81	52.76	26.74	10.97
Auto manufacturing—major	1.05	9.79	0.64	42.53	5.22	3.33	10.60	10.87	10.62
Beverage (soft drink)	1.37	7.56	0.60	63.50	11.43	6.84	31.06	45.66	17.92
Electronics—diversified	2.17	4.65	0.59	27.54	13.96	8.20	16.04	39.84	13.16
Food wholesalers	1.42	14.53	3.11	75.06	1.95	6.06	39.19	24.33	11.63
Grocery stores	0.85	13.44	3.23	67.11	1.32	4.26	23.72	13.21	7.16
Health services—specialized	1.45	8.61	0.96	81.41	5.90	5.65	45.05	38.02	8.24
Lodging	0.64	6.88	0.77	68.35	5.51	4.24	21.04	28.01	13.37
Newspapers	1.22	10.13	0.75	33.77	6.13	4.63	11.84	20.20	8.02
Paper and paper products	1.43	6.38	0.71	63.64	4.81	3.43	16.92	17.64	8.90
Railroad	0.98	7.56	0.35	44.75	21.75	7.61	21.64	8.67	11.56
Restaurant	1.18	23.38	0.87	101.46	21.41	18.54	−17,557.55	24.33	13.84
Retail (department stores)	1.28	2.68	1.23	53.27	2.71	3.34	14.37	15.34	9.47
Scientific and technical instruments	1.41	4.56	0.42	39.39	11.30	4.71	9.87	43.86	11.66
Sporting goods	0.84	21.94	0.46	31.03	18.14	8.30	15.92	32.68	11.68
Steel and iron	1.48	5.01	0.81	21.88	5.18	4.20	8.78	11.49	8.44
Tobacco (cigarettes)	1.05	1.57	0.57	103.50	45.55	25.90	−1,149.89	5.77	15.31

Notes:

[a]The ratios presented are averages for each industry. Ratios for the individual companies are also available.

[b]The inventory turnover ratio in this table is calculated as the company's latest 12 months of cost of sales divided by the average of its inventory for the last quarter and the comparable year earlier quarter.

[c]LT debt/LT capital is calculated as LT debt/(LT debt + Equity) by using MSN's Debt/Equity ratio as follows:

$$\frac{D/E}{(1 + D/E)}$$

[d]Information was obtained from NYU Stern School of Business. Data current as of January 2018, pages.stern.nyu.edu/~adamodar/New_Home_Page/datafile/vebitda.html.

Sources: Data for all ratios except enterprise value multiples obtained from MSN Money Analysis (www.msn.com/en-us/money/markets/), April 9, 2018; and enterprise value multiples obtained from Aswath Damodaran, NYU Stern School of Business, January 2018.

data, security analysts can and do generate comparative ratios tailored to their specific needs.

Each of the data-supplying organizations uses a somewhat different set of ratios designed for its own purposes. For example, D&B deals mainly with small firms, many of which are proprietorships, and it sells its services primarily to banks and other lenders. Therefore, D&B is concerned largely with the creditor's viewpoint, and its ratios emphasize current assets and liabilities, not market value ratios. So, when you select a comparative data source, you should be sure that your emphasis is similar to that of the agency whose ratios you plan to use. Additionally, there are often definitional differences in the ratios presented by different sources, so before using a source, be sure to verify the exact definitions of the ratios to ensure consistency with your own work.

4-9C TREND ANALYSIS

As a final comparison, Allied compares its ratios to its own past levels. It is important to analyze trends in ratios as well as their absolute levels, for trends give clues as to whether a firm's financial condition is likely to improve or to deteriorate. To

FIGURE 4.1 Rate of Return on Common Equity, 2015–2019

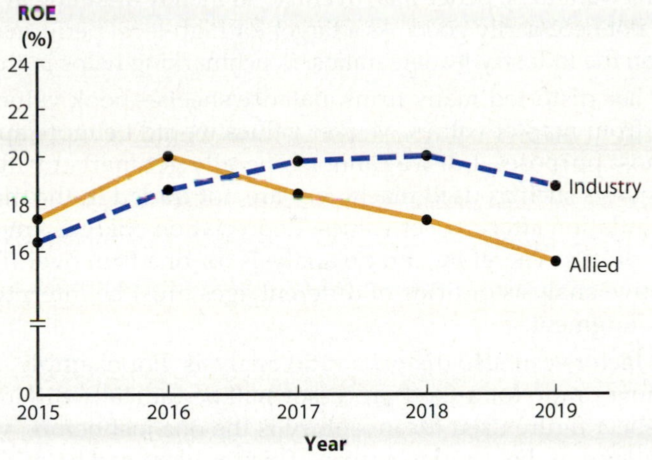

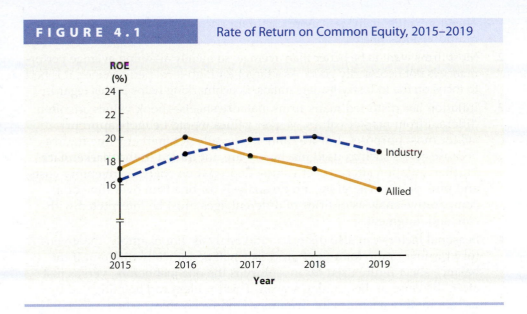

do a **trend analysis**, simply plot a ratio over time, as shown in Figure 4.1. This graph shows that Allied's ROE has been declining since 2016 even though the industry average has been relatively stable. All the other ratios could be analyzed similarly, and such an analysis can be quite useful in gaining insights as to why the ROE behaved as it did.

Trend Analysis
An analysis of a firm's financial ratios over time; used to estimate the likelihood of improvement or deterioration in its financial condition.

Self*Test*

Why might railroads have such low total assets turnovers and food wholesalers and grocery stores such high turnovers?

If competition causes all companies to have similar ROEs in the long run, would companies with high turnovers tend to have high or low profit margins? Explain your answer.

Why are comparative ratio analyses useful?

How does one do a trend analysis?

What important information does a trend analysis provide?

4-10 Uses and Limitations of Ratios

As noted earlier, ratio analysis is used by three main groups: (1) *managers,* who use ratios to help analyze, control, and thus improve their firms' operations; (2) *credit analysts,* including bank loan officers and bond rating analysts, who analyze ratios to help judge a company's ability to repay its debts; and (3) *stock analysts,* who are interested in a company's efficiency, risk, and growth prospects. In later chapters, we will look more closely at the basic factors that underlie each ratio. Note, though, that while ratio analysis can provide useful information concerning a company's operations and financial condition, it does have limitations. Some potential problems are listed here:

1. Many firms have divisions that operate in different industries; for such companies, it is difficult to develop a meaningful set of industry averages.

*To find information about a company quickly, link to **reuters.com/finance**. You can enter the company name or ticker symbol at the search symbol (on the top right of the screen) to find company profiles and snapshots, and stock price quotes, as well as share information, key ratios, and comparative ratios.*

Therefore, ratio analysis is more useful for narrowly focused firms than for multidivisional ones.

2. Most firms want to be better than average, so merely attaining average performance is not necessarily good. As a target for high-level performance, it is best to focus on the industry leaders' ratios. Benchmarking helps in this regard.
3. Inflation has distorted many firms' balance sheets—book values are often different from market values. Market values would be more appropriate for most purposes, but we cannot generally get market value figures because assets such as used machinery are not traded in the marketplace. Further, inflation affects asset values, depreciation charges, inventory costs, and thus profits. Therefore, a ratio analysis for one firm over time or a comparative analysis of firms of different ages must be interpreted with care and judgment.
4. Seasonal factors can also distort a ratio analysis. For example, the inventory turnover ratio for a food processor will be radically different if the balance sheet figure used for inventory is the one just before, versus just after, the close of the canning season. This problem can be mitigated by using monthly averages for inventory (and receivables) when calculating turnover ratios.

"Window Dressing" Techniques
Techniques employed by firms to make their financial statements look better than they really are.

5. Firms can employ **"window dressing" techniques** to improve their financial statements. To illustrate, people tend to think that larger hedge funds got large because their high returns attracted many investors. However, we learned in 2007 that some funds simply borrowed and invested money to increase their apparent size. One fund, Wharton Asset Management, reported $2 billion "under management," but it had actually attracted less than $100 million of investors' capital.
6. Different accounting practices can distort comparisons. As noted earlier, inventory valuation and depreciation methods can affect financial statements and thus distort comparisons among firms. Also, in the past, it has sometimes been hard to compare firms that purchase their equipment (often with debt) to those that lease their equipment, since leased assets have often not appeared on the balance sheet. Consequently, firms with leased assets tended to have both lower assets and lower reported debt levels, both of which can distort comparisons. However, the accounting profession has taken steps to reduce this problem. It recently added a new guideline (ASC 842), which starting in 2019 will eliminate off-balance sheet financing for long-term leases.
7. It is difficult to generalize about whether a particular ratio is "good" or "bad." For example, a high current ratio may indicate a strong liquidity position, which is good, but it can also indicate excessive cash, which is bad because excess cash in the bank is a nonearning asset. Similarly, a high fixed assets turnover ratio may indicate that the firm uses its assets efficiently, but it could also indicate that the firm is short of cash and cannot afford to make needed fixed asset investments.
8. Firms often have some ratios that look "good" and others that look "bad," making it difficult to tell whether the company is, on balance, strong or weak. To deal with this problem, banks and other lending organizations often use statistical procedures to analyze the *net effects* of a set of ratios and to classify firms according to their probability of getting into financial trouble.[21]

---

[21]The technique used is discriminant analysis. The seminal work on this subject was undertaken by Edward I. Altman, "Financial Ratios, Discriminant Analysis, and the Prediction of Corporate Bankruptcy," *Journal of Finance*, vol. 23, no. 4 (September 1968), pp. 589–609.

LOOKING FOR WARNING SIGNS WITHIN THE FINANCIAL STATEMENTS

Financial scandals have spurred a renewed interest in financial accounting, and analysts now scour companies' financial statements to see if trouble is lurking. This renewed interest has led to a list of red flags to consider when reviewing a company's financial statements. For example, after conferring with New York University accounting professor Baruch Lev, *Fortune* magazine's Shawn Tully identified the following warning signs:

- Year after year a company reports restructuring charges and/or write-downs. This practice raises concerns because companies can use write-downs to mask operating expenses, which results in overstated earnings.
- A company's earnings have been propped up through a series of acquisitions. Acquisitions can increase earnings if the acquiring company has a higher P/E ratio than the acquired firm, but such "growth" cannot be sustained over the long run.
- A company depreciates its assets more slowly than the industry average. Lower depreciation boosts current earnings, but again this cannot be sustained because eventually depreciation must be recognized.
- A company routinely has high earnings but low cash flow. As Tully points out, this warning sign would have exposed Enron's problems. In the second quarter of 2001 (a few months before its problems began to unfold), Enron reported earnings of $423 million versus a cash flow of minus $527 million.

Along similar lines, after consulting with various professionals, Ellen Simon of the *Newark Star Ledger* came up with her list of red flags:

- You wouldn't buy the stock at today's price.
- You don't really understand the company's financial statements.
- The company is in a business that lends itself to "creative accounting."
- The company keeps taking nonrecurring charges.
- Accounts receivable and inventory are increasing faster than sales revenues.
- The company's insiders are selling their stock.
- The company is making aggressive acquisitions, especially in unrelated fields.

There is some overlap between these two lists. Also, none of these items automatically means there is something wrong with the company—instead, the items should be viewed as warning signs that cause you to take a closer look at the company' performance before making an investment.

We see then that ratio analysis is useful, but analysts should be aware of the problems just listed and make adjustments as necessary. Ratio analysis conducted in a mechanical, unthinking manner is dangerous, but used intelligently and with good judgment, it can provide useful insights into firms' operations. Your judgment in interpreting ratios is bound to be weak at this point, but it will improve as you go through the remainder of the book.

Self*Test*

List three types of users of ratio analysis. Would the different users emphasize the same or different types of ratios? Explain.

List several potential difficulties with ratio analysis.

4-11 Looking Beyond the Numbers

Working through this chapter should increase your ability to understand and interpret financial statements. This is critically important for anyone making business decisions or forecasting stock prices. However, sound financial analysis involves more than just numbers—good analysis requires that certain qualitative factors also be considered. These factors, as summarized by the American Association of Individual Investors (AAII), include the following:

Students might want to refer to AAII's educational website at ***aaii.com****. The site provides information on investing basics, financial planning, and portfolio management, so that individuals can manage their own assets more effectively.*

1. Are the company's revenues tied to one key customer? If so, the company's performance may decline dramatically if that customer goes elsewhere. On the other hand, if the customer has no alternative to the company's products, this might actually stabilize sales.
2. To what extent are the company's revenues tied to one key product? Firms that focus on a single product are often efficient, but a lack of diversification also increases risk because having revenues from several products stabilizes profits and cash flows in a volatile world.
3. To what extent does the company rely on a single supplier? Depending on a single supplier may lead to an unanticipated shortage and a hit to sales and profits.
4. What percentage of the company's business is generated overseas? Companies with a large percentage of overseas business are often able to realize higher growth and larger profit margins. However, overseas operations may expose the firm to political risks and exchange rate problems.
5. How much competition does the firm face? Increases in competition tend to lower prices and profit margins; so when forecasting future performance, it is important to assess the likely actions of current competitors and the entry of new ones.
6. Is it necessary for the company to continually invest in research and development? If so, its future prospects will depend critically on the success of new products in the pipeline. For example, investors in a pharmaceutical company want to know whether the company has a strong pipeline of potential blockbuster drugs and whether those products are doing well in the required tests.
7. Are changes in laws and regulations likely to have important implications for the firm? For example, when the future of electric utilities is forecasted, it is crucial to factor in the effects of proposed regulations affecting the use of coal, nuclear, and gas-fired plants.

As a good illustration of the need to look beyond the numbers, consider the recent rise of Netflix. In early 2013, its stock price was right around $100 a share. Two years later in late February 2015, its shares were trading at $483. In fact, its share price continued to soar, so management split the shares 7-to-1 in July 2015. As of early April 2018, Netflix stock was around $289 per share—having increased in value 319 percent during the last 3 years. Although Netflix's financial statements have improved over time, the rapid improvement in the company's stock price is mostly due to dramatic positive shifts in the market's expectations regarding its future prospects. Investors have been impressed with the company's ability to successfully take advantage of changing technology, as an increased number of households have used Netflix to access movies directly through streaming video. Netflix has also greatly benefited from the creation of its own content. At the same time, Netflix's future success is far from guaranteed. The company continues to confront (and hopefully take advantage of) ever-changing technology and stiff competition from on-demand offerings from cable companies and from other sources, such as Apple's iTunes. It will be interesting for both consumers and Netflix's shareholders to see how this plays out in the years ahead.

Self*Test*

What are some qualitative factors that analysts should consider when evaluating a company's likely future financial performance?

TYING IT ALL TOGETHER

In the last chapter, we discussed the key financial statements; in this chapter, we described how ratios are used to analyze the statements to identify weaknesses that need to be strengthened to maximize the stock price. Ratios are grouped into five categories:

- **Liquidity**
- **Asset management**
- **Debt management**
- **Profitability**
- **Market value**

The firm's ratios are compared with averages for its industry and with the leading firms in the industry (benchmarking), and these comparisons are used to help formulate policies that will lead to improved future performance. Similarly, the firm's own ratios can be analyzed over time to see if its financial situation is getting better or worse (trend analysis).

The single most important ratio over which management has control is the ROE—the other ratios are also important, but mainly because they affect the ROE. One tool used to show how ROE is determined is the DuPont equation: ROE = Profit margin × Total assets turnover × Equity multiplier. If the firm's ROE is below the industry average and that of the benchmark companies, a DuPont analysis can help identify problem areas that should be strengthened. In later chapters, we consider specific actions that can be taken to improve ROE and thus a firm's stock price. One closing note: Although ratio analysis is useful, it must be applied with care and good judgment. Actions taken to improve one ratio can have negative effects on other ratios. For example, it might be possible to improve the ROE by using more debt, but the risk of the additional debt may lead to a decrease in the P/E ratio and thus in the firm's stock price. Quantitative analysis such as ratio analysis can be useful, but thinking through the results is even more important.

Self-Test Questions And Problems

(Solutions Appear in Appendix A)

ST-1 **KEY TERMS** Define each of the following terms:

a. Liquid asset
b. Liquidity ratios: current ratio; quick (acid test) ratio
c. Asset management ratios: inventory turnover ratio; days sales outstanding (DSO); fixed assets turnover ratio; total assets turnover ratio
d. Debt management ratios: total debt to total capital; times-interest-earned (TIE) ratio
e. Profitability ratios: operating margin; profit margin; return on total assets (ROA); return on common equity (ROE); return on invested capital (ROIC); basic earning power (BEP) ratio
f. Market value ratios: price/earnings (P/E) ratio; market/book (M/B) ratio; enterprise value/EBITDA ratio

g. DuPont equation; benchmarking; trend analysis
h. "Window dressing" techniques

ST-2 **TOTAL DEBT TO TOTAL CAPITAL** Last year K. Billingsworth & Co. had earnings per share of \$4 and dividends per share of \$2. Total retained earnings increased by \$12 million during the year, while book value per share at year-end was \$40. Billingsworth has no preferred stock, and no new common stock was issued during the year. If its year-end total debt was \$120 million, what was the company's year-end total debt to total capital ratio?

ST-3 **RATIO ANALYSIS** The following data apply to A.L. Kaiser & Company (millions of dollars):

Cash and equivalents	\$ 100.00
Fixed assets	283.50
Sales	1,000.00
Net income	50.00
Current liabilities	105.50
Notes payable to bank	20.00
Current ratio	3.00×
DSO[a]	40.55 days
ROE	12.00%

[a]This calculation is based on a 365-day year.

Kaiser has no preferred stock—only common equity, current liabilities, and long-term debt.

a. Find Kaiser's (1) accounts receivable, (2) current assets, (3) total assets, (4) ROA, (5) common equity, (6) quick ratio, and (7) long-term debt.
b. In part a, you should have found that Kaiser's accounts receivable (A/R) = \$111.1 million. If Kaiser could reduce its DSO from 40.55 days to 30.4 days while holding other things constant, how much cash would it generate? If this cash were used to buy back common stock (at book value), thus reducing common equity, how would this affect (1) the ROE, (2) the ROA, and (3) the total debt/total capital ratio?

Questions

4-1 Financial ratio analysis is conducted by three main groups of analysts: credit analysts, stock analysts, and managers. What is the primary emphasis of each group, and how would that emphasis affect the ratios on which they focus?

4-2 Why would the inventory turnover ratio be more important for someone analyzing a grocery store chain than an insurance company?

4-3 Over the past year, M.D. Ryngaert & Co. had an increase in its current ratio and a decline in its total assets turnover ratio. However, the company's sales, cash and equivalents, DSO, and fixed assets turnover ratio remained constant. What balance sheet accounts must have changed to produce the indicated changes?

4-4 Profit margins and turnover ratios vary from one industry to another. What differences would you expect to find between the turnover ratios, profit margins, and DuPont equations for a grocery chain and a steel company?

4-5 How does inflation distort ratio analysis comparisons for one company over time (trend analysis) and for different companies that are being compared? Are only balance sheet items or both balance sheet and income statement items affected?

4-6 If a firm's ROE is low and management wants to improve it, explain how using more debt might help.

4-7 Give some examples that illustrate how (a) seasonal factors and (b) different growth rates might distort a comparative ratio analysis. How might these problems be alleviated?

4-8 Why is it sometimes misleading to compare a company's financial ratios with those of other firms that operate in the same industry?

4-9 Suppose you were comparing a discount merchandiser with a high-end merchandiser. Suppose further that both companies had identical ROEs. If you applied the DuPont equation to both firms, would you expect the three components to be the same for each company? If not, explain what balance sheet and income statement items might lead to the component differences.

4-10 Refer to an online finance source such as Yahoo! Finance or Google Finance to look up the P/E ratios for Alphabet Inc. (the parent company of Google), and Walmart. Which company has the higher P/E ratio? What factors could explain this?

4-11 Differentiate between ROE and ROIC.

4-12 Indicate the effects of the transactions listed in the following table on total current assets, current ratio, and net income. Use (+) to indicate an increase, (−) to indicate a decrease, and (0) to indicate either no effect or an indeterminate effect. Be prepared to state any necessary assumptions and assume an initial current ratio of more than 1.0. (Note: A good accounting background is necessary to answer some of these questions; if yours is not strong, answer the questions you can.)

		Total Current Assets	Current Ratio	Effect on Net Income
a.	Cash is acquired through issuance of additional common stock.	____	____	____
b.	Merchandise is sold for cash.	____	____	____
c.	Federal income tax due for the previous year is paid.	____	____	____
d.	A fixed asset is sold for less than book value.	____	____	____
e.	A fixed asset is sold for more than book value.	____	____	____
f.	Merchandise is sold on credit.	____	____	____
g.	Payment is made to trade creditors for previous purchases.	____	____	____
h.	A cash dividend is declared and paid.	____	____	____
i.	Cash is obtained through short-term bank loans.	____	____	____
j.	Short-term notes receivable are sold at a discount.	____	____	____
k.	Marketable securities are sold below cost.	____	____	____
l.	Advances are made to employees.	____	____	____
m.	Current operating expenses are paid.	____	____	____
n.	Short-term promissory notes are issued to trade creditors in exchange for past due accounts payable.	____	____	____
o.	10-year notes are issued to pay off accounts payable.	____	____	____
p.	A fully depreciated asset is retired.	____	____	____
q.	Accounts receivable are collected.	____	____	____
r.	Equipment is purchased with short-term notes.	____	____	____
s.	Merchandise is purchased on credit.	____	____	____
t.	The estimated taxes payable are increased.	____	____	____

Problems

Easy Problems 1-6

4-1 **DAYS SALES OUTSTANDING** Baxley Brothers has a DSO of 23 days, and its annual sales are $3,650,000. What is its accounts receivable balance? Assume that it uses a 365-day year.

4-2 **DEBT TO CAPITAL RATIO** Kaye's Kitchenware has a market/book ratio equal to 1. Its stock price is $12 per share and it has 4.8 million shares outstanding. The firm's total capital is $110 million and it finances with only debt and common equity. What is its debt-to-capital ratio?

4-3 **DuPONT ANALYSIS** Henderson's Hardware has an ROA of 11%, a 6% profit margin, and an ROE of 23%. What is its total assets turnover? What is its equity multiplier?

4-4 **MARKET/BOOK AND EV/EBITDA RATIOS** Edelman Engines has $17 billion in total assets—of which cash and equivalents total $100 million. Its balance sheet shows $1.7 billion in current liabilities—of which the notes payable balance totals $1 billion. The firm also has $10.2 billion in long-term debt and $5.1 billion in common equity. It has 300 million shares of common stock outstanding, and its stock price is $20 per share. The firm's EBITDA totals $1.368 billion. Assume the firm's debt is priced at par, so the market value of its debt equals its book value. What are Edelman's market/book and its EV/EBITDA ratios?

4-5 **PRICE/EARNINGS RATIO** A company has an EPS of $2.40, a book value per share of $21.84, and a market/book ratio of 2.7×. What is its P/E ratio?

4-6 **DuPONT AND ROE** A firm has a profit margin of 3% and an equity multiplier of 1.9. Its sales are $150 million, and it has total assets of $60 million. What is its ROE?

Intermediate Problems 7-19

4-7 **ROE AND ROIC** Baker Industries's net income is $24,000, its interest expense is $5,000, and its tax rate is 25%. Its notes payable equals $27,000, long-term debt equals $75,000, and common equity equals $250,000. The firm finances with only debt and common equity, so it has no preferred stock. What are the firm's ROE and ROIC?

4-8 **DuPONT AND NET INCOME** Precious Metal Mining has $17 million in sales, its ROE is 17%, and its total assets turnover is 3.2×. Common equity on the firm's balance sheet is 50% of its total assets. What is its net income?

4-9 **BEP, ROE, AND ROIC** Broward Manufacturing recently reported the following information:

Net income	$615,000
ROA	10%
Interest expense	$202,950
Accounts payable and accruals	$950,000

Broward's tax rate is 25%. Broward finances with only debt and common equity, so it has no preferred stock. 40% of its total invested capital is debt, and 60% of its total invested capital is common equity. Calculate its basic earning power (BEP), its return on equity (ROE), and its return on invested capital (ROIC).

4-10 **M/B, SHARE PRICE, AND EV/EBITDA** You are given the following information: Stockholders' equity as reported on the firm's balance sheet = $6.5 billion, price/earnings ratio = 9, common shares outstanding = 180 million, and market/book ratio = 2.0. The firm's market value of total debt is $7 billion, the firm has cash and equivalents totaling $250 million, and the firm's EBITDA equals $2 billion. What is the price of a share of the company's common stock? What is the firm's EV/EBITDA?

4-11 **RATIO CALCULATIONS** Assume the following relationships for the Caulder Corp.:

Sales/Total assets	1.3×
Return on assets (ROA)	4.0%
Return on equity (ROE)	8.0%

Calculate Caulder's profit margin and debt-to-capital ratio assuming the firm uses only debt and common equity, so total assets equal total invested capital.

4-12 **RATIO CALCULATIONS** Thomson Trucking has $12 billion in assets, and its tax rate is 25%. Its basic earning power (BEP) ratio is 10%, and its return on assets (ROA) is 5.25%. What is its times-interest-earned (TIE) ratio?

4-13 **TIE AND ROIC RATIOS** The W.C. Pruett Corp. has $600,000 of interest-bearing debt outstanding, and it pays an annual interest rate of 7%. In addition, it has $600,000 of common stock on its balance sheet. It finances with only debt and common equity, so it has no preferred stock. Its annual sales are $2.7 million, its average tax rate is 25%, and its profit margin is 7%. What are its TIE ratio and its return on invested capital (ROIC)?

4-14 **RETURN ON EQUITY** Pacific Packaging's ROE last year was only 5%, but its management has developed a new operating plan that calls for a debt-to-capital ratio of 40%, which will result in annual interest charges of $561,000. The firm has no plans to use preferred stock and total assets equal total invested capital. Management projects an EBIT of $1,870,000 on sales of $17,000,000, and it expects to have a total assets turnover ratio of 2.1. Under these conditions, the tax rate will be 25%. If the changes are made, what will be the company's return on equity?

4-15 **RETURN ON EQUITY AND QUICK RATIO** Lloyd Inc. has sales of $200,000, a net income of $15,000, and the following balance sheet:

Cash	$ 10,000	Accounts payable	$ 30,000
Receivables	50,000	Notes payable to bank	20,000
Inventories	150,000	Total current liabilities	$ 50,000
Total current assets	$ 210,000	Long-term debt	50,000
Net fixed assets	90,000	Common equity	200,000
Total assets	$ 300,000	Total liabilities and equity	$300,000

The new owner thinks that inventories are excessive and can be lowered to the point where the current ratio is equal to the industry average, 2.5×, without affecting sales or net income. If inventories are sold and not replaced (thus reducing the current ratio to 2.5×), if the funds generated are used to reduce common equity (stock can be repurchased at book value), and if no other changes occur, by how much will the ROE change? What will be the firm's new quick ratio?

4-16 **RETURN ON EQUITY** Commonwealth Construction (CC) needs $3 million of assets to get started, and it expects to have a basic earning power ratio of 35%. CC will own no securities, all of its income will be operating income. If it so chooses, CC can finance up to 30% of its assets with debt, which will have an 8% interest rate. If it chooses to use debt, the firm will finance using only debt and common equity, so no preferred stock will be used. Assuming a 25% tax rate on taxable income, what is the *difference* between CC's expected ROE if it finances these assets with 30% debt versus its expected ROE if it finances these assets entirely with common stock?

4-17 **CONCEPTUAL: RETURN ON EQUITY** Which of the following statements is most correct? (*Hint:* Work Problem 4-16 before answering 4-17, and consider the solution setup for 4-16 as you think about 4-17.)

a. If a firm's expected basic earning power (BEP) is constant for all of its assets and exceeds the interest rate on its debt, adding assets and financing them with debt will raise the firm's expected return on common equity (ROE).
b. The higher a firm's tax rate, the lower its BEP ratio, other things held constant.
c. The higher the interest rate on a firm's debt, the lower its BEP ratio, other things held constant.
d. The higher a firm's debt ratio, the lower its BEP ratio, other things held constant.
e. Statement a is false, but statements b, c, and d are true.

4-18 **TIE RATIO** MPI Incorporated has $6 billion in assets, and its tax rate is 25%. Its basic earning power (BEP) ratio is 11%, and its return on assets (ROA) is 6%. What is MPI's times-interest-earned (TIE) ratio?

4-19 **CURRENT RATIO** The Stewart Company has $2,392,500 in current assets and $1,076,625 in current liabilities. Its initial inventory level is $526,350, and it will raise funds as additional notes payable and use them to increase inventory. How much can its short-term debt (notes payable) increase without pushing its current ratio below 2.0?

Challenging Problems 20–24

4-20 **DSO AND ACCOUNTS RECEIVABLE** Ingraham Inc. currently has $205,000 in accounts receivable, and its days sales outstanding (DSO) is 71 days. It wants to reduce its DSO to 20 days by pressuring more of its customers to pay their bills on time. If this policy is adopted, the company's average sales will fall by 15%. What will be the level of accounts receivable following the change? Assume a 365-day year.

4-21 **P/E AND STOCK PRICE** Ferrell Inc. recently reported net income of $8 million. It has 540,000 shares of common stock, which currently trades at $21 a share. Ferrell continues to expand and anticipates that 1 year from now its net income will be $13.2 million. Over the next year, it also anticipates issuing an additional 81,000 shares of stock so that 1 year from now it will have 621,000 shares of common stock. Assuming Ferrell's price/earnings ratio remains at its current level, what will be its stock price 1 year from now?

4-22 **BALANCE SHEET ANALYSIS** Complete the balance sheet and sales information using the following financial data:

Total assets turnover: 1.5×
Days sales outstanding: 36.5 days[a]
Inventory turnover ratio: 5×
Fixed assets turnover: 3.0×
Current ratio: 2.0×
Gross profit margin on sales: (Sales − Cost of goods sold)/Sales = 25%

[a]Calculation is based on a 365-day year.

Balance Sheet

Cash		Current liabilities	
Accounts receivable		Long-term debt	60,000
Inventories		Common stock	
Fixed assets		Retained earnings	97,500
Total assets	$300,000	Total liabilities and equity	
Sales		Cost of goods sold	

4-23 **RATIO ANALYSIS** Data for Barry Computer Co. and its industry averages follow. The firm's debt is priced at par, so the market value of its debt equals its book value. Since dollars are in thousands, number of shares are shown in thousands too.

a. Calculate the indicated ratios for Barry.
b. Construct the DuPont equation for both Barry and the industry.
c. Outline Barry's strengths and weaknesses as revealed by your analysis.
d. Suppose Barry had doubled its sales as well as its inventories, accounts receivable, and common equity during 2019. How would that information affect the validity of your ratio analysis? (*Hint:* Think about averages and the effects of rapid growth on ratios if averages are not used. No calculations are needed.)

Barry Computer Company:
Balance Sheet as of December 31, 2019 (in Thousands)

Cash	$ 77,500	Accounts payable	$129,000
Receivables	336,000	Other current liabilities	117,000
Inventories	241,500	Notes payable to bank	84,000
Total current assets	$ 655,000	Total current liabilities	$330,000
		Long-term debt	256,500
Net fixed assets	292,500	Common equity (36,100 shares)	361,000
Total assets	$ 947,500	Total liabilities and equity	$947,500

Barry Computer Company: Income Statement for Year Ended December 31, 2019 (in Thousands)

Sales		$1,607,500
Cost of goods sold		
Materials	$717,000	
Labor	453,000	
Heat, light, and power	68,000	
Indirect labor	113,000	
Depreciation	41,500	1,392,500
Gross profit		$ 215,000
Selling expenses		115,000
General and administrative expenses		30,000
Earnings before interest and taxes (EBIT)		$ 70,000
Interest expense		21,000
Earnings before taxes (EBT)		$ 49,000
Federal and state income taxes (25%)		12,250
Net income		$ 36,750
Earnings per share		$ 1.018
Price per share on December 31, 2019		$ 12.00

Ratio	Barry	Industry Average
Current	____	2.0×
Quick	____	1.3×
Days sales outstanding[a]	____	35 days
Inventory turnover	____	6.7×
Total assets turnover	____	3.0×
Profit margin	____	1.6%
ROA	____	4.8%
ROE	____	12.1%
ROIC	____	9.4%
TIE	____	3.5×
Debt/Total capital	____	47.0%
M/B	____	4.22×
P/E	____	13.27
EV/EBITDA	____	9.14

[a]Calculation is based on a 365-day year.

4-24 **DuPONT ANALYSIS** A firm has been experiencing low profitability in recent years. Perform an analysis of the firm's financial position using the DuPont equation. The firm has no lease payments but has a $2 million sinking fund payment on its debt. The most recent industry average ratios and the firm's financial statements are as follows:

Industry Average Ratios

Current ratio	3×	Fixed assets turnover	6×
Debt-to-capital ratio	20%	Total assets turnover	3×
Times interest earned	7×	Profit margin	3.75%
EBITDA coverage	9×	Return on total assets	11.25%
Inventory turnover	10×	Return on common equity	16.10%
Days sales outstanding[a]	24 days	Return on invested capital	14.40%

[a]Calculation is based on a 365-day year.

Balance Sheet as of December 31, 2019 (millions of dollars)

Cash and equivalents	$ 78	Accounts payable	$ 45
Accounts receivable	66	Other current liabilities	11
Inventories	159	Notes payable	29
Total current assets	$303	Total current liabilities	$ 85
		Long-term debt	50
		Total liabilities	$135
Gross fixed assets	225	Common stock	114
Less depreciation	78	Retained earnings	201
Net fixed assets	$147	Total stockholders' equity	$315
Total assets	$450	Total liabilities and equity	$450

Income Statement for Year Ended December 31, 2019 (millions of dollars)

Net sales	$795.00
Cost of goods sold	660.00
Gross profit	$135.00
Selling expenses	73.50
EBITDA	$ 61.50
Depreciation expense	12.00
Earnings before interest and taxes (EBIT)	$ 49.50
Interest expense	4.50
Earnings before taxes (EBT)	$ 45.00
Taxes (25%)	11.25
Net income	$ 33.75

a. Calculate the ratios you think would be useful in this analysis.
b. Construct a DuPont equation, and compare the company's ratios to the industry average ratios.
c. Do the balance sheet accounts or the income statement figures seem to be primarily responsible for the low profits?
d. Which specific accounts seem to be most out of line relative to other firms in the industry?
e. If the firm had a pronounced seasonal sales pattern or if it grew rapidly during the year, how might that affect the validity of your ratio analysis? How might you correct for such potential problems?

Comprehensive/Spreadsheet Problem

4-25 **RATIO ANALYSIS** The Corrigan Corporation's 2018 and 2019 financial statements follow, along with some industry average ratios. Corrigan is exempt from the interest deduction limitation because its average gross revenues for the prior 3 years was less than $25 million. So 100% of its interest expense is deductible.

a. Assess Corrigan's liquidity position, and determine how it compares with peers and how the liquidity position has changed over time.
b. Assess Corrigan's asset management position, and determine how it compares with peers and how its asset management efficiency has changed over time.
c. Assess Corrigan's debt management position, and determine how it compares with peers and how its debt management has changed over time.
d. Assess Corrigan's profitability ratios, and determine how they compare with peers and how its profitability position has changed over time.
e. Assess Corrigan's market value ratios, and determine how its valuation compares with peers and how it has changed over time. Assume the firm's debt is priced at par, so the market value of its debt equals its book value.

f. Calculate Corrigan's ROE as well as the industry average ROE, using the DuPont equation. From this analysis, how does Corrigan's financial position compare with the industry average numbers?

g. What do you think would happen to its ratios if the company initiated cost-cutting measures that allowed it to hold lower levels of inventory and substantially decreased the cost of goods sold? No calculations are necessary. Think about which ratios would be affected by changes in these two accounts.

Corrigan Corporation: Balance Sheets as of December 31

	2019	2018
Cash	$ 72,000	$ 65,000
Accounts receivable	439,000	328,000
Inventories	894,000	813,000
Total current assets	$ 1,405,000	$ 1,206,000
Land and building	238,000	271,000
Machinery	132,000	133,000
Other fixed assets	61,000	57,000
Total assets	$ 1,836,000	$ 1,667,000
Accounts payable	$ 80,000	$ 72,708
Accrued liabilities	45,010	40,880
Notes payable	476,990	457,912
Total current liabilities	$ 602,000	$ 571,500
Long-term debt	399,688	258,898
Common stock	575,000	575,000
Retained earnings	259,312	261,602
Total liabilities and equity	$1,836,000	$ 1,667,000

Corrigan Corporation: Income Statements for Years Ending December 31

	2019	2018
Sales	$4,240,000	$ 3,635,000
Cost of goods sold	3,680,000	2,980,000
Gross operating profit	$ 560,000	$ 655,000
General administrative and selling expenses	303,320	297,550
Depreciation	159,000	154,500
EBIT	$ 97,680	$ 202,950
Interest	67,000	43,000
Earnings before taxes (EBT)	$ 30,680	$ 159,950
Taxes (25%)	7,670	39,988
Net income	$ 23,010	$ 119,963

Per-Share Data

	2019	2018
EPS	$ 1.00	$ 5.22
Cash dividends	$ 1.10	$ 0.95
Market price (average)	$12.34	$23.57
P/E ratio	12.33×	4.52×
Number of shares outstanding	23,000	23,000

Industry Financial Ratios[a]

	2019
Current ratio	2.7×
Inventory turnover[b]	7.0×
Days sales outstanding[c]	32.0 days
Fixed assets turnover[b]	13.0×
Total assets turnover[b]	2.6×
Return on assets	11.4%
Return on equity	18.2%
Return on invested capital	14.5%
Profit margin	4.4%
Debt-to-capital ratio	50.0%
P/E ratio	6.0×
M/B ratio	1.5
EV/EBITDA ratio	6.0

[a]Industry average ratios have been constant for the past 4 years.
[b]Based on year-end balance sheet figures.
[c]Calculation is based on a 365-day year.

INTEGRATED CASE

D'LEON INC., PART II

4-26 FINANCIAL STATEMENTS AND TAXES Part I of this case, presented in Chapter 3, discussed the situation of D'Leon Inc., a regional snack foods producer, after an expansion program. D'Leon had increased plant capacity and undertaken a major marketing campaign in an attempt to "go national." Thus far, sales have not been up to the forecasted level, costs have been higher than were projected, and a large loss occurred in 2019 rather than the expected profit. As a result, its managers, directors, and investors are concerned about the firm's survival.

Donna Jamison was brought in as assistant to Fred Campo, D'Leon's chairman, who had the task of getting the company back into a sound financial position. D'Leon's 2018 and 2019 balance sheets and income statements, together with projections for 2020, are given in Tables IC 4.1 and IC 4.2. Note that D'Leon is exempt from the interest deduction limitation because its average gross receipts for the prior 3 years was less than $25 million. So 100% of its interest expense is deductible. Also, many of D'Leon's assets have lives greater than 20 years and thus qualify for the alternative depreciation system (straight line) rather than the 100% bonus depreciation. In addition, Table IC 4.3 gives the company's 2018 and 2019 financial ratios, together with industry average data. The 2020 projected financial statement data represent Jamison's and Campo's best guess for 2020 results, assuming that some new financing is arranged to get the company "over the hump."

Jamison examined monthly data for 2019 (not given in the case), and she detected an improving pattern during the year. Monthly sales were rising, costs were falling, and large losses in the early months had turned to a small profit by December. Thus, the annual data look somewhat worse than final monthly data. Also, it appears to be taking longer for the advertising program to get the message out, for the new sales offices to generate sales, and for the new manufacturing facilities to operate efficiently. In other words, the lags between spending money and deriving benefits were longer than D'Leon's managers had anticipated. For these reasons, Jamison and Campo see hope for the company—provided it can survive in the short run.

Jamison must prepare an analysis of where the company is now, what it must do to regain its financial health, and what actions should be taken. Your assignment is to help her answer the following questions. Provide clear explanations, not yes or no answers.

a. Why are ratios useful? What are the five major categories of ratios?

b. Calculate D'Leon's 2020 current and quick ratios based on the projected balance sheet and income statement data. What can you say about the company's liquidity positions in 2018, in 2019, and as projected for 2020? We often think of ratios as being useful (1) to managers to help run the business, (2) to bankers for credit analysis, and (3) to stockholders for stock valuation. Would these different types of analysts have an equal interest in the company's liquidity ratios? Explain your answer.

c. Calculate the 2020 inventory turnover, days sales outstanding (DSO), fixed assets turnover, and total assets turnover. How does D'Leon's utilization of assets stack up against other firms in the industry?

d. Calculate the 2020 debt-to-capital and times-interest-earned ratios. How does D'Leon compare with the industry with respect to financial leverage? What can you conclude from these ratios?

e. Calculate the 2020 operating margin, profit margin, basic earning power (BEP), return on assets (ROA), return on equity (ROE), and return on invested capital (ROIC). What can you say about these ratios?

f. Calculate the 2020 price/earnings ratio and market/book ratio. Do these ratios indicate that investors are expected to have a high or low opinion of the company?

g. Use the DuPont equation to provide a summary and overview of D'Leon's financial condition as projected for 2020. What are the firm's major strengths and weaknesses?

h. Use the following simplified 2020 balance sheet to show, in general terms, how an improvement in the DSO would tend to affect the stock price. For example, if the company could improve its collection procedures and thereby lower its DSO from 45.6 days to the 32-day industry average without affecting sales, how would that change "ripple through" the financial statements (shown in thousands in the following table) and influence the stock price?

Accounts receivable	$ 878	Current liabilities	$ 845
Other current assets	1,802	Debt	700
Net fixed assets	817	Equity	1,952
Total assets	$3,497	Liabilities plus equity	$3,497

i. Does it appear that inventories could be adjusted? If so, how should that adjustment affect D'Leon's profitability and stock price?

j. In 2019, the company paid its suppliers much later than the due dates; also, it was not maintaining financial ratios at levels called for in its bank loan agreements. Therefore, suppliers could cut the company off, and its bank could refuse to renew the loan when it comes due in 90 days. On the basis of data provided, would you, as a credit manager, continue to sell to D'Leon on credit? (You could demand cash on delivery—that is, sell on terms of COD—but that might cause D'Leon to stop buying from your company.) Similarly, if you were the bank loan officer, would you recommend renewing the loan or demanding its repayment? Would your actions be influenced if, in early 2020, D'Leon showed you its 2020 projections along with proof that it was going to raise more than $1.2 million of new equity?

k. In hindsight, what should D'Leon have done in 2018?

l. What are some potential problems and limitations of financial ratio analysis?

m. What are some qualitative factors that analysts should consider when evaluating a company's likely future financial performance?

TABLE IC 4.1 Balance Sheets

	2020E	2019	2018
Assets			
Cash	$ 85,632	$ 7,282	$ 57,600
Accounts receivable	878,000	632,160	351,200
Inventories	1,716,480	1,287,360	715,200
Total current assets	$2,680,112	$1,926,802	$ 1,124,000
Net fixed assets	817,040	939,790	344,800
Total assets	$3,497,152	$2,866,592	$ 1,468,800
Liabilities and Equity			
Accounts payable	$ 436,800	$ 524,160	$ 145,600
Accruals	408,000	489,600	136,000
Notes payable	300,000	636,808	200,000
Total current liabilities	$1,144,800	$1,650,568	$ 481,600
Long-term debt	400,000	723,432	323,432
Common stock	1,718,986	460,000	460,000
Retained earnings	233,366	32,592	203,768
Total equity	$1,952,352	$ 492,592	$ 663,768
Total liabilities and equity	$3,497,152	$2,866,592	$ 1,468,800

Note: E indicates estimated. The 2020 data are forecasts.

TABLE IC 4.2 Income Statements

	2020E	2019	2018
Sales	$ 6,900,600	$ 6,126,796	$ 3,432,000
Cost of goods sold	5,875,992	5,528,000	2,864,000
Other expenses	550,000	519,988	358,672
Total operating costs excluding depreciation and amortization	$ 6,425,992	$ 6,047,988	$ 3,222,672
EBITDA	$ 474,608	$ 78,808	$ 209,328
Depreciation and amortization	116,960	116,960	18,900
EBIT	$ 357,648	($ 38,152)	$ 190,428
Interest expense	70,008	122,024	43,828
EBT	$ 287,640	($ 160,176)	$ 146,600
Taxes (25%)	31,866[a]	0[a]	36,650
Net income	$ 255,774	($ 160,176)	$ 109,950
EPS	$ 1.023	($ 1.602)	$ 1.100
DPS	$ 0.220	$ 0.110	$ 0.275
Book value per share	$ 7.809	$ 4.926	$ 6.638
Stock price	$ 12.17	$ 2.25	$ 8.50
Shares outstanding	250,000	100,000	100,000
Tax rate	25.00%	25.00%	25.00%
Lease payments	$ 40,000	$ 40,000	$ 40,000
Sinking fund payments	0	0	0

Note: E indicates estimated. The 2020 data are forecasts.

[a]The firm had sufficient taxable income in 2020 (the 2019 loss wasn't greater than 80% of its 2020 taxable income before the loss was deducted) to carry forward its 2019 loss in its entirety. As a result, its 2020 taxes were reduced by 0.25× the loss amount.

TABLE IC 4.3 Ratio Analysis

	2020E	2019	2018	Industry Average
Current		1.2×	2.3×	2.7×
Quick		0.4×	0.8×	1.0×
Inventory turnover		4.8×	4.8×	6.1×
Days sales outstanding (DSO)[a]		37.7	37.4	32.0
Fixed assets turnover		6.5×	10.0×	7.0×
Total assets turnover		2.1×	2.3×	2.6×
Debt-to-capital ratio		73.4%	44.1%	40.0%
TIE		−0.3×	4.3×	6.2×
Operating margin		−0.6%	5.5%	7.3%
Profit margin		−2.6%	3.2%	4.3%
Basic earning power		−1.3%	13.0%	19.1%
ROA		−5.6%	7.5%	11.2%
ROE		−32.5%	16.6%	18.2%
ROIC		−1.5%	12.0%	16.5%
Price/earnings		−1.4×	7.7×	14.2×
Market/book		0.5×	1.3×	2.4×
Book value per share		$4.93	$6.64	n.a.
EV/EBITDA		20.02	6.29	8.0

Note: E indicates estimated. The 2020 data are forecasts.

[a]Calculation is based on a 365-day year.

TAKING A CLOSER LOOK

Conducting a Financial Ratio Analysis on HP Inc.

Use online resources to work on this chapter's questions. Please note that website information changes over time, and these changes may limit your ability to answer some of these questions.

In Chapter 3, we looked at Dunkin' Brands' financial statements. In this chapter, we will use a financial Internet website, www.morningstar.com, to analyze HP Inc., a computer hardware company. Once on the website, you simply enter HP Inc.'s ticker symbol (HPQ) to obtain the financial information needed. We will also perform a trend analysis, where we evaluate changes in key ratios over time.

Through the Morningstar website, you can find the firm's financials (Income Statement, Balance Sheet, and Cash Flow) on an annual or quarterly basis for the five most recent time periods. In addition, the site contains Key Ratios (Profitability, Growth, Cash Flow, Financial Health, and Efficiency) for 10 years. We will use the Key Ratios on this site to conduct the firm's trend analysis. (At the bottom of the screen you will see that you can click "Glossary" to find definitions for the different ratios. For example, Morningstar's Financial Leverage ratio is the same as the Equity multiplier that we use in the textbook.)

Discussion Questions

1. Looking at Morningstar's Financial Health ratios, what has happened to HP's liquidity position over the past 10 years?
2. Looking at Morningstar's Financial Health ratios, what has happened to HP's financial leverage position (looking at both its financial leverage and debt/equity ratios) over the past 10 years?
3. Looking at Morningstar's Profitability ratios, what has happened to HP's profit margin (net margin %) over the past 10 years? What has happened to its return on assets (ROA) and return on equity (ROE) over the past 10 years?
4. Looking at Morningstar's Efficiency ratios, how well has it managed its assets (as measured by days sales outstanding, inventory turnover, fixed assets turnover, and total assets turnover) over the past 10 years?

Time Value of Money

CHAPTER 5

Goodluz/Shutterstock.com

Will You Be Able to Retire?

*For an interesting website that looks at global savings rates, refer to **www.gfmag.com/global-data/economic-data/916lqg-household-saving-rates**.*

Your reaction to that question is probably, "First things first! I'm worried about getting a job, not about retiring!" However, understanding the retirement situation can help you land a job because (1) this is an important issue today; (2) employers like to hire people who know what's happening in the real world; and (3) professors often test on the time value of money with problems related to saving for future purposes (including retirement).

A recent study by the Employee Benefit Research Institute suggests that many U.S. workers are not doing enough to prepare for retirement. The survey found that 47% of workers had less than $25,000 in savings and investments (not including the values of their homes and defined benefit plans). Equally concerning, 16% of those surveyed said they were not at all confident that they would be able to retire comfortably.[1] Unfortunately, there is no easy solution. In order to reach their retirement goals, many current workers will need to work longer, spend less and save more, and hopefully earn higher returns on their current savings.

Historically, many Americans have relied on Social Security as an important source of their retirement income. However, given current demographics, it is likely that this important program will need to be restructured down the road in order to maintain its viability. Although the average personal savings rate in the United States had edged up in recent years, in January 2018 it was still at a fairly low level of 3.2%.[2] In addition, the ratio of U.S.

[1]Refer to Lisa Greenwald et al., "The 2017 Retirement Confidence Survey: Many Workers Lack Retirement Confidence and Feel Stressed about Retirement Preparations," Employee Benefit Research Institute, no. 431, March 21, 2017, ebri.org/pdf/surveys/rcs/2017/IB.431.Mar17.RCS17..21Mar17.pdf.

[2]Refer to the U.S. Bureau of Economic Analysis, *Personal Saving Rate: January 1, 1959–January 1, 2018,* fred.stlouisfed.org/series/PSAVERT.

workers to retirees has steadily declined over the past half century. In 1955, there were 8.6 workers supporting each retiree, but by 1975, that number had declined to 3.2 workers for every one retiree. From 1975 through 2016, the ratio remained between 2.8 and 3.4 workers for every retiree. Current projections show this ratio significantly declining in the years ahead—the forecast is for 2.2 workers per retiree in 2035 and 2.0 workers per retiree in 2095.[3] With so few people paying into the Social Security system and so many drawing funds out, Social Security is going to be in serious trouble. In fact, for the first time since its inception, in 2010 (and 7 years ahead of schedule), Social Security was in the red—paying out more in benefits than it received in payroll tax revenues. Considering these facts, many people may have trouble maintaining a reasonable standard of living after they retire, and many of today's college students will have to support their parents.

This is an important issue for millions of Americans, but many don't know how to deal with it. Most Americans have been ignoring what is most certainly going to be a huge personal and social problem. However, if you study this chapter carefully, you can use the tools and techniques presented here to avoid the trap that has caught, and is likely to catch, so many people.

PUTTING THINGS IN PERSPECTIVE

Time value analysis has many applications, including planning for retirement, valuing stocks and bonds, setting up loan payment schedules, and making corporate decisions regarding investing in new plants and equipment. *In fact, of all financial concepts, time value of money is the single most important concept. Indeed, time value analysis is used throughout the book; so it is vital that you understand this chapter before continuing.*

You need to understand basic time value concepts, but conceptual knowledge will do you little good if you can't do the required calculations. Therefore, this chapter is heavy on calculations. Most students studying finance have a financial or scientific calculator; some also own or have access to a computer. One of these tools is necessary to work many finance problems in a reasonable length of time. However, when students begin reading this chapter, many of them don't know how to use the time value functions on their calculator or computer. If you are in that situation, you will find yourself simultaneously studying concepts and trying to learn how to use your calculator, and you will need more time to cover this chapter than you might expect.[4]

When you finish this chapter, you should be able to do the following:

- **Explain how the time value of money works and discuss why it is such an important concept in finance.**
- **Calculate the present value and future value of lump sums.**
- **Identify the different types of annuities, calculate the present value and future value of both an ordinary annuity and an annuity due, and calculate the relevant annuity payments.**

*Excellent retirement calculators are available at **www.msn.com/en-us/money/tools/retirementplanner**, **ssa.gov/retire**, and **choosetosave.org/calculators**. These calculators allow you to input hypothetical retirement savings information; the program then shows if current retirement savings will be sufficient to meet retirement needs.*

[3]Refer to the U.S. Social Security Administration, *2017 Annual Report of the Board of Trustees of the Federal Old-Age and Survivors Insurance and Federal Disability Insurance Trust Funds*, Table IV. B3, pp. 61–62.

[4]Calculator manuals tend to be long and complicated, partly because they cover a number of topics that aren't required in the basic finance course. We provide tutorials for the most commonly used calculators on the student companion site for this textbook and you can access these by going to cengage.com. The tutorials are keyed to this chapter, and they show exactly how to do the required calculations. If you don't know how to use your calculator, go to the student companion site, find the relevant tutorial, and work through it as you study the chapter.

- **Calculate the present value and future value of an uneven cash flow stream. You will use this knowledge in later chapters that show how to value common stocks and corporate projects.**
- **Explain the difference between nominal, periodic, and effective interest rates. An understanding of these concepts is necessary when comparing rates of returns on alternative investments.**
- **Discuss the basics of loan amortization and develop a loan amortization schedule that you might use when considering an auto loan or home mortgage loan.**

5-1 Time Lines

Time Line
An important tool used in time value analysis; it is a graphical representation used to show the timing of cash flows.

The first step in time value analysis is to set up a **time line**, which will help you visualize what's happening in a particular problem. As an illustration, consider the following diagram, where PV represents $100 that is on hand today, and FV is the value that will be in the account on a future date:

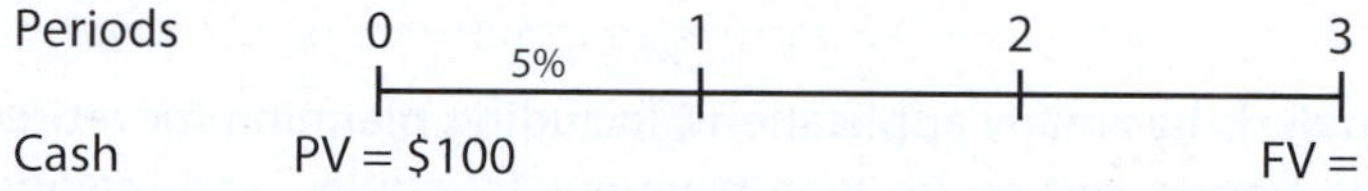

The intervals from 0 to 1, 1 to 2, and 2 to 3 are time periods such as years or months. Time 0 is today, and it is the beginning of Period 1; Time 1 is one period from today, and it is both the end of Period 1 and the beginning of Period 2; and so forth. Although the periods are often years, periods can also be quarters or months or even days. Note that each tick mark corresponds to both the *end* of one period and the *beginning* of the next one. Thus, if the periods are years, the tick mark at Time 2 represents the *end* of Year 2 and the *beginning* of Year 3.

Cash flows are shown directly below the tick marks, and the relevant interest rate is shown just above the time line. Unknown cash flows, which you are trying to find, are indicated by question marks. Here the interest rate is 5%; a single cash outflow, $100, is invested at Time 0; and the Time 3 value is an unknown inflow. In this example, cash flows occur only at Times 0 and 3, with no flows at Times 1 or 2. Note that in our example, the interest rate is constant for all three years. That condition is generally true, but if it were not, we would show different interest rates for the different periods.

Time lines are essential when you are first learning time value concepts, but even experts use them to analyze complex finance problems—and we use them throughout the book. We begin each problem by setting up a time line to illustrate the situation, after which we provide an equation that must be solved to find the answer. Then we explain how to use a regular calculator, a financial calculator, and a spreadsheet to find the answer.

Self*Test*

Do time lines deal only with years, or can other time periods be used?

Set up a time line to illustrate the following situation: You currently have $2,000 in a 3-year certificate of deposit (CD) that pays a guaranteed 4% annually.

5-2 Future Values

A dollar in hand today is worth more than a dollar to be received in the future because if you had it now, you could invest it, earn interest, and own more than a dollar in the future. The process of going to **future value (FV)** from **present value (PV)** is called **compounding**. For an illustration, refer back to our 3-year time line, and assume that you plan to deposit $100 in a bank that pays a guaranteed 5% interest each year. How much would you have at the end of Year 3? We first define some terms, and then we set up a time line to show how the future value is calculated.

Future Value (FV)
The amount to which a cash flow or series of cash flows will grow over a given period of time when compounded at a given interest rate.

Present Value (PV)
The value today of a future cash flow or series of cash flows.

Compounding
The arithmetic process of determining the final value of a cash flow or series of cash flows when compound interest is applied.

PV = Present value, or beginning amount. In our example, PV = $100.

FV_N = Future value, or ending amount, of your account after N periods. Whereas PV is the value now, or the *present value*, FV_N is the value N periods into the *future*, after the interest earned has been added to the account.

CF_t = Cash flow. Cash flows can be positive or negative. The cash flow for a particular period is often given as a subscript, CF_t, where t is the period. Thus, CF_0 = PV = the cash flow at Time 0, whereas CF_3 is the cash flow at the end of Period 3.

I = Interest rate earned per year. Sometimes a lowercase i is used. Interest earned is based on the balance at the beginning of each year, and we assume that it is paid at the end of the year. Here I = 5% or, expressed as a decimal, 0.05. Throughout this chapter, we designate the interest rate as I because that symbol (or I/YR, for interest rate per year) is used on most financial calculators. Note, though, that in later chapters, we use the symbol r to denote rates because r (for rate of return) is used more often in the finance literature. Note too that in this chapter we generally assume that interest payments are guaranteed by the U.S. government; hence, they are certain. In later chapters, we consider risky investments, where the interest rate earned might differ from its expected level.

INT = Dollars of interest earned during the year = Beginning amount × I. In our example, INT = $100(0.05) = $5.

N = Number of periods involved in the analysis. In our example, N = 3. Sometimes the number of periods is designated with a lowercase n, so both N and n indicate the number of periods involved.

We can use four different procedures to solve time value problems.[5] These methods are described in the following sections.

[5]A fifth procedure, using tables that show "interest factors," was used before financial calculators and computers became available. Now, though, calculators and spreadsheet applications such as Microsoft Excel are programmed to calculate the specific factor needed for a given problem and then to use it to find the FV. This is more efficient than using the tables. Moreover, calculators and spreadsheets can handle fractional periods and fractional interest rates, such as the FV of $100 after 3.75 years when the interest rate is 5.375%, whereas tables provide numbers only for whole periods and rates. For these reasons, tables are not used in business today; hence, we do not discuss them in the text.

5-2A STEP-BY-STEP APPROACH

The time line used to find the FV of \$100 compounded for 3 years at 5%, along with some calculations, is shown. Multiply the initial amount and each succeeding amount by $(1 + I) = (1.05)$:

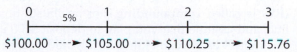

Time	0	1	2	3
	5%			
Amount at beginning of period	\$100.00 ---→	\$105.00 ---→	\$110.25 ---→	\$115.76

You start with \$100 in the account—this is shown at $t = 0$:

- You earn \$100(0.05) = \$5 of interest during the first year, so the amount at the end of Year 1 (or $t = 1$) is \$100 + \$5 = \$105.
- You begin the second year with \$105, earn 0.05(\$105) = \$5.25 on the now larger beginning-of-period amount, and end the year with \$110.25. Interest during Year 2 is \$5.25, and it is higher than the first year's interest, \$5.00, because you earned \$5(0.05) = \$0.25 interest on the first year's interest. This is called compounding, and interest earned on interest is called compound interest.
- This process continues, and because the beginning balance is higher each successive year, the interest earned each year increases.
- The total interest earned, \$15.76, is reflected in the final balance, \$115.76.

The step-by-step approach is useful because it shows exactly what is happening. However, this approach is time-consuming, especially when a number of years are involved; so streamlined procedures have been developed.

5-2B FORMULA APPROACH

In the step-by-step approach, we multiply the amount at the beginning of each period by $(1 + I) = (1.05)$. If $N = 3$, we multiply by $(1 + I)$ three different times, which is the same as multiplying the beginning amount by $(1 + I)^3$. This concept can be extended, and the result is this key equation:

Compound Interest
Occurs when interest is earned on prior periods' interest.

Simple Interest
Occurs when interest is not earned on interest.

$$FV_N = PV(1 + I)^N \qquad 5.1$$

We can apply Equation 5.1 to find the FV in our example:

$$FV_3 = \$100(1.05)^3 = \$115.76$$

Equation 5.1 can be used with any calculator that has an exponential function, making it easy to find FVs no matter how many years are involved.

SIMPLE VERSUS COMPOUND INTEREST

Interest earned on the interest earned in prior periods, as was true in our example and is always true when we apply Equation 5.1, is called **compound interest**. If interest is not earned on interest, we have **simple interest**. The formula for FV with simple interest is $FV = PV + PV(I)(N)$; so in our example, FV would have been \$100 + \$100(0.05)(3) = \$100 + \$15 = \$115 based on simple interest. Most financial contracts are based on compound interest, but in legal proceedings, the law often specifies that simple interest must be used. For example, Maris Distributing, a company founded by home-run king Roger Maris, won a lawsuit against Anheuser-Busch (A-B) because A-B had breached a contract and taken away Maris's franchise to sell Budweiser beer. The judge awarded Maris \$50 million plus interest at 10% from 1997 (when A-B breached the contract) until the payment was actually made. The interest award was based on simple interest, which as of 2005 (when a settlement was reached between A-B and the Maris family) had raised the total from \$50 million to \$50 million + 0.10(\$50 million)(8 years) = \$90 million. (No doubt the sheer size of this award and the impact of the interest, even simple interest, influenced A-B to settle.) If the law had allowed compound interest, the award would have totaled (\$50 million) × $(1.10)^8$ = \$107.18 million, or \$17.18 million more. This legal procedure dates back to the days before calculators and computers. The law moves slowly!

5-2C FINANCIAL CALCULATORS

Financial calculators are extremely helpful in working time value problems. Their manuals explain calculators in detail; on the student companion site, we provide summaries of the features needed to work the problems in this book for several popular calculators. Also see the box titled, "Hints on Using Financial Calculators," on page 155, for suggestions that will help you avoid common mistakes. If you are not yet familiar with your calculator, we recommend that you work through the tutorial as you study this chapter.

First, note that financial calculators have five keys that correspond to the five variables in the basic time value equations. We show the inputs for our text example above the respective keys and the output, the FV, below its key. Because there are no periodic payments, we enter 0 for PMT. We describe the keys in more detail after this calculation.

3	5	−100	0	
N	I/YR	PV	PMT	FV
				115.76

Where:

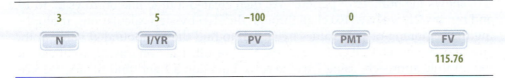

N = Number of periods. Some calculators use n rather than N.

I/YR = Interest rate per period. Some calculators use i or I rather than I/YR.

PV = Present value. In our example, we begin by making a deposit, which is an outflow (the cash leaves our wallet and is deposited at one of many financial institutions); so the PV should be entered with a negative sign. On most calculators, you must enter the 100, then press the +/− key to switch from +100 to −100. If you enter −100 directly, 100 will be subtracted from the last number in the calculator, giving you an incorrect answer.

PMT = Payment. This key is used when we have a series of equal, or constant, payments. Because there are no such payments in our illustrative problem, we enter PMT = 0. We will use the PMT key when we discuss annuities later in this chapter.

FV = Future value. In this example, the FV is positive because we entered the PV as a negative number. If we had entered the 100 as a positive number, the FV would have been negative.

As noted in our example, you enter the known values (N, I/YR, PV, and PMT) and then press the FV key to get the answer, 115.76. Again, note that if you enter the PV as 100 without a minus sign, the FV will be shown on the calculator display as a negative number. The calculator *assumes* that either the PV or the FV is negative. This should not be confusing if you think about what you are doing. When PMT is zero, it doesn't matter what sign you enter for PV as your calculator will automatically assign the opposite sign to FV. We will discuss this point in greater detail later in the chapter when we cover annuities.

5-2D SPREADSHEETS[6]

Students generally use calculators for homework and exam problems, but in business, people generally use spreadsheets for problems that involve the time value

[6]If you have never worked with spreadsheets, you may choose to skip this section. However, you might want to read through it and refer to this chapter's Excel model to get an idea of how spreadsheets work.

of money (TVM). Spreadsheets show in detail what is happening, and they help reduce both conceptual and data-entry errors. The spreadsheet discussion can be skipped without loss of continuity, but if you understand the basics of Excel and have access to a computer, we recommend that you read through this section. Even if you aren't familiar with spreadsheets, the discussion will still give you an idea of how they operate.

resource

Students can download the Excel chapter models from the student companion site on cengage.com. Once downloaded onto your computer, retrieve the Chapter 5 Excel model and follow along as you read this chapter.

We used Excel to create Table 5.1, which is part of the spreadsheet model that corresponds to this chapter. Table 5.1 summarizes the four methods of finding the FV and shows the spreadsheet formulas toward the bottom. Note that spreadsheets can be used to do calculations, but they can also be used like a word processor to create exhibits like Table 5.1, which includes text, drawings, and calculations. The letters across the top designate columns; the numbers to the left designate rows; and the rows and columns jointly designate cells. Thus, C14 is the cell in which we specify the −\$100 investment; C15 shows the interest rate; and C16 shows the number of periods. We then created a time line on rows 17 to 19, and on row 21, we have Excel go through the step-by-step calculations, multiplying the beginning-of-year values by $(1 + I)$ to find the compounded value at the end of each period. Cell G21 shows the final result. Then on row 23, we illustrate the formula approach, using Excel to solve Equation 5.1 and find the FV, \$115.76. Next, on rows 25 to 27, we show a picture of the calculator solution. Finally, on rows 30 and 31, we use Excel's built-in FV function to find the answers given in cells G30 and G31. The G30 answer is based on fixed inputs, while the G31 answer is based on cell references, which makes it easy to change inputs and see the effects on the output.

For example, if you want to quickly see how the future value changes if the interest rate is 7% instead of 5%, all you need to do is change cell C15 to 7%. Looking at cell G31, you will immediately see that the future value is now \$122.50.

TABLE 5.1 Summary of Future Value Calculations

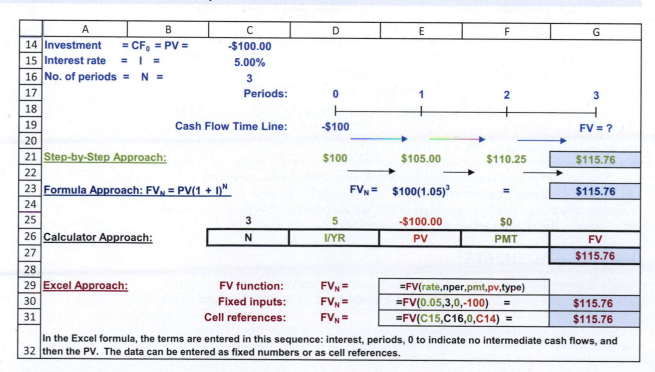

	A	B	C	D	E	F	G
14	Investment	$= CF_0 = PV =$	-\$100.00				
15	Interest rate	$= I =$	5.00%				
16	No. of periods =	N =	3				
17			Periods:	0	1	2	3
18							
19			Cash Flow Time Line:	-\$100			FV = ?
20							
21	Step-by-Step Approach:			\$100	\$105.00	\$110.25	\$115.76
22							
23	Formula Approach: $FV_N = PV(1 + I)^N$			$FV_N =$	$\$100(1.05)^3$	=	\$115.76
24							
25			3	5	-\$100.00	\$0	
26	Calculator Approach:		N	I/YR	PV	PMT	FV
27							\$115.76
28							
29	Excel Approach:		FV function:	$FV_N =$	=FV(rate,nper,pmt,pv,type)		
30			Fixed inputs:	$FV_N =$	=FV(0.05,3,0,-100)	=	\$115.76
31			Cell references:	$FV_N =$	=FV(C15,C16,0,C14)	=	\$115.76
32	In the Excel formula, the terms are entered in this sequence: interest, periods, 0 to indicate no intermediate cash flows, and then the PV. The data can be entered as fixed numbers or as cell references.						

Hints on Using Financial Calculators

When using a financial calculator, make sure it is set up as indicated here. Refer to your calculator manual or to our calculator tutorial on the student companion site for information on setting up your calculator.

- *One payment per period.* Many calculators "come out of the box," assuming that 12 payments are made per year; that is, monthly payments. However, in this book, we generally deal with problems in which only one payment is made each year. *Therefore, you should set your calculator at one payment per year and leave it there. See our tutorial or your calculator manual if you need assistance.*
- *End mode.* With most contracts, payments are made at the end of each period. However, some contracts call for payments at the beginning of each period. You can switch between "End Mode" and "Begin Mode," depending on the problem you are solving. *Because most of the problems in this book call for end-of-period payments, you should return your calculator to End Mode after you work a problem where payments are made at the beginning of periods.*
- *Negative sign for outflows.* Outflows must be entered as negative numbers. This generally means typing the outflow as a positive number and then pressing the +/− key to convert from + to − before hitting the enter key.
- *Decimal places.* With most calculators, you can specify from 0 to 11 decimal places. When working with dollars, we generally specify two decimal places. When dealing with interest rates, we generally specify two places after the decimal when the rate is expressed as a percentage (e.g., 5.25%), but we specify four decimal places when the rate is expressed as a decimal (e.g., 0.0525).
- *Interest rates.* For arithmetic operations with a nonfinancial calculator, 0.0525 must be used, but with a financial calculator and its TVM keys, you must enter 5.25, not 0.0525, because financial calculators assume that rates are stated as percentages.

If you are using Excel, there are a few things to keep in mind:

- When calculating time value of money problems in Excel, interest rates are entered as percentages or decimals (e.g., 5% or .05). However, when using the time value of money function on most financial calculators you generally enter the interest rate as a whole number (e.g., 5).
- When calculating time value of money problems in Excel, the abbreviation for the number of periods is nper, whereas for most financial calculators the abbreviation is simply N. Throughout the text, we will use these terms interchangeably.
- When calculating time value of money problems in Excel, you will often be prompted to enter Type. Type refers to whether the payments come at the end of the year (in which case Type = 0, or you can just omit it), or at the beginning of the year (in which case Type = 1). Most financial calculators have a BEGIN/END mode function that you toggle on or off to indicate whether the payments come at the beginning or at the end of the period.

Table 5.1 demonstrates that all four methods get the same result, but they use different calculating procedures. It also shows that with Excel, all inputs are shown in one place, which makes checking data entries relatively easy. Finally, it shows that Excel can be used to create exhibits, which are quite important in the real world. In business, it's often as important to explain what you are doing as it is to "get the right answer," because if decision makers don't understand your analysis, they may reject your recommendations.

5-2E GRAPHIC VIEW OF THE COMPOUNDING PROCESS

Figure 5.1 shows how a $1 investment grows over time at different interest rates. We made the curves by solving Equation 5.1 with different values for N and I. The interest rate is a growth rate: If a sum is deposited and earns 5% interest per year,

FIGURE 5.1 Growth of $1 at Various Interest Rates and Time Periods

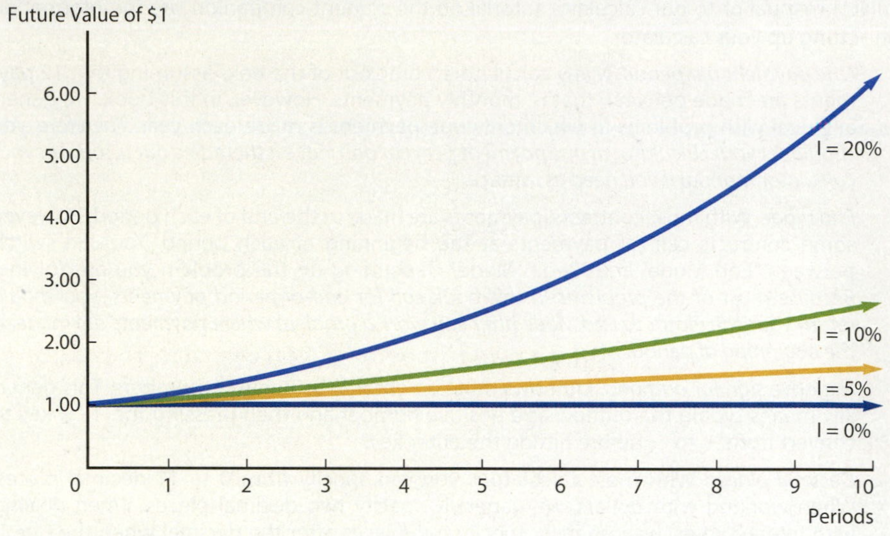

the funds on deposit will grow by 5% per year. Note also that time value concepts can be applied to anything that grows—sales, population, earnings per share, or future salary.

quick question

QUESTION:

At the beginning of your freshman year, your favorite aunt and uncle deposit $10,000 into a 4-year bank certificate of deposit (CD) that pays 5% annual interest. You will receive the money in the account (including the accumulated interest) if you graduate with honors in 4 years. How much will there be in the account after 4 years?

ANSWER:

Using the formula approach, we know that $FV_N = PV(1 + I)^N$. In this case, you know that N = 4, PV = $10,000, and I = 0.05. It follows that the future value after 4 years will be $FV_4 = \$10{,}000(1.05)^4 =$ **$12,155.06**. Alternatively, using the calculator approach we can set the problem up as follows:

4	5	−10000	0	
N	I/YR	PV	PMT	FV
				12,155.06

Finally, we can use Excel's FV function:

=FV(0.05,4,0,−10000)

FV(rate, nper, pmt, [pv], [type])

Here we find that the future value equals **$12,155.06**.

Self*Test*

Explain why this statement is true: A dollar in hand today is worth more than a dollar to be received next year.

What is compounding? What's the difference between simple interest and compound interest? What would the future value of \$100 be after 5 years at 10% *compound* interest? At 10% *simple* interest? **(\$161.05, \$150.00)**

Suppose you currently have \$2,000 and plan to purchase a 3-year certificate of deposit (CD) that pays 4% interest compounded annually. How much will you have when the CD matures? How would your answer change if the interest rate were 5% or 6% or 20%? **(\$2,249.73, \$2,315.25, \$2,382.03, \$3,456.00. *Hint:* With a calculator, enter N = 3, I/YR = 4, PV = −2000, and PMT = 0; then press FV to get 2,249.73. Enter I/YR = 5 to override the 4%, and press FV again to get the second answer. In general, you can change one input at a time to see how the output changes.)**

A company's sales in 2019 were \$100 million. If sales grow at 8%, what will they be 10 years later, in 2029? **(\$215.89 million)**

How much would \$1 growing at 5% per year be worth after 100 years? What would the FV be if the growth rate were 10%? **(\$131.50, \$13,780.61)**

5-3 Present Values

Finding a present value is the reverse of finding a future value. Indeed, we simply solve Equation 5.1, the formula for the future value, for the PV to produce the basic present value formula, Equation 5.2:

$$\text{Future value} = FV_N = PV(1 + I)^N \quad (5.1)$$

$$\text{Present value} = PV = \frac{FV_N}{(1 + I)^N} \quad (5.2)$$

We illustrate PVs with the following example. A broker offers to sell you a Treasury bond that will pay \$115.76 three years from now. Banks are currently offering a guaranteed 5% interest on 3-year certificates of deposit (CDs), and if you don't buy the bond, you will buy a CD. The 5% rate paid on the CDs is defined as your **opportunity cost**, or the rate of return you could earn on an alternative investment of similar risk. Given these conditions, what's the most you should pay for the bond? We answer this question using the four methods discussed in the last section—step-by-step, formula, calculator, and spreadsheet. Table 5.2 summarizes the results.

Opportunity Cost
The rate of return you could earn on an alternative investment of similar risk.

First, recall from the future value example in the last section that if you invested \$100 at 5%, it would grow to \$115.76 in 3 years. You would also have \$115.76 after 3 years if you bought the T-bond. Therefore, the most you should pay for the bond is \$100—this is its "fair price." If you could buy the bond for *less than* \$100, you should buy it rather than invest in the CD. Conversely, if its price was *more than* \$100, you should buy the CD. If the bond's price was exactly \$100, you should be indifferent between the T-bond and the CD.

The \$100 is defined as the present value, or PV, of \$115.76 due in 3 years when the appropriate interest rate is 5%. In general, *the present value of a cash*

TABLE 5.2 Summary of Present Value Calculations

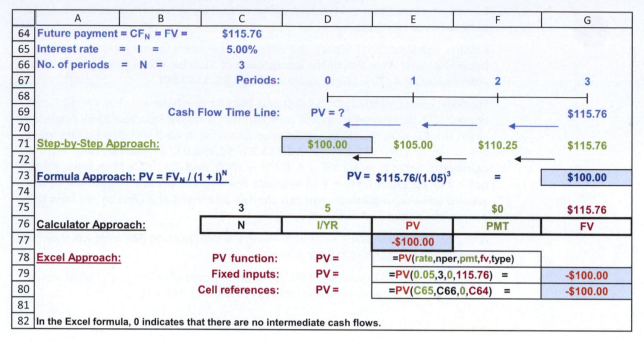

	A	B	C	D	E	F	G
64	Future payment = CF_N = FV =		$115.76				
65	Interest rate = I =		5.00%				
66	No. of periods = N =		3				
67			Periods:	0	1	2	3
68							
69		Cash Flow Time Line:		PV = ?			$115.76
70				←	←	←	
71	Step-by-Step Approach:			$100.00	$105.00	$110.25	$115.76
72				←	←	←	
73	Formula Approach: PV = $FV_N / (1 + I)^N$			PV = $115.76/(1.05)^3$		=	$100.00
74							
75			3	5		$0	$115.76
76	Calculator Approach:		N	I/YR	PV	PMT	FV
77					-$100.00		
78	Excel Approach:		PV function:	PV =	=PV(rate,nper,pmt,fv,type)		
79			Fixed inputs:	PV =	=PV(0.05,3,0,115.76)	=	-$100.00
80			Cell references:	PV =	=PV(C65,C66,0,C64)	=	-$100.00
81							
82	In the Excel formula, 0 indicates that there are no intermediate cash flows.						

Discounting
The process of finding the present value of a cash flow or a series of cash flows; discounting is the reverse of compounding.

flow due N years in the future is the amount which, if it were on hand today, would grow to equal the given future amount. Because $100 would grow to $115.76 in 3 years at a 5% interest rate, $100 is the present value of $115.76 due in 3 years at a 5% rate. Finding present values is called **discounting**, and as previously noted, it is the reverse of compounding—if you know the PV, you can compound to find the FV, while if you know the FV, you can discount to find the PV.

The top section of Table 5.2 calculates the PV using the step-by-step approach. When we found the future value in the previous section, we worked from left to right, multiplying the initial amount and each subsequent amount by (1 + I). To find present values, we work backward, or from right to left, dividing the future value and each subsequent amount by (1 + I). This procedure shows exactly what's happening, which can be quite useful when you are working complex problems. However, it's inefficient, especially when you are dealing with a large number of years.

With the formula approach, we use Equation 5.2, simply dividing the future value by $(1 + I)^N$. This is more efficient than the step-by-step approach, and it gives the same result. Equation 5.2 is built into financial calculators, and as shown in Table 5.2, we can find the PV by entering values for N, I/YR, PMT, and FV and then pressing the PV key. Finally, Excel's PV function can be used:

=PV(0.05,3,0,–115.76)
PV(rate, nper, pmt, [fv], [type])

It is essentially the same as the calculator and solves Equation 5.2.

The fundamental goal of financial management is to maximize the firm's value, and the value of a business (or any asset, including stocks and bonds) is the *present value* of its expected future cash flows. Because present value lies at

FIGURE 5.2 Present Value of $1 at Various Interest Rates and Time Periods

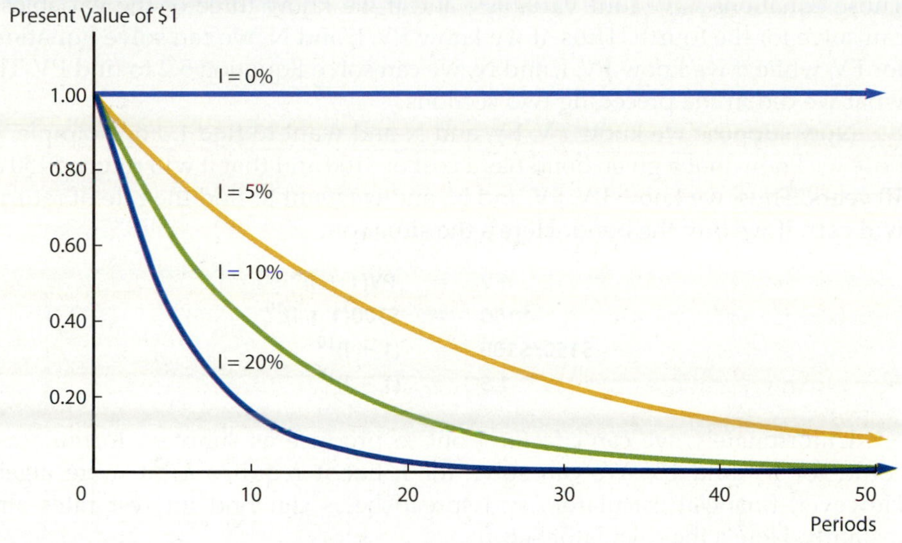

the heart of the valuation process, we will have much more to say about it in the remainder of this chapter and throughout the book.

5-3A GRAPHIC VIEW OF THE DISCOUNTING PROCESS

Figure 5.2 shows that the present value of a sum to be received in the future decreases and approaches zero as the payment date is extended further into the future and that the present value falls faster at higher interest rates. At relatively high rates, funds due in the future are worth very little today, and even at relatively low rates, present values of sums due in the very distant future are quite small. For example, at a 20% discount rate, $1 million due in 100 years would be worth only $0.0121 today. This is because $0.0121 would grow to $1 million in 100 years when compounded at 20%.

Self*Test*

What is discounting, and how is it related to compounding? How is the future value equation (Equation 5.1) related to the present value equation (Equation 5.2)?

How does the present value of a future payment change as the time to receipt is lengthened? As the interest rate increases?

Suppose a U.S. government bond promises to pay $2,249.73 three years from now. If the going interest rate on 3-year government bonds is 4%, how much is the bond worth today? How much is it worth today if the bond matured in 5 years rather than 3? How much is it worth today if the interest rate on the 5-year bond was 6% rather than 4%? **($2,000, $1,849.11, $1,681.13)**

How much would $1,000,000 due in 100 years be worth today if the discount rate was 5%? If the discount rate was 20%? **($7,604.49, $0.0121)**

5-4 Finding the Interest Rate, I

Thus far we have used Equations 5.1 and 5.2 to find future and present values. Those equations have four variables, and if we know three of the variables, we can solve for the fourth. Thus, if we know PV, I, and N, we can solve Equation 5.1 for FV, while if we know FV, I, and N, we can solve Equation 5.2 to find PV. That's what we did in the preceding two sections.

Now suppose we know PV, FV, and N and want to find I. For example, suppose we know that a given bond has a cost of $100 and that it will return $150 after 10 years. Thus, we know PV, FV, and N, and we want to find the rate of return we will earn if we buy the bond. Here's the situation:

$$
\begin{aligned}
FV &= PV(1 + I)^N \\
\$150 &= \$100(1 + I)^{10} \\
\$150/\$100 &= (1 + I)^{10} \\
1.5 &= (1 + I)^{10}
\end{aligned}
$$

Unfortunately, we can't factor I out to produce as simple a formula as we could for FV and PV. We can solve for I, but it requires a bit more algebra.[7] However, financial calculators and spreadsheets can find interest rates almost instantly. Here's the calculator setup:

10		−100	0	150
N	I/YR	PV	PMT	FV
	4.14			

Enter N = 10, PV = −100, PMT = 0, because there are no payments until the security matures, and FV = 150. Then when you press the I/YR key, the calculator gives the answer, 4.14%. You would get this same answer using the RATE function in Excel:

```
=RATE(10,0,–100,150)
 RATE(nper, pmt, pv, [fv], [type], [guess])
```

Here we find that the interest rate is equal to 4.14%.[8]

Self*Test*

The U.S. Treasury offers to sell you a bond for $585.43. No payments will be made until the bond matures 10 years from now, at which time it will be redeemed for $1,000. What interest rate would you earn if you bought this bond for $585.43? What rate would you earn if you could buy the bond for $550? For $600? **(5.5%, 6.16%, 5.24%)**

Microsoft earned $1.42 per share in 2007. Ten years later in 2017 it earned $3.08. What was the growth rate in Microsoft's earnings per share (EPS) over the 10-year period? If EPS in 2017 had been $2.40 rather than $3.08, what would the growth rate have been? **(8.05%, 5.39%)**

[7]Raise the left side of the equation, the 1.5, to the power 1/N = 1/10 = 0.1, getting 1.0414. That number is 1 plus the interest rate, so the interest rate is 0.0414 = 4.14%.

[8]The RATE function prompts you to make a guess. In many cases, you can leave this blank, but if Excel is unable to find a solution to the problem, you should enter a reasonable guess, which will help the program converge to the correct solution.

5-5 Finding the Number of Years, N

We sometimes need to know how long it will take to accumulate a certain sum of money, given our beginning funds and the rate we will earn on those funds. For example, suppose we believe that we could retire comfortably if we had $1 million. We want to find how long it will take us to acquire $1 million, assuming we now have $500,000 invested at 4.5%. We cannot use a simple formula—the situation is like that with interest rates. We can set up a formula that uses logarithms, but calculators and spreadsheets find N very quickly. Here's the calculator setup:

	4.5	−500000	0	1000000
N	I/YR	PV	PMT	FV
15.7473				

Enter I/YR = 4.5, PV = −500000, PMT = 0, and FV = 1000000. Then when you press the N key, you get the answer, 15.7473 years. If you plug N = 15.7473 into the FV formula, you can prove that this is indeed the correct number of years:

$$FV = PV(1 + I)^N = \$500{,}000(1.045)^{15.7473} = \$1{,}000{,}000$$

You can also use Excel's NPER function:

```
=NPER(0.045,0,–500000,1000000)
NPER(rate, pmt, pv, [fv], [type])
```

Here we find that it will take 15.7473 years for $500,000 to double at a 4.5% interest rate.

Self*Test*

How long would it take $1,000 to double if it was invested in a bank that paid 6% per year? How long would it take if the rate was 10%? **(11.9 years, 7.27 years)**

Microsoft's 2017 earnings per share were $3.08, and its growth rate during the prior 10 years was 8.05% per year. If that growth rate was maintained, how long would it take for Microsoft's EPS to double? **(8.95 years)**

5-6 Annuities

Thus far we have dealt with single payments, or "lump sums." However, many assets provide a series of cash inflows over time, and many obligations, such as auto, student, and mortgage loans, require a series of payments. When the payments are equal and are made at fixed intervals, the series is an **annuity**. For example, $100 paid at the end of each of the next 3 years is a 3-year annuity. If the payments occur at the *end* of each year, the annuity is an **ordinary** (or **deferred**) **annuity**. If the payments are made at the *beginning* of each year, the annuity is an **annuity due**. Ordinary annuities are more common in finance; so when we use the term *annuity* in this book, assume that the payments occur at the ends of the periods unless otherwise noted.

Annuity
A series of equal payments at fixed intervals for a specified number of periods.

Ordinary (Deferred) Annuity
An annuity whose payments occur at the end of each period.

Annuity Due
An annuity whose payments occur at the beginning of each period.

Here are the time lines for a $100, 3-year, 5% ordinary annuity and for an annuity due. With the annuity due, each payment is shifted to the left by one year. A $100 deposit will be made each year, so we show the payments with minus signs:

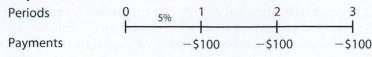

Ordinary Annuity:

Periods	0 (5%)	1	2	3
Payments		−$100	−$100	−$100

Annuity Due:

Periods	0 (5%)	1	2	3
Payments	−$100	−$100	−$100	

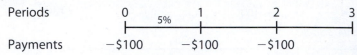

As we demonstrate in the following sections, we can find an annuity's future and present values, the interest rate built into annuity contracts, and the length of time it takes to reach a financial goal using an annuity. Keep in mind that annuities must have *constant payments* at *fixed intervals* for a *specified number of periods.* If these conditions don't hold, then the payments do not constitute an annuity.

Self*Test*

What's the difference between an ordinary annuity and an annuity due?

Why would you prefer to receive an annuity due for $10,000 per year for 10 years than an otherwise similar ordinary annuity?

5-7 Future Value of an Ordinary Annuity

FVA_N
The future value of an annuity over N periods.

The future value of an annuity can be found using the step-by-step approach or using a formula, a financial calculator, or a spreadsheet. As an illustration, consider the ordinary annuity diagrammed earlier, where you deposit $100 at the end of each year for 3 years and earn 5% per year. How much will you have at the end of the third year? The answer, $315.25, is defined as the future value of the annuity, $\mathbf{FVA_N}$; it is shown in Table 5.3.

As shown in the step-by-step section of the table, we compound each payment out to Time 3, then sum those compounded values to find the annuity's FV, FVA_3 = $315.25. The first payment earns interest for two periods, the second payment earns interest for one period, and the third payment earns no interest at all because it is made at the end of the annuity's life. This approach is straightforward, but if the annuity extends out for many years, the approach is cumbersome and time-consuming.

As you can see from the time line diagram, with the step-by-step approach, we apply the following equation, with N = 3 and I = 5%:

$$\begin{aligned} FVA_N &= PMT(1 + I)^{N-1} + PMT(1 + I)^{N-2} + PMT(1 + I)^{N-3} \\ &= \$100(1.05)^2 + \$100(1.05)^1 + \$100(1.05)^0 \\ &= \$315.25 \end{aligned}$$

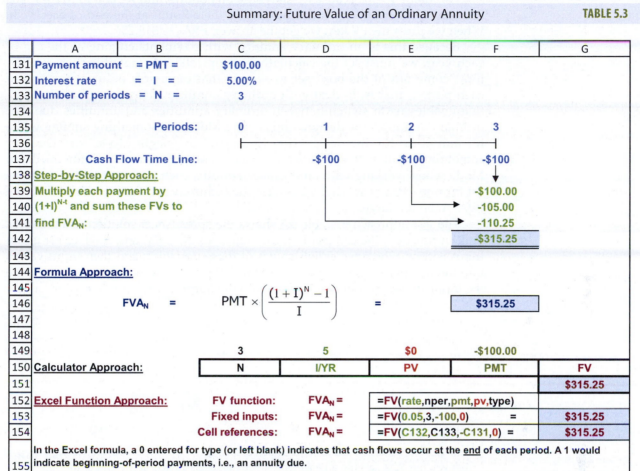

Summary: Future Value of an Ordinary Annuity **TABLE 5.3**

	A	B	C	D	E	F	G
131	Payment amount	= PMT =	$100.00				
132	Interest rate	= I =	5.00%				
133	Number of periods	= N =	3				
134							
135		Periods:	0	1	2	3	
136							
137		Cash Flow Time Line:		-$100	-$100	-$100	
138	Step-by-Step Approach:						
139	Multiply each payment by					-$100.00	
140	$(1+I)^{N-t}$ and sum these FVs to					-105.00	
141	find FVA_N:					-110.25	
142						-$315.25	
143							
144	Formula Approach:						
145							
146		FVA_N =	$PMT \times \left(\frac{(1+I)^N - 1}{I}\right)$		=	$315.25	
147							
148							
149			3	5	$0	-$100.00	
150	Calculator Approach:		N	I/YR	PV	PMT	FV
151							$315.25
152	Excel Function Approach:		FV function:	FVA_N =	=FV(rate,nper,pmt,pv,type)		
153			Fixed inputs:	FVA_N =	=FV(0.05,3,-100,0)	=	$315.25
154			Cell references:	FVA_N =	=FV(C132,C133,-C131,0)	=	$315.25
155	In the Excel formula, a 0 entered for type (or left blank) indicates that cash flows occur at the end of each period. A 1 would indicate beginning-of-period payments, i.e., an annuity due.						

We can generalize and streamline the equation as follows:

$$FVA_N = PMT(1+I)^{N-1} + PMT(1+I)^{N-2} + PMT(1+I)^{N-3} + \cdots + PMT(1+I)^0$$
$$= PMT\left[\frac{(1+I)^N - 1}{I}\right] \qquad 5.3$$

The first line shows the equation in its long form. It can be transformed to the second form on the last line, which can be used to solve annuity problems with a nonfinancial calculator.[9] This equation is also built into financial calculators and spreadsheets. With an annuity, we have recurring payments; hence, the PMT key is used. Here's the calculator setup for our illustrative annuity:

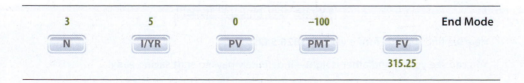

3	5	0	−100		End Mode
N	I/YR	PV	PMT	FV	
				315.25	

[9]The long form of the equation is a geometric progression that can be reduced to the second form.

We enter PV = 0 because we start off with nothing, and we enter PMT = −100 because we plan to deposit this amount in the account at the end of each year. When we press the FV key, we get the answer, FVA_3 = 315.25.

Because this is an ordinary annuity, with payments coming at the *end* of each year, we must set the calculator appropriately. As noted earlier, calculators "come out of the box" set to assume that payments occur at the end of each period, that is, to deal with ordinary annuities. However, there is a key that enables us to switch between ordinary annuities and annuities due. For ordinary annuities the designation is "End Mode" or something similar, while for annuities due the designation is "Begin" or "Begin Mode" or "Due" or something similar. If you make a mistake and set your calculator on Begin Mode when working with an ordinary annuity, each payment will earn interest for one extra year. That will cause the compounded amounts, and thus the FVA, to be too large.

The last approach in Table 5.3 shows the spreadsheet solution using Excel's built-in function. We can put in fixed values for N, I, PV, and PMT or set up an Input Section where we assign values to those variables, and then input values into the function as cell references. Using cell references makes it easy to change the inputs to see the effects of changes on the output.

quick question

QUESTION:

Your grandfather urged you to begin a habit of saving money early in your life. He suggested that you put $5 a day into an envelope. If you follow his advice, at the end of the year you will have $1,825 (365 × $5). Your grandfather further suggested that you take that money at the end of the year and invest it in an online brokerage mutual fund account that has an annual expected return of 8%.

You are 18 years old. If you start following your grandfather's advice today, and continue saving in this way the rest of your life, how much do you expect to have in the brokerage account when you are 65 years old?

ANSWER:

This problem is asking you to calculate the future value of an ordinary annuity. More specifically, you are making 47 payments of $1,825, where the annual interest rate is 8%.

To quickly find the answer, enter the following inputs into a financial calculator: N = 47; I/YR = 8; PV = 0; and PMT = −1825. Then solve for the FV of the ordinary annuity by pressing the FV key, FV = **$826,542.78**.

In addition, we can use Excel's FV function:

```
=FV(0.08,47,–1825,0)
    FV(rate, nper, pmt, [pv], [type])
```

Here we find that the future value is **$826,542.78**.

You can see your grandfather is right—it definitely pays to start saving early!

Self*Test*

For an ordinary annuity with five annual payments of $100 and a 10% interest rate, how many years will the first payment earn interest? What will this payment's value be at the end? Answer this same question for the fifth payment. **(4 years, $146.41, 0 years, $100)**

Assume that you plan to buy a condo 5 years from now, and you estimate that you can save $2,500 per year. You plan to deposit the money in a bank account that pays 4% interest, and you will make the first deposit at the end of the year. How much will you have after 5 years? How much will you have if the interest rate is increased to 6% or lowered to 3%? **($13,540.81, $14,092.73, $13,272.84)**

5-8 Future Value of an Annuity Due

Because each payment occurs one period earlier with an annuity due, all of the payments earn interest for one additional period. Therefore, the FV of an annuity due will be greater than that of a similar ordinary annuity. If you went through the step-by-step procedure, you would see that our illustrative annuity due has an FV of $331.01 versus $315.25 for the ordinary annuity.

With the formula approach, we first use Equation 5.3; however, because each payment occurs one period earlier, we multiply the Equation 5.3 result by (1 + I):

$$FVA_{due} = FVA_{ordinary}(1 + I) \quad (5.4)$$

Thus, for the annuity due, $FVA_{due} = \$315.25(1.05) = \$331.01$, which is the same result when the period-by-period approach is used. With a calculator, we input the variables just as we did with the ordinary annuity, but now we set the calculator to Begin Mode to get the answer, $331.01.

Self*Test*

Why does an annuity due always have a higher future value than an ordinary annuity?

If you calculated the value of an ordinary annuity, how could you find the value of the corresponding annuity due?

Assume that you plan to buy a condo 5 years from now, and you need to save for a down payment. You plan to save $2,500 per year (with the first deposit made *immediately*), and you will deposit the funds in a bank account that pays 4% interest. How much will you have after 5 years? How much will you have if you make the deposits at the end of each year? **($14,082.44, $13,540.81)**

5-9 Present Value of an Ordinary Annuity

PVA_N
The present value of an annuity of N periods.

The present value of an annuity, **PVA_N**, can be found using the step-by-step, formula, calculator, or spreadsheet method. Look back at Table 5.3. To find the FV of the annuity, we compounded the deposits. To find the PV, we discount them, dividing each payment by $(1 + I)^t$. The step-by-step procedure is diagrammed as follows:

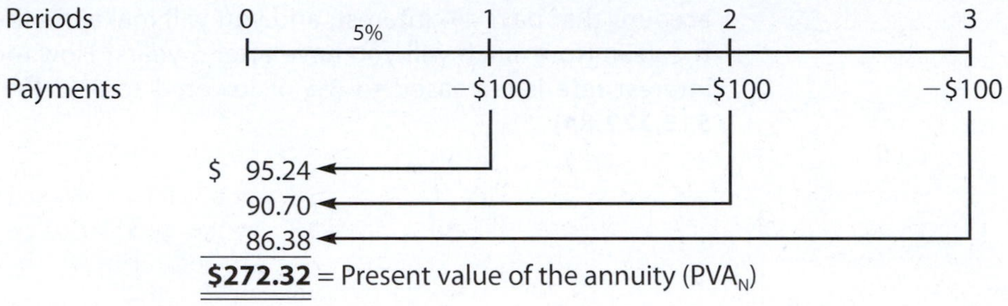

Equation 5.5 expresses the step-by-step procedure in a formula. The bracketed form of the equation can be used with a scientific calculator, and it is helpful if the annuity extends out for a number of years:

$$PVA_N = PMT/(1 + I)^1 + PMT/(1 + I)^2 + \ldots + PMT/(1 + I)^N \tag{5.5}$$

$$= PMT\left[\frac{1 - \frac{1}{(1 + I)^N}}{I}\right]$$

$$= \$100 \times [1 - 1/(1.05)^3]/0.05 = \$272.32$$

Calculators are programmed to solve Equation 5.5, so we merely input the variables and press the PV key, *making sure the calculator is set to End Mode.* The calculator setup follows for both an ordinary annuity and an annuity due. Note that the PV of the annuity due is larger because each payment is discounted back one less year. Note too that you can find the PV of the ordinary annuity and then multiply by $(1 + I) = 1.05$, calculating $272.32(1.05) = $285.94, the PV of the annuity due.

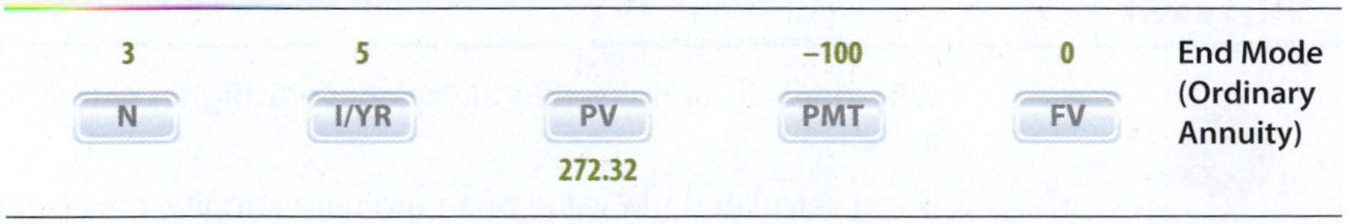

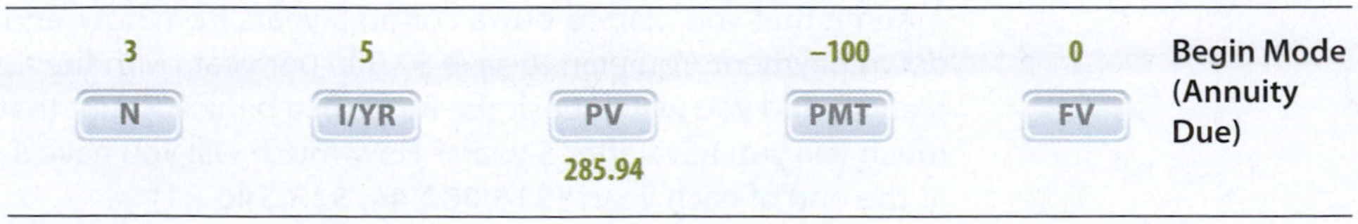

quick question

QUESTION:

You just won the Florida lottery. To receive your winnings, you must select ONE of the two following choices:

1. You can receive $1,000,000 a year at the end of each of the next 30 years.
2. You can receive a one-time payment of $15,000,000 today.

Assume that the current interest rate is 6%. Which option is most valuable?

ANSWER:

The most valuable option is the one with the largest present value. You know that the second option has a present value of $15,000,000, so we need to determine whether the present value of the $1,000,000, 30-year ordinary annuity exceeds $15,000,000.

Using the formula approach, we see that the present value of the annuity is

$$PVA_N = PMT\left[\frac{1 - \frac{1}{(1+I)^N}}{I}\right]$$

$$= \$1{,}000{,}000\left[\frac{1 - \frac{1}{(1.06)^{30}}}{0.06}\right]$$

$$= \mathbf{\$13{,}764{,}831.15}$$

Alternatively, using the calculator approach, we can set up the problem as follows:

30	**6**		**−1000000**	**0**
N	I/YR	PV	PMT	FV
		13,764,831.15		

Finally, we can use Excel's PV function:

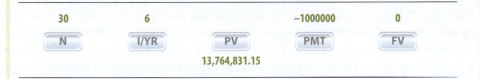

=PV(0.06,30,–1000000,0)

PV(rate, nper, pmt, [fv], [type])

Here we find that the present value is **$13,764,831.15**.

Because the present value of the 30-year annuity is less than $15,000,000, you should choose to receive your winnings as a one-time up-front payment.

Self*Test*

Why does an annuity due have a higher present value than a similar ordinary annuity?

If you know the present value of an ordinary annuity, how can you find the PV of the corresponding annuity due?

What is the PVA of an ordinary annuity with 10 payments of $100 if the appropriate interest rate is 10%? What would the PVA be if the interest rate was 4%? What if the interest rate was 0%? How much would the PVA values be if we were dealing with annuities due? **($614.46, $811.09, $1,000.00, $675.90, $843.53, $1,000.00)**

Assume that you are offered an annuity that pays $100 at the end of each year for 10 years. You could earn 8% on your money in other investments with equal risk. What is the most you should pay for the annuity? If the payments began immediately, how much would the annuity be worth? **($671.01, $724.69)**

5-10 Finding Annuity Payments, Periods, and Interest Rates

We can find payments, periods, and interest rates for annuities. Here five variables come into play: N, I, PMT, FV, and PV. If we know any four, we can find the fifth.

5-10A FINDING ANNUITY PAYMENTS, PMT

Suppose we need to accumulate $10,000 and have it available 5 years from now. Suppose further that we can earn a return of 6% on our savings, which are currently zero. Thus, we know that FV = 10,000, PV = 0, N = 5, and I/YR = 6. We can enter these values in a financial calculator and press the PMT key to find how large our deposits must be. The answer will, of course, depend on whether we make deposits at the end of each year (ordinary annuity) or at the beginning (annuity due). Here are the results for each type of annuity:

Ordinary Annuity:

5	6	0		10000	
N	I/YR	PV	PMT	FV	**End Mode (Ordinary Annuity)**
			−1,773.96		

We can also use Excel's PMT function:

```
=PMT(0.06,5,0,10000
PMT(rate, nper, pv, [fv], [type])
```

Because the deposits are made at the end of the year, we can leave "type" blank. Here we find that an annual deposit of $1,773.96 is needed to reach your goal.

Annuity Due:

5	6	0		10000	Begin Mode (Annuity Due)
N	I/YR	PV	PMT	FV	
			−1,673.55		

Alternatively, Excel's PMT function can be used to calculate the annual deposit for the annuity due:

=PMT(0.06,5,0,10000,1)

PMT(rate, nper, pv, [fv], [type])

Because the deposits are now made at the beginning of the year, enter 1 for type. Here we find that an annual deposit of $1,673.55 is needed to reach your goal.

Thus, you must save $1,773.96 per year if you make deposits at the *end* of each year, but only $1,673.55 if the deposits begin *immediately.* Note that the required annual deposit for the annuity due can also be calculated as the ordinary annuity payment divided by (1 + I): $1,773.96/1.06 = $1,673.55.

5-10B FINDING THE NUMBER OF PERIODS, N

Suppose you decide to make end-of-year deposits, but you can save only $1,200 per year. Again assuming that you would earn 6%, how long would it take to reach your $10,000 goal? Here is the calculator setup:

	6	0	−1200	10000	End Mode
N	I/YR	PV	PMT	FV	
6.96					

With these smaller deposits, it would take 6.96 years to reach your $10,000 goal. If you began the deposits immediately, you would have an annuity due, and N would be a bit smaller, 6.63 years.

You can also use Excel's NPER function to arrive at both of these answers. If we assume end-of-year payments, Excel's NPER function looks like this:

=NPER(0.06,−1200,0,10000)

NPER(rate, pmt, pv, [fv], [type])

Here we find that it will take 6.96 years to reach your goal.

If we assume beginning-of-year payments, Excel's NPER function looks like this:

=NPER(0.06,−1200,0,10000,1)

NPER(rate, pmt, pv, [fv], [type])

Here we find that it will take only 6.63 years to reach your goal.

5-10C FINDING THE INTEREST RATE, I

Now suppose you can save only $1,200 annually, but you still need the $10,000 in 5 years. What rate of return would enable you to achieve your goal? Here is the calculator setup:

5		0	−1200	10000	End Mode
N	I/YR	PV	PMT	FV	
	25.78				

Excel's RATE function will arrive at the same answer:

```
=RATE(5,–1200,0,10000)
RATE(nper, pmt, pv, [fv], [type], [guess])
```

Here we find that the interest rate is 25.78%.

You must earn a whopping 25.78% to reach your goal. About the only way to earn such a high return would be to invest in speculative stocks or head to the casinos in Las Vegas. Of course, investing in speculative stocks and gambling aren't like making deposits in a bank with a guaranteed rate of return, so there's a good chance you'd end up with nothing. You might consider changing your plans—save more, lower your $10,000 target, or extend your time horizon. It might be appropriate to seek a somewhat higher return, but trying to earn 25.78% in a 6% market would require taking on more risk than would be prudent.

It's easy to find rates of return using a financial calculator or a spreadsheet. However, to find rates of return without one of these tools, you would have to go through a trial-and-error process, which would be very time-consuming if many years were involved.

Self*Test*

Suppose you inherited $100,000 and invested it at 7% per year. What is the most you could withdraw at the *end* of each of the next 10 years and have a zero balance at Year 10? How much could you withdraw if you made withdrawals at the *beginning* of each year? **($14,237.75, $13,306.31)**

If you had $100,000 that was invested at 7% and you wanted to withdraw $10,000 at the end of each year, how long would your funds last? How long would they last if you earned 0%? How long would they last if you earned the 7% but limited your withdrawals to $7,000 per year? **(17.8 years, 10 years, forever)**

Your uncle named you beneficiary of his life insurance policy. The insurance company gives you a choice of $100,000 today or a 12-year annuity of $12,000 at the end of each year. What rate of return is the insurance company offering? **(6.11%)**

Assume that you just inherited an annuity that will pay you $10,000 per year for 10 years, with the first payment being made today. A friend of your mother offers to give you $60,000 for the annuity. If you sell it, what rate of return would your mother's friend earn on his investment? If you think a "fair" return would be 6%, how much should you ask for the annuity? **(13.70%, $78,016.92)**

5-11 Perpetuities

Perpetuity
A stream of equal payments at fixed intervals expected to continue forever.

A **perpetuity** is simply an annuity with an extended life. Because the payments go on forever, you can't apply the step-by-step approach. However, it's easy to find the PV of a perpetuity with a formula found by solving Equation 5.5 with N set at infinity:

$$\text{PV of a perpetuity} = \frac{\text{PMT}}{\text{I}} \qquad (5.6)$$

Let's say, for example, that you buy preferred stock in a company that pays you a fixed dividend of $2.50 each year the company is in business. If we assume that the company will go on indefinitely, the preferred stock can be valued as a perpetuity. If the discount rate on the preferred stock is 10%, the present value of the perpetuity, the preferred stock, is $25:

$$\text{PV of a perpetuity} = \frac{\$2.50}{0.10} = \$25$$

Self*Test*

What's the present value of a perpetuity that pays $1,000 per year beginning 1 year from now, if the appropriate interest rate is 5%? What would the value be if payments on the annuity began immediately? **($20,000, $21,000. *Hint:* Just add the $1,000 to be received immediately to the value of the annuity.)**

5-12 Uneven Cash Flows

The definition of an annuity includes the words *constant payment*—in other words, annuities involve payments that are equal in every period. Although many financial decisions involve constant payments, many others involve **uneven**, or **nonconstant, cash flows.** For example, the dividends on common stocks typically increase over time, and investments in capital equipment almost always generate uneven cash flows. Throughout the book, we reserve the term **payment (PMT)** for annuities with their equal payments in each period and use the term **cash flow (CF_t)** to denote uneven cash flows, where t designates the period in which the cash flow occurs.

Uneven (Nonconstant) Cash Flows
A series of cash flows where the amount varies from one period to the next.

Payment (PMT)
This term designates equal cash flows coming at regular intervals.

Cash Flow (CF_t)
This term designates a cash flow that's not part of an annuity.

There are two important classes of uneven cash flows: (1) a stream that consists of a series of annuity payments plus an additional final lump sum and (2) all other uneven streams. Bonds represent the best example of the first type, while stocks and capital investments illustrate the second type. Here are numerical examples of the two types of flows:

1. Annuity plus additional final payment:

Periods	0 (I = 12%)	1	2	3	4	5
Cash flows	$0	$100	$100	$100	$100	$ 100
						1,000
						$1,100

2. Irregular cash flows:

Periods	0 (I = 12%)	1	2	3	4	5
Cash flows	$0	$100	$300	$300	$300	$500

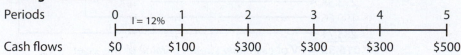

We can find the PV of either stream by using Equation 5.7 and following the step-by-step procedure, where we discount each cash flow and then sum them to find the PV of the stream:

$$PV = \frac{CF_1}{(1+I)^1} + \frac{CF_2}{(1+I)^2} + \cdots + \frac{CF_N}{(1+I)^N} = \sum_{t=1}^{N} \frac{CF_t}{(1+I)^t} \quad 5.7$$

If we did this, we would find the PV of Stream 1 to be $927.90 and the PV of Stream 2 to be $1,016.35.

The step-by-step procedure is straightforward; however, if we have a large number of cash flows, it is time-consuming. However, financial calculators speed up the process considerably. First, consider Stream 1; notice that we have a 5-year, 12% ordinary annuity plus a final payment of $1,000. We could find the PV of the annuity, and then find the PV of the final payment and sum them to obtain the PV of the stream. Financial calculators do this in one simple step—use the five TVM keys; enter the data as shown below and press the PV key to obtain the answer, $927.90.

5	12		100	1000
N	I/YR	PV	PMT	FV
		−927.90		

The solution procedure is different for the second uneven stream. Here we must use the step-by-step approach, as shown in Figure 5.3. Even calculators and spreadsheets solve the problem using the step-by-step procedure, but they do it quickly and efficiently. First, you enter all of the cash flows and the interest rate; then the calculator or computer discounts each cash flow to find its present value and sums these PVs to produce the PV of the stream. You must enter each cash flow in the calculator's "cash flow register," enter the interest rate, and then press the NPV key to find the PV of the stream. NPV stands for "net present value." We cover the calculator mechanics in the calculator tutorial, and we discuss the process in more detail in Chapters 9 and 11, where we use the NPV calculation to analyze stocks and proposed capital budgeting projects. If you don't know how to do the calculation with your calculator, it would be worthwhile to review the tutorial or your calculator manual, learn the steps, and make sure you can do this calculation. Because you will have to learn to do it eventually, now is a good time to begin.

FIGURE 5.3 PV of an Uneven Cash Flow Stream

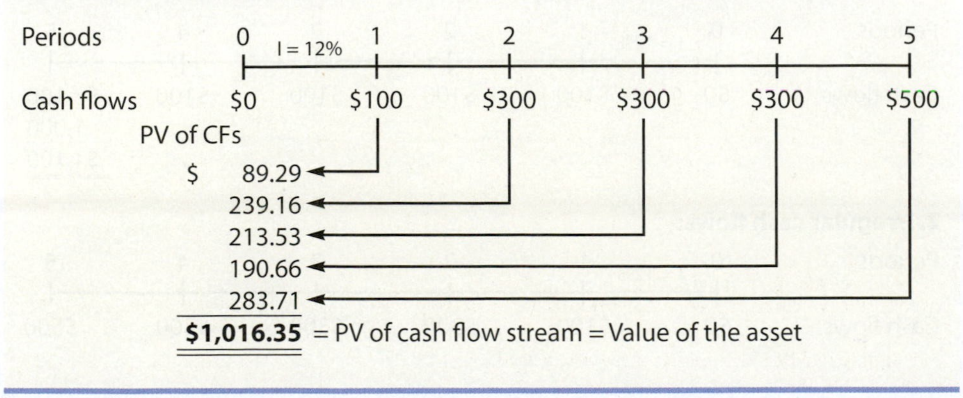

Self*Test*

How could you use Equation 5.2 to find the PV of an uneven stream of cash flows?

What's the present value of a 5-year ordinary annuity of $100 plus an additional $500 at the end of Year 5 if the interest rate is 6%? What is the PV if the $100 payments occur in Years 1 through 10 and the $500 comes at the end of Year 10? **($794.87, $1,015.21)**

What's the present value of the following uneven cash flow stream: $0 at Time 0, $100 in Year 1 (or at Time 1), $200 in Year 2, $0 in Year 3, and $400 in Year 4 if the interest rate is 8%? **($558.07)**

Would a typical common stock provide cash flows more like an annuity or more like an uneven cash flow stream? Explain.

5-13 Future Value of an Uneven Cash Flow Stream

We find the future value of uneven cash flow streams by compounding rather than discounting. Consider Cash Flow Stream 2 in the preceding section. We discounted those cash flows to find the PV, but we would compound them to find the FV. Figure 5.4 illustrates the procedure for finding the FV of the stream, using the step-by-step approach.

The values of all financial assets—stocks, bonds, and business capital investments—are found as the present values of their expected future cash flows. Therefore, we need to calculate present values very often, far more often than future values. As a result, all financial calculators provide automated functions for finding PVs, but they generally do not provide automated FV functions. On the relatively few occasions when we need to find the FV of an uneven cash flow stream, we generally use the step-by-step procedure shown in Figure 5.4. That approach works for all cash flow streams, even those for which some cash flows are zero or negative.[10]

FIGURE 5.4 FV of an Uneven Cash Flow Stream

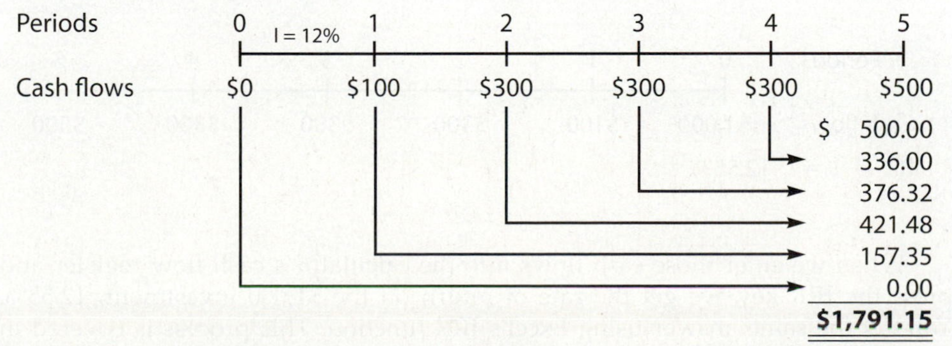

[10]The HP 10bII+ calculator provides a shortcut to finding the FV of a cash flow stream. Enter the cash flows into the cash flow register; input the interest rate; and calculate the net present value of the stream. Once the NPV of the stream is calculated, simply press SWAP, and the calculator will display the FV of the cash flow stream.

Self*Test*

Why are we more likely to need to calculate the PV of cash flow streams than the FV of streams?

What is the future value of this cash flow stream: $100 at the end of 1 year, $150 due after 2 years, and $300 due after 3 years, if the appropriate interest rate is 15%? **($604.75)**

5-14 Solving for I with Uneven Cash Flows[11]

Before financial calculators and spreadsheets existed, it was *extremely difficult* to find I when the cash flows were uneven. With spreadsheets and financial calculators, however, it's relatively easy to find I. If you have an annuity plus a final lump sum, you can input values for N, PV, PMT, and FV into the calculator's TVM registers and then press the I/YR key. Here is the setup for Stream 1 from Section 5-12, assuming we must pay $927.90 to buy the asset. The rate of return on the $927.90 investment is 12%.

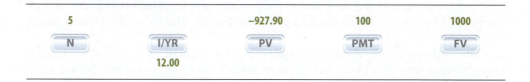

5		–927.90	100	1000
N	I/YR	PV	PMT	FV
	12.00			

Finding the interest rate for an uneven cash flow stream such as Stream 2 is a bit more complicated. First, note that there is no simple procedure—finding the rate requires a trial-and-error process, which means that a financial calculator or a spreadsheet is needed. With a calculator, we enter each CF into the cash flow register and then press the IRR key to get the answer. IRR stands for "internal rate of return," and it is the rate of return the investment provides. The investment is the cash flow at Time 0, and it must be entered as a negative value. As an illustration, consider the cash flows given here, where $CF_0 = -\$1{,}000$ is the cost of the asset.

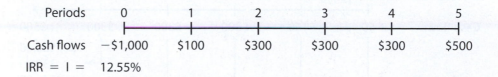

Periods	0	1	2	3	4	5
Cash flows	−$1,000	$100	$300	$300	$300	$500
IRR = I =	12.55%					

When we enter those cash flows into the calculator's cash flow register and press the IRR key, we get the rate of return on the $1,000 investment, 12.55%. You get the same answer using Excel's IRR function. This process is covered in the calculator tutorial; it is also discussed in Chapter 11, where we study capital budgeting.

[11]This section is relatively technical. It can be deferred at this point, but the calculations will be required in Chapter 11.

Self*Test*

An investment costs \$465 and is expected to produce cash flows of \$100 at the end of each of the next 4 years, then an extra lump sum payment of \$200 at the end of the fourth year. What is the expected rate of return on this investment? **(9.05%)**

An investment costs \$465 and is expected to produce cash flows of \$100 at the end of Year 1, \$200 at the end of Year 2, and \$300 at the end of Year 3. What is the expected rate of return on this investment? **(11.71%)**

5-15 Semiannual and Other Compounding Periods

In all of our examples thus far, we assumed that interest was compounded once a year, or annually. This is called **annual compounding**. Suppose, however, that you deposit \$100 in a bank that pays a 5% annual interest rate but credits interest each 6 months. So in the second 6-month period, you earn interest on your original \$100 plus interest on the interest earned during the first 6 months. This is called **semiannual compounding**. Note that banks generally pay interest more than once a year; virtually all bonds pay interest semiannually; and most mortgages, student loans, and auto loans require monthly payments. Therefore, it is important to understand how to deal with nonannual compounding.

Annual Compounding
The arithmetic process of determining the final value of a cash flow or series of cash flows when interest is added once a year.

Semiannual Compounding
The arithmetic process of determining the final value of a cash flow or series of cash flows when interest is added twice a year.

For an illustration of semiannual compounding, assume that we deposit \$100 in an account that pays 5% and leave it there for 10 years. First, consider again what the future value would be under *annual* compounding:

$$FV_N = PV(1 + I)^N = \$100(1.05)^{10} = \$162.89$$

We would, of course, get the same answer using a financial calculator or a spreadsheet.

How would things change in this example if interest was paid semiannually rather than annually? First, whenever payments occur more than once a year, you must make two conversions: (1) Convert the stated interest rate into a "periodic rate." (2) Convert the number of years into "number of periods." The conversions are done as follows, where I is the stated annual rate, M is the number of compounding periods per year, and N is the number of years:

$$\text{Periodic rate } (I_{PER}) = \frac{\text{Stated annual rate}}{\text{Number of payments per year}} = I/M \qquad 5.8$$

With a stated annual rate of 5%, compounded semiannually, the periodic rate is 2.5%:

$$\text{Periodic rate} = 5\%/2 = 2.5\%$$

The number of compounding periods is found with Equation 5.9:

$$\text{Number of periods} = (\text{Number of years})(\text{Periods per year}) = NM \qquad 5.9$$

With 10 years and semiannual compounding, there are 20 periods:

$$\text{Number of periods} = 10(2) = 20 \text{ periods}$$

Under semiannual compounding, our \$100 investment will earn 2.5% every 6 months for 20 semiannual periods, not 5% per year for 10 years. The periodic rate and number of periods, not the annual rate and number of years, must be shown on time lines and entered into the calculator or spreadsheet whenever you are working with nonannual compounding.[12]

With this background, we can find the value of \$100 after 10 years if it is held in an account that pays a stated annual rate of 5.0%, but with semiannual compounding. Here's the time line and the future value:

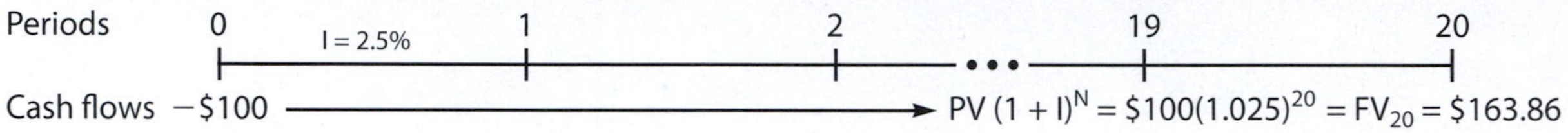

With a financial calculator, we get the same result using the periodic rate and number of periods:

The future value under semiannual compounding, \$163.86, exceeds the FV under annual compounding, \$162.89, because interest starts accruing sooner; thus, you earn more interest on interest.

How would things change in our example if interest was compounded quarterly or monthly or daily? With quarterly compounding, there would be NM = 10(4) = 40 periods and the periodic rate would be I/M = 5%/4 = 1.25% per quarter. Using those values, we would find FV = \$164.36. If we used monthly compounding, we would have 10(12) = 120 periods, the monthly rate would be 5%/12 = 0.416667%, and the FV would rise to \$164.70. If we went to daily compounding, we would have 10(365) = 3,650 periods, the daily rate would be 5%/365 = 0.0136986% per day, and the FV would be \$164.87 (based on a 365-day year).

The same logic applies when we find present values under semiannual compounding. Again, we use Equation 5.8 to convert the stated annual rate to the periodic (semiannual) rate and Equation 5.9 to find the number of semiannual periods. We then use the periodic rate and number of periods in the calculations. For example, we can find the PV of \$100 due after 10 years when the stated annual rate is 5%, with semiannual compounding:

$$\textbf{Periodic rate} = 5\%/2 = 2.5\% \text{ per period}$$
$$\textbf{Number of periods} = 10(2) = 20 \text{ periods}$$
$$\textbf{PV of \$100} = \$100/(1.025)^{20} = \$61.03$$

[12]With some financial calculators, you can enter the annual (nominal) rate and the number of compounding periods per year rather than make the conversions we recommend. We prefer the conversions because they must be used on time lines and because it is easy to forget to reset your calculator after you change its settings, which may lead to an error on your next calculations.

We would get this same result with a financial calculator:

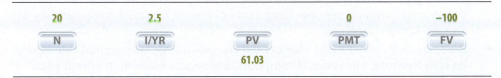

20	2.5		0	−100
N	I/YR	PV	PMT	FV
		61.03		

If we increased the number of compounding periods from 2 (semiannual) to 12 (monthly), the PV would decline to \$60.72; if we went to daily compounding, the PV would fall to \$60.66.

Self*Test*

Would you rather invest in an account that pays 7% with annual compounding or 7% with monthly compounding? Would you rather borrow at 7% and make annual or monthly payments? Why?

What's the *future value* of \$100 after 3 years if the appropriate interest rate is 8% compounded annually? Compounded monthly? **(\$125.97, \$127.02)**

What's the *present value* of \$100 due in 3 years if the appropriate interest rate is 8% compounded annually? Compounded monthly? **(\$79.38, \$78.73)**

5-16 Comparing Interest Rates

Different compounding periods are used for different types of investments. For example, bank accounts generally pay interest daily; most bonds pay interest semiannually; stocks pay dividends quarterly; and mortgages, auto loans, and other instruments require monthly payments.[13] If we are to compare investments or loans with different compounding periods properly, we need to put them on a common basis. Here are some terms you need to understand:

- The **nominal interest rate (I_{NOM}),** also called the *annual percentage rate* **(APR)**, is the quoted, or stated, rate that credit card companies, student loan officers, auto dealers, and other lenders tell you they are charging on loans. Note that if two banks offer loans with a stated rate of 8%, but one requires monthly payments and the other quarterly payments, they are not charging the same "true" rate. The one that requires monthly payments is charging more than the one with quarterly payments because it will receive your money sooner. So to compare loans across lenders, or interest rates earned on different securities, you should calculate effective annual rates as described here.[14]

Nominal Interest Rate (APR), I_{NOM}
The contracted interest rate.

[13]Some banks even pay interest compounded continuously. Continuous compounding is discussed in Web Appendix 5A.

[14]Note, though, that if you are comparing two bonds that both pay interest semiannually, it's okay to compare their nominal rates. Similarly, you can compare the nominal rates on two money funds that pay interest daily. But don't compare the nominal rate on a semiannual bond with the nominal rate on a money fund that compounds daily because that will make the money fund look worse than it really is.

Effective (Equivalent) Annual Rate (EFF% or EAR)
The annual rate of interest actually being earned, as opposed to the quoted rate.

- The **effective annual rate**, abbreviated **EFF%**, is also called the **equivalent annual rate (EAR).** This is the rate that would produce the same future value under annual compounding as would more frequent compounding at a given nominal rate.
- If a loan or an investment uses annual compounding, its nominal rate is also its effective rate. However, if compounding occurs more than once a year, the EFF% is higher than I_{NOM}.
- To illustrate, a nominal rate of 10% with semiannual compounding is equivalent to a rate of 10.25% with annual compounding because both rates will cause $100 to grow to the same amount after 1 year. The top line in the following diagram shows that $100 will grow to $110.25 at a nominal rate of 10.25%. The lower line shows the situation if the nominal rate is 10% but semiannual compounding is used.

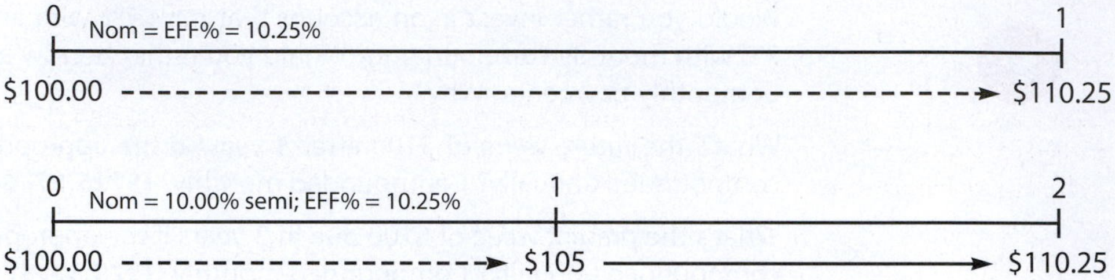

Given the nominal rate and the number of compounding periods per year, we can find the effective annual rate with this equation:

$$\text{Effective annual rate (EFF\%)} = \left[1 + \frac{I_{NOM}}{M}\right]^{M} - 1.0 \qquad \textbf{5.10}$$

Here I_{NOM} is the nominal rate expressed as a decimal and M is the number of compounding periods per year. In our example, the nominal rate is 10%. But with semiannual compounding, I_{NOM} = 10% = 0.10 and M = 2. This results in EFF% = 10.25%:

$$\text{Effective annual rate (EFF\%)} = \left[1 + \frac{0.10}{2}\right]^{2} - 1 = 0.1025 = 10.25\%$$

We can also use the EFFECT function in Excel to solve for the effective rate:

=EFFECT (0.1,2)

EFFECT(nominal_rate, npery)

Here we find that the effective rate is 10.25%. NPERY refers to the number of payments per year. Likewise, if you know the effective rate and want to solve for the nominal rate, you can use the NOMINAL function in Excel.[15] Thus, if one investment promises to pay 10% with semiannual compounding, and an equally risky

[15]Most financial calculators are programmed to find the EFF% or, given the EFF%, to find the nominal rate. This is called *interest rate conversion.* You enter the nominal rate and the number of compounding periods per year and then press the EFF% key to find the effective annual rate. However, we generally use Equation 5.10 because it's as easy to use as the interest rate conversion feature, and the equation reminds us of what we are really doing. If you use the interest rate conversion feature on your calculator, don't forget to reset your calculator settings. Interest rate conversion is discussed in the calculator tutorials.

investment promises 10.25% with annual compounding, we would be indifferent between the two.

quick question

QUESTION:

You just received your first credit card and decided to purchase a new Apple iPad. You charged the iPad's \$500 purchase price on your new credit card. Assume that the nominal interest rate on the credit card is 18% and that interest is compounded monthly.

The minimum payment on the credit card is only \$10 a month. If you pay the minimum and make no other charges, how long will it take you to fully pay off the credit card?

ANSWER:

Here we are given that the nominal interest rate is 18%. It follows that the monthly periodic rate is 1.5% (18%/12). Using a financial calculator, we can solve for the number of months that it takes to pay off the credit card.

	1.5	500	−10	0
N	I/YR	PV	PMT	FV
93.11				

We can also use Excel's NPER function:

=NPER(0.015,–10,500,0)

NPER(rate, pmt, pv, [fv], [type])

Here we find that it will take **93.11** months to pay off the credit card.

Note that it would take you almost 8 years to pay off your iPad purchase. Now, you see why you can quickly get into financial trouble if you don't manage your credit cards wisely!

Self*Test*

Define the terms *annual percentage rate (APR), effective annual rate (EFF%), and nominal interest rate* (I_{NOM}).

A bank pays 5% with daily compounding on its savings accounts. Should it advertise the nominal or effective rate if it is seeking to attract new deposits?

By law, credit card issuers must print their annual percentage rate on their monthly statements. A common APR is 18% with interest paid monthly. What is the EFF% on such a loan? **(EFF% = $[1 + 0.18/12]^{12} - 1 = 0.1956$ = 19.56%)**

Fifty years ago, banks didn't have to reveal the rates they charged on credit cards. Then Congress passed the Truth in Lending Act that required banks to publish their APRs. Is the APR really the most truthful rate, or would the EFF% be more truthful? Explain.

5-17 Fractional Time Periods

Thus far we have assumed that payments occur at the beginning or the end of periods but not *within* periods. However, we often encounter situations that require compounding or discounting over fractional periods. For example, suppose you deposited $100 in a bank that pays a nominal rate of 10% but adds interest daily, based on a 365-day year. How much would you have after 9 months? The answer is $107.79, found as follows:[16]

$$\text{Periodic rate} = I_{PER} = 0.10/365 = 0.000273973 \text{ per day}$$
$$\text{Number of days} = (9/12)(365) = 0.75(365) = 273.75, \text{ rounded to } 274$$
$$\text{Ending amount} = \$100(1.000273973)^{274} = \$107.79$$

Now suppose you borrow $100 from a bank whose nominal rate is 10% per year simple interest, which means that interest is not earned on interest. If the loan is outstanding for 274 days, how much interest would you have to pay? Here we would calculate a daily interest rate, I_{PER}, as just shown, but multiply it by 274 rather than use the 274 as an exponent:

$$\text{Interest owed} = \$100(0.000273973)(274) = \$7.51$$

You would owe the bank a total of $107.51 after 274 days. This is the procedure that most banks use to calculate interest on loans, except that they require borrowers to pay the interest on a monthly basis rather than after 274 days.

Self*Test*

Suppose a company borrowed $1 million at a rate of 9% simple interest, with interest paid at the end of each month. The bank uses a 360-day year. How much interest would the firm have to pay in a 30-day month? What would the interest be if the bank used a 365-day year? **([0.09/360] [30] [$1,000,000] = $7,500 interest for the month. For the 365-day year, [0.09/365][30][$1,000,000] = $7,397.26 of interest. The use of a 360-day year raises the interest cost by $102.74, which is why banks like to use it on loans.)**

Suppose you deposited $1,000 in a credit union account that pays 7% with daily compounding and a 365-day year. What is the EFF%, and how much could you withdraw after 7 months, assuming this is seven-twelfths of a year? **(EFF% = $[1 + 0.07/365]^{365} - 1 = 0.07250098$ = 7.250098%. Thus, your account would grow from $1,000 to $1,000 $[1.07250098]^{0.583333}$ = $1,041.67, and you could withdraw that amount.)**

5-18 Amortized Loans[17]

An important application of compound interest involves loans that are paid off in installments over time. Included are automobile loans, home mortgage loans, student loans, and many business loans. A loan that is to be repaid in

[16]Bank loan contracts specifically state whether they are based on a 360- or a 365-day year. If a 360-day year is used, the daily rate is higher, which means that the effective rate is also higher. Here we assumed a 365-day year. Also note that in real-world calculations, banks' computers have built-in calendars, so they can calculate the exact number of days, taking account of 30-day, 31-day, and 28- or 29-day months.

[17]Amortized loans are important, but this section can be omitted without loss of continuity.

TABLE 5.4 Loan Amortization Schedule, $100,000 at 6% for 5 Years

Amount borrowed: $100,000
Years: 5
Rate: 6%
PMT: −$23,739.64

Year	Beginning Amount (1)	Payment (2)	Interest[a] (3)	Repayment of Principal[b] (4)	Ending Balance (5)
1	$100,000.00	$23,739.64	$6,000.00	$17,739.64	$82,260.36
2	82,260.36	23,739.64	4,935.62	18,804.02	63,456.34
3	63,456.34	23,739.64	3,807.38	19,932.26	43,524.08
4	43,524.08	23,739.64	2,611.44	21,128.20	22,395.89
5	22,395.89	23,739.64	1,343.75	22,395.89	0.00

Notes:
[a]Interest in each period is calculated by multiplying the loan balance at the beginning of the year by the interest rate. Therefore, interest in Year 1 is $100,000(0.06) = $6,000; in Year 2, it is $4,935.62; and so forth.
[b]Repayment of principal is equal to the payment of $23,739.64 minus the interest charge for the year.

equal amounts on a monthly, quarterly, or annual basis is called an **amortized loan.**[18]

Amortized Loan
A loan that is repaid in equal payments over its life.

Table 5.4 illustrates the amortization process. A homeowner borrows $100,000 on a mortgage loan, and the loan is to be repaid in five equal payments at the end of each of the next 5 years.[19] The lender charges 6% on the balance at the beginning of each year. Our first task is to determine the payment the homeowner must make each year. Here's a picture of the situation:

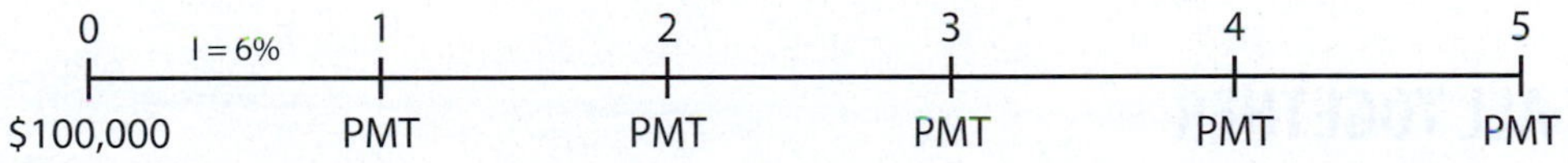

The payments must be such that the sum of their PVs equals $100,000:

$$\$100{,}000 = \frac{PMT}{(1.06)^1} + \frac{PMT}{(1.06)^2} + \frac{PMT}{(1.06)^3} + \frac{PMT}{(1.06)^4} + \frac{PMT}{(1.06)^5} = \sum_{t=1}^{5} \frac{PMT}{(1.06)^t}$$

We could insert values into a calculator as shown on the next page to get the required payments, $23,739.64:[20]

[18]The word *amortized* comes from the Latin *mors,* meaning "death"; so an amortized loan is one that is "killed off" over time.

[19]Most mortgage loans call for monthly payments over 10 to 30 years, but we use a shorter period to reduce the calculations.

[20]You could also factor out the PMT term; find the value of the remaining summation term (4.212364), and divide it into the $100,000 to find the payment, $23,739.64.

N	I/YR	PV	PMT	FV
5	6	100000		0
			−23,739.64	

Amortization Schedule
A table showing precisely how a loan will be repaid. It gives the required payment on each payment date and a breakdown of the payment, showing how much is interest and how much is repayment of principal.

Therefore, the borrower must pay the lender $23,739.64 per year for the next 5 years.

Each payment will consist of two parts—interest and repayment of principal. This breakdown is shown on an **amortization schedule**, such as the one in Table 5.4. The interest component is relatively high in the first year, but it declines as the loan balance decreases. For tax purposes, the borrower would deduct the interest component, and the lender would report the same amount as taxable income.

Self*Test*

Suppose you borrowed $30,000 on a student loan at a rate of 8% and must repay it in three equal installments at the end of each of the next 3 years. How large would your payments be; how much of the first payment would represent interest, how much would be principal; and what would your ending balance be after the first year? **(PMT = $11,641.01; Interest = $2,400; Principal = $9,241.01; Balance at end of Year 1 = $20,758.99)**

TYING IT ALL TOGETHER

In this chapter, we worked with single payments, ordinary annuities, annuities due, perpetuities, and uneven cash flow streams. One fundamental equation, Equation 5.1, is used to calculate the future value of a given amount. The equation can be transformed to Equation 5.2 and then used to find the present value of a given future amount. We used time lines to show when cash flows occur, and we saw that time value of money problems can be solved in a step-by-step manner when we work with individual cash flows, with formulas that streamline the approach, with financial calculators, and with spreadsheets.

As we noted at the outset, TVM is the single most important concept in finance, and the procedures developed in Chapter 5 are used throughout this book. Time value analysis is used to find the values of stocks, bonds, and capital budgeting projects. It is also used to analyze personal finance problems, such as the retirement issue set forth in the opening vignette. You will become more familiar with time value analysis as you go through the book, but we *strongly recommend* that you get a good handle on Chapter 5 before you continue.

Self-Test Questions and Problems

(Solutions Appear in Appendix A.)

ST-1 KEY TERMS Define each of the following terms:

a. Time line
b. FV_N; PV; I; INT; N; FVA_N; PMT; PVA_N
c. Compounding; discounting
d. Simple interest; compound interest
e. Opportunity cost
f. Annuity; ordinary (deferred) annuity; annuity due; perpetuity
g. Uneven (nonconstant) cash flow; payment (PMT); cash flow (CF_t)
h. Annual compounding; semiannual compounding
i. Nominal (quoted) interest rate; annual percentage rate (APR); effective (equivalent) annual rate (EAR or EFF%)
j. Amortized loan; amortization schedule

ST-2 FUTURE VALUE It is now January 1, 2019. Today you will deposit $1,000 into a savings account that pays 8%.

a. If the bank compounds interest annually, how much will you have in your account on January 1, 2022?
b. What will your January 1, 2022, balance be if the bank uses quarterly compounding?
c. Suppose you deposit $1,000 in three payments of $333.333 each on January 1 of 2020, 2021, and 2022. How much will you have in your account on January 1, 2022, based on 8% annual compounding?
d. How much will be in your account if the three payments begin on January 1, 2019?
e. Suppose you deposit three equal payments into your account on January 1 of 2020, 2021, and 2022. Assuming an 8% interest rate, how large must your payments be to have the same ending balance as in part a?

ST-3 TIME VALUE OF MONEY It is now January 1, 2019, and you will need $1,000 on January 1, 2023, in 4 years. Your bank compounds interest at an 8% annual rate.

a. How much must you deposit today to have a balance of $1,000 on January 1, 2023?
b. If you want to make four equal payments on each January 1 from 2020 through 2023 to accumulate the $1,000, how large must each payment be? (Note that the payments begin a year from today.)
c. If your father offers to make the payments calculated in part b ($221.92) or to give you $750 on January 1, 2020 (a year from today), which would you choose? Explain.
d. If you have only $750 on January 1, 2020, what interest rate, compounded annually for 3 years, must you earn to have $1,000 on January 1, 2023?
e. Suppose you can deposit only $200 each January 1 from 2020 through 2023 (4 years). What interest rate, with annual compounding, must you earn to end up with $1,000 on January 1, 2023?
f. Your father offers to give you $400 on January 1, 2020. You will then make six additional equal payments each 6 months from July 2020 through January 2023. If your bank pays 8% compounded semiannually, how large must each payment be for you to end up with $1,000 on January 1, 2023?
g. What is the EAR, or EFF%, earned on the bank account in part f? What is the APR earned on the account?

ST-4 EFFECTIVE ANNUAL RATES Bank A offers loans at an 8% nominal rate (its APR) but requires that interest be paid quarterly; that is, it uses quarterly compounding. Bank B wants to charge the same effective rate on its loans, but it wants to collect interest on a monthly basis, that is, to use monthly compounding. What nominal rate must Bank B set?

Questions

5-1 What is an *opportunity cost?* How is this concept used in TVM analysis, and where is it shown on a time line? Is a single number used in all situations? Explain.

5-2 Explain whether the following statement is true or false: $100 a year for 10 years is an annuity, but $100 in Year 1, $200 in Year 2, and $400 in Years 3 through 10 does *not* constitute an annuity. However, the second series *contains* an annuity.

5-3 If a firm's earnings per share grew from $1 to $2 over a 10-year period, the *total growth* would be 100%, but the *annual growth rate* would be *less than* 10%. True or false? Explain. (*Hint:* If you aren't sure, plug in some numbers and check it out.)

5-4 Would you rather have a savings account that pays 5% interest compounded semiannually or one that pays 5% interest compounded daily? Explain.

5-5 To find the present value of an uneven series of cash flows, you must find the PVs of the individual cash flows and then sum them. Annuity procedures can never be of use, even when some of the cash flows constitute an annuity, because the entire series is not an annuity. True or false? Explain.

5-6 The present value of a perpetuity is equal to the payment on the annuity, PMT, divided by the interest rate, I : PV = PMT/I. What is the *future value* of a perpetuity of PMT dollars per year? (*Hint:* The answer is infinity, but explain why.)

5-7 Banks and other lenders are required to disclose a rate called the APR. What is this rate? Why did Congress require that it be disclosed? Is it the same as the effective annual rate? If you were comparing the costs of loans from different lenders, could you use their APRs to determine the loan with the lowest effective interest rate? Explain.

5-8 What is a loan amortization schedule, and what are some ways these schedules are used?

Problems

Easy Problems 1-8

5-1 **FUTURE VALUE** If you deposit $2,000 in a bank account that pays 6% interest annually, how much will be in your account after 5 years?

5-2 **PRESENT VALUE** What is the present value of a security that will pay $29,000 in 20 years if securities of equal risk pay 5% annually?

5-3 **FINDING THE REQUIRED INTEREST RATE** Your parents will retire in 19 years. They currently have $350,000 saved, and they think they will need $800,000 at retirement. What annual interest rate must they earn to reach their goal, assuming they don't save any additional funds?

5-4 **TIME FOR A LUMP SUM TO DOUBLE** If you deposit money today in an account that pays 4% annual interest, how long will it take to double your money?

5-5 **TIME TO REACH A FINANCIAL GOAL** You have $33,556.25 in a brokerage account, and you plan to deposit an additional $5,000 at the end of every future year until your account totals $220,000. You expect to earn 12% annually on the account. How many years will it take to reach your goal?

5-6 **FUTURE VALUE: ANNUITY VERSUS ANNUITY DUE** What's the future value of a 5%, 5-year ordinary annuity that pays $800 each year? If this was an annuity due, what would its future value be?

5-7 **PRESENT AND FUTURE VALUES OF A CASH FLOW STREAM** An investment will pay $150 at the end of each of the next 3 years, $250 at the end of Year 4, $300 at the end of Year 5, and $500 at the end of Year 6. If other investments of equal risk earn 11% annually, what is its present value? Its future value?

5-8 **LOAN AMORTIZATION AND EAR** You want to buy a car, and a local bank will lend you $40,000. The loan will be fully amortized over 5 years (60 months), and the nominal interest rate will be 8% with interest paid monthly. What will be the monthly loan payment? What will be the loan's EAR?

Intermediate Problems 9-26

5-9 **PRESENT AND FUTURE VALUES FOR DIFFERENT PERIODS** Find the following values *using the equations* and then a financial calculator. Compounding/discounting occurs annually.

a. An initial $600 compounded for 1 year at 6%
b. An initial $600 compounded for 2 years at 6%
c. The present value of $600 due in 1 year at a discount rate of 6%
d. The present value of $600 due in 2 years at a discount rate of 6%

5-10 **PRESENT AND FUTURE VALUES FOR DIFFERENT INTEREST RATES** Find the following values. Compounding/discounting occurs annually.

a. An initial $200 compounded for 10 years at 4%
b. An initial $200 compounded for 10 years at 8%
c. The present value of $200 due in 10 years at 4%
d. The present value of $1,870 due in 10 years at 8% and at 4%
e. Define *present value* and illustrate it using a time line with data from part d. How are present values affected by interest rates?

5-11 **GROWTH RATES** Sawyer Corporation's 2018 sales were $5 million. Its 2013 sales were $2.5 million.

a. At what rate have sales been growing?
b. Suppose someone made this statement: "Sales doubled in 5 years. This represents a growth of 100% in 5 years; so dividing 100% by 5, we find the growth rate to be 20% per year." Is the statement correct?

5-12 **EFFECTIVE RATE OF INTEREST** Find the interest rates earned on each of the following:

a. You *borrow* $720 and promise to pay back $792 at the end of 1 year.
b. You *lend* $720 and the borrower promises to pay you $792 at the end of 1 year.
c. You *borrow* $65,000 and promise to pay back $98,319 at the end of 14 years.
d. You *borrow* $15,000 and promise to make payments of $4,058.60 at the end of each year for 5 years.

5-13 **TIME FOR A LUMP SUM TO DOUBLE** How long will it take $300 to double if it earns the following rates? Compounding occurs once a year.

a. 6%
b. 13%
c. 21%
d. 100%

5-14 **FUTURE VALUE OF AN ANNUITY** Find the *future values* of these *ordinary annuities.* Compounding occurs once a year.

a. $500 per year for 8 years at 14%
b. $250 per year for 4 years at 7%
c. $700 per year for 4 years at 0%
d. Rework parts a, b, and c assuming they are *annuities due.*

5-15 **PRESENT VALUE OF AN ANNUITY** Find the *present values* of these *ordinary annuities.* Discounting occurs once a year.

a. $600 per year for 12 years at 8%
b. $300 per year for 6 years at 4%
c. $500 per year for 6 years at 0%
d. Rework parts a, b, and c assuming they are *annuities due.*

5-16 **PRESENT VALUE OF A PERPETUITY** What is the present value of a $600 perpetuity if the interest rate is 5%? If interest rates doubled to 10%, what would its present value be?

5-17 **EFFECTIVE INTEREST RATE** You borrow $230,000; the annual loan payments are $20,430.31 for 30 years. What interest rate are you being charged?

5-18 UNEVEN CASH FLOW STREAM

a. Find the present values of the following cash flow streams at a 5% discount rate.

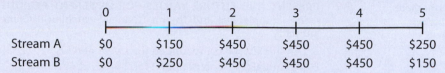

	0	1	2	3	4	5
Stream A	$0	$150	$450	$450	$450	$250
Stream B	$0	$250	$450	$450	$450	$150

b. What are the PVs of the streams at a 0% discount rate?

5-19 FUTURE VALUE OF AN ANNUITY Your client is 26 years old. She wants to begin saving for retirement, with the first payment to come one year from now. She can save $8,000 per year, and you advise her to invest it in the stock market, which you expect to provide an average return of 10% in the future.

a. If she follows your advice, how much money will she have at 65?

b. How much will she have at 70?

c. She expects to live for 20 years if she retires at 65 and for 15 years if she retires at 70. If her investments continue to earn the same rate, how much will she be able to withdraw at the end of each year after retirement at each retirement age?

5-20 PV OF A CASH FLOW STREAM A rookie quarterback is negotiating his first NFL contract. His opportunity cost is 7%. He has been offered three possible 4-year contracts. Payments are guaranteed, and they would be made at the end of each year. Terms of each contract are as follows:

	1	2	3	4
Contract 1	$3,000,000	$3,000,000	$3,000,000	$3,000,000
Contract 2	$2,000,000	$3,000,000	$4,500,000	$5,500,000
Contract 3	$7,000,000	$1,000,000	$1,000,000	$1,000,000

As his adviser, which contract would you recommend that he accept?

5-21 EVALUATING LUMP SUMS AND ANNUITIES Kristina just won the lottery, and she must choose among three award options. She can elect to receive a lump sum today of $62 million, to receive 10 end-of-year payments of $9.5 million, or to receive 30 end-of-year payments of $5.6 million.

a. If she thinks she can earn 7% annually, which should she choose?

b. If she expects to earn 8% annually, which is the best choice?

c. If she expects to earn 9% annually, which option would you recommend?

d. Explain how interest rates influence her choice.

5-22 LOAN AMORTIZATION Jan sold her house on December 31 and took a $10,000 mortgage as part of the payment. The 10-year mortgage has a 10% nominal interest rate, but it calls for semiannual payments beginning next June 30. Next year Jan must report on Schedule B of her IRS Form 1040 the amount of interest that was included in the two payments she received during the year.

a. What is the dollar amount of each payment Jan receives?

b. How much interest was included in the first payment? How much repayment of principal was included? How do these values change for the second payment?

c. How much interest must Jan report on Schedule B for the first year? Will her interest income be the same next year?

d. If the payments are constant, why does the amount of interest income change over time?

5-23 FUTURE VALUE FOR VARIOUS COMPOUNDING PERIODS Find the amount to which $500 will grow under each of these conditions:

a. 12% compounded annually for 5 years

b. 12% compounded semiannually for 5 years

c. 12% compounded quarterly for 5 years

d. 12% compounded monthly for 5 years

e. 12% compounded daily for 5 years

f. Why does the observed pattern of FVs occur?

5-24 **PRESENT VALUE FOR VARIOUS DISCOUNTING PERIODS** Find the present value of $500 due in the future under each of these conditions:

a. 12% nominal rate, semiannual compounding, discounted back 5 years
b. 12% nominal rate, quarterly compounding, discounted back 5 years
c. 12% nominal rate, monthly compounding, discounted back 1 year
d. Why do the differences in the PVs occur?

5-25 **FUTURE VALUE OF AN ANNUITY** Find the future values of the following ordinary annuities:

a. FV of $400 paid each 6 months for 5 years at a nominal rate of 12% compounded semiannually
b. FV of $200 paid each 3 months for 5 years at a nominal rate of 12% compounded quarterly
c. These annuities receive the same amount of cash during the 5-year period and earn interest at the same nominal rate, yet the annuity in part b ends up larger than the one in part a. Why does this occur?

5-26 **PV AND LOAN ELIGIBILITY** You have saved $4,000 for a down payment on a new car. The largest monthly payment you can afford is $350. The loan will have a 12% APR based on end-of-month payments. What is the most expensive car you can afford if you finance it for 48 months? For 60 months?

Challenging Problems 27-40

5-27 **EFFECTIVE VERSUS NOMINAL INTEREST RATES** Bank A pays 2% interest compounded annually on deposits, while Bank B pays 1.75% compounded daily.

a. Based on the EAR (or EFF%), which bank should you use?
b. Could your choice of banks be influenced by the fact that you might want to withdraw your funds during the year as opposed to at the end of the year? Assume that your funds must be left on deposit during an entire compounding period in order to receive any interest.

5-28 **NOMINAL INTEREST RATE AND EXTENDING CREDIT** As a jewelry store manager, you want to offer credit, with interest on outstanding balances paid monthly. To carry receivables, you must borrow funds from your bank at a nominal 9%, monthly compounding. To offset your overhead, you want to charge your customers an EAR (or EFF%) that is 3% more than the bank is charging you. What APR rate should you charge your customers?

5-29 **BUILDING CREDIT COST INTO PRICES** Your firm sells for cash only, but it is thinking of offering credit, allowing customers 90 days to pay. Customers understand the time value of money, so they would all wait and pay on the 90th day. To carry these receivables, you would have to borrow funds from your bank at a nominal 9%, daily compounding based on a 360-day year. You want to increase your base prices by exactly enough to offset your bank interest cost. To the closest whole percentage point, by how much should you raise your product prices?

5-30 **REACHING A FINANCIAL GOAL** Allison and Leslie, who are twins, just received $10,000 each for their 25th birthday. They both have aspirations to become millionaires. Each plans to make a $5,000 annual contribution to her "early retirement fund" on her birthday, beginning a year from today. Allison opened an account with the Safety First Bond Fund, a mutual fund that invests in high-quality bonds whose investors have earned 8% per year in the past. Leslie invested in the New Issue Bio-Tech Fund, which invests in small, newly issued bio-tech stocks and whose investors have earned an average of 13% per year in the fund's relatively short history.

a. If the two women's funds earn the same returns in the future as in the past, how old will each be when she becomes a millionaire?
b. How large would Allison's annual contributions have to be for her to become a millionaire at the same age as Leslie, assuming their expected returns are realized?
c. Is it rational or irrational for Allison to invest in the bond fund rather than in stocks?

5-31 **REQUIRED LUMP SUM PAYMENT** Starting next year, you will need $5,000 annually for 4 years to complete your education. (One year from today you will withdraw the first $5,000.) Your uncle deposits an amount *today* in a bank paying 6% annual interest, which will provide the needed $5,000 payments.

a. How large must the deposit be?
b. How much will be in the account immediately after you make the first withdrawal?

5-32 REACHING A FINANCIAL GOAL Six years from today you need $10,000. You plan to deposit $1,500 annually, with the first payment to be made a year from today, in an account that pays a 5% effective annual rate. Your last deposit, which will occur at the end of Year 6, will be for less than $1,500 if less is needed to reach $10,000. How large will your last payment be?

5-33 FV OF UNEVEN CASH FLOW You want to buy a house within 3 years, and you are currently saving for the down payment. You plan to save $9,000 at the end of the first year, and you anticipate that your annual savings will increase by 5% annually thereafter. Your expected annual return is 8%. How much will you have for a down payment at the end of Year 3?

5-34 AMORTIZATION SCHEDULE

a. Set up an amortization schedule for a $19,000 loan to be repaid in equal installments at the end of each of the next 3 years. The interest rate is 8% compounded annually.

b. What percentage of the payment represents interest and what percentage represents principal for each of the 3 years? Why do these percentages change over time?

5-35 AMORTIZATION SCHEDULE WITH A BALLOON PAYMENT You want to buy a house that costs $140,000. You have $14,000 for a down payment, but your credit is such that mortgage companies will not lend you the required $126,000. However, the realtor persuades the seller to take a $126,000 mortgage (called a seller take-back mortgage) at a rate of 5%, provided the loan is paid off in full in 3 years. You expect to inherit $140,000 in 3 years, but right now all you have is $14,000, and you can afford to make payments of no more than $22,000 per year given your salary. (The loan would call for monthly payments, but assume end-of-year annual payments to simplify things.)

a. If the loan was amortized over 3 years, how large would each annual payment be? Could you afford those payments?

b. If the loan was amortized over 30 years, what would each payment be? Could you afford those payments?

c. To satisfy the seller, the 30-year mortgage loan would be written as a balloon note, which means that at the end of the third year, you would have to make the regular payment plus the remaining balance on the loan. What would the loan balance be at the end of Year 3, and what would the balloon payment be?

5-36 NONANNUAL COMPOUNDING

a. You plan to make five deposits of $1,000 each, one every 6 months, with the first payment being made in 6 months. You will then make no more deposits. If the bank pays 6% nominal interest, compounded semiannually, how much will be in your account after 3 years?

b. One year from today you must make a payment of $4,000. To prepare for this payment, you plan to make two equal quarterly deposits (at the end of Quarters 1 and 2) in a bank that pays 6% nominal interest compounded quarterly. How large must each of the two payments be?

5-37 PAYING OFF CREDIT CARDS Simon recently received a credit card with an 18% nominal interest rate. With the card, he purchased an Apple iPhone 7 for $372.71. The minimum payment on the card is only $10 per month.

a. If Simon makes the minimum monthly payment and makes no other charges, how many months will it be before he pays off the card? Round to the nearest month.

b. If Simon makes monthly payments of $35, how many months will it be before he pays off the debt? Round to the nearest month.

c. How much more in total payments will Simon make under the $10-a-month plan than under the $35-a-month plan? Make sure you use three decimal places for N.

5-38 PV AND A LAWSUIT SETTLEMENT It is now December 31, 2018 (t = 0), and a jury just found in favor of a woman who sued the city for injuries sustained in a January 2017 accident. She requested recovery of lost wages plus $300,000 for pain and suffering plus $60,000 for legal expenses. Her doctor testified that she has been unable to work since the accident and that she will not be able to work in the future. She is now 62, and the jury decided that she would have worked for another 3 years. She was scheduled to have earned $36,000 in 2017. (To simplify this problem, assume that the entire annual salary amount would have been received on December 31, 2017.) Her employer testified that she probably would have received raises of 3% per year. The actual payment for the jury award will be made on December 31, 2019. The judge stipulated that all dollar amounts are to be adjusted to a present value basis on December 31, 2019, using an 8% annual interest rate and using compound, not simple, interest. Furthermore, he stipulated that the pain and suffering and legal expenses should be based on a December 31, 2018, date. How large a check must the city write on December 31, 2019?

5-39 **REQUIRED ANNUITY PAYMENTS** Your father is 50 years old and will retire in 10 years. He expects to live for 25 years after he retires, until he is 85. He wants a fixed retirement income that has the same purchasing power at the time he retires as $50,000 has today. (The real value of his retirement income will decline annually after he retires.) His *retirement income will begin the day he retires,* 10 years from today, at which time he will receive 24 additional annual payments. Annual inflation is expected to be 4%. He currently has $90,000 saved, and he expects to earn 8% annually on his savings. How much must he save during each of the next 10 years (end-of-year deposits) to meet his retirement goal?

5-40 **REQUIRED ANNUITY PAYMENTS** A father is now planning a savings program to put his daughter through college. She is 13, plans to enroll at the university in 5 years, and should graduate 4 years later. Currently, the annual cost (for everything—food, clothing, tuition, books, transportation, and so forth) is $12,000, but these costs are expected to increase by 6% annually. The college requires total payment at the start of the year. She now has $10,000 in a college savings account that pays 9% annually. Her father will make six equal annual deposits into her account; the first deposit today and the sixth on the day she starts college. How large must each of the six payments be? (*Hint:* Calculate the cost (inflated at 6%) for each year of college and find the total present value of those costs, discounted at 9%, as of the day she enters college. Then find the compounded value of her initial $10,000 on that same day. The difference between the PV of costs and the amount that would be in the savings account must be made up by the father's deposits, so find the six equal payments that will compound to the required amount.)

Comprehensive/Spreadsheet Problem

5-41 **TIME VALUE OF MONEY** Answer the following questions:

a. Assuming a rate of 10% annually, find the FV of $1,000 after 5 years.

b. What is the investment's FV at rates of 0%, 5%, and 20% after 0, 1, 2, 3, 4, and 5 years?

c. Find the PV of $1,000 due in 5 years if the discount rate is 10%.

d. What is the rate of return on a security that costs $1,000 and returns $2,000 after 5 years?

e. Suppose California's population is 36.5 million people and its population is expected to grow by 2% annually. How long will it take for the population to double?

f. Find the PV of an ordinary annuity that pays $1,000 each of the next 5 years if the interest rate is 15%. What is the annuity's FV?

g. How will the PV and FV of the annuity in part f change if it is an annuity due?

h. What will the FV and the PV be for $1,000 due in 5 years if the interest rate is 10%, semiannual compounding?

i. What will the annual payments be for an ordinary annuity for 10 years with a PV of $1,000 if the interest rate is 8%? What will the payments be if this is an annuity due?

j. Find the PV and the FV of an investment that pays 8% annually and makes the following end-of-year payments:

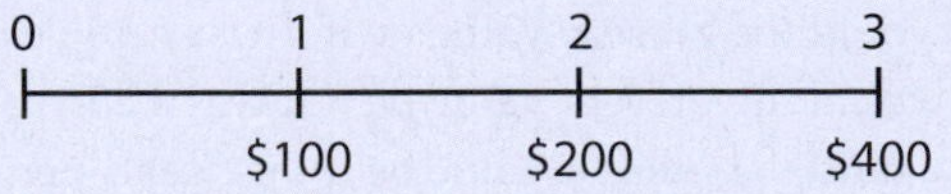

k. Five banks offer nominal rates of 6% on deposits, but A pays interest annually, B pays semiannually, C pays quarterly, D pays monthly, and E pays daily.

1. What effective annual rate does each bank pay? If you deposit $5,000 in each bank today, how much will you have in each bank at the end of 1 year? 2 years?
2. If all of the banks are insured by the government (the FDIC) and thus are equally risky, will they be equally able to attract funds? If not (and the TVM is the only consideration), what nominal rate will cause all of the banks to provide the same effective annual rate as Bank A?
3. Suppose you don't have the $5,000 but need it at the end of 1 year. You plan to make a series of deposits—annually for A, semiannually for B, quarterly for C, monthly for

D, and daily for E—with payments beginning today. How large must the payments be to each bank?

4. Even if the five banks provided the same effective annual rate, would a rational investor be indifferent between the banks? Explain.

l. Suppose you borrow $15,000. The loan's annual interest rate is 8%, and it requires four equal end-of-year payments. Set up an amortization schedule that shows the annual payments, interest payments, principal repayments, and beginning and ending loan balances.

INTEGRATED CASE

FIRST NATIONAL BANK

5-42 **TIME VALUE OF MONEY ANALYSIS** You have applied for a job with a local bank. As part of its evaluation process, you must take an examination on time value of money analysis covering the following questions:

a. Draw time lines for (1) a $100 lump sum cash flow at the end of Year 2; (2) an ordinary annuity of $100 per year for 3 years; and (3) an uneven cash flow stream of −$50, $100, $75, and $50 at the end of Years 0 through 3.

b. 1. What's the future value of $100 after 3 years if it earns 4%, annual compounding?

2. What's the present value of $100 to be received in 3 years if the interest rate is 4%, annual compounding?

c. What annual interest rate would cause $100 to grow to $119.10 in 3 years?

d. If a company's sales are growing at a rate of 10% annually, how long will it take sales to double?

e. What's the difference between an ordinary annuity and an annuity due? What type of annuity is shown here? How would you change it to the other type of annuity?

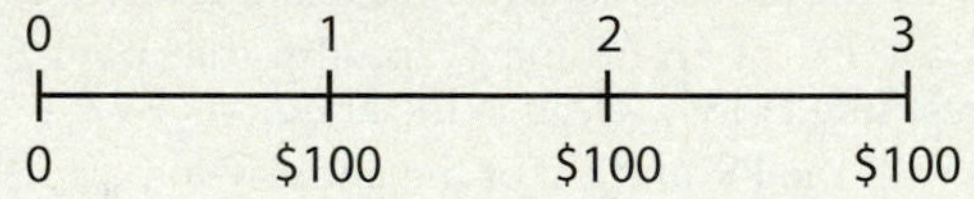

f. 1. What is the future value of a 3-year, $100 ordinary annuity if the annual interest rate is 4%?

2. What is its present value?

3. What would the future and present values be if it was an annuity due?

g. A 5-year, $100 ordinary annuity has an annual interest rate of 4%.

1. What is its present value?

2. What would the present value be if it was a 10-year annuity?

3. What would the present value be if it was a 25-year annuity?

4. What would the present value be if this was a perpetuity?

h. A 20-year-old student wants to save $5 a day for her retirement. Every day she places $5 in a drawer. At the end of each year, she invests the accumulated savings ($1,825) in a brokerage account with an expected annual return of 8%.

1. If she keeps saving in this manner, how much will she have accumulated at age 65?

2. If a 40-year-old investor began saving in this manner, how much would he have at age 65?

3. How much would the 40-year-old investor have to save each year to accumulate the same amount at 65 as the 20-year-old investor?

i. What is the present value of the following uneven cash flow stream? The annual interest rate is 4%.

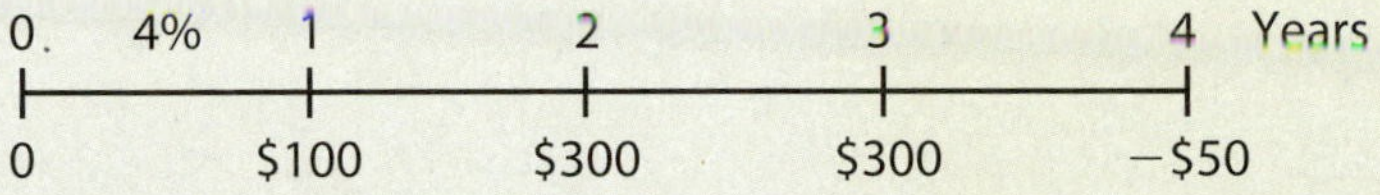

j. 1. Will the future value be larger or smaller if we compound an initial amount more often than annually (e.g., semiannually, holding the stated (nominal) rate constant)? Why?

2. Define (a) the stated (or quoted or nominal) rate, (b) the periodic rate, and (c) the effective annual rate (EAR or EFF%).

3. What is the EAR corresponding to a nominal rate of 4% compounded semiannually? Compounded quarterly? Compounded daily?

4. What is the future value of $100 after 3 years under 4% semiannual compounding? Quarterly compounding?

k. When will the EAR equal the nominal (quoted) rate?

l. 1. What is the value at the end of Year 3 of the following cash flow stream if interest is 4% compounded semiannually? (*Hint:* You can use the EAR and treat the cash flows as an ordinary annuity or use the periodic rate and compound the cash flows individually.)

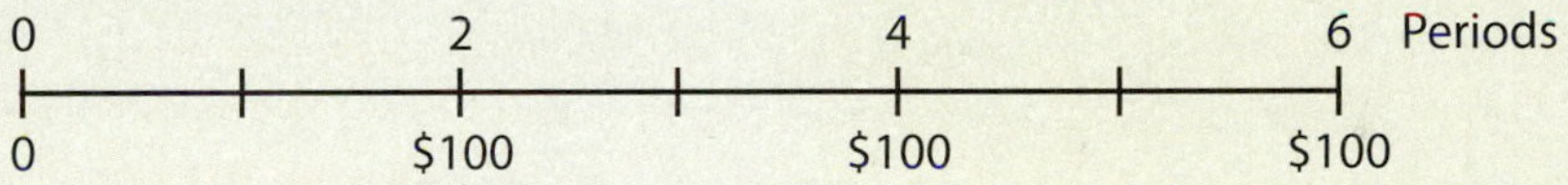

2. What is the PV?

3. What would be wrong with your answer to parts (1) and (2) if you used the nominal rate, 4%, rather than the EAR or the periodic rate, $I_{NOM}/2 = 4\%/2 = 2\%$, to solve the problems?

m. 1. Construct an amortization schedule for a $1,000, 4% annual interest loan with three equal installments.

2. What is the annual interest expense for the borrower and the annual interest income for the lender during Year 2?

part 3

Financial Assets

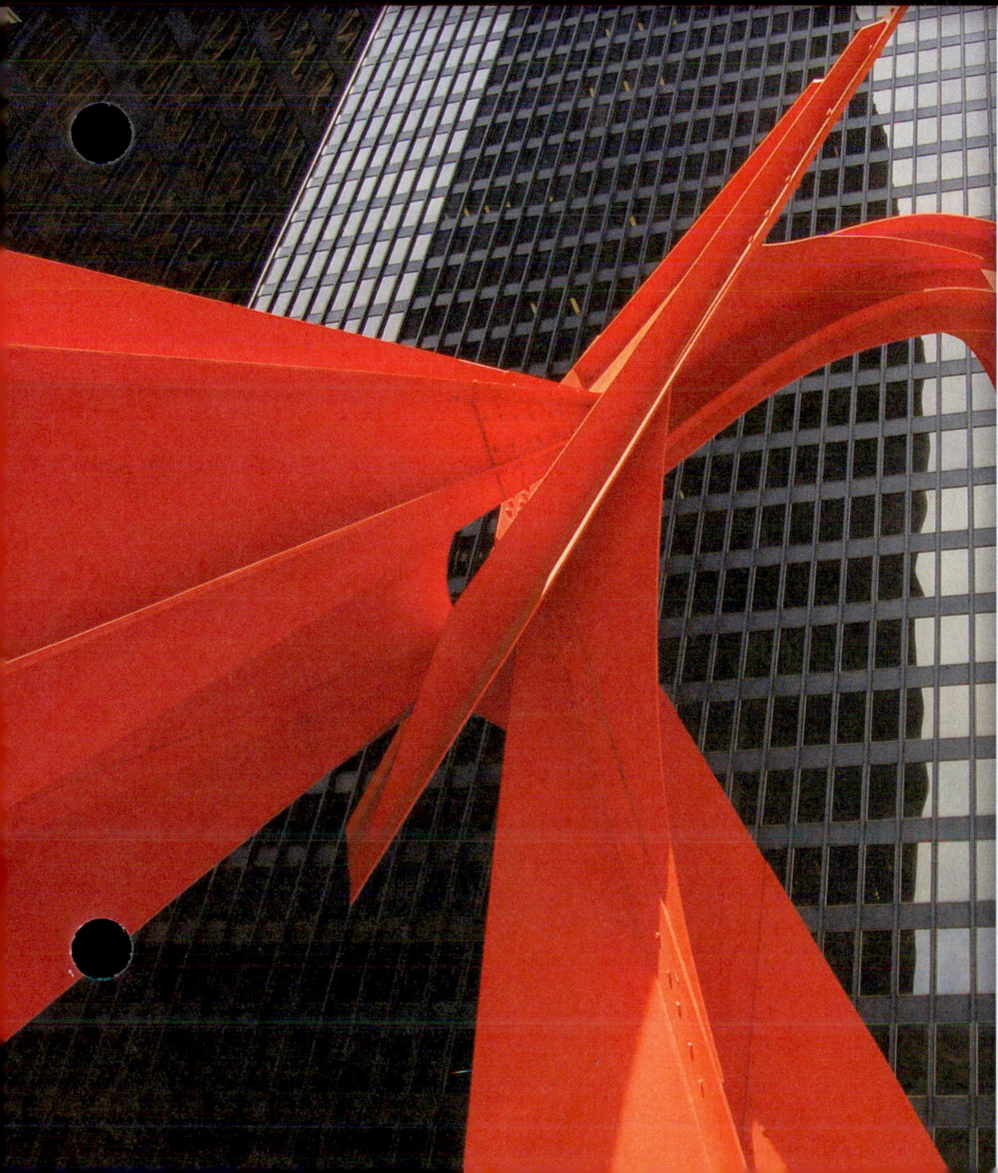

CHAPTERS

Interest Rates

CHAPTER

6

ZUMA Press, Inc./Alamy Stock Photo

The Fed Shifts Course

The Federal Reserve often confronts a difficult balancing act. If their policies are too restrictive, the accompanying sharp rise in interest rates may lead to an economic slowdown. On the other hand, if they make credit too available, there is the risk of stimulating higher inflation. The ultimate goal is to find the so-called Goldilocks policy, which keeps the economy strong without triggering inflation.

Despite ever present fears about signs in early 2018 that the economy had indeed reached a bliss point, in the midst of a growing economy, low unemployment, and low to moderate inflation levels, Jerome Powell took over as the Federal Reserve Board chair in February 2018. Under his leadership, the Fed has continued its plans to slowly increase interest rates to keep the improving economy from overheating. In the face of continued good news, the Federal Reserve in May 2018 reaffirmed its commitment to slow and steady rate increases.

Following the Fed's May statements, *The Wall Street Journal* offered the following summary and quote from a leading practitioner:

> *After years of aggressive, postcrisis interventions to heal labor markets, and delayed rate rises to spur inflation, central bank officials now have the economy largely where they want it.*
>
> *Labor markets are strong. Wages are rising. And inflation has reached the central bank's 2% target but with little evidence of a breakout.*
>
> *"Mission accomplished, for now," said Michael Feroli, chief U.S. economist at JPMorganChase, in a research note Wednesday.*

To be sure, the Fed's recent policy shifts are a dramatic departure from what we observed a decade earlier. To keep the economy afloat after the financial crisis of 2008–2009, the Federal Reserve established extremely low interest rates. The hope was that the lower cost of capital would encourage business investment, help repair a damaged housing market, and prop up stock and bond markets, all of which would help stimulate the overall economy. Looking back, after the crisis, it appears that policymakers successfully kept the economy from immediately collapsing, but the economy was still weak, and unemployment remained stubbornly high.

In response to the economy's continued sluggishness, the Federal Reserve redoubled its efforts to strengthen the economy with its policy of "quantitative easing." Through this policy, the Fed has systematically purchased large amounts of longer-term financial assets from leading financial institutions. The Fed paid for these assets by injecting new funds into the economy, which helped put downward pressure on interest rates. As a result of their actions, the 10-year Treasury rate was pushed below 2%, and shorter-term Treasury rates were close to zero. However, as the economy began to show limited signs of life, there were concerns that the Federal Reserve's stimulative policies would eventually trigger a rise in inflation. Trying to maintain a delicate balance, the Fed reaffirmed its policy of quantitative easing. However, the Federal Reserve also suggested that in the months ahead it might "taper" its aggressive bond-buying program.

In early 2014, Janet Yellen succeeded Ben Bernanke as Chair of the Federal Reserve, and immediately supported the Fed's balancing act. Over the next year and a half, the economy showed signs of slow improvement, but the Fed resisted raising rates until December 2015. In arguing against rate hikes, many Fed leaders pointed out that despite improvement, the economy was still far from robust and that there were few signs of rising inflation. However, other policymakers promoted rate increases, arguing that it was important to restore a "normal" rate environment and to respond before inflation increased. A month after the 2016 election, the Fed once again raised their short-term interest rate target, and, as just described, in the year and a half since then, has continued its policy of slowly increasing rates.

Although the Federal Reserve has a tremendous influence on interest rates, other factors have helped keep interest rates low. Most notably, inflation remains low and foreign investors have maintained a strong willingness to purchase U.S. securities. Looking ahead, there is a concern that some of these forces may start working in reverse. Moreover, if inflation does pick up, this would also likely lead to a drop in the value of the U.S. dollar. At the same time, federal budget deficits also put upward pressure on interest rates. To the extent that deficits and inflation fears combine with a weakening dollar, foreign investors may sell U.S. bonds, which would put even more upward pressure on rates.

Because corporations and individuals are greatly affected by interest rates, this chapter takes a closer look at the major factors that determine those rates. As we will see, there is no single interest rate—various factors determine the rate that each borrower pays—and in some cases, rates on different types of debt move in different directions. With these issues in mind, we will also consider the various factors influencing the spreads between long- and short-term interest rates and between Treasury and corporate bonds.

Sources: Nick Timiraos, "Fed Holds Rates Steady, but Indicates Increases Will Continue," *The Wall Street Journal* (www.wsj.com), May 2, 2018; John Hilsenrath and Victoria McGrane, "Yellen Stakes Out a Flexible Policy Path," *The Wall Street Journal* (www.wsj.com), April 16, 2014; Jeff Cox, "Fed to Keep Easing, Sets Target for Rates," *CNBC* (www.cnbc.com), December 12, 2012; Eric Morath, "Brisk Jobs Growth Puts Fed on Notice," *The Wall Street Journal Weekend*, March 7–8, 2015, pp. A1–A2; and Patti Domm, "Fed Surprises with Three Rate Hikes Next Year—And It Could Need to Do More," *CNBC* (www.cnbc.com), December 14, 2016.

PUTTING THINGS IN PERSPECTIVE

Companies raise capital in two main forms: debt and equity. In a free economy, capital, like other items, is allocated through a market system, where funds are transferred and prices are established. The interest rate is the price that lenders receive and borrowers pay for debt capital. Similarly, equity investors expect to receive dividends and capital gains, the sum of which represents the cost of equity. We take up the cost of equity in a later chapter, but our focus in this chapter is on the cost of debt. We begin by examining the factors that affect the supply of and demand for capital, which in turn affects the cost of money. We will see that there is no single interest rate—interest rates on different types of debt vary depending on

the borrower's risk, the use of the funds borrowed, the type of collateral used to back the loan, and the length of time the money is needed. In this chapter, we concentrate mainly on how these various factors affect the cost of debt for individuals, but in later chapters, we delve into the cost of debt for a business and its role in investment decisions. As you will see in Chapters 7 and 9, the cost of debt is a key determinant of bond and stock prices; it is also an important component of the cost of corporate capital, which we cover in Chapter 10.

When you finish this chapter, you should be able to do the following:

- **List the various factors that influence the cost of money.**
- **Discuss how market interest rates are affected by borrowers' need for capital, expected inflation, different securities' risks, and securities' liquidity.**
- **Explain what the yield curve is, what determines its shape, and how you can use the yield curve to help forecast future interest rates.**

6-1 The Cost of Money

Production Opportunities
The investment opportunities in productive (cash generating) assets.

Time Preferences for Consumption
The preferences of consumers for current consumption as opposed to saving for future consumption.

Risk
In a financial market context, the chance that an investment will provide a low or negative return.

Inflation
The amount by which prices increase over time.

The four most fundamental factors affecting the cost of money are (1) **production opportunities**, (2) **time preferences for consumption**, (3) **risk**, and (4) **inflation**. To see how these factors operate, visualize an isolated island community where people live on fish. They have a stock of fishing gear that permits them to survive reasonably well, but they would like to have more fish. Now suppose one of the island's inhabitants, Mr. Crusoe, had a bright idea for a new type of fishnet that would enable him to double his daily catch. However, it would take him a year to perfect the design, build the net, and learn to use it efficiently. Mr. Crusoe would probably starve before he could put his new net into operation. Therefore, he might suggest to Ms. Robinson, Mr. Friday, and several others that if they would give him one fish each day for a year, he would return two fish a day the next year. If someone accepted the offer, the fish that Ms. Robinson and the others gave to Mr. Crusoe would constitute *savings*, these savings would be *invested* in the fishnet, and the extra fish the net produced would constitute a *return on the investment*.

Obviously, the more productive Mr. Crusoe thought the new fishnet would be, the more he could afford to offer potential investors for their savings. In this example, we assume that Mr. Crusoe thought he would be able to pay (and thus he offered) a 100% rate of return—he offered to give back two fish for every one he received. He might have tried to attract savings for less—for example, he might have offered only 1.5 fish per day next year for every one he received this year, which would represent a 50% rate of return to Ms. Robinson and the other potential savers.

How attractive Mr. Crusoe's offer appeared to a potential saver would depend in large part on the saver's *time preference for consumption*. For example, Ms. Robinson might be thinking of retirement, and she might be willing to trade fish today for fish in the future on a one-for-one basis. On the other hand, Mr. Friday might have a wife and several young children and need his current fish; so he might be unwilling to "lend" a fish today for anything less than three fish next year. Mr. Friday would be said to have a high time preference for current consumption, and Ms. Robinson, a low time preference. Note also that if the entire population were living right at the subsistence level, time preferences for current consumption would necessarily be high; aggregate savings would be low; interest rates would be high; and capital formation would be difficult.

The *risk* inherent in the fishnet project (and thus in Mr. Crusoe's ability to repay the loan) also affects the return that investors require: The higher the perceived risk, the higher the required rate of return. Also, in a more complex society, there are many businesses like Mr. Crusoe's, many goods other than fish, and many savers like Ms. Robinson and Mr. Friday. Therefore, people use money as a medium of exchange rather than barter with fish. When money is used, its value in the future, which is affected by *inflation*, comes into play: The higher the expected rate of inflation, the larger the required dollar return. We discuss this point in detail later in the chapter.

Thus, we see that the interest rate paid to savers depends (1) on the rate of return that producers expect to earn on invested capital, (2) on savers' time preferences for current versus future consumption, (3) on the riskiness of the loan, and (4) on the expected future rate of inflation. Producers' expected returns on their business investments set an upper limit to how much they can pay for savings, while consumers' time preferences for consumption establish how much consumption they are willing to defer and hence how much they will save at different interest rates.[1] Higher risk and higher inflation also lead to higher interest rates.

Self*Test*

What is the price paid to borrow debt capital called?

What are the two items whose sum is the cost of equity?

What four fundamental factors affect the cost of money?

Which factor sets an upper limit on how much can be paid for savings?

Which factor determines how much will be saved at different interest rates?

How do risk and inflation impact interest rates in the economy?

6-2 Interest Rate Levels

Borrowers bid for the available supply of debt capital using interest rates: The firms with the most profitable investment opportunities are willing and able to pay the most for capital, so they tend to attract it away from inefficient firms and firms whose products are not in demand. At the same time, government policy can also influence the allocation of capital and the level of interest rates. For example, the federal government has agencies that help designated individuals or groups obtain credit on favorable terms. Among those eligible for this kind of assistance are small businesses, certain minorities, and firms willing to build plants in areas with high unemployment. Still, most capital in the United States is allocated through the price system, where the interest rate is the price.

Figure 6.1 shows how supply and demand interact to determine interest rates in two capital markets. Markets L and H represent two of the many capital markets in existence. The supply curve in each market is upward sloping, which indicates that investors are willing to supply more capital the higher the interest rate they receive on their capital. Likewise, the downward-sloping demand curve indicates that borrowers will borrow more if interest rates are lower. The interest rate in each market is the point where the supply and demand curves intersect. The going interest rate, designated as r, is initially 5% for the low-risk securities in Market L. Borrowers whose credit is strong enough to participate in this market can obtain funds at a cost of 5%, and investors who want to put their money to work without much risk can obtain a 5% return. Riskier borrowers must obtain higher cost funds in Market H, where investors who are more willing to take risks expect to earn a 7%

[1]The term *producers* in this example is too narrow. A better word might be *borrowers,* which would include corporations, home purchasers, people borrowing to go to college, and even people borrowing to buy autos or to pay for vacations. Also, the wealth of a society and its demographics influence its people's ability to save and thus their time preferences for current versus future consumption.

FIGURE 6.1 Interest Rates as a Function of Supply and Demand for Funds

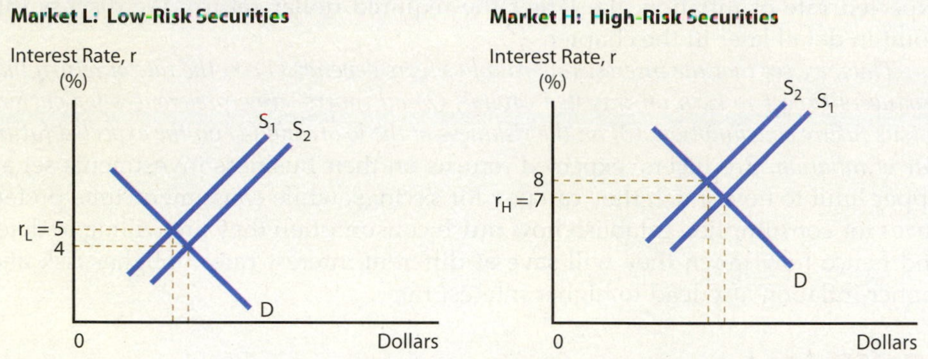

return but also realize that they might receive much less. In this scenario, investors are willing to accept the higher risk in Market H in exchange for a *risk premium* of 7% − 5% = 2%.

Now let's assume that because of changing market forces, investors perceive that Market H has become relatively more risky. This changing perception will induce many investors to shift toward safer investments—referred to as a "flight to quality." As investors move their money from Market H to Market L, the supply of funds is increased in Market L from S_1 to S_2, and the increased availability of capital will push down interest rates in this market from 5% to 4%. At the same time, as investors move their money out of Market H, there will be a decreased supply of funds in that market, and tighter credit in that market will force interest rates up from 7% to 8%. In this new environment, money is transferred from Market H to Market L and the risk premium rises from 2% to 8% − 4% = 4%.

There are many capital markets in the United States, and Figure 6.1 highlights the fact that they are interconnected. U.S. firms also invest and raise capital throughout the world, and foreigners both borrow and lend in the United States. There are markets for home loans; farm loans; business loans; federal, state, and local government loans; and consumer loans. Within each category, there are regional markets as well as different types of submarkets. For example, in real estate, there are separate markets for first and second mortgages and for loans on single-family homes, apartments, office buildings, shopping centers, and vacant land. And, of course, there are separate markets for prime and subprime mortgage loans. Within the business sector, there are dozens of types of debt securities and there are several different markets for common stocks.

There is a price for each type of capital, and these prices change over time as supply and demand conditions change. Figure 6.2 shows how long- and short-term interest rates to business borrowers have varied since the early 1970s. Notice that short-term interest rates are especially volatile, rising rapidly during booms and falling equally rapidly during recessions. (The shaded areas of the chart indicate recessions.) When the economy is expanding, firms need capital, and this demand pushes rates up. Inflationary pressures are strongest during business booms, also exerting upward pressure on rates. Conditions are reversed during recessions: Slack business reduces the demand for credit, inflation falls, and the Federal Reserve increases the supply of funds to help stimulate the economy. The result is a decline in interest rates.

These tendencies do not always hold exactly, as demonstrated by the period after 1984. Oil prices fell dramatically in 1985 and 1986, reducing inflationary pressures on other prices and easing fears of serious long-term inflation.

FIGURE 6.2 Long- and Short-Term Interest Rates, 1972–2018

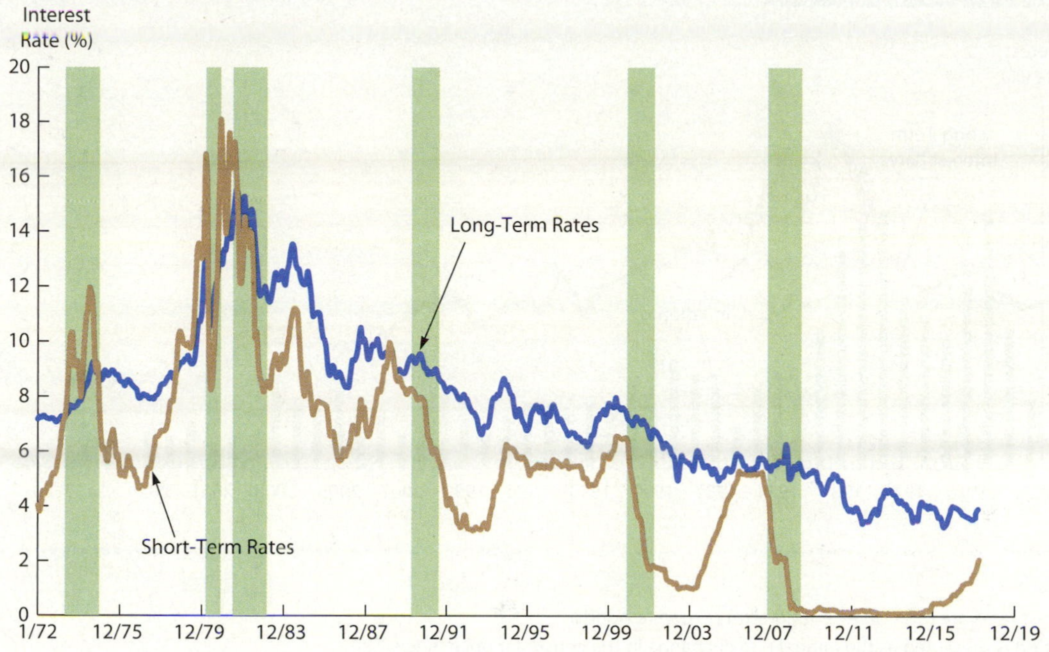

Notes:

1. The shaded areas designate business recessions.
2. Short-term rates are measured by 3- to 6-month loans to very large, strong corporations; long-term rates are measured by AAA corporate bonds.

Sources: St. Louis Federal Reserve FRED database, fred.stlouisfed.org/series/AAA and fred.stlouisfed.org/series/CPN3M.

Earlier these fears had pushed interest rates to record levels. The economy from 1984 to 1987 was strong, but the declining fears of inflation more than offset the normal tendency for interest rates to rise during good economic times; the net result was lower interest rates.[2]

The relationship between inflation and long-term interest rates is highlighted in Figure 6.3, which plots inflation over time along with long-term interest rates. In the early 1960s, inflation averaged 1% per year and interest rates on high-quality long-term bonds averaged 4%. Then the Vietnam War heated up, leading to an increase in inflation, and interest rates began an upward climb. When the war ended in the early 1970s, inflation dipped a bit, but then the 1973 Arab oil embargo led to rising oil prices, much higher inflation rates, and sharply higher interest rates.

Inflation peaked at about 13% in 1980. But interest rates continued to increase into 1981 and 1982, and they remained quite high until 1985 because people feared another increase in inflation. Thus, the "inflationary psychology" created during the 1970s persisted until the mid-1980s. People gradually realized that the Federal Reserve was serious about keeping inflation down, that global competition was keeping U.S. auto producers and other corporations from raising prices as they had in the past, and that constraints on corporate price increases were diminishing labor unions' ability to push through cost-increasing wage hikes. As these realizations set in, interest rates declined.

The current interest rate minus the current inflation rate (which is also the gap between the inflation bars and the interest rate curve in Figure 6.3) is defined as

[2]Short-term rates are responsive to current economic conditions, whereas long-term rates primarily reflect long-run expectations for inflation. As a result, short-term rates are sometimes above and sometimes below long-term rates. The relationship between long- and short-term rates is called the *term structure of interest rates*, and it is discussed later in this chapter.

FIGURE 6.3 Relationship Between Annual Inflation Rates and Long-Term Interest Rates, 1972–2018

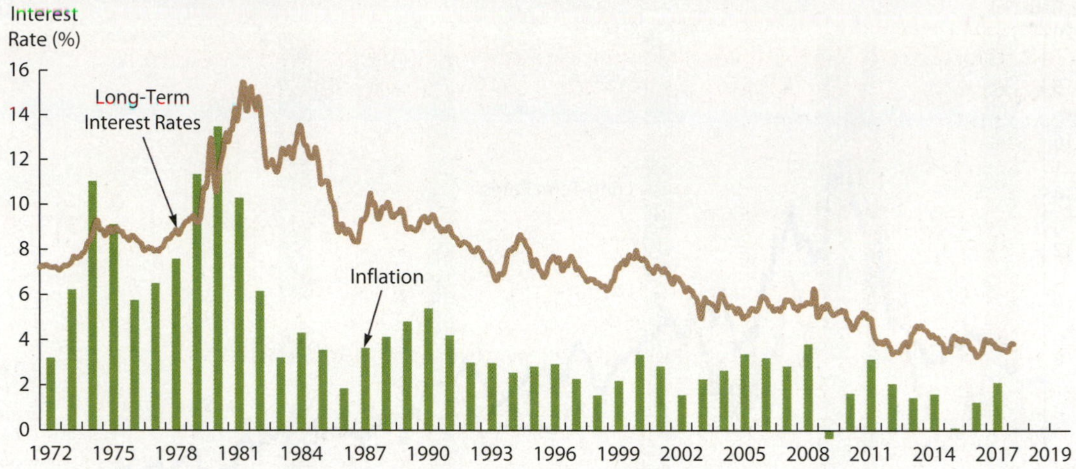

Notes:

1. Interest rates are rates on AAA long-term corporate bonds.
2. Inflation is measured as the annual rate of change in the consumer price index (CPI).

Sources: St. Louis Federal Reserve, FRED database (fred.stlouisfed.org/series/AAA) and Department of Labor, Bureau of Labor Statistics, CPI-All Urban Consumers (Current Series), 1982–1984 = 100 (data.bls.gov/cgi-bin/surveymost?cu).

the "current real rate of interest." It is called a "real rate" because it shows how much investors really earned after the effects of inflation are removed. The real rate was extremely high during the mid-1980s, but it has generally been in the range of 1% to 4% since 1987.[3]

In recent years, inflation has been quite low, averaging about 2% a year, and it was even negative in 2009, as prices fell in the midst of the deep recession. However, long-term interest rates have been volatile because investors are not sure if inflation is truly under control or is about to jump back to the higher levels of the 1980s. In the years ahead, we can be sure of two things: (1) Interest rates will vary. (2) Interest rates will increase if inflation appears to be headed higher or decrease if inflation is expected to decline.

Self*Test*

What role do interest rates play in allocating capital to different potential borrowers?

What happens to market-clearing, or equilibrium, interest rates in a capital market when the supply of funds declines? What happens when expected inflation increases or decreases?

How does the price of capital tend to change during a boom? During a recession?

How does risk affect interest rates?

If inflation during the last 12 months was 2% and the interest rate during that period was 5%, what was the real rate of interest? If inflation is expected to average 4% during the next year and the real rate is 3%, what should the current interest rate be? **(3%; 7%)**

[3]Refer to Carmen M. Reinhart and Kenneth S. Rogoff, *This Time Is Different: Eight Centuries of Financial Folly* (Princeton, NJ: Princeton University Press, 2009).

6-3 The Determinants of Market Interest Rates

In general, the quoted (or nominal) interest rate on a debt security, r, is composed of a real risk-free rate, r^*, plus several premiums that reflect inflation, the security's risk, its liquidity (or marketability), and the years to its maturity. This relationship can be expressed as follows:

$$\text{Quoted interest rate} = r = r^* + IP + DRP + LP + MRP \qquad (6.1)$$

resource

Students can download the Excel chapter models from the textbook's student companion site on cengage.com. Once downloaded onto your computer, retrieve the Chapter 6 Excel model and follow along as you read this chapter.

Where:

r = the quoted, or nominal, rate of interest on a given security.[4]

r^* = the real risk-free rate of interest, r^* is pronounced "r-star," and it is the rate that would exist on a riskless security in a world where no inflation was expected.

r_{RF} = r^* + IP. It is the quoted rate on a risk-free security such as a U.S. Treasury bill, which is very liquid and is free of most types of risk. Note that the premium for expected inflation, IP, is included in r_{RF}.

IP = inflation premium. IP is equal to the average expected rate of inflation over the life of the security. The expected future inflation rate is not necessarily equal to the current inflation rate, so IP is not necessarily equal to current inflation, as shown in Figure 6.3.

DRP = default risk premium. This premium reflects the possibility that the issuer will not pay the promised interest or principal at the stated time. DRP is zero for U.S. Treasury securities, but it rises as the riskiness of the issuer increases.

LP = liquidity (or marketability) premium. This is a premium charged by lenders to reflect the fact that some securities cannot be converted to cash on short notice at a "reasonable" price. LP is very low for Treasury securities and for securities issued by large, strong firms, but it is relatively high on securities issued by small, privately held firms.

MRP = maturity risk premium. As we will explain later, longer-term bonds, even Treasury bonds, are exposed to a significant risk of price declines due to increases in inflation and interest rates, and a maturity risk premium is charged by lenders to reflect this risk.

Because $r_{RF} = r^* + IP$, we can rewrite Equation 6.1 as follows:

$$\text{Nominal, or quoted, rate} = r = r_{RF} + DRP + LP + MRP$$

We discuss the components whose sum makes up the quoted, or nominal, rate on a given security in the following sections.

6-3A THE REAL RISK-FREE RATE OF INTEREST, r*

The **real risk-free rate of interest, r***, is the interest rate that would exist on a riskless security if no inflation were expected. It may be thought of as the rate of interest on short-term U.S. Treasury securities in an inflation-free world. The real

Real Risk-Free Rate of Interest, r*
The rate of interest that would exist on default-free U.S. Treasury securities if no inflation were expected.

[4]The term *nominal* as it is used here means the *stated* rate as opposed to the *real* rate, where the real rate is adjusted to remove inflation's effects. If you had bought a 30-year Treasury bond in May 2018, the quoted, or nominal, rate would have been about 3.1%. But if inflation averages 2.0% over the next 30 years, the real rate would turn out to be about 3.1% − 2.0% = 1.1%. Also note that in later chapters, when we discuss both debt and equity, we use the subscripts *d* and *s* to designate returns on debt and stock, that is, r_d and r_s.

risk-free rate is not static—it changes over time, depending on economic conditions, especially on (1) the rate of return that corporations and other borrowers expect to earn on productive assets and (2) people's time preferences for current versus future consumption. Borrowers' expected returns on real assets set an upper limit on how much borrowers can afford to pay for funds, whereas savers' time preferences for consumption establish how much consumption savers will defer—hence, the amount of money they will lend at different interest rates.

It is difficult to measure the real rate precisely, but most experts believe that r^* typically fluctuates in the range of 1% to 3%.[5] Perhaps the best estimate of r^* is the rate of return on indexed Treasury bonds, which are discussed later in the chapter. It is interesting to note that between 2011 and 2018, the rate on indexed Treasury bonds has often been negative. These negative real rates of interest have arisen largely because of Federal Reserve policies that have pushed interest rates on Treasury securities below the rate of expected inflation.

6-3B THE NOMINAL, OR QUOTED, RISK-FREE RATE OF INTEREST, $r_{RF} = r^* + IP$

Nominal (Quoted) Risk-Free Rate, r_{RF}
The rate of interest on a security that is free of all risk; r_{RF} is proxied by the T-bill rate or the T-bond rate; r_{RF} includes an inflation premium.

The **nominal,** or **quoted, risk-free rate,** r_{RF}, is the real risk-free rate plus a premium for expected inflation: $r_{RF} = r^* + IP$. To be strictly correct, the risk-free rate should be the interest rate on a totally risk-free security—one that has no default risk, no maturity risk, no liquidity risk, no risk of loss if inflation increases, and no risk of any other type. However, as the recent downgrade of U.S. Treasuries illustrates, there is no such security; hence, there is no observable truly risk-free rate. However, one security is free of most risks—a Treasury Inflation Protected Security (TIPS), whose value increases with inflation. Short-term TIPS are free of default, maturity, and liquidity risks and of risk due to changes in the general level of interest rates. However, they are not free of changes in the real rate.[6]

If the term *risk-free rate* is used without the modifiers *real* or *nominal,* people generally mean the quoted (or nominal) rate, and we follow that convention in this book. Therefore, when we use the term *risk-free rate,* r_{RF}, we mean the nominal risk-free rate, which includes an inflation premium equal to the average expected inflation rate over the remaining life of the security. In general, we use the T-bill rate to approximate the short-term risk-free rate and the T-bond rate to approximate the long-term risk-free rate. So whenever you see the term *risk-free rate,* assume that we are referring to the quoted U.S. T-bill rate or to the quoted T-bond rate. Our definition of the risk-free rate assumes that, despite the recent downgrade, Treasury securities have no meaningful default risk. For convenience, we will assume in our subsequent problems and examples that Treasury securities have no default risk.

6-3C INFLATION PREMIUM (IP)

Inflation has a major impact on interest rates because it erodes the real value of what you receive from an investment. To illustrate, suppose you have saved $10,000 to purchase a car. Rather than buying a car today, you could invest the money with

---

[5]The real rate of interest as discussed here is different from the *current* real rate as discussed in connection with Figure 6.3. The current real rate is the current interest rate minus the current (or latest past) inflation rate, while the real rate (without the word *current*) is the current interest rate minus the *expected future* inflation rate over the life of the security. For example, suppose the current quoted rate for a 1-year Treasury bill is 2.0%, inflation during the latest year was 1.0%, and inflation expected for the coming year is 1.5%. The *current* real rate would be 2.0% − 1.0% = 1.0%, but the *expected* real rate would be 2.0% − 1.5% = 0.5%. The rate on a 10-year bond would be related to the average expected inflation rate over the next 10 years, and so on. In the press, the term *real rate* generally means the current real rate, but in economics and finance (hence, in this book unless otherwise noted), the real rate means the one based on *expected* inflation rates.

[6]Indexed Treasury securities are the closest things we have to a riskless security, but even they are not totally riskless because r^* can change and cause a decline in the prices of these securities.

the hope of buying a better car 1 year from now. If you decide to invest in a 1-year Treasury bill that pays a 1% interest rate, you will have a little bit more money ($10,100—your original money plus $100 in interest) at the end of the year. Now suppose that the overall inflation rate increased by 3% that year. In this case, a similar version of the $10,000 car that you would have purchased at the beginning of the year would cost 3% more ($10,300) at the end of the year. Notice, in this case, the additional interest that you earn on the Treasury bill is not enough to compensate for the expected increase in the price of the car. In real terms you are worse off because the nominal interest rate is less than the expected inflation rate.

Investors are well aware of all this; so when they lend money, they build an **inflation premium (IP)** equal to the average expected inflation rate over the life of the security into the rate they charge. As discussed previously, the actual interest rate on a short-term default-free U.S. Treasury bill, $r_{T\text{-bill}}$, would be the real risk-free rate, r^*, plus the inflation premium (IP):

Inflation Premium (IP)
A premium equal to expected inflation that investors add to the real risk-free rate of return.

$$r_{T\text{-bill}} = r_{RF} = r^* + IP$$

Therefore, if the real risk-free rate was $r^* = 1.7\%$ and if inflation was expected to be 1.5% (and hence IP = 1.5%) during the next year, the quoted rate of interest on 1-year T-bills would be 1.7% + 1.5% = 3.2%.

It is important to note that the inflation rate built into interest rates is the *inflation rate expected in the future,* not the rate experienced in the past. Thus, the latest reported figures might show an annual inflation rate of 3% over the past 12 months, but that is for the *past* year. If people, on average, expect a 4% inflation rate in the future, 4% would be built into the current interest rate. Note also that the inflation rate reflected in the quoted interest rate on any security is the *average inflation rate expected over the security's life.* Thus, the inflation rate built into a 1-year bond is the expected inflation rate for the next year, but the inflation rate built into a 30-year bond is the average inflation rate expected over the next 30 years.[7]

Expectations for future inflation are closely, but not perfectly, correlated with past inflation rates. Therefore, if the inflation rate reported for last month increased, people would tend to raise their expectations for future inflation, and this change in expectations would increase current rates. Also, consumer prices change with a lag following changes at the producer level. Thus, if the price of oil increases this month, gasoline prices are likely to increase in the coming months. This lagged situation between final product and producer goods prices exists throughout the economy.

Students should go to ***Bloomberg.com/markets/rates-bonds*** *to find current interest rates in the United States as well as in Great Britain, Germany, Japan, and Australia.*

Note that Switzerland has, over the past several years, had lower inflation rates than the United States; hence, its interest rates have generally been lower than those of the United States. South Africa, Mexico, and most South American countries have experienced higher inflation, so their rates have been higher than those of the United States.

Students should go to ***tradingeconomics.com*** *for information on a number of economic indicators such as interest rates, inflation, and GDP.*

6-3D DEFAULT RISK PREMIUM (DRP)

The risk that a borrower will *default,* which means the borrower will not make scheduled interest or principal payments, also affects the market interest rate on a bond: The greater the bond's risk of default, the higher the market rate. Once

[7]To be theoretically precise, we should use a *geometric average.* Also, because millions of investors are active in the market, it is impossible to determine exactly the consensus-expected inflation rate. Survey data are available, however, that give us a reasonably good idea of what investors expect over the next few years. For example, in 1980, the University of Michigan's Survey Research Center reported that people expected inflation during the next year to be 11.9% and that the average rate of inflation expected over the next 5 to 10 years was 10.5%. Those expectations led to record-high interest rates. However, the economy cooled thereafter, and as Figure 6.3 showed, actual inflation dropped sharply. This led to a gradual reduction in the *expected future* inflation rate, and as inflationary expectations dropped, so did quoted market interest rates.

again, we are assuming that Treasury securities have no default risk; hence, they carry the lowest interest rates on taxable securities in the United States. For corporate bonds, bond ratings are often used to measure default risk. The higher the bond's rating, the lower its default risk and, consequently, the lower its interest rate.[8] The difference between the quoted interest rate on a T-bond and that on a corporate bond with similar maturity, liquidity, and other features is the **default risk premium (DRP)**. The average default risk premiums vary over time, and tend to get larger when the economy is weaker and borrowers are more likely to have a hard time paying off their debts.

Default Risk Premium (DRP)
The difference between the interest rate on a U.S. Treasury bond and a corporate bond of equal maturity and marketability.

6-3E LIQUIDITY PREMIUM (LP)

Liquidity Premium (LP)
A premium added to the equilibrium interest rate on a security if that security cannot be converted to cash on short notice and at close to its "fair market value."

A "liquid" asset can be converted to cash quickly at a "fair market value." Real assets are generally less liquid than financial assets, but different financial assets vary in their liquidity. Because they prefer assets that are more liquid, investors include a **liquidity premium (LP)** in the rates charged on different debt securities. Although it is difficult to measure liquidity premiums accurately, we can get some sense of an asset's liquidity by looking at its trading volume. Assets with higher trading volume are generally easier to sell and are therefore more liquid. The average liquidity premiums also vary over time. During the recent financial crisis, the liquidity premiums on many assets soared. The market for many assets that were once highly liquid suddenly dried up as everyone rushed to sell them at the same time. The liquidity of real assets also varies over time. For example, at the height of the housing boom, many homes in "hot" real estate markets were often sold the first day they were listed. After the bubble burst, homes in these same markets often sat unsold for months.

6-3F INTEREST RATE RISK AND THE MATURITY RISK PREMIUM (MRP)

Despite a few recent concerns about the Treasury's long-run ability to service its growing debt, we generally assume that U.S. Treasury securities are free of default risk in the sense that one can be virtually certain that the federal government will pay interest on its bonds and pay them off when they mature. Therefore, we assume that the default risk premium on Treasury securities is zero. Further, active markets exist for Treasury securities, so we assume that their liquidity premium is also zero.[9] Thus, as a first approximation, the rate of interest on a Treasury security should be the risk-free rate, r_{RF}, which is the real risk-free rate plus an inflation premium, $r_{RF} = r^* + IP$. However, the prices of long-term bonds decline whenever interest rates rise, and because interest rates can and do occasionally rise, all long-term bonds, even Treasury bonds, have an element of risk called **interest rate risk**. As a general rule, the bonds of any organization have more interest rate risk the longer the maturity of the bond.[10] Therefore, a **maturity risk premium (MRP)**, which is higher the greater the years to maturity, is included in the required interest rate.

Interest Rate Risk
The risk of capital losses to which investors are exposed because of changing interest rates.

Maturity Risk Premium (MRP)
A premium that reflects interest rate risk.

[8]Bond ratings and bonds' riskiness in general are discussed in detail in Chapter 7. For now, merely note that bonds rated AAA are judged to have less default risk than bonds rated AA, AA bonds are less risky than A bonds, and so forth. Ratings are designated AAA or Aaa, AA or Aa, and so forth, depending on the rating agency. In this book, the designations are used interchangeably.

[9]Although it is a reasonable approximation to assume that the liquidity premium is zero for Treasury securities, in reality some Treasury securities are more liquid than others. In particular, bonds tend to be less liquid if it has been a long time since the bonds were originally issued.

[10]For example, if someone had bought a 20-year Treasury bond for $1,000 in October 1998, when the long-term interest rate was 5.3%, and sold it in May 2002, when long-term T-bond rates were about 5.8%, the value of the bond would have declined to about $942. That would represent a loss of 5.8%, and it demonstrates that long-term bonds, even U.S. Treasury bonds, are not riskless. However, had the investor purchased short-term T-bills in 1998 and subsequently reinvested the principal each time the bills matured, he or she would still have had the original $1,000. This point is discussed in detail in Chapter 7.

AN ALMOST RISKLESS TREASURY BOND

Investors who purchase bonds must constantly worry about inflation. If inflation turns out to be greater than expected, bonds will provide a lower-than-expected real return. To protect themselves against expected increases in inflation, investors build an inflation risk premium into their required rate of return. This raises borrowers' costs.

To provide investors with an inflation-protected bond and to reduce the cost of debt to the government, the U.S. Treasury issues Treasury Inflation Protected Securities (TIPS), which are bonds that are indexed to inflation. For example, in 2009, the Treasury issued 10-year TIPS with a $2^1/_8$% coupon. These bonds pay an interest rate of $2^1/_8$% plus an additional amount that is just sufficient to offset inflation. At the end of each 6-month period, the principal (originally set at par or $1,000) is adjusted by the inflation rate. To understand how TIPS work, consider that during the first 6-month interest period, inflation (as measured by the CPI) declined by 0.55% (1/15/09 CPI = 214.69971 and 7/15/09 CPI = 213.51819). The inflation-adjusted principal was then calculated as $1,000 (1 − 0.0055) = $1,000 × 0.9945 = $994.50. So on July 15, 2009, each bond paid interest of (0.02125/2) × $994.50 = $10.57. Note that the interest rate is divided by 2 because interest on Treasury (and most other) bonds is paid twice a year. This same adjustment process will continue each year until the bonds mature on January 15, 2019, at which time they will pay the adjusted maturity value. On January 15, 2018, the CPI from when the bonds were originally issued increased by 14.8887%. The inflation-adjusted principal was calculated as $1,000 × 1.148887 = $1,148.89. So on January 15, 2018, each bond paid interest of (0.02125/2) × $1,148.89 = $12.21. Thus, the cash income provided by the bonds rises and falls by exactly enough to cover inflation or a decline in inflation, producing a real inflation-adjusted rate of $2^1/_8$% for those who hold the bond from its original issue date until its maturity. Further, because the principal also rises and falls by the inflation rate or its decline, it too is protected from inflation.

Both the annual interest received and the increase in principal are taxed each year as interest income, even though cash from the appreciation will not be received until the bond matures. Therefore, these bonds are not good for accounts subject to current income taxes, but they are excellent for individual retirement accounts (IRAs) and 401(k) plans, which are not taxed until funds are withdrawn.

The Treasury regularly conducts auctions to issue indexed bonds. The $2^1/_8$% coupon rate was based on the relative supply and demand for the issue, and it will remain fixed over the life of the bond. However, after the bonds are issued, they continue to trade in the open market, and their price will vary as investors' perceptions of the real rate of interest changes. The following graph shows that real rates steadily declined during 2009–2012, but they began to increase after the early part of 2013. Confirming the point we made earlier, the graph also shows that real rates have been negative in recent years. Finally, as we see in the graph, the real rate of interest has varied quite a bit since this TIPS was issued, and as the real rate changes, so does the price of the bond. Thus, despite their protection against inflation, indexed bonds are not completely riskless. The real rate can change, and if r^* rises, the prices of indexed bonds will decline. This confirms again that there is no such thing as a free lunch or a riskless security.

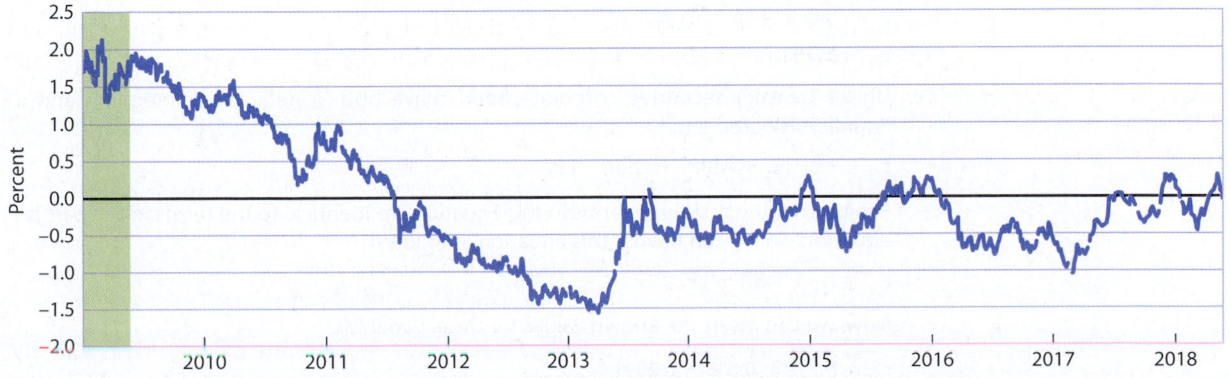

Sources: Dow Jones & Company, Haver Analytics, and St. Louis Federal Reserve, FRED database, fred.stlouisfed.org.

The effect of maturity risk premiums is to raise interest rates on long-term bonds relative to those on short-term bonds. This premium, like the others, is difficult to measure, but (1) it varies somewhat over time, rising when interest rates are more volatile and uncertain, and then falling when interest rates are more stable; and (2) in recent years, the maturity risk premium on 20-year T-bonds has generally been in the range of one to two percentage points.[11]

Reinvestment Rate Risk
The risk that a decline in interest rates will lead to lower income when bonds mature and funds are reinvested.

We should also note that although long-term bonds are heavily exposed to interest rate risk, short-term bills are heavily exposed to **reinvestment rate risk**. When short-term bills mature and the principal must be reinvested, or "rolled over," a decline in interest rates would necessitate reinvestment at a lower rate, which would result in a decline in interest income. To illustrate, suppose you had $100,000 invested in T-bills and you lived on the income. In 1981, short-term Treasury rates were about 15%, so your income would have been about $15,000.

quick question

QUESTION:

An analyst evaluating securities has obtained the following information. The real rate of interest is 2% and is expected to remain constant for the next 3 years. Inflation is expected to be 3% next year, 3.5% the following year, and 4% the third year. The maturity risk premium is estimated to be $0.1 \times (t - 1)\%$, where t = number of years to maturity. The liquidity premium on relevant 3-year securities is 0.25% and the default risk premium on relevant 3-year securities is 0.6%.

a. What is the yield on a 1-year T-bill?

b. What is the yield on a 3-year T-bond?

c. What is the yield on a 3-year corporate bond?

ANSWER:

a. A Treasury security has no default risk premium or liquidity risk premium. Therefore,

$$r_{T1} = r^* + IP_1 + MRP_1$$
$$r_{T1} = 2\% + 3\% + 0.1(1 - 1)\%$$
$$r_{T1} = \mathbf{5\%}.$$

b. A Treasury security has no default risk premium or liquidity risk premium. Therefore,

$$r_{T3} = r^* + IP_3 + MRP_3$$
$$r_{T3} = 2\% + [(3\% + 3.5\% + 4\%)/3] + 0.1(3 - 1)\%$$
$$r_{T3} = 2\% + 3.5\% + 0.2\%$$
$$r_{T3} = \mathbf{5.7\%}.$$

c. Unlike Treasury securities, corporate bonds have both a default risk premium and a liquidity risk premium.

$$r_{C3} = r^* + IP_3 + MRP_3 + DRP + LP.$$

Realize that the first three terms in this equation are identical to the terms in the part b equation. So we can rewrite this equation as follows:

$$r_{C3} = r_{T3} + DRP + LP.$$

Now, we can insert the known values for these variables.

$$r_{C3} = 5.7\% + 0.6\% + 0.25\%$$
$$r_{C3} = \mathbf{6.55\%}.$$

---

[11]The MRP for long-term bonds has averaged 1.6% between 1926 and 2017. See Roger G. Ibbotson, *Stocks, Bonds, Bills, and Inflation: 2018 Yearbook* (Chicago, IL: Duff & Phelps, 2018).

However, your income would have declined to about $9,000 by 1983 and to just $2,300 by May 2018. Had you invested your money in long-term T-bonds, your income (but not the value of the principal) would have been stable.[12] Thus, although "investing short" preserves one's principal, the interest income provided by short-term T-bills is less stable than that on long-term bonds.

Self*Test*

Write an equation for the nominal interest rate on any security.

Distinguish between the *real* risk-free rate of interest, r^*, and the *nominal,* or *quoted,* risk-free rate of interest, r_{RF}.

How do investors deal with inflation when they determine interest rates in the financial markets?

Does the interest rate on a T-bond include a default risk premium? Explain.

Distinguish between liquid and illiquid assets, and list some assets that are liquid and some that are illiquid.

Briefly explain the following statement: Although long-term bonds are heavily exposed to interest rate risk, short-term T-bills are heavily exposed to reinvestment rate risk. The maturity risk premium reflects the net effects of those two opposing forces.

Assume that the real risk-free rate is $r^* = 2\%$ and the average expected inflation rate is 3% for each future year. The DRP and LP for Bond X are each 1%, and the applicable MRP is 2%. What is Bond X's interest rate? Is Bond X (1) a Treasury bond or a corporate bond and (2) more likely to have a 3-month or a 20-year maturity? **(9%, corporate, 20-year)**

6-4 The Term Structure of Interest Rates

The **term structure of interest rates** describes the relationship between long- and short-term rates. The term structure is important to corporate treasurers deciding whether to borrow by issuing long- or short-term debt and to investors who are deciding whether to buy long- or short-term bonds. Therefore, both borrowers and lenders should understand (1) how long- and short-term rates relate to each other and (2) what causes shifts in their relative levels.

Term Structure of Interest Rates
The relationship between bond yields and maturities.

Interest rates for bonds with different maturities can be found in a variety of publications, including *The Wall Street Journal* and the *Federal Reserve Bulletin,* and on a number of websites, including those of Bloomberg, Yahoo!, CNN Money, and the Federal Reserve Board. Using interest rate data from these sources, we can determine the term structure at any given point in time. For example, the table section of Figure 6.4 presents interest rates for different maturities on three different dates. The set of data for a given date, when plotted on a graph such as Figure 6.4, is called the **yield curve** for that date.

Yield Curve
A graph showing the relationship between bond yields and maturities.

[12] Most long-term bonds also have some reinvestment rate risk. If a person is saving and investing for some future purpose (say, to buy a house or to retire), to actually earn the quoted rate on a long-term bond, each interest payment must be reinvested at the quoted rate. However, if interest rates fall, the interest payments would be reinvested at a lower rate; so the realized return would be less than the quoted rate. Note, though, that reinvestment rate risk is lower on long-term bonds than on short-term bonds because only the interest payments (rather than interest plus principal) on a long-term bond are exposed to reinvestment rate risk. Noncallable zero coupon bonds, which are discussed in Chapter 7, are completely free of reinvestment rate risk during their lifetime.

FIGURE 6.4 U.S. Treasury Bond Interest Rates on Different Dates

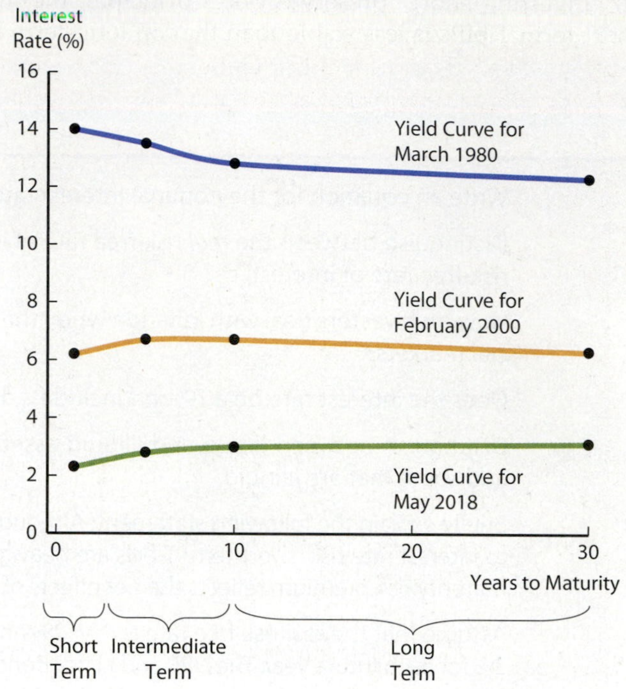

	INTEREST RATE		
Term to Maturity	**March 1980**	**February 2000**	**May 2018**
1 year	14.0%	6.2%	2.3%
5 years	13.5	6.7	2.8
10 years	12.8	6.7	3.0
30 years	12.3	6.3	3.1

As the figure shows, the yield curve changes in position and in slope over time. In March 1980, all rates were quite high because high inflation was expected. However, the rate of inflation was expected to decline; so short-term rates were higher than long-term rates, and the yield curve was thus *downward sloping*. By February 2000, inflation had indeed declined; thus, all rates were lower, and the yield curve had become *humped*—intermediate-term rates were higher than either short- or long-term rates. By May 2018, all rates had fallen below the 2000 levels, and because short-term rates had dropped below long-term rates, the yield curve was *upward sloping*.

Figure 6.4 shows yield curves for U.S. Treasury securities, but we could have constructed curves for bonds issued by GE, IBM, Delta Air Lines, or any other company that borrows money over a range of maturities. Had we constructed such corporate yield curves and plotted them on Figure 6.4, they would have been above those for Treasury securities because corporate yields include default risk premiums and somewhat higher liquidity premiums. Even so, the corporate yield curves would have had the same general shape as the Treasury curves. Also, the riskier the corporation, the higher its yield curve. For example, in May 2018, Microsoft Corporation's bonds with a 5-year maturity were rated AAA by both

Moody's and S&P and yielded 2.955%, whereas The Fresh Market, Inc. had 5-year bonds outstanding that were rated CCC and had a yield of 22.195%. At the same point in time, 5-year Treasury securities had an interest rate of 2.80%.

Historically, long-term rates are generally above short-term rates because of the maturity risk premium; so all yield curves usually slope upward. For this reason, people often call an upward-sloping yield curve a **"normal" yield curve** and a yield curve that slopes downward an **inverted or "abnormal" yield curve**. Thus, in Figure 6.4, the yield curve for March 1980 was inverted, while the one for May 2018 was normal. However, the February 2000 yield curve is humped—a **humped yield curve**—which means that interest rates on intermediate-term maturities were higher than rates on both short- and long-term maturities. We will explain in detail why an upward slope is the normal situation. Briefly, however, the reason is that short-term securities have less interest rate risk than longer-term securities; hence, they have smaller MRPs. So short-term rates are normally lower than long-term rates.

"Normal" Yield Curve
An upward-sloping yield curve.

Inverted ("Abnormal") Yield Curve
A downward-sloping yield curve.

Humped Yield Curve
A yield curve where interest rates on intermediate-term maturities are higher than rates on both short- and long-term maturities.

Self*Test*

What is a yield curve, and what information would you need to draw this curve?

Distinguish among the shapes of a "normal" yield curve, an "abnormal" curve, and a "humped" curve.

If the interest rates on 1-, 5-, 10-, and 30-year bonds are 4%, 5%, 6%, and 7%, respectively, how would you describe the yield curve? If the rates were reversed, how would you describe it?

6-5 What Determines the Shape of the Yield Curve?

Because maturity risk premiums are positive, if other things were held constant, long-term bonds would always have higher interest rates than short-term bonds. However, market interest rates also depend on expected inflation, default risk, and liquidity, each of which can vary with maturity.

Expected inflation has an especially important effect on the yield curve's shape, especially the curve for U.S. Treasury securities. Treasuries have essentially no default or liquidity risk, so the yield on a Treasury bond that matures in t years can be expressed as follows:

$$\text{T-bond yield} = r_t^* + IP_t + MRP_t \qquad 6.2$$

Although the real risk-free rate, r^*, varies somewhat over time because of changes in the economy and demographics, these changes are random rather than predictable. Therefore, the best forecast for the future value of r^* is its current value. However, the inflation premium, IP, varies significantly over time and in a somewhat predictable manner. Recall that the inflation premium is the average level of expected inflation over the life of the bond. Thus, if the market expects inflation to increase in the future (say, from 3% to 4% to 5% over the next 3 years), the inflation premium will be higher on a 3-year bond than on a 1-year bond. On the other hand, if the market expects inflation to decline in the future, long-term bonds will have a smaller inflation premium than will short-term bonds. Finally, because investors consider long-term bonds to be riskier than short-term bonds because of interest rate risk, the maturity risk premium always increases with maturity.

FIGURE 6.5 Illustrative Treasury Yield Curves

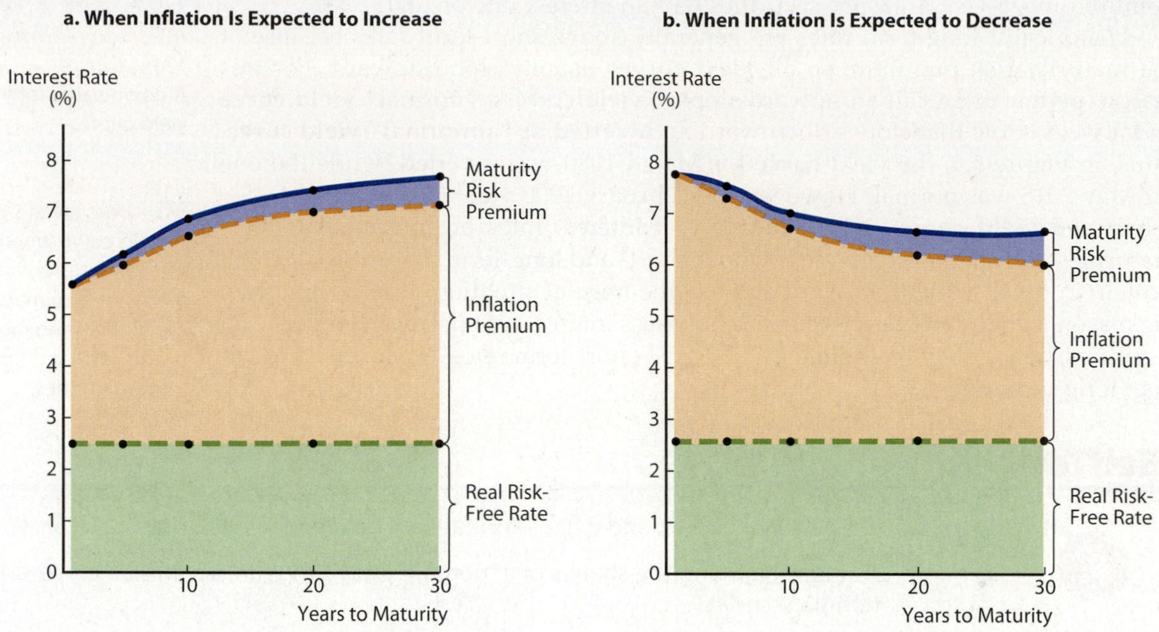

With Inflation Expected to Increase

Maturity	r*	IP	MRP	Yield
1 year	2.50%	3.00%	0.00%	5.50%
5 years	2.50	3.40	0.18	6.08
10 years	2.50	4.00	0.28	6.78
20 years	2.50	4.50	0.42	7.42
30 years	2.50	4.67	0.53	7.70

With Inflation Expected to Decrease

Maturity	r*	IP	MRP	Yield
1 year	2.50%	5.00%	0.00%	7.50%
5 years	2.50	4.60	0.18	7.28
10 years	2.50	4.00	0.28	6.78
20 years	2.50	3.50	0.42	6.42
30 years	2.50	3.33	0.53	6.36

Figure 6.5 shows two illustrative yield curves—one where inflation is expected to increase over time and another where inflation is expected to decrease. Note that these hypothetical interest rates are similar to historical rates, but they are much higher than current interest rates. Panel a shows the Treasury yield curve when inflation is expected to increase. Here long-term bonds have higher yields for two reasons: (1) Inflation is expected to be higher in the future. (2) There is a positive maturity risk premium. Panel b shows the yield curve when inflation is expected to decline. Such a downward-sloping yield curve often foreshadows an economic downturn because weaker economic conditions generally lead to declining inflation, which in turn results in lower long-term rates.[13]

Now let's consider the yield curve for corporate bonds. Recall that corporate bonds include a default risk premium (DRP) and a liquidity premium (LP).

[13] Note that yield curves tend to rise or fall relatively sharply over the first 5 to 10 years and then flatten out. One reason this occurs is that when forecasting future interest rates, people often predict relatively high or low inflation for the next few years, after which they assume an average long-run inflation rate. Consequently, the short end of the yield curve tends to have more curvature, and the long end of the yield curve tends to be more stable.

THE LINKS BETWEEN EXPECTED INFLATION AND INTEREST RATES: A CLOSER LOOK

Throughout the text, we use the following equation to describe the link between expected inflation and the nominal risk-free rate of interest, r_{RF}:

$$r_{RF} = r^* + IP$$

Recall that r^* is the real risk-free interest rate and IP is the corresponding inflation premium. This equation suggests that there is a simple link between expected inflation and nominal interest rates.

It turns out, however, that this link is a bit more complex. To fully understand this relationship, first recognize that individuals get utility through the consumption of real goods and services such as bread, water, haircuts, pizza, and textbooks. When we save money, we are giving up the opportunity to consume these goods today in return for being able to consume more of them in the future. Our gain from waiting is measured by the real rate of interest, r^*.

To illustrate this point, consider the following example. Assume that a loaf of bread costs \$1 today. Also assume that the real rate of interest is 3% and that inflation is expected to be 5% over the next year. The 3% real rate indicates that the average consumer is willing to trade 100 loaves of bread today for 103 loaves next year. If a "bread bank" were available, consumers who wanted to defer consumption until next year could deposit 100 loaves today and withdraw 103 loaves next year. In practice, most of us do not directly trade real goods such as bread—instead, we purchase these goods with money because in a well-functioning economy, it is more efficient to exchange money than goods. However, when we lend money over time, we worry that borrowers might pay us back with dollars that aren't worth as much due to inflation. To compensate for this risk, lenders build in a premium for expected inflation.

With these concerns in mind, let's compare the dollar cost of 100 loaves of bread today to the cost of 103 loaves next year. Given the current price, 100 loaves of bread today would cost \$100. Because expected inflation is 5%, this means that a loaf of bread is expected to cost \$1.05 next year. Consequently, 103 loaves of bread are expected to cost \$108.15 next year (103 × \$1.05). So if consumers were to deposit \$100 in a bank today, they would need to earn 8.15% to realize a real return of 3%.

Putting this all together, we see that the 1-year nominal interest rate can be calculated as follows:

$$\begin{aligned} r_{RF} &= (1 + r^*)(1 + IP) - 1 \\ &= (1.03)(1.05) - 1 = 0.0815 = 8.15\% \end{aligned}$$

Note that this expression can be rewritten as follows:

$$r_{RF} = r^* + IP + (r^* \times IP)$$

That equation is identical to our original expression for the nominal risk-free rate except that it includes a "cross-term," $r^* \times IP$. When real interest rates and expected inflation are relatively low, the cross-term turns out to be quite small and thus is often ignored. Because it is normally insignificant, we disregard the cross-term in the text unless stated otherwise. (When working problems, we will tell you when to include the cross-term; otherwise, ignore this term when solving problems.)

One last point—you should recognize that while it may be reasonable to ignore the cross-term when interest rates are low (as they are in the United States today), it is a mistake to do so when investing in a market where interest rates and inflation are quite high, as is often the case in many emerging markets. In these markets, the cross-term can be significant and thus should not be disregarded.

Therefore, the yield on a corporate bond that matures in t years can be expressed as follows:

$$\text{Corporate bond yield} = r^*_t + IP_t + MRP_t + DRP_t + LP_t \quad (6.3)$$

Comparing the Treasury bond yield in Equation 6.2 and the corporate bond yield in Equation 6.3, we can calculate the corporate bond yield spread:

$$\text{Corporate bond yield spread} = \text{Corporate bond yield} - \text{Treasury bond yield} = DRP_t + LP_t$$

One recent study estimates that both the default risk premium and liquidity premium vary over time, and that the majority of the corporate bond yield spread can be attributed to default risk.[14] Corporate bonds' default and liquidity risks are affected by their maturities. For example, the default risk on Coca-Cola's

[14] Refer to Francis A. Longstaff, Sanjay Mithal, and Eric Neis, "Corporate Yield Spreads: Default Risk or Liquidity? New Evidence from the Credit Default Swap Market," *Journal of Finance*, vol. 60, no. 5 (October 2005), pp. 2213–2253.

short-term debt is very small because there is almost no chance that Coca-Cola will go bankrupt over the next few years. However, Coke has some bonds that have a maturity of almost 75 years, and although the odds of Coke defaulting on those bonds might not be very high, there is still a higher probability of default risk on Coke's long-term bonds than on its short-term bonds.

Longer-term corporate bonds also tend to be less liquid than shorter-term bonds. Because short-term debt has less default risk, someone can buy a short-term bond without doing as much credit checking as would be necessary for a long-term bond. Thus, people can move in and out of short-term corporate debt relatively rapidly. As a result, a corporation's short-term bonds are typically more liquid and thus have lower liquidity premiums than its long-term bonds.

Figure 6.6 shows yield curves for two hypothetical corporate bonds—an AA-rated bond with minimal default risk and a BBB-rated bond with more default risk—along with the yield curve for Treasury securities taken from panel a of Figure 6.5. Here we assume that inflation is expected to increase, so the Treasury yield curve is upward sloping. Because of their additional default and liquidity risk, corporate bonds yield more than Treasury bonds with the same maturity and BBB-rated bonds yield more than AA-rated bonds. Finally, note that

FIGURE 6.6 Illustrative Corporate and Treasury Yield Curves

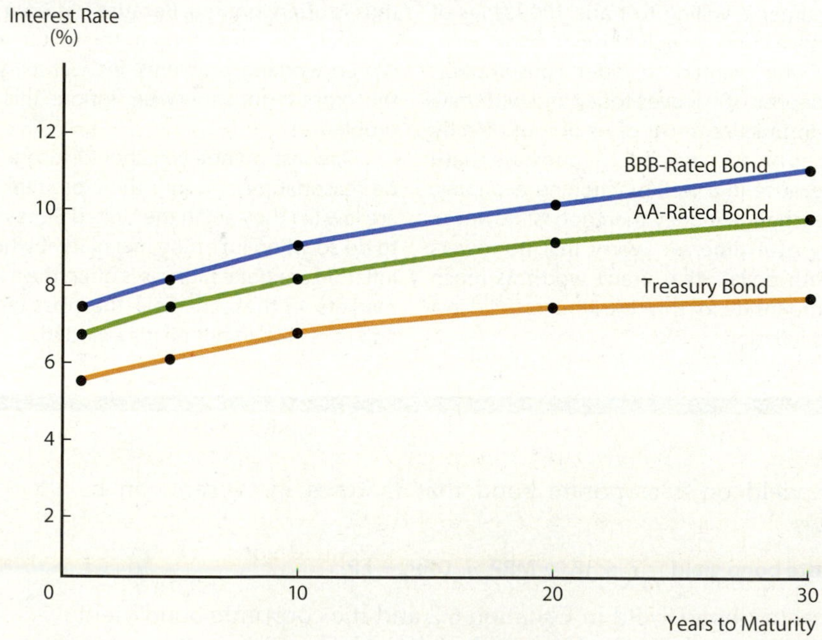

	Interest Rate		
	Treasury Bond	**AA-Rated Bond**	**BBB-Rated Bond**
1 year	5.5%	6.7%	7.4%
5 years	6.1	7.4	8.1
10 years	6.8	8.2	9.1
20 years	7.4	9.2	10.2
30 years	7.7	9.8	11.1

the yield spread between corporate and Treasury bonds is larger the longer the maturity. This occurs because longer-term corporate bonds have more default and liquidity risk than shorter-term bonds, and both of these premiums are absent in Treasury bonds.

Self*Test*

How do maturity risk premiums affect the yield curve?

If the inflation rate is expected to increase, would this increase or decrease the slope of the yield curve?

If the inflation rate is expected to remain constant at the current level in the future, would the yield curve slope up, slope down, or be horizontal? Consider all factors that affect the yield curve, not just inflation.

Explain why corporate bonds' default and liquidity premiums are likely to increase with their maturity.

Explain why corporate bonds always yield more than Treasury bonds and why BBB-rated bonds always yield more than AA-rated bonds.

6-6 Using the Yield Curve to Estimate Future Interest Rates[15]

In the last section, we saw that the slope of the yield curve depends primarily on two factors: (1) expectations about future inflation and (2) effects of maturity on bonds' risk. We also saw how to calculate the yield curve, given inflation and maturity-related risks. Note, though, that people can reverse the process: They can look at the yield curve and use information embedded in it to estimate the market's expectations regarding future inflation, risk, and short-term interest rates. For example, suppose a company is in the midst of a 5-year expansion program and the treasurer knows that she will need to borrow short-term funds a year from now. She knows the current cost of 1-year money, read from the yield curve, but she wants to know the cost of 1-year money next year. That information can be "backed out" by analyzing the current yield curve, as will be discussed.

The estimation process is straightforward provided we (1) focus on Treasury bonds and (2) assume that Treasury bonds contain no maturity risk premiums.[16] This position has been called the **pure expectations theory** of the term structure of interest rates, often simply referred to as the "expectations theory." The expectations theory assumes that bond traders establish bond prices and interest rates strictly on the basis of expectations for future interest rates and that they are indifferent to maturity because they do not view long-term bonds as being riskier than

Pure Expectations Theory
A theory that states that the shape of the yield curve depends on investors' expectations about future interest rates.

[15]This section is relatively technical, but instructors can omit it without loss of continuity.

[16]Although most evidence suggests that there is a positive maturity risk premium, some academics and practitioners contend that this second assumption is reasonable, at least as an approximation. They argue that the market is dominated by large bond traders who buy and sell securities of different maturities each day, that these traders focus only on short-term returns, and that they are not concerned with maturity risk. According to this view, a bond trader is just as willing to buy a 20-year bond to pick up a short-term profit as he or she is to buy a 3-month security. Proponents of this view argue that the shape of the Treasury yield curve is therefore determined only by market expectations about future interest rates. Later in this section, we show what happens when we include the effects of maturity risk premiums.

short-term bonds. If this were true, the maturity risk premium (MRP) would be zero, and long-term interest rates would simply be a weighted average of current and expected future short-term interest rates.

To illustrate the pure expectations theory, assume that a 1-year Treasury bond currently yields 5.00%, and a 2-year bond yields 5.50%. Investors who want to invest for a 2-year horizon have two primary options:

Option 1: *Buy a 2-year security and hold it for 2 years.*
Option 2: *Buy a 1-year security, hold it for 1 year, and then at the end of the year reinvest the proceeds in another 1-year security.*

If they select Option 1, for every dollar they invest today, they will have accumulated $1.113025 by the end of Year 2:

$$\text{Funds at end of Year 2} = \$1 \times (1.055)^2 = \$1.113025$$

If they select Option 2, they should end up with the same amount, but this equation is used to find the ending amount:

$$\text{Funds at end of Year 2} = \$1 \times (1.05) \times (1 + X)$$

Here X is the expected interest rate on a 1-year Treasury security 1 year from now.

If the expectations theory is correct, each option must provide the same amount of cash at the end of 2 years, which implies the following:

$$(1.05)(1 + X) = (1.055)^2$$

We can rearrange this equation and then solve for X:

$$\begin{aligned} 1 + X &= (1.055)^2/1.05 \\ &= (1.055)^2/1.05 - 1 = 0.0600238 = 6.00238\% \end{aligned}$$

Therefore, X, the 1-year rate 1 year from today, must be 6.00238%; otherwise, one option will be better than the other, and the market will not be in equilibrium. However, if the market is not in equilibrium, buying and selling will quickly bring about equilibrium. For example, suppose investors expect the 1-year Treasury rate to be 6.00238% a year from now but a 2-year bond now yields 5.25%, not the 5.50% rate required for equilibrium. Bond traders could earn a profit by adopting the following strategy:

1. Borrow money for 2 years at the 2-year rate, 5.25% per year.
2. Invest the money in a series of 1-year securities, expecting to earn 5.00% this year and 6.00238% next year, for an overall expected return over the 2 years of $[1.05 \times 1.0600238]^{1/2} - 1 = 5.50\%$.

Borrowing at 5.25% and investing to earn 5.50% is a good deal, so bond traders would rush to borrow money (demand funds) in the 2-year market and invest (or supply funds) in the 1-year market.

Recall from Figure 6.1 that a decline in the supply of funds raises interest rates, while an increase in the supply lowers rates. Likewise, an increase in the demand for funds raises rates, while a decline in demand lowers rates. Therefore, bond traders would push up the 2-year yield and simultaneously lower the yield on 1-year bonds. This buying and selling would cease when the 2-year rate becomes a weighted average of expected future 1-year rates.[17]

---

[17]In our calculations, we used the geometric average of the current and expected 1-year rates: $[1.05 \times 1.0600238]^{1/2} - 1 = 0.055$ or 5.50%. The arithmetic average of the two rates is $(5\% + 6.00238\%)/2 = 5.50119\%$. The geometric average is theoretically correct, but the difference is only 0.00119%. With interest rates at the levels they have been in the United States and most other nations in recent years, the geometric and arithmetic averages are so close that many people use the arithmetic average, especially given the other assumptions that underlie the estimation of future 1-year rates.

Let's suppose that the yield curve looks as follows:

1-year T-bond: 5.00%
2-year T-bond: 5.50%
4-year T-bond: 6.25%

An investor would like to purchase a 1-year T-bond today and then to invest in a 3-year T-bond 1 year from now. What yield would this investor expect to earn on the 3-year T-bond 1 year from now? You have enough information from the preceding yield curve to determine the expected yield on the 3-year T-bond 1 year from today. Here's the equation setup:

$$(1.0625)^4 = (1.05) \times (1 + X)^3$$
$$(1.0625)^4/1.05 = (1 + X)^3$$
$$1.213742 = (1 + X)^3$$
$$(1.213742)^{1/3} = 1 + X$$
$$1.0667 = 1 + X, \text{ so } X = 6.67\%$$

To eliminate the exponent, each side of the equation is raised to the 1/3 power.

The investor would expect to earn one year from today a yield of 6.67% for 3 years on the 3-year T-bond. Note that the investor would expect to earn the same yield investing in a 4-year T-bond today as he would be investing in a 1-year T-bond today and then investing in a 3-year T-bond 1 year from now.

The preceding analysis was based on the assumption that the maturity risk premium is zero. However, most evidence suggests that a positive maturity risk premium exists. For example, assume once again that 1- and 2-year maturities yield 5.00% and 5.50%, respectively; so we have a rising yield curve. However, now assume that the maturity risk premium on the 2-year bond is 0.20% versus zero for the 1-year bond. This premium means that in equilibrium, the expected annual return on a 2-year bond (5.50%) must be 0.20% higher than the expected return on a series of two 1-year bonds (5.00% and X%). Therefore, the expected return on the series must be 5.50% − 0.20% = 5.30%:

$$\text{Expected return on 2-year series} = \text{Rate on 2-year bond} - \text{MRP}$$
$$= 0.055 - 0.002 = 0.053 = 5.30\%$$

Now recall that the annual expected return from the series of two 1-year bonds can be expressed as follows, where X is the 1-year rate next year:

$$(1.05)(1 + X) = (1 + \text{Expected return on 2-year series})^2 = (1.053)^2$$
$$1.05X = (1.053)^2 - 1.05$$
$$X = \frac{0.0588090}{1.05} = 0.0560086 = 5.60086\%.$$

Under these conditions, equilibrium requires that market participants expect the 1-year rate next year to be 5.60086%.

Note that the rate read from the yield curve rises by 0.50% when the years to maturity increase from one to two: 5.50% − 5.00% = 0.50%. Of this 0.50% increase, 0.20% is attributable to the MRP, and the remaining 0.30% is due to the increase in expected 1-year rates next year.

Putting all of this together, we see that one can use the yield curve to estimate what the market expects the short-term rate to be next year. However, this requires an estimate of the maturity risk premium, and if our estimated MRP is incorrect, then so will our yield-curve-based interest rate forecast. Thus, though the yield curve can be used to obtain insights into what the market thinks future interest rates will be, the preceding calculations (although they appear to be precise) will only approximate these expectations unless the pure expectations theory holds or we know with certainty the exact maturity risk premium. Because neither of these conditions holds, it is difficult to know for sure what the market is forecasting.

Note too that even if we could determine the market's consensus forecast for future rates, the market is not always right. So a forecast of next year's rate based on the yield curve could be wrong. Therefore, obtaining an accurate forecast of interest rates for next year—or even for next month—is extremely difficult.

Self*Test*

What key assumption underlies the pure expectations theory?

Assuming that the pure expectations theory is correct, how are expected short-term rates used to calculate expected long-term rates?

According to the pure expectations theory, what would happen if long-term rates were not an average of expected short-term rates?

Most evidence suggests that a positive maturity risk premium exists. How would this affect your calculations when determining interest rates?

Assume that the interest rate on a 1-year T-bond is currently 7% and the rate on a 2-year bond is 9%. If the maturity risk premium is zero, what is a reasonable forecast of the rate on a 1-year bond next year? What would the forecast be if the maturity risk premium on the 2-year bond was 0.5% versus zero for the 1-year bond? **(11.04%; 10.02%)**

6-7 Macroeconomic Factors That Influence Interest Rate Levels

*The home page for the Board of Governors of the Federal Reserve System can be found at **federalreserve.gov**. You can access general information about the Federal Reserve, including press releases, speeches, and monetary policy.*

We described how key components such as expected inflation, default risk, maturity risk, and liquidity concerns influence the level of interest rates over time and across different markets. On a day-to-day basis, a variety of macroeconomic factors may influence one or more of these components; hence, macroeconomic factors have an important effect on both the general level of interest rates and the shape of the yield curve. The primary factors are (1) Federal Reserve policy, (2) the federal budget deficit or surplus, (3) international factors, including the foreign trade balance and interest rates in other countries, and (4) the level of business activity.

6-7A FEDERAL RESERVE POLICY

As you probably learned in your economics courses, (1) the money supply has a significant effect on the level of economic activity, inflation, and interest rates. (2) In the United States, the Federal Reserve Board controls the money supply. If the Fed wants to stimulate the economy, it increases the money supply. The Fed buys and sells short-term securities, so the initial effect of a monetary easing would be to cause short-term rates to decline. However, a larger money supply might lead to an increase in expected future inflation, which would cause long-term rates to rise even as short-term rates fell. The reverse holds if the Fed tightens the money supply. The Fed's job is to promote economic growth while keeping inflation at bay. This is a delicate balancing act.

As you can see from Figure 6.2, interest rates in recent years have been relatively low, with short-term rates especially low during the last 8 years shown (January 2010 through May 2018). As we discussed in the opening vignette to this chapter, the Federal Reserve has recently taken modest steps to increase rates. However, despite these recent movements, rates still remain quite low compared to historical standards.

It is also important to recognize that actions that lower short-term rates won't necessarily lower long-term rates. Lower rates could cause foreigners to sell their holdings of U.S. bonds. These investors would be paid with dollars, which they would then sell to buy their own currencies. The sale of dollars and the purchase of other currencies would lower the value of the dollar relative to other currencies, which would make U.S. goods less expensive, which would help manufacturers and thus lower the trade deficit. Note also that during periods when the Fed is actively intervening in the markets, the yield curve may be temporarily distorted. Short-term rates may be driven below the long-run equilibrium level if the Fed is easing credit and above the equilibrium rate if the Fed is tightening credit. Long-term rates are not affected as much by Fed intervention.

6-7B FEDERAL BUDGET DEFICITS OR SURPLUSES

If the federal government spends more than it takes in as taxes, it runs a deficit, and that deficit must be covered by additional borrowing (selling more Treasury bonds) or by printing money. If the government borrows, this increases the demand for funds and thus pushes up interest rates. If the government prints money, investors recognize that with "more money chasing a given amount of goods," the result will be increased inflation, which will also increase interest rates. So the larger the federal deficit, other things held constant, the higher the level of interest rates.

Over the past several decades, the federal government has generally run large budget deficits. There were some surpluses in the late 1990s, but the September 11, 2001, terrorist attacks, the subsequent recession, and the Iraq war all boosted government spending and caused the deficits to return. These concerns have been boosted by the 2017 tax bill, which has been forecasted to further increase deficits.

6-7C INTERNATIONAL FACTORS

Businesses and individuals in the United States buy from and sell to people and firms all around the globe. If they buy more than they sell (that is, if there are more imports than exports), they are said to be running a **foreign trade deficit**. When trade deficits occur, they must be financed, and this generally means borrowing from nations with export surpluses. Thus, if the United States imported $200 billion of goods but exported only $100 billion, it would run a trade deficit of $100 billion, and other countries would have a $100 billion trade surplus. The United States would probably borrow the $100 billion from the surplus nations.[18] At any rate, the larger the trade deficit, the higher the tendency to borrow. Note that foreigners will hold U.S. debt if and only if the rates on U.S. securities are competitive with rates in other countries. This causes U.S. interest rates to be highly dependent on rates in other parts of the world.

Foreign Trade Deficit
The situation that exists when a country imports more than it exports.

All this interdependency limits the ability of the Federal Reserve to use monetary policy to control economic activity in the United States. For example, if the Fed attempts to lower U.S. interest rates and this causes rates to fall below rates abroad, foreigners will begin selling U.S. bonds. Those sales will depress bond prices, which will push up rates in the United States. Thus, the large U.S. trade deficit (and foreigners' holdings of U.S. debt that resulted from many years of deficits) hinders the Fed's ability to combat a recession by lowering interest rates.

For about 25 years following World War II, the United States ran large trade surpluses, and the rest of the world owed it many billions of dollars. However,

[18]The deficit could also be financed by selling assets, including gold, corporate stocks, entire companies, and real estate. The United States has financed its massive trade deficits by all of these means in recent years. Although the primary method has been by borrowing from foreigners, in recent years, there has been a sharp increase in foreign purchases of U.S. assets, especially oil exporters' purchases of U.S. businesses.

the situation changed, and the United States has been running trade deficits since the mid-1970s. (The U.S. annual 2017 international trade deficit for goods and services was $568 billion, which was up 12.6% from the prior year.) The cumulative effect of these deficits has been to change the United States from being the largest creditor nation to being the largest debtor nation of all time. As a result, interest rates are very much influenced by interest rates in other countries—higher or lower rates abroad lead to higher or lower U.S. rates. Because of all of this, U.S. corporate treasurers and everyone else who is affected by interest rates should keep up with developments in the world economy.

6-7D BUSINESS ACTIVITY

You can examine Figure 6.2 to see how business conditions influence interest rates. Here are the key points revealed by the graph:

1. Because inflation increased from 1972 to 1981, the general tendency during that period was toward higher interest rates. However, since the 1981 peak, the trend has generally been downward.
2. The shaded areas in the graph represent recessions, during which (a) the demand for money and the rate of inflation tended to fall and (b) the Federal Reserve tended to increase the money supply in an effort to stimulate the economy. As a result, there is a tendency for interest rates to decline during recessions. For example, the economy began to slow down in 2000, and the country entered a mild recession in 2001. In response, the Federal Reserve cut interest rates. In 2004, the economy began to rebound; so the Fed began to raise rates. However, the subprime debacle hit in 2007; so the Fed began lowering rates in September 2007. By February 2008, the Fed's target rate had fallen from 5.25% to 3.00%—eventually lowering rates to near zero in the midst of the financial crisis. The Fed has increased rates six times since the financial crisis—having increased them in December 2015 and 2016, March, June, and December 2017, and again in March 2018, making its target short-term interest rate range 1.50% to 1.75%. The Fed expects to increase rates two more times in 2018 for interest rates to return to more normal levels.[19]
3. During recessions, short-term rates decline more sharply than long-term rates. This occurs for two reasons: (a) The Fed operates mainly in the short-term sector, so its intervention has the strongest effect there. (b) Long-term rates reflect the average expected inflation rate over the next 20 to 30 years, and this expectation generally does not change much, even when the current inflation rate is low because of a recession or high because of a boom. So short-term rates are more volatile than long-term rates. Taking another look at Figure 6.2, we see that short-term rates did decline recently by much more than long-term rates.

Self*Test*

Identify some macroeconomic factors that influence interest rates and explain the effects of each.

How does the Fed stimulate the economy? How does the Fed affect interest rates?

Does the Fed have complete control over U.S. interest rates? That is, can it set rates at any level it chooses? Why or why not?

[19]Refer to Jim Tankersley, "Fed Raises Interest Rates for Sixth Time since Financial Crisis," *The New York Times* (www.nytimes.com), March 21, 2018.

6-8 Interest Rates and Business Decisions

As you might expect, companies look carefully at the level of interest rates and the shape of the yield curve when making important business decisions. For example, assume that Leading Edge Co. is considering building a new plant with a 30-year life that will cost $1 million, and it plans to raise the $1 million by borrowing rather than by issuing new stock. At the time of its decision in May 2018, the company faces an upward-sloping yield curve. If it borrows on a short-term basis from a bank—say for 1 year—its annual interest cost would be only 2.5%, or $25,000. On the other hand, if it issued long-term bonds, then its annual cost would be 4.7%, or $47,000. Therefore, at first glance, it would seem that Leading Edge should use short-term debt.

However, this could prove to be a horrible mistake. If it used short-term debt, it will have to renew its loan every year, and the rate charged on each new loan will reflect the then-current short-term rate. Interest rates could dramatically increase, in which case the company's interest payments would soar over time. Those high interest payments would cut into and perhaps eliminate its profits. Even more concerning, if at some point in time the company's lenders refused to renew the loan and demanded its repayment, as they would have every right to do, Leading Edge might have to sell assets at a loss, which could result in bankruptcy. On the other hand, if the company used long-term financing in 2018, its interest costs would remain constant at $47,000 per year; so it would not be directly hurt if interest rates in the economy increased over time.

Does all of this suggest that firms should avoid short-term debt? Not at all. If inflation falls over the next few years, so will interest rates. If Leading Edge had borrowed on a long-term basis in May 2018, it would be at a disadvantage if it was locked into 4.7% debt while its competitors (who used short-term debt in 2018) had a borrowing cost of only 2.5%.

Financing decisions would be easy if we could make accurate forecasts of future interest rates. Unfortunately, predicting interest rates with consistent accuracy is nearly impossible. However, although it is difficult to predict future interest rate *levels*, it is easy to predict that interest rates will *fluctuate*—they always have, and they always will. That being the case, sound financial policy calls for using a mix of long- and short-term debt as well as equity to position the firm so that it can survive in any interest rate environment. Further, the optimal financial policy depends in an important way on the nature of the firm's assets—the easier it is to sell assets to generate cash, the more feasible it is to use more short-term debt. This makes it logical for a firm to finance current assets such as inventories and receivables with short-term debt and to finance fixed assets such as buildings and equipment with long-term debt. We return to this issue later in the book when we discuss capital structure and financing policy.

Changes in interest rates also have implications for savers. For example, if you had a 401(k) plan—and someday most of you will—you would probably want to invest some of your money in a bond mutual fund. You could choose a fund that had an average maturity of 25 years, 20 years, or on down to only a few months (a money market fund). How would your choice affect your investment results and hence your retirement income? First, your decision would affect your annual interest income. For example, if the yield curve was upward sloping, as it normally is, you would earn more interest if you chose a fund that held long-term bonds. Note, though, that if you chose a long-term fund and interest rates then rose, the market value of your fund would decline. For example, as we will see in Chapter 7, if you had $100,000 in a fund whose average bond had a maturity of 25 years and a coupon rate of 6%, and if interest rates then rose from 6% to 10%, the market value of your fund would decline from $100,000 to about $63,500. On the other hand, if rates declined, your fund would increase in value. If you invested in a short-term fund, its value would be more stable, but it would probably provide less interest income per year. In any event, your choice of maturity would have a major effect on your investment performance and therefore on your future income.

Self*Test*

If short-term interest rates are lower than long-term rates, why might a borrower still choose to finance with long-term debt?

Explain the following statement: The optimal financial policy depends in an important way on the nature of the firm's assets.

TYING IT ALL TOGETHER

In this chapter, we discussed the way interest rates are determined, the term structure of interest rates, and some of the ways interest rates affect business decisions. We saw that the interest rate on a given bond, r, is based on this equation:

$$r = r^* + IP + DRP + LP + MRP$$

Here r* is the real risk-free rate, IP is the premium for expected inflation, DRP is the premium for potential default risk, LP is the premium for lack of liquidity, and MRP is the premium to compensate for the risk inherent in bonds with long maturities. Both r* and the various premiums can and do change over time, depending on economic conditions, Federal Reserve actions, and the like. Because changes in these factors are difficult to predict, it is hard to forecast the future direction of interest rates.

The yield curve, which relates bonds' interest rates to their maturities, usually has an upward slope, but it can slope up or down, and both its slope and level change over time. The main determinants of the slope of the curve are expectations for future inflation and the MRP. We can analyze yield curve data to estimate what market participants think future interest rates are likely to be. We will use the insights gained from this chapter in later chapters when we analyze the values of bonds and stocks and examine various corporate investment and financing decisions.

Self-Test Questions And Problems

(Solutions Appear in Appendix A)

ST-1 KEY TERMS Define each of the following terms:

a. Production opportunities; time preferences for consumption; risk; inflation
b. Real risk-free rate of interest, r^*; nominal (quoted) risk-free rate of interest, r_{RF}
c. Inflation premium (IP)
d. Default risk premium (DRP)
e. Liquidity premium (LP); maturity risk premium (MRP)
f. Interest rate risk; reinvestment rate risk
g. Term structure of interest rates; yield curve
h. "Normal" yield curve; inverted ("abnormal") yield curve; humped yield curve
i. Pure expectations theory
j. Foreign trade deficit

ST-2 INFLATION AND INTEREST RATES The real risk-free rate of interest, r^*, is 3%, and it is expected to remain constant over time. Inflation is expected to be 2% per year for the next 3 years and 4% per year for the next 5 years. The maturity risk premium is equal to 0.1 × (t − 1)%, where t = the bond's maturity. The default risk premium for a BBB-rated bond is 1.3%.

a. What is the average expected inflation rate over the next 4 years?
b. What is the yield on a 4-year Treasury bond?
c. What is the yield on a 4-year BBB-rated corporate bond with a liquidity premium of 0.5%?
d. What is the yield on an 8-year Treasury bond?
e. What is the yield on an 8-year BBB-rated corporate bond with a liquidity premium of 0.5%?
f. If the yield on a 9-year Treasury bond is 7.3%, what does that imply about expected inflation in 9 years?

ST-3 **PURE EXPECTATIONS THEORY** The yield on 1-year Treasury securities is 6%, 2-year securities yield 6.2%, 3-year securities yield 6.3%, and 4-year securities yield 6.5%. There is no maturity risk premium. Using expectations theory and geometric averages, forecast the yields on the following securities:

a. A 1-year security, 1 year from now
b. A 1-year security, 2 years from now
c. A 2-year security, 1 year from now
d. A 3-year security, 1 year from now

Questions

6-1 Suppose interest rates on residential mortgages of equal risk are 5.5% in California and 7.0% in New York. Could this differential persist? What forces might tend to equalize rates? Would differentials in borrowing costs for businesses of equal risk located in California and New York be more or less likely to exist than differentials in residential mortgage rates? Would differentials in the cost of money for New York and California firms be more likely to exist if the firms being compared were very large or if they were very small? What are the implications of all of this with respect to nationwide branching?

6-2 Which fluctuate more—long-term or short-term interest rates? Why?

6-3 Suppose you believe that the economy is just entering a recession. Your firm must raise capital immediately, and debt will be used. Should you borrow on a long-term or a short-term basis? Why?

6-4 Suppose the population of Area Y is relatively young, and the population of Area O is relatively old, but everything else about the two areas is the same.

a. Would interest rates likely be the same or different in the two areas? Explain.
b. Would a trend toward nationwide branching by banks and the development of nationwide diversified financial corporations affect your answer to part a? Explain.

6-5 Suppose a new process was developed that could be used to make oil out of seawater. The equipment required is quite expensive, but it would in time lead to low prices for gasoline, electricity, and other types of energy. What effect would this have on interest rates?

6-6 Suppose a new and more liberal Congress and administration are elected. Their first order of business is to take away the independence of the Federal Reserve System and to force the Fed to greatly expand the money supply. What effect will this have:

a. On the level and slope of the yield curve immediately after the announcement?
b. On the level and slope of the yield curve that would exist 2 or 3 years in the future?

6-7 It is a fact that the federal government (1) encouraged the development of the savings and loan industry, (2) virtually forced the industry to make long-term fixed-interest-rate mortgages, and (3) forced the savings and loans to obtain most of their capital as deposits that were withdrawable on demand.

a. Would the savings and loans have higher profits in a world with a "normal" or an inverted yield curve? Explain your answer.
b. Would the savings and loan industry be better off if the individual institutions sold their mortgages to federal agencies and then collected servicing fees or if the institutions held the mortgages that they originated?

6-8 Suppose interest rates on Treasury bonds rose from 5% to 9% as a result of higher interest rates in Europe. What effect would this have on the price of an average company's common stock?

6-9 What does it mean when it is said that the United States is running a trade deficit? What impact will a trade deficit have on interest rates?

6-10 Suppose you have noticed that the slope of the corporate yield curve has become steeper over the past few months. What factors might explain the change in the slope?

Problems

Easy Problems 1–7

6-1 **YIELD CURVES** Assume that yields on U.S. Treasury securities were as follows:

Term	Rate
6 months	4.69%
1 year	5.49
2 years	5.66
3 years	5.71
4 years	5.89
5 years	6.05
10 years	6.12
20 years	6.64
30 years	6.76

a. Plot a yield curve based on these data.
b. What type of yield curve is shown?
c. What information does this graph tell you?
d. Based on this yield curve, if you needed to borrow money for longer than 1 year, would it make sense for you to borrow short term and renew the loan or borrow long term? Explain.

6-2 **REAL RISK-FREE RATE** You read in *The Wall Street Journal* that 30-day T-bills are currently yielding 5.8%. Your brother-in-law, a broker at Safe and Sound Securities, has given you the following estimates of current interest rate premiums:

- Inflation premium = 3.25%
- Liquidity premium = 0.6%
- Maturity risk premium = 1.85%
- Default risk premium = 2.15%

On the basis of these data, what is the real risk-free rate of return?

6-3 **EXPECTED INTEREST RATE** The real risk-free rate is 2.25%. Inflation is expected to be 2.5% this year and 4.25% during the next 2 years. Assume that the maturity risk premium is zero. What is the yield on 2-year Treasury securities? What is the yield on 3-year Treasury securities?

6-4 **DEFAULT RISK PREMIUM** A Treasury bond that matures in 10 years has a yield of 5.75%. A 10-year corporate bond has a yield of 8.75%. Assume that the liquidity premium on the corporate bond is 0.35%. What is the default risk premium on the corporate bond?

6-5 **MATURITY RISK PREMIUM** The real risk-free rate is 2.5% and inflation is expected to be 2.75% for the next 2 years. A 2-year Treasury security yields 5.55%. What is the maturity risk premium for the 2-year security?

6-6 **INFLATION CROSS-PRODUCT** An analyst is evaluating securities in a developing nation where the inflation rate is very high. As a result, the analyst has been warned not to ignore the cross-product between the real rate and inflation. If the real risk-free rate is 5% and inflation is expected to be 18% each of the next 4 years, what is the yield on a 4-year security with no maturity, default, or liquidity risk? (*Hint:* Refer to "The Links Between Expected Inflation and Interest Rates: A Closer Look" on page 211.)

6-7 **EXPECTATIONS THEORY** One-year Treasury securities yield 4.85%. The market anticipates that 1 year from now, 1-year Treasury securities will yield 5.2%. If the pure expectations theory is correct, what is the yield today for 2-year Treasury securities? Calculate the yield using a geometric average.

Intermediate Problems 8–16

6-8 **EXPECTATIONS THEORY** Interest rates on 4-year Treasury securities are currently 6.7%, while 6-year Treasury securities yield 7.25%. If the pure expectations theory is correct, what does the market believe that 2-year securities will be yielding 4 years from now? Calculate the yield using a geometric average.

6-9 **EXPECTED INTEREST RATE** The real risk-free rate is 2.05%. Inflation is expected to be 3.05% this year, 4.75% next year, and 2.3% thereafter. The maturity risk premium is estimated to be $0.05 \times (t - 1)\%$, where t = number of years to maturity. What is the yield on a 7-year Treasury note?

6-10 **INFLATION** Due to a recession, expected inflation this year is only 3.25%. However, the inflation rate in Year 2 and thereafter is expected to be constant at some level above 3.25%. Assume that the expectations theory holds and the real risk-free rate (r^*) is 2.5%. If the yield on 3-year Treasury bonds equals the 1-year yield plus 1.5%, what inflation rate is expected after Year 1?

6-11 **DEFAULT RISK PREMIUM** A company's 5-year bonds are yielding 7% per year. Treasury bonds with the same maturity are yielding 5.2% per year, and the real risk-free rate (r^*) is 2.75%. The average inflation premium is 2.05%, and the maturity risk premium is estimated to be $0.1 \times (t - 1)\%$, where t = number of years to maturity. If the liquidity premium is 0.7%, what is the default risk premium on the corporate bonds?

6-12 **MATURITY RISK PREMIUM** An investor in Treasury securities expects inflation to be 2.1% in Year 1, 2.7% in Year 2, and 3.65% each year thereafter. Assume that the real risk-free rate is 1.95% and that this rate will remain constant. Three-year Treasury securities yield 5.20%, while 5-year Treasury securities yield 6.00%. What is the difference in the maturity risk premiums (MRPs) on the two securities; that is, what is $MRP_5 - MRP_3$?

6-13 **DEFAULT RISK PREMIUM** The real risk-free rate, r^*, is 1.7%. Inflation is expected to average 1.5% a year for the next 4 years, after which time inflation is expected to average 4.8% a year. Assume that there is no maturity risk premium. An 11-year corporate bond has a yield of 8.7%, which includes a liquidity premium of 0.3%. What is its default risk premium?

6-14 **EXPECTATIONS THEORY AND INFLATION** Suppose 2-year Treasury bonds yield 4.1%, while 1-year bonds yield 3.2%. r^* is 1%, and the maturity risk premium is zero.

a. Using the expectations theory, what is the yield on a 1-year bond, 1 year from now? Calculate the yield using a geometric average.
b. What is the expected inflation rate in Year 1? Year 2?

6-15 **EXPECTATIONS THEORY** Assume that the real risk-free rate is 2% and that the maturity risk premium is zero. If a 1-year Treasury bond yield is 5% and a 2-year Treasury bond yields 7%, what is the 1-year interest rate that is expected for Year 2? Calculate this yield using a geometric average. What inflation rate is expected during Year 2? Comment on why the average interest rate during the 2-year period differs from the 1-year interest rate expected for Year 2.

6-16 **INFLATION CROSS-PRODUCT** An analyst is evaluating securities in a developing nation where the inflation rate is very high. As a result, the analyst has been warned not to ignore the cross-product between the real rate and inflation. A 6-year security with no maturity, default, or liquidity risk has a yield of 20.84%. If the real risk-free rate is 6%, what average rate of inflation is expected in this country over the next 6 years? (*Hint:* Refer to "The Links Between Expected Inflation and Interest Rates: A Closer Look" on page 211.)

Challenging Problems 17–19

6-17 **INTEREST RATE PREMIUMS** A 5-year Treasury bond has a 5.2% yield. A 10-year Treasury bond yields 6.4%, and a 10-year corporate bond yields 8.4%. The market expects that inflation will average 2.5% over the next 10 years ($IP_{10} = 2.5\%$). Assume that there is no maturity risk premium (MRP = 0) and that the annual real risk-free rate, r^*, will remain constant over the next 10 years. (*Hint:* Remember that the default risk premium and the liquidity premium are zero for Treasury securities: DRP = LP = 0.) A 5-year corporate bond has the same default risk premium and liquidity premium as the 10-year corporate bond described. What is the yield on this 5-year corporate bond?

6-18 **YIELD CURVES** Suppose the inflation rate is expected to be 7% next year, 5% the following year, and 3% thereafter. Assume that the real risk-free rate, r^*, will remain at 2% and that maturity risk premiums on Treasury securities rise from zero on very short-term bonds (those that mature in a few days) to 0.2% for 1-year securities. Furthermore, maturity risk premiums increase 0.2% for each year to maturity, up to a limit of 1.0% on 5-year or longer-term T-bonds.

a. Calculate the interest rate on 1-, 2-, 3-, 4-, 5-, 10-, and 20-year Treasury securities and plot the yield curve.
b. Suppose a AAA-rated company (which is the highest bond rating a firm can have) had bonds with the same maturities as the Treasury bonds. Estimate and plot what you believe a AAA-rated company's yield curve would look like on the same graph with the Treasury bond yield curve. (*Hint:* Think about the default risk premium on its long-term versus its short-term bonds.)
c. On the same graph, plot the approximate yield curve of a much riskier lower-rated company with a much higher risk of defaulting on its bonds.

6-19 INFLATION AND INTEREST RATES In late 1980, the U.S. Commerce Department released new data showing inflation was 15%. At the time, the prime rate of interest was 21%, a record high. However, many investors expected the new Reagan administration to be more effective in controlling inflation than the Carter administration had been. Moreover, many observers believed that the extremely high interest rates and generally tight credit, which resulted from the Federal Reserve System's attempts to curb the inflation rate, would lead to a recession, which, in turn, would lead to a decline in inflation and interest rates. Assume that, at the beginning of 1981, the expected inflation rate for 1981 was 13%; for 1982, 9%; for 1983, 7%; and for 1984 and thereafter, 6%.

a. What was the average expected inflation rate over the 5-year period 1981–1985? (Use the arithmetic average.)
b. Over the 5-year period, what average *nominal* interest rate would be expected to produce a 2% real risk-free return on 5-year Treasury securities? Assume MRP = 0.
c. Assuming a real risk-free rate of 2% and a maturity risk premium that equals 0.1 × (t)%, where t is the number of years to maturity, estimate the interest rate in January 1981 on bonds that mature in 1, 2, 5, 10, and 20 years. Draw a yield curve based on these data.
d. Describe the general economic conditions that could lead to an upward-sloping yield curve.
e. If investors in early 1981 expected the inflation rate for every future year to be 10% (i.e., $I_t = I_{t+1}$ = 10% for t = 1 to ∞), what would the yield curve have looked like? Consider all the factors that are likely to affect the curve. Does your answer here make you question the yield curve you drew in part c?

Comprehensive/Spreadsheet Problem

6-20 INTEREST RATE DETERMINATION AND YIELD CURVES

a. What effect would each of the following events likely have on the level of nominal interest rates?
   1. Households dramatically increase their savings rate.
   2. Corporations increase their demand for funds following an increase in investment opportunities.
   3. The government runs a larger-than-expected budget deficit.
   4. There is an increase in expected inflation.

b. Suppose you are considering two possible investment opportunities: a 12-year Treasury bond and a 7-year, A-rated corporate bond. The current real risk-free rate is 4%, and inflation is expected to be 2% for the next 2 years, 3% for the following 4 years, and 4% thereafter. The maturity risk premium is estimated by this formula: MRP = 0.02(t − 1)%. The liquidity premium (LP) for the corporate bond is estimated to be 0.3%. You may determine the default risk premium (DRP), given the company's bond rating, from the following table. Remember to subtract the bond's LP from the corporate spread given in the table to arrive at the bond's DRP. What yield would you predict for each of these two investments?

	Rate	Corporate Bond Yield Spread = DRP + LP
U.S. Treasury	0.83%	———
AAA corporate	0.93	0.10%
AA corporate	1.29	0.46
A corporate	1.67	0.84

c. Given the following Treasury bond yield information, construct a graph of the yield curve.

Maturity	Yield
1 year	5.37%
2 years	5.47
3 years	5.65
4 years	5.71
5 years	5.64
10 years	5.75
20 years	6.33
30 years	5.94

d. Based on the information about the corporate bond provided in part b, calculate yields and then construct a new yield curve graph that shows both the Treasury and the corporate bonds.

e. Which part of the yield curve (the left side or right side) is likely to be most volatile over time?

f. Using the Treasury yield information in part c, calculate the following rates using geometric averages:

1. The 1-year rate, 1 year from now
2. The 5-year rate, 5 years from now
3. The 10-year rate, 10 years from now
4. The 10-year rate, 20 years from now

INTEGRATED CASE

MORTON HANDLEY & COMPANY

6-21 INTEREST RATE DETERMINATION Maria Juarez is a professional tennis player, and your firm manages her money. She has asked you to give her information about what determines the level of various interest rates. Your boss has prepared some questions for you to consider.

a. What are the four most fundamental factors that affect the cost of money, or the general level of interest rates, in the economy?

b. What is the real risk-free rate of interest (r^*) and the nominal risk-free rate (r_{RF})? How are these two rates measured?

c. Define the terms *inflation premium (IP)*, *default risk premium (DRP)*, *liquidity premium (LP)*, and *maturity risk premium (MRP)*. Which of these premiums is included in determining the interest rate on (1) short-term U.S. Treasury securities, (2) long-term U.S. Treasury securities, (3) short-term corporate securities, and (4) long-term corporate securities? Explain how the premiums would vary over time and among the different securities listed.

d. What is the term structure of interest rates? What is a yield curve?

e. Suppose most investors expect the inflation rate to be 5% next year, 6% the following year, and 8% thereafter. The real risk-free rate is 3%. The maturity risk premium is zero for bonds that mature in 1 year or less and 0.1% for 2-year bonds; then the MRP increases by 0.1% per year thereafter for 20 years, after which it is stable. What is the interest rate on 1-, 10-, and 20-year Treasury bonds? Draw a yield curve with these data. What factors can explain why this constructed yield curve is upward sloping?

f. At any given time, how would the yield curve facing a AAA-rated company compare with the yield curve for U.S. Treasury securities? At any given time, how would the yield curve facing a

BB-rated company compare with the yield curve for U.S. Treasury securities? Draw a graph to illustrate your answer.

g. What is the pure expectations theory? What does the pure expectations theory imply about the term structure of interest rates?

h. Suppose you observe the following term structure for Treasury securities:

Maturity	Yield
1 year	6.0%
2 years	6.2
3 years	6.4
4 years	6.5
5 years	6.5

Assume that the pure expectations theory of the term structure is correct. (This implies that you can use the yield curve provided to "back out" the market's expectations about future interest rates.) What does the market expect will be the interest rate on 1-year securities, 1 year from now? What does the market expect will be the interest rate on 3-year securities, 2 years from now? Calculate these yields using geometric averages.

i. Describe how macroeconomic factors affect the level of interest rates. How do these factors explain why interest rates have been lower in recent years?

TAKING A CLOSER LOOK

Using The New York Times Bond Market Page to Understand Interest Rates

Use online resources to work on this chapter's questions. Please note that website information changes over time, and these changes may limit your ability to answer some of these questions.

In Chapter 6, we looked at the determinants of market interest rates. The following questions are designed to aid with your understanding of interest rates. Here, we will access The New York Times Bonds Market Page website (markets.on.nytimes.com/research/markets/bonds/bonds.asp) to answer these questions:

1. Plot the most recent yield curve for Treasury bonds.
2. How does the current yield curve for Treasury bonds compare to the yield curve 1 month ago? 1 year ago?
3. What is the 52-week total return for the Investment Grade Corporate Bond Index? From the graph shown, what has happened to this return over the past year?
4. What is the 52-week total return for the High Yield Corporate Bond Index? From the graph shown, what has happened to this return over the past year?
5. List several investment grade corporate issues—noting the issuer, coupon rate, maturity, credit rating, and yield information.
6. List several high yield corporate issues—noting the issuer, coupon rate, maturity, credit rating, and yield information.

Bonds and Their Valuation

CHAPTER 7

John Clark/Shutterstock.com

Sizing Up Risk in the Bond Market

Many people view Treasury securities as a lackluster but ultrasafe investment. From a default standpoint, Treasuries are indeed our safest investments, but their prices can still decline in any given year if interest rates increase. This is especially true for long-term Treasury bonds, which lost nearly 15% in 2009. However, bonds can also perform well—Treasury bonds earned a return of over 27% in 2011, and they outgained stocks in 8 of the 18 years between 2000 and 2017.

Not all bonds are alike, and they don't always move in the same direction. For example, corporate bonds are often callable, and issuers can default on them, whereas Treasury bonds are not exposed to these risks. To compensate investors for these additional risks, corporate bonds typically have higher yields. When the economy is strong, corporate bonds generally produce higher returns than Treasuries because their promised returns are higher, and most make their promised payments because few go into default. However, when the economy weakens, concerns about defaults rise, which lead to declines in corporate bond prices. Furthermore, at any point in time, there are widespread differences among corporate bonds. For example, in May 2018, outstanding bonds issued by Johnson & Johnson, with an AAA credit rating, maturing in 2033, were trading at a yield to maturity of 3.734%. At the same point in time, bonds issued by Genworth Financial Inc., with a B credit rating, maturing in 2034, were trading at a yield to maturity of 9.133%.

A 2009 article in *The Wall Street Journal* highlighted the concerns that bond investors face in today's environment. The article offers what it refers to as "five key pointers":

1. *Watch Out for Defaults.* Investors should be wary of low-rated corporate bonds on the edge of default. The article cautions investors about increased default risk in the municipal market as state and local governments struggle to balance their budgets.

2. *Limit Your Rate Risk.* Rates are likely to increase over time as the economy continues to recover. As we see in this chapter, increasing interest rates reduce the value of bonds, and this effect is particularly important for investors of long-term bonds. For this reason, *The Wall Street Journal* writer suggests that some bond investors may want to gradually shift away from longer-maturity bonds.
3. *Consider a Passive Strategy.* This advice is directed specifically to investors in bond mutual funds. Rather than investing in actively managed funds, where the portfolio manager is constantly moving in and out of different bonds, the author suggests that investors invest in index funds or exchange-traded funds (ETFs) that track a broad index of bonds.
4. *Have an Inflation Hedge.* Many analysts worry that down the road, higher government spending and a relaxed monetary policy will ultimately lead to higher levels of inflation. As we will see in this chapter, one way to hedge against rising inflation is to invest in Treasury securities that are indexed to inflation.
5. *Don't Try to Time the Market.* As we have seen in recent years, bond prices can move quickly and dramatically, which makes it difficult to effectively bet on where the market is heading next. Rather than trying to time the next move in the market, the article urges investors to adopt a more steady long-term strategy when it comes to bonds.

Although these pointers are relevant in today's market, in many ways the advice is timeless. In the face of similar risks in 2001, a *BusinessWeek Online* article gave investors the following similar advice, which is still applicable today:

> Take the same diversified approach to bonds as you do with stocks. Blend in U.S. government, corporate—both high-quality and high-yield—and perhaps even some foreign government debt. If you're investing taxable dollars, consider tax-exempt municipal bonds. And it doesn't hurt to layer in some inflation-indexed bonds.

Sources: Michael A. Pollack, "The New Bond Equation," *The Wall Street Journal* (www.wsj.com), August 3, 2009; Scott Patterson, "Ahead of the Tape: Junk Yields Flashing Back to '01 Slump," *The Wall Street Journal*, January 30, 2008, p. C1; Roger G. Ibbotson, *Stocks, Bonds, Bills, and Inflation: 2018 Yearbook* ((Chicago, IL: Duff & Phelps, 2018); Susan Scherreik, "Getting the Most Bang Out of Your Bonds," *BusinessWeek Online* (businessweek.com), November 12, 2001; and FINRA (finra-markets.morningstar.com/BondCenter/), May 30, 2018.

PUTTING THINGS IN PERSPECTIVE

In previous chapters, we noted that companies raise capital in two main forms: debt and equity. In this chapter, we examine the characteristics of bonds and discuss the various factors that influence bond prices. In Chapter 9, we will turn our attention to stocks and their valuation.

If you skim through *The Wall Street Journal*, you will see references to a wide variety of bonds. This variety may seem confusing, but in actuality, only a few characteristics distinguish the various types of bonds.

When you finish this chapter, you should be able to do the following:

- **Identify the different features of corporate and government bonds.**
- **Discuss how bond prices are determined in the market, what the relationship is between interest rates and bond prices, and how a bond's price changes over time as it approaches maturity.**
- **Calculate a bond's yield to maturity and yield to call if it is callable, and determine the "true" yield.**
- **Explain the different types of risk that bond investors and issuers face, and discuss how a bond's terms and collateral can be changed to affect its interest rate.**

7-1 Who Issues Bonds?

A **bond** is a long-term contract under which a borrower agrees to make payments of interest and principal on specific dates to the holders of the bond. Bonds are issued by corporations and government agencies that are looking for long-term debt capital. For example, on January 4, 2019, Allied Food Products borrowed $170 million by issuing $170 million of bonds. For convenience, we assume that Allied sold 170,000 individual bonds for $1,000 each. Actually, it could have sold one $170 million bond, 17 bonds each with a $10 million face value, or any other combination that totaled $170 million. In any event, Allied received the $170 million, and in exchange, it promised to make annual interest payments and to repay the $170 million on a specified maturity date.

Bond
A long-term debt instrument.

Until the 1970s, most bonds were beautifully engraved pieces of paper and their key terms, including their face values, were spelled out on the bonds. Today, though, virtually all bonds are represented by electronic data stored in secure computers, much like the "money" in a bank checking account.

Bonds are grouped in several ways. One grouping is based on the issuer: the U.S. Treasury, corporations, state and local governments, and foreigners. Each bond differs with respect to risk and consequently its expected return.

Treasury bonds, generally called Treasuries and sometimes referred to as government bonds, are issued by the federal government.[1] It is reasonable to assume that the U.S. government will make good on its promised payments, so Treasuries have no default risk. However, these bonds' prices do decline when interest rates rise; so they are not completely riskless.

Treasury Bonds
Bonds issued by the federal government, sometimes referred to as government bonds.

Corporate bonds are issued by business firms. Unlike Treasuries, corporates are exposed to default risk—if the issuing company gets into trouble, it may be unable to make the promised interest and principal payments and bondholders may suffer losses. Corporate bonds have different levels of default risk depending on the issuing company's characteristics and the terms of the specific bond. Default risk is often referred to as "credit risk," and as we saw in Chapter 6, the larger this risk, the higher the interest rate investors demand.

Corporate Bonds
Bonds issued by corporations.

Municipal bonds, or munis, are bonds issued by state and local governments. Like corporates, munis are exposed to some default risk, but they have one major advantage over all other bonds: As we discussed in Chapter 3, the interest earned on most munis is exempt from federal taxes and from state taxes if the holder is a resident of the issuing state. Consequently, the market interest rate on a muni is considerably lower than on a corporate bond of equivalent risk.

Municipal Bonds
Bonds issued by state and local governments.

Foreign bonds are issued by a foreign government or a foreign corporation. All foreign corporate bonds are exposed to default risk, as are some foreign government bonds. Indeed, recently, concerns have risen about possible defaults in many countries, including Greece, Ireland, Portugal, and Spain. An additional risk exists when the bonds are denominated in a currency other than that of the investor's home currency. Consider, for example, a U.S. investor who purchases a corporate bond denominated in Japanese yen. At some point, the investor will want to close out his investment and convert the yen back to U.S. dollars. If the Japanese yen unexpectedly falls relative to the dollar, the investor will have fewer dollars than he originally expected to receive. Consequently, the investor could still lose money even if the bond does not default.

Foreign Bonds
Bonds issued by foreign governments or by foreign corporations.

---

[1]The U.S. Treasury actually calls its debt "bills," "notes," or "bonds." T-bills generally have maturities of 1 year or less at the time of issue, notes generally have original maturities of 2 to 7 years, and bonds originally mature in 8 to 30 years. There are technical differences between bills, notes, and bonds, but they are not important for our purposes. So we generally call all Treasury securities "bonds." Note too that a 30-year T-bond at the time of issue becomes a 29-year bond the next year, and it is a 1-year bond after 29 years.

Self*Test*

What is a bond?

What are the four main issuers of bonds?

Why are U.S. Treasury bonds not completely riskless?

In addition to default risk, what key risk do investors in foreign bonds face? Explain.

7-2 Key Characteristics of Bonds

*An excellent website on bonds is **finra-markets.morningstar.com/BondCenter/**. It provides extensive information about the bond market, and allows you to quickly search for a particular bond or to perform an advanced search based on select criteria.*

Although all bonds have some common characteristics, different types of bonds can have different contractual features. For example, most corporate bonds have provisions that allow the issuer to pay them off early ("call" features), but the specific call provisions vary widely among different bonds. Similarly, some bonds are backed by specific assets that must be turned over to the bondholders if the issuer defaults, while other bonds have no such collateral backup. Differences in contractual provisions (and in the fundamental underlying financial strength of the companies backing the bonds) lead to differences in bonds' risks, prices, and expected returns. To understand bonds, it is essential that you understand the following terms.

7-2A PAR VALUE

Par Value
The face value of a bond.

The **par value** is the stated face value of the bond; for illustrative purposes, we generally assume a par value of $1,000, although any multiple of $1,000 (e.g., $10,000 or $10 million) can be used. The par value generally represents the amount of money the firm borrows and promises to repay on the maturity date.

7-2B COUPON INTEREST RATE

Coupon Payment
The specified number of dollars of interest paid each year.

Allied Food Products's bonds require the company to pay a fixed number of dollars of interest each year. This payment, generally referred to as the **coupon payment**, is set at the time the bond is issued and remains in force during the bond's life.[2] Typically, at the time a bond is issued, its coupon payment is set at a level that will induce investors to buy the bond at or near its par value. Most of the examples and problems throughout this text focus on bonds with fixed coupon rates.

Coupon Interest Rate
The stated annual interest rate on a bond.

When this annual coupon payment is divided by the par value, the result is the **coupon interest rate**. For example, Allied's bonds have a $1,000 par value, and they pay $80 in interest each year. The bond's coupon payment is $80, so its coupon interest rate is $80/$1,000 = 8%. In this regard, the $80 is the annual income that an investor receives when he or she invests in the bond.

[2]Back when bonds were engraved pieces of paper rather than electronic information stored on a computer, each bond had a number of small (1/2- by 2-inch) dated coupons attached to it. On each interest payment date, the owner would "clip the coupon" for that date, send it to the company's paying agent, and receive a check for the interest. A 30-year semiannual bond would start with 60 coupons, whereas a 5-year annual payment bond would start with only 5 coupons. Today no physical coupons are involved, and interest checks are mailed or deposited automatically to the bonds' registered owners on the payment date. Even so, people continue to use the terms *coupon* and *coupon interest rate* when discussing bonds. You can think of the coupon interest rate as the *promised rate*.

Allied's bonds are **fixed-rate bonds** because the coupon rate is fixed for the life of the bond. In some cases, however, a bond's coupon payment is allowed to vary over time. These **floating-rate bonds** work as follows: The coupon rate is set for an initial period, often 6 months, after which it is adjusted every 6 months based on some open market rate. For example, the bond's rate may be adjusted so as to equal the 10-year Treasury bond rate plus a "spread" of 1.5 percentage points. Other provisions can be included in corporate bonds. For example, some can be converted at the holders' option into fixed-rate debt, and some floaters have upper limits (caps) and lower limits (floors) on how high or low the rate can go.

Fixed-Rate Bonds
Bonds whose interest rate is fixed for their entire life.

Floating-Rate Bonds
Bonds whose interest rate fluctuates with shifts in the general level of interest rates.

Some bonds pay no coupons at all but are offered at a discount below their par values and hence provide capital appreciation rather than interest income. These securities are called **zero coupon bonds** (*zeros*). Other bonds pay some coupon interest, but not enough to induce investors to buy them at par. In general, any bond originally offered at a price significantly below its par value is called an **original issue discount (OID) bond**. Some of the details associated with issuing or investing in zero coupon bonds are discussed more fully in Web Appendix 7A.

Zero Coupon Bonds
Bonds that pay no annual interest but are sold at a discount below par, thus compensating investors in the form of capital appreciation.

Original Issue Discount (OID) Bond
Any bond originally offered at a price below its par value.

7-2C MATURITY DATE

Bonds generally have a specified **maturity date** on which the par value must be repaid. Allied's bonds, which were issued on January 4, 2019, will mature on January 3, 2034; thus, they had a 15-year maturity at the time they were issued. Most bonds have an **original maturity** (the maturity at the time the bond is issued) ranging from 10 to 40 years, but any maturity is legally permissible.[3] Of course, the effective maturity of a bond declines each year after it has been issued. Thus, Allied's bonds had a 15-year original maturity. But in 2020, a year later, they will have a 14-year maturity; a year after that, they will have a 13-year maturity; and so on.

Maturity Date
A specified date on which the par value of a bond must be repaid.

Original Maturity
The number of years to maturity at the time a bond is issued.

7-2D CALL PROVISIONS

Many corporate and municipal bonds contain a **call provision** that gives the issuer the right to call the bonds for redemption. The call provision generally states that the issuer must pay the bondholders an amount greater than the par value if they are called. The additional sum, which is termed a *call premium*, is often equal to 1 year's interest. For example, the call premium on a 10-year bond with a 10% annual coupon and a par value of $1,000 might be $100, which means that the issuer would have to pay investors $1,100 (the par value plus the call premium) if it wanted to call the bonds. In most cases, the provisions in the bond contract are set so that the call premium declines over time as the bonds approach maturity. Also, although some bonds are immediately callable, in most cases, bonds are often not callable until several years after issue, generally 5 to 10 years. This is known as a *deferred call*, and such bonds are said to have *call protection*.

Call Provision
A provision in a bond contract that gives the issuer the right to redeem the bonds under specified terms prior to the normal maturity date.

Companies are not likely to call bonds unless interest rates have declined significantly since the bonds were issued. Suppose a company sold bonds when interest rates were relatively high. Provided the issue is callable, the company

[3]In July 1993, The Walt Disney Company, attempting to lock in a low interest rate, stretched the meaning of "long-term bond" by issuing the first 100-year bonds sold by any borrower in modern times. Soon after, Coca-Cola became the second company to sell 100-year bonds. Other companies that have issued 100-year bonds include Columbia/HCA Healthcare Corporation, BellSouth Telecommunications, J.C. Penney, Wisconsin Electric Power Company, and IBM.

could sell a new issue of low-yielding securities if and when interest rates drop, use the proceeds of the new issue to retire the high-rate issue, and thus reduce its interest expense. This process is called a *refunding operation*. Thus, the call privilege is valuable to the firm but detrimental to long-term investors, who will need to reinvest the funds they receive at the new and lower rates. Accordingly, the interest rate on a new issue of callable bonds will exceed that on the company's new noncallable bonds. For example, on May 30, 2019, Pacific Timber Company sold a bond issue yielding 6% that was callable immediately. On the same day, Northwest Milling Company sold an issue with similar risk and maturity that yielded only 5.5%, but its bonds were noncallable for 10 years. Investors were willing to accept a 0.5% lower coupon interest rate on Northwest's bonds for the assurance that the 5.5% interest rate would be earned for at least 10 years. Pacific, on the other hand, had to incur a 0.5% higher annual interest rate for the option of calling the bonds in the event of a decline in rates.

Note that the refunding operation is similar to a homeowner refinancing his or her home mortgage after a decline in interest rates. Consider, for example, a homeowner with an outstanding mortgage at 7%. If mortgage rates fall to 4%, the homeowner will probably find it beneficial to refinance the mortgage. There may be some fees involved in the refinancing, but the lower rate may be more than enough to offset those fees. The analysis required is essentially the same for homeowners and corporations.

7-2E SINKING FUNDS

Sinking Fund Provision
A provision in a bond contract that requires the issuer to retire a portion of the bond issue each year.

Some bonds include a **sinking fund provision** that facilitates the orderly retirement of the bond issue. Years ago firms were required to deposit money with a trustee that invested the funds and then used the accumulated sum to retire the bonds when they matured. Today, though, sinking fund provisions require the issuer to buy back a specified percentage of the issue each year. A failure to meet the sinking fund requirement constitutes a default, which may throw the company into bankruptcy. Therefore, a sinking fund is a mandatory payment.

Suppose a company issued $100 million of 20-year bonds and it is required to call 5% of the issue, or $5 million of bonds, each year. In most cases, the issuer can handle the sinking fund requirement in either of two ways:

1. It can call in for redemption, at par value, the required $5 million of bonds. The bonds are numbered serially, and those called for redemption would be determined by a lottery administered by the trustee.
2. The company can buy the required number of bonds on the open market.

The firm will choose the least-cost method. If interest rates have fallen since the bond was issued, the bond will sell for more than its par value. In this case, the firm will use the call option. However, if interest rates have risen, the bonds will sell at a price below par, and so the firm can and will buy $5 million par value of bonds in the open market for less than $5 million. Note that a call for sinking fund purposes is generally different from a refunding call because most sinking fund calls require no call premium. However, only a small percentage of the issue is normally callable in a given year.

Although sinking funds are designed to protect investors by ensuring that the bonds are retired in an orderly fashion, these funds work to the detriment of bondholders if the bond's coupon rate is higher than the current market rate. For example, suppose the bond has a 10% coupon, but similar bonds now yield only 7.5%. A sinking fund call at par would require a long-term investor to give up a bond that pays $100 of interest and then to reinvest in a bond that pays only $75 per year. This is an obvious disadvantage to those bondholders whose bonds are called. On balance, however, bonds that have a sinking fund are regarded as being safer than those without such a provision; so at the time they are issued, sinking fund bonds have lower coupon rates than otherwise similar bonds without sinking funds.

7-2F OTHER FEATURES

Several other types of bonds are used sufficiently often to warrant mention. First, **convertible bonds** are bonds that are exchangeable into shares of common stock at a fixed price at the option of the bondholder. Convertibles offer investors the chance for capital gains if the stock price increases, but that feature enables the issuing company to set a lower coupon rate than on nonconvertible debt with similar credit risk. Bonds issued with **warrants** are similar to convertibles, but instead of giving the investor an option to exchange the bonds for stock, warrants give the holder an option to buy stock for a stated price, thereby providing a capital gain if the stock's price rises. Because of this factor, bonds issued with warrants, like convertibles, carry lower coupon rates than otherwise similar nonconvertible bonds.

While callable bonds give the *issuer* the right to retire the debt prior to maturity, **putable bonds** allow *investors* to require the company to pay in advance. If interest rates rise, investors will put the bonds back to the company and reinvest in higher coupon bonds. Yet another type of bond is the **income bond**, which pays interest only if the issuer has earned enough money to pay the interest. Thus, income bonds cannot bankrupt a company; however, from an investor's standpoint, they are riskier than "regular" bonds. Yet another bond is the **indexed,** or **purchasing power, bond**. The interest rate is based on an inflation index such as the consumer price index (CPI), so the interest paid rises automatically when the inflation rate rises, thus protecting bondholders against inflation. As we mentioned in Chapter 6, the U.S. Treasury is the main issuer of indexed bonds.

Convertible Bonds
Bonds that are exchangeable at the option of the holder for the issuing firm's common stock.

Warrants
Long-term options to buy a stated number of shares of common stock at a specified price.

Putable Bonds
Bonds with a provision that allows investors to sell them back to the company prior to maturity at a prearranged price.

Income Bond
A bond that pays interest only if it is earned.

Indexed (Purchasing Power) Bond
A bond that has interest payments based on an inflation index so as to protect the holder from inflation.

Self*Test*

Define floating-rate bonds, zero coupon bonds, callable bonds, putable bonds, income bonds, convertible bonds, and inflation-indexed bonds (TIPS).

Which is riskier to an investor, other things held constant—a callable bond or a putable bond? Explain.

In general, how is the rate on a floating-rate bond determined?

What are the two ways sinking funds can be handled? Which alternative will be used if interest rates have risen? If interest rates have fallen?

7-3 Bond Valuation

The value of any financial asset—a stock, a bond, a lease, or even a physical asset such as an apartment building or a piece of machinery—is the present value of the cash flows the asset is expected to produce. The cash flows for a standard coupon bearing bond, like those of Allied Food, consist of interest payments during the bond's 15-year life plus the amount borrowed (generally the par value) when the bond matures. In the case of a floating-rate bond, the interest payments vary over time. For zero coupon bonds, there are no interest payments, so the only cash

resource

Students can download the Excel chapter models from the textbook's student companion site on cengage.com. Once downloaded onto your computer, retrieve the Chapter 7 Excel model and follow along as you read this chapter.

flow is the face amount when the bond matures. For a "regular" bond with a fixed coupon, like Allied's, here is the situation:

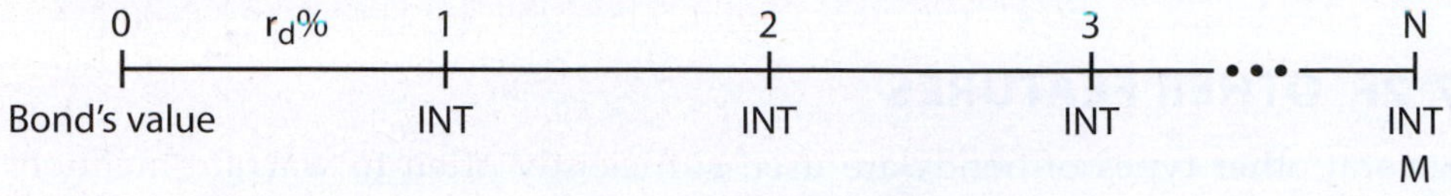

Where:

r_d = the market rate of interest on the bond, 8%. This is the discount rate used to calculate the present value of the cash flows, which is also the bond's price. In Chapter 6, we discussed in detail the various factors that determine market interest rates. Note that r_d is *not* the coupon interest rate. However, r_d is equal to the coupon rate at times, especially the day the bond is issued; when the two rates are equal, as in this case, the bond sells at par.

N = the number of years before the bond matures = 15. N declines over time after the bond has been issued, so a bond that had a maturity of 15 years when it was issued (original maturity = 15) will have N = 14 after 1 year, N = 13 after 2 years, and so forth. At this point, we assume that the bond pays interest once a year, or annually; so N is measured in years. Later on we will analyze semiannual payment bonds, which pay interest every 6 months.

INT = dollars of interest paid each year = Coupon rate × Par value = 0.08($1,000) = $80. In calculator terminology, INT = PMT = 80. If the bond had been a semiannual payment bond, the payment would have been $40 every 6 months. The payment would have been zero if Allied had issued zero coupon bonds, and it would have varied over time if the bond had been a "floater."

M = the par, or maturity, value of the bond = $1,000. This amount must be paid at maturity. Back in the 1970s and before, when paper bonds with paper coupons were used, most bonds had a $1,000 value. Now with computer-entry bonds, the par amount purchased can vary, but in the text we use $1,000 for simplicity.

We can now redraw the time line to show the numerical values for all variables except the bond's value (and price, assuming an equilibrium exists), V_B:

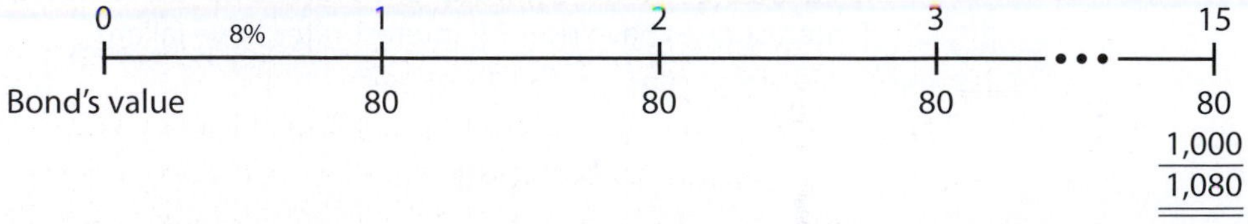

The following general equation can be solved to find the value of any bond:

$$\text{Bond's value} = V_B = \frac{INT}{(1 + r_d)^1} + \frac{INT}{(1 + r_d)^2} + \cdots + \frac{INT}{(1 + r_d)^N} + \frac{M}{(1 + r_d)^N}$$
$$= \sum_{t=1}^{N} \frac{INT}{(1 + r_d)^t} + \frac{M}{(1 + r_d)^N} \quad \textbf{7.1}$$

Inserting values for the Allied bond, we have

$$V_B = \sum_{t=1}^{15} \frac{\$80}{(1.08)^t} + \frac{\$1{,}000}{(1.08)^{15}}$$

The cash flows consist of an annuity of N years plus a lump sum payment at the end of Year N, and this fact is reflected in Equation 7.1.

We could simply discount each cash flow back to the present and sum those PVs to find the bond's value; see Figure 7.1 for an example. However, this procedure is not very efficient, especially when the bond has many years to maturity. Therefore, we use a financial calculator to solve the problem. Here is the setup:

15	8		80	1000
N	I/YR	PV	PMT	FV
		= −1,000		

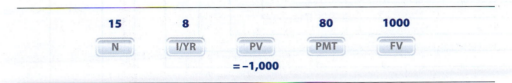

Simply input N = 15, r_d = I/YR = 8, INT = PMT = 80, and M = FV = 1000; then press the PV key to find the bond's value, \$1,000.[4] Because the PV is an outflow to the investor, it is shown with a negative sign. The calculator is programmed to solve Equation 7.1. It finds the PV of an annuity of \$80 per year for 15 years discounted at 8%; then it finds the PV of the \$1,000 maturity value; then it adds those two PVs to find the bond's value. In this Allied example, the bond is selling at a price equal to its par value.

Whenever the bond's market, or going, rate, r_d, is equal to its coupon rate, a *fixed-rate* bond will sell at its par value. Normally, the coupon rate is set at the going rate in the market the day a bond is issued, causing it to sell at par initially.

The coupon rate remains fixed after the bond is issued, but interest rates in the market move up and down. Looking at Equation 7.1, we see that an *increase* in the market interest rate (r_d) causes the price of an outstanding bond to *fall*, whereas a *decrease* in the rate causes the bond's price to *rise*. For example, if the market interest rate on Allied's bond increased to 12% immediately after it was issued, we would recalculate the price with the new market interest rate as follows:

15	12		80	1000
N	I/YR	PV	PMT	FV
		= −727.57		

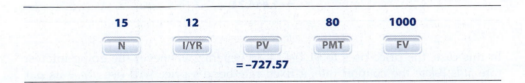

The bond's price would fall to \$727.57, well below par, as a result of the increase in interest rates. Whenever the going rate of interest *rises above* the coupon rate,

[4]Spreadsheets can also be used to solve for the bond's value. The PV of this bond can be calculated using Excel's PV function:

```
=PV(0.08,15,80,1000)
PV(rate, nper, pmt, [fv], [type])
```

This gives the bond's value as \$1,000. Note that type is left blank because cash flows occur at year-end.

FIGURE 7.1 Time Line for Allied Food Products' Bonds, 8% Interest Rate

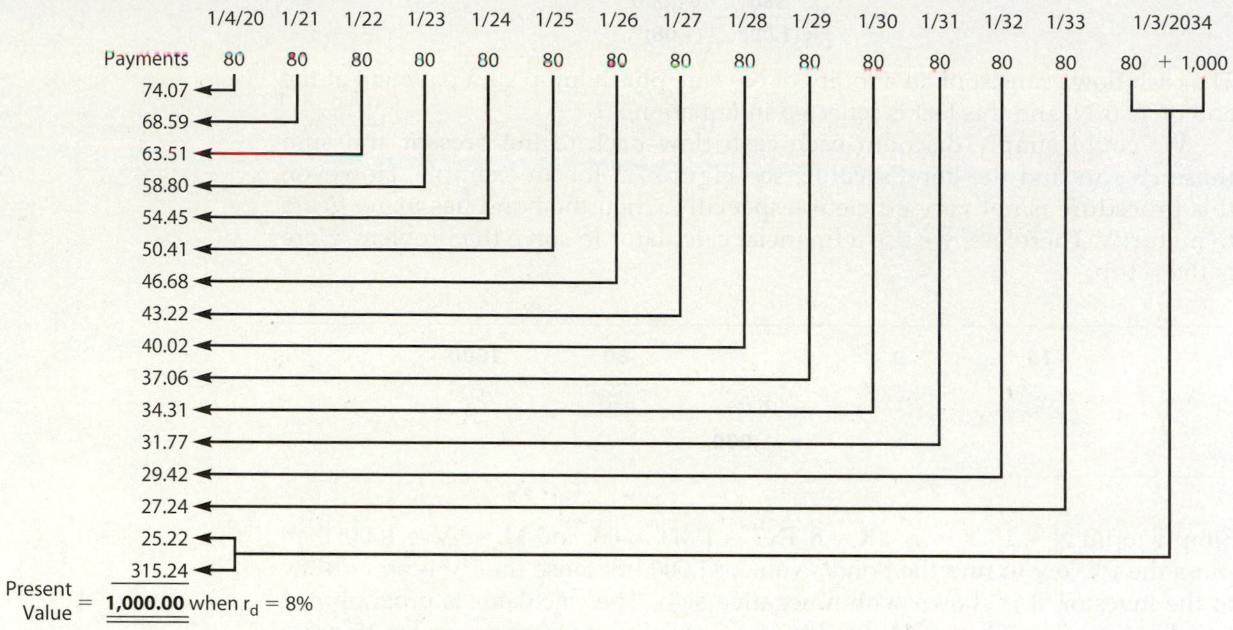

a fixed-rate bond's price will fall *below* its par value; this type of bond is called a **discount bond**.

Discount Bond
A bond that sells below its par value; occurs whenever the going rate of interest is above the coupon rate.

On the other hand, bond prices rise when market interest rates fall. For example, if the market interest rate on Allied's bond decreased to 4% immediately after it was issued, we would once again recalculate its price as follows:

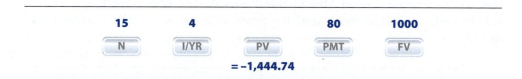

15	4		80	1000
N	I/YR	PV	PMT	FV
		= −1,444.74		

In this case, the price rises to $1,444.74. In general, whenever the going interest rate *falls below* the coupon rate, a fixed-rate bond's price will rise *above* its par value; this type of bond is called a **premium bond**.

Premium Bond
A bond that sells above its par value; occurs whenever the going rate of interest is below the coupon rate.

To summarize, here is the situation:

r_d = coupon rate, fixed-rate bond sells at par; hence, it is a *par bond*.
$r_d >$ coupon rate, fixed-rate bond sells below par; hence, it is a *discount bond*.
$r_d <$ coupon rate, fixed-rate bond sells above par; hence, it is a *premium bond*.

quick question

QUESTION:

A friend of yours just invested in an outstanding bond with a 5% annual coupon and a remaining maturity of 10 years. The bond has a par value of $1,000, and the market interest rate is currently 7%. How much did your friend pay for the bond? Is it a par, premium, or discount bond?

ANSWER:

Using a financial calculator, we can determine that your friend paid **$859.53** for the bond.

10	7		50	1000
N	I/YR	PV	PMT	FV
		= −859.53		

Using Excel's PV function, we solve for the bond's value as follows:

= PV(0.07,10,50,1000)

PV(rate, nper, pmt, [fv], [type])

Here we find that the bond's value is equal to **$859.53**.

Because the bond's coupon rate (5%) is less than the current market interest rate (7%), the bond is a discount bond—reflecting that interest rates have increased since this bond was originally issued.

Self*Test*

A bond that matures in 8 years has a par value of $1,000 and an annual coupon payment of $70; its market interest rate is 9%. What is its price? **($889.30)**

A bond that matures in 12 years has a par value of $1,000 and an annual coupon rate of 10%; the market interest rate is 8%. What is its price? **($1,150.72)**

Which of those two bonds is a discount bond, and which is a premium bond? Explain.

7-4 Bond Yields

If you examine the bond market table of *The Wall Street Journal* or a price sheet put out by a bond dealer, you will typically see information regarding each bond's maturity date, price, and coupon interest rate. You will also see a reported yield. Unlike the coupon interest rate, which is fixed, the bond's yield varies from day to day, depending on current market conditions.

To be most useful, the bond's yield should give us an estimate of the rate of return we would earn if we purchased the bond today and held it over its remaining life. If the bond is not callable, its remaining life is its years to maturity. If it is callable, its remaining life is the years to maturity if it is not called or the years to the call if it is called. In the following sections, we explain how to calculate those two possible yields and which one is likely to be earned by an investor.

7-4A YIELD TO MATURITY

Yield to Maturity (YTM)
The rate of return earned on a bond if it is held to maturity.

Suppose you were offered a 14-year, 8% annual coupon, $1,000 par value bond at a price of $1,422.52. What rate of interest would you earn on your investment if you bought the bond, held it to maturity, and received the promised interest payments and maturity value? This rate is called the bond's **yield to maturity (YTM)**, and it is the interest rate generally discussed by investors when they talk about rates of return and the rate reported by *The Wall Street Journal* and other publications. To find the YTM, all you need to do is solve Equation 7.1 for r_d as follows:

$$V_B = \frac{INT}{(1 + r_d)^1} + \frac{INT}{(1 + r_d)^2} + \cdots + \frac{INT}{(1 + r_d)^N} + \frac{M}{(1 + r_d)^N}$$

$$\$1{,}422.52 = \frac{\$80}{(1 + r_d)^1} + \cdots + \frac{\$80}{(1 + r_d)^{14}} + \frac{\$1{,}000}{(1 + r_d)^{14}}$$

You can substitute values for r_d until you find a value that "works" and force the sum of the PVs in the equation to equal $1,422.52. However, finding r_d = YTM by trial and error would be a tedious, time-consuming process. However, as you might guess, the calculation is easy with a financial calculator.[5] Here is the setup:

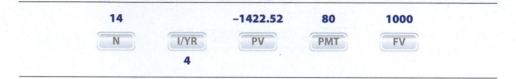

N	I/YR	PV	PMT	FV
14		−1422.52	80	1000
	4			

Simply enter N = 14, PV = −1422.52, PMT = 80, and FV = 1000; then press the I/YR key. The answer, 4%, will appear.

quick question

QUESTION:

You have just purchased an outstanding 15-year bond with a par value of $1,000 for $1,145.68. Its annual coupon payment is $75. What is the bond's yield to maturity?

ANSWER:

Using a financial calculator, we can determine that the bond's YTM is **6%**.

N	I/YR	PV	PMT	FV
15		−1145.68	75	1000
	6			

(continued)

[5]You can also find the YTM with a spreadsheet. In Excel, you use the RATE function:

= RATE(14,80,−1422.52,1000)
RATE(nper, pmt, pv, [fv], [type], [guess])

This gives the YTM as 4%. Note that we didn't need to specify a value for type (because the cash flows occur at the end of the year) or guess.

Using Excel's RATE function, we solve for the bond's YTM as follows:

=RATE(15,75,–1145.68,1000)

RATE(nper, pmt, pv, [fv], [type], [guess])

Here we find the bond's YTM is equal to **6%**.

Because the bond's coupon rate ($75/$1,000 = 7.5%) is greater than its YTM (6%), the bond is a premium bond—Indicating that interest rates have declined since the bond was originally issued.

The yield to maturity can also be viewed as the bond's *promised rate of return*, which is the return that investors will receive if all of the promised payments are made. However, the yield to maturity equals the *expected rate of return* only when (1) the probability of default is zero and (2) the bond cannot be called. If there is some default risk or the bond may be called, there is some chance that the promised payments to maturity will not be received, in which case the calculated yield to maturity will exceed the expected return.

Note also that a bond's calculated yield to maturity changes whenever interest rates in the economy change, which is almost daily. An investor who purchases a bond and holds it until it matures will receive the YTM that existed on the purchase date, but the bond's calculated YTM will change frequently between the purchase date and the maturity date.

7-4B YIELD TO CALL

If you purchase a bond that is callable and the company calls it, you do not have the option of holding it to maturity. Therefore, the yield to maturity would not be earned. For example, if Allied's 8% coupon bonds were callable and if interest rates fell from 8% to 4%, the company could call in the 8% bonds, replace them with 4% bonds, and save $80 − $40 = $40 interest per bond per year. This would be beneficial to the company, but not to its bondholders.

If current interest rates are well below an outstanding bond's coupon rate, a callable bond is likely to be called, and investors will estimate its most likely rate of return as the **yield to call (YTC)** rather than the yield to maturity. To calculate the YTC, we modify Equation 7.1, using years to call as N and the call price rather than the maturity value as the ending payment. Here's the modified equation:

Yield to Call (YTC)
The rate of return earned on a bond when it is called before its maturity date.

$$\text{Price of bond} = \sum_{t=1}^{N} \frac{\text{INT}}{(1 + r_d)^t} + \frac{\text{Call price}}{(1 + r_d)^N} \qquad 7.2$$

Here N is the number of years until the company can call the bond, call price is the price the company must pay in order to call the bond (it is often set equal to the par value plus 1 year's interest), and r_d is the YTC.

To illustrate, suppose Allied's bonds had a deferred call provision that permitted the company, if it desired, to call them 10 years after their issue date at a price of $1,080. Suppose further that interest rates had fallen and that 1 year after issuance the going interest rate had declined, causing their price to rise to $1,422.52. Here is the time line and the setup for finding the bonds' YTC with a financial calculator:

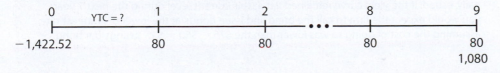

0	YTC = ? 1	2	•••	8	9
−1,422.52	80	80		80	80 1,080

9		−1422.52	80	1080
N	I/YR	PV	PMT	FV
	3.28			

The YTC is 3.28%—this is the return you would earn if you bought an Allied bond at a price of $1,422.52 and it was called 9 years from today. (It could not be called until 10 years after issuance because of its deferred call provision. One year has gone by, so there are 9 years left until the first call date.)

A company is more likely to call its bonds if they are able to replace their current high-coupon debt with less expensive financing. Broadly speaking, a bond is more likely to be called if its price is above par—because a price above par means that the going market interest rate (the yield to maturity) is less than the coupon rate. So, do you think Allied *will* call its 8% bonds when they become callable? Allied's action will depend on what the going interest rate is when they become callable. If the going rate remains at $r_d = 4\%$, Allied could save $8\% - 4\% = 4\%$, or $40 per bond per year; so it would call the 8% bonds and replace them with a new 4% issue. There would be some cost to the company to refund the bonds, but because the interest savings would most likely be worth the cost, Allied would probably refund them. Therefore, you should expect to earn the YTC = 3.28% rather than the YTM = 4% if you purchased the bond under the indicated conditions.

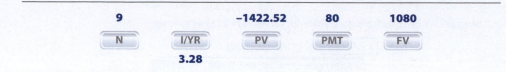

quick question

QUESTION:

You have just purchased an outstanding 15-year bond with a par value of $1,000 for $1,145.68. Its annual coupon payment is $75. We calculated the YTM of this bond (6%) in the Quick Question box on page 238. Now, assume that this bond is callable in 7 years at a price of $1,075. What is the bond's YTC? If the yield curve remains flat at its current level during this time period, would you expect to earn the YTM or YTC?

ANSWER:

Using a financial calculator, we can determine that the bond's YTC is **5.81%**.

7		−1145.68	75	1075
N	I/YR	PV	PMT	FV
	5.81			

Using Excel's RATE function, we solve for the bond's YTC as follows:

= RATE(7,75,–1145.68,1075)

RATE(nper, pmt, pv, [fv], [type], [guess])

Here we find the bond's YTC is equal to **5.81%**.

This bond sells at a premium, so interest rates have declined since the bond was originally issued. If the yield curve remained flat at this current level during the next 7 years, you would expect the firm to call the bond and issue bonds at the lower 6% interest rate, assuming the cost of doing so was lower than the $75 − $60 = $15 savings per bond.

In the balance of this chapter, we assume that bonds are not callable unless otherwise noted. However, some of the end-of-chapter problems deal with yield to call.[6]

Self*Test*

Explain the difference between yield to maturity (YTM) and yield to call (YTC).

Halley Enterprises's bonds currently sell for $975. They have a 7-year maturity, an annual coupon of $90, and a par value of $1,000. What is their yield to maturity? **(9.51%)**

The Henderson Company's bonds currently sell for $1,275. They pay a $120 annual coupon, have a 20-year maturity, and a par value of $1,000, but they can be called in 5 years at $1,120. What are their YTM and their YTC, and if the yield curve remained flat, which rate would investors expect to earn? **(8.99%, 7.31%, YTC)**

7-5 Changes in Bond Values over Time

When a coupon bond is issued, the coupon is generally set at a level that causes the bond's market price to equal its par value. If a lower coupon were set, investors would not be willing to pay $1,000 for the bond, but if a higher coupon were set, investors would clamor for it and bid its price up over $1,000. Investment bankers can judge quite precisely the coupon rate that will cause a bond to sell at its $1,000 par value.

A bond that has just been issued is known as a *new issue*. Once it has been issued, it is an *outstanding bond*, also called a *seasoned issue*. Newly issued bonds generally sell at prices very close to par, but the prices of outstanding bonds can vary widely from par. Except for floating-rate bonds, coupon payments are constant; so when economic conditions change, a bond with an $80 coupon that sold at its $1,000 par value when it was issued will sell for more or less than $1,000 thereafter.

Among its outstanding bonds, Allied currently has three equally risky issues that will mature in 15 years:

- Allied's just-issued 15-year bonds have an 8% annual coupon. They were issued at par, which means that the market interest rate on their issue date was also 8%. Because the coupon rate equals the market interest rate, these bonds are trading at par, or $1,000.
- Five years ago Allied issued 20-year bonds with a 5% annual coupon. These bonds currently have 15 years remaining until maturity. They were originally issued at par, which means that 5 years ago the market interest rate was 5%. Currently, this bond's coupon rate is less than the 8% market rate, so they sell at a discount. Using a financial calculator or spreadsheet, we can quickly find that they have a price of $743.22. (Set

[6]Brokerage houses occasionally report a bond's *current yield*, defined as the annual interest payment divided by the current price. For example, if Allied's 8% coupon bonds were selling for $981.60, the current yield would be $80/$981.60 = 8.15%. Unlike the YTM or YTC, the current yield *does not* represent the actual return that investors should expect because it does not account for the capital gain or loss that will be realized if the bond is held until it matures or is called. The current yield was popular before calculators and computers came along because it was easy to calculate. However, it can be misleading, and now it's easy enough to calculate the YTM and YTC.

N = 15, I/YR = 8, PMT = 50, and FV = 1000, and solve for the PV to calculate the price.)

- Ten years ago Allied issued 25-year bonds with an 11% annual coupon. These bonds currently have 15 years remaining until maturity. They were originally issued at par, which means that 10 years ago the market interest rate must have been 11%. Because their coupon rate is greater than the current market rate, they sell at a premium. Using a financial calculator or spreadsheet, we can find that their price is $1,256.78. (Set N = 15, I/YR = 8, PMT = 110, and FV = 1000, and solve for the PV to determine the price.)

Each of these three bonds has a 15-year maturity, each has the same credit risk, and thus each has the same market interest rate, 8%. However, the bonds have different prices because of their different coupon rates.

Now let's consider what would happen to the prices of these three bonds over the 15 years until they mature, assuming that market interest rates remain constant at 8% and Allied does not default on its payments. Table 7.1 demonstrates how the prices of each of these bonds will change over time if market interest rates remain at 8%. One year from now each bond will have a maturity of 14 years—that is, N = 14. With a financial calculator, override N = 15 with N = 14, and press the PV key; that gives you the value of each bond 1 year from now. Continuing, set N = 13, N = 12, and so forth, to see how the prices change over time.

Table 7.1 also shows the current yield (which is the coupon interest divided by the bond's price), the capital gains yield, and the total return over time. For any given year, the *capital gains yield* is calculated as the bond's annual change in price divided by the beginning-of-year price. For example, if a bond was selling for $1,000 at the beginning of the year and $1,035 at the end of the year, its capital gains yield for the year would be $35/$1,000 = 3.5%. (If the bond was selling at a premium, its price would decline over time. Then the capital gains yield would be negative, but it would be offset by a high current yield.) A bond's total return is equal to the current yield plus the capital gains yield. In the absence of default risk and assuming market equilibrium, the total return is also equal to YTM and the market interest rate, which in our example is 8%.

Figure 7.2 plots the three bonds' predicted prices as calculated in Table 7.1. Notice that the bonds have very different price paths over time but that at maturity all three will sell at their par value of $1,000. Here are some points about the prices of the bonds over time:

- The price of the 8% coupon bond trading at par will remain at $1,000 if the market interest rate remains at 8%. Therefore, its current yield will remain at 8%, and its capital gains yield will be zero each year.
- The 5% bond trades at a discount; however, at maturity, it must sell at par because that is the amount the company will pay its bondholders. Therefore, its price must rise over time.
- The 11% coupon bond trades at a premium. However, its price must be equal to its par value at maturity; so the price must decline over time.

Although the prices of the 5% and 11% coupon bonds move in opposite directions over time, each bond provides investors with the same total return, 8%, which is also the total return on the 8% coupon par value bond. The discount bond has a low coupon rate (and therefore a low current yield), but it provides a capital gain

TABLE 7.1 Calculation of Current Yields, Capital Gains Yields, and Total Returns for 5%, 8%, and 11% Coupon Bonds When the Market Rate Remains Constant at 8%

	5% COUPON BOND				8% COUPON BOND				11% COUPON BOND			
Number of Years Until Maturity	Price[a]	Expected Current Yield[b]	Expected Capital Gains Yield[c]	Expected Total Return[d]	Price[a]	Expected Current Yield[b]	Expected Capital Gains Yield[c]	Expected Total Return[d]	Price[a]	Expected Current Yield[b]	Expected Capital Gains Yield[c]	Expected Total Return[d]
15	$ 743.22	6.7%	1.3%	8.0%	$1,000.00	8.0%	0.0%	8.0%	$1,256.78	8.8%	−0.8%	8.0%
14	752.67	6.6	1.4	8.0	1,000.00	8.0	0.0	8.0	1,247.33	8.8	−0.8	8.0
13	762.89	6.6	1.4	8.0	1,000.00	8.0	0.0	8.0	1,237.11	8.9	−0.9	8.0
12	773.92	6.5	1.5	8.0	1,000.00	8.0	0.0	8.0	1,226.08	9.0	−1.0	8.0
11	785.83	6.4	1.6	8.0	1,000.00	8.0	0.0	8.0	1,214.17	9.1	−1.1	8.0
10	798.70	6.3	1.7	8.0	1,000.00	8.0	0.0	8.0	1,201.30	9.2	−1.2	8.0
9	812.59	6.2	1.8	8.0	1,000.00	8.0	0.0	8.0	1,187.41	9.3	−1.3	8.0
8	827.60	6.0	2.0	8.0	1,000.00	8.0	0.0	8.0	1,172.40	9.4	−1.4	8.0
7	843.81	5.9	2.1	8.0	1,000.00	8.0	0.0	8.0	1,156.19	9.5	−1.5	8.0
6	861.31	5.8	2.2	8.0	1,000.00	8.0	0.0	8.0	1,138.69	9.7	−1.7	8.0
5	880.22	5.7	2.3	8.0	1,000.00	8.0	0.0	8.0	1,119.78	9.8	−1.8	8.0
4	900.64	5.6	2.4	8.0	1,000.00	8.0	0.0	8.0	1,099.36	10.0	−2.0	8.0
3	922.69	5.4	2.6	8.0	1,000.00	8.0	0.0	8.0	1,077.31	10.2	−2.2	8.0
2	946.50	5.3	2.7	8.0	1,000.00	8.0	0.0	8.0	1,053.50	10.4	−2.4	8.0
1	972.22	5.1	2.9	8.0	1,000.00	8.0	0.0	8.0	1,027.78	10.7	−2.7	8.0
0	1,000.00				1,000.00				1,000.00			

Notes:

[a] Using a financial calculator, the price of each bond is calculated by entering the data for N, I/YR, PMT, and FV, then solving for PV = the bond's value.

[b] The expected current yield is calculated as the annual interest divided by the price of the bond.

[c] The expected capital gains yield is calculated as the difference between the end-of-year bond price and the beginning-of-year bond price divided by the beginning-of-year bond price.

[d] The expected total return is the sum of the expected current yield and the expected capital gains yield.

FIGURE 7.2 Time Paths of 5%, 8%, and 11% Coupon Bonds When the Market Rate Remains Constant at 8%

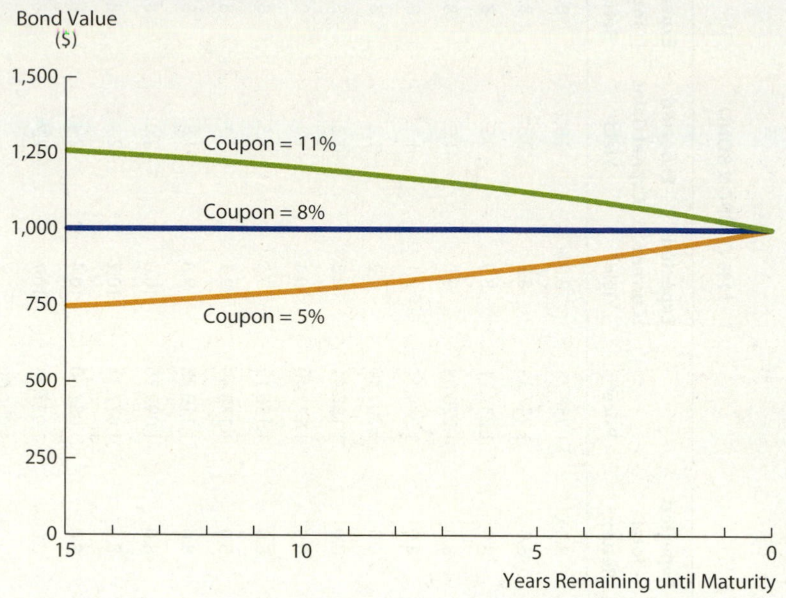

each year. In contrast, the premium bond has a high current yield, but it has an expected capital loss each year.[7]

Self*Test*

What is meant by the terms *new issue* and *seasoned issue?*

Last year a firm issued 20-year, 8% annual coupon bonds at a par value of $1,000.

a. Suppose that 1 year later the going market interest rate drops to 6%. What is the new price of the bonds, assuming they now have 19 years to maturity? **($1,223.16)**

b. Suppose that 1 year after issue, the going market interest rate is 10% (rather than 6%). What would the price have been? **($832.70)**

Why do the prices of fixed-rate bonds fall if expectations for inflation rise?

7-6 Bonds with Semiannual Coupons

Although some bonds pay interest annually, the vast majority actually make payments semiannually. To evaluate semiannual bonds, we must modify the valuation model (Equation 7.1) as follows:

1. Divide the annual coupon interest payment by 2 to determine the dollars of interest paid each 6 months.

[7]In this example (and throughout the text), we ignore the tax effects associated with purchasing different types of bonds. For coupon bonds, under the current Tax Code (May 2018), coupon payments are taxed as ordinary income, whereas long-term capital gains are taxed at the long-term capital gains tax rate. As we mentioned in Chapter 3, for most investors, the long-term capital gains tax rate is lower than the personal tax rate. Moreover, although coupon payments are taxed each year, capital gains taxes are deferred until the bond is sold or matures. Consequently, all else equal, investors end up paying lower taxes on discount bonds because a greater percentage of their total return comes in the form of capital gains. For details on the tax treatment of zero coupon bonds, see Web Appendix 7A.

2. Multiply the years to maturity, N, by 2 to determine the number of semiannual periods.
3. Divide the nominal (quoted) interest rate, r_d, by 2 to determine the periodic (semiannual) interest rate.

On a time line, there would be twice as many payments, but each would be half as large as with an annual payment bond. Making the indicated changes results in the following equation for finding a semiannual bond's value:

$$V_B = \sum_{t=1}^{2N} \frac{INT/2}{(1 + r_d/2)^t} + \frac{M}{(1 + r_d/2)^{2N}} \quad \text{7.1a}$$

To illustrate, assume that Allied Food's 15-year bonds, as discussed in Section 7-3, pay \$40 of interest each 6 months rather than \$80 at the end of each year. Thus, each interest payment is only half as large but there are twice as many of them. We would describe the coupon rate as "8% with semiannual payments."[8]

When the going (nominal) rate is $r_d = 4\%$ with semiannual compounding, the value of a 15-year, 8% semiannual coupon bond that pays \$40 interest every 6 months is found as follows:

30	2		40	1000
N	I/YR	PV	PMT	FV
		= −1,447.93		

Enter N = 30, r_d = I / YR = 2, PMT = 40, and FV = 1000; then press the PV key to obtain the bond's value, \$1,447.93. The value with semiannual interest payments is slightly larger than \$1,444.74, the value when interest is paid annually as we calculated in Section 7-3. This higher value occurs because each interest payment is received somewhat faster under semiannual compounding.

Alternatively, when we know the price of a semiannual bond, we can easily back out the bond's nominal yield to maturity. In the previous example, if you were told that a 15-year bond with an 8% semiannual coupon was selling for \$1,447.93, you could solve for the bond's periodic interest rate as follows:

30		−1447.93	40	1000
N	I/YR	PV	PMT	FV
	2			

[8]In this situation, the coupon rate of "8% paid semiannually" is the rate that bond dealers, corporate treasurers, and investors generally discuss. Of course, if this bond were issued at par, its *effective annual rate* would be higher than 8%:

$$\text{EAR} = \text{EFF\%} = \left(1 + \frac{r_{NOM}}{M}\right)^M - 1 = \left(1 + \frac{0.08}{2}\right)^2 - 1 = (1.04)^2 - 1 = 8.16\%$$

Because 8% with annual payments is quite different from 8% with semiannual payments, we have assumed a change in effective rates in this section from the situation in Section 7-3, where we assumed 8% with annual payments.

In this case, enter N = 30, PV = −1447.93, PMT = 40, and FV = 1000; then press the I/YR key to obtain the interest rate per semiannual period, 2%. Multiplying by 2, we calculate the bond's nominal yield to maturity to be 4%.[9]

quick question

QUESTION:

You have just purchased an outstanding noncallable, 15-year bond with a par value of $1,000. Assume that this bond pays interest of 7.5%, with semiannual compounding. If the going (nominal) annual rate is 6%, what price did you pay for this bond? How does the price compare to the price of the annual coupon bond?

ANSWER:

Using a financial calculator, we can determine that the bond's price is **$1,147.00**.

30	3		37.50	1000
N	I/YR	PV	PMT	FV
		= −1,147.00		

Using Excel's PV function, we solve for the semiannual bond's price as follows:

= PV(0.03,30,37.5,1000)

PV(rate, nper, pmt, [fv], [type])

Here we find that the bond's value is equal to **$1,147.00**.

In the Quick Question box on page 238 we calculated the YTM on this annual bond whose price was $1,145.68. Notice that the semiannual bond's price is $1,147.00 − $1,145.68 = $1.32 greater due to the interest payments being received semiannually rather than on an annual basis.

Self*Test*

Describe how the annual payment bond valuation formula is changed to evaluate semiannual coupon bonds, and write the revised formula.

Hartwell Corporation's bonds have a 20-year maturity, an 8% semiannual coupon, and a face value of $1,000. The going nominal annual interest rate (r_d) is 7%. What is the bond's price? **($1,106.78)**

7-7 Assessing a Bond's Riskiness

In this section, we identify and explain the two key factors that impact a bond's riskiness. Once those factors are identified, we differentiate between them and discuss how you can minimize these risks.

[9]We can use a similar process to calculate the nominal yield to call for a semiannual bond. The only difference would be that N should represent the number of semiannual periods until the bond is callable, and FV should be the bond's call price rather than its par value.

7-7A PRICE RISK

As we saw in Chapter 6, interest rates fluctuate over time, and when they rise, the value of outstanding bonds decline. This risk of a decline in bond values due to an increase in interest rates is called **price risk** (or **interest rate risk**). To illustrate, refer back to Allied's bonds; assume once more that they have an 8% annual coupon, and assume that you bought one of these bonds at its par value, \$1,000. Shortly after your purchase, the going interest rate rises from 8% to 12%.[10] As we saw in Section 7-3, this interest rate increase would cause the bond's price to fall from \$1,000 to \$727.57, so you would have a loss of \$272.43 on the bond.[11] Because interest rates can and do rise, rising rates cause losses to bondholders; people or firms who invest in bonds are exposed to risk from increasing interest rates.

Price (Interest Rate) Risk
The risk of a decline in a bond's price due to an increase in interest rates.

Price risk is higher on bonds that have long maturities than on bonds that will mature in the near future.[12] This follows because the longer the maturity, the longer before the bond will be paid off and the bondholder can replace it with another bond with a higher coupon. This point can be demonstrated by showing how the value of a 1-year bond with an 8% annual coupon fluctuates with changes in r_d and then comparing those changes with changes on a 15-year bond. The 1-year bond's values at different interest rates are shown here:

Value of a 1-year bond at:

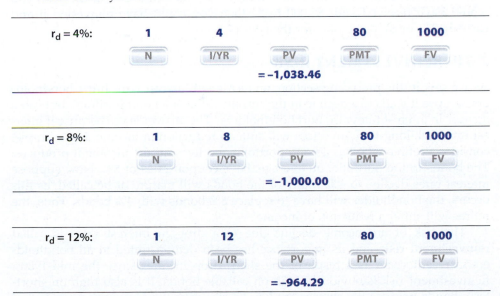

$r_d = 4\%$:	1	4		80	1000
	N	I/YR	PV	PMT	FV
			= −1,038.46		

$r_d = 8\%$:	1	8		80	1000
	N	I/YR	PV	PMT	FV
			= −1,000.00		

$r_d = 12\%$:	1	12		80	1000
	N	I/YR	PV	PMT	FV
			= −964.29		

[10] An immediate increase in rates from 8% to 12% would be quite unusual, and it would occur only if something quite bad were revealed about the company or happened in the economy. Smaller but still significant rate increases that adversely affect bondholders do occur fairly often.

[11] You would have an accounting (and tax) loss only if you sold the bond; if you held it to maturity, you would not have such a loss. However, even if you did not sell, you would still have suffered a real economic loss in an opportunity cost sense because you would have lost the opportunity to invest at 12% and would be stuck with an 8% bond in a 12% market. In an economic sense, "paper losses" are just as bad as realized accounting losses.

[12] Actually, a bond's maturity and coupon rate both affect price risk. Low coupons mean that most of the bond's return will come from repayment of principal, whereas on a high-coupon bond with the same maturity, more of the cash flows will come in during the early years due to the relatively large coupon payments.

You would obtain the first value with a financial calculator by entering N = 1, I/YR = 4, PMT = 80, and FV = 1000 and then pressing PV to get $1,038.46. With all the data still in your calculator, enter I/YR = 8 to override the old I/YR = 4, and press PV to find the bond's value at an 8% rate; it drops to $1,000. Then enter I/YR = 12, and press the PV key to find the last bond value, $964.29.

The effects of increasing rates on the 15-year bond value as found earlier in Section 7-3 can be compared with the just-calculated effects for the 1-year bond. This comparison is shown in Figure 7.3, where we show bond prices at several rates and then plot those prices on the graph. Compared to the 1-year bond, the 15-year bond is far more sensitive to changes in rates. At an 8% interest rate, both the 15-year and 1-year bonds are valued at $1,000. When rates rise to 12%, the 15-year bond falls to $727.57, but the 1-year bond falls only to $964.29. The price decline for the 1-year bond is only 3.57%, while that for the 15-year bond is 27.24%.

For bonds with similar coupons, this differential interest rate sensitivity always holds true—the longer a bond's maturity, the more its price changes in response to a given change in interest rates. Thus, even if the risk of default on two bonds is exactly the same, the one with the longer maturity is typically exposed to more risk from a rise in interest rates.[13]

The logical explanation for this difference in price risk is simple. Suppose you bought a 15-year bond that yielded 8%, or $80 a year. Now suppose interest rates on comparable-risk bonds rose to 12%. You would be stuck receiving only $80 of interest for the next 15 years. On the other hand, had you bought a 1-year bond, you would have earned a low return for only 1 year. At the end of the year, you would have received your $1,000 back; then you could have reinvested it and earned 12%, or $120 per year, for the next 14 years.

7-7B REINVESTMENT RISK

As we saw in the preceding section, an *increase* in interest rates hurts bondholders because it leads to a decline in the current value of a bond portfolio. But can a *decrease* in interest rates also hurt bondholders? The answer is yes because if interest rates fall, long-term investors will suffer a reduction in income. For example, consider a retiree who has a bond portfolio and lives off the income it produces. The bonds in the portfolio, on average, have coupon rates of 8%. Now suppose interest rates decline to 4%. Many of the bonds will mature or be called; as this occurs, the bondholder will have to replace 8% bonds with 4% bonds. Thus, the retiree will suffer a reduction of income.[14]

Reinvestment Risk
The risk that a decline in interest rates will lead to a decline in income from a bond portfolio.

The risk of an income decline due to a drop in interest rates is called **reinvestment risk**, and its importance has been demonstrated to all bondholders in recent years as a result of the sharp drop in rates since the mid-1980s. Reinvestment risk is obviously high on callable bonds. It is also high on short-term bonds because the shorter the bond's maturity, the fewer the years before the relatively high old coupon bonds will be replaced with the new low-coupon issues. Thus, retirees whose primary holdings are short-term bonds or other debt securities will be hurt badly by a decline in rates, but holders of noncallable long-term bonds will continue to enjoy the old high rates.

---

[13]If a 10-year bond were plotted on the graph in Figure 7.3, its curve would lie between those of the 15-year and the 1-year bonds. The curve of a 1-month bond would be almost horizontal, indicating that its price would change very little in response to an interest rate change, but a 100-year bond would have a very steep slope, and the slope of a perpetuity would be even steeper. Also, a zero coupon bond's price is quite sensitive to interest rate changes, and the longer its maturity, the greater its price sensitivity. Therefore, a 30-year zero coupon bond would have a huge amount of price risk.

[14]Charles Schwab makes this point in an opinion piece in *The Wall Street Journal*, where he argues that continued low interest rates have had a devastating effect on many senior citizens who live off of the interest generated from their investments. For additional information, refer to Charles Schwab, "Low Interest Rates Are Squeezing Seniors," *The Wall Street Journal* (www.wsj.com), March 30, 2010.

FIGURE 7.3 Values of Long- and Short-Term 8% Annual Coupon Bonds at Different Market Interest Rates

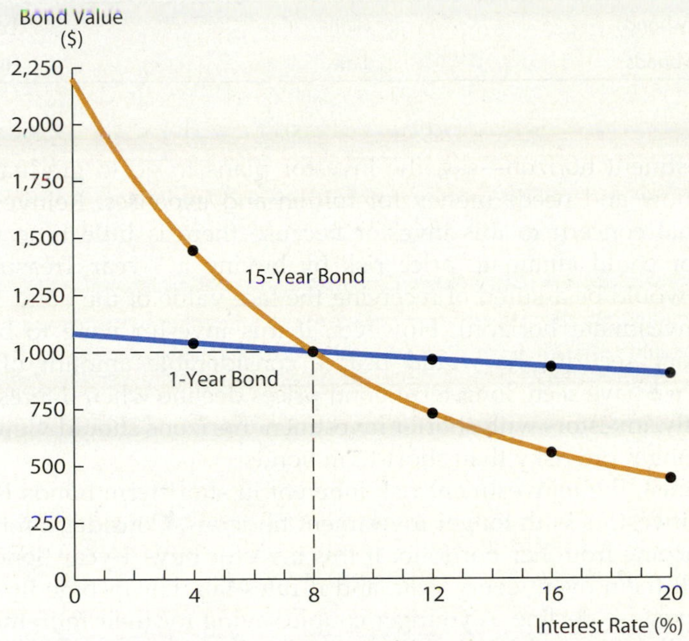

Current Market Interest Rate, r_d	Value of 1-Year Bond	Value of 15-Year Bond
4%	$1,038.46	$1,444.74
8	1,000.00	1,000.00
12	964.29	727.57
16	931.03	553.96
20	900.00	438.94

Note: Bond values were calculated using a financial calculator assuming annual, or once-a-year, compounding.

7-7C COMPARING PRICE RISK AND REINVESTMENT RISK

Note that price risk relates to the *current market value* of the bond portfolio, while reinvestment risk relates to the *income* the portfolio produces. If you hold long-term bonds, you will face significant price risk because the value of your portfolio will decline if interest rates rise, but you will not face much reinvestment risk because your income will be stable. On the other hand, if you hold short-term bonds, you will not be exposed to much price risk, but you will be exposed to significant reinvestment risk. Table 7.2 summarizes how a bond's maturity and coupon rate affect its price risk and reinvestment risk. For example, a long-term zero coupon bond will have a very high level of price risk and relatively little reinvestment risk. In contrast, a short-term bond with a high coupon rate will have low price risk but considerable reinvestment risk.

Which type of risk is "more relevant" to a given investor depends on how long the investor plans to hold the bonds—this is often referred to as his or her **investment horizon**. To illustrate, consider an investor who has a relatively short

Investment Horizon
The period of time an investor plans to hold a particular investment.

TABLE 7.2 Comparing Price Risk and Reinvestment Risk

Bond	Level of Price Risk	Level of Reinvestment Risk
Longer-maturity bonds	High	Low
Higher-coupon bonds	Low	High

1-year investment horizon—say, the investor plans to go to graduate school a year from now and needs money for tuition and expenses. Reinvestment risk is of minimal concern to this investor because there is little time to reinvest. The investor could eliminate price risk by buying a 1-year Treasury security because he would be assured of receiving the face value of the bond 1 year from now (the investment horizon). However, if this investor were to buy a long-term Treasury security, he would bear a considerable amount of price risk because, as we have seen, long-term bond prices decline when interest rates rise. Consequently, investors with shorter investment horizons should view long-term bonds as being more risky than short-term bonds.

By contrast, the reinvestment risk inherent in short-term bonds is especially relevant to investors with longer investment horizons. Consider a retiree who is living on income from her portfolio. If this investor buys 1-year bonds, she will have to "roll them over" every year, and if rates fall, her income in subsequent years will likewise decline. A younger couple saving for their retirement or their children's college costs, for example, would be affected similarly because if they buy short-term bonds, they too will have to roll over their portfolio at possibly much lower rates. Because of the uncertainty today about the rates that will be earned on these reinvested cash flows, long-term investors should be especially concerned about the reinvestment risk inherent in short-term bonds.

Duration
The weighted average of the time it takes to receive each of the bond's cash flows.

To account for the effects related to both a bond's maturity and coupon, many analysts focus on a measure called **duration**. A bond's duration is the weighted average of the time it takes to receive each of the bond's cash flows. It follows that a zero coupon bond whose only cash flow is paid at maturity has a duration equal to its maturity. On the other hand, a coupon bond will have a duration that is less than its maturity. You can use Excel's DURATION function to calculate a bond's duration. We discuss duration in greater detail in Web Appendix 7B.

One way to manage both price and reinvestment risk is to buy a zero coupon Treasury bond with a duration equal to the investor's investment horizon. A very simple way to do this is to buy a zero coupon bond with a maturity that matches the investment horizon. For example, assume your investment horizon is 10 years. If you buy a 10-year zero, you will receive a guaranteed payment in 10 years equal to the bond's face value.[15] Moreover, as there are no coupons to reinvest, there is no reinvestment risk. This explains why investors with specific goals often invest in zero coupon bonds.[16]

[15]Note that in this example, the 10-year zero technically has a considerable amount of price risk because its *current* price is highly sensitive to changes in interest rates. However, the year-to-year movements in price should not be of great concern to an investor with a 10-year investment horizon because the investor knows that, regardless of what happens to interest rates, the bond's price will still be $1,000 when it matures.

[16]Two words of caution about zeros are in order. First, as we show in Web Appendix 7A, investors in zeros must pay taxes each year on their accrued gain in value, even though the bonds don't pay any cash until they mature. Second, buying a zero coupon bond with a maturity equal to your investment horizon enables you to lock in a nominal cash payoff, but the *real* value of that payment still depends on what happens to inflation during your investment horizon.

Recall from Chapter 6 that maturity risk premiums are generally positive.[17] Moreover, a positive maturity risk premium implies that investors, on average, regard longer-term bonds as being riskier than shorter-term bonds. That, in turn, suggests that the average investor is more concerned with price risk. Still, it is appropriate for each investor to consider his or her own situation, to recognize the risks inherent in bonds with different maturities, and to construct a portfolio that deals best with the investor's most relevant risk.

Self*Test*

Differentiate between price risk and reinvestment risk.

To which type of risk are holders of long-term bonds more exposed? Short-term bondholders?

What type of security can be used to minimize both price risk and reinvestment risk for an investor with a fixed investment horizon? Does this security protect the real payoff? Explain.

7-8 Default Risk

Potential default is another important risk that bondholders face. If the issuer defaults, investors will receive less than the promised return. Recall from Chapter 6 that the quoted interest rate includes a default risk premium—the higher the probability of default, the higher the premium and thus the yield to maturity. Default risk on Treasuries is zero, but this risk is substantial for lower-grade corporate and municipal bonds.

To illustrate, suppose two bonds have the same promised cash flows—their coupon rates, maturities, liquidity, and inflation exposures are identical—but one has more default risk than the other. Investors will naturally pay more for the one with less chance of default. As a result, bonds with higher default risk have higher market rates: $r_d = r^* + IP + DRP + LP + MRP$. If a bond's default risk changes, r_d and thus the price will be affected. Thus, if the default risk on Allied's bonds increases, their price will fall and the yield to maturity (YTM $= r_d$) will increase.

7-8A Various Types of Corporate Bonds

Default risk is influenced by the financial strength of the issuer and the terms of the bond contract, including whether collateral has been pledged to secure the bond. The characteristics of some key types of bonds are described in this section.

Mortgage Bonds

Under a **mortgage bond**, the corporation pledges specific assets as security for the bond. To illustrate, in 2019, Billingham Corporation needed $10 million to build a regional distribution center. Bonds in the amount of $4 million, secured by a *first mortgage* on the property, were issued. (The remaining $6 million was financed with equity capital.) If Billingham defaults on the bonds, the bondholders can foreclose on the property and sell it to satisfy their claims.

Mortgage Bond
A bond backed by fixed assets. First mortgage bonds are senior in priority to claims of second mortgage bonds.

[17]The fact that maturity risk premiums are positive suggests that most investors have relatively short investment horizons, or at least worry about short-term changes in their net worth. See Roger G. Ibbotson, *Stocks, Bonds, Bills, and Inflation: 2018 Yearbook* (Chicago, IL: Duff & Phelps, 2018), which finds that the maturity risk premium for long-term bonds has averaged 1.6% over the past 92 years.

If Billingham had chosen to, it could have issued *second mortgage bonds* secured by the same $10 million of assets. In the event of liquidation, the holders of the second mortgage bonds would have a claim against the property, but only after the first mortgage bondholders had been paid in full. Thus, second mortgages are sometimes called *junior mortgages* because they are junior in priority to the claims of *senior mortgages*, or *first mortgage bonds*.

Indenture
A formal agreement between the issuer and the bondholders.

All mortgage bonds are subject to an **indenture**, which is a legal document that spells out in detail the rights of the bondholders and the corporation. The indentures of many major corporations were written 20, 30, 40, or more years ago. These indentures are generally "open ended," meaning that new bonds can be issued from time to time under the same indenture. However, the amount of new bonds that can be issued is usually limited to a specified percentage of the firm's total "bondable property," which generally includes all land, plant, and equipment. And, of course, the coupon interest rate on newly issued bonds changes over time, along with the market rate on the older bonds.

Debentures

Debenture
A long-term bond that is not secured by a mortgage on specific property.

A **debenture** is an unsecured bond, and as such, it provides no specific collateral as security for the obligation. Therefore, debenture holders are general creditors whose claims are protected by property not otherwise pledged. In practice, the use of debentures depends on the nature of the firm's assets and on its general credit strength. Extremely strong companies such as General Electric and Exxon Mobil can use debentures because they do not need to put up property as security for their debt. Debentures are also issued by weak companies that have already pledged most of their assets as collateral for mortgage loans. In this case, the debentures are quite risky, and that risk will be reflected in their interest rates.

Subordinated Debentures

Subordinated Debentures
Bonds having a claim on assets only after the senior debt has been paid in full in the event of liquidation.

The term *subordinate* means "below" or "inferior to," and in the event of bankruptcy, subordinated debt has a claim on assets only after senior debt has been paid in full. **Subordinated debentures** may be subordinated to designated notes payable (usually bank loans) or to all other debt. In the event of liquidation or reorganization, holders of subordinated debentures receive nothing until all senior debt, as named in the debentures' indenture, has been paid. Precisely how subordination works and how it strengthens the position of senior debtholders are explained in detail in Web Appendix 7C.

7-8B BOND RATINGS

Investment-Grade Bonds
Bonds rated triple-B or higher; many banks and other institutional investors are permitted by law to hold only investment-grade bonds.

Junk Bonds
High-risk, high-yield bonds.

Since the early 1900s, bonds have been assigned quality ratings that reflect their probability of going into default. The three major rating agencies are Moody's Investors Service (Moody's), Standard & Poor's Corporation (S&P), and Fitch Investors Service. Moody's and S&P's rating designations are shown in Table 7.3.[18] The triple-A and double-A bonds are extremely safe. Single-A and triple-B bonds are also strong enough to be called **investment-grade bonds**, and they are the lowest-rated bonds that many banks and other institutional investors are permitted by law to hold. Double-B and lower bonds are speculative-grade bonds (**junk bonds**), and they have a significant probability of going into default.

[18]In the discussion to follow, reference to the S&P rating is intended to imply the Moody's and Fitch's ratings as well. Thus, triple-B bonds mean both BBB and Baa bonds, double-B bonds mean both BB and Ba bonds, and so forth.

TABLE 7.3 Bond Ratings, Default Risk, and Yields

Rating Agency[a]		**Percent Defaulting within:**[b]		**Median Ratios**[c]		**Percent Upgraded or Downgraded in 2017**[b]		
S&P and Fitch (1)	**Moody's (2)**	**1 year (3)**	**5 years (4)**	**Return on Capital (5)**	**Total Debt/ Total Capital (6)**	**Down (7)**	**Up (8)**	**Yield**[d] **(9)**
Investment-grade bonds								
AAA	Aaa	0.12%	0.67%	27.6%	12.4%	0.00%	NA%	2.95%
AA	Aa	0.05	0.06	27.0	28.3	6.99	0.00	2.78
A	A	0.05	0.51	17.5	37.5	3.20	0.51	3.04
BBB	Baa	0.14	1.52	13.4	42.5	4.26	2.05	3.59
Junk bonds								
BB	Ba	0.70	5.39	11.3	53.7	3.80	5.31	4.42
B	B	2.02	9.60	8.7	75.9	4.25	2.83	5.90
CCC	Caa	21.05	35.42	3.2	113.5	17.31	21.15	10.53

Notes:

[a]The ratings agencies also use "modifiers" for bonds rated below triple-A. S&P and Fitch use a plus and minus system; thus, A+ designates the strongest A-rated bonds and A− the weakest. Moody's uses a 1, 2, or 3 designation, with 1 denoting the strongest and 3 the weakest; thus, within the double-A category, Aa1 is the best, Aa2 is average, and Aa3 is the weakest.

[b]Default data, downgrades, and upgrades are from Fitch Ratings Global Corporate Finance 2017 Transition and Default Study, March 28, 2018. See www.fitchratings.com/site/re/10024297. Default data are for the period 1990–2017. (A free registration is required to access the Fitch report.)

[c]Median ratios are from Standard & Poor's 2006 Corporate Ratings Criteria, April 23, 2007. See standardandpoors.com/en_US /web/guest/article/-/view/type/HTML/id/785022. You must register (which is free) and log in to get access to this report.

[d]Data are from BofA Merrill Lynch, retrieved from FRED, Federal Reserve Bank of St. Louis, fred.stlouisfed.org, December 31, 2017.

Consistent with these arguments, Table 7.3 shows that lower-rated bonds generally have higher default rates. These numbers are based on an underlying sample of bonds rated by Fitch Ratings over the past several years. For example, 0.51% of A-rated bonds defaulted within the first 5 years of being issued, whereas 35.42% of C-rated bonds defaulted within 5 years. The numbers in this table also illustrate that (as expected) lower-rated bonds have higher yields and their issuing companies have higher debt ratios.

Bond Rating Criteria

The framework used by rating agencies examines both qualitative and quantitative factors. Quantitative factors relate to financial risk—examining a firm's financial ratios, such as those discussed in Chapter 4. Published ratios are, of course, historical—they show the firm's condition in the past, whereas bond investors are more interested in the firm's condition in the future. Qualitative factors considered include an analysis of a firm's business risk, such as its competitiveness within its industry and the quality of its management. Determinants of bond ratings include the following:

1. *Financial Ratios.* All of the ratios are potentially important, but those related to financial risk are key. The rating agencies' analysts perform a financial

analysis along the lines discussed in Chapter 4 and forecast future ratios along the lines described in Chapter 16.

2. *Qualitative Factors: Bond Contract Terms.* Every bond is covered by a contract, often called an indenture, between the issuer and the bondholders. The indenture spells out all the terms related to the bond. Included in the indenture are the maturity, the coupon interest rate, a statement of whether the bond is secured by a mortgage on specific assets, any sinking fund provisions, and a statement of whether the bond is guaranteed by some other party with a high credit ranking. Other provisions might include *restrictive covenants* such as requirements that the firm not let its debt ratio exceed a stated level and that it keep its times-interest-earned ratio at or above a given level. Some bond indentures are hundreds of pages long, while others are quite short and cover just the terms of the loan.
3. *Miscellaneous Qualitative Factors.* Included here are issues like the sensitivity of the firm's earnings to the strength of the economy, the way it is affected by inflation, a statement of whether it is having or likely to have labor problems, the extent of its international operations (including the stability of the countries in which it operates), potential environmental problems, and potential antitrust problems. Today the most important factor is exposure to subprime loans, including the difficulty to determine the extent of this exposure as a result of the complexity of the assets backed by such loans.

We see that bond ratings are determined by a great many factors, some quantitative and some qualitative (or subjective). Also, the rating process is dynamic—at times, one factor is of primary importance; at other times, some other factor is key. Table 7.4 provides a summary of the criteria a rating agency examines when rating a company's bonds. Panel a shows how business and financial risk determine the "anchor" for establishing the underlying bond rating. Panel b further illustrates how this anchor is combined with a comprehensive set of other factors to determine the issuer's final credit rating.

Importance of Bond Ratings

Bond ratings are important to both firms and investors. First, because a bond's rating is an indicator of its default risk, the rating has a direct, measurable influence on the bond's interest rate and the firm's cost of debt. Second, most bonds are purchased by institutional investors rather than individuals, and many institutions are restricted to investment-grade securities. Thus, if a firm's bonds fall below BBB, it will have a difficult time selling new bonds because many potential purchasers will not be allowed to buy them.

As a result of their higher risk and more restricted market, lower-grade bonds have higher required rates of return, r_d, than high-grade bonds. Figure 7.4 illustrates this point. In each of the years shown on the graph, U.S. government bonds have had the lowest yields, AAA bonds have been next, and BBB bonds have had the highest yields. The figure also shows that the gaps between yields on the three types of bonds vary over time, indicating that the cost differentials, or yield spreads, fluctuate from year to year. Most recently there was a dramatic increase in the yield spreads between corporate and Treasury securities in the aftermath of the recent financial crisis. In the years since the crisis, these spreads have narrowed as investors have slowly become once again more willing to hold riskier securities. This point is highlighted in Figure 7.5, which gives the yields on the three types of bonds and the yield spreads for AAA and BBB bonds over

TABLE 7.4 Bond Rating Criteria

Panel a: Combining the Business and Financial Risk Profiles to Determine the Anchor

	Financial Risk Profile					
Business Risk Profile	**Minimal**	**Modest**	**Intermediate**	**Significant**	**Aggressive**	**Highly Leveraged**
Excellent	AAA/AA+	AA	A+/A	A–	BBB	BBB–/BB+
Strong	AA/AA–	A+/A	A–/BBB+	BBB	BB+	BB
Satisfactory	A/A–	BBB+	BBB/BBB–	BBB–/BB+	BB	B+
Fair	BBB/BBB–	BBB–	BB+	BB	BB–	B
Weak	BB+	BB+	BB	BB–	B+	B/B–
Vulnerable	BB–	BB–	BB–/B+	B+	B	B–

Panel b: Issuer and Issue Credit Rating

Issuer and Issue Credit Rating

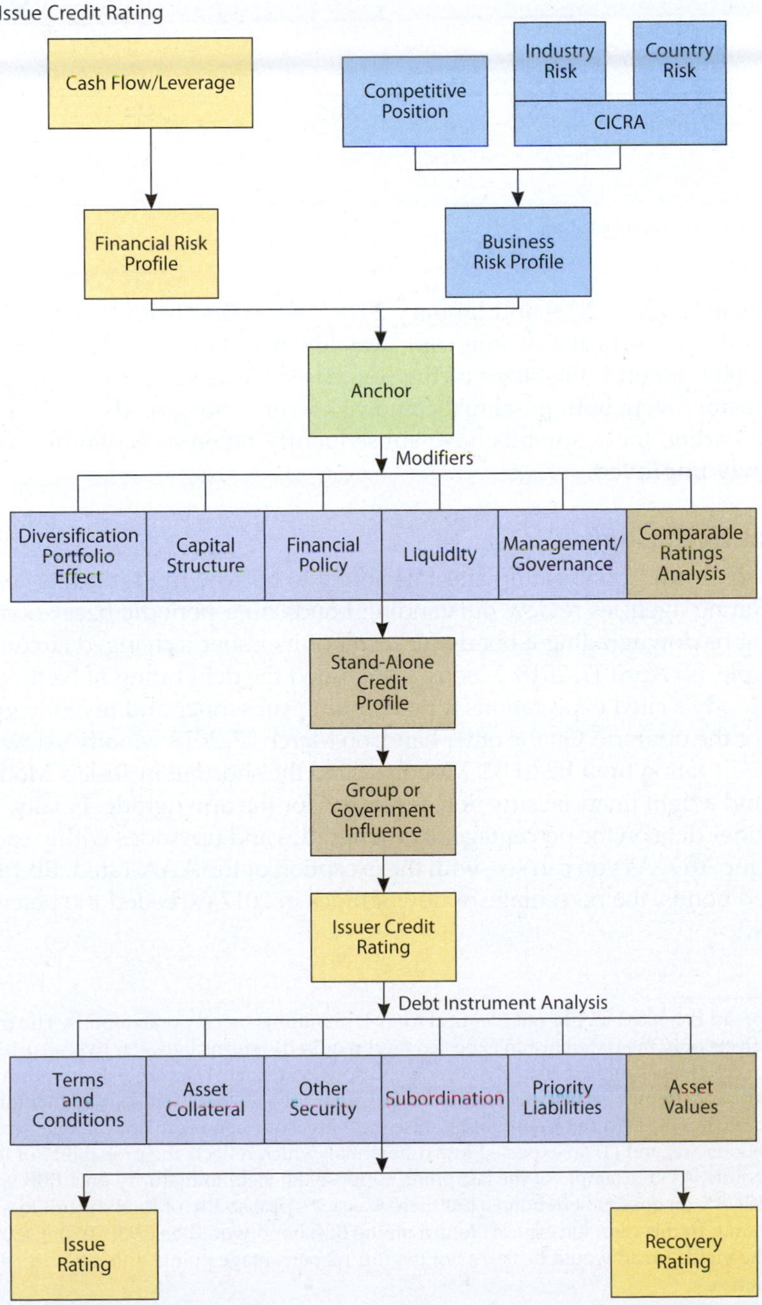

Source: "Corporate Ratings Methodology," Standard & Poor's Ratings Services (McGraw-Hill Financial), April 2014.

FIGURE 7.4 Yields on Selected Long-Term Bonds, 1994–2018

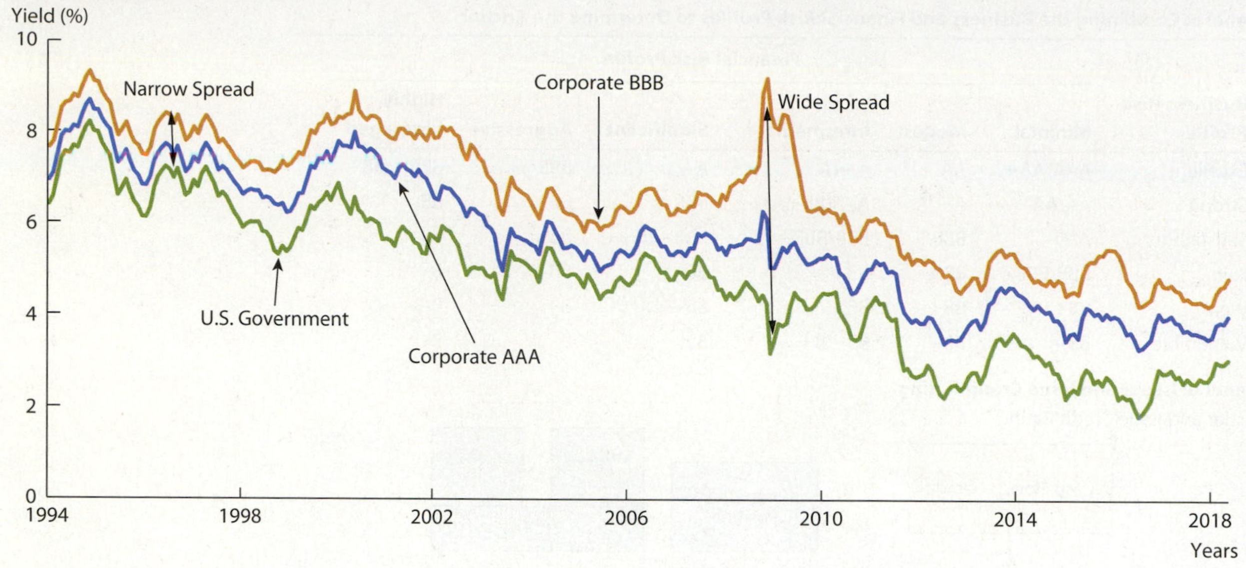

Source: FRED Economic Data, Federal Reserve Bank of St. Louis, fred.stlouisfed.org.

Treasuries in January 2009 and January 2018.[19] Note first from Figure 7.5 that the risk-free rate, or vertical axis intercept, was lower in January 2018 than it was in January 2009. Second, the slope of the line has decreased. In the crisis period of 2009, investors were both pessimistic and risk-averse, so spreads were quite high. As noted earlier, these spreads have subsequently fallen as economic conditions have slowly improved.

Changes in Ratings

Changes in a firm's bond rating affect its ability to borrow funds and its cost of that capital. Rating agencies review outstanding bonds on a periodic basis, occasionally upgrading or downgrading a bond as a result of its issuer's changed circumstances. For example, on April 11, 2018, Moody's upgraded the debt rating of Netflix from B1 to Ba3. Moody's cited expectations for continuing subscriber and revenue growth as reasons for the upgrade. On the other hand, on March 27, 2018, Moody's downgraded Tesla's credit rating from B2 to B3. Moody's cited the shortfall in Tesla's Model 3 production and a tight financial situation as reasons for the downgrade. Finally, Table 7.3 also provides data on the percentage of downgrades and upgrades within each rating category for 2017. As you can see, with the exception of the AAA-rated, BB-rated, and CCC-rated bonds, the percentage of downgrades in 2017 exceeded the percentage of upgrades.

---

[19]A yield spread is related to, but not identical to, risk premiums on corporate bonds. The true *risk premium* reflects only the difference in expected (and required) returns between two securities that results from differences in their risk. However, yield spreads reflect (1) a true risk premium; (2) a liquidity premium, which reflects the fact that U.S. Treasury bonds are more readily marketable than most corporate bonds; (3) a call premium because most Treasury bonds are not callable, whereas corporate bonds are; and (4) an expected loss differential, which reflects the probability of loss on the corporate bonds. As an example of the last point, suppose the yield to maturity on a BBB bond was 6.0% versus 4.8% on government bonds, but there was a 5% probability of total default loss on the corporate bond. In this case, the *expected* return on the BBB bond would be 0.95(6.0%) + 0.05(0%) = 5.7% and the yield spread would be 0.9%, not the full 1.2 percentage points difference in "promised" yields to maturity.

FIGURE 7.5 Relationship between Bond Ratings and Bond Yields, 2009 and 2018

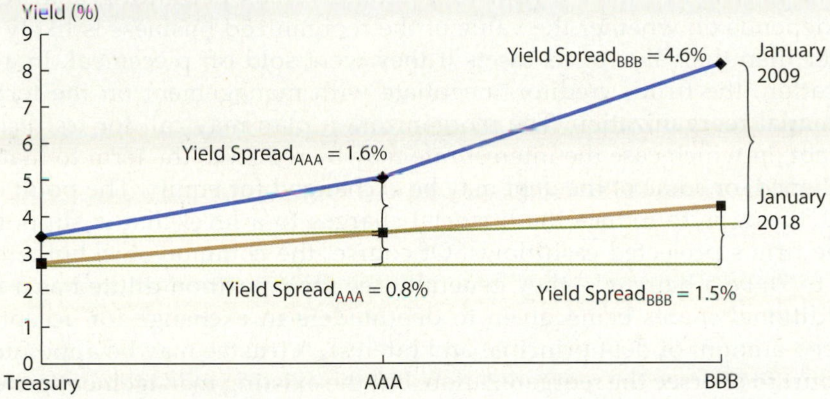

	Long-Term Government Bonds (Default-Free) (1)	AAA Corporate Bonds (2)	BBB Corporate Bonds (3)	Yield Spreads AAA (4) = (2) − (1)	Yield Spreads BBB (5) = (3) − (1)
January 2009	3.5%	5.1%	8.1%	1.6%	4.6%
January 2018	2.7	3.5	4.2	0.8	1.5

Source: FRED Economic Data, Federal Reserve Bank of St. Louis, fred.stlouisfed.org.

Over the long run, rating agencies have done a reasonably good job of measuring the average credit risk of bonds and of changing ratings whenever there is a significant change in credit quality. However, it is important to understand that ratings do not adjust immediately to changes in credit quality, and in some cases, there can be a considerable lag between a change in credit quality and a change in rating. For example, Enron's bonds still carried an investment-grade rating on a Friday in December 2001, but the company declared bankruptcy 2 days later, on Sunday. More recently, the rating agencies have come under considerable fire for significantly underestimating the risks of many of the securities that were backed by subprime mortgages. Many worry that rating agencies don't have the proper incentives to measure risk because they are paid by the issuing firms. In response to these concerns, the Dodd-Frank Act, which was enacted in 2010, directed the SEC to put in place stronger oversight of the rating agencies. The exact nature of this oversight remains a work in progress.[20]

7-8C BANKRUPTCY AND REORGANIZATION

When a business becomes *insolvent*, it doesn't have enough cash to meet its interest and principal payments. A decision must then be made whether to dissolve the firm through *liquidation* or to permit it to *reorganize* and thus

[20]For an overview of the SEC's current policy, see the SEC's website www.sec.gov/spotlight/dodd-frank.shtml. Relatedly, a *New York Times* article discusses the difficulties involved in drafting these new regulations. Refer to Gretchen Morgenson, "The Stone Unturned: Credit Ratings," *The New York Times* (www.nytimes.com), March 22, 2014.

continue to operate. These issues are addressed in Chapter 7 and Chapter 11 of the federal bankruptcy statutes, and the final decision is made by a federal bankruptcy court judge.

The decision to force a firm to liquidate versus permitting it to reorganize depends on whether the value of the reorganized business is likely to be greater than the value of its assets if they were sold off piecemeal. In a reorganization, the firm's creditors negotiate with management on the terms of a potential reorganization. The reorganization plan may call for *restructuring* the debt, in which case the interest rate may be reduced; the term to maturity, lengthened; or some of the debt may be exchanged for equity. The point of the restructuring is to reduce the financial charges to a level that is supportable by the firm's projected cash flows. Of course, the common stockholders also have to "take a haircut"—they generally see their position diluted as a result of additional shares being given to debtholders in exchange for accepting a reduced amount of debt principal and interest. A trustee may be appointed by the court to oversee the reorganization, but the existing management generally is allowed to retain control.

Liquidation occurs if the company is deemed to be worth more "dead" than "alive." If the bankruptcy court orders a liquidation, assets are auctioned off and the cash obtained is distributed as specified in Chapter 7 of the Bankruptcy Act. Web Appendix 7C provides an illustration of how a firm's assets are distributed after liquidation. For now, this is what you need to know: (1) The federal bankruptcy statutes govern reorganization and liquidation. (2) Bankruptcies occur frequently. (3) A priority of the specified claims must be followed when the assets of a liquidated firm are distributed. (4) Bondholders' treatment depends on the terms of the bond. (5) Stockholders generally receive little in reorganizations and nothing in liquidations because the assets are usually worth less than the amount of debt outstanding.

Self*Test*

Differentiate between mortgage bonds and debentures.

Name the major rating agencies, and list some factors that affect bond ratings.

Why are bond ratings important to firms and investors?

Do bond ratings adjust immediately to changes in credit quality? Explain.

Differentiate between Chapter 7 liquidations and Chapter 11 reorganizations. In general, when should each be used?

7-9 Bond Markets

Corporate bonds are traded primarily in the over-the-counter market. Most bonds are owned by and traded among large financial institutions (e.g., life insurance companies, mutual funds, hedge funds, and pension funds, all of which deal in very large blocks of securities), and it is relatively easy for over-the-counter bond dealers to arrange the transfer of large blocks of bonds among the relatively few holders of the bonds. It would be more difficult to conduct similar operations in the stock market among the literally millions of

ACCRUED INTEREST AND THE PRICING OF COUPON BONDS

In this chapter, we have demonstrated the various factors that influence bond prices. But in practice, how much you are willing to pay for a bond also depends on when the next coupon payment is due. Clearly, all else equal, you would be willing to pay more for a bond the day before a coupon is paid, than you would the day after it has been paid. So, if you purchase a bond between coupon payments, you also have to pay what is called *accrued interest*. Accrued interest represents the amount of interest that has accumulated between coupon payments, and it can be calculated as follows:

$$\text{Accrued interest} = \text{Coupon payment} \times \frac{\text{Number of days since the last coupon payment}}{\text{Number of days in the coupon period}}$$

Let's consider, for example, a corporate bond that was issued on May 31, 2018. The bond has an 8% semiannual coupon and a par value of $1,000—which means six months later, on November 30, 2018, the bond will pay its first $40 coupon, and on May 31, 2019, it will pay its second $40 coupon. If you buy the bond on August 19, 2019 (79 days since the bond's last coupon payment on May 31), you will have to pay the seller $17.56 in accrued interest:[21]

$$\text{Accrued interest} = \$40 \times (79/180) = \$17.56$$

In most cases, bonds are quoted net of accrued interest—in what is often referred to as a *clean price*. The actual invoice price you pay (often referred to as the *dirty price*) is the clean price plus accrued interest. In the case of the preceding bond, let's assume that the bond's nominal yield to maturity is the same as it was when the bond was issued (8%), which means that excluding accrued interest the bond continues to trade at par. It follows that

$$\text{Clean price (quoted price)} = \$1{,}000$$
$$\text{Accrued interest} = \$17.56$$
$$\text{Dirty price (invoice price)} = \text{Clean price} + \text{Accrued interest} = \$1{,}017.56$$

You can also use the Accrued Interest function in Excel (ACCRINT) to easily calculate a bond's accrued interest.[22] As a final point, in the examples we use in the text, when we refer to a bond's price we are referring to the bond's quoted, or clean, price. But you should keep in mind that if you buy or sell a bond, the actual price paid or received is the dirty price, which includes accrued interest.

large and small stockholders, so a higher percentage of stock trades occur on the exchanges.

A number of leading business publications and websites routinely report key developments in the Treasury, corporate, and municipal bond markets. For example, *The Wall Street Journal* provides a list of bonds whose yield spreads (relative to Treasury securities) widened and narrowed the most in the previous day. Table 7.5 reprints a portion of this data for a given day in May 2018. The table also reports the company's previous day's stock performance, which enables an investor to easily see how recent news has affected both the company's stock price and the interest rate on its debt. As part of its reported data, *The Wall Street Journal* also includes interesting data regarding a number of bond indices and a snapshot of government bond rates in different countries. Other helpful sources include the bond sections of Bloomberg.com and Finra-markets.morningstar.com.

---

[21]If you look up accrued interest in Yahoo! Finance's glossary, you will see more details regarding the payment of accrued interest. Most notably, it points out that accrued interest is calculated slightly differently for corporate and Treasury bonds:

> Interest on most bonds and fixed-income securities is paid twice a year. On corporate and municipal bonds, interest is calculated on 30-day months and a 360-day year. For government bonds, interest is calculated on actual days and a 365-day year.

[22]Refer to the Accrued Interest tab on the Chapter 7 Excel Model. In the ACCRINT Excel function for this example, we used Actual days/360 as the day count basis, which is entered as 2.

TABLE 7.5 *The Wall Street Journal* Corporate Debt Section, May 31, 2018

Corporate Debt

Investment-grade spreads that tightened the most...

Issuer	Symbol	Coupon (%)	Maturity	Spread*, in basis points: Current	Spread*, in basis points: One-day change	Last week	Stock Performance: Close ($)	Stock Performance: %chg
Intesa Sanpaolo Spa	**ISPIM**	4.375	Jan. 12, '48	**269**	–29	237	...	...
Societe Generale S.A.	**SOCGEN**	7.375	Sept. 13, '49	**316**	–26	n.a.	...	...
BNP Paribas	**BNP**	6.750	March 14, '49	**319**	–23	242	...	...
HSBC Holdings	**HSBC**	6.250	March 23, '49	**317**	–23	303	48.38	**–0.53**
Credit Agricole S.A.	**ACAFP**	7.875	Jan. 23, '49	**393**	–13	n.a.	...	...
Bank of America NA	**BAC**	6.000	Oct. 15, '36	**130**	–13	115	...	...
Wyndham Worldwide	**WYN**	3.900	March 1, '23	**244**	–12	230	108.44	**–2.15**
Australia And New Zealand Banking	**ANZ**	2.300	June 1, '21	**65**	–11	63	...	...

...And spreads that widened the most

Issuer	Symbol	Coupon (%)	Maturity	Spread*, in basis points: Current	Spread*, in basis points: One-day change	Last week	Stock Performance: Close ($)	Stock Performance: %chg
Deutsche Bank AG	**DB**	7.500	April 30, '49	**623**	54	472	11.08	**–4.24**
Bank of New York Mellon	**BK**	4.500	June 20, '49	**293**	28	249	54.75	**–1.17**
PepsiCo	**PEP**	2.000	April 15, '21	**28**	11	29	100.25	**–0.65**
American Express Credit	**AXP**	2.600	Sept. 14, '20	**64**	9	50	...	...
Northern Trust	**NTRS**	4.600	Oct. 1, '49	**202**	9	174	102.52	**–1.16**
Aviation Capital	**PACLIF**	3.875	May 1, '23	**127**	9	114	...	...
DXC Technology	**DXC**	4.750	April 15, '27	**167**	8	144	92.11	**–0.60**
Becton Dickinson And Co	**BDX**	2.894	June 6, '22	**99**	7	91	221.59	**–0.86**

High-yield issues with the biggest price increases...

Issuer	Symbol	Coupon (%)	Maturity	Bond Price as % of face value: Current	Bond Price as % of face value: One-day change	Last week	Stock Performance: Close ($)	Stock Performance: % chg
APX	**APXSEC**	7.625	Sept. 1, '23	**87.750**	4.50	85.000	...	...
Telecom Italia Capital	**TTTIM**	6.375	Nov. 15, '33	**102.000**	2.88	103.500	...	...
Intelsat Luxembourg S.A.	**INTEL**	8.125	June 1, '23	**77.063**	2.69	75.000	...	...
Videotron	**QBRCN**	5.125	April 15, '27	**99.750**	2.50	n.a.	...	...
Staples	**SPLS**	8.500	Sept. 15, '25	**93.250**	2.50	90.500	...	...
Goodyear Tire & Rubber	**GT**	4.875	March 15, '27	**94.610**	2.11	91.625	24.43	**–0.73**
Banco Bilbao Vizcaya Argentaria S.A.	**BBVASM**	6.125	Nov. 16, '49	**91.000**	1.75	93.125	...	...
MidContinent Communications Investor	**MIDCON**	6.875	Aug. 15, '23	**107.500**	1.75	105.750	...	...

...And with the biggest price decreases

Issuer	Symbol	Coupon (%)	Maturity	Bond Price as % of face value: Current	Bond Price as % of face value: One-day change	Last week	Stock Performance: Close ($)	Stock Performance: % chg
MEG Energy	**MEGCN**	7.000	March 31, '24	**90.500**	–1.63	93.875	...	...
Halcon Resources	**HKUS**	6.750	Feb. 15, '25	**94.000**	–1.50	97.000	...	...
AECOM*	**ACM**	5.125	March 15, '27	**91.830**	–1.30	93.875	33.00	**–1.35**
Cincinnati Bell	**CBB**	7.000	July 15, '24	**90.000**	–1.02	92.625	12.30	**–2.77**
EP Energy	**EPENEG**	8.000	Feb. 15, '25	**72.500**	–1.00	75.000	...	...
Radiate Holdco	**RADIAT**	6.875	Feb. 15, '23	**95.000**	–1.00	96.998	...	...
SM Energy	**SM**	5.000	Jan. 15, '24	**93.750**	–0.88	95.480	26.20	**–1.50**
Ensco	**ESV**	7.750	Feb. 1, '26	**95.250**	–0.81	97.000	6.50	**–0.46**

*Estimated spread over 2-year, 3-year, 5-year, 10-year or 30-year hot-run Treasury; 100 basis points = one percentage pt; change in spread shown is for Z-spread.
Note: Data are for the most active issue of bonds with maturities of two years or more.

Sources: MarketAxess Corporate Bond Ticker; WSJ Market Data Group; Corporate Debt Section, *The Wall Street Journal* (www.wsj.com), June 1, 2018, p. B6.

Self*Test*

Why do most bond trades occur in the over-the-counter market?

How is accrued interest calculated?

What is meant by the terms *clean price* and *dirty price*?

TYING IT ALL TOGETHER

This chapter described the different types of bonds governments and corporations issue, explained how bond prices are established, and discussed how investors estimate rates of return on bonds. It also discussed various types of risks that investors face when they purchase bonds.

When an investor purchases a company's bonds, the investor is providing the company with capital. Moreover, when a firm issues bonds, *the return that investors require on the bonds represents the cost of debt capital to the firm*. This point is extended in Chapter 10, where the ideas developed in this chapter are used to help determine a company's overall cost of capital, which is a basic component of the capital budgeting process.

In recent years, many companies have used zero coupon bonds to raise billions of dollars, and bankruptcy is an important consideration for companies that issue debt and for investors. These two related issues are discussed in detail in Web Appendixes 7A and 7C. Duration, a measurement involving a weighted average of the bond's cash flows, is discussed in Web Appendix 7B. These appendixes can be accessed through the textbook's website on cengage.com.

Self-Test Questions and Problems

(Solutions Appear in Appendix A)

ST-1 **KEY TERMS** Define each of the following terms:

a. Bond; treasury bond; corporate bond; municipal bond; foreign bond
b. Par value; maturity date; original maturity
c. Coupon payment; coupon interest rate
d. Fixed-rate bond; floating-rate bond; zero coupon bond; original issue discount (OID) bond
e. Call provision; sinking fund provision
f. Convertible bond; warrant; putable bond; income bond; indexed, or purchasing power, bond
g. Discount bond; premium bond
h. Yield to maturity (YTM); yield to call (YTC)
i. Current yield; capital gains yield; total return
j. Price risk; reinvestment risk; investment horizon; default risk; duration
k. Mortgage bond; indenture; debenture; subordinated debenture
l. Investment-grade bond; junk bond

ST-2 **BOND VALUATION** The Pennington Corporation issued a new series of bonds on January 1, 1995. The bonds were sold at par ($1,000), had a 12% coupon, and mature in 30 years, on December 31, 2024. Coupon payments are made semiannually (on June 30 and December 31).

a. What was the YTM on January 1, 1995?

b. What was the price of the bonds on January 1, 2000, 5 years later, assuming that interest rates had fallen to 10%?

c. Find the current yield, capital gains yield, and total return on January 1, 2000, given the price as determined in part b.

d. On July 1, 2018, 6½ years before maturity, Pennington's bonds sold for $916.42. What were the YTM, the current yield, the capital gains yield, and the total return at that time?

e. Now assume that you plan to purchase an outstanding Pennington bond on March 1, 2018, when the going rate of interest given its risk was 15.5%. How large a check must you write to complete the transaction? (This is a difficult question.)

ST-2 **SINKING FUND** The Vancouver Development Company (VDC) is planning to sell a $100 million, 10-year, 12%, semiannual payment bond issue. Provisions for a sinking fund to retire the issue over its life will be included in the indenture. Sinking fund payments will be made at the end of each year, and each payment must be sufficient to retire 10% of the original amount of the issue. The last sinking fund payment will retire the last of the bonds. The bonds to be retired each period can be purchased on the open market or obtained by calling up to 5% of the original issue at par, at VDC's option.

a. How large must each sinking fund payment be if the company (1) uses the option to call bonds at par or (2) decides to buy bonds on the open market? For part (2), you can only answer in words.

b. What will happen to debt service requirements per year associated with this issue over its 10-year life?

c. Now consider an alternative plan where VDC sets up its sinking fund so that *equal annual amounts* are paid into a sinking fund trust held by a bank, with the proceeds being used to buy government bonds that are expected to pay 7% annual interest. The payments, plus accumulated interest, must total $100 million at the end of 10 years, when the proceeds will be used to retire the issue. How large must the annual sinking fund payments be? Is this amount known with certainty, or might it be higher or lower?

d. What are the annual cash requirements for covering bond service costs under the trusteeship arrangement described in part c? (*Note:* Interest must be paid on Vancouver's outstanding bonds but not on bonds that have been retired.) Assume level interest rates for purposes of answering this question.

e. What would have to happen to interest rates to cause the company to buy bonds on the open market rather than call them under the plan where some bonds are retired each year?

Questions

7-1 A sinking fund can be set up in one of two ways:

- The corporation makes annual payments to the trustee, who invests the proceeds in securities (frequently government bonds) and uses the accumulated total to retire the bond issue at maturity.
- The trustee uses the annual payments to retire a portion of the issue each year, calling a given percentage of the issue by a lottery and paying a specified price per bond or buying bonds on the open market, whichever is cheaper.

What are the advantages and disadvantages of each procedure from the viewpoint of the firm and the bondholders?

7-2 Can the following equation be used to find the value of a bond with N years to maturity that pays interest once a year? Assume that the bond was issued several years ago.

$$V_B = \sum_{t=1}^{N} \frac{\text{Annual interest}}{(1 + r_d)^t} + \frac{\text{Par value}}{(1 + r_d)^N}$$

7-3 The values of outstanding bonds change whenever the going rate of interest changes. In general, short-term interest rates are more volatile than long-term interest rates. Therefore, short-term bond prices are more sensitive to interest rate changes than are long-term bond prices. Is that statement true or false? Explain. (*Hint:* Make up a "reasonable" example based on a 1-year and a 20-year bond to help answer the question.)

7-4 If interest rates rise after a bond issue, what will happen to the bond's price and YTM? Does the time to maturity affect the extent to which interest rate changes affect the bond's price? (Again, an example might help you answer this question.)

7-5 Discuss the following statement: A bond's yield to maturity is the bond's promised rate of return, which equals its expected rate of return.

7-6 If you buy a *callable* bond and interest rates decline, will the value of your bond rise by as much as it would have risen if the bond had not been callable? Explain.

7-7 Assume that you have a short investment horizon (less than 1 year). You are considering two investments: a 1-year Treasury security and a 20-year Treasury security. Which of the two investments would you view as being riskier? Explain.

7-8 Indicate whether each of the following actions will increase or decrease a bond's yield to maturity:

a. The bond's price increases.
b. The bond is downgraded by the rating agencies.
c. A change in the bankruptcy code makes it more difficult for bondholders to receive payments in the event the firm declares bankruptcy.
d. The economy seems to be shifting from a boom to a recession. Discuss the effects of the firm's credit strength in your answer.
e. Investors learn that the bonds are subordinated to another debt issue.

7-9 Why is a call provision advantageous to a bond issuer? When would the issuer be likely to initiate a refunding call?

7-10 Are securities that provide for a sinking fund more or less risky from the bondholder's perspective than those without this type of provision? Explain.

7-11 What's the difference between a call for sinking fund purposes and a refunding call?

7-12 Why are convertibles and bonds with warrants typically offered with lower coupons than similarly rated straight bonds?

7-13 Explain whether the following statement is true or false: Only weak companies issue debentures.

7-14 Would the yield spread on a corporate bond over a Treasury bond with the same maturity tend to become wider or narrower if the economy appeared to be heading toward a recession? Would the change in the spread for a given company be affected by the firm's credit strength? Explain.

7-15 A bond's expected return is sometimes estimated by its YTM and sometimes by its YTC. Under what conditions would the YTM provide a better estimate, and when would the YTC be better?

7-16 Which of the following bonds has the most price risk? Explain your answer. (*Hint:* Refer to Table 7.2.)

a. 7-year bonds with a 5% coupon
b. 1-year bonds with a 12% coupon
c. 3-year bonds with a 5% coupon
d. 15-year zero coupon bonds
e. 15-year bonds with a 10% coupon

7-17 Which of the bonds has the most reinvestment risk? Explain your answer. (*Hint:* Refer to Table 7.2.)

a. 7-year bonds with a 5% coupon
b. 1-year bonds with a 12% coupon
c. 3-year bonds with a 5% coupon
d. 15-year zero coupon bonds
e. 15-year bonds with a 10% coupon

Problems

Easy Problems 1–4

7-1 **BOND VALUATION** Madsen Motors's bonds have 23 years remaining to maturity. Interest is paid annually, they have a $1,000 par value, the coupon interest rate is 9%, and the yield to maturity is 11%. What is the bond's current market price?

7-2 **YIELD TO MATURITY AND FUTURE PRICE** A bond has a $1,000 par value, 12 years to maturity, and an 8% annual coupon and sells for $980.

a. What is its yield to maturity (YTM)?

b. Assume that the yield to maturity remains constant for the next three years. What will the price be 3 years from today?

7-3 **BOND VALUATION** Nesmith Corporation's outstanding bonds have a $1,000 par value, an 8% semiannual coupon, 14 years to maturity, and an 11% YTM. What is the bond's price?

7-4 **YIELD TO MATURITY** A firm's bonds have a maturity of 8 years with a $1,000 face value, have an 11% semiannual coupon, are callable in 4 years at $1,154, and currently sell at a price of $1,283.09. What are their nominal yield to maturity and their nominal yield to call? What return should investors expect to earn on these bonds?

Intermediate Problems 5–14

7-5 **BOND VALUATION** An investor has two bonds in his portfolio that have a face value of $1,000 and pay an 11% annual coupon. Bond L matures in 12 years, while Bond S matures in 1 year.

a. What will the value of each bond be if the going interest rate is 6%, 8%, and 12%? Assume that only one more interest payment is to be made on Bond S at its maturity and that 12 more payments are to be made on Bond L.

b. Why does the longer-term bond's price vary more than the price of the shorter-term bond when interest rates change?

7-6 **BOND VALUATION** An investor has two bonds in her portfolio, Bond C and Bond Z. Each bond matures in 4 years, has a face value of $1,000, and has a yield to maturity of 8.2%. Bond C pays an 11.5% annual coupon, while Bond Z is a zero coupon bond.

a. Assuming that the yield to maturity of each bond remains at 8.2% over the next 4 years, calculate the price of the bonds at each of the following years to maturity:

Years to Maturity	Price of Bond C	Price of Bond Z
4	______	______
3	______	______
2	______	______
1	______	______
0	______	______

b. Plot the time path of prices for each bond.

7-7 **INTEREST RATE SENSITIVITY** An investor purchased the following five bonds. Each bond had a par value of $1,000 and an 8% yield to maturity on the purchase day. Immediately after the investor purchased them, interest rates fell, and each then had a new YTM of 7%. What is the percentage change in price for each bond after the decline in interest rates? Fill in the following table:

Bond	Price @8%	Price @7%	Percentage Change
10-year, 10% annual coupon	______	______	______
10-year zero	______	______	______
5-year zero	______	______	______
30-year zero	______	______	______
$100 perpetuity	______	______	______

7-8 **YIELD TO CALL** Seven years ago the Templeton Company issued 20-year bonds with an 11% annual coupon rate at their $1,000 par value. The bonds had a 7.5% call premium, with 5 years of call protection. Today Templeton called the bonds. Compute the realized rate of return for an investor who purchased the bonds when they were issued and held them until they were called. Explain why the investor should or should not be happy that Templeton called them.

7-9 **YIELD TO MATURITY** Harrimon Industries bonds have 6 years left to maturity. Interest is paid annually, and the bonds have a $1,000 par value and a coupon rate of 10%.

a. What is the yield to maturity at a current market price of (1) $865 and (2) $1,166?

b. Would you pay $865 for each bond if you thought that a "fair" market interest rate for such bonds was 12%—that is, if r_d = 12%? Explain your answer.

7-10 **CURRENT YIELD, CAPITAL GAINS YIELD, AND YIELD TO MATURITY** Pelzer Printing Inc. has bonds outstanding with 9 years left to maturity. The bonds have a 9% annual coupon rate and were issued 1 year ago at their par value of $1,000. However, due to changes in interest rates, the bond's market price has fallen to $910.30. The capital gains yield last year was –8.97%.

a. What is the yield to maturity?

b. For the coming year, what are the expected current and capital gains yields? (*Hint:* Refer to footnote 6 for the definition of the current yield and to Table 7.1.)

c. Will the actual realized yields be equal to the expected yields if interest rates change? If not, how will they differ?

7-11 **BOND YIELDS** Last year Carson Industries issued a 10-year, 13% semiannual coupon bond at its par value of $1,000. Currently, the bond can be called in 6 years at a price of $1,065 and it sells for $1,200.

a. What are the bond's nominal yield to maturity and its nominal yield to call? Would an investor be more likely to earn the YTM or the YTC?

b. What is the current yield? Is this yield affected by whether the bond is likely to be called? (*Hint:* Refer to footnote 6 for the definition of the current yield and to Table 7.1.)

c. What is the expected capital gains (or loss) yield for the coming year? Is this yield dependent on whether the bond is expected to be called? Explain your answer.

7-12 **YIELD TO CALL** It is now January 1, 2019, and you are considering the purchase of an outstanding bond that was issued on January 1, 2017. It has an 8% annual coupon and had a 30-year original maturity. (It matures on December 31, 2046.) There is 5 years of call protection (until December 31, 2021), after which time it can be called at 108—that is, at 108% of par, or $1,080. Interest rates have declined since it was issued, and it is now selling at 119.12% of par, or $1,191.20.

a. What is the yield to maturity? What is the yield to call?

b. If you bought this bond, which return would you actually earn? Explain your reasoning.

c. Suppose the bond had been selling at a discount rather than a premium. Would the yield to maturity have been the most likely return, or would the yield to call have been most likely?

7-13 **PRICE AND YIELD** A 7% semiannual coupon bond matures in 4 years. The bond has a face value of $1,000 and a current yield of 7.5401%. What are the bond's price and YTM? (*Hint:* Refer to footnote 6 for the definition of the current yield and to Table 7.1.)

7-14 **EXPECTED INTEREST RATE** Lourdes Corporation's 12% coupon rate, semiannual payment, $1,000 par value bonds, which mature in 25 years, are callable 6 years from today at $1,025. They sell at a price of $1,278.56, and the yield curve is flat. Assume that interest rates are expected to remain at their current level.

a. What is the best estimate of these bonds' remaining life?

b. If Lourdes plans to raise additional capital and wants to use debt financing, what coupon rate would it have to set in order to issue new bonds at par?

Challenging Problems 15–18

7-15 **BOND VALUATION** Bond X is noncallable and has 20 years to maturity, an 8% annual coupon, and a $1,000 par value. Your required return on Bond X is 9%; if you buy it, you plan to hold it for 5 years. You (and the market) have expectations that in 5 years, the yield to maturity on a 15-year bond with similar risk will be 7.5%. How much should you be willing to pay for Bond X today? (*Hint:* You will need to know how much the bond will be worth at the end of 5 years.)

7-16 **BOND VALUATION** You are considering a 10-year, $1,000 par value bond. Its coupon rate is 8%, and interest is paid semiannually. If you require an "effective" annual interest rate (not a nominal rate) of 7.1225%, how much should you be willing to pay for the bond?

7-17 **BOND RETURNS** Last year Janet purchased a $1,000 face value corporate bond with an 8% annual coupon rate and a 15-year maturity. At the time of the purchase, it had an expected yield to maturity of 10.45%. If Janet sold the bond today for $820.17, what rate of return would she have earned for the past year?

7-18 **YIELD TO MATURITY AND YIELD TO CALL** Kempton Enterprises has bonds outstanding with a $1,000 face value and 10 years left until maturity. They have an 11% annual coupon payment, and their current price is $1,185. The bonds may be called in 5 years at 109% of face value (Call price = $1,090).

a. What is the yield to maturity?
b. What is the yield to call if they are called in 5 years?
c. Which yield might investors expect to earn on these bonds? Why?
d. The bond's indenture indicates that the call provision gives the firm the right to call the bonds at the end of each year beginning in Year 5. In Year 5, the bonds may be called at 109% of face value, but in each of the next 4 years, the call percentage will decline by 1%. Thus, in Year 6, they may be called at 108% of face value; in Year 7, they may be called at 107% of face value; and so forth. If the yield curve is horizontal and interest rates remain at their current level, when is the latest that investors might expect the firm to call the bonds?

Comprehensive/Spreadsheet Problem

7-19 **BOND VALUATION** Clifford Clark is a recent retiree who is interested in investing some of his savings in corporate bonds. His financial planner has suggested the following bonds:

- Bond A has a 7% annual coupon, matures in 12 years, and has a $1,000 face value.
- Bond B has a 9% annual coupon, matures in 12 years, and has a $1,000 face value.
- Bond C has an 11% annual coupon, matures in 12 years, and has a $1,000 face value.

Each bond has a yield to maturity of 9%.

a. Before calculating the prices of the bonds, indicate whether each bond is trading at a premium, at a discount, or at par.
b. Calculate the price of each of the three bonds.
c. Calculate the current yield for each of the three bonds. (*Hint:* Refer to footnote 6 for the definition of the current yield and to Table 7.1.)
d. If the yield to maturity for each bond remains at 9%, what will be the price of each bond 1 year from now? What is the expected capital gains yield for each bond? What is the expected total return for each bond?
e. Mr. Clark is considering another bond, Bond D. It has an 8% semiannual coupon and a $1,000 face value (i.e., it pays a $40 coupon every 6 months). Bond D is scheduled to mature in 9 years and has a price of $1,150. It is also callable in 5 years at a call price of $1,040.
    1. What is the bond's nominal yield to maturity?
    2. What is the bond's nominal yield to call?
    3. If Mr. Clark were to purchase this bond, would he be more likely to receive the yield to maturity or yield to call? Explain your answer.
f. Explain briefly the difference between price risk and reinvestment risk. Which of the following bonds has the most price risk? Which has the most reinvestment risk?
    - A 1-year bond with a 9% annual coupon
    - A 5-year bond with a 9% annual coupon
    - A 5-year bond with a zero coupon
    - A 10-year bond with a 9% annual coupon
    - A 10-year bond with a zero coupon

g. Only do this part if you are using a spreadsheet. Calculate the price of each bond (A, B, and C) at the end of each year until maturity, assuming interest rates remain constant. Create a graph showing the time path of each bond's value, similar to that shown in Figure 7.2.
   1. What is the expected interest yield for each bond in each year?
   2. What is the expected capital gains yield for each bond in each year?
   3. What is the total return for each bond in each year?

INTEGRATED CASE

WESTERN MONEY MANAGEMENT INC.

7-20 BOND VALUATION Robert Black and Carol Alvarez are vice presidents of Western Money Management and codirectors of the company's pension fund management division. A major new client, the California League of Cities, has requested that Western present an investment seminar to the mayors of the represented cities. Black and Alvarez, who will make the presentation, have asked you to help them by answering the following questions:

a. What are a bond's key features?

b. What are call provisions and sinking fund provisions? Do these provisions make bonds more or less risky?

c. How is the value of any asset whose value is based on expected future cash flows determined?

d. How is a bond's value determined? What is the value of a 10-year, $1,000 par value bond with a 10% annual coupon if its required return is 10%?

e. 1. What is the value of a 13% coupon bond that is otherwise identical to the bond described in part d? Would we now have a discount or a premium bond?
   2. What is the value of a 7% coupon bond with these characteristics? Would we now have a discount or premium bond?
   3. What would happen to the values of the 7%, 10%, and 13% coupon bonds over time if the required return remained at 10%? (*Hint:* With a financial calculator, enter PMT, I/YR, FV, and N; then change (override) N to see what happens to the PV as it approaches maturity.)

f. 1. What is the yield to maturity on a 10-year, 9% annual coupon, $1,000 par value bond that sells for $887.00? That sells for $1,134.20? What does the fact that it sells at a discount or at a premium tell you about the relationship between r_d and the coupon rate?
   2. What are the total return, the current yield, and the capital gains yield for the discount bond? Assume that it is held to maturity, and the company does not default on it. (*Hint:* Refer to footnote 6 for the definition of the current yield and to Table 7.1.)

g. What is *price risk?* Which has more price risk, an annual payment 1-year bond or a 10-year bond? Why?

h. What is *reinvestment risk?* Which has more reinvestment risk, a 1-year bond or a 10-year bond?

i. How does the equation for valuing a bond change if semiannual payments are made? Find the value of a 10-year, semiannual payment, 10% coupon bond if nominal r_d = 13%.

j. Suppose for $1,000 you could buy a 10%, 10-year, annual payment bond or a 10%, 10-year, semiannual payment bond. They are equally risky. Which would you prefer? If $1,000 is the proper price for the semiannual bond, what is the equilibrium price for the annual payment bond?

k. Suppose a 10-year, 10% semiannual coupon bond with a par value of $1,000 is currently selling for $1,135.90, producing a nominal yield to maturity of 8%. However, it can be called after 4 years for $1,050.
   1. What is the bond's *nominal yield to call (YTC)*?
   2. If you bought this bond, would you be more likely to earn the YTM or the YTC? Why?

l. Does the yield to maturity represent the promised or expected return on the bond? Explain.
m. These bonds were rated AA− by S&P. Would you consider them investment-grade or junk bonds?
n. What factors determine a company's bond rating?
o. If this firm were to default on the bonds, would the company be immediately liquidated? Would the bondholders be assured of receiving all of their promised payments? Explain.

TAKING A CLOSER LOOK

Using Online Resources to Understand the Impact of Interest Rates on Bond Valuation

Use online resources to work on this chapter's questions. Please note that website information changes over time, and these changes may limit your ability to answer some of these questions.

In Chapter 7, we looked at how interest rates impact bond valuation. The following questions are designed to help you understand how bond values are affected by different interest rate levels. Here, we will access the website finra-markets.morningstar.com/BondCenter to answer these questions:

1. Once you've accessed the Bond Center screen, click on the search tab in the middle of your screen. Do a quick search for Alphabet bonds. Remember that Alphabet is the parent company of Google. What are the bonds rated by S&P? By Moody's? What is the longest maturity of an issue displaying on the screen? What is this issue's price and yield? Is this issue selling at par, discount, or premium? What have interest rates done since the bond was issued? (*Hint:* Look at the bond's coupon rate relative to its yield to maturity.)
2. Now, run an advanced search by going back to the main Bond Center screen. Click on the search tab in the middle of your screen, and click on "Show" (next to "Advanced Search"). Search for an Industrial, Senior, Nonconvertible, Corporate Bond. Select all debt instrument types. The bond should have fixed, semiannual coupons—but don't specify the coupon rate. Be sure to exclude perpetual, callable, and putable bonds. Finally, don't specify a bond rating. Now, select "Show Results". Briefly explain how the yields to maturity of the bonds vary according to bond rating.
3. Identify the lowest-rated bond shown in your search. What is its bond rating? What are its current price and yield to maturity? When does it mature?
4. Now, select a different bond from your search. What is the bond rating by Moody's? By S&P? Is the bond an investment-grade bond? Explain.
5. Using the same bond selected for question 4, note the bond's coupon rate, maturity, current price, and yield to maturity. Based on this information, has the bond's yield to maturity increased, decreased, or stayed the same since it was issued? Is the bond currently selling at par, discount, or premium?

Risk and Rates of Return

CHAPTER

8

Blend Images/Alamy Stock Photo

Managing Risk in Difficult Times

Over the past few decades, the U.S. stock market has seen more than its share of ups and downs. To give you a quick sense of the market's recent performance, consider that in April 1993, the S&P 500 index had a value around 440. In the following 7 years, the market roared to a high of 1,516. Slightly more than 2 years later—following the 2001 terrorist attacks and the resulting recession—the index had lost nearly half of its value. Five bumpy years later, in September 2007, the market finally recovered back to where it was trading near its old highs above 1,500. But then the housing market collapsed and the financial crisis began, and by March 2009, the S&P 500 plunged to a level below 700. A little less than 9 years later, in January 2018, the market stood at a new record just below 2,900, before retreating to 2,700 four months later.

In many cases, the returns on individual stocks have been even more volatile than the S&P 500 index. For example, over a 2-year period, Netflix Inc.'s stock rose more than 500%—from a price just below $6 per share in July 2009 to more than $38 per share in July 2011. But following this incredible run-up, the stock's price subsequently plummeted to $8 per share just a little over a year later in August 2012. Afterwards, the stock took off once again, and by May 2017, Netflix's stock was trading above $156 per share.[1] Even more incredibly, the stock more than doubled in the following year and was sitting at right above $330 a share in May 2018.

As we see in this chapter, one way to reduce the risk of investing is to hold a diversified portfolio of stocks. One approach is to invest in mutual funds or exchange traded funds (ETFs) that track the overall market. An even broader

[1]Note that these prices have been adjusted to reflect a 7-to-1 stock split in July 2015.

diversification strategy is to invest in a wide range of global assets including stocks, bonds, commodities, and real estate. Although many U.S. investors are reluctant to invest in foreign stocks and bonds, many foreign markets have performed well, and their performance has not been perfectly correlated with U.S. markets. Therefore, global diversification offers U.S. investors an opportunity to increase returns and at the same time reduce risk. To be sure, however, these other investments can also be quite risky at times.

Although diversification is important, the events of the past decade show all too well that even fully diversified investors can suffer large losses in short periods of time. As a result, many have become more conservative with their money and are holding larger amounts of cash and other safe assets in their portfolios. Many are convinced that these investors won't return to the market unless they are reasonably assured that the expected returns are enough to justify the risks of stocks and other more speculative investments.

In this chapter, we explore these ideas in more detail, and specifically consider the different types of risk that investors face, the benefits of diversification, and the fundamental trade-off between risk and return. After studying the concepts in this chapter, you should be able to avoid some of the investing pitfalls that a number of investors have faced recently in their quest for wealth.

PUTTING THINGS IN PERSPECTIVE

We start this chapter from the basic premise that investors like returns and dislike risk; hence, they will invest in risky assets only if those assets offer higher expected returns. We define what risk means as it relates to investments, examine procedures that are used to measure risk, and discuss the relationship between risk and return. Investors should understand these concepts, as should corporate managers as they develop the plans that will shape their firms' futures.

Risk can be measured in different ways, and different conclusions about an asset's riskiness can be reached depending on the measure used. Risk analysis can be confusing, but it will help if you keep the following points in mind:

1. **All business assets are expected to produce *cash flows*, and the riskiness of an asset is based on the riskiness of its cash flows. The riskier the cash flows, the riskier the asset.**
2. **Assets can be categorized as *financial assets*, especially stocks and bonds, and as *real assets*, such as trucks, machines, and whole businesses. In theory, risk analysis for all types of assets is similar, and the same fundamental concepts apply to all assets. However, in practice, differences in the types of available data lead to different procedures for stocks, bonds, and real assets. Our focus in this chapter is on financial assets, especially stocks. We considered bonds in Chapter 7, and we take up real assets in the capital budgeting chapters, especially Chapter 12.**
3. **A stock's risk can be considered in two ways: (a) on a *stand-alone, or single-stock, basis*, or (b) in a *portfolio context*, where a number of stocks are combined and their consolidated cash flows are analyzed.[2] There is an important difference between stand-alone and portfolio risk, and a stock that has a great deal of risk held by itself may be much less risky when held as part of a larger portfolio.**

[2]A *portfolio* is a collection of investment securities. If you owned stock in General Motors, Exxon Mobil, and IBM, you would be holding a three-stock portfolio. Because diversification lowers risk without sacrificing much, if any, expected return, most stocks are held in portfolios.

4. **In a portfolio context, a stock's risk can be divided into two components: (a) *diversifiable risk*, which can be diversified away and is thus of little concern to diversified investors, and (b) *market risk*, which reflects the risk of a general stock market decline and cannot be eliminated by diversification (hence, does concern investors). Only market risk is *relevant* to rational investors because diversifiable risk can and will be eliminated.**
5. **A stock with high market risk must offer a relatively high expected rate of return to attract investors. Investors in general are *averse to risk*, so they will not buy risky assets unless they are compensated with high expected returns.**
6. **If investors, on average, think a stock's expected return is too low to compensate for its risk, they will start selling it, driving down its price and boosting its expected return. Conversely, if the expected return on a stock is more than enough to compensate for the risk, people will start buying it, raising its price and thus lowering its expected return. The stock will be in equilibrium, with neither buying nor selling pressure, when its expected return is exactly sufficient to compensate for its risk.**
7. **Stand-alone risk, the topic of Section 8-2, is important in stock analysis primarily as a lead-in to portfolio risk analysis. However, stand-alone risk is extremely important when analyzing real assets such as capital budgeting projects.**

When you finish this chapter, you should be able to do the following:

- **Explain the difference between stand-alone risk and risk in a portfolio context.**
- **Describe how risk aversion affects a stock's required rate of return.**
- **Discuss the difference between diversifiable risk and market risk, and explain how each type of risk affects well-diversified investors.**
- **Describe what the CAPM is, and illustrate how it can be used to estimate a stock's required rate of return.**
- **Discuss how changes in the general stock and bond markets could lead to changes in the required rate of return on a firm's stock.**
- **Discuss how changes in a firm's operations might lead to changes in the required rate of return on the firm's stock.**

8-1 The Risk-Return Trade-Off

As previously mentioned, we start from a very simple premise that investors like returns and they dislike risk. This premise suggests that there is a fundamental trade-off between risk and return: to entice investors to take on more risk, you have to provide them with higher expected returns. This trade-off is illustrated in Figure 8.1.

The slope of the risk-return line in panel a of Figure 8.1 indicates how much additional return an individual investor requires in order to take on a higher level of risk. A steeper line suggests that an investor is very averse to taking on risk, whereas a flatter line would suggest that the investor is more comfortable bearing risk. Not surprisingly, investors who are less comfortable bearing risk tend to gravitate toward lower-risk investments, while investors with a greater-risk appetite tend to put more of their money into higher-risk, higher-return investments. The average investor's willingness to take on risk also varies over time. For example, prior to the recent financial crisis, an increasing number of investors were putting their money into riskier

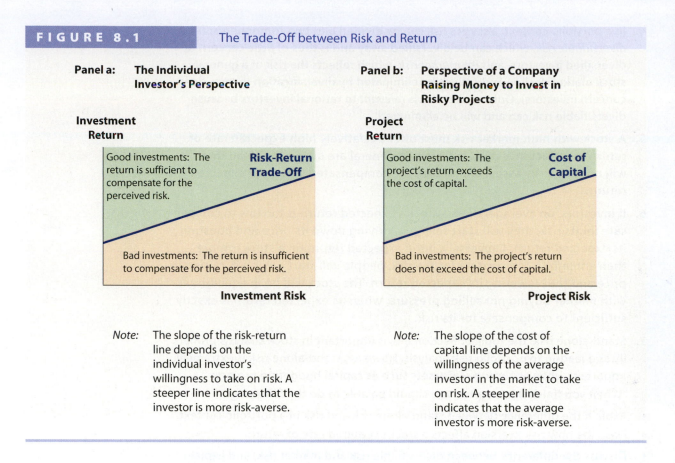

FIGURE 8.1 The Trade-Off between Risk and Return

Panel a: The Individual Investor's Perspective

Panel b: Perspective of a Company Raising Money to Invest in Risky Projects

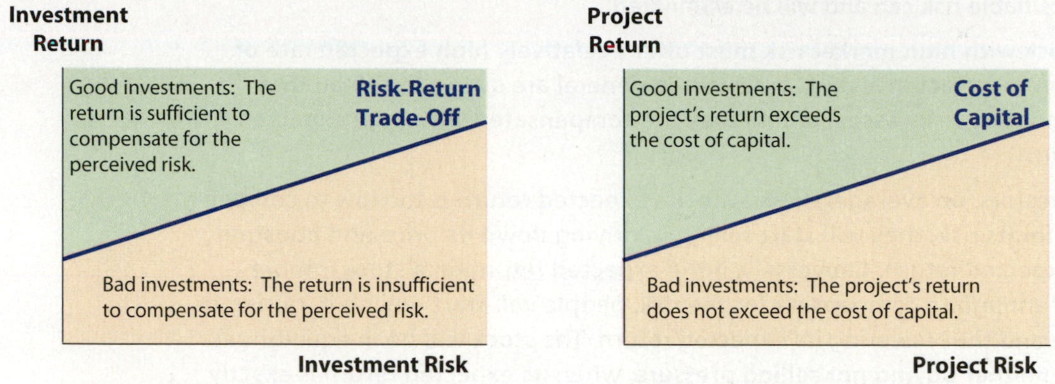
Investment Return
Good investments: The return is sufficient to compensate for the perceived risk.
Risk-Return Trade-Off
Bad investments: The return is insufficient to compensate for the perceived risk.
Investment Risk
Project Return
Good investments: The project's return exceeds the cost of capital.
Cost of Capital
Bad investments: The project's return does not exceed the cost of capital.
Project Risk

Note: The slope of the risk-return line depends on the individual investor's willingness to take on risk. A steeper line indicates that the investor is more risk-averse.

Note: The slope of the cost of capital line depends on the willingness of the average investor in the market to take on risk. A steeper line indicates that the average investor is more risk-averse.

investments that included high-growth stocks, junk bonds, and emerging market funds. In the aftermath of the crisis, there was a tremendous "flight to quality" where investors rapidly moved away from riskier investments and instead flocked toward safer investments such as Treasury securities and money market funds. At any point in time, an investor's goal should be to earn returns that are more than sufficient to compensate for the perceived risk of the investment—in other words, getting above the risk-return trade-off line illustrated in panel a of Figure 8.1.

The trade-off between risk and return is also an important concept for companies trying to create value for their shareholders. Panel b of Figure 8.1 suggests that if a company is investing in riskier projects, it must offer its investors (both bondholders and stockholders) higher expected returns. As we showed in Chapter 7, higher-risk companies must pay higher yields on their bonds to compensate bondholders for the additional default risk. Likewise, as we will see in this chapter, riskier companies trying to increase their stock price must generate higher returns to compensate their stockholders for the additional risk. It is important to understand that the returns that companies have to pay their investors represent the companies' costs of obtaining capital. Thus from a company's perspective, the risk-return line in panel b of Figure 8.1 represents its cost of obtaining capital, and the slope of the risk-return line reflects the average investor's current willingness to take on risk. As we will see in Chapters 10 through 12, companies create value by investing in projects where the returns on the investments exceed their costs of capital. Once again, this translates into operating above the risk-return trade-off line.

Throughout the rest of this chapter, we discuss these simple ideas in greater detail. We begin by discussing the concept of risk. Later we discuss returns, and we provide a model for estimating the trade-off between risk and return.

Self*Test*

Briefly explain the fundamental trade-off between risk and return.

What do the slopes of the risk-return lines illustrated in Figure 8.1 indicate?

Does the average investor's willingness to take on risk vary over time? Explain.

What do you think the average investor's risk perception is now? In what types of investments do you think the average investor is investing currently?

Should companies completely avoid high-risk projects? Explain.

8-2 Stand-Alone Risk

Risk is defined by *Webster's Dictionary* as "a hazard; a peril; exposure to loss or injury." Thus, risk refers to the chance that some unfavorable event will occur. If you engage in skydiving, you are taking a chance with your life—skydiving is risky. If you bet on the horses, you are risking your money.

Risk
The chance that some unfavorable event will occur.

As we saw in previous chapters, individuals and firms invest funds today with the expectation of receiving additional funds in the future. Bonds offer relatively low returns, but with relatively little risk—at least if you stick to Treasury and high-grade corporate bonds. Stocks offer the chance of higher returns, but stocks are generally riskier than bonds. If you invest in speculative stocks (or, really, *any* stock), you are taking a significant risk in the hope of making an appreciable return.

An asset's risk can be analyzed in two ways: (1) on a stand-alone basis, where the asset is considered by itself and (2) on a portfolio basis, where the asset is held as one of a number of assets in a portfolio. Thus, an asset's **stand-alone risk** is the risk an investor would face if he or she held only this one asset. Most financial assets, and stocks in particular, are held in portfolios, but it is necessary to understand stand-alone risk to understand risk in a portfolio context.

Stand-Alone Risk
The risk an investor would face if he or she held only one asset.

To illustrate stand-alone risk, suppose an investor buys $100,000 of short-term Treasury bills with an expected return of 5%. In this case, the investment's return, 5%, can be estimated quite precisely, and the investment is defined as being essentially *risk-free*. This same investor could also invest the $100,000 in the stock of a company just being organized to prospect for oil in the mid-Atlantic. Returns on the stock would be much harder to predict. In the worst case, the company would go bankrupt, and the investor would lose all of his or her money, in which case the return would be −100%. In the best-case scenario, the company would discover huge amounts of oil, and the investor would receive a 1,000% return. When evaluating this investment, the investor might analyze the situation and conclude that the *expected* rate of return, in a statistical sense, is 20%, but the *actual* rate of return could range from, say, +1,000% to −100%. Because there is a significant danger of earning much less than the expected return, such a stock would be relatively risky.

No investment should be undertaken unless the expected rate of return is high enough to compensate for the perceived risk. In our example, it is clear that few if any investors would be willing to buy the oil exploration stock if its expected return didn't exceed that of the T-bill. This is an extreme example. Generally, things are much less obvious, and we need to measure risk in order to decide whether a potential investment should be undertaken. Therefore, we need to define risk more precisely.

As you will see, the risk of an asset is different when the asset is held by itself versus when it is held as a part of a group, or portfolio, of assets. We look at stand-alone risk in this section, and then at portfolio risk in later sections. It's necessary to know something about stand-alone risk in order to understand portfolio risk. Also, stand-alone risk is important to the owners of small businesses and in our examination of physical assets in the capital budgeting chapters. For stocks and most financial assets, though, it is portfolio risk that is most important. Still, you need to understand the key elements of both types of risk.

resource

Students can download the Excel chapter models from the textbook's student companion site on cengage.com. Once downloaded onto your computer, retrieve the Chapter 8 Excel model and follow along as you read this chapter.

8-2A STATISTICAL MEASURES OF STAND-ALONE RISK

This is not a statistics book, and we won't spend a great deal of time on statistics. However, you do need an intuitive understanding of the relatively simple statistics presented in this section. All of the calculations can be done easily with a calculator or with Excel, and though we show pictures of the Excel setup, Excel is not needed for the calculations.

Here are the six key items that are covered:

1. Probability distributions
2. Expected rates of return, $\hat{r}$ ("r hat")
3. Historical, or past realized, rates of return, $\bar{r}$ ("r bar")
4. Standard deviation, σ (sigma)
5. Coefficient of variation (CV)
6. Sharpe ratio

Probability Distributions
Listings of possible outcomes or events with a probability (chance of occurrence) assigned to each outcome.

Table 8.1 gives the **probability distributions** for Martin Products, which makes engines for long-haul trucks (18-wheelers), and for U.S. Water, which supplies an essential product and thus has very stable sales and profits. Three possible states of the economy are shown in column 1, and the probabilities of these outcomes, expressed as decimals rather than percentages, are given in column 2 and then repeated in column 5. There is a 30% chance of a strong economy and thus strong demand, a 40% probability of normal demand, and a 30% probability of weak demand.

Columns 3 and 6 show the returns for the two companies under each state of the economy. Returns are relatively high when demand is strong and low when demand is weak. Notice, though, that Martin's rate of return could vary far more widely than U.S. Water's. Indeed, there is a fairly high probability that Martin's stock will suffer a 60% loss, though at worst, U.S. Water should have a 5% return.[3]

Columns 4 and 7 show the products of the probabilities times the returns under the different demand levels. When we sum these products, we obtain the

TABLE 8.1 Probability Distributions and Expected Returns

	A	B	C	D	E	F	G	H
16			Martin Products				U.S. Water	
17			Rate of				Rate of	
18	Economy,	Probability	Return			Probability	Return	
19	Which	of this	if this			of this	if this	
20	Affects	Demand	Demand	Product		Demand	Demand	Product
21	Demand	Occurring	Occurs	(2) × (3)		Occurring	Occurs	(5) × (6)
22	(1)	(2)	(3)	(4)		(5)	(6)	(7)
23	Strong	0.30	80%	24%		0.30	15%	4.5%
24	Normal	0.40	10%	4%		0.40	10%	4.0%
25	Weak	0.30	–60%	–18%		0.30	5%	1.5%
26		1.00	Expected return =	10%		1.00	Expected return =	10.0%
27								

[3]Although this example is illustrative, it is also somewhat unrealistic. In reality, most stocks have at least some chance of producing a negative return.

Expected Rate of Return, $\hat{r}$
The rate of return expected to be realized from an investment; the weighted average of the probability distribution of possible results.

expected rate of return, $\hat{r}$ ("r-hat"), for each stock. Both stocks have an expected return of 10%.[4]

We can graph the data in Table 8.1 as shown in Figure 8.2. The height of each bar indicates the probability that a given outcome will occur. The range of possible returns for Martin is from −60% to +80%, and the expected return is 10%. The expected return for U.S. Water is also 10%, but its possible range (and thus maximum loss) is much narrower.

In Figure 8.2, we assumed that only three economic states could occur: strong, normal, and weak. Actually, the economy can range from a deep depression to a fantastic boom, with an unlimited number of possibilities in between. Suppose we had the time and patience to assign a probability to each possible level of demand (with the sum of the probabilities still equaling 1.0) and to assign a rate of return to each stock for each level of demand. We would have a table similar to Table 8.1 except that it would have many more demand levels. This table could be used to calculate expected rates of return as shown previously, and the probabilities and outcomes could be represented by continuous curves such as those shown in Figure 8.3. Here we changed the assumptions so that there is essentially no chance that Martin's return will

FIGURE 8.2 Probability Distributions of Martin Products's and U.S. Water's Rates of Return

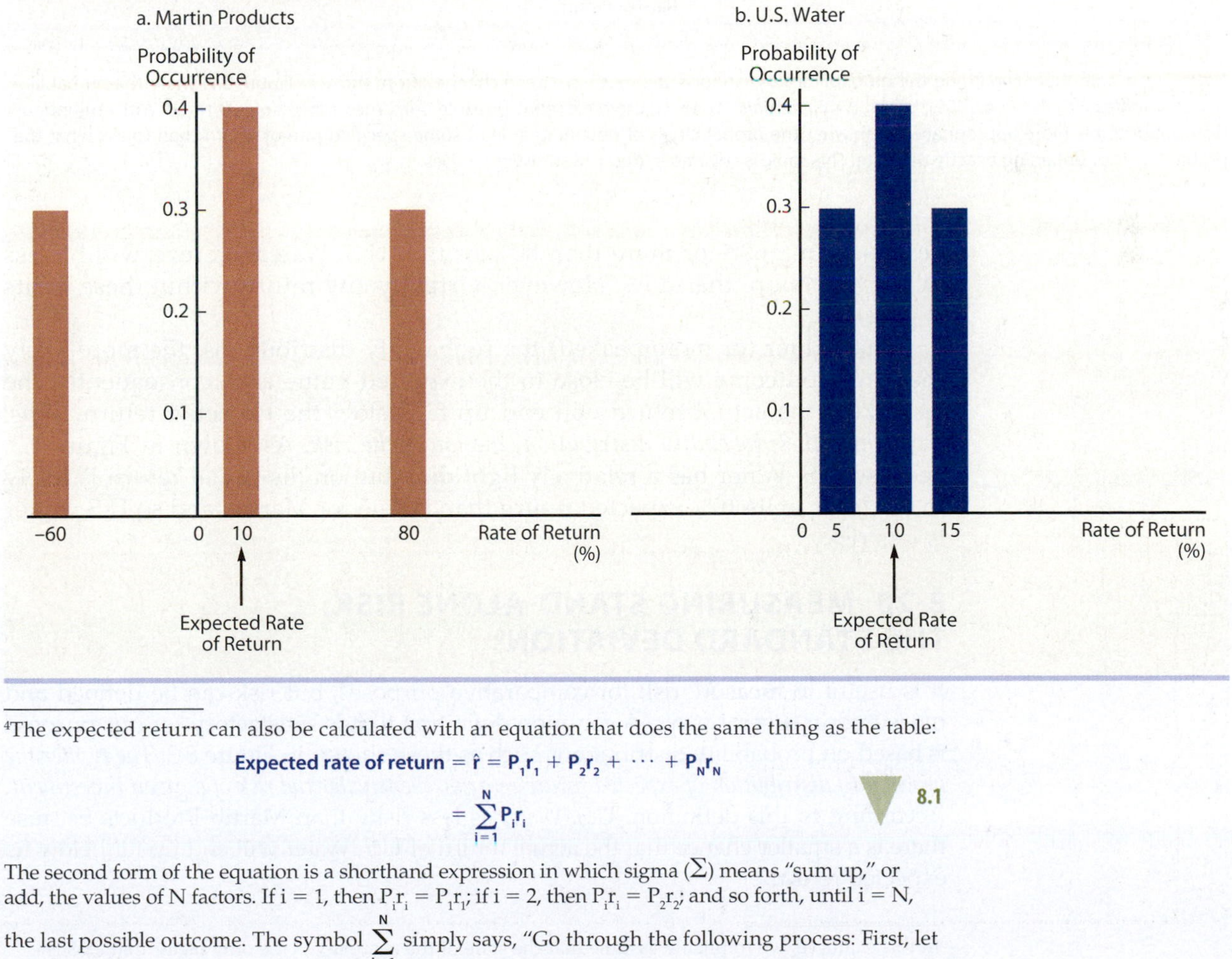

[4]The expected return can also be calculated with an equation that does the same thing as the table:

$$\text{Expected rate of return} = \hat{r} = P_1r_1 + P_2r_2 + \cdots + P_Nr_N = \sum_{i=1}^{N} P_ir_i \qquad 8.1$$

The second form of the equation is a shorthand expression in which sigma (Σ) means "sum up," or add, the values of N factors. If i = 1, then $P_ir_i = P_1r_1$; if i = 2, then $P_ir_i = P_2r_2$; and so forth, until i = N, the last possible outcome. The symbol $\sum_{i=1}^{N}$ simply says, "Go through the following process: First, let i = 1 and find the first product; then let i = 2 and find the second product; then continue until each individual product up to N has been found. Add these individual products to find the expected rate of return."

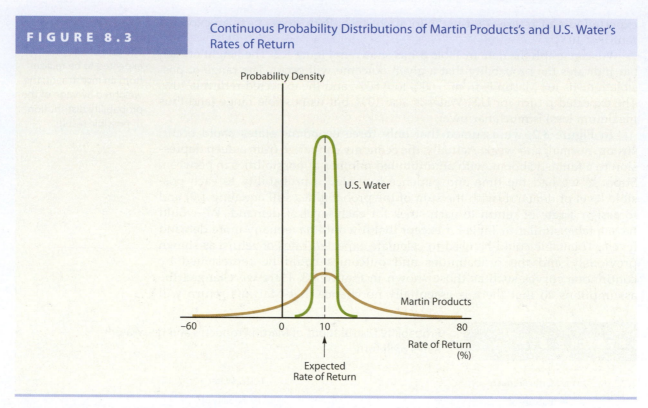

FIGURE 8.3 Continuous Probability Distributions of Martin Products's and U.S. Water's Rates of Return

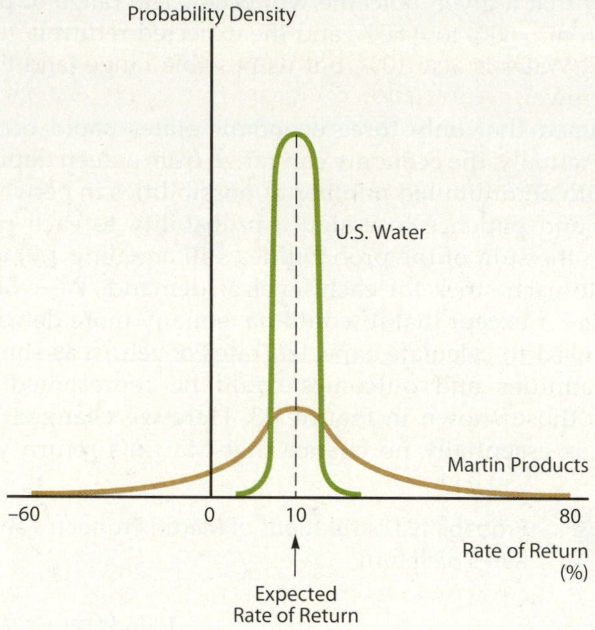

Note: The assumptions regarding the probabilities of various outcomes have been changed from those in Figure 8.2. There the probability of obtaining exactly 10% was 40%; here it is *much smaller* because there are many possible outcomes instead of just three. With continuous distributions, it is more appropriate to ask what the probability is of obtaining at least some specified rate of return than to ask what the probability is of obtaining exactly that rate. This topic is covered in detail in statistics courses.

be less than −60% or more than 80% or that U.S. Water's return will be less than 5% or more than 15%. However, virtually any return within these limits is possible.

The tighter (or more peaked) the probability distributions, the more likely the actual outcome will be close to the expected value and, consequently, the less likely the actual return will end up far below the expected return. *Thus, the tighter the probability distribution, the lower the risk.* As shown in Figure 8.3, because U.S. Water has a relatively tight distribution, its actual return is likely to be closer to its 10% expected return than is true for Martin, and so U.S. Water is less risky.[5]

8-2B MEASURING STAND-ALONE RISK: THE STANDARD DEVIATION[6]

It is useful to measure risk for comparative purposes, but risk can be defined and measured in several ways. A common definition that is satisfactory for our purpose is based on probability distributions such as those shown in Figure 8.3: *The tighter the probability distribution of expected future returns, the smaller the risk of a given investment.* According to this definition, U.S. Water is less risky than Martin Products because there is a smaller chance that the actual return of U.S. Water will end up far below its expected return.

[5]In this example, we implicitly assume that the state of the economy is the only factor that affects returns. In reality, many factors, including labor, materials, and development costs, influence returns. This is discussed at greater length in the chapters on capital budgeting.

[6]This section is relatively technical, but it can be omitted without loss of continuity.

We can use the standard deviation (σ, pronounced "sigma") to quantify the tightness of the probability distribution.[7] The smaller the standard deviation, the tighter the probability distribution and, accordingly, the lower the risk. We calculate Martin's σ in Table 8.2. We picked up columns 1, 2, and 3 from Table 8.1. Then in column 4, we find the deviation of the return in each demand state from the expected return: Actual return − Expected 10% return. The deviations are squared and shown in column 5. Each squared deviation is then multiplied by the relevant probability and shown in column 6. The sum of the products in column 6 is the *variance* of the distribution. Finally, we find the square root of the variance—this is the *standard deviation*, and it is shown at the bottom of column 6 both as a fraction and a percentage.[8]

The **standard deviation, σ**, is a measure of how far the actual return is likely to deviate from the expected return. Martin's standard deviation is 54.22%, so its actual return is likely to be quite different from the expected 10%.[9] U.S. Water's standard deviation is 3.87%, so its actual return should be much closer to the expected return of 10%. The average publicly traded firm's σ has been in the range of 20% to 30% in recent years, so Martin is more risky than most stocks, and U.S. Water is less risky.

Standard Deviation, σ
A statistical measure of the variability of a set of observations.

8-2C USING HISTORICAL DATA TO MEASURE RISK[10]

In the last section, we found the mean and standard deviation based on a subjective probability distribution. If we had actual historical data instead, the standard

TABLE 8.2 Calculating Martin Products's Standard Deviation

	A	B	C	D	E	F	G	H
33			Rate of	Deviation:				
34	Economy,	Probability	Return	Actual –				
35	Which	of this	if this	10%			Squared	
36	Affects	Demand	Demand	Expected		Deviation	Deviation	
37	Demand	Occurring	Occurs	Return		Squared	× Prob.	
38	(1)	(2)	(3)	(4)		(5)	(6)	
39	Strong	0.30	80%	70%		0.4900	0.1470	
40	Normal	0.40	10%	0%		0.0000	0.0000	
41	Weak	0.30	−60%	−70%		0.4900	0.1470	
42		1.00				Σ = Variance:	0.2940	
43			Standard deviation = square root of variance: σ =				0.5422	
44			Standard deviation expressed as a percentage: σ =				54.22%	

[7]There are actually two types of standard deviations, one for complete distributions and one for situations that involve only a sample. Different formulas and notations are used. Also, the standard deviation should be modified if the distribution is not normal, or bell-shaped. Because our purpose is simply to get the general idea across, we leave the refinements to advanced finance and statistics courses.

[8]This formula summarizes what we did in Table 8.2:

$$\text{Standard deviation} = \sigma = \sqrt{\sum_{i=1}^{N}(r_i - \hat{r})^2 P_i} \qquad 8.2$$

[9]With a normal (bell-shaped) distribution, the actual return should be within one σ about 68% of the time.

[10]Again, this section is relatively technical, but it can be omitted without loss of continuity.

deviation of returns could be found as shown in Table 8.3.[11] Because past results are often repeated in the future, the historical σ is often used as an estimate of future risk.[12] A key question that arises when historical data is used to forecast the future is how far back in time we should go. Unfortunately, there is no simple answer. Using a longer historical time series has the benefit of giving more information, but some of that information may be misleading if you believe that the level of risk in the future is likely to be very different from the level of risk in the past.

All financial calculators (and Excel) have easy-to-use functions for finding σ based on historical data.[13] Simply enter the rates of return and press the key marked S (or S_x) to obtain the standard deviation. However, neither calculators nor Excel have a built-in formula for finding σ where probabilistic data are involved. In those cases, you must go through the process outlined in Table 8.2.

8-2D OTHER MEASURES OF STAND-ALONE RISK: THE COEFFICIENT OF VARIATION AND THE SHARPE RATIO

If a choice has to be made between two investments that have the same expected returns but different standard deviations, most people would choose the one with the lower standard deviation and therefore the lower risk. Similarly, given a choice between two investments with the same risk (standard deviation) but

TABLE 8.3 Finding σ Based on Historical Data

	A	B	C	D	E	F	G	H
73				Deviation				
74				from			Squared	
75	Year	Return		Average			Deviation	
76	(1)	(2)		(3)			(4)	
77	2016	30.0%		19.8%			0.0390	
78	2017	−10.0%		−20.3%			0.0410	
79	2018	−19.0%		−29.3%			0.0856	
80	2019	40.0%		29.8%			0.0885	
81	Average	10.3%		Sum of Squared Devs (SSDevs):			0.2541	
82				SSDevs/(N − 1) = SSDevs/3:			0.0847	
83				Standard deviation = Square root of SSDevs/3: σ =			29.10%	
84				Excel Function: STDEV(B77:B80) σ =			29.10%	

[11]The 4 years of historical data are considered to be a "sample" of the full (but unknown) set of data, and the procedure used to find the standard deviation is different from the one used for probabilistic data. Here is the equation for sample data, and it is the basis for Table 8.3:

$$\textbf{Estimated } \sigma = \sqrt{\frac{\sum_{t=1}^{N}(\bar{r}_t - \bar{r}_{Avg})^2}{N-1}} \quad \textbf{8.2a}$$

Here $\bar{r}_t$ ("r bar t") denotes the past realized rate of return in period t, and $\bar{r}_{Avg}$ is the average annual return earned over the last N years.

[12]The average return for the past period (10.3% in our example) may also be used as an estimate of future returns, but this is problematic because the average historical return varies widely depending on the period examined. In our example, if we went from 2016 to 2018, we would get a different average from the 10.3%. The average historical return stabilizes with more years of data, but that brings into question whether data from many years ago are still relevant today.

[13]See our tutorials on the textbook's student companion site on cengage.com, or your calculator manual for instructions on calculating historical standard deviations.

different expected returns, investors would generally prefer the investment with the higher expected return. To most people, this is common sense—return is "good" and risk is "bad"; consequently, investors want as much return and as little risk as possible. But how do we choose between two investments if one has the higher expected return but the other has the lower standard deviation? To help answer that question, analysts often use other measures of risk. One measure, the **coefficient of variation (CV)**, is the standard deviation divided by the expected return:

Coefficient of Variation (CV)
The standardized measure of the risk per unit of return; calculated as the standard deviation divided by the expected return.

$$\text{Coefficient of variation} = \text{CV} = \frac{\sigma}{\hat{r}} \qquad 8.3$$

The coefficient of variation shows the risk per unit of return, and it provides a more meaningful risk measure when the expected returns on two alternatives are not the same. Because U.S. Water and Martin Products have the same expected return, the coefficient of variation is not necessary in this case. In this example, the firm with the larger standard deviation, Martin, must also have the larger coefficient of variation. In fact, the coefficient of variation for Martin is 54.22/10 = 5.42, and the coefficient of variation for U.S. Water is 3.87/10 = 0.39. Thus, Martin is about 14 times riskier than U.S. Water on the basis of this criterion.

Another alternative risk measure is the **Sharpe ratio**, which was developed by the Nobel Prize-winning economist William Sharpe. The Sharpe ratio compares the asset's realized excess return to its standard deviation over a specified period:

Sharpe Ratio
A measure of stand-alone risk that compares the asset's realized excess return to its standard deviation over a specified period. An investment with a higher ratio has performed better than one with a lower ratio.

$$\text{Sharpe ratio} = (\text{Return} - \text{Risk-free rate})/\sigma$$

Depending on the circumstances, an analyst may calculate the Sharpe ratio using historical returns and standard deviation, or they may base their calculations on forward-looking estimates of expected returns. In either case, excess returns measure the amount that investment returns are above the risk-free rate—so investments with returns equal to the risk-free rate will have a zero Sharpe ratio. It follows that over a given time period, investments with higher Sharpe ratios performed better, because they generated higher excess returns per unit of risk. For example, if we calculate the Sharpe ratio on a forward-looking basis for U.S. Water and Martin Products, and assume that the risk-free rate is 4%, then U.S. Water will have a Sharpe ratio of 1.55 ((10% − 4%)/3.87%), while Martin will have a Sharpe ratio of 0.11 ((10% − 4%)/54.22%). So, once again we see on a risk-adjusted basis that U.S. Water is expected to perform better, because it has the same expected excess return as Martin Products but with considerably less risk.

quick question

QUESTION:

Historical returns for Stocks A and B over the past 5 years are listed here. The risk-free rate is 3%.

Years	Stock A	Stock B
1	20.0%	25.0%
2	30.0	18.0
3	−2.0	50.0
4	6.0	10.0
5	18.0	21.5

a. What are the coefficients of variation for Stocks A and B?

b. What are the Sharpe ratios for Stocks A and B? Which stock has performed better on a risk-adjusted basis? Explain.

ANSWER:

a. The average return for Stock A is 14.4% = (20.0% + 30.0% + −2.0% + 6.0% + 18.0%)/5. The standard deviation for Stock A is [((20.0% − 14.4%)^2 + (30.0% − 14.4%)^2 + (−2.0% − 14.4%)^2 + (6.0% − 14.4%)^2 + (18.0% − 14.4%)^2)/(5−1)]^0.5 = 12.52%. Stock A's coefficient of variation = 12.52%/14.4% = 0.87; **CV_A = 0.87**.

The average return for Stock B is 24.9% = (25.0% + 18.0% + 50.0% + 10.0% + 21.5%)/5. The standard deviation for Stock B is [((25.0% − 24.9%)^2 + (18.0% − 24.9%)^2 + (50.0% − 24.9%)^2 + (10.0% − 24.9%)^2 + (21.5% − 24.9%)^2)/(5−1)]^0.5 = 15.09%. Stock B's coefficient of variation = 15.09%/24.9% = 0.61; **CV_B = 0.61**.

b. The Sharpe ratio for Stock A is **0.91**, calculated as (14.4% − 3.0%)/12.52%. The Sharpe ratio for Stock B is **1.45**, calculated as (24.9% − 3.0%)/15.09%. Stock B has the lower coefficient of variation and the higher Sharpe ratio—indicating that Stock B has performed better on a risk-adjusted basis.

8-2E RISK AVERSION AND REQUIRED RETURNS

Suppose you inherited $1 million, which you plan to invest and then retire on the income. You can buy a 5% U.S. Treasury bill, and you will be sure of earning $50,000 interest. Alternatively, you can buy stock in R&D Enterprises. If R&D's research programs are successful, your stock will increase to $2.1 million. However, if the research is a failure, the value of your stock will be zero and you will be penniless. You regard R&D's chances of success or failure as 50–50, so the expected value of the stock a year from now is 0.5($0) + 0.5($2,100,000) = $1,050,000. Subtracting the $1 million cost leaves an expected $50,000 profit and a 5% rate of return, the same as for the T-bill:

$$\text{Expected rate of return} = \frac{\text{Expected ending value} - \text{Cost}}{\text{Cost}}$$

$$= \frac{\$1{,}050{,}000 - \$1{,}000{,}000}{\$1{,}000{,}000}$$

$$= \frac{\$50{,}000}{\$1{,}000{,}000} = 5\%$$

Given the choice of the sure $50,000 profit (and 5% rate of return) and the risky expected $50,000 profit and 5% return, which one would you choose? *If you choose the less risky investment, you are risk-averse. Most investors are risk-averse, and certainly the average investor is with regard to his or her "serious money." Because this is a well-documented fact, we assume* **risk aversion** *in our discussions throughout the remainder of the book.*

Risk Aversion
Risk-averse investors dislike risk and require higher rates of return as an inducement to buy riskier securities.

What are the implications of risk aversion for security prices and rates of return? *The answer is that, other things held constant, the higher a security's risk, the higher its required return, and if this situation does not hold, prices will change to bring about the required condition.* To illustrate this point, look back at Figure 8.3 and consider again the U.S. Water and Martin Products stocks. Suppose each stock sells for $100 per share and each has an expected rate of return of 10%. Investors are averse to risk; so under those conditions, there would be a general preference for U.S. Water. People with money to invest would bid for U.S. Water, and Martin's stockholders would want to sell

THE HISTORICAL TRADE-OFF BETWEEN RISK AND RETURN

The table accompanying this box summarizes the historical trade-off between risk and return for different classes of investments from 1926 through 2017. As the table shows, those assets that produced the highest average returns also had the highest standard deviations and the widest ranges of returns. For example, small-cap stocks had the highest average annual return, 16.5%, but the standard deviation of their returns, 31.7%, was also the highest. By contrast, U.S. Treasury bills had the lowest standard deviation, 3.1%, but they also had the lowest average return, 3.4%. Although there is no guarantee that history will repeat itself, the returns and standard deviations observed in the past are often used as a starting point for estimating future returns.

Selected Realized Returns, 1926–2017

	Average Return	**Standard Deviation**
Small-cap stocks	16.5%	31.7%
Large-cap stocks	12.1	19.8
Long-term corporate bonds	6.4	8.3
Long-term government bonds	6.0	9.9
U.S. Treasury bills	3.4	3.1
Portfolios:		
90% stocks/10% bonds	11.4%	17.8%
70% stocks/30% bonds	10.2	14.1

Source: Based on Roger G. Ibbotson, *Stocks, Bonds, Bills, and Inflation: 2018 Yearbook* (Chicago, IL: Duff & Phelps, 2018), pp. 2–6, 2–23.

and use the money to buy U.S. Water. Buying pressure would quickly drive U.S. Water's stock price up, and selling pressure would simultaneously cause Martin's price to fall.

These price changes, in turn, would change the expected returns of the two securities. Suppose, for example, that U.S. Water's stock price was bid up from \$100 to \$125 and Martin's stock price declined from \$100 to \$77. These price changes would cause U.S. Water's expected return to fall to 8% and Martin's return to rise to 13%.[14] The difference in returns, 13% − 8% = 5%, would be a **risk premium (RP),** which represents the additional compensation investors require for bearing Martin's higher risk.

Risk Premium (RP)
The difference between the expected rate of return on a given risky asset and that on a less risky asset.

This example demonstrates a very important principle: *In a market dominated by risk-averse investors, riskier securities compared to less risky securities must have higher expected returns as estimated by the marginal investor. If this situation does not exist, buying and selling will occur until it does exist.* Later in the chapter we will consider the question of how much higher the returns on risky securities must be, after we see how diversification affects the way risk should be measured.

[14]We assume that each stock is expected to pay shareholders \$10 a year in perpetuity. The price of this perpetuity can be found by dividing the annual cash flow by the stock's return. Thus, if the stock's expected return is 10%, the price must be \$10/0.10 = \$100. Likewise, an 8% expected return would be consistent with a \$125 stock price (\$10/0.08 = \$125) and a 13% return with a \$77 stock price (\$10/0.13 = \$77).

SelfTest

What does *investment risk* mean?

Set up an illustrative probability distribution table for an investment with probabilities for different conditions, returns under those conditions, and the expected return.

Which of the two stocks graphed in Figure 8.3 is less risky? Why?

Identify the three measures of stand-alone risk discussed in this section. Briefly explain what each measure indicates.

Explain why you agree or disagree with this statement: Most investors are risk-averse.

How does risk aversion affect rates of return?

An investment has a 50% chance of producing a 20% return, a 25% chance of producing an 8% return, and a 25% chance of producing a −12% return. What is its expected return? **(9%)**

8-3 Risk in a Portfolio Context: The CAPM

Capital Asset Pricing Model (CAPM)
A model based on the proposition that any stock's required rate of return is equal to the risk-free rate of return plus a risk premium that reflects only the risk remaining after diversification.

In this section, we discuss the risk of stocks when they are held in portfolios rather than as stand-alone assets. Our discussion is based on an extremely important theory, the **capital asset pricing model**, or **CAPM**, that was developed in the 1960s.[15] We do not attempt to cover the CAPM in detail—rather, we simply use its intuition to explain how risk should be considered in a world where stocks and other assets are held in portfolios. If you go on to take a course in investments, you will cover the CAPM in detail.

Thus far in the chapter we have considered the riskiness of assets when they are held in isolation. This is generally appropriate for small businesses, many real estate investments, and capital budgeting projects. However, the risk of a stock held in a portfolio is typically lower than the stock's risk when it is held alone. Because investors dislike risk and because risk can be reduced by holding portfolios, most stocks are held in portfolios. Banks, pension funds, insurance companies, mutual funds, and other financial institutions are required by law to hold diversified portfolios. Most individual investors—at least those whose security holdings constitute a significant part of their total wealth—also hold portfolios. Therefore, the fact that one particular stock's price increases or decreases is not important—*what is important is the return on the portfolio and the portfolio's risk. Logically, then, the risk and return of an individual stock should be analyzed in terms of how the security affects the risk and return of the portfolio in which it is held.*

To illustrate, Pay Up Inc. is a collection agency that operates nationwide through 37 offices. The company is not well known; its stock is not very liquid and its earnings have experienced sharp fluctuations in the past. This suggests that Pay Up is risky and that its required rate of return, r, should be relatively high. However, Pay Up's required return in 2019 (and all other years) was quite low in comparison to most other companies. This indicates that investors think Pay Up is a low-risk company in spite of its uncertain profits. *This counterintuitive finding has to do with diversification and its effect on risk.* Pay Up's earnings rise during recessions, whereas most other companies' earnings decline when the economy slumps. Thus, Pay Up's stock is like insurance—it pays off when other investments go bad—so adding Pay

[15]The CAPM was originated by Professor William F. Sharpe in his article "Capital Asset Prices: A Theory of Market Equilibrium under Conditions of Risk," *Journal of Finance*, vol. 19, no. 3 (1964), pp. 425–442. Literally thousands of articles exploring various aspects of the CAPM have been published subsequently, and it is very widely used in investment analysis.

Up to a portfolio of "regular" stocks stabilizes the portfolio's returns and makes it less risky.

8-3A EXPECTED PORTFOLIO RETURNS, $\hat{r}_p$

The **expected return on a portfolio, $\hat{r}_p$**, is the weighted average of the expected returns of the individual assets in the portfolio, with the weights being the percentage of the total portfolio invested in each asset:

Expected Return on a Portfolio, $\hat{r}_p$
The weighted average of the expected returns on the assets held in the portfolio.

$$\hat{r}_p = w_1\hat{r}_1 + w_2\hat{r}_2 + \cdots + w_N\hat{r}_N = \sum_{i=1}^{N} w_i\hat{r}_i \qquad (8.4)$$

Here $\hat{r}_i$ is the expected return on the *i*th stock; the w_i's are the stocks' weights, or the percentage of the total value of the portfolio invested in each stock; and N is the number of stocks in the portfolio.

Table 8.4 can be used to implement the equation. Here we assume that an analyst estimated returns on the four stocks shown in column 1 for the coming year, as shown in column 2. Suppose further that you had $100,000 and you planned to invest $25,000, or 25% of the total, in each stock. You could multiply each stock's percentage weight as shown in column 4 by its expected return, obtain the product terms in column 5, and then sum column 5 to calculate the expected portfolio return, 7.875%.

If you added a fifth stock with a higher expected return, the portfolio's expected return would increase, and vice versa if you added a stock with a lower expected return. *The key point to remember is that the expected return on a portfolio is a weighted average of expected returns on the stocks in the portfolio.*

Several additional points should be made:

1. The expected returns in column 2 would be based on a study of some type, but they would still be essentially subjective and judgmental because different analysts could look at the same data and reach different conclusions. Therefore, this type of analysis must be viewed with a critical eye. Nevertheless, it is useful, indeed necessary, if one is to make intelligent investment decisions.
2. If we added companies such as U.S. Steel Corp. and Netflix, which are generally considered to be relatively risky, their expected returns as estimated by the marginal investor would be relatively high; otherwise, investors would sell them, drive down their prices, and force the expected returns above the returns on safer stocks.
3. After the fact and a year later, the actual **realized rates of return, $\bar{r}_i$** on the individual stocks—the $\bar{r}_i$, or "r-bar," values—would almost certainly be

Realized Rates of Return, $\bar{r}$
Returns that were actually earned during some past period. Actual returns ($\bar{r}$) usually turn out to be different from expected returns ($\hat{r}$) except for riskless assets.

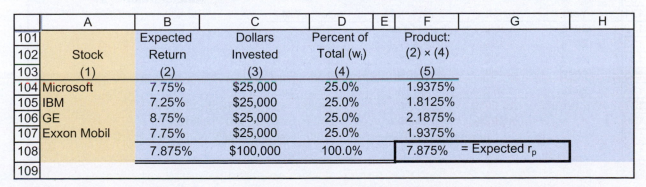

TABLE 8.4 Hypothetical Illustration: Expected Return on a Portfolio, $\hat{r}_p$

	A	B	C	D	E	F	G	H
101		Expected	Dollars	Percent of		Product:		
102	Stock	Return	Invested	Total (w_i)		(2) × (4)		
103	(1)	(2)	(3)	(4)		(5)		
104	Microsoft	7.75%	$25,000	25.0%		1.9375%		
105	IBM	7.25%	$25,000	25.0%		1.8125%		
106	GE	8.75%	$25,000	25.0%		2.1875%		
107	Exxon Mobil	7.75%	$25,000	25.0%		1.9375%		
108		7.875%	$100,000	100.0%		7.875%	= Expected r_p	
109								

different from the initial expected values. That would cause the portfolio's actual return, $\bar{r}_p$, to differ from the expected return, $\hat{r}_p = 7.875\%$. For example, Microsoft's price might double and thus provide a return of +100%, whereas IBM might have a terrible year, fall sharply, and have a return of −75%. Note, though, that those two events would be offsetting; so the portfolio's return still might be close to its expected return even though the returns on the individual stocks were far from their expected values.

8-3B PORTFOLIO RISK

Although the expected return on a portfolio is simply the weighted average of the expected returns on its individual stocks, the portfolio's risk, σ_p, is *not* the weighted average of the individual stocks' standard deviations. The portfolio's risk is generally *smaller* than the average of the stocks' σs because diversification lowers the portfolio's risk.

To illustrate this point, consider the situation in Figure 8.4. The bottom section gives data on Stocks W and M individually and data on a portfolio with 50% in each stock. The left graph plots the data in a time series format, and it shows that the returns on the individual stocks vary widely from year to year. Therefore, the individual stocks are risky. However, the portfolio's returns are constant at 15%, indicating that it is not risky at all. The probability distribution graphs to the right show the same thing—the two stocks would be quite risky if they were held in

FIGURE 8.4 Returns with Perfect Negative Correlation, ρ = −1.0

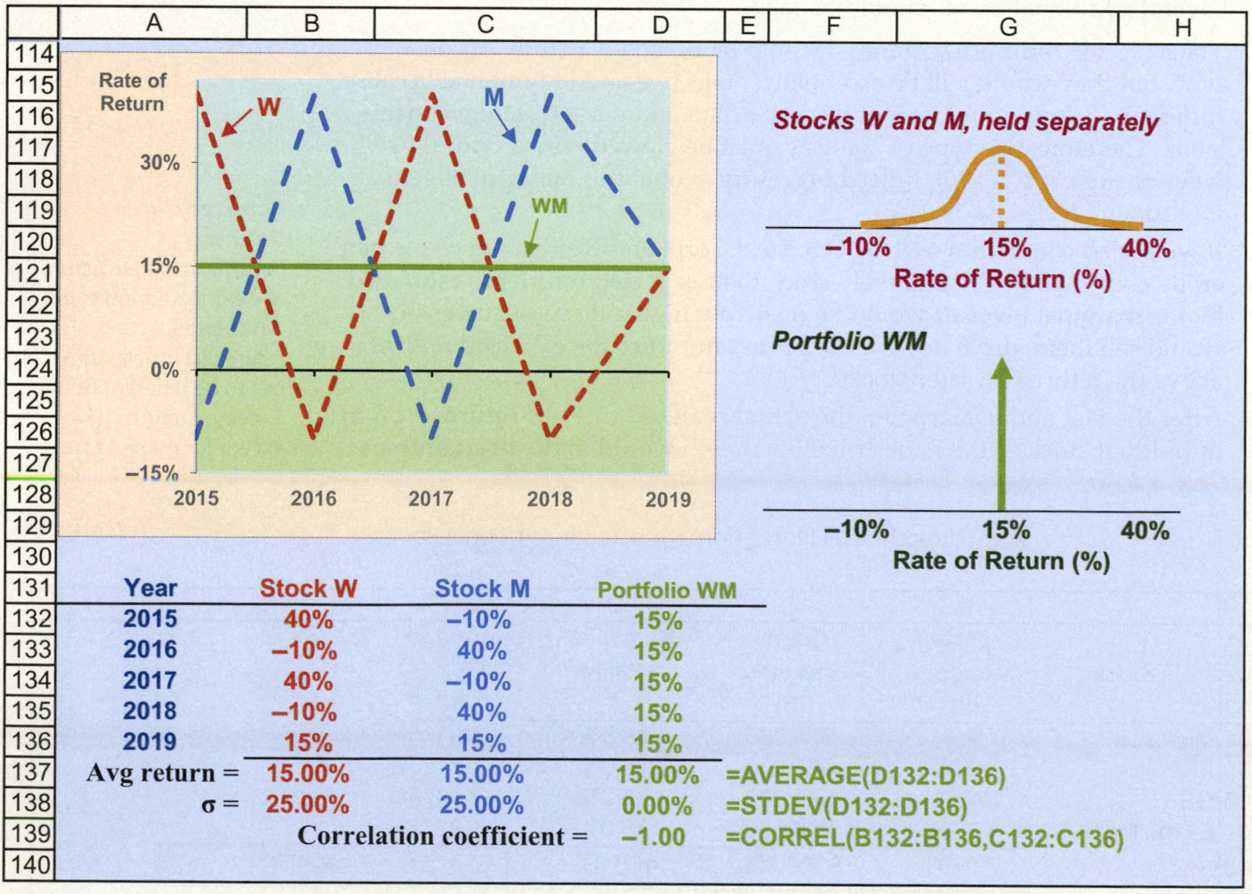

	Year	Stock W	Stock M	Portfolio WM	
131	Year	Stock W	Stock M	Portfolio WM	
132	2015	40%	−10%	15%	
133	2016	−10%	40%	15%	
134	2017	40%	−10%	15%	
135	2018	−10%	40%	15%	
136	2019	15%	15%	15%	
137	Avg return =	15.00%	15.00%	15.00%	=AVERAGE(D132:D136)
138	σ =	25.00%	25.00%	0.00%	=STDEV(D132:D136)
139			Correlation coefficient =	−1.00	=CORREL(B132:B136,C132:C136)
140					

isolation, but when they are combined to form Portfolio WM, they have no risk whatsoever.

If you invested all of your money in Stock W, you would have an expected return of 15%, but you would face a great deal of risk. The same thing would hold if you invested entirely in Stock M. However, if you invested 50% in each stock, you would have the same expected return of 15%, but with no risk whatsoever. Being rational and averse to risk, you and all other rational investors would choose to hold the portfolio, not the stocks individually.

Stocks W and M can be combined to form a riskless portfolio because their returns move countercyclically to each other—when W's fall, M's rise, and vice versa. The tendency of two variables to move together is called **correlation**, and the **correlation coefficient, ρ** (pronounced "rho"), measures this tendency.[16] In statistical terms, we say that the returns on Stocks W and M are *perfectly negatively correlated*, with $\rho = -1.0$. The opposite of perfect negative correlation is *perfect positive correlation*, with $\rho = +1.0$. If returns are not related to one another at all, they are said to be *independent* and $\rho = 0$.

Correlation
The tendency of two variables to move together.

Correlation Coefficient, ρ
A measure of the degree of relationship between two variables.

The returns on two perfectly positively correlated stocks with the same expected return would move up and down together, and a portfolio consisting of these stocks would be exactly as risky as the individual stocks. If we drew a graph like Figure 8.4, we would see just one line because the two stocks and the portfolio would have the same return at each point in time. *Thus, diversification is completely useless for reducing risk if the stocks in the portfolio are perfectly positively correlated.*

We see then that when stocks are perfectly negatively correlated ($\rho = -1.0$), all risk can be diversified away; however, when stocks are perfectly positively correlated ($\rho = +1.0$), diversification does no good. In reality, most stocks are positively correlated, but not perfectly so. Past studies have estimated that on average, the correlation coefficient between the returns of two randomly selected stocks is about 0.30.[17] *Under this condition, combining stocks into portfolios reduces risk but does not completely eliminate it.*[18] Figure 8.5 illustrates this point using two stocks whose correlation coefficient is $\rho = +0.35$. The portfolio's average return is 15%, which is the same as the average return for the two stocks, but its standard deviation is 18.62%, which is below the stocks' standard deviations and their average σ. Again, a rational, risk-averse investor would be better off holding the portfolio rather than just one of the individual stocks.

---

[16]The correlation coefficient, ρ, can range from +1.0, denoting that the two variables move up and down in perfect synchronization, to −1.0, denoting that the variables move in exactly opposite directions. A correlation coefficient of zero indicates that the two variables are not related to each other—that is, changes in one variable are independent of changes in the other. It is easy to calculate correlation coefficients with a financial calculator. Simply enter the returns on the two stocks and press a key labeled "r." For W and M, $\rho = -1.0$. See our tutorial on the textbook's student companion site on cengage.com or your calculator manual for the exact steps. Also, note that the correlation coefficient is often denoted by the term r. We use ρ here to avoid confusion with r, used to denote the rate of return.

[17]A study by Chan, Karceski, and Lakonishok (1999) estimated that the average correlation coefficient between two randomly selected stocks was 0.28, while the average correlation coefficient between two large-company stocks was 0.33. The time period of their sample was 1968 to 1998. See Louis K. C. Chan, Jason Karceski, and Josef Lakonishok, "On Portfolio Optimization: Forecasting Covariance and Choosing the Risk Model," *The Review of Financial Studies*, vol. 12, no. 5 (Winter 1999), pp. 937–974. It is important to recognize, however, that the average correlation coefficient will also shift over time. For example, the average correlation between stocks was very high immediately following the financial crisis of 2007–2009, when all stocks were heavily influenced by the same macroeconomic factors. Since then, the average correlation once again has begun to steadily decline. See Matt Jarzemsky and Tom Lauricella, "Stock Break from Herd," *The Wall Street Journal* (www.wsj.com), August 18, 2013. Finally, refer to William Watts, "This Little-Noticed Phenomenon Could Make Stock Picking Great Again," *MarketWatch* (www.marketwatch.com/story/this-chart-offers-hope-for-long-suffering-stock-pickers-2017-02-10), February 13, 2017.

[18]If we combined a large number of stocks with $\rho = 0$, we could form a riskless portfolio. However, there are not many stocks with $\rho = 0$. Stocks' returns tend to move together, not to be independent of one another.

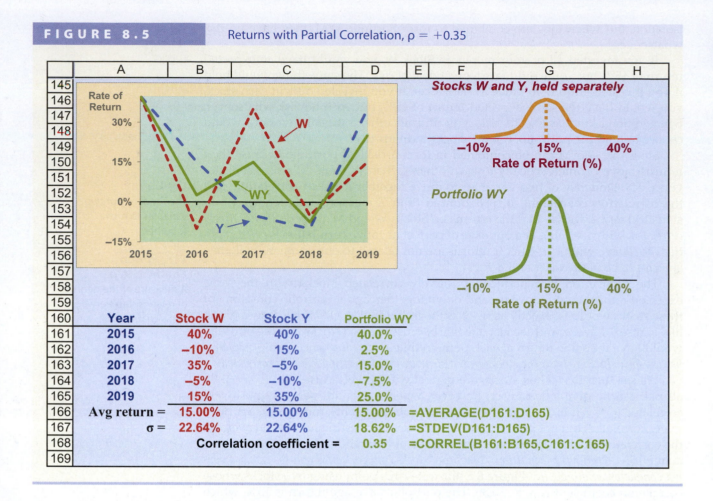

FIGURE 8.5 Returns with Partial Correlation, $\rho = +0.35$

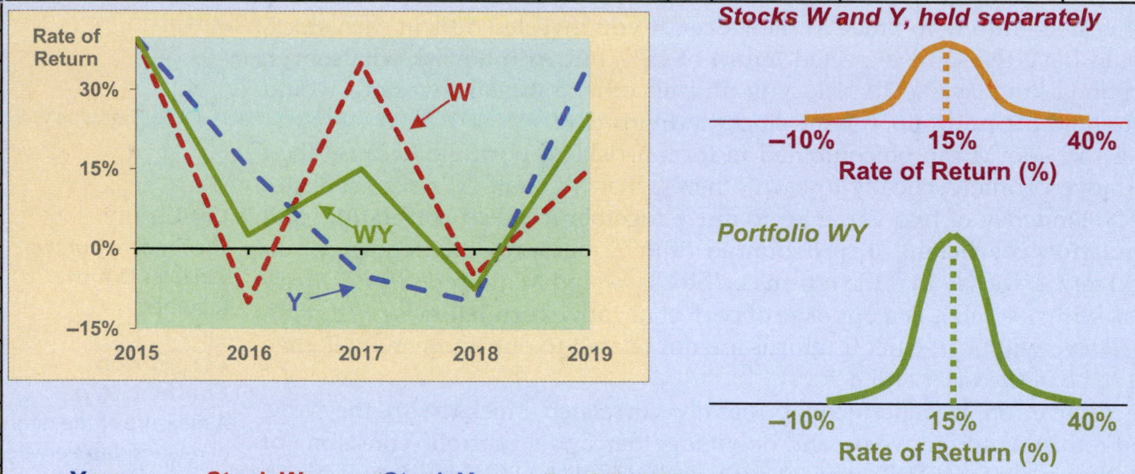

Year	Stock W	Stock Y	Portfolio WY	
2015	40%	40%	40.0%	
2016	–10%	15%	2.5%	
2017	35%	–5%	15.0%	
2018	–5%	–10%	–7.5%	
2019	15%	35%	25.0%	
Avg return =	15.00%	15.00%	15.00%	=AVERAGE(D161:D165)
σ =	22.64%	22.64%	18.62%	=STDEV(D161:D165)
	Correlation coefficient =		0.35	=CORREL(B161:B165,C161:C165)

In our examples, we considered portfolios with only two stocks. What would happen if we increased the number of stocks in the portfolio? *As a rule, on average, portfolio risk declines as the number of stocks in a portfolio increases.*

If we added enough partially correlated stocks, could we completely eliminate risk? In general, the answer is no. For an illustration, see Figure 8.6, which shows that a portfolio's risk declines as stocks are added. Here are some points to keep in mind about the figure:

Diversifiable Risk
That part of a security's risk associated with random events; it can be eliminated by proper diversification. This risk is also known as company-specific, or unsystematic, risk.

Market Risk
The risk that remains in a portfolio after diversification has eliminated all company-specific risk. This risk is also known as nondiversifiable or systematic or beta risk.

1. The portfolio's risk declines as stocks are added, but at a decreasing rate; once 40 to 50 stocks are in the portfolio, additional stocks do little to reduce risk.
2. The portfolio's total risk can be divided into two parts, **diversifiable risk** and **market risk.** Diversifiable risk is the risk that is eliminated by adding stocks. Market risk is the risk that remains even if the portfolio holds every stock in the market.
3. Diversifiable risk is caused by such random, unsystematic events as lawsuits, strikes, successful and unsuccessful marketing and R&D programs, the winning or losing of a major contract, and other events that are unique to the particular firm. Because these events are random, their effects on a portfolio can be eliminated by diversification—bad events for one firm will be offset by good events for another. Market risk, on the other hand, stems from factors that systematically affect most firms: war, inflation, recessions, high interest rates, and other macro factors. Because most stocks are affected by macro factors, market risk cannot be eliminated by diversification.

FIGURE 8.6 Effects of Portfolio Size on Risk for a Portfolio of Randomly Selected Stocks

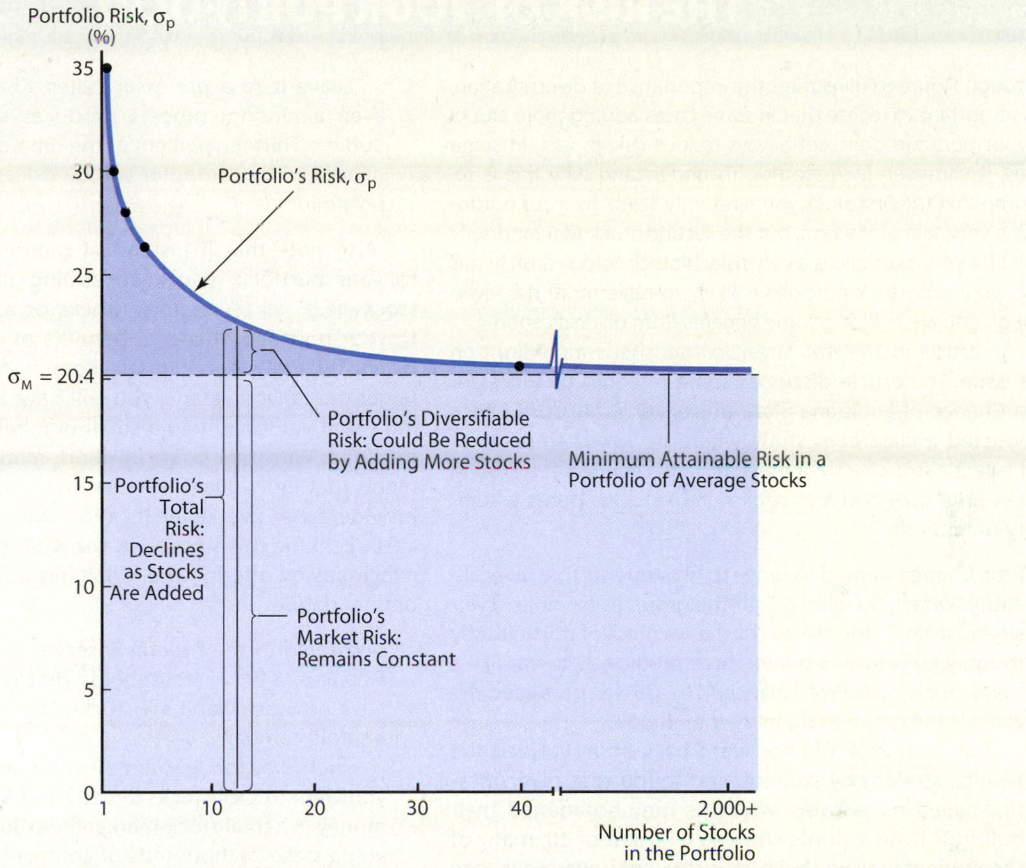

Note: This graph assumes that stocks in the portfolio are randomly selected from the universe of large, publicly traded stocks listed on the NYSE.

4. If we carefully selected the stocks included in the portfolio rather than adding them randomly, the graph would change. In particular, if we chose stocks with low correlations with one another and with low stand-alone risk, the portfolio's risk would decline faster than if random stocks were added. The reverse would hold if we added stocks with high correlations and high σs.
5. Most investors are rational in the sense that they dislike risk, other things held constant. Consequently, for many investors an ideal strategy is to hold a large diversified **market portfolio** that has low transactions costs and fees. This desire explains why low-fee index funds providing broad diversification have become so popular in recent years. That being the case, why would an investor ever hold one (or a few) stocks? In some cases, investors believe they can use their superior analysis to "beat the market"—in these instances they may focus on a small set of stocks rather than holding the broad market of stocks.

Market Portfolio
A portfolio consisting of all stocks.

6. One key question remains: How should the risk of an individual stock be measured? The standard deviation of expected returns, σ, is not appropriate because it includes risk that can be eliminated by holding the stock in a portfolio. How then should we measure a stock's risk in a world where most people hold portfolios? That's the subject of the next section.

ADDING MORE STOCKS DOESN'T ALWAYS REDUCE THE RISK OF YOUR PORTFOLIO

Although Figure 8.6 illustrates the importance of diversification, it is important to realize that in some cases adding more stocks to your portfolio does not always reduce risk. In fact, in some cases, it can even increase risk. To understand why this is so, assume that the first stock you randomly select for your portfolio is a very safe utility firm, but the second stock you randomly select for your portfolio is a very risky biotechnology firm. In this case, your two-stock portfolio is likely to have more risk, even though you are realizing some benefits from diversification.

An article in *The Wall Street Journal* sheds more light on this issue. The article discusses some research by Professor Don Chance of Louisiana State University. Professor Chance conducted a classroom study where he asked students to first select a stock for their portfolio, and then to keep adding stocks until they had a portfolio of 30 stocks. Here's a summary of his findings:

> Prof. Chance wanted to prove to his students that diversification works. On average, for the group as a whole, diversifying from 1 stock to 20 cut the riskiness of portfolios by roughly 40%, just as the research predicted. "It was like a magic trick," says Prof. Chance. "The classes produced the exact same graph that's in their textbook."
>
> But then Prof. Chance went back and analyzed the results, student by student, and found that diversification failed remarkably often. As they broadened their holdings from a single stock to a basket of 30, many of the students raised their risk instead of lowering it. One in nine times, they ended up with 30-stock portfolios that were riskier than the single company they had started with. For 23%, the final 30-stock basket fluctuated more than it had with only five stocks in it.
>
> The lesson: For any given investor, the averages mightn't apply. "We send this message out that you don't need that many stocks to diversify," says Prof. Chance, "but that's just not true." What accounts for these odd results?
>
> Leave it to a professor called Chance to show that even a random process produces seemingly unlikely outliers. Thirteen percent of the time, a 20-stock portfolio generated by computer will be riskier than a one-stock portfolio.

Also note that if instead of randomly adding stocks to your portfolio, you keep adding the same types of stocks (e.g., all technology stocks or all financial stocks) to your portfolio, then the benefits of diversification will be considerably less dramatic. Keep in mind, however, the larger point. On average, you will have a hard time reducing risk if you only hold a small number of stocks in your portfolio. With this point in mind, many analysts recommend that individual investors invest in index funds that provide extensive diversification with low transactions costs. Echoing this argument, *The Wall Street Journal* article concludes by offering the following observation and recommendation:

> According to the Federal Reserve's Survey of Consumer Finances, 84% of households that own shares directly have no more than nine stocks; 36% hold shares in only a single company.
>
> That's way too few. But 30 or 40 isn't enough either. If you want to pick stocks directly, put 90% to 95% of your money in a total stock-market index fund, which will give you a stake in thousands of companies at low cost. Put the rest in three to five stocks, at most, that you can follow closely and hold patiently. Beyond a handful, more companies may well leave you less diversified.

You should note that Figure 8.6 shows what happens on *average* if you *randomly* add more stocks to your portfolio. But although the picture shows what happens on average, there is certainly no guarantee that every time you add stocks to your portfolio the portfolio's risk will decline.

Source: Jason Zweig, "More Stocks May Not Make a Portfolio Safer," *The Wall Street Journal* (www.wsj.com), November 26, 2009.

8-3C RISK IN A PORTFOLIO CONTEXT: THE BETA COEFFICIENT

When a stock is held by itself, its risk can be measured by the standard deviation of its expected returns. However, σ is not appropriate when the stock is held in a portfolio, as stocks generally are. So how do we measure a stock's **relevant risk** in a portfolio context?

Relevant Risk
The risk that remains once a stock is in a diversified portfolio is its contribution to the portfolio's market risk. It is measured by the extent to which the stock moves up or down with the market.

First, note that all risk except that related to broad market movements can and will be diversified away by most investors—rational investors will hold enough stocks to move down the risk curve in Figure 8.6 to the point where only market risk remains in their portfolios.

The risk that remains once a stock is in a diversified portfolio is its contribution to the portfolio's market risk, and that risk can be measured by the extent to which the stock moves up or down with the market.

The tendency of a stock to move with the market is measured by its **beta coefficient, b.** Ideally, when estimating a stock's beta, we would like to have a crystal ball that tells us how the stock is going to move relative to the overall stock market in the future. But because we can't look into the future, we often use historical data and assume that the stock's historical beta will give us a reasonable estimate of how the stock will move relative to the market in the future.

Beta Coefficient, b
A metric that shows the extent to which a given stock's returns move up and down with the stock market. Beta measures market risk.

To illustrate the use of historical data, consider Figure 8.7, which shows the historical returns on three stocks and a market index. In Year 1, "the market," as defined by a portfolio containing all stocks, had a total return (dividend yield plus capital gains yield) of 10%, as did the three individual stocks. In Year 2, the market went up sharply, and its return was 20%. Stock H (for high) soared to 30%; A (for average) returned 20%, the same as the market; and L (for low) returned 15%. In Year 3, the market dropped sharply; its return was −10%. The three stocks' returns also fell—H's return was −30%, A's was −10%, and L broke even with a 0% return. In Years 4 and 5, the market returned 0% and 5%, respectively, and the three stocks' returns were as shown in the figure.

A plot of the data shows that the three stocks moved up or down with the market but that H was twice as volatile as the market, A was exactly as volatile as the market, and L had only half the market's volatility. It is apparent that the steeper the line, the greater the stock's volatility and thus the larger its loss in a down market. *The slopes of the lines are the stocks' beta coefficients.* We see in the figure that the slope coefficient for H is 2.0; for A, it is 1.0; and for L, it is 0.5.[19] Thus, beta measures a given stock's volatility relative to the market, and an **average stock's beta, b_A** = 1.0.

Average Stock's Beta, b_A
By definition, $b_A = 1$ because an average-risk stock is one that tends to move up and down in step with the general market.

Stock A is defined as an *average-risk stock* because it has a beta of b = 1.0 and thus moves up and down in step with the general market. Thus, an average stock will, in general, move up by 10% when the market moves up by 10% and fall by 10% when the market falls by 10%. A large portfolio of such b = 1.0 stocks would (1) have all of its diversifiable risk removed but (2) still move up and down with the broad market averages and thus have a degree of risk.

Stock H, which has b = 2.0, is twice as volatile as an average stock, which means that it is twice as risky. The value of a portfolio consisting of b = 2.0 stocks could double—or halve—in a short time, and if you held such a portfolio, you could quickly go from being a millionaire to being a pauper. Stock L, on the other hand, with b = 0.5, is only half as volatile as the average stock, and a portfolio of such stocks would rise and fall only half as rapidly as the market. Thus, its risk would be half that of an average-risk portfolio with b = 1.0.

Betas for literally thousands of companies are calculated and published by Value Line, Yahoo!, Google, and numerous other organizations, and the beta coefficients of some well-known companies are shown in Table 8.5. Most stocks have betas in the range of 0.50 to 1.50, and the average beta for all stocks is 1.0, which indicates that the average stock moves in sync with the market.[20]

If a stock whose beta is greater than 1.0 (say, 1.5) is added to a $b_p = 1.0$ portfolio, the portfolio's beta and consequently its risk will increase. Conversely, if a stock whose beta is less than 1.0 is added to a $b_p = 1.0$ portfolio, the portfolio's beta and risk will decline. *Thus, because a stock's beta reflects its contribution to the riskiness of a portfolio, beta is the theoretically correct measure of the stock's riskiness.*

[19]For more on calculating betas, see Eugene F. Brigham and Phillip R. Daves, *Intermediate Financial Management,* 13th edition (Mason, OH: Cengage Learning, 2019), Chapters 2 and 3.

[20]Although fairly uncommon, it is possible for a stock to have a negative beta. In that case, the stock's returns would tend to rise whenever the returns on other stocks fell.

FIGURE 8.7 Betas: Relative Volatility of Stocks H, A, and L

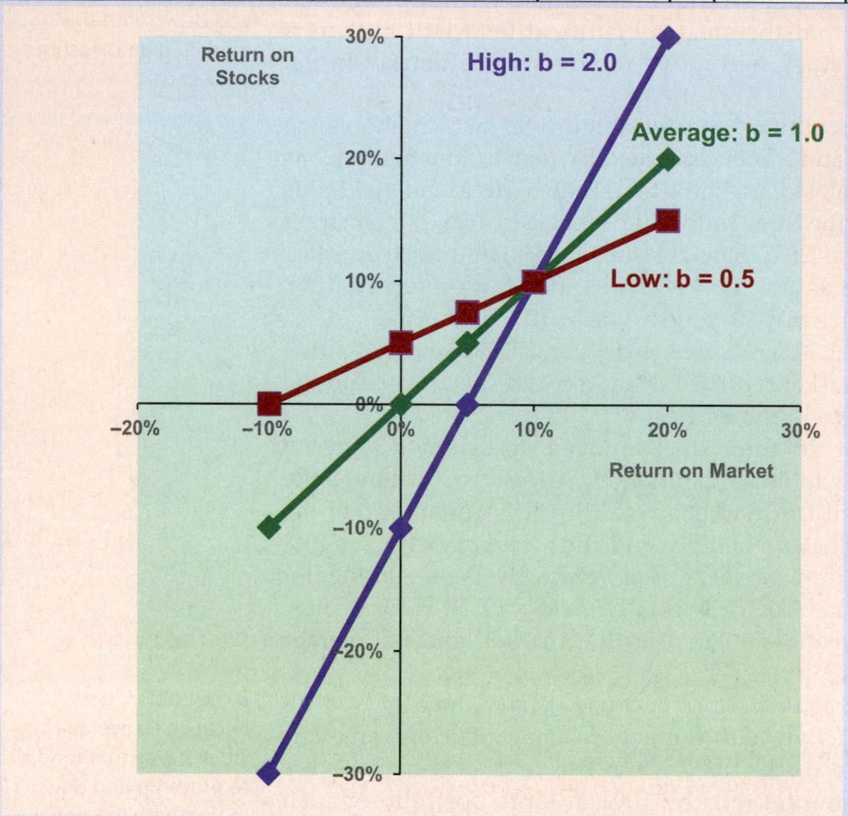

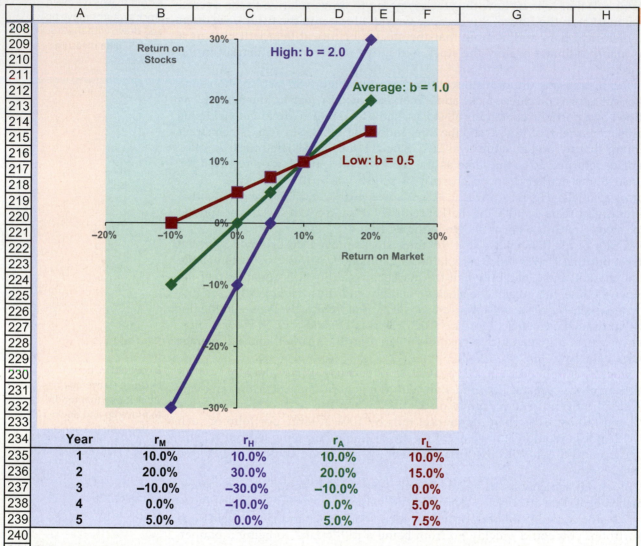

Year	r_M	r_H	r_A	r_L
1	10.0%	10.0%	10.0%	10.0%
2	20.0%	30.0%	20.0%	15.0%
3	–10.0%	–30.0%	–10.0%	0.0%
4	0.0%	–10.0%	0.0%	5.0%
5	5.0%	0.0%	5.0%	7.5%

Calculating beta:

1. Rise-Over-Run. Divide the vertical axis change that results from a given change on the horizontal axis, i.e., the change in the stock's return divided by the change in the market return. For Stock H, when the Market rises from –10% to +20%, or by 30%, the stock's return goes from –30% to +30%, or by 60%. Thus, beta H by the rise-over-run method is 60/30 = 2.0. In the same way, we find beta A to be 1.0 and beta L to be 0.5. This procedure is easy in our example because all the points lie on a straight line, but if the points were scattered around the trend line, we could not calculate an exact beta in this manner.

2. Financial Calculator. Financial calculators have a built-in function that can be used to calculate beta. The procedure differs somewhat from calculator to calculator. See our tutorial on the textbook's student companion site at cengage.com for instructions on several calculators.

3. Excel. Excel's Slope function can be used to calculate betas. Here are the functions for our three stocks:

$Beta_H$	**2.0**	**=SLOPE(C235:C239,B235:B239)**
$Beta_A$	**1.0**	**=SLOPE(D235:D239,B235:B239)**
$Beta_L$	**0.5**	**=SLOPE(F235:F239,B235:B239)**

List of Selected Company Beta Coefficients **TABLE 8.5**

Stock	Beta
NCR Corporation	1.40
American Airlines	1.30
Bank of America	1.20
Daimler AG	1.15
Best Buy	1.10
Harley-Davidson	1.10
Netflix	1.05
eBay	1.00
Exxon Mobil	1.00
General Electric	1.00
Microsoft	1.00
Facebook	0.95
Chipotle Mexican Grill	0.90
Coca-Cola	0.70
Procter & Gamble	0.65

Source: Adapted from *Value Line Investment Survey* (www.valueline.com), June 2018.

We can summarize our discussion up to this point as follows:

1. A stock's risk has two components, diversifiable risk and market risk.
2. Diversifiable risk can be eliminated, and most investors do eliminate it, either by holding very large portfolios or by buying shares in a mutual fund. We are left, then, with market risk, which is caused by general movements in the stock market and reflects the fact that most stocks are systematically affected by events such as wars, recessions, and inflation. Market risk is the only risk that should matter to a rational, diversified investor. In many cases, companies that have high stand-alone risk also have higher betas. For example, in the opening vignette to the chapter we highlighted the wild swings in Netflix's stock price over the past several years, and as we see in Table 8.5 Netflix has an above-average beta.
3. Investors must be compensated for bearing risk—the greater the risk of a stock, the higher its required return. However, compensation is required only for risk that cannot be eliminated by diversification. If risk premiums existed on a stock due to its diversifiable risk, that stock would be a bargain to well-diversified investors. They would start buying it and bid up its price, and the stock's final (equilibrium) price would be consistent with an expected return that reflected only its market risk.

To illustrate this point, suppose half of Stock B's risk is market risk (it occurs because the stock moves up and down with the market), and the other half is diversifiable. You are thinking of buying Stock B and holding it in a one-stock portfolio, so you would be exposed to all of its risk. As compensation for bearing so much risk, you want a risk premium of 8% over the 3% T-bond rate, so your required return is $r_B = 3\% + 8\% = 11\%$. But other investors, including your professor, are well diversified. They are also looking at Stock B, but they would hold it in diversified portfolios, eliminate its diversifiable risk, and thus be exposed to only half as much risk as you are. Therefore, their required risk premium would be half as large as yours, and their required rate of return would be $r_B = 3\% + 4\% = 7\%$.

If the stock was priced to yield the 11% you require, those diversified investors, including your professor, would buy it, push its price up and its yield down, and prevent you from purchasing the stock at a price low enough to provide the 11% return. In the end, you would have to accept a 7% return or keep your money in the bank.

4. The market risk of a stock is measured by its beta coefficient, which is an index of the stock's relative volatility. Here are some benchmark betas:

   b = 0.5: Stock is only half as volatile, or risky, as an average stock.

   b = 1.0: Stock is of average risk.

   b = 2.0: Stock is twice as risky as an average stock.

5. A portfolio consisting of low-beta stocks will also have a low beta because the beta of a portfolio is a weighted average of its individual securities' betas, found using this equation:

$$b_p = w_1b_1 + w_2b_2 + \cdots + w_Nb_N = \sum_{i=1}^{N} w_ib_i \quad (8.5)$$

Here b_p is the beta of the portfolio, and it shows how volatile the portfolio is relative to the market; w_i is the fraction of the portfolio invested in the *i*th stock; and b_i is the beta coefficient of the *i*th stock. To illustrate, if an investor holds a $100,000 portfolio consisting of $33,333.33 invested in each of three stocks and if each of the stocks has a beta of 0.70, the portfolio's beta will be $b_p = 0.70$:

$$b_p = 0.333(0.70) + 0.333(0.70) + 0.333(0.70) = 0.70$$

Such a portfolio would be less risky than the market, so it should experience relatively narrow price swings and have relatively small rate-of-return fluctuations. In terms of Figure 8.7, the slope of its regression line would be 0.70, which is less than that for a portfolio of average stocks.

Now suppose one of the existing stocks is sold and replaced by a stock with $b_i = 2.00$. This action will increase the portfolio's beta from $b_{p1} = 0.70$ to $b_{p2} = 1.13$:

$$b_{p2} = 0.333(0.70) + 0.333(0.70) + 0.333(2.00) = 1.13$$

Had a stock with $b_i = 0.20$ been added, the portfolio's beta would have declined from 0.70 to 0.53. Adding a low-beta stock would therefore reduce the portfolio's riskiness. Consequently, changing the stocks in a portfolio can change the riskiness of that portfolio.

6. Because a stock's beta coefficient determines how the stock affects the riskiness of a diversified portfolio, beta is, in theory, the most relevant measure of a stock's risk.

quick question

QUESTION:

Portfolio P consists of two stocks: 50% is invested in Stock A and 50% is invested in Stock B. Stock A has a standard deviation of 25% and a beta of 1.2, and Stock B has a standard deviation of 35% and a beta of 0.80. The correlation between these stocks is 0.4.

a. What is the standard deviation of Portfolio P?
   1. Less than 30%
   2. 30%
   3. More than 30%

b. What is the beta of Portfolio P?

c. Which stock is riskier to a diversified investor?

ANSWER:

a. No calculation is needed to answer this question. Remember that the standard deviation of a portfolio of two stocks is less than the weighted average of the individual stocks' standard deviations, as long as the correlation between the stocks is less than 1.0. So, in this case because the correlation is 0.4, we know that the standard deviation of Portfolio P is **less than 30%.**

b. $b_p = 0.5(1.2) + 0.5(0.8)$

   $b_p = \mathbf{1.0}$

   The beta of a portfolio is equal to the weighted average of the individual stocks' betas.

c. The relevant measure of risk to a diversified investor is beta. It follows that a diversified investor would view the higher beta stock (**Stock A**) as being more risky.

GLOBAL PERSPECTIVES

The Benefits of Diversifying Overseas

The increasing availability of international securities is making it possible to achieve a better risk-return trade-off than could be obtained by investing only in U.S. securities. So investing overseas might result in a portfolio with less risk but a higher expected return. This result occurs because of low correlations between the returns on U.S. and international securities, along with potentially high returns on overseas stocks.

Figure 8.6, presented earlier, demonstrated that an investor can reduce the risk of his or her portfolio by holding a number of stocks. Investors may be able to reduce risk even further by holding a portfolio of stocks from all around the world, given the fact that the returns on domestic and international stocks are not perfectly correlated.

Even though foreign stocks represent roughly 50% of the worldwide equity market and despite the apparent benefits from investing overseas, the typical U.S. investor still puts less than 10% of his or her money in foreign stocks. One possible explanation for this reluctance to invest overseas is that investors prefer domestic stocks because of lower transactions costs. However, this explanation is questionable because recent studies reveal that investors buy and sell overseas stocks more frequently than they trade their domestic stocks.

Other explanations for the domestic bias include the additional risks from investing overseas (e.g., exchange rate risk) and the fact that the typical U.S. investor is uninformed about international investments and/or thinks that international investments are extremely risky. It has been argued that world capital markets have become more integrated, causing the correlation of returns between different countries to increase, which reduces the benefits from international diversification. In addition, U.S. corporations are investing more internationally, providing U.S. investors with international diversification even if they purchase only U.S. stocks.

Given the benefits of global diversification, many analysts recommend that U.S. investors hold a significant percentage of foreign assets in their portfolio. A recent report in *The Wall Street Journal* asked a team of top investment advisors their thoughts regarding the optimal allocation of foreign assets. As you might expect, their opinions varied—but there seemed to be a fairly broad consensus that the average U.S. investor should hold somewhere between 30% and 40% of foreign assets in his or her portfolio. The analysts also pointed out that the optimal target varies over time and across individuals.

Sources: George Sisti, "Should You Own International Stocks?" *MarketWatch* (www.marketwatch.com), July 25, 2016; "The Experts: How Much Should You Invest Abroad?" *The Wall Street Journal* (www.wsj.com), June 10, 2013; and Kenneth Kasa, "Measuring the Gains from International Portfolio Diversification," *Federal Reserve Bank of San Francisco Weekly Letter*, no. 94-14, April 8, 1994.

SelfTest

Explain the following statement: An asset held as part of a portfolio is generally less risky than the same asset held in isolation.

What is meant by *perfect positive correlation, perfect negative correlation,* and *zero correlation?*

In general, can the riskiness of a portfolio be reduced to zero by increasing the number of stocks in the portfolio? Explain.

What is an average-risk stock? What is the beta of such a stock?

Why is it argued that beta is the best measure of a stock's risk?

An investor has a two-stock portfolio with $25,000 invested in Stock X and $50,000 invested in Stock Y. X's beta is 1.50, and Y's beta is 0.60. What is the beta of the investor's portfolio? **(0.90)**

8-4 The Relationship between Risk and Rates of Return

The preceding section demonstrated that under the CAPM theory, beta is the most appropriate measure of a stock's relevant risk. The next issue is this: For a given level of risk as measured by beta, what rate of return is required to compensate investors for bearing that risk? To begin, let us define the following terms:

$\hat{r}_i$ = *expected* rate of return on the *i*th stock.

r_i = *required* rate of return on the *i*th stock. Note that if $\hat{r}_i$ is less than r_i, the typical investor will not purchase this stock or will sell it if he or she owns it. If $\hat{r}_i$ is greater than r_i, the investor will purchase the stock because it looks like a bargain. Investors will be indifferent if $\hat{r}_i = r_i$. Buying and selling by investors tends to force the expected return to equal the required return, although the two can differ from time to time before the adjustment is completed.

$\bar{r}_i$ = realized, after-the-fact return. A person obviously does not know $\bar{r}_i$ at the time he or she is considering the purchase of a stock.

r_{RF} = risk-free rate of return. In this context, r_{RF} is generally measured by the return on U.S. Treasury securities. Some analysts recommend that short-term T-bills be used; others recommend long-term T-bonds. We generally use T-bonds because their maturity is closer to the average investor's holding period for stocks.

b_i = beta coefficient of the *i*th stock. The beta of an average stock is $b_A = 1.0$.

r_M = required rate of return on a portfolio consisting of all stocks, which is called the *market portfolio*. r_M is also the required rate of return on an average ($b_A = 1.0$) stock.

$RP_M = (r_M - r_{RF})$ = risk premium on "the market" and the premium on an average stock. This is the additional return over the risk-free rate required to compensate an average investor for assuming an average amount of risk. Average risk means a stock where $b_i = b_A = 1.0$.

$RP_i = (r_M - r_{RF})b_i = (RP_M)b_i$ = risk premium on the *i*th stock. A stock's risk premium will be less than, equal to, or greater than the premium on an average stock, RP_M, depending on whether its beta is less than, equal to, or greater than 1.0. If $b_i = b_A = 1.0$, then $RP_i = RP_M$.

Market Risk Premium, RP_M
The additional return over the risk-free rate needed to compensate investors for assuming an average amount of risk.

The **market risk premium, RP_M**, shows the premium that investors require for bearing the risk of an average stock. The size of this premium depends on how risky investors think the stock market is and on their degree of risk aversion. Let us assume that at the current time, Treasury bonds yield r_{RF} = 3%, and an average share of stock has a required rate of return of r_M = 8%. Therefore, the market risk premium is 5%, calculated as follows:

$$RP_M = r_M - r_{RF} = 8\% - 3\% = 5\%$$

It should be noted that the risk premium of an average stock, $r_M - r_{RF}$, is hard to measure because it is impossible to obtain a precise estimate of the expected future return of the market, r_M.[21] Given the difficulty of estimating future market returns, analysts often look to historical data to estimate the market risk premium. Historical data suggest that the market risk premium varies somewhat from year to year due to changes in investors' risk aversion but that it has generally ranged from 4% to 8%.

Although historical estimates might be a good starting point for estimating the market risk premium, those estimates would be misleading if investors' attitudes toward risk changed considerably over time. (See "Estimating the Market Risk Premium" box on page 296.) Indeed, many analysts have argued that the market risk premium has fallen in recent years. If this claim is correct, the market risk premium is considerably lower than one based on historical data.

The risk premium on individual stocks varies in a systematic manner from the market risk premium. For example, if one stock is twice as risky as another stock as measured by their beta coefficients, its risk premium should be twice as high. Therefore, if we know the market risk premium, RP_M, and the stock's beta, b_i, we can find its risk premium as the product $(RP_M)b_i$. For example, if beta for Stock L = 0.5 and RP_M = 5%, RP_L will be 2.5%:

$$\begin{aligned}\text{Risk premium for Stock L} = RP_L &= (RP_M)b_L \\ &= (5\%)(0.5) \\ &= 2.5\%\end{aligned} \quad \textbf{8.6}$$

As the discussion in Chapter 6 implied, the required return for any stock can be found as follows:

$$\text{Required return on a stock} = \text{Risk-free return} + \text{Premium for the stock's risk}$$

Here the risk-free return includes a premium for expected inflation; if we assume that the stocks under consideration have similar maturities and liquidity, the required return on Stock L can be found using the **security market line (SML) equation:**

Security Market Line (SML) Equation
An equation that shows the relationship between risk as measured by beta and the required rates of return on individual securities.

$$\begin{aligned}\text{Required return on Stock L} &= \text{Risk-free return} + \left(\text{Market risk premium}\right)\left(\text{Stock L's beta}\right) \\ r_L &= r_{RF} + (r_M - r_{RF})b_L \\ &= r_{RF} + (RP_M)b_L \\ &= 3\% + (8\% - 3\%)(0.5) \\ &= 3\% + 2.5\% \\ &= 5.5\%\end{aligned} \quad \textbf{8.7}$$

Stock H had b_H = 2.0, so its required rate of return is 13%:

$$r_H = 3\% + (5\%)2.0 = 13\%$$

---

[21]This concept, as well as other aspects of the CAPM, is discussed in more detail in Chapter 3 of Eugene F. Brigham and Phillip R. Daves, *Intermediate Financial Management*, 13th edition (Mason, OH: Cengage Learning, 2019). That chapter also discusses the assumptions embodied in the CAPM framework. Some of those assumptions are unrealistic; because of this, the theory does not hold exactly.

ESTIMATING THE MARKET RISK PREMIUM

The capital asset pricing model (CAPM) is more than a theory describing the trade-off between risk and return—it is also widely used in practice. As we will see later, investors use the CAPM to determine the discount rate for valuing stocks, and corporate managers use it to estimate the cost of equity capital.

The market risk premium is a key component of the CAPM, and it should be the difference between the *expected future return on the overall stock market and the expected future return on a riskless investment.* However, we cannot obtain investors' expectations; instead, academicians and practitioners often use a historical risk premium as a proxy for the expected risk premium. The historical premium is found by taking the difference between the actual return on the overall stock market and the risk-free rate during a number of different years and then averaging the annual results. Roger Ibbotson (through *Stocks, Bonds, Bills, and Inflation* Annual Yearbooks) may provide the most comprehensive estimates of historical risk premiums. It reports that the annual premiums have averaged 7% over the past 92 years.

There are three potential problems with historical risk premiums. First, what is the proper number of years over which to compute the average? Ibbotson goes back to 1926, when good data first became available, but that is an arbitrary choice, and the starting and ending points make a major difference in the calculated premium.

Second, historical premiums are likely to be misleading at times when the market risk premium is changing. To illustrate, the stock market was very strong from 1995 through 1999, *in part because investors were becoming less risk-averse, which means that they applied a lower risk premium when they valued stocks.* The strong market resulted in stock returns of about 30% per year, and when bond yields were subtracted from the high stock returns, the calculated risk premiums averaged 22.3% a year. When those high numbers were added to data from prior years, they caused the long-run historical risk premium as reported by Ibbotson to increase. Thus, a declining "true" risk premium led to very high stock returns, which in turn led to an increase in the calculated historical risk premium. That's a worrisome result, to say the least.

The third concern is that historical estimates may be biased upward because they include only the returns of firms that have survived—they do not reflect the losses incurred on investments in failed firms. Stephen Brown, William Goetzmann, and Stephen Ross discussed the implications of this *survivorship bias* in a 1995 *Journal of Finance* article. Putting these ideas into practice, Tim Koller, Marc Goedhart, and David Wessels recently suggested that survivorship bias increases historical returns by 1% to 2% a year. Therefore, they suggest that practitioners subtract 1% to 2% from the historical estimates to obtain the risk premium for use in the CAPM.

A 2018 survey of more than 4,368 academics, analysts, and practitioners in 59 countries provides further insights into the required market risk premium. For the United States, responses from academics, analysts, and practitioners indicated an average required market risk premium of 5.4%. Respondents from Venezuela indicated an average required market risk premium of 16.9%, and respondents from New Zealand indicated an average required market risk premium of 5.8%.

Sources: Roger G. Ibbotson, *Stocks, Bonds, Bills, and Inflation: 2018 Yearbook* (Chicago, IL: Duff & Phelps, 2018), p. 10–7; Pablo Fernandez, Vitaly Pershin, and Isabel Fernandez Acín, "Market Risk Premium and Risk-Free Rate Used for 59 Countries in 2018: A Survey," *Social Science Research Network*, April 4, 2018, ssrn.com/abstract=3155709; John R. Graham and Campbell R. Harvey, "The Equity Risk Premium in 2013," *Social Science Research Network*, January 28, 2013, ssrn.com/abstract=2206538; Stephen J. Brown, William N. Goetzmann, and Stephen A. Ross, "Survival," *Journal of Finance*, vol. 50, no. 3 (July 1995), pp. 853–873; and Tim Koller, Marc Goedhart, and David Wessels, *Valuation: Measuring and Managing the Value of Companies*, 5th edition (New York: McKinsey & Company, 2010).

An average stock, with b = 1.0, would have a required return of 8%, the same as the market return:

$$r_A = 3\% + (5\%)1.0 = 8\% = r_M$$

The SML equation is plotted in Figure 8.8 using the data shown below the graph on Stocks L, A, and H and assuming that $r_{RF} = 3\%$ and $r_M = 8\%$. Note the following points:

1. Required rates of return are shown on the vertical axis, and risk as measured by beta is shown on the horizontal axis. This graph is quite different from the one shown in Figure 8.7, where we calculated betas. In the earlier graph, the returns on individual stocks were plotted on the vertical axis, and returns on the market index were shown on the horizontal axis. The betas found in Figure 8.7 were then plotted as points on the horizontal axis of Figure 8.8.

FIGURE 8.8 The Security Market Line (SML)

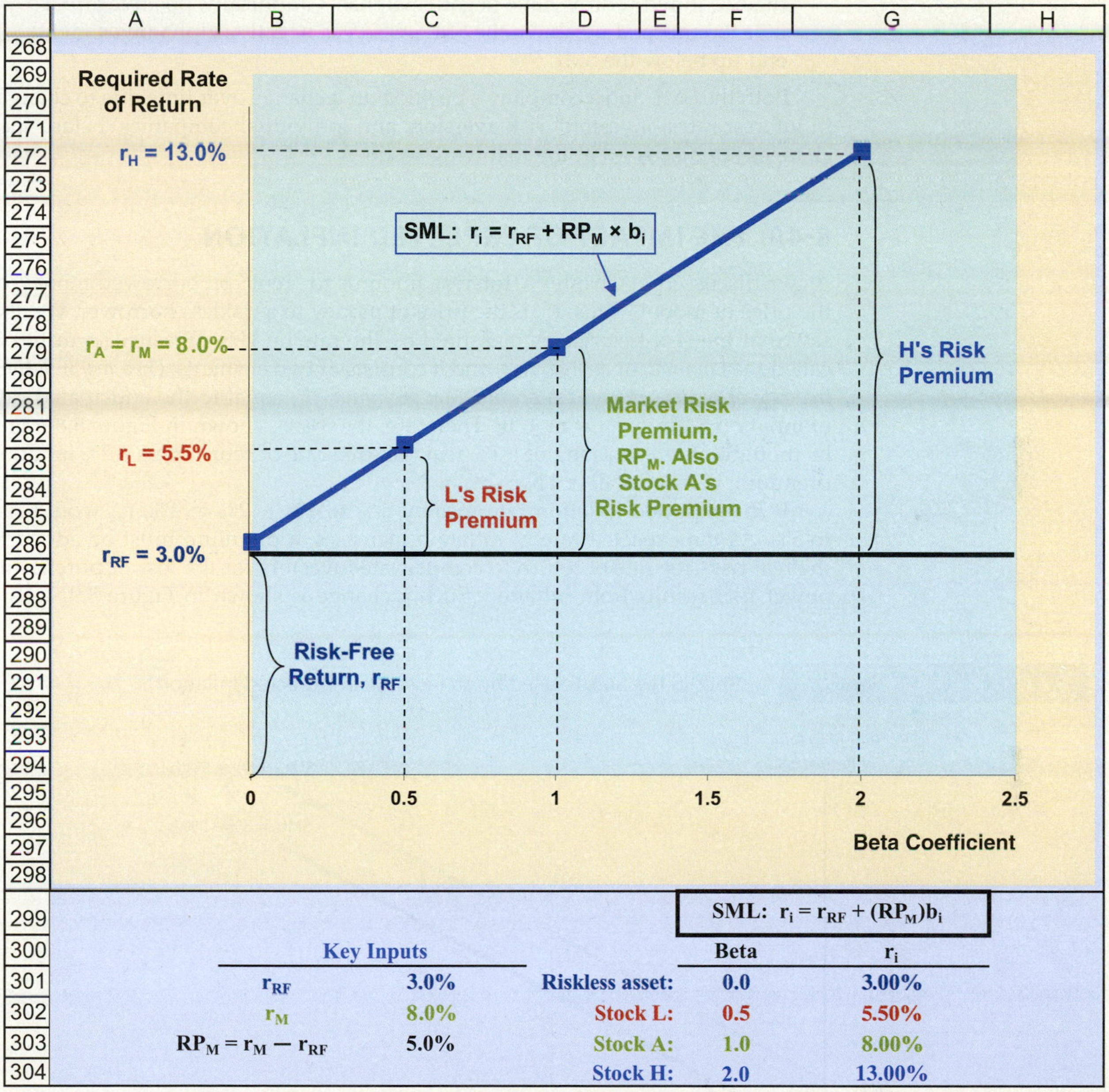

SML: $r_i = r_{RF} + (RP_M)b_i$

Key Inputs			Beta	r_i
r_{RF}	3.0%	Riskless asset:	0.0	3.00%
r_M	8.0%	Stock L:	0.5	5.50%
$RP_M = r_M - r_{RF}$	5.0%	Stock A:	1.0	8.00%
		Stock H:	2.0	13.00%

2. Riskless securities have $b_i = 0$—so the return on the riskless asset, $r_{RF} = 3\%$, is shown as the vertical axis intercept in Figure 8.8.
3. The slope of the SML in Figure 8.8 can be found using the rise-over-run procedure. When beta goes from 0 to 1.0, the required return goes from 3% to 8%, or 5%—so the slope is 5%/1.0 = 5%. Thus, a 1-unit increase in beta causes a 5% increase in the required rate of return.
4. The slope of the SML reflects the degree of risk aversion in the economy—the greater the average investor's risk aversion, (a) the steeper the slope of the line and (b) the greater the risk premium for all stocks—hence, the higher the required rate of return on all stocks.
5. Once again, the SML shows the required returns for a given level of risk. Investments outperform the market when they earn realized returns that

are greater than these required returns—doing so is often referred to as generating positive *alpha*. Similarly, investments with realized returns below their required returns have negative alphas. Graphically, positive alpha investments end up above the SML, whereas negative alpha investments end up below the SML.[22]

Both the SML and a company's position on it change over time due to changes in interest rates, investors' risk aversion, and individual companies' betas. Such changes are discussed in the following sections.

8-4A THE IMPACT OF EXPECTED INFLATION

As we discussed in Chapter 6, interest amounts to "rent" on borrowed money, or the price of money. Thus, r_{RF} is the price of money to a riskless borrower. We also saw that the risk-free rate as measured by the rate on U.S. Treasury securities is called the *nominal*, or *quoted, rate*, and it consists of two elements: (1) a *real inflation-free rate of return, r** and (2) an *inflation premium, IP*, equal to the anticipated rate of inflation.[23] Thus, $r_{RF} = r^* + IP$. Therefore, the 3% r_{RF} shown in Figure 8.8 might be thought of as consisting of a 1% real risk-free rate of return plus a 2% inflation premium: $r_{RF} = r^* + IP = 1\% + 2\% = 3\%$.

If the expected inflation rate rose by 2%, to 2% + 2% = 4%, r_{RF} would rise to 5%. As the expected rate of inflation increases, a premium must be added to the real risk-free rate of return to compensate investors for the loss of purchasing power that results from inflation. Such a change is shown in Figure 8.9. Notice

FIGURE 8.9 Shift in the SML Caused by an Increase in Expected Inflation

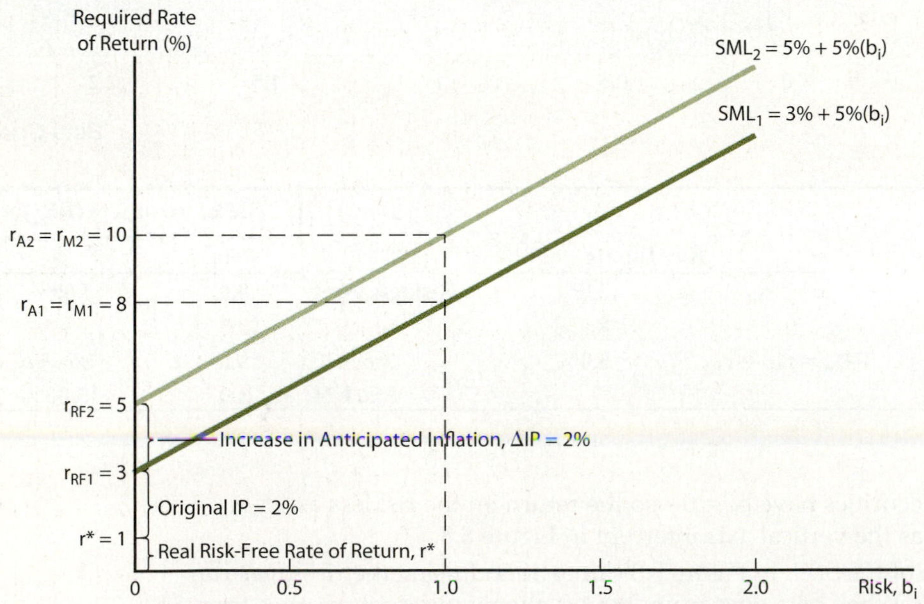

[22]Alpha can be more broadly defined to include any time an investment outperforms its stated benchmark. In this example, the stated benchmark is the required return calculated from the CAPM. But, in other cases, analysts apply other benchmarks. For example, if a mutual fund outperforms other mutual funds with the same risk profile, an analyst may characterize the fund as generating positive alpha.

[23]Long-term Treasury bonds also contain a maturity risk premium, MRP. We include the MRP in r* to simplify the discussion.

that the increase in r_{RF} leads to an equal increase in the rates of return on all risky assets because the same inflation premium is built into required rates of return on both riskless and risky assets.[24] Therefore, the rate of return on our illustrative average stock, r_A, increases from 8% to 10%. Other risky securities' returns also rise by 2 percentage points.

8-4B CHANGES IN RISK AVERSION

The slope of the SML reflects the extent to which investors are averse to risk—the steeper the slope of the line, the more the average investor requires as compensation for bearing risk. Suppose investors were indifferent to risk; that is, they were not at all risk-averse. If r_{RF} was 3%, risky assets would also have a required return of 3% because if there were no risk aversion, there would be no risk premium. In that case, the SML would plot as a horizontal line. However, because investors are risk-averse, there is a risk premium, and the greater the risk aversion, the steeper the slope of the SML.

Figure 8.10 illustrates an increase in risk aversion. The market risk premium rises from 5% to 7.5%, causing r_M to rise from $r_{M1} = 8\%$ to $r_{M2} = 10.5\%$. The returns on other risky assets also rise, and the effect of this shift in risk aversion is more pronounced on riskier securities. For example, the required return on Stock L with b = 0.5 increases by only 1.25 percentage points, from 5.5% to 6.75%, whereas the required return on a stock with a beta of 1.5 increases by 3.75 percentage points, from 10.5% to 14.25%.

FIGURE 8.10 Shift in the SML Caused by Increased Risk Aversion

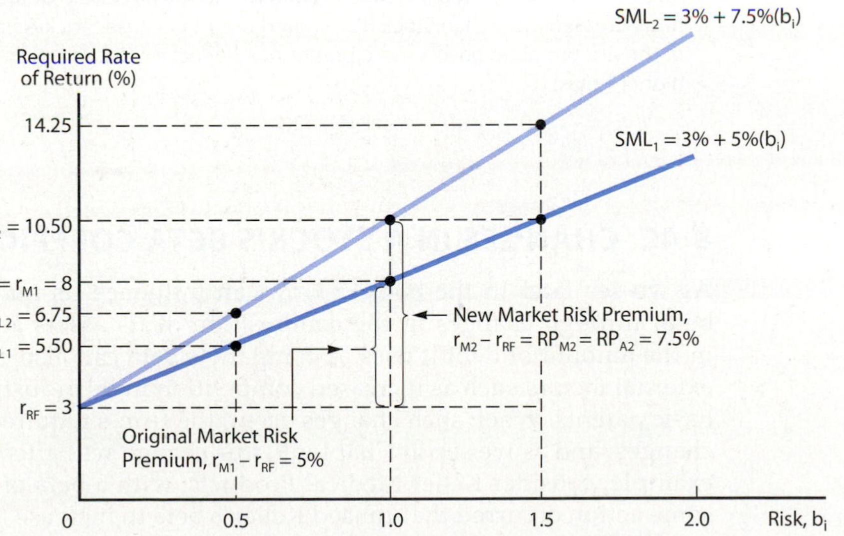

[24]Recall that the inflation premium for any asset is the average expected rate of inflation over the asset's life. Thus, in this analysis, we must assume that all securities plotted on the SML graph have the same life or that the expected rate of future inflation is constant.

It should also be noted that r_{RF} in a CAPM analysis can be proxied by either a long-term rate (the T-bond rate) or a short-term rate (the T-bill rate). Traditionally, the T-bill rate was used; however, in recent years, there has been a movement toward use of the T-bond rate because there is a closer relationship between T-bond yields and stocks' returns than between T-bill yields and stocks' returns.

quick question

QUESTION:

The risk-free rate is 3%, and the market risk premium ($r_M - r_{RF}$) is 4%. Stock A has a beta of 1.2, and Stock B has a beta of 0.8.

a. What is the required rate of return on each stock?

b. Assume that investors become less willing to take on risk (i.e., they become more risk-averse), so the market risk premium rises from 4% to 6%. Assume that the risk-free rate remains constant. What effect will this have on the required rates of return on the two stocks?

ANSWER:

a. $RP_M = r_M - r_{RF} = 4\%$

$$\begin{aligned} r_A &= r_{RF} + RP_M(b_A) \\ &= 3\% + 4\%(1.2) \\ &= \mathbf{7.8\%} \\ r_B &= r_{RF} + RP_M(b_B) \\ &= 3\% + 4\%(0.8) \\ &= \mathbf{6.2\%} \end{aligned}$$

b. RP_M rises from 4% to 6% but r_{RF} remains at 3%.

$$\begin{aligned} r_A &= 3\% + 6\%(1.2) \\ &= \mathbf{10.2\%} \\ r_B &= 3\% + 6\%(0.8) \\ &= \mathbf{7.8\%} \end{aligned}$$

Thus, the required rate of return on Stock A increases from **7.8%** to **10.2%**, and the required rate of return on Stock B increases from **6.2%** to **7.8%**. Note that Stock A's required return has increased more than Stock B's required return because Stock A has a higher beta. Shifts in the risk premium have a more pronounced effect on riskier stocks (i.e., those stocks with higher betas).

8-4C CHANGES IN A STOCK'S BETA COEFFICIENT

As we see later in the book, a firm can influence its market risk (hence, its beta) through changes in the composition of its assets and through changes in the amount of debt it uses. A company's beta can also change as a result of external factors such as increased competition in its industry and expiration of basic patents. When such changes occur, the firm's required rate of return also changes, and as we see in Chapter 9, this change will affect its stock price. For example, consider Keller Medical Products, with a beta of 1.20. Now suppose some action occurred that caused Keller's beta to increase from 1.2 to 2.0. If the conditions depicted in Figure 8.8 held, Keller's required rate of return would increase from

$$\begin{aligned} \mathbf{r_1} &= \mathbf{r_{RF} + (r_M - r_{RF})b_i} \\ &= \mathbf{3\% + (8\% - 3\%)1.20} \\ &= \mathbf{9\%} \end{aligned}$$

to

$$\begin{aligned} \mathbf{r_2} &= \mathbf{3\% + (8\% - 3\%)2.0} \\ &= \mathbf{13\%} \end{aligned}$$

As we will see in Chapter 9, increases in beta have a negative effect on a firm's stock price.[25]

SelfTest

Differentiate between a stock's expected rate of return ($\hat{r}$), required rate of return (r), and realized, after-the-fact historical return ($\bar{r}$). Which would have to be larger to induce you to buy the stock, $\hat{r}$ or r? At a given point in time, would $\hat{r}$, r, and $\bar{r}$ typically be the same or different? Explain.

What are the differences between the relative volatility graph (Figure 8.7), where "betas are made," and the SML graph (Figure 8.8), where "betas are used"? Explain how both graphs are constructed and what information they convey.

What is meant by the term, positive alpha? Negative alpha?

What would happen to the SML graph in Figure 8.8 if expected inflation increased or decreased?

What happens to the SML graph when risk aversion increases or decreases?

What would the SML look like if investors were indifferent to risk, that is, if they had zero risk aversion?

How can a firm influence the size of its beta?

A stock has a beta of 1.2. Assume that the risk-free rate is 4.5%, and the market risk premium is 5%. What is the stock's required rate of return? **(10.5%)**

8-5 Some Concerns about Beta and the CAPM[26]

The capital asset pricing model (CAPM) is more than just an abstract theory described in textbooks—it has great intuitive appeal and is widely used by analysts, investors, and corporations. However, a number of recent studies have raised concerns about its validity. For example, a study by Eugene Fama of the University of Chicago and Kenneth French of Dartmouth found no historical relationship between stocks' returns and their market betas, confirming a position long held by some professors and stock market analysts.[27]

Kenneth French's website, ***mba.tuck.dartmouth.edu/pages/faculty/ken.french/index.html****, is an excellent resource for information regarding factors related to stock returns.*

As an alternative to the traditional CAPM, researchers and practitioners are developing models with more explanatory variables than just beta. These multivariable models represent an attractive generalization of the traditional CAPM model's insight that market risk—risk that cannot be diversified away—underlies

[25]The concepts covered in this chapter are obviously important to investors, but they are also important for managers in two key ways. First, as we see in the next chapter, the risk of a stock affects the required rate of return on equity capital, and that feeds directly into the important subject of capital budgeting. Second, and also related to capital budgeting, the "true" risk of individual projects is impacted by their correlation with the firm's other projects and with other assets that the firm's stockholders might hold. We discuss these topics in later chapters.

[26]This section presents a brief overview regarding alternative models to the CAPM. For a more detailed discussion on this topic refer to Eugene F. Brigham and Phillip R. Daves, *Intermediate Financial Management*, 13th edition (Mason, OH: Cengage Learning, 2019), Chapter 3.

[27]See Eugene F. Fama and Kenneth R. French, "The Cross-Section of Expected Stock Returns," *Journal of Finance*, vol. 47, no. 2 (June 1992), pp. 427–465; and Eugene F. Fama and Kenneth R. French, "Common Risk Factors in the Returns on Stocks and Bonds," *Journal of Financial Economics*, vol. 33, no. 1 (February 1993), pp. 3–56. Fama and French found that stock returns are related to firm size and market/book ratios. Small firms and firms with low market/book ratios had higher returns; however, they found no relationship between returns and beta.

the pricing of assets. In the multivariable models, risk is assumed to be caused by a number of different factors, whereas the CAPM gauges risk only relative to returns on the market portfolio. These multivariable models represent a potentially important step forward in finance theory; however, they also have some deficiencies when applied in practice. As a result, the basic CAPM is still the most widely used method for estimating required rates of return on stocks.

SelfTest

Have there been any studies that question the validity of the CAPM? Explain.

8-6 Some Concluding Thoughts: Implications for Corporate Managers and Investors

The connection between risk and return is an important concept, and it has numerous implications for both corporate managers and investors. As we will see in later chapters, corporate managers spend a great deal of time assessing the risk and returns on individual projects. Indeed, given their concerns about the risk of individual projects, it might be fair to ask why we spend so much time discussing the riskiness of stocks. Why not begin by looking at the riskiness of such business assets as plant and equipment? *The reason is that for management whose primary goal is stock price maximization, the overriding consideration is the riskiness of the firm's stock, and the relevant risk of any physical asset must be measured in terms of its effect on the stock's risk as seen by investors.* For example, suppose Goodyear, the tire company, is considering a major investment in a new product, recapped tires. Sales of recaps (hence, earnings on the new operation) are highly uncertain; so on a stand-alone basis, the new venture appears to be quite risky. However, suppose returns in the recap business are negatively correlated with Goodyear's other operations—when times are good and people have plenty of money, they buy new cars with new tires, but when times are bad, they tend to keep their old cars and buy recaps for them. Therefore, returns would be high on regular operations and low on the recap division during good times, but the opposite would be true during recessions. The result might be a pattern like that shown earlier in Figure 8.4 for Stocks W and M. Thus, what appears to be a risky investment when viewed on a stand-alone basis might not be very risky when viewed within the context of the company as a whole.

This analysis can be extended to the corporation's stockholders. Because Goodyear's stock is owned by diversified stockholders, the real issue each time management makes an investment decision is this: How will this investment affect the risk of our stockholders? Again, the stand-alone risk of an individual project may look quite high; however, viewed in the context of the project's effect on stockholder risk, it may not be very large. We address this issue again in Chapter 12, where we examine the effects of capital budgeting on companies' beta coefficients and thus on stockholders' risks.

Although these concepts are obviously important for individual investors, they are also important for corporate managers. We summarize some key ideas that all investors should consider:

1. There is a trade-off between risk and return. The average investor likes higher returns but dislikes risk. It follows that higher-risk investments need to offer investors higher expected returns. Put another way—if you are seeking higher returns, you must be willing to assume higher risks.
2. Diversification is crucial. By diversifying wisely, investors can dramatically reduce risk without reducing their expected returns. Don't put all of your

money in one or two stocks or in one or two industries. A huge mistake that many people make is to invest a high percentage of their funds in their employer's stock. If the company goes bankrupt, they not only lose their job but also their invested capital. Although no stock is completely riskless, you can smooth out the bumps by holding a well-diversified portfolio.

3. Real returns are what matters. All investors should understand the difference between nominal and real returns. When assessing performance, the real return (what remains after inflation) is what matters. It follows that as expected inflation increases, investors need to receive higher nominal returns.
4. The risk of an investment often depends on how long you plan to hold the investment. Common stocks, for example, can be extremely risky for short-term investors. However, over the long haul, the bumps tend to even out; thus, stocks are less risky when held as part of a long-term portfolio. Indeed, in his best-selling book *Stocks for the Long Run*, Jeremy Siegel of the University of Pennsylvania concludes that "the safest long-term investment for the preservation of purchasing power has clearly been stocks, not bonds."
5. Although the past gives us insights into the risk and returns on various investments, there is no guarantee that the future will repeat the past. Stocks that have performed well in recent years might tumble, while stocks that have struggled may rebound. The same thing may hold true for the stock market as a whole. Even Jeremy Siegel, who has preached that stocks have historically been good long-term investments, also has argued that there is no assurance that returns in the future will be as strong as they have been in the past. More importantly, when purchasing a stock, you always need to ask, "Is this stock fairly valued, or is it currently priced too high?" We discuss this issue more completely in the next chapter.

Self*Test*

Explain the following statement: The stand-alone risk of an individual corporate project may be quite high, but viewed in the context of its effect on stockholders' risk, the project's true risk may not be very large.

How does the correlation between returns on a project and returns on the firm's other assets affect the project's risk?

What are some important concepts for individual investors to consider when evaluating the risk and returns of various investments?

TYING IT ALL TOGETHER

In this chapter, we described the relationship between risk and return. We discussed how to calculate risk and return for individual assets and for portfolios. In particular, we differentiated between stand-alone risk and risk in a portfolio context, and we explained the benefits of diversification. We also discussed the CAPM, which describes how risk should be measured and how risk affects rates of return. In the chapters that follow, we give you the tools needed to estimate the required rates of return on a firm's common stock and explain how that return and the yield on its bonds are used to develop the firm's cost of capital. As you will see, the cost of capital is a key element in the capital budgeting process.

Self-Test Questions and Problems

(Solutions Appear in Appendix A)

ST-1 **KEY TERMS** Define each of the following terms using graphs or equations to illustrate your answers whenever feasible:

a. Risk; stand-alone risk; probability distribution
b. Expected rate of return, $\hat{r}$
c. Standard deviation, σ; coefficient of variation (CV); Sharpe ratio
d. Risk aversion; risk premium (RP); realized rate of return, $\bar{r}$
e. Risk premium for Stock i, RP_i; market risk premium, RP_M
f. Expected return on a portfolio, $\hat{r}_p$; market portfolio
g. Correlation; correlation coefficient, ρ
h. Market risk; diversifiable risk; relevant risk
i. Capital asset pricing model (CAPM)
j. Beta coefficient, b; average stock's beta, b_A
k. Security market line (SML) equation

ST-2 **REALIZED RATES OF RETURN** Stocks A and B have the following historical returns:

Year	Stock A's Returns, r_A	Stock B's Returns, r_B
2014	(24.25%)	5.50%
2015	18.50	26.73
2016	38.67	48.25
2017	14.33	(4.50)
2018	39.13	43.86

a. Calculate the average rate of return for each stock during the period 2014 through 2018. Assume that someone held a portfolio consisting of 50% of Stock A and 50% of Stock B. What would the realized rate of return on the portfolio have been in each year from 2014 through 2018? What would the average return on the portfolio have been during that period?
b. Calculate the standard deviation of returns for each stock and for the portfolio. Use Equation 8.2a.
c. Assume the risk-free rate during this time was 3.5%. What are the Sharpe ratios for Stocks A and B and the portfolio over this time period using their average returns?
d. Looking at the annual returns on the two stocks, would you guess that the correlation coefficient between the two stocks is closer to +0.8 or to −0.8?
e. If more randomly selected stocks had been included in the portfolio, which of the following is the most accurate statement of what would have happened to σ_p?
   1. σ_p would have remained constant.
   2. σ_p would have been in the vicinity of 20%.
   3. σ_p would have declined to zero if enough stocks had been included.

ST-3 **BETA AND THE REQUIRED RATE OF RETURN** ECRI Corporation is a holding company with four main subsidiaries. The percentage of its capital invested in each of the subsidiaries (and their respective betas) is as follows:

Subsidiary	Percentage of Capital	Beta
Electric utility	60%	0.70
Cable company	25	0.90
Real estate development	10	1.30
International/special projects	5	1.50

a. What is the holding company's beta?

b. If the risk-free rate is 4% and the market risk premium is 5%, what is the holding company's required rate of return?

c. ECRI is considering a change in its strategic focus; it will reduce its reliance on the electric utility subsidiary, so the percentage of its capital in this subsidiary will be reduced to 50%. At the same time, it will increase the firm's reliance on the international/special projects division, so the percentage of its capital in that subsidiary will rise to 15%. What will the company's required rate of return be after these changes?

Questions

8-1 Suppose you owned a portfolio consisting of $250,000 of long-term U.S. government bonds.

a. Would your portfolio be riskless? Explain.

b. Now suppose the portfolio consists of $250,000 of 30-day Treasury bills. Every 30 days your bills mature, and you will reinvest the principal ($250,000) in a new batch of bills. You plan to live on the investment income from your portfolio, and you want to maintain a constant standard of living. Is the T-bill portfolio truly riskless? Explain.

c. What is the least risky security you can think of? Explain.

8-2 The probability distribution of a less risky expected return is more peaked than that of a riskier return. What shape would the probability distribution be for (a) completely certain returns and (b) completely uncertain returns?

8-3 A life insurance policy is a financial asset, with the premiums paid representing the investment's cost.

a. How would you calculate the expected return on a 1-year life insurance policy?

b. Suppose the owner of a life insurance policy has no other financial assets—the person's only other asset is "human capital," or earnings capacity. What is the correlation coefficient between the return on the insurance policy and the return on the human capital?

c. Life insurance companies must pay administrative costs and sales representatives' commissions; hence, the expected rate of return on insurance premiums is generally low or even negative. Use portfolio concepts to explain why people buy life insurance in spite of low expected returns.

8-4 Is it possible to construct a portfolio of real-world stocks that has a required return equal to the risk-free rate? Explain.

8-5 Stock A has an expected return of 7%, a standard deviation of expected returns of 35%, a correlation coefficient with the market of −0.3, and a beta coefficient of −0.5. Stock B has an expected return of 12%, a standard deviation of returns of 10%, a 0.7 correlation with the market, and a beta coefficient of 1.0. Which security is riskier? Why?

8-6 A stock had a 12% return last year, a year when the overall stock market declined. Does this mean that the stock has a negative beta and thus very little risk if held in a portfolio? Explain.

8-7 If investors' aversion to risk increased, would the risk premium on a high-beta stock increase by more or less than that on a low-beta stock? Explain.

8-8 If a company's beta were to double, would its required return also double?

8-9 In Chapter 7, we saw that if the market interest rate, r_d, for a given bond increased, the price of the bond would decline. Applying this same logic to stocks, explain (a) how a decrease in risk aversion would affect stocks' prices and earned rates of return, (b) how this would affect risk premiums as measured by the historical difference between returns on stocks and returns on bonds, and (c) what the implications of this would be for the use of historical risk premiums when applying the SML equation.

8-10 Suppose you own Stocks A and B. Based on data over the past decade, the Sharpe ratio for Stock A is 1.3, while the Sharpe ratio for Stock B is 0.8. Briefly explain which stock has performed better.

8-11 ABC Company's stock earned a return of 10% this past year. Investors' required return for this stock based on the SML equation was 9%. Where would this stock plot on the SML? What can you say about this investment's alpha? Explain.

Problems

Easy Problems 1-5

8-1 **EXPECTED RETURN** A stock's returns have the following distribution:

Demand for the Company's Products	Probability of this Demand Occurring	Rate of Return if this Demand Occurs
Weak	0.1	(30%)
Below average	0.1	(14)
Average	0.3	11
Above average	0.3	20
Strong	0.2	45
	1.0	

Assume the risk-free rate is 2%. Calculate the stock's expected return, standard deviation, coefficient of variation, and Sharpe ratio.

8-2 **PORTFOLIO BETA** An individual has \$20,000 invested in a stock with a beta of 0.6 and another \$75,000 invested in a stock with a beta of 2.5. If these are the only two investments in her portfolio, what is her portfolio's beta?

8-3 **REQUIRED RATE OF RETURN** Assume that the risk-free rate is 5.5% and the required return on the market is 12%. What is the required rate of return on a stock with a beta of 2?

8-4 **EXPECTED AND REQUIRED RATES OF RETURN** Assume that the risk-free rate is 3.5% and the market risk premium is 4%. What is the required return for the overall stock market? What is the required rate of return on a stock with a beta of 0.8?

8-5 **BETA AND REQUIRED RATE OF RETURN** A stock has a required return of 9%, the risk-free rate is 4.5%, and the market risk premium is 3%.

a. What is the stock's beta?

b. If the market risk premium increased to 5%, what would happen to the stock's required rate of return? Assume that the risk-free rate and the beta remain unchanged.

Intermediate Problems 6-12

8-6 **EXPECTED RETURNS** Stocks A and B have the following probability distributions of expected future returns:

Probability	A	B
0.1	(10%)	(35%)
0.2	2	0
0.4	12	20
0.2	20	25
0.1	38	45

a. Calculate the expected rate of return, $\hat{r}_B$, for Stock B ($\hat{r}_A$ = 12%).

b. Calculate the standard deviation of expected returns, σ_A, for Stock A (σ_B = 20.35%). Now calculate the coefficient of variation for Stock B. Is it possible that most investors will regard Stock B as being less risky than Stock A? Explain.

c. Assume the risk-free rate is 2.5%. What are the Sharpe ratios for Stocks A and B? Are these calculations consistent with the information obtained from the coefficient of variation calculations in part b? Explain.

8-7 **PORTFOLIO REQUIRED RETURN** Suppose you are the money manager of a \$4.82 million investment fund. The fund consists of four stocks with the following investments and betas:

Stock	Investment	Beta
A	\$ 460,000	1.50
B	500,000	(0.50)
C	1,260,000	1.25
D	2,600,000	0.75

If the market's required rate of return is 8% and the risk-free rate is 4%, what is the fund's required rate of return?

8-8 **BETA COEFFICIENT** Given the following information, determine the beta coefficient for Stock L that is consistent with equilibrium: $\hat{r}_L = 10.5\%$; $r_{RF} = 3.5\%$; $r_M = 9.5\%$.

8-9 **REQUIRED RATE OF RETURN** Stock R has a beta of 2.0, Stock S has a beta of 0.45, the required return on an average stock is 10%, and the risk-free rate of return is 5%. By how much does the required return on the riskier stock exceed the required return on the less risky stock?

8-10 **CAPM AND REQUIRED RETURN** Beale Manufacturing Company has a beta of 1.1, and Foley Industries has a beta of 0.30. The required return on an index fund that holds the entire stock market is 11%. The risk-free rate of interest is 4.5%. By how much does Beale's required return exceed Foley's required return?

8-11 **CAPM AND REQUIRED RETURN** Calculate the required rate of return for Mudd Enterprises assuming that investors expect a 3.6% rate of inflation in the future. The real risk-free rate is 1.0%, and the market risk premium is 6.0%. Mudd has a beta of 1.5, and its realized rate of return has averaged 8.5% over the past 5 years.

8-12 **REQUIRED RATE OF RETURN** Suppose $r_{RF} = 4\%$, $r_M = 10\%$, and $b_i = 1.4$.

a. What is r_i, the required rate of return on Stock i?

b. Now suppose that r_{RF} (1) increases to 5% or (2) decreases to 3%. The slope of the SML remains constant. How would this affect r_M and r_i?

c. Now assume that r_{RF} remains at 4%, but r_M (1) increases to 12% or (2) falls to 9%. The slope of the SML does not remain constant. How would these changes affect r_i?

Challenging Problems 13-21

8-13 **CAPM, PORTFOLIO RISK, AND RETURN** Consider the following information for Stocks A, B, and C. The returns on the three stocks are positively correlated, but they are not perfectly correlated. (That is, each of the correlation coefficients is between 0 and 1.)

Stock	Expected Return	Standard Deviation	Beta
A	9.55%	15%	0.9
B	10.45	15	1.1
C	12.70	15	1.6

Fund P has one-third of its funds invested in each of the three stocks. The risk-free rate is 5.5%, and the market is in equilibrium. (That is, required returns equal expected returns.)

a. What is the market risk premium ($r_M - r_{RF}$)?

b. What is the beta of Fund P?

c. What is the required return of Fund P?

d. Would you expect the standard deviation of Fund P to be less than 15%, equal to 15%, or greater than 15%? Explain.

8-14 **PORTFOLIO BETA** Suppose you held a diversified portfolio consisting of a \$7,500 investment in each of 20 different common stocks. The portfolio's beta is 1.25. Now suppose you decided to sell one of the stocks in your portfolio with a beta of 1.0 for \$7,500 and use the proceeds to buy another stock with a beta of 0.80. What would your portfolio's new beta be?

8-15 **CAPM AND REQUIRED RETURN** HR Industries (HRI) has a beta of 1.6; LR Industries's (LRI) beta is 0.8. The risk-free rate is 6%, and the required rate of return on an average stock is 13%. The expected rate of inflation built into r_{RF} falls by 1.5 percentage points, the real risk-free rate remains constant, the required return on the market falls to 10.5%, and all betas remain constant. After all of these changes, what will be the difference in the required returns for HRI and LRI?

8-16 **CAPM AND PORTFOLIO RETURN** You have been managing a \$5 million portfolio that has a beta of 1.15 and a required rate of return of 11.475%. The current risk-free rate is 4%. Assume that you receive another \$500,000. If you invest the money in a stock with a beta of 0.85, what will be the required return on your \$5.5 million portfolio?

8-17 **PORTFOLIO BETA** A mutual fund manager has a \$20 million portfolio with a beta of 1.7. The risk-free rate is 4.5%, and the market risk premium is 7%. The manager expects to receive an additional \$5 million, which she plans to invest in a number of stocks. After investing the additional funds, she wants the fund's required return to be 15%. What should be the average beta of the new stocks added to the portfolio?

8-18 **EXPECTED RETURNS** Suppose you won the lottery and had two options: (1) receiving \$0.5 million or (2) taking a gamble in which, at the flip of a coin, you receive \$1 million if a head comes up but receive zero if a tail comes up.

a. What is the expected value of the gamble?

b. Would you take the sure \$0.5 million or the gamble?

c. If you chose the sure \$0.5 million, would that indicate that you are a risk averter or a risk seeker?

d. Suppose the payoff was actually \$0.5 million—that was the only choice. You now face the choice of investing it in a U.S. Treasury bond that will return \$537,500 at the end of a year or a common stock that has a 50–50 chance of being worthless or worth \$1,150,000 at the end of the year.

   1. The expected profit on the T-bond investment is \$37,500. What is the expected dollar profit on the stock investment?
   2. The expected rate of return on the T-bond investment is 7.5%. What is the expected rate of return on the stock investment?
   3. Would you invest in the bond or the stock? Why?
   4. Exactly how large would the expected profit (or the expected rate of return) have to be on the stock investment to make you invest in the stock, given the 7.5% return on the bond?
   5. How might your decision be affected if, rather than buying one stock for \$0.5 million, you could construct a portfolio consisting of 100 stocks with \$5,000 invested in each? Each of these stocks has the same return characteristics as the one stock—that is, a 50–50 chance of being worth zero or \$11,500 at year-end. Would the correlation between returns on these stocks matter? Explain.

8-19 **EVALUATING RISK AND RETURN** Stock X has a 10% expected return, a beta coefficient of 0.9, and a 35% standard deviation of expected returns. Stock Y has a 12.5% expected return, a beta coefficient of 1.2, and a 25% standard deviation. The risk-free rate is 6%, and the market risk premium is 5%.

a. Calculate each stock's coefficient of variation.

b. Which stock is riskier for a diversified investor?

c. Calculate each stock's required rate of return.

d. On the basis of the two stocks' expected and required returns, which stock would be more attractive to a diversified investor?

e. Calculate the required return of a portfolio that has \$7,500 invested in Stock X and \$2,500 invested in Stock Y.

f. If the market risk premium increased to 6%, which of the two stocks would have the larger increase in its required return?

8-20 **REALIZED RATES OF RETURN** Stocks A and B have the following historical returns:

Year	Stock A's Returns, r_A	Stock B's Returns, r_B
2014	(18.00%)	(14.50%)
2015	33.00	21.80
2016	15.00	30.50
2017	(0.50)	(7.60)
2018	27.00	26.30

a. Calculate the average rate of return for each stock during the period 2014 through 2018.

b. Assume that someone held a portfolio consisting of 50% of Stock A and 50% of Stock B. What would the realized rate of return on the portfolio have been each year? What would the average return on the portfolio have been during this period?

c. Calculate the standard deviation of returns for each stock and for the portfolio.

d. Calculate the coefficient of variation for each stock and for the portfolio.

e. Assuming you are a risk-averse investor, would you prefer to hold Stock A, Stock B, or the portfolio? Why?

8-21 **SECURITY MARKET LINE** You plan to invest in the Kish Hedge Fund, which has total capital of $500 million invested in five stocks:

Stock	Investment	Stock's Beta Coefficient
A	$160 million	0.5
B	120 million	1.2
C	80 million	1.8
D	80 million	1.0
E	60 million	1.6

Kish's beta coefficient can be found as a weighted average of its stocks' betas. The risk-free rate is 6%, and you believe the following probability distribution for future market returns is realistic:

Probability	Market Return
0.1	−28%
0.2	0
0.4	12
0.2	30
0.1	50

a. What is the equation for the security market line (SML)? (*Hint:* First, determine the expected market return.)

b. Calculate Kish's required rate of return.

c. Suppose Rick Kish, the president, receives a proposal from a company seeking new capital. The amount needed to take a position in the stock is $50 million, it has an expected return of 15%, and its estimated beta is 1.5. Should Kish invest in the new company? At what expected rate of return should Kish be indifferent to purchasing the stock?

Comprehensive/Spreadsheet Problem

8-22 **EVALUATING RISK AND RETURN** Bartman Industries's and Reynolds Inc.'s stock prices and dividends, along with the Winslow 5000 Index, are shown here for the period 2013–2018. The Winslow 5000 data are adjusted to include dividends.

	Bartman Industries		Reynolds Inc.		Winslow 5000
Year	**Stock Price**	**Dividend**	**Stock Price**	**Dividend**	**Includes Dividends**
2018	$17.25	$1.15	$48.75	$3.00	$11,663.98
2017	14.75	1.06	52.30	2.90	8,785.70
2016	16.50	1.00	48.75	2.75	8,679.98
2015	10.75	0.95	57.25	2.50	6,434.03
2014	11.37	0.90	60.00	2.25	5,602.28
2013	7.62	0.85	55.75	2.00	4,705.97

a. Use the data to calculate annual rates of return for Bartman, Reynolds, and the Winslow 5000 Index. Then calculate each entity's average return over the 5-year period. (*Hint:* Remember, returns are calculated by subtracting the beginning price from the ending price to get the capital gain or loss, adding the dividend to the capital gain or loss, and dividing the result by the beginning price. Assume that dividends are already included in the index. Also, you cannot calculate the rate of return for 2013 because you do not have 2012 data.)

b. Calculate the standard deviations of the returns for Bartman, Reynolds, and the Winslow 5000. (*Hint:* Use the sample standard deviation formula, Equation 8.2a in this chapter, which corresponds to the STDEV function in Excel.)

c. Calculate the coefficients of variation for Bartman, Reynolds, and the Winslow 5000.

d. Assume the risk-free rate during this time was 3%. Calculate the Sharpe ratios for Bartman, Reynolds, and the Index over this period using their average returns.

e. Construct a scatter diagram that shows Bartman's and Reynolds's returns on the vertical axis and the Winslow 5000 Index's returns on the horizontal axis.

f. Estimate Bartman's and Reynolds's betas by running regressions of their returns against the index's returns. (*Hint:* Refer to Web Appendix 8A.) Are these betas consistent with your graph?

g. Assume that the risk-free rate on long-term Treasury bonds is 4.5%. Assume also that the average annual return on the Winslow 5000 is *not* a good estimate of the market's required return—it is too high. So use 10% as the expected return on the market. Use the SML equation to calculate the two companies' required returns.

h. If you formed a portfolio that consisted of 50% Bartman and 50% Reynolds, what would the portfolio's beta and required return be?

i. Suppose an investor wants to include Bartman Industries's stock in his portfolio. Stocks A, B, and C are currently in the portfolio, and their betas are 0.769, 0.985, and 1.423, respectively. Calculate the new portfolio's required return if it consists of 25% of Bartman, 15% of Stock A, 40% of Stock B, and 20% of Stock C.

INTEGRATED CASE

MERRILL FINCH INC.

8-23 **RISK AND RETURN** Assume that you recently graduated with a major in finance. You just landed a job as a financial planner with Merrill Finch Inc., a large financial services corporation. Your first assignment is to invest $100,000 for a client. Because the funds are to be invested in a business at the end of 1 year, you have been instructed to plan for a 1-year holding period. Further, your boss has restricted you to the investment alternatives in the following table, shown with their probabilities and associated outcomes. (For now, disregard the items at the bottom of the data; you will fill in the blanks later.)

Returns on Alternative Investments

		Estimated Rate of Return					
State of the Economy	**Probability**	**T-Bills**	**High Tech**	**Collections**	**U.S. Rubber**	**Market Portfolio**	**Two-Stock Portfolio**
Recession	0.1	3.0%	(29.5%)	24.5%	3.5%[a]	(19.5%)	(2.5%)
Below average	0.2	3.0	(9.5)	10.5	(16.5)	(5.5)	
Average	0.4	3.0	12.5	(1.0)	0.5	7.5	5.8
Above average	0.2	3.0	27.5	(5.0)	38.5	22.5	
Boom	0.1	3.0	42.5	(20.0)	23.5	35.5	11.3
$\hat{r}$				1.2%	7.3%	8.0%	
σ		0.0		11.2	18.8	15.2	4.6
CV				9.8	2.6	1.9	0.8
Sharpe ratio		—		−0.16			0.54
b				−0.50	0.88		

Note:

[a]The estimated returns of U.S. Rubber do not always move in the same direction as the overall economy. For example, when the economy is below average, consumers purchase fewer tires than they would if the economy was stronger. However, if the economy is in a flat-out recession, a large number of consumers who were planning to purchase a new car may choose to wait and instead purchase new tires for the car they currently own. Under these circumstances, we would expect U.S. Rubber's stock price to be higher if there is a recession than if the economy is just below average.

Merrill Finch's economic forecasting staff has developed probability estimates for the state of the economy, and its security analysts developed a sophisticated computer program to estimate the rate of return on each alternative under each state of the economy. High Tech Inc. is an electronics firm, Collections Inc. collects past-due debts, and U.S. Rubber manufactures tires and various other rubber and plastics products. Merrill Finch also maintains a "market portfolio" that owns a market-weighted fraction of all publicly traded stocks; you can invest in that portfolio and thus obtain average stock market results. Given the situation described, answer the following questions:

a. 1. Why is the T-bill's return independent of the state of the economy? Do T-bills promise a completely risk-free return? Explain.

   2. Why are High Tech's returns expected to move with the economy, whereas Collections's are expected to move counter to the economy?

b. Calculate the expected rate of return on each alternative, and fill in the blanks on the row for $\hat{r}$ in the previous table.

c. You should recognize that basing a decision solely on expected returns is appropriate only for risk-neutral individuals. Because your client, like most people, is risk-averse, the riskiness of each alternative is an important aspect of the decision. One possible measure of risk is the standard deviation of returns.

   1. Calculate this value for each alternative and fill in the blank on the row for σ in the table.

   2. What type of risk is measured by the standard deviation?

3. Draw a graph that shows *roughly* the shape of the probability distributions for High Tech, U.S. Rubber, and T-bills.

d. Suppose you suddenly remembered that the coefficient of variation (CV) is generally regarded as being a better measure of stand-alone risk than the standard deviation when the alternatives being considered have widely differing expected returns. Calculate the missing CVs, and fill in the blanks on the row for CV in the table. Does the CV produce the same risk rankings as the standard deviation? Explain.

e. Someone mentioned that you might also want to calculate the Sharpe ratio as a measure of stand-alone risk. Calculate the missing ratios and fill in the blanks on the row for the Sharpe ratio in the table. Briefly explain what the Sharpe ratio actually measures.

f. Suppose you created a two-stock portfolio by investing $50,000 in High Tech and $50,000 in Collections.

1. Calculate the expected return ($\hat{r}_p$), the standard deviation (σ_p), the coefficient of variation (CV_P), and the Sharpe ratio for this portfolio, and fill in the appropriate blanks in the table.
2. How does the riskiness of this two-stock portfolio compare with the riskiness of the individual stocks if they were held in isolation?

g. Suppose an investor starts with a portfolio consisting of one randomly selected stock.

1. What would happen to the riskiness and to the expected return of the portfolio as more randomly selected stocks were added to the portfolio?
2. What is the implication for investors? Draw a graph of the two portfolios to illustrate your answer.

h. 1. Should the effects of a portfolio impact the way investors think about the riskiness of individual stocks?

2. If you decided to hold a one-stock portfolio (and consequently were exposed to more risk than diversified investors), could you expect to be compensated for all of your risk; that is, could you earn a risk premium on the part of your risk that you could have eliminated by diversifying?

i. The expected rates of return and the beta coefficients of the alternatives supplied by an independent analyst are as follows:

Security	Return, $\hat{r}$	Risk (Beta)
High Tech	9.9%	1.31
Market	8.0	1.00
U.S. Rubber	7.3	0.88
T-bills	3.0	0.00
Collections	1.2	(0.50)

1. What is a beta coefficient, and how are betas used in risk analysis?
2. Do the expected returns appear to be related to each alternative's market risk?
3. Is it possible to choose among the alternatives on the basis of the information developed thus far? Use the data given at the start of the problem to construct a graph that shows how the T-bill's, High Tech's, and the market's beta coefficients are calculated. Then discuss what betas measure and how they are used in risk analysis.

j. The yield curve is currently flat; that is, long-term Treasury bonds also have a 3.0% yield. Consequently, Merrill Finch assumes that the risk-free rate is 3.0%.

1. Write out the security market line (SML) equation; use it to calculate the required rate of return on each alternative, and graph the relationship between the expected and required rates of return.
2. How do the expected rates of return compare with the required rates of return?
3. Does the fact that Collections has an expected return that is less than the T-bill rate make any sense? Explain.
4. What would be the market risk and the required return of a 50-50 portfolio of High Tech and Collections? Of High Tech and U.S. Rubber?

k. 1. Suppose investors raised their inflation expectations by 3 percentage points over current estimates as reflected in the 3.0% risk-free rate. What effect would higher inflation have on the SML and on the returns required on high- and low-risk securities?

2. Suppose instead that investors' risk aversion increased enough to cause the market risk premium to increase by 3 percentage points. (Inflation remains constant.) What effect would this have on the SML and on returns of high- and low-risk securities?

TAKING A CLOSER LOOK

Using Past Information to Estimate Required Returns

Use online resources to work on this chapter's questions. Please note that website information changes over time, and these changes may limit your ability to answer some of these questions.

Chapter 8 discussed the basic trade-off between risk and return. In the capital asset pricing model (CAPM) discussion, beta was identified as the correct measure of risk for diversified shareholders. Recall that beta measures the extent to which the returns of a given stock move with the stock market. When using the CAPM to estimate required returns, we would like to know how the stock will move with the market in the future, but because we don't have a crystal ball, we generally use historical data to estimate this relationship with beta.

As mentioned in Web Appendix 8A, beta can be estimated by regressing the individual stock's returns against the returns of the overall market. As an alternative to running our own regressions, we can rely on reported betas from a variety of sources. These published sources make it easy for us to readily obtain beta estimates for most large publicly traded corporations. However, a word of caution is in order. Beta estimates can often be quite sensitive to the time period in which the data are estimated, the market index used, and the frequency of the data used. Therefore, it is not uncommon to find a wide range of beta estimates among the various Internet websites.

Discussion Questions

1. Begin by looking at the historical performance of the overall stock market. Typically, on most of the financial websites you can enter S&P 500 and go right to the index's summary page. You will see a quick summary of the market's performance over the past 24 hours and 12 months. How has the market performed over the past year?
2. On the summary screen, you should see an interactive chart. Typically, you can chart performance over the last 24 hours, 1 month, 6 months—up to 5 years, or even longer. Select different time periods and watch how the graph changes. On this screen you should also see a menu to select historical prices (historical data). Some websites will not only show daily activity but also weekly or monthly activity. In addition, some websites will allow you to download the data into an Excel spreadsheet.
3. Now let's take a closer look at the stocks of four companies: Colgate Palmolive (Ticker = CL), McDonald's (MCD), Microsoft (MSFT), and Tiffany & Co (TIF). Before looking at the data, which of these companies would you expect to have a relatively high beta (greater than 1.0) and which of these companies would you expect to have a relatively low beta (less than 1.0)?
4. Select one of the four stocks listed in question 3 by entering the company's ticker symbol on the financial website you have chosen. On the screen you should see the interactive chart. Select the six-month time period and compare the stock's performance to the S&P 500's performance on the graph by adding the S&P 500 to the interactive chart. Has the stock outperformed or underperformed the overall market during this time period?
5. Go back to the summary page to see an estimate of the company's beta. What is the company's beta? What was the source of the estimated beta? Realize that if you go to another website, the beta shown could be different due to measurement differences.
6. What is the company's current dividend yield? What has been its total return to investors over the past year? Over the past 3 years? (Remember that total return includes the dividend yield plus any capital gains or losses.) You will have to go to more than one website to find this information. MSN Money (www.msn.com/en-us/money/markets) gives DPS information over the past 4 years on the detailed Income Statement Financials page. (Be sure to enter the ticker symbol in the quote search box located in the middle of your screen—not the web search box at the top of your screen.) You can use the price information to calculate dividend yield and capital gains yield. Yahoo! Finance provides historical price information.
7. Assume that the risk-free rate is 4% and the market risk premium is 5%. What is the required return on the company's stock?
8. Repeat the same exercise for each of the three remaining companies. Do the reported betas confirm your earlier intuition? In general, do you find that the higher-beta stocks tend to do better in up markets and worse in down markets? Explain.

Stocks and Their Valuation

CHAPTER 9

newphotoservice/Shutterstock.com

Searching for the Right Stock

Over the long run, returns in the U.S. stock market have been quite strong, averaging approximately 12% per year. However, these returns are far from certain, and there is considerable variation in the market's performance from year to year.

As we discussed in Chapter 8, the returns of individual stocks are even more volatile than the returns of the overall market. For example, in 2017, Boeing's stock price increased 94.71%, Align Technology's stock price increased 131.13%, and NRG Energy's stock price rose by 133.70%. Even with the S&P 500 up 21.83% in 2017, not all stocks fared well. On the down side, Mattel's stock price decreased by 41.85%, GE's stock price declined by 42.05%, and Under Armour's stock price fell 47.08%. This wide range in individual stocks' performance shows, first, that diversification is important and, second, that when it comes to picking stocks, it is not enough to simply pick a good company—the stock must also be "fairly" priced.

To determine whether a stock is fairly priced, you first need to estimate the stock's true value, or "intrinsic value," a concept first discussed in Chapter 1. With this objective in mind, in this chapter we describe some models that analysts have used to estimate intrinsic values. As you will see, though it is difficult to predict stock prices, we are not completely in the dark. Indeed, after studying this chapter, you should have a reasonably good understanding of the factors that influence stock prices; with that knowledge—plus a little luck—you should be able to successfully navigate the market's often treacherous ups and downs.

PUTTING THINGS IN PERSPECTIVE

In Chapter 7, we examined bonds and their valuation. We now turn to stocks, both common and preferred. Because the cash flows provided by bonds are set by contract, it is generally easy to predict their cash flows. Preferred stock dividends are also set by contract, which makes them similar to bonds, and they are valued in much the same way. However, common stock dividends are not contractual—they depend on the firm's earnings, which in turn depend on many random factors, making their valuation more difficult. Two fairly straightforward models are used to estimate stocks' intrinsic (or "true") values: (1) the discounted dividend model and (2) the corporate valuation model. A stock should, of course, be bought if its price is less than its estimated intrinsic value and sold if its price exceeds its intrinsic value.

By the time you finish this chapter, you should be able to do the following:

- **Discuss the legal rights of stockholders.**
- **Explain the distinction between a stock's price and its intrinsic value.**
- **Identify the two models that can be used to estimate a stock's intrinsic value: the discounted dividend model and the corporate valuation model.**
- **List the key characteristics of preferred stock, and describe how to estimate the value of preferred stock.**

Stock valuation is interesting in its own right, but you also need to understand valuation when estimating a firm's cost of capital for use in its capital budgeting analysis, which is probably a firm's most important task.

Key trends in the securities industry are listed and explained at ***sifma.org/resources/archive/research/***.

9-1 Legal Rights and Privileges of Common Stockholders

A corporation's common stockholders are the owners of the corporation, and as such, they have certain rights and privileges, as discussed in this section.

9-1A CONTROL OF THE FIRM

A firm's common stockholders have the right to elect its directors, who in turn elect the officers who manage the business. In a small firm, usually the major stockholder is also the president and chair of the board of directors. In large, publicly owned firms, the managers typically have some stock, but their personal holdings are generally insufficient to give them voting control. Thus, the managements of most publicly owned firms can be removed by the stockholders if the management team is not effective.

State and federal laws stipulate how stockholder control is to be exercised. First, corporations must hold elections of directors periodically, usually once a year, with the vote taken at the annual meeting. Typically, each share of stock has one vote; thus, the owner of 1,000 shares has 1,000 votes for each director.[1] Stockholders can appear at the annual meeting and vote in person, but they

[1]In the situation described, a 1,000-share stockholder could cast 1,000 votes for each of three directors if there were three contested seats on the board. An alternative procedure that may be prescribed in the corporate charter calls for *cumulative voting.* There the 1,000-share stockholder would get 3,000 votes if there were three vacancies, and he or she could cast all of them for one director. Cumulative voting helps small groups obtain representation on the board.

Proxy
A document giving one person the authority to act for another, typically the power to vote shares of common stock.

Proxy Fight
An attempt by a person or group to gain control of a firm by getting its stockholders to grant that person or group the authority to vote its shares to replace the current management.

Takeover
An action whereby a person or group succeeds in ousting a firm's management and taking control of the company.

more often transfer their right to vote to another person by means of a **proxy**. Management always solicits stockholders' proxies and usually receives them. However, if performance is poor and stockholders are dissatisfied, an outside group may solicit the proxies in an effort to overthrow management and take control of the business. This is known as a **proxy fight**. In other cases, another corporation may attempt to take the firm over by purchasing a majority of the outstanding stock. These actions are called **takeovers**. Some well-known examples of takeover battles in past years include KKR's acquisition of RJR Nabisco, Chevron's acquisition of Gulf Oil, and the QVC/Viacom fight to take over Paramount. In November 2009, Kraft Foods made a hostile takeover bid of $16.7 billion for Cadbury, the British chocolate and gum manufacturer. On January 19, 2010, Cadbury's management accepted Kraft's revised $21.8 billion buyout offer and agreed to recommend the offer to its shareholders. Interestingly, Kraft continued its deal-making in March 2015, when it announced plans to merge with Heinz, in a deal that was partially financed by the Brazilian private equity firm 3G Capital and Warren Buffett's Berkshire Hathaway. The merger was finalized in July 2015, and the firm is now known as The Kraft Heinz Company.

Managers without more than 50% of their firms' stock are very concerned about proxy fights and takeovers, and many of them have attempted to obtain stockholder approval for changes in their corporate charters that would make takeovers more difficult. For example, a number of companies have persuaded their stockholders to agree (1) to elect only one-third of the directors each year (rather than electing all directors each year), (2) to require 75% of the stockholders (rather than 50%) to approve a merger, and (3) to vote in a "poison pill" provision that would allow the stockholders of a firm that is taken over by another firm to buy shares in the second firm at a reduced price. The poison pill makes the acquisition unattractive and thus helps ward off hostile takeover attempts. Managers seeking such changes generally cite a fear that the firm will be picked up at a bargain price, but it often appears that the managers' concern about their own positions is the primary consideration.

Managers' moves to make takeovers more difficult have been countered by stockholders, especially large institutional stockholders, who do not like barriers erected to protect incompetent managers. To illustrate, the California Public Employees Retirement System (CalPERS), which is one of the largest institutional investors, has led proxy fights with several corporations whose financial performances were poor in CalPERS's judgment. CalPERS wants companies to increase outside (nonmanagement) directors' ability to force managers to be more responsive to stockholder complaints.

Managers' pay is another contentious issue. It has been asserted that in some cases CEOs receive excessive compensation because they are too closely aligned with the company's board of directors. At the same time, enlightened boards want to reward CEOs when they act in shareholders' interests, but also hold them accountable for poor performance. CalPERS and other institutional investors have further encouraged firms to make their compensation packages more transparent and aligned with shareholders' interests. Similarly, the Dodd-Frank bill imposed a Say-on-Pay provision, which provides shareholders the ability to vote on executive compensation. Although this provision is nonbinding it imposes some pressure on managers who don't want to see shareholders voting to disapprove of their pay package. For example, in 2014, Coca-Cola adjusted the compensation package of its senior executives after receiving negative feedback from Warren Buffett and other shareholders.[2] In fact, in April 2018, 75% of voting shareholders of Ameriprise Financial Inc., a financial planning, asset management, and insurance product firm, rejected the

[2]For a discussion about this, refer to Anupreeta Das, Mike Esterl, and Joann S. Lublin, "Buffett Pressures Coca-Cola over Executive Pay," *The Wall Street Journal* (www.wsj.com), April 30, 2014; and Mark Melin, "Coca-Cola Changes Pay Plan, Warren Buffett Influence Credited," *ValueWalk* (www.valuewalk.com), October 1, 2014.

firm's 2017 compensation plan. The vote was nonbinding; however, the firm's board will consider the vote and reassess its compensation package to better align it with shareholder value creation.[3]

For many years, SEC rules prohibited large investors such as CalPERS from getting together to force corporate managers to institute policy changes. However, the SEC began changing its rules in 1993, and now large investors can work together to force management changes. These rulings have helped keep managers focused on stockholder concerns. Indeed, there is no sign that activist investors are slowing down. A May 2017 front-page article in *The Wall Street Journal* reported that "so far, in 2017, activists have started 9 campaigns targeting top management, the fastest pace on record, according to FactSet."[4] In 2017, activist investors helped remove the CEOs of General Electric, American International Group, Arconic Inc., CSX, Pandora Media Inc., Perrigo, and Buffalo Wild Wings.[5]

9-1B THE PREEMPTIVE RIGHT

Common stockholders often have the right, called the **preemptive right**, to purchase on a pro rata basis any additional shares sold by the firm. In some states, the preemptive right is automatically included in every corporate charter; in other states, it must be specifically inserted into the charter.

Preemptive Right
A provision in the corporate charter or bylaws that gives common stockholders the right to purchase on a pro rata basis new issues of common stock (or convertible securities).

The purpose of the preemptive right is twofold. First, it prevents the management of a corporation from issuing a large number of additional shares and purchasing those shares itself. Management could use this tactic to seize control of the corporation and frustrate the will of the current stockholders. The second, and far more important, reason for the preemptive right is to protect stockholders from a dilution of value. For example, suppose 1,000 shares of common stock, each with a price of $100, were outstanding, making the total market value of the firm $100,000. If an additional 1,000 shares were sold at $50 a share, or for $50,000, this would raise the firm's total market value to $150,000. When the new total market value is divided by the 2,000 total shares now outstanding, a value of $75 a share is obtained. The old stockholders would thus lose $25 per share, and the new stockholders would have an instant profit of $25 per share. Thus, selling common stock at a price below the market value would dilute a firm's price and transfer wealth from its present stockholders to those who were allowed to purchase the new shares. The preemptive right prevents this.

Self*Test*

Identify some actions that companies have taken to make takeovers more difficult.

What is the preemptive right, and what are the two primary reasons for its existence?

9-2 Types of Common Stock

Although most firms have only one type of common stock, in some instances, **classified stock** is used to meet special needs. Generally, when special classifications are used, one type is designated *Class A*, another *Class B*, and so forth. Small,

Classified Stock
Common stock that is given a special designation such as Class A or Class B to meet special needs of the company.

[3]Mark Reilly, "Ameriprise Shareholders Revolt over Pay for Top Executives," *Minneapolis/St. Paul Business Journal* (www.bizjournals.com), April 30, 2018.

[4]Refer to David Benoit, "Activist Investors Have a New Bloodlust: CEOs," *The Wall Street Journal* (www.wsj.com), May 16, 2017.

[5]Refer to Ronald Orol, "Activists Forced CEOs to Leave These Huge Companies This Year," *The Street* (www.thestreet.com), July 8, 2017.

ARE "SMART BETA" FUNDS A SMART IDEA?

In Chapter 8, we demonstrated the benefits of diversification. These benefits lead many experts to recommend that investors regularly hold some portion of their wealth in well-diversified index funds. These index funds have the benefit of providing diversification with low transactions costs. For example, a Vanguard fund that tracks the S&P 500 has total transactions costs that are less than 0.20% of the total amount invested.

In effect, these funds are holding a portfolio of S&P 500 stocks, where each stock's weight in the portfolio is determined by its current market capitalization (which is its stock price multiplied by the number of shares outstanding). So, for example, if a stock's market capitalization equals 1% of the total market capitalization of the S&P 500, then an S&P 500 index fund or exchange traded fund would have 1% invested in that stock.

While generally applauded, some analysts have expressed concern that index funds may typically overinvest in "overvalued" stocks. Here's the idea: As stocks become overvalued, their market capitalization rises (to levels above what should be given their intrinsic value), and this increase automatically results in an index fund holding a larger percentage of the overvalued stock. To address these concerns, fund investments have arisen that use portfolio weights that are based on approaches other than market capitalization. Oftentimes these alternatives are characterized as "smart beta" or "strategic beta" funds.

These funds typically use a variety of different approaches for weighting the index. For example, some use an equal weighted approach where each stock in the index has the same weight regardless of market capitalization. Others weight the stocks according to some "fundamentals" such as dividends or earnings that are believed to be correlated with intrinsic value. In a recent article on CNBC.com, a Morningstar analyst highlighted the rapid growth of smart beta products and summarized them in the following way:

> "What investors are getting here is an active bet, and no two products are the same even if they have the same strategy," said Morningstar analyst Alex Bryan. "Fees are usually considerably lower than [those associated with] actively managed funds, but more than with traditional index funds."

As you might expect, not all analysts think that smart beta is a smart idea. Even an early proponent of these products who has been characterized by *The Wall Street Journal* as the "godfather of smart beta" has raised concerns about the valuation and underlying risk of some of the newer products. Others point out that you are still paying higher fees to try to outguess the market, something which has been notoriously hard to do for many funds. Perhaps not surprisingly, Jack Bogle, Vanguard's founder and a long-time champion of index funds, has characterized smart beta investing as "stupid."

Sources: "Do 'Smart Beta' Funds Outperform Index Funds?" finance.yahoo.com, March 16, 2015; and Aaron Kuriloff, "Rob Arnott, 'Godfather of Smart Beta,' Tells Investors: You're Doing it Wrong," *The Wall Street Journal* (www.wsj.com), April 28, 2017.

new companies seeking funds from outside sources frequently use different types of common stock. For example, when Google went public, it sold Class A stock to the public while its Class B stock was retained by the company's insiders. The key difference is that the Class B stock has 10 votes per share while the Class A stock has 1 vote per share. Google's Class B shares are predominantly held by the company's two founders and its current CEO. Taking things a step further, when Snap went public in 2017, its newly issued shares had zero voting rights. More broadly, Jay Ritter, an expert on IPOs at the University of Florida, has estimated that 19% of the tech companies that went public between 2012 and 2016, issued multiple classes of stock.[6]

Founders' Shares
Stock owned by the firm's founders that enables them to maintain control over the company without having to own a majority of stock.

The use of classified stock enables the company's founders to maintain control over the company without having to own a majority of the common stock. For this reason, Class B stock of this type is sometimes called **founders' shares**. Because *dual-class* share structures of this type give special voting privileges to key insiders, these structures are sometimes criticized because they may enable insiders to make decisions that are counter to the interests of the majority of stockholders. With these concerns in mind, S&P Dow Jones Indices recently

[6]Refer to Maureen Farrell, "In Snap IPO, New Investors to Get Zero Votes, While Founders Keep Control," *The Wall Street Journal* (www.wsj.com), January 16, 2017.

announced that it would no longer allow companies with dual-class shares to be added to the S&P 500 Index.[7]

Note that "Class A," "Class B," and so forth have no standard meanings. Most firms have no classified shares, but a firm that does could designate its Class B shares as founders' shares and its Class A shares as those sold to the public, while another could reverse those designations. Still other firms could use stock classifications for entirely different purposes. For example, when General Motors acquired Hughes Aircraft for $5 billion, it paid in part with a new Class H common, GMH, which had limited voting rights and whose dividends were tied to Hughes's performance as a GM subsidiary. The reasons for the new stock were that (1) GM wanted to limit voting privileges on the new classified stock because of management's concern about a possible takeover and (2) Hughes's employees wanted to be rewarded more directly on Hughes's own performance than would have been possible through regular GM stock. These Class H shares disappeared in 2003 when GM decided to sell off the Hughes unit.

SelfTest

What are some reasons a company might use classified stock?

9-3 Stock Price versus Intrinsic Value

We saw in Chapter 1 that a manager should seek to maximize the value of his or her firm's stock. In that chapter, we also emphasized the difference between stock price and intrinsic value. The stock price is simply the current market price, and it is easily observed for publicly traded companies. By contrast, intrinsic value, which represents the "true" value of the company's stock, cannot be directly observed and must instead be estimated. Figure 9.1 illustrates once again the connection between stock price and intrinsic value.

As the figure suggests, market equilibrium occurs when the stock's price equals its intrinsic value. If the stock market is reasonably efficient, gaps between the stock price and intrinsic value should not be very large, and they should not persist for very long. However, in some cases, an individual company's stock may trade for an extended period of time at a price much higher or lower than its intrinsic value. As we discussed in Chapter 2, behavioral finance theory has used principles from psychology to try to understand why investors' irrationality at times can lead investors to systematically misevaluate the quality and risk of certain investments for a sustained period of time.[8] As a notable example, several years leading up to the credit crunch of 2007–2008, most of the large investment banks were reporting record profits and selling at record prices. However, much of those earnings were illusory because they did not reflect the huge risks that existed in the mortgage-backed securities that these firms were purchasing. So with hindsight, we now know that the market prices of most financial firms' stocks exceeded their intrinsic values just prior to 2007. Then when the market

[7]Refer to Chris Dieterich, Maureen Farrell, and Sarah Krouse, "Stock Indexes Push Back Against Dual-Class Listings," *The Wall Street Journal* (www.wsj.com), August 2, 2017; and Ken Brown, "Indexers Push Back Against Wall Street," *The Wall Street Journal* (www.wsj.com), August 1, 2017.

[8]More recently, Professor Andrew Lo has put forward the *adaptive markets* hypothesis. In his analysis, he uses principles of evolution to explain how market participants often use simple rules of thumb to adapt to changing environments. His work provides an interesting bridge between behavioral finance and market efficiency. For further details refer to Andrew W. Lo, *Adaptive Markets: Financial Evolution at the Speed of Thought* (Princeton, NJ: Princeton University Press, 2017).

FIGURE 9.1 Determinants of Intrinsic Values and Stock Prices

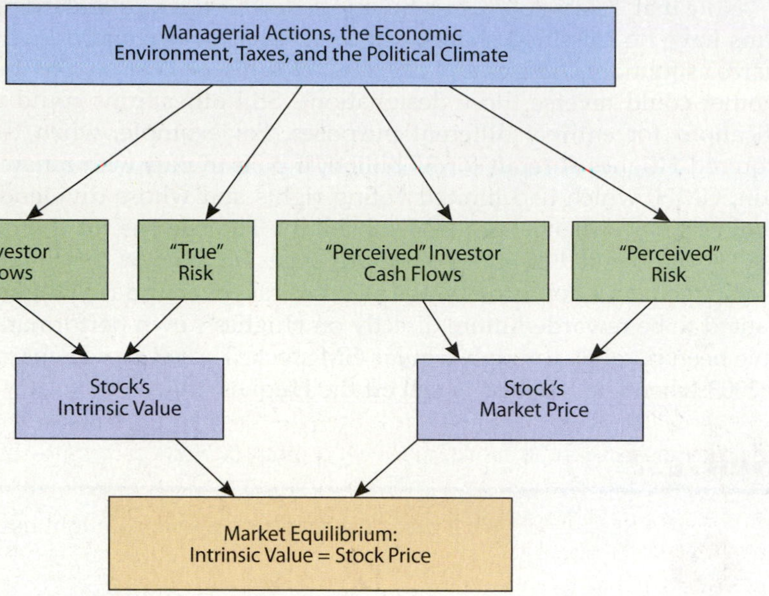

realized what was happening, those stock prices crashed. Citigroup, Merrill Lynch, and others lost more than 60% of their value in a few short months, and Bear Stearns, at that time the fifth-largest investment bank, saw its stock price drop from $171 in 2007 to $2 just before its ultimate collapse in mid-March 2008. It clearly pays to question market prices at times!

9-3A WHY DO INVESTORS AND COMPANIES CARE ABOUT INTRINSIC VALUE?

The remainder of this chapter focuses primarily on different approaches for estimating a stock's intrinsic value. Before these approaches are described, it is worth asking why it is important for investors and companies to understand how to calculate intrinsic value.

When investing in common stocks, one's goal is to purchase stocks that are undervalued (i.e., the price is below the stock's intrinsic value) and avoid stocks that are overvalued. Consequently, Wall Street analysts, institutional investors who control mutual funds and pension funds, and many individual investors are interested in finding reliable models that help predict a stock's intrinsic value.

Investors obviously care about intrinsic value, but managers also need to understand how intrinsic value is estimated. First, managers need to know how alternative actions are likely to affect stock prices; the models of intrinsic value that we cover help demonstrate the connection between managerial decisions and firm value. Second, managers should consider whether their stock is significantly undervalued or overvalued before making certain decisions. For example, firms should consider carefully the decision to issue new shares if they believe their stock is undervalued; an estimate of their stock's intrinsic value is the key to such decisions.

Two basic models are used to estimate intrinsic values: the *discounted dividend model* and the *corporate valuation model.* The dividend model focuses on dividends, while the corporate model goes beyond dividends and focuses on sales, costs, and free cash flows. In the following sections, we describe these approaches in more detail.

Self*Test*

What is the difference between a stock's price and its intrinsic value?

Why do investors and managers need to understand how to estimate a firm's intrinsic value?

What are two commonly used approaches for estimating a stock's intrinsic value? How do they differ in their focus?

9-4 The Discounted Dividend Model

The value of a share of common stock depends on the cash flows it is expected to provide, and those flows consist of two elements: (1) the dividends the investor receives each year while he or she holds the stock and (2) the price received when the stock is sold. The final price includes the original price paid plus an expected capital gain. Keep in mind that there are many different investors in the market and thus many different sets of expectations. Therefore, investors will have different opinions about a stock's true intrinsic value and thus its proper price. The analysis as performed by the **marginal investor**, whose actions actually determine the equilibrium stock price, is critical, but every investor, marginal or not, implicitly goes through the same type of analysis.

Marginal Investor
A representative investor whose actions reflect the beliefs of those people who are currently trading a stock. It is the marginal investor who determines a stock's price.

The following terms are used in our analysis:[9]

D_t = the dividend a stockholder expects to receive at the end of each Year t. D_0 is the last dividend the company paid. Because it has already been paid, a buyer of the stock will not receive D_0. The first dividend a new buyer will receive is D_1, which is paid at the end of Year 1. D_2 is the dividend expected at the end of Year 2; D_3, at the end of Year 3; and so forth. D_0 is known with certainty, but D_1, D_2, and all other future dividends are *expected values*, and different investors can have different expectations.[10] Our primary concern is with D_t as forecasted by the *marginal investor*.

P_0 = actual **market price** of the stock today. $\mathbf{P_0}$ is known with certainty, but predicted future prices are subject to uncertainty.

Market Price, P_0
The price at which a stock sells in the market.

$\hat{P}_t$ = both the expected price and the expected intrinsic value of the stock at the end of each Year t (pronounced "P hat t") as seen by the investor doing

[9]Many terms are described here, and students sometimes get concerned about having to memorize all of them. We tell our students that we will provide formula sheets for use on exams, so they don't have to try to memorize everything. With their minds thus eased, they end up learning what the terms actually mean rather than memorizing formulas.

[10]Stocks generally pay dividends quarterly, so theoretically we should evaluate them on a quarterly basis. However, most analysts actually work with annual data because forecasted stock data are not precise enough to warrant the use of a quarterly model. For additional information on the quarterly model, see Charles M. Linke and J. Kenton Zumwalt, "Estimation Biases in Discounted Cash Flow Analysis of Equity Capital Costs in Rate Regulation," *Financial Management*, vol. 13, no. 3 (Autumn 1984), pp. 15–21.

the analysis. $\hat{P}_t$ is based on the investor's estimates of the dividend stream and the riskiness of that stream. There are many investors in the market, so there can be many estimates for $\hat{P}_t$. However, for the marginal investor, P_0 must equal $\hat{P}_0$. Otherwise, a disequilibrium would exist, and buying and selling in the market would soon result in P_0 equaling $\hat{P}_0$ as seen by the marginal investor.

Growth Rate, g
The expected rate of growth in dividends per share.

g = expected **growth rate g** in dividends as predicted by an investor. If dividends are expected to grow at a constant rate, g should also equal the expected growth rate in earnings and the stock's price. Different investors use different g's to evaluate a firm's stock, but the market price, P_0, is based on g as estimated by the marginal investor.

Required Rate of Return, r_s
The minimum rate of return on a common stock that a stockholder considers acceptable.

r_s = **required**, or minimum acceptable, **rate of return** on the stock considering its riskiness and the returns available on other investments. Different investors typically have different opinions, but the key is again the marginal investor. The determinants of $\mathbf{r_s}$ include factors discussed in Chapter 8, including the real rate of return, expected inflation, and risk.

Expected Rate of Return, $\hat{r}_s$
The rate of return on a common stock that a stockholder expects to receive in the future.

$\hat{r}_s$ = **expected rate of return** (pronounced "r hat s") that an investor believes the stock will provide in the future. The expected return can be above or below the required return, but a rational investor will buy the stock if $\mathbf{\hat{r}_s}$ exceeds r_s, sell the stock if $\hat{r}_s$ is less than r_s, and simply hold the stock if these returns are equal. Again, the key is the marginal investor, whose views determine the actual stock price.

Actual (Realized) Rate of Return, $\bar{r}_s$
The rate of return on a common stock actually received by stockholders in some past period; $\bar{r}_s$ may be greater or less than $\hat{r}_s$ and/or r_s.

$\bar{r}_s$ = **actual**, or **realized**, *after-the-fact* **rate of return**, pronounced "r bar s." You can *expect* to obtain a return of $\mathbf{\bar{r}_s}$ = 10% if you buy a stock today, but if the market declines, you may earn an actual realized return that is much lower, perhaps even negative.

Dividend Yield
The expected dividend divided by the current price of a share of stock.

D_1/P_0 = **dividend yield** expected during the coming year. If Company X's stock is expected to pay a dividend of D_1 = \$1 during the next 12 months and if X's current price is P_0 = \$20, the expected dividend yield will be \$1/\$20 = 0.05 = 5%. Different investors could have different expectations for D_1, but again, the marginal investor is the key.

Capital Gains Yield
The capital gain during a given year divided by the beginning price.

$(\hat{P}_1 - P_0)/P_0$ = expected **capital gains yield** on the stock during the coming year. If the stock sells for \$20.00 today and if it is expected to rise to \$21.00 by the end of the year, the expected capital gain will be $\hat{P}_1 - P_0$ = \$21.00 − \$20.00 = \$1.00 and the expected capital gains yield will be \$1.00/\$20.00 = 0.05 = 5%. Different investors can have different expectations for $\hat{P}_1$, but the marginal investor is key.

Expected Total Return
The sum of the expected dividend yield and the expected capital gains yield.

Expected total return = $\hat{r}_s$ = expected dividend yield (D_1/P_0) plus expected capital gains yield $[(\hat{P}_1 - P_0)/P_0]$. In our example, the **expected total return** = 5% + 5% = 10%.

All active investors hope to achieve better-than-average returns—they hope to identify stocks whose intrinsic values exceed their current prices and whose expected returns (expected by this investor) exceed their required rates of return. Note, though, that about half of all investors are likely to be disappointed. A good understanding of the points made in this chapter can help you avoid being disappointed.

9-4A EXPECTED DIVIDENDS AS THE BASIS FOR STOCK VALUES

In our discussion of bonds, we used Equation 7.1 to find the value of a bond; the equation is the present value of interest payments over the bond's life plus the present value of its maturity (or par) value:

$$V_B = \frac{INT}{(1 + r_d)^1} + \frac{INT}{(1 + r_d)^2} + \cdots + \frac{INT}{(1 + r_d)^N} + \frac{M}{(1 + r_d)^N}$$

Stock prices are likewise determined as the present value of a stream of cash flows, and the basic stock valuation equation is similar to the one for bonds. What are the cash flows that a corporation will provide to its stockholders? To answer that question, think of yourself as an investor who purchases the stock of a company that is expected to exist indefinitely (e.g., GE). You intend to hold it (in your family) forever. In this case, all you (and your heirs) will receive is a stream of dividends, and the value of the stock today can be calculated as the present value of an infinite stream of dividends:

$$\begin{aligned} \text{Value of stock} = \hat{P}_0 &= \text{PV of expected future dividends} \\ &= \frac{D_1}{(1 + r_s)^1} + \frac{D_2}{(1 + r_s)^2} + \cdots + \frac{D_\infty}{(1 + r_s)^\infty} \\ &= \sum_{t=1}^{\infty} \frac{D_t}{(1 + r_s)^t} \end{aligned} \quad \textbf{9.1}$$

What about the more typical case, where you expect to hold the stock for a finite period and then sell it—what will be the value of $\hat{P}_0$ in this case? Unless the company is likely to be liquidated or sold and thus disappears, *the value of the stock is again determined by Equation 9.1.* To see this, recognize that for any individual investor, the expected cash flows consist of expected dividends plus the expected sale price of the stock. However, the sale price to the current investor depends on the dividends some future investor expects, and that investor's expected sale price is also dependent on some future dividends, and so forth. Therefore, for all present and future investors in total, expected cash flows must be based on expected future dividends. Put another way, unless a firm is liquidated or sold to another concern, the cash flows it provides to its stockholders will consist only of a stream of dividends. Therefore, the value of a share of stock must be established as the present value of the stock's expected dividend stream.[11]

---

[11]The general validity of Equation 9.1 can also be confirmed by asking yourself the following question: Suppose I buy a stock and expect to hold it for 1 year. I will receive dividends during the year plus the value $\hat{P}_1$ when I sell it at the end of the year. But what will determine the value of $\hat{P}_1$? The answer is that it will be determined as the present value of the dividends expected during Year 2 plus the stock price at the end of that year, which in turn will be determined as the present value of another set of future dividends and an even more distant stock price. This process can be continued ad infinitum, and the ultimate result is Equation 9.1.

We should note that investors periodically lose sight of the long-run nature of stocks as investments and forget that in order to sell a stock at a profit, one must find a buyer who will pay the higher price. If you analyze a stock's value in accordance with Equation 9.1, conclude that the stock's market price exceeds a reasonable value, and buy the stock anyway, you would be following the *"bigger fool" theory of investment*—you think you may be a fool to buy the stock at its excessive price, but you also believe that when you get ready to sell it, you can find someone who is an even bigger fool. The bigger fool theory was widely followed in the summer of 2000, just before the stock market crashed.

Self*Test*

Explain the following statement: Whereas a bond contains a promise to pay interest, a share of common stock typically provides an expectation of, but no promise of, dividends plus capital gains.

What are the two parts of most stocks' expected total return?

If $D_1 = \$2.00$, $g = 6\%$, and $P_0 = \$40.00$, what are the stock's expected dividend yield, capital gains yield, and total expected return for the coming year? **(5%, 6%, 11%)**

Is it necessary for all investors to have the same expectations regarding a stock for the stock to be in equilibrium?

What would happen to a stock's price if the "marginal investor" examined a stock and concluded that its intrinsic value was greater than its current market price?

9-5 Constant Growth Stocks

Equation 9.1 is a generalized stock valuation model in the sense that the time pattern of D_t can be anything: D_t can be rising, falling, or fluctuating randomly, or it can be zero for several years. Equation 9.1 can be applied in any of these situations, and with a computer spreadsheet, we can easily use the equation to find a stock's intrinsic value—provided we have an estimate of the future dividends. However, it is not easy to obtain accurate estimates of future dividends.

Still, for many companies it is reasonable to predict that dividends will grow at a constant rate. In this case, Equation 9.1 may be rewritten as follows:

$$\hat{P}_0 = \frac{D_0(1+g)^1}{(1+r_s)^1} + \frac{D_0(1+g)^2}{(1+r_s)^2} + \cdots + \frac{D_0(1+g)^\infty}{(1+r_s)^\infty} = \frac{D_0(1+g)}{r_s - g} = \frac{D_1}{r_s - g} \quad (9.2)$$

Constant Growth (Gordon) Model Used to find the value of a constant growth stock.

The last term of Equation 9.2 is the **constant growth**, or **Gordon, model**, named after Myron J. Gordon, who did much to develop and popularize it.[12]

The term r_s in Equation 9.2 is the *required rate of return*, which is a riskless rate plus a risk premium. However, we know that if the stock is in equilibrium, the required rate of return must equal the expected rate of return, which is the expected dividend yield plus an expected capital gains yield. So we can solve Equation 9.2 for r_s, but now using the hat to indicate that we are dealing with an expected rate of return:[13]

$$\text{Expected rate of return} = \text{Expected dividend yield} + \text{Expected growth rate, or capital gains yield} \quad (9.3)$$

$$\hat{r}_s = \frac{D_1}{P_0} + g$$

We illustrate Equations 9.2 and 9.3 in the following section.

[12]The last term in Equation 9.2 is derived in the Web Extension of Chapter 8 of Eugene F. Brigham and Phillip R. Daves, *Intermediate Financial Management*, 13th edition (Mason, OH: Cengage Learning, 2019). In essence, Equation 9.2 is the sum of a geometric progression, and the final result is the solution value of the progression.

[13]The r_s value in Equation 9.2 is a *required* rate of return, but when we transform Equation 9.2 to obtain Equation 9.3, we solve for an *expected* rate of return. Obviously, the transformation requires that $r_s = \hat{r}_s$. This equality must hold if the stock is in equilibrium, as most normally are.

9-5A ILLUSTRATION OF A CONSTANT GROWTH STOCK

Table 9.1 presents an analysis of Keller Medical Products's stock as performed by a security analyst after a meeting for analysts and other investors presided over by Keller's CFO. The table looks complicated, but it is really quite straightforward.[14] Part I, in the upper left corner, provides some basic data. The last dividend, which was just paid, was \$1.00; the stock's last closing price was \$20.80; and it is in equilibrium. Based on an analysis of Keller's history and likely future, the analyst forecasts that earnings and dividends will grow at a constant rate of 4% per year and that the stock's price will grow at this same rate. Moreover, the analyst believes that the most appropriate required rate of return is 9%. Different analysts might use different inputs, but we

resource

Students can download the Excel chapter models from the textbook's student companion site on cengage.com. Once downloaded onto your computer, retrieve the Chapter 9 Excel model and follow along as you read this chapter.

Analysis of a Constant Growth Stock **TABLE 9.1**

	A	B	C–G	H–I
3				
4	**I. Basic Information:**		**II. Formulas Used in the Analysis:**	
5	D_0 =	\$1.00	Dividend in Year t, D_t, in column 2	$D_{t-1}(1 + g)$
6	P_0 =	\$20.80	Intrinsic value (and price) in Year t, P_t, in column 3	$D_{t+1} / (r_s - g)$
7	g =	4.00%	Dividend yield (constant) in column 4	D_t / P_{t-1}
8	r_s =	9.00%	Capital gains yield (constant) in column 5	$(P_t - P_{t-1}) / P_{t-1}$
9			Total return (constant) in column 6	Div. yield + CG yield
10			PV of dividends discounted at 9% in column 7	$D_t / (1 + r_s)^t$

11	**III. Examples:**			
12		column 2	D_1 = \$1.00(1.04)	\$1.04
13		column 3	P_0 = \$1.04 / (0.09 − 0.04)	\$20.80
14		column 4	Dividend yield, Year 1: \$1.04 / \$20.80	5.0%
15		column 5	Cap gains yield, Year 1: (\$21.63 − \$20.80) / \$20.80	4.0%
16		column 6	Total return, Year 1: 5.0% + 4.0%	9.0%
17		column 7	PV of D_1 discounted at 9.0%	\$0.95
18				

	IV. Forecasted Results over Time:						
20–22	At end of year: (1)	Dividend (2)	Price* (3)	Dividend yield (4)	Capital gains yield (5)	Total return (6)	PV of dividend at 9.0% (7)
23	2019	\$1.00	\$20.80				
24	2020	\$1.04	\$21.63	5.0%	4.0%	9.0%	\$0.95
25	2021	\$1.08	\$22.50	5.0%	4.0%	9.0%	\$0.91
26	2022	\$1.12	\$23.40	5.0%	4.0%	9.0%	\$0.87
27	2023	\$1.17	\$24.33	5.0%	4.0%	9.0%	\$0.83
28	2024	\$1.22	\$25.31	5.0%	4.0%	9.0%	\$0.79
29	2025	\$1.27	\$26.32	5.0%	4.0%	9.0%	\$0.75
30	2026	\$1.32	\$27.37	5.0%	4.0%	9.0%	\$0.72
31	2027	\$1.37	\$28.47	5.0%	4.0%	9.0%	\$0.69
32	2028	\$1.42	\$29.60	5.0%	4.0%	9.0%	\$0.66
33	2029	\$1.48	\$30.79	5.0%	4.0%	9.0%	\$0.63
34	↓						↓
35	∞			Sum of PVs from 1 to ∞ = P_0 =			**\$20.80** = Value on 1/1/2020
36							

37 *Because this is a constant growth stock, we could have found the value for P_t as $P_{t-1}(1 + g)$. For example, P_1 = \$20.80(1.04) = \$21.63.

[14]You may notice some minor "errors" in the table. These are not errors—they are simply differences caused by rounding.

assume for now that because this analyst is widely followed, her results represent those of the marginal investor.

Look at part IV, where we show the predicted stream of dividends and stock prices along with annual values for the dividend yield, the capital gains yield, and the expected total return. Notice that the total return shown in column 6 is equal to the required rate of return shown in part I. This indicates that the stock analyst thinks that the stock is fairly priced; hence, it is in equilibrium. She forecasted data for 10 years, but she could have forecasted out to infinity.

Part II shows the formulas used to calculate the data in part IV, and part III gives examples of the calculations. For example, D_1, the first dividend a purchaser would receive, is forecasted to be $D_1 = \$1.00(1.04) = \$1.04$, and the other forecasted dividends in column 2 were calculated similarly. The estimated intrinsic values shown in column 3 are based on Equation 9.2, the constant growth model: $P_0 = D_1/(r_s - g) = \$1.04/(0.09 - 0.04) = \$20.80$, $\hat{P}_1 = \$21.63$, and so forth.

Column 4 shows the dividend yield, which for 2020 is $D_1/P_0 = 5.0\%$, and this number is constant thereafter. The capital gain expected during 2020 is $\hat{P}_1 - P_0 = \$21.63 - \$20.80 = \$0.83$, which when divided by P_0 gives the expected capital gains yield, $\$0.83/\$20.80 = 4.0\%$. The total return is found as the dividend yield plus the capital gains yield, 9.0%, and it is both constant and equal to the required rate of return given in part I.

Finally, look at column 7 in the table. Here we find the present value of each of the dividends shown in column 2, discounted at the required rate of return. For example, the PV of $D_1 = \$1.04/(1.09)^1 = \$0.95$, the PV of $D_2 = \$1.08/(1.09)^2 = \$0.91$, and so forth. If you extended the table out to about 170 years (with Excel, this is easy), then summed the PVs of the dividends, you would obtain the same value as that found using Equation 9.2, \$20.80.[15] Figure 9.2 shows graphically what's happening. We extended the table out 20 years and then plotted dividends from column 2 in the upper step function curve and the PV of those dividends in the lower curve. The sum of the PVs is an estimate of the stock's forecasted intrinsic value.

Note that in Table 9.1, the forecasted intrinsic value is equal to the current stock price, and the expected total return is equal to the required rate of return. In this situation, the analyst would call the stock a "Hold" and would recommend that investors not buy or sell it. However, if the analyst were somewhat more optimistic and thought the growth rate would be 5.0% rather than 4.0%, the forecasted intrinsic value would be (by Equation 9.2) \$26.25 and the analyst would call it a "Buy." At $g = 3.0\%$, the intrinsic value would be \$17.17 and the stock would be a "Sell." Changes in the required rate of return would produce similar changes in the forecasted intrinsic value and thus the equilibrium current price.

9-5B DIVIDENDS VERSUS GROWTH

The discounted dividend model as expressed in Equation 9.2 shows that, other things held constant, a higher value for D_1 increases a stock's price. However, Equation 9.2 shows that a higher growth rate also increases the stock's price. But now recognize the following:

- Dividends are paid out of earnings.
- Therefore, growth in dividends requires growth in earnings.

[15]The dividends get quite large, but the discount rate exceeds the growth rate, and so the PVs of the dividends become quite small. In theory, you would have to go out to infinity to find the exact price of a constant growth stock, but the difference between the Equation 9.2 value and the sum of the PVs can't be seen out to two decimal places if you extend the analysis to 170 periods.

FIGURE 9.2 Present Values of Dividends of a Constant Growth Stock Where $D_0 = \$1.00$, $g = 4.0\%$, $r_s = 9.0\%$

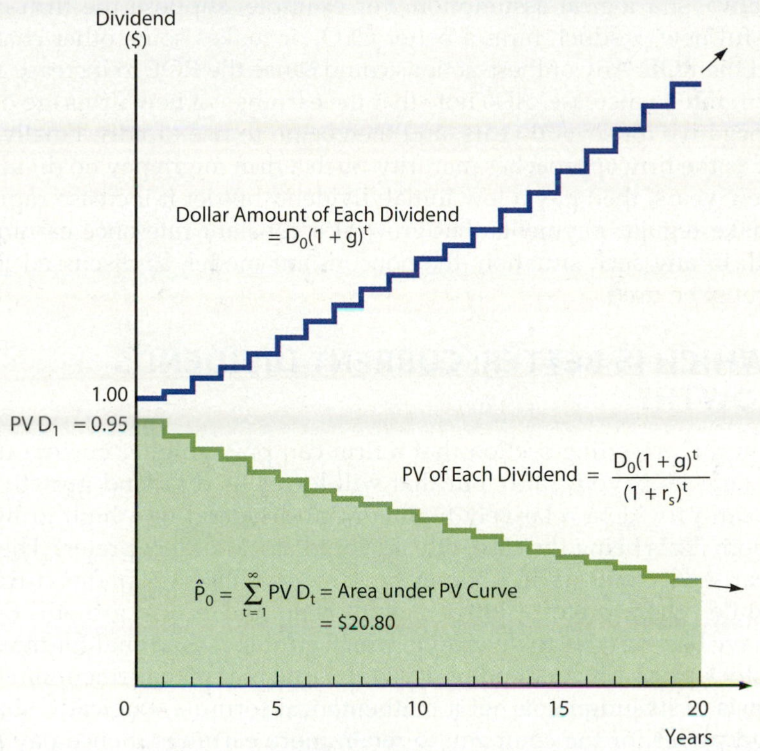

- Earnings growth in the long run occurs primarily because firms retain earnings and reinvest them in the business.
- Therefore, the higher the percentage of earnings retained, the higher the growth rate.

To illustrate this, suppose you inherit a business that has \$1,000,000 of assets and no debt, thus \$1,000,000 of equity. The expected return on equity (ROE) equals 10.0%, so its expected earnings for the coming year are (0.10)(\$1,000,000) = \$100,000. You could take out the entire \$100,000 of earnings in dividends, or you could reinvest some or all of the \$100,000 in the business. If you pay out all the earnings, you will have \$100,000 of dividend income this year, but dividends will not grow because assets, and therefore earnings, will not grow.

However, suppose you decide to have the firm pay out 60% and retain 40%. Now your dividend income in Year 1 will be \$60,000, but assets will rise by \$40,000, and earnings and dividends will likewise increase:

Next year's earnings = Prior earnings + ROE(Retained earnings)
= \$100,000 + 0.1(\$40,000)
= \$104,000
Next year's dividends = 0.6(\$104,000) = \$62,400

Moreover, your dividend income will continue to grow by 4% per year thereafter:

$$\text{Growth rate} = (1 - \text{Payout ratio})\text{ROE} = (1 - 0.6)10.0\% = 0.4(10.0\%) = 4.0\% \quad (9.4)$$

This demonstrates that in the long run, growth in dividends depends primarily on the firm's payout ratio and its ROE.

In our example, we assumed that other things remain constant. This is often, but not always, a logical assumption. For example, suppose the firm develops a successful new product, hires a better CEO, or makes some other change that increased the ROE. Any of these actions could cause the ROE to increase and thus the growth rate to increase. Also note that the earnings of new firms are often low or even negative for several years, and then begin to rise rapidly. Finally, growth levels off as the firm approaches maturity. Such a firm might pay no dividends for its first few years, then pay a low initial dividend but let it increase rapidly, and finally make regular payments that grow at a constant rate once earnings have stabilized. In any such situation, the nonconstant model, as discussed in a later section, must be used.

9-5C WHICH IS BETTER: CURRENT DIVIDENDS OR GROWTH?

We saw in the preceding section that a firm can pay a higher current dividend by increasing its payout ratio, but that will lower its dividend growth rate. So the firm can provide a relatively high current dividend or a high growth rate, but not both. This being the case, which would stockholders prefer? The answer is not clear. As we will see in Chapter 14, some stockholders prefer current dividends while others prefer a lower payout ratio and future growth. Empirical studies have been unable to determine which strategy is optimal for maximizing a firm's stock price. So dividend policy is an issue that management must decide on the basis of its judgment, not a mathematical formula. Logically, shareholders should prefer for the company to retain more earnings (hence pay less current dividends) if the firm has exceptionally good investment opportunities; however, shareholders should prefer a high payout if investment opportunities are poor. In spite of this, taxes and other factors complicate the situation. We will discuss all this in detail in Chapter 14; for now, just assume that the firm's management has decided on a payout policy and uses that policy to determine the actual dividend.

9-5D REQUIRED CONDITIONS FOR THE CONSTANT GROWTH MODEL

Several conditions are necessary for Equation 9.2 to be used. First, the required rate of return, r_s, must be greater than the long-run growth rate, g. *If the equation is used in situations where g is greater than r_s, the results will be wrong, meaningless, and misleading.* For example, if the forecasted growth rate in our example were 10% and thus exceeded the 9.0% required rate of return, stock price as calculated by Equation 9.2 would be a *negative* \$110.00. That would be nonsense—stocks can't have negative prices. Moreover, in Table 9.1, the PV of each future dividend would exceed that of the prior year. If this situation were graphed in Figure 9.2, the stepfunction curve for the PV of dividends would be increasing, not decreasing; therefore, the sum would be infinitely high, which would indicate an infinitely high stock price. Obviously, stock prices cannot be either infinite or negative, so Equation 9.2 cannot be used unless $r_s > g$.

Second, the constant growth model as expressed in Equation 9.2 is not appropriate unless a company's growth rate is expected to remain constant in the future. This condition almost never holds for new start-up firms, but it does exist for many mature companies. Indeed, mature firms such as Keller, Allied, and GE are generally expected to grow at about the same rate as nominal gross domestic product (i.e., real GDP plus inflation). On this basis, one might expect the dividends of an average, or "normal," company to grow at a rate of 3% to 6% a year.

Note too that Equation 9.2 is sufficiently general to handle the case of a **zero growth stock**, where the dividend is expected to remain constant over time. If g = 0, Equation 9.2 reduces to Equation 9.5:

Zero Growth Stock
A common stock whose future dividends are not expected to grow at all; that is, g = 0.

$$\hat{P}_0 = \frac{D}{r_s} \quad (9.5)$$

This is the same equation as the one we developed in Chapter 5 for a perpetuity, and it is simply the current dividend divided by the required rate of return.

Finally, as we discuss later in the chapter, most firms, even rapidly growing start-ups and others that pay no dividends at present, can be expected to pay dividends at some point in the future, at which time the constant growth model will be appropriate. For such firms, Equation 9.2 is used as one part of a more complicated valuation equation that we discuss next.

Self*Test*

Write out and explain the valuation formula for a constant growth stock.

Describe how the formula for a zero growth stock can be derived from the formula for a normal constant growth stock.

Firm A is expected to pay a dividend of $1.00 at the end of the year. The required rate of return is $r_s = 11\%$. Other things held constant, what would the stock's price be if the growth rate was 5%? What if g was 0%? **($16.67, $9.09)**

Firm B has a 12% ROE. Other things held constant, what would its expected growth rate be if it paid out 25% of its earnings as dividends? 75%? **(9%, 3%)**

If Firm B had a 75% payout ratio but then lowered it to 25%, causing its growth rate to rise from 3% to 9%, would that action necessarily increase the price of its stock? Why or why not?

9-6 Valuing Nonconstant Growth Stocks

For many companies, it is not appropriate to assume that dividends will grow at a constant rate. Indeed, most firms go through *life cycles* where they experience different growth rates during different parts of the cycle. In their early years, most firms grow much faster than the economy as a whole; then they match the economy's growth; and finally they grow at a slower rate than the economy.[16] Automobile manufacturers in the 1920s, computer software firms such as Microsoft in the 1990s, and Google in the 2000s are examples of firms in the early part of their cycle. These firms are defined as **supernormal**, or **nonconstant, growth**, firms.

Supernormal (Nonconstant) Growth
The part of the firm's life cycle in which it grows much faster than the economy as a whole.

[16]The concept of life cycles could be broadened to *product cycle*, which would include both small start-up companies and large companies such as Microsoft and Procter & Gamble, which periodically introduce new products that give sales and earnings a boost. We should also mention *business cycles*, which alternately depress and boost sales and profits. The growth rate just after a major new product has been introduced (or just after a firm emerges from the depths of a recession) is likely to be much higher than the "expected long-run average growth rate," which is the proper number for use in the discounted dividend model.

Figure 9.3 illustrates nonconstant growth and compares it with normal growth, zero growth, and negative (or declining) growth.[17]

In the figure, the dividends of the supernormal growth firm are expected to grow at a 10% rate for 3 years, after which the growth rate is expected to fall to 4%, the assumed average for the economy. The value of this firm's stock, like any other asset, is the present value of its expected future dividends as determined by Equation 9.1. When D_t is growing at a constant rate, we can simplify Equation 9.1 to Equation 9.2, $\hat{P}_0 = D_1/(r_s - g)$. In the supernormal case, however, the expected growth rate is not a constant. In our example, there are two distinctly different rates.

Horizon (Terminal) Date
The date when the growth rate becomes constant. At this date, it is no longer necessary to forecast the individual dividends.

Because Equation 9.2 requires a constant growth rate, we obviously cannot use it to value stocks that are not growing at a constant rate. However, assuming that a company currently enjoying supernormal growth will eventually slow down and become a constant growth stock, we can combine Equations 9.1 and 9.2 to construct a new formula, Equation 9.6, for valuing the stock.

Horizon (Continuing) Value
The value at the horizon date of all dividends expected thereafter.

First, we assume that the dividend will grow at a nonconstant rate (generally a relatively high rate) for N periods, after which it will grow at a constant rate, g. N is often called the **horizon**, or **terminal, date**. Second, we can use the constant growth formula, Equation 9.2, to determine what the stock's **horizon**, or **continuing, value** will be N periods from today:

$$\text{Horizon value} = \hat{P}_N = \frac{D_{N+1}}{r_s - g}$$

FIGURE 9.3 Illustrative Dividend Growth Rates

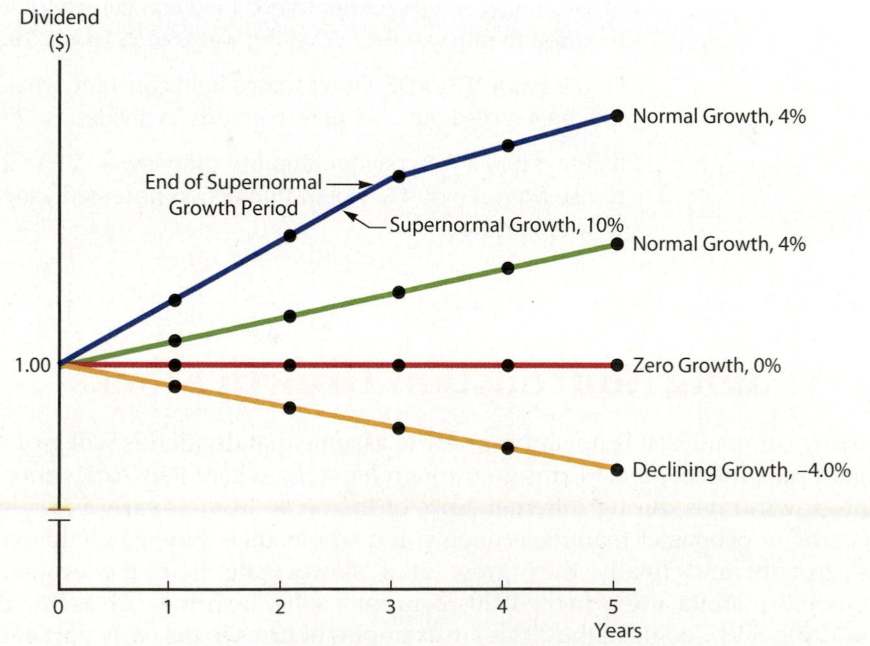

[17]A negative growth rate indicates a declining company. A mining company whose profits are falling because of a declining ore body is an example. Someone purchasing stock in such a company would expect its earnings (and consequently its dividends and stock price) to decline each year, which would lead to capital losses rather than capital gains. Obviously, a declining-growth company's stock price is relatively low, and its dividend yield must be high enough to offset the expected capital loss and still produce a competitive total return. Students sometimes argue that they would never be willing to buy a stock whose price was expected to decline. However, if the present value of the expected dividends exceeds the stock price, the stock is still a good investment that would provide a good return.

The stock's intrinsic value today, $\hat{P}_0$, is the present value of the dividends during the nonconstant growth period plus the present value of the horizon value:

$$\hat{P}_0 = \underbrace{\frac{D_1}{(1+r_s)^1} + \frac{D_2}{(1+r_s)^2} + \cdots + \frac{D_N}{(1+r_s)^N}}_{\substack{\text{PV of dividends during the}\\ \text{nonconstant growth}\\ \text{period, } t = 1, \cdots N}} + \underbrace{\frac{D_{N+1}}{(1+r_s)^{N+1}} + \cdots + \frac{D_\infty}{(1+r_s)^\infty}}_{\substack{\text{Horizon value} = \text{PV of dividends}\\ \text{during the constant growth}\\ \text{period, } t = N+1, \cdots \infty}}$$

$$\hat{P}_0 = \underbrace{\frac{D_1}{(1+r_s)^1} + \frac{D_2}{(1+r_s)^2} + \cdots + \frac{D_N}{(1+r_s)^N}}_{\substack{\text{PV of dividends during the}\\ \text{nonconstant growth period}\\ t = 1, \cdots N}} + \underbrace{\frac{\hat{P}_N}{(1+r_s)^N}}_{\substack{\text{PV of horizon}\\ \text{value, } \hat{P}_N:\\ \frac{[(D_{N+1})/(r_s - g)]}{(1+r_s)^N}}} \quad \textbf{9.6}$$

To implement Equation 9.6, we go through the following three steps:

1. Find the PV of each dividend during the period of nonconstant growth and sum them.
2. Find the expected stock price at the end of the nonconstant growth period. At this point it has become a constant growth stock, so it can be valued with the constant growth model. Discount this price back to the present.
3. Add these two components to find the stock's intrinsic value, $\hat{P}_0$.

Figure 9.4 illustrates the process for valuing nonconstant growth stocks. Here we use a new company, Firm M, and we assume the following information:

r_s = stockholders' required rate of return = 9.0%. This rate is used to discount the cash flows.
N = years of nonconstant growth = 3.
g_s = rate of growth in both earnings and dividends during the nonconstant growth period = 10%. This rate is shown directly on the time line. (*Note:* The growth rate during the nonconstant growth period could vary from year to year. Also, there could be several different nonconstant growth periods—e.g., 10% for 3 years, 8% for the next 3 years, and a constant 4% thereafter.)
g_n = rate of normal, constant growth after the nonconstant period = 4.0%. This rate is also shown on the time line, after Year 3, when it is in effect.
D_0 = last dividend the company paid = $1.00.

The valuation process diagrammed in Figure 9.4 is explained in the steps set forth below the time line. The value of the nonconstant growth stock is calculated as $24.43.

Note that in this example, we assumed a relatively short 3-year horizon to keep things simple. When evaluating stocks, most analysts use a longer horizon (e.g., 10 years) to estimate intrinsic values. This requires a few more calculations, but because analysts use spreadsheets, the arithmetic is not a problem. In practice, the real limitation is obtaining reliable forecasts for future growth.

FIGURE 9.4 Finding the Value of a Nonconstant Growth Stock

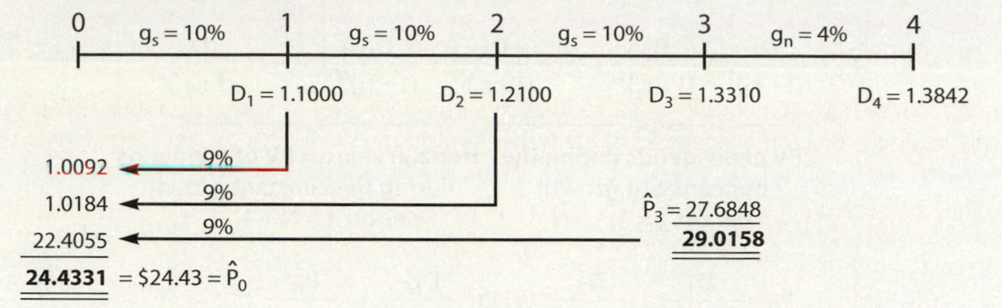

Notes:

Step 1. Calculate the dividends expected at the end of each year during the nonconstant growth period. Calculate the first dividend, $D_1 = D_0(1 + g_s) = \$1.00(1.10) = \$1.1000$. Here g_s is the growth rate during the 3-year nonconstant growth period, 10%. Show the \$1.1000 on the time line as the cash flow at Time 1. Calculate $D_2 = D_1(1 + g_s) = \$1.1000(1.10) = \$1.2100$, then $D_3 = D_2(1 + g_s) = \$1.2100(1.10) = \$1.3310$. Show these values on the time line as the cash flows at Time 2 and Time 3. Note that D_0 is used only to calculate D_1.

Step 2. The price of the stock is the PV of dividends from Time 1 to infinity; so in theory, we could project each future dividend, with the normal growth rate, $g_n = 4\%$, used to calculate D_4 and subsequent dividends. However, we know that after D_3 has been paid at Time 3, the stock becomes a constant growth stock. Therefore, we can use the constant growth formula to find $\hat{P}_3$, which is the PV of the dividends from Time 4 to infinity as evaluated at Time 3.

First, we determine $D_4 = \$1.3310(1.04) = \$1.3842$ for use in the formula; then we calculate $\hat{P}_3$ as follows:

$$\hat{P}_3 = \frac{D_4}{r_s - g_n} = \frac{\$1.3842}{0.09 - 0.04} = \$27.6848$$

We show this \$27.6848 on the time line as a second cash flow at Time 3. The \$27.6848 is a Time 3 cash flow in the sense that the stockholder could sell the stock for \$27.6848 at Time 3 and in the sense that \$27.6848 is the present value of the dividend cash flows from Time 4 to infinity. Note that the total cash flow at Time 3 consists of the sum of $D_3 + \hat{P}_3 = \$1.3310 + \$27.6848 = \$29.0158$.

Step 3. Now that the cash flows have been placed on the time line, we can discount each cash flow at the required rate of return, $r_s = 9.0\%$. We could discount each cash flow by dividing by $(1.09)^t$, where t = 1 for Time 1, t = 2 for Time 2, and t = 3 for Time 3. This produces the PVs shown to the left below the time line, and the sum of the PVs is the value of the nonconstant growth stock, \$24.43.

With a financial calculator, you can find the PV of the cash flows as shown on the time line with the cash flow (CFLO) register of your calculator. Enter 0 for CF_0 because you receive no cash flow at Time 0, $CF_1 = 1.10$, $CF_2 = 1.21$, and $CF_3 = 1.3310 + 27.6848 = 29.0158$. Then enter I/YR = 9.0 and press the NPV key to find the value of the stock, \$24.43.

Self*Test*

Explain how one would find the value of a nonconstant growth stock.

Explain what is meant by horizon (terminal) date and horizon (continuing) value.

EVALUATING STOCKS THAT DON'T PAY DIVIDENDS

The discounted dividend model assumes that the firm is currently paying a dividend. However, many firms, even highly profitable ones, including Google, have never paid a dividend. If a firm is expected to begin paying dividends in the future, we can modify the equations presented in the chapter and use them to determine the value of the stock.

A new business often expects to have low sales during its first few years of operation as it develops its product. Then if the product catches on, sales will grow rapidly for several years. Sales growth brings with it the need for additional assets—a firm cannot increase sales without also increasing its assets, and asset growth requires an increase in liability and/or equity accounts. Small firms can generally obtain some bank credit, but they must maintain a reasonable balance between debt and equity. Thus, additional bank borrowings require increases in equity, and getting the equity capital needed to support growth can be difficult for small firms. They have limited access to the capital markets, and even when they can sell common stock, their owners are reluctant to do so for fear of losing voting control. Therefore, the best source of equity for most small businesses is retained earnings; for this reason most small firms pay no dividends during their rapid growth years. Eventually, though, successful small firms do pay dividends, and those dividends generally grow rapidly at first, but slow down to a sustainable constant rate once the firm reaches maturity.

If a firm currently pays no dividends but is expected to pay future dividends, the value of its stock can be found as follows:

1. Estimate at what point dividends will be paid, the amount of the first dividend, the growth rate during the supernormal growth period, the length of the supernormal period, the long-run (constant) growth rate, and the rate of return required by investors.
2. Use the constant growth model to determine the stock price after the firm reaches a stable growth situation.
3. Set out on a time line the cash flows (dividends during the supernormal growth period and the stock price once the constant growth state is reached); then find the present value of these cash flows. That present value represents the value of the stock today.

To illustrate this process, consider the situation for Marvel-Lure Inc., a company that was set up in 2018 to produce and market a new high-tech fishing lure. Marvel-Lure's sales are currently growing at a rate of 200% per year. The company expects to experience a high but declining rate of growth in sales and earnings during the next 10 years, after which analysts estimate that it will grow at a steady 10% per year. The firm's management has announced that it will pay no dividends for 5 years but that if earnings materialize as forecasted, it will pay a dividend of \$0.20 per share at the end of Year 6, \$0.30 in Year 7, \$0.40 in Year 8, \$0.45 in Year 9, and \$0.50 in Year 10. After Year 10, current plans are to increase dividends by 10% per year.

Marvel-Lure's investment bankers estimate that investors require a 15% return on similar stocks. Therefore, we find the value of a share of Marvel-Lure's stock as follows:

$$\hat{P}_0 = \frac{\$0}{(1.15)^1} + \cdots + \frac{\$0}{(1.15)^5} + \frac{\$0.20}{(1.15)^6} + \frac{\$0.30}{(1.15)^7} + \frac{\$0.40}{(1.15)^8}$$
$$+ \frac{\$0.45}{(1.15)^9} + \frac{\$0.50}{(1.15)^{10}} + \left(\frac{\$0.50(1.10)}{0.15 - 0.10}\right)\left(\frac{1}{(1.15)^{10}}\right)$$
$$= \$3.30$$

The last term finds the expected stock price in Year 10 and then finds the present value of that price. Thus, we see that the discounted dividend model can be applied to firms that currently pay no dividends, provided we can estimate future dividends with a fair degree of confidence. However, in many cases, we can have more confidence in the forecasts of free cash flows, and in these situations, it is better to use the corporate valuation model, which we discuss next.

9-7 Enterprise-Based Approach to Valuation[18]

Thus far we have discussed the discounted dividend model for valuing a firm's common stock. This procedure is widely used, but it is based on the assumption that the analyst can forecast future dividends reasonably well. This is often true for mature companies that have a history of steadily growing dividends. However, dividends are dependent on earnings, so a reliable dividend forecast must be based on an underlying forecast of the firm's future sales, costs, and capital requirements.

[18]The corporate valuation model presented in this section is widely used by analysts, and it is in many respects superior to the discounted dividend model. However, it is rather involved as it requires the estimation of future sales, costs, and cash flows before the discounting process is begun. Therefore, in the introductory course, some instructors may prefer to omit Section 9-7 and skip to Section 9-8.

Corporate Valuation Model
A valuation model used as an alternative to the discounted dividend model to determine a firm's value, especially one with no history of dividends, or the value of a division of a larger firm. The corporate model first calculates the firm's free cash flows, then finds their present values to determine the firm's value.

This recognition has led to an alternative stock valuation approach, the **corporate valuation model**.

Rather than starting with a forecast of dividends, the corporate valuation model focuses on the firm's future free cash flows (FCFs). We discussed FCF in Chapter 3, where we developed the following equation:

$$\text{FCF} = \left[\text{EBIT}(1 - \text{T}) + \begin{matrix}\text{Depreciation}\\ \text{and amortization}\end{matrix}\right] - \left[\begin{matrix}\text{Capital}\\ \text{expenditures}\end{matrix} + \begin{matrix}\Delta\text{Net operating}\\ \text{working capital}\end{matrix}\right]$$

EBIT is earnings before interest and taxes, and free cash flow represents the cash generated from current operations less the cash that must be spent on investments in fixed assets and working capital to support future growth.

Consider the case of Home Depot (HD). The first term in brackets in the preceding equation represents the amount of cash that HD is generating from its existing stores. The second term represents the amount of cash the company plans to spend this period to construct new stores. To open a new store, HD must spend cash to purchase the land and construct the building—these are the capital expenditures, and they lead to a corresponding increase in the firm's fixed assets, as shown on the balance sheet. But HD also needs to increase its working capital, especially inventory. Putting everything together, HD generates positive free cash flow for its investors if and only if the money from its existing stores exceeds the money required to build and equip its new stores.

9-7A THE CORPORATE VALUATION MODEL

In Chapter 3, we explained that a firm's value is determined by its ability to generate cash flow both now and in the future. Therefore, the market value of a company's operations can be expressed as follows:

$$\begin{aligned}\text{Market value of company's operations} &= V_{\text{Company's operations}} = \text{PV of expected future free cash flows} \\ &= \frac{\text{FCF}_1}{(1+\text{WACC})^1} + \frac{\text{FCF}_2}{(1+\text{WACC})^2} + \cdots + \frac{\text{FCF}_\infty}{(1+\text{WACC})^\infty}\end{aligned} \quad \textbf{9.7}$$

Here FCF_t is the free cash flow in Year t and the discount rate, the WACC, is the weighted average cost of all the firm's capital. When thinking about the WACC, note these two points:

1. The firm finances with debt, preferred stock, and common equity. The WACC is the weighted average of these three types of capital, and we will discuss it in detail in Chapter 10.
2. Free cash flow is the cash generated *before any payments are made to any investors, so it must be used to compensate common stockholders, preferred stockholders, and bondholders*. Moreover, each type of investor has a required rate of return, and the weighted average of those returns is the WACC, which is used to discount the free cash flows.

Free cash flows are generally forecasted for 5 to 10 years, after which it is assumed that the final explicitly forecasted FCF will grow at some long-run constant rate. Once the company reaches its horizon date, when cash flows begin to grow at a constant rate, we can use the following formula to calculate the market value of the company's operations as of that date:

$$\text{Horizon value} = V_{\text{Company's operations at t=N}} = \text{FCF}_{N+1}/(\text{WACC} - g_{\text{FCF}}) \quad \textbf{9.8}$$

In addition to their operating assets, some companies may also have significant non-operating assets that are not captured in the estimated free cash flows. These non-operating assets should be included as part of the company's total corporate value. Examples may include large holdings of excess cash, real estate holdings outside of its main operations, or a company's minority stake in another business. Consequently, the overall market value of the company can be estimated as follows:

$$\text{Market value of company} = \text{Market value of company's operations} + \text{Market value of company's non-operating assets} \quad \textbf{9.9}$$

$$\text{Market value of company} = \frac{FCF_1}{(1 + WACC)^1} + \frac{FCF_2}{(1 + WACC)^2} + \cdots + \frac{FCF_\infty}{(1 + WACC)^\infty} + \text{Market value of company's non-operating assets}$$

For example, if we wanted to value Microsoft, we would first forecast the present value of the company's future free cash flows, which includes the cash it expects to generate from current products such as its Microsoft Windows line of operating systems and Microsoft Office Suite, as well as the cash expected to be generated from its future products. This forecast would give us an estimate of the company's operations. We would then estimate the value of any non-operating assets. In the case of Microsoft, the most notable non-operating asset is the company's excess cash. Indeed, in March 2018, Microsoft had over $132 billion of cash on hand—the overwhelming majority of which could be viewed as excess cash.

The corporate model is applied internally by the firm's financial staff and by outside security analysts. For illustrative purposes, we discuss Allied's free cash flow valuation analysis conducted by Susan Buskirk, senior food analyst for the investment banking firm Morton Staley and Company. Her analysis is summarized in Table 9.2, which was reproduced from the chapter Excel model.

- Based on Allied's history and Buskirk's knowledge of the firm's business plan, she estimated sales, costs, and cash flows on an annual basis for 5 years. Growth will vary during those years, but she assumes that things will stabilize, and growth will be constant after the fifth year. She would have made explicit forecasts for more years if she thought it would take longer to reach a steady-state, constant growth situation.
- For each of the first 5 years, Buskirk paid particular attention to the key variables that influence free cash flow. Specifically, she focused on EBIT, required capital expenditures, and the anticipated changes in net operating working capital (NOWC).
- Buskirk next calculated the expected free cash flows (FCFs) for each of the 5 nonconstant growth years, and she found the PV of those cash flows discounted at the WACC.
- After Year 5, she assumed that FCF growth would be constant; hence, the constant growth model could be used to find Allied's market value of operations at Year 5. This "horizon, or continuing, value" is the sum of the PVs of the FCFs from Year 6 on out into the future, discounted back to Year 5 at the WACC. It follows that: Horizon $\text{Value}_{t=5} = FCF_6/(WACC - g_{FCF})$, where g_{FCF} represents the long-run growth rate of the free cash flow.
- Next, she discounted the Year 5 horizon value back to the present to find its PV at Year 0.
- She then summed all the PVs, the annual cash flows during the nonconstant period plus the PV of the horizon value, to find the firm's estimated market value of the company's operations.

TABLE 9.2 Analysis of a Constant Growth Stock

	A	B	C	D	E	F	G	H
135	Part 1. Key Inputs			Forecasted Years				
136				2020	2021	2022	2023	2024
137	Sales growth rate			10.0%	9.0%	8.0%	7.0%	7.0%
138	Operating costs as a % of sales			87.0%	87.0%	86.0%	85.0%	85.0%
139	Growth in net fixed assets			8.0%	8.0%	8.0%	7.0%	7.0%
140	Growth in NOWC			8.0%	8.0%	8.0%	7.0%	7.0%
141	Depr'n as a % of operating capital			6.0%	8.0%	7.0%	7.0%	7.0%
142	Tax rate			25%				
143	WACC			10%				
144	Long-run FCF growth, g_{FCF}			4.0%				
145								
146	Part 2. Forecast of Cash Flows During Period of Nonconstant Growth							
147			Historical	Forecasted Years				
148			2019	2020	2021	2022	2023	2024
149								
150	Sales		*$3,000.0*	$3,300.0	$3,597.0	$3,884.8	$4,156.7	$4,447.7
151	Operating costs		*2,622.0*	2,871.0	3,129.4	3,340.9	3,533.2	3,780.5
152	DEP = Depreciation		*100.0*	116.6	168.0	158.7	169.8	181.7
153	EBIT		*$278.0*	$312.4	$299.6	$385.1	$453.7	$485.4
154	EBIT x (1 − T)		*208.5*	234.3	224.7	288.9	340.3	364.1
155	EBIT x (1 − T) + DEP		*308.5*	350.9	392.7	447.6	510.1	545.8
156								
157	Net fixed assets		*$1,000.0*	$1,080.0	$1,166.4	$1,259.7	$1,347.9	$1,442.2
158	Net oper. working capital (NOWC)		*800.0*	864.0	933.1	1,007.8	1,078.3	1,153.8
159	Total operating capital		*$1,800.0*	$1,944.0	$2,099.5	$2,267.5	$2,426.2	$2,596.0
160	Net CAPEX = Change in net fixed assets		*130.0*	80.0	86.4	93.3	88.2	94.4
161	CAPEX = Gross capital expenditures = Net CAPEX + DEP		*230.0*	196.6	254.4	252.0	258.0	276.1
162	ΔNOWC		*150.0*	64.0	69.1	74.6	70.5	75.5
163								
164	Free Cash Flow, FCF = EBIT(1 − T) + DEP − CAPEX − ΔNOWC		-$71.5	$90.3	$69.2	$120.9	$181.5	$194.2
165	*PV of FCFs*		*N.A.*	*$82.1*	*$57.2*	*$90.8*	*$124.0*	*$120.6*
166								
167	Part 3. Horizon Value and Intrinsic Value Estimation							
168	*Estimated Value at the Horizon, 2024*							
169	Free Cash Flow (2025)			$202.0 ←		$FCF_{2024}(1+g_{FCF})$		
170	Horizon Value at 2024, HV_{2024}			$3,366.7 ←		$HV_{2024} = \frac{FCF_{2025}}{WACC - g_{FCF}}$		
171	PV of HV_{2024}			$2,090.5 ←		$HV_{2024} / (1+WACC)^N$		
172								
173	*Calculation of Firm's Intrinsic Value*							
174	Sum of PVs of FCFs, 2020-2024			$474.7				
175	PV of HV_{2024}			2,090.5				
176	MV of nonoperating assets			0.0				
177	Total corporate value			$2,565.2				
178	Less: market value of debt and preferred			860.0				
179	Intrinsic value of common equity			$1,705.2				
180	Shares outstanding (millions)			75.0				
181								
182	Intrinsic Value Per Share			$22.74				

- Next, she would add her estimate of the value of any non-operating assets. In this case, Buskirk assumes that Allied does not have any meaningful non-operating assets, so she concludes that the total market value of the firm equals the market value of its operations. Allied's total market value would obviously be higher if the company had positive non-operating assets.[19]
- From her estimate of the company's total market value, she then subtracted the current market value of the debt and preferred stock to find the value of Allied's common equity.

[19]Let's assume instead that Allied has $100 million of unspecified non-operating assets. Its total corporate value without these assets is $2,565.2 million, so when non-operating assets are considered, its total corporate value increases to $2,665.2 million, and its intrinsic value of common equity increases to $1,805.2 million. Therefore, its intrinsic value increases by $1.33 per share to $24.07 = $1,805.2/75.

Finally, she divided the equity value by the number of shares outstanding, and the result was her estimate of Allied's intrinsic value per share. This value was quite close to the stock's market price, so she concluded that Allied's stock is priced at its equilibrium level. Consequently, she issued a "Hold" recommendation on the stock. If the estimated intrinsic value had been significantly below the market price, she would have issued a "Sell" recommendation; if the estimated intrinsic value had been well above the market price, she would have called the stock a "Buy."

In practice, the corporate valuation model can be further extended to take into account a variety of other factors. An analyst may need to account for significant non-operating liabilities such as an underfunded pension liability or contingencies related to future litigation. Another example is executive stock options—to the extent these options are valuable, it means that the company's executives will receive some portion of the company's future gains. For some companies, these other factors can be quite important, and often quite complicated. Consequently, we will leave a more detailed discussion of these issues to more advanced finance courses that focus more specifically on valuation.

9-7B COMPARING THE CORPORATE VALUATION AND DISCOUNTED DIVIDEND MODELS

Analysts use both the discounted dividend model and the corporate valuation model when valuing mature, dividend-paying firms, and they generally use the corporate model when valuing divisions and firms that do not pay dividends. In principle, we should find the same intrinsic value using either model, but differences are often observed. When a conflict exists, the assumptions embedded in the corporate model can be reexamined, and once the analyst is convinced they are reasonable, the results of that model are used.

In practice, intrinsic value estimates based on the two models normally deviate from one another and from actual stock prices, leading different analysts to reach different conclusions about the attractiveness of a given stock. The better the analyst, the more often his or her valuations turn out to be correct; no one can make perfect predictions, however, because too many things can change randomly and unpredictably in the future. Given all this, does it matter whether you use the corporate model or the dividend model to value stocks? We would argue that it does. If we had to value, for example, 100 mature companies whose dividends were expected to grow steadily in the future, we would probably use the discounted dividend model. Here we would estimate only the growth rate in dividends, not the entire set of pro forma financial statements; hence, it would be more feasible to use the dividend model.

However, if we were studying just one company or a few companies, especially companies still in the high-growth stage of their life cycles, we would want to project future financial statements before estimating future dividends. Because we would already have projected future financial statements, we would go ahead and apply the corporate valuation model. Intel, which pays a dividend of $1.20 versus earnings of about $2.31, is an example of a company where either model could be used, but we believe the corporate model is better.

Now suppose you were trying to estimate the value of a company such as Snap that to date has never paid a dividend or a private firm such as Uber or Airbnb that has yet to go public. In either situation, you would be better off using the corporate valuation model. Actually, even if a company is paying steady dividends, much can be learned from the corporate valuation model so analysts today use it for all types of valuations. The process of projecting future financial statements can reveal a great deal about a company's operations and financing needs. Also, such an analysis can provide insights into actions that might be taken to increase the company's value; for this reason, it is integral to the planning and forecasting process, as we discuss in a later chapter.

OTHER APPROACHES TO VALUING COMMON STOCKS

Although the dividend growth and the corporate valuation models presented in this chapter are the most widely used methods for valuing common stocks, they are by no means the only approaches. Analysts often use a number of different techniques to value stocks. Three of these alternative approaches are described here.

The P/E Multiple Approach

Investors have long looked for simple rules of thumb to determine whether a stock is fairly valued. One such approach is to look at the stock's price-to-earnings (P/E) ratio. Recall from Chapter 4 that a company's P/E ratio shows how much investors are willing to pay for each dollar of reported earnings. As a starting point, you might conclude that stocks with low P/E ratios are undervalued because their price is "low" given current earnings, whereas stocks with high P/E ratios are overvalued.

Unfortunately, however, valuing stocks is not that simple. We should not expect all companies to have the same P/E ratio. P/E ratios are affected by risk—investors discount the earnings of riskier stocks at a higher rate. Thus, all else equal, riskier stocks should have lower P/E ratios. In addition, when you buy a stock, you have a claim not only on current earnings but also on all future earnings. All else equal, companies with stronger growth opportunities will generate larger future earnings and thus should trade at higher P/E ratios. Therefore, in and of itself, a high P/E ratio does not mean that a stock is overvalued.

Nevertheless, P/E ratios can provide a useful starting point in stock valuation. If a stock's P/E ratio is well above its industry average and if the stock's growth potential and risk are similar to other firms in the industry, the stock's price may be too high. Likewise, if a company's P/E ratio falls well below its historical average, the stock may be undervalued—particularly if the company's growth prospects and risk are unchanged and if the overall P/E for the market has remained constant or increased.

One obvious drawback of the P/E approach is that it depends on reported accounting earnings. For this reason, some analysts choose to rely on other multiples to value stocks. For example, some analysts look at a company's price-to-cash-flow ratio, whereas others look at the price-to-sales ratio.

Enterprise-Based Multiples Approach

Other analysts like to focus on broader multiples that are based on a company's Enterprise Value to EBITDA ratio (EV/EBITDA). Recall from Chapter 4 that a company's enterprise value is calculated as follows:

$$\text{Enterprise value (EV)} = \text{Market value of equity} + \text{Market value of total debt} + \text{Market value of other financial claims} - (\text{Cash and equivalents})$$

For example, TripleJ Corporation's forecasted EBITDA is \$3 billion. Also, assume that the average company in TripleJ's industry has an EV/EBITDA ratio of 10, and that TripleJ's estimated risk and growth opportunities are the same as the average firm in its industry. It follows that a reasonable estimate of TripleJ's enterprise value is \$30 billion, calculated as Industry EV × TripleJ's EBITDA = 10 × \$3 billion.

TripleJ currently has \$11 billion of debt (at market value), \$6 billion of cash and equivalents on its balance sheet, and 1 billion shares of common stock outstanding. Given this information, an analyst can then use the estimated enterprise value to back out an estimate of the market value of the company's equity:

$$\text{Market value of equity} = \text{EV} - \text{Market value of debt} + (\text{Cash and equivalents})$$

$$\text{Market value of equity} = \$30 \text{ billion} - \$11 \text{ billion} + \$6 \text{ billion} = \$25 \text{ billion.}$$

Finally, if an analyst wanted to forecast the intrinsic value of the company's share price, she would simply divide the estimated market value of the company (\$25 billion) by the number of common shares outstanding (1 billion), to come up with an estimated share price of \$25.

The EVA Approach

In recent years, analysts have looked for more rigorous alternatives to the discounted dividend model. More than a quarter of all stocks listed on the NYSE pay no dividends. This proportion is even higher on NASDAQ. Although the discounted dividend model can still be used for these stocks (see "Evaluating Stocks That Don't Pay Dividends"), this approach requires that analysts forecast when the stock will begin paying dividends, what the dividend will be once it is established, and what the future dividend growth rate will be. In many cases, these forecasts contain considerable errors.

An alternative approach is based on the concept of Economic Value Added (EVA), which we discussed in Chapter 3 and in the Chapter 4 box "Economic Value Added (EVA) versus Net Income," that can be written as follows:

$$\text{EVA} = (\text{Equity capital})(\text{ROE} - \text{Cost of equity capital})$$

This equation suggests that companies can increase their EVA by investing in projects that provide shareholders with returns that are above their cost of equity capital, which is the return they could expect to earn on alternative investments with the same level of risk. When you purchase stock in a company, you receive more than just the book value of equity—you also receive a claim on all future value that is created by the firm's managers (the present value of all future EVAs). It follows that a company's market value of equity can be written as follows:

$$\text{Market value of equity} = \text{Book value} + \text{PV of all future EVAs}$$

We can find the "fundamental" value of the stock, P_0, by simply dividing the preceding expression by the number of shares outstanding.

As is the case with the discounted dividend model, we can simplify the expression by assuming that at some point in time, annual EVA becomes a perpetuity, or grows at some constant rate over time. Presented here is a simplified version of what is often referred to as the Edwards-Bell-Ohlson (EBO) model. For a more complete description of this technique and an excellent summary of how it can be used in practice, read the article "Measuring Wealth," by Charles M. C. Lee, in *CA Magazine*, April 1996, pp. 32–37.

Self*Test*

Write out the equation for free cash flows and explain it.

Why might someone use the corporate valuation model for companies that have a history of paying dividends?

What steps are taken to find a stock price using the corporate valuation model?

Why might the calculated intrinsic value differ from the stock's current market price? Which would be "correct," and what does "correct" mean?

9-8 Preferred Stock[20]

Preferred stock is a *hybrid*—it is similar to a bond in some respects and to common stock in others. This hybrid nature becomes apparent when we try to classify preferred stock in relation to bonds and common stock. Like bonds, preferred stock has a par value and a fixed dividend that must be paid before dividends can be paid on the common stock. However, the directors can omit (or "pass") the preferred dividend without throwing the company into bankruptcy. So although preferred stock calls for a fixed payment like bonds, skipping the payment will not lead to bankruptcy.

As noted earlier, a preferred stock entitles its owners to regular, fixed dividend payments. If the payments last forever, the issue is a *perpetuity* whose value, V_p, is found as follows:

$$V_p = \frac{D_p}{r_p} \qquad \textbf{9.10}$$

V_p is the value of the preferred stock, D_p is the preferred dividend, and r_p is the required rate of return on the preferred. Allied Food has no preferred outstanding, but discussions about such an issue suggested that its preferred should pay a dividend of $10 per year. If its required return was 10.3%, the preferred's value would be $97.09, found as follows:

$$V_p = \frac{\$10.00}{0.103} = \$97.09$$

In equilibrium, the expected return, $\hat{r}_p$, must be equal to the required return, r_p. Thus, if we know the preferred's current price and dividend, we can solve for the expected rate of return as follows:

$$\hat{r}_p = \frac{D_p}{V_p} \qquad \textbf{9.10a}$$

Some preferreds have a stated maturity, often 50 years. Assume that our illustrative preferred matured in 50 years, paid a $10 annual dividend, and had a required return of 8%. We could then find its price as follows: Enter N = 50, I/YR = 8, PMT = 10, and FV = 100. Then press PV to find the price, V_p = $124.47. If r_p rose to 10%, you would change I/YR to 10, in which case V_p = PV = $100. If you know the price of a share of preferred stock, you can solve for I/YR to find the expected rate of return, $\hat{r}_p$.

Self*Test*

Explain the following statement: Preferred stock is a hybrid security.

Is the equation used to value preferred stock more like the one used to value a bond or the one used to value a "normal" constant growth common stock? Explain.

[20]Refer to Chapter 20 of Eugene F. Brigham and Phillip R. Daves, *Intermediate Financial Management*, 13th edition (Mason, OH: Cengage Learning, 2019).

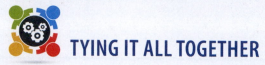

TYING IT ALL TOGETHER

Corporate decisions should be analyzed in terms of how alternative courses of action are likely to affect a firm's value. However, it is necessary to know how stock prices are established before attempting to measure how a given decision will affect a specific firm's value. This chapter discussed the rights and privileges of common stockholders, showed how stock values are determined, and explained how investors estimate stocks' intrinsic values and expected rates of return.

Two types of stock valuation models were discussed: the discounted dividend model and the corporate valuation model. The discounted dividend model is useful for mature, stable companies. It is easier to use, but the corporate valuation model is more flexible and better for use with companies that do not pay dividends or whose dividends would be especially hard to predict.

We also discussed preferred stock, which is a hybrid security that has some characteristics of a common stock and some of a bond. Preferreds are valued using models similar to those for perpetual and "regular" bonds.

Self-Test Questions and Problems

(Solutions Appear in Appendix A)

ST-1 **KEY TERMS** Define the following terms:

a. Proxy; proxy fight; takeover
b. Preemptive right
c. Classified stock; founders' shares
d. Marginal investor; intrinsic value ($\hat{P}_0$); market price (P_0)
e. Required rate of return, r_s; expected rate of return, $\hat{r}_s$; actual (realized) rate of return, $\bar{r}_s$
f. Capital gains yield; dividend yield; expected total return; growth rate, g
g. Zero growth stock
h. Constant growth (Gordon) model; supernormal (nonconstant) growth
i. Corporate valuation model
j. Horizon (terminal) date; horizon (continuing) value
k. Preferred stock

ST-2 **CONSTANT GROWTH STOCK VALUATION** Fletcher Company's current stock price is \$36.00, its last dividend was \$2.40, and its required rate of return is 12%. If dividends are expected to grow at a constant rate, g, in the future, and if r_s is expected to remain at 12%, what is Fletcher's expected stock price 5 years from now?

ST-3 **NONCONSTANT GROWTH STOCK VALUATION** Snyder Computers Inc. is experiencing rapid growth. Earnings and dividends are expected to grow at a rate of 15% during the next 2 years, at 13% the following year, and at a constant rate of 6% during Year 4 and thereafter. Its last dividend was \$1.15, and its required rate of return is 12%.

a. Calculate the value of the stock today.
b. Calculate $\hat{P}_1$ and $\hat{P}_2$.
c. Calculate the dividend and capital gains yields for Years 1, 2, and 3.

ST-4 **CORPORATE VALUATION** Shome Industries retains and reinvests all its earnings. So, Shome does not pay any dividends, and it has no plans to pay dividends any time soon. A major pension fund is interested in purchasing Shome's stock. The pension fund manager has estimated Shome's free cash flows for the next 3 years as follows: \$5 million, \$9 million, and \$12 million. After Year 3, free cash flow is projected to grow at a constant 4%. Shome's

WACC is 10%, the market value of its debt and preferred stock totals $27.2727 million, Shome has $10 million in non-operating assets, and it has 5 million shares of common stock outstanding. What is an estimate of Shome's stock price?

Questions

9-1 It is frequently stated that the one purpose of the preemptive right is to allow individuals to maintain their proportionate share of the ownership and control of a corporation.

a. How important do you suppose control is for the average stockholder of a firm whose shares are traded on the New York Stock Exchange?

b. Is the control issue likely to be of more importance to stockholders of publicly owned or closely held (private) firms? Explain.

9-2 Is the following equation correct for finding the value of a constant growth stock? Explain.

$$\hat{P}_0 = \frac{D_0}{r_s + g}$$

9-3 If you bought a share of common stock, you would probably expect to receive dividends plus an eventual capital gain. Would the distribution between the dividend yield and the capital gains yield be influenced by the firm's decision to pay more dividends rather than to retain and reinvest more of its earnings? Explain.

9-4 Two investors are evaluating GE's stock for possible purchase. They agree on the expected value of D_1 and on the expected future dividend growth rate. Further, they agree on the riskiness of the stock. However, one investor normally holds stocks for 2 years, while the other holds stocks for 10 years. On the basis of the type of analysis done in this chapter, should they both be willing to pay the same price for GE's stock? Explain.

9-5 A bond that pays interest forever and has no maturity is a perpetual bond. In what respect is a perpetual bond similar to a no-growth common stock? Are there preferred stocks that are evaluated similarly to perpetual bonds and other preferred issues that are more like bonds with finite lives? Explain.

9-6 Discuss the similarities and differences between the discounted dividend and corporate valuation models.

9-7 This chapter discusses the discounted dividend and corporate valuation models for valuing common stocks. Three alternative approaches, the P/E multiple, Enterprise Values, and EVA approaches, were presented. Explain each approach and how you might use each one to value a common stock.

9-8 How do non-operating assets impact a firm's valuation using the corporate valuation model?

Problems

Easy Problems 1-6

9-1 **DPS CALCULATION** Weston Corporation just paid a dividend of $1.00 a share (i.e., D_0 = $1.00). The dividend is expected to grow 12% a year for the next 3 years and then at 5% a year thereafter. What is the expected dividend per share for each of the next 5 years?

9-2 **CONSTANT GROWTH VALUATION** Tresnan Brothers is expected to pay a $1.80 per share dividend at the end of the year (i.e., D_1 = $1.80). The dividend is expected to grow at a constant rate of 4% a year. The required rate of return on the stock, r_s, is 10%. What is the stock's current value per share?

9-3 **CONSTANT GROWTH VALUATION** Holtzman Clothiers's stock currently sells for $38.00 a share. It just paid a dividend of $2.00 a share (i.e., D_0 = $2.00). The dividend is expected to grow at a constant rate of 5% a year. What stock price is expected 1 year from now? What is the required rate of return?

9-4 **NONCONSTANT GROWTH VALUATION** Holt Enterprises recently paid a dividend, D_0, of $2.75. It expects to have nonconstant growth of 18% for 2 years followed by a constant rate of 6% thereafter. The firm's required return is 12%.

a. How far away is the horizon date?

b. What is the firm's horizon, or continuing, value?

c. What is the firm's intrinsic value today, $\hat{P}_0$?

9-5 **CORPORATE VALUATION** Scampini Technologies is expected to generate $25 million in free cash flow next year, and FCF is expected to grow at a constant rate of 4% per year indefinitely. Scampini has no debt or preferred stock, its WACC is 10%, and it has zero non-operating assets. If Scampini has 40 million shares of stock outstanding, what is the stock's value per share?

9-6 **PREFERRED STOCK VALUATION** Farley Inc. has perpetual preferred stock outstanding that sells for $30 a share and pays a dividend of $2.75 at the end of each year. What is the required rate of return?

Intermediate Problems 7–15

9-7 **PREFERRED STOCK RATE OF RETURN** What will be the nominal rate of return on a perpetual preferred stock with a $100 par value, a stated dividend of 10% of par, and a current market price of (a) $61, (b) $90, (c) $100, and (d) $138?

9-8 **PREFERRED STOCK VALUATION** Earley Corporation issued perpetual preferred stock with an 8% annual dividend. The stock currently yields 7%, and its par value is $100.

a. What is the stock's value?

b. Suppose interest rates rise and pull the preferred stock's yield up to 9%. What is its new market value?

9-9 **PREFERRED STOCK RETURNS** Avondale Aeronautics has perpetual preferred stock outstanding with a par value of $100. The stock pays a quarterly dividend of $1.00 and its current price is $45.

a. What is its nominal annual rate of return?

b. What is its effective annual rate of return?

9-10 **VALUATION OF A DECLINING GROWTH STOCK** Maxwell Mining Company's ore reserves are being depleted, so its sales are falling. Also, because its pit is getting deeper each year, its costs are rising. As a result, the company's earnings and dividends are declining at the constant rate of 6% per year. If D_0 = $3 and r_s = 10%, what is the value of Maxwell Mining's stock?

9-11 **VALUATION OF A CONSTANT GROWTH STOCK** A stock is expected to pay a dividend of $2.75 at the end of the year (i.e., D_1 = $2.75), and it should continue to grow at a constant rate of 5% a year. If its required return is 15%, what is the stock's expected price 4 years from today?

9-12 **VALUATION OF A CONSTANT GROWTH STOCK** Investors require an 8% rate of return on Mather Company's stock (i.e., r_s = 8%).

a. What is its value if the previous dividend was D_0 = $1.25 and investors expect dividends to grow at a constant annual rate of (1) −2%, (2) 0%, (3) 3%, or (4) 5%?

b. Using data from part a, what would the Gordon (constant growth) model value be if the required rate of return was 8% and the expected growth rate was (1) 8% or (2) 12%? Are these reasonable results? Explain.

c. Is it reasonable to think that a constant growth stock could have $g > r_s$? Why or why not?

9-13 **CONSTANT GROWTH** You are considering an investment in Justus Corporation's stock, which is expected to pay a dividend of $2.25 a share at the end of the year (D_1 = $2.25) and has a beta of 0.9. The risk-free rate is 4.9%, and the market risk premium is 5%. Justus currently sells for $46.00 a share, and its dividend is expected to grow at some constant rate, g. Assuming the market is in equilibrium, what does the market believe will be the stock price at the end of 3 years? (That is, what is $\hat{P}_3$?)

9-14 **NONCONSTANT GROWTH** Computech Corporation is expanding rapidly and currently needs to retain all of its earnings; hence, it does not pay dividends. However, investors expect Computech to begin paying dividends, beginning with a dividend of $0.50 coming 3 years from today. The dividend should grow rapidly—at a rate of 35% per year—during Years 4 and 5, but after Year 5, growth should be a constant 7% per year. If the required return on Computech is 13%, what is the value of the stock today?

9-15 **CORPORATE VALUATION** Dantzler Corporation is a fast-growing supplier of office products. Analysts project the following free cash flows (FCFs) during the next 3 years, after which FCF is expected to grow at a constant 5% rate. Dantzler's WACC is 11%.

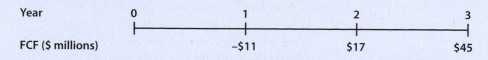

Year	0	1	2	3
FCF ($ millions)		-$11	$17	$45

a. What is Dantzler's horizon, or continuing, value? (*Hint:* Find the value of all free cash flows beyond Year 3 discounted back to Year 3.)

b. What is the firm's market value today? Assume that Dantzler has zero non-operating assets.

c. Suppose Dantzler has $112.60 million of debt and 25 million shares of stock outstanding. What is your estimate of the current price per share?

Challenging Problems 16–21

9-16 **NONCONSTANT GROWTH** Carnes Cosmetics Co.'s stock price is $30, and it recently paid a $1.00 dividend. This dividend is expected to grow by 30% for the next 3 years, then grow forever at a constant rate, g; and r_s = 9%. At what constant rate is the stock expected to grow after Year 3?

9-17 **CONSTANT GROWTH** Your broker offers to sell you some shares of Bahnsen & Co. common stock that paid a dividend of $2.00 yesterday. Bahnsen's dividend is expected to grow at 5% per year for the next 3 years. If you buy the stock, you plan to hold it for 3 years and then sell it. The appropriate discount rate is 12%.

a. Find the expected dividend for each of the next 3 years; that is, calculate D_1, D_2, and D_3. Note that D_0 = $2.00.

b. Given that the first dividend payment will occur 1 year from now, find the present value of the dividend stream; that is, calculate the PVs of D_1, D_2, and D_3, and then sum these PVs.

c. You expect the price of the stock 3 years from now to be $34.73; that is, you expect $\hat{P}_3$ to equal $34.73. Discounted at a 12% rate, what is the present value of this expected future stock price? In other words, calculate the PV of $34.73.

d. If you plan to buy the stock, hold it for 3 years, and then sell it for $34.73, what is the most you should pay for it today?

e. Use Equation 9.2 to calculate the present value of this stock. Assume that g = 5% and that it is constant.

f. Is the value of this stock dependent upon how long you plan to hold it? In other words, if your planned holding period was 2 years or 5 years rather than 3 years, would this affect the value of the stock today, $\hat{P}_0$? Explain.

9-18 **NONCONSTANT GROWTH STOCK VALUATION** Taussig Technologies Corporation (TTC) has been growing at a rate of 20% per year in recent years. This same growth rate is expected to last for another 2 years, then decline to g_n = 6%.

a. If D_0 = $1.60 and r_s = 10%, what is TTC's stock worth today? What are its expected dividend, and capital gains yields at this time, that is, during Year 1?

b. Now assume that TTC's period of supernormal growth is to last for 5 years rather than 2 years. How would this affect the price, dividend yield, and capital gains yield? Answer in words only.

c. What will TTC's dividend and capital gains yields be once its period of supernormal growth ends? (*Hint:* These values will be the same regardless of whether you examine the case of 2 or 5 years of supernormal growth; the calculations are very easy.)

d. Explain why investors are interested in the changing relationship between dividend and capital gains yields over time.

9-19 **CORPORATE VALUATION** Brandtly Industries invests a large sum of money in R&D; as a result, it retains and reinvests all of its earnings. In other words, Brandtly does not pay any dividends, and it has no plans to pay dividends in the near future. A major pension fund is interested in purchasing Brandtly's stock. The pension fund manager has estimated Brandtly's free cash flows for the next 4 years as follows: $3 million, $6 million, $8 million, and $16 million. After the fourth year, free cash flow is projected to grow at a constant 3%. Brandtly's WACC is 9%, the market value of its debt and preferred stock totals $75 million, the firm has $15 million in non-operating assets, and it has 7.5 million shares of common stock outstanding.

a. What is the present value of the free cash flows projected during the next 4 years?

b. What is the firm's horizon, or continuing, value?

c. What is the market value of the company's operations? What is the firm's total market value today?

d. What is an estimate of Brandtly's price per share?

9-20 **CORPORATE VALUE MODEL** Assume that today is December 31, 2019, and that the following information applies to Abner Airlines:

- After-tax operating income [EBIT(1 − T)] for 2020 is expected to be $400 million.
- The depreciation expense for 2020 is expected to be $140 million.
- The capital expenditures for 2020 are expected to be $225 million.

- No change is expected in net operating working capital.
- The free cash flow is expected to grow at a constant rate of 6% per year.
- The required return on equity is 14%.
- The WACC is 10%.
- The firm has $200 million of non-operating assets.
- The market value of the company's debt is $3.875 billion.
- 200 million shares of stock are outstanding.

Using the corporate valuation model approach, what should be the company's stock price today?

9-21 **NONCONSTANT GROWTH** Assume that it is now January 1, 2020. Wayne-Martin Electric Inc. (WME) has developed a solar panel capable of generating 200% more electricity than any other solar panel currently on the market. As a result, WME is expected to experience a 15% annual growth rate for the next 5 years. Other firms will have developed comparable technology by the end of 5 years, and WME's growth rate will slow to 5% per year indefinitely. Stockholders require a return of 12% on WME's stock. The most recent annual dividend (D_0), which was paid yesterday, was $1.75 per share.

a. Calculate WME's expected dividends for 2020, 2021, 2022, 2023, and 2024.

b. Calculate the value of the stock today, $\hat{P}_0$. Proceed by finding the present value of the dividends expected at the end of 2020, 2021, 2022, 2023, and 2024 plus the present value of the stock price that should exist at the end of 2024. The year end 2024 stock price can be found by using the constant growth equation. Notice that to find the December 31, 2024, price, you must use the dividend expected in 2025, which is 5% greater than the 2024 dividend.

c. Calculate the expected dividend yield (D_1/P_0), capital gains yield, and total return (dividend yield plus capital gains yield) expected for 2020. (Assume that $\hat{P}_0 = P_0$ and recognize that the capital gains yield is equal to the total return minus the dividend yield.) Then calculate these same three yields for 2025.

d. How might an investor's tax situation affect his or her decision to purchase stocks of companies in the early stages of their lives, when they are growing rapidly, versus stocks of older, more mature firms? When does WME's stock become "mature" for purposes of this question?

e. Suppose your boss tells you she believes that WME's annual growth rate will be only 12% during the next 5 years and that the firm's long-run growth rate will be only 4%. Without doing any calculations, what general effect would these growth rate changes have on the price of WME's stock?

f. Suppose your boss also tells you that she regards WME as being quite risky and that she believes the required rate of return should be 14%, not 12%. Without doing any calculations, determine how the higher required rate of return would affect the price of the stock, the capital gains yield, and the dividend yield. Again, assume that the long-run growth rate is 4%.

Comprehensive/Spreadsheet Problem

9-22 **NONCONSTANT GROWTH AND CORPORATE VALUATION** Rework Problem 9-18, parts a, b, and c, using a spreadsheet model. For part b, calculate the price, dividend yield, and capital gains yield as called for in the problem. After completing parts a through c, answer the following additional question, using the spreadsheet model:

d. TTC recently introduced a new line of products that has been wildly successful. On the basis of this success and anticipated future success, the following free cash flows were projected:

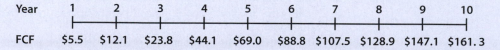

Year	1	2	3	4	5	6	7	8	9	10
FCF	$5.5	$12.1	$23.8	$44.1	$69.0	$88.8	$107.5	$128.9	$147.1	$161.3

After the 10th year, TTC's financial planners anticipate that its free cash flow will grow at a constant rate of 6%. Also, the firm concluded that the new product caused the WACC to fall to 9%. The market value of TTC's debt is $1,200 million, it uses no preferred stock, it has zero non-operating assets; and there are 20 million shares of common stock outstanding. Use the corporate valuation model to value the stock.

INTEGRATED CASE

MUTUAL OF CHICAGO INSURANCE COMPANY

9-23 **STOCK VALUATION** Robert Balik and Carol Kiefer are senior vice presidents of the Mutual of Chicago Insurance Company. They are codirectors of the company's pension fund management division, with Balik having responsibility for fixed-income securities (primarily bonds) and Kiefer being responsible for equity investments. A major new client, the California League of Cities, has requested that Mutual of Chicago present an investment seminar to the mayors of the represented cities, and Balik and Kiefer, who will make the actual presentation, have asked you to help them.

To illustrate the common stock valuation process, Balik and Kiefer have asked you to analyze the Bon Temps Company, an employment agency that supplies word-processor operators and computer programmers to businesses with temporarily heavy workloads. You are to answer the following questions:

a. Describe briefly the legal rights and privileges of common stockholders.

b. 1. Write a formula that can be used to value any stock, regardless of its dividend pattern.
   2. What is a constant growth stock? How are constant growth stocks valued?
   3. What are the implications if a company forecasts a constant g that exceeds its r_s? Will many stocks have expected $g > r_s$ in the short run (i.e., for the next few years)? In the long run (i.e., forever)?

c. Assume that Bon Temps has a beta coefficient of 1.2, that the risk-free rate (the yield on T-bonds) is 3%, and that the required rate of return on the market is 8%. What is Bon Temps's required rate of return?

d. Assume that Bon Temps is a constant growth company whose last dividend (D_0, which was paid yesterday) was $2.00 and whose dividend is expected to grow indefinitely at a 4% rate.
   1. What is the firm's expected dividend stream over the next 3 years?
   2. What is its current stock price?
   3. What is the stock's expected value 1 year from now?
   4. What are the expected dividend yield, capital gains yield, and total return during the first year?

e. Now assume that the stock is currently selling at $40.00. What is its expected rate of return?

f. What would the stock price be if its dividends were expected to have zero growth?

g. Now assume that Bon Temps's dividend is expected to grow 30% the first year, 20% the second year, 10% the third year, and return to its long-run constant growth rate of 4%. What is the stock's value under these conditions? What are its expected dividend and capital gains yields in Year 1? In Year 4?

h. Suppose Bon Temps is expected to experience zero growth during the first 3 years and then resume its steady-state growth of 4% in the fourth year. What would be its value then? What would be its expected dividend and capital gains yields in Year 1? In Year 4?

i. Finally, assume that Bon Temps's earnings and dividends are expected to decline at a constant rate of 4% per year, that is, $g = -4\%$. Why would anyone be willing to buy such a stock, and at what price should it sell? What would be its dividend and capital gains yields in each year?

j. Suppose Bon Temps embarked on an aggressive expansion that requires additional capital. Management decided to finance the expansion by borrowing $40 million and by halting dividend payments to increase retained earnings. Its WACC is now 7%, and the projected free cash flows for the next three years are −$5 million, $10 million, and $20 million. After Year 3, free cash flow is projected to grow at a constant 5%. What is Bon Temps's market value of operations? If it has 10 million shares of stock, $40 million of debt and preferred stock combined, and $5 million of non-operating assets, what is the price per share?

k. Suppose Bon Temps decided to issue preferred stock that would pay an annual dividend of $5.00 and that the issue price was $100.00 per share. What would be the stock's expected return? Would the expected rate of return be the same if the preferred was a perpetual issue or if it had a 20-year maturity?

TAKING A CLOSER LOOK

Estimating Exxon Mobil Corporation's Intrinsic Stock Value

Use online resources to work on this chapter's questions. Please note that website information changes over time, and these changes may limit your ability to answer some of these questions.

In this chapter, we described the various factors that influence stock prices and the approaches that analysts use to estimate a stock's intrinsic value. By comparing these intrinsic value estimates to the current price, an investor can assess whether it makes sense to buy or sell a particular stock. Stocks trading at a price far below their estimated intrinsic values may be good candidates for purchase, whereas stocks trading at prices far in excess of their intrinsic value may be good stocks to avoid or sell. Although estimating a stock's intrinsic value is a complex exercise that requires reliable data and good judgment, we can use the Internet to find financial data in order to arrive at a quick "back-of-the-envelope" calculation of intrinsic value.

Discussion Questions

1. For purposes of this exercise, let's take a closer look at the stock of Exxon Mobil Corporation (XOM). Use websites such as Yahoo! Finance, Google Finance, MSN Money (www.msn.com/en-us/money/markets), and Morningstar to find the company's current stock price and see its performance relative to the overall market in recent months. What is Exxon Mobil's current stock price? How has the stock performed relative to the market over the past few months?
2. Check recent headlines on the website to see the company's recent news stories. Have there been any recent events impacting the company's stock price, or have things been relatively quiet?
3. To provide a starting point for gauging a company's relative valuation, analysts often look at a company's price-to-earnings (P/E) ratio. Go to the website's summary quote or key statistics screen to see XOM's forward P/E ratio, which uses XOM's next 12-month estimate of earnings in the calculation, and to see its current P/E ratio. What are the firm's forward and current P/E ratios?
4. To put XOM's P/E ratio in perspective, it is useful to see how this ratio has varied over time. (If you go to Morningstar and click on the valuation tab, you should see a 10-year summary of its P/E ratio. In addition, it shows Exxon Mobil's 5-year average.) Is XOM's current P/E ratio well above or well below its 5-year average? Explain why the current P/E deviates from its historical trend. On the basis of this information, does XOM's current P/E suggest that the stock is undervalued or overvalued? Explain.
5. In the text, we discussed using the discounted dividend model to estimate a stock's intrinsic value. To keep things as simple as possible, let's assume at first that XOM's dividend is expected to grow at a constant rate of 4% annually over time. So, $g = 4\%$. If so, the intrinsic value equals $D_1/(r_s - g)$, where D_1 is the expected annual dividend 1 year from now, r_s is the stock's required rate of return, and g is the dividend's constant growth rate. Go back to the statistics screen and find XOM's current (trailing) annual dividend. Multiply this dividend by $1 + g$ to arrive at an estimate of D_1.
6. The required return on equity, r_s, is the final input needed to estimate intrinsic value. For our purposes, you can assume a number (say, 9% or 10%) or you can use the CAPM to calculate an estimate of the cost of equity, using the data available on the Internet. (For more details, look at the Taking a Closer Look exercise for Chapter 8.) Having decided on your best estimates for D_1, r_s, and g, you can calculate XOM's intrinsic value. Be careful to make sure that the long-run growth rate is less than the required rate of return. How does this estimate compare with the current stock price? Does your preliminary analysis suggest that XOM is undervalued or overvalued? Explain.

7. It is often useful to perform a sensitivity analysis, where you show how your estimate of intrinsic value varies according to different estimates of D_1, r_s, and g. To do so, recalculate your intrinsic value estimate for a range of different estimates for each of these key inputs. One convenient way to do this is to set up a simple data table in Excel. On the basis of this analysis, what inputs justify the current stock price?

8. Until now, we have assumed that XOM's dividend will grow at a long-run constant rate of 4%. To gauge whether this is a reasonable assumption, it's helpful to look at XOM's dividend history. If you go to the MSN Money website (www.msn.com/en-us/money/markets) and go to the annual income statement financials screen, you should see the firm's annual dividend over the past 4 years. On the basis of this information, what has been the average annual dividend growth rate?

   On the basis of the dividend history and your assessment of XOM's future dividend payout policies, do you think it is reasonable to assume that the constant growth model is a good proxy for intrinsic value? If not, how would you use the available data on the Internet to estimate intrinsic value using the nonconstant growth model?

9. Finally, you can also use the information on the Internet to value the entire corporation. This approach requires that you estimate XOM's annual free cash flows. Once you estimate the value of the firm's operations and the value of any non-operating assets, you subtract the value of debt and preferred stock to arrive at an estimate of the company's equity value. By dividing this value by the number of shares of common stock outstanding, you calculate an alternative estimate of the stock's intrinsic value. Although this approach may take additional time and involves more judgment concerning forecasts of future free cash flows, you can use the financial statements and growth forecasts on the Internet as useful starting points.

   If you go to the annual cash flow statement financials screen, you will find historical annual free cash flow values. These numbers are useful as a starting point to arrive at an estimate for the next year. Note that you can also obtain historical free cash flows over a 5-year period from Morningstar. After entering the company's ticker symbol, simply select the Financials tab, click on All Financials Data, select Cash flow, and make sure the annual dialog box is selected. (To find any definitions on Morningstar, scroll down to the bottom of the main screen page, and select Glossary. On the next screen you will see an alphabetic index; just click the first letter of the term for the definition you're interested in.)

Appendix 9A

Stock Market Equilibrium

Recall that r_X, the required return on Stock X, can be found using the security market line (SML) equation from the capital asset pricing model (CAPM), as discussed in Chapter 8:

$$r_X = r_{RF} + (r_M - r_{RF})b_X = r_{RF} + (RP_M)b_X$$

If the risk-free rate is 3%, the market risk premium is 5%, and Stock X has a beta of 2, the marginal investor will require a return of 13% on the stock:

$$r_X = 3\% + (5\%)2.0$$
$$= 13\%$$

This 13% required return is shown as the point on the SML in Figure 9A.1 associated with beta = 2.0. A marginal investor will purchase Stock X if its expected return is more than 13%, will sell it if the expected return is less than 13%, and will be indifferent (will hold it, but not buy or sell it) if the expected return is exactly 13%.

9A-1 An Illustration

Now suppose the investor's portfolio contains Stock X; he or she analyzes its prospects and concludes that its earnings, dividends, and price can be expected to grow at a constant rate of 4% per year. The last dividend was D_0 = \$1.9231, so the next expected dividend is as follows:

$$D_1 = \$1.9231(1.04) = \$2.00$$

The investor observes that the stock price, P_0, is \$25. Should he or she buy more of Stock X, sell the stock, or maintain the present position?

The investor can calculate Stock X's *expected rate of return* as follows:

$$\hat{r}_X = \frac{D_1}{P_0} + g = \frac{\$2}{\$25} + 4\% = 12\%$$

FIGURE 9A.1 Expected and Required Returns on Stock X

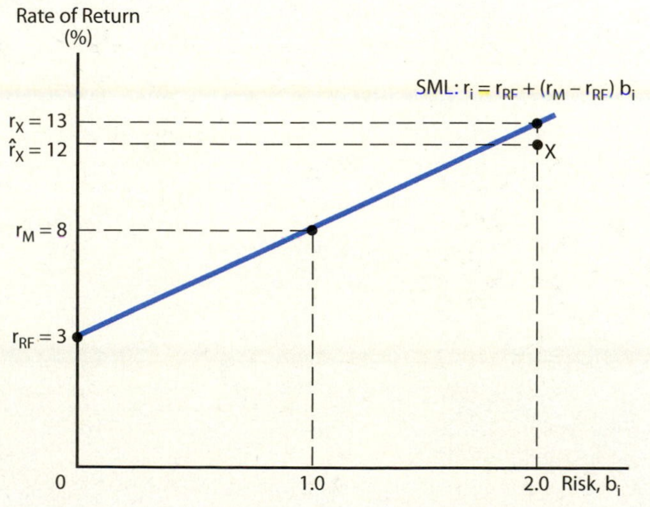

This value is plotted on Figure 9A.1 as point X, which is below the SML. Because the expected rate of return is less than the required return, he or she (and many other investors) would want to sell the stock. However, few people would want to buy at the $25 price, so the present owners would be unable to find buyers unless they reduced the stock price. Thus, the price would decline, and the decline would continue until the price hit $22.22. At that point, the stock would be in **equilibrium**, defined as the price at which the expected rate of return, 13%, is equal to the required rate of return:

Equilibrium
The condition under which the expected return on a security is just equal to its required return, $\hat{r}_i = r_i$. Also, $P_0 = \hat{P}_0$, and the price is stable.

$$\hat{r}_x = \frac{\$2.00}{\$22.22} + 4\% = 9\% + 4\% = 13\% = r_x$$

Had the stock initially sold for less than $22.22 (say, $20), events would have been reversed. Investors would have wanted to purchase the stock because its expected rate of return would have exceeded its required rate of return, buy orders would have come in, and the stock's price would have been driven up to $22.22.

To summarize, in equilibrium, two related conditions must hold:

1. A stock's expected rate of return as seen by the marginal investor must equal its required rate of return: $\hat{r}_i = r_i$.
2. The actual market price of the stock must equal its intrinsic value as estimated by the marginal investor: $P_0 = \hat{P}_0$.

Of course, some individual investors may believe that $\hat{r}_i > r_i$ and $\hat{P}_0 > P_0$ (hence, they would invest most of their funds in the stock), while other investors might have an opposite view and sell all of their shares. However, investors at the margin establish the actual market price; and for these investors, we must have $\hat{r}_i = r_i$ and $\hat{P}_0 = P_0$. If these conditions do not hold, trading will occur until they do.

9A-2 Changes in Equilibrium Stock Prices

Stock prices are not constant—they undergo violent changes at times. For example, during the week of October 6, 2008, through October 10, 2008, the Dow Jones Industrial Average fell more than 1,874 points, representing an 18% decline. On October 27, 1997, the Dow Jones Industrial fell 554 points, a 7.18% drop in value. Even worse, on October 19, 1987, the Dow lost 508 points, causing an average stock to lose 23% of its value on that one day, and some individual stocks lost more than 70%. More recently, on February 5, 2018, the Dow lost 1,175 points, representing a 4.60% drop in value.

To see what could cause such changes to occur, assume that Stock X is in equilibrium, selling at a price of $22.22 per share. If all expectations were met exactly, during the next year the price would gradually rise to $23.11, or by 4%. However, suppose conditions changed as indicated in the second column of the following table:

	Variable Value	
	Original	**New**
Risk-free rate, r_{RF}	3%	2%
Market risk premium, $r_M - r_{RF}$	5%	4%
Stock X's beta coefficient, b_X	2.0	1.25
Stock X's expected growth rate, g_X	4%	5%
D_0	$1.9231	$1.9231
Price of Stock X	$22.22	?

Now give yourself a test: How would the change in each variable, by itself, affect the price, and what new price would result?

Every change, taken alone, would lead to an *increase* in the price. The first three changes together lower r_X, which declines from 13% to 7%:

$$\text{Original } r_X = 3\% + 5\%(2.0) = 13\%$$
$$\text{New } r_X = 2\% + 4\%(1.25) = 7\%$$

Using these values, together with the new g, we find that $\hat{P}_0$ rises from \$22.22 to \$100.96, or by approximately 354%:[1]

$$\text{Original } \hat{P}_0 = \frac{\$1.9231(1.04)}{0.13 - 0.04} = \frac{\$2.00}{0.09} = \$22.22$$

$$\text{New } \hat{P}_0 = \frac{\$1.9231(1.05)}{0.07 - 0.05} = \frac{\$2.0193}{0.02} = \$100.96$$

Note too that at the new price, the expected and required rates of return will be equal:[2]

$$\hat{r}_X = \frac{\$2.0193}{\$100.96} + 5\% = 7\% = r_X$$

Evidence suggests that stocks, especially those of large companies, adjust rapidly when their fundamental positions change. Such stocks are followed closely by a number of security analysts, so as soon as things change, so does the stock price. Consequently, equilibrium ordinarily exists for any given stock, and required and expected returns are generally close to equal. Stock prices certainly change, sometimes violently and rapidly, but this simply reflects changing conditions and expectations. There are, of course, times when a stock will continue to react for several months to unfolding favorable or unfavorable developments. However, this does not signify a long adjustment period; it simply indicates that as more new information about the situation becomes available, the market adjusts to it.

Questions

9A-1 For a stock to be in equilibrium, what two conditions must hold?

9A-2 If a stock is not in equilibrium, explain how financial markets adjust to bring it into equilibrium.

Problems

9A-1 **RATES OF RETURN AND EQUILIBRIUM** Stock C's beta coefficient is $b_C = 0.4$, and Stock D's is $b_D = -0.5$. (Stock D's beta is negative, indicating that its return rises when returns on most other stocks fall. There are very few negative beta stocks, although collection agency stocks are sometimes cited as an example.)

a. If the risk-free rate is 7% and the required rate of return on an average stock is 11%, what are the required rates of return on Stocks C and D?

b. For Stock C, suppose the current price, P_0, is \$25.00; the next expected dividend, D_1, is \$1.50; and the stock's expected constant growth rate is 4%. Is the stock in equilibrium? Explain and describe what will happen if the stock is not in equilibrium.

---

[1]A price change of this magnitude is by no means rare. The prices of *many* stocks double or halve during a year. For example, in 2017, NRG Energy's stock price increased by 133.70%. On the other hand, Under Armour's stock price declined by 47.08%.

[2]It should be obvious by now that actual realized rates of return are not necessarily equal to expected and required returns. Thus, an investor might have expected to receive a return of 12% if he or she had purchased NRG Energy's or Under Armour's stock in 2017, but after the fact, the realized return on NRG Energy was far above 12%, whereas the return on Under Armour was far below 12%.

9A-2 **EQUILIBRIUM STOCK PRICE** The risk-free rate of return, r_{RF}, is 6%; the required rate of return on the market, r_M, is 10%, and Upton Company's stock has a beta coefficient of 1.5.

a. If the dividend expected during the coming year, D_1, is \$2.25 and if g = a constant 5%, at what price should Upton's stock sell?

b. Now suppose the Federal Reserve Board increases the money supply, causing the risk-free rate to drop to 5% and r_M to fall to 9%. What would happen to Upton's price?

c. In addition to the change in part b, suppose investors' risk aversion declines and this, combined with the decline in r_{RF}, causes r_M to fall to 8%. Now what is Upton's price?

d. Suppose Upton has a change in management. The new group institutes policies that increase the expected constant growth rate from 5% to 6%. Also, the new management smoothes out fluctuations in sales and profits, causing beta to decline from 1.5 to 1.3. Assume that r_{RF} and r_M are equal to the values in part c. After all these changes, what is its new equilibrium price? (*Note:* D_1 is now \$2.27.)

9A-3 **BETA COEFFICIENTS** Suppose Chance Chemical Company's management conducted a study and concluded that if it expands its consumer products division (which is less risky than its primary business, industrial chemicals), its beta will decline from 1.2 to 0.9. However, consumer products have a somewhat lower profit margin, and this would cause its constant growth rate in earnings and dividends to fall from 6% to 4%. The following also apply: r_M = 9%, r_{RF} = 6%, and D_0 = \$2.00.

a. Should management expand the consumer products division? Explain.

b. Assume all the facts given except the change in the beta coefficient. How low would the beta have to fall to cause the expansion to be a good one? (*Hint:* Set $\hat{P}_0$ under the new policy equal to $\hat{P}_0$ under the old one, and find the new beta that will produce this equality.)

part 4

Investing in Long-Term Assets: Capital Budgeting

CHAPTERS

The Cost of Capital

CHAPTER 10

Jonathan Weiss/Shutterstock.com

Creating Value at Disney

Walt Disney Co. (DIS) is one of the world's most successful companies. Despite a tough economic environment over the past few years, Disney's managers have worked hard to create value for shareholders by investing in assets that earn more than the cost of the capital used to acquire them. For example, if a project earns 20%, but the capital invested in it costs only 10%, taking on the project will increase the firm's value and thus its stock price.

Capital is obtained in three primary forms: debt, preferred stock, and common equity, with equity acquired by retaining earnings and issuing new stock. The investors who provide capital to Disney expect to earn at least their required rate of return on that capital, and the required return represents the firm's cost of capital.[1]

A variety of factors influence the cost of capital. Some—including interest rates, state and federal tax policies, and general economic conditions—are outside the firm's control. However, the firm's decisions regarding how it raises capital and how it invests those funds also have a profound effect on its cost of capital. For example, in the summer of 2018, Disney was in a battle with Comcast to acquire a significant portion of 21st Century Fox. If Disney successfully acquires these assets, then it will likely see a change in the riskiness of its assets and perhaps also a change in both its organizational structure and capital structure.

Estimating the cost of capital for a company such as Disney is conceptually straightforward. Disney's capital comes from debt plus common

[1]Recall from earlier chapters that expected and required returns as seen by the marginal investor must be equal; otherwise, the security will not be in equilibrium. Therefore, buying and selling will force this equality to hold, except for short periods immediately following the release of new information. Because expected and required returns are normally equal, we use the two terms interchangeably.

equity, so its cost of capital depends largely on the level of interest rates in the economy and the marginal stockholder's required rate of return on equity. However, Disney operates many different divisions throughout the world, so the corporation is similar to a portfolio that contains a number of different stocks, each with a different risk. Recall that portfolio risk is a weighted average of the relevant risks of the different stocks in the portfolio.

Similarly, each of Disney's divisions has its own level of risk and hence its own cost of capital. Therefore, Disney's overall cost of capital is a weighted average of its divisions' costs. For example, Disney's Media Networks segment (which includes ABC and ESPN) probably has a different cost of capital than its Parks and Resorts unit (which includes Disney World Resort, Disneyland, the Disney Cruise Line, and Disney Vacation Club); even projects within divisions have different costs because some projects are riskier than others. Moreover, its overseas projects may have different risks and thus different costs of capital than similar domestic projects. As we will see in this chapter, the cost of capital is an essential element in a firm's capital budgeting process. This process is the primary determinant of the firm's long-run stock price.

PUTTING THINGS IN PERSPECTIVE

In the last four chapters, we explained how risk influences prices and required rates of return on bonds and stocks. A firm's primary objective is to maximize its shareholders' value. The principal way value is increased is by investing in projects that earn more than their cost of capital. In the next two chapters, we will see that a project's future cash flows can be forecasted and that those cash flows can be discounted to find their present value. Then if the PV of the future cash flows exceeds the project's cost, the firm's value will increase if the project is accepted. However, we need a discount rate to find the PV of these future cash flows, and that discount rate is the firm's cost of capital. Finding the cost of the capital required to take on new projects is the primary focus of this chapter.[2]

Most formulas used in this chapter were developed earlier, when we examined the required rates of return on bonds and stocks in Chapters 7 and 9. *Indeed, the rates of return that investors require on bonds and stocks represent the costs of those securities to the firm.* As we shall see, companies estimate the required returns on their securities, calculate a weighted average of the costs of their different types of capital, and use this average cost for capital budgeting purposes.

When you finish this chapter, you should be able to do the following:

- **Explain why the weighted average cost of capital (WACC) is used in capital budgeting.**
- **Estimate the costs of different capital components—debt, preferred stock, retained earnings, and common stock.**
- **Combine the different component costs to determine the firm's WACC.**

These concepts are necessary to understand the firm's capital budgeting process.

[2]If projects differ in risk, risk-adjusted costs of capital should be used, not one single corporate cost of capital. We will discuss this point later in Section 10-9.

resource

Students can download the Excel chapter models from the textbook's student companion site on cengage.com. Once downloaded onto your computer, retrieve the Chapter 10 Excel model and follow along as you read this chapter.

10-1 An Overview of the Weighted Average Cost of Capital (WACC)

Table 10.1 shows Allied Food Products's balance sheet as presented in Chapter 3, with three additions: (1) the actual capital supplied by investors (banks, bondholders, and stockholders), calculated using the accounting-based book values, (2) the market values of the investor-supplied capital, and (3) the target capital structure that Allied plans to use in the future.

When calculating the WACC, our concern is with capital that must be provided by *investors*—interest-bearing debt, preferred stock, and common equity. Accounts payable and accruals, which arise spontaneously when capital budgeting projects are undertaken, are not included as part of investor-supplied capital because they do not come directly from investors. Looking at column 1 of Table 10.1, we see that using the accounting-based book values, Allied's capital consists of 47.8% debt and 52.2% equity.

Although these accounting-based measures are important, Allied's investors are more concerned about the current market value of the company's debt and equity, which are shown in column 2 of Table 10.1. To keep things relatively simple, we assume that the market value of Allied's debt is equal to its book value (i.e., we assume that its average outstanding debt is trading at its par value).[3] The market value of equity is the number of shares of stock outstanding multiplied by the current stock price. Recall from Chapter 3 that Allied has 75 million shares

TABLE 10.1 Allied Food Products: Capital Structure Used to Calculate the WACC (dollars in millions)

Assets and Claims Against Assets at Book Value on 12/31/19					Investor-Supplied Capital: Payables and Accruals Are Excluded Because They Come from Operations, Not from Investors				
Assets		Claims			Book Value (1)		Market Value (2)		Target (3)
Cash	$ 10	Accounts payable	$ 60	3.0%					
Receivables	375	Accruals	140	7.0%					
Inventories	615	Notes payable	110	5.5%	$ 110		$ 110		
Total C.A.	$1,000	Total C.L.	$ 310	15.5%					
Net fixed assets	$1,000	Long-term debt	750	37.5%	750		750		
		Total liabilities	$1,060	53.0%	$ 860	47.8%	$ 860	33.2%	33.0%
		Preferred stock	-	0.0%	-	0.0%	-	0.0%	2.0%
		Common stock	130	6.5%	130				
		Retained earnings	810	40.5%	810				
		Total common equity	$ 940	47.0%	$ 940	52.2%	$1,730	66.8%	65.0
Total	$2,000	Total	$2,000	100.0%	$1,800	100.0%	$2,590	100.0%	100.0%

Notes:

1. The market value calculations assume that the company's debt is trading at par, so the market value of debt equals the book value of debt.
2. The market value of equity is the share price of common stock multiplied by the number of shares outstanding. At 12/31/19, the firm has 75 million shares outstanding, and its stock sold for $23.06 per share.

[3]In practice, the market value of debt may be somewhat higher or lower than its book value, depending on whether the outstanding bonds are trading at a premium or at a discount. Again, to keep things simple, for our purposes we will generally assume that the market value of debt equals the book value of debt when calculating the WACC.

of common stock outstanding, and the company's stock currently trades at $23.06 per share, which means that the market value of its equity is $1.73 billion. Because the market value of its equity exceeds the book value of its equity, we see that Allied's market-based capital structure has a higher percentage of equity (66.8%) than the capital structure that was calculated using its accounting-based book values (52.2%).

Although these market-based numbers are a useful starting point, what ultimately matters is the **target capital structure**, which refers to how Allied plans to raise capital to fund its future projects. In Chapter 13, we explore in more detail how companies determine their target capital structure. As we will see, there is an optimal capital structure—one where the percentages of debt, preferred stock, and common equity maximize the firm's value. As shown in column 3 of Table 10.1, Allied Food has concluded that its target capital structure should include 33% debt, 2% preferred stock, and 65% common equity, and in the future it plans to raise capital in those proportions. Therefore, we use those target weights when we calculate Allied's WACC. It follows that Allied's overall cost of capital is a weighted average of the costs of the various types of capital it uses, where the weights correspond to the company's target capital structure.

Target Capital Structure
The mix of debt, preferred stock, and common equity the firm plans to raise to fund its future projects.

Self*Test*

When calculating WACC, what capital is excluded and why?

When calculating a company's WACC, should book value, market value, or target weights be used? Explain.

Why might the weights of capital be different depending on whether book values, market values, or target values are used?

10-2 Basic Definitions

The investor-supplied items—debt, preferred stock, and common equity—are called **capital components**. Increases in assets must be financed by increases in these capital components. The cost of each component is called its *component* cost; for example, Allied can borrow money at 8%, so its component cost of debt is 8%.[4] These costs are then combined to form a WACC, which is used in the firm's capital budgeting analysis. Throughout this chapter, we concentrate on the three major capital components. The following symbols identify the cost and weight of each:

Capital Components
One of the types of capital used by firms to raise funds.

r_d = interest rate on the firm's new debt = before-tax component cost of debt. It can be found in several ways, including calculating the yield to maturity on the firm's currently outstanding bonds.

[4]We will see shortly that there is a before-tax and an after-tax cost of debt; for now, it is sufficient to know that 8% is the before-tax component cost of debt. Also, for simplicity, we assume that long- and short-term debt have the same cost; hence, we deal with just one type of debt. Finally, realize that Allied's cost of each capital component is meant to be illustrative. As we see in real-world examples, Allied's numbers are higher than current real-world numbers but closer in line with long-run averages.

$r_d(1 - T)$ = after-tax component cost of debt, where T is the firm's marginal tax rate. *$r_d(1-T)$ is the debt cost used to calculate the weighted average cost of capital.* As we shall see, the after-tax cost of debt is lower than its before-tax cost because interest is tax deductible.

r_p = component cost of preferred stock, found as the yield investors expect to earn on the preferred stock. Preferred dividends are not tax deductible; hence, the before- and after-tax costs of preferred are equal.

r_s = component cost of common equity raised by retaining earnings, or *internal equity*. It is the r_s developed in Chapters 8 and 9 and defined there as the rate of return that investors require on a firm's common stock. Most firms, once they have become well established, obtain all of their new equity as retained earnings; hence, r_s is their cost of all new equity.

r_e = component cost of *external equity*, or common equity raised by issuing new stock. As we will see, r_e is equal to r_s plus a factor that reflects the cost of issuing new stock. Note, though, that established firms such as Allied Food rarely issue new stock; hence, r_e is rarely a relevant consideration except for very young, rapidly growing firms.

w_d, w_p, w_c = target weights of debt, preferred stock, and common equity (which includes retained earnings, internal equity, and new common stock, external equity). The weights are the percentages of the different types of capital the firm plans to use when it raises capital in the future. Target weights may differ from actual current weights.[5]

WACC = the firm's weighted average, or overall, cost of capital.

Weighted Average Cost of Capital (WACC)
A weighted average of the component costs of debt, preferred stock, and common equity.

The target proportions of debt (w_d), preferred stock (w_p), and common equity (w_c), along with the costs of those components, are used to calculate the firm's **weighted average cost of capital, WACC**. We assume at this point that all new common equity is raised as retained earnings, as is true for most companies; hence, the cost of common equity is r_s:

$$\text{WACC} = \left(\begin{array}{c}\%\\ \text{of}\\ \text{debt}\end{array}\right)\left(\begin{array}{c}\text{After-tax}\\ \text{cost of}\\ \text{debt}\end{array}\right) + \left(\begin{array}{c}\%\text{ of}\\ \text{preferred}\\ \text{stock}\end{array}\right)\left(\begin{array}{c}\text{Cost of}\\ \text{preferred}\\ \text{stock}\end{array}\right) + \left(\begin{array}{c}\%\text{ of}\\ \text{common}\\ \text{equity}\end{array}\right)\left(\begin{array}{c}\text{Cost of}\\ \text{common}\\ \text{equity}\end{array}\right)$$

$$= w_d r_d(1 - T) + w_p r_p + w_c r_s \quad \text{10.1}$$

Note that only debt has a tax adjustment factor (1 − T). As discussed in the next section, this is because interest on debt is tax deductible, but preferred dividends and the returns on common stock (dividends and capital gains) are not.

These definitions and concepts are discussed in the remainder of the chapter, using Allied Food for illustrative purposes. Later in Chapter 13, we extend the discussion to show how the optimal mix of securities minimizes the firm's cost of capital and maximizes its value.

---

[5]In Chapter 13, we will discuss in more detail how firms determine their target weights of debt, preferred stock, and common equity. As we indicate in the text, these target weights may differ from actual current weights. The current weights can be estimated using either book or market values. Book values follow directly from the company's balance sheet, whereas market values depend on current market prices for the company's debt, preferred stock, and common equity. For example, the market value of equity equals the number of shares outstanding multiplied by the current stock price. From a theoretical perspective, most analysts believe that market value provides a better assessment of the company's current capital structure. However, bond rating agencies and security analysts will sometimes also consider the company's book weights when assessing the company's position.

Self*Test*

Identify the firm's three major capital structure components, and give their respective component cost and weight symbols.

Why might there be two different component costs for common equity? Which one is generally relevant, and for what type of firm is the second one likely to be relevant?

If a firm now has a debt ratio of 50% but plans to finance with only 40% debt in the future, what should it use as w_d when it calculates its WACC? Explain.

10-3 Cost of Debt, $r_d(1-T)$

The interest rate a firm must pay on its *new* debt is defined as its **before-tax cost of debt, r_d**. Firms can estimate r_d by asking their bankers what it will cost to borrow or by finding the yield to maturity on their currently outstanding debt (as we illustrated in Chapter 7). *However, the* **after-tax cost of debt, $r_d(1-T)$**, *should be used to calculate the weighted average cost of capital*. This is the interest rate on new debt, r_d, less the tax savings that result because interest is tax deductible:[6]

Before-Tax Cost of Debt, r_d
The interest rate the firm must pay on new debt.

After-Tax Cost of Debt, $r_d(1-T)$
The relevant cost of new debt, taking into account the tax deductibility of interest; used to calculate the WACC.

$$\begin{aligned}\text{After-tax cost of debt} &= \text{Interest rate on new debt} - \text{Tax savings} \\ &= r_d - r_dT \\ &= r_d(1-T)\end{aligned} \qquad (10.2)$$

In effect, the government pays part of the cost of debt because interest is tax deductible. Therefore, if Allied can borrow at an interest rate of 8%, and its marginal federal-plus-state tax rate is 25%, its after-tax cost of debt will be 6%:[7]

$$\begin{aligned}\text{After-tax cost of debt} &= r_d(1-T) \\ &= 8\%(1.0-0.25) \\ &= 8\%(0.75) \\ &= 6.0\%\end{aligned}$$

We use the after-tax cost of debt in calculating the WACC because we are interested in maximizing the value of the firm's stock, and the stock price depends on *after-tax* cash flows. Because we are concerned with after-tax cash flows and because cash flows and rates of return should be calculated on a comparable basis, we adjust the interest rate downward due to debt's preferential tax treatment.[8]

It is important to emphasize that the cost of debt is the interest rate on *new* debt, not outstanding debt. We are interested in the cost of new debt because

[6]If Allied borrowed $100,000 at 8%, it would have to write a check for $8,000 to pay annual interest charges. However, that $8,000 would be a tax deduction, which at a 25% tax rate would save $2,000 annually in taxes. The tax rate is *zero* for a firm with losses. Therefore, for a company that does not pay taxes, the cost of debt is not reduced. In Equation 10.2, if the tax rate is zero, the after-tax cost of debt is not reduced and is simply equal to the before-tax cost of debt.

[7]Note that in 2018, the federal tax rate for corporations is a single flat rate of 21%. However, most corporations are also subject to state income taxes, so for illustrative purposes, we assume that the effective federal-plus-state tax rate on marginal income is 25%.

[8]Strictly speaking, the after-tax cost of debt should reflect the *expected* cost of debt. Although Allied's bonds have a promised return of 8%, there is some chance of default, so its bondholders' expected return (and consequently Allied's cost) is a bit less than 8%. For a relatively strong company such as Allied, this difference is quite small. As we discuss later in the chapter, Allied must also incur flotation costs when it issues debt, but like the difference between the promised and the expected rates of return, flotation costs for debt are generally small. Finally, note that these two factors tend to offset one another—not including the possibility of default leads to an overstatement of the cost of debt, but not including flotation costs leads to an understatement. For all these reasons, r_d is generally a good approximation of the before-tax cost of debt capital and $r_d(1-T)$ of the after-tax cost.

our primary concern with the cost of capital is its use in capital budgeting decisions. For example, would a new machine earn a return greater than the cost of the capital needed to acquire the machine? The rate at which the firm has borrowed in the past is irrelevant when answering this question because we need to know the cost of *new capital. For these reasons, the yield to maturity on outstanding debt (which reflects current market conditions) is a better measure of the cost of debt than the coupon rate.* Note that if the yield curve is upward or downward sloping, the cost of long- and short-term debt will differ. In these cases, the yield to maturity on the company's long-term debt is generally used to calculate the cost of debt because, more often than not, the capital is being raised to fund long-term projects.[9] However, as we see in Chapter 15, some companies regularly use a mix of short-term and long-term debt to finance their projects. When calculating their costs of debt, these companies may choose to calculate an average of their debt costs based on the proportion of long- and short-term debt that they plan to use.

Self*Test*

Why is the after-tax cost of debt rather than the before-tax cost used to calculate the WACC?

Why is the relevant cost of debt the interest rate on *new* debt, not that on already outstanding, or *old*, debt?

How can the yield to maturity on a firm's outstanding debt be used to estimate its before-tax cost of debt?

A company has outstanding 20-year noncallable bonds with a face value of $1,000, an 11% annual coupon, and a market price of $1,294.54. If the company was to issue new debt, what would be a reasonable estimate of the interest rate on that debt? If the company's tax rate is 25%, what is its after-tax cost of debt? **(8.0%, 6.0%)**

10-4 Cost of Preferred Stock, r_p

Cost of Preferred Stock, r_p
The rate of return investors require on the firm's preferred stock; r_p is calculated as the preferred dividend, D_p, divided by the current price, P_p.

The component **cost of preferred stock, r_p,** used to calculate the WACC is the preferred dividend, D_p, divided by the current price of the preferred stock, P_p:

$$\text{Component cost of preferred stock} = r_p = \frac{D_p}{P_p} \qquad (10.3)$$

Allied does not have any preferred stock outstanding, but the company plans to issue some in the future and therefore has included it in its target capital structure. Allied would sell this stock to a few large hedge funds, the stock would have a $10.00 dividend per share, and it would be priced at $97.50 a share. Therefore, Allied's cost of preferred stock would be 10.3%:[10]

$$r_p = \$10.00/\$97.50 = 10.3\%$$

[9]To get a true measure of the cost of debt, you should use the yield to maturity on outstanding debt that is noncallable and not convertible to common stock.

[10]This preferred stock would be sold directly to a group of hedge funds, so no flotation costs would be incurred. If significant flotation costs were involved, the cost of the preferred should be adjusted upward, as we explain in a later section.

As we can see from Equation 10.3, calculating the cost of preferred stock is easy. This is particularly true for traditional "plain vanilla" preferred that pays a fixed dividend in perpetuity. However, in Chapter 9, we noted that some preferred issues have a specified maturity date and we described how to calculate the expected return on these issues. Also, preferred stock may include an option to convert to common stock, which adds another layer of complexity. We leave these more complicated situations for advanced classes. Finally, note that no tax adjustments are made when calculating r_p because preferred dividends, unlike interest on debt, are *not* tax deductible, so no tax savings are associated with preferred stock.

Self*Test*

Is a tax adjustment made to the cost of preferred stock? Why or why not?

A company's preferred stock currently trades at $80 per share and pays a $6 annual dividend per share. Ignoring flotation costs, what is the firm's cost of preferred stock? **(7.50%)**

10-5 Cost of Retained Earnings, r_s

The costs of debt and preferred stock are based on the returns that investors require on these securities. Similarly, the cost of common equity is based on the rate of return that investors require on the company's common stock. Note, though, that new common equity is raised in two ways: (1) by retaining some of the current year's earnings and (2) by issuing new common stock.[11] We use the symbol r_s to designate the **cost of retained earnings** and r_e to designate the **cost of new common stock**, or external equity. Equity raised by issuing stock has a higher cost than equity from retained earnings due to the flotation costs required to sell new common stock. Therefore, once firms get beyond the start-up stage, they normally obtain all of their new equity by retaining earnings.

Cost of Retained Earnings, r_s
The rate of return required by stockholders on a firm's common stock.

Cost of New Common Stock, r_e
The cost of external equity; based on the cost of retained earnings, but increased for flotation costs necessary to issue new common stock.

Some have argued that retained earnings should be "free" because they represent money that is "left over" after dividends are paid. Although it is true that no direct costs are associated with retained earnings, this capital still has a cost, an *opportunity cost*. The firm's after-tax earnings belong to its stockholders. Bondholders are compensated by interest payments; preferred stockholders, by preferred dividends. But the net earnings remaining after paying interest and preferred dividends belong to the common stockholders, and these earnings serve to compensate them for the use of their capital. The managers, who work for the stockholders, can either pay out earnings in the form of dividends or retain earnings for reinvestment in the business. When managers make this decision, they should recognize that there is an opportunity cost involved—stockholders could have received the earnings as dividends and invested this money in other stocks, in bonds, in real estate, or in

[11]The term *retained earnings* can be interpreted to mean the balance sheet account *retained earnings*, consisting of all the earnings retained in the business throughout its history or the income statement item *addition to retained earnings*. The income statement item is relevant in this chapter. For our purpose, *retained earnings* refers to that part of the current year's earnings not paid as dividends (hence, available for reinvestment in the business this year). If this is not clear, look back at Allied's balance sheet shown in Table 3.1 and note that at the end of 2018, Allied had $750 million of retained earnings, but that figure rose to $810 million by the end of 2019. Then look at the 2019 income statement, where you will see that Allied retained $60 million of its 2019 income. This $60 million was the new equity from retained earnings that was used, along with some additional debt, to fund the 2019 capital budgeting projects. Also, you can see from the 2018 and 2019 balance sheets that Allied had $130 million of common stock at the end of both years. This indicates that it did not issue (sell) any new common stock to raise capital during 2019.

anything else. *Therefore, the firm needs to earn at least as much on any earnings retained as the stockholders could earn on alternative investments of comparable risk.*

What rate of return can stockholders expect to earn on equivalent-risk investments? First, recall from Chapter 9 that stocks are normally in equilibrium, with expected and required rates of return equal: $\hat{r}_s = r_s$. Thus, Allied's stockholders expect to be able to earn r_s on their money. *Therefore, if the firm cannot invest retained earnings to earn at least r_s, it should pay those funds to its stockholders and let them invest directly in stocks or other assets that will provide that return.*

Whereas debt and preferred stocks are contractual obligations whose costs are clearly stated within the contracts, stocks have no comparable stated cost rate. That makes it difficult to measure r_s. However, we can employ the techniques developed in Chapters 8 and 9 to produce reasonably good estimates of the cost of equity from retained earnings. To begin, recall that if a stock is in equilibrium, its *required rate of return*, r_s, must be equal to its *expected rate of return*, $\hat{r}_s$. Further, its *required return* is equal to a risk-free rate, r_{RF}, plus a risk premium, RP, whereas the *expected return* on the stock is its expected dividend yield, D_1/P_0, plus its expected growth rate, g. Thus, we can write the following equation and estimate r_s using the left term, the right term, or both terms:

Required rate of return = Expected rate of return

$$r_s = r_{RF} + RP = D_1/P_0 + g = \hat{r}_s \qquad \textbf{10.4}$$

The left term is based on the capital asset pricing model (CAPM) as discussed in Chapter 8, and the right term is based on the discounted dividend model as developed in Chapter 9. We discuss these two procedures, in addition to one based on the firm's own cost of debt, in the following sections.

10-5A CAPM APPROACH

The most widely used method for estimating the cost of common equity is the capital asset pricing model (CAPM) as developed in Chapter 8.[12] Here are the steps used to find r_s:

Step 1: Estimate the risk-free rate, r_{RF}. We generally use the 10-year Treasury bond rate as the measure of the risk-free rate, but some analysts use the short-term Treasury bill rate.

Step 2: Estimate the stock's beta coefficient, b_i, and use it as an index of the stock's risk. The *i* signifies the *i*th company's beta.

Step 3: Estimate the market risk premium. Recall that the market risk premium is the difference between the return that investors require on an average stock and the risk-free rate.[13]

[12] A survey by John Graham and Campbell Harvey indicates that the CAPM approach is most often used to estimate the cost of equity. More than 70% of the surveyed firms used the CAPM approach. In some cases, they used beta from the CAPM as one determinant of r_s, but they also added other factors thought to improve the estimate. For more details, see John R. Graham and Campbell R. Harvey, "The Theory and Practice of Corporate Finance: Evidence from the Field," *Journal of Financial Economics*, vol. 60, nos. 2 and 3 (May–June 2001), pp. 187–243. For further survey evidence regarding techniques that companies use to estimate their costs of capital, refer to W. Todd Brotherson, Kenneth Eades, Robert Harris, and Robert Higgins, "'Best Practices' in Estimating the Cost of Capital: An Update," *Journal of Applied Finance: Theory, Practice, Education*, vol. 23, no. 1 (2013), pp. 15–33.

[13] It is important to be consistent in the use of a long-term versus a short-term rate for r_{RF} and for the market risk premium. The market risk premium ($RP_M = r_M - r_{RF}$) depends on the measure used for the risk-free rate. The yield curve is normally upward-sloping, so the 10-year Treasury bond rate normally exceeds the short-term Treasury bill rate. In this case, it follows that one will obtain a lower estimate of the market risk premium if the higher longer-term bond rate is used as the risk-free rate. At any rate, the r_{RF} used to find the market risk premium should be the same as the r_{RF} used as the first term in the CAPM equation.

Step 4: Substitute the preceding values in the CAPM equation to estimate the required rate of return on the stock in question:

$$\begin{aligned} r_s &= r_{RF} + (RP_M)b_i \\ &= r_{RF} + (r_M - r_{RF})b_i \end{aligned} \qquad 10.5$$

Thus, the CAPM estimate of r_s is equal to the risk-free rate, r_{RF}, plus a risk premium that is equal to the risk premium on an average stock, $(r_M - r_{RF})$, scaled up or down to reflect the particular stock's risk as measured by its beta coefficient, b_i.

Assume that in today's market, $r_{RF} = 4.5\%$, the market risk premium is $RP_M = 5.0\%$, and Allied's beta is 1.50. Using the CAPM approach, Allied's cost of equity is estimated to be 12.0%:

$$\begin{aligned} r_s &= 4.5\% + (5.0\%)(1.50) \\ &= 12.0\% \end{aligned}$$

Although the CAPM appears to produce an accurate, precise estimate of r_s, several potential problems exist. First, as we saw in Chapter 8, if a firm's stockholders are not well diversified, they may be concerned with *stand-alone risk* rather than just market risk. In that case, the firm's true investment risk would not be measured by its beta and the CAPM estimate would understate the correct value of r_s. Further, even if the CAPM theory is valid, it is hard to obtain accurate estimates of the required inputs because (1) there is controversy about whether to use long-term or short-term Treasury yields for r_{RF}, (2) it is hard to estimate the beta that investors expect the company to have in the future, and (3) it is difficult to estimate the proper market risk premium. As we indicated earlier, the CAPM approach is used most often, but because of the just-noted problems, analysts also estimate the cost of equity using the other approaches discussed in the following sections.

10-5B BOND-YIELD-PLUS-RISK-PREMIUM APPROACH

In situations where reliable inputs for the CAPM approach are not available, as would be true for a closely held company, analysts often use a somewhat subjective procedure to estimate the cost of equity. Empirical studies suggest that the risk premium on a firm's stock over its own bonds generally ranges from 3 to 5 percentage points.[14] Based on this evidence, one might simply add a judgmental risk premium of 3% to 5% to the interest rate on the firm's own long-term debt to estimate its cost of equity. Firms with risky, low-rated, and consequently high-interest-rate debt also have risky, high-cost equity, and the procedure of basing the cost of equity on the firm's own readily observable debt cost utilizes this logic. For example, given that Allied's bonds yield 8%, its cost of equity might be estimated as follows:

$$r_s = \text{Bond yield} + \text{Risk premium} = 8.0\% + 4.0\% = 12.0\%$$

The bonds of a riskier company might have a higher yield, 12%, in which case the estimated cost of equity would be 16%:

$$r_s = 12.0\% + 4.0\% = 16.0\%$$

[14] Roger G. Ibbotson has calculated the historical returns on common stocks and on corporate bonds and used the differential as an estimate of the *historical risk premium* of stocks over corporate bonds. Historical risk premiums vary from year to year, but a range of 3% to 5% is common. Also, analysts have calculated the CAPM required return on equity for publicly traded firms in a given industry, averaged them, subtracted those firms' average bond yield, and used the differential as an *expected risk premium*. Again, these risk premium estimates are often generally in the 3% to 5% range.

Because the 4% risk premium is an estimate based on judgment, the estimated value of r_s is also judgmental. Therefore, one might use a range of 3% to 5% for the risk premium and obtain a range of 11% to 13% for Allied. Although this method does not produce a precise cost of equity, it should "get us in the right ballpark."

10-5C DIVIDEND-YIELD-PLUS-GROWTH-RATE, OR DISCOUNTED CASH FLOW (DCF), APPROACH

In Chapter 9, we saw that both the price and the expected rate of return on a share of common stock depend, ultimately, on the stock's expected cash flows. For companies that are expected to remain in business indefinitely, the cash flows are the dividends; on the other hand, if investors expect the firm to be acquired by some other company or to be liquidated, the cash flows will be dividends for some number of years plus a price at the horizon date when the firm is expected to be acquired or liquidated. Like most firms, Allied is expected to continue indefinitely, in which case the following equation applies:

$$P_0 = \frac{D_1}{(1 + r_s)^1} + \frac{D_2}{(1 + r_s)^2} + \cdots + \frac{D_\infty}{(1 + r_s)^\infty} \quad \textbf{10.6}$$

$$= \sum_{t=1}^{\infty} \frac{D_t}{(1 + r_s)^t}$$

Here P_0 is the current stock price, D_t is the dividend expected to be paid at the end of Year t, and r_s is the required rate of return. If dividends are expected to grow at a constant rate, as we saw in Chapter 9, Equation 10.6 reduces to this important formula:[15]

$$P_0 = \frac{D_1}{r_s - g} \quad \textbf{10.7}$$

We can solve for r_s to obtain the required rate of return on common equity, which for the marginal investor is also equal to the expected rate of return:

$$r_s = \hat{r}_s = \frac{D_1}{P_0} + \text{Expected } g \quad \textbf{10.8}$$

Thus, investors expect to receive a dividend yield, D_1/P_0, plus a capital gain, g, for a total expected return of $\hat{r}_s$; in equilibrium, this expected return is also equal to the required return, r_s. This method of estimating the cost of equity is called the *discounted cash flow,* or *DCF, method.* Henceforth, we will assume that equilibrium exists, which permits us to use the terms r_s and $\hat{r}_s$ interchangeably.

It is easy to calculate the dividend yield, but because stock prices fluctuate, the yield varies from day to day, which leads to fluctuations in the DCF cost of equity. Also, it is difficult to determine the proper growth rate. If past growth rates in earnings and dividends have been relatively stable, and if investors expect a continuation of past trends, g may be based on the firm's historic growth rate. *However, if the company's past growth has been abnormally high or low due to a unique situation or because of general economic fluctuations, investors will not project historical growth rates into the future.* In this case, which applies to Allied, g must be obtained in some other manner.

Security analysts regularly forecast growth rates for earnings and dividends, looking at such factors as projected sales, profit margins, and competition. For example, *Value Line Investment Survey,* which is available in most libraries,

---

[15]If the growth rate is not expected to be constant, the DCF procedure can still be used to estimate r_s, but in this case, it is necessary to calculate an average growth rate using the procedures described in this chapter's Excel model.

provides growth rate forecasts for 1,700 companies; Citigroup, UBS, Credit Suisse, Morgan Stanley, and other organizations make similar forecasts. Averages of these forecasts are available on Yahoo! Finance and other websites. Therefore, someone estimating a firm's cost of equity can obtain analysts' forecasts and use them as a proxy for the growth expectations of investors in general. Then he or she can combine this g with the current dividend yield to estimate $\hat{r}_s$:

$$\hat{r}_s = \frac{D_1}{P_0} + \text{Growth rate as projected by security analysts}$$

Again, note that this estimate of $\hat{r}_s$ is based on the assumption that g is expected to remain constant in the future. Otherwise, we must use an average of expected future rates.[16]

To illustrate the DCF approach, Allied's stock sells for \$23.06, its next expected dividend is \$1.21, and analysts expect its growth rate to be 5.5%. Thus, Allied's expected and required rates of return (hence, its cost of retained earnings) are estimated to be 10.7%:

$$\begin{aligned}\hat{r}_s = r_s &= \frac{\$1.21}{\$23.06} + 5.5\% \\ &= 5.2\% + 5.5\% \\ &= 10.7\%\end{aligned}$$

Based on the DCF method, 10.7% is the minimum rate of return that should be earned on retained earnings to justify plowing earnings back into the business rather than paying them out to shareholders as dividends. Put another way, because investors are thought to have an *opportunity* to earn 10.7% if earnings are paid out as dividends, the *opportunity cost* of equity from retained earnings is 10.7%.

10-5D AVERAGING THE ALTERNATIVE ESTIMATES

In our examples, Allied's estimated cost of equity was 12.0% by the CAPM, 12.0% by the bond-yield-plus-risk premium method, and 10.7% by the DCF method. Which method should the firm use? If management has confidence in one method, it would probably use that method's estimate alone. Otherwise, it might use some weighted average of the three methods.

As consultants, we have estimated companies' costs of capital on numerous occasions. We generally take into account all three methods, but we rely most heavily on the method that seems best under the circumstances. Judgment is important and comes into play here, as is true for most decisions in finance. Also, we recognize that our final estimate will almost certainly be incorrect to some extent.[17] Therefore, we try to provide a range and state that in our judgment, the cost of equity is within that range. Allied's management prefers to use the CAPM and therefore has elected to use the CAPM estimate of 12.0% for use in the firm's WACC calculation.

---

[16]Analysts' growth rate forecasts are usually for 5 years into the future, and the rates provided represent the average growth rate over that 5-year horizon.

[17]Investment bankers are generally regarded as experts on concepts such as the cost of capital, and they are paid big salaries for their analyses. But those investment bankers aren't always accurate. To illustrate, the stock price of the fifth-largest investment bank at that time, Bear Stearns, closed on Friday, March 14, 2008, at \$30. Its employees owned 33% of the stock. On Sunday, in a special meeting, its board of directors agreed to sell the company to J.P. Morgan for \$2 per share. Bear Stearns was eventually sold to J.P. Morgan for \$10 per share in 2008, and it has since discontinued the use of the Bear Stearns name. As you can see, even investment bankers don't always get it right, so don't expect precision unless you are given a set of numbers and told to do some relatively simple calculations.

Self*Test*

Why must a cost be assigned to retained earnings?

What three approaches are used to estimate the cost of common equity? Which approach is most commonly used in practice?

Identify some potential problems with the CAPM.

Which of the two components of the DCF formula, the dividend yield or the growth rate, do you think is more difficult to estimate? Why?

What's the logic behind the bond-yield-plus-risk-premium approach?

Suppose you are an analyst with the following data: $r_{RF} = 5.5\%$, $r_M - r_{RF} = 6\%$, $b = 0.8$, $D_1 = \$1.00$, $P_0 = \$25.00$, $g = 6\%$, and r_d = firm's bond yield = 6.5%. What is this firm's cost of equity using the CAPM, DCF, and bond-yield-plus-risk-premium approaches? Use the midrange of the judgmental risk premium for the bond-yield-plus-risk-premium approach. **(CAPM = 10.3%, DCF = 10%, Bond yield + RP = 10.5%)**

10-6 Cost of New Common Stock, r_e

Companies generally use an investment banker when they issue new common stock and sometimes when they issue preferred stock or bonds. In return for a fee, investment bankers help the company structure the terms, set a price for the issue, and sell the issue to investors. The bankers' fees are called *flotation costs*, and the total cost of the capital raised is the investors' required return plus the flotation cost.

For most firms at most times, equity flotation costs are not an issue, because most equity comes from retained earnings. Therefore, in our discussion to this point, we have ignored flotation costs. However, flotation costs can often be substantial. So if a firm does plan to issue new stock, these costs should not be ignored. When firms use investment bankers to raise capital, two approaches can be used to account for flotation costs.[18] We describe them in the next two sections.

10-6A ADD FLOTATION COSTS TO A PROJECT'S COST

In the next chapter, we show that capital budgeting projects typically involve an initial cash outlay followed by a series of cash inflows. One approach to handling flotation costs, found as the sum of the flotation costs for the debt, preferred, and common stock used to finance the project, is to add this sum to the initial investment cost. Because the investment cost is increased, the project's expected rate of return is reduced. For example, consider a 1-year project with an initial cost (not including flotation costs) of \$100 million. After 1 year, the project is expected to produce an inflow of \$115 million. Therefore, its expected rate of return is $\$115/\$100 - 1 = 0.15 = 15.0\%$. However, if the project requires the company to raise \$100 million of new capital and incur \$2 million of flotation costs, the total upfront cost will rise to \$102 million, which will lower the expected rate of return to $\$115/\$102 - 1 = 0.1275 = 12.75\%$.

[18]A more complete discussion of flotation cost adjustments can be found in Chapter 11 of Eugene F. Brigham and Phillip R. Daves, *Intermediate Financial Management*, 13th edition (Mason, OH: Cengage Learning, 2019), and other advanced texts.

10-6B INCREASE THE COST OF CAPITAL

The second approach involves adjusting the cost of capital rather than increasing the project's investment cost. If the firm plans to continue using the capital in the future, as is generally true for equity, this second approach theoretically will be better. The adjustment process is based on the following logic. If there are flotation costs, the issuing firm receives only a portion of the capital provided by investors, with the remainder going to the underwriter. To provide investors with their required rate of return on the capital they contributed, each dollar the firm actually receives must "work harder"; that is, each dollar must earn a higher rate of return than the investors' required rate of return. For example, suppose investors require a 10.7% return on their investment, but flotation costs represent 10% of the funds raised. Therefore, the firm actually keeps and invests only 90% of the amount that investors supplied. In that case, the firm must earn about 11.3% on the available funds in order to provide investors with a 10.7% return on their investment. This higher rate of return is the flotation-adjusted cost of equity.

The DCF approach can be used to estimate the effects of flotation costs. Here is the equation for the *cost of new common stock*, r_e:

$$\text{Cost of equity from new stock} = r_e = \frac{D_1}{P_0(1 - F)} + g \qquad (10.9)$$

Here **F** is the percentage **flotation cost** required to sell the new stock, so $P_0(1 - F)$ is the net price per share received by the company.

Flotation Cost, F The percentage cost of issuing new common stock.

Assuming that Allied has a flotation cost of 10%, its cost of new common equity, r_e, would be calculated as follows:

$$r_e = \frac{\$1.21}{\$23.06(1 - 0.10)} + 5.5\%$$
$$= \frac{\$1.21}{\$20.75} + 5.5\%$$
$$= 5.8\% + 5.5\% = 11.3\%$$

This is 0.6% higher than the previously estimated 10.7% DCF cost of equity, so the **flotation cost adjustment** is 0.6%:

Flotation Cost Adjustment The amount that must be added to r_s to account for flotation costs to find r_e.

$$\text{Flotation cost adjustment} = \text{Adjusted DCF cost} - \text{Pure DCF cost} = 11.3\% - 10.7\% = 0.6\%$$

The 0.6% flotation cost adjustment can be added to the previously estimated r_s = 12.0% (Allied management's estimate of its cost of equity considering the CAPM approach), resulting in a cost of equity from new common stock, or external equity, of 12.6%:

$$\text{Cost of external equity} = r_s + \text{Flotation cost adjustment} = 12.0\% + 0.6\% = 12.6\%$$

If Allied earns 12.6% on funds obtained from selling new stock, the investors who purchased that stock will end up earning 12.0%, their required rate of return, on the money they invested. If Allied earns more than 12.6%, its stock price should rise, but the price should fall if Allied earns less than 12.6%.[19]

[19]Flotation costs for preferred stock and bonds are handled similarly to common stock. In both cases, the dollars of flotation costs are deducted from the price of the security, P_p for preferred stock and $1,000 for bonds issued at par. Then for preferred, the cost is found using Equation 10.9 with g = 0. For bonds, we find the YTM based on the net proceeds received, $1,000 − Flotation costs, for example, the net proceeds would be $970 if flotation costs are 3% of the issue price.

10-6C WHEN MUST EXTERNAL EQUITY BE USED?

Because of flotation costs, dollars raised by selling new stock must "work harder" than dollars raised by retaining earnings. Moreover, because no flotation costs are involved, retained earnings cost less than new stock. Therefore, firms should utilize retained earnings to the greatest extent possible. However, if a firm has more good investment opportunities than can be financed with retained earnings plus the debt and preferred stock supported by those retained earnings, it may need to issue new common stock. The total amount of capital that can be raised before new stock must be issued is defined as the **retained earnings breakpoint**, and it can be calculated as follows:

Retained Earnings Breakpoint
The amount of capital raised beyond which new common stock must be issued.

$$\text{Retained earnings breakpoint} = \frac{\text{Addition to retained earnings for the year}}{\text{Equity fraction}} \qquad \textbf{10.10}$$

Allied's addition to retained earnings in 2020 is expected to be $66 million (as we will see later in Chapter 16), and its target capital structure consists of 33% debt, 2% preferred, and 65% equity. Therefore, its retained earnings breakpoint for 2020 is as follows:

$$\text{Retained earnings breakpoint} = \$66/0.65 = \$101.5 \text{ million}$$

To prove that this is correct, note that a capital budget of $101.5 million could be financed as 0.33($101.5) = $33.5 million of debt, 0.02($101.5) = $2.0 million of preferred stock, and 0.65($101.5) = $66 million of equity raised from retained earnings. Up to a total of $101.5 million of new capital raised for the capital budget will not exhaust the addition to retained earnings, so equity would have a cost of r_s = 12.0%. However, if the capital budget exceeded $101.5 million, the addition to retained earnings would be exhausted, and Allied would have to obtain equity by issuing new common stock at a cost of r_e = 12.6%.[20]

Self*Test*

What are the two approaches that can be used to adjust for flotation costs?

Would a firm that has many good investment opportunities be likely to have a higher or a lower dividend payout ratio than a firm with few good investment opportunities? Explain.

A firm's common stock has D_1 = $1.50, P_0 = $30.00, g = 5%, and F = 4%. If the firm must issue new stock, what is its cost of new external equity? **(10.21%)**

Suppose Firm A plans to retain $100 million of earnings for the year. It wants to finance its capital budget using a target capital structure of 46% debt, 3% preferred, and 51% common equity. How large could its capital budget be before it must issue new common stock? **($196.08 million)**

[20]This breakpoint is only suggested—it is not written in stone. For example, rather than issuing new common stock, the company could use more debt (hence, increase its debt ratio) or it could increase its addition to retained earnings by reducing its dividend payout ratio. Both actions would change the retained earnings breakpoint. Also, breakpoints could occur due to increases in the costs of debt and preferred. Indeed, a number of changes could occur, and the end result would be a large number of potential breakpoints.

10-7 Composite, or Weighted Average, Cost of Capital, WACC

Allied's target capital structure calls for 33% debt, 2% preferred stock, and 65% common equity. Earlier we saw that its before-tax cost of debt is 8.0%; its after-tax cost of debt is $r_d(1 - T) = 8\%(0.75) = 6.0\%$; its cost of preferred stock is 10.3%; its cost of common equity from retained earnings is 12.0%, and its marginal tax rate is 25%. Equation 10.1, presented earlier, can be used to calculate its WACC when all of the new common equity comes from retained earnings:

$$\begin{aligned} \text{WACC} &= w_d r_d(1 - T) + w_p r_p + w_c r_s \\ &= 0.33(8\%)(0.75) + 0.02(10.3\%) + 0.65(12.0\%) \\ &= 10.0\% \text{ if equity comes from retained earnings} \end{aligned}$$

Under these conditions, every dollar of new capital that Allied raises would consist of 33 cents of debt with an after-tax cost of 6%, 2 cents of preferred stock with a cost of 10.3%, and 65 cents of common equity from additions to retained earnings with a cost of 12.0%. The average cost of each whole dollar, or the WACC, would be 10.0%.

This estimate of Allied's WACC assumes that common equity comes exclusively from retained earnings. If, instead, Allied had to issue new common stock, its WACC would be slightly higher because of the additional flotation costs:

$$\begin{aligned} \text{WACC} &= w_d r_d(1 - T) + w_p r_p + w_c r_e \\ &= 0.33(8\%)(0.75) + 0.02(10.3\%) + 0.65(12.6\%) \\ &= 10.4\% \text{ with equity raised by selling new stock} \end{aligned}$$

In Web Appendix 10A, we discuss in more detail the connection between the firm's WACC and the costs of issuing new common stock.

Self*Test*

Write the equation for the WACC.

Firm A has the following data: Target capital structure of 46% debt, 3% preferred, and 51% common equity; tax rate = 25%; $r_d = 7\%$; $r_p = 7.5\%$; $r_s = 11.5\%$; and $r_e = 12.5\%$. What is the firm's WACC if it does not issue any new stock? **(8.51%)**

What is Firm A's WACC if it issues new common stock? **(9.02%)**

Firm A has 11 equally risky capital budgeting projects, each costing $19.608 million and each having an expected rate of return of 8.25%. Firm A's retained earnings breakpoint is $196.08 million. The firm's WACC using retained earnings is 8.0% but increases to 8.5% if new equity must be issued. The company invests in projects where the expected return exceeds the cost of capital. How much capital should Firm A raise and invest? Why? **($196.08 million; the 11th project would have a higher WACC than its expected rate of return.)**

10-8 Factors That Affect the WACC

The cost of capital is affected by a number of factors. Some are beyond the firm's control, but others can be influenced by its financing and investment decisions.

10-8A FACTORS THE FIRM CANNOT CONTROL

The three most important factors that the firm cannot directly control are *interest rates in the economy, the general level of stock prices, and tax rates.* If interest rates in the economy rise, the cost of debt increases because the firm must pay bondholders more when it borrows. Similarly, if stock prices in general decline, pulling the firm's stock price down, its cost of equity will rise. Also, because tax rates are used in the calculation of the component cost of debt, they have an important effect on the firm's cost of capital. Taxes also affect the cost of capital in other less apparent ways. For example, when tax rates on dividends and capital gains were lowered relative to rates on interest income, stocks became relatively more attractive than debt; consequently, the cost of equity and WACC declined.

SOME REAL-WORLD ESTIMATES OF THE WACC

In the following table, we have summarized quick estimates (done in June 2018) of the WACC for some leading companies. Our calculations were based on the following assumptions:

1. We did not have access to the company's internal target capital structure forecasts, so we used the current market-value weights for debt and equity as the capital structure weights. For simplicity, we assumed that the market value of the company's debt equaled the book value of debt (as estimated by *Value Line Investment Survey*). The market value of equity is the company's stock price multiplied by the number of shares outstanding. The market equity weight and the market debt weight are the percentage of capital (on a market basis) coming from equity and debt, respectively. Note that the firms in this table do not use preferred stock, so we can eliminate the preferred stock term in the WACC equation.
2. The yield to maturity of the company's debt was compiled from Morningstar or Financial Industry Regulatory Authority's (FINRA's) Bond Center. Where available, we selected an outstanding bond issue with a maturity of 10 years or more. The income tax rate was the 2018 forecasted rate obtained from *Value Line Investment Survey*. The after-tax cost of debt is the yield to maturity multiplied by one minus the company's tax rate.
3. The risk-free rate approximates the yield to maturity on 10-year government debt. We assumed a market risk premium of 6.0%, and we used the CAPM to estimate the cost of equity. The stock's betas were obtained from *Value Line Investment Survey*.
4. The WACC was calculated as follows:

$$\text{WACC} = (\text{Market debt weight}) \times (\text{After-tax cost of debt}) + (\text{Market equity weight}) \times (\text{CAPM cost of equity})$$

As expected, companies in more stable businesses (Coca-Cola, Walmart, and Campbell Soup) have the lowest WACC estimates, whereas companies in riskier industries (Southwest Airlines and Boeing) have higher WACC estimates. Although these quick estimates can give you a broad sense of the WACC for each of these companies, you should recognize that these calculations are very sensitive to changes in the underlying assumptions. For example, if we assume a higher or lower market risk premium, or use a different source to estimate betas, we can often arrive at significantly different estimates for these WACCs.

2018 Sample Data: Cost of Capital Analytics Table—Some Real-World Estimates of the WACC

Company	Market Equity Weight	Market Debt Weight	Yield to Maturity on Existing Debt	Income Tax Rate	After-Tax Cost of Debt	Risk-Free Rate	Market Risk Premium	Value Line Beta	CAPM Cost of Equity	WACC
Coca-Cola	79.71%	20.29%	4.47%	21.0%	3.53%	2.83%	6.00%	0.70	7.03%	6.32%
Walmart	84.80	15.20	4.12	25.5	3.07	2.83	6.00	0.70	7.03	6.43
Campbell Soup	76.62	23.38	5.46	26.0	4.04	2.83	6.00	0.75	7.33	6.56
Merck & Co.	85.58	14.42	4.09	19.0	3.31	2.83	6.00	0.85	7.93	7.26
Wyndham Worldwide	65.79	34.21	6.04	30.0	4.23	2.83	6.00	1.10	9.43	7.65
Apple Inc.	88.22	11.78	4.13	19.0	3.35	2.83	6.00	0.95	8.53	7.92
Disney (Walt)	85.15	14.85	4.32	21.0	3.41	2.83	6.00	1.00	8.83	8.03
Exxon Mobil Corp.	89.48	10.52	4.02	34.0	2.65	2.83	6.00	1.00	8.83	8.18
Home Depot	90.00	10.00	4.26	26.0	3.15	2.83	6.00	1.00	8.83	8.26
Microsoft Corp.	90.44	9.56	3.89	16.5	3.25	2.83	6.00	1.00	8.83	8.30
Southwest Airlines	89.43	10.57	4.10	23.0	3.16	2.83	6.00	1.15	9.73	9.04
Boeing	94.28	5.72	4.72	16.0	3.97	2.83	6.00	1.10	9.43	9.12

10-8B FACTORS THE FIRM CAN CONTROL

A firm can directly affect its cost of capital in three primary ways: (1) by changing its *capital structure*, (2) by changing its *dividend payout ratio*, and (3) by *altering its capital budgeting decision rules* to accept projects with more or less risk than projects previously undertaken.

Capital structure impacts a firm's cost of capital. So far we have assumed that Allied has a given target capital structure, and we used the target weights to calculate its WACC. However, if the firm changes its target capital structure, the weights used to calculate the WACC will change. Other things held constant, an increase in the target debt ratio tends to lower the WACC (and vice versa if the debt ratio is lowered) because the after-tax cost of debt is lower than the cost of equity. However, other things are not likely to remain constant. An increase in the use of debt will increase the riskiness of both the debt and the equity, and these increases in component costs might more than offset the effects of the changes in the weights and raise the WACC. In Chapter 13, we discuss how a firm can try to balance these effects to reach its optimal capital structure.

Dividend policy affects the amount of retained earnings available to the firm and thus the need to sell new stock and incur flotation costs. This suggests that the higher the dividend payout ratio, the smaller the addition to retained earnings, the higher the cost of equity, and therefore the higher the firm's WACC will be. However, investors may prefer dividends to retained earnings, in which case reducing dividends might lead to an increase in both r_s and r_e. As we will see in Chapter 14, the optimal dividend policy is a complicated issue, but one that can have an important effect on the cost of capital.

The firm's capital budgeting decisions can also affect its cost of capital. When we estimate the firm's cost of capital, we use as the starting point the required rates of return on its outstanding stock and bonds. These cost rates reflect the riskiness of the firm's existing assets. Therefore, we have been implicitly assuming that new capital will be invested in assets that have the same risk as existing assets. This assumption is generally correct, as most firms do invest in assets similar to ones they currently operate. However, if the firm decides to invest in an entirely new and risky line of business, its component costs of debt and equity (and thus its WACC) will increase.

Self*Test*

Name three factors that affect the cost of capital and are beyond the firm's control.

What are three factors under the firm's control that can affect its cost of capital?

Suppose interest rates in the economy increase. How would such a change affect the costs of both debt and common equity based on the CAPM?

10-9 Adjusting the Cost of Capital for Risk

As you will see in Chapters 11 and 12, the cost of capital is a key element in the capital budgeting process. Projects should be accepted if and only if their estimated returns exceed their costs of capital. Thus, the cost of capital is a "hurdle rate"—a project's expected rate of return must "jump the hurdle" for it to be accepted. Moreover, investors require higher returns on riskier investments. Consequently, companies that are raising capital to take on risky projects will have higher costs of capital than companies that are investing in safer projects.

FIGURE 10.1 Risk and the Cost of Capital

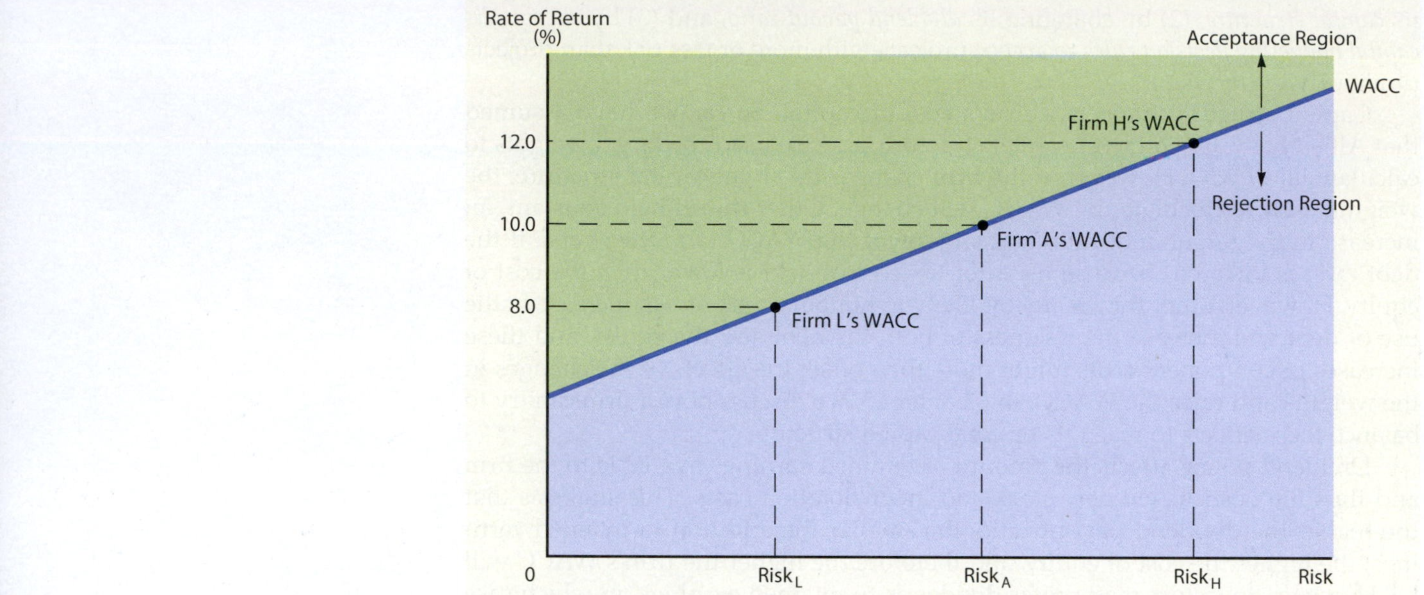

Figure 10.1 illustrates the trade-off between risk and the cost of capital. Firm L is in a low-risk business and has a WACC of 8%. Firm A is an average-risk business with a WACC of 10%, whereas Firm H's business is exposed to greater risk and consequently has a WACC of 12%. Thus, Firm L will accept a typical project if its expected return is above 8%. Firm A's hurdle rate is 10%, whereas the corresponding hurdle rate for Firm H is 12%.

It's important to remember that the costs of capital for Firms L, A, and H in Figure 10.1 represent the overall, or composite, WACCs for the three firms and thus apply only to "typical" projects for each firm. However, different projects often have different risks, even for a given firm. *Therefore, each project's hurdle rate should reflect the risk of the project, not the risk associated with the firm's average project as reflected in its composite WACC.* Empirical studies do indicate that firms consider the risks of individual projects, but the studies also indicate that most firms regard most projects as having about the same risk as the firm's average existing assets. Therefore, the WACC is used to evaluate most projects, but if a project has especially high or low risk, the WACC will be adjusted up or down to account for the risk differential.

For example, assume that Firm A (the average-risk firm with a composite WACC of 10%) has two divisions, L and H. Division L has relatively little risk, and if it were operated as a separate firm, its WACC would be 7%. Division H has higher risk, and its divisional cost of capital is 13%. Because the two divisions are of equal size, Firm A's composite WACC is calculated as 0.50(7%) + 0.50(13%) = 10%. However, it would be a mistake to use this 10% WACC for either division. To see this point, assume that Division L is considering a relatively low-risk project with an expected return of 9%, and Division H is considering a higher-risk project with an expected return of 11%. As shown in Figure 10.2, Division L's project should be accepted because its return is above its risk-based cost of capital, whereas Division H's project should be rejected. If the 10% corporate WACC was used by each division, the decision would be reversed: Division H would incorrectly accept its project, and Division L would incorrectly reject its project. In general, failing to adjust for differences in risk would lead the firm to accept too many risky projects and reject too many safe ones. Over time, the firm would become riskier, its WACC

FIGURE 10.2 Firm A's Divisional Costs of Capital

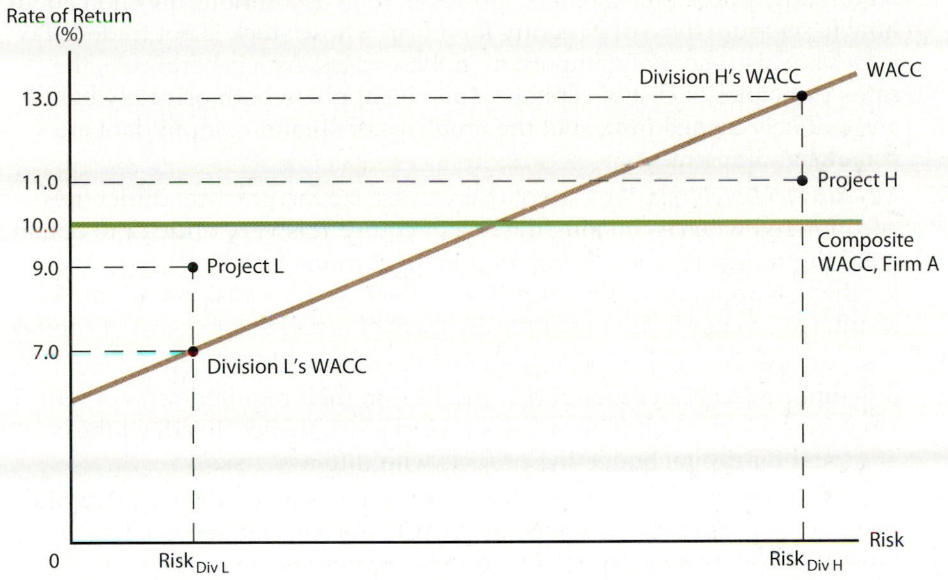

would increase, and its shareholder value would suffer. We return to these issues in Chapter 12, when we consider different approaches for measuring project risk.

Self*Test*

Why is the cost of capital sometimes referred to as a "hurdle rate"?

How should firms evaluate projects with different risks?

Should all divisions within the same firm use the firm's composite WACC for evaluating all capital budgeting projects? Explain.

10-10 Some Other Problems with Cost of Capital Estimates

A number of issues related to the cost of capital have not been mentioned or were glossed over in this chapter. These topics are covered in advanced finance courses, but they deserve mention now to alert you to potential dangers and to provide a preview of some matters covered in advanced courses.

1. *Depreciation-generated funds.*[21] The largest single source of capital for many firms is depreciation, yet we have not discussed how the cost of this capital is determined. In brief, depreciation cash flows can either be reinvested or returned to investors (stockholders *and* creditors). The cost of depreciation-generated funds is thus an opportunity cost, and it is approximately equal to the WACC from retained earnings, preferred stock, and debt. Therefore, we can ignore it in our estimate of the WACC.

[21]See Table 3.3, the statement of cash flows, for an illustration of the cash flows provided from depreciation. Refer to advanced finance textbooks for a discussion on the treatment of depreciation-generated funds.

2. *Privately owned firms*. Our discussion of the cost of equity focused on publicly owned corporations, and we have concentrated on the rate of return required by public stockholders. However, there is a serious question about how to measure the cost of equity for a firm whose stock is not traded. Tax issues are also especially important in these cases. As a general rule, the same principles of cost of capital estimation apply to both privately held and publicly owned firms, but the problems of obtaining input data are somewhat different.
3. *Measurement problems*. We cannot overemphasize the practical difficulties encountered when estimating the cost of equity. It is very difficult to obtain good input data for the CAPM, for g in the formula $\hat{r}_s = D_1/P_0 + g$, and for the risk premium in the formula r_s = Bond yield + Risk premium. As a result, we can never be sure of the accuracy of our estimated cost of capital.
4. *Costs of capital for projects of differing risk*. We touched briefly on the fact that different projects can differ in risk and thus in their required rates of return. However, it is difficult to measure a project's risk (hence, to adjust the cost of capital for capital budgeting projects with different risks).
5. *Capital structure weights*. In this chapter, we took as given the target capital structure and used it to calculate the WACC. As we shall see in Chapter 13, establishing the target capital structure is a major task in itself.

Although this list of problems appears formidable, the state of the art in cost of capital estimation is not in bad shape. The procedures outlined in this chapter can be used to obtain costs of capital estimates that are sufficiently accurate for practical purposes, so the problems listed previously merely indicate the desirability of refinements. The refinements are not unimportant, but the problems noted do not invalidate the usefulness of the procedures outlined in this chapter.

Self*Test*

Identify some problem areas in cost of capital analysis. Do these problems invalidate the cost of capital procedures discussed in this chapter? Explain.

TYING IT ALL TOGETHER

We began this chapter by discussing the concept of the weighted average cost of capital. We then discussed the three major capital components (debt, preferred stock, and common equity) and the procedures used to estimate each component's cost. Next, we calculated the WACC, which is a key element in capital budgeting. A key issue here is the weights that should be used to find the WACC. In general, companies consider a number of factors and then establish a target capital structure that is used to calculate the WACC. We will discuss the target capital structure and its affect on the WACC in more detail in Chapter 13.

The cost of capital is a key element in capital budgeting decisions, our focus in the following chapters. Indeed, capital budgeting as it should be done is impossible without a good estimate of the cost of capital, so you need to have a good understanding of cost of capital concepts before you continue to the next chapter, where we discuss capital budgeting basics.

Self-Test Questions and Problems

(Solutions Appear in Appendix A)

ST-1 **KEY TERMS** Define each of the following terms:

a. Target capital structure; capital components
b. Before-tax cost of debt, r_d; after-tax cost of debt, $r_d(1 - T)$
c. Cost of preferred stock, r_p
d. Cost of retained earnings, r_s; cost of new common stock, r_e
e. Weighted average cost of capital, WACC
f. Flotation cost, F; flotation cost adjustment; retained earnings breakpoint

ST-2 **WACC** Lancaster Engineering Inc. (LEI) has the following capital structure, which it considers to be optimal:

Debt	25%
Preferred stock	15
Common equity	60
	100%

LEI's expected net income this year is \$34,285.72, its established dividend payout ratio is 30%, its federal-plus-state tax rate is 25%, and investors expect future earnings and dividends to grow at a constant rate of 9%. LEI paid a dividend of \$3.60 per share last year, and its stock currently sells for \$54.00 per share. LEI can obtain new capital in the following ways: (1) New preferred stock with a dividend of \$11.00 can be sold to the public at a price of \$95.00 per share. (2) Debt can be sold at an interest rate of 12%.

a. Determine the cost of each capital component.
b. Calculate the WACC.
c. LEI has the following investment opportunities that are average-risk projects:

Project	Cost at t = 0	Rate of Return
A	\$10,000	17.4%
B	20,000	16.0
C	10,000	14.2
D	20,000	13.2
E	10,000	12.0

Which projects should LEI accept? Why? Assume that LEI does not want to issue any new common stock.

Questions

10-1 How would each of the following scenarios affect a firm's cost of debt, $r_d(1 - T)$; its cost of equity, r_s; and its WACC? Indicate with a plus (+), a minus (−), or a zero (0) whether the factor would raise, lower, or have an indeterminate effect on the item in question. Assume for each answer that other things are held constant, even though in some instances this would probably not be true. Be prepared to justify your answer but recognize that several of the parts have no single correct answer. These questions are designed to stimulate thought and discussion.

	Effect on		
	$r_d(1 - T)$	r_s	WACC
a. The corporate tax rate is lowered.	____	____	____
b. The Federal Reserve tightens credit.	____	____	____
c. The firm uses more debt; that is, it increases its debt ratio.	____	____	____
d. The dividend payout ratio is increased.	____	____	____
e. The firm doubles the amount of capital it raises during the year.	____	____	____
f. The firm expands into a risky new area.	____	____	____
g. The firm merges with another firm whose earnings are counter-cyclical both to those of the first firm and to the stock market.	____	____	____
h. The stock market falls drastically, and the firm's stock price falls along with the rest.	____	____	____
i. Investors become more risk-averse.	____	____	____
j. The firm is an electric utility with a large investment in nuclear plants. Several states are considering a ban on nuclear power generation.	____	____	____

10-2 Assume that the risk-free rate increases, but the market risk premium remains constant. What impact would this have on the cost of debt? What impact would it have on the cost of equity?

10-3 How should the capital structure weights used to calculate the WACC be determined?

10-4 Suppose a firm estimates its WACC to be 10%. Should the WACC be used to evaluate all of its potential projects, even if they vary in risk? If not, what might be "reasonable" costs of capital for average-, high-, and low-risk projects?

10-5 The WACC is a weighted average of the costs of debt, preferred stock, and common equity. Would the WACC be different if the equity for the coming year came solely in the form of retained earnings versus some equity from the sale of new common stock? Would the calculated WACC depend in any way on the size of the capital budget? How might dividend policy affect the WACC?

Problems

Easy Problems 1-5

10-1 **AFTER-TAX COST OF DEBT** The Holmes Company's currently outstanding bonds have an 8% coupon and a 10% yield to maturity. Holmes believes it could issue new bonds at par that would provide a similar yield to maturity. If its marginal tax rate is 25%, what is Holmes' after-tax cost of debt?

10-2 **COST OF PREFERRED STOCK** Torch Industries can issue perpetual preferred stock at a price of $57.00 a share. The stock would pay a constant annual dividend of $6.00 a share. What is the company's cost of preferred stock, r_p?

10-3 **COST OF COMMON EQUITY** Pearson Motors has a target capital structure of 30% debt and 70% common equity, with no preferred stock. The yield to maturity on the company's outstanding bonds is 9%, and its tax rate is 25%. Pearson's CFO estimates that the company's WACC is 10.50%. What is Pearson's cost of common equity?

10-4 **COST OF EQUITY WITH AND WITHOUT FLOTATION** Jarett & Sons's common stock currently trades at $30.00 a share. It is expected to pay an annual dividend of $1.00 a share at the end of the year (D_1 = $1.00), and the constant growth rate is 4% a year.

a. What is the company's cost of common equity if all of its equity comes from retained earnings?

b. If the company issued new stock, it would incur a 10% flotation cost. What would be the cost of equity from new stock?

10-5 **PROJECT SELECTION** Midwest Water Works estimates that its WACC is 10.5%. The company is considering the following capital budgeting projects:

Project	Size	Rate of Return
A	$1 million	12.0%
B	2 million	11.5
C	2 million	11.2
D	2 million	11.0
E	1 million	10.7
F	1 million	10.3
G	1 million	10.2

Assume that each of these projects is just as risky as the firm's existing assets and that the firm may accept all the projects or only some of them. Which set of projects should be accepted? Explain.

Intermediate Problems 6-13

10-6 **COST OF COMMON EQUITY** The future earnings, dividends, and common stock price of Callahan Technologies Inc. are expected to grow 6% per year. Callahan's common stock currently sells for $22.00 per share, its last dividend was $2.00, and it will pay a $2.12 dividend at the end of the current year.

a. Using the DCF approach, what is its cost of common equity?

b. If the firm's beta is 1.2, the risk-free rate is 6%, and the average return on the market is 13%, what will be the firm's cost of common equity using the CAPM approach?

c. If the firm's bonds earn a return of 11%, based on the bond-yield-plus-risk-premium approach, what will be r_s? Use the midpoint of the risk premium range discussed in Section 10-5 in your calculations.

d. If you have equal confidence in the inputs used for the three approaches, what is your estimate of Callahan's cost of common equity?

10-7 **COST OF COMMON EQUITY WITH AND WITHOUT FLOTATION** The Evanec Company's next expected dividend, D_1, is $3.18; its growth rate is 6%; and its common stock now sells for $36.00. New stock (external equity) can be sold to net $32.40 per share.

a. What is Evanec's cost of retained earnings, r_s?

b. What is Evanec's percentage flotation cost, F?

c. What is Evanec's cost of new common stock, r_e?

10-8 **COST OF COMMON EQUITY AND WACC** Palencia Paints Corporation has a target capital structure of 35% debt and 65% common equity, with no preferred stock. Its before-tax cost of debt is 8%, and its marginal tax rate is 25%. The current stock price is P_0 = $22.00. The last dividend was D_0 = $2.25, and it is expected to grow at a 5% constant rate. What is its cost of common equity and its WACC?

10-9 **WACC** The Paulson Company's year-end balance sheet is shown here. Its cost of common equity is 14%, its before-tax cost of debt is 10%, and its marginal tax rate is 25%. Assume that the firm's long-term debt sells at par value. The firm's total debt, which is the sum of the company's short-term debt and long-term debt, equals $1,167. The firm has 576 shares of common stock outstanding that sell for $4.00 per share. Calculate Paulson's WACC using market-value weights.

Assets		Liabilities and Equity	
Cash	$ 120	Accounts payable and accruals	$ 10
Accounts receivable	240	Short-term debt	47
Inventories	360	Long-term debt	1,120
Plant and equipment, net	2,160	Common equity	1,703
Total assets	$2,880	Total liabilities and equity	$2,880

10-10 **WACC** Olsen Outfitters Inc. believes that its optimal capital structure consists of 55% common equity and 45% debt, and its tax rate is 25%. Olsen must raise additional capital to fund its upcoming expansion. The firm will have $4 million of retained earnings with a cost of r_s = 11%. New common stock in an amount up to $8 million would have a cost of r_e = 12.5%. Furthermore, Olsen can raise up to $4 million of debt at an interest rate of r_d = 9% and an additional $5 million of debt at r_d = 13%. The CFO estimates that a proposed expansion would require an investment of $8.2 million. What is the WACC for the last dollar raised to complete the expansion?

10-11 **WACC AND PERCENTAGE OF DEBT FINANCING** Hook Industries's capital structure consists solely of debt and common equity. It can issue debt at r_d = 11%, and its common stock currently pays a $2.00 dividend per share (D_0 = $2.00). The stock's price is currently $24.75, its dividend is expected to grow at a constant rate of 7% per year, its tax rate is 25%, and its WACC is 13.95%. What percentage of the company's capital structure consists of debt?

10-12 **WACC** Empire Electric Company (EEC) uses only debt and common equity. It can borrow unlimited amounts at an interest rate of r_d = 9% as long as it finances at its target capital structure, which calls for 35% debt and 65% common equity. Its last dividend (D_0) was $2.20, its expected constant growth rate is 6%, and its common stock sells for $26. EEC's tax rate is 25%. Two projects are available: Project A has a rate of return of 12.5% and Project B's return is 11.5%. These two projects are equally risky and about as risky as the firm's existing assets.

a. What is its cost of common equity?
b. What is the WACC?
c. Which projects should Empire accept?

10-13 **COST OF COMMON EQUITY WITH FLOTATION** Banyan Co.'s common stock currently sells for $46.75 per share. The growth rate is a constant 6%, and the company has an expected dividend yield of 5%. The expected long-run dividend payout ratio is 20%, and the expected return on equity (ROE) is 7.5%. New stock can be sold to the public at the current price, but a flotation cost of 5% would be incurred. What would be the cost of new equity?

Challenging Problems 14-20

10-14 **COST OF PREFERRED STOCK INCLUDING FLOTATION** Travis Industries plans to issue perpetual preferred stock with an $11.00 dividend. The stock is currently selling for $108.50, but flotation costs will be 5% of the market price, so the net price will be $103.08 per share. What is the cost of the preferred stock, including flotation?

10-15 **WACC AND COST OF COMMON EQUITY** Kahn Inc. has a target capital structure of 60% common equity and 40% debt to fund its $10 billion in operating assets. Furthermore, Kahn Inc. has a WACC of 13%, a before-tax cost of debt of 10%, and a tax rate of 25%. The company's retained earnings are adequate to provide the common equity portion of its capital budget. Its expected dividend next year (D_1) is $3, and the current stock price is $35.

a. What is the company's expected growth rate?
b. If the firm's net income is expected to be $1.1 billion, what portion of its net income is the firm expected to pay out as dividends? (***Hint:*** Refer to Equation 9.4 in Chapter 9.)

10-16 **COST OF COMMON EQUITY** The Bouchard Company's EPS was $6.50 in 2019, up from $4.42 in 2014. The company pays out 40% of its earnings as dividends, and its common stock sells for $36.00.

a. Calculate the past growth rate in earnings. (***Hint:*** This is a 5-year growth period.)
b. The last dividend was D_0 = 0.4($6.50) = $2.60. Calculate the next expected dividend, D_1, assuming that the past growth rate continues.
c. What is Bouchard's cost of retained earnings, r_s?

10-17 **CALCULATION OF g AND EPS** Sidman Products's common stock currently sells for $60.00 a share. The firm is expected to earn $5.40 per share this year and to pay a year-end dividend of $3.60, and it finances only with common equity.

a. If investors require a 9% return, what is the expected growth rate?
b. If Sidman reinvests retained earnings in projects whose average return is equal to the stock's expected rate of return, what will be next year's EPS? (***Hint:*** Refer to Equation 9.4 in Chapter 9.)

10-18 **WACC AND OPTIMAL CAPITAL BUDGET** Adamson Corporation is considering four average-risk projects with the following costs and rates of return:

Project	Cost	Expected Rate of Return
1	$2,000	16.00%
2	3,000	15.00
3	5,000	13.75
4	2,000	12.50

The company estimates that it can issue debt at a rate of $r_d = 10\%$, and its tax rate is 25%. It can issue preferred stock that pays a constant dividend of $5.00 per year at $50.00 per share. Also, its common stock currently sells for $38.00 per share; the next expected dividend, D_1, is $4.25, and the dividend is expected to grow at a constant rate of 5% per year. The target capital structure consists of 75% common stock, 15% debt, and 10% preferred stock.

a. What is the cost of each of the capital components?

b. What is Adamson's WACC?

c. Only projects with expected returns that exceed WACC will be accepted. Which projects should Adamson accept?

10-19 **ADJUSTING COST OF CAPITAL FOR RISK** Ziege Systems is considering the following independent projects for the coming year:

Project	Required Investment	Rate of Return	Risk
A	$4 million	14.0%	High
B	5 million	11.5	High
C	3 million	9.5	Low
D	2 million	9.0	Average
E	6 million	12.5	High
F	5 million	12.5	Average
G	6 million	7.0	Low
H	3 million	11.5	Low

Ziege's WACC is 10%, but it adjusts for risk by adding 2% to the WACC for high-risk projects and subtracting 2% for low-risk projects.

a. Which projects should Ziege accept if it faces no capital constraints?

b. If Ziege can only invest a total of $13 million, which projects should it accept, and what would be the dollar size of its capital budget?

c. Suppose Ziege can raise additional funds beyond the $13 million, but each new increment (or partial increment) of $5 million of new capital will cause the WACC to increase by 1%. Assuming that Ziege uses the same method of risk adjustment, which projects should it now accept, and what would be the dollar size of its capital budget?

10-20 **WACC** The following table gives Foust Company's earnings per share for the last 10 years. The common stock, 7.8 million shares outstanding, is now (1/1/20) selling for $65.00 per share. The expected dividend at the end of the current year (12/31/20) is 55% of the 2019 EPS. Because investors expect past trends to continue, g may be based on the historical earnings growth rate. (Note that 9 years of growth are reflected in the 10 years of data.)

Year	EPS	Year	EPS
2010	$3.90	2015	$5.73
2011	4.21	2016	6.19
2012	4.55	2017	6.68
2013	4.91	2018	7.22
2014	5.31	2019	7.80

The current interest rate on new debt is 9%; Foust's marginal tax rate is 25%, and its target capital structure is 40% debt and 60% equity.

a. Calculate Foust's after-tax cost of debt and common equity. Calculate the cost of equity as $r_s = D_1/P_0 + g$.

b. Find Foust's WACC.

Comprehensive/Spreadsheet Problem

10-21 **CALCULATING THE WACC** Here is the condensed 2019 balance sheet for Skye Computer Company (in thousands of dollars):

	2019
Current assets	$2,000
Net fixed assets	3,000
Total assets	$5,000
Accounts payable and accruals	$ 900
Short-term debt	100
Long-term debt	1,100
Preferred stock (10,000 shares)	250
Common stock (50,000 shares)	1,300
Retained earnings	1,350
Total common equity	$2,650
Total liabilities and equity	$5,000

Skye's earnings per share last year were $3.20. The common stock sells for $55.00, last year's dividend (D_0) was $2.10, and a flotation cost of 10% would be required to sell new common stock. Security analysts are projecting that the common dividend will grow at an annual rate of 9%. Skye's preferred stock pays a dividend of $3.30 per share, and its preferred stock sells for $30.00 per share. The firm's before-tax cost of debt is 10%, and its marginal tax rate is 25%. The firm's currently outstanding 10% annual coupon rate, long-term debt sells at par value. The market risk premium is 5%, the risk-free rate is 6%, and Skye's beta is 1.516. The firm's total debt, which is the sum of the company's short-term debt and long-term debt, equals $1.2 million.

a. Calculate the cost of each capital component, that is, the after-tax cost of debt, the cost of preferred stock, the cost of equity from retained earnings, and the cost of newly issued common stock. Use the DCF method to find the cost of common equity.

b. Now calculate the cost of common equity from retained earnings, using the CAPM method.

c. What is the cost of new common stock based on the CAPM? (***Hint:*** Find the difference between r_e and r_s as determined by the DCF method, and add that differential to the CAPM value for r_s.)

d. If Skye continues to use the same market-value capital structure, what is the firm's WACC assuming that (1) it uses only retained earnings for equity and (2) if it expands so rapidly that it must issue new common stock?

INTEGRATED CASE

COLEMAN TECHNOLOGIES INC.

10-22 COST OF CAPITAL Coleman Technologies is considering a major expansion program that has been proposed by the company's information technology group. Before proceeding with the expansion, the company must estimate its cost of capital. Suppose you are an assistant to Jerry Lehman, the financial vice president. Your first task is to estimate Coleman's cost of capital. Lehman has provided you with the following data, which he believes may be relevant to your task.

- The firm's tax rate is 25%.
- The current price of Coleman's 12% coupon, semiannual payment, noncallable bonds with 15 years remaining to maturity, is $1,153.72. Coleman does not use short-term, interest-bearing debt on a permanent basis. New bonds would be privately placed with no flotation cost.
- The current price of the firm's 10%, $100.00 par value, quarterly dividend, perpetual preferred stock is $111.10.
- Coleman's common stock is currently selling for $50.00 per share. Its last dividend (D_0) was $4.19, and dividends are expected to grow at a constant annual rate of 5% in the foreseeable future. Coleman's beta is 1.2, the yield on T-bonds is 7%, and the market risk premium is estimated to be 6%. For the bond-yield-plus-risk-premium approach, the firm uses a risk premium of 4%.
- Coleman's target capital structure is 30% debt, 10% preferred stock, and 60% common equity.

To structure the task somewhat, Lehman has asked you to answer the following questions:

a. 1. What sources of capital should be included when you estimate Coleman's WACC?
   2. Should the component costs be figured on a before-tax or an after-tax basis?
   3. Should the costs be historical (embedded) costs or new (marginal) costs?

b. What is the market interest rate on Coleman's debt and its component cost of debt?

c. 1. What is the firm's cost of preferred stock?
   2. Coleman's preferred stock is riskier to investors than its debt, yet the preferred's yield to investors is lower than the yield to maturity on the debt. Does this suggest that you have made a mistake? (*Hint:* Think about taxes.)

d. 1. Why is there a cost associated with retained earnings?
   2. What is Coleman's estimated cost of common equity using the CAPM approach?

e. What is the estimated cost of common equity using the DCF approach?

f. What is the bond-yield-plus-risk-premium estimate for Coleman's cost of common equity?

g. What is your final estimate for r_s?

h. Explain in words why new common stock has a higher cost than retained earnings.

i. 1. What are two approaches that can be used to adjust for flotation costs?
   2. Coleman estimates that if it issues new common stock, the flotation cost will be 15%. Coleman incorporates the flotation costs into the DCF approach. What is the estimated cost of newly issued common stock, considering the flotation cost?

j. What is Coleman's overall, or weighted average, cost of capital (WACC)? Ignore flotation costs.

k. What factors influence Coleman's composite WACC?

l. Should the company use the composite WACC as the hurdle rate for each of its projects? Explain.

TAKING A CLOSER LOOK

CALCULATING 3M'S COST OF CAPITAL

Use online resources to work on this chapter's questions. Please note that website information changes over time, and these changes may limit your ability to answer some of these questions.

In this chapter, we described how to estimate a company's WACC, which is the weighted average of its costs of debt, preferred stock, and common equity. Most of the data we need to do this can be found from various data sources on the Internet. Here we walk through the steps used to calculate Minnesota Mining & Manufacturing's (MMM) WACC.

DISCUSSION QUESTIONS

1. As a first step, we need to estimate what percentage of MMM's capital comes from debt, preferred stock, and common equity. This information can be found on the firm's latest annual balance sheet. (As of year end 2017, MMM had no preferred stock.) Total debt includes all interest-bearing debt and is the sum of short-term debt and long-term debt.
   a. Recall that the weights used in the WACC are based on the company's target capital structure. If we assume that the company wants to maintain the same mix of capital that it currently has on its balance sheet, what weights should you use to estimate the WACC for MMM?
   b. Find MMM's market capitalization, which is the market value of its common equity. Using the sum of its short-term debt and long-term debt from the balance sheet (we assume that the market value of its debt equals its book value) and its market capitalization, recalculate the firm's debt and common equity weights to be used in the WACC equation. These weights are approximations of market-value weights. Be sure not to include accruals in the debt calculation.
2. Once again we can use the CAPM to estimate MMM's cost of equity. From the Internet, you can find a number of different sources for estimates of beta—select the measure that you think is best, and combine this with your estimates of the risk-free rate and the market risk premium to obtain an estimate of its cost of equity. (See the Taking a Closer Look problem in Chapter 8 for more details.) What is your estimate for MMM's cost of equity? Why might it not make much sense to use the DCF approach to estimate MMM's cost of equity?
3. Next, we need to calculate MMM's cost of debt. We can use different approaches to estimate it. One approach is to take the company's interest expense and divide it by total debt (which is the sum of short-term debt and long-term debt). This approach only works if the historical cost of debt equals the yield to maturity in today's market (i.e., if MMM's outstanding bonds are trading at close to par). This approach may produce misleading estimates in years in which MMM issues a significant amount of new debt. For example, if a company issues a great deal of debt at the end of the year, the full amount of debt will appear on the year-end balance sheet, yet we still may not see a sharp increase in annual interest expense because the debt was outstanding for only a small portion of the entire year. When this situation occurs, the estimated cost of debt will likely understate the true cost of debt. Another approach is to try to find this number in the notes to the company's annual report by accessing the company's home page and its Investor Relations section. Finally, you can go to FINRA's Bond Center (finra-markets.morningstar.com/BondCenter/) and do a quick search for MMM's bond issues. A longer-term issue's YTM could provide an estimate of the firm's current cost of debt to be used in the WACC calculation. Remember that you need the after-tax cost of debt to calculate a firm's WACC, so you will need MMM's tax rate (which is forecasted to be 22%). What is your estimate of MMM's after-tax cost of debt?
4. a. What is your estimate of MMM's WACC using the book-value weights calculated in Question 1a?
   b. What is your estimate of MMM's WACC using the market-value weights calculated in Question 1b?
   c. Explain the difference between the two WACC estimates. Which estimate do you prefer? Explain your answer.
   d. How confident are you in the estimate chosen in part c? Explain your answer.

The Basics of Capital Budgeting

CHAPTER 11

Ivan Cholakov/Shutterstock.com

Competition in the Aircraft Industry: Airbus versus Boeing

Changing technology and market conditions often present executives with opportunities to invest in major projects, the success of which may go a long way toward determining their company's future success. For example, in recent years, Ford made the dramatic decision to shift to an aluminum base for its immensely popular F-150 pick-up; Apple decided after much fanfare to produce its Apple Watch; and Boeing and Airbus (a unit of the European Aeronautic Defence & Space Co., EADS) both have unveiled a series of new aircraft projects.

As you might expect, these projects require billions of dollars of capital to develop, and along the way the companies make many detailed calculations when forecasting crucial factors such as development costs, operating costs, and anticipated demand. These forecasts are further complicated by the fact that market conditions can dramatically change, and that companies don't operate in a vacuum—their key competitors are often making similar decisions, and the future cash flows will typically depend on who "wins the game" by developing the best product or service. Among these notable battles is the contest between Samsung, Apple, and others to develop smartphone technology, the steps that many tech and automotive companies are taking today to develop driverless cars, and the ongoing clash between Airbus and Boeing, where both companies have recently made major commitments toward investing in the next generation of aircraft.

Typically in these types of projects, Boeing and Airbus project negative cash flows for the first few years, followed by hopefully a long series of positive cash flows. Given their forecasted cash flows, both managements then decide whether taking on a given project would increase each company's intrinsic value. But given the inherent risks in this business and the fact that the planes will compete with one another, both Boeing's and Airbus's financial analysts recognize that their forecasts are subject to considerable errors. Moreover, as highlighted in a recent *New York Times* article, the two companies often develop different strategies when deciding what type of planes to build.

While these large-scale projects receive a great deal of attention, many companies also make a great many routine investment decisions every year, ranging from buying new trucks or machinery to purchasing computers and software to optimize inventory management. Although each project has its own unique characteristics, the same techniques described in this chapter are used to analyze projects of all types and sizes.

Sources: "Airbus Unveils First Passenger-Ready A350 XWB Plane," *CNN* (www.cnn.com), January 2, 2014; Jack Harty, "Countdown to Launch: The Airbus A350 XWB," *Airways News* (airwaysnews.com/blog), May 8, 2013; Peter Sanders and Daniel Michaels, "Winds of Change for Boeing, Airbus," *The Wall Street Journal* (www.wsj.com), March 16, 2010; and Jad Mouawad, "Oversize Expectations for the Airbus A380," *The New York Times* (www.nytimes.com), August 9, 2014.

PUTTING THINGS IN PERSPECTIVE

In the last chapter, we discussed the cost of capital. Now we turn to investment decisions involving fixed assets, or *capital budgeting*. Here *capital* refers to long-term assets used in production, while a *budget* is a plan that outlines projected expenditures during some future period. Thus, the *capital budget* is a summary of planned investments in long-term assets, and capital budgeting is the whole process of analyzing projects and deciding which ones to include in the capital budget. Boeing, Airbus, and other companies use the techniques in this chapter when deciding to accept or reject proposed capital expenditures.

Capital Budgeting
The process of planning expenditures on assets with cash flows that are expected to extend beyond 1 year.

When you finish this chapter, you should be able to do the following:

- **Discuss capital budgeting.**
- **Calculate and use the major capital budgeting decision criteria, which are NPV, IRR, MIRR, and payback.**
- **Explain why NPV is the best criterion and how it overcomes problems inherent in the other methods.**

With an understanding of the theory of capital budgeting developed in this chapter, which uses simplified examples, you will be ready for the next chapter, where we discuss how cash flows are estimated, how risk is measured, and how capital budgeting decisions are made.

11-1 An Overview of Capital Budgeting

The same concepts used in security valuation are also used in capital budgeting, but there are two major differences. First, stocks and bonds exist in the security markets, and investors select from the available set; firms, however, create capital budgeting projects. Second, for most securities, investors have no influence on the cash flows produced by their investments, whereas corporations have a major influence on projects' results. Still, in both security valuation and capital budgeting, we forecast a set of cash flows, find the present value of those flows, and make the investment only if the PV of the inflows exceeds the investment's cost.

A firm's growth, and even its ability to remain competitive and to survive, depends on a constant flow of ideas relating to new products, to improvements in existing products, and to ways of operating more efficiently. Accordingly, well-managed firms go to great lengths to develop good capital budgeting proposals. For example, the executive vice president of one successful corporation said that his company takes the following steps to generate projects:

Our R&D department constantly searches for new products and ways to improve existing products. In addition, our Executive Committee, which consists of senior executives in marketing, production, and finance, identifies the products and markets in which our company should compete, and the Committee sets long-run targets for each division. These targets, which are spelled out in the corporation's **strategic business plan**, *provide a general guide to the operating executives who must meet them. The operating executives then seek new products, set expansion plans for existing products, and look for ways to reduce production and distribution costs. Because bonuses and promotions are based on each unit's ability to meet or exceed its targets, these economic incentives encourage our operating executives to seek out profitable investment opportunities.*

Although our senior executives are judged and rewarded on the basis of how well their units perform, people further down the line are given bonuses and stock options for suggestions that lead to profitable investments. Additionally, a percentage of our corporate profit is set aside for distribution to nonexecutive employees, and we have an Employees' Stock Ownership Plan (ESOP) to provide further incentives. Our objective is to encourage employees at all levels to keep an eye out for good ideas, especially those that lead to capital investments.

Strategic Business Plan
A long-run plan that outlines in broad terms the firm's basic strategy for the next 5 to 10 years.

Analyzing capital expenditure proposals is not costless—benefits can be gained, but analysis does have a cost. For certain types of projects, an extremely detailed analysis may be warranted, while for other projects, simpler procedures are adequate. Accordingly, firms generally categorize projects and then analyze them in each category somewhat differently:

1. *Replacement: needed to continue current operations*. One category consists of expenditures to replace worn-out or damaged equipment required in the production of profitable products. The only questions here are should the operation be continued and if so, should the firm continue to use the same production processes? If the answers are yes, the project will be approved without going through an elaborate decision process.
2. *Replacement: cost reduction*. This category includes expenditures to replace serviceable but obsolete equipment and thereby to lower costs. These decisions are discretionary, and a fairly detailed analysis is generally required.
3. *Expansion of existing products or markets.* These are expenditures to increase output of existing products or to expand retail outlets or distribution facilities in markets now being served. Expansion decisions are more complex because they require an explicit forecast of growth in demand, so a more detailed analysis is required. The go/no-go decision is generally made at a higher level within the firm.
4. *Expansion into new products or markets.* These investments relate to new products or geographic areas, and they involve strategic decisions that could change the fundamental nature of the business. Invariably, a detailed analysis is required, and the final decision is generally made at the top level of management.
5. *Safety and/or environmental projects.* Expenditures necessary to comply with government orders, labor agreements, or insurance policy terms fall into this

category. How these projects are handled depends on their size, with small ones being treated much like the Category 1 projects.

6. *Other projects.* This catch-all includes items such as office buildings, parking lots, and executive aircraft. How they are handled varies among companies.
7. *Mergers.* In a merger, one firm buys another one. Buying a whole firm is different from buying an asset such as a machine or investing in a new airplane, but the same principles are involved. The concepts of capital budgeting underlie merger analysis.

In general, relatively simple calculations, and only a few supporting documents, are required for replacement decisions, especially maintenance investments in profitable plants. More detailed analyses are required for cost-reduction projects, for expansion of existing product lines, and especially for investments in new products or areas. Also, within each category, projects are grouped by their dollar costs: Larger investments require increasingly detailed analysis and approval at higher levels. Thus, a plant manager might be authorized to approve maintenance expenditures up to $10,000 using a relatively unsophisticated analysis, but the full board of directors might have to approve decisions that involve amounts greater than $1 million or expansions into new products or markets.

If a firm has capable and imaginative executives and employees and if its incentive system is working properly, many ideas for capital investment will be advanced. Some ideas will be good ones, but others will not. Therefore, procedures must be established for screening projects. Companies use, and we discuss, the following criteria for deciding to accept or reject projects:[1]

1. Net present value (NPV)
2. Internal rate of return (IRR)
3. Modified internal rate of return (MIRR)
4. Regular payback
5. Discounted payback

The NPV is the best method, primarily because it addresses directly the central goal of financial management—maximizing shareholder wealth. However, all of the methods provide useful information, and all are used in practice at least to some extent.

Self*Test*

How is capital budgeting similar to security valuation? How is it different?

What are some ways that firms generate ideas for capital projects?

Identify the major project classification categories, and explain how and why they are used.

What is the single best capital budgeting decision criterion? Explain.

11-2 Net Present Value (NPV)

We saw in Chapter 3 that there is a difference between cash flows and accounting income, and we noted that investors are particularly concerned with *free cash flow*. Recall that free cash flow represents the net amount of cash that is available for

[1]Two other rarely used criteria, the Profitability Index and the Accounting Rate of Return, are covered in Chapter 12 and Web Extension 12A of Eugene F. Brigham and Phillip R. Daves, *Intermediate Financial Management*, 13th edition (Mason, OH: Cengage Learning, 2019).

all investors after taking into account the necessary investments in fixed assets (capital expenditures) and net operating working capital.

In Chapter 9, we demonstrated that the value of the firm is equal to the present value of the free cash flows the firm produces for its investors over time. Similarly, the value of a project is equal to its **net present value (NPV),** which is simply the present value of the project's free cash flows discounted at the cost of capital. The NPV tells us how much a project contributes to shareholder wealth; the larger the NPV, the more value the project adds—and added value means a higher stock price.[2] Thus, NPV is the best selection criterion.

Net Present Value (NPV)
A method of ranking investment proposals using the NPV, which is equal to the present value of the project's free cash flows discounted at the cost of capital.

The most difficult aspect of capital budgeting is estimating the relevant cash flows. For simplicity, the cash flows are treated as given in this chapter, which allows us to focus on the rules for making capital budgeting decisions. However, in Chapter 12, we discuss cash flow estimation in detail.

We use the data for Projects S and L shown in Table 11.1 to illustrate the calculation. The S stands for *short*; the L, for *long*. Project S is a short-term project in the sense that more of its cash inflows come early, while L has more total cash inflows but they come in later in its life. The projects are equally risky, and they both have a 10% cost of capital. Furthermore, the cash flows have been adjusted to reflect depreciation, taxes, and salvage values. The investment outlays shown as CF_0 include fixed assets and any necessary investments in working capital, and cash flows come in at the end of the year. Finally, we show the table with an "Excel look," which simply means adding row and column headings to a "regular" table. All of the calculations can be done easily with a financial calculator; however, because some students may want to work with Excel, we show how problems would be set up in Excel. Do keep in mind, though, that Excel is not necessary.

resource

Students can download the Excel chapter models from the textbook's student companion site on cengage.com. Once downloaded onto your computer, retrieve the Chapter 11 Excel model and follow along as you read this chapter.

We find the NPVs as follows:

1. The present value of each cash flow is calculated and discounted at the project's risk-adjusted cost of capital, r = 10% in our example.
2. The sum of the discounted cash flows is defined as the project's NPV.

The equation for the NPV, set up with input data for Project S, is as follows:

$$\text{NPV} = CF_0 + \frac{CF_1}{(1+r)^1} + \frac{CF_2}{(1+r)^2} + \cdots + \frac{CF_N}{(1+r)^N} = \sum_{t=0}^{N} \frac{CF_t}{(1+r)^t} \quad \textbf{11.1}$$

$$\text{NPV}_S = -\$1{,}000 + \frac{\$500}{(1.10)^1} + \frac{\$400}{(1.10)^2} + \frac{\$300}{(1.10)^3} + \frac{\$100}{(1.10)^4}$$

$$= -\$1{,}000 + \$454.55 + \$330.58 + \$225.39 + \$68.30$$

$$= \$78.82$$

Here CF_t is the expected cash flow at Time t, r is the project's risk-adjusted cost of capital (or WACC), and N is its life. Projects generally require an initial investment—for example, developing the product, buying the equipment needed to manufacture it, building a factory, and stocking inventory. The initial investment is a negative cash flow. For Projects S and L, only CF_0 is negative, but for large projects such as Boeing's Dreamliner or Airbus's A350 XWB, outflows occur for several years before cash inflows ever begin.

Figure 11.1 shows the cash flow time line for Project S, the PV of each cash flow, and the sum of the PVs, which is by definition the NPV. The cost, at t = 0, is −$1,000.

[2] We could divide the NPV by the number of shares outstanding to estimate a project's effect on the stock price. However, given the lag between project acceptance and visible effects on earnings, this is rarely done for routine projects. However, for major projects, this procedure is useful.

TABLE 11.1 Data on Projects S and L

	A	B	C	D	E	F	G
13	WACC for both projects =		10%				
14		Initial Cost	After-Tax, End-of-Year Cash Inflows, CF_t				Total
15	Year	0	1	2	3	4	Inflows
16	Project S	–$1,000	$500	$400	$300	$100	$1,300
17	Project L	–$1,000	$100	$300	$400	$675	$1,475

The first positive cash flow is $500, and with a regular calculator, you could find its PV as $\$500/(1.10)^1 = \$454.55$. You could also find the PV of the $500 with a financial calculator. Other PVs could be found similarly, and the end result would be the numbers in the left column of the diagram. When we sum those numbers, the result is $78.82, which is NPV_S. Note that the initial cost, the −$1,000, is not discounted because it occurs at Time 0. The NPV for Project L, $100.40, could be found similarly.

The step-by-step procedure shown in Figure 11.1 is useful for illustrating how the NPV is calculated, but in practice (and on exams), it is far more efficient to use a financial calculator or Excel. Different calculators are set up somewhat differently, but as we discussed in Chapter 5, they all have a "cash flow register" that can be used to evaluate uneven cash flows such as those for Projects S and L. Equation 11.1 is programmed into these calculators, and all you must do is enter the cash flows (with the correct signs) along with r = I/YR = 10. Once the data have been entered and you press the NPV key, the answer, 78.82, appears on the screen.[3]

FIGURE 11.1 Finding the NPV for Projects S and L

	A	B	C	D	E	F	G
22	Project S	0 r = 10%	1	2	3	4	
23		−1,000.00	500	400	300	100	
24		454.55 ←					
25		330.58 ←					
26		225.39 ←					
27		68.30 ←					
28	NPV_S =	$78.82	Sum = NPV for Project S				
29							
30	NPV_L =	$100.40	=NPV(C13,C17:F17)+B17		NPV$_L$ found using Excel's NPV function		
31							

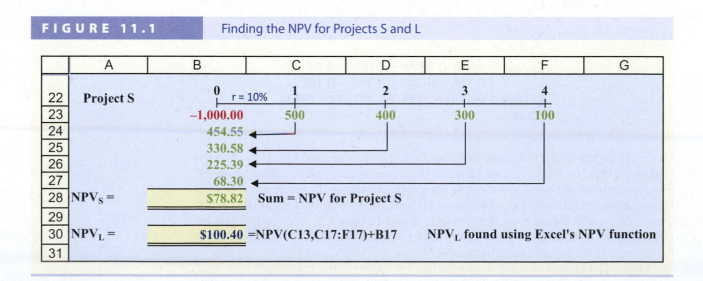

[3]The keystrokes for finding the NPV are shown for several calculators in the calculator tutorials provided on the textbook's student companion site, and you can access them by going to cengage.com.

If you are familiar with Excel, you can use Excel's NPV function to find the NPVs for S and L:[4]

$$NPV_S = \$78.82$$
$$NPV_L = \$100.40$$

The calculations used to obtain these values are provided in the chapter's Excel model, as shown in Figure 11.1. If you want to know something about Excel, you should review the model because this is the way most people in practice find NPVs.

Before using these NPVs in the decision process, we need to know whether Projects S and L are **independent** or **mutually exclusive**. Independent projects are projects whose cash flows are not affected by one another. If Walmart was considering a new store in Boise and another in Atlanta, the projects would be independent—and if both had positive NPVs, Walmart should accept both. Mutually exclusive projects, on the other hand, are projects where if one project is accepted, the other must be rejected. A conveyor belt system to move goods in a warehouse and a fleet of forklifts used for the same purpose would be mutually exclusive—accepting one implies rejecting the other.

Independent Projects
Projects with cash flows that are not affected by the acceptance or nonacceptance of other projects.

Mutually Exclusive Projects
A set of projects where only one can be accepted.

quick question

Projects X and Y have the following cash flows:

End-of-Year Cash Flows

	0	1	2	3	**WACC = r = 10%**
X	−$700	$500	$300	$100	
Y	−$700	$100	$300	$600	

QUESTION:

a. If a 10% cost of capital is appropriate for both projects, what are their NPVs?

b. Which project(s) would you accept if X and Y are (1) independent or (2) mutually exclusive?

ANSWER:

a. $NPV_X = -\$700 + \$500/(1.10)^1 + \$300/(1.10)^2 + \$100/(1.10)^3$
$= -\$700 + \$454.55 + \$247.93 + \$75.13$
$= \mathbf{\$77.61}$

$NPV_Y = -\$700 + \$100/(1.10)^1 + \$300/(1.10)^2 + \$600/(1.10)^3$
$= -\$700 + \$90.91 + \$247.93 + \$450.79$
$= \mathbf{\$89.63}$

b. (1) If the two projects are independent, then both projects would be accepted because both have positive NPVs.

(2) If the two projects are mutually exclusive, then Project Y would be accepted because it has the larger positive NPV.

[4]Excel's NPV function has the following format: = NPV (rate, CF_1 to CF_N). Notice that the NPV function (shown in Figure 11.1) does not include the initial outlay at Time 0. Excel's NPV function assumes that the first cell reference in the cash flow range given refers to the cash flow at Time 1. Thus, the initial outlay must be subtracted from the value obtained using Excel's NPV function to calculate the project's NPV.

What should be the decision if Projects S and L are independent? In this case, both should be accepted because both have positive NPVs and thus add value to the firm. However, if they are mutually exclusive, Project L should be chosen because it has the higher positive NPV and thus adds more value than S. Here is a summary of the NPV decision rules:

- *Independent projects.* If NPV exceeds zero, accept the project.
- *Mutually exclusive projects.* Accept the project with the highest positive NPV. If no project has a positive NPV, reject them all.

Because projects must be either independent or mutually exclusive, one or the other of these rules applies to every project.

Self*Test*

Why is the NPV the primary capital budgeting decision criterion?

Differentiate between independent and mutually exclusive projects.

11-3 Internal Rate of Return (IRR)

In Chapter 7, we discussed the yield to maturity (YTM) on a bond, and we explained that if you hold it to maturity, you will earn the YTM on your investment. The YTM is found as the discount rate that forces the PV of the cash inflows to equal the price of the bond. This same concept is involved in capital budgeting when we calculate a project's **internal rate of return (IRR)**:

Internal Rate of Return (IRR)
The discount rate that forces a project's NPV to equal zero.

A project's IRR is the discount rate that forces the PV of its inflows to equal its cost. This is equivalent to forcing the NPV to equal zero. The IRR is an estimate of the project's rate of return, and it is comparable to the YTM on a bond.

To calculate the IRR, we begin with Equation 11.1 for the NPV, replace r in the denominator with the term IRR, and set the NPV equal to zero. This transforms Equation 11.1 into Equation 11.2, the one used to find the IRR. The rate that forces NPV to equal zero is the IRR:[5]

$$\text{NPV} = \text{CF}_0 + \frac{\text{CF}_1}{(1+\text{IRR})^1} + \frac{\text{CF}_2}{(1+\text{IRR})^2} + \cdots + \frac{\text{CF}_N}{(1+\text{IRR})^N} = 0 \qquad \textbf{11.2}$$

$$0 = \sum_{t=0}^{N} \frac{\text{CF}_t}{(1+\text{IRR})^t}$$

$$\text{NPV}_S = 0 = -\$1{,}000 + \frac{\$500}{(1+\text{IRR})^1} + \frac{\$400}{(1+\text{IRR})^2} + \frac{\$300}{(1+\text{IRR})^3} = \frac{\$100}{(1+\text{IRR})^4}$$

Figure 11.2 illustrates the process of finding the IRR for Project S. Three procedures can be used:

1. *Trial and error.* We could use a trial-and-error procedure—try a discount rate, see if the equation solves to zero, and if it doesn't, try a different rate. We could then continue until we found the rate that forces the NPV to zero; that rate would be the IRR. For Project S, the IRR is 14.489%. Note, though, that the trial-and-error procedure is so time consuming that before computers and financial calculators were available, the IRR was rarely used. It's

[5]For a large, complex project like Boeing's Dreamliner, costs are incurred for several years before cash inflows begin. That means that we have a number of negative cash flows before the positive cash flows start.

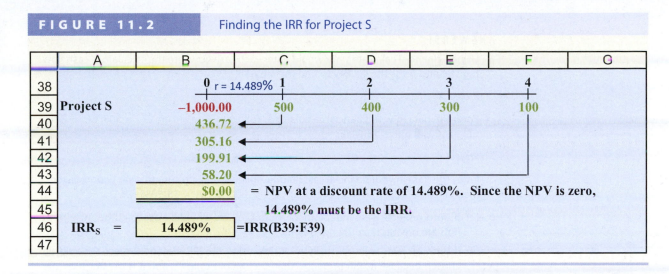

FIGURE 11.2 Finding the IRR for Project S

	A	B	C	D	E	F	G
38		0 r = 14.489%	1	2	3	4	
39	Project S	−1,000.00	500	400	300	100	
40		436.72 ←					
41		305.16 ←					
42		199.91 ←					
43		58.20 ←					
44		$0.00	= NPV at a discount rate of 14.489%. Since the NPV is zero,				
45			14.489% must be the IRR.				
46	IRR_S =	14.489%	=IRR(B39:F39)				
47							

useful to think about the trial-and-error procedure, but it's far better to use a calculator or Excel to do the actual calculations.

2. *Calculator solution.* Enter the cash flows in the calculator's cash flow register just as we did to find the NPV; then press the calculator key labeled "IRR." Instantly, you get the IRR. Here are the values for Projects S and L:[6]

$$IRR_S = 14.489\%$$
$$IRR_L = 13.549\%$$

3. *Excel solution.* It is even easier to find IRRs using Excel's IRR function, as we demonstrate in the chapter model and illustrate in Figure 11.2.

quick question

The cash flows for Projects X and Y are as follows:

End-of-Year Cash Flows

	0	1	2	3	
X	−$700	$500	$300	$100	
Y	−$700	$100	$300	$600	

WACC = r = 10%

QUESTIONS:

a. What are the projects' IRRs?
b. Which project(s) would the IRR method select if the firm had a 10% cost of capital and the projects were (1) independent or (2) mutually exclusive?

[6] See the calculator tutorials on the textbook's student companion site, which you can access by going to cengage.com. Note that once the cash flows have been entered in the cash flow register, you can find the NPV and the IRR. To find the NPV, enter the interest rate (I/YR) and then press the NPV key. Then with no further entries, press the IRR key to find the IRR. Thus, once you set up the calculator to find the NPV, it is easy to find the IRR. This is one reason most firms calculate both the NPV and the IRR. If you calculate one, it is easy to calculate the other; both provide information that decision makers find useful. The same is true with Excel.

ANSWERS:

a. Using a financial calculator, you would enter each cash flow into the calculator's cash flow register and press the IRR key to find the answer.

Project X

Enter the data in your financial calculator as follows: $CF_0 = -700$; $CF_1 = 500$; $CF_2 = 300$; $CF_3 = 100$; ■ IRR = **18.01%**.

Project Y

Enter the data in your financial calculator as follows, making sure to clear your registers first: $CF_0 = -700$; $CF_1 = 100$; $CF_2 = 300$; $CF_3 = 600$; ■ IRR = **15.56%**.

b. (1) If both projects were independent, both projects would be accepted because both IRRs are greater than the firm's WACC.

(2) If both projects were mutually exclusive, using the IRR method Project X would be chosen because its IRR is greater than the IRR of Project Y, and it is greater than the firm's WACC. *Note:* This may not be the correct choice for maximizing shareholder wealth, which we will discuss later in Section 11-7.

Why is the discount rate that causes a project's NPV to equal zero so special? The reason is that the IRR is an estimate of the project's rate of return. If this return exceeds the cost of the funds used to finance the project, the difference will be an additional return (in a sense a "bonus") that goes to the firm's stockholders and causes the stock price to rise. Project S has an estimated return of 14.489% versus a 10% cost of capital, so it provides an additional return of 4.489% above its cost of capital. On the other hand, if the IRR is less than the cost of capital, stockholders must make up the shortfall, which will hurt the stock price.

Note again that the IRR formula, Equation 11.2, is simply the NPV formula, Equation 11.1, solved for the particular discount rate that forces the NPV to equal zero. Thus, the same basic equation is used for both methods. The only difference is that with the NPV method the discount rate is given, and we find the NPV; with the IRR method the NPV is set equal to zero, and we find the interest rate that produces this equality.

As we noted earlier, projects should be accepted or rejected depending on whether their NPVs are positive. However, the IRR is sometimes used (improperly we believe) to rank projects and make capital budgeting decisions. When this is done, here are the decision rules:

- *Independent projects.* If IRR exceeds the project's WACC, accept the project. If IRR is less than the project's WACC, reject it.
- *Mutually exclusive projects.* Accept the project with the highest IRR, provided that IRR is greater than WACC. Reject all projects if the best IRR does not exceed WACC.

The IRR is logically appealing—it is useful to know the rates of return on proposed investments. However, as we demonstrate in Section 11-7, NPV and IRR can produce conflicting conclusions when a choice is being made between mutually exclusive projects, and when conflicts occur, the NPV is generally better.

Self*Test*

In what sense is a project's IRR similar to the YTM on a bond?

WHY NPV IS BETTER THAN IRR

Buffett University recently hosted a seminar on business methods for managers. A finance professor covered capital budgeting, explaining how to calculate the NPV and stating that it should be used to screen potential projects. In the Q&A session, Ed Wilson, the treasurer of an electronics firm, said that his firm used the IRR primarily because the CFO and the directors understood the selection of projects based on their rates of return but didn't understand the NPV. Ed had tried to explain why the NPV was better, but he simply confused everyone, so the company stuck with the IRR. Now a meeting on the firm's capital budget is approaching, and Ed asked the professor for a simple way to explain why the NPV is better.

The professor recommended the following extreme example. A firm with adequate access to capital and a 10% WACC is choosing between two equally risky, mutually exclusive projects. Project Large calls for investing $100,000 and then receiving $50,000 per year for 10 years, while Project Small calls for investing $1 and receiving $0.60 per year for 10 years. Each project's NPV and IRR are shown in the table in the top right column. The IRR says choose S, but the NPV says take L. Intuitively, it's obvious that the firm would be better off choosing the large project in spite of its lower IRR. With a cost of capital of only 10%, a 49% rate of return on a $100,000 investment is more profitable than a 59% return on a $1 investment.

Project Large (L)	Project Small (S)
$CF_0 = -\$100{,}000$	$CF_0 = -\$1.00$
$CF_{1-10} = \$50{,}000$	$CF_{1-10} = \$0.60$
I/YR = 10	I/YR = 10
NPV = $207,228.36	NPV = $2.69
IRR = 49.1%	IRR = 59.4%

When Ed gave this example in his firm's executive meeting on the capital budget, the CFO argued that this example was extreme and unrealistic, and that no one would choose S in spite of its higher IRR. Ed agreed, but he asked the CFO where the line should be drawn between realistic and unrealistic examples. When Ed received no answer, he went on to say that (1) it's hard to draw this line and (2) the NPV is always better because it tells us how much value each project will add to the firm, and value is what the firm should maximize. The president was listening, and he declared Ed the winner. The company switched from using IRR to NPV, and Ed is now the CFO.

11-4 Multiple Internal Rates of Return[7]

A problem with the IRR is that under certain conditions a project may have more than one IRR. First, note that a project is said to have *normal* cash flows if it has one or more cash outflows (costs) followed by a series of cash inflows. If, however, a cash *outflow* occurs sometime after the inflows have commenced, meaning that the signs of the cash flows change *more than once*, the project is said to have *non-normal* cash flows. Examples follow:

Normal:	−	+	+	+	+	+	**or**	−	−	−	+	+	+	+	+
Non-normal:	−	+	+	+	+	−	**or**	−	+	+	+	−	+	+	+

An example of a project with non-normal cash flows would be a strip coal mine where the company spends money to purchase the property and prepare the site for mining, has positive inflows for several years, and then the company spends more money to return the land to its original condition. In such a case, the project might have two IRRs, that is, **multiple IRRs.**[8]

Multiple IRRs
The situation where a project has two or more IRRs.

[7]This section is relatively technical, but it can be omitted without loss of continuity.

[8]Equation 11.2 is a polynomial of degree n, so it has n different roots, or solutions. All except one of the roots is an imaginary number when investments have normal cash flows (one or more cash outflows followed by cash inflows). So in the normal case, only one value of IRR appears. However, the possibility of multiple real roots (hence multiple IRRs) arises when negative cash flows occur after the project has been placed in operation.

To illustrate multiple IRRs, suppose a firm is considering a potential strip mine (Project M) that has a cost of $1.6 million and will produce a cash flow of $10 million at the end of Year 1. Then at the end of Year 2, the firm must spend $10 million to restore the land to its original condition. Therefore, the project's expected cash flows (in millions) are as follows:

	Year 0	End of Year 1	End of Year 2
Cash flows	−$1.6	+$10	−$10

We can substitute these values into Equation 11.2 and solve for the IRR:

$$\text{NPV} = \frac{-\$1.6 \text{ million}}{(1 + \text{IRR})^0} + \frac{\$10 \text{ million}}{(1 + \text{IRR})^1} + \frac{-\$10 \text{ million}}{(1 + \text{IRR})^2} = 0$$

NPV equals 0 when IRR = 25%, but it also equals 0 when IRR = 400%.[9] Therefore, Project M has an IRR of 25% and another of 400%, and we don't know which one to use. This relationship is depicted graphically in Figure 11.3.[10] The graph is constructed by plotting the project's NPV at different discount rates.

FIGURE 11.3 Graph for Multiple IRRs: Project M

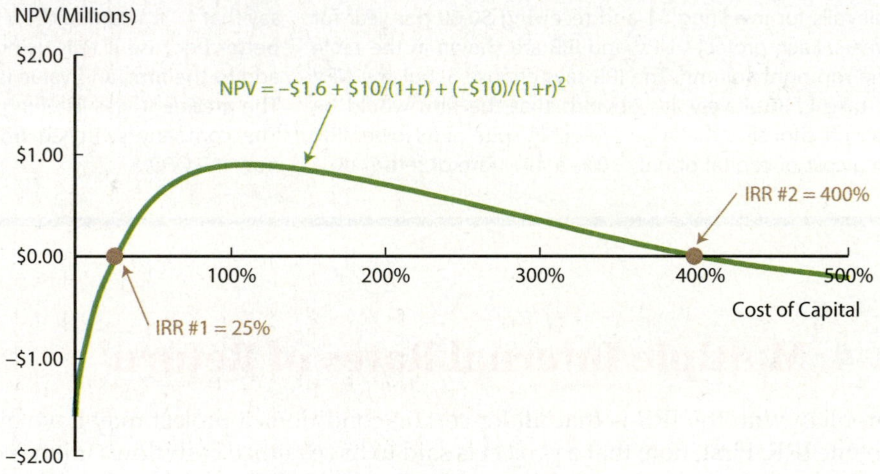

WACC = 10%

Discount Rate	NPV	
0%	−$1.6000	
10	−0.7736	
25	0.0000	= IRR #1
110	0.8943	
400	0.0000	= IRR #2
500	−0.2111	

[9]If you attempt to find Project M's IRR with an HP calculator, you will get an error message, while TI calculators give only the IRR that's closest to zero. When you encounter either situation, you can find the approximate IRRs by calculating NPVs using several different values for r = I/YR, plotting NPV on the vertical axis with the corresponding discount rate on the horizontal axis of a graph, and seeing about where NPV = 0. The intersection with the X-axis provides a rough idea of the IRRs' values. With some calculators and with Excel, you can find both IRRs by entering guesses, as explained in the calculator and Excel tutorials on the textbook's student companion site, which you can access by going to cengage.com.

[10]Figure 11.3 is called an NPV profile. Profiles are discussed in more detail in Section 11-7.

Note that no dilemma regarding Project M would arise if the NPV method was used; we would simply find the NPV and use it to evaluate the project. We would see that if Project M's cost of capital was 10%, its NPV would be −$0.7736 million, and the project should be rejected. However, if r was between 25% and 400%, NPV would be positive, but those numbers would not be realistic or useful for anything.

Self*Test*

What condition regarding cash flows would cause more than one IRR to exist?

Project MM has the following cash flows:

End-of-Year Cash Flows

0	1	2	3
−$1,000	$2,000	$2,000	−$3,350

Calculate MM's NPV at discount rates of 0%, 10%, 12.2258%, 25%, 122.1470%, and 150%. What are MM's IRRs? If the cost of capital is 10%, should the project be accepted or rejected? **(NPVs range from −$350 to +$164.8 and then back down to −$94.4; the IRRs are 12.23% and 122.15%. At a 10% WACC, the project's NPV is negative, so reject the project.)**

11-5 Reinvestment Rate Assumptions[11]

The NPV calculation is based on the assumption that cash inflows can be reinvested at the project's risk-adjusted WACC, whereas the IRR calculation is based on the assumption that cash flows can be reinvested at the IRR. To see why this is so, consider the following diagram, which was first used in Chapter 5 to illustrate the future value of $100 when the interest rate was 5%.

0 — 5% — 1 — 5% — 2 — 5% — 3

Going from PV to FV: PV = $100.00 ⟶ $105.00 ⟶ $110.25 ⟶ $115.76 = FV

Observe that the FV calculation assumes that the interest earned during each year can be reinvested to earn the same 5% in each succeeding year.

Now recall that when we found the PV, we reversed the process, discounting rather than compounding at the 5% rate. This diagram was used to demonstrate this point:

0 — 5% — 1 — 5% — 2 — 5% — 3

Going from FV to PV: PV = $100.00 ⟵ $105.00 ⟵ $110.25 ⟵ $115.76 = FV

This led to the following conclusion: *When we calculate a present value, we are implicitly assuming that cash flows can be reinvested at a specified interest rate, 5% in our example.* This applies to Projects S and L: When we calculated their NPVs, we discounted at the WACC, 10%, which means that we were assuming that their cash flows could be reinvested at 10%.

Now consider the IRR. In Section 11-3, we presented a cash flow diagram set up to show the PVs of the cash flows when discounted at the IRR. We saw that

[11] This section gives a theoretical explanation of the key difference between NPV and IRR. However, it is relatively technical, so if time is a constraint, professors may decide to have students skip it and just read the box titled "Why NPV Is Better Than IRR," which appears in Section 11-3.

for Project S the sum of the PVs is equal to the cost at a discount rate of 14.489%; so by definition, 14.489% is the IRR for Project S. Now we can ask this question: What reinvestment rate is built into the IRR?

Because discounting at a given rate assumes that cash flows can be reinvested at that same rate, the IRR assumes that cash flows are reinvested at the IRR.

The NPV assumes reinvestment at the WACC, while the IRR assumes reinvestment at the IRR. Which assumption is more reasonable? For most firms, assuming reinvestment at the WACC is more reasonable for the following reasons:

- If a firm has reasonably good access to the capital markets, it can raise all the capital it needs at the going rate, which in our example is 10%.
- Because the firm can obtain capital at 10%, if it has investment opportunities with positive NPVs, it should take them on, and it can finance them at a 10% cost.
- If the firm uses internally generated cash flows from past projects rather than external capital, this will save it the 10% cost of capital. Thus, 10% is the *opportunity cost* of the cash flows, and that is the effective return on reinvested funds.

To illustrate, suppose a project's IRR is 50%, the firm's WACC is 10%, and the firm has adequate access to the capital markets. Thus, the firm can raise the capital it needs at the 10% rate. Unless the firm is a monopoly, the 50% return would attract competition, which would make it difficult to find new projects with similar high returns, which is what the IRR assumes. Moreover, even if the firm does find such projects, it could take them on with external capital that costs 10%. The logical conclusion is that the original project's cash flows will save the 10% cost of the external capital, and that is the effective return on those flows.

If a firm does not have good access to external capital and if it has many potential projects with high IRRs, it might be reasonable to assume that a project's cash flows could be reinvested at a rate close to its IRR. However, that situation rarely exists: Firms with good investment opportunities generally do have good access to debt and equity markets.

Our conclusion is that the assumption built into the IRR—that cash flows can be reinvested at the IRR—is flawed, whereas the assumption built into the NPV—that cash flows can be reinvested at the WACC—is generally correct. Moreover, if the true reinvestment rate is less than the IRR, the true rate of return on the investment must be less than the calculated IRR; thus, the IRR is misleading as a measure of a project's profitability. This point is discussed further in the next section.

Self*Test*

Why is it true that a reinvestment rate is implicitly assumed whenever we find the present value of a future cash flow? Would it be possible to find the PV of a FV without specifying an implicit reinvestment rate?

What reinvestment rate is built into the NPV calculation? The IRR calculation?

For a firm that has adequate access to capital markets, is it more reasonable to assume reinvestment at the WACC or the IRR? Explain.

11-6 Modified Internal Rate of Return (MIRR)[12]

It is logical for managers to want to know the expected rate of return on investments, and this is what the IRR is supposed to tell them. However, the IRR is based on the assumption that projects' cash flows can be reinvested at the IRR. *This assumption is generally incorrect, and this causes the IRR to overstate the project's*

[12]Again, this section is relatively technical; it too can be omitted without loss of continuity.

true return.[13] Given this fundamental flaw, is there a percentage evaluator that is better than the regular IRR? The answer is yes—we can modify the IRR to make it a better measure of profitability.

This new measure, the **modified IRR (MIRR)**, is illustrated for Project S in Figure 11.4. It is similar to the regular IRR except that it is based on the assumption that cash flows are reinvested at the WACC (or some other explicit rate if that is a more reasonable assumption). Refer to Figure 11.4 as you read about its construction.

Modified IRR (MIRR)
The discount rate at which the present value of a project's cost is equal to the present value of its terminal value, where the terminal value is found as the sum of the future values of the cash inflows, compounded at the firm's cost of capital.

1. Project S has just one outflow, a negative \$1,000 at t = 0. Because it occurs at Time 0, it is not discounted and its PV is −\$1,000. If the project had additional outflows, we would find the PV at t = 0 for each one and sum them to arrive at the PV of total costs for use in the MIRR calculation.
2. Next, we find the future value of each *inflow* compounded at the WACC out to the "terminal year," which is the year the last inflow is received. We assume that cash flows are reinvested at the WACC. For Project S, the first cash flow, \$500, is compounded at WACC = 10% for 3 years and it grows to \$665.50. The second inflow, \$400, grows to \$484.00; the third inflow grows to \$330.00. The last inflow is received at the end, so it is not compounded at all. The sum of the future values, \$1,579.50, is called the "terminal value," or TV.
3. We now have the cost at t = 0, −\$1,000, and the TV at Year 4, \$1,579.50. There is some discount rate that will cause the PV of the terminal value to equal the cost. *That interest rate is defined as the MIRR.* Using your financial calculator, enter N = 4, PV = −1000, PMT = 0, and FV = 1579.50. Then when you press the I/YR key, you get the MIRR, 12.11%.
4. The MIRR can be found in a number of ways. Figure 11.4 illustrates how the MIRR is calculated: We compound each cash inflow, sum them to determine the TV, and then find the rate that causes the PV of the TV to equal the cost. That rate is calculated as 12.11%. However, some of the better calculators have a built-in MIRR function that streamlines the process. In Excel, you can use either the RATE function or MIRR function to calculate the MIRR, as shown in Figure 11.4.[14] We explain how to use the calculator function in the calculator tutorials, and we explain how to find MIRR with Excel in the chapter Excel model.[15]

---

[13]The IRR overstates the expected return for accepted projects because cash flows cannot generally be reinvested at the IRR. Therefore, the average IRR for accepted projects is greater than the true expected rate of return. This imparts an upward bias on corporate projections based on IRRs.

[14]Excel's MIRR function allows you to enter a different reinvestment rate from the WACC for the cash inflows. However, we assume reinvestment at the WACC, so the WACC is entered twice in the Excel MIRR function, shown in Figure 11.4.

[15]Equation 11.2a summarizes these steps.

$$\sum_{t=0}^{N}\frac{COF_t}{(1+r)^t}=\frac{\sum_{t=0}^{N}CIF_t(1+r)^{N-t}}{(1+MIRR)^N} \qquad \mathbf{11.2a}$$

$$\text{PV costs}=\frac{TV}{(1+MIRR)^N}$$

COF_t is the cash outflow at time t, and CIF_t is the cash inflow at time t. The left term is the PV of the investment outlays when discounted at the cost of capital; the numerator of the second term is the compounded value of the inflows, assuming the inflows are reinvested at the cost of capital. The MIRR is the discount rate that forces the PV of the TV to equal the PV of the costs.

Also, note that there are alternative definitions for the MIRR. One difference relates to whether negative cash flows, after the positive cash flows begin, should be compounded and treated as part of the TV or discounted and treated as a cost. A related issue is whether negative and positive flows in a given year should be netted or treated separately. For a complete discussion, see William R. McDaniel, Daniel E. McCarty, and Kenneth A. Jessell, "Discounted Cash Flow with Explicit Reinvestment Rates: Tutorial and Extension," *The Financial Review*, vol. 23, no. 3 (August 1988), pp. 369–385; and David M. Shull, "Interpreting Rates of Return: A Modified Rate of Return Approach," *Financial Practice and Education*, vol. 10 (Fall 1993), pp. 67–71.

FIGURE 11.4 Finding the MIRR for Project S, WACC = 10%

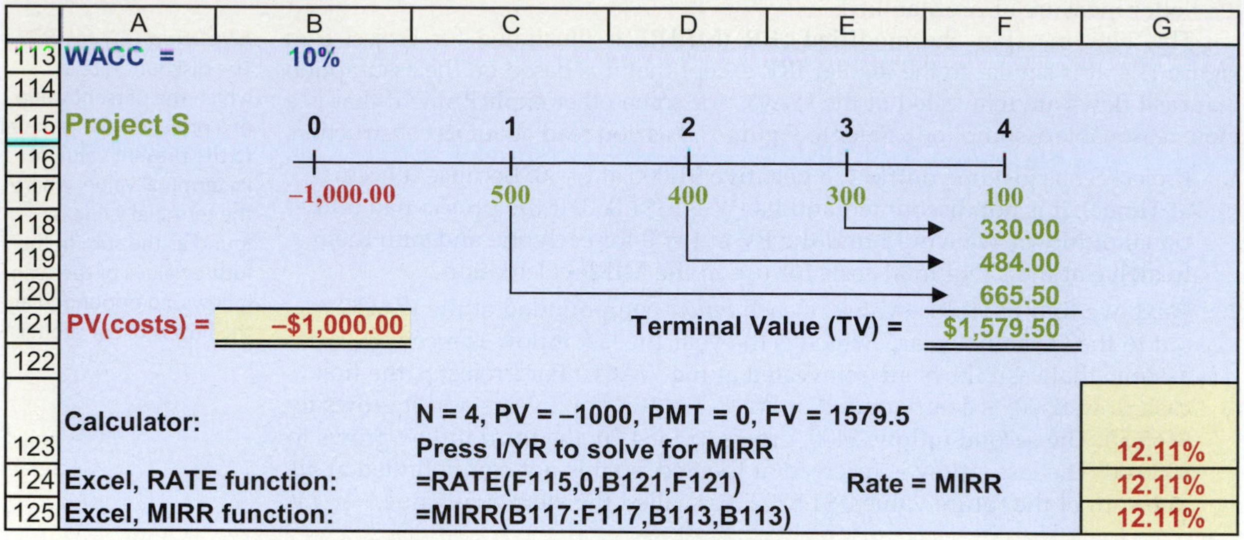
A B C D E F G
113 WACC = 10%
114
115 Project S 0 1 2 3 4
116
117 −1,000.00 500 400 300 100
118 330.00
119 484.00
120 665.50
121 PV(costs) = −$1,000.00 Terminal Value (TV) = $1,579.50
122
123 Calculator: N = 4, PV = −1000, PMT = 0, FV = 1579.5
Press I/YR to solve for MIRR 12.11%
124 Excel, RATE function: =RATE(F115,0,B121,F121) Rate = MIRR 12.11%
125 Excel, MIRR function: =MIRR(B117:F117,B113,B113) 12.11%

The MIRR has two significant advantages over the regular IRR. First, whereas the regular IRR assumes that the cash flows from each project are reinvested at the IRR, the MIRR assumes that cash flows are reinvested at the cost of capital (or some other explicit rate). Because reinvestment at the IRR is generally not correct, the MIRR is generally a better indicator of a project's true profitability. Second, the MIRR eliminates the multiple IRR problem—there can never be more than one MIRR, and it can be compared with the cost of capital when deciding to accept or reject projects.

quick question

Projects A and B have the following cash flows:

	End-of-Year Cash Flows		
	0	**1**	**2**
Project A	−\$1,000	\$1,150	\$100
Project B	−\$1,000	\$100	\$1,300

Their cost of capital is 10%.

QUESTIONS:

a. What are the projects' NPVs, IRRs, and MIRRs?
b. Which project would each method select if the projects were mutually exclusive?

ANSWER:

a. *Project A*

$$\text{NPV}: -\$1{,}000 + \$1{,}150/(1.10)^1 + \$100/(1.10)^2 = \mathbf{\$128.10}.$$

Alternatively, enter the cash flows into the financial calculator as follows:

$CF_0 = -1000$; $CF_1 = 1150$; $CF_2 = 100$; I/YR = 10; ■ NPV = **\$128.10**.

IRR: Enter the cash flows into the financial calculator as follows:

$CF_0 = -1000$; $CF_1 = 1150$; $CF_2 = 100$; ■ IRR = **23.12%**.

MIRR:

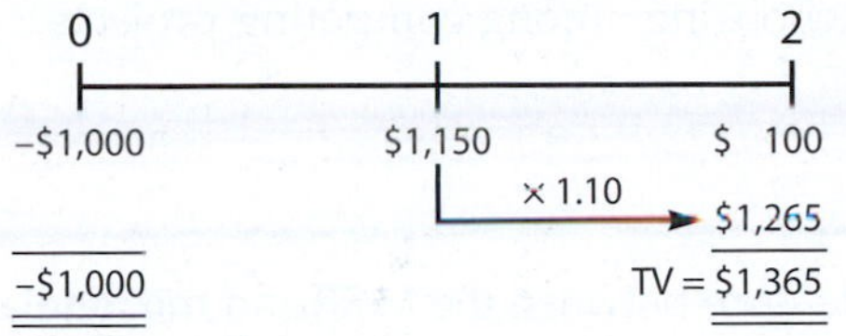

Using a financial calculator, enter the following data: N = 2; PV = –1000; PMT = 0; FV = 1365; and solve for I/YR = MIRR = **16.83%**.

Project B

NPV: $-\$1,000 + \$100/(1.10)^1 + \$1,300/(1.10)^2 =$ **$165.29**.

Alternatively, enter the cash flows into the financial calculator as follows:

$CF_0 = -1000$; $CF_1 = 100$; $CF_2 = 1300$; I/YR = 10; ■ NPV = **$165.29**.

IRR: Enter the cash flows into the financial calculator as follows:

$CF_0 = -1000$; $CF_1 = 100$; $CF_2 = 1300$; ■ IRR = **19.13%**.

MIRR:

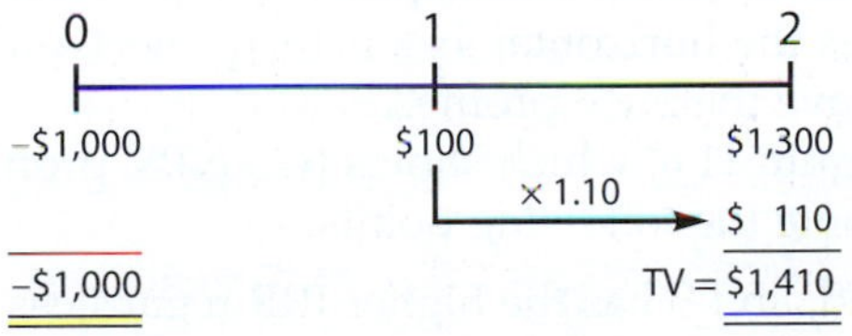

Using a financial calculator, enter the following data: N = 2; PV = –1000; PMT = 0; FV = 1410; and solve for I/YR = MIRR = **18.74%**.

b. Here's a summary of the results. The project chosen under each method is highlighted.

	Project A	Project B
NPV	$128.10	[$165.29]
IRR	[23.12 %]	19.13%
MIRR	16.83%	[18.74%]

Using the NPV and MIRR criteria, you would select Project B; however, if you use the IRR criteria, you would select Project A. Because Project B adds the most value to the firm, B should be chosen.

Our conclusion is that the MIRR is better than the regular IRR; however, this question remains: Is MIRR as good as the NPV? Here are our conclusions:

- For *independent* projects with normal cash flows, the NPV, IRR, and MIRR always reach the same accept/reject conclusion, so in these circumstances the three criteria are equally good.

- However, if projects are *mutually exclusive* and they differ in size, conflicts can arise. In such cases, the NPV is best because it selects the project that maximizes value.[16]
- Our overall conclusions are: (1) The MIRR is superior to the regular IRR as an indicator of a project's "true" rate of return. (2) NPV is better than IRR and MIRR when choosing among competing projects.

Self*Test*

What's the primary difference between the MIRR and the regular IRR?

Which provides a better estimate of a project's "true" rate of return, the MIRR or the regular IRR? Explain.

11-7 NPV Profiles

Net Present Value Profile
A graph showing the relationship between a project's NPV and the firm's cost of capital.

Figure 11.5 presents the **net present value profile** for Project S. To make the profile, we find the project's NPV at a number of different discount rates and then plot those values to create a graph. Note that at a zero cost of capital, the NPV is simply the net total of the undiscounted cash flows, \$1,300 − \$1,000 = \$300. This value is plotted as the vertical axis intercept. Also recall that the IRR is the discount rate that causes the NPV to equal zero, so the discount rate at which the profile line crosses the horizontal axis is the project's IRR. When we connect the data points, we have the NPV profile.[17]

Now consider Figure 11.6, which shows two NPV profiles—one for Project S and one for L—and note the following points:

- The IRRs are fixed, and S has the higher IRR regardless of the cost of capital.
- However, the NPVs vary depending on the actual cost of capital.
- The two NPV profile lines cross at a cost of capital of 11.975%, which is called the **crossover rate**. The crossover rate can be found by calculating the IRR of the differences in the projects' cash flows, as demonstrated here:

Crossover Rate
The cost of capital at which the NPV profiles of two projects cross and, thus, at which the projects' NPVs are equal.

	0	1	2	3	4
Project S	−\$1,000	\$500	\$400	\$300	\$100
−Project L	−\$1,000	\$100	\$300	\$400	\$675
$\Delta = CF_S - CF_L$	\$ 0	\$400	\$100	−\$100	−\$575
IRR Δ =	11.975% = Crossover rate				

- Project L has the higher NPV if the cost of capital is less than the crossover rate, but S has the higher NPV if the cost of capital is greater than that rate.

[16]See Eugene F. Brigham and Phillip R. Daves, *Intermediate Financial Management*, 13th edition (Mason, OH: Cengage Learning, 2019), Section 12-6.

[17]Notice that the NPV profile is curved—it is *not* a straight line. NPV approaches CF_0, which is the −\$1,000 project cost, as the discount rate increases toward infinity. At an infinitely high cost of capital, all the PVs of the inflows would be zero; so NPV at $r = \infty$ must be CF_0. We should also note that under certain conditions, the NPV profiles can cross the horizontal axis several times or never cross it. This point was discussed in Section 11-4.

FIGURE 11.5 NPV Profile for Project S

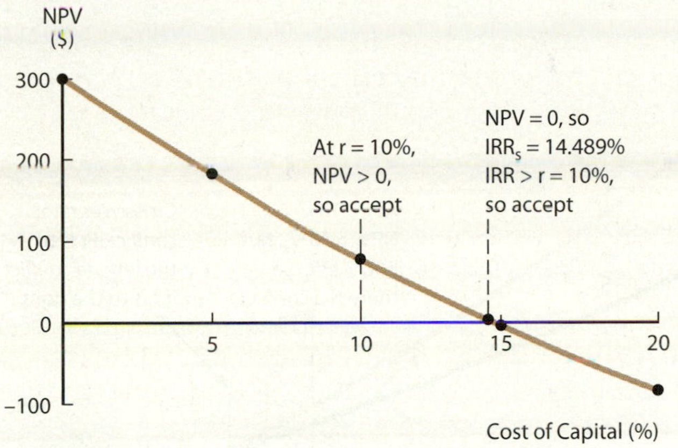

Cost of Capital	NPV_S	
0%	$300.00	
5	180.42	
10	78.82	
14.489	0.00	NPV = $0, so IRR = 14.489%
15	−8.33	
20	−83.72	

Notice that Project L has the steeper slope, indicating that a given increase in the cost of capital causes a larger decline in NPV_L than in NPV_S. To see why this is so, recall that L's cash flows come in later than those of S. Therefore, L is a long-term project and S is a short-term project. Next, recall the equation for the NPV:

$$NPV = CF_0 + \frac{CF_1}{(1 + r)^1} + \frac{CF_2}{(1 + r)^2} + \cdots + \frac{CF_N}{(1 + r)^N}$$

Now recognize that the impact of an increase in the cost of capital is much greater on distant than near-term cash flows, as we demonstrate here:

Effect of doubling r on a Year 1 cash flow:

$$\text{PV of \$100 due in 1 year @ r = 5\%: } \frac{\$100}{(1.05)^1} = \$95.24$$

$$\text{PV of \$100 due in 1 year @ r = 10\%: } \frac{\$100}{(1.10)^1} = \$90.91$$

$$\text{Percentage decline due to higher r} = \frac{\$95.24 - \$90.91}{\$95.24} = 4.5\%$$

Effect of doubling r on a Year 20 cash flow:

$$\text{PV of \$100 due in 20 years @ r = 5\%: } \frac{\$100}{(1.05)^{20}} = \$37.69$$

$$\text{PV of \$100 due in 20 years @ r = 10\%: } \frac{\$100}{(1.10)^{20}} = \$14.86$$

$$\text{Percentage decline due to higher r} = \frac{\$37.69 - \$14.86}{\$37.69} = 60.6\%$$

FIGURE 11.6 NPV Profiles for Projects S and L

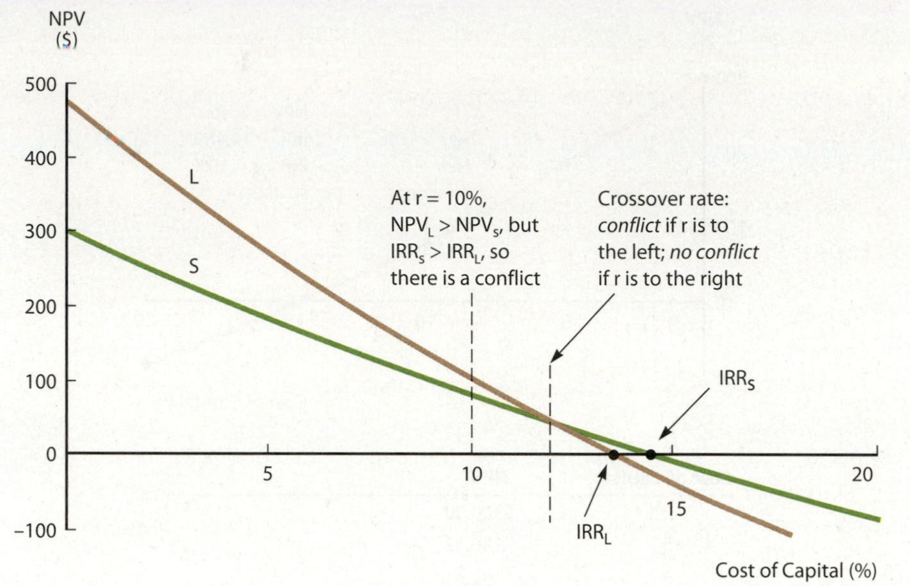

Cost of Capital	NPV_S	NPV_L
0%	$300.00	$475.00
5	180.42	268.21
10	78.82	100.40
Crossover = 11.97	42.84	42.84
IRR_L = 13.55	15.64	0.00
IRR_S = 14.49	0.00	−24.37
15	−8.33	−37.26
20	−83.72	−151.33

Thus, a doubling of the discount rate results in only a 4.5% decline in the PV of a Year 1 cash flow, but the same discount rate increase causes the PV of a Year 20 cash flow to fall by more than 60%. *Therefore, if a project has most of its cash flows coming in the later years, its NPV will decline sharply if the cost of capital increases, but a project whose cash flows come earlier will not be severely penalized by high capital costs.* Most of Project L's cash flows come in its later years, so if the cost of capital is high, L is hurt much worse than Project S. Therefore, Project L's NPV profile has the steeper slope.

Sometimes the NPV and IRR methods produce conflicting results. We can use NPV profiles to see when conflicts can and cannot arise. If an independent project with normal cash flows is being evaluated, the NPV and IRR criteria always lead to the same accept/reject decision: If NPV says accept, IRR also says accept, and vice versa. To see why this is so, look at Figure 11.5 and notice that (1) the IRR says accept if the project's cost of capital is less than (or to the left of) the IRR and (2) if the cost of capital is less than the IRR, the NPV will be positive. Thus, at any cost of capital less than 14.489%, Project S will be recommended by both the NPV and IRR criteria, and both methods reject the project if the cost of capital is greater than 14.489%. A similar graph could be used for Project L or any other normal project, and we would always reach the same conclusion: *For normal, independent projects, if the IRR says accept, so will the NPV.*

Assume that Projects S and L are mutually exclusive rather than independent. Therefore, we can choose either S or L, or we can reject both, but we can't accept both. Now look at Figure 11.6 and note these points:

- As long as the cost of capital is *greater than* the crossover rate, 11.975%, both methods agree that Project S is better: $NPV_S > NPV_L$ and $IRR_S > IRR_L$. Therefore, if r is *greater* than the crossover rate, no conflict occurs.
- However, if the cost of capital is *less than* the crossover rate, a conflict arises: NPV ranks L higher, but IRR ranks S higher.

Two basic conditions cause NPV profiles to cross and thus lead to conflicts:[18]

1. *Timing differences.* If most of the cash flows from one project come in early while most of those from the other project come in later, as occurred with Projects S and L, the NPV profiles may cross and result in a conflict.
2. *Project size (or scale) differences.* If the amount invested in one project is larger than the other, this too can lead to profiles crossing and a resulting conflict.

When size or timing differences occur, the firm will have different amounts of funds to invest in the various years depending on which of the two mutually exclusive projects it chooses. If it chooses S, it will have more funds to invest in Year 1 because S has a higher inflow that year. Similarly, if one project costs more than the other, the firm will have more money to invest at t = 0 if it selects the smaller project.

Given this situation, the rate of return at which differential cash flows can be reinvested is a critical issue. We saw earlier that the NPV assumes reinvestment at the cost of capital and that this is generally the best assumption. Therefore, *when conflicts exist between mutually exclusive projects, use the NPV method.*

Self*Test*

Describe in words how an NPV profile is constructed. How are the intercepts of the X- and Y-axes determined?

What is the crossover rate, and how does its value relative to the cost of capital determine whether a conflict exists between NPV and IRR?

What two conditions can lead to conflicts between the NPV and the IRR when evaluating mutually exclusive projects?

11-8 Payback Period

NPV is the most commonly used method for capital budgeting today; historically, however, the first selection criterion used was the **payback period**, defined as the number of years required to recover the funds invested in a project from its cash flows. Equation 11.3 is used for the calculation, and the process is diagrammed in Figure 11.7. We start with the project's cost, a negative value, and then add the cash inflow for each year until the cumulative cash flow turns positive. The payback year is the year prior to full recovery

Payback Period
The length of time required for an investment's cash flows to cover its cost.

[18]Of course, mutually exclusive projects can differ with respect to both scale and timing. Also, if mutually exclusive projects have different lives (as opposed to different cash flow patterns over a common life), this introduces further complications, and for meaningful comparisons, some mutually exclusive projects must be evaluated over a common life. This point is discussed later in Web Appendix 12E on the text's website, cengage.com.

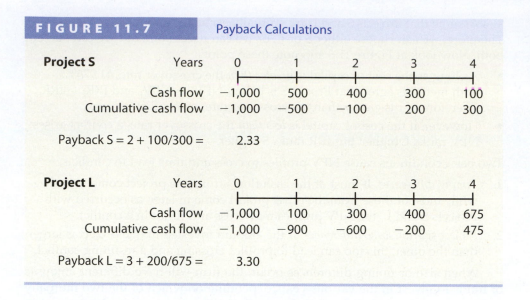

FIGURE 11.7 Payback Calculations

Project S					
Years	0	1	2	3	4
Cash flow	−1,000	500	400	300	100
Cumulative cash flow	−1,000	−500	−100	200	300
Payback S = 2 + 100/300 =	2.33				

Project L					
Years	0	1	2	3	4
Cash flow	−1,000	100	300	400	675
Cumulative cash flow	−1,000	−900	−600	−200	475
Payback L = 3 + 200/675 =	3.30				

plus a fraction equal to the shortfall at the end of that year divided by the cash flow during the full recovery year:[19]

$$\text{Payback} = \text{Number of years prior to full recovery} + \frac{\text{Unrecovered cost at start of year}}{\text{Cash flow during full recovery year}} \tag{11.3}$$

The shorter the payback, the better the project. Therefore, if the firm requires a payback of 3 years or less, S would be accepted, but L would be rejected. If the projects were mutually exclusive, S would be ranked over L because of its shorter payback.

The payback has three flaws: (1) All dollars received in different years are given the same weight (i.e., the time value of money is ignored); (2) cash flows beyond the payback year are given no consideration regardless of how large they might be; (3) unlike the NPV, which tells us how much wealth a project adds, and the IRR, which tells us how much a project yields over the cost of capital, the payback merely tells us when we will recover our investment. There is no necessary relationship between a given payback and investor wealth maximization, so we do not know what an acceptable payback is. The firm might use 2 years, 3 years, or any other number as the minimum acceptable payback; but the choice is arbitrary.

Discounted Payback
The length of time required for an investment's cash flows, discounted at the investment's cost of capital, to cover its cost.

To counter the first criticism, analysts developed the **discounted payback**. Here cash flows are discounted at the WACC; then those discounted cash flows are used to find the payback. In Figure 11.8, we calculate the discounted paybacks for S and L assuming that both have a 10% cost of capital. Each inflow is divided by $(1 + r)^t = (1.10)^t$, where t is the year in which the cash flow occurs and r is the project's cost of capital, and those PVs are used to find the payback. Project S's discounted payback is 2.95, while L's is 3.78.

Note that the payback is a "break-even" calculation in the sense that if cash flows come in at the expected rate, the project will break even. However, because the regular payback doesn't consider the cost of capital, it doesn't specify the true break-even year. The discounted payback does consider capital costs, but it still disregards cash flows beyond the payback year, which is a serious flaw. Further, if mutually exclusive projects vary in size, both payback methods can conflict with the NPV, which might lead to a poor choice. Finally, there is no way of telling how low the paybacks must be to justify project acceptance.

[19] Equation 11.3 assumes that cash flows come in uniformly during the full recovery year.

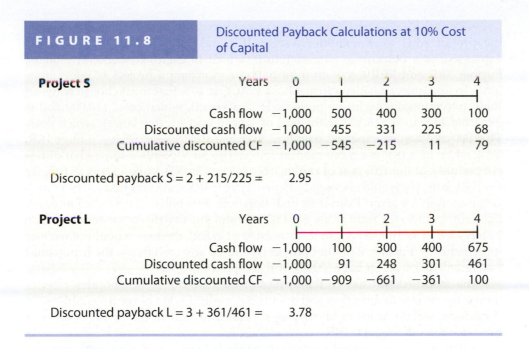

FIGURE 11.8 Discounted Payback Calculations at 10% Cost of Capital

Project S

Years	0	1	2	3	4
Cash flow	−1,000	500	400	300	100
Discounted cash flow	−1,000	455	331	225	68
Cumulative discounted CF	−1,000	−545	−215	11	79

Discounted payback S = 2 + 215/225 = 2.95

Project L

Years	0	1	2	3	4
Cash flow	−1,000	100	300	400	675
Discounted cash flow	−1,000	91	248	301	461
Cumulative discounted CF	−1,000	−909	−661	−361	100

Discounted payback L = 3 + 361/461 = 3.78

Although the payback methods have faults as ranking criteria, they do provide information about *liquidity* and *risk*. The shorter the payback, other things held constant, the greater the project's liquidity. This factor is often important for smaller firms that don't have ready access to the capital markets. Also, cash flows expected in the distant future are generally riskier than near-term cash flows, so the payback is used as one *risk indicator*.

Self*Test*

What information does the payback convey that is absent from the other capital budgeting decision methods?

What three flaws does the regular payback have? Does the discounted payback correct all of these flaws? Explain.

Project P has a cost of $1,000 and cash flows of $300 per year for 3 years plus another $1,000 in Year 4. The project's cost of capital is 15%. What are Project P's regular and discounted paybacks? **(3.10, 3.55)** If the company requires a payback of 3 years or less, would the project be accepted? Would this be a good accept/reject decision considering the NPV and/or the IRR? **(NPV = $256.72, IRR = 24.78%)**

11-9 Conclusions on Capital Budgeting Methods

We have discussed five capital budgeting decision criteria—NPV, IRR, MIRR, payback, and discounted payback. We compared these methods with one another and highlighted their strengths and weaknesses. In the process, we may have created the impression that "sophisticated" firms should use only one method, the NPV. However, virtually all capital budgeting decisions are analyzed by computer, so it is easy to calculate all five decision criteria. In making the accept/reject decision, large, sophisticated firms such as Boeing and Airbus generally calculate and consider all five measures because each provides a somewhat different piece of information about the decision.

NPV is the single best criterion because it provides a direct measure of value the project adds to shareholder wealth. IRR and MIRR measure profitability expressed as a percentage rate of return, which is useful to decision makers. Further, IRR and MIRR contain information concerning a project's "safety margin." To illustrate, consider a firm whose WACC is 10% that must choose between these two mutually exclusive projects: SS (for small), which costs $10,000 and is expected to return $16,500 at the end of 1 year, and LL (for large), which costs $100,000 and has an expected payoff of $115,550 after 1 year. SS has a huge IRR, 65%, while LL's IRR is a more modest 15.6%. The NPV paints a somewhat different picture—at the 10% cost of capital, SS's NPV is $5,000 while LL's is $5,045. By the NPV rule, we would choose LL. However, SS's IRR indicates that it has a much larger margin for error: Even if its cash flow was 39% below the $16,500 forecast, the firm would still recover its $10,000 investment. On the other hand, if LL's inflows fell by only 13.5% from its forecasted $115,550, the firm would not recover its investment. Further, if neither project generated any cash flows, the firm would lose only $10,000 on SS but $100,000 if it accepted LL.

The modified IRR has all the virtues of the IRR, but it incorporates a better reinvestment rate assumption and avoids the multiple rate of return problem. So if decision makers want to know projects' rates of return, the MIRR is a better indicator than the regular IRR.

Payback and discounted payback provide indications of a project's *liquidity* and *risk*. A long payback means that investment dollars will be locked up for a long time; hence, the project is relatively illiquid. In addition, a long payback means that cash flows must be forecasted far out into the future, and that probably makes the project riskier than one with a shorter payback. A good analogy for this is bond valuation. An investor should never compare the yields to maturity on two bonds without also considering their terms to maturity because a bond's risk is significantly influenced by the number of years remaining until its maturity. The same holds true for capital projects.

In summary, the different measures provide different types of information. Because it is easy to calculate all of them, all should be considered when capital budgeting decisions are being made. For most decisions, the greatest weight should be given to the NPV, but it would be foolish to ignore the information provided by the other criteria.

Self*Test*

Describe the advantages and disadvantages of the five capital budgeting methods discussed in this chapter.

Should capital budgeting decisions be made solely on the basis of a project's NPV? Explain.

11-10 Decision Criteria Used in Practice

Surveys designed to find out which of the criteria managers actually use have been taken over the years. Surveys prior to 1999 asked companies to indicate which method they gave the most weight, while the most recent survey, in 1999, asked what method(s) managers actually calculated and used. A summary of all these surveys is shown in Table 11.2, and it reveals some interesting trends.

First, the NPV criterion was not used significantly before 1980, but by 1999, it was close to the top in usage. Moreover, informal discussions with companies suggest that if a survey were to be taken in 2018, NPV would be at the top of this list. Second, the IRR method is widely used, but its recent growth is less dramatic than that of NPV. Third, payback was the most important criterion years ago, but its use as the primary criterion had fallen drastically by 1980. Companies still use

TABLE 11.2 Capital Budgeting Methods Used in Practice

	Primary Criterion			Calculate and Use
	1960	**1970**	**1980**	**1999**
NPV	0%	0%	15%	75%
IRR	20	60	65	76
Payback	35	15	5	57
Discounted Payback	NA	NA	NA	29
Other Methods	45	25	15	NA
Totals	100%	100%	100%	

Sources: The 1999 data are from John R. Graham and Campbell R. Harvey, "The Theory and Practice of Corporate Finance: Evidence from the Field," *Journal of Financial Economics*, vol. 60, nos. 2 and 3 (2001), pp. 187–244. Data from prior years are our estimates based on averaging data from these studies: James S. Moore and Alan K. Reichert, "An Analysis of the Financial Management Techniques Currently Employed by Large U.S. Corporations," *Journal of Business Finance and Accounting*, vol. 10, no. 4 (Winter 1983), pp. 623–645; and Marjorie T. Stanley and Stanley R. Block, "A Survey of Multinational Capital Budgeting," *The Financial Review*, vol. 19, no. 1 (March 1984), pp. 36–51.

payback because it is easy to calculate and it does provide some information, but it is rarely used today as the primary criterion. Fourth, "other methods," primarily the accounting rate of return and the profitability index, have been fading due to the increased use of IRR and especially NPV.

These trends are consistent with our evaluation of the various methods. NPV is the best single criterion, but all of the methods provide useful information and all are easy to calculate; thus, all are used, along with judgment and common sense. We will have more to say about all this in the next chapter.

Self*Test*

What trends in capital budgeting methodology can be seen from Table 11.2?

TYING IT ALL TOGETHER

In this chapter, we described five techniques—NPV, IRR, MIRR, payback, and discounted payback—that are used to evaluate proposed capital budgeting projects. NPV is the best single measure as it tells us how much value each project contributes to shareholder wealth. Therefore, NPV is the method that should be given the greatest weight in capital budgeting decisions. However, the other approaches provide useful information, and in this age of computers, it is easy to calculate all of them. Therefore, managers generally look at all five criteria when deciding to accept or reject projects and when choosing among mutually exclusive projects.

In this chapter, we took the cash flows given and used them to illustrate the different capital budgeting methods. As you will see in the next chapter, estimating cash flows is a major task. Still, the framework established in this chapter is critically important for sound capital budgeting analyses; and at this point, you should:

- **Understand capital budgeting.**
- **Know how to calculate and use the major capital budgeting decision criteria, which are NPV, IRR, MIRR, and payback.**

- **Understand why NPV is the best criterion and how it overcomes problems inherent in the other methods.**
- **Recognize that while NPV is the best method, the other methods do provide information that decision makers find useful.**

Self-Test Questions and Problems

(Solutions Appear in Appendix A)

ST-1 **KEY TERMS** Define the following terms:

a. Capital budgeting; strategic business plan
b. Net present value (NPV)
c. Internal rate of return (IRR)
d. NPV profile; crossover rate
e. Mutually exclusive projects; independent projects
f. Non-normal cash flows; normal cash flows; multiple IRRs
g. Modified internal rate of return (MIRR)
h. Payback period; discounted payback

ST-2 **CAPITAL BUDGETING CRITERIA** You must analyze two projects, X and Y. The firm's WACC is 12%, and the expected cash flows are as follows:

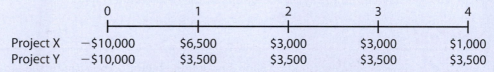

	0	1	2	3	4
Project X	−$10,000	$6,500	$3,000	$3,000	$1,000
Project Y	−$10,000	$3,500	$3,500	$3,500	$3,500

a. Calculate each project's NPV, IRR, MIRR, payback, and discounted payback.
b. Which project(s) should be accepted if they are independent?
c. Which project(s) should be accepted if they are mutually exclusive?
d. How might a change in the WACC produce a conflict between the NPV and IRR rankings of the two projects? Would there be a conflict if WACC were 5%? (*Hint:* Plot the NPV profiles. The crossover rate is 6.21875%.)
e. Why does the conflict exist?

Questions

11-1 How are project classifications used in the capital budgeting process?

11-2 What are three potential flaws with the regular payback method? Does the discounted payback method correct all three flaws? Explain.

11-3 Why is the NPV of a relatively long-term project (one for which a high percentage of its cash flows occurs in the distant future) more sensitive to changes in the WACC than that of a short-term project?

11-4 What is a mutually exclusive project? How should managers rank mutually exclusive projects?

11-5 If two mutually exclusive projects were being compared, would a high cost of capital favor the longer-term or the shorter-term project? Why? If the cost of capital declined, would that lead firms to invest more in longer-term projects or shorter-term projects? Would a decline (or an increase) in the WACC cause changes in the IRR ranking of mutually exclusive projects? Explain.

11-6 Discuss the following statement: If a firm has only independent projects, a constant WACC, and projects with normal cash flows, the NPV and IRR methods will always lead to identical capital budgeting decisions. What does this imply about the choice between IRR and NPV? If each of the assumptions were changed (one by one), how would your answer change?

11-7 Why might it be rational for a small firm that does not have access to the capital markets to use the payback method rather than the NPV method?

11-8 Project X is very risky and has an NPV of $3 million. Project Y is very safe and has an NPV of $2.5 million. They are mutually exclusive, and project risk has been properly considered in the NPV analyses. Which project should be chosen? Explain.

11-9 What reinvestment rate assumptions are built into the NPV, IRR, and MIRR methods? Give an explanation for your answer.

11-10 A firm has a $100 million capital budget. It is considering two projects, each costing $100 million. Project A has an IRR of 20% and an NPV of $9 million; it will be terminated after 1 year at a profit of $20 million, resulting in an immediate increase in EPS. Project B, which cannot be postponed, has an IRR of 30% and an NPV of $50 million. However, the firm's short-run EPS will be reduced if it accepts Project B because no revenues will be generated for several years.

a. Should the short-run effects on EPS influence the choice between the two projects?
b. How might situations like this influence a firm's decision to use payback?

Problems

Easy Problems 1-6

11-1 **NPV** Project L requires an initial outlay at t = 0 of $65,000, its expected cash inflows are $12,000 per year for 9 years, and its WACC is 9%. What is the project's NPV?

11-2 **IRR** Refer to problem 11-1. What is the project's IRR?

11-3 **MIRR** Refer to problem 11-1. What is the project's MIRR?

11-4 **PAYBACK PERIOD** Refer to problem 11-1. What is the project's payback?

11-5 **DISCOUNTED PAYBACK** Refer to problem 11-1. What is the project's discounted payback?

11-6 **NPV** Your division is considering two projects with the following cash flows (in millions):

	0	1	2	3
Project A	−$25	$5	$10	$17
Project B	−$20	$10	$9	$6

a. What are the projects' NPVs assuming the WACC is 5%? 10%? 15%?
b. What are the projects' IRRs at each of these WACCs?
c. If the WACC was 5% and A and B were mutually exclusive, which project would you choose? What if the WACC was 10%? 15%? (*Hint:* The crossover rate is 7.81%.)

Intermediate Problems 7–13

11-7 **CAPITAL BUDGETING CRITERIA** A firm with a 14% WACC is evaluating two projects for this year's capital budget. After-tax cash flows are as follows:

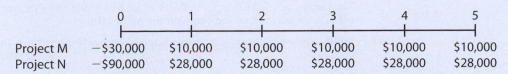

	0	1	2	3	4	5
Project M	−$30,000	$10,000	$10,000	$10,000	$10,000	$10,000
Project N	−$90,000	$28,000	$28,000	$28,000	$28,000	$28,000

a. Calculate NPV, IRR, MIRR, payback, and discounted payback for each project.
b. Assuming the projects are independent, which one(s) would you recommend?

c. If the projects are mutually exclusive, which would you recommend?
d. Notice that the projects have the same cash flow timing pattern. Why is there a conflict between NPV and IRR?

11-8 **CAPITAL BUDGETING CRITERIA: ETHICAL CONSIDERATIONS** A mining company is considering a new project. Because the mine has received a permit, the project would be legal, but it would cause significant harm to a nearby river. The firm could spend an additional $10 million at Year 0 to mitigate the environmental problem, but it would not be required to do so. Developing the mine (without mitigation) would require an initial outlay of $60 million, and the expected cash inflows would be $20 million per year for 5 years. If the firm does invest in mitigation, the annual inflows would be $21 million. The risk-adjusted WACC is 12%.

a. Calculate the NPV and IRR with and without mitigation.
b. How should the environmental effects be dealt with when this project is evaluated?
c. Should this project be undertaken? If so, should the firm do the mitigation?

11-9 **CAPITAL BUDGETING CRITERIA: ETHICAL CONSIDERATIONS** An electric utility is considering a new power plant in northern Arizona. Power from the plant would be sold in the Phoenix area, where it is badly needed. Because the firm has received a permit, the plant would be legal, but it would cause some air pollution. The company could spend an additional $40 million at Year 0 to mitigate the environmental problem, but it would not be required to do so. The plant without mitigation would require an initial outlay of $240 million, and the expected cash inflows would be $80 million per year for 5 years. If the firm does invest in mitigation, the annual inflows would be $84 million. Unemployment in the area where the plant would be built is high, and the plant would provide about 350 good jobs. The risk-adjusted WACC is 17%.

a. Calculate the NPV and IRR with and without mitigation.
b. How should the environmental effects be dealt with when evaluating this project?
c. Should this project be undertaken? If so, should the firm do the mitigation? Why or why not?

11-10 **CAPITAL BUDGETING CRITERIA: MUTUALLY EXCLUSIVE PROJECTS** A firm with a WACC of 10% is considering the following mutually exclusive projects:

	0	1	2	3	4	5
Project 1	−$200	$75	$75	$75	$190	$190
Project 2	−$650	$250	$250	$125	$125	$125

Which project would you recommend? Explain.

11-11 **CAPITAL BUDGETING CRITERIA: MUTUALLY EXCLUSIVE PROJECTS** Project S requires an initial outlay at t = 0 of $17,000, and its expected cash flows would be $5,000 per year for 5 years. Mutually exclusive Project L requires an initial outlay at t = 0 of $30,000, and its expected cash flows would be $8,750 per year for 5 years. If both projects have a WACC of 12%, which project would you recommend? Explain.

11-12 **IRR AND NPV** A company is analyzing two mutually exclusive projects, S and L, with the following cash flows:

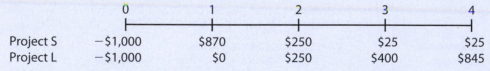

	0	1	2	3	4
Project S	−$1,000	$870	$250	$25	$25
Project L	−$1,000	$0	$250	$400	$845

The company's WACC is 8.5%. What is the IRR of the *better* project? (*Hint:* The better project may or may not be the one with the higher IRR.)

11-13 **MIRR** A firm is considering two mutually exclusive projects, X and Y, with the following cash flows:

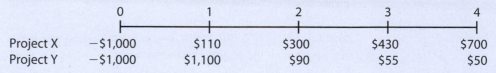

	0	1	2	3	4
Project X	−$1,000	$110	$300	$430	$700
Project Y	−$1,000	$1,100	$90	$55	$50

The projects are equally risky, and their WACC is 11%. What is the MIRR of the project that maximizes shareholder value?

Challenging Problems 14–22

11-14 **CHOOSING MANDATORY PROJECTS ON THE BASIS OF LEAST COST** Kim Inc. must install a new air conditioning unit in its main plant. Kim must install one or the other of the units; otherwise, the highly profitable plant would have to shut down. Two units are available, HCC and LCC (for high and low capital costs, respectively). HCC has a high capital cost but relatively low operating costs, while LCC has a low capital cost but higher operating costs because it uses more electricity. The costs of the units are shown here. Kim's WACC is 7%.

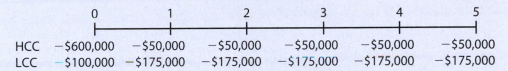

	0	1	2	3	4	5
HCC	−$600,000	−$50,000	−$50,000	−$50,000	−$50,000	−$50,000
LCC	−$100,000	−$175,000	−$175,000	−$175,000	−$175,000	−$175,000

a. Which unit would you recommend? Explain.

b. If Kim's controller wanted to know the IRRs of the two projects, what would you tell him?

c. If the WACC rose to 15%, would this affect your recommendation? Explain your answer and the reason this result occurred.

11-15 **NPV PROFILES: TIMING DIFFERENCES** An oil-drilling company must choose between two mutually exclusive extraction projects, and each requires an initial outlay at t = 0 of $12 million. Under Plan A, all the oil would be extracted in 1 year, producing a cash flow at t = 1 of $14.4 million. Under Plan B, cash flows would be $2.1 million per year for 20 years. The firm's WACC is 12%.

a. Construct NPV profiles for Plans A and B, identify each project's IRR, and show the approximate crossover rate.

b. Is it logical to assume that the firm would take on all available independent, average-risk projects with returns greater than 12%? If all available projects with returns greater than 12% have been undertaken, does this mean that cash flows from past investments have an opportunity cost of only 12% because all the company can do with these cash flows is to replace money that has a cost of 12%? Does this imply that the WACC is the correct reinvestment rate assumption for a project's cash flows? Why or why not?

11-16 **NPV PROFILES: SCALE DIFFERENCES** A company is considering two mutually exclusive expansion plans. Plan A requires a $40 million initial outlay on a large-scale integrated plant that would provide expected cash flows of $6.4 million per year for 20 years. Plan B requires a $12 million initial outlay to build a somewhat less efficient, more labor-intensive plant with expected cash flows of $2.72 million per year for 20 years. The firm's WACC is 10%.

a. Calculate each project's NPV and IRR.

b. Graph the NPV profiles for Plan A and Plan B and approximate the crossover rate.

c. Calculate the crossover rate where the two projects' NPVs are equal.

d. Why is NPV better than IRR for making capital budgeting decisions that add to shareholder value?

11-17 **CAPITAL BUDGETING CRITERIA** A company has an 11% WACC and is considering two mutually exclusive investments (that cannot be repeated) with the following cash flows:

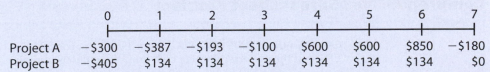

	0	1	2	3	4	5	6	7
Project A	−$300	−$387	−$193	−$100	$600	$600	$850	−$180
Project B	−$405	$134	$134	$134	$134	$134	$134	$0

a. What is each project's NPV?

b. What is each project's IRR?

c. What is each project's MIRR? (*Hint:* Consider Period 7 as the end of Project B's life.)

d. From your answers to parts a, b, and c, which project would be selected? If the WACC was 18%, which project would be selected?

e. Construct NPV profiles for Projects A and B.
f. Calculate the crossover rate where the two projects' NPVs are equal.
g. What is each project's MIRR at a WACC of 18%?

11-18 **NPV AND IRR** A store has 5 years remaining on its lease in a mall. Rent is $2,000 per month, 60 payments remain, and the next payment is due in 1 month. The mall's owner plans to sell the property in a year and wants rent at that time to be high so that the property will appear more valuable. Therefore, the store has been offered a "great deal" (owner's words) on a new 5-year lease. The new lease calls for no rent for 9 months, then payments of $2,600 per month for the next 51 months. The lease cannot be broken, and the store's WACC is 12% (or 1% per month).

a. Should the new lease be accepted? (*Hint:* Make sure you use 1% per month.)
b. If the store owner decided to bargain with the mall's owner over the new lease payment, what new lease payment would make the store owner indifferent between the new and old leases? (*Hint:* Find FV of the old lease's original cost at t = 9; then treat this as the PV of a 51-period annuity whose payments represent the rent during months 10 to 60.)
c. The store owner is not sure of the 12% WACC—it could be higher or lower. At what *nominal* WACC would the store owner be indifferent between the two leases? (*Hint:* Calculate the differences between the two payment streams; then find its IRR.)

11-19 **MULTIPLE IRRS AND MIRR** A mining company is deciding whether to open a strip mine with an initial outlay at t = 0 of $2 million. Cash inflows of $13 million would occur at the end of Year 1. The land must be returned to its natural state so there is a cash outflow of $12 million, payable at the end of Year 2.

a. Plot the project's NPV profile.
b. Should the project be accepted if WACC = 10%? If WACC = 20%? Explain your reasoning.
c. Think of some other capital budgeting situations in which negative cash flows during or at the end of the project's life might lead to multiple IRRs.
d. What is the project's MIRR at WACC = 10%? At WACC = 20%? Does MIRR lead to the same accept/reject decision for this project as the NPV method? Does the MIRR method *always* lead to the same accept/reject decision as NPV? (*Hint:* Consider mutually exclusive projects that differ in size.)

11-20 **NPV** A project has annual cash flows of $5,000 for the next 10 years and then $9,000 each year for the following 10 years. The IRR of this 20-year project is 8.52%. If the firm's WACC is 8%, what is the project's NPV?

11-21 **MIRR** Project A requires an initial outlay at t = 0 of $1,000, and its cash flows are the same in Years 1 through 10. Its IRR is 16%, and its WACC is 8%. What is the project's MIRR?

11-22 **MIRR** A project has the following cash flows:

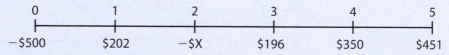

0	1	2	3	4	5
−$500	$202	−$X	$196	$350	$451

This project requires two outflows at Years 0 and 2, but the remaining cash flows are positive. Its WACC is 10%, and its MIRR is 14.14%. What is the Year 2 cash outflow?

Comprehensive / Spreadsheet Problem

11-23 **CAPITAL BUDGETING CRITERIA** Your division is considering two projects. Its WACC is 10%, and the projects' after-tax cash flows (in millions of dollars) would be as follows:

	0	1	2	3	4
Project A	−$30	$5	$10	$15	$20
Project B	−$30	$20	$10	$8	$6

a. Calculate the projects' NPVs, IRRs, MIRRs, regular paybacks, and discounted paybacks.
b. If the two projects are independent, which project(s) should be chosen?

c. If the two projects are mutually exclusive and the WACC is 10%, which project(s) should be chosen?
d. Plot NPV profiles for the two projects. Identify the projects' IRRs on the graph.
e. If the WACC was 5%, would this change your recommendation if the projects were mutually exclusive? If the WACC was 15%, would this change your recommendation? Explain your answers.
f. The crossover rate is 13.5252%. Explain what this rate is and how it affects the choice between mutually exclusive projects.
g. Is it possible for conflicts to exist between the NPV and the IRR when *independent* projects are being evaluated? Explain your answer.
h. Now look at the regular and discounted paybacks. Which project looks better when judged by the paybacks?
i. If the payback was the only method a firm used to accept or reject projects, what payback should it choose as the cutoff point, that is, reject projects if their paybacks are not below the chosen cutoff? Is your selected cutoff based on some economic criteria, or is it more or less arbitrary? Are the cutoff criteria equally arbitrary when firms use the NPV and/or the IRR as the criteria? Explain.
j. Define the MIRR. What's the difference between the IRR and the MIRR, and which generally gives a better idea of the rate of return on the investment in a project? Explain.
k. Why do most academics and financial executives regard the NPV as being the single best criterion and better than the IRR? Why do companies still calculate IRRs?

INTEGRATED CASE

ALLIED COMPONENTS COMPANY

11-24 BASICS OF CAPITAL BUDGETING You recently went to work for Allied Components Company, a supplier of auto repair parts used in the after-market with products from Daimler AG, Ford, Toyota, and other automakers. Your boss, the chief financial officer (CFO), has just handed you the estimated cash flows for two proposed projects. Project L involves adding a new item to the firm's ignition system line; it would take some time to build up the market for this product, so the cash inflows would increase over time. Project S involves an add-on to an existing line, and its cash flows would decrease over time. Both projects have 3-year lives because Allied is planning to introduce entirely new models after 3 years.

Here are the projects' after-tax cash flows (in thousands of dollars):

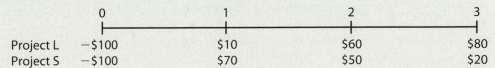

	0	1	2	3
Project L	−$100	$10	$60	$80
Project S	−$100	$70	$50	$20

Depreciation, salvage values, net operating working capital requirements, and tax effects are all included in these cash flows. The CFO also made subjective risk assessments of each project, and he concluded that both projects have risk characteristics that are similar to the firm's average project. Allied's WACC is 10%. You must determine whether one or both of the projects should be accepted.

a. What is capital budgeting? Are there any similarities between a firm's capital budgeting decisions and an individual's investment decisions?
b. What is the difference between independent and mutually exclusive projects? Between projects with normal and non-normal cash flows?

c. 1. Define the term *net present value (NPV)*. What is each project's NPV?

2. What is the rationale behind the NPV method? According to NPV, which project(s) should be accepted if they are independent? Mutually exclusive?

3. Would the NPVs change if the WACC changed? Explain.

d. 1. Define the term *internal rate of return (IRR)*. What is each project's IRR?

2. How is the IRR on a project related to the YTM on a bond?

3. What is the logic behind the IRR method? According to IRR, which project(s) should be accepted if they are independent? Mutually exclusive?

4. Would the projects' IRRs change if the WACC changed?

e. 1. Draw NPV profiles for Projects L and S. At what discount rate do the profiles cross?

2. Look at your NPV profile graph without referring to the actual NPVs and IRRs. Which project(s) should be accepted if they are independent? Mutually exclusive? Explain. Are your answers correct at any WACC less than 23.6%?

f. 1. What is the underlying cause of ranking conflicts between NPV and IRR?

2. What is the reinvestment rate assumption, and how does it affect the NPV versus IRR conflict?

3. Which method is best? Why?

g. 1. Define the term *modified IRR (MIRR)*. Find the MIRRs for Projects L and S.

2. What are the MIRR's advantages and disadvantages as compared to the NPV?

h. 1. What is the payback period? Find the paybacks for Projects L and S.

2. What is the rationale for the payback method? According to the payback criterion, which project(s) should be accepted if the firm's maximum acceptable payback is 2 years, if Projects L and S are independent? If Projects L and S are mutually exclusive?

3. What is the difference between the regular and discounted payback methods?

4. What are the two main disadvantages of discounted payback? Is the payback method useful in capital budgeting decisions? Explain.

i. As a separate project (Project P), the firm is considering sponsoring a pavilion at the upcoming World's Fair. The pavilion's initial outlay at t = 0 is \$800,000, and it is expected to result in \$5 million of incremental cash inflows during its 1 year of operation. However, it would then take another year and a \$5 million cash outflow to demolish the site and return it to its original condition. Thus, Project P's expected cash flows (in millions of dollars) look like this:

0	1	2
−\$0.8	\$5.0	−\$5.0

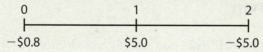

The project is estimated to be of average risk, so its WACC is 10%.

1. What is Project P's NPV? What is its IRR? Its MIRR?

2. Draw Project P's NPV profile. Does Project P have normal or non-normal cash flows? Should this project be accepted? Explain.

Cash Flow Estimation and Risk Analysis

CHAPTER 12

Rob Wilson/Shutterstock.com

Home Depot Carefully Evaluates New Investments

Home Depot (HD) has grown phenomenally over the past two decades. At the beginning of 1990, HD had 118 stores with annual sales of $2.8 billion. By early 2018, it had 2,284 stores and annual sales of just over $100 billion. Stockholders have benefited mightily from this growth as the stock's price has increased from a split-adjusted $1.87 in 1990 to $190 in May 2018.

However, during this time period, the news has not always been good. As you might expect, the company struggled in 2008 and 2009 in the midst of the financial crisis and a declining housing market. Discussing its struggles in its 2009 Annual Report, the company's management made the following observations:

> In fiscal 2008, the Company reduced its square footage growth plans to improve free cash flow, provide stronger returns for the Company, and invest in its existing stores to continue improving the customer experience. As a result of this store rationalization plan, the Company determined that it would no longer pursue the opening of approximately 50 U.S. stores that had been in its new store pipeline. The Company expects to dispose of or sublet these pipeline locations over varying periods. The Company also closed 15 underperforming U.S. stores in the second quarter of fiscal 2008, and the Company expects to dispose of or sublet those locations over varying periods.

In the years since this annual report was released, the company slowly continues to open new stores in areas it thinks the stores will thrive. For example in 2012, it opened three new stores in the United States (one of which was a relocation), it opened nine stores in Mexico, and it closed seven stores in China. Continuing this trend, in 2013, the company opened two stores and closed one store in the United States, and opened six stores in Mexico. And in 2017, Home Depot opened three new stores in the United States and three in Mexico.

It is clear that Home Depot is being very careful when it comes to evaluating new investments.

This caution is understandable: It costs several million dollars to purchase land, construct a new store, and stock it with inventory. Therefore, it is critical that the company perform a financial analysis to determine whether a potential store's expected cash flows will cover its costs.

Home Depot uses information from its existing stores to forecast the new stores' expected cash flows. Thus far, its forecasts have been outstanding, but there are always risks. First, a store's sales might be less than projected, especially if the economy weakens. Second, some of HD's customers might bypass the store altogether and buy directly from manufacturers through the Internet. Third, its new stores could "cannibalize," or take sales away from, its existing stores.

Rational expansion decisions require detailed assessments of the forecasted cash flows, along with a measure of the risk that forecasted sales might not be realized. That information can then be used to determine the risk-adjusted NPV associated with each potential project. In this chapter, we describe techniques for estimating projects' cash flows, as well as projects' risks. Companies such as Home Depot use these techniques on a regular basis when making capital budgeting decisions.

PUTTING THINGS IN PERSPECTIVE

The basic principles of capital budgeting were covered in Chapter 11. Given a project's expected cash flows, it is easy to calculate the primary decision criterion—the NPV—as well as the supplemental criteria, IRR, MIRR, payback, and discounted payback. However, in the real world, cash flow values are not just handed to you—rather, they must be estimated based on information from various sources. Moreover, uncertainty surrounds the forecasted cash flows, and some projects are more uncertain and thus riskier than others. In this chapter, we review examples that illustrate how project cash flows are estimated, discuss techniques for measuring and then dealing with risk, and discuss how projects are evaluated once they begin operations.

When you finish this chapter, you should be able to do the following:

- **Identify "relevant" cash flows that should and should not be included in a capital budgeting analysis.**
- **Estimate a project's relevant cash flows and put them into a time line format that can be used to calculate a project's NPV, IRR, and other capital budgeting metrics.**
- **Explain how risk is measured, and use this measure to adjust the firm's WACC to account for differential project riskiness.**
- **Discuss how some projects can be altered after they have been accepted and how these alterations can change a project's cash flows and thus its realized NPV.**
- **Describe the post-audit, which is an important part of the capital budgeting process and discuss its relevance in capital budgeting decisions.**

12-1 Conceptual Issues in Cash Flow Estimation

Before the cash flow estimation process is illustrated, we need to discuss several important conceptual issues. A failure to handle these issues properly can lead to calculating incorrect project NPVs, which will lead to bad capital budgeting decisions.

12-1A FREE CASH FLOW VERSUS ACCOUNTING INCOME

In the last chapter, we showed that a project's NPV is equal to the present value of its discounted free cash flows. Recall from Chapters 3 and 9 that free cash flow is defined as:

$$\text{FCF} = \left[\text{EBIT}(1-\text{T}) + \begin{matrix}\text{Depreciation}\\ \text{and amortization}\end{matrix}\right] - \left[\begin{matrix}\text{Capital}\\ \text{expenditures}\end{matrix} + \begin{matrix}\Delta\text{Net operating}\\ \text{working capital}\end{matrix}\right]$$

A typical project will require the firm to spend money upfront at t = 0 to make the necessary investments in fixed assets and net operating working capital. In some cases, the firm may also need to make continued investments throughout the life of the project, particularly for a growing project where the company needs to steadily add fixed assets and inventory over time. For simplicity, unless otherwise stated, we will assume that investments in fixed assets and net operating working capital will occur only at t = 0.

After the initial investments are made, the project will hopefully produce positive cash flows over its operating life. The first bracketed term in the free cash flow equation [EBIT(1 − T) + Depreciation and amortization] represents the project's operating cash flows. In most cases, these cash flows will vary over the life of the project.

Once the project is completed, the company sells the project's fixed assets and inventory and receives cash.[1] In some respects, we can think of the sale of fixed assets at the end of the project as a negative capital expenditure—instead of using cash to purchase fixed assets, the company is selling the assets to generate cash.

The price that the company receives for a fixed asset at the end of the project is often referred to as its *salvage value*. The company will also have to pay taxes if the asset's salvage value exceeds its book value. More specifically:

$$\text{Taxes paid on salvaged assets} = \text{Tax rate} \times (\text{Salvage value} - \text{Book value})$$

Here the book value equals the initial price for the asset minus the asset's total accumulated depreciation. Note that the preceding equation indicates that the taxes paid would be negative (i.e., the firm would receive a tax credit) if the company sold the asset for less than its book value. Although depreciation is not a cash expense, it does affect the company's taxes. For this reason, what matters is the depreciation rate that the firm's accountants use for tax purposes. In many cases, these depreciation rates and salvage values may be considerably different from the GAAP accounting values that are used to report accounting income in the firm's financial statements.

For example, the 2017 Tax Act allows firms to deduct, in many cases, all of the project's up-front fixed asset expenses at the time the costs are incurred. However, the GAAP guidelines still require the company to depreciate these costs over time. Under the new tax legislation, 100% of the cost of certain new and used business assets may be immediately expensed if placed into service after September 27, 2017, and before January 1, 2023. For assets placed into service after January 1, 2023, but before January 1, 2027, only 80% of the asset's cost may be immediately expensed. Immediate expensing is eliminated after January 1, 2027. This "bonus depreciation" is typically for assets with lives of less than 20 years. Unless we say otherwise, we will assume that the projects we examine will be eligible for this bonus depreciation, in which case, the full cost of the purchased asset will be

[1]In many cases, these fixed assets and inventory are "sold" within the company for use in other projects. In these instances, the company would establish the price that the old project would charge the new project. These "transfer prices" are important, and well-run companies work hard to make sure that they are fairly set to ensure that assets are efficiently transferred within the company.

deducted (fully depreciated) at the time of the purchase. Consequently, the book value of the asset will be zero after the time of purchase.

As we mentioned previously, a project will generally require an initial increase in NOWC. Assume that Home Depot is considering a project to open a new store. The company estimates that it will need $5 million in new inventory to stock the store; $3 million of that inventory will be financed through new accounts payable, and the remaining $2 million will be paid in cash. If all other working capital components remain constant, the project will increase the company's current operating assets by $5 million and increase the company's current operating liabilities by $3 million. The resulting change in NOWC is the $2 million in cash that is necessary to open the store. If the amount of inventory and accounts payable remain constant over time, there will be no additional changes in NOWC over the life of the project. Once the project is completed (the store is closed), the final $5 million in inventory will be sold, and the company will pay off its remaining $3 million in accounts payable. The firm will receive the remaining $2 million in cash, which corresponds to the investment made for the change in NOWC that was required when the project began.

12-1B TIMING OF CASH FLOWS

In theory, capital budgeting analyses should deal with cash flows exactly when they occur; therefore, daily cash flows theoretically would be better than annual flows. However, it would be costly to estimate and analyze daily cash flows, and they would probably be no more accurate than annual estimates because we simply cannot accurately forecast at a daily level out 10 years or so into the future. Therefore, we generally assume that all cash flows occur at the end of the year. Note, however, for projects with highly predictable cash flows, it might be useful to assume that cash flows occur at midyear (or even quarterly or monthly). But for most purposes, we assume end-of-year flows.

12-1C INCREMENTAL CASH FLOWS

Incremental Cash Flows
Cash flows that will occur if and only if the firm takes on a project.

Incremental cash flows are flows that will occur *if and only if* some specific event occurs. In capital budgeting, the event is the firm's acceptance of a project and the project's incremental cash flows are ones that occur as a result of this decision. Cash flows such as investments in buildings, equipment, and working capital needed for the project are obviously incremental, as are sales revenues and operating costs associated with the project. However, some items are not so obvious, as we explain later in this section.

12-1D REPLACEMENT PROJECTS

Two types of projects can be distinguished: expansion projects, where the firm makes an investment, such as a new Home Depot store, and replacement projects, where the firm replaces existing assets, generally to reduce costs. For example, suppose Home Depot is considering replacing some of its delivery trucks. The benefit would be lower fuel and maintenance expenses, and the shiny new trucks also might improve the company's image and reduce pollution. Replacement analysis is complicated by the fact that almost all of the cash flows are incremental, found by subtracting the new cost numbers from the old numbers. Thus, the fuel bill for a more efficient new truck might be $10,000 per year versus $15,000 for the old truck. The $5,000 savings is the incremental cash flow that would be used in the replacement analysis. Similarly, we would need to find the difference in depreciation and other factors that affect cash flows. Once we have found the incremental cash flows, we use them in a "regular" NPV analysis to decide whether to replace the asset or to continue using it.

12-1E SUNK COSTS

A **sunk cost** is an outlay that was incurred in the past and cannot be recovered in the future regardless of whether the project under consideration is accepted. In capital budgeting, we are concerned with *future incremental cash flows*—we want to know if the *new* investment will produce enough incremental cash flow to justify the incremental investment. *Because sunk costs were incurred in the past and cannot be recovered regardless of whether the project is accepted or rejected, they are not relevant in the capital budgeting analysis.*

Sunk Cost
A cash outlay that has already been incurred and that cannot be recovered regardless of whether the project is accepted or rejected.

To illustrate this concept, suppose Home Depot spent $2 million to investigate a potential new store and obtain the permits required to build it. That $2 million would be a sunk cost—the money is gone, and it won't come back regardless of whether or not the new store is built.

Not handling sunk costs properly can lead to incorrect decisions. For example, suppose Home Depot completed the analysis and found that it must spend an additional $17 million, on top of the $2 million site study, to open the store. Suppose it then used as the required investment $19 million and calculated the new store's projected NPV as *negative* $1 million. This would indicate that HD should reject the new store. *However, that would be a bad decision.* The real issue is whether the *incremental* $17 million would result in *incremental* cash inflows sufficient to produce a positive NPV. If the $2 million sunk cost is disregarded, as it should be, the new store's true NPV will be a *positive* $1 million. Therefore, the failure to deal properly with the sunk cost would lead to turning down a project that would add $1 million to stockholders' value.

12-1F OPPORTUNITY COSTS ASSOCIATED WITH ASSETS THE FIRM OWNS

Another issue relates to **opportunity costs** associated with assets the firm already owns. For example, suppose Home Depot owns land with a market value of $2 million and that land will be used for the new store if HD decides to build it. If HD decides to go forward with the project, only another $15 million will be required, not the typical $17 million because HD would not need to buy the required land. Does this mean that HD should use $15 million as the cost of the new store? The answer is no. If the new store is not built, HD could sell the land and receive a cash flow of $2 million. This $2 million is an *opportunity cost*—something that HD would not receive if the land was used for the new store. Therefore, the $2 million must be charged to the new project, and a failure to do so would artificially and incorrectly increase the new project's NPV.

Opportunity Costs
The best return that could be earned on assets the firm already owns if those assets are not used for the new project.

Consider further the following example. Assume that a firm owns a building and equipment with a market (resale) value of $10 million. The property is not being used, and the firm is considering using it for a new project. The only required additional investment would be $100,000 for working capital, and the new project would produce a cash inflow of $50,000 forever. If the firm has a WACC of 10% and evaluates the project using only the $100,000 of working capital as the required investment, it would find an NPV of $50,000/0.10 − $100,000 = $500,000 − $100,000 = $400,000. Does this mean that the project is a good one? The answer is no. The firm can sell the property for $10 million, which is a much larger amount than $400,000.

12-1G EXTERNALITIES

Another potential problem involves **externalities**, which are defined as the effects of a project on other parts of the firm or the environment. The three types of externalities—negative within-firm externalities, positive within-firm externalities, and environmental externalities—are explained next.

Externalities
Effects on the firm or the environment that are not reflected in the project's cash flows.

Negative Within-Firm Externalities

As noted earlier, when retailers such as Home Depot open new stores that are too close to their existing stores, this takes customers away from their existing stores. In this case, even though the new store has positive cash flows, its existence reduces some of the firm's current cash flows. This type of externality is called **cannibalization** because the new business eats into the company's existing business. For example, when it considers whether to open a new store, Starbucks takes into account the extent the proposed store will reduce the sales of its existing coffee shops in the surrounding area. Those lost cash flows should be taken into account, and that means charging them as a cost when analyzing the proposed new store.

Cannibalization
The situation when a new project reduces cash flows that the firm would otherwise have had.

Dealing properly with negative externalities can be tricky. If Starbucks decides not to open the new store because of its cannibalization effects, might another competitor consider opening a new store in the same location, causing the existing coffee shops to lose sales regardless of whether Starbucks builds the new store? Logically, Starbucks must examine the total situation, which is more than a simple mechanical analysis. Experience and knowledge of the industry are required to make good decisions.

One of the best examples of a company's misstep from dealing incorrectly with cannibalization effects was IBM's response when transistors made personal computers possible in the 1970s. IBM's mainframe computers were the biggest game in town, and they generated huge profits. But IBM also had the technology for PCs, entered the PC market, and for a time was the leading PC company. However, top management decided to rein back the PC division because managers were afraid it would hurt the more profitable mainframe business. That decision opened the door for Microsoft, Intel, Dell, Hewlett-Packard, and others; IBM went from being the most profitable firm in the world to one whose very survival was threatened. To its credit, IBM has been able to successfully shift its emphasis to where it now focuses on a broad range of technology and business services. Nevertheless, this experience highlights the fact that while it is essential to understand the theory of finance, it is equally important to understand the business environment, including how competitors are likely to react to a firm's actions. A great deal of judgment goes into making good financial decisions.

Positive Within-Firm Externalities

Cannibalization occurs when new products compete with old ones. However, a new project also can be *complementary* to an old one, in which case cash flows in the old operation will be *increased* when the new one is introduced. For example, Apple's iPod was a profitable product, but when Apple made an investment in another project, its iTunes music store, that investment boosted sales of the iPod. So if an analysis of the proposed music store indicated a negative NPV, the analysis would not have been complete unless the incremental cash flows that would occur in the iPod division were credited to the music store. That might well change the project's NPV from negative to positive.

Environmental Externalities

The most common type of negative externality is a project's impact on the environment. Government rules and regulations constrain what companies can do, but firms have some flexibility in dealing with the environment. For example, suppose a manufacturer is studying a proposed new plant. The company could meet the environmental regulations at a cost of $1 million, but the plant would still emit fumes that might cause ill feelings in its neighborhood. Those ill feelings would not show up in the cash flow analysis, but they still should be considered. Perhaps a relatively small additional expenditure would reduce the emissions substantially, make the plant look good relative to other plants in the area, and provide goodwill that in the future would help the firm's sales and negotiations with governmental agencies.

Of course, everyone's profits depend on the earth remaining healthy, so companies have an incentive to do things to protect the environment even though those actions are not required. However, if one firm decides to take actions that are good for the environment but costly, its products must reflect those higher costs. If its competitors decide to get by with less costly but less environment friendly processes, they can price their products lower and make more money. Of course, more environment friendly companies can advertise their environmental efforts, and this might—or might not—offset their higher costs. All of this illustrates why government regulations are necessary, both nationally and internationally. Finance, politics, and the environment are all interconnected.

Self*Test*

Why should companies use a project's free cash flows rather than accounting income when determining a project's NPV?

Explain the following terms: incremental cash flow, sunk cost, opportunity cost, externality, and cannibalization.

Provide an example of a "good" externality, that is, one that increases a project's true NPV.

12-2 Analysis of an Expansion Project

In Chapter 11, we analyzed two projects, S and L. We were given the cash flows and used them to illustrate how the NPV, IRR, MIRR, and payback are calculated. In the real world, a project's cash flows are rarely just given to you; instead, the finance staff will need to assemble the relevant information. Frequently, this information comes from a variety of sources within the company. For example, the marketing department may provide sales projections, the company's engineers may estimate costs, and the accounting staff may provide information about taxes and depreciation.

To illustrate, let's assume that Allied is considering a new expansion project, which is Project S that we introduced in Chapter 11. Project S is a new health-food product that Allied is considering introducing to the market. Along the way, Allied's finance staff has received a lot of information, the highlights of which are summarized here:

- Project S will require Allied to purchase $1,200,000 of equipment in 2020 (t = 0).
- Inventory will increase by $175,000 and accounts payable will rise by $75,000. All other working capital components will stay the same, so the change in net operating working capital (NOWC) is $100,000 at t = 0.
- The project will last for 4 years. The company forecasts the following sales: 2,720,000 units in 2021; 2,640,000 units in 2022; 2,515,000 units in 2023; and 2,430,000 units in 2024. Each unit will sell for $2.
- The fixed cost of producing the product is $2 million each year, and the variable cost of producing each unit will rise from $1.0196 in 2021 to $1.1973 in 2024.
- The estimated tax rate is 25%.
- This equipment is eligible for 100% bonus depreciation, so the after-tax cost of the equipment is $1,200,000 × (1 − T) = $1,200,000(0.75) = $900,000.

- When the project is completed in 2024 (t = 4), the company expects that it will be able to salvage the equipment for $50,000 and that it will fully recover the NOWC of $100,000. Because the equipment will be 100% expensed in 2020, the book value of the equipment is zero, so the entire $50,000 received in 2024 is subject to depreciation recapture and will be taxed.
- Based on the perceived risk, the project's WACC is estimated to be 10%.

To keep things straight, the finance staff has organized all of the key data in a spreadsheet, which is shown in Table 12.1. Note that unit sales and dollars (except for unit sales price and variable cost per unit) are in thousands; we omitted three zeros to streamline the presentation.

Table 12.1 divides the project's cash flows into three components:

1. The initial investments that are required at t = 0. These include the after-tax capital expenditures and changes in net operating working capital (ΔNOWC). Note that the after-tax capital expenditures are calculated assuming that the project is eligible for bonus depreciation, and therefore the full cost of the equipment can be deducted at t = 0.
2. The operating cash flows the company receives over the life of the project.
3. The terminal cash flows that are realized when the project is completed. These cash flows include the after-tax salvage value of the equipment and the recovery of the NOWC.

resource

Students can download the Excel chapter models from the textbook's student companion site on cengage.com. Once downloaded onto your computer, retrieve the Chapter 12 Excel model and follow along as you read this chapter.

Excel was used to create Table 12.1. We recommend that anyone with a computer and some familiarity with Excel access the model and work through it to see how the table was generated. Anyone doing real-world capital budgeting today would use such a model, and our model provides a good template, or starting point, if and when you need to analyze an actual project.

The column headers in the table, A through I, and the row headers, 12 through 45, designate cells, which contain the project data. For example, the equipment needed for Project S will cost $1,200, but it is eligible for 100% bonus depreciation so the after-tax cost of the equipment is $900, and that number is shown in cell E14 as a negative number. The equipment is expected to have a salvage value of $50 at the end of the project's 4-year life; this is shown in cell I31.[2] The new project will require $100 of net operating working capital; this is shown in cell E15 as a negative number because it is a cost, and then it is shown as a positive number in cell I34 because it is recovered at the end of Year 4. The total investment at Time 0 is $1,000, which is shown in cell E35.

Unit sales of Project S are shown on row 17; they are expected to decline somewhat over the project's 4-year life. The sales price, a constant $2, is shown on row 18. The projected variable cost per unit is given on row 19; it generally increases over time due to expected increases in materials and labor. Sales revenues, which are calculated as units multiplied by price, are given on row 20. Variable costs, equal to units multiplied by VC/unit, are given on row 21; fixed costs excluding depreciation, which are a constant $2,000, are shown on row 22.

Annual depreciation is shown on row 23. However, under the new tax law, this equipment is fully depreciated at t = 0, so no annual depreciation amounts are shown on row 23. However, if for some reason the firm decided to use straight-line depreciation, it could write off a constant $300 per year (calculated as $1,200/4). Its total cash flows over the entire 4 years would be the same as under immediate expensing, but under straight line, the depreciation cash flows are spread out over 4 years, while under immediate expensing, the depreciation cash flows are received immediately. We discuss depreciation in more detail in Web Appendix 12A.

[2] Because the equipment is fully depreciated at t = 0, the $50 estimated salvage value will exceed the book value, which will be zero. This $50 gain is classified as a recapture of depreciation, and it is taxed at the same rate as ordinary income, which is 25%.

TABLE 12.1 Cash Flow Estimation and Analysis for Expansion Project S

	A	B	C	D	E	F	G	H	I
12					0	1	2	3	4
13	*Investment Outlays at Time = 0*								
14	CAPEX = Equipment = Cost (1 − T)				-$900				
15	ΔNOWC = Additional net operating working capital needed				-100				
16	*Operating Cash Flows Over the Project's Life (Time = 1 - 4)*								
17	Unit sales					2,720	2,640	2,515	2,430
18	Sales price					$2.00	$2.00	$2.00	$2.00
19	Variable cost per unit					$1.0196	$1.0404	$1.0457	$1.1973
20	Sales revenues = Units × Price					$5,440	$5,280	$5,030	$4,860
21	Variable costs = Units × Cost/unit					2,773	2,747	2,630	2,909
22	Fixed operating costs except depr'n					2,000	2,000	2,000	2,000
23	Depreciation: 100% Bonus Depreciation in Year 0					0	0	0	0
24	Total operating costs					$4,773	$4,747	$4,630	$4,909
25	EBIT (or Operating income)					$667	$533	$400	-$49
26	Taxes on operating income			25%		167	133	100	-12
27	EBIT (1 − T) = After-tax project operating income					$500	$400	$300	-$37
28	Add back depreciation					0	0	0	0
29	EBIT (1 − T) + Depreciation					$500	$400	$300	-$37
30	*Terminal Cash Flows at Time = 4*								
31	Salvage value (taxed as ordinary income)								50
32	Tax on salvage value = 0.25 × (SV − BV of equipment at t = 4)								13
33	After-tax salvage value								37
34	ΔNOWC = Recovery of net operating working capital								100
35	Project free cash flows = EBIT(1 − T) + DEP − CAPEX − ΔNOWC				-$1,000	$500	$400	$300	$100
36									
37	*Alternative depreciation*			Straight line		0	2	3	4
38		Cost:	$1,200	Rate		25%	25%	25%	25%
39				Depreciation		$300	$300	$300	$300
40	*Project Evaluation @ WACC =*			*10%*					
41			Bonus Depreciation	Formulas			Straight line		
42		NPV	$78.82	=NPV(D40,F35:I35)+E35			$16.56		
43		IRR	14.489%	=IRR(E35:I35)			10.700%		
44		MIRR	12.106%	=MIRR(E35:I35,D40,D40)			10.349%		
45		Payback	2.33	=G12+(-E35-F35-G35)/H35			2.67		

Notes:

1. Under the new tax legislation, 100% of the cost of certain new and used business assets may be immediately expensed if placed into service after September 27, 2017, and before January 1, 2023. For assets placed into service after January 1, 2023, but before January 1, 2027, only 80% of the asset's cost may be immediately expensed. Immediate expensing is eliminated after January 1, 2027. This bonus depreciation is typically for assets with lives of fewer than 20 years. We have assumed this equipment is eligible for bonus depreciation.
2. If the firm owned assets that would be used for the project but would be sold if the project is not accepted, the after-tax value of those assets would be shown as an "opportunity cost" in the "Investment Outlays" section.
3. If this project would reduce sales and cash flows from one of the firm's other divisions, then the after-tax cannibalization effect, or "externality," would be deducted from the operating cash flows shown on row 29.
4. If the firm had previously incurred costs associated with this project, but those costs could not be recovered regardless of whether this project is accepted, then they are "sunk costs" and should not enter the analysis.

We calculate the annual cash flows for Project S over the 4 years in columns F, G, H, and I, with operating cash flows shown on row 29. On rows 31–34, we include the terminal cash flows in Year 4 to arrive at the project's free cash flows on row 35. These numbers are identical to the cash flows used in Chapter 11 for Project S. Because the numbers are the same, the NPV, IRR, MIRR, and payback shown in cells C42 through C45 are identical to those we calculated in Chapter 11.

12-2A EFFECT OF DIFFERENT DEPRECIATION RATES

If Congress repealed the new tax legislation and instead required straight-line depreciation, the equipment would no longer be fully depreciated at $t = 0$ but rather would be depreciated by a constant $300 per year. The result would be a free cash flow time line on row 35 that has the same total flows. However, under the straight-line method, the depreciation cash flows are spread out over 4 years, while under immediate expensing, the depreciation cash flows are received immediately. Because of the time value of money, dollars received earlier have a higher present value than dollars received later. Therefore, Project S's NPV is higher if the firm immediately depreciates the equipment. The exact effect is shown in the Project Evaluation section of Table 12.1—the NPV is $78.82 under bonus depreciation and $16.56, or 79% less, with straight line.

12-2B CANNIBALIZATION

Project S does not involve any cannibalization effects. Suppose, however, that Project S would reduce the after-tax cash flows of another division by $50 per year. No other firm would take on this project if our firm turns it down. In this case, we would add a row at about row 28 and deduct $50 for each year. If this were done, Project S would now have a negative NPV; hence, it would be rejected. On the other hand, if Project S would cause additional flows in some other division (a positive externality), those after-tax inflows should be attributed to Project S.

12-2C OPPORTUNITY COSTS

Now suppose the $900 after-tax cost shown in Table 12.1 was based on the assumption that the project would save money by using some equipment the company now owns and that equipment would be sold for $100, after taxes, if the project is rejected. The $100 is an opportunity cost, and it should be reflected in our calculations. We would add $100 to the project's cost. The result would be an NPV of $78.82 − $100 = −$21.18, so the project would now be rejected.

12-2D SUNK COSTS

Now suppose the firm had spent $150 on a marketing study to estimate potential sales. This $150 could not be recovered regardless of whether the project is accepted or rejected. Should the $150 be charged to Project S when determining its NPV for capital budgeting purposes? The answer is no. We are interested only in *incremental costs*. The $150 is not an incremental cost; it is a *sunk cost*. Therefore, it should not enter into the analysis.

One additional point should be made about sunk costs. If the $150 expenditure was actually made, in the final analysis Project S would turn out to be a loser: Its NPV would be $78.82 − $150 = −$71.18. If we could somehow back up and reconsider the project *before* the $150 had been spent, we would see that the project should be rejected. However, we can't back up—at this point, we can either abandon the project or spend $1,000 and go forward with it. If we go forward, we will receive an incremental NPV of $78.82, which would reduce the loss from −$150 to −$71.18.

12-2E OTHER CHANGES TO THE INPUTS

Variables other than depreciation also could be varied, and these changes would alter the calculated cash flows and thus NPV and IRR. For example, we could increase or decrease the projected unit sales, the sales price, the variable and/or the fixed costs, the initial investment cost, the working capital requirements, the salvage value, and even the tax rate if we thought Congress was likely to raise or lower taxes. Such changes could be made easily in an Excel model, making it possible to see the resulting changes in NPV and IRR immediately. This is called *sensitivity analysis*, and we will discuss it in Section 12-5 when we take up procedures for measuring projects' risks.

Self*Test*

In what ways is the setup for finding a project's cash flows similar to the projected income statements for a new single-product firm? In what ways would the two statements be different?

Would a project's NPV for a typical firm be higher or lower if the firm used bonus depreciation rather than straight-line depreciation? Explain.

How could the analysis in Table 12.1 be modified to consider cannibalization, opportunity costs, and sunk costs?

Why does net operating working capital (NOWC) appear as both a negative and a positive number in Table 12.1?

12-3 Replacement Analysis[3]

In the last section, we assumed that Project S was an entirely new project. So all of its cash flows were incremental—they occurred only if the firm accepted the project. This is true for expansion projects, but for replacement projects, we must find cash flow *differentials* between the new and old projects, and these differentials are the incremental cash flows that we analyze.

We evaluate a replacement decision in Table 12.2, which is set up much like Table 12.1, but with data on both a new, highly efficient machine (which will be fully depreciated at t = 0) and the old machine (which is being depreciated on a straight-line basis). Here we find the firm's cash flows when it continues using the old machine and the cash flows when it decides to purchase a new machine. Finally, we subtract the old flows from the new to arrive at the *incremental cash flows*. We used Excel in our analysis (refer to the "Replacement Analysis" tab in the chapter model), but again, we could have used a calculator or pencil and paper. Here are the key inputs used in the analysis. No additional operating working capital is needed.

Data applicable to both machines:	
Sales revenues, which would remain constant	$ 2,500
Expected life of the new and old machines	4 years
WACC for the analysis	10%
Tax rate	25%
Data for old machine:	
Market (salvage = book) value of the old machine today	$ 400
Old labor, materials, and other costs per year	$ 1,140
Old machine's annual depreciation	$ 100
Data for new machine:	
After-tax cost of new machine	$ 2,000
New labor, materials, and other costs per year	$ 400

[3]This section is somewhat technical, but it can be omitted without a loss of continuity.

TABLE 12.2 Cash Flow Analysis for Replacement Project R

	A	B	C	D	E	F	G	H	I
12					0	1	2	3	4
13	*Part I. Free Cash Flows Before Replacement:* *Old Machine (CAPEX and ΔNOWC = 0)*								
14	Sales revenues					$2,500	$2,500	$2,500	$2,500
15	Operating costs except depreciation					1,140	1,140	1,140	1,140
16	Depreciation					100	100	100	100
17	Total operating costs					$1,240	$1,240	$1,240	$1,240
18	EBIT (or Operating income)					$1,260	$1,260	$1,260	$1,260
19	Taxes 25%					315	315	315	315
20	EBIT (1 − T) = After-tax operating income					$945	$945	$945	$945
21	Add back depreciation					100	100	100	100
22	Free cash flows before replacement EBIT(1 − T) + DEP − CAPEX − ΔNOWC					$1,045	$1,045	$1,045	$1,045
23	*Part II. Free Cash Flows After Replacement:* *New Machine (ΔNOWC = 0)*								
24	New machine invest. after 100% bonus depr.				-$2,000				
25	After-tax salvage value, old machine				400				
26	CAPEX, after taxes				-$1,600				
27	Sales revenues					$2,500	$2,500	$2,500	$2,500
28	Costs except depreciation					400	400	400	400
29	Depreciation					0	0	0	0
30	Total operating costs					$400	$400	$400	$400
31	EBIT (or Operating income)					$2,100	$2,100	$2,100	$2,100
32	Taxes 25%					525	525	525	525
33	EBIT(1 − T) = After-tax operating income					$1,575	$1,575	$1,575	$1,575
34	Add back depreciation					0	0	0	0
35	Free cash flows after replacement EBIT(1 − T) + DEP − CAPEX − ΔNOWC				-$1,600	$1,575	$1,575	$1,575	$1,575
36	Part III. Incremental Cash Flows and Evaluation								
37	*Incremental CFs = CF After — CF Before*				-$1,600	$530	$530	$530	$530
38									
39	*Project Evaluation @ WACC =*			*10%*					
40				NPV =	$80.03				
41				IRR =	12.29%				
42				*MIRR =*	11.35%				
43				*Payback =*	3.02				
44	*Part IV. Alternative (Streamlined) Calculation for Incremental CFs*								
45		New machine invest. after bonus depr.			-$2,000				
46		Salvage value, old machine			400				
47		Net cost of new machine			-$1,600				
48	Cost savings = Old — New					$740	$740	$740	$740
49	A-T savings = Cost savings × (1 — Tax rate)					555	555	555	555
50	Δ Depreciation = (New — Old)					-100	-100	-100	-100
51	Depr'n tax savings (cost) = Δ Depreciation × Tax rate					-25	-25	-25	-25
52	Incremental CFs = A-T cost savings + Depr'n tax savings (cost)				-$1,600	$530	$530	$530	$530
53									

The key here is to find the *incremental* cash flows. As noted previously, we find the cash flows from the operation with the old machine, and then find the cash flows with the new machine, then find the differences in the cash flows. This is what we do in Parts I, II, and III of Table 12.2. Because there will be an additional expenditure to purchase the new machine, that cost is shown in cell E24. The amount shown here is the after-tax cost of the machine assuming it is fully depreciated at $t = 0$. However, we can sell the old machine at its book value for $400, so that is shown as an inflow in cell E25. The cash outlay at Time 0 is $1,600, as shown in cell E35.

The cash flows based on the old machine are shown on row 22, and those for the new one are on row 35. Then on row 37, we show the differences in the cash flows with and without replacement—these are the incremental cash flows used to find the replacement NPV. When we evaluate the incremental cash flows, we see that the replacement has an NPV of $80.03, so the old machine should be replaced.[4]

In some instances, replacements add capacity as well as lower operating costs. When this is the case, sales revenues in Part II would be increased, and if that led to an increase in net operating working capital, that number would be shown as a Time 0 expenditure along with its recovery at the end of the project's life. These changes would, of course, be reflected in the differential cash flows on row 37.

Self*Test*

What role do incremental cash flows play in a replacement analysis?

If you were analyzing a replacement project and you suddenly learned that the old equipment could be sold for $1,000 rather than $100, would this new information make the replacement look better or worse?

In Table 12.2, we assumed that output would not change if the old machine was replaced. Suppose output would actually double. How would this change be dealt with in the framework of Table 12.2?

12-4 Risk Analysis in Capital Budgeting[5]

Projects differ in risk, and risk should be reflected in capital budgeting decisions. However, it is difficult to measure risk, especially for new projects where no history exists. For this reason, managers deal with risk in many different ways, ranging from almost totally subjective adjustments to highly sophisticated analyses that involve computer simulation and complex statistics.

Three separate and distinct types of risk are involved:

1. **Stand-alone risk**, which is a project's risk assuming (a) that it is the only asset the firm has and (b) that the firm is the only stock in each investor's portfolio. Stand-alone risk is measured by the variability of the project's expected returns. *Diversification is totally ignored.*
2. **Corporate, or within-firm, risk**, which is a project's risk to the corporation as opposed to its investors. Within-firm risk takes account of the fact that the project is only one asset in the firm's portfolio of assets; hence, some of its risk will be eliminated by diversification within the firm. This type of risk is measured by the project's impact on uncertainty about the firm's future returns.
3. **Market, or beta, risk**, which is the riskiness of the project as seen by a well-diversified stockholder who recognizes (a) that the project is only one of the firm's assets and (b) that the firm's stock is but one part of his or her stock portfolio. The project's market risk is measured by its effect on the firm's beta coefficient.

Stand-Alone Risk
The risk an asset would have if it were a firm's only asset and if investors owned only one stock. It is measured by the variability of the asset's expected returns.

Corporate (Within-Firm) Risk
Risk considering the firm's diversification, but not stockholder diversification. It is measured by a project's effect on uncertainty about the firm's expected future returns.

Market (Beta) Risk
Considers both firm and stockholder diversification. It is measured by the project's beta coefficient.

[4]We could have found the incremental cash flows by calculating the differences in the only factors that change, the after-tax cost of the new machine, operating cost savings reduced for the taxes, and the after-tax differences in depreciation. This procedure is shown in Part IV of the table. The two procedures produce the same incremental cash flows and NPV, as they must.

[5]Some professors may choose to cover some of the risk sections (12-4 through 12-6) and skip others. We offer a range of choices, and we tried to make the exposition clear enough that interested and self-motivated students can read these sections on their own, even if the sections are not assigned.

Taking on a project with a great deal of stand-alone or corporate risk will not necessarily affect the firm's beta. However, if the project has high stand-alone risk and if its returns are highly correlated with returns on the firm's other assets and with returns on most other stocks in the economy, the project will have a high degree of all three types of risk. Market risk is theoretically the most relevant of the three because it is the one reflected in stock prices. Unfortunately, market risk is also the most difficult to estimate, primarily because new projects don't have "market prices" that can be related to stock market returns. Therefore, most decision makers do a *quantitative* analysis of stand-alone risk and then consider the other two risk measures in a *qualitative* manner.

Risk-Adjusted Cost of Capital
The cost of capital appropriate for a given project, given the riskiness of that project. The greater the risk, the higher the cost of capital.

Projects are generally classified into several categories. Then with the firm's overall WACC as a starting point, a **risk-adjusted cost of capital** is assigned to each category. For example, a firm might establish three risk classes, assign the corporate WACC to average-risk projects, add a 5% risk premium for higher-risk projects, and subtract 2% for low-risk projects. Under this setup, if the company's overall WACC was 10%, 10% would be used to evaluate average-risk projects, 15% for high-risk projects, and 8% for low-risk projects. Although this approach is probably better than not making any risk adjustments, these adjustments are highly subjective and difficult to justify. Unfortunately, there's no perfect way to specify how high or low the adjustments should be.[6]

Self*Test*

What are the three types of project risk?

Which type is theoretically the most relevant? Why?

What is one classification scheme that firms often use to obtain risk-adjusted costs of capital?

12-5 Measuring Stand-Alone Risk

A project's stand-alone risk reflects uncertainty about its cash flows. The required investment, unit sales, sales prices, and operating costs shown in Table 12.1 for Project S are subject to uncertainty. First-year sales were projected at 2,720 units (actually, 2,720,000, but we shortened it to 2,720 to streamline the analysis) to be sold at a price of $2 per unit. However, unit sales would almost certainly be somewhat higher or lower than 2,720, and the price would probably turn out to be different from the projected $2 per unit. Similarly, the other variables would probably differ from their indicated values. *Indeed, all the inputs are expected values, and actual values can vary from expected values.*

Three techniques are used to assess stand-alone risk: (1) sensitivity analysis, (2) scenario analysis, and (3) Monte Carlo simulation. We will discuss them in the following sections.

12-5A SENSITIVITY ANALYSIS

Sensitivity Analysis
Percentage change in NPV resulting from a given percentage change in an input variable, other things held constant.

Intuitively, we know that a change in a key input variable such as units sold or sales price will cause the NPV to change. **Sensitivity analysis** *measures the percentage change in NPV that results from a given percentage change in an input, other variables held at their expected values.* This is by far the most commonly used type of risk

[6]We should note that the CAPM approach can be used for projects provided there are specialized publicly traded firms in the same business as that of the project under consideration. For further information on estimating the risk-adjusted cost of capital, see Web Appendix 12C. And for more information on measuring market (or beta) risk, see Web Appendix 12D.

analysis, and it is used by most firms. It begins with a *base-case* situation, where the project's NPV is found using the base-case value for each input variable. Here's a list of the key inputs for Project S:

- Equipment cost
- Change in net operating working capital
- Unit sales
- Sales price
- Variable cost per unit
- Fixed operating costs
- Tax rate
- WACC

The data we used back in Table 12.1 were the *most likely*, or *base-case*, values, and the resulting NPV, $78.82, is the **base-case NPV**. It's easy to imagine changes in the inputs, and those changes would result in different NPVs.

Base-Case NPV
The NPV when sales and other input variables are set equal to their most likely (or base-case) values.

When senior managers review capital budgeting studies, they are interested in the base-case NPV, but they always go on to ask the financial analyst a series of what-if questions: What if unit sales turn out to be 25% below the base-case level? What if market conditions force us to price the product at $1.80, not $2? What if variable costs are higher than we forecasted? Sensitivity analysis is designed to provide answers to such questions. Each variable is increased or decreased from its expected value, holding other variables constant at their base-case levels. Then the NPV is calculated using the changed input. Finally, the resulting set of NPVs is plotted to show how sensitive NPV is to changes in each variable.

Figure 12.1 shows Project S's sensitivity graph for six key variables. The table following the graph gives the NPVs based on different values of the inputs, and those NPVs were then plotted to make the graph. Figure 12.1 shows that as unit sales and price increase, the project's NPV increases, whereas the opposite is true for the other four input variables. An increase in variable costs, fixed costs, equipment costs, and WACC lowers the project's NPV. The ranges shown at the bottom of the table and the slopes of the lines in the graph indicate how sensitive NPV is to changes in each input. When the data are plotted in Figure 12.1, the slopes of the lines in the graph indicate how sensitive NPV is to each input: *The larger the range, the steeper the variable's slope and the more sensitive the NPV is to changes in this variable*. We see that NPV is very sensitive to changes in the sales price, fairly sensitive to changes in variable costs, a bit less sensitive to units sold and fixed costs, but not very sensitive to changes in the equipment cost or the WACC.

If we were comparing two projects, the one with the steeper sensitivity lines would be riskier, other things held constant, because relatively small changes in the input variables would produce large changes in the NPV. Thus, sensitivity analysis provides useful insights into a project's risk.[7]

12-5B SCENARIO ANALYSIS

In sensitivity analysis, we change one variable at a time. However, it is useful to know what would happen to the project's NPV if all of the inputs turned out to be better or worse than expected. Also, we can assign probabilities to the good, bad, and most likely (or base-case) scenarios, then find the expected value and the

[7]Sensitivity analysis is tedious using a regular calculator but easy using a spreadsheet. We used the chapter's Excel model to calculate the NPVs and to draw the graph in Figure 12.1. To conduct such an analysis by hand would be quite time consuming, and if the basic data were changed even slightly—say, the cost of the equipment was increased slightly—all of the calculations would have to be redone. With a spreadsheet, by simply typing over the old input with the new one, the analysis is changed instantaneously.

FIGURE 12.1 Sensitivity Graph for Project S

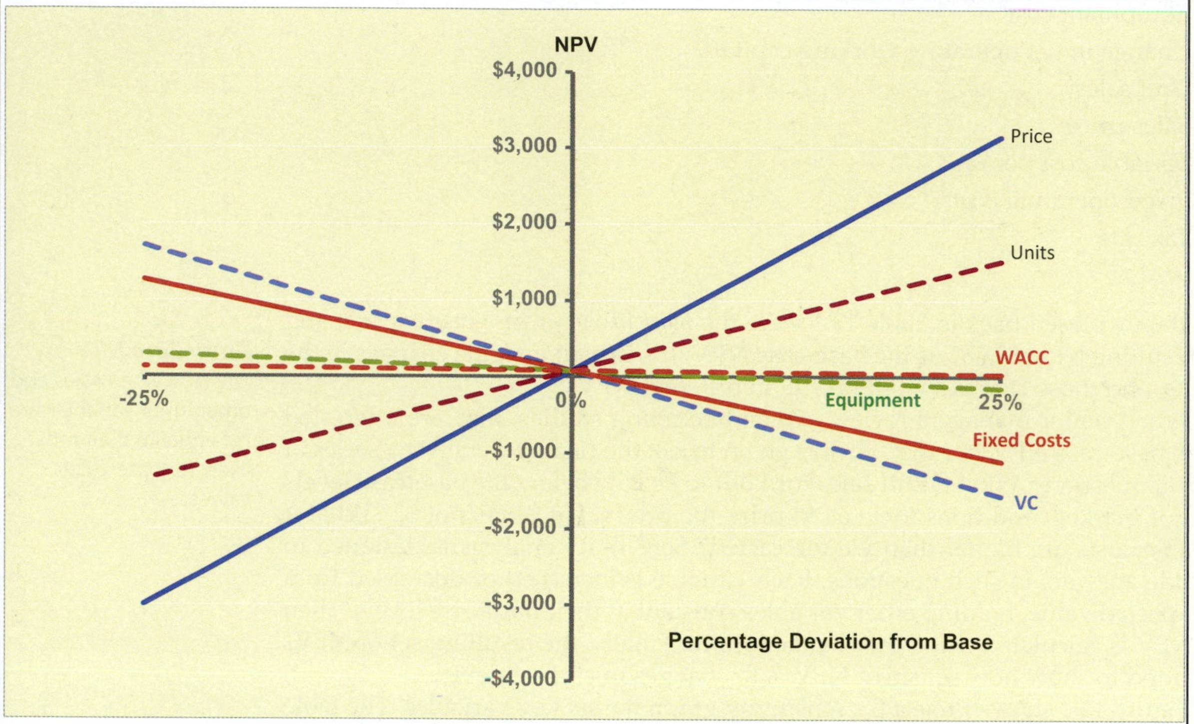

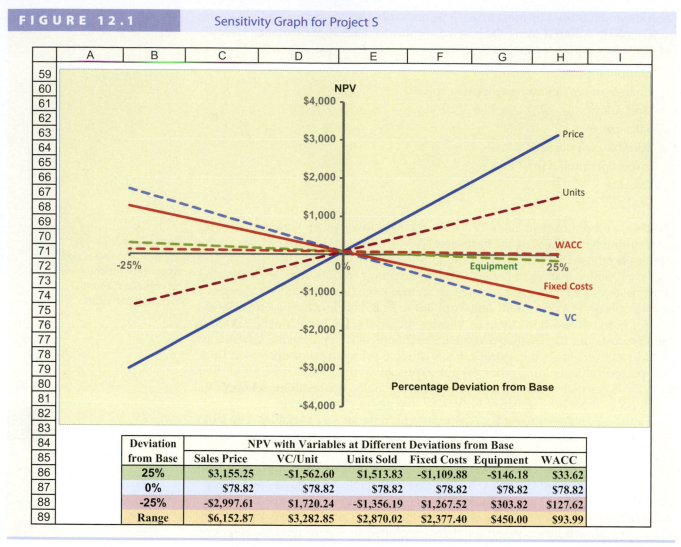

Deviation from Base	NPV with Variables at Different Deviations from Base					
	Sales Price	VC/Unit	Units Sold	Fixed Costs	Equipment	WACC
25%	$3,155.25	-$1,562.60	$1,513.83	-$1,109.88	-$146.18	$33.62
0%	$78.82	$78.82	$78.82	$78.82	$78.82	$78.82
-25%	-$2,997.61	$1,720.24	-$1,356.19	$1,267.52	$303.82	$127.62
Range	$6,152.87	$3,282.85	$2,870.02	$2,377.40	$450.00	$93.99

Notes:

1. When all of the inputs are set at their base-case levels, their deviations from base are all zero, and the NPV is $78.82. So, the vertical axis intercept is at $78.82.
2. If the sales price is set 25% above its expected $2 price and all other variables are set at their expected values, then the NPV will be +$3,155.25. If the price is set 25% below its expected $2 price, then the NPV will be −$2,997.61. All the other NPVs shown in the table were found similarly. Excel Data Tables were used to streamline the calculations.
3. Note that the best- and worst-case NPVs are different from those in the next section, which shows scenario analysis. In scenario analysis, all the variables are 25% above or below their expected levels, so the best- and worst-case NPVs are much higher or lower than those in the sensitivity analysis, where only one variable is set at its best or worst level.

Scenario Analysis
A risk analysis technique in which "bad" and "good" sets of financial circumstances are compared with a most likely, or base-case, situation.

Base-Case Scenario
An analysis in which all of the input variables are set at their most likely values.

standard deviation of the NPV. **Scenario analysis** allows for these extensions—it allows us to change more than one variable at a time, and it incorporates the probabilities of changes in the key variables.

In a scenario analysis, we begin with the **base-case scenario**, which uses the most likely set of input values. We then ask marketing, engineering, and other operating managers to specify a **worst-case scenario** (low unit sales, low sales price, high variable costs, and so forth) and a **best-case scenario**. Often the best and worst cases are defined as having a 25% probability of conditions being that good or bad, with a 50% probability for the base-case conditions. Obviously, conditions can take on more than three values, but such a scenario setup is useful to help understand the project's riskiness.

The best-case, base-case, and worst-case values for Project S are shown in Figure 12.2, along with plots of the data. If the project is highly successful, the combination of a high sales price, low production costs, and high unit sales will result in a very high NPV, $9,354.43. However, if things turn out badly, the NPV will be a negative $6,049.17. The graphs show the wide range of possibilities, suggesting that this is a risky project. If the bad conditions materialize, the company will not go bankrupt—this is just one project for a large company. Still, losing $6,049.17 (or $6,049,170, as we are working in thousands of dollars) would hurt the company's stock price.

If we multiply each scenario's probability by the NPV under that scenario and then sum the products, we will have the project's expected NPV, $865.73, as shown in Figure 12.2. Note that the *expected* NPV differs from the *base-case* NPV. This is not an error—mathematically, they are not equal. We also calculate the standard deviation of the expected NPV; it is $5,502.55. When we divide the standard deviation by the expected NPV, we calculate the coefficient of variation, 6.36, which is a measure of stand-alone risk. The firm's average-risk project has a coefficient of variation of about 2.0, so the CV of 6.36 indicates that this project is much riskier than most of the firm's other projects.

Worst-Case Scenario
An analysis in which all of the input variables are set at their worst reasonably forecasted values.

Best-Case Scenario
An analysis in which all of the input variables are set at their best reasonably forecasted values.

FIGURE 12.2 Scenario Analysis for Project S

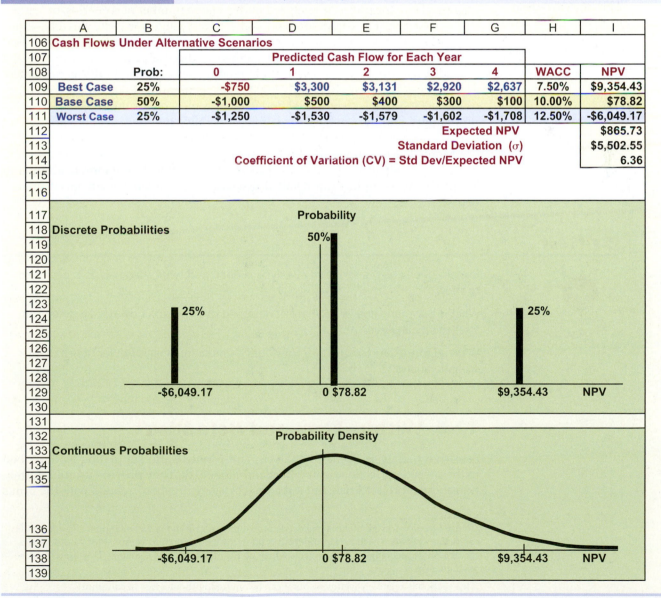

	A	B	C	D	E	F	G	H	I
106	**Cash Flows Under Alternative Scenarios**								
107					**Predicted Cash Flow for Each Year**				
108		**Prob:**	**0**	**1**	**2**	**3**	**4**	**WACC**	**NPV**
109	**Best Case**	**25%**	**-$750**	**$3,300**	**$3,131**	**$2,920**	**$2,637**	**7.50%**	**$9,354.43**
110	**Base Case**	**50%**	**-$1,000**	**$500**	**$400**	**$300**	**$100**	**10.00%**	**$78.82**
111	**Worst Case**	**25%**	**-$1,250**	**-$1,530**	**-$1,579**	**-$1,602**	**-$1,708**	**12.50%**	**-$6,049.17**
112						**Expected NPV**			**$865.73**
113						**Standard Deviation (σ)**			**$5,502.55**
114				**Coefficient of Variation (CV) = Std Dev/Expected NPV**					**6.36**
115									
116									

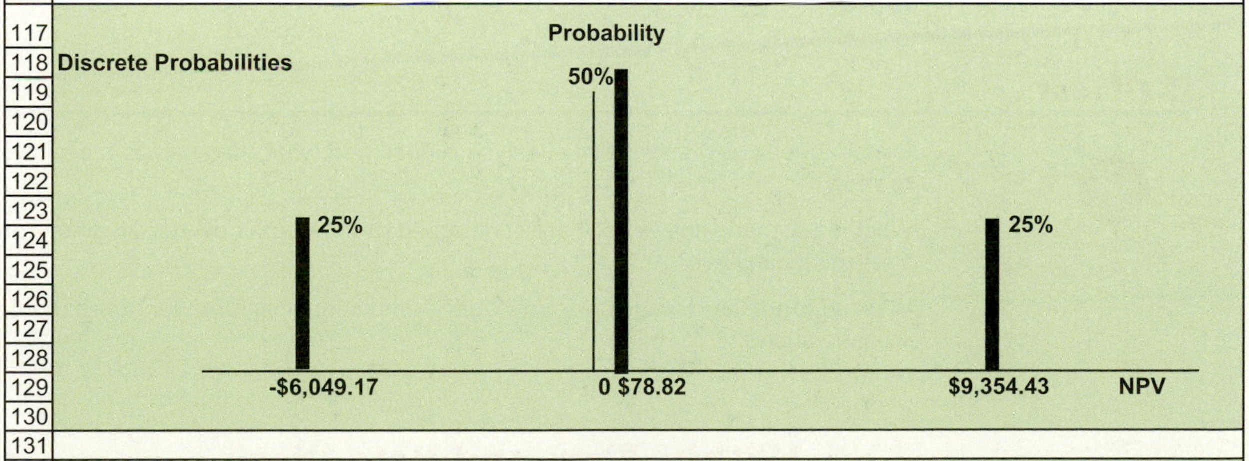

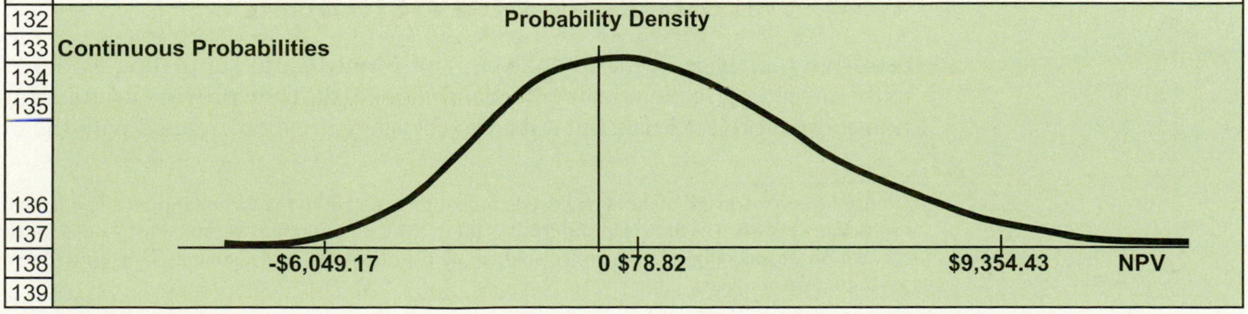

Our firm's WACC is 10%, so that rate should be used to find the NPV of an average-risk project. Project S is riskier than average, so a higher discount rate should be used to find its NPV. There is no way to determine the "correct" discount rate—this is a judgment call. However, some firms increase the corporate WACC when they evaluate projects deemed to be relatively risky and reduce it for low-risk projects. When the NPV was recalculated using a 12.5% WACC, the base-case NPV fell from $78.82 to $33.62, so the project still had a positive NPV when its expected cash flows were discounted at the risk-adjusted WACC.

Note that the base-case results are the same in our sensitivity and scenario analyses, but in the scenario analysis, the worst case is much worse than in the sensitivity analysis and the best case is much better. In scenario analysis, all of the variables are set at their best or worst values, while in sensitivity analysis, only one variable is adjusted, and all the others are left at their base-case values.

12-5C MONTE CARLO SIMULATION

Monte Carlo Simulation
A risk analysis technique in which probable future events are simulated on a computer, generating estimated rates of return and risk indexes.

Monte Carlo simulation, so named because this type of analysis grew out of work on the mathematics of casino gambling, is a sophisticated version of scenario analysis. Here the project is analyzed under a large number of scenarios, or "runs." In the first run, the computer randomly picks a value for each variable—units sold, sales price, variable costs per unit, and so forth. Those values are then used to calculate an NPV, and that NPV is stored in the computer's memory. Next, a second set of input values is selected at random, and a second NPV is calculated. This process is repeated perhaps 1,000 times, generating 1,000 NPVs. The mean of the 1,000 NPVs is determined and used as a measure of the project's expected profitability, and the standard deviation (or perhaps the coefficient of variation) of the NPVs is used as a measure of risk.

Monte Carlo simulation is technically more complex than scenario analysis, but simulation software makes the process manageable. Simulation is useful, but because of its complexity, a detailed discussion is best left for advanced finance courses.[8]

Self*Test*

Explain briefly how a sensitivity analysis is done and what the analysis is designed to show.

What is a scenario analysis? What is it designed to show, and how does it differ from a sensitivity analysis?

What is Monte Carlo simulation? How does a simulation analysis differ from a regular scenario analysis?

12-6 Within-Firm and Beta Risk[9]

Sensitivity analysis, scenario analysis, and Monte Carlo simulation as described in the preceding section dealt with stand-alone risk. They provide useful information about a project's risk, but if the project is negatively correlated with the firm's

[8]To use Monte Carlo simulation, one needs probability distributions for the inputs and correlation coefficients between each pair of inputs. It is often difficult to obtain "reasonable" values for the correlations, especially for new projects where no historical data are available. This limits the use of simulation analysis.

[9]This section is relatively technical, but it can be omitted without a loss of continuity.

other projects, it might stabilize the firm's total earnings and thus be relatively safe. Similarly, if a project is negatively correlated with returns on most stocks, it might reduce the firm's beta and thus be correctly evaluated with a relatively low WACC. So in theory, we should be more concerned with within-firm and beta risk than with stand-alone risk.

Although managers recognize the importance of within-firm and beta risk, they generally end up dealing with these risks subjectively, or judgmentally, rather than quantitatively. The problem is that to measure diversification's effects on risk, we need the *correlation coefficient between a project's returns and returns on the firm's other assets*, which requires historical data that obviously do not exist for new projects. Experienced managers generally have a "feel" for how a project's returns will relate to returns on the firm's other assets. Generally, positive correlation is expected, and if the correlation is high, stand-alone risk will be a good proxy for within-firm risk. Similarly, managers can make judgmental estimates about whether a project's returns will be high when the economy and the stock market are strong (thus, what the project's beta should be). But for the most part, those estimates are subjective, not based on actual data.

However, projects occasionally involve an entirely new product line, such as a steel company going into iron ore mining. In such cases, the firm may be able to obtain betas for "pure-play" companies in the new area. For example, this steel company might get the average beta for a group of mining companies such as Rio Tinto and BHP Billiton, assume that its mining subsidiary has similar characteristics, and use the average beta of the "comparables" to calculate a WACC for the mining subsidiary. Although the pure-play approach makes sense for some projects, its use is rare. Just think about it. How would you find a pure-play proxy for a new inventory control system, machine tool, truck, or most other projects? The answer is, you couldn't. We discuss techniques for measuring beta risk in Web Appendix 12D.

Our conclusions regarding risk analysis are as follows:

- It is very difficult, if not impossible, to quantitatively measure projects' within-firm and beta risks.
- Most projects' returns are positively correlated with returns on the firm's other assets and with returns on the stock market. This being the case, because stand-alone risk is correlated with within-firm and market risk, not much is lost by focusing just on stand-alone risk.
- Experienced managers make many judgmental assessments, including those related to risk, and they work them into the capital budgeting process. Introductory students like neat, precise answers, and they want to make decisions on the basis of calculated NPVs. Experienced managers consider quantitative NPVs, but they also bring subjective judgment into the decision process.
- If a firm does not use the types of analyses covered in this book, it will have trouble. On the other hand, if a firm tries to quantify everything and let a computer make its decisions, it too will have trouble. Good managers understand and use the theory of finance, but they apply it with judgment.

Self*Test*

Is it easier to measure the stand-alone, within-firm, or beta risk for projects such as a new delivery truck or a Home Depot warehouse?

If a firm cannot measure a potential project's risk with precision, should it abandon the project? Explain your answer.

12-7 Real Options[10]

Traditional discounted cash flow (DCF) analysis—where cash flows are estimated and then discounted to obtain the expected NPV—has been the cornerstone of capital budgeting since the 1950s. However, in recent years it has been shown that DCF techniques do not always lead to proper capital budgeting decisions.

DCF techniques were originally developed to value securities such as stocks and bonds. These are *passive* investments—once the investment has been made, most investors can take no actions that influence the cash flows they produce.[11] However, capital budgeting projects are not passive investments—managers can often take *positive actions* after the investment has been made that alter the cash flow stream. Opportunities for such actions are called **real options**—"real" to distinguish them from financial options like an option to purchase shares of Boeing stock, and "options" because they offer the right but not the obligation to take the future action to increase cash flows. Real options are valuable, but this value is not captured by conventional NPV analysis. Therefore, a project's real options must be considered separately.

Real Options
The right but not the obligation to take some future action.

12-7A Types of Real Options

There are several types of real options, including (1) *abandonment*, where the project can be shut down if its cash flows are low; (2) *timing*, where a project can be delayed until more information about demand and/or costs can be obtained; (3) *expansion*, where the project can be expanded if demand turns out to be stronger than expected; (4) *output flexibility*, where the output can be changed if market conditions change; and (5) *input flexibility*, where the inputs used in the production process (say, coal versus natural gas for generating electricity) can be changed if input prices and/or availability change. We illustrate abandonment options here in the text and we cover other types of options in Web Appendix 12F.

12-7B Abandonment Options

In capital budgeting we generally assume that a project will be operated for its full physical life. However, this is not always the best course of action. If the firm has the option to abandon a project during its operating life, this **abandonment option** can lower its risk, increase its expected profitability, and raise its calculated NPV.

Abandonment Option
The option to shut down a project if operating cash flows turn out to be lower than expected. This option can both raise expected profitability and lower project risk.

Decision Tree
A diagram that lays out different branches that are the result of different decisions made or the result of different economic situations.

Table 12.3 gives a picture of the **decision tree** for Project S. In the scenario analysis in Section 12-5, we examined Project S under the Best Case, Base Case, and Worst Case assumptions. In the worst-case situation, the project has negative cash flows for its full 4-year life. However, if the company can abandon the project after Year 1, when it sees that it is not a success, then its expected NPV can be improved. The earlier analysis is reproduced in the top section of Table 12.3, labeled "No Abandonment." In Column C, which is Time 0, we see that the firm must invest between $750 and $1,250. Columns D through G show the annual cash flows under each scenario, and in Column H we show the WACCs for each scenario. Then, in Column I, we show the NPV under each scenario when the cash flows are discounted at their respective WACCs. The sum of the products obtained by multiplying each probability times each branch NPV is the expected NPV, which is $865.73. The standard deviation and the

[10]This section is relatively technical, but it can be omitted without a loss of continuity if there is insufficient time to cover it.

[11]Large investors such as Warren Buffett and some hedge fund operators can purchase stock in companies and then influence the firms' operations and cash flows. However, the average stockholder does not have this influence.

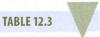

Decision Tree for Abandonment Option (Dollars in Thousands) **TABLE 12.3**

	A	B	C	D	E	F	G	H	I	J
21	**Situation 1. No Abandonment**									
22			**Predicted Cash Flow for Each Year**							
23		**Prob.**	**0**	**1**	**2**	**3**	**4**	**WACC**	**NPV**	
24	**Best Case**	**25%**	**-$750**	**$3,300**	**$3,131**	**$2,920**	**$2,637**	**7.50%**	**$9,354.43**	
25	**Base**	**50%**	**-$1,000**	**$500**	**$400**	**$300**	**$100**	**10.00%**	**$78.82**	
26	**Worst Case**	**25%**	**-$1,250**	**-$1,530**	**-$1,579**	**-$1,602**	**-$1,708**	**12.50%**	**-$6,049.17**	
27							**Expected NPV**		**$865.73**	
28							**Standard Deviation (σ)**		**$5,502.55**	
29			**Coefficient of Variation (CV) = Std Dev/Expected NPV**						**6.36**	
30										
31	**Situation 2. Can Abandon**									
32			**Predicted Cash Flow for Each Year**							
33		**Prob.**	**0**	**1**	**2**	**3**	**4**	**WACC**	**NPV**	
34	**Best Case**	**25%**	**-$750**	**$3,300**	**$3,131**	**$2,920**	**$2,637**	**7.50%**	**$9,354.43**	
35	**Base**	**50%**	**-$1,000**	**$500**	**$400**	**$300**	**$100**	**10.00%**	**$78.82**	
36	**Worst #1**	**0%**	**-$1,250**	**-$1,530**	**-$1,579**	**-$1,602**	**-$1,708**	**12.50%**	**-$6,049.17**	**Don't use**
37	**Worst #2**	**25%**	**-$1,250**	**-$1,530**	**$0**	**$0**	**$0**	**12.50%**	**-$2,610.00**	**Use**
38			**Expected NPV (includes #2, excludes #1)**						**$1,725.52**	
39							**Standard Deviation (σ)**		**$4,539.28**	
40			**Coefficient of Variation (CV) = Std Dev/Expected NPV**						**2.63**	
41										
42			**Value of the Real Option to Abandon**							
43			**Expected NPV with Abandonment**						**$1,725.52**	
44			**Expected NPV without Abandonment**						**$865.73**	
45			**Difference = Value of the Option**						**$859.79**	
46										

coefficient of variation are also calculated to provide an idea of the project's risk. This project has a positive expected NPV; hence, by the NPV criterion it should be accepted.

Now suppose the company could make a second decision, at t = 1, to abandon (or shut down) the project if things go badly during Year 1. To see what would happen then, we add another branch to the tree, as shown in the Worst #2 row in Table 12.3 under the "Can Abandon" situation. Here we assume that the company abandons the project at the end of Year 1, when information about the actual production costs and demand conditions become available. If things were going well, the project would be continued. However, if things were going badly, the firm would close the operation and not suffer the indicated losses during the next 3 years.[12]

Given the "Can Abandon" option, the firm would clearly prefer to abandon the project than to continue it under the worst-case scenario. Therefore, we assign a zero probability to continuing after a bad start. Therefore, the 25% probability associated with the worst case is used for "Worst #2" and a 0% probability is assigned to "Worst #1."

The option to abandon raises the expected NPV from $865.73 to $1,725.52, and it also lowers the standard deviation. Those changes combine to lower the coefficient of variation from 6.36 to 2.63. The coefficient of variation is still above the

[12]If the assets devoted to the project could be sold, then this after-tax amount would be a cash inflow at the time of the sale, presumably at the end of Year 1.

GOOGLE PUTS A TIME LIMIT ON ITS R&D PROJECTS

The quality of their research and development projects drives the success of many firms. The connection between R&D and performance is particularly strong for high-growth technology and pharmaceutical firms that require frequent investment in new products.

By their very nature, many R&D projects are highly speculative. Successful projects can produce enormous returns, but the batting average for success is often quite low. As you might imagine, picking winners is often difficult, but managers can help things along by doing their best to control expenditures and to pull the plug as quickly as possible when it appears that a project is going to be unsuccessful.

The principles outlined in this chapter are directly relevant for evaluating R&D projects. When deciding whether to initially invest in an R&D project, a company uses capital budgeting techniques to estimate cash flows, evaluate risk, and to ultimately assess whether the project has a positive NPV. Real option analysis is also relevant. Many R&D projects involve several stages that are similar to a series of "growth options"; in other cases, companies have important "timing options" when it comes to deciding whether to proceed with the investment or wait to collect additional information. Finally, most R&D projects have an implicit "abandonment" option, which allows them to shut down a project that is deemed unsuccessful.

A 2015 article in *The Wall Street Journal* highlights how Google has placed a time limit on many of its projects to create urgency, enhance efficiency, and avoid scenarios where unsuccessful projects continue to drain cash for long periods of time. Recognizing this concern, Google has looked for ways to make quicker decisions. Given this emphasis, the article goes on to describe how the company operates its Advanced Technology and Projects Group, which focuses heavily on mobile-related research:

> Hence the new emphasis on Advanced Technology and Projects, which upends some Google traditions. Most projects are limited to two years, after which they are killed, moved into Google, spun off into independent firms or licensed to others. The group jettisons project leaders after two years and hires mostly outside experts.

One fan of this policy, Eric Schmidt, who at the time was serving as Google's executive chairman, offered the following quote:

> We like this model because it puts pressure on people to perform and do relevant things or stop. I've spent an awful lot of time on projects that never end and products that would never ship.

Assuming Google continues this policy, it will be quite interesting to see how this unit performs down the road.

Source: Alistair Barr, "Google Lab Puts a Time Limit on Innovations," *The Wall Street Journal* (online.wsj.com), March 31, 2015.

Option Value
The difference between the expected NPVs with and without the relevant option. It is the value that is not accounted for in a traditional NPV analysis. A positive option value expands the firm's opportunities.

company's average CV of 2.0, which indicates that the project is still more risky than most, even after the abandonment option has been considered. Therefore, the 12.50% WACC is still appropriate for discounting this project's free cash flows. Also, note that the difference between the expected NPVs with and without abandonment represents the **option value** to abandon this project. As shown in the lower part of Table 12.3, this option is worth $859.79. If the NPV of the "No Abandonment" situation had been negative, then the value of the option would simply have been the NPV of the "Can Abandon" situation.

With this project, the ability to abandon it makes the NPV look better, but it does not reverse the accept/reject decision. However, it often turns out that if we fail to consider abandonment, the bad case is so bad that the expected NPV is negative, but when abandonment is considered, the expected NPV becomes positive. Clearly, abandonment must be considered to obtain valid assessments for different projects, and the opportunity to abandon a project is an important way to limit downside losses.

Note too that it might be necessary for the firm to arrange things so that it has the possibility of abandonment when it is making the initial decision about a project. This might require contractual arrangements with suppliers, customers, and its union, and there might be some costs to obtaining these advance permissions. Any such costs could be compared with the value of the option as we calculated it, and this could enter into the initial decision.

Self*Test*

Why might DCF techniques not always lead to proper capital budgeting decisions?

What is a real option?

What are some types of real options? Briefly explain each one.

Would you expect an abandonment option to increase or decrease a project's NPV and its risk as measured by the coefficient of variation? Why?

How can the value of an option be estimated?

12-8 The Optimal Capital Budget

Thus far, we have described various factors that managers consider when they evaluate individual projects. For planning purposes, managers must also forecast the total capital budget, because the amount of capital raised affects the WACC and thus influences projects' NPVs. We use Data Devices Inc. (DDI), a manufacturer and distributor of storage devices, to illustrate how this process works.

Step 1. The treasurer obtains an estimate of the firm's overall composite WACC. As we discussed in Chapter 10, this composite WACC is based on market conditions, the firm's capital structure, and the riskiness of its assets. DDI's projects are roughly similar from year to year in terms of their risks.

Step 2. The corporate WACC is scaled up or down for each of the firm's divisions to reflect the division's risk. DDI, for example, assigns a factor of 0.9 to its stable, low-risk replacement battery division, but a factor of 1.1 to its large disk drives, which it sells to computer manufacturers and whose business is extremely competitive. Therefore, if the corporate cost of capital is determined to be 10.50%, the cost of capital for the battery division is 0 9(10.50%) = 9.45%, while that for the disk-drive division is 1.1(10.50%) = 11.55%.

Step 3. Financial managers within each of the firm's divisions estimate the relevant cash flows and risks of each of their potential projects. The estimated cash flows should explicitly consider any embedded real options. Then, within each division, projects are classified into one of three groups—high risk, average risk, and low risk—and the same 0.9 and 1.1 factors are used to adjust the divisional cost of capital estimates. (A factor of 1.0 would be used for an average-risk project.) For example, a low-risk project in the battery division would be assigned a cost of capital of 0.9(9.45%) = 8.51%, while a high-risk project in the disk-drive division would have a cost of 1.1(11.55%) = 12.71%.

Step 4. Each project's NPV is then determined, using its risk-adjusted cost of capital. The optimal capital budget consists of all independent projects with positive NPVs plus those mutually exclusive projects with the highest positive NPVs.

In estimating its **optimal capital budget**, we assumed that DDI can obtain financing for all of its profitable projects. This assumption is reasonable for large, mature firms with good track records. However, smaller firms, new firms, and firms with dubious track records may have difficulties raising capital, even for projects that the firm concludes would have highly positive NPVs. In such circumstances, the size of the capital budget may be constrained, a situation called

Optimal Capital Budget
The annual investment in long-term assets that maximizes the firm's value.

Capital Rationing
The situation in which a firm can raise only a specified, limited amount of capital regardless of how many good projects it has.

capital rationing. If capital is limited, it should be used in the most efficient way possible. Procedures have been developed for allocating capital so as to maximize the aggregate NPV subject to the constraint that the capital rationing ceiling is not exceeded. However, these procedures are extremely complicated, so they are best left for advanced finance courses.

The procedures discussed in this section cannot be implemented with precision. However, they do force the firm to think carefully about each division's relative risk, about the risk of each project within the divisions, and about the relationship between the total amount of capital raised and the cost of that capital. Further, the process forces the firm to adjust its capital budget to reflect capital market conditions. If the costs of debt and equity rise, this fact will be reflected in the cost of capital used to evaluate projects, and projects that would be marginally acceptable when capital costs were low would (correctly) be ruled unacceptable when capital costs become high.

Self*Test*

Explain how a financial manager might estimate his or her firm's optimal capital budget.

What is capital rationing?

Is a firm's optimal capital budget dynamic or static over time? Explain.

What factors must be considered when a firm is developing its optimal capital budget?

How does a firm's annual capital budget reflect market conditions?

12-9 The Post-Audit

A final aspect of the capital budgeting process is the post-audit, which involves (1) comparing actual results with those predicted by the project's sponsors and (2) explaining why any differences occurred. For example, many firms require that the operating divisions send a monthly report for the first six months after a project goes into operation and a quarterly report thereafter, until the project's results meet expectations. From then on, reports on the operation are reviewed on a regular basis like those of other operations. The post-audit has two main purposes:

1. *Improve forecasts*. When decision makers are forced to compare their projections with actual outcomes, there is a tendency for estimates to improve. Conscious or unconscious biases are observed and eliminated; new forecasting methods are sought as the need for them becomes apparent; and people simply tend to do everything better, including forecasting, if they know that their actions are being monitored.
2. *Improve operations*. Businesses are run by people, and people can perform at higher or lower levels of efficiency. When a divisional team has made a forecast about an investment, the team members are, in a sense, putting their reputations on the line. Accordingly, if costs are above and sales below predicted levels, then executives in production, marketing, and other areas will strive to improve operations and to bring results into line with forecasts. In a discussion related to this point, one executive made this statement: "You academicians only worry about making good decisions. In business, we also worry about making decisions good."

The post-audit is not a simple process. First, we must recognize that each element of the cash flow forecast is subject to uncertainty, so a percentage of all projects undertaken by any reasonably aggressive firm will necessarily go awry. This fact must be considered when appraising the performances of the operating executives who sponsor projects. Second, projects sometimes fail to meet expectations for reasons beyond the control of their sponsors and for reasons that no one could be expected to anticipate. Third, it is often difficult to separate the operating results of one investment from those of a larger system. Although some projects stand alone and permit ready identification of costs and revenues, the cost savings that result from assets like new computers may be very hard to measure. Fourth, it is often hard to hand out blame or praise because the executives who were responsible for launching a given investment have moved on by the time the results are known.

Because of these difficulties, some firms tend to play down the importance of the post-audit. However, observations of both businesses and governmental units suggest that the best-run and most successful organizations put a lot of emphasis on post-audits. Accordingly, we regard the post-audit as an important element in a good capital budgeting system.

SelfTest

What is done in the post-audit?

Identify several benefits of the post-audit.

What are some factors that complicate the post-audit process?

TYING IT ALL TOGETHER

This chapter focused on estimating the free cash flows that are used in a capital budgeting analysis, appraising the riskiness of those flows, finding NPVs when risk is present, and determining the values of real options, which can raise expected returns and lower risks. Here is a summary of our primary conclusions:

- **Some cash flows are *relevant* (thus should be included in a capital budgeting analysis), while others should not be included. The key question is this: Is the cash flow *incremental* in the sense that it will occur if and only if the project is accepted?**
- ***Sunk costs* are not incremental costs—they are not affected by accepting or rejecting the project. *Cannibalization* and other *externalities*, on the other hand, are incremental—they will occur if and only if the project is accepted.**
- **The cash flows used to analyze a project are different from a project's *net income*.**
- **Many projects require additional *net operating working capital*. An increase in net operating working capital is an additional outlay when the project is started but is an inflow at the end of the project's life, when the capital is recovered (i.e., the investment in operating working capital is reduced when the project is completed).**
- **We considered two types of projects, expansion and replacement. For a replacement project, we find the difference in the free cash flows when the firm continues to use the old asset versus the new asset. If the NPV of the differential flows is positive, the replacement should be made.**

- **The forecasted free cash flows (and thus NPV and other outputs) are only estimates—they may turn out to be incorrect, and this means *risk*.**
- **There are three types of risk: *stand-alone, within-firm*, and *market* (or *beta*) *risk*. In theory, market risk is most relevant; but because it cannot be measured for most projects, stand-alone risk is the one on which we generally focus. However, firms subjectively consider within-firm and market risk, which they definitely should not ignore. Note, though, that because the three types of risk are generally positively correlated, stand-alone risk is often a good proxy for the other risks.**
- **Stand-alone risk can be analyzed using *sensitivity analysis, scenario analysis,* and/or *Monte Carlo simulation*.**
- **Once a decision has been made about a project's relative risk, we determine a *risk-adjusted WACC* for evaluating it.**
- ***Real options* enable firms to take actions to alter the originally forecasted cash flows after a project is in operation. These options can increase NPVs and reduce risk.**
- **The *post-audit*, which compares the project's actual performance to its expected results, is an important part of the capital budgeting process.**

Self-Test Questions and Problems

(Solutions Appear in Appendix A)

ST-1 **KEY TERMS** Define the following terms:

a. Incremental cash flow; sunk cost; opportunity cost; externality; cannibalization
b. Stand-alone risk; corporate (within-firm) risk; market (beta) risk
c. Risk-adjusted cost of capital
d. Sensitivity analysis; base-case NPV
e. Scenario analysis; base-case scenario; worst-case scenario; best-case scenario
f. Monte Carlo simulation
g. Real option; abandonment option; decision tree
h. Option value
i. Optimal capital budget; capital rationing
j. Post-audit

ST-2 **PROJECT AND RISK ANALYSIS** As a financial analyst, you must evaluate a proposed project to produce printer cartridges. The purchase price of the equipment, including installation, is $65,000, and the equipment will be fully depreciated at t = 0. Annual sales would be 4,000 units at a price of $50 per cartridge, and the project's life would be 3 years. Current assets would increase by $5,000 and payables by $3,000. At the end of 3 years, the equipment could be sold for $10,000. Variable costs would be 70% of sales revenues, fixed costs would be $30,000 per year, the marginal tax rate is 25%, and the corporate WACC is 11%.

a. What is the required investment after bonus depreciation is considered, that is, the Year 0 project cash flow?
b. What are the project's annual cash flows?
c. If the project is of average risk, what is its NPV? Should it be accepted?
d. Management is uncertain about the exact unit sales. What would the project's NPV be if unit sales turned out to be 20% below forecast, but other inputs were as forecasted? Would this change the decision? Explain.

e. The CFO asks you to do a scenario analysis using these inputs:

	Probability	Unit Sales	VC%
Best case	25%	4,800	65%
Base case	50	4,000	70
Worst case	25	3,200	75

Other variables are unchanged. What are the expected NPV, its standard deviation, and the coefficient of variation? (*Hint:* To do the scenario analysis, you must change unit sales and VC% to the values specified for each scenario, get the scenario cash flows, and then find each scenario's NPV. Then you must calculate the project's expected NPV, standard deviation (σ), and coefficient of variation [CV]. This is not difficult, but it would require a lot of calculations. You might want to look at the answer in Appendix A at the back of the text, but make sure you understand how it was calculated.)

f. The firm's project CVs generally range from 1.0 to 1.5. A 3% risk premium is added to the WACC if the initial CV exceeds 1.5, and the WACC is reduced by 0.5% if the CV is 0.75 or less. Then a revised NPV is calculated. What WACC should be used for this project when project risk has been properly considered? What are the revised values for the NPV, standard deviation, and coefficient of variation? Would you recommend that the project be accepted? Why or why not?

Questions

12-1 Operating cash flows rather than accounting income are listed in Table 12.1. Why do we focus on cash flows as opposed to net income in capital budgeting?

12-2 Explain why sunk costs should not be included in a capital budgeting analysis but opportunity costs and externalities should be included. Give an example of each.

12-3 Explain why net operating working capital is included in a capital budgeting analysis and how it is recovered at the end of a project's life.

12-4 Why are interest charges not deducted when a project's cash flows for use in a capital budgeting analysis are calculated?

12-5 Most firms generate cash inflows every day, not just once at the end of the year. In capital budgeting, should we recognize this fact by estimating daily project cash flows and then using them in the analysis? If we do not, are our results biased? If so, would the NPV be biased up or down? Explain.

12-6 What are some differences in the analysis for a replacement project versus that for a new expansion project?

12-7 Distinguish among beta (or market) risk, within-firm (or corporate) risk, and stand-alone risk for a project being considered for inclusion in the capital budget.

12-8 In theory, market risk should be the only "relevant" risk. However, companies focus as much on stand-alone risk as on market risk. What are the reasons for the focus on stand-alone risk?

12-9 Define (a) sensitivity analysis, (b) scenario analysis, and (c) simulation analysis. If GE were considering two projects (one for $500 million to develop a satellite communications system and the other for $30,000 for a new truck), on which would the company be more likely to use a simulation analysis?

12-10 If you were the CFO of a company that had to decide on hundreds of potential projects every year, would you want to use sensitivity analysis and scenario analysis as described in the chapter, or would the amount of arithmetic required take too much time and thus not be cost-effective? What involvement would non-financial people such as those in marketing, accounting, and production have in the analysis?

12-11 What is a post-audit? Why do firms use them? What problems can arise when they are used?

Problems

Easy Problems 1-5

12-1 **REQUIRED INVESTMENT** Tannen Industries is considering an expansion. The necessary equipment would be purchased for $18 million and will be fully depreciated at the time of purchase, and the expansion would require an additional $2 million investment in net operating working capital. The tax rate is 25%.

a. What is the initial investment outlay after bonus depreciation is considered?
b. The company spent and expensed $20,000 on research related to the project last year. Would this change your answer? Explain.
c. Suppose the company plans to use a building that it owns to house the project. The building could be sold for $1 million after taxes and real estate commissions. How would that fact affect your answer?

12-2 **PROJECT CASH FLOW** Colsen Communications is trying to estimate the first-year cash flow (at Year 1) for a proposed project. The assets required for the project were fully depreciated at the time of purchase. The financial staff has collected the following information on the project:

Sales revenues	$15 million
Operating costs	13.5 million
Interest expense	1 million

The company has a 25% tax rate, and its WACC is 11%.

a. What is the project's cash flow for the first year (t = 1)?
b. If this project would cannibalize other projects by $0.5 million of cash flow before taxes per year, how would this change your answer to part a?

12-3 **AFTER-TAX SALVAGE VALUE** Karsted Air Services is now in the final year of a project. The equipment originally cost $29 million, of which 100% has been depreciated. Karsted can sell the used equipment today for $8 million, and its tax rate is 25%. What is the equipment's after-tax salvage value?

12-4 **REPLACEMENT ANALYSIS** The Oviedo Company is considering the purchase of a new machine to replace an obsolete one. The machine being used for the operation has a book value and a market value of zero. However, the machine is in good working order and will last at least another 10 years. The proposed replacement machine will perform the operation so much more efficiently that Oviedo's engineers estimate that it will produce after-tax cash flows (labor savings) of $8,000 per year. The after-tax cost of the new machine is $45,000, and its economic life is estimated to be 10 years. It has zero salvage value. The firm's WACC is 10%, and its marginal tax rate is 25%. Should Oviedo buy the new machine?

12-5 **OPTIMAL CAPITAL BUDGET** Marble Construction estimates that its WACC is 10% if equity comes from retained earnings. However, if the company issues new stock to raise new equity, it estimates that its WACC will rise to 10.8%. The company believes that it will exhaust its retained earnings at $2,500,000 of capital due to the number of highly profitable projects available to the firm and its limited earnings. The company is considering the following seven investment projects:

Project	Size	IRR
A	$ 650,000	14.0%
B	1,050,000	13.5
C	1,000,000	11.2
D	1,200,000	11.0
E	500,000	10.7
F	650,000	10.3
G	700,000	10.2

Assume that each of these projects is independent and that each is just as risky as the firm's existing assets. Which set of projects should be accepted, and what is the firm's optimal capital budget?

Intermediate Problems 6-12

12-6 DEPRECIATION METHODS Charlene is evaluating a capital budgeting project that should last for 4 years. The project requires $800,000 of equipment and is eligible for 100% bonus depreciation. She is unsure whether immediately expensing the equipment or using straight-line depreciation is better for the analysis. Under straight-line depreciation, the cost of the equipment would be depreciated evenly over its 4-year life. The company's WACC is 8%, and its tax rate is 25%.

a. What would the depreciation expense be each year under each method?

b. Which depreciation method would produce the higher NPV, and how much higher would it be?

12-7 SCENARIO ANALYSIS Huang Industries is considering a proposed project whose estimated NPV is $12 million. This estimate assumes that economic conditions will be "average." However, the CFO realizes that conditions could be better or worse, so she performed a scenario analysis and obtained these results:

Economic Scenario	Probability of Outcome	NPV
Recession	0.05	($70 million)
Below average	0.20	(25 million)
Average	0.50	12 million
Above average	0.20	20 million
Boom	0.05	30 million

Calculate the project's expected NPV, standard deviation, and coefficient of variation.

12-8 NEW PROJECT ANALYSIS You must evaluate the purchase of a proposed spectrometer for the R&D department. The purchase price of the spectrometer including modifications is $170,000, and the equipment will be fully depreciated at the time of purchase. The equipment would be sold after 3 years for $60,000. The equipment would require an $8,000 increase in net operating working capital (spare parts inventory). The project would have no effect on revenues, but it should save the firm $50,000 per year in before-tax labor costs. The firm's marginal federal-plus-state tax rate is 25%.

a. What is the initial investment outlay for the spectrometer after bonus depreciation is considered, that is, what is the Year 0 project cash flow?

b. What are the project's annual cash flows in Years 1, 2, and 3?

c. If the WACC is 10%, should the spectrometer be purchased? Explain.

12-9 NEW PROJECT ANALYSIS You must evaluate a proposal to buy a new milling machine. The purchase price of the milling machine, including shipping and installation costs, is $143,000, and the equipment will be fully depreciated at the time of purchase. The machine would be sold after 3 years for $94,500. The machine would require a $5,000 increase in net operating working capital (increased inventory less increased accounts payable). There would be no effect on revenues, but pretax labor costs would decline by $52,000 per year. The marginal tax rate is 25%, and the WACC is 8%. Also, the firm spent $4,500 last year investigating the feasibility of using the machine.

a. How should the $4,500 spent last year be handled?

b. What is the initial investment outlay for the machine for capital budgeting purposes after the 100% bonus depreciation is considered, that is, what is the Year 0 project cash flow?

c. What are the project's annual cash flows during Years 1, 2, and 3?

d. Should the machine be purchased? Explain your answer.

12-10 REPLACEMENT ANALYSIS The Dauten Toy Corporation currently uses an injection molding machine that was purchased prior to the new tax legislation. This machine is being depreciated on a straight-line basis, and it has 6 years of remaining life. Its current book value is $2,100, and it can be sold for $2,500 at this time. Thus, the annual depreciation expense is $2,100/6 = $350 per year. If the old machine is not replaced, it can be sold for $500 at the end of its useful life.

Dauten is offered a replacement machine which has a cost of $8,000, an estimated useful life of 6 years, and an estimated salvage value of $800. The replacement machine is eligible for 100% bonus depreciation at the time of purchase. The replacement machine would permit an output expansion, so sales would rise by $1,000 per year; even so, the new machine's much greater efficiency would cause operating expenses to decline by $1,500 per year. The new machine would require that inventories be increased by $2,000, but accounts payable would simultaneously increase by $500. Dauten's marginal federal-plus-state tax rate is 25%, and its WACC is 11%. Should it replace the old machine?

12-11 **REPLACEMENT ANALYSIS** St. Johns River Shipyards is considering the replacement of an 8-year-old riveting machine with a new one that will increase earnings from $24,000 to $46,000 per year. The new machine will cost $80,000, and it will have an estimated life of 8 years and no salvage value. The new riveting machine is eligible for 100% bonus depreciation at the time of purchase. The applicable corporate tax rate is 25%, and the firm's WACC is 10%. The old machine has been fully depreciated and has no salvage value. Should the old riveting machine be replaced by the new one? Explain your answer.

12-12 **PROJECT RISK ANALYSIS** The Butler-Perkins Company (BPC) must decide between two mutually exclusive projects. Each project has an initial outflow of $6,750 and has an expected life of 3 years. Annual project cash flows begin 1 year after the initial investment and are subject to the following probability distributions:

Project A		Project B	
Probability	**Cash Flows**	**Probability**	**Cash Flows**
0.2	$6,000	0.2	$ 0
0.6	6,750	0.6	6,750
0.2	7,500	0.2	18,000

BPC has decided to evaluate the riskier project at 12% and the less-risky project at 10%.

a. What is each project's expected annual cash flow? Project B's standard deviation (σ_B) is $5,798, and its coefficient of variation (CV_B) is 0.76. What are the values of σ_A and CV_A?
b. Based on the risk-adjusted NPVs, which project should BPC choose?
c. If you knew that Project B's cash flows were negatively correlated with the firm's other cash flows, but Project A's cash flows were positively correlated, how might this affect the decision? If Project B's cash flows were negatively correlated with gross domestic product (GDP), while A's cash flows were positively correlated, would that influence your risk assessment?

Challenging Problems 13-17

12-13 **NEW PROJECT ANALYSIS** Holmes Manufacturing is considering a new machine that costs $285,000 and would reduce pretax manufacturing costs by $90,000 annually. The new machine will be fully depreciated at the time of purchase. Management thinks the machine would have a value of $23,000 at the end of its 5-year operating life. Net operating working capital would increase by $25,000 initially, but it would be recovered at the end of the project's 5-year life. Holmes's marginal tax rate is 25%, and a 10% WACC is appropriate for the project.

a. Calculate the project's NPV, IRR, MIRR, and payback.
b. Assume management is unsure about the $90,000 cost savings—this figure could deviate by as much as plus or minus 20%. What would the NPV be under each of these situations?
c. Suppose the CFO wants you to do a scenario analysis with different values for the cost savings, the machine's salvage value, and the net operating working capital (NOWC) requirement. She asks you to use the following probabilities and values in the scenario analysis:

Scenario	Probability	Cost Savings	Salvage Value	NOWC
Worst case	0.35	$ 72,000	$18,000	$30,000
Base case	0.35	90,000	23,000	25,000
Best case	0.30	108,000	28,000	20,000

Calculate the project's expected NPV, its standard deviation, and its coefficient of variation. Would you recommend that the project be accepted? Why or why not?

12-14 **REPLACEMENT ANALYSIS** The Darlington Equipment Company purchased a machine 5 years ago at a cost of $85,000. The machine had an expected life of 10 years at the time of purchase, and it is being depreciated by the straight-line method by $8,500 per year. If the machine is not replaced, it can be sold for $15,000 at the end of its useful life.

A new machine can be purchased for $170,000, including installation costs. During its 5-year life, it will reduce cash operating expenses by $40,000 per year. Sales are not expected to change. At the end of its useful life, the machine is estimated to be worthless. The new machine is eligible for 100% bonus depreciation at the time of purchase.

The old machine can be sold today for $55,000. The firm's tax rate is 25%. The appropriate WACC is 9%.

a. If the new machine is purchased, what is the amount of the initial cash flow at Year 0 after bonus depreciation is considered?
b. What are the incremental cash flows that will occur at the end of Years 1 through 5?
c. What is the NPV of this project? Should Darlington replace the old machine? Explain.

12-15 **REPLACEMENT ANALYSIS** The Bigbee Bottling Company is contemplating the replacement of one of its bottling machines with a newer and more efficient one. The old machine was purchased prior to the new tax legislation, has a book value of $600,000, and a remaining useful life of 5 years. The firm does not expect to realize any return from scrapping the old machine in 5 years, but it can sell it now to another firm in the industry for $265,000. The old machine is being depreciated by $120,000 per year, using the straight-line method.

The new machine has a purchase price of $1,175,000, an estimated useful life of 5 years, and an estimated salvage value of $145,000. The new machine is eligible for 100% bonus depreciation at the time of purchase. It is expected to economize on electric power usage, labor, and repair costs, as well as to reduce the number of defective bottles. In total, an annual savings before taxes of $220,000 will be realized if the new machine is installed. The company's marginal tax rate is 25% and it has a 12% WACC.

a. What initial cash outlay is required for the new machine after bonus depreciation is considered?
b. Calculate the change in the annual depreciation expense if the replacement is made.
c. What are the incremental cash flows in Years 1 through 5?
d. Should the firm purchase the new machine? Support your answer.
e. In general, how would each of the following factors affect the investment decision, and how should each be treated?
   1. The expected life of the existing machine decreases.
   2. The WACC is not constant, but is increasing as Bigbee adds more projects into its capital budget for the year.

12-16 **ABANDONMENT OPTION** The Sorensen Supplies Company recently purchased a new delivery truck. The initial cash outflow for the new truck is $22,500, and it is expected to generate after-tax cash flows of $5,875 per year. The truck has a 5-year expected life. The expected year-end abandonment values (after-tax salvage values) for the truck are given here. The company's WACC is 9%.

Year	Annual After-Tax Cash Flow	Abandonment Value
0	($22,500)	—
1	5,875	$17,000
2	5,875	15,000
3	5,875	9,000
4	5,875	4,750
5	5,875	0

a. Should the firm operate the truck until the end of its 5-year physical life; if not, what is the truck's optimal economic life?
b. Would the introduction of abandonment values, in addition to operating cash flows, ever *reduce* the expected NPV and/or IRR of a project? Explain.

12-17 **OPTIMAL CAPITAL BUDGET** Hampton Manufacturing estimates that its WACC is 12.5%. The company is considering the following seven investment projects:

Project	Size	IRR
A	$ 750,000	14.0%
B	1,250,000	13.5
C	1,250,000	13.2
D	1,250,000	13.0
E	750,000	12.7
F	750,000	12.3
G	750,000	12.2

a. Assume that each of these projects is independent and that each is just as risky as the firm's existing assets. Which set of projects should be accepted, and what is the firm's optimal capital budget?

b. Now assume that Projects C and D are mutually exclusive. Project D has an NPV of $400,000, whereas Project C has an NPV of $350,000. Which set of projects should be accepted, and what is the firm's optimal capital budget?

c. Ignore Part b and assume that each of the projects is independent but that management decides to incorporate project risk differentials. Management judges Projects B, C, D, and E to have average risk; Project A to have high risk; and Projects F and G to have low risk. The company adds 2% to the WACC of those projects that are significantly more risky than average, and it subtracts 2% from the WACC of those projects that are substantially less risky than average. Which set of projects should be accepted, and what is the firm's optimal capital budget?

Comprehensive/Spreadsheet Problem

12-18 **NEW PROJECT ANALYSIS** You must analyze a potential new product—a caulking compound that Cory Materials' R&D people developed for use in the residential construction industry. Cory's marketing manager thinks the company can sell 115,000 tubes per year at a price of $3.25 each for 3 years, after which the product will be obsolete. The purchase price of the required equipment, including shipping and installation costs, is $175,000, and the equipment is eligible for 100% bonus depreciation at the time of purchase. Current assets (receivables and inventories) would increase by $35,000, while current liabilities (accounts payable and accruals) would rise by $15,000. Variable cost per unit is $1.95, and fixed costs would be $70,000 per year. When production ceases after 3 years, the equipment should have a market value of $15,000. Cory's tax rate is 25%, and it uses a 10% WACC for average-risk projects.

a. Find the required Year 0 investment outlay after bonus depreciation is considered and the project's annual cash flows. Then calculate the project's NPV, IRR, MIRR, and payback. Assume at this point that the project is of average risk.

b. Suppose you now learn that R&D costs for the new product were $30,000 and that those costs were incurred and expensed for tax purposes last year. How would this affect your estimate of NPV and the other profitability measures?

c. If the new project would reduce cash flows from Cory's other projects and if the new project would be housed in an empty building that Cory owns and could sell, how would those factors affect the project's NPV?

d. Are this project's cash flows likely to be positively or negatively correlated with returns on Cory's other projects and with the economy, and should this matter in your analysis? Explain.

e. **Spreadsheet assignment: at instructor's option** Construct a spreadsheet that calculates the cash flows, NPV, IRR, payback, and MIRR.

f. The CEO expressed concern that some of the base-case inputs for the caulking compound might be too optimistic or too pessimistic, and he wants to know how the NPV would be affected if these six variables were 20% above or 20% below the base-case levels: unit sales, sales price, variable cost, fixed costs, WACC, and equipment cost. Hold other things constant when you consider each variable and construct a sensitivity graph to illustrate your results.

g. Do a scenario analysis based on the assumption that there is a 25% probability that each of the six variables itemized in part f will turn out to have their best-case values as calculated in part f, a 50% probability that all will have their base-case values, and a 25% probability that all will have their worst-case values. The other variables remain at base-case levels. Calculate the expected NPV, the standard deviation of NPV, and the coefficient of variation.

h. Does Cory's management use the risk-adjusted discount rate to adjust for project risk? Explain.

INTEGRATED CASE

ALLIED FOOD PRODUCTS

12-19 CAPITAL BUDGETING AND CASH FLOW ESTIMATION Allied Food Products is considering expanding into the fruit juice business with a new fresh lemon juice product. Assume that you were recently hired as assistant to the director of capital budgeting, and you must evaluate the new project.

The lemon juice would be produced in an unused building adjacent to Allied's Fort Myers plant; Allied owns the building, which is fully depreciated. The purchase price of the required equipment is $280,000, including shipping and installation costs, and the equipment is eligible for 100% bonus depreciation at the time of purchase. In addition, inventories would rise by $25,000, while accounts payable would increase by $5,000. All of these costs would be incurred at t = 0.

The project is expected to operate for 4 years, at which time it will be terminated. The cash inflows are assumed to begin 1 year after the project is undertaken, or at t = 1, and to continue out to t = 4. At the end of the project's life (t = 4), the equipment is expected to have a salvage value of $25,000.

Unit sales are expected to total 100,000 units per year, and the expected sales price is $2.00 per unit. Cash operating costs for the project are expected to total 60% of dollar sales. Allied's tax rate is 25%, and its WACC is 10%. Tentatively, the lemon juice project is assumed to be of equal risk to Allied's other assets.

You have been asked to evaluate the project and to make a recommendation as to whether it should be accepted or rejected. To guide you in your analysis, your boss gave you the following set of tasks/questions:

a. Allied has a standard form that is used in the capital budgeting process. (See Table IC 12.1.) Part of the table has been completed, but you must replace the blanks with the missing numbers. Complete the table using the following steps:
   1. Fill in the blanks under Year 0 for the initial investment outlays: CAPEX × (1 − T) and ΔNOWC.
   2. Complete the table for unit sales, sales price, total revenues, and operating costs.
   3. Complete the table down to after-tax operating income and then down to the project's operating cash flows, EBIT (1 − T) + DEP.
   4. Fill in the blanks under Year 4 for the terminal cash flows and complete the project free cash flow line. Discuss the recovery of net operating working capital. What would have happened if the machinery had been sold for less than its book value?

b. 1. Allied uses debt in its capital structure, so some of the money used to finance the project will be debt. Given this fact, should the projected cash flows be revised to show projected interest charges? Explain.
   2. Suppose you learned that Allied had spent $50,000 to renovate the building last year, expensing these costs. Should this cost be reflected in the analysis? Explain.
   3. Suppose you learned that Allied could lease its building to another party and earn $25,000 per year. Should that fact be reflected in the analysis? If so, how?
   4. Assume that the lemon juice project would take profitable sales away from Allied's fresh orange juice business. Should that fact be reflected in your analysis? If so, how?

c. Disregard all the assumptions made in part b and assume there is no alternative use for the building over the next 4 years. Now calculate the project's NPV, IRR, MIRR, and payback. Do these indicators suggest that the project should be accepted? Explain.

d. If this project had been a replacement rather than an expansion project, how would the analysis have changed? Think about the changes that would have to occur in the cash flow table.

TABLE IC 12.1 Allied's Lemon Juice Project (in thousands)

End of Year:	0	1	2	3	4
I. Investment Outlays					
CAPEX × (1 − T)					
Increase in inventory					
Increase in accounts payable					
ΔNOWC					
II. Project Operating Cash Flows					
Unit sales (thousands)			100		
Price/unit		$ 2.00	$ 2.00		
Total revenues					$ 200.0
Operating costs			$ 120.0		
Depreciation: 100% Bonus Depreciation in Year 0		0.0	0.0	0.0	0.0
Total costs		$ 120.0	$ 120.0		
EBIT (or operating income)				$ 80.0	
Taxes on operating income (25%)		20.0			20.0
EBIT (1 − T) = After-tax operating income				$ 60.0	
Add back depreciation		0.0		0.0	
EBIT (1 − T) + DEP	$ 0.0	$ 60.0			$ 60.0
III. Project Termination Cash Flows					
Salvage value (taxed as ordinary income)					
Tax on salvage value (25%)					
After-tax salvage value					
ΔNOWC = Recovery of NOWC					
Project free cash flows = EBIT(1 − T) + DEP − CAPEX − ΔNOWC	($230.0)				$ 98.8
IV. Results					
NPV =					
IRR =					
MIRR =					

e. 1. What three levels, or types, of project risk are normally considered?
   2. Which type is most relevant?
   3. Which type is easiest to measure?
   4. Are the three types of risk generally highly correlated?

f. 1. What is sensitivity analysis?
   2. How would you perform a sensitivity analysis on the unit sales, salvage value, and WACC for the project? Assume that each of these variables deviates from its base-case, or expected, value by plus or minus 10%, 20%, and 30%. Explain how you would calculate the NPV, IRR, MIRR, and payback for each case, but don't do the analysis unless your instructor asks you to.
   3. What is the primary weakness of sensitivity analysis? What are its primary advantages?

Work out quantitative answers to the remaining questions only if your instructor asks you to. Also note that it will take a *long time* to do the calculations unless you are using an Excel model.

g. Assume that inflation is expected to average 5% over the next 4 years and that this expectation is reflected in the WACC. Moreover, inflation is expected to increase revenues and variable costs by this same 5%. Does it appear that inflation has been dealt with properly in the initial analysis to this point? If not, what should be done and how would the required adjustment affect the decision?

h. The expected cash flows, considering inflation (in thousands of dollars), are given in Table IC 12.2. Allied's WACC is 10%. Assume that you are confident about the estimates of all the variables that affect the cash flows except unit sales. If product acceptance is poor, sales would be only 75,000 units a year, while a strong consumer response would produce sales of 125,000 units. In either

Allied's Lemon Juice Project Considering 5% Inflation (in thousands)

TABLE IC 12.2

	Year				
	0	1	2	3	4
Investment Outlays					
CAPEX × (1 − T)	($210)				
ΔNOWC	(20)				
Project Operating Cash Flows					
Units sales (thousands)		100	100	100	100
Sales price (dollars)		$ 2.100	$ 2.205	$ 2.315	$ 2.431
Total revenues		$ 210.0	$220.5	$ 231.5	$243.1
Cash operating costs (60%)		126.0	132.3	138.9	145.9
Depreciation: 100% Bonus Depreciation in Year 0		0.0	0.0	0.0	0.0
EBIT (or operating income)		$ 84.0	$ 88.2	$ 92.6	$ 97.2
Taxes on operating income (25%)		21.0	22.1	23.2	24.3
EBIT(1 − T) = After-tax operating income		$ 63.0	$ 66.2	$ 69.5	$ 72.9
Plus depreciation		0.0	0.0	0.0	0.0
EBIT(1 − T) + DEP		$ 63.0	$ 66.2	$ 69.5	$ 72.9
Terminal Cash Flows					
Salvage value					25.0
Tax on SV (25%)					6.2
After-tax salvage value					18.8
ΔNOWC					20.0
Project free cash flows	($230.0)	$ 63.0	$ 66.2	$ 69.5	$111.7
Cumulative cash flows for payback:	(230.0)	(167.0)	(100.8)	(31.4)	80.3
Compounded inflows for MIRR:		83.9	80.0	76.4	111.7
Sum of compounded inflows:					352.0
NPV = $10.4					
IRR = 11.9%					
MIRR = 11.2%					

case, cash costs would still amount to 60% of revenues. You believe that there is a 25% chance of poor acceptance, a 25% chance of excellent acceptance, and a 50% chance of average acceptance (the base case). Provide numbers only if you are using a computer model.

1. What is the worst-case NPV? The best-case NPV?
2. Use the worst-case, most likely case (or base-case), and best-case NPVs with their probabilities of occurrence, to find the project's expected NPV, standard deviation, and coefficient of variation.

i. Assume that Allied's average project has a coefficient of variation (CV) in the range of 1.25 to 1.75. Would the lemon juice project be classified as high risk, average risk, or low risk? What type of risk is being measured here?

j. Based on common sense, how highly correlated do you think the project would be with the firm's other assets? (Give a correlation coefficient or range of coefficients, based on your judgment.)

k. How would the correlation coefficient and the previously calculated σ combine to affect the project's contribution to corporate, or within-firm, risk? Explain.

l. Based on your judgment, what do you think the project's correlation coefficient would be with respect to the general economy and thus with returns on "the market"? How would correlation with the economy affect the project's market risk?

m. Allied typically adds or subtracts 4% to its WACC to adjust for risk. After adjusting for risk, should the lemon juice project be accepted? Should any subjective risk factors be considered before the final decision is made? Explain.

n. In recent months, Allied's group has begun to focus on real option analysis.

1. What is real option analysis?
2. What are some examples of projects with embedded real options?

part 5

Capital Structure and Dividend Policy

CHAPTERS

Capital Structure and Leverage

CHAPTER 13

AP Images/Laurent Cipriani

Debt: Rocket Booster or Anchor? Caterpillar Inc.

If it is to grow, a firm needs capital, and capital comes primarily in the form of debt or equity. Debt financing has two important advantages: (1) Interest paid is tax deductible, whereas dividends are not deductible, and this lowers debt's relative cost to equity. (2) The return on debt is fixed, so stockholders do not have to share the firm's profits if the company turns out to be extremely successful.

However, debt also has disadvantages: (1) Using more debt increases the firm's risk, and that raises the costs of both its debt and equity. (2) If the company falls on hard times and its operating income is not sufficient to cover interest charges, then the firm may go bankrupt. Good times may be just around the corner, but too much debt can bankrupt the company before it reaches that corner.

Because of the additional risk from using debt, companies with volatile earnings and operating cash flows tend to limit its use. On the other hand, companies with low business risk and stable operating cash flows can benefit from taking on more debt. Firms realize that when bad times hit, interest must be paid, so they must become "leaner" to strengthen their financial position and keep their credit rating from declining. In 2009, Caterpillar Inc. (CAT), the world's largest producer of earthmoving equipment, found itself in this precise situation.

At year-end 2008, Caterpillar's book value capital structure consisted of 89% debt (debt over capital) and 11% equity. An 89% debt ratio is quite high, and Caterpillar's management was well aware that excessive debt can push an otherwise well-regarded company into bankruptcy. Indeed, the country was in the middle of a recession that spilled over into global markets. Because Caterpillar's foreign sales made up 67% of its revenues, the company was hit hard. As a result, the firm's sales fell in 2009.

Accordingly, Caterpillar's management began to get its "financial house in order" by lowering its working capital, reducing overhead costs, and paying down its investor-supplied debt. In fact, from the first quarter of 2009 through the end of 2013, Caterpillar steadily reduced its reliance on debt financing. At the same time, as part of its renewed focus, the company was also interested in returning cash to its shareholders. With this goal in mind, Caterpillar announced, in early 2014, plans for a new $10 billion stock buy-back program that would expire in 2018. Of course, by reducing its outstanding equity, this buy-back pushed up its debt-to-capital ratio to 78% by the end of 2017.[1] For many companies, a 78% debt ratio would still be too high.

However, if we examine Caterpillar's capital structure in more detail, it soon becomes apparent that there is more here than meets the eye. At year-end, on a book-value basis, Caterpillar had about $47.4 billion of investor-supplied debt versus equity of $13.7 billion, but its market capitalization (stock price times the number of shares outstanding) was approximately $94.2 billion. From a market-value perspective, Caterpillar's debt-to-capital ratio was only $47.4/($47.4 + $94.2) ≈ 33%, which was considerably lower than the 78% calculated on a book-value basis. This helps explain why the company continued to have an A bond rating.

Caterpillar and other companies can finance with either debt or equity. Is one better than the other? If so, should firms finance either with all debt or all equity? Or, if the best solution is some mix of debt and equity, what is the optimal mix? As you read this chapter, think about these questions and consider how you would answer them.

[1]Under its plan, Caterpillar elected to repurchase stock in 2014 and 2015, but it declined to do so in 2016 and in 2017. If it had repurchased additional shares in 2016 and 2017, its book debt-to-capital ratio would have been even higher.

PUTTING THINGS IN PERSPECTIVE

When we calculated the weighted average cost of capital (WACC) in Chapter 10, we assumed that the firm had a specific target capital structure. However, target capital structures often change over time, such changes affect the risk and cost of each type of capital, and all this can change the WACC. Moreover, a change in the WACC will affect capital budgeting decisions and, ultimately, the stock price.

Many factors influence capital structure decisions, and, as we will see, determining the optimal capital structure is not an exact science. Therefore, even firms in the same industry often have dramatically different capital structures. In this chapter, we consider the effects of debt on risk and on the optimal capital structure.

When you finish this chapter, you should be able to do the following:

- **Explain why there may be differences in a firm's capital structure when measured on a book-value basis, a market-value basis, or a target basis.**
- **Distinguish between business risk and financial risk, and explain the effects that debt financing has on the firm's expected return and risk.**
- **Discuss the analytical framework used when determining the optimal capital structure.**
- **Discuss capital structure theory, and use it to explain why firms in different industries tend to have different capital structures.**

13-1 Book, Market, or "Target" Weights?

Capital
Investor-supplied funds such as long- and short-term loans from individuals and institutions, preferred stock, common stock, and retained earnings.

The term **capital** refers to *investor-supplied funds*—debt, preferred stock, common stock, and retained earnings.[2] Accounts payable and accruals are *not* included in our definition of capital because they are not provided by investors—they come

[2]Capital is frequently defined to include only long-term debt, that is, debt due in more than a year. However, many companies use short-term loans from banks on a permanent basis, and for this reason we include short-term debt that is *provided by investors* in our definition of "capital."

Capital Structure
The mix of debt, preferred stock, and common equity that is used to finance the firm's assets.

Optimal Capital Structure
The capital structure that maximizes a stock's intrinsic value.

resource

Students can download the Excel chapter models from the textbook's student companion site on cengage.com. Once downloaded onto your computer, retrieve the Chapter 13 Excel model and follow along as you read this chapter. Refer to the relevant tabs for tables and figures discussed.

from suppliers, workers, and taxing authorities as a result of normal operations, not as investments by investors. A firm's **capital structure** is typically defined as the percentage of each type of investor-supplied capital, with the total being 100%. The **optimal capital structure** is the mix of debt, preferred stock, and common equity that maximizes the stock's intrinsic value. As we will see, the capital structure that maximizes the intrinsic value also minimizes the WACC.

13-1A MEASURING THE CAPITAL STRUCTURE

To begin, we must answer this question: How should the capital structure be measured? Should we work with book values as provided by accountants and shown on the balance sheet; with the market values of the debt, preferred stock, and common equity; or with some other set of numbers? To see what's involved, consider Table 13.1, which compares the book and market values for Caterpillar (CAT) from a recent financial statement.[3]

1. In this case, as is generally true, the market value of the debt was fairly close to its book value, so, for simplicity, we show the same dollars of debt in both the book and market columns.
2. However at the time of this analysis, the common stock sold for $157.58 per share versus its $23.03 book value. There were 597.63 million shares outstanding, so the market value of the equity was $94.2 billion, calculated as $157.58(597,630,000) = $94.2 billion, versus a $13.7 billion book value.
3. For capital structure purposes, no distinction is made between common equity raised by issuing stock versus retaining earnings. Stockholders

TABLE 13.1 "Snapshot" of 12/31/17 Caterpillar Inc.'s Book Value, Market Value, and Target Capital Structure (billions of dollars)

Condensed Balance Sheet Assets and Claims against Assets at Book Values					Investor-supplied capital: Payables and accruals are excluded because they come from operations, not from investors				
	Assets		Claims		Book Value		Market Value		Target %
Cash	$ 8.3	Accounts payable	$10.2	13.2%	–	–	–	–	–
Receivables	16.1	Accruals	5.7	7.4%	–	–	–	–	–
Inventories	10.0								
Other C.A.	1.8	Notes payable (ST debt)	11.0	14.4%	$11.0	18%	$11.0	8%	5%
Total C.A.	$36.2	Total C.L.	$26.9	35.0%					
		Long-term debt	36.4	47.3%	36.4	60%	36.4	25%	35%
Fixed assets	$40.8	Total liabilities	$63.3	82.2%	$47.4	78%	$47.4	33%	40%
		Common stock	$ 5.6	7.3%	$ 5.6				
		Retained earnings	8.1	10.5%	8.1				
		Total common equity	$13.7	17.8%	$13.7	22%	$94.2	67%	60%
Total assets	$77.0	Total claims	$77.0	100%	$61.1	100%	$141.6	100%	100%

Note: At the time of this analysis, CAT had 597.63 million shares outstanding; its book value per share was $23.03, and its market price was $157.58 per share. *We do not know its management-determined target capital structure. The 40% debt ratio is just our estimate of what a reasonable target might be.* The procedure illustrated in Section 13-3 shows how CAT *might* go about establishing its target capital structure.

[3]CAT's actual balance sheet is broken down into so many elements that it is several pages long. For convenience, we compress it into the categories shown in Table 13.1. The data used in the table are from its December 31, 2017, balance sheet.

provided both components, either by purchasing newly issued shares or by allowing management to retain earnings rather than to distribute them as dividends.

4. Caterpillar does not use preferred stock, but if it did, the market value of preferred would be calculated in the same way as we calculated the market value of its common equity.
5. According to most financial theorists, it is better to use market values than book values. However, most financial analysts report data on a book-value basis, and bond rating agencies report book values and seem to give them at least as much weight as market values. Also, stock prices are quite volatile; therefore, if we use market values, then the weights used to calculate the WACC will also be volatile. For all these reasons, some analysts argue for the use of book values.
6. In a perfect world, a firm would identify its optimal capital structure based on market values, raise capital so as to maintain that structure, and use the optimal percentages to calculate its WACC. However, the world is not perfect. It is impossible to identify a precisely optimal structure, and given the volatility inherent in financial markets, it would be impossible to remain on target over time even if the optimal structure could be identified. As a result, most firms focus on a *target debt ratio range* as opposed to a single number.[4]
7. Generally, a firm's CFO considers the capital structures of the firms against which it benchmarks and performs an analysis similar to what we do in the remainder of this chapter.
8. Assume that Caterpillar's management concluded that the firm's optimal capital structure has 40% debt and set its target debt range at 35% to 45%. The equity range is thus (1 − % Debt), or between 55% and 65% equity. Now, for simplicity, assume that the average interest rate on both short-term and long-term debt is 5%, the cost of equity is 11%, and its corporate tax rate is approximately 25%. Using weights from Table 13.1, the following calculations show that the choice of capital structure makes a significant difference in the WACC estimates:

$$\begin{aligned}\text{WACC}_{\text{Book}} &= w_{d(\text{Book})}(r_d)(1 - T) + w_{c(\text{Book})}(r_s)\\ &= 0.78(5\%)(1 - 0.25) + 0.22(11\%) = 0.0293 + 0.0242 = 5.35\%\\ \text{WACC}_{\text{Market}} &= w_{d(\text{Market})}(r_d)(1 - T) + w_{c(\text{Market})}(r_s)\\ &= 0.33(5\%)(1 - 0.25) + 0.67(11\%) = 0.0124 + 0.0737 = 8.61\%\\ \text{WACC}_{\text{Target}} &= w_{d(\text{Target})}(r_d)(1 - T) + w_{c(\text{Target})}(r_s)\\ &= 0.40(5\%)(1 - 0.25) + 0.60(11\%) = 0.0150 + 0.0660 = 8.10\%\end{aligned}$$

   The greater the difference between the stock's book value and market value, the greater the difference between the alternative WACCs.
9. Using the 40% midpoint target debt ratio, our estimate of CAT's WACC for an average-risk project would be 8.10%.

If the actual debt ratio were significantly below the target range, the firm would probably raise capital by issuing debt, whereas if the debt ratio were above the target range, equity would probably be used. Note also that the target range is likely to change over time as conditions change.

---

[4]A study by Graham and Harvey surveyed corporate managers and asked whether their firms established a target capital structure. Eighty-one percent of the respondents indicated that their firms did have target capital structures. Ten percent said that they had strict target debt ratios, 34% indicated that they had a somewhat tight range for their target debt ratios, and 37% indicated that they had flexible targets. See John R. Graham and Campbell R. Harvey, "The Theory and Practice of Corporate Finance: Evidence from the Field," *Journal of Financial Economics*, vol. 60, nos. 2 and 3 (May–June 2001), pp. 187–243.

13-1B CAPITAL STRUCTURE CHANGES OVER TIME

Firms' actual capital structures change over time, and for two quite different reasons:

1. *Deliberate actions:* If a firm is not currently at its target, it may deliberately raise new money in a manner that moves the actual structure toward the target.
2. *Market actions:* The firm could incur high profits or losses that lead to significant changes in book value equity as shown on its balance sheet and to a decline in its stock price. Similarly, although the book value of its debt would probably not change, interest rate changes due to changes in the general level of rates and/or changes in the firm's default risk could cause significant changes in its debt's market value. Such changes in the market value of the debt and/or equity could result in large changes in its measured capital structure.

Still, at any given moment, most firms have a specific target range in mind.[5] If the actual debt ratio has surpassed the target, a firm can sell a large stock issue and use the proceeds to retire debt. Or, if the stock price has increased and pushed the debt ratio below the target, it can issue bonds and use the proceeds to repurchase stock. And, of course, a firm can gradually move toward its target through its annual financings to support its capital budget.[6]

Self*Test*

Define the terms "book-value capital structure," "market-value capital structure," and "target capital structure," and explain why they differ from one another.

Would the market-value debt ratio tend to be higher than the book-value debt ratio during a stock market boom or a recession? Explain.

Why would the WACC based on market values tend to be higher than the one based on book values if the stock price exceeded its book value?

Which would you expect to be more stable over time, a firm's book-value or market-value capital structure? Explain.

13-2 Business and Financial Risk

In Chapter 8, we examined risk from the viewpoint of an individual investor and we distinguished between *risk on a stand-alone basis,* where an asset's cash flows are analyzed by themselves, and *risk in a portfolio context,* where cash flows from a number of assets are combined and consolidated cash flows are analyzed. In a

[5]Even if the firm concluded that its debt ratio was below the lower limit—then it could finance its entire capital budget for the year with debt—it should still use a WACC based on the target capital structure when evaluating projects for inclusion in the firm's capital budget.

[6]Firms face costs when they adjust their capital structure, and this is particularly the case if the firm has to pay an investment banker to help it raise new debt or equity. Consequently, if the benefits of moving toward their target capital structure (a lower WACC) are less than the costs of adjusting their capital structure, firms may decide not to immediately adjust their capital structure to its target level. If you are interested in more details about capital structure adjustments, see the following article, which looks at the connection between transactions costs and the speed at which firms adjust to their target capital structure: Michael W. Faulkender, Mark J. Flannery, Kristine Watson Hankins, and Jason M. Smith, "Cash Flows and Leverage Adjustments," *Journal of Financial Economics*, vol. 103, no. 3 (March 2012), pp. 632–646.

portfolio context, we saw that an asset's risk can be divided into two components: *diversifiable risk,* which can be diversified away and hence is of little concern to most investors, and *market risk,* which is measured by the beta coefficient and reflects broad market movements that cannot be eliminated by diversification and therefore is of concern to investors. Then in Chapter 12, we examined risk from the viewpoint of the corporation, and we considered how capital budgeting decisions affect the firm's riskiness.

Now we introduce two new dimensions of risk:

1. *Business risk,* which is the riskiness of the firm's assets if no debt is used.
2. *Financial risk,* which is the additional risk placed on the common stockholders as a result of using debt.

13-2A BUSINESS RISK

Business Risk
The riskiness inherent in the firm's operations if it uses no debt.

Business risk is the single most important determinant of capital structure, and it represents the amount of risk that is inherent in the firm's operations even if it uses no debt financing. A commonly used measure of business risk is the standard deviation of the firm's return on invested capital, or ROIC. Recall from Chapter 4 that ROIC is defined as follows:[7]

$$\text{ROIC} = \text{EBIT}(1 - \text{T})/\text{Total invested capital}$$

ROIC measures the after-tax return that the company provides for all of its investors. Because ROIC does not vary with changes in capital structure, the standard deviation of ROIC (σ_{ROIC}) measures the underlying risk of the firm before considering the effects of debt financing, thereby providing a good measure of business risk.[8]

We use Bigbee Electronics, a *debt-free (unlevered)* firm, to illustrate business risk. The top graph in Figure 13.1 shows the trend in Bigbee's return on invested capital, or ROIC, from 2010 through 2018. Graphs like this show security analysts and managers how much ROIC has varied in the past and thus might vary in the future. The lower graph shows the probability distribution of Bigbee's ROIC, based on the 2010–2018 data given in the top section.

Bigbee's ROIC fluctuations were caused by many factors—booms and recessions in the economy, successful new products introduced by Bigbee and its competitors, labor strikes, a fire in Bigbee's main plant, and so on. Similar events will doubtless occur in the future, and when they do, the realized ROIC will be higher or lower than the expected 9.0%. Further, there is always the possibility that a long-term disaster will strike, permanently depressing the company's earning power. For example, a competitor might introduce a new product that makes Bigbee's products totally obsolete and puts the company out of business—much like what happened to buggy manufacturers when automobiles were invented.

The more uncertainty there is about future EBIT and thus ROIC, the greater the company's *business risk.* Bigbee uses no debt, so its stockholders currently face only business risk. However, if it issues debt, its stockholders would face the existing business risk plus some additional financial risk. Business risk varies from industry to industry and also among firms in a given industry. Further, a firm's business risk can change over time. For example, the electric utilities were

[7]Also note that EBIT(1 − T) is the after-tax income the firm would have if it used no debt. Similarly, ROIC is the ROE the firm would have if it were debt-free.

[8]At the outset, we assume that changes in capital structure have no effect on the firm's operating performance. Later in the chapter, we discuss some circumstances when the level of debt financing may affect the company's operating performance (EBIT); in these circumstances, ROIC would vary with different debt levels.

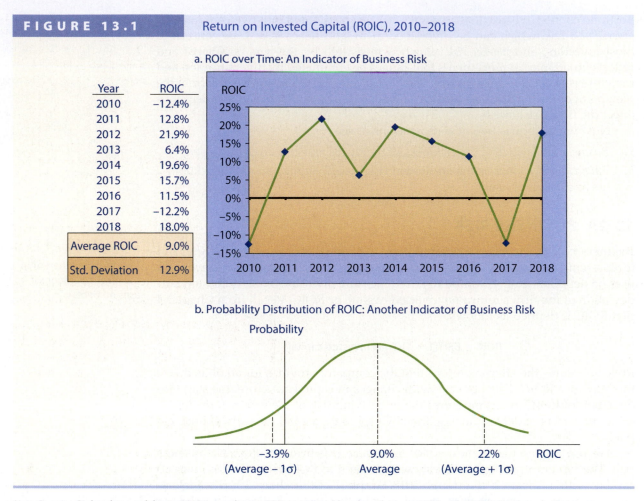

FIGURE 13.1 Return on Invested Capital (ROIC), 2010–2018

Year	ROIC
2010	−12.4%
2011	12.8%
2012	21.9%
2013	6.4%
2014	19.6%
2015	15.7%
2016	11.5%
2017	−12.2%
2018	18.0%
Average ROIC	9.0%
Std. Deviation	12.9%

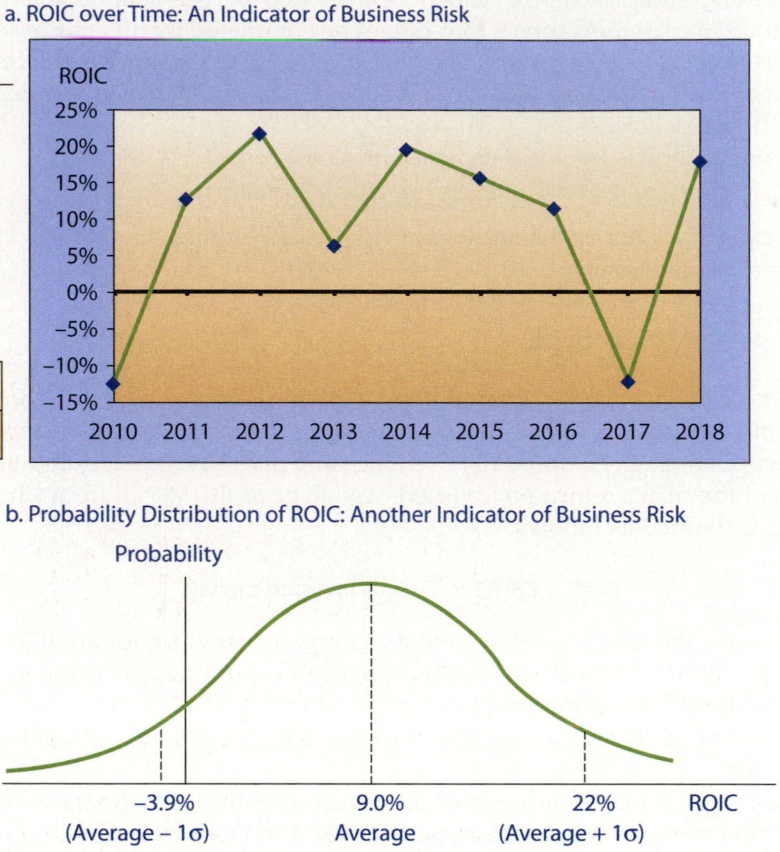

Note: Because Bigbee has no debt, its ROIC is equal to its ROE, so we could replace the term ROIC with ROE. Note, though, that as soon as debt is issued, ROE and ROIC will differ.

for many years regarded as having little business risk, but over the past few decades, utilities have faced increased competition and greater uncertainty regarding potential environmental regulations, both of which have somewhat increased the industry's risk. Today, food processors like Kraft Heinz and Pillsbury illustrate companies with low business risk, while cyclical manufacturers such as steel companies, as well as new start-up companies, have high business risk.[9]

13-2B FACTORS THAT AFFECT BUSINESS RISK

Business risk depends on a number of factors, including the following:

1. *Competition.* If a firm has a monopoly on a necessary product, it will have little risk from competition and thus have stable sales and sales prices. However, monopolistic firms' prices are often regulated, and they may not be able to raise prices enough to cover rising costs. Still, other things held constant, less competition lowers business risk.

[9]We have avoided any discussion of market versus company-specific risk in this section. We note now (1) that any action that increases business risk in the sense of stand-alone risk will generally increase a firm's beta coefficient and (2) that a part of business risk as we define it will generally be company specific and hence subject to elimination as a result of diversification by the firm's stockholders.

2. *Demand variability.* The more stable the demand for a firm's products, other things held constant, the lower its business risk.
3. *Sales price variability.* Firms whose products are sold in volatile markets are exposed to more business risk than firms whose output prices are stable, other things held constant.
4. *Input cost variability.* Firms whose input costs are uncertain have higher business risk.
5. *Product obsolescence.* Firms in high-tech industries like pharmaceuticals and computers depend on a constant stream of new products. The faster its products become obsolete, the greater a firm's business risk.
6. *Foreign risk exposure.* Firms that generate a high percentage of their earnings overseas are subject to earnings declines due to exchange rate fluctuations. They are also exposed to political risk.
7. *Regulatory risk and legal exposure.* Firms that operate in highly regulated industries such as financial services and utilities are subject to changes in the regulatory environment that may have a profound effect on the company's current and future profitability. Other companies face significant legal exposure that could damage the company if they are forced to pay large settlements. For example in April 2016, in the aftermath of the Deepwater Horizon oil spill in the Gulf of Mexico, BP agreed to a $5.5 billion settlement for civil damages that will be paid over a period of 16 years. BP previously reached a settlement related to criminal fines and penalties. Tobacco companies and pharmaceutical companies have also incurred huge legal costs after being sued for damages created by their products.
8. *The extent to which costs are fixed: operating leverage.* If a high percentage of its costs are fixed and thus do not decline when demand falls, this increases the firm's business risk. This factor is called *operating leverage,* and it is discussed in the next section.

Each of these factors is determined partly by industry characteristics and partly by managerial decisions. For example, Bigbee could reduce input cost volatility by negotiating long-term labor and supply contracts, but it might have to pay more than the current spot price to obtain such contracts.[10]

13-2C OPERATING LEVERAGE

As noted earlier, business risk depends in part on the extent to which a firm builds fixed costs into its operations—if fixed costs are high, even a small decline in sales can lead to a large decline in ROIC. So other things held constant, the higher a firm's fixed costs, the greater its business risk. Higher fixed costs are generally associated with more highly automated, capital-intensive firms and industries. However, businesses that employ highly skilled workers who must be retained and paid even during recessions also have relatively high fixed costs, as do firms with high product development costs, because the amortization of development costs is a fixed cost.

When a high percentage of total costs are fixed, the firm is said to have a high degree of **operating leverage**. In physics, leverage implies the use of a lever to raise a heavy object with a small force. In politics, if people have leverage, their smallest word or action can accomplish a great deal. *In business terminology, a high degree of operating leverage, other factors held constant, implies that a relatively small change in sales results in a large change in ROIC.*

Operating Leverage
The extent to which fixed costs are used in a firm's operations.

[10]*Hedging,* which involves actions that lock in future costs or prices, can also be used to reduce business risk. For example, a jewelry company like Tiffany might buy gold futures to freeze the price it must pay for gold, while a gold mining firm like Newmont Mining might *sell* gold futures to lock in the price it will earn on the gold it produces.

Figure 13.2 illustrates the concept of operating leverage by comparing the results that Bigbee could expect if it used different degrees of operating leverage. Plan A calls for a relatively small amount of fixed costs, $25,000. Here the firm would not have much automated equipment, so its depreciation, maintenance, property taxes, and so forth would be low. However, the total operating costs line has a relatively steep slope, indicating that variable costs per unit are higher than they would be if the firm used more operating leverage. Plan B calls for a higher level of fixed costs, $70,000. Here the firm uses automated equipment (with which one operator can turn out a few or many units at the same labor cost) to a much larger extent. The break-even point is higher under Plan B—breakeven occurs at 70,000 units under Plan B versus only 50,000 units under Plan A.

Operating Breakeven
The output quantity at which EBIT = 0.

We can calculate the break-even quantity by recognizing that **operating breakeven** occurs when earnings before interest and taxes (EBIT) = 0:[11]

$$\text{EBIT} = \text{PQ} - \text{VQ} - \text{F} = 0 \qquad \textbf{13.1}$$

Here P is average sales price per unit of output, Q is units of output, V is variable cost per unit, and F is fixed operating costs. If we solve for the break-even quantity, Q_{BE}, we get this expression:

$$Q_{BE} = \frac{F}{P - V} \qquad \textbf{13.1a}$$

Thus, for Plan A:

$$Q_{BE} = \frac{\$25{,}000}{\$2.00 - \$1.50} = 50{,}000 \text{ units}$$

And for Plan B:

$$Q_{BE} = \frac{\$70{,}000}{\$2.00 - \$1.00} = 70{,}000 \text{ units}$$

How does operating leverage affect business risk? *Other things held constant, the higher a firm's operating leverage, the higher its business risk.* This point is demonstrated in Figure 13.3, where we develop probability distributions for ROIC under Plans A and B.

The top section of Figure 13.3 graphs the probability distribution of sales that was presented in tabular form in Figure 13.2. The sales probability distribution depends on how demand for the product varies, not on whether the product is manufactured by Plan A or by Plan B. Therefore, the same sales probability distribution applies to both production plans. This distribution has expected sales of $200,000; it ranges from zero to about $400,000, with a standard deviation of σ_{Sales} = $98,793.

We use the sales probability distribution, together with the operating costs at each sales level, to develop graphs of the ROIC probability distributions under Plans A and B. These are shown in the lower section of Figure 13.3. Plan B has a higher expected ROIC, but this plan also entails a much higher probability of losses. Plan B, the one with more fixed costs and a higher degree of operating leverage, is clearly riskier. *In general, holding other factors constant, the higher the degree of operating leverage, the greater the firm's business risk.* In the discussion that

[11]This definition of breakeven does not include any fixed financial costs. If there were fixed financial costs, the firm would suffer an accounting loss at the operating break-even point. We introduce financial costs shortly.

FIGURE 13.2 Illustration of Operating Leverage

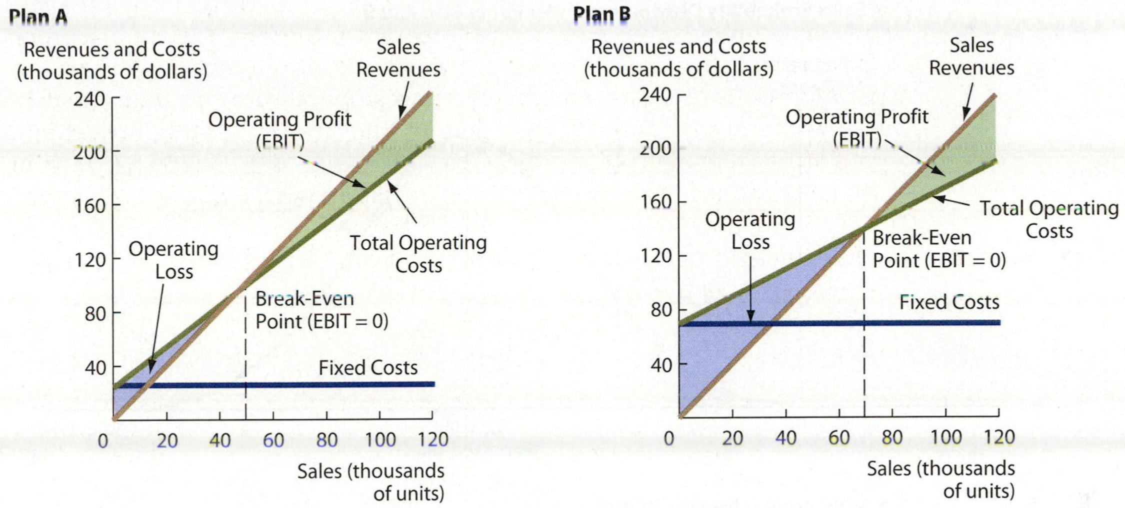

	Plan A	Plan B
Price	\$ 2.00	\$ 2.00
Variable costs	\$ 1.50	\$ 1.00
Fixed costs	\$ 25,000	\$ 70,000
Invested capital	\$200,000	\$200,000
Tax rate	25%	25%

				Plan A				Plan B			
Demand	**Probability**	**Units Sold**	**Dollar Sales**	**Operating Costs**	**Operating Profit (EBIT)**	**EBIT(1 − T)**	**ROIC**	**Operating Costs**	**Operating Profit (EBIT)**	**EBIT(1 − T)**	**ROIC**
Terrible	0.05	0	\$ 0	\$ 25,000	(\$25,000)	(\$18,750)	(9.38)%	\$ 70,000	(\$ 70,000)	(\$52,500)	(26.25)%
Poor	0.20	40,000	80,000	85,000	(5,000)	(3,750)	(1.88)	110,000	(30,000)	(22,500)	(11.25)
Normal	0.50	100,000	200,000	175,000	25,000	18,750	9.38	170,000	30,000	22,500	11.25
Good	0.20	160,000	320,000	265,000	55,000	41,250	20.63	230,000	90,000	67,500	33.75
Wonderful	0.05	200,000	400,000	325,000	75,000	56,250	28.13	270,000	130,000	97,500	48.75
Expected value		100,000	\$200,000	\$175,000	\$ 25,000	\$ 18,750	9.38%	\$ 170,000	\$ 30,000	\$22,500	11.25%
Standard deviation					\$ 24,698		9.26%		\$ 49,396		18.52%
Coefficient of variation					0.99		0.99		1.65		1.65

Notes:
a. Operating costs = Variable costs + Fixed costs
b. Because the company has no debt, Net Income = EBIT(1 − T) and ROE = ROIC, but these equations would no longer hold once the company had outstanding debt.
c. The break-even sales levels for Plans A and B are not shown in the table, but it is 50,000 units or \$100,000 for A and 70,000 units or \$140,000 for B.
d. The expected values, standard deviations, and coefficients of variation were found using procedures discussed in Chapter 8.

follows, we assume that Bigbee has decided to go ahead with Plan B because its management believes that the higher expected return is sufficient to compensate for the higher risk.

To what extent can firms control their operating leverage? To a large extent, operating leverage is determined by technology. Electric utilities, telephone companies, airlines, steel mills, and chemical companies must have

FIGURE 13.3 Analysis of Business Risk

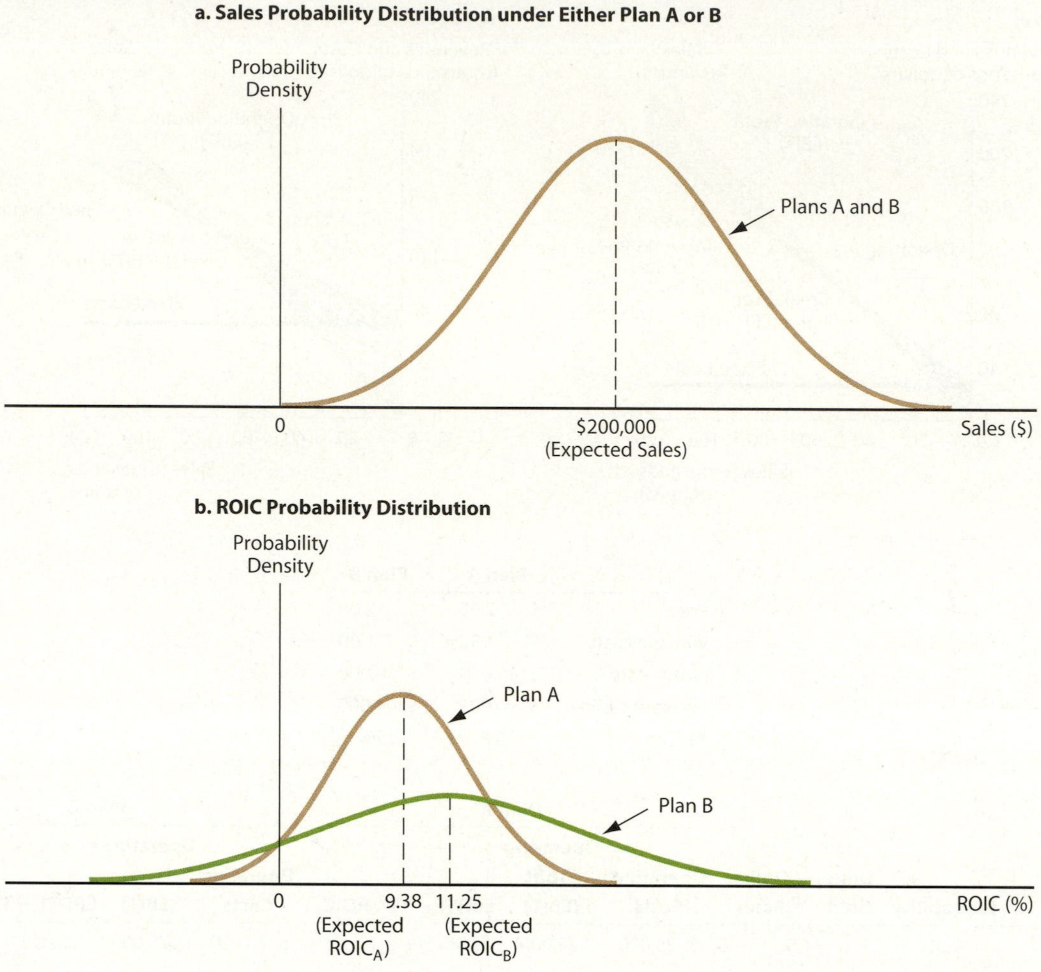

Note: We are using continuous distributions to approximate the discrete distributions contained in Figure 13.2.

large investments in fixed assets, and this results in high fixed costs and operating leverage. Similarly, pharmaceutical, auto, computer, and other companies must spend heavily to develop new products, and product-development costs increase operating leverage. Grocery stores and service businesses such as accounting and consulting firms, on the other hand, generally have significantly lower fixed costs and therefore lower operating leverage. Still, although industry factors do exert a major influence, all firms have some control over their operating leverage. For example, an electric utility can expand its generating capacity by building either gas-fired or nuclear plants. Nuclear plants would require larger investments and would have higher fixed costs, but their variable operating costs would be relatively low. Gas-fired plants, on the other hand, would require smaller investments and would have lower fixed costs, but the variable costs (for gas) would be high. So, by its capital budgeting decisions, a utility (or any other company) can influence its operating leverage and hence its business risk.

The concept of operating leverage was originally developed for use in capital budgeting. Mutually exclusive projects that involve alternative production methods for a given product often have different degrees of operating leverage and thus different break-even points and different degrees of risk. Bigbee Electronics and many other companies regularly undertake a type of break-even analysis (the sensitivity analysis discussed in Chapter 12) for each proposed project as a part of their regular capital budgeting process. Still, once a corporation's operating leverage has been established, this factor exerts a major influence on its capital structure decision.

13-2D FINANCIAL RISK

Financial Risk
An increase in stockholders' risk, over and above the firm's basic business risk, resulting from the use of financial leverage.

Financial risk is the additional risk placed on the common stockholders as a result of the decision to finance with debt. Conceptually, stockholders face a certain amount of risk that is inherent in the firm's operations—this is its business risk, defined as the uncertainty inherent in projections of future operating income. If a firm uses debt (financial leverage), this concentrates the business risk on common stockholders. To illustrate, suppose 10 people decide to form a corporation to own and operate a large apartment complex. There is a certain amount of business risk in the operation. If the firm is capitalized only with common equity and if each person buys 10% of the stock, each investor will share equally in the business risk. However, suppose the firm is capitalized with 50% debt and 50% equity, with five of the investors putting up their capital as debt and the other five putting up their money as equity. The debtholders will receive a fixed payment, and it will come before the stockholders receive anything. Also, if the firm goes bankrupt, the debtholders must be paid off before the stockholders receive anything. In this case, the five investors who put up the equity will have to bear all of the business risk, so the common stock will be twice as risky as it would have been had the firm been financed only with equity. *Thus, the use of debt, or* **financial leverage**, *concentrates the firm's business risk on the stockholders.* (In Web Appendix 13A, we describe in more detail the interaction between operating leverage and financial leverage.)

Financial Leverage
The extent to which fixed-income securities (debt and preferred stock) are used in a firm's capital structure.

To illustrate the business risk concentration, we can extend the Bigbee Electronics example. To date, the company has never used debt, but the treasurer is now considering a possible change in its capital structure.[12] As we mentioned earlier, changes in debt will not affect ROIC, but it will affect the proportion of risk borne by the firm's stockholders. More specifically, changes in the use of debt would cause changes in earnings per share (EPS) as well as changes in risk—both would affect the stock price. To understand the relationship between financial leverage and EPS, first consider Table 13.2, which shows how Bigbee's cost of debt would vary if it used different amounts of debt to finance a fixed amount of capital.

TABLE 13.2 Interest Rates for Bigbee with Different Debt/Capital Ratios

Amount Borrowed[a]	Debt/Capital Ratio	Interest Rate, r_d, on All Debt
$20,000	10%	4.0%
40,000	20	4.3
60,000	30	5.0
80,000	40	5.8
100,000	50	7.2
120,000	60	10.0

Note:
[a] We assume that the firm must borrow in increments of $20,000. We also assume that Bigbee is unable to borrow more than $120,000, which is 60% of its total capital, due to restrictions in its corporate charter.

[12] The 2017 Tax Act limits the corporate interest deduction on debt to 30% of income (measured as EBITDA for 2018–2021 and as EBIT thereafter). To simplify things in this example, we assume Bigbee Electronics is a small company with average sales of $25 million or less during the past 3 years, so it is exempt from the interest deduction limitation.

The higher the percentage of debt in the capital structure, the riskier the debt and, for that reason, the higher the interest rate lenders would charge.

For now, assume that only two financing choices are being considered—remain at 100% equity or shift to 50% debt and 50% equity. We also assume that with no debt, Bigbee has 10,000 shares of common stock outstanding, and if it decides to change its capital structure, common stock would be repurchased at the $20 current stock price. Now consider Table 13.3, which shows how the financing choice would affect Bigbee's profitability and risk.

First, focus on Section I, which assumes that Bigbee uses no debt. Because debt is zero, interest is also zero; hence net income is equal to EBIT(1−T). ROIC is calculated as EBIT(1−T) divided by invested capital. Bigbee's invested capital, which is $200,000, equals equity because it has no debt. Net income is then divided by the $200,000 of equity to calculate ROE. For simplicity, we have assumed that the company receives a full tax credit the year in which any losses occur. In reality, these losses would have to be carried forward to be applied against any future gains.[13] The ROE at each sales level is then multiplied by the probability of that sales level to calculate the 11.25% expected ROE. Note that this 11.25% is the same as that found in Figure 13.2 for Plan B. Finally, because there is no debt, the percentages calculated in the ROIC column are identical to those in the ROE column.

Section I of the table also calculates Bigbee's EPS for each scenario, under the assumption that the company continues to use no debt. Net income is divided by the 10,000 common shares outstanding to obtain EPS. If demand is terrible, the EPS will be −$5.25, but if demand is wonderful, the EPS will rise to $9.75. The EPS at each sales level is then multiplied by the probability of that level to calculate the expected EPS, which is $2.25 if Bigbee uses no debt. We also calculate the standard deviation of EPS and the coefficient of variation as indicators of the firm's risk at a zero debt ratio: σ_{EPS} = \$3.70 and CV_{EPS} = 1.65.

Now look at Section II, the situation if Bigbee decides to use 50% debt with an interest rate of 7.2%. Neither sales nor operating costs will be affected—the EBIT, the EBIT(1 − T), and the ROIC columns are the same, whether Bigbee has zero debt or 50% debt. However, the company now has $100,000 of debt with a cost of 7.2%; thus, its interest expense is $7,200. This interest must be paid regardless of the state of the economy—if it is not paid, the company will be forced into bankruptcy, and stockholders will be wiped out. Therefore, we show a $7,200 cost in column 6 as a fixed number for all sales levels. Column 7 shows the resulting net income. When net income is divided by the equity investment—which now is only $100,000 because $100,000 of the $200,000 invested capital was financed with debt—we find the ROE under each demand state. If demand is terrible and sales are zero, a very large loss will be incurred, and the ROE will be −57.90%. However, if demand is wonderful, ROE will be 92.10%. The expected ROE is the probability-weighted average, which is 17.10% if the company uses 50% debt. Note that when debt is added to the firm's capital structure, ROE and ROIC are no longer equal.

Typically, using debt increases the expected rate of return for an investment. However, debt also increases risk to the common stockholders. This situation holds with our example—financial leverage raises the expected ROE from 11.25% to 17.10%, but it also increases the risk of the investment as measured by the coefficient of variation of ROE, which rises from 1.65 to 2.17. Figure 13.4 graphs the data in Table 13.3. It demonstrates that using financial leverage increases the expected ROE but that it also flattens out the probability distribution, increases the probability of a large loss, and thus increases the risk borne by stockholders.

---

[13]As we discuss in Chapter 3, Section 3-9B of this text, the process of carrying forward losses to future gains is more complicated than simply offsetting losses against gains because the amount carried forward in any one year is limited to 80% of taxable income. A more precise calculation would require an estimate of the company's future earnings, while also taking into account current limitations on the amount of the losses that are able to be carried forward in a single year.

Effects of Financial Leverage: Bigbee Electronics Financed with Zero Debt or 50% Debt

TABLE 13.3

Section I. Zero Debt

Debt/Capital ratio	0%
Tax rate	25%
Invested capital	$200,000
Debt	$ 0
Equity	$200,000
Shares outstanding	10,000

Demand for Product (1)	Probability (2)	EBIT (3)	EBIT(1 − T) (4)	ROIC (5)	Interest (6)	Net Income = (EBIT − I)(1 − T) (7)	ROE (8)	EPS[a] (9)
Terrible	0.05	($ 70,000)	($52,500)	(26.25)%	$0	($52,500)	(26.25)%	($5.25)
Poor	0.20	(30,000)	(22,500)	(11.25)	0	(22,500)	(11.25)	(2.25)
Normal	0.50	30,000	22,500	11.25	0	22,500	11.25	2.25
Good	0.20	90,000	67,500	33.75	0	67,500	33.75	6.75
Wonderful	0.05	130,000	97,500	48.75	0	97,500	48.75	9.75
Expected value		$ 30,000	$22,500	11.25%	$0	22,500	11.25%	$2.25
Standard deviation							18.52%	$3.70
Coefficient of variation							1.65	1.65

Section II. 50% Debt

Debt/Capital ratio	50%
Tax rate	25%
Invested capital	$200,000
Debt	$100,000
Interest rate	7.2%
Equity	$100,000
Shares outstanding	5,000

Demand for Product (1)	Probability (2)	EBIT (3)	EBIT(1 − T) (4)	ROIC (5)	Interest (6)	Net Income = (EBIT − I)(1 − T) (7)	ROE (8)	EPS[a] (9)
Terrible	0.05	($ 70,000)	($52,500)	(26.25)%	$7,200	($57,900)	(57.90)%	($11.58)
Poor	0.20	(30,000)	(22,500)	(11.25)	7,200	(27,900)	(27.90)	(5.58)
Normal	0.50	30,000	22,500	11.25	7,200	17,100	17.10	3.42
Good	0.20	90,000	67,500	33.75	7,200	62,100	62.10	12.42
Wonderful	0.05	130,000	97,500	48.75	7,200	92,100	92.10	18.42
Expected value		$ 30,000	$22,500	11.25%	$7,200	$17,100	17.10%	$3.42
Standard deviation							37.05%	$7.41
Coefficient of variation							2.17	2.17

Assumptions:

1. In terms of its operating leverage, Bigbee has chosen Plan B. The probability distribution and EBIT are obtained from Figure 13.2.
2. Sales and operating costs (and thus EBIT) are not affected by the financing decision. Therefore, EBIT, EBIT(1 − T), and ROIC under both financing plans are identical and are taken from Figure 13.2.
3. For simplicity, we have assumed that the company receives a full tax credit the year in which any losses occur. In reality, these losses would have to be carried forward to be applied against any future gains. Consequently, a more precise calculation would require an estimate of the company's future earnings, while also taking into account current limitations on the amount of the losses that are able to be carried forward in a single year.

[a]The EPS figures can also be obtained using the following formula in which the numerator amounts to an income statement at a given sales level displayed horizontally:

$$\text{EPS} = \frac{(\text{Sales} - \text{Fixed costs} - \text{Variable costs} - \text{Interest})(1 - \text{Tax rate})}{\text{Shares outstanding}} = \frac{(\text{EBIT} - \text{I})(1 - \text{T})}{\text{Shares outstanding}}$$

For example, with zero debt and sales = $200,000, EPS is $2.25:

$$\text{EPS}_{D/(D+E)=0\%} = \frac{(\$200{,}000 - \$70{,}000 - \$100{,}000 - \$0)(0.75)}{10{,}000} = \$2.25$$

With 50% debt and sales = $200,000, EPS is $3.42:

$$\text{EPS}_{D/(D+E)=50\%} = \frac{(\$200{,}000 - \$70{,}000 - \$100{,}000 - \$7{,}200)(0.75)}{5{,}000} = \$3.42$$

Refer to the tabular data given in Figure 13.2 to arrive at sales, fixed costs, and variable costs that are used in the preceding equations.

Note: Because the demand for the product has a normal distribution, the probability distribution is symmetrical. Consequently, the expected values equal the values under normal demand. This would not occur under an asymmetrical probability distribution.

FIGURE 13.4 ROE Probability Distributions for Bigbee Electronics, with and without Financial Leverage

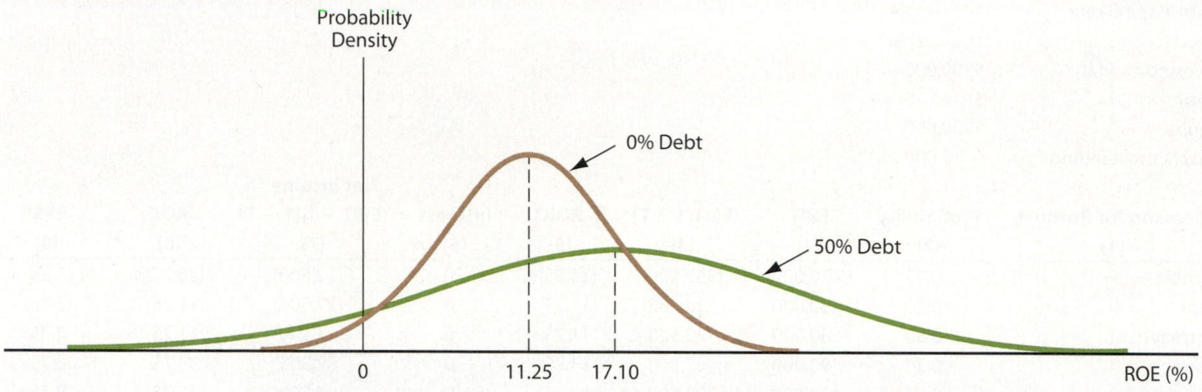

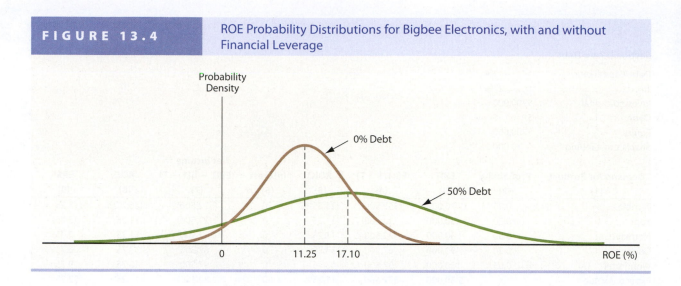

We can also calculate Bigbee's EPS if it uses 50% debt. With Debt = \$0, 10,000 shares would be outstanding, but if half the equity was replaced by debt (Debt = \$100,000), only 5,000 shares would be outstanding. We can determine the EPS that would result at each of the possible demand levels under the different capital structures.[14] With no debt, EPS would be −\$5.25 if demand was terrible, \$2.25 if demand was normal, and \$9.75 if demand was wonderful. With 50% debt, EPS would be −\$11.58 if demand was terrible, \$3.42 if demand was normal, and \$18.42 if demand was wonderful. Expected EPS would be \$2.25 with no debt but \$3.42 with 50% financial leverage. Although expected EPS would be much higher if financial leverage was employed, the risk of low, or even negative, EPS would also be higher if debt was used.

Another view of the relationships among expected EPS, risk, and financial leverage is presented in Figure 13.5. The tabular data in the lower section were calculated in the manner set forth in Table 13.3, and the graphs plot these data. Here we see that expected EPS rises until the firm is financed with 50% debt. Interest charges rise, but this effect is more than offset by the declining number of shares outstanding as debt is substituted for equity. However, EPS peaks at a debt ratio of 50%, beyond which interest rates rise so rapidly that EPS falls in spite of the falling number of shares outstanding.[15] The right graph in Figure 13.5 shows that risk, as measured by the coefficient of variation of EPS, rises continuously and at an increasing rate as debt is substituted for equity.

These examples make it clear that using leverage has both positive and negative effects: Higher leverage increases expected EPS (in this example, until the Debt/Capital ratio equals 50%), but it also increases risk. When determining its optimal capital structure, Bigbee needs to balance these positive and negative effects of leverage. This issue is discussed in the following sections.

---

[14]We assume in this example that the firm could change its capital structure by repurchasing common stock at its book value of \$100,000/5,000 shares = \$20 per share. However, the firm may have to pay a higher price to repurchase its stock on the open market. If Bigbee had to pay \$22 per share, it could repurchase only \$100,000/\$22 = 4,545 shares, and in this case, expected EPS would be only \$17,100/(10,000 − 4,545) = \$17,100/5,455 = \$3.13 rather than \$3.42.

[15]In this context and in the remainder of this chapter, the debt ratio we are referring to is the Debt/Capital ratio.

FIGURE 13.5 Relationships among Expected EPS, Risk, and Financial Leverage

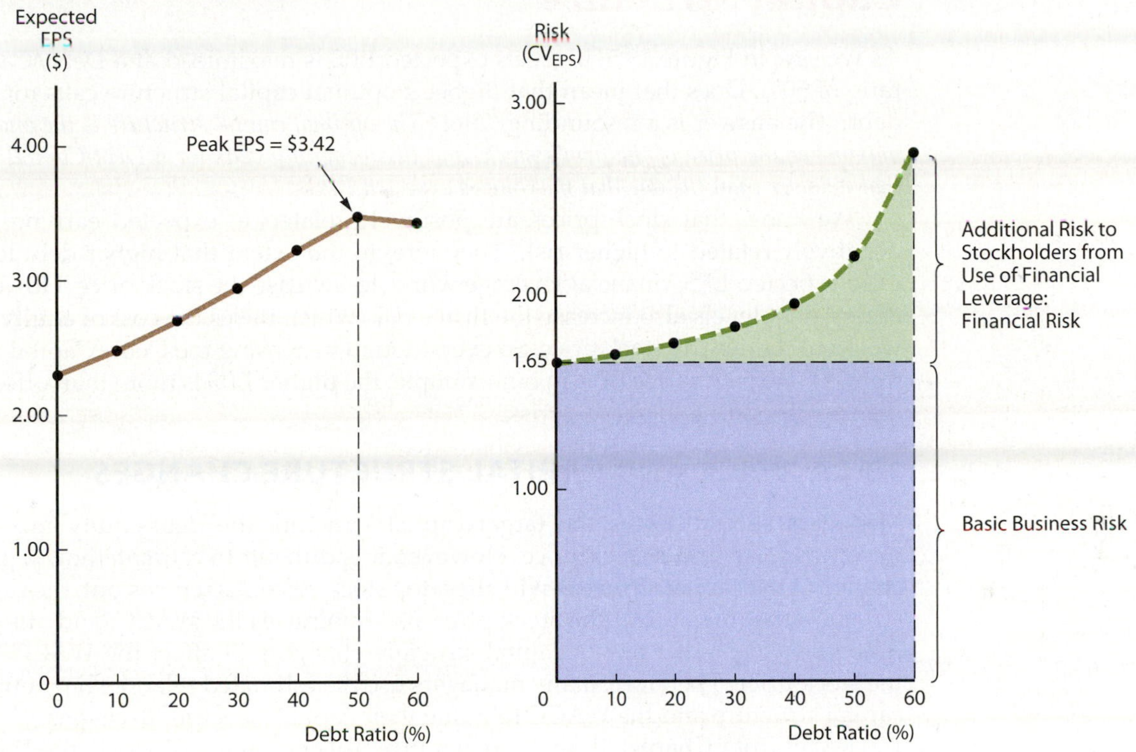

Debt/Capital	Expected EPS	Standard Deviation of EPS	Coefficient of Variation
0%[a]	$2.25[a]	$3.70[a]	1.65[a]
10	2.43	4.12	1.69
20	2.65	4.63	1.75
30	2.89	5.29	1.83
40	3.17	6.17	1.95
50[a]	3.42[a]	7.41[a]	2.17[a]
60	3.38	9.26	2.74

Note:
[a]Values for Debt/Capital = 0% and 50% are taken from Table 13.3. Values at other Debt/Capital ratios were calculated similarly.

Self*Test*

What is business risk, and how can it be measured?

What are some determinants of business risk?

Why does business risk vary from industry to industry?

What is operating leverage?

How does operating leverage affect business risk?

What is financial risk, and how does it arise?

Explain this statement: Using financial leverage has both good and bad effects.

13-3 Determining the Optimal Capital Structure

As we saw in Figure 13.5, Bigbee's expected EPS is maximized at a Debt/Capital ratio of 50%. Does that mean that Bigbee's optimal capital structure calls for 50% debt? The answer is a resounding "No!" *The optimal capital structure is the one that maximizes the price of the firm's stock, and this generally calls for a Debt/Capital ratio that is lower than the one that maximizes expected EPS.*

We know that stock prices are positively related to expected earnings but negatively related to higher risk. Therefore, to the extent that higher debt levels raise expected EPS, financial leverage works to increase the stock price. However, higher debt levels also increase the firm's risk, which raises the cost of equity and works to reduce the stock price. So even though increasing the Debt/Capital ratio from 40% to 50% raises EPS, in our example, the higher EPS is more than offset by the corresponding increase in risk.

13-3A WACC AND CAPITAL STRUCTURE CHANGES

Managers should set as the target capital structure the debt-equity mix that maximizes the firm's stock price. However, it is difficult to estimate how a given change in the capital structure will affect the stock price. As it turns out, the capital structure that maximizes the stock price also minimizes the WACC, and at times, it is easier to predict how a capital structure change will affect the WACC than the stock price. Therefore, many managers use the estimated relationship between capital structure and the WACC to guide their capital structure decisions.

Recall from Chapter 10 that when a firm uses no preferred stock, the WACC is found as follows:

$$\text{WACC} = w_d(r_d)(1 - T) + w_c(r_s)$$

In this expression, w_d and w_c represent the percentage of debt and equity in the firm's capital structure, respectively, and they must sum to 1.0. Note that in Table 13.4, an increase in the Debt/Capital ratio increases the costs of both debt and equity. [The cost of debt, r_d, is taken from Table 13.2 but multiplied by $(1 - T)$ to put it on an after-tax basis.] Bondholders recognize that if a firm has a higher Debt/Capital ratio, this increases the risk of financial distress, which leads to higher interest rates.

In practice, financial managers use financial statement forecasting models to determine how changes in the debt-to-capital ratio will affect the current ratio, times-interest-earned (TIE) ratio, and EBITDA coverage ratio.[16] They then discuss their projected ratios with bankers and bond rating agencies, which ask probing questions and may make their own adjustments to the firm's forecasts. The bankers and rating agencies compare the firm's ratios with those of other firms in its industry and arrive at a "what if" rating and corresponding interest rate. Moreover, if the company plans to issue bonds to the public, the SEC requires that it inform investors what the coverages will be after the new bonds have been sold. Recognizing all this, sophisticated financial managers use their forecasted ratios to predict how bankers and other lenders will judge their firms' risks and thus their costs of debt. Experienced financial managers and investment bankers can judge quite accurately the effects of capital structure on the cost of debt.

13-3B THE HAMADA EQUATION

Increasing the debt ratio increases the risk that bondholders face and thus the cost of debt. More debt also raises the risk borne by stockholders, which raises the cost of

[16]We will discuss financial statement forecasts in Chapter 16.

Bigbee's Stock Price and WACC Estimates with Different Debt/Capital Ratios **TABLE 13.4**

w_d = Debt/Capital (1)	Debt/Equity[a] (2)	$r_d(1-T)$ (3)	Expected EPS (and DPS)[b] (4)	Estimated Beta[c] (5)	$r_s = [r_{RF} + (RP_M)b]$[d] (6)	Estimated Price[e] (7)	Resulting P/E Ratio (8)	WACC[f] (9)
0%	0.00%	3.00%	$2.25	1.375	11.25%	$20.00	8.89×	11.25%
10	11.11	3.00	2.43	1.490	11.94	20.38	8.38	11.04
20	25.00	3.23	2.65	1.633	12.80	20.72	7.81	10.88
30	42.86	3.75	2.89	1.817	13.90	20.81	7.19	10.86
40	66.67	4.35	3.17	2.063	15.38	20.62	6.50	10.97
50	100.00	5.40	3.42	2.406	17.44	19.61	5.73	11.42
60	150.00	7.50	3.38	2.922	20.53	16.44	4.87	12.71

Notes:

[a]$D/E = \frac{w_d}{1 - w_d}$, where w_d = Debt/(Debt + Equity) = Debt/Capital.

[b]Bigbee pays all of its earnings out as dividends, so EPS = DPS.

[c]The firm's unlevered beta, b_U, is 1.375. The remaining betas were calculated using the Hamada equation, given the unlevered beta, tax rate, and D/E ratio as inputs.

[d]We assume that r_{RF} = 3% and RP_M = 6%. Therefore, at Debt/Capital = 0, r_s = 3% + (6%)1.375 = 11.25%. Other values of r_s are calculated similarly.

[e]Because all earnings are paid out as dividends, no retained earnings will be reinvested in the business and growth in EPS and DPS will be zero. Hence, the zero growth stock price model developed in Chapter 9 can be used to estimate the price of Bigbee's stock. For example, at Debt/Capital = 0,

$$P_0 = \frac{DPS}{r_s} = \frac{\$2.25}{0.1125} = \$20$$

Other prices were calculated similarly.

[f]Column 9 values are found with the weighted average cost of capital (WACC) equation developed in Chapter 10:

$$WACC = w_d(r_d)(1 - T) + w_c(r_s)$$

For example, at Debt/Capital = 30%,

$$WACC = 0.3(5.0\%)(0.75) + 0.7(13.90\%) = 10.86\%$$

equity, r_s. It is harder to quantify leverage's effects on the cost of equity, but a theoretical formula can help measure the effect.

To begin, recall from Chapter 8 that a stock's beta is the relevant measure of risk for a diversified investor. Moreover, beta increases with financial leverage. Robert Hamada formulated the following equation to quantify this effect:[17]

$$b_L = b_U[1 + (1 - T)(D/E)] \quad (13.2)$$

Here b_L is the firm's current beta, which we now assume is based on the existence of some financial leverage, and b_U is the firm's beta if the firm were debt-free, or unlevered.[18] If the firm were debt-free, its beta would depend entirely on its business risk and thus would be a measure of the firm's "basic business risk." D/E is

[17]See Robert S. Hamada, "Portfolio Analysis, Market Equilibrium, and Corporation Finance," *Journal of Finance*, vol. 24, no. 1 (March 1969), pp. 13–31.

[18]Note that Equation 13.2 is the original equation that Hamada put forward, and it was based on a set of assumptions. The most notable were (a) that the beta of the company's debt is zero, (b) that the level of debt is constant, and (c) that the values of the company's interest tax shields are discounted at the before-tax cost of debt. Other researchers have derived alternative equations that are based on different assumptions. For example, one commonly used alternative assumes that the company's debt ratio remains constant and that the interest tax shields are discounted at the unlevered cost of equity. In this case, the resulting equation is as follows:

$$b_L = b_U(1 + D/E)$$

the measure of financial leverage as used in the Hamada equation, and T is the corporate tax rate.[19]

Now recall the CAPM version of the cost of equity:

$$r_s = r_{RF} + (RP_M)b_i$$

Note that beta is the only variable in the equity cost equation that is under management's control. The other two variables, r_{RF} and RP_M, are determined by market forces that are beyond the firm's control, but b_L is determined by the firm's operating decisions, which as we saw earlier affect its basic business risk, and by its capital structure decisions as reflected in its debt (or D/E) ratio.

Unlevered Beta, b_U The firm's beta coefficient if it has no debt.

We can solve Equation 13.2 to find the **unlevered beta, b_U**, obtaining Equation 13.2a:

$$b_U = b_L/[1 + (1 - T)(D/E)] \qquad \textbf{13.2a}$$

Because the current (levered) beta is known, as are the tax rate and the debt/equity ratio, we can insert values for these known variables and find the unlevered beta. The unlevered beta can then be used in Equation 13.2 with different debt levels to find the levered betas that would exist at those different debt levels. The resulting betas can be used to find the cost of equity at different debt levels.

We can illustrate this with Bigbee Electronics. First, assume that the risk-free rate of return, r_{RF}, is 3% and that the market risk premium, RP_M, is 6%. Next, we need the unlevered beta, b_U. Because Bigbee has no debt, its D/E = 0. Therefore, its current 1.375 beta is also its unlevered beta; hence, b_U = 1.375. With b_U, r_{RF}, and RP_M specified, we can use Equation 13.2 to estimate Bigbee's betas at different degrees of financial leverage and its resulting cost of equity at each debt ratio.

Bigbee's betas at different debt/equity ratios are shown in column 5 of Table 13.4. The current cost of equity is 11.25% as shown on the first line of column 6:

$$\begin{aligned} r_s &= r_{RF} + \text{Risk premium} \\ &= 3\% + (6\%)(1.375) \\ &= 3\% + 8.25\% = 11.25\% \end{aligned}$$

From this equation, we see that 3% is the risk-free rate and 8.25% is the firm's risk premium. Because Bigbee currently uses no debt, it has no financial risk. Therefore, the 8.25% risk premium is attributable entirely to business risk.

If Bigbee changes its capital structure by adding debt, this would increase the risk stockholders would have to bear. That, in turn, would result in a higher risk premium. Conceptually, a firm's cost of equity consists of the following components:

$$r_s = r_{RF} + \text{Premium for business risk} + \text{Premium for financial risk}$$

Figure 13.6, which is based on data shown in column 6 of Table 13.4, graphs Bigbee's costs of equity at different debt ratios. As the figure shows, r_s consists of the 3% risk-free rate, a constant 8.25% premium for business risk, and a premium for financial risk that starts at zero but rises at an increasing rate as the firm's debt ratio increases.

[19]Note that w_d is equal to the percentage of debt in the firm's capital structure, and it is equal to Debt/Capital = D/(D + E). So it follows that

$$\frac{D}{E} = \frac{w_d}{1 - w_d}$$

For example, if the firm has \$30 of debt and \$70 of equity, w_d = D/(D + E) = \$30/(\$30 + \$70) = 0.3. Therefore,

$$\frac{D}{E} = \frac{0.3}{1 - 0.3} = \frac{0.3}{0.7} = 0.4286$$

Note also that Hamada's equation assumes that debt and equity are reported at market values rather than accounting book values. This point is discussed at length in Chapter 16 of Eugene F. Brigham and Phillip R. Daves, *Intermediate Financial Management,* 13th edition (Mason, OH: Cengage Learning, 2019), where feedbacks among capital structure, stock prices, and capital costs are examined.

FIGURE 13.6 Bigbee's Required Rates of Return on Equity at Different Debt Levels

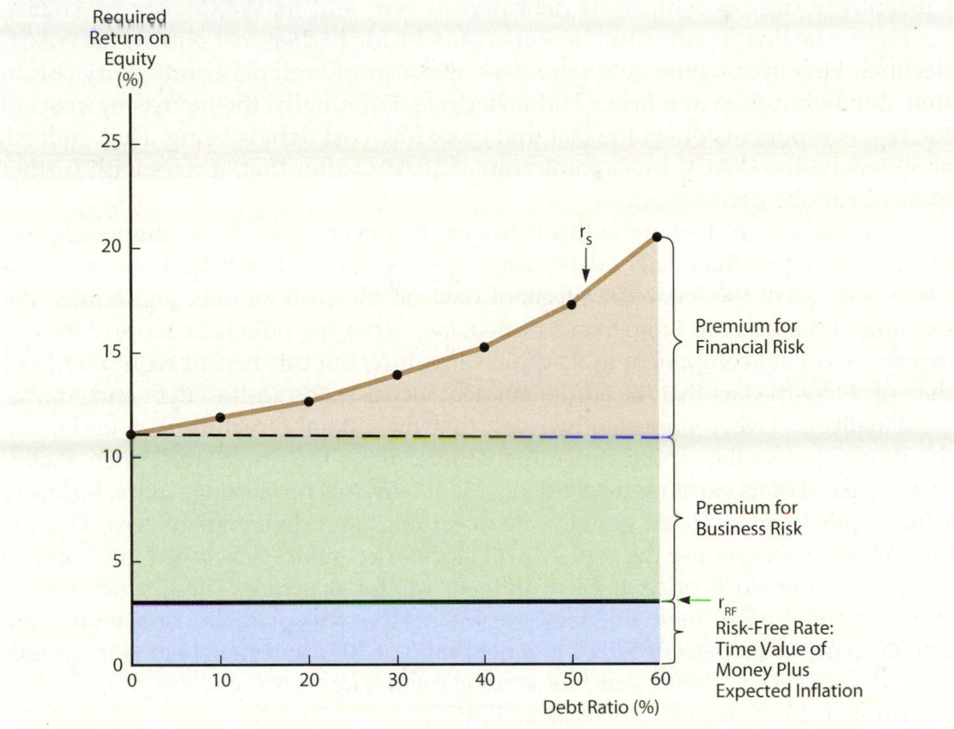

quick question

QUESTION:

Barnes Co. currently has a capital structure that consists of 40% debt and 60% common equity. The company has a 25% tax rate. Currently the levered beta (b_L) on the company's stock is 1.5.

a. What is the company's unlevered beta (b_U)?

b. What would be the company's levered beta (b_L) if Barnes changed its capital structure to 20% debt and 80% common equity?

ANSWER:

a. The company's unlevered beta is calculated as follows:

$$b_U = b_L/[1 + (1 - T)(D/E)]$$
$$b_U = 1.5/[1 + (0.75)(0.4/0.6)]$$
$$b_U = \mathbf{1.0}$$

Notice that $b_U < b_L$; b_U is the firm's beta if it had no debt. Beta is a measure of risk, so with no debt one would anticipate $b_U < b_L$.

b. Using the unlevered beta calculated in part a, the company's new levered beta under the changed capital structure of 20% debt and 80% equity is calculated as follows:

$$b_L = b_U[1 + (1 - T)(D/E)]$$
$$b_L = 1.0[1 + (0.75)(0.2/0.8)]$$
$$b_L = \mathbf{1.1875}$$

Again, notice that the new $b_L <$ original b_L. This result is consistent with the reduction in debt level. The risk is lower, and this is reflected in the new lower levered beta.

13-3C THE OPTIMAL CAPITAL STRUCTURE

Column 9 of Table 13.4 also shows Bigbee's WACCs at different capital structures. Currently, it has no debt, so its debt ratio is zero and its WACC is r_s = 11.25%. As Bigbee begins to substitute lower-cost debt for higher-cost equity, its WACC declines. However, as the debt ratio rises, the costs of both debt and equity rise, at first slowly but then at a faster and faster rate. Eventually, the increasing costs of the two components offset the fact that more low-cost debt is being used. Indeed, at 30% debt, the WACC hits a minimum of 10.86%; after that, it rises with further increases in the debt ratio.

Another way of looking at this is to note that even though the component cost of equity is higher than that of debt, using only lower-cost debt would not maximize value because of the feedback effects of debt on the costs of debt and equity. For example, if Bigbee used more than 30% debt (say, 40%), it would have more of the less expensive capital component in its capital structure, but this benefit would be more than offset by the fact that the additional debt increases the costs of debt and equity.

Finally, and very importantly, recall that the capital structure that minimizes the WACC is also the capital structure that maximizes the firm's stock price. Bigbee distributes all of its earnings as dividends, so it reinvests no earnings in the business, which leads to an expected growth rate in earnings and dividends of zero. Thus, in Bigbee's case, we can use the zero growth stock price model developed in Chapter 9 to estimate the stock price at each different capital structure. These estimates are shown in column 7 of Table 13.4. Here we see that the stock price first rises with financial leverage, hits a peak of $20.81 at a debt ratio of 30%, and then begins to decline. *Thus, Bigbee's optimal capital structure occurs at a debt ratio of 30%, and that debt ratio both maximizes its stock price and minimizes its WACC.*[20]

The EPS, cost of capital, and stock price data shown in Table 13.4 are plotted in Figure 13.7. As the graph shows, the debt ratio that maximizes Bigbee's expected EPS is 50%. However, the expected stock price is maximized, and the WACC is minimized at a 30% debt ratio. Thus, Bigbee's optimal capital structure calls for 30% debt and 70% equity. Management should set its target capital structure at these ratios, and if the existing ratios are off target, it should move toward that target when new securities are issued.

Self*Test*

What happens to the component costs of debt and equity when the debt ratio is increased? Why does this occur?

Using the Hamada equation, explain the effects of financial leverage on beta.

What is the equation for calculating a firm's unlevered beta?

Use the Hamada equation to calculate the unlevered beta for Firm X with the following data: b_L = 1.25, T = 25%, Debt/Capital = 0.42, and Equity/Capital = 0.58. **(b_U = 0.8101)**

What would be the cost of equity for Firm X at Equity/Capital ratios of 1.0 (no debt) and 0.58 assuming that r_{RF} = 5% and RP_M = 4%? **(8.24%,10%)**

Using a graph and illustrative data, discuss the premiums for financial risk and business risk at different debt levels. Do these premiums vary depending on the debt level? Explain.

Is expected EPS generally maximized at the optimal capital structure? Explain.

[20]We could also estimate the stock price if some earnings were retained and the expected growth rate were positive. However, this would complicate the analysis, and it is another reason we generally analyze the optimal capital structure decision using the WACC rather than the stock price.

FIGURE 13.7 Effects of Capital Structure on EPS, Cost of Capital, and Stock Price

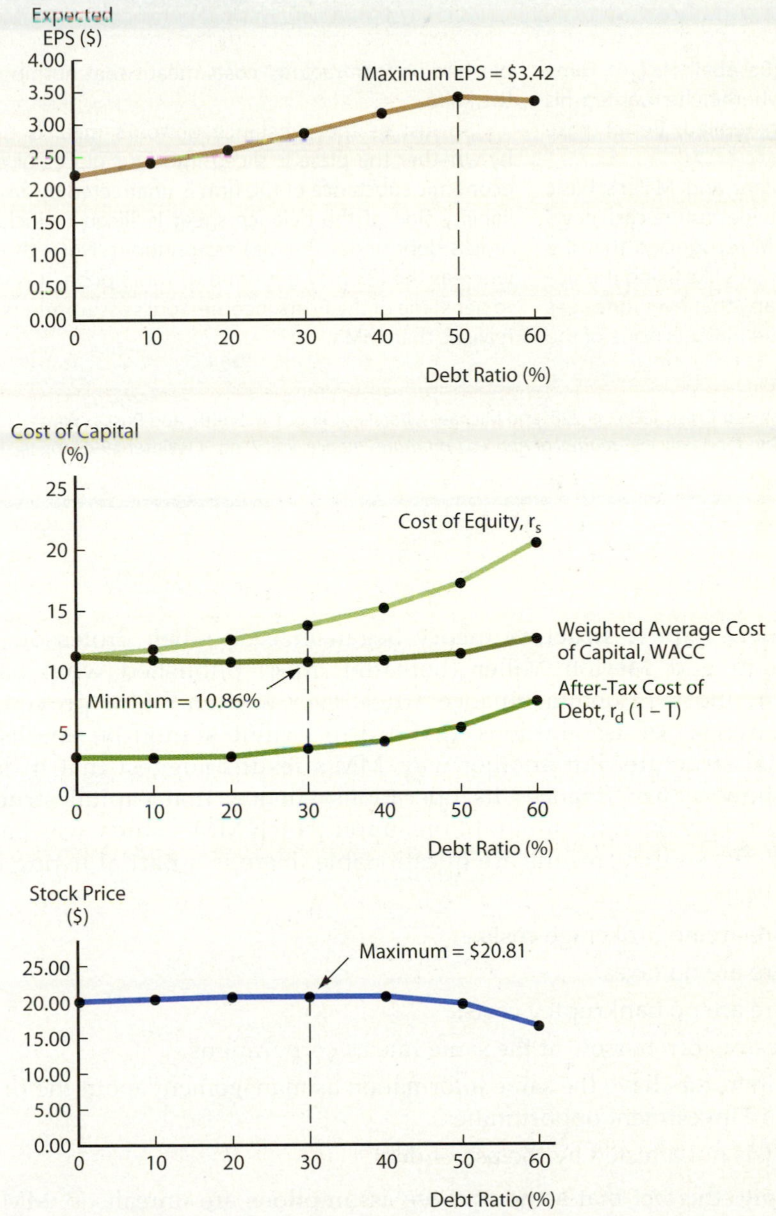

13-4 Capital Structure Theory

Business risk is an important determinant of the optimal capital structure. Moreover, firms in different industries have different business risks. So we would expect capital structures to vary considerably across industries, and this is the case. For example, biotechnology companies generally have very different capital structures than food processors. In addition, capital structures vary among firms within a given industry, which is a bit harder to explain. What factors can explain these differences? In an attempt to answer that question, academics and practitioners have developed a number of theories.

YOGI BERRA ON THE MM PROPOSITION

When a waitress asked Yogi Berra (Baseball Hall of Fame catcher for the New York Yankees) whether he wanted his pizza cut into four pieces or eight, Yogi replied: "Better make it four. I don't think I can eat eight."

Yogi's quip helps convey Modigliani and Miller's basic insight. The firm's choice of leverage divides future cash flows in a way that's like slicing a pizza. MM recognized that if a company's future investments are fixed, it's like fixing the size of the pizza: No information costs means that everyone sees the same pizza, no taxes means that the IRS gets none of the pie, and no "contracting" costs means that nothing sticks to the knife.

So just as the substance of Yogi's meal is unaffected by whether the pizza is sliced into four pieces or eight, the economic substance of the firm is unaffected by whether the liability side of the balance sheet is sliced to include more or less debt under the MM assumptions. Note, though, that whereas the IRS may get none of Yogi's pizza, it is very likely to get some of the firm's income. Yogi's assumptions are more realistic than MM's.

Sources: Lee Green, *Sportswit* (New York: Fawcett Crest, 1984), p. 228; and Michael J. Barclay, Clifford W. Smith, and Ross L. Watts, "The Determinants of Corporate Leverage and Dividend Policies," *Journal of Applied Corporate Finance*, vol. 7, no. 4 (Winter 1995), pp. 4–19.

Modern capital structure theory began in 1958 when Professors Franco Modigliani and Merton Miller (hereafter, MM) published what has been called the most influential finance article ever written.[21] MM proved, under a restrictive set of assumptions, that a firm's value should be unaffected by its capital structure. Put another way, MM's results suggest that it does not matter how a firm finances its operations—hence, that capital structure is irrelevant. However, the assumptions upon which MM's study was based are not realistic, so their results are questionable. Here is a partial listing of their assumptions:

1. There are no brokerage costs.
2. There are no taxes.
3. There are no bankruptcy costs.
4. Investors can borrow at the same rate as corporations.
5. All investors have the same information as management about the firm's future investment opportunities.
6. EBIT is not affected by the use of debt.

Despite the fact that some of these assumptions are unrealistic, MM's irrelevance result is extremely important. By indicating the conditions under which capital structure is irrelevant, MM provided clues about what is required to make capital structure relevant and, therefore, to affect a firm's value. MM's work marked the beginning of modern capital structure research, and subsequent research has focused on relaxing the MM assumptions to develop a more robust and realistic theory. Research in this area is quite extensive, but the highlights are summarized in the following sections.

[21]Franco Modigliani and Merton H. Miller, "The Cost of Capital, Corporation Finance, and the Theory of Investment," *American Economic Review*, vol. 48, no. 3 (June 1958), pp. 261–297. Both Modigliani and Miller won Nobel Prizes for their work.

13-4A THE EFFECT OF TAXES[22]

MM's original 1958 paper was criticized harshly, and they published a follow-up in 1963 that relaxed the assumption of no corporate taxes.[23] They recognized that the Tax Code allows corporations to deduct interest payments as an expense, but dividend payments to stockholders are not deductible. This differential treatment encourages corporations to use debt in their capital structures. Indeed, MM demonstrated that if all their other assumptions hold, this differential treatment leads to an optimal capital structure of 100% debt.

MM's 1963 work was modified several years later by Merton Miller (this time without Modigliani), when he brought in the effects of personal taxes.[24] Miller noted that bonds pay interest, which is taxed as personal income at rates going up to 37%, while income from stocks comes partly from dividends and partly from capital gains. Further, long-term capital gains are taxed at a maximum rate of 15% (20% in 2018 for high-income taxpayers), and this tax can be deferred until the stock is sold and the gain realized. If a stock is held until the owner dies, no capital gains tax must be paid. So on balance, returns on common stocks are taxed at lower effective rates than returns on debt.[25]

Because of the tax situation, Miller argued that investors are willing to accept relatively low before-tax returns on stocks as compared to the before-tax returns on bonds. For example, an investor in the 37% tax bracket might require a 10% pretax return on Bigbee's bonds, which would result in a 10%(1 − T) = 10%(0.63) = 6.30% after-tax return. Bigbee's stock is riskier than its bonds, so the investor would require a higher after-tax return (say, 8%) on the stock. Because the stock's returns (either dividends or capital gains) would be taxed at 20%, a pretax return of 8%/(1 − T) = 8.0%/0.80 = 10.0% would provide the required 8.0% after-tax return. In this example, the interest rate on the bonds would be 10%, the same as the required return on the stock, r_s. Thus, the more favorable treatment of income on the stock would cause investors to accept the same before-tax returns on the stock and on the bond.[26]

As Miller pointed out, (1) the *deductibility of interest* favors the use of debt financing. (2) The *more favorable tax treatment of income from stocks* lowers the required rates of return on stocks and thus favors the use of equity. It is difficult to specify the net effect of these two factors. However, most observers believe that interest deductibility has a stronger effect and hence that our tax system favors the corporate use of debt. Still, that effect is certainly reduced by the lower taxes on stock income. Duke University professor John Graham estimated the overall tax benefits of debt financing.[27] He concluded that the tax benefits associated with debt financing represent about 7% of the average

---

[22]This section is relatively technical, and it can be omitted without a loss of continuity.

[23]Franco Modigliani and Merton H. Miller, "Corporate Income Taxes and the Cost of Capital: A Correction," *American Economic Review*, vol. 53, no. 3 (June 1963), pp. 433–443.

[24]Merton H. Miller, "Debt and Taxes," *Journal of Finance*, vol. 32, no. 2 (May 1977), pp. 261–275.

[25]When Miller wrote his article, dividends were taxed at a maximum rate of 70% and capital gains at a much lower rate. Today (2018) dividends and capital gains are taxed at a maximum rate of 20% for high-income taxpayers, but interest is taxed at a maximum rate of 37%. [Capital gains can be caught by the Alternative Minimum Tax (AMT), in which case they are taxed at either 26% or 28% depending on one's income bracket.] These tax law changes would not affect Miller's final conclusion.

[26]The situation here is similar to that involving tax-exempt municipal bonds versus taxable bonds.

[27]John R. Graham, "How Big Are the Tax Benefits of Debt?" *Journal of Finance*, vol. 55, no. 5 (October 2000), pp. 1901–1941; and John R. Graham, "Estimating the Tax Benefits of Debt," *Journal of Applied Corporate Finance*, vol. 14, no. 1 (Spring 2001), pp. 42–54.

firm's value, so if a leverage-free firm decided to use an average amount of debt, its value would rise by 7%.

13-4B THE EFFECT OF POTENTIAL BANKRUPTCY

MM's irrelevance results also depend on the assumption that firms don't go bankrupt and hence that bankruptcy costs are irrelevant. However, in practice, bankruptcy exists, and it can be quite costly. Firms in bankruptcy have high legal and accounting expenses, and they have a hard time retaining customers, suppliers, and employees. Moreover, bankruptcy often forces a firm to liquidate assets for less than they would be worth if the firm continued to operate. Assets such as plant and equipment are often illiquid because they are configured to a company's individual needs and because they are difficult to disassemble and move.

Note too that the *threat of bankruptcy,* not just bankruptcy per se, brings about these problems. If they become concerned about the firm's future, key employees start "jumping ship," suppliers start refusing to grant credit, customers begin seeking more stable suppliers, and lenders start demanding higher interest rates and imposing stricter loan covenants.

Bankruptcy-related problems are likely to increase the more debt a firm has in its capital structure. Therefore, bankruptcy costs discourage firms from pushing their use of debt to excessive levels. Note too that bankruptcy-related costs have two components: (1) the probability of their occurrence and (2) the costs that will be incurred if financial distress arises. A firm whose earnings are relatively volatile, all else equal, faces a greater chance of bankruptcy and thus should use less debt than a more stable firm. This is consistent with our earlier point that firms with high operating leverage (and thus greater business risk) should limit their use of financial leverage. Likewise, firms whose assets are illiquid and would have to be sold at "fire sale" prices should limit their use of debt financing.

13-4C TRADE-OFF THEORY

Trade-Off Theory
The capital structure theory that states that firms trade off the tax benefits of debt financing against problems caused by potential bankruptcy.

The preceding arguments led to the development of what is called "the trade-off theory of leverage." This theory states that firms trade off the tax benefits of debt financing against problems caused by potential bankruptcy. A summary of the **trade-off theory** is expressed graphically in Figure 13.8. Here are some observations about the figure:

1. The fact that interest paid is a deductible expense makes debt less expensive than common or preferred stock. In effect, the government pays part of the cost of debt—or to put it another way, debt provides *tax shelter benefits.* As a result, using more debt reduces taxes and thus allows more of the firm's operating income (EBIT) to flow through to investors. This factor, on which MM focused, tends to raise the stock's price. Indeed, under the assumptions of MM's original paper, the stock price would be maximized at 100% debt. The line labeled "MM Result Incorporating the Effects of Corporate Taxation" in Figure 13.8 expresses the relationship between stock prices and debt under their assumptions.
2. In the real world, firms have target debt ratios that call for less than 100% debt to limit the adverse effects of potential bankruptcy.
3. There is some threshold level of debt, labeled D_1 in Figure 13.8, below which the probability of bankruptcy is so low as to be immaterial. Beyond D_1, however, bankruptcy-related costs become increasingly important, and they begin to offset the tax benefits of debt. In the range from D_1 to D_2, bankruptcy-related costs reduce but do not completely offset the tax benefits of debt, so the firm's stock price continues to rise (but at a decreasing rate) as its debt ratio increases. However, beyond D_2, bankruptcy-related costs exceed the tax benefits, so from this point on, increasing the debt ratio lowers the stock price. Therefore, D_2 is

FIGURE 13.8 Effect of Financial Leverage on the Value of Bigbee's Stock

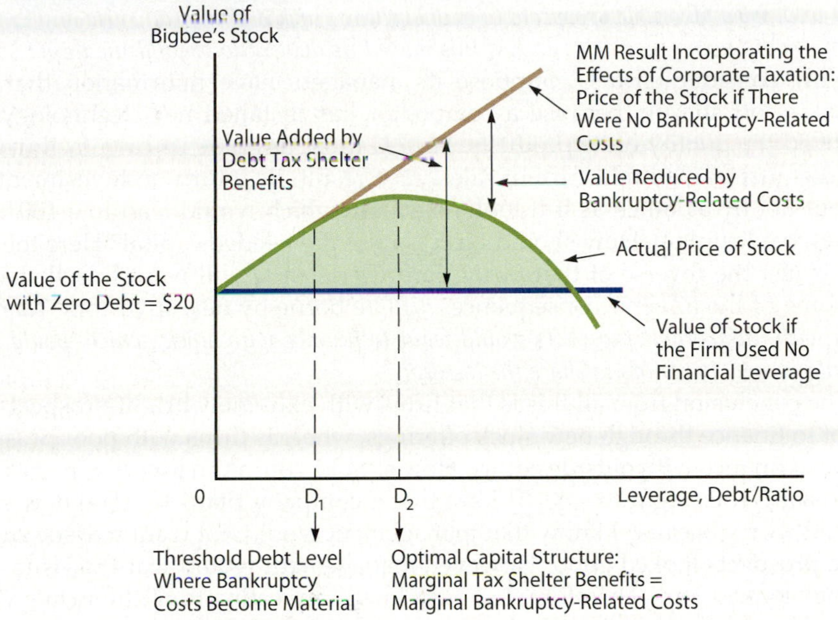

the optimal capital structure, the one where the stock price is maximized. Of course, D_1 and D_2 vary from firm to firm depending on business risk and bankruptcy costs, and they can change for a given firm over time.

4. Although theoretical and empirical work supports the general shape of the curves in Figures 13.7 and 13.8, these graphs must be taken as approximations, not as precisely defined functions. The numbers in Figure 13.7 are rounded to two decimal places, but that is merely for illustrative purposes—the numbers are not nearly that accurate because the graph is based on estimates.
5. Another disturbing aspect of capital structure theory expressed in Figure 13.8 is the fact that many large, successful firms such as Intel and Microsoft use far less debt than the theory suggests. This point led to the development of signaling theory, which is discussed in the next section.

13-4D SIGNALING THEORY

MM assumed that everyone—investors and managers alike—has the same information about a firm's prospects. This is called **symmetric information**. However, in fact, managers often have better information than outside investors. This is called **asymmetric information**, and it has an important effect on the optimal capital structure. To see why, consider two situations, one where the company's managers know that its prospects are extremely favorable (Firm F) and one where the managers know that the future looks unfavorable (Firm U).

Symmetric Information
The situation where investors and managers have identical information about firms' prospects.

Asymmetric Information
The situation where managers have different (better) information about firms' prospects than do investors.

Now suppose Firm F's R&D labs have just discovered a nonpatentable cure for the common cold. They want to keep the new product a secret as long as possible to delay competitors' entry into the market. New plants must be built to make the new product, so capital must be raised. But how should Firm F raise the needed capital? If it sells stock, when profits from the new product start flowing in, the price of the stock will rise sharply, and purchasers of the new stock will make a bonanza. The current stockholders (including the managers) also will do well, but not as well as they would have done if the company had not sold stock before the price increased. In that case, they would not have had to share the benefits of the new product with the new stockholders. *Therefore, we would expect a firm with very favorable prospects to avoid selling stock and instead raise any required new capital by using new debt, even if this moved its debt ratio beyond the target level.*[28]

Now consider Firm U. Suppose its managers have information that new orders are off sharply because a competitor has installed new technology that improved the quality of its products. Firm U must upgrade its own facilities at a high cost just to maintain current sales. As a result, its return on investment will fall (but not by as much as if it took no action, which would lead to a 100% loss through bankruptcy). How should Firm U raise the needed capital? Here the situation is just the reverse of that facing Firm F—Firm U will want to sell stock so that some of the adverse consequences will be borne by new investors. *Therefore, a firm with unfavorable prospects would want to finance with stock, which would mean bringing in new investors to share the losses.*[29]

The conclusion from all this is that firms with extremely bright prospects prefer not to finance through new stock offerings, whereas firms with poor prospects do like to finance with outside equity. How should you, as an investor, react to this conclusion? You ought to say, "If I see that a company plans to issue new stock, I should worry because I know that management would not want to issue stock if future prospects looked good. However, management would want to issue stock if things looked bad. Therefore, I should lower my estimate of the firm's value, other things held constant, if it plans to issue new stock."

If you gave that answer, your views are consistent with those of sophisticated portfolio managers. *In a nutshell, the announcement of a stock offering is generally taken as a* **signal** *that the firm's prospects as seen by its management are not bright.* This, in turn, suggests that when a firm announces a new stock offering, more often than not, the price of its stock will decline.[30] Empirical studies have shown that this situation does exist.[31]

Signal
An action taken by a firm's management that provides clues to investors about how management views the firm's prospects.

What are the implications of all this for capital structure decisions? Issuing stock emits a negative signal and thus tends to depress the stock price; even if the company's prospects are bright, a firm should, in normal times, maintain a **reserve borrowing capacity** that can be used in the event that some especially good investment opportunity comes along. *This means that firms should, in normal times, use more equity and less debt than is suggested by the tax benefit/bankruptcy cost trade-off model illustrated in Figure 13.8.*

Reserve Borrowing Capacity
The ability to borrow money at a reasonable cost when good investment opportunities arise. Firms often use less debt than specified by the MM optimal capital structure in "normal" times to ensure that they can obtain debt capital later if necessary.

13-4E USING DEBT FINANCING TO CONSTRAIN MANAGERS

In Chapter 1, we stated that conflicts of interest may arise if managers and shareholders have different objectives. Such conflicts are particularly likely when the firm has more cash than is needed to support its core operations. Managers often use excess cash to finance their pet projects or for perquisites such as plush offices, corporate jets, and skyboxes at sports arenas, all of which may do little to benefit stock prices.[32] By contrast, managers with more limited free cash flow are less able to make wasteful expenditures.

---

[28]It would be illegal for Firm F's managers to personally purchase more shares on the basis of their inside knowledge of the new product. They could be sent to jail if they did.

[29]Of course, Firm U would have to make certain disclosures when it offered new shares to the public, but it might be able to meet the legal requirements without fully disclosing management's worst fears.

[30]Stock issues are more of a negative signal for mature companies than for new, rapidly growing firms, where investors expect rapid growth to require additional equity.

[31]See Paul Asquith and David W. Mullins Jr., "The Impact of Initiating Dividend Payments on Shareholders' Wealth," *Journal of Business*, vol. 56, no. 1 (January 1983), pp. 77–96.

[32]If you don't believe that corporate managers can waste money, read Bryan Burrough, *Barbarians at the Gate: The Fall of RJR Nabisco* (New York: Harper & Row, 1990), the story of the takeover of RJR Nabisco.

Firms can reduce excess cash flow in a variety of ways. One way is to funnel some of it back to shareholders through higher dividends or stock repurchases. Another alternative is to tilt the target capital structure toward more debt in the hope that higher debt service requirements will force managers to become more disciplined. If debt is not serviced as required, the firm will be forced into bankruptcy, in which case its managers would lose their jobs. Therefore, a manager is less likely to buy an expensive corporate jet if the firm has large debt service requirements.

A leveraged buyout (LBO) is a good way to reduce excess cash flow. In an LBO, debt is used to finance the purchase of a high percentage of the company's shares. Indeed, the projected savings from reducing frivolous waste has motivated quite a few LBOs. As noted, high debt payments after the LBO force managers to conserve cash by eliminating unnecessary expenditures.

Of course, increasing debt and reducing free cash flow has its downside: It increases the risk of bankruptcy. Economist Ben Bernanke (who is the former Federal Reserve chairman) has argued that adding debt to a firm's capital structure is like putting a dagger into the steering wheel of a car.[33] The dagger—which points toward your chest—motivates you to drive more carefully, but you may get stabbed if someone runs into you, even if you are being careful. The analogy applies to corporations in the following sense: Higher debt forces managers to be more careful with shareholders' money, but even well-run firms can face bankruptcy (get stabbed) if some event beyond their control, such as a war, an earthquake, a strike, or a recession, occurs. To complete the analogy, the capital structure decision comes down to deciding how big a dagger stockholders should use to keep managers in line.

If you find the discussion of capital structure theory imprecise and somewhat confusing, you're not alone. In truth, not even the former chairman of the Federal Reserve knows how to identify a firm's precise optimal capital structure or how to measure the effects of capital structure changes on stock prices and the cost of capital. In practice, capital structure decisions must be made using a combination of judgment and numerical analysis. Still, an understanding of the theoretical issues presented here can help you make better judgments about capital structure issues.

13-4F PECKING ORDER HYPOTHESIS

Yet another factor that may influence capital structures is the idea that managers have a preferred **pecking order** when it comes to raising capital and that this pecking order affects capital structure decisions.[34] We know that firms often finance in the following order: Their first source of funds is accounts payable and accruals. Retained earnings generated during the current year would be the next source. Then, if the amount of retained earnings is not sufficient to cover capital requirements, firms issue debt. Finally, and only as a last resort, they issue new common stock.

Pecking Order
The sequence in which firms prefer to raise capital: first spontaneous credit, then retained earnings, then other debt, and finally new common stock.

Why might it be logical for a firm to follow this pecking order? First, no flotation costs are incurred to raise capital as spontaneous credit or retained earnings, and costs are relatively low when issuing new debt. However, flotation costs for new stock issues are quite high, and the existence of asymmetric information/signaling effects makes it even more undesirable to finance with new common stock. So, the pecking order theory is logical, and it can influence a firm's capital structure, although there is still some debate about its relative importance.[35]

---

[33]Ben Bernanke, "Is There Too Much Corporate Debt?" Federal Reserve Bank of Philadelphia, *Business Review* (September/October 1989), pp. 3–13.

[34]See Jonathan Baskin, "An Empirical Investigation of the Pecking Order Hypothesis," *Financial Management*, vol. 18 (Spring 1989), pp. 26–35.

[35]See Murray Z. Frank and Vidhan K. Goyal, "Testing the Pecking Order Theory of Capital Structure," *Journal of Financial Economics*, vol. 67, no. 2 (February 2003), pp. 217–248.

13-4G WINDOWS OF OPPORTUNITY

Windows of Opportunity
The occasion where a company's managers adjust its firm's capital structure to take advantage of certain market situations.

If a company's stock is selling for a price different than its intrinsic value, the company's managers can adjust the firm's capital structure to take advantage of this mispricing. When a company's stock is overvalued (trading for more than its intrinsic value), its managers can take the opportunity to issue new equity at a time when its market value is relatively high. Likewise, managers may choose to repurchase stock when the firm's stock is undervalued. A study by Malcolm Baker and Jeffrey Wurgler documents that many companies take advantage of these **windows of opportunity**, and they argue that these attempts to time the market have had a profound effect on these companies' capital structures.[36]

Self*Test*

Why does MM's theory with taxes lead to 100% debt?

How would an increase in corporate taxes tend to affect an average firm's capital structure? What about an increase in the personal tax rate?

Explain what asymmetric information means, and how signals affect capital structure decisions.

What is meant by reserve borrowing capacity, and why is it important to firms?

How can the use of debt serve to discipline managers?

What is the pecking order hypothesis, and how does it influence firms' capital structures?

How do "windows of opportunity" impact a firm's capital structure?

13-5 Checklist for Capital Structure Decisions

In addition to the types of analyses discussed previously, firms generally consider the following factors when making capital structure decisions:

1. *Sales stability.* A firm whose sales are relatively stable can safely take on more debt and incur higher fixed charges than a company with unstable sales. Utility companies, because of their stable demand, historically have been able to use more financial leverage than can industrial firms.
2. *Asset structure.* Many companies also take their desired cash holdings into account when setting their target capital structure. Holding other factors constant, a company is able to take on more debt if it has more cash on the balance sheet. For this reason, some analysts also evaluate an alternative measure, **net debt**, which subtracts cash and equivalent securities from the company's total debt:

Net Debt
Equal to short-term debt plus long-term debt less cash and equivalents. Companies often look at this measure when setting their target capital structure.

$$\text{Net debt} = \text{Short-term debt} + \text{Long-term debt} - \text{Cash and equivalents}$$

Looking at Table 13.1, we see that Caterpillar has \$39.1 billion in net debt (\$47.4 billion in total debt minus \$8.3 billion in cash and equivalents). Holding other factors constant, firms that have more cash or other assets that are suitable as security for loans tend to use debt relatively heavily. General-purpose assets that can be used by many businesses make good collateral, whereas special-purpose assets do not. Thus, real estate companies

[36]See Malcolm Baker and Jeffrey Wurgler, "Market Timing and Capital Structure," *Journal of Finance*, vol. 57, no. 1 (February 2002), pp. 1–32.

are usually highly leveraged, whereas companies involved in technological research are not.[37]

3. *Operating leverage.* Other things the same, a firm with less operating leverage is better able to employ financial leverage because it will have less business risk.
4. *Growth rate.* Other things the same, faster-growing firms must rely more heavily on external capital. Further, the flotation cost involved in selling common stock exceeds that incurred when selling debt, which encourages rapidly growing firms to rely more heavily on debt. At the same time, however, those firms often face higher uncertainty, which tends to reduce their willingness to use debt.
5. *Profitability.* It is often observed that firms with very high rates of return on investment use relatively little debt. Although there is no theoretical justification for this fact, one practical explanation is that very profitable firms such as Intel, Microsoft, and Google do not need to do much debt financing. Their high rates of return enable them to do most of their financing with internally generated funds.
6. *Taxes.* Interest is a deductible expense, and deductions are most valuable to firms with high tax rates. Therefore, the higher a firm's tax rate, the greater the advantage of debt. However, with the passage of new tax legislation, the corporate tax rate is a flat 21%. The lower tax rate reduces the value of the tax deduction associated with debt financing.
7. *Control.* The effect of debt versus stock on a management's control position can influence capital structure. If management currently has voting control (more than 50% of the stock) but is not in a position to buy any more stock, it may choose debt for new financings. On the other hand, management may decide to use equity if the firm's financial situation is so weak that the use of debt might subject it to serious risk of default. The reason? If the firm goes into default, managers will probably lose their jobs. However, if too little debt is used, management runs the risk of a takeover. Thus, control considerations can lead to the use of debt or equity because the type of capital that best protects management varies from situation to situation. In any event, if management is at all insecure, it will consider the control situation.
8. *Management attitudes.* No one can prove that one capital structure will lead to higher stock prices than another. Management, then, can exercise its own judgment about the proper capital structure. Some managers tend to be relatively conservative and thus use less debt than an average firm in the industry, whereas aggressive managers use a relatively high percentage of debt in their quest for higher profits.
9. *Lender and rating agency attitudes.* Regardless of a manager's analysis of the proper leverage factors for his or her firm, the attitudes of lenders and rating agencies frequently influence financial structure decisions. Corporations often discuss their capital structures with lenders and rating agencies and give much weight to their advice. For example, Moody's and Standard & Poor's recently told one large utility that its bonds would be downgraded if it issued more bonds. This influenced its decision, and its next financing was with common equity.

---

[37]Two capital structure issues that we do not address in this chapter relate to how long-term leases and convertible securities impact the financing mix. Leases are de facto a substitute for debt, so it would be appropriate to determine the present value of the firm's future lease payments and treat them as debt. Convertibles are bonds (or preferred stocks) that can be converted into common stock at the option of the holder. Before conversion, these securities technically increase the firm's financial leverage, but immediately after conversion leverage declines. For a precise examination of a firm's leverage, it would be useful to estimate the likely timing of conversion and take it into account. However, such an analysis goes beyond the scope of an introductory text.

10. *Market conditions.* Conditions in the stock and bond markets undergo long- and short-run changes that can have an important bearing on a firm's optimal capital structure. For example, during a recent credit crunch, the junk bond market dried up and there simply was no market at a "reasonable" interest rate for any new long-term bonds rated below BBB. Therefore, low-rated companies in need of capital were forced to go to the stock market or to the short-term debt market, regardless of their target capital structures. When conditions eased, however, these companies sold long-term bonds to get their capital structures back on target.
11. *The firm's internal condition.* A firm's own internal condition can also have a bearing on its target capital structure. For example, suppose a firm just successfully completed an R&D program and forecasts higher earnings in the immediate future. However, the new earnings are not yet anticipated by investors and are not reflected in the stock price. This company would not want to issue stock—it would prefer to finance with debt until the higher earnings materialize and are reflected in the stock price. Then it could sell an issue of common stock, use the proceeds to retire the debt, and return to its target capital structure. This point was discussed earlier in connection with asymmetric information and signaling.
12. *Financial flexibility.* An astute corporate treasurer made this statement to the authors:

    Our company can earn a lot more money from good capital budgeting and operating decisions than from good financing decisions. Indeed, we are not sure exactly how financing decisions affect our stock price, but we know for sure that having to turn down promising ventures because funds are not available will reduce our long-run profitability. For this reason, my primary goal as treasurer is to always be in a position to raise the capital needed to support operations.

    We also know that when times are good, we can raise capital with either stocks or bonds, but when times are bad, suppliers of capital are much more willing to make funds available if we give them a stronger position, and this means debt. Further, when we sell a new issue of stock, this sends a negative "signal" to investors, so stock sales by a mature company such as ours are not desirable.

    Combining these thoughts gives rise to the goal of maintaining financial flexibility, which from an operational viewpoint means maintaining adequate "reserve borrowing capacity." Determining the "adequate" reserve is based on judgment, but it clearly depends on the firm's forecasted need for funds, predicted capital market conditions, management's confidence in its forecasts, and the consequences of a capital shortage.

Self*Test*

How does sales stability affect the target capital structure?

How do the types of assets used affect a firm's capital structure?

How do taxes affect the target capital structure?

How do the attitudes of lenders and rating agencies affect capital structure?

How does the firm's internal condition affect its actual capital structure?

What is financial flexibility, and is it increased or decreased by a high debt ratio? Explain.

13-6 Variations in Capital Structures

As might be expected, wide variations in the use of financial leverage occur across industries and among the individual firms in each industry. Table 13.5 illustrates differences for selected companies in different industries, the ranking is in ascending order of the company's long-term debt ratio.[38]

Petroleum, biotechnology, and steel companies use relatively little debt because their industries tend to be cyclical, oriented toward research, or subject to huge product liability suits. On the other hand, grocery stores, utility companies, and airlines use debt relatively heavily because their fixed assets make good security for mortgage bonds and their relatively stable sales make it safe to carry more than average debt.

The TIE ratio gives an indication of how vulnerable the company is to financial distress. This ratio depends on three factors: (1) the percentage of debt, (2) the interest rate on the debt, and (3) the company's profitability. Generally, low-leveraged companies such as Alphabet Inc. and Eli Lilly have high coverage ratios, whereas companies like Southern Company and Kroger, which have financed heavily with debt, have lower coverage ratios.

Wide variations in capital structures also exist among firms in given industries. This can be seen from Table 13.5. For example, although the average ratio of long-term debt to total capital in 2018 for the aerospace industry was 58.51%, Rockwell Collins had a ratio of 49.24%. Thus, factors unique to individual firms,

TABLE 13.5 Capital Structure Percentages, 2018: Selected Companies Ranked by Company Long-Term Debt Ratios[a]

	Company		Industry		
Name	**Long-Term Debt Ratio**	**Times-Interest-Earned Ratio**	**Description**	**Long-Term Debt Ratio**	**Times-Interest-Earned Ratio**
Alphabet	1.96%	272.20	Internet Content	2.91%	204.63
NUCOR	26.47	10.48	Steel	21.26	6.98
BP	34.64	6.93	Petroleum	21.88	8.96
Eli Lilly	39.39	15.93	Pharmaceuticals	36.71	12.41
ConAgra Foods	46.81	6.38	Food Processing	35.48	5.59
Rockwell Collins	49.24	4.89	Aerospace	58.51	13.89
CSX	49.49	7.56	Railroads	40.48	9.83
United Continental Holdings	60.94	5.40	Airlines	52.15	9.30
Kroger	63.37	6.96	Grocery Stores	62.83	6.91
Southern Company	64.29	1.65	Electric Utilities	49.75	3.54
Ford	74.29	7.92	Automobiles	41.18	29.03
Wendy's	85.71	1.70	Restaurants	107.40	12.18

Note:
[a]Long-term debt ratios are calculated as a percentage of total capital, where total capital is defined as long-term debt plus equity, with both measured at book value. Note that this ratio understates the debt ratio as we define it in this textbook, as short-term debt is not included in either the numerator or the denominator.
Source: *MSN Money* (www.msn.com/en-us/money/markets), July 24, 2018.

[38]Information on capital structures and financial strength is available from a multitude of sources. We used *MSN Money* (www.msn.com) to develop Table 13.5, but published sources include *The Value Line Investment Survey, Risk Management Association Annual Statement Studies,* and *Dun & Bradstreet Key Business Ratios.*

including managerial attitudes, play an important role in setting target capital structures. At the same time, research by Harry DeAngelo and Richard Roll shows that many companies have considerable instability in debt ratios over time.[39] Their findings suggest that a lot of companies do not establish a fixed target capital structure, and that there are a lot of interesting dynamics over time. From a broader perspective, recent research by John Graham, Mark Leary, and Michael Roberts traces average debt ratios of U.S. companies over the past century. Their work demonstrates that leverage ratios have dramatically increased since World War II, and they offer a number of possible explanations for the shifts in capital structure trends over time.[40] However, with the passage of the 2017 Tax Act, the lower corporate tax rate reduces the value of the tax deduction associated with debt financing. In addition, the new tax legislation limits the interest deduction of debt to 30% of income. The impact of these two provisions will likely be a reduction in the percentage of debt financing and will lead to an increase in the average company's cost of capital.

Self*Test*

Why do wide variations in the use of financial leverage occur across industries and among individual firms in each industry?

What is the likely impact of the 2017 Tax Act on the average company' capital structure?

TYING IT ALL TOGETHER

When we studied the cost of capital in Chapter 10, we took the firm's capital structure as given and calculated the cost of capital based on that structure. Then in Chapters 11 and 12, we described capital budgeting techniques, which use the cost of capital as input. Capital budgeting decisions determine the types of projects that a firm accepts, which affect the nature of the firm's assets and its business risk. In this chapter, we reverse the process, taking the firm's assets and business risk as given and then seeking to determine the best way to finance those assets. More specifically, in this chapter, we examined the effects of financial leverage on earnings per share, stock prices, and the cost of capital and we discussed various capital structure theories.

The different theories lead to different conclusions about the optimal capital structure, and no one has been able to prove that one theory is better than the others. Therefore, we cannot estimate a firm's optimal capital structure with much precision. Accordingly, financial executives generally treat the optimal capital structure as a range—for example, 30% to 40% debt—rather than as a precise point, such as 35% debt. The concepts discussed in this chapter are used as a guide, and they help managers understand the factors to consider when they are setting the target capital structures of their firms.

---

[39]See Harry DeAngelo and Richard Roll, "How Stable Are Corporate Capital Structures?" *Journal of Finance,* vol. 70, no. 1 (February 2015), pp. 373–418. A shorter, less technical version of this paper can also be found in "Capital Structure Instability," *Journal of Applied Corporate Finance*, vol. 28, no. 4 (Fall 2016), pp. 38–52.

[40]See John R. Graham, Mark T. Leary, and Michael R. Roberts, "A Century of Capital Structure: The Leveraging of Corporate America," *Journal of Financial Economics*, vol. 118, no. 3 (December 2015), pp. 658–683. Once again, a shorter, less technical version of this paper can be found in "The Leveraging of Corporate America: A Long-Run Perspective on Changes in Capital Structure," *Journal of Applied Corporate Finance*, vol. 28, no. 4 (Fall 2016), pp. 29–37.

Self-Test Questions and Problems

(Solutions Appear in Appendix A)

ST-1 KEY TERMS Define each of the following terms:

a. Capital; capital structure; optimal capital structure
b. Business risk; financial risk
c. Financial leverage; operating leverage; operating breakeven
d. Hamada equation; unlevered beta
e. Symmetric information; asymmetric information
f. Modigliani-Miller theories
g. Trade-off theory; signaling theory
h. Reserve borrowing capacity; pecking order
i. Windows of opportunity; net debt

ST-2 OPERATING LEVERAGE AND BREAK-EVEN ANALYSIS Olinde Electronics Inc. produces stereo components that sell at P = $100 per unit. Olinde's fixed costs are $200,000, variable costs are $50 per unit, 5,000 components are produced and sold each year, EBIT is currently $50,000, and Olinde's assets (all equity-financed) are $500,000. Olinde can change its production process by adding $400,000 to assets and $50,000 to fixed operating costs. This change would (1) reduce variable costs per unit by $10 and (2) increase output by 2,000 units, but (3) the sales price on all units would have to be lowered to $95 to permit sales of the additional output. Olinde has tax loss carry-forwards that cause its tax rate to be zero, it uses no debt, and its average cost of capital is 10%.

a. Should Olinde make the change? Why or why not?
b. Would Olinde's break-even point increase or decrease if it made the change?
c. Suppose Olinde was unable to raise additional equity financing and had to borrow the $400,000 at an interest rate of 10% to make the investment. Use the DuPont equation to find the expected ROA of the investment. Should Olinde make the change if debt financing must be used? Explain.

ST-3 OPTIMAL CAPITAL STRUCTURE Carlisle Industries is trying to determine its optimal capital structure, which now consists of only common equity. The firm will add debt to its capital structure if it minimizes its WACC, but the firm has no plans to use preferred stock in its capital structure. In addition, the firm's size will remain the same, so funds obtained from debt issued will be used to repurchase stock. The percentage of shares repurchased will be equal to the percentage of debt added to the firm's capital structure. (In other words, if the firm's debt-to-capital ratio increases from 0 to 25%, then 25% of the shares outstanding will be repurchased.) Carlisle is a small firm with average sales of $25 million or less during the past 3 years, so it is exempt from the interest deduction limitation.

Its treasury staff has consulted with investment bankers. On the basis of those discussions, the staff has created the following table showing the firm's debt cost at different debt levels:

Debt-to-Capital Ratio (w_d)	Equity-to-Capital Ratio (w_c)	Debt-to-Equity Ratio (D/E)	Bond Rating	Before-Tax Cost of Debt (r_d)
0.00	1.00	0.0000	AA	5.0%
0.25	0.75	0.3333	A	6.0
0.50	0.50	1.0000	BBB	8.3
0.75	0.25	3.0000	BB	11.0

The firm has total capital of $5 million and 200,000 shares of common stock outstanding. Its EBIT is $500,000 and will not change if debt, at any of the levels shown in the preceding table, is added to the firm's capital structure. Carlisle uses the CAPM to estimate its cost of common equity, r_s. It estimates that the risk-free rate is 3.5%, the market risk premium is 4.5%, and its tax rate is 25%. Carlisle's current beta, which is b_U because it has no debt, is 1.25.

a. Calculate the firm's interest expense, net income, shares outstanding, and EPS for each of the capital structures shown in the preceding table.

b. At what capital structure is EPS maximized, and what is the firm's EPS at this capital structure?
c. Calculate the after-tax cost of debt [$r_d(1 - T)$], beta (b_L), cost of equity (r_s), and WACC for each of the capital structures shown in the preceding table.
d. Considering only the capital structures shown, at what capital structure is WACC minimized and what is the WACC at this capital structure?
e. At what capital structure does the firm maximize shareholder value? Is this the same capital structure selected in parts b and d? Explain why it is, or why it isn't the same.
f. As an analyst, what is your recommendation to the firm's management regarding Carlisle's capital structure?

Questions

13-1 Changes in sales cause changes in profits. Would the profit change associated with sales changes be larger or smaller if a firm increased its operating leverage? Explain your answer.

13-2 Would each of the following increase, decrease, or have an indeterminant effect on a firm's break-even point (unit sales)?

a. The sales price increases with no change in unit costs.
b. An increase in fixed costs is accompanied by a decrease in variable costs.
c. Variable labor costs decline; other things are held constant.

13-3 Discuss the following statement: All else equal, firms with relatively stable sales are able to carry relatively high debt ratios. Is the statement true or false? Why?

13-4 If Congress increased the personal tax rate on interest, dividends, and capital gains but simultaneously reduced the rate on corporate income, what effect would this have on the average company's capital structure?

13-5 Which of the following would likely encourage a firm to increase the debt in its capital structure?

a. The corporate tax rate increases.
b. The personal tax rate increases.
c. Due to market changes, the firm's assets become less liquid.
d. Changes in the bankruptcy code make bankruptcy less costly to the firm.
e. The firm's sales and earnings become more volatile.

13-6 Why do public utilities generally use different capital structures than biotechnology companies?

13-7 Why is EBIT generally considered independent of financial leverage? Why might EBIT actually be affected by financial leverage at high debt levels?

13-8 Is the debt level that maximizes a firm's expected EPS the same as the debt level that maximizes its stock price? Explain.

13-9 If a firm goes from zero debt to successively higher levels of debt, why would you expect its stock price to rise first, then hit a peak, and then begin to decline?

13-10 When the Bell System was broken up, the old AT&T was split into a new AT&T and seven regional telephone companies. The specific reason for forcing the breakup was to increase the degree of competition in the telephone industry. AT&T had a monopoly on local service, long distance, and the manufacture of all equipment used by telephone companies, and the breakup was expected to open most of those markets to competition. In the court order that set the terms of the breakup, the capital structures of the surviving companies were specified and much attention was given to the increased competition telephone companies could expect in the future. Do you think the optimal capital structure after the breakup was the same as the pre-breakup optimal capital structure? Explain your position.

13-11 A firm is about to double its assets to serve its rapidly growing market. It must choose between a highly automated production process and a less automated one. It also must choose a capital structure for financing the expansion. Should the asset investment and financing decisions be jointly determined, or should each decision be made separately? How would these decisions affect one another? How could the leverage concept be used to help management analyze the situation?

Problems

Easy Problems 1-5

13-1 **BREAK-EVEN ANALYSIS** A company's fixed operating costs are $430,000, its variable costs are $2.95 per unit, and the product's sales price is $4.50. What is the company's break-even point; that is, at what unit sales volume will its income equal its costs?

13-2 **OPTIMAL CAPITAL STRUCTURE** Terrell Trucking Company is in the process of setting its target capital structure. The CFO believes that the optimal debt-to-capital ratio is somewhere between 20% and 50%, and her staff has compiled the following projections for EPS and the stock price at various debt levels:

Debt/Capital Ratio	Projected EPS	Projected Stock Price
20%	$3.10	$34.25
30	3.55	36.00
40	3.70	35.50
50	3.55	34.00

Assuming that the firm uses only debt and common equity, what is Terrell's optimal capital structure? At what debt-to-capital ratio is the company's WACC minimized?

13-3 **RISK ANALYSIS**

a. Given the following information, calculate the expected value for Firm C's EPS. Data for Firms A and B are as follows: $E(EPS_A) = \$5.10$, $\sigma_A = \$3.61$, $E(EPS_B) = \$4.20$, and $\sigma_B = \$2.96$.

	Probability				
	0.1	**0.2**	**0.4**	**0.2**	**0.1**
Firm A: EPS_A	($1.50)	$1.80	$5.10	$8.40	$11.70
Firm B: EPS_B	(1.20)	1.50	4.20	6.90	9.60
Firm C: EPS_C	(2.40)	1.35	5.10	8.85	12.60

b. You are given that $\sigma_C = \$4.11$. Discuss the relative riskiness of the three firms' earnings.

13-4 **UNLEVERED BETA** Hartman Motors has $18 million in assets, which were financed with $6 million of debt and $12 million in equity. Hartman's beta is currently 1.3, and its tax rate is 25%. Use the Hamada equation to find Hartman's unlevered beta, b_U.

13-5 **FINANCIAL LEVERAGE EFFECTS** Firms HL and LL are identical except for their financial leverage ratios and the interest rates they pay on debt. Each has $20 million in invested capital, has $4 million of EBIT, and is in the 25% federal-plus-state tax bracket. Both firms are small with average sales of $25 million or less during the past 3 years, so both are exempt from the interest deduction limitation. Firm HL, however, has a debt-to-capital ratio of 50% and pays 12% interest on its debt, whereas LL has a 30% debt-to-capital ratio and pays only 10% interest on its debt. Neither firm uses preferred stock in its capital structure.

a. Calculate the return on invested capital (ROIC) for each firm.
b. Calculate the return on equity (ROE) for each firm.

c. Observing that HL has a higher ROE, LL's treasurer is thinking of raising the debt-to-capital ratio from 30% to 60% even though that would increase LL's interest rate on all debt to 15%. Calculate the new ROE for LL.

Intermediate Problems 6-9

13-6 **BREAK-EVEN ANALYSIS** The Warren Watch Company sells watches for $26, fixed costs are $155,000, and variable costs are $13 per watch.

a. What is the firm's gain or loss at sales of 9,000 watches? At 15,000 watches?

b. What is the break-even point? Illustrate by means of a chart.

c. What would happen to the break-even point if the selling price was raised to $33? What is the significance of this analysis?

d. What would happen to the break-even point if the selling price was raised to $33 but variable costs rose to $24 a unit?

13-7 **FINANCIAL LEVERAGE EFFECTS** The Neal Company wants to estimate next year's return on equity (ROE) under different financial leverage ratios. Neal's total capital is $14 million, it currently uses only common equity, it has no future plans to use preferred stock in its capital structure, and its federal-plus-state tax rate is 25%. Neal is a small firm with average sales of $25 million or less during the past 3 years, so it is exempt from the interest deduction limitation. The CFO has estimated next year's EBIT for three possible states of the world: $4.2 million with a 0.2 probability, $2.8 million with a 0.5 probability, and $700,000 with a 0.3 probability. Calculate Neal's expected ROE, standard deviation, and coefficient of variation for each of the following debt-to-capital ratios; then evaluate the results:

Debt/Capital Ratio	Interest Rate
0%	—
10	9%
50	11
60	14

13-8 **HAMADA EQUATION** Situational Software Co. (SSC) is trying to establish its optimal capital structure. Its current capital structure consists of 25% debt and 75% equity; however, the CEO believes that the firm should use more debt. The risk-free rate, r_{RF}, is 4%; the market risk premium, RP_M, is 5%; and the firm's tax rate is 25%. Currently, SSC's cost of equity is 12%, which is determined by the CAPM. What would be SSC's estimated cost of equity if it changed its capital structure to 40% debt and 60% equity?

13-9 **RECAPITALIZATION** Tartan Industries currently has total capital equal to $4 million, has zero debt, is in the 25% federal-plus-state tax bracket, has a net income of $1 million, and distributes 40% of its earnings as dividends. Net income is expected to grow at a constant rate of 3% per year, 200,000 shares of stock are outstanding, and the current WACC is 12.30%.

The company is considering a recapitalization where it will issue $2 million in debt and use the proceeds to repurchase stock. Investment bankers have estimated that if the company goes through with the recapitalization, its before-tax cost of debt will be 10% and its cost of equity will rise to 15.5%.

a. What is the stock's current price per share (before the recapitalization)?

b. Assuming that the company maintains the same payout ratio, what will be its stock price following the recapitalization? Assume that shares are repurchased at the price calculated in part a.

Challenging Problems 10-13

13-10 **BREAKEVEN AND OPERATING LEVERAGE**

a. Given the following graphs, calculate the total fixed costs, variable costs per unit, and sales price for Firm A. Firm B's fixed costs are $120,000, its variable costs per unit are $4, and its sales price is $8 per unit.

b. Which firm has the higher operating leverage at any given level of sales? Explain.

c. At what sales level, in units, do both firms earn the same operating profit?

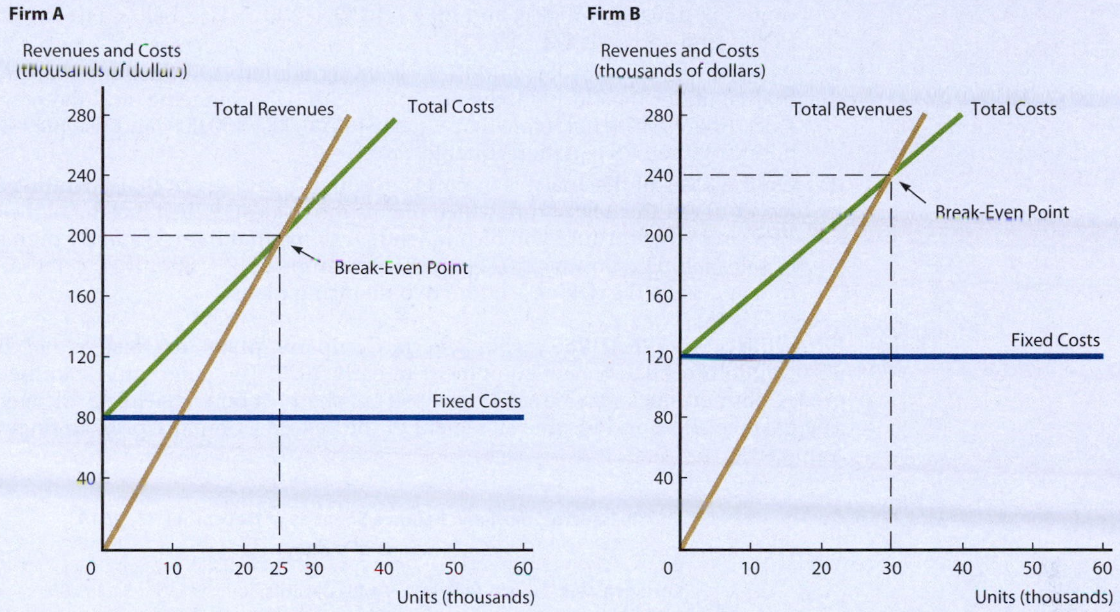

13-11 **RECAPITALIZATION** Currently, Forever Flowers Inc. has a capital structure consisting of 25% debt and 75% equity. Forever's debt currently has a 7% yield to maturity. The risk-free rate (r_{RF}) is 6%, and the market risk premium ($r_M - r_{RF}$) is 7%. Using the CAPM, Forever estimates that its cost of equity is currently 14.5%. The company has a 25% tax rate.

a. What is Forever's current WACC?
b. What is the current beta on Forever's common stock?
c. What would Forever's beta be if the company had no debt in its capital structure? (That is, what is Forever's unlevered beta, b_U?)

Forever's financial staff is considering changing its capital structure to 40% debt and 60% equity. If the company went ahead with the proposed change, the yield to maturity on the company's bonds would rise to 10.5%. The proposed change will have no effect on the company's tax rate.

d. What would be the company's new cost of equity if it adopted the proposed change in capital structure?
e. What would be the company's new WACC if it adopted the proposed change in capital structure?
f. Based on your answer to part e, would you advise Forever to adopt the proposed change in capital structure? Explain.

13-12 **BREAKEVEN AND LEVERAGE** Wingler Communications Corporation (WCC) produces premium stereo headphones that sell for $28.80 per set, and this year's sales are expected to be 450,000 units. Variable production costs for the expected sales under present production methods are estimated at $10,200,000, and fixed production (operating) costs at present are $1,560,000. WCC has $4,800,000 of debt outstanding at an interest rate of 8%. There are 240,000 shares of common stock outstanding, and there is no preferred stock. The dividend payout ratio is 70%, and WCC is in the 25% federal-plus-state tax bracket. WCC is a small company with average sales of $25 million or less during the past 3 years, so it is exempt from the interest deduction limitation.

The company is considering investing $7,200,000 in new equipment. Sales would not increase, but variable costs per unit would decline by 20%. Also, fixed operating costs would increase from $1,560,000 to $1,800,000. WCC could raise the required capital by borrowing $7,200,000 at 10% or by selling 240,000 additional shares of common stock at $30 per share.

a. What would be WCC's EPS (1) under the old production process, (2) under the new process if it uses debt, and (3) under the new process if it uses common stock?
b. At what unit sales level would WCC have the same EPS assuming it undertakes the investment and finances it with debt or with stock? {*Hint:* V = variable cost per

unit = \$8,160,000/450,000, and EPS = [(PQ − VQ − F − I)(1 − T)]/N. Set EPS_{Stock} = EPS_{Debt} and solve for Q.}

c. At what unit sales level would EPS = 0 under the three production/financing setups—that is, under the old plan, the new plan with debt financing, and the new plan with stock financing? (*Hint:* Note that V_{old} = \$10,200,000/450,000, and use the hints for part b, setting the EPS equation equal to zero.)

d. On the basis of the analysis in parts a through c, and given that operating leverage is lower under the new setup, which plan is the riskiest, which has the highest expected EPS, and which would you recommend? Assume that there is a fairly high probability of sales falling as low as 250,000 units. Determine EPS_{Debt} and EPS_{Stock} at that sales level to help assess the riskiness of the two financing plans.

13-13 FINANCING ALTERNATIVES The Severn Company plans to raise a net amount of \$270 million to finance new equipment in early 2020. Two alternatives are being considered: Common stock may be sold to net \$60 per share, or bonds yielding 9% may be issued. The balance sheet and income statement of the Severn Company prior to financing are as follows:

The Severn Company: Balance Sheet as of December 31, 2019 (millions of dollars)

Current assets	\$ 900.00	Notes payable	\$ 255.00
Net fixed assets	450.00	Long-term debt (7%)	697.50
		Common stock, \$1 par	60.00
		Retained earnings	337.50
Total assets	\$1,350.00	Total liabilities and equity	\$1,350.00

The Severn Company: Income Statement for Year Ended December 31, 2019 (millions of dollars)

Sales	\$2,475.00
Operating costs	2,103.75
Earnings before interest and taxes (15%)	\$ 371.25
Interest on short-term debt	10.50
Interest on long-term debt	48.83
Earnings before taxes	\$ 311.92
Federal-plus-state taxes (25%)	77.98
Net income	\$ 233.94

The probability distribution for annual sales is as follows:

Probability	Annual Sales (millions of dollars)
0.30	\$2,250
0.40	2,700
0.30	3,150

Assuming that EBIT equals 15% of sales, calculate earnings per share (EPS) under the debt financing and the stock financing alternatives at each possible sales level. Then calculate expected EPS and σ_{EPS} under both debt and stock financing alternatives. Also calculate the debt-to-capital ratio and the times-interest-earned (TIE) ratio at the expected sales level under each alternative. The old debt will remain outstanding. Which financing method do you recommend? (*Hint:* Notes payable should be included in both the numerator and the denominator of the debt-to-capital ratio.)

Comprehensive/Spreadsheet Problem

13-14 WACC AND OPTIMAL CAPITAL STRUCTURE Elliott Athletics is trying to determine its optimal capital structure, which now consists of only debt and common equity. The firm does not currently use preferred stock in its capital structure, and it does not plan to do so in the future. Its treasury staff has consulted with investment bankers. On the basis of those discussions, the staff has created the following table showing the firm's debt cost at different debt levels:

Debt-to-Capital Ratio (w_d)	Equity-to-Capital Ratio (w_c)	Debt-to-Equity Ratio (D/E)	Bond Rating	Before-Tax Cost of Debt (r_d)
0.0	1.0	0.00	A	7.0%
0.2	0.8	0.25	BBB	8.0
0.4	0.6	0.67	BB	10.0
0.6	0.4	1.50	C	12.0
0.8	0.2	4.00	D	15.0

Elliott uses the CAPM to estimate its cost of common equity, r_s, and estimates that the risk-free rate is 5%, the market risk premium is 6%, and its tax rate is 25%. Elliott estimates that if it had no debt, its "unlevered" beta, b_U, would be 1.2.

a. What is the firm's optimal capital structure, and what would be its WACC at the optimal capital structure?

b. If Elliott's managers anticipate that the company's business risk will increase in the future, what effect would this likely have on the firm's target capital structure?

c. If Congress were to dramatically increase the corporate tax rate, what effect would this likely have on Elliott's target capital structure?

d. Plot a graph of the after-tax cost of debt, the cost of equity, and the WACC versus (1) the debt/capital ratio and (2) the debt/equity ratio.

INTEGRATED CASE

CAMPUS DELI INC.

13-15 OPTIMAL CAPITAL STRUCTURE Assume that you have just been hired as business manager of Campus Deli (CD), which is located adjacent to the campus. Sales were $1,100,000 last year, variable costs were 60% of sales, and fixed costs were $40,000. Therefore, EBIT totaled $400,000. Because the university's enrollment is capped, EBIT is expected to be constant over time. Because no expansion capital is required, CD distributes all earnings as dividends. Invested capital is $2 million, and 80,000 shares are outstanding. The management group owns about 50% of the stock, which is traded in the over-the-counter market.

CD currently has no debt—it is an all-equity firm—and its 80,000 shares outstanding sell at a price of $25 per share, which is also the book value. The firm's federal-plus-state tax rate is 25%. On the basis of statements made in your finance text, you believe that CD's shareholders would be better off if some debt financing were used. When you suggested this to your new boss, she encouraged you to pursue the idea but to provide support for the suggestion. Note that CD is a small firm, so it is exempt from the interest deduction limitation.

In today's market, the risk-free rate, r_{RF}, is 7.5%, and the market risk premium, RP_M, is 6%. CD's unlevered beta, b_U, is 1.25. CD currently has no debt, so its cost of equity (and WACC) is 15%. If the firm was recapitalized, debt would be issued, and the borrowed funds would be used to repurchase stock. Stockholders, in turn, would use funds provided by the repurchase to buy equities in other fast-food companies similar to CD. You plan to complete your report by asking and then answering the following questions.

a. 1. What is business risk? What factors influence a firm's business risk?
   2. What is operating leverage, and how does it affect a firm's business risk?
   3. What is the firm's return on invested capital (ROIC)?

b. 1. What do the terms *financial leverage* and *financial risk* mean?
   2. How does financial risk differ from business risk?

c. To develop an example that can be presented to CD's management as an illustration, consider two small hypothetical firms: Firm U with zero debt financing and Firm L with $10,000 of 12% debt. Both firms have $20,000 in invested capital and a 25% federal-plus-state tax rate, and they have the following EBIT probability distribution for next year:

Probability	EBIT
0.25	$2,000
0.50	3,000
0.25	4,000

   1. Complete the partial income statements and the firms' ratios in Table IC 13.1.
   2. Be prepared to discuss each entry in the table and to explain how this example illustrates the effect of financial leverage on expected rate of return and risk.

d. After speaking with a local investment banker, you obtain the following estimates of the cost of debt at different debt levels (in thousands of dollars):

Amount Borrowed	Debt/Capital Ratio	D/E Ratio	Bond Rating	r_d
$ 0	0	0	—	—
250	0.125	0.1429	AA	8.0%
500	0.250	0.3333	A	9.0
750	0.375	0.6000	BBB	11.5
1,000	0.500	1.0000	BB	14.0

Now consider the optimal capital structure for CD.
   1. To begin, define the terms *optimal capital structure* and *target capital structure.*
   2. Why does CD's bond rating and cost of debt depend on the amount of money borrowed?
   3. Assume that shares could be repurchased at the current market price of $25 per share. Calculate CD's expected EPS and TIE at debt levels of $0, $250,000, $500,000, $750,000, and $1,000,000. How many shares would remain after recapitalization under each scenario?
   4. Using the Hamada equation, what is the cost of equity if CD recapitalizes with $250,000 of debt? $500,000? $750,000? $1,000,000?
   5. Considering only the levels of debt discussed, what is the capital structure that minimizes CD's WACC?
   6. What would be the new stock price if CD recapitalizes with $250,000 of debt? $500,000? $750,000? $1,000,000? Recall that the payout ratio is 100%, so $g = 0$.
   7. Is EPS maximized at the debt level that maximizes share price? Why or why not?
   8. Considering only the levels of debt discussed, what is CD's optimal capital structure?
   9. What is the WACC at the optimal capital structure?

e. Suppose you discovered that CD had more business risk than you originally estimated. Describe how this would affect the analysis. How would the analysis be affected if the firm had less business risk than originally estimated?

f. What are some factors a manager should consider when establishing his or her firm's target capital structure?

TABLE IC 13.1 Income Statements and Ratios

	Firm U			Firm L		
Total capital	$20,000	$20,000	$20,000	$20,000	$20,000	$20,000
Equity	$20,000	$20,000	$20,000	$10,000	$10,000	$10,000
Probability	0.25	0.50	0.25	0.25	0.50	0.25
Sales	$ 6,000	$ 9,000	$12,000	$ 6,000	$ 9,000	$12,000
Operating costs	4,000	6,000	8,000	4,000	6,000	8,000
Earnings before interest and taxes	$ 2,000	$ 3,000	$ 4,000	$ 2,000	$ 3,000	$ 4,000
Interest (12%)	0	0	0	1,200		1,200
Earnings before taxes	$ 2,000	$ 3,000	$ 4,000	$ 800	$	$ 2,800
Taxes (25%)	500	750	1,000	200		700
Net income	$ 1,500	$ 2,250	$ 3,000	$ 600	$	$ 2,100
ROIC	7.5%	11.25%	15.0%	%	%	%
ROE	7.5%	11.25%	15.0%	6.0%	%	21.0%
TIE	∞	∞	∞	1.7×	×	3.3×
Expected ROIC		11.25%			%	
Expected ROE		11.25%			13.50%	
Expected TIE		∞			2.5×	
σ_{ROIC}		2.65%			%	
σ_{ROE}		2.65%			5.30%	
σ_{TIE}		0			0.6×	

g. Put labels on Figure IC 13.1 and then discuss the graph as you might use it to explain to your boss why CD might want to use some debt.

h. How does the existence of asymmetric information and signaling affect capital structure?

FIGURE IC 13.1 Relationship between Capital Structure and Stock Price

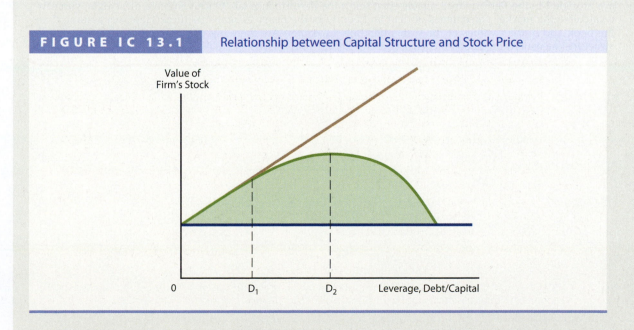

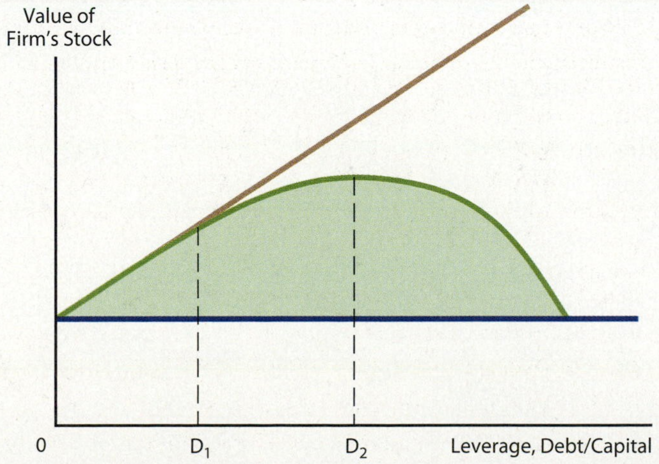

TAKING A CLOSER LOOK

Exploring the Capital Structures for Four Restaurant Companies

Use online resources to work on this chapter's questions. Please note that website information changes over time, and these changes may limit your ability to answer some of these questions.

This chapter provides an overview of the effects of leverage and describes the process that firms use to determine their optimal capital structure. The chapter also indicates that capital structures tend to vary across industries and across countries. If you are interested in exploring these differences in more detail, the Morningstar website provides information about the capital structures of each of the companies it follows. The following discussion questions demonstrate how we can use this information to evaluate the capital structures for four restaurant companies: Cheesecake Factory (CAKE), Chipotle Mexican Grill (CMG), BJ's Restaurants Inc. (BJRI), and Darden Restaurants Inc. (DRI).

Discussion Questions

1. To get an overall picture of each company's capital structure, it is helpful to look at the Key Ratios screen by selecting Full Key Ratios Data and then selecting the Financial Health tab. Common size balance sheet data are provided over a 10-year period. What, if any, are the major trends that emerge when you're looking at these data? Do these companies tend to have relatively high or relatively low levels of debt? Do these companies have significant levels of current liabilities? Have their capital structures changed over time?
2. Repeat this procedure for the other three companies. Do you find similar capital structures for each of the four companies? Do you find that the capital structures have moved in the same direction over the past 5 years, or have the different companies changed their capital structures in different ways over the past 5 years?
3. The financial ratios investigated thus far are based on book values of debt and equity. Determine whether using the market value of equity makes a significant difference in the firm's capital structure. To make these calculations, you will have to use the balance sheet information (5 years of data are shown) provided in the Financials screen by selecting All Financials Data and selecting Balance Sheet. The market capitalization data are provided in the Performance screen—just select the Performance tab. Once you have these data, you can recalculate the market percentages of debt and equity in the firm's capital structure. (Here, we assume that the book and market values of the firm's debt are the same.) Are there big differences between the capital structures measured on a book or market basis? Explain your answer.

Distributions to Shareholders: Dividends and Share Repurchases

CHAPTER 14

Africa Studio/Shutterstock.com

Apple Shifts Gears and Begins to Unload Part of Its Vast Cash Hoard

Profitable companies regularly face three important questions: (1) How much of our free cash flow should we pass on to shareholders? (2) Should we provide this cash to stockholders by raising the dividend or by repurchasing stock? (3) Should we maintain a stable, consistent payment policy, or should we let the payments vary as conditions change?

In this chapter, we discuss many of the issues that affect firms' cash distribution policies. As we will see, mature companies with stable cash flows and limited growth opportunities tend to return a significant amount of their cash to shareholders either by paying dividends or by repurchasing common stock. By contrast, rapidly growing companies with good investment opportunities are prone to invest most of their available cash in new projects rather than paying dividends or repurchasing stock. Apple Inc., which has been regarded over the past decade as the epitome of a growth company, illustrates this tendency. Its sales grew from $6.2 billion in 2003 to $229.2 billion in 2017, which translates to an annual growth rate of 29%. Much of this growth came from large, long-term investments in new products and technology; given the firm's emphasis on growth, it had long been reluctant to pay dividends.

Demonstrating this viewpoint at a shareholders' meeting in early 2010, Apple's legendary co-founder and CEO Steve Jobs strongly reaffirmed that the company had no intentions to start paying a dividend, even though Apple had more than $50 billion in cash and short-term securities on its balance sheet. According to *The Wall Street Journal,* Jobs said "that he preferred 'to leave the powder dry' for future acquisitions, though none were in the offing. He added that the cash 'will come in handy.'"

However, after Steve Jobs died in late 2011, the company faced increased pressure to return some of its cash to shareholders. Since then, the company's cash holdings have continued to balloon, while at the same time there are growing concerns that Apple's growth engine may be slowing down.

Well aware of the new environment, the company's new CEO Tim Cook shifted gears; in early 2012, Apple established a dividend and also announced a plan to repurchase shares of its common stock. In the years since, Apple has aggressively followed through on its plan to return cash to its shareholders. Summarizing these changes in its May 2018 press release, the company reported, "From the inception of its capital return program in August 2012 through March 2018, Apple has returned over $275 billion to shareholders, including $200 billion in share repurchases."

Despite this important shift in policy, Apple continues to generate a great deal of cash. Indeed, CNBC reported in early 2018 that the company still had $285 billion in cash, a large percentage of which has been held overseas. Notably, in response to the 2017 tax reform bill that gave companies increased incentives to repatriate cash they have generated from foreign earnings, Apple has also announced plans to repatriate a significant portion of its overseas cash. This money will undoubtedly be used in part to return more cash to its investors over time.

More broadly, when managers decide how and when to distribute cash to shareholders, they face a fundamental question: Could we earn more on the available cash if we kept it in the firm and used it to invest in new projects, or would shareholders earn more if they received the cash and invested it in alternative investments with the same risk? If the company could earn more, it would make sense to retain the cash. However, if investors could earn more, the company would increase shareholder value by paying out more dividends and/or by repurchasing more shares.

Sources: "Apple Reports Second Quarter Results," *Apple Press Release* (www.apple.com/newsroom/archive), May 1, 2018; Jack Nicas, "Apple Says It Will Buy Back $100 Billion in Stock," *The New York Times* (www.nytimes.com), May 1, 2018; Tae Kim, "Apple's Vow to Put $163 Billion in Cash to Work Could Ease the Blow for Shareholders During Sell-Off," *CNBC* (www.cnbc.com/2018/02/02/apple-vows-to-cut-its-163-billion-in-net-cash-to-zero.html), February 2, 2018; Steven Russolillo, "Apple Announces Massive Cash Plans," *The Wall Street Journal* (www.wsj.com), April 23, 2013; and Ben Charny, "Jobs Defends Apple's Cash Hoard," *The Wall Street Journal* (www.wsj.com), February 25, 2010.

PUTTING THINGS IN PERSPECTIVE

Successful companies earn income. That income can be reinvested in operating assets, used to retire debt, or distributed to stockholders. If the decision is made to distribute income to stockholders, three key issues arise: (1) How much should be distributed? (2) Should the distribution be in the form of dividends, or should the cash be passed on to shareholders by buying back stock? (3) How stable should the distribution be? That is, should the funds paid out from year to year be stable and dependable, which stockholders like, or should they be varied depending on the firms' cash flows and investment requirements, which managers tend to like?

Those three issues are the primary focus of this chapter. By the time you complete it, you should be able to do the following:

- **Explain why some investors like the firm to pay more dividends while other investors prefer reinvestment and the resulting capital gains.**
- **Discuss the various trade-offs that companies face when trying to establish their optimal dividend policy.**
- **Differentiate between stock splits and stock dividends.**
- **List the advantages and disadvantages of stock repurchases vis-à-vis dividends from both investors' and companies' perspectives.**

14-1 Dividends versus Capital Gains: What Do Investors Prefer?

When deciding how much cash to distribute, financial managers must keep in mind that the firm's objective is to maximize shareholder value. Consequently, the **target payout ratio**—defined as the percentage of net income to be paid out as cash dividends—should be based in large part on investors' preferences for dividends versus capital gains: Do investors prefer to receive dividends, or would they rather have the firm plow the cash back into the business, which presumably will produce capital gains? This preference can be considered in terms of the constant growth stock valuation model:

Target Payout Ratio
The target percentage of net income paid out as cash dividends.

$$\hat{P}_0 = \frac{D_1}{r_s - g}$$

If the company increases the payout ratio, this will raise D_1, which, taken alone, will cause the stock price to rise. However, if D_1 is raised, less money will be available for reinvestment, which will cause the expected growth rate to decline, and that will tend to lower the stock's price. Therefore, any change in the payout policy will have two opposing effects. As a result, the **optimal dividend policy** must strike the balance between current dividends and future growth that maximizes the stock price. In the following sections, we discuss the major theories that have been advanced to explain how investors regard current dividends versus future growth.

Optimal Dividend Policy
The dividend policy that strikes a balance between current dividends and future growth and maximizes the firm's stock price.

14-1A DIVIDEND IRRELEVANCE THEORY

Professors Merton Miller and Franco Modigliani (MM) advanced the **dividend irrelevance theory**, which stated that dividend policy has no effect on either the price of a firm's stock or its cost of capital.[1] MM developed their theory under a stringent set of assumptions, and under those assumptions, they proved that a firm's value is determined only by its basic earning power and its business risk. In other words, the value of the firm depends only on the income produced by its assets, not on how that income is split between dividends and retained earnings. Note, though, that MM assumed, among other things, that no taxes are paid on dividends, that stocks can be bought and sold with no transactions costs, and that everyone—investors and managers alike—has the same information regarding firms' future earnings.

Dividend Irrelevance Theory
The theory that a firm's dividend policy has no effect on either its value or its cost of capital.

Given their assumptions, MM argued that each shareholder can construct his or her own dividend policy. For example, if a firm does not pay dividends, a shareholder who wants a 5% dividend can "create" it by selling 5% of his or her stock. Conversely, if a company pays a higher dividend than an investor wants, the investor can use the unwanted dividends to buy additional shares of the company's stock. Note, though, that in the real world, individual investors who want additional dividends would have to incur transactions costs to sell shares, and investors who do not want dividends would have to pay taxes on the unwanted dividends and then incur transactions costs to purchase shares with the after-tax dividends. Because taxes and transactions costs do exist, dividend policy may well be relevant, and investors may prefer policies that help them reduce taxes and transactions costs.

In defense of their theory, MM noted that many stocks are owned by institutional investors who pay no taxes and who can buy and sell stocks with very low

[1]Merton H. Miller and Franco Modigliani, "Dividend Policy, Growth, and the Valuation of Shares," *Journal of Business*, October 1961, pp. 411–433.

transactions costs. For such investors, dividend policy might well be irrelevant, and if these investors dominate the market and represent the "marginal investor," MM's theory could be valid in spite of its unrealistic assumptions. Note too that for tax-paying investors, the taxes and transactions costs depend on what the individual investor's income is and how long he or she plans to hold the stock. As a result, when it comes to investors' preferences for dividends, one size does not fit all. Next, we discuss why some investors prefer dividends whereas others prefer capital gains.

14-1B REASONS SOME INVESTORS PREFER DIVIDENDS

The principal conclusion of MM's dividend irrelevance theory is that dividend policy does not affect either stock prices or the required rate of return on equity, r_s. Early critics of MM's theory suggested that investors preferred a sure dividend today to an uncertain future capital gain. In particular, Myron Gordon and John Lintner argued that r_s declines as the dividend payout is increased because investors are less certain of receiving the capital gains that should result from retaining earnings than they are of receiving dividend payments.[2]

MM disagreed. They argued that r_s is independent of dividend policy, which implies that investors are indifferent between dividends and capital gains, that is, between D_1/P_0 and g. MM called the Gordon–Lintner argument the **bird-in-the-hand fallacy** because in MM's view, most investors plan to reinvest their dividends in the stock of the same or similar firms and, in any event, the riskiness of the firm's cash flows to investors in the long run is determined by the riskiness of operating cash flows, not by dividend payout policy.

Bird-in-the-Hand Fallacy
MM's name for the Gordon–Lintner theory that a firm's value will be maximized by setting a high dividend payout ratio.

Keep in mind, however, that MM's theory relied on the assumption that there are no taxes or transactions costs, which means that investors who prefer dividends could simply create their own dividend policy by selling a percentage of their stock each year. In reality, most investors face transactions costs when they sell stock, so investors who are looking for a steady stream of income would logically prefer that companies pay regular dividends. For example, retirees who have accumulated wealth over time and now want annual income from their investments probably prefer dividend-paying stocks.

14-1C REASONS SOME INVESTORS PREFER CAPITAL GAINS

While dividends reduce transactions costs for investors who are looking for steady income from their investments, dividends increase transactions costs for other investors who are less interested in income and more interested in saving money for the long-term future. These long-term investors want to reinvest their dividends, and that creates transactions costs. Given this concern, a number of companies have established dividend reinvestment plans that help investors automatically reinvest their dividends. (We discuss dividend reinvestment plans in Section 14-4.)

In addition (and perhaps more importantly), the Tax Code encourages many individual investors to prefer capital gains to dividends. One key advantage is that taxes must be paid on dividends the year they are received, but taxes on capital gains are not paid until the stock is sold. Due to time value effects, a dollar of taxes paid in the future has a lower effective cost than a dollar of taxes

[2]Myron J. Gordon, "Optimal Investment and Financing Policy," *Journal of Finance*, vol. 18, no. 2 (May 1963), pp. 264–272; and John Lintner, "Dividends, Earnings, Leverage, Stock Prices, and the Supply of Capital to Corporations," *Review of Economics and Statistics*, vol. 44, no. 3 (August 1962), pp. 243–269.

paid today.[3] Apart from this advantage, the tax rate on dividends has often been higher than the tax rate on capital gains. For example, prior to 2003, dividends were taxed at the ordinary income tax rate, which went up to 38.6%, versus a rate of 20% on long-term capital gains. These differential rates were eliminated in 2003, when the maximum tax rate on dividends and long-term capital gains was set at 15%.[4] However, in early 2013, Congress increased the maximum tax rate on dividends and long-term capital gains to 20% for high-income taxpayers.[5]

Self*Test*

Explain briefly the ideas behind the dividend irrelevance theory.

What did Modigliani and Miller assume about taxes and brokerage costs when they developed their dividend irrelevance theory?

Why did MM refer to the Gordon–Lintner dividend argument as the bird-in-the-hand fallacy?

Why do some investors prefer high-dividend-paying stocks?

Why might other investors prefer low-dividend-paying stocks?

14-2 Other Dividend Policy Issues

Before we discuss how dividend policy is set in practice, we need to examine two other issues that affect dividend policy: (1) the *information content*, or *signaling, hypothesis* and (2) the *clientele effect.*

14-2A INFORMATION CONTENT, OR SIGNALING, HYPOTHESIS

An increase in the dividend is often accompanied by an increase in the stock price, while a dividend cut generally leads to a stock price decline. This observation was used to refute MM's irrelevance theory—their opponents argued that stock price actions after changes in dividend payouts demonstrate that investors prefer dividends to capital gains. However, MM argued differently. They noted that corporations are reluctant to cut dividends and thus that corporations do not raise dividends unless they anticipate higher earnings in the future to support the higher dividends. Thus, MM argued that a higher than expected dividend

[3]Moreover, if a stock is held by someone until he or she dies, there is no capital gains tax at all—the beneficiaries who receive the stock can use the stock's value on the date of death as their cost basis, which permits them to escape the capital gains tax completely.

[4]However, long-term capital gains are classified as income subject to the Alternative Minimum Tax (AMT), and the AMT rate is 26% or 28%, depending on your income bracket. The AMT was supposed to hit only the very wealthy, but prior to 2013 it was not indexed for inflation. So by 2012, many not-so-wealthy individuals were being hit. However, Congress fixed this problem with new tax legislation, and beginning in 2013, the AMT exemption amounts are indexed to inflation.

[5]Effective January 1, 2013, long-term capital gains and dividend tax rates increased to 20% for high-income taxpayers in the top tax bracket (39.6% marginal tax rate). Short-term capital gains on assets held for 1 year or less are taxed as ordinary income. On January 1, 2018, long-term capital gains and dividend tax rates increased to 20% for single individual taxpayers with income greater than $425,800 and for married taxpayers with income greater than $479,000.

increase is a signal to investors that management forecasts good future earnings.[6] Conversely, a dividend reduction, or a smaller than expected increase, is a signal that management forecasts poor future earnings. If the MM position is correct, stock price changes after dividend increases or decreases do not demonstrate a preference for dividends over retained earnings. Rather, such price changes simply indicate that dividend announcements have **information (signaling) content** about future earnings.

Information (Signaling) Content
The theory that investors regard dividend changes as signals of management's earnings forecasts.

Managers often have better information about future prospects for dividends than public stockholders, so there is clearly some information content in dividend announcements. However, it is difficult to tell whether the stock price changes that follow dividend increases or decreases reflect only signaling effects (as MM argue) or both signaling and dividend preference. Still, a firm should consider signaling effects when it is contemplating a change in dividend policy. For example, if a firm has good long-term prospects but also has a need for cash to fund current investments, it might be tempted to cut the dividend to increase funds available for investment. However, this action might cause the stock price to decline because the dividend reduction is taken as a signal that future earnings are likely to decline, when just the reverse is actually true. So managers should consider signaling effects when they set dividend policy.

14-2B CLIENTELE EFFECT

Clienteles
Different groups of stockholders who prefer different dividend payout policies.

As we indicated earlier, different groups, or **clienteles**, of stockholders prefer different dividend payout policies. For example, retired individuals, pension funds, and university endowment funds generally prefer cash income, so they often want the firm to distribute a high percentage of its earnings. Such investors are frequently in low or even zero tax brackets, so taxes are of little concern. On the other hand, stockholders in their peak earning years might prefer reinvestment because they have less need for current investment income and simply reinvest dividends received after incurring income taxes and brokerage costs.

If a firm retains and reinvests income rather than paying dividends, those stockholders who need current income will be disadvantaged. The value of their stock might increase, but they will be forced to go to the trouble and expense of selling some of their shares to obtain cash. Also, some institutional investors (or trustees for individuals) might be legally precluded from selling stock and then "spending capital." On the other hand, stockholders who are saving rather than spending dividends favor the low-dividend policy: The less the firm pays out in dividends, the less these stockholders have to pay in current taxes and the less trouble and expense they must go through to reinvest their after-tax dividends. Therefore, investors who want current investment income should own shares in high-dividend-payout firms, while investors with no need for current investment income should own shares in low-dividend-payout firms. For example, investors seeking high cash income might invest in Duke Energy, an electric utility that paid a dividend of $3.71 for a dividend payout of 79% in mid-2018, while investors favoring growth could invest in Adobe Systems, a computer software company that had no dividend payout.

---

[6]Stephen Ross has suggested that managers can use capital structure as well as dividends to give signals concerning a firm's future prospects. For example, a firm with good earnings prospects can carry more debt than a similar firm with poor earnings prospects. This theory, called *incentive signaling*, rests on the premise that signals with cash-based variables (either debt interest or dividends) cannot be mimicked by unsuccessful firms because those firms do not have the future cash-generating power to maintain the announced interest or dividend payment. Thus, investors are more likely to believe a glowing verbal report when it is accompanied by a dividend increase or a debt-financed expansion program. See Stephen A. Ross, "The Determination of Financial Structure: The Incentive-Signaling Approach," *The Bell Journal of Economics*, vol. 8, no. 1 (Spring 1977), pp. 23–40.

All of this suggests that a **clientele effect** exists, which means that firms have different clienteles and that the clienteles have different preferences; hence, a change in dividend policy might upset the majority clientele and have a negative effect on the stock's price.[7] This suggests that a company should follow a stable, dependable dividend policy so as to avoid upsetting its clientele.

Clientele Effect
The tendency of a firm to attract a set of investors who like its dividend policy.

Borrowing from the ideas of *behavioral finance,* some recent research suggests that investors' preferences for dividends vary over time. Malcolm Baker and Jeffrey Wurgler have proposed a **catering theory** for dividends where investors sometimes have strong preferences for safety and high-dividend-paying stocks, whereas at other times they are more aggressive and seek low-dividend-paying stocks with greater potential for capital gains. Baker and Wurgler argue that corporate managers who accommodate the shifting preferences of investors are more likely to initiate dividends when dividend-paying stocks are in favor with investors, and are more likely to omit dividends when investors demonstrate a greater preference for capital gains.[8]

Catering Theory
A theory that suggests investors' preferences for dividends vary over time and that corporations adapt their dividend policies to cater to the current desires of investors.

SelfTest

Define (1) information content and (2) the clientele effect, and explain how they affect dividend policy.

What is catering theory, and how does it impact a firm's dividend policy?

14-3 Establishing the Dividend Policy in Practice

Investors may or may not prefer dividends to capital gains; however, because of the clientele effect, they almost certainly prefer *predictable* dividends. Given this situation, how should firms set their basic dividend policies? In particular, how should a company establish the specific percentage of earnings it will distribute, the form of that distribution, and the stability of its distributions over time? In this section, we describe how most firms answer those questions.

resource

Students can download the Excel chapter models from the textbook's student companion site on cengage.com. Once downloaded onto your computer, retrieve the Chapter 14 Excel model and follow along as you read this chapter.

14-3A SETTING THE TARGET PAYOUT RATIO: THE RESIDUAL DIVIDEND MODEL[9]

When a firm is deciding how much cash to distribute to stockholders, it should consider two points: (1) The overriding objective is to maximize shareholder value. (2) The firm's cash flows really belong to its shareholders, so management should not retain income unless they can reinvest those earnings at higher rates of return than shareholders can earn themselves. On the other hand, recall from

[7]For example, see R. Richardson Pettit, "Taxes, Transactions Costs and the Clientele Effect of Dividends," *Journal of Financial Economics,* vol. 5, no. 3 (December 1977), pp. 419–436.

[8]See Malcolm Baker and Jeffrey Wurgler, "A Catering Theory of Dividends," *Journal of Finance,* vol. 59, no. 3 (June 2004), pp. 1125–1165.

[9]The term *payout ratio* can be interpreted in two ways: (1) in the conventional way, as the percentage of net income paid out as *cash dividends* or (2) as the percentage of net income distributed to stockholders *through dividends and share repurchases.* In this section, we assume that no repurchases occur. Increasingly, though, firms are using the residual model to determine "distributions to shareholders" and then making a separate decision as to the form of those distributions. Further, over time, an increasing percentage of the total distribution has been in the form of share repurchases as we discuss in Section 14-7.

Chapter 10 that internal equity (retained earnings) is less expensive than external equity (new common stock), so if good investments are available, it is better to finance them with retained earnings than with new stock.

When a dividend policy is established, one size does not fit all. Some firms produce a large amount of cash but have limited investment opportunities—this is true for firms in profitable but mature industries where few growth opportunities exist. Such firms typically distribute a large percentage of their cash to shareholders, thereby attracting investor clienteles who prefer high dividends. Other firms have many good investment opportunities but currently generate little or no excess cash. Such firms generally distribute few or no cash dividends but enjoy rising earnings and stock prices, thereby attracting investors who prefer capital gains.

The past few decades have seen increasing numbers of young, high-growth firms trading on the stock exchanges. A study by Eugene Fama and Kenneth French showed that the proportion of firms paying dividends has fallen sharply over time. In 1978, 66.5% of firms on the major stock exchanges paid dividends. By 1999, that proportion had fallen to 20.8%. Fama and French's analysis suggested that part of this decline was due to the changing composition of firms on the exchanges. However, their analysis also indicated that all firms, new and old, have become less likely to pay dividends.[10]

As a result of the 2003 tax changes, which lowered the tax rate on dividends, many companies initiated dividends or increased their payouts. For example, in 2002, only 113 companies raised or initiated dividends; however, in 2003 that number doubled to 229. Previously, those companies would have been more inclined to repurchase shares. As of August 2018, 422 companies in the S&P 500 paid dividends.

As Table 14.1 suggests, dividend payouts and dividend yields for large corporations vary considerably. Generally, firms in stable, cash-producing

TABLE 14.1 Dividend Payouts in 2018

Company	Industry	Dividend Payout	Dividend Yield
I. Companies That Pay High Dividends			
Gannett	Newspaper	834.90%	6.13%
Southern Company	Electric utilities	210.91	4.96
AstraZeneca	Pharmaceuticals	126.37	7.07
Philip Morris International	Tobacco	105.58	5.15
Anheuser Busch Inbev	Beverage	98.42	4.34
II. Companies That Pay No Dividends			
Adobe Systems	Computer software	0.00%	0.00%
Amazon	Online retail	0.00	0.00
Biogen	Biotechnology	0.00	0.00
eBay	Internet services	0.00	0.00
Unisys	Computers	0.00	0.00

Source: *Yahoo! Finance* (finance.yahoo.com), August 10, 2018.

[10]Eugene F. Fama and Kenneth R. French, "Disappearing Dividends: Changing Firm Characteristics or Lower Propensity to Pay?" *Journal of Applied Corporate Finance*, vol. 14, no. 1 (Spring 2001), pp. 67–79; and "Disappearing Dividends: Changing Firm Characteristics or Lower Propensity to Pay?" *Journal of Financial Economics*, vol. 60, no. 1 (April 2001), pp. 3–43. The latter citation is a longer and more technical version of the first paper cited.

industries such as utilities and food pay relatively high dividends, whereas companies in rapidly growing industries such as computer software and biotechnology tend to pay lower dividends. Average dividends also differ significantly across countries. Higher payout ratios in some countries can be partially explained by lower tax rates on earnings distributed as cash dividends relative to applicable rates on reinvested income. This biases the dividend policy toward higher payouts.

For a given firm, the optimal payout ratio is a function of four factors: (1) management's opinion about its investors' preferences for dividends versus capital gains, (2) the firm's investment opportunities, (3) the firm's target capital structure, and (4) the availability and cost of external capital. These factors are combined in what we call the **residual dividend model**. First, under this model, we assume that investors are indifferent between dividends and capital gains. Then the firm follows these four steps to establish its target payout ratio: (1) It determines the optimal capital budget. (2) Given its target capital structure, it determines the amount of equity needed to finance that budget. (3) It uses retained earnings to meet equity requirements to the extent possible. (4) It pays dividends only if more earnings are available than are needed to support the optimal capital budget. The word *residual* implies "leftover," and the residual policy implies that dividends are paid out of "leftover" earnings.

Residual Dividend Model
A model in which the dividend paid is set equal to net income minus the amount of retained earnings necessary to finance the firm's optimal capital budget.

If a firm rigidly follows the residual dividend policy, dividends paid in any given year can be expressed in the following equation:

$$\text{Dividends} = \text{Net income} - \text{Retained earnings required to help finance new investments}$$

$$= \text{Net income} - [(\text{Target equity ratio})(\text{Total capital budget})]$$

For example, suppose the company has \$100 million of earnings, it has a target equity ratio of 60%, and it plans to spend \$50 million on capital projects. In that case, it would need \$50(0.6) = \$30 million of common equity plus \$20 million of new debt to finance the capital budget. That would leave \$100 − \$30 = \$70 million available for dividends, which would result in a 70% payout ratio.

Note that the amount of equity needed to finance the capital budget might exceed net income. In the preceding example, if the capital budget was \$100/Equity percentage = \$100/0.6 = \$166.67 million, no dividends would be paid. If the capital budget exceeded \$166.67 million, the company would have to issue new common stock in order to maintain its target capital structure.

Most firms have a target capital structure that calls for at least some debt, so new financing is done partly with debt and partly with equity. As long as a firm finances with the optimal mix of debt and equity and uses only internally generated equity (retained earnings), the marginal cost of each new dollar of capital will be minimized. So internally generated equity is available for financing a certain amount of new investment; beyond that amount, however, the firm must turn to more expensive new common stock. At the point where new stock must be sold, the cost of equity (and consequently the marginal cost of capital) rises.

To illustrate these points, consider the case of Texas and Western (T&W) Transport Company. T&W's overall composite cost of capital is 10%. However, this cost assumes that all new equity comes from retained earnings. If the company must issue new stock, its cost of capital will be higher. T&W has \$60 million of net income and a target capital structure with 60% equity and 40% debt. Provided it does not pay any cash dividends, T&W could make net investments (investments in addition to asset replacements from depreciation) of \$100 million, consisting of $60 million from retained earnings plus $40 million of new debt supported by the retained earnings, at a 10% marginal cost of capital. If the capital budget exceeded $100 million, the required equity component would exceed net income, which is, of course, the maximum possible amount of retained earnings. In this case, T&W would have to issue new common stock, thereby pushing its cost of capital above 10%.[11]

At the beginning of its planning period, T&W's financial staff considers all proposed projects for the upcoming period. All independent projects are accepted if their estimated IRRs exceed their risk-adjusted costs of capital. In choosing among mutually exclusive projects, the project with the highest positive NPV is accepted. The capital budget represents the amount of capital that is required to finance all accepted projects. If T&W follows a strict residual dividend policy, we can see from Table 14.2 that the estimated capital budget will have a profound effect on its dividend payout ratio. If investment opportunities are poor, the capital budget will be only $40 million. To maintain the target capital structure, 0.6($40) = $24 million must be equity, with the remaining $16 million as debt. If T&W followed a strict residual policy, it would pay out $60 − $24 = $36 million as dividends; hence, its payout ratio would be $36/$60 = 0.6 = 60%.

If the company's investment opportunities were average, its capital budget would be $70 million. This would require $42 million of equity, so dividends would be $60 − $42 = $18 million, for a payout of $18/$60 = 30%. Finally, if investment opportunities were good, the capital budget would be $150 million and 0.6($150) = $90 million of equity would be required. Therefore, all of the net income would be retained, dividends would be zero, and the company would have to issue some new common stock to maintain the target capital structure.

We see then that under the residual model, dividends and the payout ratio would vary with investment opportunities. Dividend variations would also occur if earnings fluctuated. Because investment opportunities and earnings vary from year to year, strict adherence to the residual dividend policy would

TABLE 14.2 T&W's Dividend Payout Ratio with $60 Million of Net Income When Faced with Different Investment Opportunities (dollars in millions)

	Investment Opportunities		
	Poor	Average	Good
Capital budget	$40	$70	$150
Net income (NI)	60	60	60
Required equity (0.6 × Capital budget)	24	42	90
Dividends paid (NI − Required equity)	$36	$18	($ 30)[a]
Dividend payout ratio (Dividends/NI)	60%	30%	0%

Note:
[a]With a $150 million capital budget, T&W would retain all of its earnings and also issue $30 million of new common stock.

[11]If T&W does not retain all of its earnings, its cost of capital will rise above 10% before its capital budget reaches $100 million. For example, if T&W chose to retain $36 million, its cost of capital would increase once the capital budget exceeded $36/0.6 = $60 million. To understand this point, note that a capital budget of $60 million would require $36 million of equity. If the capital budget rose above $60 million, the company's required equity capital would exceed its retained earnings, thereby requiring it to issue new common stock.

result in unstable dividends. One year the firm might pay zero dividends because it needed the money to finance good investment opportunities, but the next year it might pay high dividends because investment opportunities were poor and it didn't need to retain as much. Similarly, fluctuating earnings would also lead to variable dividends, even if investment opportunities were stable. *Therefore, following the residual dividend policy would almost certainly lead to fluctuating, unstable dividends.* This would not be bad if investors were not bothered by fluctuating dividends, but because investors prefer stable, dependable dividends, it would not be optimal to strictly follow the residual model each year. One possible strategy that firms could use to balance these concerns is to:

1. Estimate earnings and investment opportunities, on average, over the next 5 or so years.
2. Use the forecasted information to find the average dividends that would be paid using the residual model (and the corresponding payout ratio) during the planning period.
3. Set a target payout policy based on the projected data.

Thus, firms should use the residual policy to help set their long-run target payout ratios, but not as a guide to the payout in any one year.

Most large companies use the residual dividend model in a conceptual sense and then implement it with a computerized financial forecasting model. Information on projected capital expenditures and working capital requirements is entered into the model, along with sales forecasts, profit margins, depreciation, and the other elements required to forecast cash flows. The target capital structure is also specified; the model then generates the amount of debt and equity that will be required to meet the capital budgeting requirements while maintaining the target capital structure.

Dividend payments are introduced, and the higher the payout ratio, the greater the required external equity. Most companies use the model to find a dividend payout over the forecast period (generally 5 years) that will provide sufficient equity to support the capital budget without having to sell new common stock or taking the capital structure ratios outside the optimal range. This chapter's Excel model includes an illustration of this process. In addition, Web Appendix 14A discusses this approach in more detail. The end result might be a memo such as the following from the CFO to the chairperson of the board:

We forecasted the total market demand for our products, what our share of the market is likely to be, and our required investments in capital assets and working capital. Using this information, we developed projected balance sheets and income statements for the period 2020–2024.

Our 2019 dividends totaled $50 million, or $2.00 per share. On the basis of projected earnings, cash flows, and capital requirements, we can increase the dividend by 6% per year. This would be consistent with a payout ratio of 42%, on average, over the forecast period. Any faster dividend growth rate would require us to sell common stock, cut the capital budget, or raise the debt ratio. Any slower growth rate would lead to increases in the common equity ratio. Therefore, I recommend that the Board increase the dividend for 2020 by 6%, to $2.12, and that it plan for similar increases in the future.

Events over the next 5 years will undoubtedly lead to differences between our forecasts and actual results. If and when such events occur, we should reexamine our position. However, I am confident that we can meet random cash shortfalls by increasing our borrowings—we have unused debt capacity that gives us flexibility in this regard.

We ran the corporate model under several scenarios. If the economy totally collapses, our earnings will not cover the dividend. However, in all likely scenarios our cash flows would cover the recommended dividend. I know the Board does not want to push the dividend up to a level where we would have to cut it under poor economic conditions. Our model runs indicate, though, that the $2.12 dividend could be maintained under any reasonable set of forecasts. Only if we increased the dividend to more than $3.00 would we be seriously exposed to the danger of having to reduce it.

I might also note that most analysts' reports are forecasting that our dividends will grow in the 5% to 6% range. Thus, if we go to $2.12, we will be at the high end of the forecast range, which should give our stock a boost. With takeover rumors so widespread, getting the stock price up a bit would make us all breathe a little easier.

Finally, we considered distributing cash to shareholders through a stock repurchase program. Here we would reduce the dividend payout ratio and use the funds generated to buy our stock on the open market. Such a program has several advantages, but it would also have drawbacks. I do not recommend that we institute a stock repurchase program at this time. However, if our free cash flows exceed our forecasts, I would recommend that we use these surpluses to buy back stock. Also, I plan to continue looking into a regular repurchase program, and I may recommend such a program in the future.

This company has very stable operations, so it can plan its dividends with a fairly high degree of confidence. Other companies, especially those in cyclical industries, have difficulty maintaining a dividend in bad times that would be too low in good times. Such companies often set a very low "regular" dividend and then supplement it with an "extra" dividend when times are good, which is known as a **low-regular-dividend-plus-extras** dividend policy. The company announces a low regular dividend that it is confident it can maintain "come hell or high water," one that stockholders could count on under all conditions. Then when times are good and profits and cash flows are high, the company pays a clearly designated extra dividend. Because investors recognize that the extras might not be maintained in the future, they don't interpret them as a signal that the companies' earnings are permanently higher, nor do they take the elimination of the extra as a negative signal.

Low-Regular-Dividend-Plus-Extras
The policy of announcing a low, regular dividend that can be maintained no matter what and then, when times are good, paying a designated "extra" dividend.

Alternately, companies may temporarily suspend paying dividends because of a short-run need for cash, but the hope is that they will be able to restore the dividend when its situation returns to normal. For example, during the Deepwater Horizon oil spill crisis, BP bowed to political pressure and suspended a series of dividend payments for the first three quarters of 2010, using the cash to pay for part of its clean-up operations. BP resumed paying dividends in the fourth quarter of 2010 (although at a smaller amount than it had been paying prior to the oil spill).

14-3B EARNINGS, CASH FLOWS, AND DIVIDENDS

We normally think of earnings as being the primary determinant of dividends, but cash flows are actually more important. This is demonstrated in Figure 14.1, which plots data for Exxon Mobil Corporation from 1998 through 2017. Panel a shows that Exxon Mobil's dividends per share (DPS) rose slowly but steadily from 1998 to 2017. Earnings per share (EPS) also grew slowly, but they were more volatile, rising and falling with the price of oil. The earnings payout ratio (defined as DPS/EPS) averaged about 46% over the entire 20 years, but it exceeded 100% once during this time period—in 2016.

FIGURE 14.1 Exxon Mobil Corporation: Earnings, Cash Flows, and Dividends, 1998–2017

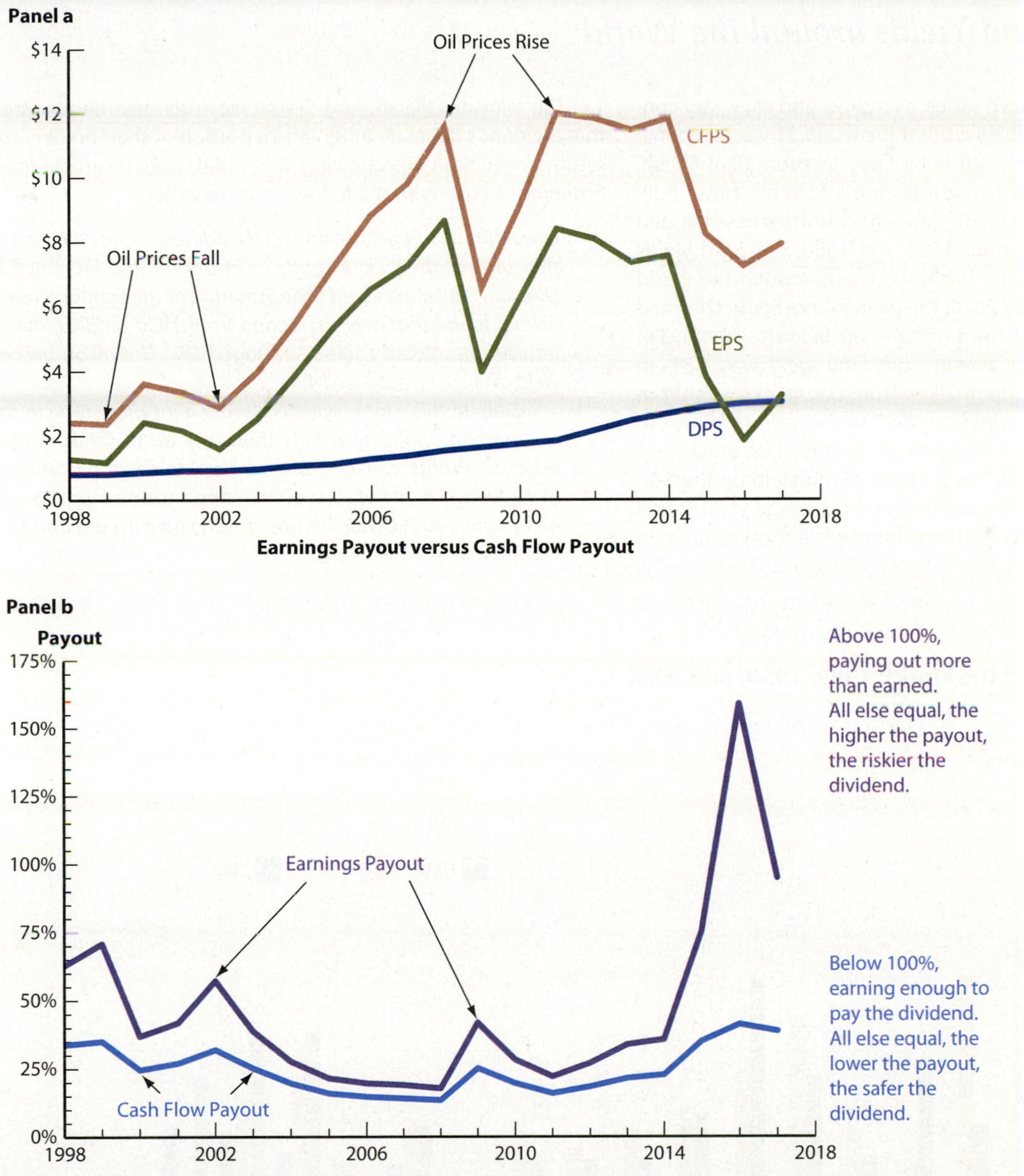

Note: For consistency, data have been adjusted for two-for-one splits in 1994 and 2004.
Source: Adapted from *Value Line Investment Survey*, various issues.

Cash flow per share (CFPS) tracked EPS very closely—the two were correlated at 0.93. However, CFPS was always higher than EPS, and it always exceeded the dividend by a substantial margin. Moreover, cash dividends are paid in cash, so even when earnings were insufficient to cover the dividend, cash flows took up the slack and enabled the company to maintain a stable dividend policy.

GLOBAL PERSPECTIVES

Dividend Yields around the World

Average dividend yields have varied over time, and they vary considerably in different countries around the world. The accompanying graph, obtained from a study by Elroy Dimson, Paul Marsh, and Mike Staunton of the London Business School, shows how the average dividend yield for 16 different countries has changed over the past century. In both 1900 and 1950, dividend yields varied from nation to nation, but the average around the world was about 5%. However, by 2004, the yield in most countries had declined significantly and the average had fallen to about 3%. For the United States, the average dividend yield was 4.3% in 1900, 7.2% in 1950, and 1.7% in 2004. Thus, U.S. stocks went from having one of the highest yields in 1950 to the second lowest in 2004. Since then, the average dividend yield for U.S. stocks has increased somewhat. In July 2018, the dividend yield on the S&P 500 was 1.81%, a level that is still below the average yield found in many other countries. As further evidence, we show a table on the next page that summarizes selected country dividend yields in early 2017.

The Dimson, Marsh, and Staunton study also demonstrates that dividends generate a significant portion of shareholders' total returns over time. Recognizing this point, a 2010 article in *The Economist* began with the following observation:

> *Dividends do not get the respect they deserve. Over the long run they provide the bulk of equity investors' returns. Work by Elroy Dimson, Paul Marsh, and Mike Staunton of the London Business School found that over the period from 1900 to 2005, the real return from global equities averaged 5%. The mean dividend yield over that period was 4.5%.*
>
> *Despite this, stock markets devote a lot more time to forecasting and analyzing profits than they do to thinking about payouts. Profits can be easily manipulated and come in a bewildering variety of forms (operating, reported, posttax, pre-exceptional, etc.). Dividends are (mostly) paid in cash and so are hard to fake.*

Dividend Yields around the World: 1900, 1950, and 2004

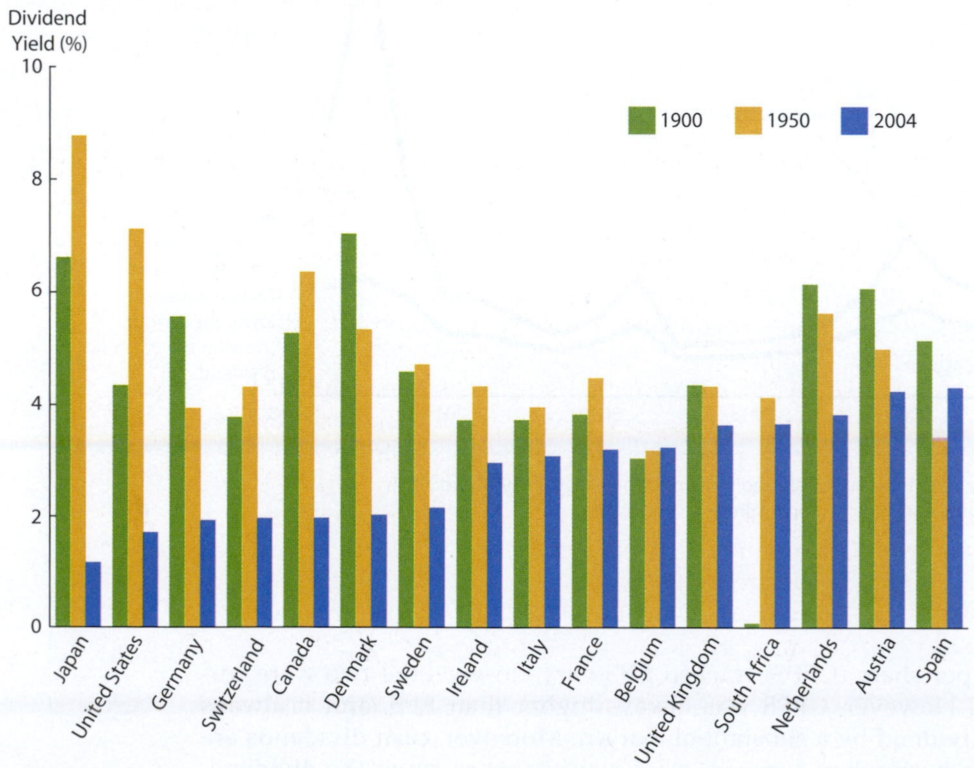

Sample of Dividend Yields around the World as of January 2017

Country	Dividend Yield
Turkey	4.15%
Australia	3.98
Italy	3.58
United Kingdom	3.41
Saudi Arabia	3.39
South Africa	2.93
Russia	2.91
Brazil	2.89
France	2.88
Germany	2.65
China	2.64
Japan	2.48
Canada	2.41
United States	1.93
Indonesia	1.80
South Korea	1.47
Mexico	1.46
Argentina	1.43
India	0.99

Note: Data obtained from Aswath Damodaran, Dividend and Cash Return, by Country Dataset (dividendcountry2017.xls).

Sources: Aswath Damodaran, "January 2017 Data Update 9: Dividends and Buybacks," aswathdamodaran.blogspot.com/2017/02/January-2017-data-update-9-dividends.html, January 2017; "Divvying Up Returns," *The Economist* (www.economist.com), September 2, 2010; and Elroy Dimson, Paul Marsh, and Mike Staunton, *Triumph of the Optimists* (Princeton, NJ: Princeton University Press, 2002).

Now look at panel b. Here we see that the earnings payout is extremely volatile, but the cash flow payout (defined as DPS/CFPS) is relatively stable and always below 100%. Those stable (and high) cash flows indicate that Exxon Mobil's dividend is relatively safe, and investors can count on receiving it going forward. Indeed, given the very high cash flows per share, continued substantial dividend increases (or large share repurchases) are likely—provided something bad doesn't happen in the oil market.

Exxon Mobil is typical of most large, strong companies. Its dividend is dependable, and it grows at a steady rate. Earnings are relatively volatile, but cash flows are more stable, and those stable cash flows are responsible for the steady dividends. When earnings change dramatically, either up or down, dividends are likely to follow with a lag while management determines whether the earnings change is likely to continue. Thus, the dip in Exxon Mobil's earnings in 2001 and 2002 turned out to be temporary, so the dividend was increased slightly during those years. The huge earnings and cash flow gains after 2002 continued into 2008. Earnings and cash flows declined in 2009 during the economic slowdown and returned to even higher levels during 2010 and 2011, but declined in 2012 and 2013. In 2014, earnings and cash flow increased slightly, but they were still below the 2011 levels. Earnings and cash flow declined in 2015 and 2016, but cash flow was above the 2009 level. In 2017, earnings and cash flow increased from 2016 levels, but only cash flow was still above the 2009 level. However, with the exception of 2016, Exxon Mobil's DPS is still well below its CFPS and EPS, which suggests that dividends, repurchases, and profitable new investments will continue on into the future. But Exxon Mobil does deal with oil, and with that commodity, strange things can happen!

14-3C PAYMENT PROCEDURES

Companies normally pay dividends quarterly, and if conditions permit, the dividend is increased once each year. For example, Katz Corporation paid $0.50 per quarter in 2019, an annual rate of $2.00. In common financial parlance, we say that Katz's 2019 *regular quarterly dividend* was $0.50 and its *annual dividend* was $2.00. In late 2019, Katz's board of directors met, reviewed projections for 2020, and decided to keep the 2020 dividend at $2.00. The directors announced the $2.00 rate, so stockholders can count on receiving it unless unanticipated operating problems arise.

The actual payment procedure is as follows:

Declaration Date
The date on which a firm's directors issue a statement declaring a dividend.

1. *Declaration date.* On the **declaration date**—say, November 4—the directors meet and declare the regular dividend, issuing a statement similar to the following: "On November 4, 2019, the directors of Katz Corporation met and declared the regular quarterly dividend of 50 cents per share, payable to holders of record at the close of business on December 5, payment to be made on January 2, 2020." For accounting purposes, the declared dividend becomes an actual liability on the declaration date. If a balance sheet was constructed, the amount ($0.50 × Number of shares outstanding) would appear as a current liability and retained earnings would be reduced by a like amount.

Holder-of-Record Date
If the company lists the stockholder as an owner on this date, then the stockholder receives the dividend.

2. *Holder-of-record date.* At the close of business on the **holder-of-record date**, December 5, the company closes its stock transfer books and makes up a list of shareholders as of that date. If Katz Corporation is notified of the sale before the close of business on December 5, the new owner will receive the dividend. However, if notification is received on or after December 6, the previous owner will receive the dividend check.

Ex-Dividend Date
The date on which the right to the current dividend no longer accompanies a stock; it is usually two business days prior to the holder-of-record date.

3. *Ex-dividend date.* Suppose Jean Buyer buys 100 shares of stock from John Seller on December 2. Will the company be notified of the transfer in time to list Buyer as the new owner and thus pay the dividend to her? To avoid conflict, the securities industry has set up a convention under which the right to the dividend remains with the stock until two business days prior to the holder-of-record date; on the second business day before that date, the right to the dividend no longer goes with the shares. The date when the right to the dividend leaves the stock is called the **ex-dividend date**. In this case, the ex-dividend date is two business days prior to December 5, or December 3:

Dividend goes with stock if it is bought on or before this date	December 2
Ex-dividend date: Buyer does not receive the dividend	December 3
Buyer does not receive the dividend	December 4
Holder-of-record date; not normally of concern to stockholder	December 5

Therefore, if Buyer is to receive the dividend, Buyer must buy the stock on or before December 2. If Buyer buys it on December 3 or later, Seller will receive the dividend because he or she will be the official holder of record.

*For additional information regarding when you're entitled to dividends and when you're not, visit **www.sec.gov/fast-answers/answers-dividenhtm.html**.*

Katz's dividend amounts to $0.50, so the ex-dividend date is important. Barring fluctuations in the stock market, we would normally expect the price of a stock to drop by approximately the amount of the dividend on the ex-dividend date. Thus, if Katz closed at $30.50 on December 2, it would probably open at about $30 on December 3.[12]

4. *Payment date.* The company actually mails the checks to the holders of record on January 2, the **payment date.**

Payment Date
The date on which a firm actually mails dividend checks.

Self*Test*

Explain the logic of the residual dividend model, the steps a firm would take to implement it, and the reason it is more likely to be used to establish a long-run payout target than to set the actual year-by-year payout ratio.

How do firms use long-run planning models to help set dividend policy?

Which are more critical to the dividend decision, earnings or cash flow? Explain.

Explain the procedures used to actually pay the dividend.

What is the ex-dividend date, and why is it important to investors?

A firm has a capital budget of $30 million, net income of $35 million, and a target capital structure of 45% debt and 55% equity. If the residual dividend policy is used, what is the firm's dividend payout ratio? **(52.86%)**

14-4 Dividend Reinvestment Plans

During the 1970s, most large companies instituted **dividend reinvestment plans (DRIPs)**, under which stockholders can automatically reinvest their dividends in the stock of the paying corporation.[13] Today most large companies offer DRIPs, but participation rates vary considerably. There are two types of DRIPs: (1) plans that involve only old, already outstanding stock and (2) plans that involve newly issued stock. In either case, the stockholder must pay taxes on the amount of the dividends even though stock rather than cash is received.

Dividend Reinvestment Plans (DRIPs)
Plans that enable stockholders to automatically reinvest dividends received back into the stocks of the paying firms.

Under both types of DRIPs, stockholders choose between continuing to receive dividend checks versus having the company use the dividends to buy

[12]Tax effects cause the price decline, on average, to be less than the full amount of the dividend. If you bought Katz's stock on December 2, you would receive the dividend, but you would almost immediately pay 15% (20% if you were a high-income taxpayer) of it in taxes. Thus, you would want to wait until December 3 to buy the stock if you thought you could get it for $0.50 less per share. Your reaction (and that of others) would influence stock prices around dividend payment dates. Here is what would happen:

1. Other things held constant, a stock's price should rise during the quarter, with the daily price increase (for Katz) equal to $0.50/90 = $0.005556. Therefore, if the price started at $30 just after its last ex-dividend date, it would rise to $30.50 on December 2.
2. In the absence of taxes, the stock's price would fall to $30 on December 3 and then start up as the next dividend accrual period began. Thus, over time, if everything else was held constant, the stock's price would follow a sawtooth pattern if it was plotted on a graph.
3. Because of taxes, the stock's price would neither rise by the full amount of the dividend nor fall by the full dividend amount when it goes ex-dividend.
4. The amount of the rise and subsequent fall would be the Dividend (1 – T), where generally T = 15%, the tax rate on individual dividends (unless you are a high-income taxpayer then T = 20%).

See Edwin J. Elton and Martin J. Gruber, "Marginal Stockholder Tax Rates and the Clientele Effect," *Review of Economics and Statistics*, vol. 5, no. 3 (February 1970), pp. 68–74, for an interesting discussion of the subject.

[13]See Richard H. Pettway and R. Phil Malone, "Automatic Dividend Reinvestment Plans," *Financial Management*, vol. 2, no. 4 (Winter 1973), pp. 11–18, for an old but still excellent discussion of the subject.

more stock in the corporation for the investor. Under an "old stock" plan, the company gives the money that stockholders who elect to use the DRIP would have received to a bank, which acts as a trustee. The bank then uses the money to purchase the corporation's stock on the open market and allocates the shares purchased to the participating stockholders' accounts on a pro rata basis. The transactions costs of buying shares (brokerage costs) are low because of volume purchases, so these plans benefit small stockholders who do not need current cash dividends.

A "new stock" DRIP invests the dividends in newly issued stock; hence, these plans raise new capital for the firm. AT&T, Xerox, and many other companies have used new stock plans to raise substantial amounts of equity. No fees are charged to stockholders, and some companies have offered stock at discounts of 1% to 10% below the actual market price. The companies offer discounts because they would have incurred flotation costs if the new stock had been raised through investment banks.

One interesting aspect of DRIPs is that they are forcing corporations to reexamine their basic dividend policies. A high participation rate in a DRIP suggests that stockholders might be better served if the firm simply reduced cash dividends, which would save stockholders some personal income taxes. Quite a few firms have surveyed their stockholders to learn more about their preferences and to find out how they would react to a change in dividend policy. A more rational approach to basic dividend policy decisions may emerge from this research. Companies switch from old stock to new stock DRIPs depending on their need for equity capital.

Currently (August 2018), of the 30 stocks making up the Dow Jones Industrial Average, 26 offer dividend reinvestment programs. The four companies not offering a DRIP are Apple, Goldman Sachs, UnitedHealth Group, and VISA.[14] Many companies offering DRIPs have expanded their programs by moving to "open enrollment," whereby anyone can purchase the firm's stock directly and thus bypass brokers' commissions. As of January 2017, there are nearly 1,300 dividend-paying companies that offer DRIPs.[15]

Many companies have taken even broader steps to encourage investors to buy their shares. For example, Exxon Mobil not only allows investors to buy their initial shares at no fee but also lets them pick up additional shares through automatic bank account withdrawals. Several plans, including Exxon Mobil's, offer dividend reinvestment for individual retirement accounts, and some allow participants to invest weekly or monthly rather than on the quarterly dividend schedule. With all of these plans (and many others), stockholders can invest more than the dividends they are forgoing—they simply send a check to the company and buy shares without a brokerage commission.

Self*Test*

What are dividend reinvestment plans?

What are their advantages and disadvantages from both stockholders' and firms' perspectives?

---

[14]See Charles Carlson, "DJIA Turns 120 Years Old," *DRIP Investor* (www.dripinvestor.com/totw/totw436.asp), June 20, 2016.

[15]Refer to Vita Nelson, "Ten Dividend Stocks to Own Forever and Get Rich Slowly," *Forbes* (www.forbes.com), January 18, 2017.

14-5 Summary of Factors Influencing Dividend Policy

In earlier sections, we described the theories of investors' preferences for dividends and the potential effects of dividend policy on the value of a firm. We also discussed the residual dividend model for setting a firm's long-run target payout ratio. In this section, we discuss several other factors that affect the dividend decision. These factors may be grouped into four broad categories: (1) constraints on dividend payments, (2) investment opportunities, (3) availability and cost of alternative sources of capital, and (4) effects of dividend policy on r_s. We discuss these factors next.

14-5A CONSTRAINTS

1. *Bond indentures.* Debt contracts often limit dividend payments to earnings generated after the loan was granted. Also, debt contracts often stipulate that no dividends can be paid unless the current ratio, times-interest-earned ratio, and other safety ratios exceed stated minimums.
2. *Regulatory requirements.* Companies in regulated industries may face direct or indirect limitations on their ability to return cash to shareholders. Most notably, the Dodd-Frank Act mandates that banks have to pass a series of "stress tests" before they are able to pay dividends or repurchase stock.
3. *Preferred stock restrictions.* Typically, common dividends cannot be paid if the company has omitted its preferred dividend. The preferred arrearages must be satisfied before common dividends can be resumed.
4. *Impairment of capital rule.* Dividend payments cannot exceed the balance sheet item "retained earnings." This legal restriction, known as the impairment of capital rule, is designed to protect creditors. Without the rule, a company that is in trouble might distribute most of its assets to stockholders and leave its debtholders out in the cold. (Liquidating dividends can be paid out of capital, but they must be indicated as such, and they must not reduce capital below the limits stated in debt contracts.)
5. *Availability of cash.* Cash dividends can be paid only with cash. Thus, a shortage of cash in the bank can restrict dividend payments. However, the ability to borrow can offset this factor.
6. *Penalty tax on improperly accumulated earnings.* To prevent wealthy individuals from using corporations to avoid personal taxes, the Tax Code provides for a special surtax on improperly accumulated income. Thus, if the IRS can demonstrate that a firm's dividend payout ratio is deliberately being held down to help its stockholders avoid personal taxes, the firm is subject to heavy penalties. This factor is relevant primarily to privately owned firms.

14-5B INVESTMENT OPPORTUNITIES

1. *Number of profitable investment opportunities.* As we saw in our discussion of the residual dividend model, if a firm has a large number of profitable investment opportunities, this will tend to produce a low target payout ratio and vice versa if the firm has few good investment opportunities.
2. *Possibility of accelerating or delaying projects.* The ability to accelerate or postpone projects permits a firm to adhere more closely to a stable dividend policy.

14-5C ALTERNATIVE SOURCES OF CAPITAL

1. *Cost of selling new stock.* If a firm needs to finance a given level of investment, it can obtain equity by retaining earnings or by issuing new common stock. If flotation costs (including any negative signaling effects of a stock offering) are high, r_e will be well above r_s, making it better to set a low payout ratio and to finance through retention rather than through the sale of new common stock. On the other hand, a high dividend payout ratio is more feasible for a firm whose flotation costs are low. Flotation costs differ among firms—for example, the flotation percentage is especially high for small firms, so they tend to set low payout ratios.
2. *Ability to substitute debt for equity.* A firm can finance a given level of investment with debt or equity. As noted, low stock flotation costs permit a more flexible dividend policy because equity can be raised by retaining earnings or by selling new stock. A similar situation holds for debt policy: If the firm can adjust its debt ratio without raising its WACC sharply, it can pay the expected dividend, even if earnings fluctuate, by additional borrowing.
3. *Control.* If management is concerned about maintaining control, it may be reluctant to sell new stock; hence, the company may retain more earnings than it otherwise would. However, if stockholders want higher dividends and a proxy fight looms, the dividend might be increased.

14-5D EFFECTS OF DIVIDEND POLICY ON r_s

The effects of dividend policy on r_s may be considered in terms of four factors: (1) stockholders' desire for current versus future income, (2) the perceived riskiness of dividends versus capital gains, (3) the tax advantage of capital gains, and (4) the information (signaling) content of dividends. We discussed each of those factors earlier, so we only note here that the importance of each factor varies from firm to firm depending on the makeup of its current and possible future stockholders.

It should be apparent that dividend policy decisions are based more on informed judgment than on quantitative analysis. Even so, to make rational dividend decisions, financial managers must take into account all the points discussed in the preceding sections.

Self*Test*

Identify the four broad sets of factors that affect dividend policy.

What constraints affect dividend policy?

How do investment opportunities affect dividend policy?

How does the availability and cost of outside capital affect dividend policy?

14-6 Stock Dividends and Stock Splits

Stock dividends were originally used in lieu of regular cash dividends by firms that were short of cash. Today, though, the primary purpose of stock dividends is to increase the number of shares outstanding and thus to lower the stock's price in the market. Stock splits have a similar purpose.

Stock dividends and splits can be explained best through an example. We use Porter Electronic Controls Inc., a $700 million electronic components manufacturer, for this purpose. Since its inception, Porter's markets have been expanding and the company has enjoyed growth in sales and earnings. Some of its earnings have been paid out in dividends, but some also were retained each year, causing its EPS and the stock price to grow. The company began its life with only a few thousand shares outstanding, and, after some years of growth, each of Porter's shares had a very high EPS and DPS. When a "normal" P/E ratio was applied, the resulting market price was so high that few people could afford to buy a "round lot" of 100 shares. This high market price limited demand for the stock and thus kept the firm's total market value below what it would have been if more shares at a lower price had been outstanding. To correct this situation, Porter "split its stock," as described in the next section.

14-6A STOCK SPLITS

Although there is little empirical evidence to support the contention, there is nevertheless a widespread belief in financial circles that an *optimal price range* exists for stocks. *Optimal* means that if the price is within this range, the price/earnings ratio (and hence the firm's value) will be maximized. Many observers, including Porter's management, believe that the best range for most stocks is from $20 to $80 per share. Accordingly, if the price of Porter's stock rose to $80, management would probably declare a two-for-one **stock split**, thus doubling the number of shares outstanding, halving the EPS and DPS, and thereby lowering the stock price. Each stockholder would have more shares, but each share would be worth less. In Yogi Berra's terms (refer to the feature box "Yogi Berra on the MM Proposition" in Chapter 13), a stock split just divides the corporate value pie into more slices. If the post-split price was $40, Porter's stockholders would be exactly as well off as they were before the split. However, if the stock price stabilized above $40, stockholders would be better off. Stock splits can be split in varying proportions—for example, the stock can be split two-for-one, three-for-one, one-and-a-half-for-one, or any other way.[16]

Stock Split
An action taken by a firm to increase the number of shares outstanding, such as doubling the number of shares outstanding by giving each stockholder two new shares for each one formerly held.

14-6B STOCK DIVIDENDS

Stock dividends are similar to stock splits because they "divide the pie into smaller slices" without affecting the fundamental position of the current stockholders. On a 5% stock dividend, the holder of 100 shares would receive an additional 5 shares (without cost); on a 20% stock dividend, the same holder would receive 20 new shares; and so forth. Again, the total number of shares is increased, so, holding all other things constant, earnings, dividends, and price per share all decline.

Stock Dividends
A dividend paid in the form of additional shares of stock rather than in cash.

If a firm wants to reduce its stock price, should it use a stock split or a stock dividend? Stock splits are generally used after a sharp price run-up to produce a large price reduction. Stock dividends used on a regular annual basis keep the stock price more or less constrained. For example, if a firm's earnings and dividends were growing at about 10% per year, its stock price would tend to increase at about that same rate, and it would soon be outside the desired trading range. A 10% annual stock dividend would maintain the stock price within the optimal trading range. Note, however, that because small stock dividends create

[16]*Reverse splits,* which reduce the shares outstanding, also can be used. For example, a company whose stock sells for $5 might employ a one-for-five reverse split, exchanging one new share for five old ones and raising the value of the shares to about $25, which is within the optimal price range. LTV Corporation did this after several years of losses had driven its stock price below the optimal range.

bookkeeping problems and unnecessary expenses, firms use stock splits far more often than stock dividends.[17]

14-6C EFFECT ON STOCK PRICES

If a company splits its stock or declares a stock dividend, will this increase the market value of its stock? From a pure economic standpoint, stock dividends and splits are just additional pieces of paper. However, they provide management with a relatively low-cost way of signaling that the firm's prospects look good. Further, we should note that few large, publicly owned stocks sell at prices above several hundred dollars; therefore, we simply do not know what the effect would be if, for example, Exxon Mobil, Chevron, Microsoft, Xerox, HP, and other highly successful firms had never split their stocks and consequently sold at prices in the thousands or even millions of dollars per share.

A recent *BloombergBusiness* article notes that stock splits have become a lot less popular in recent years. The article suggests that one possible reason for this shift is that individual investors have increasingly moved from buying shares of individual companies and have instead navigated toward mutual funds. Consequently, institutional investors (such as mutual funds) have become relatively more important. These institutional investors are less concerned about whether a stock's price is above or below a particular range, and they are less likely to value stock splits.[18] Similarly, a 2014 article in *The Wall Street Journal* reports that "S&P 500 companies have been splitting around a dozen times annually in recent years, down from 100 or more at the heights of the 1980s and 1990s stock bull markets, according to Howard Silverblatt of S&P Dow Jones Indices."[19] In mid-2018, the three top stock splits were done by AFLAC, Trex, and Herbalife Nutrition. According to data from S&P Dow Jones Indices, the minimum number of stock splits came in 2017, when there were only 5 stock splits.[20] And, after decades of "mostly remaining in a range between $25 and $50, the average stock in the S&P 500 is now trading above $98, the highest ever, according to Birinyi Associates."[21]

Despite the drop in the frequency of stock splits, a number of high profile firms continue to employ stock splits. In 2014, Apple announced a seven-for-one stock split, and in 2015, Netflix also announced a seven-for-one stock split. Ball Corporation is one of the two S&P 500 companies that split its shares in 2017 and increased its dividend to signal to investors that its cash flow was strong. Finally, it is also worth pointing out that Warren Buffett, Chairman and CEO of Berkshire Hathaway, had long resisted the use of stock splits, but he shifted gears in early 2010. After Berkshire Hathaway acquired Burlington Northern Santa Fe, the

---

[17]Accountants treat stock splits and stock dividends somewhat differently. For example, in a two-for-one stock split, the number of shares outstanding is doubled and the par value is halved, and that is about all there is to it. With a stock dividend, a bookkeeping entry is made transferring "retained earnings" to "common stock." For example, if a firm had 1,000,000 shares outstanding, if the stock price was $10, and if it wanted to pay a 10% stock dividend, (1) each stockholder would be given 1 new share of stock for each 10 shares held, and (2) the accounting entries would involve showing 100,000 more shares outstanding and transferring 100,000($10) = $1,000,000 from "retained earnings" to "common stock." The retained earnings transfer limits the size of stock dividends, but that is not important because companies can split their stock any way they choose.

[18]Refer to Whitney Kisling and Alex Barinka, "Stock Splits Lose Their Allure for Companies Trading Above $100," *BloombergBusiness* (www.bloomberg.com), August 22, 2013.

[19]Daisuke Wakabayashi, "Apple Boosts Buyback, Splits Stock to Reward Investors," *The Wall Street Journal* (www.wsj.com), April 23, 2014.

[20]Refer to Dan Caplinger, "The 3 Top Stock Splits of 2018," *The Motley Fool* (www.fool.com/investing/2018/06/15/the-3-top-stock-splits-of-2018.aspx), June 15, 2018; and Kinsey Grant, "Why Aren't Companies Splitting Their Stocks Anymore? *The Street* (www.thestreet.com/markets/why-arent-companies-splitting-stock-anymore--14584642), May 9, 2018.

[21]Erik Holm and Ben Eisen, "Amazon's Brush with $1,000 Signals the Death of the Stock Split," *Fox Business* (www.foxbusiness.com), May 26, 2017.

company announced a 50-for-1 split for its Class B shares. Prior to the announcement, the stock traded around $3,500 per share. After the split, the stock traded around $70 per share.

Self*Test*

What are stock dividends and stock splits?

How do stock dividends and splits affect stock prices?

In what situation should a firm pay a stock dividend?

In what situation should a firm split its stock?

Suppose you have 100 common shares of Tillman Industries. The EPS is $4.00, the DPS is $2.00, and the stock sells for $60 per share. Now Tillman announces a two-for-one split. Immediately after the split, how many shares will you have, what will be the adjusted EPS and DPS, and what would you expect the stock price to be? **(200 shares, $2.00, $1.00, probably a little over $30)**

14-7 Stock Repurchases

Several years ago, a *Fortune* article entitled "Beating the Market by Buying Back Stock" reported that during a 1-year period, more than 600 major corporations repurchased significant amounts of their own stock. It also gave illustrations of some specific companies' repurchase programs and the effects of these programs on stock prices. The article's conclusion was that "buybacks have made a mint for shareholders who stay with the companies carrying them out."

More recently, as we noted in the opening vignette, Apple Inc. has repurchased a large number of shares of its common stock since 2012. Apple's recent actions are part of a larger trend in which many leading companies have repurchased stock. In July 2018, *The Wall Street Journal* reported that U.S. corporations were buying back stock at a record pace. However, the report also noted that the market's response to the 2018 buybacks has not always been stellar: "57% of the more than 350 companies in the S&P 500 that bought back shares so far this year are trailing the index's 3.2% increase. That is the highest percentage of companies to fall short of the benchmark's gain since the onset of the financial crisis in 2008."[22] One explanation for this relatively poor market response is that many companies may be buying back their shares at overvalued prices. Beyond their effect on shareholders, others criticize buybacks because they prefer to see the companies use the money to reinvest in new projects or pay higher wages to their workers. With these issues in mind, we discuss in the remainder of this section two important questions: How do stock repurchase programs work, and why have they become so prevalent over the past several years?

There are three principal types of **stock repurchases**: (1) situations where the firm has cash available for distribution to its stockholders, and it distributes this cash by repurchasing shares rather than by paying cash dividends; (2) situations where the firm concludes that its capital structure is too heavily weighted with equity, and it sells debt and uses the proceeds to buy back its stock; and (3) situations where the firm has issued options to employees, and it uses open market repurchases to obtain stock for use when the options are exercised.

Stock Repurchases
Transactions in which a firm buys back shares of its own stock, thereby decreasing shares outstanding, increasing EPS, and, often, increasing the stock price.

Stock that has been repurchased by a firm is called *treasury stock*. If some of the outstanding stock is repurchased, fewer shares will remain outstanding. Assuming

[22]Refer to Michael Wursthorn, "Stock Buybacks Are Booming, but Share Prices Aren't Budging," *The Wall Street Journal* (www.wsj.com), July 8, 2018.

that the repurchase does not adversely affect the firm's future earnings, the earnings per share on the remaining shares will increase, resulting in a higher market price per share. As a result, capital gains will have been substituted for dividends.

14-7A THE EFFECTS OF STOCK REPURCHASES

Many companies have been repurchasing their stock in recent years. As mentioned in the opening vignette, between 2012 and March 2018, Apple repurchased \$200 billion. *The Wall Street Journal* recently reported that between 2006 and early 2013, DirecTV repurchased 57% of its shares, which is the highest proportion of shares repurchased among the stocks in the S&P 500 over this time period.[23] In the past, other large repurchases have been made by Procter & Gamble, Dell, Home Depot, Texas Instruments, IBM, Coca-Cola, Teledyne, Atlantic Richfield, Goodyear, and Xerox. Indeed, share repurchases have soared in recent years—in fact, S&P 500 companies are on track to repurchase as much as \$800 billion in stock in 2018.[24] In one respect, this is good news for shareholders, since as we mentioned earlier, share prices tend to rise after announced repurchases. At the same time, some critics are concerned that companies are relying too much on repurchases, and they argue that companies are not investing enough in future projects.[25]

The effects of a repurchase can be illustrated with data on American Development Corporation (ADC). The company expects to earn \$4.4 million in 2019, and it plans to use 50% of this amount (or \$2.2 million) to repurchase shares of its common stock. There are 1.1 million shares outstanding, and the market price is \$20 a share. ADC believes that it can use the \$2.2 million to repurchase 110,000 of its shares at the current price of \$20 per share.[26]

The effect of the repurchase on the EPS and market price per share of the remaining stock can be analyzed as follows:

1. $\text{Current EPS} = \dfrac{\text{Total earnings}}{\text{Number of shares}} = \dfrac{\$4.4\text{ million}}{1.1\text{ million}} = \$4.00\text{ per share}$

2. $\text{P/E ratio} = \dfrac{\$20}{\$4} = 5\times$

3. $\text{EPS after repurchasing 110,000 shares} = \dfrac{\$4.4\text{ million}}{0.99\text{ million}} = \$4.44\text{ per share}$

4. $\text{P/E ratio after repurchase} = \dfrac{\$20}{\$4.44} = 4.50\times$

It should be noted from this example that we assumed that the shares were repurchased at the current stock price of \$20 per share. In this example, the company's EPS increased, but there was a corresponding drop in its P/E ratio. One reason

[23]Refer to Vipal Monga, "DirecTV Tops in Buying Back Stock Since 2006," *The Wall Street Journal* (www.wsj.com), May 9, 2013.

[24]Refer to Michael Wursthorn, "Stock Buybacks Are Booming, but Share Prices Aren't Budging," *The Wall Street Journal* (www.wsj.com), July 8, 2018.

[25]See "The Repurchase Revolution," *The Economist* (www.economist.com), September 12, 2014.

[26]Stock repurchases are generally made in one of three ways: (1) A publicly owned firm can simply buy its own stock through a broker on the open market. (2) It can make a *tender offer,* under which it permits stockholders to send in (i.e., "tender") their shares to the firm in exchange for a specified price per share. In this case, the firm generally indicates that it will buy up to a specified number of shares within a particular time period (usually about 2 weeks); if more shares are tendered than the company wants to purchase, purchases are made on a pro rata basis. (3) The firm can purchase a block of shares from one large holder on a negotiated basis. If a negotiated purchase is employed, care must be taken to ensure that this one stockholder does not receive preferential treatment over other stockholders, or that any preference given can be justified by "sound business reasons." A number of years ago Texaco's management was sued by stockholders who were unhappy over the company's repurchase of about \$600 million of stock from the Bass Brothers at a substantial premium over the market price. The suit charged that Texaco's management, afraid the Bass Brothers would attempt a takeover, used the buyback to "get them off its back." Such payments have been dubbed *greenmail.*

the P/E ratio may drop is that the repurchase works to increase the company's debt ratio (as there are now fewer shares of stock outstanding). Because of the higher debt ratio, shareholders may consider the stock to be riskier. As a result, the future earnings are discounted at a higher rate, which reduces the P/E ratio.

In reality, companies often have to pay a premium in order to get shareholders to sell their shares back to the company. If instead, ADC had to pay $22 per share to repurchase the stock, it would only be able to repurchase 100,000 shares. In this case, the EPS would be somewhat lower ($4.40 = $4.4 million/1 million shares), and the P/E ratio would again be 5.0×. (This assumes that the market price of the stock remains at $22 following the repurchase.)

For a variety of reasons, the stock's price might change as a result of the repurchase operation, rising if investors viewed it favorably and falling if they viewed it unfavorably. Some of these factors are considered next.

14-7B ADVANTAGES OF REPURCHASES

The advantages of repurchases are as follows:

1. A repurchase announcement may be viewed as a positive signal by investors because repurchases are often motivated by managements' belief that their firms' shares are undervalued.
2. The stockholders have a choice when the firm distributes cash by repurchasing stock—they can sell or not sell. With a cash dividend, on the other hand, stockholders must accept a dividend payment and pay the tax. Thus, those stockholders who need cash can sell back some of their shares, while those who do not want additional cash can simply retain their stock. From a tax standpoint, a repurchase permits both types of stockholders to get what they want.
3. A repurchase can remove a large block of stock that is "overhanging" the market and keeping the price per share down.
4. Dividends are "sticky" in the short run because managements are reluctant to raise the dividend if the increase cannot be maintained in the future—managements dislike cutting cash dividends because of the negative signal a cut gives. Therefore, if excess cash flows are expected to be temporary, managements may prefer to make distributions as share repurchases rather than to declare increased cash dividends that cannot be maintained.
5. Companies can use the residual dividend model to set a target cash distribution level, then divide the distribution into a *dividend component* and a *repurchase component*. The dividend payout ratio will be relatively low, but the dividend itself will be relatively secure, and it will grow as a result of the declining number of shares outstanding. This gives the company more flexibility in adjusting the total distribution than if the entire distribution were in the form of cash dividends because repurchases can be varied from year to year without sending adverse signals. This procedure has much to recommend it, and it is an important reason for the dramatic increase in the volume of share repurchases. IBM, NextEra Energy (formerly FPL Group), Walmart, and most other large companies use repurchases in this manner.
6. Repurchases can be used to produce large-scale changes in capital structure. For example, a number of years ago Consolidated Edison decided that its debt ratio was so low that it was not minimizing its WACC. It then borrowed $400 million and used the funds to repurchase shares of its common stock. This resulted in an immediate shift from a non-optimal to an optimal capital structure.
7. Companies that use stock options as an important component of employee compensation can repurchase shares and then reissue those shares when employees exercise their options. This avoids having to issue new shares, which dilutes EPS. Microsoft and other high-tech companies have used this procedure in recent years.

14-7C DISADVANTAGES OF REPURCHASES

Disadvantages of repurchases include the following:

1. Stockholders may not be indifferent between dividends and capital gains, and the stock price might benefit more from cash dividends than from repurchases. Cash dividends are generally dependable, but repurchases are not.
2. The *selling* stockholders may not be fully aware of all the implications of a repurchase, or they may not have all the pertinent information about the corporation's present and future activities. This is especially true in situations where management has good reason to believe that the stock price is well below its intrinsic value. However, firms generally announce repurchase programs before embarking on them to avoid potential stockholder suits.
3. The corporation may pay too high a price for the repurchased stock, to the disadvantage of remaining stockholders. If its shares are not actively traded and if the firm seeks to acquire a relatively large number of shares of its stock, the price may be bid above its intrinsic value and then fall after the firm ceases its repurchase operations.

14-7D CONCLUSIONS ON STOCK REPURCHASES

When all the pros and cons on stock repurchases have been totaled, where do we stand? Our conclusions may be summarized as follows:

1. Because of the deferred tax on capital gains, repurchases have a tax advantage over dividends as a way to distribute income to stockholders. This advantage is reinforced by the fact that repurchases provide cash to stockholders who want cash but also allow those who do not need current cash to delay its receipt. On the other hand, dividends are more dependable and are thus better suited for those who need a steady source of income.
2. Because of signaling effects, companies should not pay fluctuating dividends—that would lower investors' confidence in the company and adversely affect its cost of equity and its stock price. However, cash flows vary over time, as do investment opportunities, so the "proper" dividend in the residual dividend model sense varies. To get around this problem, a company can set its dividend at a level low enough to keep dividend payments from constraining operations and then use repurchases on a more or less regular basis to distribute excess cash. Such a procedure would provide regular, dependable dividends in addition to supplemental cash flows to those stockholders who want it.
3. Repurchases are also useful when a firm wants to make a large, rapid shift in its capital structure, to distribute cash from a one-time event such as the sale of a division, or to obtain shares for use in an employee stock option plan.

In earlier editions of this book, we argued that companies ought to be doing more repurchasing and distributing less cash as dividends. Increases in the size and frequency of repurchases in recent years suggest that companies have finally reached this same conclusion.

SelfTest

Explain how repurchases can (1) help stockholders limit taxes and (2) help firms change their capital structures.

What is treasury stock?

What are three procedures a firm can use to repurchase its stock?

What are some advantages and disadvantages of stock repurchases?

How can stock repurchases help a company operate in accordance with the residual dividend model?

TYING IT ALL TOGETHER

Once a company becomes profitable, it must decide what to do with the cash it generates. It may choose to retain cash and use it to purchase additional operating assets, to repay outstanding debt, or to acquire other companies. Alternatively, it may choose to return cash to shareholders. Keep in mind that every dollar that management chooses to retain is a dollar that shareholders could have received and invested elsewhere. Therefore, managers should retain earnings if and only if they can invest the money within the firm, and earn more than stockholders can earn outside the firm. Consequently, high-growth companies with many good projects tend to retain a high percentage of their earnings, whereas mature companies with a great deal of cash but limited investment opportunities tend to have generous cash distribution policies.

Self-Test Questions and Problems

(Solutions Appear in Appendix A)

ST-1 **KEY TERMS** Define each of the following terms:

a. Target payout ratio; optimal dividend policy
b. Dividend irrelevance theory; bird-in-the-hand fallacy
c. Information content (signaling) hypothesis; clienteles; clientele effect
d. Catering theory; residual dividend model
e. Low-regular-dividend-plus-extras
f. Declaration date; holder-of-record date; ex-dividend date; payment date
g. Dividend reinvestment plan (DRIP)
h. Stock split; stock dividend
i. Stock repurchase

ST-2 **ALTERNATIVE DIVIDEND POLICIES** Components Manufacturing Corporation (CMC) has an all-common-equity capital structure. It has 200,000 shares of $2 par value common stock outstanding. When CMC's founder, who was also its research director and most successful inventor, retired unexpectedly to the South Pacific in late 2019, CMC was left suddenly and permanently with materially lower growth expectations and relatively few attractive new investment opportunities. Unfortunately, there was no way to replace the founder's contributions to the firm. Previously, CMC found it necessary to reinvest most of its earnings to finance growth, which averaged 12% per year. Future growth at a 6% rate is considered realistic, but that level would call for an increase in the dividend payout. Further, it now appears that new investment projects, with at least the 14% rate of return required by CMC's stockholders (r_s = 14%), would total only $800,000 for 2020, compared to a projected net income of $2,000,000. If the existing 20% dividend payout was continued, retained earnings would be $1.6 million in 2020, but as noted, only $800,000 of investments would yield the 14% cost of capital.

The one encouraging point is that the high earnings from existing assets are expected to continue, and net income of $2 million is still expected for 2020. Given the dramatically changed circumstances, CMC's management is reviewing the firm's dividend policy.

a. Assuming that the acceptable 2020 investment projects would be financed entirely by earnings retained during the year, and assuming that CMC uses the residual dividend model, calculate DPS in 2020.
b. What payout ratio does your answer to part a imply for 2020?

c. If a 60% payout ratio is maintained for the foreseeable future, what is your estimate of the present market price for the common stock? How does this compare with the market price that should have prevailed under the assumptions existing just before the news about the founder's retirement? If the two values of P_0 are different, comment on why they are different.

d. What would happen to the stock price if the old 20% payout was continued? Assume that if this payout is maintained, the average rate of return on the retained earnings will fall to 7.5% and the new growth rate will be as follows:

$$\begin{aligned} g &= (1.0 - \text{Payout ratio})(\text{ROE}) \\ &= (1.0 - 0.2)(7.5\%) \\ &= (0.8)(7.5\%) = 6.0\% \end{aligned}$$

Questions

14-1 Discuss the pros and cons of having the directors formally announce a firm's future dividend policy.

14-2 The cost of retained earnings is less than the cost of new outside equity capital. Consequently, it is totally irrational for a firm to sell a new issue of stock and to pay cash dividends during the same year. Discuss the meaning of those statements.

14-3 Would it ever be rational for a firm to borrow money in order to pay cash dividends? Explain.

14-4 Modigliani and Miller (MM), on the one hand, and Gordon and Lintner (GL), on the other hand, have expressed strong views regarding the effect of dividend policy on a firm's cost of capital and value.

a. In essence, what are MM's and GL's views regarding the effect of dividend policy on the cost of capital and stock prices?
b. How could MM use the information content, or signaling, hypothesis to counter their opponents' arguments? If you were debating MM, how would you counter them?
c. How could MM use the clientele effect concept to counter their opponents' arguments? If you were debating MM, how would you counter them?

14-5 How would each of the following changes tend to affect aggregate (i.e., the average for all corporations) payout ratios, other things held constant? Explain your answers.

a. An increase in the personal income tax rate
b. A liberalization of depreciation for federal income tax purposes—that is, faster tax write-offs
c. An increase in interest rates
d. An increase in corporate profits
e. A decline in investment opportunities
f. Permission for corporations to deduct dividends for tax purposes as they now deduct interest expense
g. A change in the Tax Code so that realized and unrealized long-term capital gains in any year are taxed at the same rate as ordinary income

14-6 One position expressed in the financial literature is that firms set their dividends as a residual after using income to support new investment.

a. Explain what a residual dividend policy implies, illustrating your answer with a table showing how different investment opportunities can lead to different dividend payout ratios.
b. Think back to Chapter 13 where we considered the relationship between capital structure and the cost of capital. If the WACC-versus-debt-ratio plot was shaped like a sharp V, would this have a different implication for the importance of setting dividends according to the residual policy than if the plot was shaped like a shallow bowl (a flattened U)?

14-7 Executive salaries have been shown to be more closely correlated to the size of the firm than to its profitability. If a firm's board of directors is controlled by management rather than outside directors, this might result in the firm's retaining more earnings than can be justified from the stockholders' point of view. Discuss those statements, being sure (1) to discuss the interrelationships among cost of capital, investment opportunities, and new investment and (2) to explain the implied relationship between dividend policy and stock prices.

14-8 What is the difference between a stock dividend and a stock split? As a stockholder, would you prefer to see your company declare a 100% stock dividend or a two-for-one split? Assume that either action is feasible.

14-9 Most firms like to have their stock selling at a high P/E ratio, and they also like to have extensive public ownership (many different shareholders). Explain how stock dividends or stock splits may help achieve those goals.

14-10 Indicate whether the following statements are true or false. If the statement is false, explain why.

a. If a firm repurchases its stock in the open market, the shareholders who tender the stock are subject to capital gains taxes.
b. If you own 100 shares in a company's stock and the company's stock splits two-for-one, you will own 200 shares in the company following the split.
c. Some dividend reinvestment plans increase the amount of equity capital available to the firm.
d. The Tax Code encourages companies to pay a large percentage of their net income in the form of dividends.
e. If your company has established a clientele of investors who prefer large dividends, the company is unlikely to adopt a residual dividend policy.
f. If a firm follows a residual dividend policy, holding all else constant, its dividend payout will tend to rise whenever the firm's investment opportunities improve.

14-11 What is meant by catering theory, and how might it impact a firm's dividend policy?

Problems

Easy Problems 1-3

14-1 **RESIDUAL DIVIDEND MODEL** Altamonte Telecommunications has a target capital structure that consists of 45% debt and 55% equity. The company anticipates that its capital budget for the upcoming year will be $1,000,000. If Altamonte reports net income of $1,200,000 and it follows a residual dividend payout policy, what will be its dividend payout ratio?

14-2 **STOCK SPLIT** Emergency Medical's stock trades at $145 a share. The company is contemplating a 3-for-2 stock split. Assuming that the stock split will have no effect on the market value of its equity, what will be the company's stock price following the stock split?

14-3 **STOCK REPURCHASES** Gamma Industries has net income of $3,800,000, and it has 1,490,000 shares of common stock outstanding. The company's stock currently trades at $67 a share. Gamma is considering a plan in which it will use available cash to repurchase 10% of its shares in the open market at the current $67 stock price. The repurchase is expected to have no effect on net income or the company's P/E ratio. What will be its stock price following the stock repurchase?

Intermediate Problems 4-6

14-4 **STOCK SPLIT** After a 5-for-l stock split, Tyler Company paid a dividend of $1.15 per new share, which represents a 7% increase over last year's pre-split dividend. What was last year's dividend per share?

14-5 **EXTERNAL EQUITY FINANCING** Coastal Carolina Heating and Cooling Inc. has a 6-month backlog of orders for its patented solar heating system. To meet this demand, management plans to expand production capacity by 45% with a $20 million investment in plant and machinery. The firm wants to maintain a 35% debt level in its capital structure. It also wants to maintain its past dividend policy of distributing 55% of last year's net income. In 2019, net income was $5 million. How much external equity must Coastal Carolina seek at the beginning of 2020 to expand capacity as desired? Assume that the firm uses only debt and common equity in its capital structure.

14-6 **RESIDUAL DIVIDEND MODEL** Walsh Company is considering three independent projects, each of which requires a $4 million investment. The estimated internal rate of return (IRR) and cost of capital for these projects are presented here:

Project H (high risk):	Cost of capital = 16%	IRR = 19%
Project M (medium risk):	Cost of capital = 12%	IRR = 13%
Project L (low risk):	Cost of capital = 9%	IRR = 8%

Note that the projects' costs of capital vary because the projects have different levels of risk. The company's optimal capital structure calls for 40% debt and 60% common equity, and it expects to have net income of $7,500,000. If Walsh establishes its dividends from the residual dividend model, what will be its payout ratio?

Challenging Problems 7-9

14-7 **DIVIDENDS** Brooks Sporting Inc. is prepared to report the following 2019 income statement (shown in thousands of dollars).

Sales	$12,570
Operating costs including depreciation	10,056
EBIT	$ 2,514
Interest	330
EBT	$ 2,184
Taxes (25%)	546
Net income	$ 1,638

Prior to reporting this income statement, the company wants to determine its annual dividend. The company has 320,000 shares of common stock outstanding, and its stock trades at $37 per share.

a. The company had a 25% dividend payout ratio in 2018. If Brooks wants to maintain this payout ratio in 2019, what will be its per-share dividend in 2019?
b. If the company maintains this 25% payout ratio, what will be the current dividend yield on the company's stock?
c. The company reported net income of $1.35 million in 2018. Assume that the number of shares outstanding has remained constant. What was the company's per-share dividend in 2018?
d. As an alternative to maintaining the same dividend payout ratio, Brooks is considering maintaining the same per-share dividend in 2019 that it paid in 2018. If it chooses this policy, what will be the company's dividend payout ratio in 2019?
e. Assume that the company is interested in dramatically expanding its operations and that this expansion will require significant amounts of capital. The company would like to avoid transactions costs involved in issuing new equity. Given this scenario, would it make more sense for the company to maintain a constant dividend payout ratio or to maintain the same per-share dividend? Explain.

14-8 **ALTERNATIVE DIVIDEND POLICIES** Rubenstein Bros. Clothing is expecting to pay an annual dividend per share of $0.75 out of annual earnings per share of $2.25. Currently, Rubenstein Bros.' stock is selling for $12.50 per share. Adhering to the company's target capital structure, the firm has $10 million in total invested capital, of which 40% is funded by debt. Assume that the firm's book value of equity equals its market value. In past years, the firm has earned a return on equity (ROE) of 18%, which is expected to continue this year and into the foreseeable future.

a. Based on this information, what long-run growth rate can the firm be expected to maintain? (*Hint:* $g = \text{Retention rate} \times \text{ROE}$.)
b. What is the stock's required return?
c. If the firm changed its dividend policy and paid an annual dividend of $1.50 per share, financial analysts would predict that the change in policy will have no effect on the firm's stock price or ROE. Therefore, what must be the firm's new expected long-run growth rate and required return?

d. Suppose instead that the firm has decided to proceed with its original plan of disbursing $0.75 per share to shareholders, but the firm intends to do so in the form of a stock dividend rather than a cash dividend. The firm will allot new shares based on the current stock price of $12.50. In other words, for every $12.50 in dividends due to shareholders, a share of stock will be issued. How large will the stock dividend be relative to the firm's current market capitalization? (*Hint:* Remember that market capitalization = $P_0 \times$ number of shares outstanding.)

e. If the plan in part d is implemented, how many new shares of stock will be issued, and by how much will the company's earnings per share be diluted?

14-9 **ALTERNATIVE DIVIDEND POLICIES** In 2018, Keenan Company paid dividends totaling $3,600,000 on net income of $10.8 million. Note that 2018 was a normal year and that for the past 10 years, earnings have grown at a constant rate of 10%. However, in 2019, earnings are expected to jump to $14.4 million and the firm expects to have profitable investment opportunities of $8.4 million. It is predicted that Keenan will not be able to maintain the 2019 level of earnings growth because the high 2019 earnings level is attributable to an exceptionally profitable new product line introduced that year. After 2019, the company will return to its previous 10% growth rate. Keenan's target capital structure is 40% debt and 60% equity.

a. Calculate Keenan's total dividends for 2019 assuming that it follows each of the following policies:
   1. Its 2019 dividend payment is set to force dividends to grow at the long-run growth rate in earnings.
   2. It continues the 2018 dividend payout ratio.
   3. It uses a pure residual dividend policy (40% of the $8.4 million investment is financed with debt and 60% with common equity).
   4. It employs a regular-dividend-plus-extras policy, with the regular dividend being based on the long-run growth rate and the extra dividend being set according to the residual dividend policy.

b. Which of the preceding policies would you recommend? Restrict your choices to the ones listed but justify your answer.

c. Assume that investors expect Keenan to pay total dividends of $9,000,000 in 2019 and to have the dividend grow at 10% after 2019. The stock's total market value is $180 million. What is the company's cost of equity?

d. What is Keenan's long-run average return on equity? [*Hint:* g = Retention rate $\times$ ROE = (1.0 − Payout rate)(ROE)]

e. Does a 2019 dividend of $9,000,000 seem reasonable in view of your answers to parts c and d? If not, should the dividend be higher or lower? Explain your answer.

Comprehensive/Spreadsheet Problem

14-10 **RESIDUAL DIVIDEND MODEL** Buena Terra Corporation is reviewing its capital budget for the upcoming year. It has paid a $3.00 dividend per share (DPS) for the past several years, and its shareholders expect the dividend to remain constant for the next several years. The company's target capital structure is 60% equity and 40% debt, it has 1,000,000 shares of common equity outstanding, and its net income is $8 million. The company forecasts that it will require $10 million to fund all of its profitable (i.e., positive NPV) projects for the upcoming year.

a. If Buena Terra follows the residual dividend model, how much retained earnings will it need to fund its capital budget?

b. If Buena Terra follows the residual dividend model, what will be the company's dividend per share and payout ratio for the upcoming year?

c. If Buena Terra maintains its current $3.00 DPS for next year, how much retained earnings will be available for the firm's capital budget?

d. Can the company maintain its current capital structure, the $3.00 DPS, and a $10 million capital budget without having to raise new common stock?

e. Suppose that Buena Terra's management is firmly opposed to cutting the dividend; that is, it wants to maintain the $3.00 dividend for the next year. Also, assume that the company was committed to funding all profitable projects and was willing to issue more debt (along with the available retained earnings) to help finance the company's capital budget. Assume that the resulting change in capital structure has a minimal effect on the company's composite cost of capital so that the capital budget remains at $10 million. What portion of this year's capital budget would have to be financed with debt?

f. Suppose once again that Buena Terra's management wants to maintain the $3.00 DPS. In addition, the company wants to maintain its target capital structure (60% equity and 40% debt) and its $10 million capital budget. What is the minimum dollar amount of new common stock that the company would have to issue to meet each of its objectives?

g. Now consider the case where Buena Terra's management wants to maintain the $3.00 DPS and its target capital structure, but it wants to avoid issuing new common stock. The company is willing to cut its capital budget to meet its other objectives. Assuming that the company's projects are divisible, what will be the company's capital budget for the next year?

h. What actions can a firm that follows the residual dividend model take when its forecasted retained earnings are less than the retained earnings required to fund its capital budget?

INTEGRATED CASE

SOUTHEASTERN STEEL COMPANY

14-11 DIVIDEND POLICY Southeastern Steel Company (SSC) was formed 5 years ago to exploit a new continuous casting process. SSC's founders, Donald Brown and Margo Valencia, had been employed in the research department of a major integrated-steel company, but when that company decided against using the new process (which Brown and Valencia had developed), they decided to strike out on their own. One advantage of the new process was that it required relatively little capital compared to the typical steel company, so Brown and Valencia have been able to avoid issuing new stock and thus own all of the shares. However, SSC has now reached the stage in which outside equity capital is necessary if the firm is to achieve its growth targets yet still maintain its target capital structure of 60% equity and 40% debt. Therefore, Brown and Valencia have decided to take the company public. Until now, Brown and Valencia have paid themselves reasonable salaries but routinely reinvested all after-tax earnings in the firm, so the firm's dividend policy has not been an issue. However, before talking with potential outside investors, they must decide on a dividend policy.

Assume that you were recently hired by Arthur Adamson & Company (AA), a national consulting firm, which has been asked to help SSC prepare for its public offering. Martha Millon, the senior AA consultant in your group, has asked you to make a presentation to Brown and Valencia in which you review the theory of dividend policy and discuss the following questions:

a. 1. What is meant by the term *dividend policy*?

2. Explain briefly the dividend irrelevance theory that was put forward by Modigliani and Miller. What were the key assumptions underlying their theory?

3. Why do some investors prefer high-dividend-paying stocks, while other investors prefer stocks that pay low or nonexistent dividends?

b. Discuss (1) the information content, or signaling, hypothesis, (2) the clientele effect, (3) catering theory, and (4) their effects on dividend policy.

c. 1. Assume that SSC has an $800,000 capital budget planned for the coming year. You have determined that its present capital structure (60% equity and 40% debt) is optimal, and its net income is forecasted at $600,000. Use the residual dividend model to determine SSC's total dollar dividend and payout ratio. In the process, explain how the residual dividend model works. Then explain what would happen if expected net income was $400,000 or $800,000.

2. In general terms, how would a change in investment opportunities affect the payout ratio under the residual dividend model?

3. What are the advantages and disadvantages of the residual policy? (*Hint:* Don't neglect signaling and clientele effects.)

d. Describe the series of steps that most firms take in setting dividend policy in practice.
e. What is a dividend reinvestment plan (DRIP), and how does it work?
f. What are stock dividends and stock splits? What are the advantages and disadvantages of stock dividends and stock splits?
g. What are stock repurchases? Discuss the advantages and disadvantages of a firm repurchasing its own shares.

TAKING A CLOSER LOOK

Apple's Dividend Policy

Use online resources to work on this chapter's questions. Please note that website information changes over time, and these changes may limit your ability to answer some of these questions.

In this chapter's opening vignette, we discussed Apple's decision to establish a dividend payout policy in 2012 and the establishment of a share repurchase program that has returned $200 billion to shareholders. Let's find out what has happened to Apple's (AAPL) dividend policy since the time of its original announcement. We can address this issue by relying on data provided on Internet financial websites such as Yahoo! Finance, Morningstar.com, and MSN Money (www.msn.com/en-us/money/markets). You will have to use a combination of these sites to answer these questions.

Discussion Questions

1. What has happened to Apple's dividend per share, dividend yield, and dividend payout over the past 4 years? Provide an explanation for what took place.
2. Manually plot earnings per share, dividends per share, and cash flow per share over time. In the text, we point out that dividends are often more stable than earnings, that cash flows track earnings very closely, and that cash flow per share exceeds dividends per share by a safe margin. Do you see a similar pattern for Apple? Explain. (Note that Morningstar.com provides cash flow information for a 10-year period.)
3. Identify the dividend declared date, the ex-dividend date, the holder-of-record date, and the dividend payment date. From the ex-dividend date and industry convention, you should be able to determine the holder-of-record date. Explain the significance of those dates. Now, go to the interactive price chart on the website. Can you observe price shifts around these dates? Explain what price shifts you might expect to see.
4. Investors are more concerned with future dividends than historical dividends. Look at analysts' earnings estimates for the next year and the 5-year annual growth estimates. On the basis of these data, what would you expect Apple's payout policy to be over the next 5 years? (Your answer will only be a guess based on current data.)
5. Review the firm's annual cash flow statements. Has Apple been repurchasing stock, or has it been issuing new stock?
6. What has happened to its year-end market capitalization over this 4-year period? (To calculate the firm's market capitalization, you will need to multiply the adjusted closing price at its fiscal year-end (September 30th) by the number of weighted average shares outstanding. You will have to go to the firm's website to find its annual 10-K filings for the number of shares outstanding in prior years.)

part

6

Working Capital Management, Forecasting, and Multinational Financial Management

CHAPTERS

Working Capital Management

CHAPTER 15

Jirapong Manustrong/Shutterstock.com

Successful Firms Efficiently Manage Their Working Capital

Working capital management involves finding the optimal levels for cash, marketable securities, accounts receivable, and inventory, and then financing that working capital at the least cost. Effective working capital management can generate considerable amounts of cash.

As any owner of a small business can tell you, one way to generate cash is to have your customers pay you more quickly than you pay your suppliers. Recognizing this point on a much larger scale, Amazon has created strong competitive advantages through its effective use of working capital management. When customers order books online from Amazon, they must provide a credit card number. Amazon then receives next-day cash, even before the product is shipped and before it has paid its suppliers.

Another key component of working capital management is efficient inventory usage. Best Buy, the large consumer electronics retailer, pays particular attention to inventories. To maintain sales, its stores must be well stocked with the goods customers are seeking at the time they are shopping. This involves determining what new products are hot, finding where they can be obtained at the lowest cost, and delivering them to stores in a timely manner. Dramatic improvements in communications and computer technology have transformed the way Best Buy manages its inventories. It collects real-time data from each store on how each product is selling, and its computers place orders automatically to keep the shelves full. Moreover, if sales of an item are slipping, prices are lowered to reduce stocks of that item before the situation deteriorates to the point that drastic price cuts are necessary.

Working capital management has become particularly difficult in the declining economic environment following the 2007–2009 financial crisis. Some companies have been stuck with unused inventory, while others are reluctant to purchase additional inventory until they see clear evidence that consumer spending has rebounded. Still other companies have found it more difficult to obtain short-term loans from financial institutions, so they have increasingly relied on trade credit from their suppliers as a substitute form of financing. At the same time, many suppliers are faced with a dilemma—in order to generate new sales they find it necessary to provide their customers with generous payment terms—but in doing so, they worry that in a weak economy many of these customers may not be able to pay them back in a timely fashion.

As you can see, effective working capital management is a continual balancing act that has an important influence on the company's value. After studying this chapter, you should understand how working capital should be managed so as to maximize profits and stock prices.

PUTTING THINGS IN PERSPECTIVE

About 50% of the typical industrial or retail firm's assets are held as working capital, and many students' first jobs focus on working capital management. This is particularly true in smaller businesses, where the majority of new jobs are being created.

When you finish this chapter, you should be able to do the following:

- **Explain how different amounts of current assets and current liabilities affect firms' profitability and thus their stock prices.**
- **Explain how companies decide on the proper amount of each current asset—cash, marketable securities, accounts receivable, and inventory.**
- **Discuss how the cash conversion cycle is determined, how the cash budget is constructed, and how each is used in working capital management.**
- **Discuss how companies set their credit policies, and explain the effect of credit policy on sales and profits.**
- **Describe how the costs of trade credit, bank loans, and commercial paper are determined and how that information impacts decisions for financing working capital.**
- **Explain how companies use security to lower their costs of short-term credit.**

15-1 Background on Working Capital

The term *working capital* originated with the old Yankee peddler who would load up his wagon and go off to peddle his wares. The merchandise was called "working capital" because it was what he actually sold, or "turned over," to produce his profits. The wagon and horse were his fixed assets. He generally owned the horse and wagon (so they were financed with "equity" capital), but he bought his merchandise on credit (that is, by borrowing from his supplier) or with money borrowed from a bank. Those loans were called *working capital loans,* and they had to be repaid after each trip to demonstrate that the peddler was solvent and worthy of a new loan. Banks that followed this procedure were said to be employing "sound banking practices." The more trips the peddler took per year, the faster his working capital turned over and the greater his profits.

resource

Students can download the Excel chapter models from the textbook's student companion site on cengage.com. Once downloaded onto your computer, retrieve the Chapter 15 Excel model and follow along as you read the chapter.

This concept can be applied to modern businesses, as we demonstrate in this chapter. We begin with a review of three basic definitions that were first covered in Chapter 3:

1. *Working capital.* Current assets are often called *working capital* because these assets "turn over" (i.e., are used and then replaced during the year).[1]
2. *Net working capital* is defined as current assets minus current liabilities. Recall from Chapter 3 that Allied Food Products has $690 million in net working capital:

$$\begin{aligned}\textbf{Net working capital} &= \textbf{Current assets} - \textbf{Current liabilities}\\ &= \$1{,}000 - \$310 = \$690 \textbf{ million}\end{aligned}$$

3. *Net operating working capital* (NOWC) represents the working capital that is used for operating purposes. As we saw in Chapters 9 and 12, NOWC is an important component of the firm's free cash flow. NOWC differs from net working capital because interest-bearing notes payable are deducted from current liabilities in the calculation of NOWC. The reason for this distinction is that most analysts view interest-bearing notes payable as a financing cost (similar to long-term debt) that is not part of the company's operating free cash flows. In contrast, the other current liabilities (accounts payable and accruals) are treated as part of the company's operations, and therefore are included as part of free cash flow.[2] Once again, here is the 2019 net operating working capital for Allied Food Products, the firm we discussed in Chapter 3:

$$\begin{aligned}\text{Net operating working capital (NOWC)} &= \text{Operating current assets} - \text{Operating current liabilities}\\ &= \left(\text{Current assets} - \text{Excess cash}\right) - \left(\text{Current liabilities} - \text{Notes payable}\right)\\ &= (\$1{,}000 - \$0) - (\$310 - \$110) = \$800 \text{ million}\end{aligned}$$

Self*Test*

How did the term working capital originate?

Differentiate between working capital and net working capital.

Differentiate between net working capital and net operating working capital.

15-2 Current Assets Investment Policies

In this section, we discuss how the amount of current assets held affects profitability. To begin, Figure 15.1 shows three alternative policies regarding the size of current asset holdings. The top line has the steepest slope, which indicates that the firm holds a great deal of cash, marketable securities, receivables, and inventories relative to its sales. When receivables are high, the firm has a liberal credit policy, which

[1]Any current assets not used in normal operations, such as excess cash held to pay for a plant under construction, are deducted and thus not included in working capital. Allied Food Products uses all of its current assets in operations.

[2]As we mentioned in Chapter 3, we assumed that all of Allied's current assets are used for normal operating purposes. In practice, if a financial analyst believes that some of a company's current assets are held for non-operating purposes, they would be subtracted from its current assets when calculating net operating working capital. The most common case occurs when a company holds large amounts of "excess cash" on its balance sheet.

FIGURE 15.1 Current Assets Investment Policies (millions of dollars)

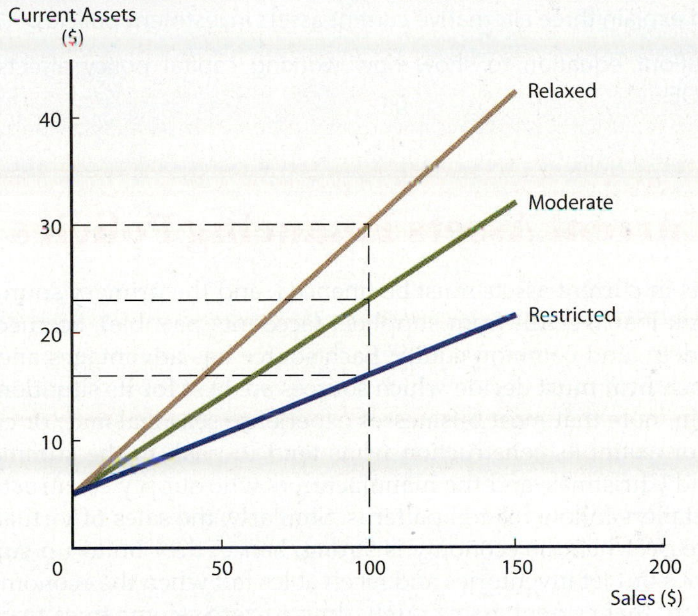

Note: The sales/current assets relationship is shown here as being linear, but the relationship could be curvilinear.

results in a high level of accounts receivable. This is a **relaxed investment policy**. On the other hand, when a firm has a **restricted** (or *tight* or *"lean-and-mean"*) **investment policy**, holdings of current assets are minimized. A **moderate investment policy** lies between the two extremes.

Relaxed Investment Policy
Relatively large amounts of cash, marketable securities, and inventories are carried, and a liberal credit policy results in a high level of receivables.

Restricted Investment Policy
Holdings of cash, marketable securities, inventories, and receivables are constrained.

Moderate Investment Policy
An investment policy that is between the relaxed and restricted policies.

We can use the DuPont equation to demonstrate how working capital management affects ROE:

$$\text{ROE} = \text{Profit margin} \times \text{Total assets turnover} \times \text{Equity multiplier}$$
$$= \frac{\text{Net income}}{\text{Sales}} \times \frac{\text{Sales}}{\text{Assets}} \times \frac{\text{Assets}}{\text{Equity}}$$

A restricted (lean-and-mean) policy indicates a low level of assets (hence, a high total assets turnover ratio), which results in a high ROE, other things held constant. However, this policy also exposes the firm to risks because shortages can lead to work stoppages, unhappy customers, and serious long-run problems. The relaxed policy minimizes such operating problems, but it results in a low turnover, which in turn lowers ROE. The moderate policy falls between the two extremes. The optimal strategy is the one that maximizes the firm's long-run earnings and the stock's intrinsic value.

Note that changing technologies can lead to changes in the optimal policy. For example, when a new technology makes it possible for a manufacturer to produce a given product in 5 rather than 10 days, work-in-progress inventories can be cut in half. Similarly, retailers typically have inventory management systems in which bar codes on all merchandise are read at the cash register. This information is transmitted electronically to a computer that records the remaining stock of each item, and the computer automatically places an order with the supplier's computer when the stock falls to a specified level. This process lowers the "safety stocks" that would otherwise be necessary to avoid running out of stock, which lowers inventories to profit-maximizing levels.

Self*Test*

Identify and explain three alternative current assets investment policies.

Use the DuPont equation to show how working capital policy affects a firm's expected ROE.

15-3 Current Assets Financing Policies

Investments in current assets must be financed, and the primary sources of funds include bank loans, credit from suppliers (accounts payable), accrued liabilities, long-term debt, and common equity. Each source has advantages and disadvantages, so each firm must decide which sources are best for its situation.

To begin, note that most businesses experience seasonal and/or cyclical fluctuations. For example, construction firms tend to peak in the summer, retailers peak around Christmas, and the manufacturers who supply construction companies and retailers follow related patterns. Similarly, the sales of virtually all businesses increase when the economy is strong; hence, they build up current assets at those times but let inventories and receivables fall when the economy weakens. Note, though, that current assets rarely drop to zero—companies maintain some **permanent current assets**, which are the current assets needed at the low point of the business cycle. Then as sales increase during an upswing, current assets are increased, and these extra current assets are defined as **temporary current assets** as opposed to permanent current assets. The manner in which these two types of current assets are financed is called the firm's **current assets financing policy**.

Permanent Current Assets
Current assets that a firm must carry even at the trough of its cycles.

Temporary Current Assets
Current assets that fluctuate with seasonal or cyclical variations in sales.

Current Assets Financing Policy
The manner in which current assets are financed.

Maturity Matching, or "Self-Liquidating," Approach
A financing policy that matches the maturities of assets and liabilities. This is a moderate policy.

15-3A MATURITY MATCHING, OR "SELF-LIQUIDATING," APPROACH

The **maturity matching, or "self-liquidating," approach** calls for matching asset and liability maturities as shown in panel a of Figure 15.2. All of the fixed assets plus the permanent current assets are financed with long-term capital, but temporary current assets are financed with short-term debt. Inventory expected to be sold in 30 days would be financed with a 30-day bank loan; a machine expected to last for 5 years would be financed with a 5-year loan; a 20-year building would be financed with a 20-year mortgage bond; and so forth. Actually, two factors prevent an exact maturity matching: (1) There is uncertainty about the lives of assets. For example, a firm might finance inventories with a 30-day bank loan, expecting to sell the inventories and use the cash to retire the loan. But if sales are slow, the cash would not be forthcoming, and the firm might not be able to pay off the loan when it matures. (2) Some common equity must be used, and common equity has no maturity. Still, when a firm attempts to match asset and liability maturities, this is defined as a *moderate current assets financing policy.*

15-3B AGGRESSIVE APPROACH

Panel b of Figure 15.2 illustrates the situation for a more aggressive firm that finances some of its permanent assets with short-term debt. Note that we used the term *relatively* in the title of panel b because there can be different *degrees* of aggressiveness. For example, the dashed line in panel b could have been drawn *below* the line designating fixed assets, indicating that all of the current assets—both permanent and temporary—and part of the fixed assets were financed with short-term credit. This policy would be a highly aggressive, extremely non-conservative position, and the firm would be subject to dangers from loan renewal as well as

FIGURE 15.2 Alternative Current Assets Financing Policies

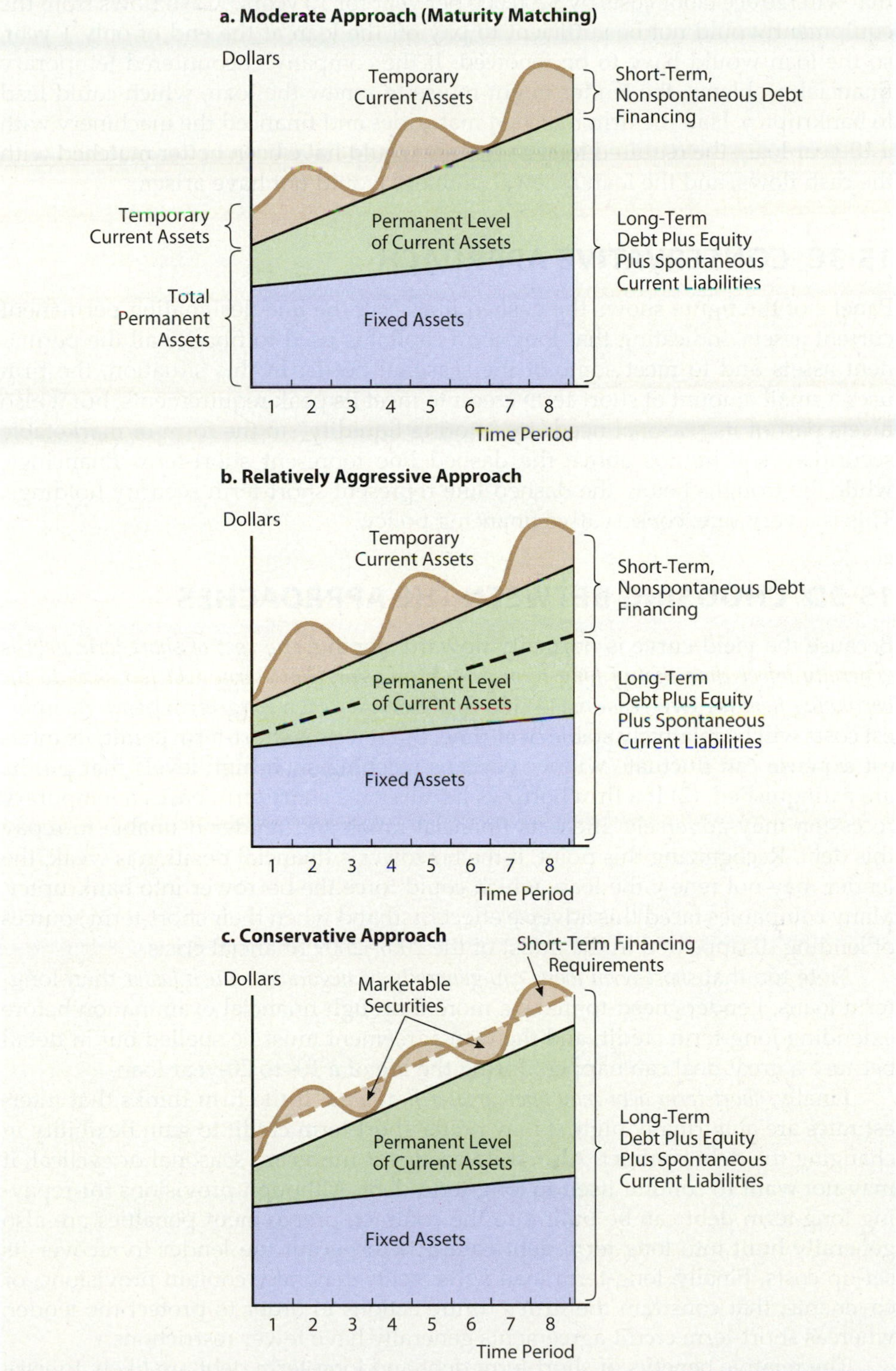

problems with rising interest rates. However, short-term interest rates are generally lower than long-term rates, and some firms are willing to sacrifice some safety for the chance of higher profits.

The reason for adopting the aggressive policy is to take advantage of the fact that the yield curve is generally upward sloping; hence, short-term rates are generally lower than long-term rates. However, a strategy of financing long-term assets with short-term debt is really quite risky. To illustrate, suppose a company borrows $1 million on a 1-year basis and uses the funds to purchase machinery that will reduce labor costs by $200,000 per year for 10 years.[3] Cash flows from the equipment would not be sufficient to pay off the loan at the end of only 1 year, so the loan would have to be renewed. If the company encountered temporary financial problems, the lender might refuse to renew the loan, which could lead to bankruptcy. Had the firm matched maturities and financed the machinery with a 10-year loan, the required loan payments would have been better matched with the cash flows, and the loan renewal problem would not have arisen.

15-3C CONSERVATIVE APPROACH

Panel c of the figure shows the dashed line *above* the line designating permanent current assets, indicating that long-term capital is used to finance all the permanent assets and to meet some of the seasonal needs. In this situation, the firm uses a small amount of short-term credit to meet its peak requirements, but it also meets part of its seasonal needs by "storing liquidity" in the form of marketable securities. The humps above the dashed line represent short-term financings, while the troughs below the dashed line represent short-term security holdings. This is a very safe, conservative financing policy.

15-3D CHOOSING BETWEEN THE APPROACHES

Because the yield curve is normally upward sloping, the *cost of short-term debt is generally lower than that of long-term debt.* However, *short-term debt is riskier to the borrowing firm* for two reasons: (1) If a firm borrows on a long-term basis, its interest costs will be relatively stable over time. But if it uses short-term credit, its interest expense can fluctuate widely, perhaps reaching such high levels that profits are extinguished. (2) If a firm borrows heavily on a short-term basis, a temporary recession may adversely affect its financial ratios and render it unable to repay this debt. Recognizing this point, if the borrower's financial position is weak, the lender may not renew the loan, which could force the borrower into bankruptcy. Many companies faced this adverse effect firsthand when their short-term sources of lending disappeared in the midst of the 2007–2009 financial crisis.

Note too that *short-term loans can generally be negotiated much faster* than long-term loans. Lenders need to make a more thorough financial examination before extending long-term credit, and the loan agreement must be spelled out in detail because a great deal can happen during the life of a 10- to 20-year loan.

Finally, *short-term debt may offer greater flexibility.* If the firm thinks that interest rates are abnormally high, it may prefer short-term credit to gain flexibility in changing the debt contract. Also, if its needs for funds are seasonal or cyclical, it may not want to commit itself to long-term debt. Although provisions for repaying long-term debt can be built into the contract, prepayment penalties are also generally built into long-term debt contracts to permit the lender to recover its set-up costs. Finally, long-term loan agreements generally contain provisions, or covenants, that constrain the firm's future actions in order to protect the lender, whereas short-term credit agreements generally have fewer restrictions.

The relative benefits of short-term debt and long-term debt are likely to vary over time. For example, in the credit crunch following the 2007–2009 financial crisis, many companies found it difficult to roll over their short-term loans coming due. We suspect that many of these companies had wished that they had instead

[3]We are over-simplifying here. Few lenders would explicitly lend money for 1 year to finance a 10-year asset. What would actually happen is that the firm would borrow on a 1-year basis for "general corporate purposes" and then use the money to purchase the 10-year machinery.

adopted a much more conservative approach toward managing their working capital. However, prior to the crisis, overly conservative firms relying on long-term debt often found themselves at a competitive disadvantage because short-term debt was consistently cheaper than long-term debt, and the rollover risk was minimal because credit was readily available.

All things considered, it is not possible to state that long-term or short-term financing is better than the other. The firm's specific conditions will affect the choice, as will the preferences of managers. Optimistic and/or aggressive managers will probably lean more toward short-term credit to gain an interest cost advantage, while more conservative managers will lean toward long-term financing to avoid potential loan renewal problems. The factors discussed here should be considered, but the final decision will reflect managers' personal preferences and judgments.

Self*Test*

Differentiate between permanent current assets and temporary current assets.

What does maturity matching mean, and what is the advantage of this financing policy?

What are the advantages and disadvantages of short-term versus long-term debt as identified in this section?

15-4 The Cash Conversion Cycle

All firms follow a "working capital cycle" in which they purchase or produce inventory, hold it for a time, and then sell it and receive cash. This process is similar to the Yankee peddler's trips, and it is known as the **cash conversion cycle (CCC)**.

Cash Conversion Cycle (CCC)
The length of time funds are tied up in working capital, or the length of time between paying for working capital and collecting cash from the sale of the working capital.

15-4A CALCULATING THE TARGETED CCC

Assume that Great Fashions Inc. (GFI) is a start-up business that buys ladies' golf outfits from a manufacturer in China and sells them through pro shops at high-end golf clubs in the United States, Canada, and Mexico. The company's business plan calls for it to purchase $100,000 of merchandise at the start of each month and have the merchandise sold within 60 days. The company will have 40 days to pay its suppliers, and it will give its customers 60 days to pay for their purchases. GFI expects to just break even during its first few years, so its monthly sales will be $100,000, the same as its purchases. Any funds required to support operations will be obtained from the bank, and those loans must be repaid as soon as cash is available. This information can be used to calculate GFI's cash conversion cycle, which nets out the three time periods described below:[4]

1. **Inventory conversion period**. For GFI, this is the 60 days it takes to sell the merchandise.[5]

Inventory Conversion Period
The average time required to convert raw materials into finished goods and then to sell them.

[4]See Verlyn D. Richards and Eugene J. Laughlin, "A Cash Conversion Cycle Approach to Liquidity Analysis," *Financial Management*, vol. 9, no. 1 (Spring 1980), pp. 32–38.

[5]If GFI were a manufacturer, the inventory conversion period would be the time required to convert raw materials into finished goods and then to sell those goods.

Average Collection Period (ACP)
The average length of time required to convert the firm's receivables into cash, that is, to collect cash following a sale.

Payables Deferral Period
The average length of time between the purchase of materials and labor and the payment of cash for them.

2. **Average collection period (ACP).** This is the length of time customers are given to pay for goods following a sale. The ACP is also called the *days sales outstanding (DSO).* GFI's business plan calls for an ACP of 60 days, which is consistent with its 60-day credit terms.
3. **Payables deferral period.** This is the length of time GFI's suppliers give GFI to pay for its purchases (40 days in our example).

On Day 1, GFI buys merchandise and expects to sell the goods and thus convert them to accounts receivable in 60 days. It should take another 60 days to collect the receivables, making a total of 120 days between receiving merchandise and collecting cash. However, GFI is able to defer its own payments for only 40 days. We combine these three periods to find the planned cash conversion cycle, shown here as an equation and in Figure 15.3 as an illustration:

$$\begin{matrix}\text{Inventory} & & \text{Average} & & \text{Payables} & & \text{Cash} \\ \text{conversion} & + & \text{collection} & - & \text{deferral} & = & \text{conversion} \\ \text{period} & & \text{period} & & \text{period} & & \text{cycle} \\ 60 & + & 60 & - & 40 & = & 80\text{ days}\end{matrix} \quad \textbf{15.1}$$

Although GFI must pay $100,000 to its suppliers after 40 days, it will not receive any cash until 60 + 60 = 120 days into the cycle. Therefore, it will have to borrow the $100,000 cost of the merchandise from its bank on Day 40, and it will not be able to repay the loan until it collects from customers on Day 120. Thus, for 120 − 40 = 80 days—which is the cash conversion cycle (CCC)—it will owe the bank $100,000 and will pay interest on this debt. The shorter the cash conversion cycle, the better because that will lower interest charges. Note that if GFI could sell goods faster, collect receivables faster, or defer its payables longer without hurting sales or increasing operating costs, its CCC would decline, its interest expense would be reduced, and its profits and stock price would be improved.

15-4B CALCULATING THE CCC FROM FINANCIAL STATEMENTS

The preceding section illustrates the CCC in theory, but in practice we would calculate the CCC based on the firm's financial statements. Moreover, the actual CCC would almost certainly differ from the theoretically forecasted value because of real-world complexities such as shipping delays, sales slowdowns, and customer delays in making payments. Moreover, a firm such as GFI would start a new cycle before the earlier one ended, and this too would muddy the waters.

To see how the CCC is calculated in practice, assume that GFI has been in business for several years and is now in a stable position—placing orders,

FIGURE 15.3 The Cash Conversion Cycle

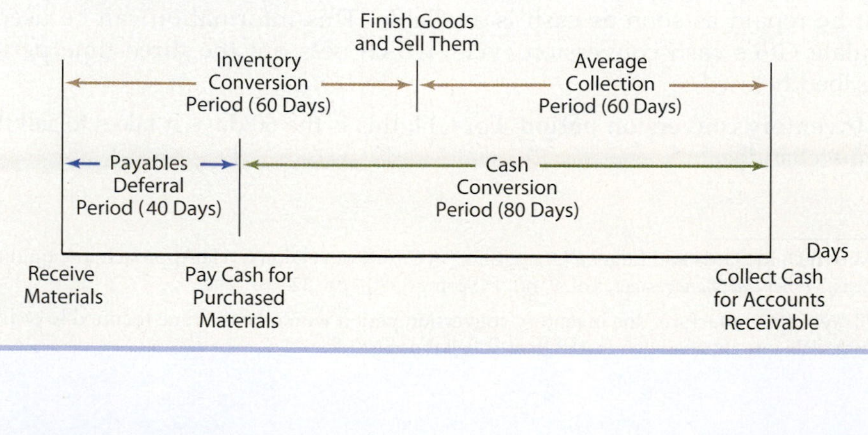

SOME REAL-WORLD EXAMPLES OF THE CASH CONVERSION CYCLE

The table below summarizes some recent estimates of the cash conversion cycle (CCC) for 12 companies in six industries. As you would expect, the CCC tends to be higher in retailing industries that require more inventory. On the plus side, many retail companies benefit from a low DSO because most of their customers pay with cash or credit cards that are quickly collected. Large differences in CCC can also arise within a given industry. For example, Pepsi's inventory conversion period is almost half that of Coke's inventory conversion period, and Pepsi has a 20% larger payables deferral period than Coke, which leads to Pepsi's much lower CCC. In fact, Pepsi has a negative CCC, which means that instead of using cash, working capital provides cash to the firm. Apple and HP also have a negative CCC.

Likewise, taking a look at the three firms in the clothing retail business, we see that Abercrombie & Fitch has an abnormally high CCC because of its relatively large inventory holdings. This is no doubt a concern to the company's management.

Cash Conversion Cycle: Real World Examples, 2018

Company	Industry	Inventory Conversion Period[a]	Average Collection Period = DSO[a]	Payables Deferral Period[a]	Cash Conversion Cycle (CCC)
Coca-Cola	Beverages	73.38	38.77	68.42	43.73
PepsiCo Inc.	Beverages	35.95	33.51	81.69	−12.23
Abercrombie & Fitch	Clothing retail	106.76	9.05	46.10	69.71
American Eagle Outfitters	Clothing retail	56.94	5.44	36.34	26.04
Gap	Clothing retail	71.35	7.10	45.19	33.26
Best Buy	Computer retail	56.96	10.37	55.74	11.60
Apple Inc.	Computers and peripherals	9.04	26.77	111.72	−75.91
HP Inc.	Computers and peripherals	44.12	29.90	104.75	−30.73
CVS Health Corp.	Food and staples retailing	35.11	25.03	19.64	40.51
Walmart	Food and staples retailing	42.44	4.18	42.78	3.84
Alcoa Corp.	Metal manufacturing	52.57	23.16	67.45	8.28
U.S. Steel Corp.	Metal manufacturing	55.62	32.02	62.12	25.51

Note:

[a]*Morningstar* uses an average of the beginning and ending balances of the balance sheet accounts in their ratio calculations.

Source: Data for company's latest fiscal year-end obtained from www.morningstar.com, August 15, 2018.

generating sales, collecting cash receipts, and paying vendors on a recurring basis. The following data were taken from its latest financial statements:

Annual sales	$1,216,666
Cost of goods sold	1,013,889
Inventory	250,000
Accounts receivable	300,000
Accounts payable	150,000

We begin with the inventory conversion period:

$$\text{Inventory conversion period} = \frac{\text{Inventory}}{\text{Cost of goods sold per day}}$$

$$= \frac{\$250,000}{\$1,013,889/365} = 90 \text{ days} \qquad 15.2$$

Thus, it takes GFI an average of 90 days to sell its merchandise, not the 60 days called for in its business plan. Note also that inventory is carried at cost, so the denominator of the equation is the cost of goods sold, not sales.

The average collection period (or DSO) is calculated next:

$$\text{Average collection period} = \text{ACP (or DSO)} = \frac{\text{Receivables}}{\text{Sales}/365} \quad \textbf{15.3}$$

$$= \frac{\$300{,}000}{\$1{,}216{,}666/365} = 90 \text{ days}$$

Note that it takes GFI 90 days after a sale to receive cash, not the 60 days called for in its business plan. Because receivables are recorded at the sales price, we use sales rather than cost of goods sold in the denominator.

The payables deferral period is found as follows, again using cost of goods sold in the denominator because payables are recorded at cost:

$$\text{Payables deferral period} = \frac{\text{Payables}}{\text{Purchases per day}} = \frac{\text{Payables}}{\text{Cost of goods sold}/365} \quad \textbf{15.4}$$

$$= \frac{\$150{,}000}{\$1{,}013{,}889/365} = 54 \text{ days}$$

GFI is supposed to pay its suppliers after 40 days, but it is a slow payer, delaying payment on average until Day 54.

We can combine the three periods to calculate GFI's actual cash conversion cycle:

$$\text{Cash conversion cycle (CCC)} = 90 \text{ days} + 90 \text{ days} - 54 \text{ days} = 126 \text{ days}$$

GFI's actual 126-day CCC is quite different from the planned 80 days. It takes longer than planned to sell merchandise, customers don't pay as quickly as they should, and GFI pays its suppliers slower than it should. The end result is a CCC of 126 days versus the planned 80 days.

Although the planned 80-day CCC is "reasonable," the actual 126 days is too high. The CFO should push salespeople to speed up sales and the credit manager to accelerate collections. Also, the purchasing department should try to get longer payment terms. If GFI could take those steps without hurting its sales and operating costs, the firm would improve its profits and stock price.

Two professors, Hyun-Han Shin and Luc Soenen, studied more than 2,900 companies over a 20-year period. They found that shortening the cash conversion cycle resulted in higher profits and better stock price performances.[6] Their study demonstrates that good working capital management is important to a firm's financial position and performance.

quick question

QUESTION:

Direct Furnishings Inc. has the following data:

Annual sales	$10,000,000
Cost of goods sold	6,000,000
Inventory	2,547,945
Accounts receivable	1,643,836
Accounts payable	1,200,000

What is the firm's cash conversion cycle?

[6] See Hyun-Han Shin and Luc Soenen, "Efficiency of Working Capital Management and Corporate Profitability," *Financial Practice and Education*, vol. 8, no. 2 (Fall/Winter 1998), pp. 37–45.

ANSWER:

We must first calculate the firm's inventory conversion period, its average collection period, and its payables deferral period before we can calculate its cash conversion cycle.

$$\text{Inventory conversion period} = \frac{\text{Inventory}}{\text{Cost of goods sold per day}}$$

$$= \frac{\$2{,}547{,}945}{\$6{,}000{,}000/365} = 155 \text{ days}$$

$$\text{Average collection period} = \frac{\text{Accounts receivable}}{\text{Sales}/365}$$

$$= \frac{\$1{,}643{,}836}{\$10{,}000{,}000/365} = 60 \text{ days}$$

$$\text{Payables deferral period} = \frac{\text{Accounts payable}}{\text{Cost of goods sold}/365}$$

$$= \frac{\$1{,}200{,}000}{\$6{,}000{,}000/365} = 73 \text{ days}$$

$$\text{Cash conversion cycle} = \begin{matrix}\text{Inventory}\\ \text{conversion}\\ \text{period}\end{matrix} + \begin{matrix}\text{Average}\\ \text{collection}\\ \text{period}\end{matrix} - \begin{matrix}\text{Payables}\\ \text{deferral}\\ \text{period}\end{matrix}$$

$$= 155 + 60 - 73 = \mathbf{142\ days}$$

SelfTest

Define the following terms: inventory conversion period, average collection period, and payables deferral period. Explain how these terms are used to form the cash conversion cycle.

How would a reduction in the cash conversion cycle increase profitability?

What are some actions a firm can take to shorten its cash conversion cycle?

15-5 The Cash Budget

Firms need to forecast their cash flows. If they are likely to need additional cash, they should line up funds well in advance. On the other hand, if they are likely to generate surplus cash, they should plan for its productive use. The primary forecasting tool is the **cash budget**, illustrated in Table 15.1, which is a printout from the chapter's Excel model.

Cash Budget
A table that shows cash receipts, disbursements, and balances over some period.

Cash budgets can be of any length, but firms typically develop a monthly cash budget like Table 15.1, for the coming year and a daily cash budget at the start of each month. The monthly budget is good for annual planning, while the daily budget gives a more precise picture of the actual cash flows and is good for scheduling actual payments on a day-by-day basis.

The monthly cash budget begins with a sales forecast for each month and a projection of when actual collections will occur. Then there is a forecast of materials purchases, followed by forecasted payments for materials, labor, leases, new equipment, taxes, and other expenses. When the forecasted payments are subtracted from the forecasted collections, the result is the expected net cash gain or loss for each month. This gain or loss is added to or subtracted from the beginning cash balance, and the result is the amount of cash the firm would have on hand at the end of the month if it neither borrowed nor invested.

TABLE 15.1 Allied Food Products 2020 Cash Budget (dollars in millions)

Row	Item	Value	Comment
5	**Input Data**		
6	Collections during month of sale	20%	Assumed constant. Don't change.
7	Collections during 1st month after sale	70%	Assumed constant. Don't change.
8	Collections during 2nd month after sale	10%	Equal to 100% – (20% + 70%) – Bad debt %
9	Percent bad debts	0%	Can change to see effects
10	Discount on first month collections	2%	Can change to see effects
11	Purchases as a % of next month's sales	70%	Can change to see effects
12	Lease payments	$ 15	Can change to see effects
13	Construction cost for new plant (Oct)	$ 100	Can change to see effects
14	Target cash balance	$ 10	Can change to see effects
15	Sales adjustment factor (change from base)	0%	% increase or decrease from base to see effects
16			
17			

Row	THE CASH BUDGET	May	June	July	August	Sept	Oct	Nov	Dec
20	*Sales (gross)*	$200	$250	$300	$400	$500	$350	$250	$200
21	*Collections*								
22	During month of sale: 0.2(Sales)(0.98)			$59	$78	$98	$69	$49	$39
23	During 1st month after sale: 0.7(prior month's sales)			175	210	280	350	245	175
24	During 2nd month after sale: 0.1(sales 2 months ago)			20	25	30	40	50	35
25	Total collections			$254	$313	$408	$459	$344	$249
26	*Purchases: 70% of next month's sales*		$210	$280	$350	$245	$175	$140	
27	*Payments*								
28	Payment for materials: Last month's purchases			$210	$280	$350	$245	$175	$140
29	Wages and salaries			30	40	50	40	30	30
30	Lease payments			15	15	15	15	15	15
31	Other expenses			10	15	20	15	10	10
32	Taxes					15			10
33	Payment for plant construction						100		
34	Total payments			$265	$350	$450	$415	$230	$205
35	*Net cash flows:*								
36	Net cash flow (NCF) for month: row 25 minus row 34			($11)	($37)	($42)	$44	$114	$44
37	Cumulative NCF: Prior month's cum. NCF plus this month's NCF			($11)	($48)	($90)	($46)	$68	$112
38	*Cash surplus (or loan requirement)*								
39	Target cash balance			$10	$10	$10	$10	$10	$10
40	Surplus cash (or loan needed): row 37 – row 39			($21)	($58)	($100)	($56)	$58	$102
41	Maximum required loan (shown as a negative)			($100)					
42	Maximum available for investment			$102					

Notes:

1. Although the budget period is July through December, sales and purchases data for May and June are needed to determine collections and payments during July and August.
2. Firms can both borrow and pay off commercial loans on a daily basis. So the $21 million loan shown for July would likely be borrowed gradually on a daily basis as needed, and during October the $100 million loan that existed at the beginning of the month would be reduced daily to the $56 million ending balance, which, in turn, would be completely paid off sometime during November.

We use Allied Food to illustrate cash budgets. To shorten the example, we deal only with the last half of 2020. Allied sells mainly to grocery chains, and its projected 2020 sales are $3,300 million. As Table 15.1 shows, sales increase during the summer, peak in September, and then decline during the fall. All sales are on terms of 2/10, net 30, meaning that a 2% discount is allowed if payment is made within 10 days. But if the discount is not taken, the full amount is due in 30 days. However, like most companies, Allied finds that some customers pay late. Experience shows that 20% of customers pay during the month of the sale—these are the discount customers. Another 70% pay during the month immediately following the sale, and 10% are late, paying in the second month after the sale.[7]

The costs to Allied for foodstuffs, spices, preservatives, and packaging materials average 70% of sales revenues. Purchases are generally made 1 month before the firm expects to sell the finished products, but Allied's suppliers allow it to delay payments for 30 days. July sales are forecasted at $300 million, so purchases during June should amount to $210 million, and this amount must be paid in July.

Wages and lease payments are also built into the cash budget, as are Allied's estimated tax payments—$15 million due September 15 and $10 million due December 15. Also, a $100 million payment for a new plant must be made in October, and miscellaneous other required payments are shown in the budget. Allied's **target cash balance** is $10 million, and it plans to borrow to meet this target or to invest surplus funds if it generates more cash than is needed.

Target Cash Balance
The desired cash balance that a firm plans to maintain in order to conduct business.

We use the information at the top of Table 15.1 to forecast monthly cash surpluses or shortfalls from July through December, along with the amount Allied will need to borrow or will have available to invest so as to keep the end-of-month cash balance at the target level. Inputs used in the forecast—which are assumptions that may not be correct—are given in rows 6 through 15. These values are used in the calculations shown here. Row 20 gives the sales forecast for the period May through December. May and June sales are needed to determine collections for July and August. Rows 22 through 25 relate to collections. Row 22 shows that 20% of the sales during any given month are collected during that month. However, customers who pay the first month take the discount, so collections for that month are reduced by 2%. For example, collections for July are calculated as 20% of the $300 million sales for that month minus the 2% discount, or 0.2($300) − 0.2($300)(0.02) = $58.8 million, rounded to $59 million. Row 23 shows the collections for the previous month's sales. For example, in July, 70% of the $250 million June sales, or $175 million, should be collected. Row 24 shows collections from sales 2 months earlier. Thus, in July, collections for May sales should be (0.10)($200) = $20 million. The collections during each month are summed and shown on row 25. Thus, the July collections include 20% of July sales (minus the discount) and 70% of June sales plus 10% of May sales, or $254 million in total.

Raw material costs, which are 70% of next month's sales, are shown on row 26. July sales are forecasted at $300 million, so June purchases are 0.7($300) = $210 million. The $210 million must be paid in July, so that amount is shown on row 28. Continuing, forecasted sales for August are $400 million, so Allied must purchase 0.7($400) = $280 million of materials in July, and that amount must be paid in August. Other required payments—labor costs, lease payments, taxes, construction costs, and miscellaneous expenses—are shown on rows 29 through 33, and the total of all payments is shown on row 34.

Next, on row 36, we show the net cash flow (NCF) for each month, calculated as total collections on row 25 minus total payments on row 34. The NCF for July is −$11 million, and cash flows remain negative due to the fall harvest and processing until October, when positive cash flows begin.

The monthly cash flows are then used to calculate the cumulative NCF as shown on row 37. Here we add the NCF for each month to the cumulative NCF from the prior month. Because there was no prior cumulative NCF at the beginning of July, the cumulative NCF for July is simply the NCF for that month, −$11 million. For August, we add the NCF for that month, −$37 million, to the prior cumulative NCF, the −$11 million at the end of July, to get the −$48 million cumulative NCF at the end of August. There is another negative cash flow during September, so the cumulative

[7]A negligible percentage of sales results in bad debts. The low bad debt losses result from Allied's careful screening of customers and its generally tight credit policies. However, the cash budget model can show the effects of bad debts, so Allied's CFO could show top management how cash flows would be affected if the firm relaxed its credit policy to stimulate sales.

NCF rises to a peak of −$90 million. However, in October, the NCF is positive, so the cumulative figure declines to −$46 million, and it changes from a negative amount to a positive amount in November and remains positive in December.

Allied's target cash balance is $10 million—it wants to maintain that balance at all times. It plans to borrow $10 million at the start of the analysis, and we show that amount on row 39. Because there is a projected cash loss of $11 million during July and because Allied borrowed $10 million at the start of the month, at the end of July, its loan outstanding will total $21 million, as shown on row 40.[8] It will incur additional cash shortfalls in August and September, and the required loan will continue to increase, peaking at $100 million at the end of September. However, positive cash flows begin in October, and they will be used to reduce the loan, which will be completely paid off by the end of November, at which time the company will have funds to invest. Indeed, by the end of December, Allied should have no loans outstanding and $102 million available for investment.

For the 6-month period shown, row 41 shows the maximum required loan, $100 million, and row 42 shows the maximum projected surplus, $102 million. Allied's treasurer will need to arrange a line of credit so that the firm can borrow up to $100 million, increasing the loan over time as funds are needed and repaying it later when cash flows become positive. The treasurer would show the cash budget to the bankers when negotiating for the line of credit. Lenders would want to know how much Allied expects to need, when the funds will be needed, and when the loan will be repaid. The lenders—and Allied's top executives—would question the treasurer about the budget. They would want to know how the forecasts would be affected if sales were higher or lower than those projected, how changes would affect the forecasts when customers pay, and the like. The questioning would focus on these two questions: *How accurate is the forecast likely to be? What would be the effects of significant errors?*

Note that if cash inflows and outflows do not occur uniformly during each month, the actual funds needed might be quite different from the indicated amounts. The data in Table 15.1 show the situation on the last day of each month, and we see that the maximum projected loan is $100 million. However, if all payments had to be made on the 1st of the month, but most collections came on the 30th, Allied would have to make $265 million, of payments in July before it received the $254 million from collections. In that case, the firm would need to borrow about $275 million, not the $21 million shown in Table 15.1. A daily cash budget would reveal that situation.

Table 15.1 was prepared using Excel, which makes it easy to change the assumptions. Therefore, we could examine the cash flow effects of changes in sales, the target cash balance, customers' payments, and so forth. Also, the effects of changes in credit policy and inventory management could be examined through the cash budget.

Self*Test*

How could the cash budget be used when the terms of a bank loan are negotiated?

Suppose a firm's cash flows do not occur uniformly throughout the month. What effect would this have on the accuracy of the forecasted borrowing requirements based on a monthly cash budget? How could the firm deal with this problem?

15-6 Cash and Marketable Securities

When most people use the term *cash,* they mean currency (paper money and coins) in addition to bank demand deposits. However, when corporate treasurers use the term, they often mean currency and demand deposits *in addition to very*

[8] If Allied had begun with a positive cash balance, that amount would have been deducted from the initial loan needed. Note too that our cash budget is simplified because it does not show interest expense for the loan or interest income on investments. Those items could be added easily to the cash budget.

safe, highly liquid, marketable securities that can be sold quickly at a predictable price, and thus be converted to bank deposits.[9] Therefore, "cash" as reported on balance sheets generally includes short-term securities, which are also called "cash equivalents."

Note that a firm's marketable security holdings can be divided into two categories: (1) *operating short-term securities,* which are held primarily to provide liquidity and are bought and sold as needed to provide funds for operations, and (2) *other short-term securities,* which are holdings in excess of the amount needed to support normal operations. Highly profitable firms such as Microsoft often hold far more securities than are needed for liquidity purposes. Those securities will eventually be liquidated, and the cash will be used for such things as paying a large one-time dividend, repurchasing stock, retiring debt, acquiring other firms, or financing major expansions. This breakdown is not reported on the balance sheet, but financial managers know how much of their securities will be needed for operating versus other purposes. In our discussion of net working capital, the focus is on securities held to provide operating liquidity.

15-6A CURRENCY

Fast-food operators, casinos, hotels, movie theaters, and a few other businesses hold substantial amounts of currency, but the importance of currency has decreased over time due to the rise of credit cards, debit cards, and other payment mechanisms. Companies such as McDonald's need to hold enough currency to support operations, but if they held more, this would raise capital costs and tempt robbers. Each firm decides its own optimal level, but even for retailers, currency generally represents a small part of total cash holdings.[10]

15-6B DEMAND DEPOSITS

Demand (or checking) deposits are far more important than currency for most businesses. These deposits are used for *transactions*—paying for labor and raw materials, purchasing fixed assets, paying taxes, servicing debt, paying dividends, and so forth. However, commercial demand deposits typically earn no interest, so firms try to minimize their holdings while still ensuring that they are able to pay suppliers promptly, take trade discounts, and take advantage of bargain purchases. The following techniques are used to optimize demand deposit holdings:

1. *Hold marketable securities rather than demand deposits to provide liquidity.* When the firm holds marketable securities, the need for demand deposits is reduced. For example, if a large bill requiring immediate payment comes in unexpectedly, the treasurer can simply call a securities dealer, sell some securities, and have funds deposited in the firm's checking account that same day. Securities pay interest, whereas demand deposits do not, so holding securities in lieu of demand deposits increases profits.
2. *Borrow on short notice.* Firms can establish lines of credit under which they can borrow with just a telephone call if and when they need extra cash. Note, though, that they may have to pay fees for those commitments, and the cost of those fees must be considered when deciding to use borrowing capacity rather than securities to provide liquidity.

[9]The reason corporate treasurers think of cash as they do is that, from their perspective, there is little difference between demand deposits and liquid marketable securities. They can call a dealer, sell securities, and have the proceeds deposited in the firm's bank account in an hour or so. Also, many types of short-term securities are available. Treasury bills are an obvious example, but as we discussed in Chapter 2, there are many other safe, liquid, short-term, marketable securities.

[10]In the "olden days," currency was also held as a store of value, for use during emergencies, for use in making bargain purchases, and the like. That is true today only in undeveloped parts of the world.

3. *Forecast payments and receipts better.* The better the firm can forecast its cash inflows and outflows, the smaller its needs for funds to meet unexpected requirements. Therefore, improving inflow/outflow forecasts lessens the need to hold liquid assets and thus reduces the required amount of working capital. The cash budget is the key tool used to improve cash forecasts.
4. *Speed up payments.* Firms can take actions to obtain their cash receipts faster. For example, they can use **lockboxes**, which are post office boxes operated by banks. Suppose a New York firm sells to customers all across the country. If it sends out bills and has customers make payments to its New York headquarters, time will be lost in waiting on the mail, opening envelopes, depositing checks in the bank, and waiting for the bank to clear the checks to make sure they are good. To speed up this process, the firm can direct customers to send payments to a post office box in the customer's local area, then have a bank empty the box several times each day and start the collection process. If a firm's receipts average $1 million per day and if the use of lockboxes can reduce the delay in obtaining usable cash from 5 days to 1 day, the firm will reduce funds in transit from $5 million to $1 million and thus receive an effective cash infusion of $4 million. This is a one-time benefit, but the firm will be earning a continuing return on the $4 million.[11]

Lockboxes
Post office boxes operated by a bank to which payments are sent. Used to speed up effective receipt of cash.

5. *Use credit cards, debit cards, wire transfers, and direct deposits.* If a firm switches from selling on credit to accepting credit or debit cards, it will receive next-day cash and thus the same cash flow benefits as described earlier. Similarly, requiring customers to pay via wire deposits speeds up collections, increases free cash flows, and reduces required cash holdings. Many companies have taken advantage of changing technology, which allows them to use products such as PayPal, Square, and Apple Pay to get paid more efficiently at the point of sale. In other cases, companies have developed their own products to encourage mobile payments—for example, Starbucks' mobile payment app has been hugely successful.
6. *Synchronize cash flows.* If a firm can synchronize its cash inflows and outflows, the firm will reduce its need for cash balances. For example, utilities, oil companies, department stores, and the like generally use "billing cycles" under which different customers are billed on different days, causing cash to flow in evenly during the month. These firms can then set up their own payment schedules to match their inflows. This reduces average cash balances, just as your personal average monthly balance can be reduced when your income comes in at the same time as your required payments.

Banks have experts who help firms optimize their cash management procedures. The banks charge a fee for this service, but the benefits of a good cash management system are well worth the cost.

15-6C MARKETABLE SECURITIES

Marketable securities held for operations are managed in conjunction with demand deposits—the management of one requires coordination with the other. Firms also purchase marketable securities as cash builds up from operations and then sell those securities when they need cash. Recently, to maintain flexibility and/or to have

[11]We should mention the term *float*, as it often comes up in connection with cash management. If you write a check and it takes 5 days for the recipient to receive and deposit the check and for it to be deducted from your account, you have 5 days of float, or the use of the money for 5 days before you have to deposit funds in your account. That's *payment float*. On the other hand, if someone sends you a check and it takes 4 days for you to receive and deposit it and for the bank to clear the funds, that's 4 days of *collection float*. Your *net float* would be 1 day. Positive net float is good, but negative net float is bad from the standpoint of minimizing required cash holdings.

funds available to withstand a future economic decline, many companies have continued to hold large amounts of cash and marketable securities. The Federal Reserve reported in September 2011 that cash and marketable securities held by non-financial companies totaled more than $2 trillion—an amount which represented more than 7% of all assets that these companies reported on their balance sheets.[12] Today, many large companies continue to hold vast amounts of cash and securities; for example, Microsoft, Apple, Oracle, and Cisco Systems have all recently held more than $50 billion in cash and marketable securities. In recent years, a significant portion of this cash has been held overseas. In September 2016, U.S. companies were holding $2.5 trillion in cash overseas—equivalent to nearly 14% of total U.S. gross domestic product.[13] Notably, many companies were holding cash overseas in markets with lower corporate tax rates. Arguably, the Tax Cuts and Jobs Act of 2017 provides incentives for these companies to return much of this cash to the United States.[14]

Given the size and importance of marketable securities holdings, how they are managed can have a significant effect on profits. A trade-off between risk and return is involved—the firm wants to earn high returns, but because most marketable securities are held to provide liquidity, treasurers want to hold securities that can be sold very quickly at a known price. That means high-quality, short-term instruments. Long-term Treasury bonds are safe, but they are not well suited for the marketable securities portfolio because their prices decline when interest rates rise. Similarly, short-term securities issued by risky companies are not suitable because their prices decline when the issuers' problems grow worse. Treasury bills, most commercial paper (discussed in Section 15-11), bank certificates of deposit, and money market funds are suitable holdings.

It's worth noting that so-called safe securities don't always turn out to be safe. In 2007, billions of dollars of Aaa-rated commercial paper were actually backed by subprime mortgages; when those mortgages started defaulting, this commercial paper caused their holders a great deal of trouble. One issue of commercial paper was downgraded from Aaa to Ba in just 1 day, and those people holding what they thought was safe and highly liquid paper found it to be totally illiquid and of doubtful value. As you might guess, before it defaulted, the mortgage-backed commercial paper paid a somewhat higher return, about 3.505% versus about 3.467% for paper backed by T-bills. Those seeking higher returns generally have to accept more risk.

A firm's relationship with its bank—especially its ability to borrow on short notice—can have a significant effect on its need for both demand deposits and marketable securities. If a company has a firmly committed line of credit under which it can obtain funds with a simple telephone call, it won't need much in the way of liquid reserves. Indeed, many argue that growing concerns about banks' willingness to provide credit has caused some companies to increase their holdings of cash and marketable securities.

Finally, larger corporations shop for securities all around the world, buying wherever risk-adjusted rates are highest. This shopping tends to equalize worldwide rates—if interest rates in Europe are higher than rates in the United States

---

[12]Refer to the following article, Ben Casselman and Justin Lahart, "Companies Shun Investment, Hoard Cash," *The Wall Street Journal* (www.wsj.com), September 17, 2011.

[13]Refer to the following article, Jeff Cox, "US Companies Are Hoarding $2.5 Trillion in Cash Overseas," *CNBC* (www.cnbc.com), September 20, 2016.

[14]Included in the new tax law is a provision for a one-time tax charge to repatriate overseas cash or funds. Overseas profits brought back to the United States (that normally would be taxed at 35%) would be taxed at 8% for profits invested in real estate and equipment and at 15.5% for profits in cash, stock, and other liquid assets. No additional taxes would be owed on these profits. Refer to Lisa Marie Segarra, "Apple Leads These Companies with Massive Overseas Cash Repatriation Tax Bills," *Fortune* (fortune.com), January 18, 2018, for the repatriation tax impact on some of the larger U.S. corporations.

for equally risky securities, companies will buy European securities, driving their prices up and their yields down, until an equilibrium has been established. We truly live in a global economy.[15]

SelfTest

What two definitions of cash are commonly encountered?

Differentiate between marketable securities held for operating (transactions) purposes and securities held for other reasons.

How has the development of credit and debit cards affected firms' currency holdings?

How would the use of credit cards affect a firm's cash conversion cycle assuming it previously allowed customers 30 days to pay for their purchases?

How does a firm's ability to borrow affect its optimal holdings of cash and securities?

Common stocks that are traded on the NYSE are liquid in the sense that they can be sold and converted to cash on short notice. Are stocks a good choice for a firm's marketable securities portfolio? Explain.

15-7 Inventories

Inventories, which can include (1) *supplies,* (2) *raw materials,* (3) *work in process*, and (4) *finished goods*, are an essential part of virtually all business operations. Optimal inventory levels depend on sales, so sales must be forecasted before target inventories can be established. Moreover, because errors in setting inventory levels lead to lost sales or excessive carrying costs, inventory management is quite important. Therefore, firms use sophisticated computer systems to monitor their inventory holdings.

Retailers typically use computers to keep track of each inventory item by size, shape, and color; and bar code information collected at checkout updates inventory records. When inventories shown in the computer decline to a set level, the computer sends an order to the supplier's computer, specifying exactly what is needed. The computer also reports how fast items are moving. If an item is moving too slowly, the computer will suggest a price cut to lower the inventory stock before the item becomes obsolete. Manufacturers use similar systems to keep track of items and to place orders as they are needed.

Although inventory management is important, it is under the operational control of production managers and marketing people rather than financial managers. Still, financial managers are involved in several ways. First, it is expensive to install and maintain the computer systems used to track inventories, and the capital budgeting analysis discussed earlier in the text must be used to determine which system is best. Second, if the firm decides to increase its inventory holdings, the financial manager must raise the capital needed to acquire the additional inventory. And third, the financial manager is responsible for identifying any area of weakness that affects the firm's overall profitability, using ratios and other procedures for comparing the firm to its benchmark companies. Therefore, the CFO will compare the firm's inventory-to-sales ratio with those of its benchmarks to see if things look "reasonable." Because inventory management is outside the mainstream of finance, we cover it in Web Appendix 15A rather than in this chapter.

[15]Companies can also buy securities that are denominated in different currencies. Thus, if a firm's treasurer thinks that the euro is likely to appreciate against the dollar, he or she might purchase securities denominated in euros; if things work out as expected, the firm will earn interest and enjoy an additional gain from the change in exchange rates. Again, these actions help to keep world financial markets in equilibrium.

SelfTest

What are the three primary tasks of the financial manager regarding inventory management?

15-8 Accounts Receivable

Although some sales are made for cash, today the vast majority of sales are on credit. Thus, in the typical situation, goods are shipped, inventories are reduced, and an **account receivable** is created.[16] Eventually, the customer pays, the firm receives cash, and its receivables decline. The firm's credit policy is the primary determinant of accounts receivable, and it is under the administrative control of the CFO. Moreover, credit policy is a key determinant of sales, so sales and marketing executives are concerned with this policy. Therefore, we begin our discussion of accounts receivable by discussing credit policy.

Account Receivable
Funds due from a customer.

15-8A CREDIT POLICY

Credit policy consists of these four variables:

Credit Policy
A set of rules that include the firm's credit period, discounts, credit standards, and collection procedures offered.

Credit Period
The length of time customers have to pay for purchases.

Discounts
Price reductions given for early payment.

1. **Credit period** is the length of time buyers are given to pay for their purchases. For example, the credit period might be 30 days. Customers prefer longer credit periods, so lengthening the period will stimulate sales. However, a longer credit period lengthens the cash conversion cycle; hence, it ties up more capital in receivables, which is costly. Also, the longer a receivable is outstanding, the higher the probability that the customer will default and that the account will end up as a bad debt.
2. **Discounts** are price reductions given for early payment. The discount specifies what the percentage reduction is and how rapidly payment must be made to be eligible for the discount. For example, a 2% discount is often given if the customer pays within 10 days. Offering discounts has two benefits. First, the discount amounts to a price reduction, which stimulates sales. Second, discounts encourage customers to pay earlier than they otherwise would, which shortens the cash conversion cycle. However, discounts also mean lower prices—and lower revenues unless the quantity sold increases by enough to offset the price reduction. The benefits and costs of discounts must be balanced when credit policy is being established.
3. **Credit standards** refer to the required financial strength of acceptable credit customers. With regard to credit standards, factors considered for business customers include ratios such as the customer's debt and interest coverage ratios, the customer's credit history (whether the customer has paid on time in the past or tended to be delinquent), and the like. For individual customers, their credit score as developed by credit rating agencies is the key item. In both cases, the key question is this: Is the customer likely to be willing and able to make the required payment on schedule? Note that when standards are set too low, bad debt losses will be too high; on the other hand, when standards are set too high, the firm loses sales and thus profits. So a balance must be struck between the costs and benefits of tighter credit standards.

Credit Standards
The financial strength customers must exhibit to qualify for credit.

[16]Whenever goods are sold on credit, two accounts are created—an asset item titled *account receivable* appears on the books of the selling firm, and a liability item called an *account payable* appears on the purchaser's books. At this point, we are analyzing the transaction from the viewpoint of the seller, so we are focusing on the variables under the seller's control—in this case, receivables. In Section 15-9, we examine the transaction from the purchaser's viewpoint when we discuss accounts payable as a source of funds and consider their cost relative to the cost of funds obtained from other sources.

Collection Policy
Degree of toughness in enforcing the credit terms.

4. **Collection policy** refers to the procedures used to collect past due accounts, including the toughness or laxity used in the process. At one extreme, the firm might write a series of polite letters after a fairly long delay; at the other extreme, delinquent accounts may be turned over to a collection agency relatively quickly. Companies should be somewhat firm, but excessive pressure can lead customers whose business is profitable to take their business elsewhere. Again, a balance must be struck between the costs and benefits of different collection policies.

Credit Terms
Statement of the credit period and discount policy.

Firms generally publish their **credit terms**, defined as a statement of their credit period and discount policy. Thus, Allied Food might have stated credit terms of 2/10, net 30, which means that it allows a 2% discount if payment is received within 10 days of the purchase; if the discount is not taken then, the full amount is due in 30 days. Credit standards and collection policies are relatively subjective, so they are not generally discussed in the published credit terms.

15-8B SETTING AND IMPLEMENTING THE CREDIT POLICY

Credit policy is important for three main reasons: (1) It has a major effect on sales. (2) It influences the amount of funds tied up in receivables. (3) It affects bad debt losses. Because of the importance of the policy, the firm's executive committee (which normally consists of the president in addition to the vice presidents of finance and marketing) has the final say on setting the credit policy. Once the policy has been established, the credit manager, who typically works under the CFO, must implement it and monitor its effects. Managing a credit department requires fast, accurate, and up-to-date information. Several organizations, including Experian, Equifax, and TransUnion, use computer-based networks to collect, store, and distribute credit information. For businesses, Dun & Bradstreet provides detailed credit reports over the Internet for a fee. The reports include the following types of information:

1. A summary balance sheet and income statement
2. A number of key ratios with trend information
3. Data obtained from the firm's suppliers telling whether it pays promptly or slowly and whether it has recently failed to make any payments
4. A verbal description of the physical condition of the firm's operations
5. A verbal description of the backgrounds of the firm's owners, including any previous bankruptcies, lawsuits, or divorce settlement problems
6. A summary rating ranging from A for the best credit risks down to F for those firms that are deemed likely to default

Credit Scores
Numerical scores that indicate the likelihood that people or businesses will pay on time.

Credit scores are numerical scores that are based on a statistical analysis and provide a summary assessment of the likelihood that a potential customer will default on a required payment. Computerized analytical systems assist in making better credit decisions, but in the final analysis, most credit decisions are exercises in informed judgment.[17]

We have emphasized the costs of granting credit. *However, if it is possible to sell on credit and to impose a carrying charge on the receivables that are outstanding, credit*

[17]Credit analysts use procedures ranging from highly sophisticated computerized *credit-scoring* systems, which calculate the statistical probability that a given customer will default, to informal procedures, which involve going through a checklist of factors that should be considered when a credit application is processed. The credit-scoring systems use various financial ratios, such as the current ratio and the debt ratio (for businesses), and income, years with the same employer, and the like (for individuals), to determine the statistical probability of default. Credit is then granted to those with low default probabilities. The informal procedures often involve examining the "5 Cs of Credit": character, capacity, capital, collateral, and conditions. Character is obvious; capacity is a subjective estimate of ability to repay; capital means how much net worth the borrower has; collateral means assets pledged to secure the loan; and conditions refers to business conditions, which affect ability to repay.

sales can actually be more profitable than cash sales. This is especially true for consumer durables (e.g., automobiles and appliances), but it is also true for certain types of industrial equipment.[18] Some companies actually earn more on credit than cash sales, and their salespeople earn higher commissions when they make a credit sale.

The carrying charges on outstanding consumer credit are generally about 18% on a nominal basis: 1.5% per month, so 1.5% × 12 = 18%. This is equivalent to an effective annual rate of $(1.015)^{12} - 1.0 = 19.6\%$. Having receivables outstanding that earn more than 18% is highly profitable unless there are too many bad debt losses.

Legal considerations must also be considered when setting credit policy. Under the Robinson–Patman Act, it is illegal for a firm to charge prices that discriminate between customers unless the different prices are cost-justified. The same holds true for credit—it is illegal to offer more favorable credit terms to one customer or class of customers than to another unless the differences are cost-justified.

15-8C MONITORING ACCOUNTS RECEIVABLE

The total amount of accounts receivable outstanding at any given time is determined by the volume of credit sales and the average length of time between sales and collections. For example, suppose Boston Lumber Company (BLC), a wholesale distributor of lumber products, has sales of $1,000 per day (all on credit) and it requires payment after 10 days. BLC has no bad debts or slow-paying customers. Under those conditions, it must have the capital to carry $10,000 of receivables:

$$\text{Accounts receivable} = \text{Sales per day} \times \text{Length of collection period} = \$1{,}000 \times 10 \text{ days} = \$10{,}000 \tag{15.5}$$

If either sales or the collection period changes, so will accounts receivable. For example, if sales doubled to $2,000/day, receivables would also double, and the firm would need an additional $10,000 to finance this increase. Similarly, if the collection period lengthened to 20 days, this too would double the receivables and require additional capital.

If management is not careful, the collection period will creep up as good customers take longer to pay and as sales are made to weaker customers who tend to pay slowly or not at all and thus create bad debts. So it is important to monitor receivables. One easy-to-use monitoring technique employs the DSO. Here's Allied Food's DSO as calculated in Chapter 4:

$$\text{DSO} = \begin{matrix}\text{Days}\\ \text{sales}\\ \text{outstanding}\end{matrix} = \frac{\text{Receivables}}{\text{Average sales per day}} = \frac{\text{Receivables}}{\text{Annual sales/365}}$$

$$= \frac{\$375}{\$3{,}000/365} = \frac{\$375}{\$8.2192} = 45.625 \text{ days} \approx 46 \text{ days}$$

$$\text{Industry average} = 36 \text{ days}$$

Allied has average daily sales (ADS) of $8.2192 million, and those sales are outstanding for 45.625 days. If we multiply the DSO by the average daily sales, we determine the capital tied up in receivables:

$$\text{Receivables} = (\text{ADS})(\text{DSO}) = (\$8.2192)(45.625) = \$375 \text{ million}$$

[18]Companies that do a large volume of sales financing typically set up subsidiary companies called *captive finance companies* to do the actual financing. For example, Ford, Sears, and IBM have captive finance companies.

Note, though, that if Allied collected its receivables faster and reduced its DSO to the 36-day industry average, its receivables would decline to $295.89 million, or by $79.11 million. The DSO can also be compared to the firm's own credit terms. Allied sells on terms of net 30, so its DSO should be no greater than 30 days. Obviously, some customers are paying late, so there is room for improvement in its collection policy and practices.[19]

Self*Test*

What are credit terms?

What are the four credit policy variables?

Define days sales outstanding (DSO). What can be learned from it, and how is it affected by seasonal sales fluctuations?

What is credit quality, and how is it assessed?

How does collection policy influence sales, the collection period, and the bad debt loss percentage?

How can cash discounts be used to influence sales volume and the DSO?

How do legal considerations affect a firm's credit policy?

15-9 Accounts Payable (Trade Credit)

Trade Credit
Debt arising from credit sales and recorded as an account receivable by the seller and as an account payable by the buyer.

Firms generally make purchases from other firms on credit and record the debt as an *account payable.* Accounts payable, or **trade credit**, is the largest single category of short-term debt, representing about 40% of the average corporation's current liabilities. This credit is a spontaneous source of financing in the sense that *it arises spontaneously from ordinary business transactions.* For example, if a firm makes a purchase of $1,000 on terms of net 30, it must pay for goods 30 days after the invoice date. This instantly and spontaneously provides $1,000 of credit for 30 days. If the firm purchases $1,000 of goods each day, on average, it will be receiving 30 times $1,000, or $30,000, of credit from its suppliers. If sales, and consequently purchases, double, its accounts payable also will double, to $60,000. So simply by growing, the firm spontaneously generates another $30,000 of financing. Similarly, if the terms under which it buys are extended from 30 to 40 days, its accounts payable will expand from $30,000 to $40,000. Thus, expanding sales and lengthening the credit period generate additional financing.

Trade credit may be free, or it may be costly. If the seller does not offer discounts, the credit is free in the sense that there is no cost for using it. However, if discounts are available, a complication arises. To illustrate, suppose PCC Inc. buys 20 microchips each day, with a list price of $100 per chip on terms of 2/10, net 30. Under those terms, the "true" price of the chips is 0.98($100) = $98 because the chips can be purchased for only $98 by paying within 10 days. Thus, the $100 list price has two components:

List price = $98 "true" price + $2 finance charge

[19]Another technique used to monitor receivables is the *Aging Schedule*, which shows the dollar amount and percentage of receivables that have been outstanding for different lengths of time. See Chapter 21, "Supply Chains and Working Capital," in Eugene F. Brigham and Phillip R. Daves, *Intermediate Financial Management*, 13th edition (Mason, OH: Cengage Learning, 2019).

If PCC decides to take the discount, it will pay at the end of Day 10 and show \$19,600 of accounts payable:[20]

$$\text{Accounts payable}_{\text{(Take discounts)}} = \text{(10 days)(20 chips)(\$98 per chip)} = \$19{,}600$$

If it decides to delay payment until the 30th day, its trade credit will be \$58,800:

$$\text{Accounts payable}_{\text{(No discounts)}} = \text{(30 days)(20 chips)(\$98 per chip)} = \$58{,}800$$

By not taking discounts, PCC can obtain an additional \$39,200 of trade credit, *but this \$39,200 is costly credit because the firm must forgo the discounts to receive it.* Therefore, PCC must answer this question: Could we obtain the additional \$39,200 at a lower cost from some other source (for example, a bank)?

To illustrate the situation, assume that PCC operates 365 days per year and buys 20 chips per day at a "true" price of \$98 per chip. Therefore, its total chip purchases are 20(\$98)(365) = \$715,400 per year. If it does not take discounts, its chips will cost 20(\$100)(365) = \$730,000, or an additional \$14,600. *This \$14,600 is the annual cost of the \$39,200 of extra credit.* Dividing the \$14,600 cost by the \$39,200 additional credit yields the nominal annual cost of the additional trade credit, 37.24%:

$$\text{Nominal annual cost of trade credit} = \frac{\$14{,}600}{\$39{,}200} = 37.24\%$$

If PCC can borrow from its bank or some other source for less than 37.24%, it should take the discount and use only \$19,600 of trade credit.

The same result can be obtained with the following equation:

$$\text{Nominal annual cost of trade credit} = \frac{\text{Discount \%}}{100 - \text{Discount \%}} \times \frac{365}{\text{Days credit is outstanding} - \text{Discount period}} \quad \textbf{15.6}$$

$$= \frac{2}{98} \times \frac{365}{20} = 2.04\% \times 18.25 = 37.24\%$$

The numerator of the first term, Discount %, is the cost per dollar of credit, while the denominator, 100 − Discount %, represents the funds made available by not taking the discount. Thus, the first term, 2.04%, is the cost per period for the trade credit. The denominator of the second term is the number of days of extra credit obtained by not taking the discount. So the entire second term shows how many times per year the cost is incurred, 18.25 times in this example.[21]

---

[20]A question arises here: Should accounts payable reflect gross purchases or purchases net of discounts? Generally accepted accounting principles permit either treatment if the difference is not material, but if the discount is material, the account payable must be recorded net of discounts, or at the "true" price. Then the cost of not taking discounts is reported as an additional expense called "discounts lost." This procedure highlights the often high cost of not taking discounts. In PCC's case, it would record payables of 20(\$98) = \$1,960, not \$2,000, per day, and if it did not take the discount and had to pay the full \$2,000, it would show the \$40 discount lost per day as an expense.

[21]The nominal annual cost formula does not consider compounding, and in effective annual interest terms, the cost of trade credit is even higher. The discount is equivalent to interest; with terms of 2/10, net 30, the firm gains the use of funds for 30 − 10 = 20 days. So there are 365/20 = 18.25 "interest periods" per year. Remember that the first term in Equation 15.6, (Discount%)/(100 − Discount%) = 0.02/0.98 = 0.0204, is the periodic interest rate. That rate is paid 18.25 times each year, so the effective annual cost of trade credit is 44.6%:

$$\text{Effective annual rate} = (1.0204)^{18.25} - 1.0 = 1.4459 - 1.0 = 44.6\%$$

Thus, the 37.2% nominal cost calculated with Equation 15.6 understates the effective cost.

A DIFFICULT BALANCING ACT

During tough economic times, many companies find it harder to obtain loans to finance their working capital, so they increasingly rely on trade credit. Often times, suppliers are very willing to provide this trade credit because it helps maintain a valuable customer relationship.

But as an article in *CFO* magazine points out, suppliers frequently face a difficult balancing act when their customers are slow to pay them back. On the one hand, you don't want to push too hard to force payment, for fear that you may lose the customer. But on the other hand, the longer the customer takes to pay, the more your cash is tied up, and the greater the risk that you will never get paid.

The article quotes, among others, Pam Krank, who is president of an outsourcing firm, The Credit Department. Krank recommends keeping a close eye on your customer's DSO to gauge the timeliness of payments. She points out, "If your customer doesn't get paid by its customer for 80 days, you won't get paid in 30." At the same time, Krank argues that while you have to be vigilant with slow payers, you can't just walk away from doing business with them, particularly during tough times. She asserts, "You can't just say they're high risk so we can't sell to them." Echoing Krank's viewpoint, Jerry Flum, the chief executive of CreditRiskMonitor, also argues that you sometimes have to keep doing business with slow payers, especially if your company is earning high profit margins from the sales.

Looking at a similar issue, a 2009 *Wall Street Journal* article demonstrates that during the 2007–2009 slowdown, large companies and small companies balanced these concerns in different ways. During the slowdown, companies with sales over $5 billion collected their bills slightly faster (the average bill was collected in 41 days in 2009 compared to 41.9 days in 2008), but they took longer to pay their bills (55.8 days in 2009 compared to 53.2 days in 2008). In contrast, the reverse pattern holds for companies with sales less than $500 million. These companies paid their bills more quickly in 2009 (40.1 days compared to 42.9 days in 2008), but their customers were much slower paying them (58.9 days in 2009 compared to 54.4 days in 2008).

Summarizing these trends, the article provides the following assessment:

> "There's a power struggle going on as the credit crunch has moved to Main Street," says Sung Won Sohn, a former chief economist at Wells Fargo who now teaches at California State University, Channel Islands. "Big firms can force their terms on suppliers and customers. And if you're a small business or a small store in a mall, you have no bargaining power and have to take what's given, which is not much today."

Sources: Vincent Ryan, "Slow Burn: What Should You Do When Customers Are Slow to Pay?" *CFO* (www.cfo.com), April 1, 2010; and Serena Ng and Cari Tuna, "Big Firms Are Quick to Collect, Slow to Pay," *The Wall Street Journal* (www.wsj.com), August 31, 2009.

With this background, we can define two types of trade credit: free and costly.

Free Trade Credit
Credit received during the discount period.

Costly Trade Credit
Credit taken in excess of free trade credit, whose cost is equal to the discount lost.

1. **Free trade credit** is the trade credit that is obtained without a cost, and it consists of all trade credit that is available without forgoing discounts. In PCC's case, when it buys on terms of 2/10, net 30, the first 10 days of purchases, or $19,600, are free.
2. **Costly trade credit** is any trade credit over and above the free trade credit. For PCC, the additional 20 days, or $39,200, are not free because receiving the additional credit means forfeiting the discount.

Firms should always use the free component, but they should use the costly component only if they cannot obtain funds at a lower cost from another source.[22]

[22]Note that the cost of trade credit can be reduced by paying late. If PCC could get away with paying in 60 days rather than the specified 30 days, the effective credit period would become 60 − 10 = 50 days, the number of times the discount would be lost would fall to 365/50 = 7.3, and the nominal cost would drop from 37.2% to 2.04% × 7.3 = 14.9%. This is called *stretching accounts payable*, and it damages the firm's reputation and can cause problems later.

quick question

QUESTION:

Diana's Designs just recently opened as an upscale dress shop in northeast Florida. The owner is trying to decide whether to take the discount offered from her suppliers, or whether to pay at the end of the month. Diana's suppliers are offering her a 3% discount if she pays within 15 days; otherwise, the balance is due 30 days after purchase. What are Diana's nominal and effective annual costs of trade credit?

ANSWER:

$$\text{Nominal annual cost of trade credit} = \frac{\text{Discount \%}}{100 - \text{Discount \%}} \times \frac{365}{\text{Days credit is outstanding} - \text{Discount period}}$$

$$= \frac{3}{97} \times \frac{365}{30 - 15} = 3.093\% \times 24.333 = \mathbf{75.26\%}$$

$$\text{Effective annual cost of trade credit} = (1.03093)^{24.333} - 1.0 = \mathbf{109.84\%}$$

Clearly, the effective cost of trade credit is extremely high. So, if she is able to pay within the 15-day window, Diana should definitely take the 3% discount offered by her suppliers.

Self*Test*

What is trade credit?

What is the difference between free trade credit and costly trade credit?

What is the formula for finding the nominal annual cost of trade credit? Does the nominal cost of trade credit understate the effective cost? Explain.

15-10 Bank Loans

The key features of bank loans, another important source of short-term financing for businesses and individuals, are discussed in this section.

15-10A PROMISSORY NOTE

The terms of a bank loan are spelled out in a **promissory note**. Here are some key features of most promissory notes: [23]

Promissory Note A document specifying the terms and conditions of a loan, including the amount, interest rate, and repayment schedule.

1. *Amount.* The amount borrowed is indicated.
2. *Maturity.* Although banks do make longer-term loans, *the bulk of their lending is on a short-term basis*—about two-thirds of all bank loans mature in a year or less. Long-term loans always have a specific maturity date, while a short-term loan may or may not have a specified maturity. For example, a

[23]Sometimes, the note will also specify that the firm must maintain a *compensating balance* equal to 10% to 20% of the face amount of the loan. This balance generally has the effect of increasing the effective cost of the loan. Compensating balances are much less common today than they were a few years ago.

loan may mature in 30 days, 90 days, 6 months, or 1 year, or it may call for payment "on demand," in which case the loan can remain outstanding as long as the borrower wants to continue using the funds and the bank agrees. Bank loans to businesses are frequently written as 90-day notes, so the loan must be repaid or renewed at the end of 90 days. It is often expected that the loan will be renewed, but if the borrower's financial position deteriorates, the bank can refuse to renew it. This can lead to bankruptcy. Because banks usually don't demand payment unless the borrower's creditworthiness has deteriorated, some "short-term loans" remain outstanding for years, with the interest rate floating with rates in the economy.

3. *Interest rate.* The interest rate can be *fixed* or *floating.* For larger loans, it is typically indexed to the bank's prime rate, to the T-bill rate, or to the London Interbank Offered Rate (LIBOR). The note will also indicate whether the bank uses a *360-* or *365-day year* for purposes of calculating interest. The indicated rate is a *nominal rate,* and the effective annual rate is generally higher.
4. *Interest only versus amortized.* Loans are either *interest only,* meaning that only interest is paid during the life of the loan, with all principal repaid when the loan matures, or *amortized,* meaning that some of the principal is repaid on each payment date. Amortized loans are also called *installment loans.*
5. *Frequency of interest payments.* If the note is on an interest-only basis, it will indicate *how frequently interest must be paid.* Interest is typically calculated daily but paid monthly.
6. *Discount interest.* Most loans call for interest to be paid only after it has been earned, but banks also lend on a *discount basis,* where interest is paid in advance. On a discount loan, the borrower actually receives less than the face amount of the loan, and this increases its effective cost. We discuss discount loans in Web Appendix 15B.
7. *Add-on loans.* Auto loans and other consumer installment loans are generally set up on an "add-on basis," which means that interest charges over the life of the loan are calculated and then added to the face amount of the loan. Thus, the borrower signs a promissory note calling for payment of the funds received plus all interest that must be paid over the life of the loan. The add-on feature raises the effective cost of a loan.
8. *Collateral.* If a loan is secured by equipment, buildings, accounts receivable, or inventories, this fact is indicated in the note. Security for loans is discussed in more detail in Section 15-13.
9. *Restrictive covenants.* The note may also specify that the borrower must maintain certain ratios at or better than specified levels, and it spells out what happens if the borrower defaults on those covenants. Default provisions often allow the lender to demand immediate payment of the entire loan balance. Also, the interest rate on the loan might be increased.
10. *Loan guarantees.* If the borrower is a small corporation, the bank will probably insist that its larger stockholders *personally guarantee* the loan. Troubled companies' owners have been known to divert assets from the company to relatives or other entities they own, so banks protect themselves by obtaining personal guarantees.

15-10B LINE OF CREDIT

Line of Credit
An arrangement in which a bank agrees to lend up to a specified maximum amount of funds during a designated period.

A **line of credit** is an agreement between a bank and a borrower indicating the maximum amount of credit the bank will extend to the borrower. For example, in December, a bank loan officer might indicate to a financial manager that the bank regards the firm as being "good for" up to $80,000 during the coming year, provided the borrower's financial condition does not deteriorate. If on January 10 the financial manager signs a promissory note for $15,000 for 90 days, this would be called "taking down" $15,000 of the credit line. The $15,000 would be credited to the firm's checking account, and before it was repaid, the firm could borrow an additional $65,000 for a total of $80,000. Such a line of credit would be informal and nonbinding, but formal and binding lines are available, as discussed next.

15-10C REVOLVING CREDIT AGREEMENT

A **revolving credit agreement** is a formal line of credit. To illustrate, in 2019 a Texas petroleum company negotiated a revolving credit agreement for $100 million with a group of banks. The banks were formally committed for 4 years to lend the firm up to $100 million if the funds were needed. The company, in turn, paid an annual commitment fee of one-fourth of 1% on the unused balance of the commitment to compensate the banks for making the commitment. Thus, if the firm did not take down any of the $100 million commitment during a year, it would still be required to pay a $250,000 annual fee, normally in monthly installments of $20,833.33. If it borrowed $50 million on the first day of the agreement, the unused portion of the line of credit would fall to $50 million and the annual fee would fall to $125,000. Of course, interest would also have to be paid on the money the firm actually borrowed. In this case, the interest rate on the "revolver" was pegged to the LIBOR rate, being set at LIBOR minus 0.1 percentage point; so the cost of the loan would vary over time as interest rates changed.[24]

Revolving Credit Agreement
A formal, committed line of credit extended by a bank or other lending institution.

Note that a revolving credit agreement is similar to an informal line of credit, but with an important difference: The bank has a *legal obligation* to honor a revolving credit agreement, and it receives a commitment fee. Neither the legal obligation nor the fee exists under informal lines of credit.

Research by Victoria Ivashina and David Scharfstein suggests that lines of credit played an important role in the 2007–2009 financial crisis. They argued that many corporate borrowers rushed to take down loans under their lines of credit because they feared that if the crisis worsened, the banks would not be able to honor their loan commitments. In some cases, this rush to obtain credit took valuable funds from the banks at a time when they needed it most. This draining of funds arguably diminished the banks' ability to provide new loans.[25]

15-10D COSTS OF BANK LOANS

The costs of bank loans vary for different types of borrowers at any given point in time and for all borrowers over time. Interest rates are higher for riskier borrowers, and rates are higher on smaller loans because of the fixed costs involved in making and servicing loans. If a firm can qualify as a "prime credit" because of its size and financial strength, it can borrow at the **prime rate**, which at one time was the lowest rate banks charged. Rates on other loans are generally scaled up from the prime rate. But loans to large, strong customers are made at rates tied to LIBOR, and the costs of such loans are generally well below prime:

Prime Rate
A published interest rate charged by commercial banks to large, strong borrowers.

Rates on August 15, 2018: Prime: 5.00%; 3-Month LIBOR: 2.31519%

---

[24]Each bank sets its own prime rate, but because of competitive forces, most banks' prime rates are identical. Further, most banks follow the rate set by the large New York City banks.

In recent years, many banks have been lending to large, strong companies at rates below the prime rate. As we discuss in Section 15-11, larger firms have ready access to the commercial paper market; if banks want to do business with these companies, they must match (or at least come close to) the commercial paper rate.

[25]See Victoria Ivashina and David Scharfstein, "Bank Lending during the Financial Crisis of 2008," *Journal of Financial Economics*, vol. 97, no. 3 (2010), pp. 319–338.

The rate to smaller, riskier borrowers is generally stated something like "prime plus 2.5%," but for a larger borrower such as the Texas oil company, it is generally stated something like "LIBOR plus 2.5%."

Bank rates vary widely over time, depending on economic conditions and Federal Reserve policy. When the economy is weak, loan demand is usually slack, inflation is low, and the Fed makes plenty of money available to the system. As a result, rates on all types of loans are relatively low. Conversely, when the economy is booming, loan demand is typically strong, the Fed restricts the money supply to fight inflation, and the result is high interest rates. As an indication of the kinds of fluctuations that can occur, the prime rate during 1980 rose from 11% to 21% in just 4 months, and it rose from 6% to 9% during 1994.

Calculating Banks' Interest Charges: Regular (or Simple) Interest

Banks calculate interest in several different ways. In this section, we explain the procedure used for most business loans. (We discuss procedures used for consumer and small business loans in Web Appendix 15B.) For illustrative purposes, we assume a loan of $10,000 at the prime rate (currently 5.00%) with a 360-day year. Interest must be paid monthly, and the principal is payable "on demand" if and when the bank wants to end the loan. Such a loan is called a **regular, or simple, interest** loan.

Regular, or Simple, Interest
The situation when interest only is paid monthly.

We begin by dividing the nominal interest rate (5.00% in this case) by 360 to calculate the rate per day. The rate is expressed as a *decimal fraction,* not as a percentage:

$$\text{Simple interest rate per day} = \frac{\text{Nominal rate}}{\text{Days in year}}$$
$$= 0.05/360 = 0.000138889$$

To find the monthly interest payment, the daily rate is multiplied by the amount of the loan, and then by the number of days during the payment period. For our illustrative loan, the daily interest charge would be $1.388888889, and the total for a 30-day month would be $41.67:

$$\text{Interest charge for month} = (\text{Rate per day})(\text{Amount of loan})(\text{Days in month})$$
$$= (0.000138889)(\$10{,}000)(30\ \text{days}) = \$41.67$$

The *effective interest rate* on a loan depends on how frequently interest must be paid—the more frequently interest is paid, the higher the effective rate. If interest is paid once a year, the nominal rate also will be the effective rate. However, if interest must be paid monthly, the effective rate will be $(1 + 0.05/12)^{12} - 1 = 5.1162\%$.

Calculating Banks' Interest Charges: Add-On Interest

Add-On Interest
Interest that is calculated and added to funds received to determine the face amount of an installment loan.

Banks and other lenders typically use **add-on interest** for automobiles and other types of installment loans. The term *add-on* means that the interest is calculated and then added to the amount borrowed to determine the loan's face value. To illustrate, suppose you borrow $10,000 on an *add-on* basis at a nominal rate of 3.00% to buy a car, with the loan to be repaid in 12 monthly installments. At a 3.00% add-on rate, you would make total interest payments of $10,000(0.03) = $300. However, because the loan is paid off in monthly installments, you would have the use of the full $10,000 for only the first month, and the outstanding balance would decline until, during the last month, only 1/12 of the original loan was still outstanding. Thus, you would be paying $300 for the use of only about half the loan's face amount, as the average usable funds would be only about $5,000. Therefore, we can calculate the approximate annual rate as 6.0%:

$$\text{Approximate annual rate}_{\text{Add-on}} = \frac{\text{Interest paid}}{(\text{Amount received})/2} \qquad \textbf{15.7}$$
$$= \frac{\$300}{\$10{,}000/2} = 6.0\%$$

The annual percentage rate (APR) the bank would provide to the borrower would be 5.49%, and the true effective annual rate would be 5.63%. Both of those rates are far higher than the nominal 3.00%.[26]

Self*Test*

What is a promissory note, and what terms are normally included in promissory notes?

What is a line of credit? A revolving credit agreement?

What's the difference between simple interest and add-on interest as bankers use these terms?

If a firm borrowed $500,000 at a rate of 10% simple interest with monthly interest payments and a 365-day year, what would be the required interest payment for a 30-day month? If interest must be paid monthly, what would be the effective annual rate? **($4,109.59, 10.47%)**

If this loan had been made on a 10% add-on basis payable in 12 end-of-month installments, what would be the monthly payments? What is the annual percentage rate? The effective annual rate? **($45,833.33, 17.97%, 19.53%)**

How does the cost of costly trade credit generally compare with the cost of short-term bank loans?

15-11 Commercial Paper

Commercial paper is a promissory note issued by a large, strong firm—most often a financial institution—that wants to borrow on a short-term basis. Commercial paper is sold primarily to other business firms, insurance companies, pension funds, money market mutual funds, and banks, in denominations of at least $100,000. It is generally unsecured, but "asset-backed paper" secured by credit card debt and other small, short-term loans has also been issued. Also (and with very bad consequences) in 2007, subsidiaries of financial institutions such as Citigroup sold a great deal of commercial paper and used it to buy bonds backed by subprime mortgages. This created a situation in which short-term commercial paper was backed by long-term debt—and very poor quality debt at that. When the real situation was learned, holders of commercial paper refused to roll it over when it matured, and the financial institutions that had sold it were forced to sell the mortgages that backed the paper, often at huge losses. That forced Citi and other institutions to bail out their subsidiaries and to take losses in the tens of billions of dollars.

Commercial Paper
Unsecured, short-term promissory notes of large firms, usually issued in denominations of $100,000 or more with an interest rate somewhat below the prime rate.

A large majority of the commercial paper outstanding has been issued by financial institutions. Non-financial companies also issue a great deal of paper, but they generally rely more heavily on bank loans for short-term funding. For example, in July 2018, the Federal Reserve reported that commercial paper issued by non-financial firms totaled approximately $296 billion—that same month the total amount of commercial and industrial loans held by commercial banks was just over $2.2269 trillion.

Students can access economic and research data from the Federal Reserve at ***federalreserve.gov****.*

[26]To find the annual percentage rate and the effective rate on an add-on loan, we first find the payment per month, $10,300/12 = $858.33. With a financial calculator, enter N = 12, PV = 10000, PMT = −858.33, FV = 0; then press I/YR to obtain 0.457646%. This is a monthly rate, so multiply by 12 to get 5.49%, which is the APR the bank would report to the borrower. The effective annual rate would be $(1.00457646)^{12} - 1 = 5.63\%$, slightly higher than the APR.

SelfTest

What is commercial paper?

What types of companies use commercial paper to meet their short-term financing needs?

15-12 Accruals (Accrued Liabilities)

As we discussed in Chapter 3, firms generally pay employees on a weekly, biweekly, or monthly basis, so the balance sheet typically shows some accrued wages. Similarly, the firm's own estimated income taxes, Social Security and income taxes withheld from employee payrolls, and sales taxes collected are generally paid on a weekly, monthly, or quarterly basis. Therefore, the balance sheet typically shows some accrued wages and taxes, which we refer to as **accruals**.

Accruals
Continually recurring short-term liabilities, especially accrued wages and accrued taxes.

Spontaneous Funds
Funds that are generated spontaneously as the firm expands.

Accruals arise automatically from a firm's operations; hence, they are **spontaneous funds**. For example, if sales grow by 50%, accrued wages and taxes should also grow by about 50%. Accruals are "free" in the sense that no interest is paid on them. However, firms cannot control their accruals because the timing of wage payments is set by contract or industry custom and tax payments are set by law. Thus, firms use all the accruals they can, but they have little control over their levels.

SelfTest

What types of short-term credit are classified as accrued liabilities?

What is the cost of accrued liabilities? If accruals have such a low cost, why don't firms use them even more?

15-13 Use of Security in Short-Term Financing

Secured Loans
A loan backed by collateral, often inventories or accounts receivable.

Other things held constant, borrowers prefer to use unsecured short-term debt because the bookkeeping costs associated with **secured loans** are high. However, firms may find that they can borrow only if they put up collateral to protect the lender or that securing the loan enables them to borrow at a lower rate.

Stocks and bonds, equipment, inventory, accounts receivable, land, and buildings can be used as collateral. However, few firms that need loans hold portfolios of stocks and bonds. Land, buildings, and equipment are good forms of collateral, but they are generally used to secure long-term loans rather than short-term working capital loans. Therefore, most secured short-term business loans use accounts receivable and inventories as collateral.

To understand the use of security, consider the case of a Chicago hardware dealer who wanted to modernize and expand his store. He requested a $200,000 loan.

After examining his financial statements, the bank indicated that it would lend him a maximum of $100,000 on an unsecured basis and that the interest rate would be 10%. However, the company had about $300,000 of accounts receivable that could be used as collateral; with the receivables as security, the bank agreed to lend the full $200,000 and at the prime rate of 5.00%. Processing costs for administering the loan were fairly high, but even so, the secured loan was less expensive than an unsecured loan would have been.[27]

When the collateral securing a loan is to be kept on the borrower's premises, a form called a UCC-1 (Uniform Commercial Code Form 1) is filed with the secretary of the state in which the collateral is located, along with a *Security Agreement* (also part of the Uniform Commercial Code) that describes the nature of the agreement. The UCC-1 prevents the borrower from using the same collateral to secure loans from different lenders, and the security agreement spells out conditions under which the lender can seize the collateral.

Self*Test*

From the borrower's standpoint, what are the advantages and disadvantages of securing a loan?

What two types of current assets are frequently used as security for short-term loans?

How could borrowers take advantage of lenders if UCC-1s did not exist?

TYING IT ALL TOGETHER

This chapter discussed the management of current assets, including cash, marketable securities, inventory, and receivables. Current assets are essential, but there are costs associated with holding them. So if a company can reduce its current assets without hurting sales, this will increase its profitability. The investment in current assets must be financed, and this financing can be in the form of long-term debt, common equity, and/or short-term credit. Firms typically use trade credit and accruals; they also may use bank debt or commercial paper.

Although current assets and procedures for financing them can be analyzed as we did in this chapter, decisions are normally made within the context of the firm's overall financial plan. We take up financial planning in the next chapter; hence, we continue our discussion of working capital there.

[27]The term *asset-based financing* is often used as a synonym for *secured financing*. In recent years, accounts receivable have been used as security for long-term bonds, which has permitted corporations to borrow from lenders such as pension funds rather than being restricted to banks and other traditional short-term lenders.

Self-Test Questions and Problems

(Solutions Appear in Appendix A)

ST-1 **KEY TERMS** Define each of the following terms:

a. Working capital; net working capital; net operating working capital
b. Relaxed investment policy; restricted investment policy; moderate investment policy
c. Permanent current assets; temporary current assets
d. Current assets financing policy; maturity matching (self-liquidating) approach
e. Cash conversion cycle (CCC); inventory conversion period; average collection period; payables deferral period
f. Cash budget; target cash balance
g. Lockbox; account receivable
h. Credit policy; credit period; discounts; credit standards; collection policy; credit terms; credit score
i. Trade credit; free trade credit; costly trade credit
j. Promissory note; line of credit; revolving credit agreement
k. Prime rate; regular, or simple interest; add-on interest
l. Commercial paper; accruals; spontaneous funds
m. Secured loan

ST-2 **CURRENT ASSETS INVESTMENT POLICY** Calgary Company is thinking of modifying its current assets investment policy. Fixed assets are $600,000, sales are projected at $3 million, the EBIT/Sales ratio is projected at 15%, the interest rate is 10% on all debt, the federal-plus-state tax rate is 25%, and Calgary plans to maintain a 50% debt-to-assets ratio. Three alternative current assets investment policies are under consideration: 40%, 50%, and 60% of projected sales. What is the expected return on equity under each alternative?

ST-3 **CURRENT ASSETS FINANCING** Vanderheiden Press Inc. and Herrenhouse Publishing Company had the following balance sheets as of December 31, 2019 (thousands of dollars):

	Vanderheiden Press	Herrenhouse Publishing
Current assets	$ 100,000	$ 80,000
Fixed assets (net)	100,000	120,000
Total assets	$ 200,000	$ 200,000
Short-term debt	$ 20,000	$ 80,000
Long-term debt	80,000	20,000
Common stock	50,000	50,000
Retained earnings	50,000	50,000
Total liabilities and equity	$ 200,000	$ 200,000

Earnings before interest and taxes for both firms are $30 million, and the effective federal-plus-state tax rate is 25%.

a. What is the return on equity for each firm if the interest rate on short-term debt is 2% and the rate on long-term debt is 5%?
b. Assume that the short-term rate rises to 9%. Although the rate on new long-term debt rises to 7%, the rate on existing long-term debt remains unchanged. What would be the returns on equity for Vanderheiden Press and Herrenhouse Publishing under these conditions?
c. Which company is in a riskier position? Why?

Questions

15-1 What are some pros and cons of holding high levels of current assets in relation to sales? Use the DuPont equation to help explain your answer.

15-2 Define the cash conversion cycle (CCC) and explain why, holding other things constant, a firm's profitability would increase if it lowered its CCC.

15-3 What are the two definitions of cash, and why do corporate treasurers often use the second definition?

15-4 What is a cash budget, and how can this statement be used to help reduce the amount of cash that a firm needs to carry? What are the advantages and disadvantages of daily over monthly cash budgets, and how might a cash budget be used when a firm is negotiating a loan from its bank?

15-5 What are the four key factors in a firm's credit policy? How would a relaxed policy differ from a restrictive policy? Give examples of how the four factors might differ between the two policies. How would the relaxed versus the restrictive policy affect sales? Profits?

15-6 What does it mean to adopt a maturity matching approach to financing assets, including current assets? How would a more aggressive or a more conservative approach differ from the maturity matching approach, and how would each affect expected profits and risk? In general, is one approach better than the others?

15-7 Why is some trade credit called free while other credit is called costly? If a firm buys on terms of 2/10, net 30, pays at the end of the 30th day, and typically shows $300,000 of accounts payable on its balance sheet, would the entire $300,000 be free credit, would it be costly credit, or would some be free and some costly? Explain your answer. No calculations are necessary.

15-8 Define each of the following loan terms, and explain how they are related to one another: the prime rate, the rate on commercial paper, the simple interest rate on a bank loan calling for interest to be paid monthly, and the rate on an installment loan based on add-on interest. If the stated rate on each of these loans was 5%, would they all have equal, effective annual rates? Explain.

15-9 Why are accruals called spontaneous sources of funds, what are their costs, and why don't firms use more of them?

15-10 Indicate using a (+), (−), or (0) whether each of the following events would probably cause accounts receivable (A/R), sales, and profits to increase, decrease, or be affected in an indeterminate manner:

	A/R	Sales	Profits
The firm restricts its credit standards.	______	______	______
The terms of trade are changed from 2/10, net 30, to 3/10, net 30.	______	______	______
The terms are changed from 2/10, net 30, to 3/10, net 40.	______	______	______
The credit manager gets tough with past-due accounts.	______	______	______

Problems

Easy Problems 1-3

15-1 **CASH CONVERSION CYCLE** Parramore Corp has $12 million of sales, $3 million of inventories, $3.25 million of receivables, and $1.25 million of payables. Its cost of goods sold is 75% of sales, and it finances working capital with bank loans at an 8% rate. What is Parramore's cash conversion cycle (CCC)? If Parramore could *lower* its inventories and receivables by 10% each and increase its payables by 10%, all without affecting sales or cost of goods sold, what would be the new CCC, how much cash would be freed up, and how would that affect pretax profits?

15-2 RECEIVABLES INVESTMENT Leyton Lumber Company has sales of $12 million per year, all on credit terms calling for payment within 30 days, and its accounts receivable are $1.5 million. What is Leyton's DSO, what would it be if all customers paid on time, and how much capital would be released if Leyton could take action that led to on-time payments?

15-3 COST OF TRADE CREDIT AND BANK LOAN Lancaster Lumber buys $8 million of materials (net of discounts) on terms of 3/5, net 55, and it currently pays on the 5th day and takes discounts. Lancaster plans to expand, which will require additional financing. If Lancaster decides to forgo discounts, how much additional credit could it obtain, and what would be the nominal and effective cost of that credit? If the company could get the funds from a bank at a rate of 9%, interest paid monthly, based on a 365-day year, what would be the effective cost of the bank loan? Should Lancaster use bank debt or additional trade credit? Explain.

Intermediate Problems 4-6

15-4 CASH CONVERSION CYCLE Zane Corporation has an inventory conversion period of 64 days, an average collection period of 28 days, and a payables deferral period of 41 days.

a. What is the length of the cash conversion cycle?
b. If Zane's annual sales are $2,578,235 and all sales are on credit, what is the investment in accounts receivable?
c. How many times per year does Zane turn over its inventory? Assume that the cost of goods sold is 75% of sales. Use sales in the numerator to calculate the turnover ratio.

15-5 RECEIVABLES INVESTMENT McEwan Industries sells on terms of 3/10, net 30. Total sales for the year are $1,921,000; 40% of the customers pay on the 10th day and take discounts, while the other 60% pay, on average, 70 days after their purchases.

a. What is the days sales outstanding?
b. What is the average amount of receivables?
c. What is the percentage cost of trade credit to customers who take the discount?
d. What is the percentage cost of trade credit to customers who do not take the discount and pay in 70 days?
e. What would happen to McEwan's accounts receivable if it toughened up on its collection policy with the result that all nondiscount customers paid on the 30th day?

15-6 WORKING CAPITAL INVESTMENT Pasha Corporation produces motorcycle batteries. Pasha turns out 1,400 batteries a day at a cost of $7 per battery for materials and labor. It takes the firm 22 days to convert raw materials into a battery. Pasha allows its customers 40 days in which to pay for the batteries, and the firm generally pays its suppliers in 30 days.

a. What is the length of Pasha's cash conversion cycle?
b. At a steady state in which Pasha produces 1,400 batteries a day, what amount of working capital must it finance?
c. By what amount could Pasha reduce its working capital financing needs if it was able to stretch its payables deferral period to 33 days?
d. Pasha's management is trying to analyze the effect of a proposed new production process on its working capital investment. The new production process would allow Pasha to decrease its inventory conversion period to 17 days and to increase its daily production to 2,400 batteries. However, the new process would cause the cost of materials and labor to increase to $12. Assuming the change does not affect the average collection period (40 days) or the payables deferral period (30 days), what will be the length of its cash conversion cycle and its working capital financing requirement if the new production process is implemented?

Challenging Problems 7-10

15-7 CASH CONVERSION CYCLE Chastain Corporation is trying to determine the effect of its inventory turnover ratio and days sales outstanding (DSO) on its cash conversion cycle. Chastain's 2019 sales (all on credit) were $121,000, its cost of goods sold is 80% of sales, and it earned a net profit of 2%, or $2,420. It turned over its inventory 7 times during the year, and its DSO was 37 days. The firm had fixed assets totaling $42,000. Chastain's payables deferral period is 35 days.

a. Calculate Chastain's cash conversion cycle.
b. Assuming Chastain holds negligible amounts of cash and marketable securities, calculate its total assets turnover and ROA.
c. Suppose Chastain's managers believe that the inventory turnover can be raised to 9.9 times. What would Chastain's cash conversion cycle, total assets turnover, and ROA have been if the inventory turnover had been 9.9 for 2019?

15-8 CURRENT ASSETS INVESTMENT POLICY Rentz Corporation is investigating the optimal level of current assets for the coming year. Management expects sales to increase to approximately $2 million as a result of an asset expansion presently being undertaken. Fixed assets total $1 million, and the firm plans to maintain a 60% debt-to-assets ratio. Rentz's interest rate is currently 5% on both short- and long-term debt (which the firm uses in its permanent structure). Three alternatives regarding the projected current assets level are under consideration: (1) a restricted policy where current assets would be only 45% of projected sales, (2) a moderate policy where current assets would be 50% of sales, and (3) a relaxed policy where current assets would be 60% of sales. Earnings before interest and taxes should be 12% of total sales, and the federal-plus-state tax rate is 25%.

a. What is the expected return on equity under each current assets level?
b. In this problem, we assume that expected sales are independent of the current assets investment policy. Is this a valid assumption? Why or why not?
c. How would the firm's risk be affected by the different policies?

15-9 LOCKBOX SYSTEM Fisher-Gardner Corporation (FGC) began operations 5 years ago as a small firm serving customers in the Chicago area. However, its reputation and market area grew quickly. Today FGC has customers all over the United States. Despite its broad customer base, FGC has maintained its headquarters in Chicago, and it keeps its central billing system there. On average, it takes 7 days from the time customers mail in payments until FGC can receive, process, and deposit them. FGC would like to set up a lockbox collection system, which it estimates would reduce the time lag from customer mailing to deposit by 2 days—bringing it down to 5 days. FGC receives an average of $2,300,000 in payments per day.

a. How much free cash would FGC generate if it implemented the lockbox system? Would this be a one-time cash flow or a recurring one, assuming the company ceases to grow? How would growth affect your answer?
b. If FGC has an opportunity cost of 6%, how much is the lockbox system worth on an annual basis?
c. What is the maximum monthly charge FGC should pay for the lockbox system?

15-10 CASH BUDGETING Helen Bowers, owner of Helen's Fashion Designs, is planning to request a line of credit from her bank. She has estimated the following sales forecasts for the firm for parts of 2019 and 2020:

May 2019	$180,000
June	180,000
July	360,000
August	540,000
September	720,000
October	360,000
November	360,000
December	90,000
January 2020	180,000

Estimates regarding payments obtained from the credit department are as follows: collected within the month of sale, 10%; collected the month following the sale, 75%; collected the second month following the sale, 15%. Payments for labor and raw materials are made the month after these services were provided. Here are the estimated costs of labor plus raw materials:

May 2019	$90,000
June	90,000
July	126,000
August	882,000
September	306,000
October	234,000
November	162,000
December	90,000

General and administrative salaries are approximately $27,000 a month. Lease payments under long-term leases are $9,000 a month. Depreciation charges are $36,000 a month. Miscellaneous expenses are $2,700 a month. Income tax payments of $63,000 are due in September and December. A progress payment of $180,000 on a new design studio must be paid in October. Cash on hand on July 1 will be $132,000, and a minimum cash balance of $90,000 should be maintained throughout the cash budget period.

a. Prepare a monthly cash budget for the last 6 months of 2019.

b. Prepare monthly estimates of the required financing or excess funds—that is, the amount of money Bowers will need to borrow or will have available to invest.

c. Now suppose receipts from sales come in uniformly during the month (that is, cash receipts come in at the rate of 1/30 each day), but all outflows must be paid on the 5th. Will this affect the cash budget? That is, will the cash budget you prepared be valid under these assumptions? If not, what could be done to make a valid estimate of the peak financing requirements? No calculations are required, although if you prefer, you can use calculations to illustrate the effects.

d. Bowers' sales are seasonal, and her company produces on a seasonal basis, just ahead of sales. Without making any calculations, discuss how the company's current and debt ratios would vary during the year if all financial requirements were met with short-term bank loans. Could changes in these ratios affect the firm's ability to obtain bank credit? Explain.

Comprehensive/Spreadsheet Problem

15-11 CASH BUDGETING Rework Problem 15-10 using a spreadsheet model. After completing parts a through d, respond to the following: If Bowers' customers began to pay late, collections would slow down, thus increasing the required loan amount. If sales declined, this also would have an effect on the required loan. Do a sensitivity analysis that shows the effects of these two factors on the maximum loan requirement.

INTEGRATED CASE

SKI EQUIPMENT INC.

15-12 MANAGING CURRENT ASSETS Dan Barnes, financial manager of Ski Equipment Inc. (SKI), is excited, but apprehensive. The company's founder recently sold his 51% controlling block of stock to Kent Koren, who is a big fan of EVA (Economic Value Added). EVA is found by taking the after-tax operating profit and subtracting the dollar cost of all the capital the firm uses:

$$\begin{aligned} \text{EVA} &= \text{EBIT}(1 - \text{T}) - \text{Annual dollar cost of capital} \\ &= \text{EBIT}(1 - \text{T}) - (\text{WACC} \times \text{Capital employed}) \end{aligned}$$

If EVA is positive, the firm is creating value. On the other hand, if EVA is negative, the firm is not covering its cost of capital and stockholders' value is being eroded. Koren rewards managers handsomely if they create value, but those whose operations produce negative EVAs are soon looking for work. Koren frequently points out that if a company can generate its current level of sales with fewer assets, it will need less capital. That would, other things held constant, lower capital costs and increase EVA.

Shortly after he took control, Koren met with SKI's senior executives to tell them his plans for the company. First, he presented some EVA data that convinced everyone that SKI had not been creating value in recent years. He then stated, in no uncertain terms, that this situation must change. He noted that SKI's designs of skis, boots, and clothing are acclaimed throughout the industry but that other aspects of the company must be seriously amiss. Either costs are too high, prices are too low, or the company employs too much capital, and he expects SKI's managers to identify and correct the problem.

Barnes has long believed that SKI's working capital situation should be studied—the company may have the optimal amounts of cash, securities, receivables, and inventories, but it may also have too much or too little of these items. In the past, the production manager resisted Barnes's efforts to question his holdings of raw materials inventories, the marketing manager resisted questions about finished goods, the sales staff resisted questions about credit policy (which affects accounts receivable), and the treasurer did not want to talk about her cash and securities balances. Koren's speech made it clear that such resistance would no longer be tolerated.

Barnes also knows that decisions about working capital cannot be made in a vacuum. For example, if inventories could be lowered without adversely affecting operations, less capital would be required, the dollar cost of capital would decline, and EVA would increase. However, lower raw materials inventories might lead to production slowdowns and higher costs, while lower finished goods inventories might lead to the loss of profitable sales. So before inventories are changed, it will be necessary to study operating as well as financial effects. The situation is the same with regard to cash and receivables.

a. Barnes plans to use the ratios in Table IC 15.1 as the starting point for discussions with SKI's operating executives. He wants everyone to think about the pros and cons of changing each type of current asset and the way changes would interact to affect profits and EVA. Based on the data in Table IC 15.1, does SKI seem to be following a relaxed, moderate, or restricted current assets investment policy?

b. How can we distinguish between a relaxed but rational current assets investment policy and a situation where a firm has a large amount of current assets due to inefficiency? Does SKI's current assets investment policy seem appropriate? Explain.

c. SKI tries to match the maturity of its assets and liabilities. Describe how SKI could adopt a more aggressive or a more conservative financing policy.

d. Assume that SKI's payables deferral period is 30 days. Now calculate the firm's cash conversion cycle estimating the inventory conversion period as 365/Inventory turnover.

e. What might SKI do to reduce its cash and securities without harming operations?

In an attempt to better understand SKI's cash position, Barnes developed a cash budget. Data for the first 2 months of the year are shown in Table IC 15.2. (Note that Barnes's preliminary cash budget does not account for interest income or interest expense.) He has the figures for the other months, but they are not shown in Table IC 15.2.

f. In his preliminary cash budget, Barnes has assumed that all sales are collected and thus that SKI has no bad debts. Is this realistic? If not, how would bad debts be dealt with in a cash budgeting sense? (*Hint:* Bad debts affect collections but not purchases.)

g. Barnes's cash budget for the entire year, although not given here, is based heavily on his forecast for monthly sales. Sales are expected to be extremely low between May and September but then increase dramatically in the fall and winter. November is typically the firm's best month, when SKI ships equipment to retailers for the holiday season. Interestingly, Barnes's forecasted cash budget indicates that the company's cash holdings will exceed the targeted cash balance every month except October and November, when shipments will be high but collections will not be coming in until later. Based on the ratios in Table IC 15.1, does it appear that SKI's target cash balance is appropriate? In addition to possibly lowering the target cash balance, what actions might SKI take to better improve its cash management policies and how might that affect its EVA?

h. Is there any reason to think that SKI may be holding too much inventory? If so, how would that affect EVA and ROE?

i. If the company reduces its inventory without adversely affecting sales, what effect should this have on the company's cash position (1) in the short run and (2) in the long run? Explain in terms of the cash budget and the balance sheet.

j. Barnes knows that SKI sells on the same credit terms as other firms in the industry. Use the ratios presented in Table IC 15.1 to explain whether SKI's customers pay more or less promptly than those of its competitors. If there are differences, does that suggest that SKI should restrict or relax its credit policy? What four variables make up a firm's credit policy, and in what direction should each be changed by SKI?

k. Does SKI face any risks if it restricts its credit policy? Explain.

l. If the company reduces its DSO without seriously affecting sales, what effect will this have on its cash position (1) in the short run and (2) in the long run? Answer in terms of the cash budget and the balance sheet. What effect should this have on EVA in the long run?

m. Assume that SKI buys on terms of 1/10, net 30, but that it can get away with paying on the 40th day if it chooses not to take discounts. Also, assume that it purchases $3 million of components per year, net of discounts. How much free trade credit can the company get, how much costly trade credit can it get, and what is the percentage cost of the costly credit? Should SKI take discounts? Why or why not?

n. Suppose SKI decided to raise an additional $100,000 as a 1-year loan from its bank, for which it was quoted a rate of 8%. What is the effective annual cost rate assuming simple interest and add-on interest on a 12-month installment loan?

TABLE IC 15.1 Selected Ratios: SKI and Industry Average

	SKI	Industry
Current	1.75	2.25
Debt/Assets	58.76%	50.00%
Turnover of cash and securities	16.67	22.22
Days sales outstanding (365-day basis)	45.63 days	32.00 days
Inventory turnover	4.82	7.00
Fixed assets turnover	11.35	12.00
Total assets turnover	2.08	3.00
Profit margin	2.07%	3.50%
Return on equity (ROE)	10.45%	21.00%

TABLE IC 15.2 SKI's Cash Budget for January and February

	Nov	Dec	Jan	Feb	Mar	Apr
I. Collections and Purchases Worksheet						
(1) Sales (gross)	$71,218	$68,212	$ 65,213.00	$ 52,475.00	$42,909	$30,524
Collections						
(2) During month of sale (0.2)(0.98)(month's sales)			12,781.75	10,285.10		
(3) During first month after sale (0.7)(previous month's sales)			47,748.40	45,649.10		
(4) During second month after sale (0.1)(sales 2 months ago)			7,121.80	6,821.20		
(5) Total collections (lines 2 + 3 + 4)			$ 67,651.95	$ 62,755.40		
Purchases						
(6) (0.85)(forecasted sales 2 months from now)		$44,603.75	$ 36,472.65	$ 25,945.40		
(7) Payments (1-month lag)			44,603.75	36,472.65		
II. Cash Gain or Loss for Month						
(8) Collections (from Section I)			$ 67,651.95	$ 62,755.40		
(9) Payments for purchases (from Section I)			44,603.75	36,472.65		
(10) Wages and Salaries			6,690.56	5,470.90		
(11) Rent			2,500.00	2,500.00		
(12) Taxes						
(13) Total payments			$ 53,794.31	$ 44,443.55		
(14) Net cash gain (loss) during month (line 8 − line 13)			$ 13,857.64	$ 18,311.85		
III. Cash Surplus or Loan Requirement						
(15) Cash at beginning of month if no borrowing is done			$ 3,000.00	$ 16,857.64		
(16) Cumulative cash [cash at start + gain or − loss = (line 14 + line 15)]			$ 16,857.64	$ 35,169.49		
(17) Target cash balance			1,500.00	1,500.00		
(18) Cumulative surplus cash or loans outstanding to maintain $1,500 target cash balance (line 16 − line 17)			$ 15,357.64	$ 33,669.49		

Financial Planning and Forecasting

CHAPTER 16

DON EMMERT/AFP/Getty Images

Effective Forecasting Is an Important Component of Strong Performance

Like all other public companies, UPS delivers an annual report to its shareholders that summarizes its past performance and offers insights into what its senior executives see as the key opportunities and risks moving forward. In its 2017 Annual Report, UPS has some good news to report. The company's revenues grew 8.2% and its earnings per share grew 4.5%.

Over the past decade, many consumers have shifted large portions of their purchases online—which is good news for companies like UPS that are called on to deliver those packages. Indeed, UPS reported that it now ships on average more than 20 million packages per day.

At the same time, the massive scale of its operations requires continued investment in what it refers to as its "Smart Logistics Network." Summarizing the need for this type of investment, the company's Chairman and CEO David Abney made the following statement in his letter to shareholders:

> The cornerstone of that plan are the investments we're making to implement the most sweeping transformation of our network in decades. We are taking full advantage of the advances in artificial intelligence, machine learning, blockchain, robotics, and many other cutting-edge technologies to future-proof our network. While these investments represent a major financial commitment in the near term, the benefits to our customers and shareowners over the long run will be substantial. By implementing new technology and expanding capacity in our facilities, we are making the industry's most-efficient network

even more effective. Our digital investments give us—and our customers—more flexibility, consistency and visibility in how packages are routed and delivered.

When deciding which investments to make, the company relies heavily on financial forecasting. Effective forecasting requires a strong understanding of market and industrial trends, the competitive environment, and the strength of the overall economy. But with their eyes wide open, prudent managers recognize that things will often turn out differently than expected. UPS made a similar point in its 2017 annual report:

> Forecasting projected volume involves many factors which are subject to uncertainty, such as general economic trends, changes in governmental regulation and competition. If we do not accurately forecast our future capital investment needs, we could have excess capacity or insufficient capacity, either of which would negatively affect our revenues and profitability. In addition to forecasting our capital investment requirements, we adjust other elements of our operations and cost structure in response to adverse economic conditions; however, these adjustments may not be sufficient to allow us to maintain our operating margins in a weak economy.

As UPS knows all too well, the economic environment is always changing, which makes it difficult to develop reasonable forecasts of the company's future performance. Forecasting has become increasingly challenging given the tremendous volatility in the economy and financial markets during the past few years. With numbers changing faster than you can update your forecasts, it is tempting to throw your hands up and say, "Why bother?" Despite this urge to throw in the towel, during volatile times effective forecasting is more important than ever. Well-run companies know that you can't just operate on autopilot and assume that next year will be like last year.

Source: "Transforming UPS . . . for Today and Tomorrow," *2017 UPS Annual Report*, www.investors.ups.com/financials/annual-reports.

PUTTING THINGS IN PERSPECTIVE

Yogi Berra, the former player and manager for the New York Yankees, once said, "You've got to be very careful if you don't know where you're going, because you might not get there." That's certainly true for a company—it needs a plan, one that starts with the firm's general goals and details the steps that will be taken to get there.

When you finish this chapter, you should be able to do the following:

- **Discuss the importance of strategic planning and the central role that financial forecasting plays in the overall planning process.**
- **Explain how firms forecast sales.**
- **Use the Additional Funds Needed (or AFN) equation and discuss the relationship between asset growth and the need for funds.**
- **Explain how spreadsheets are used in the forecasting process, starting with historical statements, ending with projected statements, and including a set of financial ratios based on those projected statements.**
- **Discuss how planning is an iterative process.**

Financial planners begin with a set of assumptions, see what is likely to happen based on those assumptions, and then see if modifications can help the firm achieve better results. Although we focus on forecasting from the corporation's standpoint, top security analysts go through the same process. Analysts with hedge and private equity funds are especially active as forecasters, and they are particularly interested in the iterative process of forecasting.

16-1 Strategic Planning

Management textbooks often list the following as the key elements of a strategic plan:

- *Mission Statement.* Many but not all firms articulate a **mission statement**. For example, here is Pepsico's mission statement:[1]

  As one of the largest food and beverage companies in the world, our mission is to provide consumers around the world with delicious, affordable, convenient, and complementary foods and beverages from wholesome breakfasts to healthy and fun daytime snacks and beverages to evening treats.

  We are committed to investing in our people, our company, and the communities where we operate to help position the company for long-term, sustainable growth.

- *Corporate Scope.* **Corporate scope** defines the lines of business the firm plans to pursue and the geographic areas in which it will operate. Some firms deliberately limit their scope, on the theory that it is better for top managers to focus sharply on a narrow range of functions as opposed to spreading the company over many different types of businesses. Academics have studied which is the better choice. Some studies suggest that investors generally value focused firms more highly than diversified ones.[2] However, if a firm is successful in combining a group of diversified businesses so that they help one another, the result may be synergistic effects that raise the value of the overall enterprise.[3] In any event, the stated corporate scope should be logical and consistent with the firm's capabilities.
- *Statement of Corporate Objectives.* A firm's **statement of corporate objectives** is that part of the corporate plan that sets forth the specific goals that operating managers are expected to meet. GE is an example of another good company that has long recognized the need for effective forecasting, and has used it as a basis for evaluating investments, developing strategic plans, allocating resources among various units, and establishing targets for compensation. Like most firms, GE has both qualitative and quantitative objectives. GE has a history of selling business units that do not meet its objectives and of replacing underperforming managers, but GE also rewards managers generously when they meet their targets.
- *Corporate Strategies.* UPS has several broad **corporate strategies**. Most notably, the company offers supply chain services throughout the world,

Mission Statement
A condensed version of a firm's strategic plan.

Corporate Scope
Defines a firm's lines of business and geographic areas of operation.

Statement of Corporate Objectives
Sets forth specific goals to guide management.

Corporate Strategies
Broad approaches developed for achieving a firm's goals.

[1]Refer to Pepsico's mission statement on its website, www.pepsico.com/sustainability.

[2]See, for example, Philip G. Berger and Eli Ofek, "Diversification's Effect on Firm Value," *Journal of Financial Economics*, vol. 37, no. 1 (1995), pp. 39–66; and Larry Lang and René Stulz, "Tobin's Q, Corporate Diversification, and Firm Performance," *Journal of Political Economy*, vol. 102, no. 6 (1994), pp. 1248–1280.

[3]The dictionary definition of *synergy* is a situation where the whole is greater than the sum of the parts, and it's sometimes called the 2 + 2 = 5 effect. GE has a jet engine business and another business that produces gas turbines for electric power generation. Those businesses are similar enough so that new developments in one can benefit the other. One has to wonder, though, how GE's jet engine business benefited the NBC-Universal (NBCU) entertainment unit. GE's management argued that its diversification stabilized its revenues and profits and that this resulted in an A bond rating and a relatively low cost of capital for all its businesses. A number of academic studies dispute this conclusion, though, with the academics arguing that it is easy for stockholders to diversify and better to have top managers focus on one business. Perhaps with these concerns in mind, in 2010 GE's management reached the conclusion that some of its assets were not creating synergistic benefits, and so it sold some of those assets—including giving up a 51% ownership stake in NBCU to Comcast. In fact, by March 19, 2013, Comcast purchased the remaining 49% ownership stake, so NBC Universal is now a subsidiary of Comcast. In addition, in 2015, GE took steps to sell off the bulk of GE Capital to refocus on its manufacturing base.

and has utilized its "smart logistics" framework to help achieve earnings stability and financial strength. In its 2016 annual report, UPS highlighted how its corporate strategy will help increase the "vitality and environmental sustainability of the global economy by aggregating the shipping activity of millions of businesses into a single highly efficient logistics network."[4]

Operating Plan
Provides management detailed implementation guidance, based on the corporate strategy, to help meet the corporate objectives.

Financial Plan
The document that includes assumptions, projected financial statements, and projected ratios and ties the entire planning process together.

- *Operating Plan.* To be successful, each of UPS's units must develop a detailed **operating plan** that is consistent with the corporate strategy to help it achieve the firm's objectives. Operating plans can be developed for any time horizon, but most companies use a 5-year horizon. The plan explains in considerable detail the people responsible for each particular function, deadlines for specific tasks, sales and profit targets, and the like.
- *Financial Plan.* For most companies, financial planning is a multistep process. Likewise, Allied's **financial plan** involves four steps. First, assumptions are made about the future levels of sales, costs, interest rates, and so forth, for use in the forecast. Second, a set of projected financial statements is developed. Third, projected ratios such as those discussed in Chapter 4 are calculated and analyzed. Fourth, the entire plan is reexamined, the assumptions are reviewed, and the management team considers how additional changes in operations might improve results. This last step requires reconsideration of all the earlier parts of the overall plan, from the mission statement to the operating plan. Thus, the financial plan ties the entire planning process together.

Financial planning as described previously is often called *value-based management,* meaning that the effects of various decisions on the firm's financial position and value are studied by simulating their effects within the firm's financial model. For example, if Tesla was considering whether to build a new Gigafactory in Nevada or California, it would simulate the effects through its financial model and then make the move based on which location maximized long-run shareholder wealth.[5]

SelfTest

What are the key elements of a corporation's strategic plan?

How is the financial plan related to the other parts of a firm's overall strategic plan?

How can the financial plan be used to help management provide guidance to security analysts?

resource

Students can download the Excel chapter models from the textbook's student companion site on cengage.com. Once downloaded onto your computer, retrieve the Chapter 16 Excel model and follow along as you read this chapter.

16-2 The Sales Forecast

Financial plans generally begin with a *sales forecast,* which starts with a review of sales during the past 5 years, shown as a graph such as the one in Figure 16.1 for Allied Food. These numbers are based on Allied's financial statements, which were first presented in Chapter 3. The data below the graph show 5 years of historical sales.

[4]Refer to *UPS 2016 Annual Report*, www.investors.ups.com/financials/sec-filings, Form 10-K, p. 8.

[5]Note, however, that there would surely be political ramifications to such a move. These effects would be studied by use of the model, and the computer-generated results would be an input in the decision. However, the ultimate decision would be made by Tesla's top executives and board, not, in essence, by a computer.

FIGURE 16.1 Allied Food Products: 2020 Sales Projection (millions of dollars)

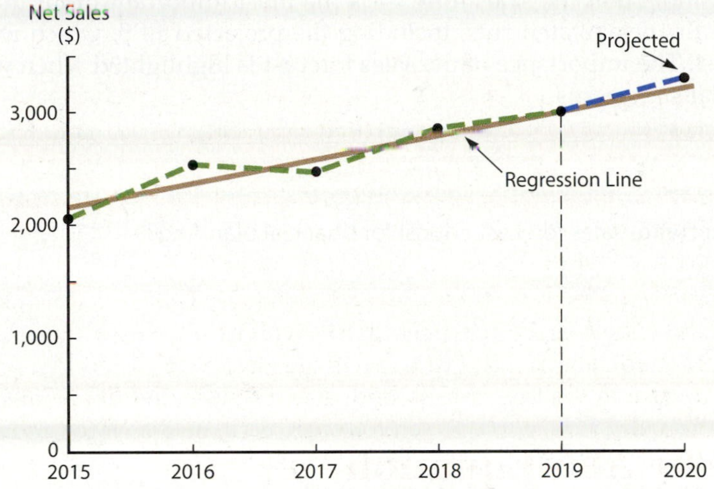

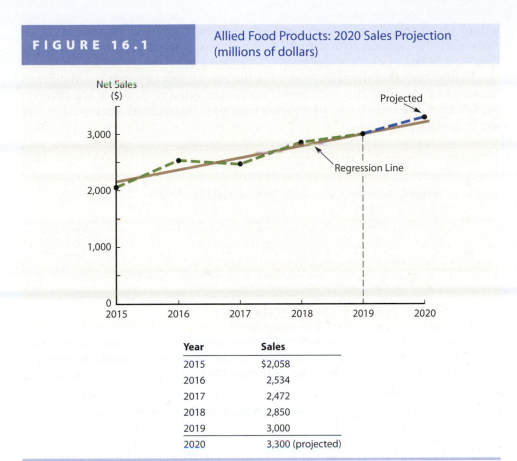

Year	Sales
2015	$2,058
2016	2,534
2017	2,472
2018	2,850
2019	3,000
2020	3,300 (projected)

Allied had its ups and downs from 2015 through 2019. In 2017, poor weather in California's fruit-producing regions resulted in below-average crops, which caused 2017 sales to fall below the 2016 level. Then a bumper crop in 2018 pushed sales up by 15%, an unusually high growth rate for a mature food processor. The compound annual growth rate over the 4-year period was 9.88%.[6] Due to planned new products, increased production, distribution capacity, a new advertising campaign, and other factors, management expects the growth rate to increase slightly, to 10%, in 2020. Therefore, sales should rise from $3,000 million to $3,300 million.

Of course, management likes higher sales growth, but not at any cost. For example, sales could be increased by cutting prices, spending more on advertising, granting easier credit, and the like. However, all of those actions would have a cost. Also, sales growth cannot occur without a concurrent increase in capacity, and that too is costly. So the sales growth must be balanced against the cost of achieving that growth.

If the sales forecast is off, the consequences can be serious. First, if the market expands by more than Allied expects, it will not be able to meet demand, its customers will buy from competitors, and it will lose market share. On the other hand, if its projections are overly optimistic, Allied could end up with too much plant, equipment, and inventory, leading to low turnover ratios, high costs for depreciation and storage, and write-offs of spoiled inventory. This

[6]Note that you need 5 years of data to find the 4-year growth rate from 2015 through 2019. Enter the inputs as follows: N = 4, PV = −2058, PMT = 0, and FV = 3000. Then, solve for I/YR = 9.88%, which is the growth rate in sales during this period.

would result in low profits and a depressed stock price. Moreover, if Allied financed its expansion with debt, high interest expenses would compound the firm's problems.

Finally, note that the sales forecast is the most important input in the firm's forecast of financial statements, including the projected EPS, which we cover in Section 16-4. The importance of the sales forecast is highlighted when we forecast the financial statements.

Self*Test*

Why is an accurate sales forecast critical for financial planning?

16-3 The AFN Equation

We saw in Chapter 3 that in 2019, Allied had assets of \$2,000 million and sales of \$3,000 million. Thus, it required \$2,000/\$3,000 = \$0.6667 of assets to generate each dollar of sales. Moreover, the company plans to increase sales by 10%, or \$300 million, in 2020:

$$\text{Increase in sales} = \Delta\text{Sales} = 0.10(\$3{,}000\text{ million}) = \$300\text{ million}$$

Assuming the assets-to-sales ratio remains constant, Allied will need an additional \$200 million of assets to support the \$300 million increase in sales:

$$\text{Required increase in assets} = 0.6667\ (\Delta\text{Sales}) = 0.6667\ (\$300) = \$200\text{ million}$$

Note that if growth is low (say, 0%), ΔSales will be zero, and there will be no required increase in assets. On the other hand, if sales grow very rapidly, the requirement for additional assets will be large. Thus, the increase in assets is fundamentally dependent on the growth rate in sales.

Naturally, if assets are to grow by \$200 million, liabilities and equity must also grow by the same amount—the balance sheet must balance. But from where will this capital come? Here are a firm's primary capital sources:

1. *Spontaneous Increases in Accounts Payable and Accruals.* Allied must make additional purchases to increase its inventories, and it must hire more workers. Its purchases will automatically lead to additional accounts payable, which amount to "loans" from its suppliers. Also, hiring more workers will automatically lead to higher accrued wages, which amount to short-term "loans" from its workers. Hence, some of the required \$200 million will come *spontaneously* from suppliers and workers—this is called **spontaneously generated funds**. Also, assuming profit margins are maintained, higher sales will mean higher profits and thus higher taxes and accrued taxes. So "spontaneous" increases in payables, accrued wages, and accrued taxes will take care of part of the required \$200 million.
2. *Addition to Retained Earnings.* Assuming Allied has positive earnings and does not pay out all of those earnings as dividends, its retained earnings will grow. The addition to retained earnings depends on the firm's profit margin and its **retention ratio**, which is the proportion of net income that is reinvested in the firm. This addition to retained earnings will help finance growth.
3. *AFN: Additional Funds Needed.* It is possible that spontaneous funds and additional retained earnings will offset the forecasted increase in assets.

Spontaneously Generated Funds
Funds that arise out of normal business operations from its suppliers, employees, and the government (such as accounts payable and accrued wages and taxes) that reduce the firm's need for external financing.

Retention Ratio
It is the proportion of net income that is reinvested in the firm, and is calculated as 1 minus the dividend payout ratio.

Normally, though, that situation does not occur—normally, there is a shortfall, called **additional funds needed (AFN)**, which has to be made up by additional borrowing and/or the sale of new stock. Note, though, that if a company is growing very slowly and thus not increasing assets very much, its spontaneous funds plus its addition to retained earnings may be larger than the required increase in assets. In that case, the AFN is negative, indicating that a surplus of capital is forecasted.

Additional Funds Needed (AFN)
The amount of external capital (interest-bearing debt and preferred and common stock) that will be necessary to acquire the required assets.

AFN Equation
An equation that shows the relationship of external funds needed by a firm to its projected increase in assets, the spontaneous increase in liabilities, and its increase in retained earnings.

We can combine these concepts to develop Equation 16.1, the **AFN equation**. AFN is the total amount of new interest-bearing debt and preferred and common stock the firm must issue to support its planned growth:[7]

$$\text{Additional funds needed, or AFN} = \text{Projected increase in assets} - \text{Spontaneous increase in liabilities} - \text{Increase in retained earnings}$$

$$= (A_0^*/S_0)\Delta S - (L_0^*/S_0)\Delta S - MS_1(1 - \text{Payout}) \quad \mathbf{16.1}$$

Allied's CFO used Equation 16.1 in the following manner. Every fall the company's Executive Committee, which includes the CEO, the CFO, and other top executives, meets to consider plans for the coming year. The meeting this year is especially important for two reasons: (1) The national credit crunch is constraining the firm's ability to raise capital, so the amounts needed and available must be determined. (2) Corporate raiders and private equity firms have targeted a number of food processors, and when they take over, heads roll in the acquired firm. Allied's executives are aware of both factors.

Allied's CFO plans to proceed in two steps. First, he will use the AFN equation to give the others an idea of how much new capital the firm will need to support the targeted 10% growth rate, assuming the various operating ratios remain constant. Second, he will present the results of a full-scale financial planning model. The model shows forecasted financial statements in addition to a set of forecasted ratios like those discussed in Chapter 4, along with an estimate of the 2020 EPS.

The CFO brought copies of Table 16.1, which is based on Equation 16.1, and data from the financial statements presented in Chapter 3 to the Executive Committee.[8] Part I of the table picks up selected data from the 2019 balance sheet and income statement. Part II uses the Part I data to calculate inputs for Equation 16.1. Note that all the calculations in Part II assume that the company's operating ratios in 2020 continue at 2019 levels. Part III uses the items calculated in Part II to calculate the AFN. To increase sales by $300 million, Allied must increase assets by $200 million. The asset increase will be supported by $20 million from spontaneous increases in payables and accruals, and another $66 million will come from retained earnings. In total, $114 million of new outside funds will be needed, and because Allied does not use preferred stock, the amount must come from interest-bearing debt in addition to new common stock.

---

[7]The term *additional funds needed* was developed to show how much additional capital a firm needs to support its planned growth. However, as we see later, a firm may be able to grow without any additional outside capital. In fact, the firm may even generate excess capital that can be used to retire debt, repurchase stock, and raise the dividend. In this case, the calculated AFN will be negative. Also, in this chapter we do quite a few calculations and generally round when we show results. This may lead to minor "rounding differences," which you should disregard.

[8]The CFO also loaded the Excel model on his laptop so he could do on-the-spot sensitivity analyses. For example, he could change the growth rate and instantly find the new AFN. Similarly, he could change the dividend payout ratio, the profit margin, and the other variables to see how those changes would affect the firm's capital requirements. Still, the analysis in Table 16.1 provided a useful starting point.

As noted, the AFN equation assumes that the 2020 ratios will remain constant at the 2019 levels.[9] If economic conditions or managerial decisions cause the ratios to change, the forecasted AFN will change. Part IV of the table shows how some specific input changes will change the forecasted AFN. For example,

TABLE 16.1 Additional Funds Needed (AFN) Model (millions of dollars)

	A	B	C	D	E	F	G	H	I
2	**Part I. 2019 Data from Chapter 3, Tables 3.1 and 3.2**								
3	A_0^* = Assets at 12/31/19. All assets were needed for 2019 sales								$2,000
4	S_0 = 2019 Sales								$3,000
5	2019 Net Income								$146.3
6	2019 Dividends								$86.3
7	L_0^* = 2019 payables + accruals, which increase spontaneously with sales								$200
8	**Part II. Data Used in the AFN Equation: 2019 Ratios Held Constant**								
9	AFN = Additional Funds Needed to buy assets needed to support growth. AFN is in addition to funds raised internally, i.e., AFN represents required external funds.								Base Case: 2019 Data
10	g = Target growth rate in sales.								10.00%
11	A_0^*/S_0 = Assets required per $1 of sales = $2,000/$3,000. When multiplied by the increase in sales shows the required new assets for the coming year. Also called the *capital intensity ratio*. The higher this ratio, the more new assets the firm will need to support a given amount of growth.								0.6667
12	S_1 = 2020 Sales = $(1+g)(S_0)$ = (1.1)($3,000)								$3,300
13	ΔS = Growth in sales = $S_1 - S_0$ = $3,300 − $3,000. Can also be found as $\Delta S = g(S_0)$								$300
14	L_0^*/S_0 = Spontaneously generated funds per dollar of new sales. When multiplied by ΔS, we find the new payables and accruals that are available to support growth.								0.0667
15	M = Profit margin on sales = 2019 net income/S_0 = $146.3/$3,000. Multiply by S_1 (not S_0) to find the net income available in 2020 for dividends or growth.								0.0488
16	1 − Dividend Payout Ratio = 1 − (Dividends/Net Income) = 1 − ($86.3/$146.3). The lower the payout rate, the more of the net income is retained to support growth.								0.4101
17	**Part III. The AFN Equation**								
18	AFN =	Required increase in assets		−	Spontaneous increase in payables and accruals	−		Funds obtained as new retained earnings Based on 2020 sales	
19	=	$(A_0^*/S_0)\Delta S$		−	$(L_0^*/S_0)\Delta S$	−		$MS_1(1 - \text{Payout})$	
20	=	0.6667($300)		−	0.0667($300)	−		0.0488($3,300)(0.4101)	
21	=	$200		−	$20	−		$66	
22	AFN =	$114 million							

(continued)

[9]This assumption helps simplify the AFN calculation, but in many instances it is not completely realistic. For example, in any given year, fixed assets may not grow at the same rate as sales. With this concern in mind, some analysts use the following alternative AFN equation:

$$\text{AFN} = (\text{Sales-driven current assets/Sales}) \times \Delta\text{Sales} + \Delta\text{Fixed assets}$$
$$- (\text{Sales-driven current liabilities/Sales}) \times \Delta\text{Sales} - \Delta\text{Retained earnings}$$

In this alternative equation, sales-driven current assets are items such as accounts receivable and inventory, both of which are likely to grow at the same rate as sales. Likewise, sales-driven current liabilities are items such as accounts payable and accruals that are also likely to grow at the same rate as sales. (These are equivalent to the spontaneous liabilities described in the standard (simplified) AFN equation.) Although slightly more complicated, this alternative equation is more flexible and arguably provides a more accurate forecasting tool than the simplified AFN equation. However, in all of our subsequent examples and end-of-chapter problems we will use the simplified AFN equation (Equation 16.1) that is presented in the text.

If you are looking for more details regarding this alternative AFN equation, see Wallace N. Davidson, III, *Financial Forecasting and Management Decisions* (New York: AICPA, 2009).

TABLE 16.1 Additional Funds Needed (AFN) Model (millions of dollars) (*Continued*)

	A	B–G	H	I
23	<u>Part IV. Sensitivity Analysis: AFN with Changed Input Values</u>		AFN (Old = $114)	
24			New	Change: New – Old
25	Higher Growth:	15%, up from 10%. With faster growth, the firm needs more new assets.	$201	$87
26	Lower Growth:	5%, down from 10%. With slower growth, the firm needs less new assets.	$27	–$87
27	A_0^*/S_0:	0.5000, down from 0.6667. This factor is called the *capital intensity ratio.* We lowered it in this example; and with a lower value, fewer assets are required for any given level of sales. If Allied's management can increase the total assets turnover ratio, the A^*/S_0 ratio will decline, and that will reduce AFN.	$64	–$50
28	L_0^*/S_0:	0.0800, up from 0.0667. Allied spontaneously generates funds from accounts payable and accruals; and the larger the L_0^*/S_0 ratio, the smaller the need for external financing. Here we increase the ratio. With a higher value, more spontaneous funds are available; so the AFN declines.	$110	–$4
29	M:	0.1000, up from 0.0488. If the profit margin increases, more earnings will be available to support growth and thus the smaller the AFN. Here we increase M and the AFN declines.	$45	–$69
30	Payout:	0.2000, down from 0.5899. If Allied lowers the dividend payout ratio, then more of its earnings will be retained and thus the smaller the AFN. Here we lower the payout, so the AFN declines.	$51	–$63
31	Change all variables simultaneously to g = 5% and the other values as indicated above. The result is a large but negative AFN, indicating that the firm is generating a substantial amount of capital.		–$189	–$303
32				
33	<u>Part V. Sustainable Growth Rate.</u> Maximum achievable growth without raising external funds, i.e., g that forces AFN = 0, holding other variables at base-case levels. Use g = 3.45% and you will see that AFN = 0.			3.45%

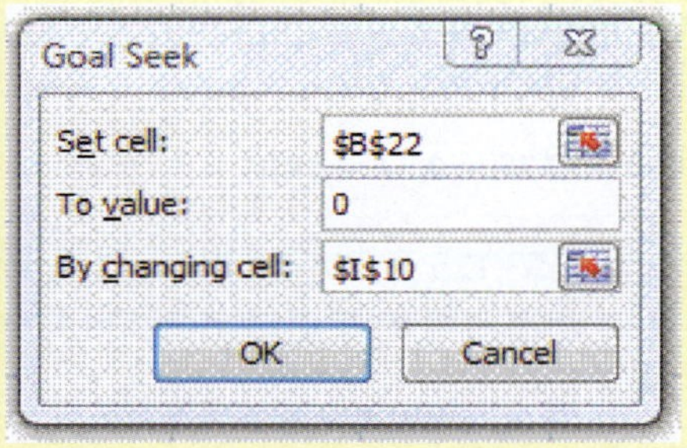

The sustainable growth rate is found using Excel's Goal Seek. AFN (calculated in Cell B22) is set to zero by changing the growth rate in Cell I10. Once you click OK, the growth rate in Cell I10 changes until AFN equals zero. You should see that this growth rate is 3.45%.

if the target growth rate was increased from 10% to 15% with other things held constant, the AFN would increase from $114 million to $201 million. On the other hand, if the target growth rate was lowered to 5%, the AFN would be only $27 million. Also, as shown in Part V, if the company grew at a rate of 3.45% while other things were held constant, AFN would be zero. Thus, 3.45% is called Allied's **sustainable growth rate**. As you can see from the model,

Sustainable Growth Rate
The maximum achievable growth rate without the firm having to raise external funds. In other words, it is the growth rate at which the firm's AFN equals zero.

the sustainable growth rate can be easily estimated using the Goal Seek tool in Excel. Finally, note that if the growth rate slowed and other inputs were changed in the manner specified in Part IV of the table, Allied would end up with a large negative AFN, indicating that retained earnings and spontaneous capital were far more than sufficient to finance the now smaller amount of additional assets needed.

16-3A EXCESS CAPACITY ADJUSTMENTS

Capital Intensity Ratio
The ratio of assets required per dollar of sales (A_0^*/S_0).

Excess Capacity Adjustments
Changes made to the existing asset forecast because the firm is not operating at full capacity.

The AFN equation includes the term A_0^*/S_0, which is called the **capital intensity ratio**. For Allied, this ratio is calculated as $2,000/$3,000 = 0.6667. When multiplied by ΔS = $300 million, this ratio indicated that Allied must increase its assets by $200 million. However, the CFO thought that in 2019, Allied had more fixed assets than it really needed; he wanted to demonstrate to the Executive Committee how **excess capacity adjustments** might affect the firm's need for external funds. He noted that Allied had $1,000 million of current assets and $1,000 million of fixed assets, so he split A_0^*/S_0 into two parts, one for fixed assets and one for current assets:

$$\text{Current assets}: A_{0\,C}^*/S_0 = \$1{,}000/\$3{,}000 = 0.333 = 33.3\%$$
$$\text{Fixed assets}: A_{0\,F}^*/S_0 = \$1{,}000/\$3{,}000 = 0.333 = 33.3\%$$

Now suppose that the current assets were used at full capacity but that fixed assets had been used at only 96% of capacity in 2019. Therefore, if fixed assets had been used to full capacity, sales could have reached $3,125 million before any additions to fixed assets were required versus the actual $3,000 million of sales. In this example, the calculated $3,125 million sales is Allied's full capacity sales:

$$\text{Full capacity sales} = \frac{\text{Actual sales}}{\text{Percentage of capacity at which fixed assets were operated}}$$
$$= \$3{,}000\text{ million}/0.96 = \$3{,}125\text{ million}$$

This indicates that Allied's Target fixed assets/Sales ratio should be 32% rather than the indicated 33.3% calculated previously:

$$\frac{\text{Target fixed assets}}{\text{Sales}} = \frac{\text{Actual fixed assets}}{\text{Full capacity sales}}$$
$$= \$1{,}000/\$3{,}125 = 0.32 = 32\%$$

Under these conditions, sales could increase to $3,125 million with no increase in fixed assets, and a sales increase to $3,300 million would require only $1,056 million of fixed assets, or an additional $56 million of fixed assets:

$$\begin{aligned}
\text{Required level of fixed assets} &= (\text{Target fixed assets/Sales})(\text{Projected sales}) \\
&= 0.32(\$3{,}300) = \$1{,}056\text{ million} \\
\text{Earlier estimate of fixed assets} &= 1.1(\$1{,}000) = \$1{,}100\text{ million} \\
\text{Difference in fixed assets needed} &= -\$44\text{ million}
\end{aligned}$$

Thus, the existence of excess capacity in its fixed assets would lower Allied's required AFN from $114 million to $114 million − $44 million = $70 million.

A similar situation could occur with respect to inventories, cash, or any other asset. Moreover, the L_0^*/S_0 ratio could be increased if the firm negotiated longer credit terms for its purchases. Similarly, it might be possible for Allied to improve its profit margin or to lower its dividend payout ratio. Because so many conditions can change, it is useful to go beyond the AFN equation analysis and construct Allied's **forecasted financial statements**, the topic of the next section. Also, we want to know how good or bad the firm's financial ratios will be and what the impact will be on its EPS. The AFN tells us nothing about those things, but the forecasted financial statements do.

Forecasted Financial Statements
Financial statements that project the company's financial position and performance over a period of years.

Self*Test*

If the key ratios are expected to remain constant, the AFN equation can be used to forecast the need for external funds. Write out the equation and explain its logic.

How would an *increase* in each of the following factors affect the AFN?

1. Payout ratio
2. Capital intensity ratio, A_0^*/S_0
3. Profit margin
4. Days sales outstanding, DSO
5. Sales growth rate

Is it possible for the AFN to be negative? If so, what would this indicate?

If excess capacity exists, how would that affect the calculated AFN?

16-4 Forecasted Financial Statements[10]

The AFN equation provides useful insights into the forecasting process—if you understand the AFN, you will find it easier to understand forecasted financial statements. Therefore, Allied's CFO used the AFN calculations in Table 16.1 as a warm up for his presentation of the forecasted 2020 financial statements. We describe how he developed the forecast presented in Table 16.2 in this section.

16-4A PART I. INPUTS

Rows 4 through 9 show the basic inputs, or assumptions, used in the forecast. The CFO had met previously with the CEO and other top executives. They had reviewed the ratio analysis developed in Chapter 4 and concluded that improvements must be made in 2020. Otherwise, a private equity buyer or hedge fund might decide to take over the firm, and if that occurred, the executives would probably lose their jobs.

Adjustable Inputs

The inputs in column C show key 2019 ratios that management controls and that may be adjusted in the future. Column D gives the values the CFO used for the initial 2020 forecast, and column E gives industry average numbers. The first input shown is the growth rate. This number can be changed, but throughout Table 16.2, a 10% growth rate is assumed. Next, we have the Operating costs/Sales ratio. Allied's ratio in 2019 was 90.73%, which is higher than the industry's

[10]This section is relatively straightforward, but it does involve a number of steps. The table can be developed with a calculator, but it's far easier to do using Excel. We recommend that everyone read the section and look at Table 16.2 while doing so. Finance majors should read the section especially carefully. It also would help if students accessed the chapter model and worked through it while reading this section.

87% ratio. A reduction toward the industry average would lead to a substantial improvement in net income, and the CFO used a ratio of 89.5% as a tentative target for 2020. Next, we saw in Chapter 4 that Allied's receivables and inventories were too high relative to its sales. If those accounts can be reduced, the result will be lower bad debts and storage costs and thus increased profits. Also, the excess capital invested in receivables and inventories can be released and used to pay off debt and/or to repurchase common stock, both of which would improve the firm's ROE and EPS. Again, the CFO set initial targets between Allied's 2019 ratios and the industry averages.

In addition, Allied's equity/assets ratio, at 47%, is significantly less than the industry average, and the firm's bankers have complained and indicated that the cost of debt would decline if this ratio were increased. Security analysts also

TABLE 16.2 Forecasted Financial Statements (total dollars and shares in millions)

	A	B	C	D	E	F	G
2	Part I. Inputs		Adjustable Inputs				
3			2019	2020	Industry	Fixed Inputs	
4		Growth rate, g	NA	10.00%	NA	Tax rate (T)	25.00%
5		Operating costs/Sales	90.73%	89.50%	87.00%	Interest rate	9.60%
6		Receivables/Sales	12.50%	11.00%	9.86%	Shares	75
7		Inventories/Sales	20.50%	19.00%	9.17%	Price per share	$23.06
8		Total liabilities/Assets ratio	53.00%	49.00%	40.00%	FA/Sales	33.33%
9		Payout ratio	58.99%	55.00%	45.00%		
10	Part II. Income Statements				2019	Change	2020
11	Sales				$ 3,000.0	(1+ g)	$ 3,300.0
12	Operating costs (includes depreciation)				2,722.0	0.895	2,953.5
13	Earnings before interest and taxes (EBIT)				$ 278.0		$ 346.5
14	Interest expense				83.0	See notes	77.7
15	Earnings before taxes (EBT)				$ 195.0		$ 268.8
16	Taxes				48.8	EBT(T)	67.2
17	Net income (NI)				$ 146.3		$ 201.6
18	Dividends				$ 86.3	NI(Payout)	$ 110.9
19	Addition to retained earnings				$ 60.0		$ 90.7
20	Part III. Balance Sheets				2019	Change	2020
21	Assets						
22	Cash (grow with sales)				$ 10.0	(1+ g)	$ 11.0
23	Accounts receivable				375.0	0.1100	363.0
24	Inventories				615.0	0.1900	627.0
25	Fixed assets (grow with sales)				1,000.0	(1+ g)	1,100.0
26	Total assets				$ 2,000.0		$ 2,101.0
27	Liabilities and Equity						
28	Payables + accruals (both grow with sales)				$ 200.0	(1+ g)	$ 220.0
29	Short-term bank loans				110.0	See notes	103.5
30	Total current liabilities				$ 310.0		$ 323.5
31	Long-term bonds				750.0	See notes	706.0
32	Total liabilities				$ 1,060.0		$ 1,029.5
33	Common stock				130.0	See notes	170.8
34	Retained earnings				810.0	$90.7	900.7
35	Total common equity				$ 940.0		$ 1,071.5
36	Total liabilities and equity				$ 2,000.0		$ 2,101.0

(continued)

Forecasted Financial Statements (total dollars and shares in millions) (*Continued*) **TABLE 16.2**

	A	B	C	D	E	F	G
37	Part IV. Ratios and EPS		2019		2020E		Industry
38	Operating costs/Sales		90.73%		89.50%		87.00%
39	Receivables/Sales		12.50%		11.00%		9.86%
40	Inventory/Sales		20.50%		19.00%		9.17%
41	Total liabilities/Assets ratio		53.00%		49.00%		40.00%
42	Payout ratio		58.99%		55.00%		45.00%
43	Inventory turnover		4.88		5.26		10.90
44	Days sales outstanding (DSO)		45.63		40.15		36.00
45	Total assets turnover		1.50		1.57		1.80
46	Assets/Equity (equity multiplier)		2.13		1.96		1.73
47	Times interest earned (TIE)		3.35		4.46		6.00
48	Profit margin		4.88%		6.11%		6.00%
49	Return on assets (ROA)		7.32%		9.60%		10.80%
50	Return on equity (ROE)		15.56%		18.81%		18.70%
51	DuPont Calculations		Profit Margin (NI/S)	Total Assets Turnover (S/A)	Equity Multiplier (A/ E)	= ROE	
52	Actual 2019		4.88%	1.50	2.13	15.6%	
53	Forecasted for 2020		6.11%	1.57	1.96	18.8%	
54	Industry average data		6.00%	1.80	1.73	18.7%	
55	**Earnings per share (EPS)**		**$1.95**		**$2.63**		
56	Part V. Notes on Calculations						
57		Assets in 2020 will change to this amount, from the balance sheet					$ 2,101.0
58		Target total liabilities/assets ratio					49.00%
59		Resulting total liabilities: (Target total liabilities/assets ratio)(2020 Assets)					$ 1,029.5
60		Less: Payables and accruals					(220.0)
61		Bank loans and bonds (= Interest-bearing debt)					$ 809.5
62		Allocated to bank loans, based on 2019 proportions				12.79%	103.5
63		Allocated to bonds, based on 2019 proportions				87.21%	$ 706.0
64		Interest expense: (Interest rate)(2020 Bank loans plus bonds)					$ 77.7
65		Target equity ratio = 1 – Target total liabilities/assets ratio					51.00%
66		Required total equity: (2020 Assets)(Target equity ratio)					$ 1,071.5
67		Retained earnings, from 2020 balance sheet					900.7
68		Required common stock = Required equity – Retained earnings					$ 170.8
69		Old shares outstanding (millions)					75.0
70		Increase in common stock = 2020 Stock – 2019 Stock					$ 40.8
71		Initial price per share from input section					$ 23.06
72		Change in shares = Change in stock/Initial price per share					1.77
73		New shares outstanding = Old shares + Δ Shares					76.77
74		Old EPS = 2019 Net income / Old shares outstanding					$ 1.95
75		New EPS = 2020 Net income / New shares outstanding					$ 2.63

have stated that Allied's stock is riskier than it would be if it had less debt, and that adversely affects its price/earnings (P/E) ratio. With these concerns in mind, Allied has established a target equity/assets ratio of 51%, which implies that Allied's target total liabilities/assets ratio is 49%.

Similarly, Allied's dividend payout ratio is higher than the industry average, and the CEO and several board members think it should be lowered. This would provide more funds to support growth, which stockholders may want.

Fixed Inputs

Some other inputs required for the forecast are not under management's direct control or are not expected to change. These inputs are shown in column G and include the tax rate, the interest rate, the shares initially outstanding, the initial stock price, and the Fixed assets/Sales ratio, which the CFO concluded was fine. The number of shares outstanding will change in 2020 depending on how much new equity the firm must raise. The amount of additional interest-bearing debt is dependent on the increase in spontaneous funds generated, the target total liabilities/assets ratio, and the increase in assets. Allied's management decided to keep the same proportion of notes payable and long-term debt in 2020 as it had in 2019. Of course, management hopes the stock price will increase as a result of the firm's actions and improved financial position, but the CFO wisely decided not to make a prediction at this point.

16-4B PART II. FORECASTED INCOME STATEMENT

The forecasted 2020 income statement starts with the 2019 income statement, but forecasts that 2020 sales will grow by 10%. Next, the assumed new operating cost ratio is multiplied by the new sales level to calculate the forecasted 2020 operating costs, which are subtracted from sales to obtain the forecasted EBIT. Interest expenses are calculated in Part V, the Notes section, after the interest-bearing debt has been determined in the balance sheet developed in Part III.[11] Once the interest expense has been calculated and entered in the income statement, the forecasted net income is determined. Dividends for 2020 are found by multiplying the target payout ratio by the 2020 forecasted net income. Dividends are then subtracted from net income to find the 2020 addition to retained earnings.

16-4C PART III. FORECASTED BALANCE SHEET

The forecasted 2020 balance sheet is developed from the 2019 balance sheet. Cash and fixed assets are multiplied by 1.10 because they increase at the same rate as sales growth. Accounts receivable are found by multiplying the assumed 11% Receivables/Sales ratio (given in Part I) by forecasted 2020 sales, and inventories are found by multiplying the 19% Inventories/Sales ratio (also given in Part I) by forecasted 2020 sales. We then sum the four asset accounts to find forecasted 2020 total assets.

On the liabilities side, because payables and accruals grow at the same rate as sales, we multiply the 2019 values by 1.10. Also, 2020 retained earnings are found by adding the 2020 addition to retained earnings from the income statement to 2019 retained earnings. To complete the balance sheet, we need to find the amounts for short-term bank loans, bonds, and new common stock. To obtain those values, we skip down to Part V, the Notes section. Here we multiply the target total liabilities/assets ratio times the forecasted 2020 total assets to obtain the forecasted total liabilities amount. We then subtract payables and accruals from

---

[11]Notes payable and the $170 million of recently issued bonds have an 8% interest rate, while the average interest rate of the remaining bonds is 10.45%. The result is an average interest rate of 9.6%, which was used in this forecasting model.

this amount to find the forecast for interest-bearing debt (which includes bank loans and bonds). Next, we multiply the interest-bearing debt by the 2019 proportions of bank debt and long-term bonds to find the forecasted amounts for those two items. Similarly, we find the required amount of 2020 total equity by multiplying (1 − target total liabilities/assets ratio) times the 2020 forecasted assets. We then subtract forecasted retained earnings to find 2020 common stock, which we insert in the balance sheet. When we sum the liability and equity accounts, the total matches the forecasted assets, which it must.

16-4D PART IV. RATIOS AND EPS

With the 2020 income statement and balance sheet forecasted, we can calculate the forecasted 2020 ratios and EPS; those calculations are done in Part IV. The first five ratios shown are the same ones given in the Part I Inputs section. We calculated them from the forecasted statement as a check on the accuracy of the model.

An interesting aspect of Part IV is the DuPont calculations. In 2019, Allied's profit margin and turnover were quite low, but its equity multiplier was relatively high. The result was a low but risky 15.6% ROE. The forecast for 2020 shows improvements in the profit margin and turnover, which boost ROE, and a lowering of the equity multiplier, which holds down the ROE but indicates less financial risk. The result is a much better and less risky 18.8% ROE, which is slightly above the industry average.

The final item in Part IV is the forecasted EPS, which jumps from $1.95 in 2019 to $2.63 in 2020. The CFO calculated the following data for use in his talk but decided not to include it in the table:

P/E ratio	**11.8 × versus 13.6 × for the industry**
Current stock price	**$23.06**

Allied's estimated 2020 stock price is then calculated by multiplying its forecasted EPS by the industry average P/E ratio:[12]

$$\$2.63(13.6) = \$35.77$$

$$\text{Percentage gain: } \$35.77/\$23.06 - 1 = 55.12\%, \text{ or approximately } 55\%$$

16-4E USING THE FORECAST TO IMPROVE OPERATIONS

Allied's CFO generated Table 16.2 with a straightforward Excel model. The table could have been worked with a calculator, but it was easier to do the work using Excel. Moreover and very importantly, once he developed the model, he could make all kinds of changes to see the forecasted results under alternative scenarios. It's easy to change the growth rate and the five key input variables in Part I. It would be easy to change the financing assumptions, perhaps using more bank loans and fewer bonds. It also would be easy to show the results of financing only with debt or only with stock. With any such input changes, the model instantly provides modified results. Indeed, the CFO had the model on his laptop, took it to the meeting, and answered a number of "what if" questions. In fact, Excel's Data Tab contains "What If" Analysis tools such as Scenario Manager, Goal Seek, and Data Tables. Throughout the Excel chapter models developed for this text, we have used Goal Seek and Data Tables.[13]

Of course, it's much easier to change inputs in a spreadsheet model than it is to change actual operations so that the forecasted results are generated. However, as we said earlier in the chapter, if you don't know where you're going, it's hard to get there. Allied's ratio analysis in Chapter 4 pointed out the firm's weaknesses, and the model shown in Table 16.2 demonstrates how improvements in the driver

[12]Refer to Table 4.2 in Chapter 4 for Allied's P/E ratio and the industry average P/E ratio.

[13]Scenario Manager is a little more complicated to use, so we leave that tool for the more advanced Excel user.

variables will affect the firm's ROE, its EPS, and (of course) its stock price. Allied's managers' compensation is partly based on the firm's financial results, including its ROE and stock price, so they are keenly interested in the model and its results. The threat of firing is also a strong motivator, and obtaining poor results while operating good assets makes the firing of management a real possibility.

Self*Test*

What advantages does the forecasted financial statement method have over the AFN equation for forecasting financial requirements?

Why should a marketing or management major be interested in financial forecasting?

Would financial forecasting be relevant for nonfinance majors when they graduate and enter the workforce? Explain.

16-5 Using Regression to Improve Forecasts[14]

Regression Analysis
A statistical technique that fits a line to observed data points so that the resulting equation can be used to forecast other data points.

In financial statement forecasts, it is often appropriate to assume that most of the assets increase at the same rate as sales. However, that is often not the case. We noted in our discussion of the AFN equation that excess capacity might exist, in which case assets would increase less rapidly than sales. Similarly, economies of scale might exist, and this too could enable sales to increase less rapidly than assets. We can use regression techniques to investigate the existence of such situations and thus improve the financial forecasts.

To illustrate **regression analysis**, consider Figure 16.2, which shows Allied's sales, inventories, and receivables during the last 5 years and scatter

FIGURE 16.2 Allied Food Products: Regression Models (millions of dollars)

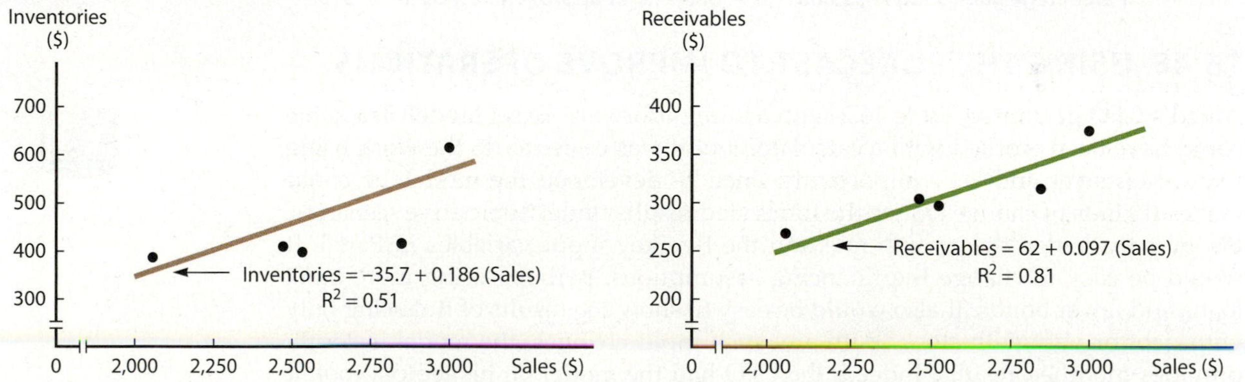

Year	Sales	Inventories	Accounts Receivable
2015	$2,058	$387	$268
2016	2,534	398	297
2017	2,472	409	304
2018	2,850	415	315
2019	3,000	615	375
2020	3,300 (projected)		

[14]This section is relatively technical, but it can be omitted without loss of continuity.

diagrams of inventories and receivables versus sales. Estimated regression equations, found with a financial calculator or spreadsheet, can be developed. For example, here is the estimated relationship between inventories and sales (in millions of dollars):

$$\text{Inventories} = -\$35.7 + 0.186(\text{Sales})$$

We can use the regression equation to estimate the 2020 inventory level. Because 2020 sales are projected at \$3,300 million, according to the regression, 2020 inventories should be \$578 million:

$$\text{Inventories} = -\$35.7 + 0.186(\$3{,}300) = \$578 \text{ million}$$

This estimate based on the regression equation is \$49 million less than the \$627 million forecast used in the projected financial statements in Part III of Table 16.2. Note also that although our graph shows a linear relationship between sales and inventories, we could have used a nonlinear regression model had we believed that such a relationship was more appropriate. Also, we could have used a multiple regression equation, which would have brought other factors that affect inventories into the picture.

Self*Test*

Examine the following statement: Using regression to predict items such as inventories is better than basing such predictions on last year's Inventory/Sales ratio because regression helps smooth out the effects of random fluctuations. Do you agree or disagree? Explain.

16-6 Analyzing the Effects of Changing Ratios

When we forecasted the 2020 financial statements, we assumed that the 2020 operating ratios would move closer to the industry averages and we based asset levels on those assumptions. However, it is often preferable to base forecasted assets on a regression analysis. Also, it is often useful to examine specific asset ratios to get a better idea of the effects on the firm's financial position given various changes to these ratios. In this section, we explore the effects of modifying receivable and inventory ratios.

16-6A MODIFYING ACCOUNTS RECEIVABLE

In Table 16.2, Allied's DSO is projected to be 40.15 days versus an industry average 36 days. Its sales per day are projected to be \$3,300/365 = \$9.04 million. If Allied could operate at the industry-average DSO, its receivables would be reduced by:

$$\begin{aligned}
\text{Receivables at 40.15 day} &= 40.15(\$9.04) = \$363.0 \text{ million}\\
\text{Receivables at 36.00 days} &= 36.00(\$9.04) = \underline{\$325.5 \text{ million}}\\
\text{Receivables reduction} = \text{Additional 2020 FCF} &= \underline{\underline{\$\ \ 37.5 \text{ million}}}
\end{aligned}$$

Thus, receivables could be reduced by another \$37.5 million if Allied's credit manager could achieve the industry-average DSO. That would mean \$37.5 million of additional free cash flow to the firm in 2020, plus additional FCF going forward as Allied grows. The CFO could use this example in a discussion with Allied's credit manager.

16-6B MODIFYING INVENTORIES

Inventories can be analyzed in a similar manner. First, note that Allied's forecasted inventory turnover is 5.26 times versus 10.9 times for the industry. Moreover, in Table 16.2, Allied's forecasted 2020 inventory is \$627 million versus \$3,300 million of sales. Given this information, we can find Allied's inventories if Allied is able to achieve the industry-average inventory turnover:

$$\text{Inventory at forecasted inventory turnover} = \$3{,}300/5.26 = \$627 \text{ million}$$
$$\text{Inventory at industry-average turnover} = \$3{,}300/10.9 = \underline{\$303 \text{ million}}$$
$$\text{Inventory reduction} = \text{Additional 2020 FCF} = \underline{\underline{\$324 \text{ million}}}$$

Thus, inventories could be reduced by another \$324 million if Allied's inventory turnover could be increased to the industry average. That would mean another \$324 million of free cash flow in 2020, plus further additions going forward. Again, the CFO could use this example in a discussion with the inventory manager.

16-6C OTHER "SPECIAL STUDIES"

Once a firm has developed a model to forecast its financial statements, it can do all types of special "what if" studies. For example, the model that Allied's CFO used to make Table 16.2 (which is part of the chapter Excel model) could be used to find the results shown in the two preceding sections for receivables and inventories. The model also could be used to estimate the effects of changing the dividend policy on the statements and on the required AFN. Indeed, the AFN equation could be modified to obtain a "quick and dirty" estimate of the effects of the dividend payout on the AFN. As we saw earlier in Section 16-3 in the discussion of the AFN equation, Allied has a payout ratio of 0.5899, and when that number was used in the equation, an AFN of \$114 million resulted:

$$\begin{aligned}\text{AFN} &= 0.6667(\Delta S) - 0.06667(\Delta S) - 0.0488(S_1)(0.4101)\\ &= 0.6667(\$300) - 0.06667(\$300) - 0.0488(\$3{,}300)(0.4101)\\ &= \$200 - \$20 - \$66\\ &= \$114 \text{ million}\end{aligned}$$

Now suppose Allied anticipated problems raising \$114 million to carry out its business plan. The CFO might then suggest to the directors a reduction of the payout ratio to 20%. That would result in an AFN of about \$51 million (shown in Part IV of Table 16.1), which is about \$63 million less than the original AFN calculated. Of course, as we saw in the dividend chapter, lowering the dividend might create problems of its own, but at times such an action may be necessary to maximize a firm's intrinsic value and long-run stock price.

TYING IT ALL TOGETHER

This chapter described techniques for forecasting financial statements, which is a crucial part of the financial planning process. Both investors and corporations regularly use forecasting techniques to help value a company's stock, to estimate the benefits of potential projects, and to estimate how changes in capital structure, dividend policy, and working capital policy influence shareholder value.

The type of forecasting described in this chapter is important for several reasons. First, if the projected operating results are unsatisfactory, management can "go back to the drawing board," reformulate its plans, and develop more reasonable targets for the coming year. Second, the funds required to meet the sales forecast simply may not be obtainable. If not, it is obviously better to know this in advance and to scale back projected operations than to suddenly run out of cash and have operations grind to an abrupt halt. And third, firms often give guidance to analysts regarding likely future earnings, so it is beneficial to be able to provide reasonably accurate forecasts.

Self-Test Questions and Problems

(Solutions Appear in Appendix A)

ST-1 **KEY TERMS** Define each of the following terms:

a. Mission statement; corporate scope; statement of corporate objectives; corporate strategies
b. Operating plan; financial plan
c. Spontaneously generated funds
d. Additional Funds Needed (AFN); AFN equation
e. Capital intensity ratio; sustainable growth rate
f. Forecasted financial statements; retention ratio
g. Excess capacity adjustments
h. Regression analysis

ST-2 **SUSTAINABLE GROWTH RATE** Weatherford Industries Inc. has the following ratios: $A_0^*/S_0 = 1.6$; $L_0^*/S_0 = 0.4$; profit margin $= 0.10$; and payout ratio $= 0.45$, or 45%. Sales last year were \$100 million. Assuming that these ratios will remain constant, use the AFN equation to determine the maximum growth rate (the sustainable growth rate) Weatherford can achieve without having to employ nonspontaneous external funds.

ST-3 **ADDITIONAL FUNDS NEEDED** Suppose Weatherford's financial consultants report (1) that the inventory turnover ratio is Sales/Inventory = 3 times versus an industry average of 4 times and (2) that Weatherford can reduce inventories and thus raise its turnover to 4 without affecting sales, the profit margin, or the other asset turnover ratios. Under those conditions, use the AFN equation to determine the amount of additional funds Weatherford will require next year if sales grow by 20%.

Questions

16-1 What are the key factors on which external financing depends, as indicated in the AFN equation?

16-2 Assume that an average firm in the office supply business has a 6% profit margin, a 40% total liabilities/assets ratio, a total assets turnover of 2 times, and a dividend payout ratio of 40%. Is it true that if such a firm is to have any sales growth ($g > 0$), it will be forced to borrow or to sell common stock (that is, it will need some nonspontaneous external capital even if g is very small)? Explain.

16-3 Would you agree that computerized corporate planning models were a fad during the 1990s but that because of a need for flexibility in corporate planning, they are no longer used by most firms? Explain.

16-4 Certain liability and net worth items generally increase spontaneously with increases in sales. Put a check mark (✓) next to those items that typically increase spontaneously.

Accounts payable	______
Notes payable to banks	______
Accrued wages	______
Accrued taxes	______
Mortgage bonds	______
Common stock	______
Retained earnings	______

16-5 Suppose a firm makes the following policy changes. If the change means that external non-spontaneous financial requirements (AFN) will increase, indicate this with a (+); indicate a decrease with a (−); and indicate an indeterminate or negligible effect with a (0). Think in terms of the immediate short-run effect on funds requirements.

a. The dividend payout ratio is increased. ______
b. Rather than produce computers in advance, a computer company decides to produce them only after an order has been received. ______
c. The firm decides to pay all suppliers on delivery, rather than after a 30-day delay, to take advantage of discounts for rapid payment. ______
d. The firm begins to sell on credit. (Previously, all sales had been on a cash basis.) ______
e. The firm's profit margin is eroded by increased competition; sales are steady. ______
f. Advertising expenditures are stepped up. ______
g. A decision is made to substitute long-term mortgage bonds for short-term bank loans. ______
h. The firm begins to pay employees on a weekly basis. (Previously, it had paid employees at the end of each month.) ______

Problems

Easy Problems 1-6

16-1 **AFN EQUATION** Carlsbad Corporation's sales are expected to increase from $5 million in 2019 to $6 million in 2020, or by 20%. Its assets totaled $3 million at the end of 2019. Carlsbad is at full capacity, so its assets must grow in proportion to projected sales. At the end of 2019, current liabilities are $1 million, consisting of $250,000 of accounts payable, $500,000 of notes payable, and $250,000 of accrued liabilities. Its profit margin is forecasted to be 3%, and the forecasted retention ratio is 30%. Use the AFN equation to forecast the additional funds Carlsbad will need for the coming year.

16-2 **AFN EQUATION** Refer to Problem 16-1. What additional funds would be needed if the company's year-end 2019 assets had been $4 million? Assume that all other numbers are the same. Why is this AFN different from the one you found in Problem 16-1? Is the company's "capital intensity" the same or different? Explain.

16-3 **AFN EQUATION** Refer to Problem 16-1 and assume that the company had $3 million in assets at the end of 2019. However, now assume that the company pays no dividends. Under these assumptions, what additional funds would be needed for the coming year? Why is this AFN different from the one you found in Problem 16-1?

16-4 **PRO FORMA INCOME STATEMENT** Austin Grocers recently reported the following 2019 income statement (in millions of dollars):

Sales	$700
Operating costs including depreciation	500
EBIT	$200
Interest	40
EBT	$160
Taxes (25%)	40
Net income	$120
Dividends	$ 40
Addition to retained earnings	$ 80

For the coming year, the company is forecasting a 25% increase in sales, and it expects that its year-end operating costs, including depreciation, will equal 70% of sales. Austin's tax rate, interest expense, and dividend payout ratio are all expected to remain constant.

a. What is Austin's projected 2020 net income?
b. What is the expected growth rate in Austin's dividends?

16-5 **EXCESS CAPACITY** Williamson Industries has $7 billion in sales and $1.944 billion in fixed assets. Currently, the company's fixed assets are operating at 90% of capacity.

a. What level of sales could Williamson Industries have obtained if it had been operating at full capacity?
b. What is Williamson's target fixed assets/sales ratio?
c. If Williamson's sales increase 15%, how large of an increase in fixed assets will the company need to meet its target fixed assets/sales ratio?

16-6 **REGRESSION AND INVENTORIES** Jasper Furnishings has $300 million in sales. The company expects that its sales will increase 12% this year. Jasper's CFO uses a simple linear regression to forecast the company's inventory level for a given level of projected sales. On the basis of recent history, the estimated relationship between inventories and sales (in millions of dollars) is as follows:

$$\text{Inventories} = \$25 + 0.125(\text{Sales})$$

Given the estimated sales forecast and the estimated relationship between inventories and sales, what are your forecasts of the company's year-end inventory level and its inventory turnover ratio?

Intermediate Problems 7-12

16-7 **PRO FORMA INCOME STATEMENT** At the end of last year, Roberts Inc. reported the following income statement (in millions of dollars):

Sales	$3,000
Operating costs excluding depreciation	2,450
EBITDA	$ 550
Depreciation	250
EBIT	$ 300
Interest	124
EBT	$ 176
Taxes (25%)	44
Net income	$ 132

Looking ahead to the following year, the company's CFO has assembled this information:

- Year-end sales are expected to be 10% higher than the $3 billion in sales generated last year.
- Year-end operating costs, excluding depreciation, are expected to equal 80% of year-end sales.
- Depreciation is expected to increase at the same rate as sales.
- Interest costs are expected to remain unchanged.
- The tax rate is expected to remain at 25%.

On the basis of that information, what will be the forecast for Roberts' year-end net income?

16-8 **LONG-TERM FINANCING NEEDED** At year-end 2019, total assets for Arrington Inc. were $1.8 million and accounts payable were $450,000. Sales, which in 2019 were $3.0 million, are expected to increase by 25% in 2020. Total assets and accounts payable are proportional to sales, and that relationship will be maintained; that is, they will grow at the same rate as sales. Arrington typically uses no current liabilities other than accounts payable. Common stock amounted to $500,000 in 2019, and retained earnings were $475,000. Arrington plans to sell new common stock in the amount of $130,000. The firm's profit margin on sales is 5%; 35% of earnings will be retained.

a. What were Arrington's total liabilities in 2019?

b. How much new long-term debt financing will be needed in 2020? (*Hint:* AFN − New stock = New long-term debt.)

16-9 **SALES INCREASE** Paladin Furnishings generated $4 million in sales during 2019, and its year-end total assets were $3.2 million. Also, at year-end 2019, current liabilities were $500,000, consisting of $200,000 of notes payable, $200,000 of accounts payable, and $100,000 of accrued liabilities. Looking ahead to 2020, the company estimates that its assets must increase by $0.80 for every $1.00 increase in sales. Paladin's profit margin is 3%, and its retention ratio is 50%. How large of a sales increase can the company achieve without having to raise funds externally?

16-10 **REGRESSION AND RECEIVABLES** Edwards Industries has $320 million in sales. The company expects that its sales will increase 12% this year. Edwards' CFO uses a simple linear regression to forecast the company's receivables level for a given level of projected sales. On the basis of recent history, the estimated relationship between receivables and sales (in millions of dollars) is as follows:

$$\text{Receivables} = \$9.25 + 0.07(\text{Sales})$$

Given the estimated sales forecast and the estimated relationship between receivables and sales, what are your forecasts of the company's year-end balance for receivables and its year-end days sales outstanding (DSO) ratio? Assume that DSO is calculated on the basis of a 365-day year.

16-11 **REGRESSION AND INVENTORIES** Charlie's Cycles Inc. has $110 million in sales. The company expects that its sales will increase 5% this year. Charlie's CFO uses a simple linear regression to forecast the company's inventory level for a given level of projected sales. On the basis of recent history, the estimated relationship between inventories and sales (in millions of dollars) is as follows:

$$\text{Inventories} = \$9 + 0.0875(\text{Sales})$$

Given the estimated sales forecast and the estimated relationship between inventories and sales, what are your forecasts of the company's year-end inventory level and its inventory turnover ratio?

16-12 **EXCESS CAPACITY** Earleton Manufacturing Company has $3 billion in sales and $787,500,000 in fixed assets. Currently, the company's fixed assets are operating at 80% of capacity.

a. What level of sales could Earleton have obtained if it had been operating at full capacity?

b. What is Earleton's target fixed assets/sales ratio?

c. If Earleton's sales increase 30%, how large of an increase in fixed assets will the company need to meet its target fixed assets/sales ratio?

Challenging Problems 13-14

16-13 **ADDITIONAL FUNDS NEEDED** Morrissey Technologies Inc.'s 2019 financial statements are shown here.

Morrissey Technologies Inc.: Balance Sheet as of December 31, 2019

Cash	$ 180,000	Accounts payable	$ 360,000
Receivables	360,000	Accrued liabilities	180,000
Inventories	720,000	Notes payable	56,000
Total current assets	$1,260,000	Total current liabilities	$ 596,000
		Long-term debt	100,000
Fixed assets	1,440,000	Common stock	1,800,000
		Retained earnings	204,000
Total assets	$2,700,000	Total liabilities and equity	$2,700,000

Morrissey Technologies Inc.: Income Statement for December 31, 2019

Sales	$3,600,000
Operating costs including depreciation	3,279,720
EBIT	$ 320,280
Interest	20,280
EBT	$ 300,000
Taxes (25%)	75,000
Net Income	$ 225,000
Per Share Data:	
Common stock price	$45.00
Earnings per share (EPS)	$ 2.25
Dividends per share (DPS)	$ 1.35

Suppose that in 2020, sales increase by 10% over 2019 sales. The firm currently has 100,000 shares outstanding. It expects to maintain its 2019 dividend payout ratio and believes that its assets should grow at the same rate as sales. The firm has no excess capacity. However, the firm would like to reduce its operating costs/sales ratio to 87.5% and increase its total liabilities-to-assets ratio to 30%. (It believes its liabilities-to-assets ratio currently is too low relative to the industry average.) The firm will raise 30% of the 2020 forecasted interest-bearing debt as notes payable, and it will issue long-term bonds for the remainder. The firm forecasts that its before-tax cost of debt (which includes both short- and long-term debt) is 12.5%. Assume that any common stock issuances or repurchases can be made at the firm's current stock price of $45.

a. Construct the forecasted financial statements assuming that these changes are made. What are the firm's forecasted notes payable and long-term debt balances? What is the forecasted addition to retained earnings?

b. If the profit margin remains at 6.25% and the dividend payout ratio remains at 60%, at what growth rate in sales will the additional financing requirements be exactly zero? In other words, what is the firm's sustainable growth rate? (*Hint:* Set AFN equal to zero and solve for g.)

16-14 EXCESS CAPACITY Krogh Lumber's 2019 financial statements are shown here.

Krogh Lumber: Balance Sheet as of December 31, 2019 (thousands of dollars)

Cash	$ 1,800	Accounts payable	$ 7,200
Receivables	10,800	Accrued liabilities	2,520
Inventories	12,600	Notes payable	3,472
Total current assets	$25,200	Total current liabilities	$13,192
		Mortgage bonds	5,000
Net fixed assets	21,600	Common stock	2,000
		Retained earnings	26,608
Total assets	$46,800	Total liabilities and equity	$46,800

Krogh Lumber: Income Statement for December 31, 2019 (thousands of dollars)

Sales	$36,000
Operating costs including depreciation	30,783
Earnings before interest and taxes	$ 5,217
Interest	1,017
Earnings before taxes	$ 4,200
Taxes (25%)	1,050
Net income	$ 3,150
Dividends (60%)	$ 1,890
Addition to retained earnings	$ 1,260

a. Assume that the company was operating at full capacity in 2019 with regard to all items *except* fixed assets; fixed assets in 2019 were being utilized to only 75% of capacity. By what percentage could 2020 sales increase over 2019 sales without the need for an increase in fixed assets?

b. Now suppose 2020 sales increase by 25% over 2019 sales. Assume that Krogh cannot sell any fixed assets. All assets other than fixed assets will grow at the same rate as sales; however, after reviewing industry averages, the firm would like to reduce its operating costs/sales ratio to 82% and increase its total liabilities-to-assets ratio to 42%. The firm will maintain its 60% dividend payout ratio, and it currently has 1 million shares outstanding. The firm plans to raise 35% of its 2020 forecasted interest-bearing debt as notes payable, and it will issue bonds for the remainder. The firm forecasts that its before-tax cost of debt (which includes both short- and long-term debt) is 11%. Any stock issuances or repurchases will be made at the firm's current stock price of $40. Develop Krogh's projected financial statements like those shown in Table 16.2. What are the balances of notes payable, bonds, common stock, and retained earnings?

Comprehensive/Spreadsheet Problem

16-15 FORECASTING FINANCIAL STATEMENTS Use a spreadsheet model to forecast the financial statements in Problems 16-13 and 16-14.

INTEGRATED CASE

NEW WORLD CHEMICALS INC.

16-16 FINANCIAL FORECASTING Sue Wilson, the new financial manager of New World Chemicals (NWC), a California producer of specialized chemicals for use in fruit orchards, must prepare a formal financial forecast for 2020. NWC's 2019 sales were $2 billion, and the marketing department is forecasting a 25% increase for 2020. Wilson thinks the company was operating at full capacity in 2019, but she is not sure. The first step in her forecast was to assume that key ratios would remain unchanged and that it would be "business as usual" at NWC. The 2019 financial statements, the 2020 initial forecast, and a ratio analysis for 2019 and the 2020 initial forecast are given in Table IC 16.1.

Assume that you were recently hired as Wilson's assistant and that your first major task is to help her develop the formal financial forecast. She asks you to begin by answering the following questions:

a. Assume (1) that NWC was operating at full capacity in 2019 with respect to all assets, (2) that all assets must grow at the same rate as sales, (3) that accounts payable and accrued liabilities also will grow at the same rate as sales, and (4) that the 2019 profit margin and dividend payout will be maintained. Under those conditions, what would the AFN equation predict the company's financial requirements to be for the coming year?

b. Consultations with several key managers within NWC, including production, inventory, and receivable managers, have yielded some very useful information.

   1. NWC's high DSO is largely due to one significant customer who battled through some hardships the past 2 years but who appears to be financially healthy again and is generating strong cash flow. As a result, NWC's accounts receivable manager expects the firm to lower receivables enough for a calculated DSO of 34 days without adversely affecting sales.
   2. NWC was operating slightly below capacity, but its forecasted growth will require a new facility, which is expected to increase NWC's net fixed assets to $700 million.
   3. A relatively new inventory management system (installed last year) has taken some time to catch on and to operate efficiently. NWC's inventory turnover improved slightly last year, but this year NWC expects even more improvement as inventories decrease and inventory turnover is expected to rise to 10×.

   Incorporate that information into the 2020 initial forecast results, as these adjustments to the initial forecast represent the final forecast for 2020. (*Hint:* Total assets do not change from the initial forecast.)

c. Calculate NWC's forecasted ratios based on its final forecast and compare them with the company's 2019 historical ratios, the 2020 initial forecast ratios, and the industry averages. How does NWC compare with the average firm in its industry, and is the company's financial position expected to improve during the coming year? Explain.

d. Based on the final forecast, calculate NWC's free cash flow for 2020. How does this FCF differ from the FCF forecasted by NWC's initial "business as usual" forecast?

e. Initially, some NWC managers questioned whether the new facility expansion was necessary, especially as it results in increasing net fixed assets from $500 million to $700 million (a 40% increase). However, after extensive discussions about NWC needing to position itself for future growth and being flexible and competitive in today's marketplace, NWC's top managers agreed that the expansion was necessary. Among the issues raised by opponents was that NWC's fixed assets were being operated at only 85% of capacity. Assuming that its fixed assets were operating at only 85% of capacity, by how much could sales have increased, both in dollar terms and in percentage terms, before NWC reached full capacity?

f. How would changes in the following items affect the AFN: (1) the dividend payout ratio, (2) the profit margin, (3) the capital intensity ratio, and (4) NWC beginning to buy from its suppliers on terms that permit it to pay after 60 days rather than after 30 days? (Consider each item separately and hold all other things constant.)

TABLE IC 16.1 Financial Statements and Other Data on NWC (millions of dollars)

A. Balance Sheets	**2019**	**2020E**
Cash and equivalents	$ 20	$ 25
Accounts receivable	240	300
Inventories	240	300
Total current assets	$ 500	$ 625
Net fixed assets	500	625
Total assets	$1,000	$1,250
Accounts payable and accrued liabilities	$ 100	$ 125
Notes payable	100	190
Total current liabilities	$ 200	$ 315
Long-term debt	100	180
Common stock	500	500
Retained earnings	200	255
Total liabilities and equity	$1,000	$1,250

B. Income Statements	**2019**	**2020E**
Sales	$2,000.00	$2,500.00
Variable costs	1,200.00	1,500.00
Fixed costs	700.00	875.00
Earnings before interest and taxes (EBIT)	$ 100.00	$ 125.00
Interest	16.00	20.00
Earnings before taxes (EBT)	$ 84.00	$ 105.00
Taxes (25%)	21.00	26.25
Net income	$ 63.00	$ 78.75
Dividends (30%)	$ 18.90	$ 23.63
Addition to retained earnings	$ 44.10	$ 55.13

C. Key Ratios	**NWC (2019)**	**NWC (2020E)**	**Industry**	**Comment**
Basic earning power	10.00%	10.00%	20.00%	
Profit margin	3.15	3.15	4.00	
Return on equity	9.00	10.43	15.60	
Days sales outstanding (365 days)	43.80 days	43.80 days	32.00 days	
Inventory turnover	8.33×	8.33×	11.00×	
Fixed assets turnover	4.00	4.00	5.00	
Total assets turnover	2.00	2.00	2.50	
Total liabilities/assets	30.00%	39.60%	36.00%	
Times interest earned	6.25×	6.25×	9.40×	
Current ratio	2.50	1.98	3.00	
Payout ratio	30.00%	30.00%	30.00%	

TAKING A CLOSER LOOK

Forecasting The Future Performance Of Abercrombie & Fitch

Use online resources to work on this chapter's questions. Please note that website information changes over time, and these changes may limit your ability to answer some of these questions.

Clothing retailer Abercrombie & Fitch enjoyed phenomenal success in the late 1990s. Between 1996 and 2000, its sales grew almost fourfold—from $335 million to more than $1.2 billion—and its stock price soared by more than 500%. However, in 2002, its growth rate had begun to slow down, and Abercrombie had a hard time meeting its quarterly earnings targets. As a result, the stock price in late 2002 was about half of what it was 3 years earlier. Abercrombie's struggles resulted from increased competition, a sluggish economy, and the challenges of staying ahead of the fashion curve. From late 2002 until November 2007, the company's stock rebounded strongly; however, its stock price declined during the 2008 economic downturn. Its stock price rebounded until late October 2011, when it began a downward trend again. Questions remain about the firm's long-term growth prospects. However, the company has been cutting costs and trying to improve productivity with its focus on the supply chain. In addition, it has been actively repurchasing shares, indicating that management believes its shares are undervalued. The company continues to steadily expand stores abroad while closing under-performing domestic stores.

Given the questions about Abercrombie's future growth rate, analysts have focused on the company's earnings reports. Financial websites such as Yahoo! Finance, Morningstar, and MSN Money (www.msn.com/en-us/money/markets) provide information on the company's recent earnings history along with a summary of analysts' earnings forecasts.

Discussion Questions

1. What is the mean forecast for Abercrombie's earnings per share over the next fiscal year?
2. Based on analysts' forecasts, what is the expected long-term (5-year) growth rate in earnings?
3. Have analysts made any significant changes to their forecasted earnings for Abercrombie & Fitch in the past few months? Explain.
4. Within the last year, have Abercrombie's reported quarterly earnings generally met, exceeded, or fallen short of analysts' forecasted earnings?
5. How has Abercrombie's stock performed this year relative to the S&P 500?

Multinational Financial Management[1]

CHAPTER 17

PotograFFE/Shutterstock.com

U.S. Firms Look Overseas to Enhance Shareholder Value

From the end of World War II until the 1970s, the United States dominated the world economy. However, that situation no longer exists. Raw materials, finished goods, services, and money flow freely across most national boundaries, as do innovative ideas and new technologies. World-class U.S. companies are making breakthroughs in foreign labs, obtaining capital from foreign investors, and putting foreign employees on the fast track to the top. Dozens of top U.S. manufacturers, including Dow Chemical, Colgate-Palmolive, IBM, and HP, sell more of their products outside the United States than they do at home. Likewise, service firms such as Citigroup, McDonald's, and AFLAC receive more than half their revenues from foreign sales.

The trend is even more pronounced in profits. In recent years, Coca-Cola and many other companies have made more money in the Pacific Rim and Western Europe than in the United States. As a result, economic events around the globe and changing exchange rates now have a profound effect on the company's bottom line. In particular, profits earned in foreign currencies are worth more when the U.S. dollar declines.

Successful global companies such as Coca-Cola must conduct business in different economies, and they must be sensitive to the many subtleties of different cultures and political systems. Accordingly, they find it useful to blend into the foreign landscape to help win product acceptance and avoid political problems. At the same time, foreign-based multinationals are arriving on American shores in ever greater numbers. Switzerland's ABB, the Netherlands's Philips, France's Thomson, and Japan's Fujitsu and Honda are all waging campaigns to be identified as companies that employ Americans, transfer technology to America, and help the U.S. trade balance.

[1]This chapter was coauthored with Professor Roy Crum of the University of Florida.

The emergence of "world companies" raises a host of questions for governments. For example, should domestic firms be favored, or does it make no difference what a company's nationality is as long as the firm provides domestic jobs? Should a company make an effort to keep jobs in its home country, or should it produce where total production costs are lowest? What nation controls the technology developed by a multinational corporation, particularly when the technology can be used in military applications? Must a multinational company adhere to rules imposed in its home country with respect to its operations outside the home country? Keep those questions in mind as you read this chapter. When you finish, you should have a better appreciation of the problems that governments face and the difficult but profitable opportunities that managers of multinational companies face.

PUTTING THINGS IN PERSPECTIVE

Managers of multinational companies must deal with a wide range of issues that are not present when a company operates in a single country. In this chapter, we highlight the key differences between multinational and domestic corporations, and we discuss the impact these differences have on the financial management of multinational businesses.

By the time you complete this chapter, you should be able to do the following:

- **Identify the primary reasons companies choose to go "global."**
- **Explain how exchange rates work and interpret different exchange rate quotations.**
- **Discuss the intuition behind interest rate parity and purchasing power parity.**
- **Explain the different opportunities and risks that investors face when they invest overseas.**
- **Identify some specific challenges that a multinational corporation faces and discuss how they influence its capital budgeting, capital structure, and working capital policies.**

17-1 Multinational, or Global, Corporations

Multinational, or Global, Corporation
A firm that operates in an integrated fashion in a number of countries.

The term **multinational, or global, corporation** describes a firm that operates in an integrated fashion in a number of countries. During the past 20 years or so, a new and fundamentally different form of international commercial activity has developed that has greatly increased worldwide economic and political interdependence. Rather than merely purchase resources from and sell goods to foreign nations, multinational firms now make direct investments in fully integrated operations—from extraction of raw materials through the manufacturing process and finally to the distribution of products to consumers throughout the world. Today multinational corporate networks control a large and growing share of the world's technological, marketing, and productive resources.

Companies, both U.S. and foreign, go "global" for seven primary reasons:

1. *To seek production efficiency.* As competition increases in their domestic marketplace and as demand increases in other markets, companies often conclude that they must produce their products overseas. Companies based in high-cost countries have strong incentives to shift production to lower-cost regions, assuming an adequate supply of labor with the requisite skills and an adequate transportation infrastructure. For example, Nike has production

resource

Students can download the Excel chapter models from the textbook's student companion site on cengage.com. Once downloaded onto your computer, retrieve the Chapter 17 Excel model and follow along as you read the chapter.

plants in 42 countries.[2] Likewise Japanese manufacturers have started to shift some of their production to lower-cost countries in the Pacific Rim and the Americas. BMW, in response to high production costs in Germany, has built assembly plants in the United States, among other countries. And just recently, Foxconn, the large Taiwanese supplier to Apple and other electronics manufacturers, broke ground on a new plant in Wisconsin. Those examples illustrate how companies strive to remain competitive by locating manufacturing facilities wherever in the world they can produce and transporting their products to meet the demand in their major markets at the lowest total unit landed costs.

2. *To avoid political, trade, and regulatory hurdles.* Governments sometimes impose tariffs, quotas, and other restrictions on imported goods and services. They often do so to raise revenues, protect domestic industries, and pursue various political and economic policy objectives. To circumvent government hurdles, firms often develop production facilities abroad. For example, the primary reason Japanese auto companies moved production to the United States was to get around U.S. import quotas. Now Honda, Nissan, Toyota, Mazda, and Mitsubishi are assembling vehicles in the United States. This was also the situation in the 1970s when India followed a development strategy to compete domestically with imported products. One reason that prompted U.S. pharmaceutical maker SmithKline and the United Kingdom's Beecham to merge was to avoid licensing and regulatory delays in their largest markets, Western Europe and the United States. GlaxoSmithKline (the result of a 2000 merger between Glaxo Wellcome and SmithKline Beecham) now identifies itself as an inside player in Europe and the United States.[3] More recently, Harley-Davidson announced plans to move some of its facilities overseas in response to new tariffs imposed by the European Union (EU) in retaliation for President Trump's announced tariffs on European goods. (See the box, "President Trump Announces New Tariffs.")
3. *To broaden markets.* After a company's home market matures, growth opportunities are often better in foreign markets. According to economic product life-cycle theory, a firm first produces in its home market, where it can better develop its product and satisfy local customers. This attracts competitors, but when the home market is expanding rapidly, new customers provide the necessary sales growth. However, as the home market matures and the growth of total demand slows, competition becomes more intense. At the same time, demand for the product develops abroad, which creates conditions favoring production in foreign countries to satisfy foreign demand and to cut production and transportation costs so that the company can remain competitive. Thus, such homegrown firms as IBM, Coca-Cola, and McDonald's have aggressively expanded into overseas markets. More recently, Netflix is rapidly expanding throughout the entire world. In mid-2018, it had over 130 million subscribers in almost 200 countries.[4] Foreign firms such as Sony and Toshiba now play an important role in the U.S. consumer electronics market. Finally, as products become more

---

[2]Refer to "Nike Manufacturing Map," manufacturingmap.nikeinc.com.

[3]There is also some recent evidence that global differences in banking regulations influence the flow of capital between countries. Refer to Joel Houston, Chen Lin, and Yue Ma, "Regulatory Arbitrage and International Bank Flows," *Journal of Finance*, vol. 67, no. 5 (October 2012), pp. 1845–1895.

[4]Refer to Felix Richter, "Netflix Reaches 130 Million Subscribers," *Statista* (www.statista.com), July 17, 2018; and Brian Stelter, "Countries Where Netflix Is Now Available," *CNNMoney* (money.cnn.com), January 6, 2016.

PRESIDENT TRUMP ANNOUNCES NEW TARIFFS

President Donald Trump has been a long-standing critic of U.S. trade policies. He has argued that many of our trading partners have imposed unfair trade barriers to U.S. goods and that these barriers have been a major contributor to the large ongoing U.S. trade deficit. Acting on these concerns, the president has used his authority to impose a wide set of tariffs against several key goods sold by our leading trading partners.

Tariffs are effectively a tax on imported goods. The initial effect is to reduce imports by making these imported goods more expensive for U.S. consumers. Moreover, the president contends that the higher cost of foreign goods will enable U.S. industries to compete more effectively internationally, which in turn will eventually increase U.S. exports. The hope is that both the reduction in imports and the increase in exports will reduce the trade deficit. All else equal, these actions would provide large benefits to targeted U.S. exporters.

Critics contend that all else isn't equal and that the long-run effects of tariffs are quite negative and that their effects can ultimately be extremely disruptive to the global economy. The main concern is that trading partners will not sit still in response to the U.S. actions and will instead respond with additional tariffs. Indeed, after President Trump's initial actions, many of our key partners immediately responded with new tariffs to match the change in U.S. policy. Many critics worry that the burgeoning trade war will dramatically increase the price of global goods and that the decline in trading will reduce growth opportunities for businesses in all the affected countries, which in turn could spur a global recession. Another serious concern is that U.S. manufacturers that sell goods abroad may move their facilities overseas to avoid any retaliatory tariffs imposed by our trade partners. For example, in June 2018, Harley-Davidson announced plans to move some of its plants overseas in response to new tariffs announced by the European Union (EU) following the president's imposed tariffs on European goods.

The president has argued that he is in favor of free trade and that he wants to use the newly imposed tariffs to spur a wide series of bilateral trade deals that ultimately lead to lower barriers and more free trade. In this regard, President Trump may be engaging in a high-wire balancing act that has significant consequences if he fails. That said, the stock market has not panicked in the months following his announced tariffs, suggesting that many in the business community believe that global tensions will eventually recede. Given the importance of trade, how these issues are ultimately resolved will have important implications for the global economy in the years ahead.

Source: Alan Rappeport, "Harley-Davidson, Blaming E.U. Tariffs, Will Move Some Production Out of U.S.," *The New York Times* (www.nytimes.com), June 25, 2018.

complex and development becomes more expensive, it is necessary to sell more units to cover overhead costs, so larger markets are critical.

4. *To seek raw materials and new technology.* Supplies of many essential raw materials are geographically dispersed, so companies must go where the materials are found, no matter how challenging it may be to operate in some of the locations. For example, major deposits of oil are located on the northern coast of Alaska, in Siberia, in the deserts of the Middle East, and in the Canadian tar sands, all of which present unique challenges. Thus, U.S. oil companies such as Exxon Mobil need major production facilities around the world to ensure access to the basic input resources needed to sustain the companies in the future. Because Exxon Mobil has refineries, distribution facilities, and oil production fields, this type of investment is referred to as a **vertically integrated investment**, whereby the firm undertakes an investment to secure its supply of inputs at stable prices.

Vertically Integrated Investment
Occurs when a firm undertakes an investment to secure its input supply at stable prices.

5. *To protect processes and products.* Firms often possess special intangible assets such as brand names, technological and marketing know-how, managerial expertise, and superior research and development (R&D) capabilities. Unfortunately, property rights involving intangible assets are often difficult to protect, particularly in foreign markets. Firms sometimes invest abroad rather than license local foreign firms, in order to protect the secrecy of their

production processes, distribution systems, or the product itself. Once a firm's formula or production process is revealed to other local firms, those firms may more easily develop similar products or processes, which will hurt the original firm's sales. For example, to protect its formula, Coca-Cola builds bottling plants and distribution networks in foreign markets but imports the concentrate or syrup required to make the product from the United States. In the 1960s, Coca-Cola faced strong pressure from the Indian government to reveal its formula in order to continue its operations in India. Rather than reveal its formula, the company withdrew its operations from India until the foreign investment climate improved.

6. *To diversify.* By establishing worldwide production facilities and markets, firms can cushion the effect of adverse economic conditions in any single country. For example, U.S. corporations with significant overseas operations benefit when there is a decline in the U.S. dollar. In general, geographic diversification of inputs and outputs works because the economic fluctuations or political vagaries of different countries are not perfectly correlated. Therefore, companies investing overseas can benefit from diversification in the same way that individuals benefit from investing in a broad portfolio of stocks. However, because individual shareholders can diversify their investments internationally on their own, it makes less sense for firms to undertake foreign investments solely for diversification purposes. Note, though, that in countries that place constraints on foreign stock ownership or that do not have internationally traded companies, corporate diversification might make sense because then companies can do something that shareholders cannot easily duplicate in their individual portfolios.
7. *To retain customers.* If a company goes abroad and establishes production or distribution operations, it will need inputs and services at the new locations. If it can obtain what it needs from a supplier that also operates in the same set of countries, managing the relationship will be much easier, and economies of scale and other synergies will likely be obtained. Therefore, suppliers of inputs or services can better retain the business of their customers who are "going global" if they follow their customers abroad. Large U.S. banks, such as Citibank and JPMorgan Chase, initially expanded abroad to supply banking services to their long-time customers, although they quickly capitalized on their global network to develop new customer relationships. The same history is also true for accounting, law, advertising, and similar service providers.

The past 20 years have seen an increasing amount of investment in the United States by foreign corporations and in foreign nations by U.S. corporations. This trend is shown in Figure 17.1, and it is important because of its implications for eroding the traditional doctrine of independence and self-reliance that has been a hallmark of U.S. policy. Just as U.S. corporations with extensive overseas operations are said to use their economic power to exert substantial economic and political influence over host governments in many parts of the world, it is feared that foreign corporations are gaining similar sway over U.S. policy. These developments suggest an increasing degree of mutual influence and interdependence among business enterprises and nations, to which the United States is not immune. Figure 17.1 also demonstrates that the level of foreign investment varies over the business cycle and generally declines as the global economy weakens. We saw this effect most recently when the level of foreign investment inside and outside of the United States declined sharply during the 2008–2009 recession. However, in 2017, the level of foreign direct investment in the United States just slightly surpassed U.S. direct investment abroad.

FIGURE 17.1 Direct Investment Positions at Market Value, 1982–2017

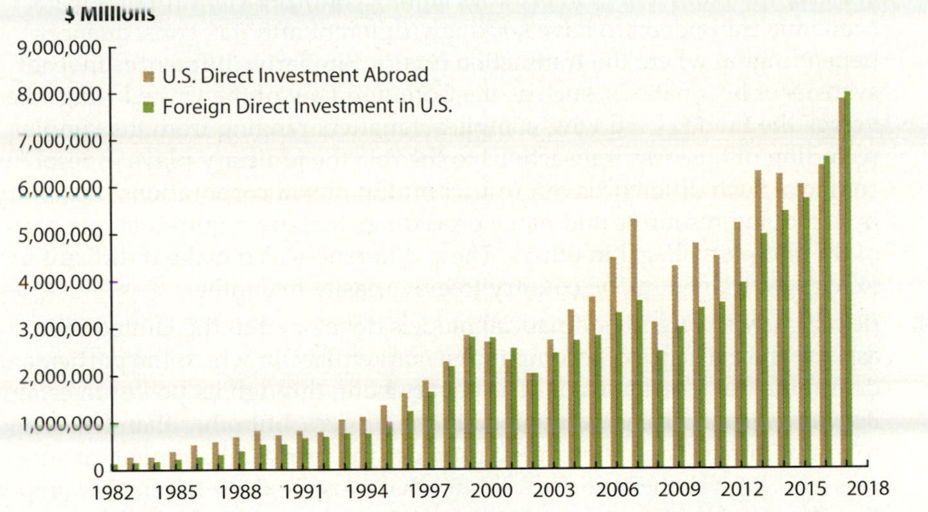

Sources: Elena L. Nguyen, "The International Investment Position of the United States at Yearend 2011," *Survey of Current Business*, vol. 92, no. 7 (July 2012), pp. 9–18; "Direct Investment Positions: Country and Industry Detail," Bureau of Economic Analysis, U.S. Department of Commerce, *Survey of Current Business*, various issues for July 2014, July 2015, July 2016, and July 2017; and "Table 2.1. U.S. Direct Investment Positions at the End of the Period," Bureau of Economic Analysis, U.S. Department of Commerce, *Survey of Current Business* (https://apps.bea.gov/scb/2018/07-july/pdf/0718-international-investment-position-tables.pdf), July 2018.

SelfTest

What is a multinational corporation?

Why do companies "go global"?

Discuss the following statement: The United States is not immune to the influence of foreign corporations over U.S. economic and political policies.

17-2 Multinational versus Domestic Financial Management

In theory, the concepts and procedures discussed in the first 16 chapters are valid for both domestic and multinational operations. However, some additional factors need to be considered when firms operate globally. Five of these factors are listed here:

1. *Different currency denominations.* Cash flows in various parts of a multinational corporate system will be denominated in different currencies. Hence, exchange rates must be included in all financial analyses.
2. *Political risk.* Nations are free to place constraints on the transfer or use of corporate resources, and they can change regulations and tax rules at any time. They can even expropriate assets within their boundaries. Therefore, political risks can take on many forms. Of course, political risks are present for companies operating in a single country. But for multinational firms, political risks exist in various forms from country to country, and they must be addressed explicitly in any financial analysis.

3. *Economic and legal ramifications.* Each country has its own unique economic and legal systems, and these differences can cause significant problems when a corporation tries to coordinate and control its worldwide operations. For example, differences in tax laws among countries can cause a given economic transaction to have strikingly different after-tax consequences depending on where the transaction occurs. Similarly, differences in legal systems of host nations, such as the Common Law of the United Kingdom versus the French Civil Law, complicate matters ranging from the simple recording of business transactions to the role the judiciary plays in resolving conflicts. Such differences can restrict multinational corporations' flexibility in deploying resources and make procedures that are required in one part of the company illegal in others. These differences also make it difficult for executives trained in one country to move easily to another.
4. *Role of governments.* Most financial models developed in the United States assume the existence of a competitive marketplace in which the participants determine the terms of trade. The government, through its power to establish basic ground rules, is involved in the process, but other than taxes, its role is minimal. Thus, the market provides the primary barometer of success, and it gives the best clues about what must be done to remain competitive. This view of the process is reasonably correct for the United States and Western Europe, but it does not accurately describe the situation in the rest of the world. Although market imperfections can complicate the decision process, they can also be valuable to the extent that they can be overcome by one firm but still serve as barriers to entry by competitors. Frequently, the terms under which companies compete, the actions that must be taken or avoided, and the terms of trade on various transactions are determined not in the marketplace, but by direct negotiation between host governments and multinational enterprises. This is essentially a political process, and it must be treated as such. Thus, traditional financial models have to be recast to include political and other noneconomic aspects of the decision.
5. *Language and cultural differences.* The ability to communicate is critical in all business transactions. In this regard, U.S. citizens are often at a disadvantage because they generally are fluent only in English. On the other hand, European and Japanese businesspeople are usually fluent in several languages, including English. At the same time, even within geographic regions that are considered relatively homogenous, different countries have unique cultural heritages that shape values and influence the conduct of business. Multinational corporations find that matters such as defining the appropriate goals of the firm, attitudes toward risk, performance evaluation and compensation systems, interactions with employees, and the ability to curtail unprofitable operations vary dramatically from one country to the next.

These five factors complicate financial management and increase the risks that multinational firms face. However, the prospects for high returns and other factors make it worthwhile for firms to accept these risks and learn how to manage them.

Self*Test*

Identify and briefly discuss five major factors that complicate financial management in multinational firms.

17-3 The International Monetary System

Every nation has a monetary system and a monetary authority. In the United States, the Federal Reserve is the monetary authority; its task is to limit inflation while promoting economic stability and growth. If countries are to trade with one another, some sort of system must be designed to facilitate payments between nations. The **international monetary system** is the framework within which exchange rates are determined, and it ties global currency, money, capital, real estate, commodity, and real asset markets into a network of institutions and instruments regulated by intergovernmental agreements and driven by each country's unique political and economic objectives.[5]

International Monetary System
The framework within which exchange rates are determined. It is the blueprint for international trade and capital flows.

17-3A INTERNATIONAL MONETARY TERMINOLOGY

In a discussion of the international monetary system, it is useful to begin by introducing some important concepts and terminology:

Exchange Rate
The number of units of a given currency that can be purchased for one unit of another currency.

1. An **exchange rate** is the price of one country's currency in terms of another country's currency. For example, on Thursday, August 30, 2018, one U.S. dollar would buy 0.7687 British pound, 0.8569 euro, or 1.2984 Canadian dollars.
2. A *spot exchange rate* is the quoted price for a unit of foreign currency to be delivered "on the spot" or within a very short period of time. The pound rate quoted, £0.7687/$, is a spot rate as of the close of business on August 30, 2018.
3. A *forward exchange rate* is the quoted price for a unit of foreign currency to be delivered at a specified date in the future. If today was August 30, 2018, and we wanted to know how many pounds we could expect to receive for a dollar on February 26, 2019, we would look at the 6-month forward rate, which was £0.7623/$ versus the £0.7687/$ spot rate. Thus, the dollar is expected to *depreciate* relative to the British pound during the next 6 months. Note also that the *forward exchange contract* on August 30 would lock in this exchange rate but no money would change hands until February 26, 2019. The spot rate on February 26 might be quite different from £0.7623, in which case we would have a profit or a loss on the forward purchase.
4. A *fixed exchange rate* for a currency is set by the government and is allowed to fluctuate only slightly (if at all) around the desired rate, which is called the *par value.* For example, Belize has fixed the exchange rate for the Belizean dollar at BZD 2.00/$1, and it has maintained this fixed rate since 1978.
5. A *floating or flexible exchange rate* is not regulated by the government, so supply and demand in the market determine the currency's value. The U.S. dollar and the euro are examples of free-floating currencies. If U.S. customers are importing more goods from Europe than they are exporting to Europe, they will have to make net purchases of euros and sales of dollars, which will cause the euro to appreciate relative to the dollar. Note, though,

For a listing of world currencies, currency symbols, and their regimes, go to the University of British Columbia Sauder School of Business Pacific Exchange Rate Service website, ***fx.sauder.ubc.ca****.*

[5]For a comprehensive history of the international monetary system and details of how it has evolved, consult one of the many economics books on the subject, including Robert Carbaugh, *International Economics*, 16th edition (Mason, OH: Cengage Learning, 2017); Mordechai Kreinin, *International Economics: A Policy Approach*, 10th edition (Mason, OH: South-Western/Thomson Learning, 2006); Beth V. Yarbrough and Robert M. Yarbrough, *The World Economy: International Trade*, 7th edition (Mason, OH: South-Western/Thomson Learning, 2006); and Joseph P. Daniels and David D. VanHoose, *Global Economic Issues and Policies*, 4th edition (London: Routledge, 2018).

that central banks do intervene in the market from time to time to nudge exchange rates up or down, even though they basically float.

6. *Devaluation* or *revaluation of a currency* is the technical term referring to the decrease or increase in the stated par value of a currency whose value is fixed. This decision is made by the government, usually without warning. For example, on July 21, 2005, the Chinese government suddenly announced that it was revaluing the yuan to make it 2.1% stronger against the U.S. dollar. (The new exchange rate was CNY 8.1097/$.) Even though it was widely believed that the yuan was significantly undervalued, this revaluation caught many by surprise because the exchange rate had been pegged at a fixed rate of CNY 8.2781/$ for nearly a decade. Just as importantly, on that date, the Chinese government abandoned the strict peg to the U.S. dollar and instead adopted a more flexible system where the yuan is now linked to a basket of trade-weighted international currencies including the dollar. Over the next 10 years, the yuan steadily appreciated relative to the U.S. dollar. During this time, the Chinese government also announced that it would gradually increase the flexibility of the exchange rate. On May 29, 2015, the exchange rate was CNY 6.2004/$; so, at that point in time, it cost 23.5% fewer yuan to buy a dollar than it did on July 21, 2005. However, just two and a half months later, the Chinese government stunned the markets when it announced over a 2-day period, a 3.5% devaluation in the Chinese currency. A few days after this devaluation, which was designed to offset weakening growth and to help bolster the collapsing Chinese stock market, the exchange rate stood at CNY 6.3948/$. China's central bank continues to manipulate the yuan's exchange rate. On July 26, 2018, the IMF mission chief for China, James Daniel, stated that the Chinese yuan is fairly valued despite recent declines against the dollar due to an escalating trade war between the United States and China. The recent fluctuations in the value of the yuan are to be expected from a flexible exchange rate.[6] On August 30, 2018, the exchange rate for the yuan was CNY 6.8448/$.
7. *Depreciation* or *appreciation of a currency* refers to a decrease or increase, respectively, in the foreign exchange value of a floating currency. These changes are caused by market forces rather than by governments.

17-3B CURRENT MONETARY ARRANGEMENTS

At the most basic level, we can divide currency regimes into two broad groups: floating rates and fixed rates. Within the two regimes, there are gradations among subregimes in terms of how rigidly they adhere to the basic positions. Looking first at the floating-rate category, the two main subgroups are as follows:

Freely Floating Regime
Occurs when the exchange rate is determined by supply and demand for the currency.

1. *Freely floating.* Here the exchange rate is determined by the supply and demand for the currency. Under a **freely floating regime**, governments may occasionally intervene in the market to buy or sell their currency to stabilize fluctuations, but they do not attempt to alter the absolute level of the rate. This policy exists at one end of the continuum of exchange-rate regimes. For example, the currencies of Australia, Brazil, and the Philippines, among many others, are allowed to float with a minimum of intervention.
2. *Managed floating.* Here there is significant government intervention to manage the exchange rate by manipulating the currency's supply and demand. For example, the governments of Colombia, Israel, and Poland manage their

[6]Huileng Tan, "The Chinese Yuan Is 'Fairly Valued' Despite Recent Weakening, Says IMF Mission Chief," *CNBC* (www.cnbc.com), July 26, 2018.

BREXIT SHAKES EUROPE

U.K. voters surprised many observers when they voted to leave the European Union (EU) in June 2016. Britain had been part of the European Community since 1973, and over the past 40 years, many have continually debated the wisdom of the United Kingdom linking itself to Europe. These tensions have notably accelerated in recent years because of the lingering debt crisis in many European countries, complaints about regulations imposed by EU leaders in Brussels, and a massive inflow of new immigrants and refugees into the European continent.

Former U.K. Prime Minister David Cameron was a strong proponent of Britain remaining within the EU. However, in the face of on-going pressure, he agreed to let the voters ultimately decide this issue, and he announced in February 2016 that a referendum would take place 4 months later in June. Despite polls that showed the vote to be close, most analysts and most of the "smart money" betting on the outcome assumed that the voters would ultimately decide to remain within the EU. These assumptions turned out to be wrong, when the "leave" forces promoting Britain's exit from the EU (Brexit) earned a narrow victory in the June referendum. Their surprise victory stunned many in the United Kingdom, Europe, and the United States. Indeed, many have suggested that the same global forces that led to Brexit also led to President Trump's surprise victory later that November.

Immediately after the Brexit vote, the British pound fell roughly 12% against the U.S. dollar and 10% against the euro. Shortly thereafter, Prime Minister Cameron resigned and was replaced by Theresa May, a Brexit proponent. Interestingly, the British stock market (the FTSE 100) has rallied since the Brexit vote, and so far, the economic impact of the vote has not been dramatic.

That said, a lot of hard work remains as the United Kingdom works to negotiate the actual details of the terms of its leaving the EU. Some have promoted a clean break, or "hard exit," while others have promoted a "soft exit." Complicating matters is the fact that EU leaders have shown little interest in accommodating U.K. leaders and have pushed Britain to accelerate its withdrawal. To be sure, it will be interesting to see how things ultimately play out both in Britain and continental Europe.

respective currency's float. Governments rarely reveal their target exchange rate levels when they use a **managed-float regime** because doing so would make it too easy for currency speculators to profit.

Most developed countries follow either a freely floating or a managed-float regime. A few developing countries do so as well, often reluctantly and as a result of a market that forces them to abandon a fixed-rate regime.

Types of fixed-exchange-rate regimes include the following:

1. *No local currency.* The most extreme position is for the country to have no local currency of its own, using another country's currency as its legal tender (such as the U.S. dollar in Ecuador and in the Turks and Caicos Islands) or belonging to a group of countries that shares a common currency (such as the euro). With this arrangement, the local government surrenders the ability to use exchange rates to tinker with its economy.
2. *Currency board arrangement.* Under a variation of the first subregime, a country technically has its own currency but commits to exchange it for a specified foreign money unit at a fixed exchange rate. This requires the country to impose domestic currency restrictions unless it has enough foreign currency reserves to cover all requested exchanges. This is called a **currency board arrangement**. Argentina had a currency board arrangement before its crisis of January 2002, when it was forced to devalue the peso and default on its debt.
3. *Fixed-peg arrangement.* In a **fixed-peg arrangement**, the country locks, or "pegs," its currency to another currency or basket of currencies at a fixed exchange rate. This allows the currency to vary only slightly from its desired rate, and if it moves outside the specified limits (often set at 1% of the target rate), its central bank intervenes to force the currency back within the limits. An example is China, where the yuan is no longer pegged to the U.S. dollar, but rather to a basket of trade-weighted international currencies. Additional examples include

Managed-Float Regime
Occurs when there is significant government intervention to control the exchange rate via manipulation of the currency's supply and demand.

Currency Board Arrangement
Occurs when a country has its own currency but commits to exchange it for a specified foreign money unit at a fixed exchange rate and legislates domestic currency restrictions, unless it has the foreign currency reserves to cover requested exchanges.

Fixed-Peg Arrangement
Occurs when a country locks its currency to a specific currency or basket of currencies at a fixed exchange rate.

Bhutan's ngultrum, which is pegged to the Indian rupee; the Falkland Islands's pound, which is pegged to the British pound sterling; and Barbados's dollar, which is pegged to the U.S. dollar. In an attempt to protect its economy from the European debt crisis, the Swiss franc was pegged to the euro on September 6, 2011. However, on January 15, 2015, the Swiss central bank abandoned this arrangement, citing that this policy was no longer needed.

Other variations have been used, and new ones are developed from time to time. A majority of the world's countries employ a system that includes a fixed-exchange rate along with occasional interventions. So while the most important currencies (as measured by volume of transactions) are allowed to float and the international monetary system is often called a floating regime, most currencies are partially fixed but occasionally are manipulated in some manner.

Self*Test*

What is the international monetary system?

What is the difference between spot and forward exchange rates?

What is the basic difference between floating and fixed exchange rates?

Differentiate between devaluation/revaluation of a currency and depreciation/ appreciation of a currency.

What are the two broad categories of the various currency regimes? What are the subgroups of those two broad categories?

17-4 Foreign Exchange Rate Quotations

For up-to-date currency quotations on the Web, visit two popular sites: ***bloomberg.com/markets/currencies*** *or* ***finance.yahoo.com/currency-investing****.*

Foreign exchange rate quotations can be found in *The Wall Street Journal* and in other leading print publications and on websites. Exchange rates are given two different ways. As shown in Table 17.1, which is an excerpt from the website of *The Wall Street Journal,* column 1 is the "USD equivalent" exchange rate, and column 2 is the "Currency per USD" exchange rate. For example, 1 Canadian dollar is worth (or can be exchanged for) 0.7702 U.S. dollar, or 1 U.S. dollar can buy 1.2984 Canadian dollars. Note that if the foreign exchange markets are in equilibrium, which is usually the case for the major traded currencies, the two quotations must be reciprocals of each other, as shown here for the Canadian dollar:

Canadian dollar: 1/0.7702 = 1.2984
1/1.2984 = 0.7702

17-4A CROSS RATES

Cross Rate
The exchange rate between any two currencies.

All of the exchange rates given in Table 17.1 are relative to the U.S. dollar. Suppose, though, that a German executive is flying to Tokyo on business. The exchange rate in which he or she is interested is not euros or yen per dollar—rather, the issue is how many yen can be purchased with a euro. This is called a **cross rate**, and it can be calculated from the following data from column 2 of Table 17.1:

	Spot Rate
Euro	€0.8569/$1
Yen	¥110.99/$1

Because the quotations have the same denominator—1 U.S. dollar—we can calculate the cross rate between these (and other) currencies by using the

TABLE 17.1

Sample Exchange Rates: Thursday, August 30, 2018

	Direct Quotation: U.S. Dollars Required to Buy One Unit of Foreign Currency (1)	Indirect Quotation: Number of Units of Foreign Currency per U.S. Dollar (2)
Australian dollar	0.7264	1.3767
Brazilian real	0.2409	4.1504
British pound	1.3009	0.7687
Canadian dollar	0.7702	1.2984
Chinese yuan	0.1461	6.8448
Danish krone	0.1565	6.3889
EMU euro	1.1670	0.8569
Hungarian forint	0.00357015	280.10
Israeli shekel	0.2767	3.6136
Japanese yen	0.00901	110.99
Mexican peso	0.0523	19.1133
South African rand	0.0679	14.7205
Swedish krona	0.1096	9.1200
Swiss franc	1.0317	0.9693
Venezuelan bolivar	0.00000403	248409.0001

Note: Column 2 equals 1.0 divided by column 1. However, rounding differences do occur.
Source: Adapted from *The Wall Street Journal* (www.wsj.com), August 30, 2018.

column 2 quotations. For our German national, the cross rates are found as follows:

$$\text{Euro/Yen exchange rate} = \frac{\text{Euro/\$}}{\text{Yen/\$}}$$

And when we cancel the dollar signs, we are left with the number of euros that 1 yen could purchase:

$$€0.8569/¥110.99 = €0.0077/¥$$

Alternatively, we could find the number of yen that 1 euro could buy:

$$\text{Yen/Euro exchange rate} = \frac{\text{Yen/\$}}{\text{Euro/\$}}$$

$$¥110.99/€0.8569 = ¥129.5250/€$$

Note that those two cross rates are reciprocals of each other.

Financial publications such as *The Wall Street Journal* and websites such as Bloomberg, Yahoo!, and www.wsj.com provide tables of key currency cross rates. Table 17.2 gives the table from *The Wall Street Journal* website for August 30, 2018. Notice that there may be slight differences when you calculate cross rates due to the rounding of individual quotations. Currency traders carry quotations out to 12 decimal places.

17-4B INTERBANK FOREIGN CURRENCY QUOTATIONS

The quotations from *The Wall Street Journal* given in Tables 17.1 and 17.2 are sufficient for many purposes. For other purposes, however, additional terminology and conventions are useful. There are two ways to state the exchange rate between two currencies, in either **American terms** or European. Accordingly, we need to designate

American Terms
The foreign exchange rate quotation that represents the number of American dollars that can be bought with one unit of local currency.

TABLE 17.2 Key Currency Cross Rates: Thursday, August 30, 2018

	USDollar (1)	Euro (2)	Pound (3)	SFranc (4)	Peso (5)	Yen (6)	CdnDlr (7)
Canada	1.2984	1.5151	1.6890	1.3395	0.0679	0.0117	—
Japan	110.9920	129.5221	144.3895	114.5074	5.8071	—	85.4870
Mexico	19.1133	22.3043	24.8645	19.7187	—	0.1722	14.7212
Switzerland	0.9693	1.1311	1.2610	—	0.0507	0.0087	0.7466
United Kingdom	0.7687	0.8970	—	0.7930	0.0402	0.0069	0.5921
Euro	0.8569	—	1.1148	0.8841	0.0448	0.0077	0.6600
United States	—	1.1670	1.3009	1.0317	0.0523	0.0090	0.7702

Note: Column 1 shows how many units of each foreign currency a U.S. dollar would buy, column 2 shows how many units a euro would buy, and so on for the other columns.

Source: Adapted from "Key Currency Cross Rates," *The Wall Street Journal* (www.wsj.com), August 30, 2018.

one of the currencies as the "home" currency and the other as the "foreign" currency. This designation is arbitrary. The *home* currency price of one unit of the *foreign* currency is called a **direct quotation**. Thus, to a person who considers the United States to be "home," American terms represent a direct quotation. On the other hand, the *foreign* currency price of one unit of the *home* currency is called an **indirect quotation**. European terms represent indirect quotations to people in the United States. Note that if the perspective changes and the "home" currency is no longer the U.S. dollar, the designations of direct and indirect will change. For the remainder of this chapter, unless specifically stated otherwise, we will assume that the United States is the "home" country and thus that the U.S. dollar is the home currency.

Direct Quotation
The home currency price of one unit of the foreign currency.

Indirect Quotation
The foreign currency price of one unit of the home currency.

Self*Test*

Explain the difference between direct and indirect quotations.

What is a cross rate?

Assume that today 1 Canadian dollar is worth 0.75 U.S. dollar. How many Canadian dollars would you receive for 1 U.S. dollar? **(1.333)**

Assume that 1 U.S. dollar can be exchanged for 105 Japanese yen or for 0.80 euro. What is the euro/yen exchange rate? **(€0.007619/¥)**

17-5 Trading in Foreign Exchange

Importers, exporters, tourists, and governments buy and sell currencies in the foreign exchange market. For example, when a U.S. trader imports automobiles from Japan, payment is probably made in Japanese yen. The importer buys yen (through its bank) in the foreign exchange market, much as one buys common stocks on the New York Stock Exchange or pork bellies on the Chicago Mercantile Exchange. However, whereas stock and commodity exchanges have organized trading floors, the foreign exchange market consists of a network of brokers and banks based in New York, London, Tokyo, and other financial centers. Most buy and sell orders are conducted by computer and telephone.[7]

[7]For a more detailed explanation of exchange rate determination and operations of the foreign exchange market, see Roy L. Crum, Eugene F. Brigham, and Joel F. Houston, *Fundamentals of International Finance* (Mason, OH: South-Western/Thomson Learning, 2005).

17-5A SPOT RATES AND FORWARD RATES

The exchange rates shown earlier in Tables 17.1 and 17.2 are known as **spot rates**, which means the rate paid for delivery of the currency "on the spot" or, in reality, no more than 2 days after the day of the trade. For most of the world's major currencies, it also is possible to buy (or sell) currencies for delivery at some agreed-upon future date, usually 30, 90, or 180 days from the day the transaction is negotiated. This rate is known as the **forward exchange rate**.

Spot Rates
Effective exchange rates of foreign currencies for delivery on (approximately) the current day.

Forward Exchange Rate
An agreed-upon price at which two currencies will be exchanged at some future date.

For example, suppose a U.S. firm must pay 500 million yen to a Japanese firm in 30 days and the current spot rate is 110.99 yen per dollar. Unless spot rates change, the U.S. firm will pay the Japanese firm the equivalent of $4.5049 million (500 million yen divided by 110.99 yen per dollar) in 30 days. But if the spot rate falls to 109 yen per dollar, for example, the U.S. firm will have to pay the equivalent of $4.5872 million. The treasurer of the U.S. firm can avoid this risk by entering into a 30-day forward exchange contract. This contract promises delivery of yen to the U.S. firm in 30 days at a guaranteed price of 110.76 yen per dollar. No cash changes hands at the time the treasurer signs the forward contract, although the U.S. firm might have to put down some collateral as a guarantee against default. Because the firm can use an interest-bearing instrument for the collateral, though, this requirement is not costly. The counterparty to the forward contract must deliver the yen to the U.S. firm in 30 days, and the U.S. firm is obligated to purchase the 500 million yen at the previously agreed-upon rate of 110.76 yen per dollar. Therefore, the treasurer of the U.S. firm is able to lock in a payment equivalent to $4.5143 million no matter what happens to spot rates. This technique is called "hedging."

Refer to ***www.investing.com/tools/forward-rates-calculator*** *that allows you to calculate the forward rates for different time periods and different currencies.*

Forward rates for 30-, 90-, and 180-day delivery, along with the current spot rates for some commonly traded currencies, are given in Table 17.3. If we can obtain *more* of the foreign currency for a dollar in the forward market than in the spot market, the forward currency is less valuable than the spot currency, and the forward currency is said to be selling at a **discount**. Conversely, if we can obtain less of the foreign currency for a dollar in the forward market than in the spot market, the forward currency is more valuable than the spot currency, and

Discount on Forward Rate
The situation when the spot rate is less than the forward rate.

TABLE 17.3

Selected Spot and Forward Exchange Rates (Number of Units of Foreign Currency per U.S. Dollar), Thursday, August 30, 2018

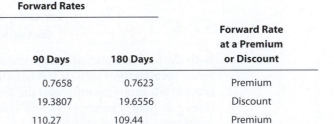

		Forward Rates			
	Spot Rate	**30 Days**	**90 Days**	**180 Days**	**Forward Rate at a Premium or Discount**
British pound	0.7687	0.7678	0.7658	0.7623	Premium
Mexican peso	19.1133	19.2050	19.3807	19.6556	Discount
Japanese yen	110.99	110.76	110.27	109.44	Premium
Swiss franc	0.9693	0.9668	0.9616	0.9530	Premium

Notes:

1. These are representative quotes as provided by a sample of New York banks. Forward rates for other currencies and for other lengths of time can often be negotiated.
2. When it takes more units of a foreign currency to buy 1 dollar in the future, the value of the foreign currency is less in the forward market than in the spot market, so the forward rate is at a discount to the spot rate. Likewise, when it takes less units of a foreign currency to buy 1 dollar in the future, the value of the foreign currency is more in the forward market than in the spot market, so the forward rate is at a premium to the spot rate.

Source: Adapted from "Forward Rates," Investing.com, https://www.investing.com/rates-bonds/forward-rates, August 30, 2018.

Premium on Forward Rate
The situation when the spot rate is greater than the forward rate.

the forward currency is said to be selling at a **premium**. Thus, because a dollar buys *fewer* pounds, yen, and Swiss francs in the forward market than in the spot market, the forward pounds, yen, and Swiss francs are selling at a premium. On the other hand, a dollar would buy more Mexican pesos in the forward market than in the spot market, so the forward Mexican pesos are selling at a discount.

Self*Test*

Explain what it means for a forward currency to sell at a discount and at a premium.

Suppose a U.S. firm must pay 200 million Swiss francs to a Swiss firm in 90 days. Briefly explain how the firm would use forward exchange rates to "lock in" the price of the payable due in 90 days.

Using data in Table 17.3, if a U.S. firm entered into a 90-day forward contract, how many dollars would be required to honor the 200 million Swiss franc obligation when it is due? **($207,986,689)**

17-6 Interest Rate Parity

Interest Rate Parity
Specifies that investors should expect to earn the same return in all countries after adjusting for risk.

Market forces determine whether a currency sells at a forward premium or discount, and the general relationship between spot and forward exchange rates is specified by a concept called "interest rate parity." **Interest rate parity** holds that investors should earn the same return on interest-bearing investments in all countries after adjusting for risk. It recognizes that when you invest in a country other than your home country, you are affected by two forces—returns on the investment itself and changes in the exchange rate. It follows that your overall return will be higher than the investment's stated return if the currency in which your investment is denominated appreciates relative to your home currency. Likewise, your overall return will be lower if the foreign currency you receive declines in value.

The relationship between spot and forward exchange rates and interest rates, which is known as interest rate parity, is expressed in the following equation:

$$\frac{\text{Forward exchange rate}}{\text{Spot exchange rate}} = \frac{(1 + r_h)}{(1 + r_f)}$$

Both the forward and spot rates are expressed in terms of the amount of home currency received per unit of foreign currency, and r_h and r_f are the periodic interest rates in the home country and the foreign country, respectively. If this relationship does not hold, currency traders will buy and sell currencies—that is, engage in *arbitrage*—until it does hold.

To illustrate interest rate parity, consider the case of a U.S. investor who can buy default-free 90-day Japanese bonds that promise a 4% nominal return. The 90-day interest rate, r_f, is 4%/4 = 1% because 90 days is one-fourth of a 360-day year. Assume also that the spot exchange rate is $0.009010, which means that you can exchange 0.009010 dollar for 1 yen, or 110.99 yen per dollar. Finally, assume that the 90-day forward exchange rate is $0.009069, which means that you can exchange 1 yen for 0.009069 dollar, or receive 110.27 yen per dollar exchanged, 90 days from now.

The U.S. investor can receive a 4% annualized return denominated in yen, but if he or she ultimately wants to consume goods in the United States, those yen must be converted to dollars. The dollar return on the investment depends, therefore, on what happens to exchange rates over the next 3 months. However, the investor can lock in the dollar return by selling the foreign currency in the forward market. For example, the investor can do the following simultaneously:

- Convert $1,000 to 110,990 yen in the spot market.
- Invest the 110,990 yen in 90-day Japanese bonds that have a 4% annualized return or a 1% quarterly return and hence will pay (110,990)(1.01) = 112,099.90 yen in 90 days.
- Agree today to exchange the 112,099.90 yen 90 days from now at the 90-day forward exchange rate of 110.27 yen per dollar, for a total of $1,016.59.

This investment, therefore, has an expected 90-day return of $16.59/$1,000 = 1.659%, which translates into a nominal return of 4(1.659%) = 6.64%. In this case, 4% of the expected 6.64% return is coming from the bond itself, and 2.64% arises because the market believes the yen will strengthen relative to the dollar. Note that by locking in the forward rate today, the investor has eliminated any exchange rate risk. And because the Japanese bond is assumed to be default-free, the investor is assured of earning a 6.64% dollar return.

Interest rate parity implies that an investment in the United States with the same risk as this Japanese bond should have an annual return of 6.64%. Solving for r_h in the parity equation, we indeed find that the predicted annual interest rate in the United States is 6.64%.

Interest rate parity shows why a particular currency might be at a forward premium or discount. Note that a currency is at a forward premium whenever domestic interest rates are higher than foreign interest rates. Discounts will prevail if domestic interest rates are lower than foreign interest rates. If these conditions do not hold, arbitrage will soon force interest rates back to parity.

Indeed, a recent study found that under normal economic conditions, interest rate parity holds remarkably well. However, significant deviations from parity did exist during the 2007–2009 financial crisis, when the lack of liquidity made it more difficult to arbitrage.[8]

quick question

QUESTION:

The nominal annual interest rate on 6-month U.S. Treasuries is 2% (i.e., the semiannual return is 1.00%). The spot rate of the British pound is $1.3009 (£0.7687 per U.S. dollar) and the 6-month forward rate of the British pound is $1.3118 (£0.7623 per U.S. dollar). If interest rate parity holds, what is the nominal annual interest rate on default-free 6-month British bonds?

ANSWER:

The interest rate parity equation is

$$\frac{\text{Forward exchange rate}}{\text{Spot exchange rate}} = \frac{(1 + r_h)}{(1 + r_f)}$$

(Continued)

[8]Tommaso Mancini-Griffoli and Angelo Ranaldo, "Limits to Arbitrage during the Crisis: Funding Liquidity Constraints and Covered Interest Parity," February 4, 2011. Available at Social Science Research Network: papers.ssrn.com/abstract=1569504.

Substituting the data given in the problem into the interest parity equation, we have

$$\frac{\$1.3118}{\$1.3009} = \frac{1.01}{(1 + r_f)}$$

This equation then reduces to the following:

$$1.008379 = \frac{1.01}{(1 + r_f)}$$

$$1.008379 + 1.008379r_f = 1.01$$

$$r_f = 0.001608$$

If interest rate parity holds, then the nominal annual interest rate on a default-free 6-month British bond would be 2 × 0.1608% = **0.3215%**.

To see the intuition behind this concept, assume that you have $1,000 and will invest in a default-free 6-month British bond. Here's what you would do:

- Convert $1,000 to £768.70 in the spot market.
- Invest the £768.70 in 6-month British bonds that have a 0.3215% nominal annual return or a 0.1608% semiannual return. They will pay (£768.70)(1.001608) = £769.94 in 6 months.
- Agree today to exchange the £769.94 six months from now at the 6-month forward exchange rate of £0.7623 per U.S. dollar, for a total of $1,010.02(£769.94/£0.7623).

The investment has an expected 6-month return of $10.02/$1,000 = 1.002% ≈ 1.00%, which translates into a nominal annual return of 2(1.00%) ≈ 2.0%. This is the identical rate that 6-month U.S. Treasuries are earning, so interest rate parity holds. (Note that there is a small rounding error in this calculation.)

Self*Test*

What is interest rate parity?

Assume that interest rate parity holds. When a currency trades at a forward premium, what does that imply about domestic rates relative to foreign interest rates? When a currency trades at a forward discount?

Assume that 90-day U.S. securities have a 3.5% annualized interest rate, whereas 90-day Canadian securities have a 4% annualized interest rate. In the spot market, 1 U.S. dollar can be exchanged for 1.4 Canadian dollars. If interest rate parity holds, what is the 90-day forward exchange rate between U.S. and Canadian dollars? **($0.7134/C$ or C$1.40173/$)**

On the basis of your answer to the previous question, is the Canadian dollar selling at a premium or discount on the forward rate?

17-7 Purchasing Power Parity

We have discussed exchange rates in some detail, and we have considered the relationship between spot and forward exchange rates. However, we have not yet addressed this fundamental question: What determines the spot level of exchange rates in each country? Although exchange rates are influenced by a multitude of factors that are difficult to predict, particularly on a day-to-day basis, over the long run, market forces work to ensure that similar goods sell for similar prices in different countries after exchange rates are taken into account. This relationship is known as "purchasing power parity."

Purchasing power parity (PPP), sometimes referred to as the *law of one price*, implies that the level of exchange rates adjusts so as to cause identical goods to cost the same amount in different countries. For example, if a pair of tennis shoes costs $100 in the United States and 50 pounds in the United Kingdom, PPP implies that the exchange rate will be $2 per pound. Consumers can purchase the shoes in the United Kingdom for 50 pounds, or they can exchange their 50 pounds for $100 and purchase the same shoes in the United States at the same effective cost, assuming no transactions or transportation costs. The equation for purchasing power parity is shown here:

Purchasing Power Parity (PPP)
The relationship in which the same products cost roughly the same amount in different countries after taking into account the exchange rate.

$$P_h = (P_f)(\text{Spot rate})$$

or

$$\text{Spot rate} = \frac{P_h}{P_f}$$

Where:

P_h = Price of the good in the home country ($100, assuming the United States is the home country)

P_f = Price of the good in the foreign country (50 pounds)

Note that the spot market exchange rate is expressed as the number of units of home currency that can be exchanged for one unit of foreign currency ($2 per pound).

quick question

QUESTION:

A U.S. consumer observes that a golf club costs $200. Currently in the spot market, 1 euro can be exchanged for $1.1670. If purchasing power parity (PPP) holds, how many euros should you expect to pay for the same golf club in Europe?

ANSWER:

From the PPP equation, we know that $P_h = (P_f)(\text{Spot rate})$. In this example, we know that the price in the home market is $200 ($P_h$ = $200). The spot rate is $1.1670 (i.e., 1euro = $1.1670, or $1 equals €0.8569). According to purchasing power parity, it follows that the price of the golf club in the European market should be **€171.3796**:

$$P_h = (P_f)(\text{Spot rate})$$
$$\$200 = P_f(\$1.1670)$$
$$P_f = \frac{\$200}{\$1.1670}$$
$$P_f = \textbf{€171.3796}$$

To further understand this, assume that the U.S. consumer has $200. She could use the $200 to buy the golf club in the U.S. market, or she could exchange her $200 for €171.3796. If the golf club cost €171.3796, then parity would hold. If instead the golf club sold for less than €171.3796, it would make sense to buy the golf club in Europe, whereas if the golf club sold for more than €171.3796, it would make sense to buy the golf club in the United States.

HUNGRY FOR A BIG MAC? GO TO EGYPT

Purchasing power parity (PPP) implies that the same product will sell for the same price in every country after adjusting for current exchange rates. One problem when testing to see if PPP holds is that it assumes that goods consumed in different countries are of the same quality. For example, if you find that a product is more expensive in Switzerland than it is in Canada, one explanation is that PPP fails to hold; however, another explanation is that the product sold in Switzerland is of a higher quality and therefore deserves a higher price.

One way to test for PPP is to find goods that have the same quality worldwide. With this in mind, *The Economist* magazine occasionally compares the prices of a well-known good whose quality is the same in 120 different countries: the McDonald's Big Mac hamburger.

The tables shown in panels a and b on the next page provide information collected during 2018. The panel a table gives the price of a Big Mac in each country's local currency and the actual dollar exchange rate when these data were collected. In panel b, the first numeric column calculates the price of the Big Mac in terms of the U.S. dollar—this is obtained by dividing the local price by the actual exchange rate at that time. For example, a Big Mac costs 42.0 kroner in Oslo, which is shown in panel a. Given an exchange rate of 8.04 kroner per dollar (as shown in panel a), this implies that the dollar price of a Big Mac is 42.0 kroner/8.04 kroner per dollar = \$5.22, shown in panel b.

The second numeric column in panel b backs out the implied exchange rate that would hold under PPP. This is obtained by dividing the price of the Big Mac in each local currency by its U.S. price. For example, as shown in panel a, a Big Mac costs 130 rubles in Russia and \$5.51 in the United States. If PPP holds, the exchange rate should be approximately 23.59 rubles per dollar (130 rubles/\$5.51), which is shown in panel b.

Comparing the implied exchange rate (shown in panel b) to the actual exchange rate (shown in panel a), we see the extent to which the local currency is under- or overvalued relative to the dollar. Given that the actual exchange rate at the time was 62.14 rubles per dollar, this rate implies that the ruble was 62% undervalued, which is shown in the next-to-last column of panel b.

The last two columns in panel b indicate the extent to which each currency is under- or overvalued relative to the dollar as suggested by the "raw" Big Mac index and as adjusted by gross domestic product (GDP) per person. A "cheap" burger doesn't necessarily indicate that a currency is undervalued relative to the dollar. One would expect average prices in poor countries to be low because labor costs are lower than in the richer industrialized countries. Researchers did a regression analysis between Big Mac prices and GDP per person and found that the difference between the price predicted (from the regression) for each country and its actual price gave a better indication of whether the currency was under- or overvalued relative to the dollar than the raw "Big Mac" Index. The final column in panel b gives the adjusted valuation from the regression analysis. Although the "raw" Big Mac Index suggested that the Russian ruble is undervalued by 62%, the regression results suggest that the ruble is undervalued by 36.6%.

The evidence suggests that strict PPP does not hold, but recent research suggests that the Big Mac test may shed some insights about where exchange rates are headed. The average price of a Big Mac in the European Monetary Union (EMU) is €4.04. This implies that the euro's PPP is €0.73; therefore, at its current rate of €0.85, the euro is undervalued by just over 14%. However, when the regression results are considered, the euro is overvalued by 5.1%. The U.S. dollar has strengthened—all currencies are undervalued relative to the dollar (from the raw Big Mac index) except the currencies of Sweden and Switzerland. When adjusted for GDP, the currencies of Brazil, Colombia, Chile, and Sweden are significantly overvalued. When adjusted for GDP, the currencies of Hong Kong, Taiwan, Egypt, Russia, Malaysia, and Turkey are significantly undervalued relative to the dollar. Consumers in these countries will find that domestic goods are less expensive than foreign imports.

One last benefit of the Big Mac test is that it tells us the cheapest places to find a Big Mac. If we look at the raw "Big Mac Index" numbers, the "cheapest" burger is in Egypt, while the most expensive burger is in Switzerland.

Panel a		Big Mac Prices in Local Currency	Actual Dollar Exchange Rate, 7/18	Panel b	Big Mac Prices in Dollars[b]	Implied PPP[c] of the Dollar	Under (−)/Over (+) Valuation against the Dollar, %: Raw Index	Under (−)/Over (+) Valuation against the Dollar, %: Adjusted for GDP per Person
United States[a]	$	5.51	—	United States[a]	$5.51	—	—	—
Argentina	Peso	75	27.73	Argentina	2.71	13.61	−50.9	−22.2
Australia	A$	6.05	1.34	Australia	4.52	1.10	−18.1	−15.4
Brazil	Real	16.9	3.84	Brazil	4.40	3.07	−20.1	34.7
Britain	£	3.19	0.75	Britain	4.23	0.58	−23.2	−8.4
Canada	C$	6.65	1.31	Canada	5.07	1.21	−8.0	4.3
Chile	Peso	2640	651.73	Chile	4.05	479.13	−26.5	15.6
China	Yuan	20.5	6.62	China	3.10	3.72	−43.8	−3.6
Colombia	Peso	11900	2874.07	Colombia	4.14	2,159.71	−24.9	33.3
Costa Rica	Colon	2290	567.80	Costa Rica	4.03	415.61	−26.8	NA
Czech Republic	Koruna	75	22.06	Czech Republic	3.40	13.61	−38.3	−8.9
Denmark	DKr	30	6.36	Denmark	4.72	5.44	−14.4	−12.2
Egypt	Pound	31.37	17.91	Egypt	1.75	5.69	−68.2	−40.3
Euro area	€	4.04	0.85	Euro area	4.74[d]	0.73	−14.1	5.1
Hong Kong	HK$	20	7.85	Hong Kong	2.55	3.63	−53.8	−48.0
Hungary	Forint	850	276.43	Hungary	3.07	154.26	−44.2	−12.7
India	Rupee	173	68.83	India	2.51	31.40	−54.4	−13.7
Indonesia	Rupiah	31500	14360.00	Indonesia	2.19	5,716.88	−60.2	−26.8
Israel	Shekel	17	3.63	Israel	4.68	3.09	−15.1	0.8
Japan	¥	390	111.25	Japan	3.51	70.78	−36.4	−23.1
Malaysia	M$	8.45	4.02	Malaysia	2.10	1.53	−61.9	−35.7
Mexico	Peso	49	19.05	Mexico	2.57	8.89	−53.3	−20.7
New Zealand	NZ	6.2	1.46	New Zealand	4.23	1.13	−23.2	−9.9
Norway	Kroner	42	8.04	Norway	5.22	7.62	−5.2	−15.9
Pakistan	Rupee	375	121.49	Pakistan	3.09	68.06	−44.0	6.7
Peru	Sol	10.5	3.27	Peru	3.21	1.91	−41.8	2.6
Philippines	Peso	140	53.49	Philippines	2.62	25.41	−52.5	−11.5
Poland	Zloty	10.1	3.69	Poland	2.74	1.83	−50.3	−20.5
Russia	Rouble	130	62.14	Russia	2.09	23.59	−62.0	−36.6
Saudi Arabia	Riyal	12	3.75	Saudi Arabia	3.20	2.18	−41.9	−15.3
Singapore	S$	5.8	1.36	Singapore	4.28	1.05	−22.4	−21.2
South Africa	Rand	31	13.36	South Africa	2.32	5.63	−57.9	−25.2
South Korea	Won	4500	1116.00	South Korea	4.03	816.70	−26.8	−3.4
Sri Lanka	Rupee	580	159.27	Sri Lanka	3.64	105.26	−33.9	NA
Sweden	SKr	51	8.75	Sweden	5.83	9.26	5.8	11.5
Switzerland	SFr	6.5	0.99	Switzerland	6.54	1.18	18.8	1.3
Taiwan	NT$	69	30.37	Taiwan	2.27	12.52	−58.8	−42.2
Thailand	Baht	119	33.17	Thailand	3.59	21.60	−34.9	15.0
Turkey	Lira	10.75	4.71	Turkey	2.28	1.95	−58.5	−30.7
UAE	Dirham	14	3.67	UAE	3.81	2.54	−30.8	NA
Ukraine	Hryvnia	50	26.20	Ukraine	1.91	9.07	−65.4	NA
Uruguay	Peso	140	31.31	Uruguay	4.47	25.41	−18.8	NA

Notes:
[a]Average of New York, Chicago, San Francisco, and Atlanta.
[b]At current exchange rate.
[c]Purchasing power parity: Local price divided by price in the United States.
[d]Weighted average of member countries.
Source: "Investors Are Gorging on American Assets," *The Economist* (www.economist.com), July 12, 2018.

PPP assumes that market forces will eliminate situations in which the same product sells at a different price overseas. For example, if the tennis shoes cost $90 in the United States, trading companies could purchase them in the United States for $90, sell them for 50 pounds in the United Kingdom, exchange the 50 pounds for $100 in the foreign exchange market, and earn a profit of $10 on every pair of shoes. Ultimately, this trading activity would increase the demand for tennis shoes in the United States and thus raise P_h, increase the supply of tennis shoes in the United Kingdom and thus reduce P_f, and increase the demand for dollars in the foreign exchange market and thus reduce the spot rate. Each of those actions works to restore PPP.

Note that PPP assumes that there are no transportation or transactions costs (or import restrictions) that would limit the ability to ship goods between countries. In many cases, these assumptions are incorrect, which explains why PPP is often violated. An additional complication, when empirically testing to see whether PPP holds, is that products in different countries are rarely identical. Frequently, there are real or perceived differences in quality, which can lead to price differences in different countries.

Still, the concepts of interest rate parity and purchasing power parity are critically important to those engaged in international activities. Companies and investors must anticipate changes in interest rates, inflation, and exchange rates, and they often try to hedge the risks of adverse movements in those factors. The parity relationships are extremely useful when anticipating future conditions.

Self*Test*

What is purchasing power parity?

A television set sells for 3,000 U.S. dollars. In the spot market, $1 = 111 Japanese yen. If purchasing power parity holds, what should be the price (in yen) of the same television set in Japan? **(¥333,000)**

Price differences in "similar" products in different countries often exist. What can explain those differences?

17-8 Inflation, Interest Rates, and Exchange Rates

Relative inflation rates, or the rates of inflation in foreign countries compared with that in the home country, have two key implications for multinational firms: (1) relative inflation rates influence future production costs at home and abroad and (2) inflation has an important effect on relative interest rates and exchange rates. Both of those factors influence multinational corporations' financing decisions and the profitability of foreign investments.

The currencies of countries with higher inflation rates than the U.S. inflation rate, by definition, *depreciate* over time against the dollar. Countries in which this has occurred include Mexico and all the South American nations. On the other hand, Switzerland has had less inflation than the United States, so the Swiss franc has *appreciated* against the dollar. *In fact, a foreign currency will, on average, depreciate or appreciate at a percentage rate approximately equal to the amount by which its inflation rate is over or under the U.S. inflation rate.*

Relative inflation also affects interest rates. Indeed, the interest rate in any country is largely determined by its inflation rate. So countries with higher inflation rates than the U.S. inflation rate also have higher interest rates, and the reverse is true for countries with lower inflation rates.

It is tempting for a multinational corporation to borrow in countries with the lowest interest rates. However, this is not always a good strategy. Suppose, for example, that interest rates in Switzerland are lower than those in the United States because of Switzerland's lower inflation rate. A U.S. multinational firm could therefore reduce its interest expense by borrowing in Switzerland. However, because of relative inflation rates, the Swiss franc will probably appreciate in the future, causing the dollar cost of annual interest and principal payments on Swiss debt to rise over time. Thus, *the lower interest rate could be more than offset by losses from currency appreciation.* Similarly, multinational corporations should not necessarily avoid borrowing in a country such as Brazil, where interest rates have been very high, because future depreciation of the Brazilian real could make such borrowing relatively inexpensive.

Self*Test*

What effects do relative inflation rates have on relative interest rates?

What happens over time to the currencies of countries with higher inflation rates than U.S. inflation rates? To the currencies of countries with lower inflation rates?

Why might a multinational corporation decide to borrow in a country such as Brazil, where interest rates are high, rather than in a country such as Switzerland, where interest rates are low?

17-9 International Money and Capital Markets

One way for U.S. citizens to invest in world markets is to buy the stocks of U.S. multinational corporations that invest directly in foreign countries. Another way is to purchase foreign securities—stocks, bonds, or money market instruments issued by foreign companies. Security investments are known as *portfolio investments,* and they are distinguished from *direct investments* in physical assets by U.S. corporations.

For a time after World War II, the U.S. capital markets dominated world markets. Today, however, the value of U.S. securities represents approximately 40% of the value of all securities. Given this situation, it is important for both corporate managers and investors to understand international markets. Moreover, these markets often offer better opportunities for raising or investing capital than are available domestically.

17-9A International Credit Markets

There are three major types of international credit markets. The first type is the market for floating-rate bank loans, called **eurocredits**, whose rates are tied to LIBOR, which stands for *London Interbank Offered Rate.* LIBOR is the interest rate offered by the largest and strongest banks on large deposits. On August 30, 2018, the 3-month LIBOR rate was 2.31263%. Eurocredits tend to be issued for a fixed term with no early repayment. The oldest example of a eurocredit is a **eurodollar** deposit, which is a U.S. dollar deposited in a bank outside the United States. Today eurocredits exist for most major trading currencies. It is notable that British regulators announced in July 2017 that they were going to

Eurocredits
Floating-rate bank loans, available in most major trading currencies, that are tied to LIBOR.

Eurodollar
A U.S. dollar deposited in a bank outside the United States.

phase out LIBOR by 2021 and replace it with a new index. These actions were in part due to the recent LIBOR price-fixing scandals that we highlighted in Chapter 1.[9]

Eurobond
An international bond underwritten by an international syndicate of banks and sold to investors in countries other than the one in whose money unit the bond is denominated.

The second type of market is the eurobond market. A **eurobond** is an international bond underwritten by an international bank and sold to investors in countries other than the one in whose currency the bond is denominated. Thus, U.S. dollar-denominated eurobonds are not sold in the United States, pound eurobonds are not sold in the United Kingdom, and yen eurobonds are not sold in Japan. These bonds are true international debt instruments and are usually issued in bearer form, which means that the owner's identity is not registered and thus is not known. To receive interest payments the owner must clip a coupon and present it for payment at one of the designated payor banks. Most eurobonds are not rated by the rating agencies such as S&P or Moody's, although a number of them are starting to be rated. Eurobonds can be issued with either a fixed-rate coupon or a floating-rate coupon, depending on the preferences of the issuer, and they have medium- or long-term maturities.

Foreign Bonds
A type of international bond issued in the domestic capital market of the country in whose currency the bond is denominated, and underwritten by investment banks from the same country; however, the borrower is headquartered in a different country.

The third type of market is the foreign bond market. **Foreign bonds** are issued in the country in whose currency the bond is denominated, and they are underwritten by investment banks in that country. However, the borrower is headquartered in a different country. For instance, a Canadian company might issue a U.S. dollar-denominated bond in New York to fund its U.S. operations. Foreign bonds issued in the United States are sometimes called "Yankee bonds." Similarly, "bulldogs" are foreign bonds issued in London, and "samurai bonds" are foreign bonds issued in Tokyo. Foreign bonds can have either a fixed-rate coupon or a floating-rate coupon, and they have the same maturities as the purely domestic bonds with which they must compete for funds.

17-9B INTERNATIONAL STOCK MARKETS

New issues of stock are sold in international markets for a variety of reasons. For example, a Turkish firm might sell an equity issue in the United States because it can tap a much larger source of capital than in its home country. Also, a U.S. firm might tap the Turkish market because it wants to create an equity market presence to accompany its operations in that country. Occasionally, large multinational companies also issue new stock simultaneously in multiple countries. For example, Alcan Aluminum, a Canadian company, simultaneously issued new stock in Canada, Europe, and the United States using different underwriting syndicates in each market.

American Depository Receipts (ADRs)
Certificates representing ownership of foreign stock held in trust.

In addition to new issues, outstanding stocks of large multinational companies are occasionally listed on several international exchanges. For example, IBM is traded on the New York Stock Exchange, the Chicago Stock Exchange, and the London Stock Exchange. Some 500 foreign stocks are listed in the United States—one example is Royal Dutch Petroleum, which is listed on the NYSE. U.S. investors also can invest in foreign companies through **American depository receipts (ADRs)**, which are certificates representing ownership of foreign stock held in trust. Many ADRs are now available in the United States, with most of them traded on the over-the-counter (OTC) market. However, more and more ADRs are being listed on the New York Stock Exchange, including the United Kingdom's British Airways, Japan's Honda Motors, and Italy's Fiat Group.

[9]Refer to Chad Bray, "Libor Brought Scandal, Cost Billions—and May Be Going Away," *The New York Times* (www.nytimes.com), July 27, 2017.

STOCK MARKET INDEXES AROUND THE WORLD

In Chapter 2, we described the major U.S. stock market indexes. Similar market indexes also exist for each major world financial center. The figure that accompanies this box compares four of these indexes (Japan, Germany, United Kingdom, and India) against the U.S. Dow Jones Industrial Average.

Hong Kong

In Hong Kong, the primary stock index is the Hang Seng. Created by HSI Services Limited, the Hang Seng Index reflects the performance of the Hong Kong stock market. It is comprised of 50 domestic stocks (accounting for about 60% of the market's capitalization), which are divided into four subindexes: Commerce and Industry, Finance, Utilities, and Properties.

Germany

The major indicator of the German stock market, the XETRA DAX, is comprised of 30 German blue chip stocks. These stocks are listed on the Frankfurt Exchange, and they are representative of the industrial structure of the German economy.

United Kingdom

The FTSE 100 Index (pronounced "footsie") is the most widely followed indicator of equity investments in the United Kingdom. It is a value-weighted index comprised of the 100 largest companies on the London Stock Exchange, and its value is calculated every minute during the trading session.

Japan

In Japan, the principal barometer of stock performance is the Nikkei 225 Index. The index's value, which is calculated every minute throughout daily trading, consists of a collection of highly liquid equity issues thought to be representative of the Japanese economy.

Chile

The Santiago Stock Exchange has three main share indexes: the General Stock Price Index (IGPA), the Selective Stock Price Index (IPSA), and the INTER-10 Index. The IPSA, which reflects the price variations of the most active stocks, is comprised of 40 of the most actively traded stocks on the exchange.

India

Of the 22 stock exchanges in India, the Bombay Stock Exchange (BSE) is the largest, with over 5,500 listed stocks and approximately two-thirds of the country's total trading volume. Established in 1875, the exchange is also the oldest in Asia. Its yardstick is the BSE Sensex (renamed S&P BSE Sensex because of its partnership with S&P Dow Jones Indices), an index of 30 publicly traded Indian stocks that account for about 40% of the BSE's market capitalization.

Spain

In Spain, the IBEX 35 is the official index for measuring equity market performance. This index is comprised of the 35 most actively traded securities on the Madrid Stock Exchange General Index.

Selected International Stock Indexes: Compound Returns Since January 1995

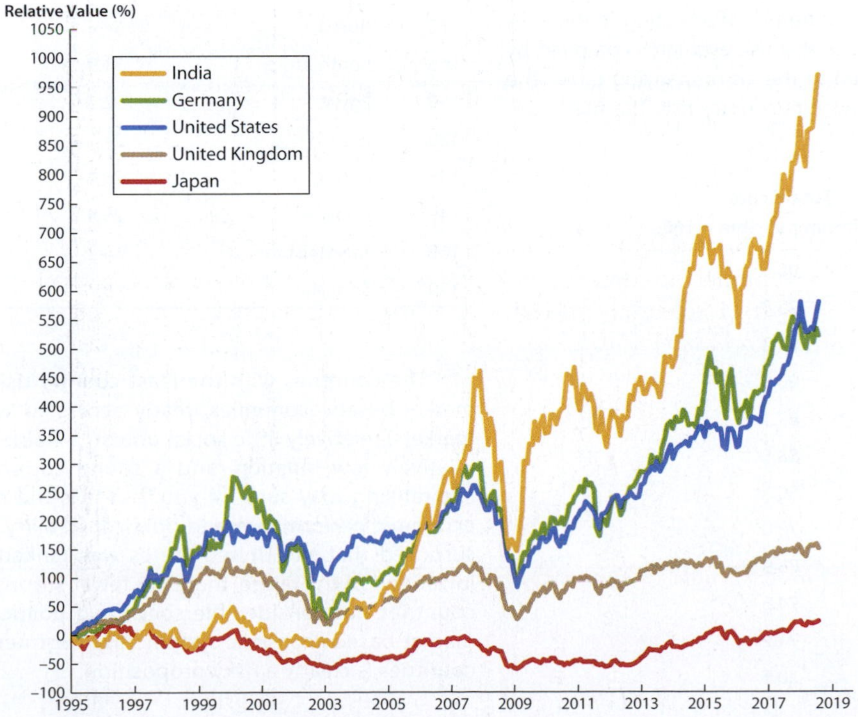

Source: Adapted from Yahoo! Finance historical quotes obtained from the website at finance.yahoo.com.

SelfTest

What are the three major types of international credit markets?

What is LIBOR?

What are ADRs?

17-10 Investing Overseas

Country Risk The risk that arises from investing or doing business in a particular country.

Investors should consider additional risk factors if they invest overseas. First, there is **country risk**, which refers to the risk involved in investing in a particular country. This risk depends on the country's economic, political, and social environment.

GLOBAL PERSPECTIVES

Measuring Country Risk

Various forecasting services measure the level of country risk in different countries and provide indexes that indicate factors such as each country's expected economic performance, access to world capital markets, political stability, and level of internal conflict. Country risk analysts use sophisticated models to measure risk, thus providing corporate managers and investors with a way to judge both the relative and absolute risk of investing in different countries. A sample of recent country risk estimates compiled by *Institutional Investor* is presented in the accompanying table. The higher a country's score, the lower its country risk. The maximum possible score is 100.

Rank	Country	Total Score (maximum possible = 100)
1	Switzerland	95.4
3	Norway	93.8
7	United States	93.3
11	Australia	90.5
14	New Zealand	87.1
18	South Korea	83.5
21	Japan	80.5
23	Chile	78.0
27	China	75.9
28	Ireland	74.6
34	Israel	71.2
36	Mexico	70.6

Rank	Country	Total Score (maximum possible = 100)
44	Colombia	62.9
57	Indonesia	56.9
59	Brazil	55.7
62	Russia	54.4
65	South Africa	51.9
100	Egypt	32.3
129	Greece	27.1
148	Iraq	21.4
149	Cuba	20.8
169	Afghanistan	14.2
179	Somalia	5.7

The countries with the least country risk all have strong, market-based economies, ready access to worldwide capital markets, relatively little social unrest, a stable political climate, relatively low inflation, and a sound currency. Switzerland's top ranking may surprise you, but it is the result of a strong economic performance and political stability. You may also be surprised that the United States was ranked seventh. At the lower end of the range, there are fewer surprises. Each of these countries has considerable social and political unrest and no market-based economic system. An investment in any of these countries is clearly a risky proposition.

Source: "The 2016 Country Credit Survey September Global Rankings," *Institutional Investor* (www.institutionalinvestor.com), September 2016.

GLOBAL PERSPECTIVES

Investing in International Stocks

At the end of 2017, the U.S. stock market represented about 40% of the world stock market, but many U.S. investors still hold at least some foreign stock. Analysts have long touted the benefits of investing overseas, arguing that foreign stocks both improve diversification and provide good growth opportunities. When investing in international stocks, you need to recognize that you are investing in both the foreign *market* and the foreign *currency*. Table 17.4 indicates how stocks in each country performed in 2017. Column 2 indicates how stocks in each country performed in terms of the U.S. dollar, while column 3 shows how the country's stocks performed in terms of its local currency. For example, in 2017 stocks in Sweden rose by 6.4%, and the Swedish krona increased by about 11.3% versus the U.S. dollar. Therefore, if a U.S. investor had bought Swedish stocks, he or she would have made 6.4% in Swedish krona terms, and those Swedish kronas would have bought 11.3% more U.S. dollars, so the effective return would have been 18.4%. Thus, the results of foreign investments depend both on the foreign market and on what happens to the exchange rate. Indeed, when you invest overseas, you are making two bets: (1) that foreign stocks will increase in their local markets and (2) that the currencies in which you will be paid will rise relative to the dollar. For the majority of countries shown in Table 17.4, the local currency increased relative to the dollar, causing local returns to be even larger when considered in dollar terms.

Global Stock Indexes in 2017 (ranked by 2017 performance in U.S. dollar terms) **TABLE 17.4**

Country	% Return in U.S. Dollars	% Return in Local Currency
Argentina	51.8	77.7
Austria	49.0	30.6
Poland	48.3	23.2
Chile	42.1	30.6
Czech Republic	41.2	17.0
Hungary	39.8	23.0
China	37.7	28.9
Turkey	37.0	47.6
India	36.2	27.9
Hong Kong	35.1	36.0
Denmark	32.3	16.1
Portugal	31.4	15.2
South Africa	30.2	17.5
Italy	29.6	13.6
Netherlands	28.6	12.7
Germany	28.4	12.5
Singapore	27.8	18.1
Belgium	25.8	10.3
Taiwan	25.8	15.0
New Zealand	25.0	22.0
Norway	25.0	18.6
Thailand	24.9	13.7
Brazil	24.7	26.9
France	24.7	9.3
Philippines	23.9	25.1
Japan	23.6	19.1
Spain	22.5	7.4
Finland	21.4	6.4
Malaysia	20.8	9.4

(Continued)

TABLE 17.4 Global Stock Indexes in 2017 (ranked by 2017 performance in U.S. dollar terms) (*Continued*)

Country	% Return in U.S. Dollars	% Return in Local Currency
Indonesia	20.5	20.0
Switzerland	19.3	14.1
Sweden	18.4	6.4
United Kingdom	17.8	7.6
Australia	16.0	7.0
Mexico	13.9	8.1
Israel	13.7	2.8
Canada	13.3	6.0
Russia	6.5	0.2
Sri Lanka	−1.1	2.3
South Korea	−86.2	21.8
Global	21.8	
Global, excluding U.S.	24.6	

Sources: "Market Data Center: International Stock Indexes," *The Wall Street Journal* (www.wsj.com), December 29, 2017; "Exchange Rates: New York Closing Snapshot," *The Wall Street Journal* (www.wsj.com), December 30, 2016; and "Exchange Rates: New York Closing Snapshot," *The Wall Street Journal* (www.wsj.com), December 29, 2017.

Some countries provide a safer investment climate and therefore less country risk than others. Examples of country risk include the risk that property will be expropriated without adequate compensation in addition to risks associated with changes in tax rates, regulations, and currency repatriation. Country risk also includes changes in host-country requirements regarding local production and employment as well as the danger of damage due to internal strife, ranging from crippling strikes to terrorism and civil war.

It is especially important to keep in mind when investing overseas that securities are often denominated in a currency other than the dollar, which means that returns on the investment depend on what happens to exchange rates. This is known as **exchange rate risk**. For example, if a U.S. investor purchases a Japanese bond, interest will probably be paid in yen, which must then be converted into dollars before the investor can spend his or her money in the United States. If the yen weakens relative to the dollar, it will buy fewer dollars, and fewer dollars will be received when funds are repatriated. However, if the yen strengthens, the effective investment return will increase. It therefore follows that returns on a foreign investment depend on the in-country performance of the foreign security and on changes in exchange rates.

Exchange Rate Risk
The risk that exchange rate changes will reduce the number of dollars provided by a given amount of a foreign currency.

Self*Test*

What is country risk?

What is exchange rate risk?

On what two factors does the return on a foreign investment depend?

17-11 International Capital Budgeting

Up to now, we have discussed the general environment in which multinational firms operate. In the remainder of the chapter, we discuss how international factors affect key corporate decisions. We begin with capital budgeting. Although the same basic principles of capital budgeting apply to both foreign and domestic operations, there are some key differences. First, cash flow estimation is more complex for overseas investments. Most multinational firms set up separate subsidiaries for each foreign country in which they operate, and the relevant cash flows for the parent company are the dividends and royalties paid by the subsidiaries to the parent. Second, these cash flows must be converted into the parent company's currency, so they are subject to exchange rate risk. For example, Coca-Cola's German subsidiary may make a profit of 100 million euros in 2019, but the value of this profit to Coca-Cola will depend on the dollar/euro exchange rate: How many *dollars* will 100 million euros buy?

The new tax law enacted in December 2017 established more of a territorial tax system where profits of non-U.S. subsidiaries earned overseas would be exempted from U.S. taxes when those profits are repatriated to the United States. Under the new law, a U.S. corporation is generally entitled to deduct the full amount of any dividend paid to it by a non-U.S. company at least 10% of whose shares are owned by the U.S. corporation. However, the new act imposed a one time tax in 2017 on earnings built up overseas prior to 2018: a 15.5% tax on accumulated earnings in cash or cash equivalents and an 8% tax on earnings reinvested in the corporation's business.[10]

A foreign government may restrict the **repatriation of earnings** to the parent company. For example, some governments place a ceiling, often stated as a percentage of the company's net worth, on the amount of cash dividends that a subsidiary can pay to its parent. Such restrictions are normally intended to force multinational firms to reinvest earnings in the foreign country, although restrictions are sometimes imposed to prevent large currency outflows that might disrupt the exchange rate.

Repatriation of Earnings
The process of sending cash flows from a foreign subsidiary back to the parent company.

Whatever the host country's motivation for blocking repatriation of profits, the result is that the parent corporation cannot use cash flows blocked in the foreign country to pay dividends to its shareholders or to invest elsewhere in the business. Hence, from the perspective of the parent organization, *the cash flows that are relevant for foreign investment analysis are those that the subsidiary is actually expected to send back to the parent.* The present value of those cash flows is found by applying an appropriate discount rate, and this present value is then compared with the parent's required investment to determine the project's NPV.

In addition to the complexities of the cash flow analysis, *the cost of capital may be different for a foreign project than for an equivalent domestic project because foreign projects may be more or less risky.* Higher risks might arise from (1) exchange rate risk and (2) political risk. A lower risk might result from the benefits of international diversification.

The foreign currency cash flows to be turned over to the parent must be converted into U.S. dollars by translating them at expected future exchange rates. An analysis should be conducted to ascertain the effects of exchange rate variations, and on the basis of this analysis, an exchange rate risk premium should be added to the domestic cost of capital to reflect this risk. It is sometimes possible to hedge against exchange rate fluctuations, but this may not be possible, especially on long-term projects. If hedging is used, the costs of doing so must be subtracted from the project's cash flows.

Political risk refers to potential actions by a host government that would reduce the value of a company's investment. It includes at one extreme the expropriation without compensation of the subsidiary's assets, but it also

Political Risk
Potential actions by a host government that would reduce the value of a company's investment.

[10]Refer to Philip Wagman, Richard Catalano, and Alan Kravitz, based on a Clifford Chance publication, "Tax Reform Implications for U.S. Businesses and Foreign Investments," *Harvard Law School Forum on Corporate Governance and Financial Regulation* (https://corpgov.law.harvard.edu/2018/01/05/tax-reform-implications-for-u-s-businesses-and-foreign-investments), January 5, 2018.

includes less drastic actions that reduce the value of the parent firm's investment in the foreign subsidiary, including higher taxes, tighter repatriation or currency controls, and restrictions on prices charged. The risk of expropriation is small in traditionally friendly and stable countries such as the United Kingdom and Switzerland. However, in Latin America, Africa, the Far East, and Eastern Europe, the risk may be substantial. Past expropriations include those of ITT and Anaconda Copper in Chile, Gulf Oil in Bolivia, Occidental Petroleum in Libya, and the assets of many companies in Iraq, Iran, and Cuba. In 2017, Venezuela expropriated a General Motors automobile plant, forcing GM to cease operations there.

Note that companies can take several steps to reduce the potential loss from expropriation: (1) finance the subsidiary with local capital, (2) structure operations so that the subsidiary has value only as a part of the integrated corporate system, and (3) obtain insurance against economic losses due to expropriation from a source such as the Overseas Private Investment Corporation (OPIC). In the latter case, insurance premiums would have to be added to the project's cost.

Several organizations rate the country risk, or the risk associated with investing in a particular country. (Refer back to the Global Perspectives box titled "Measuring Country Risk" for one source.) These ratings are based on the country's social, political, and economic environment—its **business climate**. Note that most of these studies suggest that the United States does not have the lowest level of country risk. This is particularly significant because even though people in the United States often assume that its bonds have no country risk, others do not agree. Foreign investors are concerned about how changes in U.S. policies (e.g., tax or Federal Reserve policies) might affect their investments. To the extent that these perceptions about U.S. country risk influence investors' willingness to hold U.S. securities, they will have an effect on U.S. interest rates. These issues have become increasingly relevant in the face of growing concerns about current and projected levels of U.S. government debt. These concerns dramatically came to light in August 2011 when Standard & Poor's downgraded U.S. government bonds from its long-held AAA status to AA+. (In June 2013, S&P reaffirmed the AA+ rating.) Moody's and Fitch have kept their ratings of U.S. government bonds at AAA.

Business Climate
A country's social, political, and economic environment.

Self*Test*

List some key differences in capital budgeting as applied to foreign versus domestic operations.

What are the relevant cash flows for an international investment—the cash flows produced by the subsidiary in the country in which it operates or the cash flows in dollars that it sends to its parent company? Explain.

Why might the cost of capital for a foreign project differ from that of an equivalent domestic project? Could it be lower? Explain.

What adjustments might be made to the domestic cost of capital for a foreign investment due to exchange rate risk, political risk, and country risk?

17-12 International Capital Structures

Capital structures vary across countries. For example, the Organization for Economic Cooperation and Development (OECD) reported that, on average, Japanese firms have 85% debt to total assets (in book value terms), German firms have 64%,

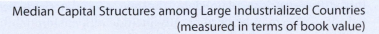

TABLE 17.5 Median Capital Structures among Large Industrialized Countries (measured in terms of book value)

Country	Total Liabilities to Total Assets (unadjusted for accounting differences) (1)	Debt to Total Assets (unadjusted for accounting differences) (2)	Total Liabilities to Total Assets (adjusted for accounting differences) (3)	Debt to Total Assets (adjusted for accounting differences) (4)	Times-Interest-Earned (TIE) Ratio (5)
Canada	56%	32%	48%	32%	1.55×
France	71	25	69	18	2.64
Germany	73	16	50	11	3.20
Italy	70	27	68	21	1.81
Japan	69	35	62	21	2.46
United Kingdom	54	18	47	10	4.79
United States	50	27	52	25	2.41
Mean	64%	26%	57%	20%	2.69×
Standard deviation	8%	7%	10%	8%	1.07×

Source: Raghuram Rajan and Luigi Zingales, "What Do We Know about Capital Structure? Some Evidence from International Data," *Journal of Finance*, vol. 50, no. 5 (December 1995), pp. 1421–1460.

and U.S. firms have 55%. One problem, however, when interpreting these numbers is that different countries often use different accounting conventions with regard to (1) reporting assets on a historical-cost versus a replacement-cost basis, (2) treating leased assets, (3) reporting pension plan liabilities, and (4) capitalizing versus expensing R&D costs. These differences make it difficult to compare capital structures.

A 1995 study by Raghuram Rajan and Luigi Zingales of the University of Chicago attempted to control for different accounting practices. In their study, Rajan and Zingales used a database that covers fewer firms than the OECD, but one that provides a more complete breakdown of balance sheet data. They concluded that differences in accounting practices can explain much but not all of the cross-country variations. More recent work has further explored the cross-country determinants of capital structure. These papers show that a firm's choice of capital structure is driven by both firm and industry characteristics as well as its country's institutional environment.[11]

Rajan and Zingales's results are summarized in Table 17.5. While somewhat dated, their study is still quite useful and highlights a number of important points. Perhaps most notably, there are a number of different ways to measure capital structure. One way is the average ratio of total liabilities to total assets—this is similar to the measure used by the OECD, and it is reported in column 1. Based on this measure, German and Japanese firms appear to be more highly leveraged than U.S. firms. However, if you look at column 2, where capital structure is measured by interest-bearing debt to total assets, it appears that German firms use less leverage than U.S. and Japanese firms. What explains this difference? Rajan and Zingales argue that much of

[11]Refer to Ali Gungoraydinoglu and Ozde Oztekin, "Firm- and Country-Level Determinants of Corporate Leverage: Some New International Evidence," *Journal of Corporate Finance*, vol. 17, no. 5 (December 31, 2011), pp. 1457–1474; and Ozde Oztekin, "Capital Structure Decisions Around the World: Which Factors Are Reliably Important?" *Journal of Financial and Quantitative Analysis*, vol. 50, no. 3 (June 2015), pp. 301–323.

this difference is explained by the way German firms account for pension liabilities. German firms generally include all pension liabilities (and their offsetting assets) on the balance sheet, whereas firms in other countries (including the United States) generally "net out" pension assets and liabilities on their balance sheets. To see the importance of this difference, consider a firm with $10 million in liabilities (not including pension liabilities) and $20 million in assets (not including pension assets). Assume that the firm has $10 million in pension liabilities that are fully funded by $10 million in pension assets. Therefore, net pension liabilities are zero. If this firm was in the United States, it would report a ratio of total liabilities to total assets equal to 50% ($10 million/$20 million). By contrast, if this firm operated in Germany, both its pension assets and liabilities would be reported on the balance sheet. The firm would have $20 million in liabilities and $30 million in assets—or a 67% ($20 million/$30 million) ratio of total liabilities to total assets. Total debt is the sum of short-term debt and long-term debt and excludes other liabilities, including pension liabilities. Therefore, the measure of total debt to total assets provides a more comparable measure of leverage across different countries.

Rajan and Zingales also make a variety of adjustments that attempt to control for other differences in accounting practices. The effects of these adjustments are reported in columns 3 and 4. Overall, the evidence suggests that companies in Germany and the United Kingdom tend to have less leverage, whereas firms in Canada appear to have more leverage relative to firms in the United States, France, Italy, and Japan. This conclusion is supported by data in the final column, which shows the average times-interest-earned ratio for firms in a number of different countries. Recall from Chapter 4 that the TIE ratio is the ratio of operating income (EBIT) to interest expense. This measure indicates how much cash the firm has available to service its interest expense. In general, firms with more leverage have a lower times-interest-earned ratio. The data indicate that this ratio is highest in the United Kingdom and Germany and lowest in Canada.

Self*Test*

Do international differences in financial leverage exist? Explain.

TYING IT ALL TOGETHER

Over the past two decades, the global economy has become increasingly integrated, and more companies generate more of their profits from overseas operations. In many respects, the concepts developed in the first 16 chapters still apply to multinational firms. However, multinational companies have more opportunities but also face different risks than do companies that operate only in their home market. The chapter discussed many of the key trends affecting the global markets today, and it described the most important differences between multinational and domestic financial management.

Self-Test Questions and Problems

(Solutions Appear in Appendix A)

ST-1 **KEY TERMS** Define each of the following terms:

a. Multinational, or global, corporation
b. Vertically integrated investment
c. International monetary system
d. Exchange rate
e. Freely floating regime; managed-float regime
f. Currency board arrangement
g. Fixed-peg arrangement
h. Cross rate
i. American terms; European terms
j. Direct quotation; indirect quotation
k. Spot rate; forward exchange rate
l. Discount on forward rate; premium on forward rate
m. Interest rate parity; purchasing power parity
n. Eurocredits; eurodollar
o. Eurobond; foreign bond
p. American depository receipts (ADRs); repatriation of earnings
q. Country risk; exchange rate risk; political risk; business climate

ST-2 **CROSS RATES** Suppose the exchange rate between the U.S. dollar and the EMU euro is €0.86 = $1.00 and the exchange rate between the U.S. dollar and the Canadian dollar is $1.00 = C$1.30. What is the cross rate of euros to Canadian dollars?

Questions

17-1 Why do U.S. corporations build manufacturing plants abroad when they can build them at home?

17-2 If the euro depreciates against the U.S. dollar, can a dollar buy more or fewer euros as a result? Explain.

17-3 If the United States imports more goods from abroad than it exports, foreigners will tend to have a surplus of U.S. dollars. What will this do to the value of the dollar with respect to foreign currencies? What is the corresponding effect on foreign investments in the United States?

17-4 Should firms require higher rates of return on foreign projects than on identical projects located at home? Explain.

17-5 Does interest rate parity imply that interest rates are the same in all countries?

17-6 Why might purchasing power parity fail to hold?

17-7 What is a eurodollar? If a French citizen deposits $10,000 in Chase Manhattan Bank in New York have eurodollars been created? What if the deposit is made in Barclay's Bank in London? In Chase Manhattan's Paris branch? Does the existence of the eurodollar market make the Federal Reserve's job of controlling U.S. interest rates easier or more difficult? Explain.

Problems

Easy Problems 1-4

17-1 **EXCHANGE RATE** If British pounds sell for $1.30 (U.S.) per pound, what should dollars sell for in pounds per dollar?

17-2 CROSS RATE A currency trader observes that in the spot exchange market, 1 U.S. dollar can be exchanged for 3.6 Israeli shekels or for 111 Japanese yen. What is the cross-exchange rate between the yen and the shekel; that is, how many yen would you receive for every shekel exchanged?

17-3 INTEREST RATE PARITY Six-month T-bills have a nominal rate of 2%, while default-free Japanese bonds that mature in 6 months have a nominal rate of 1.25%. In the spot exchange market, 1 yen equals $0.009. If interest rate parity holds, what is the 6-month forward exchange rate?

17-4 PURCHASING POWER PARITY A television costs $750 in the United States. The same television costs 637.5 euros. If purchasing power parity holds, what is the spot exchange rate between the euro and the dollar?

Intermediate Problems 5-11

17-5 EXCHANGE RATES Table 17.1 lists foreign exchange rates for August 30, 2018. On that day, how many dollars would be required to purchase 1,000 units of each of the following: British pounds, Canadian dollars, EMU euros, Japanese yen, Mexican pesos, and Swedish kronas?

17-6 EXCHANGE RATES Use the foreign exchange section of a current issue of *The Wall Street Journal* to look up the six currencies in Problem 17-5.

a. What is the current exchange rate for changing dollars into 1,000 units of pounds, Canadian dollars, euros, yen, Mexican pesos, and Swedish kronas?

b. What is the percentage gain or loss between the August 30, 2018, exchange rate and the current exchange rate for each of the currencies in part a?

17-7 CURRENCY APPRECIATION Suppose that 1 Danish krone could be purchased in the foreign exchange market today for $0.16. If the krone appreciated 4% tomorrow against the dollar, how many krones would a dollar buy tomorrow?

17-8 CROSS RATES Suppose the exchange rate between the U.S. dollar and the Swedish krona was 9.1 krona = $1, and the exchange rate between the dollar and the British pound was £1 = $1.3. What would be the exchange rate between Swedish kronas and pounds?

17-9 CROSS RATES Use the foreign exchange section of a current issue of *The Wall Street Journal* to look up the three currencies in Problem 17-8. What is the current exchange rate between Swedish kronas and pounds?

17-10 INTEREST RATE PARITY Assume that interest rate parity holds. In the spot market 1 Japanese yen = $0.00901, while in the 90-day forward market 1 Japanese yen = $0.00907. In Japan, 90-day risk-free securities yield 2%. What is the yield on 90-day risk-free securities in the United States?

17-11 PURCHASING POWER PARITY In the spot market, 19.1 Mexican pesos can be exchanged for 1 U.S. dollar. A compact disc costs $15 in the United States. If purchasing power parity (PPP) holds, what should be the price of the same disc in Mexico?

Challenging Problems 12-17

17-12 INTEREST RATE PARITY Assume that interest rate parity holds and that 90-day risk-free securities yield a nominal annual rate of 3% in the United States and a nominal annual rate of 3.5% in the United Kingdom. In the spot market, 1 pound = $1.3.

a. What is the 90-day forward rate?

b. Is the 90-day forward rate trading at a premium or a discount relative to the spot rate?

17-13 SPOT AND FORWARD RATES Arvin Australian Imports has agreed to purchase 15,000 cases of Australian wine for 4 million Australian dollars at today's spot rate. The firm's financial manager, Sarah Vintnor, has noted the following current spot and forward rates:

	U.S. Dollar/ Australian Dollar	Australian Dollar/ U.S. Dollar
Spot	0.7264	1.3767
30-day forward	0.7267	1.3761
90-day forward	0.7273	1.3749
180-day forward	0.7282	1.3732

On the same day, Vintnor agrees to purchase 15,000 more cases of wine in 3 months at the same price of 4 million Australian dollars.

a. What is the price of the wine in U.S. dollars if it is purchased at today's spot rate?
b. What is the cost in U.S. dollars of the second 15,000 cases if payment is made in 90 days and the spot rate at that time equals today's 90-day forward rate?
c. If the exchange rate for the Australian dollar is 1.30 to $1 in 90 days, how much will Vintnor have to pay for the wine (in U.S. dollars)?

17-14 **EXCHANGE GAINS AND LOSSES** You are the vice president of Worldwide InfoXchange, headquartered in Minneapolis, Minnesota. All shareholders of the firm live in the United States. Earlier this month you obtained a loan of 10 million Canadian dollars from a bank in Toronto to finance the construction of a new plant in Montreal. At the time the loan was received, the exchange rate was $0.77 to the Canadian dollar. By the end of the month, it has unexpectedly dropped to $0.70. Has your company made a gain or a loss as a result, and by how much?

17-15 **RESULTS OF EXCHANGE RATE CHANGES** Early in June 1983, it took 245 Japanese yen to equal $1. In August 2018, that exchange rate had fallen to 111 yen to $1. Assume that the price of a Japanese-manufactured automobile was $9,000 in June 1983 and that its price changes were in direct relation to exchange rates.

a. Has the price, in dollars, of the automobile increased or decreased during the 35-year period because of changes in the exchange rate?
b. What would the dollar price of the automobile be in August 2018, again assuming that the car's price changes only with exchange rates?

17-16 **FOREIGN INVESTMENT ANALYSIS** After all foreign and U.S. taxes, a U.S. corporation expects to receive 2 pounds of dividends per share from a British subsidiary this year. The exchange rate at the end of the year is expected to be $1.30 per pound, and the pound is expected to depreciate 5% against the dollar each year for an indefinite period. The dividend (in pounds) is expected to grow at 10% a year indefinitely. The parent U.S. corporation owns 10 million shares of the subsidiary. What is the present value in dollars of its equity ownership of the subsidiary? Assume a cost of equity capital of 11% for the subsidiary.

17-17 **FOREIGN CAPITAL BUDGETING** Sandrine Machinery is a Swiss multinational manufacturing company. Currently, Sandrine's financial planners are considering undertaking a 1-year project in the United States. The project's expected dollar-denominated cash flows consist of an initial investment of $2,000 and a cash inflow the following year of $2,400. Sandrine estimates that its risk-adjusted cost of capital is 10%. Currently, 1 U.S. dollar will buy 0.97 Swiss franc. In addition, 1-year risk-free securities in the United States are yielding 3%, while similar securities in Switzerland are yielding 1.50%.

a. If this project was instead undertaken by a similar U.S.-based company with the same risk-adjusted cost of capital, what would be the net present value and rate of return generated by this project?
b. What is the expected forward exchange rate 1 year from now?
c. If Sandrine undertakes the project, what is the net present value and rate of return of the project for Sandrine?

Comprehensive/Spreadsheet Problem

17-18 **MULTINATIONAL FINANCIAL MANAGEMENT** Yohe Telecommunications is a multinational corporation that produces and distributes telecommunications technology. Although its corporate headquarters are located in Maitland, Florida, Yohe usually buys its raw materials in several different foreign countries using several different foreign currencies. The matter is further complicated because Yohe often sells its products in other foreign countries. One product in particular, the SY-20 radio transmitter, draws Component X, Component Y, and Component Z (its principal components) from Switzerland, France, and the United Kingdom, respectively. Specifically, Component X costs 165 Swiss francs, Component Y costs 20 euros, and Component Z costs 105 British pounds. The largest market for the SY-20 is Japan, where the product sells for 50,000 Japanese yen. Naturally, Yohe is intimately concerned with economic conditions that could adversely affect dollar exchange rates. You will find Tables 17.1, 17.2, and 17.3 useful for completing this problem.

a. How much in dollars does it cost Yohe to produce the SY-20? What is the dollar sale price of the SY-20?
b. What is the dollar profit that Yohe makes on the sale of the SY-20? What is the percentage profit?
c. If the U.S. dollar was to weaken by 10% against all foreign currencies, what would be the dollar profit for the SY-20?
d. If the U.S. dollar was to weaken by 10% only against the Japanese yen and remained constant relative to all other foreign currencies, what would be the dollar and percentage profits for the SY-20?
e. Using the 180-day forward exchange information from Table 17.3, calculate the return on 1-year securities in Switzerland assuming the rate of return on 1-year securities in the United States is 4.9%.
f. Assuming that purchasing power parity (PPP) holds, what would be the sale price of the SY-20 if it was sold in the United Kingdom rather than Japan?

INTEGRATED CASE

CITRUS PRODUCTS INC.

17-19 MULTINATIONAL FINANCIAL MANAGEMENT Citrus Products Inc. is a medium-sized producer of citrus juice drinks with groves in Indian River County, Florida. Until now, the company has confined its operations and sales to the United States, but its CEO, George Gaynor, wants to expand into the Pacific Rim. The first step is to set up sales subsidiaries in Japan and Australia, then to set up a production plant in Japan, and finally to distribute the product throughout the Pacific Rim. The firm's financial manager, Ruth Schmidt, is enthusiastic about the plan, but she is worried about the implications of the foreign expansion on the firm's financial management process. She has asked you, the firm's most recently hired financial analyst, to develop a 1-hour tutorial package that explains the basics of multinational financial management. The tutorial will be presented at the next board of directors meeting. To get you started, Schmidt has given you the following list of questions:

a. What is a multinational corporation? Why do firms expand into other countries?
b. What are the five major factors that distinguish multinational financial management from financial management as practiced by a purely domestic firm?
c. Consider the following illustrative exchange rates:

	U.S. Dollars Required to Buy One Unit of Foreign Currency
Japanese yen	0.009
Australian dollar	0.650

1. Are these currency prices direct quotations or indirect quotations?
2. Calculate the indirect quotations for yen and Australian dollars.
3. What is a cross rate? Calculate the two cross rates between yen and Australian dollars.
4. Assume that Citrus Products can produce a liter of orange juice and ship it to Japan for $1.75. If the firm wants a 50% markup on the product, what should the orange juice sell for in Japan?
5. Now assume that Citrus Products begins producing the same liter of orange juice in Japan. The product costs 250 yen to produce and ship to Australia, where it can be sold for 6 Australian dollars. What is the U.S. dollar profit on the sale?
6. What is exchange rate risk?

d. Briefly describe the current international monetary system. What are the different types of exchange rate systems?
e. What is the difference between spot rates and forward rates? When is the forward rate at a premium to the spot rate? When is it at a discount?

f. What is interest rate parity? Currently, you can exchange 1 yen for 0.0095 U.S. dollar in the 30-day forward market, and the risk-free rate on 30-day securities is 4% in both Japan and the United States. Does interest rate parity hold? If not, which securities offer the highest expected return?

g. What is purchasing power parity (PPP)? If grapefruit juice costs $2 a liter in the United States and purchasing power parity holds, what should be the price of grapefruit juice in Australia?

h. What effect does relative inflation have on interest rates and exchange rates?

i. 1. Briefly explain the three major types of international credit markets.
   2. Briefly explain how ADRs work.

j. What is the effect of multinational operations on capital budgeting decisions?

k. To what extent do average capital structures vary across different countries?

TAKING A CLOSER LOOK

Using the Internet to Follow Exchange Rates and International Indexes

Use online resources to work on this chapter's questions. Please note that website information changes over time, and these changes may limit your ability to answer some of these questions.

From reading this chapter, it is obvious that individuals, corporations, and governments are not only impacted by what goes on in their own country but also influenced by the economies and events of other countries. To answer these questions, you will find the following websites helpful: Bloomberg, Yahoo! Finance, Investing.com, and MSN Money (www.msn.com/en-us/money/markets).

Discussion Questions

1. Recreate Table 17.1 for the following currencies: Australian dollar, British pound, Canadian dollar, Chinese yuan, EMU euro, Japanese yen, and Swiss franc. Be sure to show both the direct quotations and indirect quotations.
2. Recreate Table 17.2, which shows the currency cross rates, for the same currencies listed in Question 1.
3. Some of the websites show graphs indicating how one currency has done relative to another currency.

   a. Over the past year, how has the pound performed against the dollar? Does the dollar buy more or less pounds today than it did 1 year ago?

   b. Over the past year, how has the dollar performed against the yen? Does the dollar buy more or less yen today than it did 1 year ago?

4. Some of the websites provide information on the international indexes.

   a. How has the FTSE 100 (a U.K. stock index) performed over the past year? Calculate its return (in local currency) over the past year. (*Note:* Index value is shown in local currency.) From your answer in Question 3a, during this past year would a U.S. investor have earned more or less of a return calculated in dollars? Calculate the U.S. investor's approximate dollar return. (Assume that the U.S. investor had originally invested $1,000 in a FTSE 100 index fund at the beginning of the year but wants to liquidate the investment at the end of the year. Ignore any transactions costs.)

   b. How has the Nikkei 225 (a Japanese stock index) performed over the past year? Calculate its return (in local currency) over the past year. (*Note:* Index value is shown in local currency.) From your answer in Question 3b, during this past year would a U.S. investor have earned more or less of a return calculated in dollars? Calculate the U.S. investor's approximate dollar return. (Assume that the U.S. investor had originally invested $1,000 in a N225 index fund at the beginning of the year but wants to liquidate the investment at the end of the year. Ignore any transactions costs.)

Appendix A

Solutions to Self-Test Questions and Problems

Note: Except for Chapter 1, we do not show an answer for ST-1 problems because they are verbal rather than quantitative in nature.

Chapter 1

ST-1 Refer to the marginal glossary definitions or relevant chapter sections to check your responses.

Chapter 3

ST-2 a.

EBIT	$5,000,000
Interest	1,000,000
EBT	$4,000,000
Taxes 25%	1,000,000
Net income	$3,000,000

b. Current liabilities = Accounts payable + Accruals + Notes payable
= $3,000,000 + $1,000,000 + $2,000,000
= $6,000,000

NOWC = (Current assets − Excess cash) − (Current liabilities − Notes payable)
= ($14,000,000 − $0) − ($6,000,000 − $2,000,000)
= $10,000,000

c. NWC = Current assets − Current liabilities
= $14,000,000 − $6,000,000
= $8,000,000

d. $$\text{FCF} = (\text{EBIT}(1 - \text{T}) + \text{Depreciation}) - \left(\begin{matrix}\text{Capital}\\ \text{expenditures}\end{matrix} + \begin{matrix}\text{Increase in net operating}\\ \text{working capital}\end{matrix}\right)$$
$$= [\$5{,}000{,}000(0.75) + \$1{,}000{,}000] - [\$4{,}000{,}000 + 0]$$
$$= \$4{,}750{,}000 - \$4{,}000{,}000$$
$$= \$750{,}000$$

Note that capital expenditures are equal to the change in net plant and equipment plus the annual depreciation expense.

e. Rattner's end-of-year Statement of Stockholders' Equity is calculated as follows:

Statement of Stockholders' Equity

	Common Stock		Retained	Total Stockholders'
	Shares	Amount	Earnings	Equity
Balances, beginning of year	500,000	$5,000,000	$11,200,000	$16,200,000
Net income			3,000,000	
Cash dividends			−1,800,000	
Addition to retained earnings				1,200,000
Balances, end of year	500,000	$5,000,000	$12,400,000	$17,400,000

f. $\text{MVA} = (P_0 \times \text{Number of shares}) - \text{Book value of equity}$

$= (\$52 \times 500{,}000) - \$17{,}400{,}000$

$= \$8{,}600{,}000$

g. Before we can calculate the firm's EVA, we need to calculate the firm's total invested capital. We know that the firm uses no preferred stock, and we know that Assets = Liabilities + Equity. From the information provided in the problem, we know the following:

		Accounts payable	$ 3,000,000
		Accruals	1,000,000
		Notes payable	2,000,000
Current assets	$14,000,000	Current liabilities	$ 6,000,000
		Long-term debt	?
Net fixed assets	15,000,000	Common equity	17,400,000
Total assets	$29,000,000	Total liabilities & equity	$29,000,000

We calculated common equity in part e, so the only value we don't know on the balance sheet is long-term debt. However, we have enough information to calculate it:

$\text{Long-term debt} = \$29{,}000{,}000 - \$17{,}400{,}000 - \$6{,}000{,}000$

$\text{Long-term debt} = \$5{,}600{,}000$

Now, we can find the firm's total invested capital:

$\text{Total invested capital} = \text{Notes payable} + \text{Long-term debt} + \text{Common equity}$

$\text{Total invested capital} = \$2{,}000{,}000 + \$5{,}600{,}000 + \$17{,}400{,}000$

$\text{Total invested capital} = \$25{,}000{,}000$

Now, we can calculate the firm's EVA:

$\text{EVA} = \text{EBIT}(1 - T) - [\text{Total invested capital} \times \text{After-tax \% cost of capital}]$

$\text{EVA} = \$5{,}000{,}000(0.75) - [\$25{,}000{,}000 \times 0.09]$

$\text{EVA} = \$3{,}750{,}000 - \$2{,}250{,}000 = \$1{,}500{,}000$

Chapter 4

ST-2 Billingsworth paid $2 in dividends and retained $2 per share. Because total retained earnings rose by $12 million, there must be 6 million shares outstanding. With a book value of $40 per share, total common equity must be $40(6 million) = $240 million. Because Billingsworth has $120 million of total debt, its total debt to total capital ratio must be 33.3%:

$$\frac{\text{Total debt}}{\text{Total debt} + \text{Equity}} = \frac{\$120 \text{ million}}{\$120 \text{ million} + \$240 \text{ million}}$$
$$= 0.333 = 33.3\%$$

ST-3 a. In answering questions such as this, always begin by writing down the relevant definitional equations, and then start filling in numbers. Note that the extra zeros indicating millions have been deleted in the following calculations.

(1) $\text{DSO} = \dfrac{\text{Accounts receivable}}{\text{Sales}/365}$

$$40.55 = \frac{\text{A/R}}{\text{Sales}/365}$$

$\text{A/R} = 40.55(\$2.7397) = \$111.1 \text{ million}$

(2) $$\text{Current ratio} = \frac{\text{Current assets}}{\text{Current liabilities}} = 3.0$$
$$= \frac{\text{Current assets}}{\$105.5} = 3.0$$
$$\text{Current assets} = 3.0(\$105.5) = \$316.50 \text{ million}$$

(3) $$\text{Total assets} = \text{Current assets} + \text{Fixed assets}$$
$$= \$316.5 + \$283.5 = \$600 \text{ million}$$

(4) $$\text{ROA} = \text{Profit margin} \times \text{Total assets turnover}$$
$$= \frac{\text{Net income}}{\text{Sales}} \times \frac{\text{Sales}}{\text{Total assets}}$$
$$= \frac{\$50}{\$1{,}000} \times \frac{\$1{,}000}{\$600}$$
$$= 0.05 \times 1.667 = 0.083333 = 8.3333\%$$

(5) $$\text{ROE} = \text{ROA} \times \frac{\text{Assets}}{\text{Equity}}$$
$$12.0\% = 8.3333\% \times \frac{\$600}{\text{Equity}}$$
$$\text{Equity} = \frac{(8.3333\%)(\$600)}{12.0\%}$$
$$\text{Equity} = \$416.67 \text{ million}$$

(6) $$\text{Current assets} = \text{Cash and equivalents} + \text{Accounts receivable} + \text{Inventories}$$
$$\$316.5 = \$100.0 + \$111.1 + \text{Inventories}$$
$$\text{Inventories} = \$105.4 \text{ million}$$
$$\text{Quick ratio} = \frac{\text{Current assets} - \text{Inventories}}{\text{Current liabilities}}$$
$$= \frac{\$316.5 - \$105.4}{\$105.5} = 2.00$$

(7) $$\text{Total assets} = \text{Total claims} = \$600 \text{ million}$$
$$\text{Current liabilities} + \text{Long-term debt} + \text{Equity} = \$600 \text{ million}$$
$$\$105.5 + \text{Long-term debt} + \$416.67 = \$600 \text{ million}$$
$$\text{Long-term debt} = \$600 - \$105.5 - \$416.67 = \$77.83 \text{ million}$$

Note: We could have found equity as follows:

$$\text{ROE} = \frac{\text{Net income}}{\text{Equity}}$$
$$12.0\% = \frac{\$50}{\text{Equity}}$$
$$\text{Equity} = \$50/0.12$$
$$\text{Equity} = \$416.67 \text{ million}$$

Then we could have gone on to find long-term debt.

b. Kaiser's average sales per day were $1,000/365 = $2.74 million. Its DSO was 40.55, so A/R = 40.55($2.74) = $111.1 million. Its new DSO of 30.4 would cause A/R = 30.4($2.74) = $83.3 million. The reduction in receivables would be $111.1 − $83.3 = $27.8 million, which would equal the amount of cash generated.

(1) $$\text{New equity} = \text{Old equity} - \text{Stock bought back}$$
$$= \$416.7 - \$27.8$$
$$= \$388.9 \text{ million}$$

Thus,

$$\text{New ROE} = \frac{\text{Net income}}{\text{New equity}}$$
$$= \frac{\$50}{\$388.9}$$
$$= 12.86\% \text{ (versus old ROE of 12.0\%)}$$

(2) $$\text{New ROA} = \frac{\text{Net income}}{\text{Total assets} - \text{Reduction in A/R}}$$
$$= \frac{\$50}{\$600 - \$27.8}$$
$$= 8.74\% \text{ (versus old ROA of 8.33\%)}$$

(3) Total debt before the asset reduction is the same as total debt after the asset reduction. Neither notes payable nor long-term debt was impacted by the asset reduction. However, after the asset reduction equity has declined, so total capital has declined.

$$\text{Total debt} = \text{Notes payable} + \text{Long-term debt}$$
$$\$97.8 = \$20 + \$77.8$$

$$\text{New total assets} = \text{Old total assets} - \text{Reduction in A/R}$$
$$= \$600 - \$27.8$$
$$= \$572.2 \text{ million}$$

Before asset reduction:

$$\text{Total capital} = \text{Total debt} + \text{Old equity}$$
$$= \$97.8 + \$416.7$$
$$= \$514.5 \text{ million}$$

$$\frac{\text{Total debt}}{\text{Old total capital}} = \frac{\$97.8}{\$514.5} = 19.0\%$$

After asset reduction:

$$\text{Total capital} = \text{Total debt} + \text{New equity}$$
$$= \$97.8 + \$388.9$$
$$= \$486.7 \text{ million}$$

$$\frac{\text{Total debt}}{\text{New total capital}} = \frac{\$97.8}{\$486.7} = 20.1\%$$

Chapter 5

ST-2 a.

1/1/19	1/1/20	1/1/21	1/1/22
8%			
−1,000			FV = ?

$1,000 is being compounded for 3 years, so your balance on January 1, 2022, is $1,259.71:

$$FV_N = PV(1 + I)^N = \$1{,}000(1 + 0.08)^3 = \$1{,}259.71$$

Alternatively, using a financial calculator, input N = 3, I/YR = 8, PV = −1000, PMT = 0, and FV = ? Solve for FV = $1,259.71.

b. 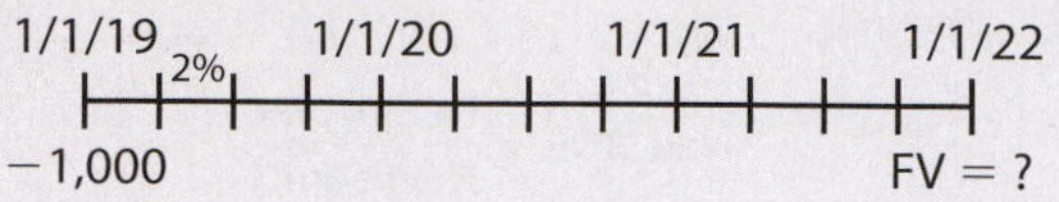

$$FV_N = PV\left(1 + \frac{I_{NOM}}{M}\right)^{MN} = FV_{12} = \$1{,}000(1.02)^{12} = \$1{,}268.24$$

Alternatively, using a financial calculator, input N = 12, I/YR = 2, PV = −1000, PMT = 0, and FV = ? Solve for FV = $1,268.24.

c. 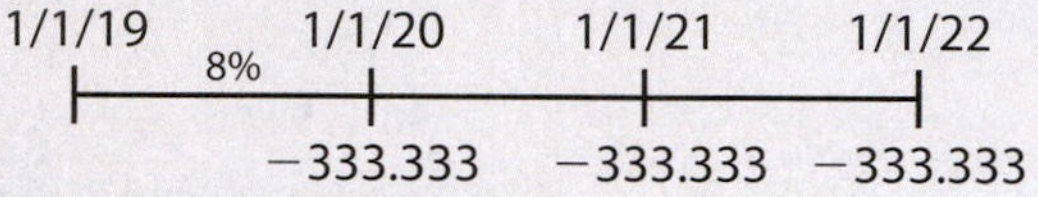

Using a financial calculator, input N = 3, I/YR = 8, PV = 0, PMT = −333.333, and FV = ? Solve for FV = $1,082.13.

d. 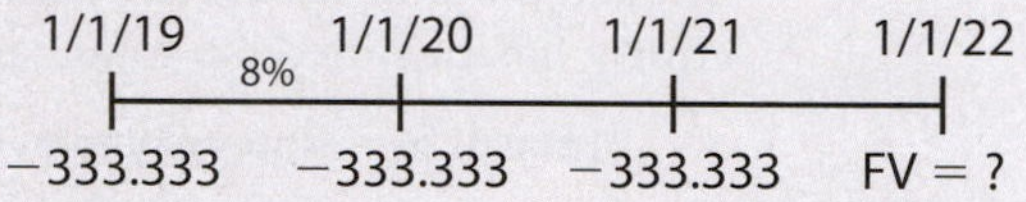

Using a financial calculator in begin mode, input N = 3, I/YR = 8, PV = 0, PMT = −333.333, and FV = ? Solve for FV = $1,168.70.

e. 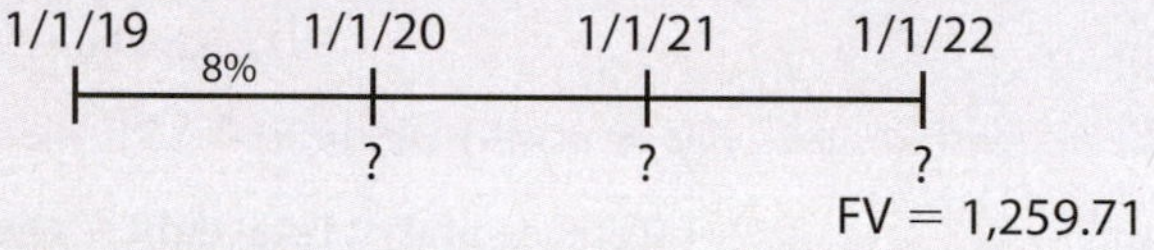

Using a financial calculator, input N = 3, I/YR = 8, PV = 0, FV = 1259.71, and PMT = ? Solve for PMT = −$388.03. Therefore, you would have to make three payments of $388.03 beginning on January 1, 2020.

ST-3 a. Set up a time line like the one in the preceding problem:

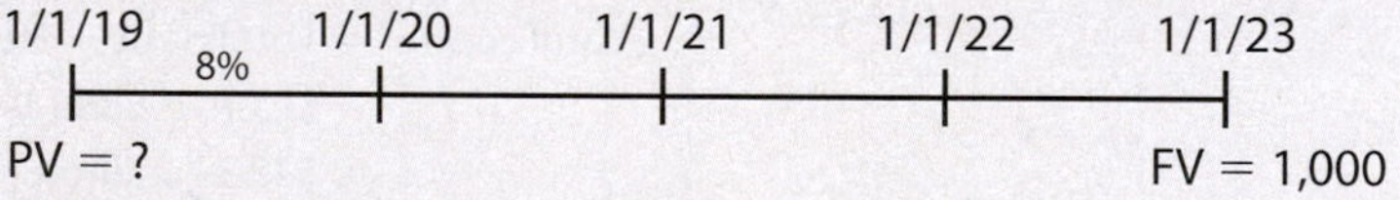

Note that your deposit will grow for 4 years at 8%. The deposit on January 1, 2019, is the PV, and the FV is $1,000. Using a financial calculator, input N = 4, I/YR = 8, PMT = 0, FV = 1000, and PV = ? Solve for PV = −$735.03.

$$PV = \frac{FV_N}{(1 + I)^N} = \frac{\$1{,}000}{(1.08)^4} = \$735.03$$

b. 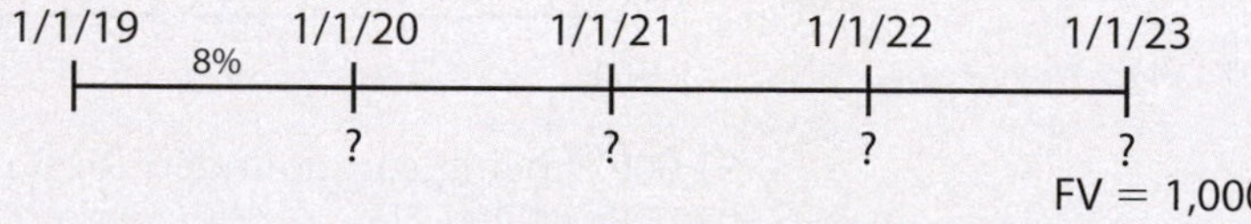

Here, we are dealing with a 4-year annuity whose first payment occurs 1 year from today, on January 1, 2020, and whose future value must equal $1,000. You should modify the time line to help visualize the situation. Using a financial calculator, input N = 4, I/YR = 8, PV = 0, FV = 1000, and PMT = ? Solve for PMT = −$221.92.

c. This problem can be approached in several ways. Perhaps the simplest is to ask this question: "If I received $750 on January 1, 2020, and deposited it to earn 8%, would I have the required $1,000 on January 1, 2023?" The answer is no.

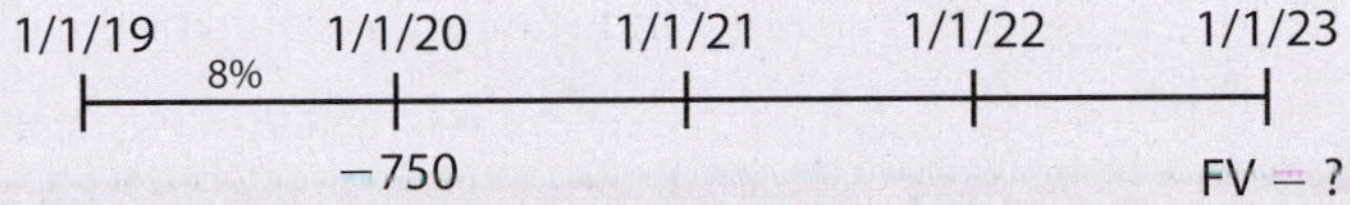

$$FV_3 = \$750(1.08)(1.08)(1.08) = \$944.78$$

This indicates that you should let your father make the payments of $221.92 rather than accept the lump sum of $750 on January 1, 2020.

You could also compare the $750 with the PV of the payments, as shown here:

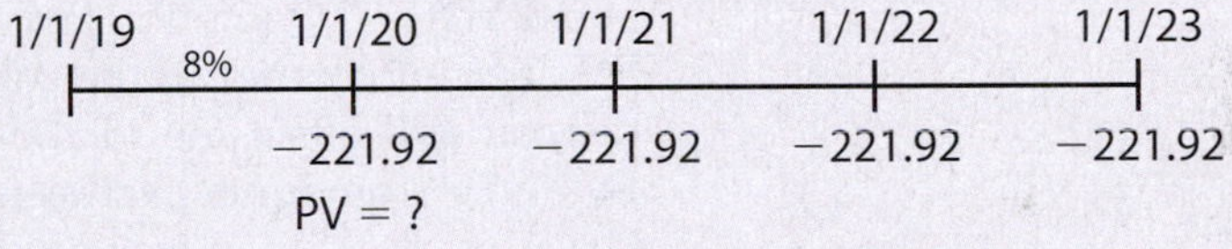

Using a financial calculator, input N = 4, I/YR = 8, PMT = −221.92, FV = 0, and PV = ? Solve for PV = $735.03.

This is less than the $750 lump sum offer, so your initial reaction might be to accept the lump sum of $750. However, this would be a mistake. The problem is that when you found the $735.03 PV of the annuity, you were finding the value of the annuity *today*, on January 1, 2019. You were comparing $735.03 today with the lump sum of $750 one year from now. This is, of course, not correct. What you should have done was take the $735.03, recognize that this is the PV of an annuity as of January 1, 2019, multiply $735.03 by 1.08 to get $793.83, and compare $793.83 with the lump sum of $750. You would then take your father's offer to make the payments of $221.92 rather than take the lump sum on January 1, 2020.

d.

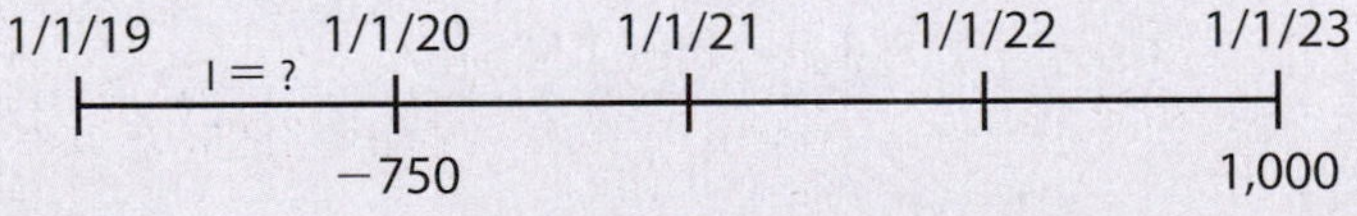

Using a financial calculator, input N = 3, PV = −750, PMT = 0, FV = 1000, and I/YR = ? Solve for I/YR = 10.0642%.

e.

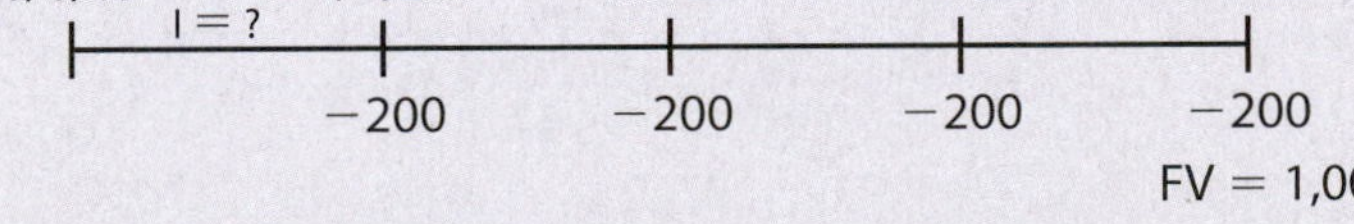

Using a financial calculator, input N = 4, PV = 0, PMT = −200, FV = 1000, and I/YR = ? Solve for I/YR = 15.09%.

You might be able to find a borrower willing to offer you a 15% interest rate, but there would be some risk involved—he or she might not actually pay you the $1,000!

f. 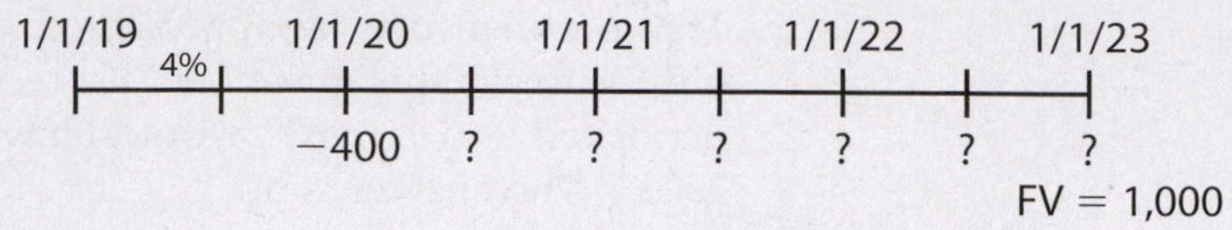

Find the future value of the original $400 deposit:

$$FV_6 = PV(1.04)^6 = \$400(1.2653) = \$506.13$$

This means that on January 1, 2023, you need an additional sum of $493.87:

$$\$1{,}000.00 - \$506.13 = \$493.87$$

This will be accumulated by making six equal payments that earn 8% compounded semiannually, or 4% each 6 months. Using a financial calculator, input N = 6, I/YR = 4, PV = 0, FV = 493.87, and PMT = ? Solve for PMT = −$74.46.

Alternatively, input N = 6, I/YR = 4, PV = −400, FV = 1000, and PMT = ? Solve for PMT = −$74.46. Note that the sign on the PV amount entered in the calculator was negative because the initial deposit will offset the total amount needed. If the signs on both the FV and PV amounts had been the same, you would have calculated a larger payment than was necessary.

g. $$\text{Effective annual rate} = \left(1 + \frac{I_{NOM}}{M}\right)^M - 1.0$$
$$= \left(1 + \frac{0.08}{2}\right)^2 - 1 = (1.04)^2 - 1$$
$$= 1.0816 - 1 = 0.0816 = 8.16\%$$

$$APR = I_{PER} \times M$$
$$= 0.04 \times 2 = 0.08 = 8\%$$

ST-4 Bank A's effective annual rate is 8.24%:

$$\text{Effective annual rate} = \left(1 + \frac{0.08}{4}\right)^4 - 1.0$$
$$= (1.02)^4 - 1$$
$$= 1.0824 - 1$$
$$= 0.0824 = 8.24\%$$

Now Bank B must have the same effective annual rate:

$$\left(1 + \frac{I_{NOM}}{12}\right)^{12} - 1.0 = 0.0824$$

$$\left(1 + \frac{I_{NOM}}{12}\right)^{12} = 1.0824$$

$$1 + \frac{I_{NOM}}{12} = (1.0824)^{1/12}$$

$$1 + \frac{I_{NOM}}{12} = 1.00662$$

$$\frac{I_{NOM}}{12} = 0.00662$$

$$I_{NOM} = 0.07944 = 7.94\%$$

Thus, the two banks have different quoted rates—Bank A's quoted rate is 8%, while Bank B's quoted rate is 7.94%; however, both banks have the same effective annual rate of 8.24%. The difference in their quoted rates is due to the difference in compounding frequency.

Chapter 6

ST-2 a. Average inflation over 4 years = (2% + 2% + 2% + 4%)/4 = 2.5%

b. $T_4 = r_{RF} + MRP_4$
$= r^* + IP_4 + MRP_4$
$= 3\% + 2.5\% + (0.1)3\%$
$= 5.8\%$

c. $C_{4,BBB} = r^* + IP_4 + MRP_4 + DRP + LP$
$= 3\% + 2.5\% + 0.3\% + 1.3\% + 0.5\%$
$= 7.6\%$

d. $T_8 = r^* + IP_8 + MRP_8$
$= 3\% + (3 \times 2\% + 5 \times 4\%)/8 + 0.7\%$
$= 3\% + 3.25\% + 0.7\%$
$= 6.95\%$

e. $C_{8,BB} = r^* + IP_8 + MRP_8 + DRP + LP$
$= 3\% + 3.25\% + 0.7\% + 1.3\% + 0.5\%$
$= 8.75\%$

f. $T_9 = r^* + IP_9 + MRP_9$

$7.3\% = 3\% + IP_9 + 0.8\%$

$IP_9 = 3.5\%$

$3.5\% = (3 \times 2\% + 5 \times 4\% + X)/9$

$31.5\% = 6\% + 20\% + X$

$5.5\% = X$

X = Inflation in Year 9 = 5.5%

ST-3 $T_1 = 6\%$; $T_2 = 6.2\%$; $T_3 = 6.3\%$; $T_4 = 6.5\%$; MRP = 0

a. Yield of 1-year security, 1 year from now, is calculated as follows:

$$(1.062)^2 = (1.06)(1 + X)$$

$$\frac{(1.062)^2}{1.06} = 1 + X$$

$$1.064 = 1 + X$$

$$6.4\% = X$$

b. Yield of 1-year security, 2 years from now, is calculated as follows:

$$(1.063)^3 = (1.062)^2(1 + X)$$

$$\frac{(1.063)^3}{(1.062)^2} = 1 + X$$

$$1.065 = 1 + X$$

$$6.5\% = X$$

c. Yield of 2-year security, 1 year from now, is calculated as follows:

$$(1.063)^3 = (1.06)(1 + X)^2$$

$$\frac{(1.063)^3}{1.06} = (1 + X)^2$$

$$1.13317 = (1 + X)^2$$

$$(1.13317)^{1/2} = 1 + X$$

$$6.45\% = X$$

d. Yield of 3-year security, 1 year from now, is calculated as follows:

$$(1.065)^4 = (1.06)(1 + X)^3$$

$$\frac{(1.065)^4}{1.06} = (1 + X)^3$$

$$1.213648 = (1 + X)^3$$

$$(1.213648)^{1/3} = 1 + X$$

$$6.67\% = X$$

Chapter 7

ST-2 a. Pennington's bonds were sold at par; therefore, the original YTM equaled the coupon rate of 12%.

b. $$V_B = \sum_{t=1}^{50} \frac{\$120/2}{\left(1 + \frac{0.10}{2}\right)^t} + \frac{\$1{,}000}{\left(1 + \frac{0.10}{2}\right)^{50}}$$

With a financial calculator, input the following: N = 50, I/YR = 5, PMT = 60, FV = 1000, and PV = ? Solve for PV = $1,182.56.

c. **Current yield = Annual coupon payment/Price**
= $120/$1,182.56
= 0.1015 = 10.15%

Capital gains yield = Total yield − Current yield
= 10% − 10.15% = −0.15%

Total return = YTM = 10%

d. With a financial calculator, input the following: N = 13, PV = −916.42, PMT = 60, FV = 1000, and $r_d/2$ = I/YR = ? Calculator solution = $r_d/2$ = 7.00%; therefore, r_d = YTM = 14.00%.

Current yield = $120/$916.42 = 13.09%

Capital gains yield = 14% − 13.09% = 0.91%

Total return = YTM = 14.00%

e. The following time line illustrates the years to maturity of the bond:

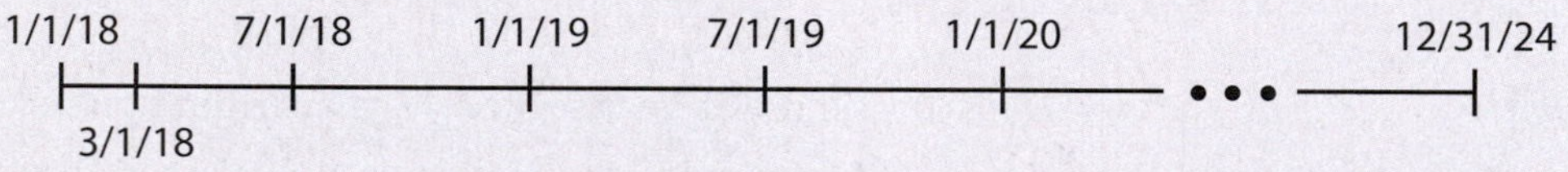

Thus, on March 1, 2018, there were 13⅔ periods left before the bond matured. Bond traders actually use the following procedure to determine the price of the bond:

(1) Find the price of the bond on the next coupon date, July 1, 2018. Using a financial calculator, input N = 13, I/YR = 7.75, PMT = 60, FV = 1000, and PV = ? Solve for PV = $859.76.

(2) Add the coupon, \$60, to the bond price to get the total value of the bond on the next interest payment date: \$859.76 + \$60.00 = \$919.76.

(3) Discount this total value back to the purchase date (March 1, 2018). Using a financial calculator, input N = 4/6, I/YR = 7.75, PMT = 0, FV = 919.76, and PV = ? Solve for PV = \$875.11.

(4) Therefore, you would have written a check for \$875.11 to complete the transaction. Of this amount, \$20 = (1/3)(\$60) would represent accrued interest and \$855.11 would represent the bond's basic value. This breakdown would affect both your taxes and those of the seller.

(5) This problem could be solved *very* easily using a spreadsheet or a financial calculator with a bond valuation function, such as the HP-12C or the HP-17BII. This is explained in the calculator manual under the heading "Bond Calculations."

ST-3 a. (1) \$100,000,000/10 = \$10,000,000 per year, or \$5 million each 6 months.

(2) VDC will purchase bonds on the open market if they're selling at less than par. So, the sinking fund payment will be less than \$5,000,000 each period.

b. The debt service requirements will decline. As the amount of bonds outstanding declines, so will the interest requirements (amounts given in millions of dollars). If the bonds are called at par, the total bond service payments are calculated as follows:

Semiannual Payment Period (1)	Sinking Fund Payment (2)	Outstanding Bonds on which Interest Is Paid (3)	Interest Payment[a] (4)	Total Debt Service (2) + (4) = (5)
1	\$5	\$100	\$6.0	\$11.0
2	5	95	5.7	10.7
3	5	90	5.4	10.4
⋮	⋮	⋮	⋮	⋮
20	5	5	0.3	5.3

[a]Interest is calculated as (0.5)(0.12)(column 3); for example, Interest in Period 2 = (0.5)(0.12)(\$95) = \$5.7.

The company's total cash bond service requirement will be \$21.7 million per year for the first year. For both options, interest will decline by 0.12(\$10,000,000) = \$1,200,000 per year for the remaining years. The total debt service requirement for the open market purchases cannot be precisely determined, but the amounts would be less than what's shown in column 5 of the preceding table.

c. Here we have a 10-year, 7% annuity whose compound value is \$100 million, and we are seeking the annual payment, PMT. The solution can be obtained with a financial calculator. Input N = 10, I/YR = 7, PV = 0, and FV = 100000000, and press the PMT key to obtain \$7,237,750. This amount is not known with certainty as interest rates over time will change, so the amount could be higher (if interest rates fall) or lower (if interest rates rise).

d. Annual debt service costs will be \$100,000,000(0.12) + \$7,237,750 = \$19,237,750.

e. If interest rates rose, causing the bond's price to fall, the company would use open market purchases. This would reduce its debt service requirements.

Chapter 8

ST-2 a. The average rate of return for each stock is calculated simply by averaging the returns over the 5-year period. The average return for Stock A is

$$r_{AVg\,A} = (-24.25\% + 18.50\% + 38.67\% + 14.33\% + 39.13\%)/5$$
$$= 17.28\%$$

The average return for Stock B is

$$r_{Avg\,B} = (5.50\% + 26.73\% + 48.25\% + -4.50\% + 43.86\%)/5$$
$$= 23.97\%$$

The realized rate of return on a portfolio made up of Stock A and Stock B would be calculated by finding the average return in each year as r_A(% of Stock A) + r_B(% of Stock B) and then averaging these annual returns:

Year	Portfolio AB's Return, r_{AB}
2014	(9.38%)
2015	22.62
2016	43.46
2017	4.92
2018	41.50
	r_{Avg} = 20.62%

b. The standard deviation of returns is estimated, using Equation 8.2a, as follows:

$$\text{Estimated } \sigma = \sqrt{\frac{\sum_{t=1}^{N}(\bar{r}_t - \bar{r}_{Avg})^2}{N-1}}$$

For Stock A, the estimated σ is 25.84%:

$$\sigma_A = \sqrt{\frac{(-24.25\% - 17.28\%)^2 + (18.50\% - 17.28\%)^2 + (38.67\% - 17.28\%)^2 + (14.33\% - 17.28\%)^2 + (39.13\% - 17.28\%)^2}{5-1}}$$
$$= 25.84\%$$

The standard deviations of returns for Stock B and for the portfolio are similarly determined, and they are as follows:

	Stock A	Stock B	Portfolio AB
Standard deviation	25.84%	23.15%	22.96%

c. The Sharpe ratio is calculated as (Return − Risk-free rate)/Standard deviation. For Stock A, we calculate the Sharpe ratio as (17.28% − 3.5%)/25.84% = 0.5333. The Sharpe ratios for Stock B and the portfolio are similarly determined, and they are as follows:

	Stock A	Stock B	Portfolio AB
Sharpe ratio	0.5333	0.8842	0.7456

d. Because the risk reduction from diversification is small (σ_{AB} falls only to 22.96%), the most likely value of the correlation coefficient is 0.8. If the correlation coefficient were −0.8, the risk reduction would be much larger. In fact, the correlation coefficient between Stocks A and B is 0.76.

e. If more randomly selected stocks were added to a portfolio, σ_p would decline to somewhere in the vicinity of 20% (see Figure 8.6); σ_p would remain constant only if the correlation coefficient were +1.0, which is most unlikely. σ_p would decline to zero only if the correlation coefficient, ρ, were equal to zero and a large number of stocks were added to the portfolio, or if the proper proportions were held in a two-stock portfolio with $\rho = -1.0$.

ST-3 a. $b = (0.6)(0.70) + (0.25)(0.90) + (0.1)(1.30) + (0.05)(1.50)$

$= 0.42 + 0.225 + 0.13 + 0.075 = 0.85$

b. $r_{RF} = 4\%$; $RP_M = 5\%$; $b = 0.85$ (calculated in part a)

$r = 4\% + (5\%)(0.85)$

$= 8.25\%$

c. $b_N = (0.5)(0.70) + (0.25)(0.90) + (0.1)(1.30) + (0.15)(1.50)$

$= 0.35 + 0.225 + 0.13 + 0.225$

$= 0.93$

$r = 4\% + (5\%)(0.93)$

$= 8.65\%$

Chapter 9

ST-2 The first step is to solve for g, the unknown variable, in the constant growth equation. Because D_1 is unknown, but D_0 is known, substitute $D_0(1 + g)$ for D_1 as follows:

$$\hat{P}_0 = P_0 = \frac{D_1}{r_s - g} = \frac{D_0(1 + g)}{r_s - g}$$

$$\$36 = \frac{\$2.40(1 + g)}{0.12 - g}$$

Solving for g, we find the growth rate to be 5%:

$$\$36(0.12 - g) = \$2.40(1 + g)$$

$$\$4.32 - \$36g = \$2.40 + \$2.40g$$

$$\$38.4g = \$1.92$$

$$g = 0.05 = 5\%$$

The next step is to use the growth rate to project the stock price 5 years hence:

$$\hat{P}_5 = \frac{D_0(1 + g)^6}{r_s - g}$$

$$= \frac{\$2.40(1.05)^6}{0.12 - 0.05}$$

$$= \frac{\$3.2162}{0.07}$$

$$= \$45.95$$

(Alternatively, $\hat{P}_5 = \$36(1.05)^5 = \$45.95$)

Therefore, the firm's expected stock price 5 years from now, $\hat{P}_5$, is \$45.95.

ST-3 a. (1) Calculate the PV of the dividends paid during the supernormal growth period:

$$D_1 = \$1.1500(1.15) = \$1.3225$$
$$D_2 = \$1.3225(1.15) = \$1.5209$$
$$D_3 = \$1.5209(1.13) = \$1.7186$$

$$\text{PV D} = \frac{\$1.3225}{1.12} + \frac{\$1.5209}{(1.12)^2} + \frac{\$1.7186}{(1.12)^3}$$
$$= \$1.1808 + \$1.2125 + \$1.2233$$
$$= \$3.6166 \approx \$3.62$$

(2) Find the PV of the firm's stock price at the end of Year 3:

$$\hat{P}_3 = \frac{D_4}{r_s - g} = \frac{D_3(1 + g)}{r_s - g}$$
$$= \frac{\$1.7186(1.06)}{0.12 - 0.06}$$
$$= \frac{\$1.8217}{0.06}$$
$$= \$30.36$$

$$\text{PV } \hat{P}_3 = \frac{\$30.36}{(1.12)^3} = \$21.61$$

(3) Sum the two components to find the value of the stock today:

$$\hat{P}_0 = \$3.62 + \$21.61 = \$25.23$$

Alternatively, the cash flows can be placed on a time line as follows:

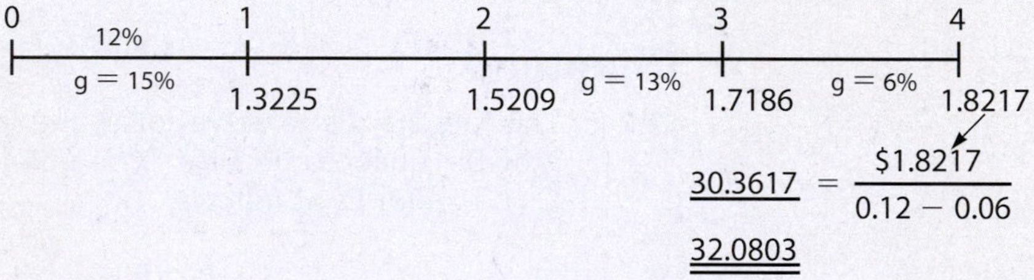

Enter the cash flows into the cash flow register (remembering that $CF_0 = 0$) and I/YR = 12, and press the NPV key to obtain $P_0 = \$25.23$.

b.
$$\hat{P}_1 = \frac{\$1.5209}{1.12} + \frac{\$1.7186}{(1.12)^2} + \frac{\$30.36}{(1.12)^2}$$
$$= \$1.3579 + \$1.3701 + \$24.2028$$
$$= \$26.9308 \approx \$26.93$$

(Calculator solution: $26.93)

$$\hat{P}_2 = \frac{\$1.7186}{1.12} + \frac{\$30.36}{1.12}$$
$$= \$1.5345 + \$27.1071$$
$$= \$28.6416 \approx \$28.64$$

(Calculator solution: $28.64)

c.

Year	Dividend Yield	+	Capital Gains Yield	=	Total Return
1	$\frac{\$1.3225}{\$25.23} \approx 5.24\%$		$\frac{\$26.93 - \$25.23}{\$25.23} \approx 6.74\%$		≈ 12%
2	$\frac{\$1.5209}{\$26.93} \approx 5.65\%$		$\frac{\$28.64 - \$26.93}{\$26.93} \approx 6.35\%$		≈ 12%
3	$\frac{\$1.7186}{\$28.64} \approx 6.00\%$		$\frac{\$30.36 - \$28.64}{\$28.64} \approx 6.00\%$		≈ 12%

ST-4

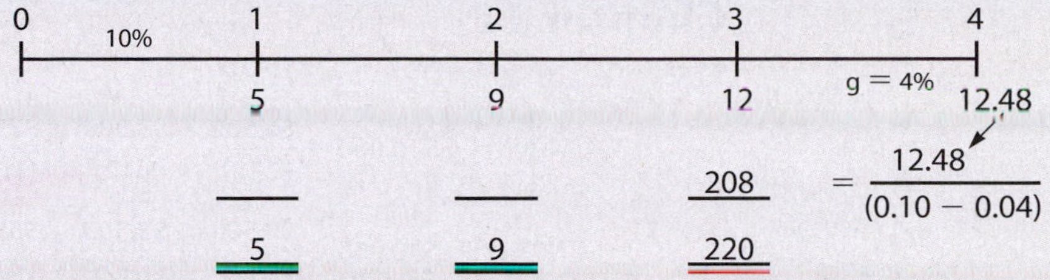

Value of company's operations $= \$5/1.10 + \$9/(1.10)^2 + \$220/(1.10)^3$

$= \$4.5454 + \$7.4380 + \$165.2893$

$= \$177.2727$ **million.**

Value of company = Value of company's operations + Market value of non-operating assets

$= \$177.2727 + \$10$

$= \$187.2727$ **million.**

Market value of equity = Value of company − Market value of debt and preferred

$= \$187.2727 - \$27.2727$

$= \$160$ **million**

$P_0 = \$160/5 = \$32.00$ **per share.**

Chapter 10

ST-2 a. Component costs are as follows:

$$\text{Common: } r_s = \frac{D_1}{P_0} + g = \frac{D_0(1 + g)}{P_0} + g$$

$$= \frac{\$3.60(1.09)}{\$54} + 0.09$$

$$= 0.0727 + 0.09 = 16.27\%$$

$$\text{Preferred: } r_p = \frac{\text{Preferred dividend}}{P_p} = \frac{\$11}{\$95} = 11.58\%$$

Debt: $r_d(1 - T) = 12\%(0.75) = 9.00\%$

b. WACC calculation:

$$\text{WACC} = w_d r_d(1 - T) + w_p r_p + w_c r_s$$

$$= 0.25(9.0\%) + 0.15(11.58\%) + 0.60(16.27\%) = 13.75\%$$

c. $$\text{Retained earnings breakpoint} = \frac{\text{Addition to retained earnings for the year}}{\text{Equity fraction}}$$

$$= \frac{0.7(\$34{,}285.72)}{0.6} = \$40{,}000$$

At a capital budget greater than $40,000, new common stock would have to be issued, and the firm's WACC would increase above 13.75%. Therefore, only Projects A, B, and C can be accepted for a total capital budget of $40,000.

Chapter 11

ST-2 a. *Net present value (NPV):*

$$NPV_X = -\$10{,}000 + \frac{\$6{,}500}{(1.12)^1} + \frac{\$3{,}000}{(1.12)^2} + \frac{\$3{,}000}{(1.12)^3} + \frac{\$1{,}000}{(1.12)^4} = \$966.01$$

$$NPV_Y = -\$10{,}000 + \frac{\$3{,}500}{(1.12)^1} + \frac{\$3{,}500}{(1.12)^2} + \frac{\$3{,}500}{(1.12)^3} + \frac{\$3{,}500}{(1.12)^4} = \$630.72$$

Alternatively, using a financial calculator, input the cash flows into the cash flow register, enter I/YR = 12, and then press the NPV key to obtain $NPV_X = \$966.01$ and $NPV_Y = \$630.72$.

Internal rate of return (IRR):

To solve for each project's IRR, find the discount rates that equate each NPV to zero:

$$IRR_X = 18.0\%$$
$$IRR_Y = 15.0\%$$

Modified internal rate of return (MIRR):

To obtain each project's MIRR, begin by finding each project's terminal value (TV) of cash inflows:

$$TV_X = \$6{,}500(1.12)^3 + \$3{,}000(1.12)^2 + \$3{,}000(1.12)^1 + \$1{,}000 = \$17{,}255.23$$
$$TV_Y = \$3{,}500(1.12)^3 + \$3{,}500(1.12)^2 + \$3{,}500(1.12)^1 + \$3{,}500 = \$16{,}727.65$$

Now, each project's MIRR is the discount rate that equates the PV of the TV to each project's cost, $10,000:

$$MIRR_X = 14.61\%$$
$$MIRR_Y = 13.73\%$$

Payback:

To determine the payback, construct the cumulative cash flows for each project:

	Cumulative Cash Flows	
Year	**Project X**	**Project Y**
0	($10,000)	($10,000)
1	(3,500)	(6,500)
2	(500)	(3,000)
3	2,500	500
4	3,500	4,000

$$Payback_X = 2 + \frac{\$500}{\$3{,}000} = 2.17 \text{ years}$$

$$Payback_Y = 2 + \frac{\$3{,}000}{\$3{,}500} = 2.86 \text{ years}$$

Discounted payback:

To determine the discounted payback, construct the cumulative discounted cash flows at the firm's WACC of 12% for each project:

Project X

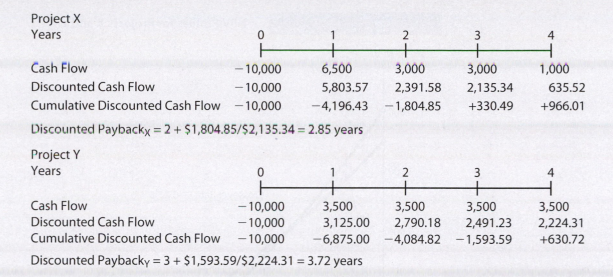

Years	0	1	2	3	4
Cash Flow	−10,000	6,500	3,000	3,000	1,000
Discounted Cash Flow	−10,000	5,803.57	2,391.58	2,135.34	635.52
Cumulative Discounted Cash Flow	−10,000	−4,196.43	−1,804.85	+330.49	+966.01

Discounted $\text{Payback}_X = 2 + \$1{,}804.85/\$2{,}135.34 = 2.85$ years

Project Y

Years	0	1	2	3	4
Cash Flow	−10,000	3,500	3,500	3,500	3,500
Discounted Cash Flow	−10,000	3,125.00	2,790.18	2,491.23	2,224.31
Cumulative Discounted Cash Flow	−10,000	−6,875.00	−4,084.82	−1,593.59	+630.72

Discounted $\text{Payback}_Y = 3 + \$1{,}593.59/\$2{,}224.31 = 3.72$ years

b. The following table summarizes the project rankings by each method:

	Project That Ranks Higher
NPV	X
IRR	X
MIRR	X
Payback	X
Discounted payback	X

Note that all methods rank Project X over Project Y. In addition, both projects are acceptable under the NPV, IRR, and MIRR criteria. Thus, both projects should be accepted if they are independent.

c. In this case, we would choose the project with the higher NPV at r = 12%, or Project X.

d. To determine the effects of changing the cost of capital, plot the NPV profiles of each project. The crossover rate occurs between 6% and 7% (≈6.22%). See the graph on the next page.

If the firm's cost of capital is less than 6.22%, a conflict exists because $NPV_Y > NPV_X$, but $IRR_X > IRR_Y$. Therefore, if r were 5%, a conflict would exist. Note, however, that when r = 5.0%, $MIRR_X = 10.64\%$ and $MIRR_Y = 10.83\%$; hence, the modified IRR ranks the projects correctly, even if r is to the left of the crossover point because the size of the projects is equal.

e. The basic cause of the conflict is differing reinvestment rate assumptions between NPV and IRR. NPV assumes that cash flows can be reinvested at the cost of capital, while IRR assumes reinvestment at the (generally) higher IRR. The high reinvestment rate assumption under IRR makes early cash flows especially valuable, and hence short-term projects look better than long-term projects under IRR.

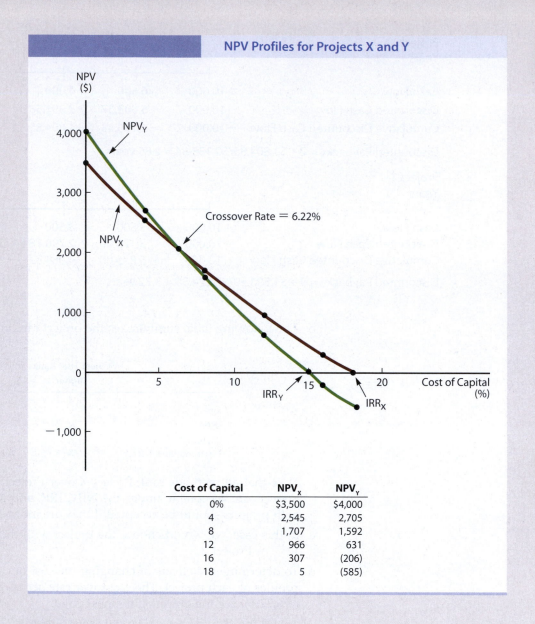

NPV Profiles for Projects X and Y

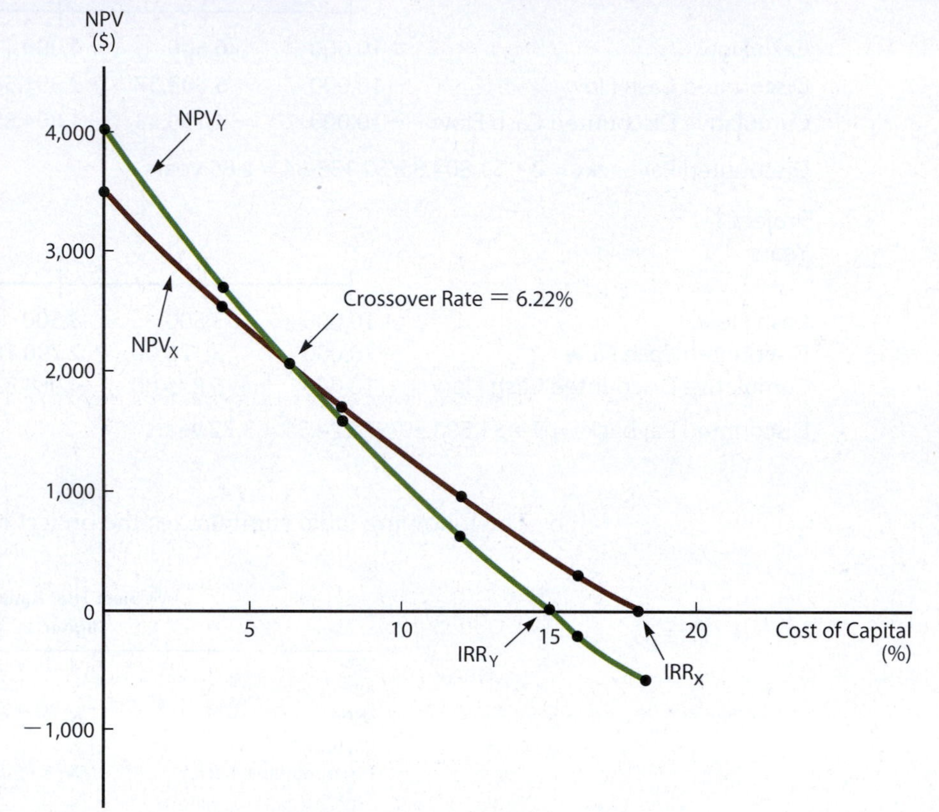

Cost of Capital	NPV$_X$	NPV$_Y$
0%	$3,500	$4,000
4	2,545	2,705
8	1,707	1,592
12	966	631
16	307	(206)
18	5	(585)

Chapter 12

ST-2 a. Estimated investment requirements:

After-tax cost of equipment	($48,750)
Change in net operating working capital	(2,000)
Total investment outlay	($50,750)

b.

	Year 0	Year 1	Year 2	Year 3
Investment Outlays:				
Equipment cost (1 − T)	($48,750)			
Change in NOWC	(2,000)			
Operating Cash Flows over Project's Life:				
Revenues (4,000 × $50)		$200,000	$200,000	$200,000
Variable costs (70%)		140,000	140,000	140,000
Fixed costs		30,000	30,000	30,000
Depreciation: 100% bonus depreciation in Year 0		0	0	0

(Continued)

	Year 0	Year 1	Year 2	Year 3
EBIT		$ 30,000	$ 30,000	$ 30,000
Taxes on operating income (25%)		7,500	7,500	7,500
AT project operating income		$ 22,500	$ 22,500	$ 22,500
Add back: Depreciation		0	0	0
EBIT(1 − T) + Depreciation		$ 22,500	$ 22,500	$ 22,500
Terminal Cash Flows:				
Salvage value				10,000
Tax on salvage value				(2,500)[a]
AT salvage value				$ 7,500
Recovery of NOWC				2,000
Project free cash flows	($50,750)	$ 22,500	$ 22,500	$ 32,000

Note:

[a]The equipment was fully depreciated at t = 0, so its remaining book value is zero. Consequently, the entire salvage value is subject to tax.

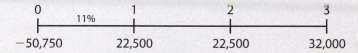

0	11%	1	2	3
−50,750		22,500	22,500	32,000

c. From the time line shown in part b, the project's NPV can be calculated as follows:

$$\text{NPV} = -\$50{,}750 + \$22{,}500/(1.11)^1 + \$22{,}500/(1.11)^2 + \$32{,}000/(1.11)^3$$
$$= \$11{,}180$$

Alternatively, using a financial calculator, you would enter the following data: $CF_0 = -50750$; $CF_1 = 22500$; $CF_2 = 22500$; $CF_3 = 32000$; I/YR = 11; and then solve for NPV = $11,180.

Because the NPV is positive, the project should be accepted.

d. Project analysis if unit sales turned out to be 20% below forecast:

Initial projection = 4,000 units; however, if unit sales turn out to be only 80% of forecast, then unit sales = 3,200.

	Year 0	Year 1	Year 2	Year 3
Investment Outlays:				
Equipment Cost (1 − T)	($48,750)			
Change in NOWC	(2,000)			
Operating Cash Flows over Project's Life:				
Revenues (3,200 × $50)		$160,000	$160,000	$160,000
Variable costs (70%)		112,000	112,000	112,000
Fixed costs		30,000	30,000	30,000
Depreciation: 100% bonus depreciation in Year 0		0	0	0
EBIT		$ 18,000	$ 18,000	$ 18,000
Taxes on operating income (25%)		4,500	4,500	4,500
AT project operating income		$ 13,500	$ 13,500	$ 13,500
Add back: Depreciation		0	0	0
EBIT(1 − T) + Depreciation		$ 13,500	$ 13,500	$ 13,500
Terminal Cash Flows:				
Salvage value				10,000
Tax on salvage value				(2,500)
AT salvage value				$ 7,500
Recovery of NOWC				2,000
Project free cash flows	($50,750)	$ 13,500	$ 13,500	$ 23,000

NPV calculation:

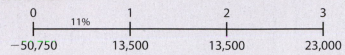

0	1	2	3
11%			
−50,750	13,500	13,500	23,000

NPV $= -\$50{,}750 + \$13{,}500/(1.11)^1 + \$13{,}500/(1.11)^2 + \$23{,}000/(1.11)^3$

$= -\$10{,}814$

Alternatively, using a financial calculator, you would enter the following data: $CF_0 = -50750$; $CF_1 = 13500$; $CF_2 = 13500$; $CF_3 = 23000$; I/YR = 11; and then solve for NPV = −$10,814.

Because the NPV is negative, the project should not be accepted. If unit sales were 20% below the forecasted level, the project would no longer be accepted.

e. *Best-case scenario:* Unit sales = 4,800; Variable cost % = 65%

	Year 0	Year 1	Year 2	Year 3
Investment Outlays:				
Equipment Cost (1 − T)	($48,750)			
Change in NOWC	(2,000)			
Operating Cash Flows over Project's Life:				
Revenues (4,800 × $50)		$240,000	$240,000	$240,000
Variable costs (65%)		156,000	156,000	156,000
Fixed costs		30,000	30,000	30,000
Depreciation: 100% bonus depreciation in Year 0		0	0	0
EBIT		$ 54,000	$ 54,000	$ 54,000
Taxes on operating income (25%)		13,500	13,500	13,500
AT project operating income		$ 40,500	$ 40,500	$ 40,500
Add back: Depreciation		0	0	0
EBIT(1 − T) + Depreciation		$ 40,500	$ 40,500	$ 40,500
Terminal Cash Flows:				
Salvage value				10,000
Tax on salvage value				(2,500)
AT salvage value				$ 7,500
Recovery of NOWC				2,000
Project free cash flows	($50,750)	$ 40,500	$ 40,500	$ 50,000

NPV calculation:

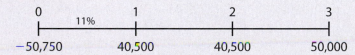

0	1	2	3
11%			
−50,750	40,500	40,500	50,000

NPV $= -\$50{,}750 + \$40{,}500/(1.11)^1 + \$40{,}500/(1.11)^2 + \$50{,}000/(1.11)^3$

$= \$55{,}167$

Alternatively, using a financial calculator, you would enter the following data: $CF_0 = -50750$; $CF_1 = 40500$; $CF_2 = 40500$; $CF_3 = 50000$; I/YR =11; and then solve for NPV = $55,167.

Base-case scenario: The NPV was calculated in part c as $11,180.

Worst-case scenario: Unit sales = 3,200; Variable cost % = 75%

	Year 0	Year 1	Year 2	Year 3
Investment Outlays:				
Equipment Cost (1 − T)	($48,750)			
Change in NOWC	(2,000)			

(Continued)

	Year 0	Year 1	Year 2	Year 3
Operating Cash Flows over Project's Life:				
Revenues (3,200 × $50)		$160,000	$160,000	$160,000
Variable costs (75%)		120,000	120,000	120,000
Fixed costs		30,000	30,000	30,000
Depreciation: 100% bonus depreciation in Year 0		0	0	0
EBIT		$ 10,000	$ 10,000	$ 10,000
Taxes on operating income (25%)		2,500	2,500	2,500
AT project operating income		$ 7,500	$ 7,500	$ 7,500
Add back: Depreciation		0	0	0
EBIT(1 − T) + Depreciation		$ 7,500	$ 7,500	$ 7,500
Terminal Cash Flows:				
Salvage value				10,000
Tax on salvage value				(2,500)
AT salvage value				$ 7,500
Recovery of NOWC				2,000
Project free cash flows	($50,750)	$ 7,500	$ 7,500	$ 17,000

NPV calculation:

0	11% → 1	2	3
−50,750	7,500	7,500	17,000

$$NPV = -\$50{,}750 + \$7{,}500/(1.11)^1 + \$7{,}500/(1.11)^2 + \$17{,}000/(1.11)^3$$
$$= -\$25{,}476$$

Alternatively, using a financial calculator, you would enter the following data: $CF_0 = -50750$; $CF_1 = 7500$; $CF_2 = 7500$; $CF_3 = 17000$; I/YR = 11; and then solve for NPV = −$25,476.

Scenario	Probability	NPV
Best case	25%	$55,167
Base case	50	11,180
Worst case	25	−25,476
	Expected NPV =	$13,013

$$\sigma_{NPV} = [0.25(\$55{,}167 - \$13{,}013)^2 + 0.50(\$11{,}180 - \$13{,}013)^2 + 0.25(-\$25{,}476 - \$13{,}013)^2]^{1/2}$$
$$\sigma_{NPV} = [\$444{,}241{,}510 + \$1{,}679{,}550 + \$370{,}341{,}254]^{1/2}$$
$$\sigma_{NPV} = \$28{,}570$$
$$CV_{NPV} = \$28{,}570/\$13{,}013 = 2.2$$

f. The project's CV = 2.2, which is larger than the firm's typical project CV. So, the WACC for this project should be adjusted upward, 11% + 3% = 14%.

To calculate the expected NPV, standard deviation, and coefficient of variation you would recalculate each scenario's NPV by discounting the project cash flows by 14% rather than 11%.

Best-case scenario:

0	14% → 1	2	3
−50,750	40,500	40,500	50,000

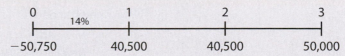

$$NPV = -\$50{,}750 + \$40{,}500/(1.14)^1 + \$40{,}500/(1.14)^2 + \$50{,}000/(1.14)^3$$
$$= \$49{,}688$$

Alternatively, using a financial calculator, you would enter the following data: $CF_0 = -50750$; $CF_1 = 40500$; $CF_2 = 40500$; $CF_3 = 50000$; I/YR = 14; and then solve for NPV = \$49,688.

Base-case scenario:

0	14%	1	2	3
−50,750		22,500	22,500	32,000

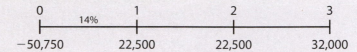

$$\text{NPV} = -\$50{,}750 + \$22{,}500/(1.14)^1 + \$22{,}500/(1.14)^2 + \$32{,}000/(1.14)^3$$
$$= \$7{,}899$$

Alternatively, using a financial calculator, you would enter the following data: $CF_0 = -50750$; $CF_1 = 22500$; $CF_2 = 22500$; $CF_3 = 32000$; I/YR = 14; and then solve for NPV = \$7,899.

Worst-case scenario:

0	14%	1	2	3
−50,750		7,500	7,500	17,000

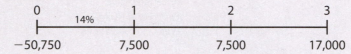

$$\text{NPV} = -\$50{,}750 + \$7{,}500/(1.14)^1 + \$7{,}500/(1.14)^2 + \$17{,}000/(1.14)^3$$
$$= -\$26{,}926$$

Alternatively, using a financial calculator, you would enter the following data: $CF_0 = -50750$; $CF_1 = 7500$; $CF_2 = 7500$; $CF_3 = 17000$; I/YR = 14; and then solve for NPV = −\$26,926.

Scenario	Probability	NPV
Best case	25%	\$49,688
Base case	50	7,899
Worst case	25	−26,926
	Expected NPV =	\$ 9,640

$$\sigma_{NPV} = [0.25(\$49{,}688 - \$9{,}640)^2 + 0.50(\$7{,}899 - \$9{,}640)^2 + 0.25(-\$26{,}926 - \$9{,}640)^2]^{1/2}$$
$$\sigma_{NPV} = [\$400{,}963{,}680 + \$1{,}515{,}932 + \$334{,}262{,}696]^{1/2}$$
$$\sigma_{NPV} = \$27{,}143$$
$$CV_{NPV} = \$27{,}143/\$9{,}640 = 2.82$$

The expected NPV of the project is still positive, so the project would still be accepted, but it is a risky project.

Chapter 13

ST-2 a. The following information is given in the problem:

Q = Units of output (sales) = 5,000

P = Average sales price per unit of output = \$100

F = Fixed operating costs = \$200,000

V = Variable costs per unit = \$50

EBIT = Operating income = \$50,000

Total assets = \$500,000

Common equity = \$500,000

(1) Determine the new EBIT level if the change is made:

$$\text{New EBIT} = P_2(Q_2) - F_2 - V_2(Q_2)$$
$$\text{New EBIT} = \$95(7{,}000) - \$250{,}000 - \$40(7{,}000)$$
$$= \$135{,}000$$

(2) Determine the incremental EBIT:

$$\Delta\text{EBIT} = \$135{,}000 - \$50{,}000 = \$85{,}000$$

(3) Estimate the approximate rate of return on the new investment:

$$\Delta ROA = \frac{\Delta EBIT}{Investment} = \frac{\$85{,}000}{\$400{,}000} = 21.25\%$$

Because the ROA exceeds Olinde's average cost of capital, this analysis suggests that the firm should go ahead and make the investment.

b. The change would increase the break-even point. Still, with a lower sales price, it might be easier to achieve the higher new break-even volume.

$$\text{Old: } Q_{BE} = \frac{F}{P - V} = \frac{\$200{,}000}{\$100 - \$50} = 4{,}000 \text{ units}$$

$$\text{New: } Q_{BE} = \frac{F_2}{P_2 - V_2} = \frac{\$250{,}000}{\$95 - \$40} = 4{,}545 \text{ units}$$

c. The incremental ROA is

$$\Delta ROA = \frac{\Delta Profit}{\Delta Sales} \times \frac{\Delta Sales}{\Delta Assets}$$

Using debt financing, the incremental profit associated with the investment is equal to the incremental profit found in part a minus the interest expense incurred as a result of the investment:

$$\begin{aligned} \Delta Profit &= \text{New profit} - \text{Old profit} - \text{Interest} \\ &= \$135{,}000 - \$50{,}000 - 0.10(\$400{,}000) \\ &= \$45{,}000 \end{aligned}$$

The incremental sales is calculated as

$$\begin{aligned} \Delta Sales &= P_2Q_2 - P_1Q_1 \\ &= \$95(7{,}000) - \$100(5{,}000) \\ &= \$665{,}000 - \$500{,}000 \\ &= \$165{,}000 \end{aligned}$$

$$\Delta ROA = \frac{\$45{,}000}{\$165{,}000} \times \frac{\$165{,}000}{\$400{,}000} = 11.25\%$$

The return on the new investment still exceeds the average cost of capital, so the firm should make the investment.

ST-3 a. Total capital = \$5,000,000 and remains the same at all levels of debt; Tax rate = 25%; Original shares outstanding = 200,000; EBIT = \$500,000 at all levels of debt.

From the data given in the problem, we can develop the following table:

w_d	w_c	r_d	EBIT	Interest[a]	Net Income[b]	Shares Outstanding[c]	EPS[d]
0.00	1.00	5.00%	\$500,000	\$ 0	\$375,000	200,000	\$1.88
0.25	0.75	6.00	500,000	75,000	318,750	150,000	2.13
0.50	0.50	8.30	500,000	207,500	219,375	100,000	2.19
0.75	0.25	11.00	500,000	412,500	65,625	50,000	1.31

Notes:

[a]Interest expense is calculated as $w_d \times$ Total capital $\times r_d$.

[b]Net income is calculated as (EBIT − Interest) (1 − T)

[c]Shares outstanding is calculated as Original shares outstanding − ($w_d \times$ Original shares outstanding).

[d]EPS is calculated as Net income divided by Shares outstanding.

b. EPS is maximized at a capital structure consisting of 50% debt and 50% equity. At that capital structure, the firm's EPS is \$2.19.

c. Tax rate = 25%; r_{RF} = 3.5%; b_U = 1.25; $r_M - r_{RF}$ = 4.5%.

From data given in the problem, we can develop the following table:

w_d	w_c	D/E	r_d	$r_d(1-T)$	b_L[a]	r_s[b]	WACC[c]
0.00	1.00	0.0000	5.00%	3.75%	1.2500	9.13%	9.13%
0.25	0.75	0.3333	6.00	4.50	1.5625	10.53	9.02
0.50	0.50	1.0000	8.30	6.23	2.1875	13.34	9.78
0.75	0.25	3.0000	11.00	8.25	4.0625	21.78	11.63

Notes:

[a]These beta estimates were calculated using the Hamada equation, $b_L = b_U[1 + (1 - T)(D/E)]$.

[b]These r_s estimates were calculated using the CAPM, $r_s = r_{RF} + (r_M - r_{RF})b$.

[c]These WACC estimates were calculated with the following equation:
$WACC = w_d(r_d)(1-T) + (w_c)(r_s)$.

d. Carlisle's WACC is minimized at a capital structure consisting of 25% debt and 75% equity. At that capital structure, the firm's WACC is 9.02%.

e. The capital structure at which the firm's WACC is minimized is the optimal capital structure, that is, the capital structure at which the firm's value is maximized. For Carlisle, this capital structure consists of 25% debt and 75% equity. This is not the same capital structure at which EPS is maximized, because the additional risk taken on is not measured in the EPS calculation, but it is measured in the WACC calculation. (That is, the costs of debt and equity increase at additional debt levels, and those component costs are used in the WACC calculation.)

f. As an analyst (on the basis of these data), the recommendation to the firm would be to issue \$1,250,000 of debt (calculated as 0.25 × \$5,000,000) with a 6% coupon rate (this is r_d at this debt level) and use these funds to repurchase 50,000 shares of common stock.

Chapter 14

ST-2 a.

Projected net income	**\$2,000,000**
Less projected capital investments	**800,000**
Available residual	**\$1,200,000**
Shares outstanding	**200,000**

DPS = \$1,200,000/200,000 shares = \$6 = D_1

b. **EPS = \$2,000,000/200,000 shares = \$10**

Payout ratio = DPS/EPS = \$6/\$10 = 60%, or

Total dividends/NI = \$1,200,000/\$2,000,000 = 60%

c. **Currently,** $$P_0 = \frac{D_1}{r_s - g} = \frac{\$6}{0.14 - 0.06} = \frac{\$6}{0.08} = \$75.00$$

Under the former circumstances, D_1 would be based on a 20% payout on an EPS of \$10, or 0.2 × \$10 = \$2. With r_s = 14% and g = 12%, we solve for P_0:

$$P_0 = \frac{D_1}{r_s - g} = \frac{\$2}{0.14 - 0.12} = \frac{\$2}{0.02} = \$100$$

Although CMC has suffered a severe setback, its existing assets will continue to provide a good income stream. More of these earnings should now be passed on to the shareholders, as the slowed internal growth has reduced the need for funds. However, the net result is a 25% decrease in the value of the shares.

d. If the payout ratio were continued at 20%, even after internal investment opportunities had declined, the price of the stock would drop to $2/(0.14 − 0.06) = $25 rather than to $75.00. Thus, an increase in the dividend payout is consistent with maximizing shareholder wealth.

Because of the diminishing nature of profitable investment opportunities, the greater the firm's level of investment, the lower the average ROE. Thus, the more money CMC retains and invests, the lower its average ROE will be. We can determine the average ROE under different conditions as follows:

Old situation (with founder active and a 20% payout):

$$g = (1.0 - \text{Payout ratio})(\text{Average ROE})$$

$$12\% = (1.0 - 0.2)(\text{Average ROE})$$

$$\text{Average ROE} = 12\%/0.8 = 15\% > r_s = 14\%$$

Note that the *average* ROE is 15%, whereas the *marginal* ROE is presumably equal to 14%.

New situation (with founder retired and a 60% payout as explained in part c):

$$g = 6\% = (1.0 - 0.6)(\text{ROE})$$

$$\text{ROE} = 6\%/0.4 = 15\% > r_s = 14\%$$

This suggests that a new payout of 60% is appropriate and that the firm is taking on investments down to the point at which marginal returns are equal to the cost of capital. Note that if the 20% payout was maintained, the *average* ROE would be only 7.5%, which would imply a marginal ROE far below the 14% cost of capital.

Chapter 15

ST-2 The Calgary Company: Alternative Balance Sheets

	Restricted (40%)	Moderate (50%)	Relaxed (60%)
Current assets	$1,200,000	$1,500,000	$1,800,000
Fixed assets	600,000	600,000	600,000
Total assets	$1,800,000	$2,100,000	$2,400,000
Debt	$ 900,000	$1,050,000	$1,200,000
Equity	900,000	1,050,000	1,200,000
Total liabilities and equity	$1,800,000	$2,100,000	$2,400,000

The Calgary Company: Alternative Income Statements

	Restricted	Moderate	Relaxed
Sales	$3,000,000	$3,000,000	$3,000,000
EBIT	450,000	450,000	450,000
Interest (10%)	90,000	105,000	120,000
Earnings before taxes	$ 360,000	$ 345,000	$ 330,000
Taxes (25%)	90,000	86,250	82,500
Net income	$ 270,000	$ 258,750	$ 247,500
ROE	30.0%	24.6%	20.6%

ST-3 a and b.

Income Statements for Year Ended December 31, 2019 (thousands of dollars)

	Vanderheiden Press		Herrenhouse Publishing	
	a	b	a	b
EBIT	\$ 30,000	\$ 30,000	\$ 30,000	\$ 30,000
Interest	4,400	5,800	2,600	8,200
Taxable income	\$ 25,600	\$ 24,200	\$ 27,400	\$ 21,800
Taxes (25%)	6,400	6,050	6,850	5,450
Net income	\$ 19,200	\$ 18,150	\$ 20,550	\$ 16,350
Equity	\$100,000	\$100,000	\$100,000	\$100,000
Return on equity	19.20%	18.15%	20.55%	16.35%

The Vanderheiden Press has a higher ROE than Herrenhouse Publishing when short-term interest rates are high, whereas Herrenhouse Publishing does better than Vanderheiden Press when rates are lower.

c. Herrenhouse's position is riskier. First, its profits and return on equity are much more volatile than Vanderheiden's. Second, Herrenhouse must renew its large short-term loan every year, and if the renewal comes up at a time when money is very tight, when its business is depressed, or both, then Herrenhouse could be denied credit, which could put it out of business.

Chapter 16

ST-2 To solve this problem, we define ΔS as the change in sales and g as the growth rate in sales, and then we use the three following equations:

$$\Delta S = S_0 g$$

$$S_1 = S_0(1 + g)$$

$$AFN = (A_0^*/S_0)(\Delta S) - (L_0^*/S_0)(\Delta S) - MS_1(1 - \text{Payout})$$

Set AFN = 0, substitute in known values for A_0^*/S_0, L_0^*/S_0, M, payout, and S_0, and then solve for g:

$$0 = 1.6(\$100g) - 0.4(\$100g) - 0.10[\$100(1 + g)](1 - 0.45)$$

$$0 = \$160g - \$40g - 0.055(\$100 + \$100g)$$

$$0 = \$160g - \$40g - \$5.5 - \$5.5g$$

$$\$114.5g = \$5.5$$

$$g = \$5.5/\$114.5 = 0.048 = 4.8\%$$

$$g = \text{Maximum growth rate without external financing}$$

ST-3 Assets consist of cash, marketable securities, receivables, inventories, and fixed assets. Therefore, we can break the A_0^*/S_0 ratio into its components—cash/sales, inventories/sales, and so forth. Then

$$\frac{A_0^*}{S_0} = \frac{A_0^* - \text{Inventories}}{S_0} + \frac{\text{Inventories}}{S_0} = 1.6$$

We know that the inventory turnover ratio is Sales/Inventories = 3 times, so Inventories/Sales = 1/3 = 0.3333. Further, if the inventory turnover ratio can be increased to 4 times, then the Inventory/Sales ratio will fall to 1/4 = 0.25, a difference of 0.3333 − 0.2500 = 0.0833. This, in turn, causes the A_0^*/S_0 ratio to fall from $A_0^*/S_0 = 1.6$ to $A_0^*/S_0 = 1.6 - 0.0833 = 1.5167$.

This change has two effects: First, it changes the AFN equation, and second, it means that Weatherford currently has excessive inventories. Because it is costly to hold excess inventories, Weatherford will want to reduce its inventory holdings by not replacing inventories until the excess amounts have been used. We can account for this by setting up the revised AFN equation (using the new A_0^*/S_0 ratio), estimating the funds that will be needed next year if no excess inventories are currently on hand, and then subtracting out the excess inventories that are currently on hand:

Present conditions:

$$\frac{\text{Sales}}{\text{Inventories}} = \frac{\$100}{\text{Inventories}} = 3$$

so

$$\text{Inventories} = \$100/3 = \$33.3 \text{ million at present}$$

New conditions:

$$\frac{\text{Sales}}{\text{Inventories}} = \frac{\$100}{\text{Inventories}} = 4$$

so

$$\text{New level of inventories} = \$100/4 = \$25 \text{ million}$$

Therefore,

$$\text{Excess inventories} = \$33.3 - \$25 = \$8.3 \text{ million}$$

Forecast of funds needed:

$$\Delta S = 0.2(\$100 \text{ million}) = \$20 \text{ million}$$

$$\begin{aligned} \text{AFN} &= 1.5167(\$20) - 0.4(\$20) - 0.1(1 - 0.45)(\$120) - \$8.3 \\ &= \$30.3 - \$8 - \$6.6 - \$8.3 \\ &= \$7.4 \text{ million} \end{aligned}$$

Chapter 17

ST-2 $$\frac{\text{Euros}}{\text{C\$}} = \frac{\text{Euros}}{\text{US\$}} \times \frac{\text{US\$}}{\text{C\$}}$$

$$= \frac{€0.86}{\$1} \times \frac{\$1}{\text{C\$}1.30} = \frac{€0.86}{\text{C\$}1.30} = €0.66154 \text{ per Canadian dollar}$$

Appendix B

Answers to Selected End-of-Chapter Problems

Note: This appendix presents some intermediate steps and final answers to selected end-of-chapter problems. Your answer may differ slightly due to rounding differences. Also, some of the problems may have more than one correct solution depending upon the assumptions made in working the problem. Finally, where the selected problems involve a verbal discussion as well as numerical calculations, the verbal answer is not provided.

3-2 \$800,000
3-4 \$34,000,000
3-6 \$22,000,000
3-8 a. \$83,379
b. 32%
c. 22.23%
3-10 \$71,600,000
3-12 a. \$62,000
b. \$72,000
3-14 a. $NOWC_{2018}$ = \$42,000; $NOWC_{2019}$ = \$50,220
b. \$22,780
c. CS = \$40,000; RE = \$46,220
d. EVA = \$21,678
e. MVA = \$13,780
3-16 a. RE_{2018} = \$1,318 million
b. \$1,600 million
c. \$15 million
d. \$620 million
3-18 a. \$16,739.50
b. \$22%
c. 16.33%

4-2 47.64%
4-4 M/B = 1.1765; EV/EBITDA = 12.5
4-6 ROE = 14.25%
4-8 NI = \$451,562.50
4-10 P_0 = \$72.22; EV/EBITDA = 9.875
4-12 TIE = 3.33×
4-14 ROE = 20.21%
4-16 ΔROE = +8.68%
4-18 TIE = 3.67×
4-20 Accounts receivable = \$49,085
4-22 Sales = \$450,000; AR = \$45,000;
Inv = \$90,000; FA = \$150,000; CL = \$75,000
4-24 a. Current ratio = 3.56×;
Debt to total capital = 20.05%;
DSO = 30.3 days; ROA = 7.50%;
ROIC = 9.42%
b. Firm: ROE = 4.24% × 1.77 × \$450/\$315
= 10.7%
Industry: ROE = 3.75% × 3 × ROE/ROA
= 3.75% × 3 × 16.1%/11.25%
= 16.1%

5-2 PV = \$10,929.80
5-4 N = 17.67 yrs.
5-6 FVA_5 = \$4,420.51; $FVA_{5\ Due}$ = \$4,641.53
5-8 PMT = \$811.06; EAR = 8.30%
5-10 a. \$296.05
b. \$431.78
c. \$135.11
d. \$866.17; \$1,263.30
5-12 a. 10%
b. 10%
c. 3%
d. 11%
5-14 a. \$6,616.38
b. \$1,109.99
c. \$2,800.00
d(1). \$7,542.67
d(2). \$1,187.68
d(3). \$2,800.00
5-16 $PV_{5\%}$ = \$12,000; $PV_{10\%}$ = \$6,000
5-18 a. Stream A: \$1,505.84;
Stream B: \$1,522.73
b. Stream A and Stream B: \$1,750
5-20 Contract 2: PV = \$12,358,739.18
5-22 a. \$802.43
b. Pymt 1: Int = \$500; Princ = \$302.43;
Pymt 2: Int = \$484.88; Princ = \$317.55
c. \$984.88
5-24 a. \$279.20
b. \$276.84
c. \$443.72
5-26 \$17,290.89; \$19,734.26
5-28 I_{NOM} = 11.729145% ≈ 11.73%
5-30 a. A = 59.89 yrs.; L = 50.08 yrs.
b. \$12,649.64
5-32 \$1,297.13
5-34 a. PMT = \$7,372.64
b. Yr.1: Int/Pymt = 20.62%; Princ/Pymt
= 79.38%;
Yr.2: Int/Pymt = 14.27%; Princ/Pymt
= 85.73%;
Yr.3: Int/Pymt = 7.41%; Princ/Pymt
= 92.59%

5-36 a. $5,468.41
b. $1,926.87

5-38 $580,191

5-40 $6,147

6-2 2.55%

6-4 2.65%

6-6 23.9%

6-8 8.36%

6-10 5.5%

6-12 0.47%

6-14 a. r_1 in Yr. 2 = 5%
b. $I_1 = 2.2\%$; $I_2 = 4\%$

6-16 14%

6-18 a. $r_{T1} = 9.20\%$; $r_{T2} = 8.40\%$; $r_{T3} = 7.60\%$; $r_{T4} = 7.30\%$; $r_{T5} = 7.20\%$; $r_{T10} = 6.60\%$; $r_{T20} = 6.30\%$

7-2 a. 8.27%
b. $983.38

7-4 YTM = $6.42%; YTC = 6.32%; most likely yield = 6.32%

7-6 a. Bond C: $1,108.82; $1,084.74; $1,058.69; $1,030.50; $1,000.00
Bond Z: $729.61; $789.44; $854.17; $924.21; $1,000.00

7-8 11.75%

7-10 a. YTM = 10.595%
b. CY = 9.887%; CGY = 0.708%

7-12 a. YTM = 6.50%; YTC = 3.72%

7-14 a. 6 yrs.
b. YTC = 6.64%

7-16 $1,071.06

7-18 a. YTM = 8.22%
b. YTC = 7.91%
c. YTC = 7.91%
d. Yr. 7; YTC = 8.20%

8-2 $b_p = 2.10$

8-4 $r_M = 7.5\%$; $r = 6.7\%$

8-6 a. $\hat{r}_B = 14\%$
b. $\sigma_A = 12.20\%$; $CV_B = 1.45$
c. Sharpe $\text{ratio}_A = 0.7787$;
Sharpe $\text{ratio}_B = 0.5651$

8-8 b = 1.1667

8-10 5.2%

8-12 a. $r_i = 12.4\%$
b(l). $r_M = 11\%$; $r_i = 13.4\%$
b(2). $r_M = 9\%$; $r_i = 11.4\%$
c(l). $r_i = 15.2\%$
c(2). $r_i = 11.0\%$

8-14 $b_N = 1.24$

8-16 $r_p = 11.30\%$

8-18 a. $0.5 million
d(l). $75,000
d(2). 15%

8-20 a. $r_A = 11.30\%$; $r_B = 11.30\%$
b. $r_{p\ Avg} = 11.30\%$
c. $\sigma_A = 20.8\%$; $\sigma_B = 20.8\%$; $\sigma_p = 20.1\%$
d. $CV_A = CV_B = 1.84$; $CV_p = 1.78$

9-2 $\hat{P}_0 = \$30.00$

9-4 a. End of Yr. 2
b. $67.65
c. $59.88

9-6 $r_p = 9.17\%$

9-8 a. $114.29
b. $88.89

9-10 $17.63

9-12 a(l). $12.25
a(2). $15.63
a(3). $25.75
a(4). $43.75
b(l). Undefined
b(2). −$35.00, which is nonsense

9-14 $P_0 = \$10.08$

9-16 2.25%

9-18 a. $P_0 = \$54.11$; $D_1/P_0 = 3.55\%$; CGY = 6.45%

9-20 $21.00

9A-2 a. $P_0 = \$32.14$
b. $P_0 = \$37.50$
c. $P_0 = \$50.00$
d. $P_0 = \$78.28$

10-2 $r_p = 10.53\%$

10-4 a. $r_s = 7.33\%$
b. $r_e = 7.70\%$

10-6 a. $r_s = 15.6\%$
b. $r_s = 14.4\%$
c. $r_s = 15\%$
d. $r_{s\ Avg} = 15.0\%$

10-8 $r_s = 15.74\%$; WACC = 12.33%

10-10 WACC = 9.91%

10-12 a. $r_s = 14.97\%$
b. WACC = 12.09%
c. Project A

10-14 10.67%

10-16 a. g = 8%
b. $D_1 = \$2.81$
c. $r_s = 15.81\%$

10-18 a. $r_d(1 - T) = 7.5\%$; $r_p = 10\%$; $r_s = 16.18\%$
b. WACC = 14.26%
c. Projects 1 and 2 will be accepted

10-20 a. $r_d(1 - T) = 6.75\%$; $r_s = 14.6\%$
b. WACC = 11.46%

11-2 IRR = 11.57%

11-4 5.42 yrs.

11-6 a. 5%: NPV_A = \$3.52; NPV_B = \$2.87
10%: NPV_A = \$0.58; NPV_B = \$1.04
15%: NPV_A = −\$1.91; NPV_B = −\$0.55
b. IRR_A = 11.10%; IRR_B = 13.18%
c. 5%: Choose A; 10%: Choose B; 15%: Do not choose either one

11-8 a. Without mitigation: NPV = \$12.10 million; IRR = 19.86%;
With mitigation: NPV = \$5.70 million; IRR = 15.24%

11-10 Project 1; NPV_1 = \$234.26

11-12 IRR_L = 12.70%

11-14 a. HCC; PV = −\$805,009.87
c. LCC; PV = −\$686,627.14

11-16 a. NPV_A = \$14,486,808; NPV_B = \$11,156,893;
IRR_A = 15.03%; IRR_B = 22.26%
c. Crossover rate ≈ 11.71%

11-18 a. No; PV_{Old} = −\$89,910.08;
PV_{New} = −\$94,611.45
b. \$2,470.80
c. 22.94%

11-20 \$2,698.89

11-22 \$250.01

12-2 a. \$1,125,000
b. \$750,000

12-4 Yes, NPV = \$4,156.54

12-6 a. SL: Deprec: = \$200,000/yr;
Bonus: \$800,000 in Year 0; \$0 in all other years
b. Bonus; \$34,393.66

12-8 a. −\$135,500
b. \$37,500; \$37,500; \$90,500
c. No, NPV = −\$2,423

12-10 Yes, NPV = \$3,384.34

12-12 a. A: \$6,750; B: \$7,650; σ_A = \$474.34;
CV_A = 0.0703
b. Project B

12-14 a. −\$75,625
b. \$27,875; \$27,875; \$27,875; \$27,875; \$16,625
c. Yes, NPV = \$25,487.30

12-16 a. 2 years; NPV_2 = \$459.98

13-2 30% debt and 70% equity

13-4 b_U = 0.9455

13-6 a(1). −\$38,000
a(2). \$40,000
b. Q_{BE} = 11,923
c. Q_{BE} = 7,750
d. Q_{BE} = 17,222

13-8 r_s = 13.60%

13-10 a. FC_A = \$80,000; V_A = \$4.80/unit;
P_A = \$8.00/unit
b. Firm B
c. 50,000 units

13-12 a. EPS_{Old} = \$2.55; New: EPS_D = \$5.93;
EPS_S = \$4.09
b. 339,750 units
c. Q_{Old} = 316,957 units;
$Q_{New, Debt}$ = 272,250 units;
$Q_{New, Stock}$ = 204,750 units

14-2 P_0 = \$96.67

14-4 D_0 = \$5.37

14-6 Payout = 36%

14-8 a. 12%
b. 18%
c. g = 6%; r_s = 18%
d. 6%
e. 28,800 new shares; \$0.13 per share

15-2 45.62 days; 30 days; \$513,698.63

15-4 a. 51 days
b. \$197,782.41 ≈ \$197,782
c. 7.60×

15-6 a. 32 days
b. \$313,600
c. \$29,400
d(1). 27 days
d(2). \$777,600

15-8 a. ROE_T = 18.06%; ROE_M = 16.88%;
ROE_R = 14.83%

15-10 a. Oct: loan = \$22,800
b. \$111,300; \$297,600; −\$155,100; −\$22,800; \$118,500; \$187,800

16-2 AFN = \$646,000

16-4 a. \$166.875 million
b. 39.06%

16-6 \$67 million; 5.01×

16-8 a. \$825,000
b. \$141,875

16-10 \$34.338 million; 34.97 ≈ 35 days

16-12 a. \$3,750,000,000
b. 21%
c. \$31,500,000

16-14 a. 33.33%
b. NP = \$3,553.2; Bonds = \$6,598.8;
Stock = \$2,095; RE = \$28,703

17-2 30.83 yen per shekel

17-4 1 euro = \$1.1765 or \$1 = 0.8500 euro

17-8 11.83 kronas per pound

17-10 $r_{NOM-U.S.}$ = 4.6770%

17-12 a. \$1.298389
b. Discount

17-14 +\$700,000

17-16 \$416,793,893

Appendix C

Selected Equations and Tables

Chapter 3

Stockholders' equity = Paid-in capital + Retained earnings

Stockholders' equity = Total assets − Total liabilities

Net working capital = Current assets − Current liabilities

Net operating working capital = Operating current assets − Operating current liabilities

$$= \left(\text{Current assets} - \text{Excess cash}\right) - \left(\text{Current liabilities} - \text{Notes payable}\right)$$

Total debt = Short-term debt + Long-term debt

Total liabilities = Total debt + Accounts payable + Accruals

Operating income (or EBIT) = Sales revenues − Operating costs

$$\text{FCF} = (\text{EBIT}(1 - T) + \text{Depreciation}) - \left(\text{Capital expenditures} + \Delta\text{Net operating working capital}\right)$$

$$\text{MVA} = (P_0 \times \text{Shares outstanding}) - \text{Book value of total common equity}$$

$$\text{EVA} = \text{EBIT}(1 - T) - \left(\text{Total invested capital} \times \text{After-tax percentage cost of capital}\right)$$

2018 Individual Tax Rates: Single Individuals

If Your Taxable Income Is	You Pay This Amount on the Base of the Bracket	Plus This Percentage on the Excess over the Base (Marginal Rate)	Average Tax Rate at Top of Bracket
Up to $9,525	$ 0	10.0%	10.0%
$9,525–$38,700	952.50	12.0	11.5
$38,700–$82,500	4,453.50	22.0	17.1
$82,500–$157,500	14,089.50	24.0	20.4
$157,500–$200,000	32,089.50	32.0	22.8
$200,000–$500,000	45,689.50	35.0	30.1
Over $500,000	150,689.50	37.0	37.0

Married Couples Filing Joint Returns

If Your Taxable Income Is	You Pay This Amount on the Base of the Bracket	Plus This Percentage on the Excess over the Base (Marginal Rate)	Average Tax Rate at Top of Bracket
Up to $19,050	0	10.0%	10.0%
$19,050–$77,400	1,905.00	12.0	11.5
$77,400–$165,000	8,907.00	22.0	17.1
$165,000–$315,000	28,179.00	24.0	20.4
$315,000–$400,000	64,179.00	32.0	22.8
$400,000–$600,000	91,379.00	35.0	26.9
Over $600,000	161,379.00	37.0	37.0

Chapter 4

$$\text{Current ratio} = \frac{\text{Current assets}}{\text{Current liabilities}}$$

$$\text{Quick, or acid test, ratio} = \frac{\text{Current assets} - \text{Inventories}}{\text{Current liabilities}}$$

$$\text{Inventory turnover} = \frac{\text{Sales}}{\text{Inventories}}$$

$$\text{Days sales outstanding (DSO)} = \frac{\text{Receivable}}{\text{Average sales per day}} = \frac{\text{Receivables}}{\text{Annual sales}/365}$$

$$\text{Fixed assets turnover} = \frac{\text{Sales}}{\text{Net fixed assets}}$$

$$\text{Total assets turnover} = \frac{\text{Sales}}{\text{Total assets}}$$

$$\text{Total-debt-to-total-capital ratio} = \frac{\text{Total debt}}{\text{Total capital}} = \frac{\text{Total debt}}{\text{Total debt} + \text{Equity}}$$

$$\text{Total-liabilities-to-assets ratio} = \frac{\text{Total liabilities}}{\text{Total assets}}$$

$$\text{Debt-to-equity ratio} = \frac{\text{Total debt}}{\text{Equity}}$$

$$\text{Times-interest-earned (TIE)} = \frac{\text{EBIT}}{\text{Interest charges}}$$

$$\text{EBITDA coverage} = \frac{\text{EBITDA} + \text{Lease payments}}{\text{Interest} + \text{Principal payments} + \text{Lease payments}}$$

$$\text{Operating margin} = \frac{\text{EBIT}}{\text{Sales}}$$

$$\text{Profit margin} = \frac{\text{Net income}}{\text{Sales}}$$

$$\text{Return on total assets (ROA)} = \frac{\text{Net income}}{\text{Total assets}}$$

$$\text{Return on common equity (ROE)} = \frac{\text{Net income}}{\text{Common equity}}$$

$$\text{Return on invested capital (ROIC)} = \frac{\text{EBIT}(1 - \text{T})}{\text{Total invested capital}} = \frac{\text{EBIT}(1 - \text{T})}{\text{Debt} + \text{Equity}}$$

$$\text{Basic earning power (BEP)} = \frac{\text{EBIT}}{\text{Total assets}}$$

$$\text{Price/Earnings (P/E)} = \frac{\text{Price per share}}{\text{Earnings per share}}$$

$$\text{Book value per share} = \frac{\text{Common equity}}{\text{Shares outstanding}}$$

$$\text{Market/Book (M/B)} = \frac{\text{Market price per share}}{\text{Book value per share}}$$

$$\text{EV/EBITDA} = [\text{MV Equity} + \text{MV Total Debt} + \text{MV Other Financial Claims} - \text{Cash and Equivalents}]/\text{EBITDA}$$

$$\begin{aligned}\text{ROE} &= \text{ROA} \times \text{Equity multiplier}\\ &= \text{Profit margin} \times \text{Total assets turnover} \times \text{Equity multiplier}\\ &= \frac{\text{Net income}}{\text{Sales}} \times \frac{\text{Sales}}{\text{Total assets}} \times \frac{\text{Total assets}}{\text{Total common equity}}\end{aligned}$$

$$\begin{aligned}\text{EVA} &= \text{Net income} - (\text{Equity} \times \text{Cost of equity})\\ &= (\text{Equity})(\text{Net income/Equity} - \text{Cost of equity})\\ &= (\text{Equity})(\text{ROE} - \text{Cost of equity})\end{aligned}$$

Chapter 5

$$\text{Future value} = FV_N = PV(1 + I)^N$$

$$\text{Present value} = PV = \frac{FV_N}{(1 + I)^N}$$

$$\begin{aligned}FVA_N &= PMT(1 + I)^{N-1} + PMT(1 + I)^{N-2} + PMT(1 + I)^{N-3} + \cdots + PMT(1 + I)^0\\ &= PMT\left[\frac{(1 + I)^N - 1}{I}\right]\end{aligned}$$

$$FVA_{due} = FVA_{ordinary}(1 + I)$$

$$\begin{aligned}PVA_N &= PMT/(1 + I)^1 + PMT/(1 + I)^2 + \cdots + PMT/(1 + I)^N\\ &= PMT\left[\frac{1 - \frac{1}{(1 + I)^N}}{I}\right]\end{aligned}$$

$$PVA_{due} = PVA_{ordinary}(1 + I)$$

$$\text{PV of a perpetuity} = \frac{PMT}{I}$$

$$\begin{aligned}PV &= \frac{CF_1}{(1 + I)^1} + \frac{CF_2}{(1 + I)^2} + \cdots + \frac{CF_N}{(1 + I)^N}\\ &= \sum_{t=1}^{N} \frac{CF_t}{(1 + I)^t}\end{aligned}$$

$$\text{Periodic rate } (I_{PER}) = \frac{\text{Stated annual rate}}{\text{Number of payments per year}} = I/M$$

$$\text{Number of periods} = (\text{Number of years})(\text{Periods per year}) = NM$$

$$\text{Effective annual rate (EFF\%)} = \left(1 + \frac{I_{NOM}}{M}\right)^M - 1.0$$

Chapter 6

$$\begin{aligned}\text{Quoted interest rate (r)} &= r^* + IP + DRP + LP + MRP\\ &= r_{RF} + DRP + LP + MRP\end{aligned}$$

$$\begin{aligned}r_{T\text{-bill}} &= r_{RF} = r^* + IP\\ r_{T\text{-bond}} &= r^*_t + IP_t + MRP_t\\ r_{C\text{-bond}} &= r^*_t + IP_t + MRP_t + DRP_t + LP_t\end{aligned}$$

$$r_{RF} \text{ with cross-product term} = r^* + IP + (r^* \times IP)$$

Chapter 7

$$\text{Bond's value} = V_B = \frac{INT}{(1+r_d)^1} + \frac{INT}{(1+r_d)^2} + \cdots + \frac{INT}{(1+r_d)^N} + \frac{M}{(1+r_d)^N}$$

$$= \sum_{t=1}^{N} \frac{INT}{(1+r_d)^t} + \frac{M}{(1+r_d)^N}$$

$$\text{Price of callable bond} = \sum_{t=1}^{N} \frac{INT}{(1+r_d)^t} + \frac{\text{Call price}}{(1+r_d)^N}$$

$$V_B = \sum_{t=1}^{2N} \frac{INT/2}{(1+r_d/2)^t} + \frac{M}{(1+r_d/2)^{2N}}$$

$$\text{Accrued interest} = \text{Coupon payment} \times \left(\frac{\text{Number of days since last coupon payment}}{\text{Number of days in coupon period}} \right)$$

Dirty price = Clean price + Accrued interest

Invoice price = Quoted price + Accrued interest

Chapter 8

$$\text{Expected rate of return} = \hat{r} = P_1r_1 + P_2r_2 + \cdots + P_Nr_N$$

$$= \sum_{i=1}^{N} P_ir_i$$

$$\text{Standard deviation} = \sigma = \sqrt{\sum_{i=1}^{N} (r_i - \hat{r})^2 P_i}$$

$$\text{Estimated } \sigma = \sqrt{\frac{\sum_{t=1}^{N} (\bar{r}_t - \bar{r}_{Avg})^2}{N-1}}$$

$$\text{Coefficient of variation} = CV = \frac{\sigma}{\hat{r}}$$

$$\text{Sharpe ratio} = \frac{(\text{Return} - \text{Risk-free rate})}{\sigma}$$

$$\hat{r}_p = w_1\hat{r}_1 + w_2\hat{r}_2 + \cdots + w_N\hat{r}_N$$

$$= \sum_{i=1}^{N} w_i\hat{r}_i$$

$$b_p = w_1b_1 + w_2b_2 + \cdots + w_Nb_N$$

$$= \sum_{i=1}^{N} w_ib_i$$

$$RP_M = r_M - r_{RF}$$

$$RP_i = (RP_M)b_i$$

$$r_i = r_{RF} + (r_M - r_{RF})b_i$$

Chapter 9

Value of stock = $\hat{P}_0$ = PV of expected future dividends

$$= \frac{D_1}{(1 + r_s)^1} + \frac{D_2}{(1 + r_s)^2} + \cdots + \frac{D_\infty}{(1 + r_s)^\infty}$$

$$= \sum_{t=1}^{\infty} \frac{D_t}{(1 + r_s)^t}$$

Constant growth stock: $\hat{P}_0 = \frac{D_0(1 + g)^1}{(1 + r_s)^1} + \frac{D_0(1 + g)^2}{(1 + r_s)^2} + \cdots + \frac{D_0(1 + g)^\infty}{(1 + r_s)^\infty}$

$$= \frac{D_0(1 + g)}{r_s - g} = \frac{D_1}{r_s - g}$$

Expected rate of return = Expected dividend yield + Expected growth rate, or capital gains yield

$$\hat{r}_s = \frac{D_1}{P_0} + g$$

Growth rate = (1 − Payout ratio) ROE

Zero growth stock: $\hat{P}_0 = \frac{D}{r_s}$

Horizon value = $\hat{P}_N = \frac{D_{N+1}}{r_s - g}$

Nonconstant growth stock: $\hat{P}_0 = \frac{D_1}{(1 + r_s)^1} + \frac{D_2}{(1 + r_s)^2} + \cdots + \frac{D_N}{(1 + r_s)^N} + \frac{D_{N+1}}{(1 + r_s)^{N+1}} + \cdots + \frac{D_\infty}{(1 + r_s)^\infty}$

$$= \frac{D_1}{(1 + r_s)^1} + \frac{D_2}{(1 + r_s)^2} + \cdots + \frac{D_N}{(1 + r_s)^N} + \frac{\hat{P}_N}{(1 + r_s)^N}$$

= PV of nonconstant dividends + PV of horizon value, $\hat{P}_N$

PV of horizon value, $\hat{P}_N = \frac{D_{N+1}/(r_s - g)}{(1 + r_s)^N}$

Market value of company's operations = $V_{\text{company's operations}}$ = PV of expected future free cash flows

$$= \frac{FCF_1}{(1 + WACC)^1} + \frac{FCF_2}{(1 + WACC)^2} + \cdots + \frac{FCF_\infty}{(1 + WACC)^\infty}$$

Horizon value = $V_{\text{Company's operations at } t=N} = FCF_{N+1}/(WACC - g_{FCF})$

Market value of company = Market value of company's operations + Market value of company's non-operating assets

Market value of equity = Enterprise value − Market value of debt + Cash and equivalents

Market value of equity = Book value + PV of all future EVAs

$$V_p = \frac{D_p}{r_p}$$

$$\hat{r}_p = \frac{D_p}{V_p}$$

Chapter 10

$$\text{WACC} = \begin{pmatrix}\%\\ \text{of}\\ \text{debt}\end{pmatrix}\begin{pmatrix}\text{After-tax}\\ \text{cost of}\\ \text{debt}\end{pmatrix} + \begin{pmatrix}\%\text{ of}\\ \text{preferred}\\ \text{stock}\end{pmatrix}\begin{pmatrix}\text{Cost of}\\ \text{preferred}\\ \text{stock}\end{pmatrix} + \begin{pmatrix}\%\text{ of}\\ \text{common}\\ \text{equity}\end{pmatrix}\begin{pmatrix}\text{Cost of}\\ \text{common}\\ \text{equity}\end{pmatrix}$$

$$= w_d r_d(1 - T) + w_p r_p + w_c r_s$$

$$\text{After-tax cost of debt} = \text{Interest rate on new debt} - \text{Tax savings}$$
$$= r_d - r_d T$$
$$= r_d(1 - T)$$

$$\text{Component cost of preferred stock} = r_p = \frac{D_p}{P_p}$$

$$\text{Required rate of return} = \text{Expected rate of return}$$

$$r_s = r_{RF} + RP = D_1/P_0 + g = \hat{r}_s$$

$$r_s = r_{RF} + (RP_M)b_i$$
$$= r_{RF} + (r_M - r_{RF})b_i$$

$$r_s = \text{Bond yield} + \text{Risk premium}$$

$$P_0 = \frac{D_1}{(1 + r_s)^1} + \frac{D_2}{(1 + r_s)^2} + \cdots + \frac{D_\infty}{(1 + r_s)^\infty}$$
$$= \sum_{t=1}^{\infty} \frac{D_t}{(1 + r_s)^t}$$

$$P_0 = \frac{D_1}{r_s - g}$$

$$r_s = \hat{r}_s = \frac{D_1}{P_0} + \text{Expected } g$$

$$\text{Cost of equity from new stock} = r_e = \frac{D_1}{P_0(1 - F)} + g$$

$$\begin{matrix}\text{Flotation cost}\\ \text{adjustment}\end{matrix} = \begin{matrix}\text{Adjusted}\\ \text{DCF cost}\end{matrix} - \begin{matrix}\text{Pure}\\ \text{DCF cost}\end{matrix}$$

$$\begin{matrix}\text{Cost of}\\ \text{external equity}\end{matrix} = r_s + \begin{matrix}\text{Flotation cost}\\ \text{adjustment}\end{matrix}$$

$$\begin{matrix}\text{Retained earnings}\\ \text{breakpoint}\end{matrix} = \frac{\text{Addition to retained earnings for the year}}{\text{Equity fraction}}$$

Chapter 11

$$\text{NPV} = CF_0 + \frac{CF_1}{(1 + r)^1} + \frac{CF_2}{(1 + r)^2} + \cdots + \frac{CF_N}{(1 + r)^N}$$
$$= \sum_{t=0}^{N} \frac{CF_t}{(1 + r)^t}$$

$$CF_0 + \frac{CF_1}{(1 + \text{IRR})^1} + \frac{CF_2}{(1 + \text{IRR})^2} + \cdots + \frac{CF_N}{(1 + \text{IRR})^N} = 0$$
$$\sum_{t=0}^{N} \frac{CF_t}{(1 + \text{IRR})^t} = 0$$

$$\sum_{t=0}^{N} \frac{COF_t}{(1 + r)^t} = \frac{\sum_{t=0}^{N} CIF_t(1 + r)^{N-t}}{(1 + \text{MIRR})^N}$$

$$\text{PV costs} = \frac{TV}{(1 + \text{MIRR})^N}$$

$$\text{Payback} = \text{Number of years prior to full recovery} + \frac{\text{Unrecovered cost at start of year}}{\text{Cash flow during full recovery year}}$$

Chapter 12

Taxes paid on salvaged assets = Tax rate × (Salvage value − Book value)

Capital Expenditures with 100% Bonus Depreciation = Cost(1 − T)

Chapter 13

$$\text{ROIC} = \frac{\text{EBIT}(1 - \text{T})}{\text{Total invested capital}}$$

Operating breakeven: EBIT = PQ − VQ − F = 0

$$Q_{BE} = \frac{F}{P - V}$$

$$b_L = b_U[1 + (1 - T)(D/E)]$$

$$b_U = b_L/[1 + (1 - T)(D/E)]$$

$$r_s = r_{RF} + \begin{matrix}\text{Premium for} \\ \text{business risk}\end{matrix} + \begin{matrix}\text{Premium for} \\ \text{financial risk}\end{matrix}$$

Net debt = Short-term debt + Long-term debt − Cash and equivalents

Chapter 14

$$\text{Dividends} = \text{Net income} - \begin{matrix}\text{Retained earnings required to help} \\ \text{finance new investments}\end{matrix}$$

$$= \text{Net income} - [(\text{Target equity ratio})(\text{Total capital budget})]$$

Chapter 15

$$\begin{matrix}\text{Inventory} \\ \text{conversion} \\ \text{period}\end{matrix} + \begin{matrix}\text{Average} \\ \text{collection} \\ \text{period}\end{matrix} - \begin{matrix}\text{Payables} \\ \text{deferral} \\ \text{period}\end{matrix} = \begin{matrix}\text{Cash} \\ \text{conversion} \\ \text{cycle}\end{matrix}$$

$$\text{Inventory conversion period} = \frac{\text{Inventory}}{\text{Cost of goods sold}/365}$$

$$\text{Average collection period} = \text{ACP (or DSO)} = \frac{\text{Receivables}}{\text{Sales}/365}$$

$$\begin{matrix}\text{Payables} \\ \text{deferral period}\end{matrix} = \frac{\text{Payables}}{\text{Purchases per day}} = \frac{\text{Payables}}{\text{Cost of goods sold}/365}$$

$$\text{Accounts receivable} = \text{Sales per day} \times \text{Length of collection period}$$
$$= (\text{ADS})(\text{DSO})$$

$$\begin{matrix}\text{Nominal annual} \\ \text{cost of} \\ \text{trade credit}\end{matrix} = \frac{\text{Discount \%}}{100 - \text{Discount \%}} \times \frac{365}{\begin{matrix}\text{Days credit is} \\ \text{outstanding}\end{matrix} - \begin{matrix}\text{Discount} \\ \text{period}\end{matrix}}$$

$$\text{Simple interest rate per day} = \frac{\text{Nominal rate}}{\text{Days in year}}$$

Interest charge for month = (Rate per day)(Amount of loan)(Days in month)

$$\text{Approximate annual rate}_{\text{Add-on}} = \frac{\text{Interest paid}}{(\text{Amount received})/2}$$

Chapter 16

$$\text{AFN} = \begin{matrix}\text{Projected}\\\text{asset}\\\text{increase}\end{matrix} - \begin{matrix}\text{Spontaneous}\\\text{liabilities}\\\text{increase}\end{matrix} - \begin{matrix}\text{Increase in}\\\text{retained}\\\text{earnings}\end{matrix}$$

$$= (A_0^*/S_0)\Delta S - (L_0^*/S_0)\Delta S - MS_1(1 - \text{Payout})$$

$$\begin{matrix}\text{Full}\\\text{capacity}\\\text{sales}\end{matrix} = \frac{\text{Actual sales}}{\begin{matrix}\text{Percentage of capacity}\\\text{at which fixed assets}\\\text{were operated}\end{matrix}}$$

$$\frac{\text{Target fixed assets}}{\text{Sales}} = \frac{\text{Actual fixed assets}}{\text{Full capacity sales}}$$

$$\begin{matrix}\text{Required level}\\\text{of fixed assets}\end{matrix} = (\text{Target fixed assets/Sales})(\text{Projected sales})$$

Chapter 17

$$\text{Direct quotation: } \frac{\text{U.S.\$ required}}{\text{1 unit of foreign currency}}$$

$$\text{Indirect quotation: } \frac{\text{Units of foreign currency}}{\text{1 U.S.\$}}$$

$$\frac{\text{Forward exchange rate}}{\text{Spot exchange rate}} = \frac{(1 + r_h)}{(1 + r_f)}$$

$$P_h = (P_f)\ (\text{Spot rate})$$

$$\text{Spot rate} = \frac{P_h}{P_f}$$

Index

Terms indicated in bold represent key terms.

J

K

L

Q

R

S